W9-BBY-214

GLENCOE

LITERATURE

The Reader's Choice

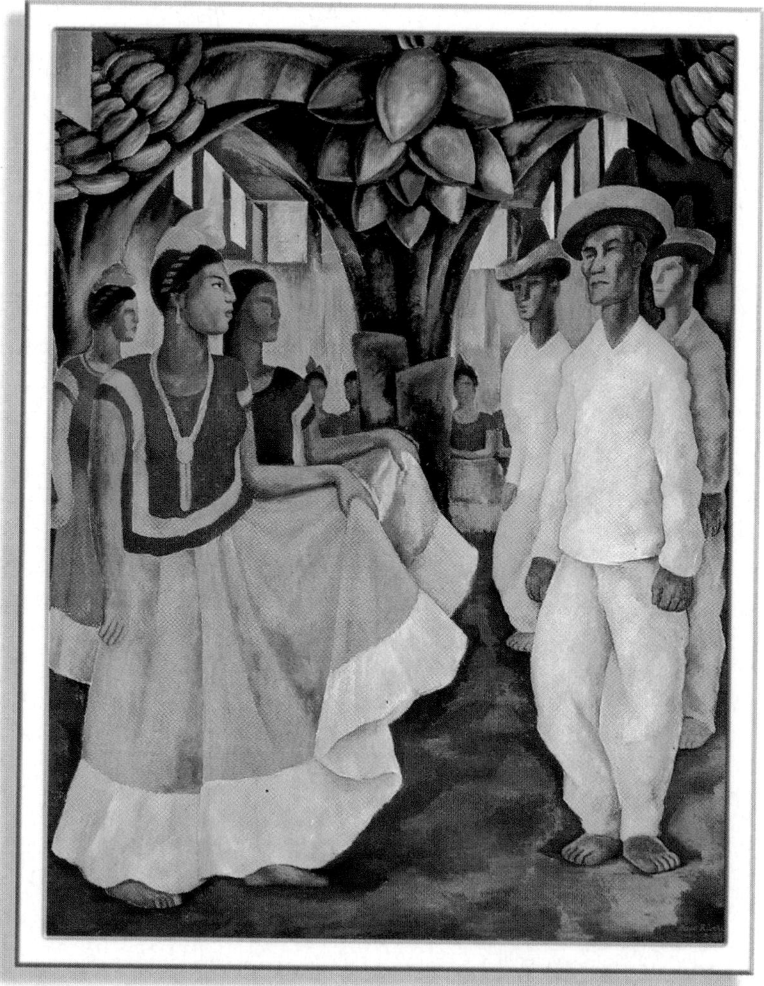

Program Consultants

Beverly Ann Chin

Denny Wolfe

Jeffrey Copeland

Mary Ann Dudzinski

William Ray

Jacqueline Jones Royster

Jeffrey Wilhelm

World Literature

New York, New York Columbus, Ohio Woodland Hills, California Peoria, Illinois

Acknowledgments

Grateful acknowledgment is given authors, publishers, photographers, museums, and agents for permission to reprint the following copyrighted material. Every effort has been made to determine copyright owners. In case of any omissions, the Publisher will be pleased to make suitable acknowledgments in future editions.

Acknowledgments continued on page R157.

The Standardized Test Practice pages in this book were written by The Princeton Review, the nation's leader in test preparation. Through its association with McGraw-Hill, The Princeton Review offers the best way to help students excel on standardized assessments.

The Princeton Review is not affiliated with Princeton University or Educational Testing Service.

Glencoe/McGraw-Hill

A Division of The **McGraw-Hill** *Companies*

Printed in the United States of America

Send all inquiries to:
Glencoe/McGraw-Hill
8787 Orion Place
Columbus, OH 43240-4027

ISBN 0-07-825112-5
(Student Edition)

ISBN 0-07-825143-5
(Teacher's Wraparound Edition)

2 3 4 5 6 7 8 9 10 058/046 05 04 03 02

Senior Program Consultants

Beverly Ann Chin is Professor of English, Director of the English Teaching Program, Director of the Montana Writing Project, and former Director of Composition at the University of Montana in Missoula. In 1995–1996, Dr. Chin served as President of the National Council of Teachers of English. She currently serves as a Member of the Board of Directors of the National Board for Professional Teaching Standards. Dr. Chin is a nationally recognized leader in English language arts standards, curriculum, and assessment. Formerly a high school English teacher and adult education reading teacher, Dr. Chin has taught in English language arts education at several universities and has received awards for her teaching and service.

Denny Wolfe, a former high school English teacher and department chair, is Professor of English Education, Director of the Tidewater Virginia Writing Project, and Director of the Center for Urban Education at Old Dominion University in Norfolk, Virginia. For the National Council of Teachers of English, he has served as Chairperson of the Standing Committee on Teacher Preparation, President of the International Assembly, member of the Executive Committee of the Council on English Education, and editor of the SLATE Newsletter. Author of more than seventy-five articles and books on teaching English, Dr. Wolfe is a frequent consultant to schools and colleges on the teaching of English language arts.

Program Consultants

Jeffrey S. Copeland is Professor and Head of the Department of English Language and Literature at the University of Northern Iowa, where he teaches children's and young adult literature courses and a variety of courses in English education. A former public school teacher, he has published many articles in the professional journals in the language arts. The twelve books he has written or edited include *Speaking of Poets: Interviews with Poets Who Write for Children and Young Adults* and *Young Adult Literature: A Contemporary Reader.*

Mary Ann Dudzinski is a former high school English teacher and recipient of the Ross Perot Award for Teaching Excellence. She also has served as a member of the core faculty for the National Endowments for the Humanities Summer Institute for Teachers of Secondary School English and History at the University of North Texas. After fifteen years of classroom experience in grades 9–12, she currently is a language arts consultant.

William Ray has taught English in the Boston Public Schools; at Lowell University; at the University of Wroclaw, Poland; and, for the last fourteen years, at Lincoln-Sudbury Regional High School in Sudbury, Massachusetts. He specializes in world literature. He has worked on a variety of educational texts, as editor, consultant, and contributing writer.

Jacqueline Jones Royster is Professor of English and Associate Dean of the College of Humanities at The Ohio State University. She is also on the faculty of the Bread Loaf School of English at Middlebury College in Middlebury, Vermont. In addition to the teaching of writing, Dr. Royster's professional interests include the rhetorical history of African American women and the social and cultural implications of literate practices.

Jeffrey Wilhelm, a former English and reading teacher, is currently an assistant professor at the University of Maine where he teaches courses in middle and secondary level literacy. He is the author or co-author of several books on the teaching of reading and literacy, including *You Gotta BE the Book* and *Boys and Books*. He also works with local schools as part of the fledgling Adolescent Literacy Project and is the director of two annual summer institutes: the Maine Writing Project and Technology as a Learning Tool.

Teacher Reviewers

Rahn Anderson
Arapahoe High School
Littleton Public Schools
Littleton, Colorado

Linda Antonowich
West Chester Area School District
West Chester, Pennsylvania

Mike Bancroft
Rock Bridge High School
Columbia, Missouri

Luella Barber
Hays High School
Hays, Kansas

Lori Beard
Cypress Creek High School
Houston, Texas

Hugh Beattie
Bergenfield Public School District
Bergenfield, New Jersey

Patricia Blatt
Centerville High School
Centerville, Ohio

Edward Blotzer III
Wilkinsburg High School
Pittsburgh, Pennsylvania

Ruby Bowker
Mt. View High School
Mt. View, Wyoming

Darolyn Brown
Osborn High School
Detroit, Michigan

Rob Bruno
Atholton High School
Columbia, Maryland

Mary Beth Crotty
Bridgetown Junior High
Cincinnati, Ohio

Susan Dawson
Sam Barlow High School
Portland, Oregon

Thomas A. Della Salla
Schenectady City School District
Schenectady, New York

Sandra Denton
East High School
Columbus, Ohio

Charles Eisele
St. John Vianney High School
St. Louis, Missouri

Mel Farberman
Benjamin Cardozo High School
Bayside, New York

Caroline Ferdinandsen
San Joaquin Memorial High School
Fresno, California

Tye Ferdinandsen
San Joaquin Memorial High School
Fresno, California

Randle Frink
East Rowan High School
Salisbury, North Carolina

Pamela Fuller
Capital High School
Charleston, West Virginia

Tara Gallagher
River Hill High School
Columbia, Maryland

June Gatewood
Rio Americano
Sacramento, California

Ellen Geisler
Mentor High School
Mentor, Ohio

Leslie Gershon
Annapolis Senior High
Mitchellville, Maryland

Kim Hartman
Franklin Heights High School
Columbus, Ohio

Charlotte Heidel
Gaylord High School
Gaylord, Michigan

Keith Henricksen
Sutton Public Schools
Sutton, Nebraska

Patricia Herigan
Central Dauphin High School
Harrisburg, Pennsylvania

Azalie Hightower
Paul Junior High School
Washington, D.C.

Bobbi Ciriza Houtchens
San Bernadino High School
San Bernadino, California

Cheri Jefferson
Atholton High School
Columbia, Maryland

Marsha Jones
Seymour High School
Seymour, Indiana

Cheryl Keast
Glendale High School
Glendale, California

Glenda Kissell
Littleton High School
Littleton, Colorado

Jan Klein
Cypress Lake High School
Fort Myers, Florida

Beth Koehler
Nathan Hale High School
West Allis, Wisconsin

Sister Mary Kay Lampert
Central Catholic High School
Portland, Oregon

Elaine Loughlin
Palo Duro High
Amarillo, Texas

Tom Mann
Franklin Heights High School
Columbus, Ohio

Carolyn Sue Mash
Westerville North High School
Westerville, Ohio

Eileen Mattingly
McDonough High School
Pomfret, Maryland

Wanda McConnell
Statesville High School
Statesville, North Carolina

Victoria McCormick
John Jay High School
San Antonio, Texas

Sandra Sue McPherson
McKeesport Area High School
McKeesport, Pennsylvania

Jill Miller
Odessa High School
Odessa, Texas

Karmen Miller
Cypress Falls High School
Houston, Texas

Catherine Morse
Shelby High School
Shelby, Ohio

Tom Omli
Rogers High School
Puyallup, Washington

John O'Toole
Solon High School
Solon, Ohio

Helen Pappas
Bridgewater-Raritan High School
Bridgewater, New Jersey

Jill Railsback
Seymour High School
Seymour, Indiana

Doug Reed
Franklin Heights High School
Columbus, Ohio

Mary Jane Reed
Solon High School
Solon, Ohio

Dorlea Rikard
Bradshaw High School
Florence, Alabama

Diane Ritzdorf
Arapahoe High School
Littleton, Colorado

Leonor Rodriguez
Breckenridge High School
San Antonio, Texas

Susanne Rubenstein
Wachusett Regional High School
Holden, Massachusetts

Steve Slagle
San Gabriel High School
San Gabriel, California

Tammy Smiley
Littleton High School
Littleton, Colorado

Carol Smith
Moses Lake School District
Moses Lake, Washington

Helen Spaith
Franklin Heights High School
Columbus, Ohio

Marsha Spampinato
High School of Enterprise,
Business, and Technology
Smithtown, New York

Nora Stephens
Huntsville High School
Huntsville, Alabama

David Stocking
Wachusett Regional High School
Holden, Massachusetts

Mark Tavernier
Norfolk Public Schools
Norfolk, Virginia

Martin Tierney
Bishop Dwenger High School
Fort Wayne, Indiana

Elysa Toler-Robinson
Detroit Public Schools
Detroit, Michigan

Megan Trow
Sprague High School
Salem, Oregon

Joseph Velten Jr.
Archbishop Wood High School
Warminster, Pennsylvania

Margaret Wildermann
McDonough High School
Pomfret, Maryland

Kathy Young
Walnut Ridge High School
Columbus, Ohio

Mary Young
Greenville High School
Greenville, Illinois

Book Overview

Reference Section

Contents

Guide to Active Reading

CONTENTS

UNIT ❦ TWO

Ancient Greece and Rome

UNIT ❧ THREE

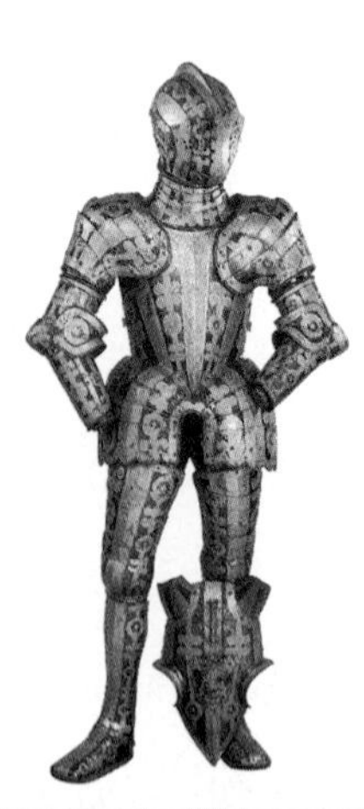

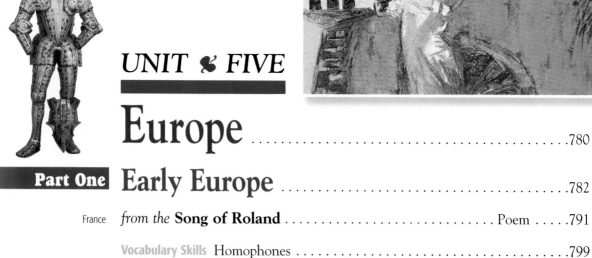

UNIT FIVE

CONTENTS

UNIT SIX

The Americas

CONTENTS

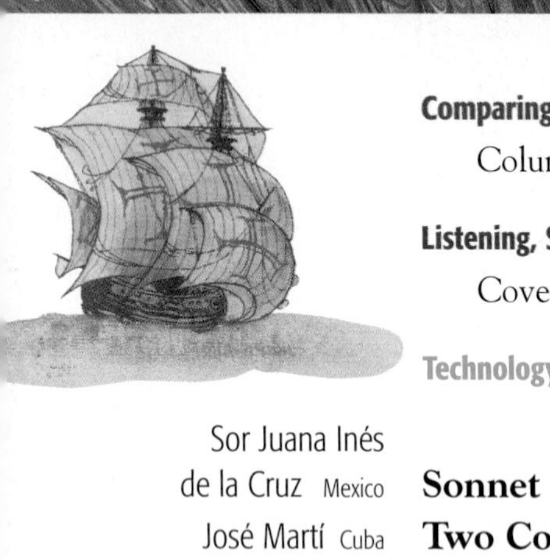

Part Two The Modern Americas

Reference Section

Selections by Genre

Short Story and Other Fiction

Nonfiction

Poetry

Drama

Epic

Fable

Folktale

Sacred Text

Electronic Media

Features

The Art of Translation

MEDIA connection

COMPARING *selections*

Genre Focus

Active Reading Strategies

Literature FOCUS

Writing Workshop

Interdisciplinary Connection

Skills

Grammar Link

Listening, Speaking, and Viewing

Reading & Thinking Skills

Technology Skills

Vocabulary Skills

Writing Skills

Genre Focus

Fiction

When you talk about computers, you use terms that relate specifically to computers: you discuss megabytes, logging on, how to boot up. When you talk about science or sports, you use different sets of terms. Likewise, when people talk about literature, they use special terms—the language of literary analysis. You will find that learning to use this language can help you discuss how a work of **fiction** is created and what qualities make it effective.

What kind of literature is fiction? A work of fiction is any narrative written in prose in which the situations and characters are invented by the writer. Novels, short stories, folktales, fairy tales, fables, and other forms of made-up stories come under the category of fiction. All works of fiction include elements described on these pages. See how a story you probably already know, the fairy tale "Cinderella," can be analyzed in terms of these elements.

ELEMENTS OF FICTION

MODEL: "Cinderella"

Setting

Setting is the time and place in which a story happens. The setting of a story includes not only physical surroundings, but also ideas, customs, values, and beliefs.

The story takes place a long time ago in a land ruled by a king and a queen.

Characters

Characters are the actors in a story's plot. They can be people, animals, robots, or whatever the writer chooses.

- The **protagonist** is the main character.
- The **antagonist** is the person or force in conflict with the main character. Not all stories have antagonists.

The main characters are Cinderella, the stepsisters, their mother, the fairy godmother, and the prince.

Protagonist: Cinderella

Antagonists: stepsisters, stepmother

Point of View

Point of view refers to the standpoint from which a story is told. The person telling the story is called the **narrator.**

- In a story told from the **first-person point of view,** the narrator is a character in the story, and uses the words *I* and *me* to tell the story.
- In **third-person point of view,** the narrator is someone who stands outside the story and describes the characters and action. **Third-person omniscient point of view** means that the narrator knows everything that goes on–including the thoughts and feelings of every character in the story. If the narrator describes events as only one character perceives them, the point of view is called **third-person limited.**

"Cinderella" is told from the third-person omniscient point of view: the narrator explains what the prince is doing as well as what is happening in Cinderella's household.

Theme

Theme is the central message of a story that readers can apply to life. Themes in fiction commonly provide perceptions about life.

- Sometimes themes are stated directly in a story.
- Usually themes are implied; the reader has to infer them by considering all the elements of a story.

The theme of "Cinderella" is implied. The reader can infer the message that if you are in a bad situation, you should do the best that you can. In the end, things will work out for you.

Plot

Plot is the sequence of events in a story. Most plots deal with a problem and develop around a conflict, a struggle between opposing forces.

- An **external conflict** is a struggle between a character and an outside force, such as another character, society, nature, or fate.
- An **internal conflict** takes place within a character who struggles with opposing feelings or with indecision about how to act.

Following are the events that make up the plot of "Cinderella."

Problem: Cinderella wants to go to the ball, but her stepsisters prevent her from going.

Conflict: The conflict is external—Cinderella versus the stepsisters and their mother.

Most plots develop in five stages.

- **Exposition** introduces the story's characters, setting, and conflict.
- **Rising action** develops the conflict with complications and suspense.
- **Climax** is the emotional high point of the story.
- **Falling action** shows what happens to the characters after the climax.
- **Resolution** shows how the conflict is resolved or the problem solved.

Active Reading Strategies

How to Read Fiction

How can you get the most from your reading? Effective readers are active readers. As they read, they have conversations with themselves about the text; they get involved. Don't be a passive reader. Use the following strategies to help you read works of fiction actively and effectively.

• For more about these and other active reading strategies, see **Reading Handbook,** pp. R82–R84.

PREDICT

Predicting helps you anticipate events and stay alert to the less obvious parts of a story. Make educated guesses about what will happen next by combining clues in the story with what you already know.

Say to yourself . . .

- From the title, I'd guess this story is about . . .
- This character will probably . . .
- The next thing that should happen is . . .
- This story is different from my original prediction. Now I think . . .

CONNECT

Draw parallels between the people, places, and events in the story and the people, places, and events in your own life.

Ask yourself . . .

- How would I act in the main character's situation?
- When have I felt the same way as this character?
- What parts of my life does this story remind me of?
- What other stories does this story remind me of?

QUESTION

Ask yourself questions to help you clarify the story as you go along.

Ask yourself . . .

- Have I understood what I've read so far?
- What's going on at this point in the story?
- Who said that?
- What does this mean?

VISUALIZE In your mind, form pictures of what is happening in the story. Pay attention to the details the writer gives you, and make them a part of your reading experience.

Ask yourself . . .

- How does this scene/character/object look?
- Who is in this scene?
- Where are the characters in relation to one another and to their surroundings?

EVALUATE Form opinions and make judgments about the story while you are reading.

Ask yourself . . .

- Does this turn of events make sense?
- Are the actions of this character consistent?
- What is particularly effective about this writer's style?
- Do I agree with this idea?

REVIEW Pause from time to time to think about your reading. Summarize events in a story or rephrase difficult language to help you understand and remember what you've read.

Say to yourself . . .

- So far, . . .
- In other words, . . .

RESPOND Respond *while* you are reading. Think about your spontaneous feelings.

Say to yourself . . .

- If I were this character, . . .
- I'd like to ask the writer why . . .
- I think this character is . . .
- Who else would enjoy this story?

Applying the Strategies

1. Read the following story, "You Are Now Entering the Human Heart," using the Active Reading Model notes in the margins.
2. Choose a work of fiction you have not yet read and practice using all of these strategies. Write comments on stick-on notes and put them in the margins of the story as you read.

New Zealand, 1983

Before You Read

You Are Now Entering the Human Heart

Meet Janet Frame

"I was in touch with the unalterable human composition that is the true basis of fiction, the great events of everyone's life and death. . . ."

As a poor, shy child growing up in New Zealand, Janet Frame dreamt of becoming a poet. As an adult, she credits writing with saving her life.

Misdiagnosed as schizophrenic, Frame spent her early adulthood in and out of mental hospitals, where she received hundreds of electroshock treatments. Even though the treatments affected her memory, she still managed to write, and she published her first book of short stories, *The Lagoon*, in 1951. Frame was scheduled to undergo a lobotomy, a brain operation used to treat mental illness, but a hospital official cancelled her operation when he discovered her book had won a literary award. Frame wrote about the experience in *An Angel at My Table*, the second of three volumes of her autobiography. Today, Frame is regarded as one of the leading writers of New Zealand.

Janet Frame was born in 1924.

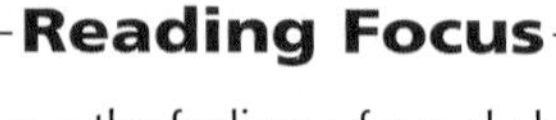

Reading Focus

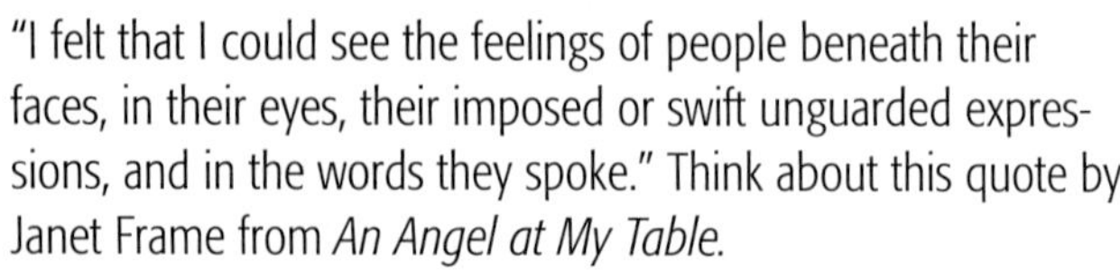

"I felt that I could see the feelings of people beneath their faces, in their eyes, their imposed or swift unguarded expressions, and in the words they spoke." Think about this quote by Janet Frame from *An Angel at My Table*.

Observing Now think about an encounter you had recently with either a stranger or someone you know, in which you could "see" the unspoken feelings of the person. What feelings did you observe from the person's expressions, gestures, or manner of speaking? Jot down a few notes about the encounter and your observations.

Setting a Purpose Read to share a character's insights into the feelings of other people.

Building Background

Science Museums in Philadelphia

The short story you are about to read is set in two science museums in Philadelphia—the Franklin Institute Science Museum and the Philadelphia Academy of Natural Sciences. Founded in 1824 and named after Benjamin Franklin, the Franklin Institute features a variety of hands-on exhibits, including a mini-earthquake and an artificial heart 220 times larger than life-size. The nearby Philadelphia Academy of Natural Sciences, founded in 1812, is a natural history museum that displays dioramas of animals in their natural habitats as well as live animals that visitors can touch.

Vocabulary Preview

askew (ə skū′) *adj.* crooked; at an angle; p. 6
persist (pər sist′) *v.* to insist, as in repeating a statement; p. 7
recoil (ri koil′) *v.* to draw back, as in fear, horror, or surprise; p. 7
petrified (pe′ trə fīd) *adj.* paralyzed with fear or horror; p. 7

Warnampi Tingari, 1980. Dick Pantimas Tjupurrula (Australia).

You Are Now Entering the Human Heart

Janet Frame

Active Reading Model

I LOOKED AT THE NOTICE. I WONDERED IF I HAD TIME BEFORE my train left Philadelphia for Baltimore in one hour. That heart, ceiling-high, occupied one corner of the large exhibition hall, and from wherever you stood in the hall you could hear its beating, *thum-thump-thum-thump*. It was a popular exhibit, and sometimes, when there were too many children about, the entrance had to be roped off, as the children loved to race up and down the blood vessels and match their cries to the heart's beating.

You Are Now Entering the Human Heart

Active Reading Model

VISUALIZE

Picture an artificial heart so large that people can walk through it.

I could see that the heart had already been punished for the day—the floor of the blood vessel was worn and dusty, the chamber walls were covered with marks, and the notice "You Are Now Taking the Path of a Blood Cell Through the Human Heart," hung askew. I wanted to see more of the Franklin Institute and the Natural Science Museum across the street, but a journey through the human heart would be fascinating. Did I have time?

Later. First, I would go across the street to the Hall of North America, among the bear and the bison, and catch up on American flora and fauna.

I made my way to the Hall. More children, sitting in rows on canvas chairs. An elementary class from a city school, under the control of an elderly teacher. A museum attendant holding a basket, and all eyes gazing at the basket.

"Oh," I said. "Is this a private lesson? Is it all right for me to be here?"

The attendant was brisk. "Surely. We're having a lesson in snake handling," he said. "It's something new. Get the children young and teach them that every snake they meet is not to be killed. People seem to think that every snake has to be knocked on the head. So we're getting them young and teaching them."

"May I watch?" I said.

"Surely. This is a common grass snake. No harm, no harm at all. Teach the children to learn the feel of them, to lose their fear."

He turned to the teacher. "Now, Miss—Mrs.—" he said.

"Miss Aitcheson."

CONNECT

How do you feel about handling snakes? How would you feel if you were the teacher?

He lowered his voice. "The best way to get through to the children is to start with teacher," he said to Miss Aitcheson. "If they see you're not afraid, then they won't be."

She must be near retiring age, I thought. A city woman. Never handled a snake in her life. Her face was pale. She just managed to drag the fear from her eyes to some place in their depths, where it lurked like a dark stain. Surely the attendant and the children noticed?

"It's harmless," the attendant said. He'd been working with snakes for years.

Miss Aitcheson, I thought again. A city woman born and bred. All snakes were creatures to kill, to be protected from, alike the rattler, the copperhead, king snake, grass snake—venom and victims. Were there not places in the South where you couldn't go into the streets for fear of the rattlesnakes?

PREDICT

What do you think the teacher will do?

Her eyes faced the lighted exit. I saw her fear. The exit light blinked, hooded. The children, none of whom had ever touched a live snake, were sitting hushed, waiting for the drama to begin; one or two looked afraid as the attendant withdrew a green snake about three feet long from the basket and with a swift movement, before the teacher could protest, draped it around her neck and stepped back, admiring and satisfied.

Vocabulary

askew (ə skū′) *adj.* crooked; at an angle

"There," he said to the class. "Your teacher has a snake around her neck and she's not afraid."

Miss Aitcheson stood rigid; she seemed to be holding her breath.

"Teacher's not afraid, are you?" the attendant persisted. He leaned forward, pronouncing judgement on her, while she suddenly jerked her head and lifted her hands in panic to get rid of the snake. Then, seeing the children watching her, she whispered, "No, I'm not afraid. Of course not." She looked around her.

"Of course not," she repeated sharply.

I could see her defeat and helplessness. The attendant seemed unaware, as if his perception had grown a reptilian covering. What did she care for the campaign for the preservation and welfare of copperheads and rattlers and common grass snakes? What did she care about someday walking through the woods or the desert and deciding between killing a snake and setting it free, as if there would be time to decide, when her journey to and from school in downtown Philadelphia held enough danger to occupy her? In two years or so, she'd retire and be in that apartment by herself and no doorman, and everyone knew what happened then, and how she'd be afraid to answer the door and to walk after dark and carry her pocketbook in the street. There was enough to think about without learning to handle and love the snakes, harmless and otherwise, by having them draped around her neck for everyone, including the children—most of all the children—to witness the outbreak of her fear.

"See, Miss Aitcheson's touching the snake. She's not afraid of it at all."

As everyone watched, she touched the snake. Her fingers recoiled. She touched it again.

"See, she's not afraid. Miss Aitcheson can stand there with a beautiful snake around her neck and touch it and stroke it and not be afraid."

The faces of the children were full of admiration for the teacher's bravery, and yet there was a cruelly persistent tension; they were waiting, waiting.

"We have to learn to love snakes," the attendant said. "Would someone like to come out and stroke teacher's snake?"

Silence.

One shamefaced boy came forward. He stood petrified in front of the teacher.

"Touch it," the attendant urged. "It's a friendly snake. Teacher's wearing it around her neck and she's not afraid."

The boy darted his hand forward, rested it lightly on the snake, and immediately withdrew his hand. Then he ran back to his seat. The children shrieked with glee.

"He's afraid," someone said. "He's afraid of the snake."

Active Reading Model

EVALUATE
What do you think of the way the attendant is acting?

REVIEW
Summarize what the narrator supposes about the teacher's situation in life and her inner feelings.

QUESTION
What are the children waiting for?

Vocabulary

persist (pər sist′) *v.* to insist, as in repeating a statement
recoil (ri koil′) *v.* to draw back, as in fear, horror, or surprise
petrified (pe′ trə fīd) *adj.* paralyzed with fear or horror

Snake Dreaming, 1989. Billy Stockman Tjapaltjarri (Australia). Acrylic on canvas, 191 x 127 cm. Corbally Stourton Contemporary Art, London.

Viewing the painting: How do the patterns and shapes in this painting contribute to its mood? How does this mood relate to the mood of the story? Explain.

The attendant soothed. "We have to get used to them, you know. Grown-ups are not afraid of them, but we can understand that when you're small you might be afraid, and that's why we want you to learn to love them. Isn't that right, Miss Aitcheson? Isn't that right? Now who else is going to be brave enough to touch teacher's snake?"

Two girls came out. They stood hand in hand side by side and stared at the snake and then at Miss Aitcheson.

I wondered when the torture would end. The two little girls did not touch the snake, but they smiled at it and spoke to it and Miss Aitcheson smiled at them and whispered how brave they were.

"Just a minute," the attendant said. "There's really no need to be brave. It's not a question of bravery. The snake is *harmless*, absolutely *harmless*. Where's the bravery when the snake is harmless?"

Suddenly the snake moved around to face Miss Aitcheson and thrust its flat head toward her cheek. She gave a scream, flung up her hands, and tore the snake from her throat and threw it on the floor, and, rushing across the room, she collapsed into a small canvas chair beside the Bear Cabinet and started to cry.

I didn't feel I should watch any longer. Some of the children began to laugh, some to cry. The attendant picked up the snake and nursed it. Miss Aitcheson, recovering, sat helplessly exposed by the small piece of useless torture. It was not her fault she was city-bred, her eyes tried to tell us. She looked at the children, trying in some way to force their admiration and respect; they were shut against her. She was evicted from them and from herself and even from her own fear-infested tomorrow, because she could not promise to love and preserve what she feared. She had nowhere, at that moment, but the small canvas chair by the Bear Cabinet of the Natural Science Museum.

I looked at my watch. If I hurried, I would catch the train from Thirtieth Street. There would be no time to make the journey through the human heart. I hurried out of the museum. It was freezing cold. The icebreakers would be at work on the Delaware and the Susquehanna; the mist would have risen by the time I arrived home. Yes, I would just catch the train from Thirtieth Street. The journey through the human heart would have to wait until some other time.

Active Reading Model

QUESTION

What is the attendant failing to acknowledge?

QUESTION

What does the narrator mean by saying Miss Aitcheson "was evicted from them and from herself and even from her own fear-infested tomorrow"?

EVALUATE

How would you judge the author's reaction to Miss Aitcheson's ordeal?

Responding to Literature

Personal Response

Did you find this story humorous? Serious? Both? Describe your impressions.

Analyzing Literature

Recall

1. What exhibit does the narrator want to view at the Franklin Institute? In what kind of condition is it?
2. Where does the narrator go, and what does she end up observing?
3. Describe what the attendant does to the teacher.
4. How does the teacher react to the situation?
5. What does the narrator do at the end?

Interpret

6. How is the exhibit at the Franklin Institute related to what happens in the rest of the story?
7. What does the narrator suppose about Miss Aitcheson's life and her inner feelings? How does the narrator gain such insights?
8. Why does the attendant ignore the teacher's fear?
9. Why does the teacher react as she does, both initially and at the end?
10. **Irony** is a contrast or discrepancy between appearance and reality (see page R6). What is ironic about the narrator's final statement, "The journey through the human heart would have to wait"?

Evaluate and Connect

11. What kind of person is the attendant? Support your opinion with evidence from the story.
12. What do you think of the children's behavior? Do you find their behavior realistic? Why or why not?
13. What do you most fear? Why?
14. How does the title fit the story?
15. What does this story suggest about the real exhibits to be observed in life? Do you agree? Give reasons for your opinion.

Literary Criticism

Commenting on Frame's fiction and autobiography, poet Fleur Adcock writes, "[Frame] can be detached and passionate at the same time." How might Adcock's comment apply to the narrator of the selection? Does the narrator seem both detached and passionate? Using specific examples from the story as evidence, explain your response in a brief paragraph.

Literary ELEMENTS

Point of View

The term **point of view** refers to the relationship of the narrator to the story. A story with **first-person point of view** is told by one of the characters who uses the pronoun *I* to refer to him- or herself. "You Are Now Entering the Human Heart" is told from the first-person point of view. However, the handling of the point of view is unusual because the narrator takes the reader into the minds of the other characters. The author manipulates the point of view so expertly that it almost seems to be shifting as the story progresses.

1. An interactive museum has exhibits that help people experience an object, a process, or an event. How does the point of view make this short story function like an interactive museum exhibit?
2. What kind of person is the narrator? How is the narrator's personality revealed?

- See **Literary Terms Handbook,** p. R9.

Literature and Writing

Writing About Literature

Examining Parallels Reread the first paragraph of the story and think about the parallels between the description of the heart exhibit and the events in the story. Note especially the condition of the heart and how the children react to it. Write a few paragraphs explaining the parallels.

Creative Writing

A Heartfelt Journey For the Reading Focus on page 4, you jotted down notes about an encounter in which you observed the unspoken feelings of another person. Use your notes to take a brief journey through that person's heart and relate the feelings you see.

Extending Your Response

Literature Groups

Questions to Ponder In your group, discuss the following questions: What does this story suggest about human fears? Is it possible to overcome deep-seated fears by confronting them? What is the source of such fears? What other questions does this story make you think about? Share a brief summary of your discussion with the rest of the class.

Performing

A Pantomime Work with a partner to prepare and stage a pantomime of the actions of Miss Aitcheson and the attendant. Remember that in a pantomime, ideas and feelings must be conveyed through facial expressions and body movements, often by exaggeration.

Internet Connection

Exploring Museums On the Internet, find the Web site of the Franklin Institute Science Museum or the Academy of Natural Sciences in Philadelphia. Explore the site and share the information you discover in an oral, written, or visual report.

Reading Further

You might enjoy reading the following stories by New Zealand writers:

"Journey," by Patricia Grace, and "Archaeology," by John Cranna, from *The Oxford Book of New Zealand Short Stories,* edited by Vincent O'Sullivan.

Save your work for your portfolio.

VOCABULARY • Prefixes

A prefix added to the beginning of a base word changes its meaning. *A* is a prefix meaning "in," "on," "to," or "at." In the word *askew,* the prefix *a* is added to the word *skew,* meaning "to swerve or twist," creating a new word meaning "at a slant" or "crooked."

PRACTICE Write the prefix used in each word below. Then write the meaning of the word, taking into account the meanings of both the prefix and the base word. You may use a dictionary.

Example: a + board = aboard, meaning "in, on, or into a ship, train, bus, or airplane"

1. precaution
2. resurge
3. converse
4. incomplete
5. commerce
6. prejudge
7. anticlimax
8. trilevel
9. misconstrue
10. impenitent

Genre Focus

Nonfiction

Nonfiction—writing about real people, events, and ideas—is the broadest category of literature. Under this term come autobiographies, biographies, memoirs, diaries, letters, essays, speeches, travelogues, news articles, reports, and many more types of writing. Like works of fiction, all types of nonfiction writing can be inventive and creative, even though they deal with real, rather than imaginary, subjects.

Narrative Nonfiction

Some works of nonfiction tell a story, just as works of fiction do. Autobiographies, memoirs, biographies, and narrative essays are types of narrative nonfiction.

- An **autobiography** presents the story of a person's life written by that person. Most autobiographies are told from the first-person point of view, using the pronoun *I*. Writers of autobiographies typically focus on themselves and events in their own lives.
- A **memoir** is also a first-person account of events in the writer's life. However, memoirs tend to emphasize subjects outside the writer's personal life, such as significant historical events the writer has been a part of or has witnessed, or other people the writer has known.
- A **biography** is an account of a person's life written by someone else. It is presented from the third-person point of view.
- A **narrative essay** is a short composition that relates a true story from either the first- or the third-person point of view.

Because they tell stories, autobiographies, memoirs, biographies, and narrative essays share many characteristics of fiction. Like fictional stories, they may include such elements as setting, character, theme, plot, and conflict. Often they are organized like fictional stories. A writer might choose to present events in **chronological order,** the order in which they occurred. Or the writer might use a **flashback,** going back in time to present incidents that happened before the beginning of the story.

Informative Nonfiction

While narrative nonfiction tells a story, informative nonfiction explains a topic or promotes an opinion. Examples of informative nonfiction include essays, speeches, reports, letters, and news articles. The differences between narrative and informative nonfiction are not always clear, however, because writers of informative works sometimes weave stories into their writing, and writers of narratives sometimes explain topics and promote opinions.

Essays are one of the most common types of literary nonfiction. An essay is a short piece of writing devoted to a single topic. Two main kinds of informative essays are expository and persuasive.

- **Expository essays** offer information about a topic–from explaining how a process works, to analyzing or commenting on a political or historical event, to reviewing a theatrical production.
- **Persuasive essays** promote an opinion or position. Commonly, persuasive essays describe a situation and then offer reasons that the reader should believe or act in a certain way regarding the issue.

Many expository and persuasive essays follow a general structure. They begin with a lead (introduction), followed by a body and a conclusion. The diagram at the top of the page shows the structure of a typical informative essay.

- The **lead,** or introduction, serves to pique the reader's interest. It also often includes the **thesis,** or main idea, of the essay. Sometimes, though, a writer saves the thesis statement for the end of the work.

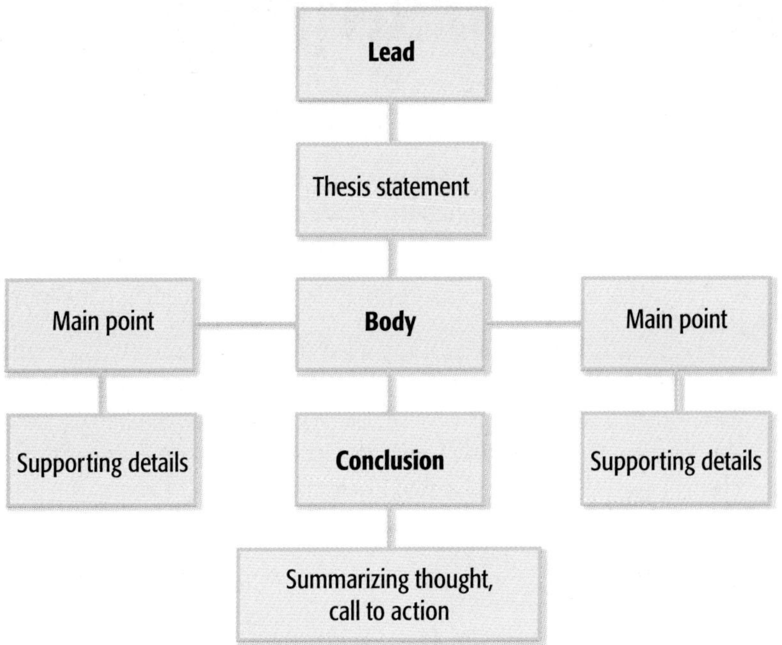

- The **body** develops and supports the thesis by providing **supporting details,** such as facts, reasons, statistics, sensory details, examples, observations, and personal experiences. This part of the work might also include quotations from expert sources and graphics, such as diagrams, graphs, and illustrations.
- The **conclusion** typically restates the thesis and provides the reader with a final or summarizing thought. A persuasive essay usually concludes by calling on readers to accept a new idea or to take a specific action.

Analyzing Nonfiction

The first step in analyzing nonfiction is to identify the type of work you are reading. By looking at the title and skimming the first few paragraphs, you can usually tell whether the work is an autobiography or a memoir, a biography, an essay, or another type of nonfiction.

As you read, you might further classify the type of work by identifying the **writer's purpose,** or reason for writing. Ask yourself what the writer is trying to achieve. Is the writer's purpose to entertain, to inform, or to persuade the reader? The answer to that question will help you classify the work you are reading.

Once you know the type of work you are reading, you will know what to look for, such as elements of fiction, a thesis and supporting details, or persuasive techniques. Be aware, however, that writers may combine various elements, and purposes, in a single work. For example, you might read a persuasive essay that is not only entertaining but also tells a story. Perhaps the best approach is to think of each work of nonfiction as a unique combination of familiar elements.

Active Reading Strategies

How to Read Nonfiction

To get the most from reading nonfiction, active readers use strategies similar to those used in reading fiction. However, as an active reader, you will need to adapt the strategies to the particular type of nonfiction you are reading.

- For more about these and other reading strategies, see **Reading Handbook,** pp. R82–R84.

PREDICT

Make educated guesses about what you are reading. Preview the work by looking at the title, skimming the text, and examining photographs, headings, illustrations, charts, and other graphics. Make predictions before beginning to read and also as you read.

Ask yourself . . .
- What will this work be about?
- What is the writer's main idea about the topic?
- What supporting evidence might the writer use?
- What point will the writer make next?

CONNECT

Make connections with what you already know about a subject.

Ask yourself . . .
- What people, events, and experiences in my own life are similar to those written about here?
- What have I heard or read about the subject?
- How does this work add to or change my understanding of the subject?
- How does this subject relate to other subjects I know about?

QUESTION

Question anything you do not understand. Reread any part that confuses you, and then read on to see if your questions are answered.

Ask yourself . . .
- Do I understand what the writer is saying here?
- Why is the writer giving me these facts?
- What does this concept have to do with what I just read?

VISUALIZE Use details the writer gives you to form mental pictures of people, places, and objects, and to see the steps in a process or how something works.

Ask yourself . . .
- What does this person look like?
- How does this scene or object look?
- Where does this part fit with the others?
- How does this step relate to the next one? the one before?

EVALUATE Make judgments about what you read.

Ask yourself . . .
- Is this a fact or an opinion?
- Does this information really support the thesis?
- Do I agree with the writer's opinions and interpretations?
- What does this action reveal about this person or situation?

REVIEW Pause often to think about and to summarize what you have read.

Say to yourself . . .
- The main idea is . . .
- Details supporting this thesis include . . .
- The steps in this process are . . .
- The writer's purpose is to . . .

RESPOND React to what you are reading. Identify and consider the spontaneous thoughts and feelings you have about what the writer is saying. Decide what you like or dislike about the work.

Say to yourself . . .
- I'd like to ask the writer why . . .
- I think this thesis is . . .
- That's pretty interesting. I'd like to know more about . . .
- Who else might benefit from learning this information?

Applying the Strategies

Read the next selection, from *Out of Africa* by Isak Dinesen, using the Active Reading Model notes in the margins. Then practice the strategies as you read another work of nonfiction.

Denmark, 1937

Before You Read

from *Out of Africa: The Iguana*

Reading Focus

Think of a time when you came to dislike something after you purchased it. Why did you change your mind about this object?

Share Ideas Describe your experience to the class.

Setting a Purpose Read "The Iguana" for insight into the elusiveness of beauty.

Meet Isak Dinesen

"I belong to an ancient, idle, wild, and useless tribe. . . . I am a storyteller."

Isak Dinesen (ē′ säk dē′ nə sən) was the pen name of Karen Blixen, a Danish author who came from an upper-class family. As a teenager she studied painting; later she said that this training taught her how to observe nature. She also wrote short stories. In 1914 she married Bror Blixen and moved to Africa. They bought a large coffee plantation near Nairobi, Kenya. By 1921 their marriage had fallen apart, so Dinesen ran the plantation by herself for another decade.

Towards the end of her stay in Africa, Dinesen renewed her interest in writing. After she returned to Denmark, she completed a volume called *Seven Gothic Tales*. The book was successful, especially in the United States, where she developed an enthusiastic following. Dinesen wrote all of her major works first in English, then in Danish. She is best known for *Out of Africa*, an account of her experiences in Kenya.

Isak Dinesen was born in 1885 and died in 1962.

Building Background

Life on the Plantation

Dinesen became an international celebrity when *Out of Africa* was published in 1937. In the memoir, she portrays incidents that occurred on the plantation, her friendships with Africans and colonists, and her relationship with an English hunter named Denys Finch-Hatton. Although *Out of Africa* is factual, Dinesen shaped her material by focusing on certain kinds of experiences and downplaying others. The book also reflects her deep love for Africa. In a letter to her mother, she expressed her romantic view of the African landscape: "A great world of poetry has revealed itself to me and taken me to itself here, and I have loved it. I have looked into the eyes of lions and slept under the Southern Cross, I have seen the grass of the great plains ablaze and covered with delicate green after the rains."

Reading Further

If you like "The Iguana," you might enjoy the following stories: "The Death of Kinanjui," "The Grave in the Hills," and "Farewell" from *Out of Africa,* Dinesen's acclaimed memoir.

Vocabulary Preview

reserve (ri zurv′) *n.* land set aside by the government for a specific purpose, such as wildlife preservation; p. 17
luminous (lo͞o′ mə nəs) *adj.* emitting light; p. 17
impetuous (im pech′ o͞o əs) *adj.* impulsive; p. 18
pulsate (pul′ sāt) *v.* to throb or beat rhythmically; p. 18
suppress (sə pres′) *v.* to keep secret; p. 18

from

Out of Africa

The Iguana

Isak Dinesen

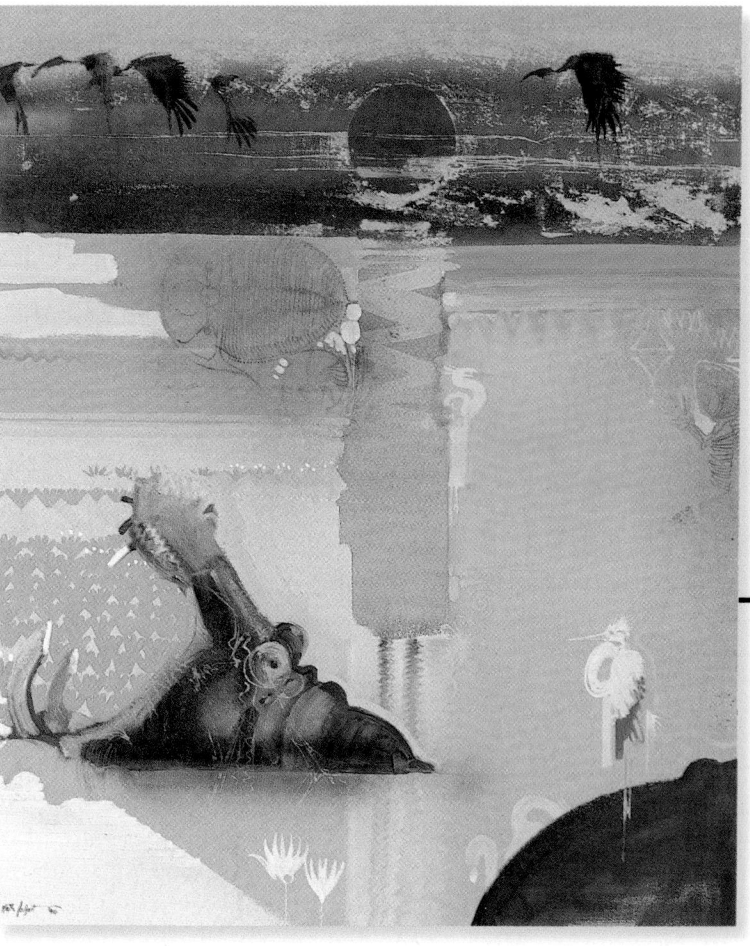

Hippo, Lake Kariba, 1994. Keith Joubert (South Africa). Oil on canvas, 102 x 86 cm. The Everard Read Gallery, Johannesburg, South Africa.

In the Reserve I have sometimes come upon the Iguana, the big lizards, as they were sunning themselves upon a flat stone in a riverbed. They are not pretty in shape, but nothing can be imagined more beautiful than their coloring. They shine like a heap of precious stones or like a pane cut out of an old church window. When, as you approach, they swish away, there is a flash of azure, green and purple over the stones, the color seems to be standing behind them in the air, like a comet's luminous tail.

Active Reading Model

VISUALIZE

From the sensory details provided, form a mental picture of the iguana.

Vocabulary

reserve (ri zurv′) *n.* land set aside by the government for a specific purpose, such as wildlife preservation

luminous (lo͞o′ mə nəs) *adj.* emitting light

from Out of Africa

Active Reading Model

Once I shot an Iguana. I thought that I should be able to make some pretty things from his skin. A strange thing happened then, that I have never afterwards forgotten. As I went up to him, where he was lying dead upon his stone, and actually while I was walking the few steps, he faded and grew pale, all color died out of him as in one long sigh, and by the time that I touched him he was gray and dull like a lump of concrete. It was the live impetuous blood pulsating within the animal, which had radiated out all that glow and splendor. Now that the flame was put out, and the soul had flown, the Iguana was as dead as a sandbag.

QUESTION

Why would Dinesen shoot an iguana again?

Often since I have, in some sort, shot an Iguana, and I have remembered the one of the Reserve. Up at Meru I saw a young Native girl with a bracelet on, a leather strap two inches wide, and embroidered all over with very small turquoise-colored beads which varied a little in color and played in green, light blue and ultramarine. It was an extraordinarily live thing; it seemed to draw breath on her arm, so that I wanted it for myself, and made Farah buy it from her. No sooner had it come upon my own arm than it gave up the ghost.[1] It was nothing now, a small, cheap, purchased article of finery. It had been the play of colors, the duet between the turquoise and the "nègre,"—that quick, sweet, brownish black, like peat[2] and black pottery, of the Native's skin,—that had created the life of the bracelet.

CONNECT

Have you ever thought that the beauty of a piece of jewelry or an article of clothing depended on the person wearing it? Explain.

In the Zoological Museum of Pietermaritzburg, I have seen, in a stuffed deep-water fish in a showcase, the same combination of coloring, which there had survived death; it made me wonder what life can well be like, on the bottom of the sea, to send up something so live and airy. I stood in Meru and looked at my pale hand and at the dead bracelet, it was as if an injustice had been done to a noble thing, as if truth had been suppressed. So sad did it seem that I remembered the saying of the hero in a book that I had read as a child: "I have conquered them all, but I am standing amongst graves."

EVALUATE

Do you agree with Dinesen's interpretation of her experiences?

In a foreign country and with foreign species of life one should take measures to find out whether things will be keeping their value when dead. To the settlers of East Africa I give the advice: "For the sake of your own eyes and heart, shoot not the Iguana."

REVIEW

What is Dinesen's purpose and thesis? What three objects does Dinesen use to explain her thesis?

1. In this context, *to give up the ghost* means "to become lifeless."
2. *Peat* is a plant-based fuel source.

Vocabulary

impetuous (im pech′ o͞o əs) *adj.* impulsive
pulsate (pul′ sāt) *v.* to throb or beat rhythmically
suppress (sə pres′) *v.* to keep secret

Responding to Literature

Personal Response

What went through your mind when you finished reading "The Iguana"? Share your response with a classmate.

Analyzing Literature

Recall and Interpret

1. What does Dinesen find beautiful about iguanas?
2. Why did Dinesen once shoot an iguana? What contrast does she draw in her description of this incident?
3. How do you interpret Dinesen's remark, "Often since I have, in some sort, shot an Iguana"?
4. Why did the bracelet lose its beauty when Dinesen put it on her arm?
5. What is Dinesen suggesting with the quotation from a book she read as a child?

Evaluate and Connect

6. A **simile** is a comparison, using the word *like* or *as,* of two things that have some quality in common (see page R11). What similes does Dinesen use to suggest the appearance of death?
7. Why might Dinesen have included the description of the stuffed fish she saw in a museum?
8. Do you think that Dinesen suggests in "The Iguana" that hunting is wrong? Why or why not?
9. What impression of Isak Dinesen did you get from reading this selection?
10. Which incidents in your own life did "The Iguana" remind you of? Explain.

Literary Criticism

Scholar Donald Hannah makes the following observation about Dinesen's writing: "There is no chance or triviality in the world she creates; all irrelevant incident and detail is either eliminated or is later shown to be an integrated and connected strand woven into the total pattern and thus contributing its part to the completed design." Do you think this statement is true of "The Iguana"? Why or why not? Discuss your answers with a partner.

Literary ELEMENTS

Theme

A **theme** is a message about life or human nature. For example, a story about a bribery in a political race might convey the theme that corruption destroys the ties that bind communities together. Some literary works, especially longer ones, have more than one theme. An author may choose to state the theme of a work directly. More often, readers must infer the theme from the author's portrayal of a subject.

1. State the theme of "The Iguana" in your own words.
2. Does Dinesen imply the theme of her essay or state it directly? Explain your response.

- See **Literary Terms Handbook,** p. R12.

Extending Your Response

Creative Writing

Consumer Culture In the Reading Focus on page 16, you were asked to describe a time when you came to dislike something after purchasing it. Write a **poem** based on this experience. Before you begin writing, consider what the experience suggests about human nature. Try to state or imply this message in your poem.

Interdisciplinary Activity

Art: Locating Beauty Find a work of art that was created for a specific location. For example, you might choose a building, an outdoor sculpture, or a painting in a cathedral. Describe the artwork to your classmates, and explain how its location enhances its appearance.

Save your work for your portfolio.

Genre Focus

Poetry

Mexican poet Octavio Paz believed that the purpose of poetry is "to create among people the possibility of wonder, admiration, enthusiasm, mystery, the sense that life is marvelous. . . . to *make* life a marvel—that is the role of poetry." Poetry conveys a sense of the mystery and marvel of life through what African American poet Quincy Troupe calls "the music of language." Understanding the basic elements of poetry will help you to hear the words sing and to sense the marvel in the poems you read.

ELEMENTS OF POETRY

Speaker

The **speaker** is the voice within a poem. It might be the poet's voice or the voice of another person, an animal, or even a thing.

MODELS

My love, you went away from
me, / . . . From dusk to dawn
I cry, / my heart has nothing
to hold on to.

from "Sudden Moods"

speaker = a lover

Lines and Stanzas

A **line** is a horizontal row of words, which may or may not form a complete sentence. A **stanza** is a group of lines forming a unit. The stanzas in a poem are separated by a line of space.

Tranquil our paths
When your hand rests on mine
in joy.
Your voice gives life, like nectar.
To see you, is more than food or
drink.

from "So small are the flowers of Seamu"

line

stanza

Rhythm and Meter

Rhythm is the pattern of sound created by the arrangement of stressed and unstressed syllables in a line. Rhythm can be regular or irregular. **Meter** is a regular pattern of stressed and unstressed syllables that sets the overall rhythm of certain poems. The basic unit in measuring rhythm is the **foot,** which usually contains a sequence of stressed syllables (ʹ) and unstressed syllables (˘).

Ĭ lívе, / Ĭ díe, / Ĭ búrn / mў sélf / ănd
drówn: /
Ĭ ám / ĕx trĕ mé / lў hót / ĭn súf fer / ĭng
cóld: /

from "Sonnet 8" by Louise Labé

Night of Sine

Léopold Sédar Senghor
Translated by John Reed & Clive Wake

Woman, lay on my forehead your perfumed hands, hands softer than fur.
Above, the swaying palm trees rustle in the high night breeze
Hardly at all. No lullaby even.
The rhythmic silence cradles us.
Listen to its song, listen to our dark blood beat, listen
To the deep pulse of Africa beating in the mist of forgotten villages.

See the tired moon comes down to her bed on the slack sea
The laughter grows weary, the story-tellers even
Are nodding their heads like a child on the back of its mother
The feet of the dancers grow heavy, and heavy the voice of the answering choirs.

It is the hour of stars, of Night that dreams
Leaning upon this hill of clouds, wrapped in its long milky cloth.
The roofs of the huts gleam tenderly. What do they say so secretly to the stars?
Inside the fire goes out among intimate smells that are acrid and sweet.

Woman, light the clear oil lamp, where the ancestors gathered around may talk as parents talk when the children are put to bed.
Listen to the voice of the ancients of Elissa. Exiled like us
They have never wanted to die, to let the torrent of their seed be lost in the sands.
Let me listen in the smoky hut where there comes a glimpse of the friendly spirits
My head on your bosom warm like a *dang* still steaming from the fire.
Let me breathe the smell of our Dead, gather and speak out again their living voice, learn to
Live before I go down, deeper than diver, into the high profundities of sleep.

Active Reading Model

LISTEN

Listen to the rhythm of the first stanza. Is it fast or slow, flowing or halting, soothing or jolting?

IMAGINE

Picture a moonlit African village by the sea, with storytellers, dancers, and singers growing weary as the night advances.

RESPOND

What is your reaction to the way the poet uses figurative language?

CLARIFY

Summarize what the speaker says about the ancestors.

INTERPRET

What does the speaker want?

Responding to Literature

Personal Response

What memories did this poem stimulate? Share your response with a classmate.

Analyzing Literature

Recall

1. What person is the speaker addressing in the poem?
2. What is the setting of the poem?
3. What activities have just occurred in the speaker's village?
4. What does the speaker think will attract his ancestors?
5. What does the speaker hope to gain from the ancestors?

Interpret

6. What is the relationship between the speaker and the listener?
7. **Personification** is a figure of speech that gives human characteristics to an object, animal, or idea (see page R9). Identify an example of personification in the description of the poem's setting.
8. What is your impression of the village described in the poem?
9. Why might the speaker refer to the ancestors as exiles?
10. How do you interpret the phrase "high profundities of sleep" in line 21?

Evaluate and Connect

11. **Tone** is the attitude that a speaker takes toward the audience, a subject, or a character (see page R12). How would you describe the speaker's tone in "Night of Sine"?
12. What values does Senghor express in the poem?
13. **Imagery** is language that appeals to the senses. Which of the senses does Senghor appeal to in the poem?
14. In the Reading Focus on page 24, you were asked to describe your feelings about night. Briefly compare your feelings with those of the speaker.
15. Which other poem does "Night of Sine" most remind you of? Why?

Literary Criticism

Scholar Janet G. Vaillant makes the following statement about Senghor's poetry: "In Senghor's imagination Eden and the Africa of his childhood are one and the same . . . Like Eden, his childhood Africa offered him a place of perfect harmony between man and his surroundings." What evidence can you find in "Night of Sine" of this perfect harmony? In what other ways does the village recall Eden? Answer in a brief essay, using evidence from the poem to support your ideas.

Literary ELEMENTS

Repetition

Repetition is the recurrence of sounds, words, phrases, lines, or stanzas in a literary work. Repetition may be used to enhance the unity of a work. It can also create a musical or rhythmic effect or emphasize an idea. One form of repetition that poets sometimes use is **alliteration**–the repetition of initial consonant sounds in words that are close together. For example, in the last line of his poem Senghor grouped together words that begin with the letter *d,* creating a musical effect:

> Live before I go down, deeper than diver, into the
> high profunditiesof sleep.

1. Which word is repeated in the first stanza of "Night of Sine"?
2. Why might Senghor have chosen to repeat this word?

- See **Literary Terms Handbook,** p. R10.

Literature and Writing

Writing About Literature

Analyzing Techniques Pick out a passage from "Night of Sine" that you found especially moving or interesting. Explain why you chose this passage, and analyze the techniques that Senghor used in it. You may wish to discuss literary elements such as imagery, figurative language, rhythm, or theme.

Creative Writing

The Listener Speaks Write a brief poem in which the woman who is addressed in "Night of Sine" offers her own impression of the night. Try using repetition to create a rhythmic effect in your poem. You may borrow images from Senghor's poem or come up with your own images.

Extending Your Response

Literature Groups

Poetic Statement Senghor used poetry to promote a positive image of Africa. Do you think that his portrait of a village in "Night of Sine" is realistic or idealized? What beliefs about Africa and Africans do you think he was reacting against when he wrote the poem? Discuss these questions in your group. When you are finished, share your conclusions with the class.

Performing

Oral Reading In a small group, perform a round-robin reading of "Night of Sine." Each student should choose a stanza or group of lines to read aloud. Before you begin reading, go over the poem together to clarify any unfamiliar words or phrases. Consider how you can vary your speed and volume to capture the rhythm of Senghor's verse.

Interdisciplinary Activity

Social Studies: African Performance The silence that the speaker describes in "Night of Sine" comes after a series of performances. In the village where Senghor spent his early years, people would gather after the evening meal to tell stories, dance, and sing. Do research to learn more about traditional African performing art. Summarize your findings for the class.

Reading Further

If you enjoyed reading "Night of Sine," the following works may be of interest to you:

Poetry: "I Awoke" from *Léopold Sédar Senghor: The Collected Poetry,* translated by Melvin Dixon.

Biography: *Black, French, and African: A Life of Léopold Sédar Senghor,* by Janet G. Vaillant.

Save your work for your portfolio.

VOCABULARY • Onomatopoeia

Writers often tailor their writing to appeal to the senses. Many use onomatopoeia to help the reader hear the sound being described. Onomatopoeia is the use of a name or word that is formed by imitating the sound associated with that object or action. For example, Senghor writes, "the palm trees *rustle*." The word *rustle* is an example of onomatopoeia.

PRACTICE Complete the following sentences with appropriate onomatopoeia.

1. The heavy crate fell off the high shelf with a startling ________ .
2. The raindrop bounced off the air conditioner with a ________ .
3. The butter ________ in the hot pan while I chopped the onions.

Phwó Mask. Early 20th century, Tshokwe, Zaire. Wood, fiber, pigments, metal, plastic, animal and plant material, height: 21 cm, width: 18 cm. Royal Museum of Central Africa, Tervuren, Belgium.

UNIT ONE

Africa

3100 B.C.–Present

Kwa mwedo gutiri irima.

On the way to one's beloved there are no hills.

—Kikuyu proverb

The Land and Its People

The continent of Africa is second only to Asia in size. Its 12 million square miles give rise to striking ecological contrasts: tropical rain forests, grasslands, and vast deserts. The earliest known humans originated in Africa, and today many different peoples live there. More than a thousand languages are spoken by hundreds of different ethnic groups, which also have distinct histories, cultures, and religious beliefs.

About five thousand years ago, one of the world's earliest civilizations developed in Egypt, at the mouth of the great Nile River. Egypt's location at the juncture of Africa, Asia, and Europe allowed for a fertile exchange of ideas and inventions. For centuries the Nile was the chief link between Egypt and that part of Africa that lies south of the vast Sahara Desert. Then, some 1,800 years ago, Africans began using camels to carry people and goods across the Sahara. As a result, an extensive trade network crossed the desert, strengthening the link between the people south of the Sahara and those living along the Mediterranean Sea.

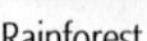

Rainforest

Savannah

Africa

- **c. 3100** Menes, the first pharaoh, unites Egypt
- **c. 3000** Earliest surviving Egyptian writing
- **2600–2200** Egyptian Old Kingdom; pyramids built
- **c. 2100–1700** Egyptian Middle Kingdom
- **c. 2000** Kingdom of Kush originates

3100 B.C. — **2250 B.C.** — **1500 B.C.**

World

- **c. 3000** Mesopotamians develop cuneiform writing
- **c. 2500–1700** Indus Valley civilization thrives
- **c. 1600** Chinese make bronze
- **c. 1500** Aryans invade India from the north

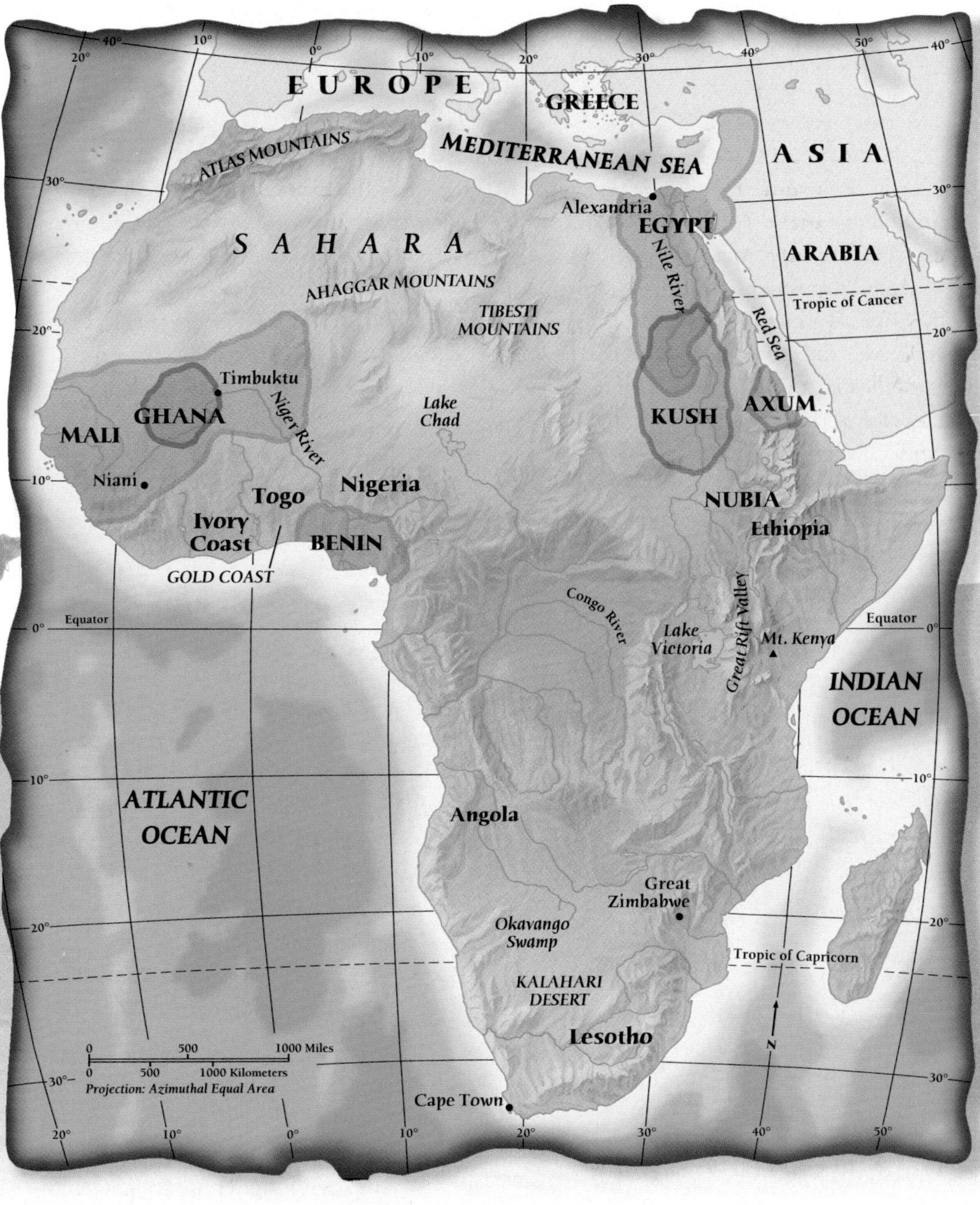

EUROPE
GREECE
MEDITERRANEAN SEA
ASIA
ATLAS MOUNTAINS
Alexandria
EGYPT
SAHARA
ARABIA
AHAGGAR MOUNTAINS
Nile River
Red Sea
Tropic of Cancer
TIBESTI MOUNTAINS
Timbuktu
GHANA
MALI
Niger River
Lake Chad
KUSH
AXUM
Niani
Togo
Nigeria
NUBIA
Ethiopia
Ivory Coast
BENIN
GOLD COAST
Congo River
Equator
Lake Victoria
Great Rift Valley
Mt. Kenya
INDIAN OCEAN
ATLANTIC OCEAN
Angola
Great Zimbabwe
Okavango Swamp
Tropic of Capricorn
KALAHARI DESERT
Lesotho
0 500 1000 Miles
0 500 1000 Kilometers
Projection: Azimuthal Equal Area
Cape Town

1500 B.C.

c. 1500–1000 Iron Age begins in Asia Minor

1500–600 Olmec civilization in Mexico

1361 King Tutankhamun begins reign

c. 1050 Nubia breaks away from Egyptian Empire

1000 David becomes king of Israel

750 B.C.

586 Babylonians destroy Jerusalem and exile Jews

552 Confucius is born

c. 550 Siddhartha Gautama, founder of Buddhism, is born

332 Greeks conquer Egypt; Alexandria founded

30 Romans conquer Egypt

1 B.C.

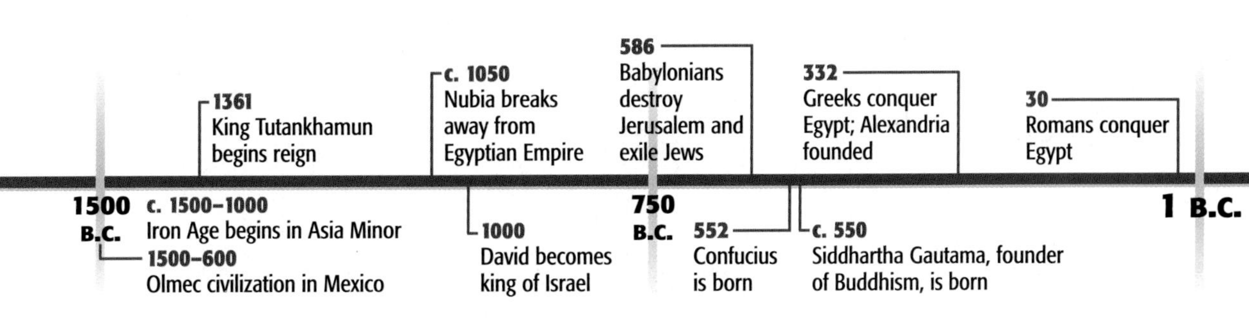

How People Lived

Ancient Egypt

The abundant gifts of the Nile allowed the ancient Egyptians to found one of the world's earliest and longest-lasting civilizations. Farmers planted their crops in the rich soil deposited by the river during its annual floods. Ships used the river to transport people and merchandise. The Egyptians developed their own form of writing, allowing them to keep records.

Three social classes existed in ancient Egyptian society: farmers and laborers at the bottom; merchants and craft workers in the middle; and landowners, government officials, scribes, and priests at the top. However, the class society was not rigid, and talented individuals could rise from one class to another. Kings, called pharaohs, came only from the royal family. Their tombs, huge stone pyramids built by thousands of workers, still stand after 4,500 years. From around 2000 B.C. Egypt spent much of its energy resisting foreign invasions by the Kushites, the Assyrians, the Persians, the Greeks, and the Romans.

Gold figures of Oskorkon II, Osiris, and Horus.

South of the Sahara

South of the Sahara most people lived in villages and grew their food on small plots nearby. However, trade created some sizable towns, including the desert city of Timbuktu, which flourished as a seat of learning as well as a commercial center. Trade gave rise to empires, as well.

Carved figure in military dress.

- Axum, in what is now Ethiopia, gained fame around 300 B.C. as the greatest trade center of northeastern Africa.
- Ghana, between the Sahara Desert and the Senegal and Niger Rivers, was the intermediary between salt traders to the north and gold and ivory producers to the south. It flourished between the ninth and thirteenth centuries A.D.
- Songhai, located in what is now Mali and parts of Niger and Nigeria, controlled the Saharan trade routes during the fifteenth and sixteenth centuries A.D.

Active Reading Strategies

Reading the Time Line

1. About how many years after Siddhartha Gautama was born did Muhammad begin preaching?
2. Put these events in chronological order. Indicate the year of each: Mansa Musa goes to Mecca; Kublai Khan founds the Mongol dynasty; Sundiata establishes the Mali Empire; the Kingdom of Ghana is at its height.

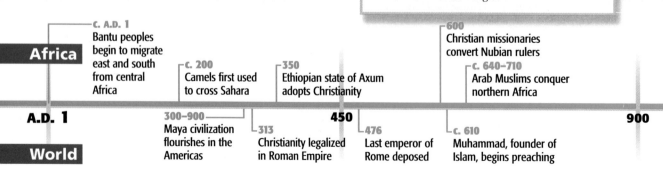

Africa

- c. A.D. 1 — Bantu peoples begin to migrate east and south from central Africa
- c. 200 — Camels first used to cross Sahara
- 350 — Ethiopian state of Axum adopts Christianity
- 600 — Christian missionaries convert Nubian rulers
- c. 640–710 — Arab Muslims conquer northern Africa

A.D. 1 — 450 — 900

World

- 300–900 — Maya civilization flourishes in the Americas
- 313 — Christianity legalized in Roman Empire
- 476 — Last emperor of Rome deposed
- c. 610 — Muhammad, founder of Islam, begins preaching

Traditions and Beliefs

Belief in the Afterlife

Ancient Egyptians made careful preparations for the life they expected to enjoy after death. The bodies of royal family members were preserved as mummies and placed in stone tombs. Their burial places contained images of all the things the dead might need in the afterlife—food, furniture, cosmetics, pets, games, and books. A primary responsibility of the king, while alive, was to intercede with the gods to maintain the order of all things and to ensure good fortune for his people. Many of the gods represented natural forces or animals, such as Re, the sun god; the falcon-headed Horus; and the cat-headed Bastet.

Sarcophagus interior.

Traditional Beliefs

The diversity of Africa resulted in hundreds of different religious systems, each with its own gods, shrines, and ceremonies. However, certain beliefs were common to many societies. Most recognized a supreme god as well as many lesser gods and spirits, which included the souls of dead ancestors. Africans believed that the present and the past, the seen and the unseen, the living and the dead, were eternally connected. People prayed to recently deceased family members to communicate with the spirits on their behalf. Men and women who were considered especially gifted at conversing with the spirit world were highly regarded in their communities.

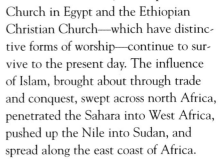

Islamic mosque lamp.

Christianity and Islam

Of the religions that originated beyond Africa, Christianity was the first to take hold there—in Egypt, Nubia, and Ethiopia. The conquest of northern Africa by Arab Muslims, which began in A.D. 639, reduced the number of Christians. However, the Coptic Church in Egypt and the Ethiopian Christian Church—which have distinctive forms of worship—continue to survive to the present day. The influence of Islam, brought about through trade and conquest, swept across north Africa, penetrated the Sahara into West Africa, pushed up the Nile into Sudan, and spread along the east coast of Africa.

900

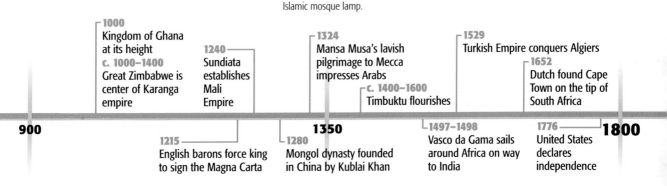

1000 Kingdom of Ghana at its height

c. 1000–1400 Great Zimbabwe is center of Karanga empire

1215 English barons force king to sign the Magna Carta

1240 Sundiata establishes Mali Empire

1280 Mongol dynasty founded in China by Kublai Khan

1324 Mansa Musa's lavish pilgrimage to Mecca impresses Arabs

1350

c. 1400–1600 Timbuktu flourishes

1497–1498 Vasco da Gama sails around Africa on way to India

1529 Turkish Empire conquers Algiers

1652 Dutch found Cape Town on the tip of South Africa

1776 United States declares independence

1800

Arts and Entertainment

Ancestor figure, Senufo culture. Beaded bracelets.

Visual Arts

Africans north and south of the Sahara created magnificent and expressive visual art for a variety of purposes:

- religious art, using forms and designs prescribed by tradition
- ceremonial art, which blended sculpture, textiles, beadwork, music, dance, and pantomime into one spectacular visual experience
- everyday art, which allowed for more freedom of expression in the carving of tables, stools, and utensils; the painting of pottery and of house exteriors; and the ornamentation of horse and camel trappings

Often a work of art would have more than one purpose; it might be both religious and ceremonial, for example.

Because the geography of Africa is so varied, the traditional arts of Africa were extremely diverse. Artists then as now used the materials at hand to create their works. For example, forest dwellers were accomplished wood carvers, while artists in areas where wood was scarce worked in other materials, such as stone or leather. Nomadic herders, who were constantly on the move, usually did not make pottery. Instead, they hollowed out gourds for containers and wove cloth for clothing on light, portable looms. In addition to the spiritual motifs used in African art, decorative motifs were used to honor the animal and plant life of a region.

Architecture

The ancient Egyptians were among the world's great architects. Lacking trees to build in wood, they mastered the use of stone, creating great pillared temples as well as the famous pyramids. Perhaps the world's first tourists were the travelers who came from Greece and Mesopotamia to see the wonders of Egypt.

The capital cities of kingdoms like Ashanti and Benin held great royal palaces; decorated with statues and carvings, these might cover several acres of ground. In Ethiopia, the Coptic Christians produced churches carved into mountainsides, with interiors richly painted with biblical scenes. In the savanna country of western Africa, Muslim mosques were built of sun-baked bricks in the local style.

Ancient mosque, Mali.

Music and Dance

Akan-type African drum.

After about A.D. 700, Africans north of the Sahara were influenced by Arab traditions of music and dance. South of the Sahara, musicians and dancers entertained at royal courts and performed at religious and other celebrations. Instruments included a wide variety of drums, harps, flutes, and xylophones. One instrument, the *mbira* (bēr′ ä), consists of metal strips attached to a wooden or gourd resonator; by plucking the strips with the thumbs, one can play melodies with harmony and counterpoint.

The drum was the most important African instrument. Some drums were made of animal skins; others were hollowed out of logs. The West African "talking drum" was designed to change pitch to imitate speech patterns.

Traditional African music was polyrhythmic. That is, musicians and dancers created complex and interlocking rhythms by beating drums, striking bells, clapping hands, and stamping feet.

Dancers incorporated into their performances movements from everyday life as well as imitations of animals. Also, dancers interpreted the polyrhythm of the drums.

Masked dancer, Dogon culture, Mali.

Masked Dances

In West Africa and some parts of central Africa, masked dances were a major part of ceremonial life. They took place on important occasions:

- events in the agricultural year, such as the first rains, planting, and harvesting
- ceremonies marking rites of passage, such as birth, adulthood, marriage, and death
- rites of secret societies
- curing the sick

Masked dances were public, but only members of the masked dance societies were allowed to see the masks except in performance or to observe dancers putting on their costumes. Dancers were accompanied by drummers and other musicians and by the singing and chanting that was sometimes done in a special language used only on that occasion.

Critical Thinking

Connecting Cultures

1. The drum is the most important instrument in African music. In a small group, discuss how drums influence our own music today.
2. In a small group, discuss how drums used in popular music today differ from the drums used in traditional African music.

Language and Literature

Early Egyptian Writing

Ancient Egyptians were among the first people in the world to develop writing. Egyptian hieroglyphics combined pictures and symbols to represent sounds. As time passed, Egyptians also developed faster writing systems for official recordkeeping. Hieroglyphics were both carved on stone and written on paper, which was made by pounding together stems of the papyrus, a reedlike plant. The less formal scripts were usually written only on papyrus. Only the upper classes in ancient Egypt could read. Writing was done by scribes, who were associated with the royal courts and temples.

Egyptian sandstone relief, 304–30 B.C.

African Languages

African cultures are often classified according to the languages people speak. Many languages are spoken throughout the continent, and millions of Africans speak two or more languages. Most African languages were not written down until the arrival of Arabic and Roman scripts.

Not including European languages introduced to Africa by colonizers, African languages can be grouped into four major language families:

- Afro-Asiatic (spoken in North Africa from the Red Sea all along the Mediterranean and south to the Sahara)
- Niger-Congo (spoken in West Africa and eastward almost to the Nile)
- Nilo-Saharan (spoken in north central Africa to Lake Victoria)
- Khoisan (click-languages, spoken in the far south)

influences

Some familiar English words and phrases can be traced to early African languages. Sometimes these words entered English through intermediate languages, such as Greek, Spanish, or French. African-inspired words include

- banjo (from *mbanya*, Kimbundu)
- okra (from *ukuruma*, Twi, West Africa)
- paper (from *papyrus*, the Greek word for the plant used by ancient Egyptians to make writing materials)
- tote (from *tota* or *tuta*, western Congo and Angola)

Responding to Literature

Personal Response

What questions would you like to ask the speakers of these poems? Share your response with the class.

Analyzing Literature

Recall and Interpret

1. According to "The Immortality of Writers," how can people benefit from books?
2. What are books compared to in "Immortality"?
3. What is the **setting** of "So small are the flowers of Seamu"?
4. Explain the last two lines in "So small are the flowers of Seamu." How do these lines suggest the speaker's attitude toward the beloved?

Evaluate and Connect

5. Why might the speaker of "Immortality" have chosen to mention specific people in the poem?
6. What kinds of books help people to be remembered?
7. Why might the speaker feel like a giant when looking at the flowers of Seamu? Have you ever had a similar feeling? Explain.
8. In the Reading Focus on page 38, you discussed your knowledge of life in ancient Egypt. What thoughts expressed in these poems surprise you the most?

Literary Criticism

In an article defining the poetic style known as Imagism, Pound writes that a poet should "compose in a sequence of the musical phrase, not in sequence of a metronome." Analyze the rhythm of "So small are the flowers of Seamu." Does the rhythm of Pound's translation seem musical (fluid) or metronomic (rigid)? Explain your answer in a brief paragraph. Use examples from the poem for support.

Literary ELEMENTS

Imagery

Imagery is language that appeals to the senses. For example, in "So small are the flowers of Seamu," the poet includes images of "perfumed flowers" and "the freshness of the north wind" to appeal to our sense of smell. Because people usually rely on sight more than the other senses, most imagery is visual. Imagery appears in all descriptive writing, but it is especially important in poetry.

1. List the images in "Immortality." What quality do the images in lines 5–8 have in common?
2. Why do you think so many love poems are filled with garden imagery?

- See **Literary Terms Handbook,** p. R6.

Extending Your Response

Personal Writing

Message for Posterity What do you want to be remembered for? Imagine that you have the opportunity to place written material in a time capsule that will be opened several centuries from now. Write a description of yourself for posterity. You might discuss your talents and accomplishments, things you like to do, or your values and ideals.

Performing

Egyptian-Style Reading Like the ancient Egyptians, many poets today use music when performing their work. Find a piece of music to accompany one of the poems. Before you decide on a musical setting, consider the poem's rhythm as well as the emotions it conveys. Bring in a recording of the music and perform the poem for the class.

Save your work for your portfolio.

Before You Read

Tselane and the Giant

Reading Focus

How are giants generally portrayed in myths and legends?

Chart It! With a partner, discuss the personality and behavior of giants you have read about. Fill in a chart such as the one shown below. Then share your conclusions with the class.

Giant	Actions	Personality Traits

Setting a Purpose Read the following tale to see the behavior of one giant.

Building Background

The Evolution of "Tselane and the Giant"

"Tselane (sə lä′ nē) and the Giant" began as an oral tale. In traditional African communities, groups of people would gather after their evening meal to share stories and other entertainment. The participants in these story circles were usually adults, although children were often invited to listen.

In its written form, "Tselane" retains some features of oral folklore, including songs, repetition, and a formal closing. Other features, such as the particulars of time and place, may have been added later as the tale gained a wider audience. For example, the first sentence indicates that the tale is set during the days of King Chaka, who ruled the Zulu people of southern Africa during the early nineteenth century.

Lesotho

Basotho woman in doorway of traditional painted house.

Lesotho is a small kingdom surrounded on all sides by the Republic of South Africa. The majority group, the Basotho, began migrating into this mountainous region during the sixteenth century. Life for many of these people has changed little since then. Thatch-roofed huts are common, and the economy is still based on farming and livestock. Lesotho has a very high literacy rate, which has helped to preserve its rich tradition of folklore. "Tselane and the Giant" is translated from Sesotho, one of the country's official languages.

Vocabulary Preview

impede (im pēd′) *v.* to hinder; to interfere with or slow the progress of; p. 44

implement (im′ plə mənt) *n.* tool, instrument, or utensil used to carry out tasks; p. 46

issue (ish′ o͞o) *v.* to come forth; to emerge; p. 46

glower (glou′ ər) *v.* to look or stare with sullen annoyance or anger; p. 47

quarry (kwôr′ ē) *n.* something that is sought or pursued; prey; p. 48

Nduu Ya Yiimu, 1997. Kivuthi MBuno (Kenya). Crayons and colors on jerrycan. Collection of the artist.

Tselane and the Giant

Translated by B. L. Leshoai

During the days of King Chaka of the Amazulu a widow lived in Lesotho at a place called Lekhalong La 'Mantsopa. Mantsopa was a Mosotho prophetess who was said to have lived sometime after Noah's great flood. There is a large imprint of an ostrich's foot on a rock in this area. It is said that during Noah's flood even the hard rocks became soft from being covered in water for such a long time. When the floods went down the animals left the Ark in search of food; and this is the time when the ostrich, whose imprint was left on the rock, went in his search for food to Mantsopa's valley.

It was in this valley that our widow lived, many years after Mantsopa's death. The valley was very far from any other place—secret and quiet, and occupied by a huge giant called Limo, who made life very miserable for the people living there. He killed their cattle and sheep and even the people themselves with his great axe. At nightfall the people locked themselves and their children behind strong doors. They shut their animals up behind well-built kraals[1] made from the wood of Mimosa trees. Even so, they did not manage to stop the evil giant from getting to the cattle and sheep when he wanted meat. Sometimes angry armed men and their vicious hunting dogs went out to fight the giant to put him to death. He waited for them to approach his cave before he rushed out to attack them with his huge axe. He always waited for them and their yelping dogs to get quite near before he appeared. Limo very much enjoyed the days when the people came to hunt him down.

Before he left the darkness of the cave he bellowed like an angry bull and the noise echoed up and down the valley. The yelping of the dogs stopped as soon as they heard this dreadful bellow. They hid their tails between their legs in great fear. The men stopped chanting their war songs as though they had already come face to face with the enemy. Limo had great fun watching what happened when he eventually appeared. The dogs were always the first to turn tail, yelping as though scalded with boiling water. As soon as the dogs ran away the men started to follow. Some dropped their heavy spears and round-headed sticks. The earth trembled under their feet. Some threw off their colorful blankets which flew in the wind and impeded their progress in the race for their lives. Their womenfolk and children, who were waiting in the hope of seeing the men return victorious with the giant's head, ran into their huts and bolted the doors behind them when they saw that they were defeated. This sight always made Limo laugh loudly. The cruel, mocking sound of his laugh upset the people even more. When they reached their homes, the dogs and the masters had to throw themselves against the strong doors. The men struck the doors with their sticks and fists. They yelled and screamed at their frightened womenfolk and children to let them in. When a door was opened or was broken down the dogs were always the first to find their way into the huts, through the men's legs. Once in, the men slammed the doors behind them and leaned against them with their backs, feet planted firmly on the floor, in an attempt to keep out the threatening giant.

Afterwards Limo would return to his cave, rocking with laughter at the foolish men and dogs. Sometimes to spite them he would follow to where their cattle and sheep were grazing and kill a few with his axe for his evening meal. Limo was a terrifying giant. His timid but kindly wife feared him like the plague. He was tall and strong, with a large round head covered with dirty, kinky hair. His face and chin were overgrown with a grizzly beard, and his huge eyes shone at night like two lights in the darkness. His large teeth always had bits of meat stuck between them. The meat rotted and so his breath had a very bad smell. His chest was big and strong, as were his thighs—larger and stronger than those of a bull! Beneath his muscular shoulders and arms was a big round and fat belly. His feet were flat and large. He ran like the wind, that one! His presence made the people of the valley feel very unsafe and one by one they began to leave. They took all their belongings and moved to a place far away. The giant began to starve

1. *Kraals* (krälz) are fenced or enclosed areas.

Vocabulary

impede (im pēd′) *v.* to hinder; to interfere with or slow the progress of because there were no longer any sheep and cattle to eat. So he began to eat human beings.

◆ ◆ ◆ ◆ ◆

Now this widow had a beautiful daughter called Tselane. Tselane refused to leave the valley with her mother because she loved the beautiful hut where she lived and the valley with its sunken lake and trees and flowers. Her mother therefore left her in the hut and promised that she would bring her bread and meat every second day. She also told Tselane that she would sing a song at the door so that Tselane would know it was her mother outside. For many days she brought her daughter food in a basket and sang at the door in her sweet and tender motherly voice:

> Tselane my child,
> Tselane my child,
> Open the door, my child,
> Open the door, my child;
> I've brought you bread to eat,
> Tselane, my child.

Tselane listened with her ear against the door and when she was certain it was her mother's voice she sang in reply:

> I hear you my mother,
> I hear you my mother.

Then she opened the door and let her mother in. When she had finished her food, Tselane let her mother out and locked the door from the inside so that no one could come in.

Limo soon discovered that Tselane had stayed behind and began to make plans to catch her. He also found out the days on which her mother visited her and what she did to be allowed into the hut. So one day, when Limo knew that her mother wasn't coming, he went to the hut carrying his hunting sack. He tiptoed quietly to the door of the hut and began to sing in his gruff voice, which shook the tiny hut:

> Tselane my child,
> Tselane my child,
> Open the door, my child,
> Open the door, my child;
> I've brought you bread to eat,
> Tselane, my child.

Tselane didn't have to put her ear against the door for she knew it was not her mother's voice. Then she said, "Go away, Limo; I know you, evil one. My mother's voice is sweet and gentle and not gruff like yours."

Limo went home very angry and nagged his wife, making her very unhappy because Tselane had been too clever for him. At night he tossed sleeplessly on his mat until he had an idea: "Aha, I've got it!" After that he slept soundly and snored loudly and his wife knew he was thinking up some mischief.

Next day Tselane's mother, after she heard her daughter's story of how Limo had tried to cheat her, attempted to persuade Tselane to go with her to her new home. But Tselane refused. On the following day Limo got up early and took his hunting sack with him. When his wife asked him where he was going he looked at her with bloodshot eyes and walked away without a word. When he was some distance from his cave he picked up a round smooth stone about the size of an ostrich's egg. He made a big fire and baked the stone. When it was red-hot he swallowed it quickly. The stone burnt his throat, though he did not feel much pain. After this he went to Tselane's hut and sang to her to open the door, but she was not deceived although his voice sounded much softer and pleasanter.

Limo went home in a very bad mood and made his wife run around doing unnecessary jobs. But this did not soothe his nerves. That night again he was unable to sleep and tossed restlessly on his mat. When his wife tried to sleep he scolded her and made her very unhappy. Towards morning, after he had been thinking and thinking, he exclaimed excitedly,

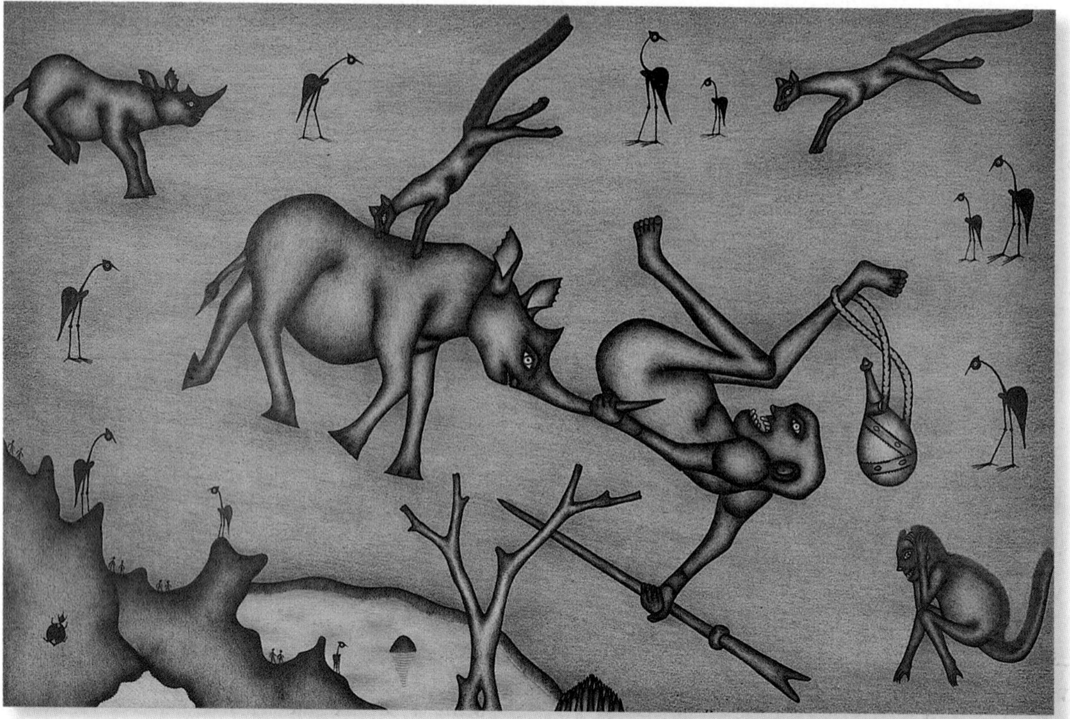

Untitled, 1997. Kivuthi MBuno (Kenya). Crayons and colors on jerrycan. Collection of the artist.

Viewing the art: Describe the qualities of the paintings in this story that remind you of a folktale or a fairy tale. In what ways do you see these qualities in the story?

"Aha, I've got it!" and immediately fell into a deep sleep, filling the cave with his heavy snores.

That day Tselane recounted her experiences to her mother, who again tried to persuade her to leave the dangerous valley. Tselane refused once more, so her mother left her with a heavy heart and wept all the way home.

Limo woke up in the late afternoon and looked for a hoe among his old implements. He put it into his hunting sack and tried to be very pleasant to his wife. She knew that when he behaved like that and tried to be nice to her he usually had some hidden plan. Next morning he was up early, with the sack over his shoulder and the hoe inside. Some distance from Tselane's hut he lit a great big fire and threw the hoe into it until it was white-hot. Then he snatched it up and swallowed it quickly. The hoe burnt his throat and a great smoke issued from his mouth. His throat was so sore that he could not sing loudly. His voice was now soft and sweet like Tselane's mother's voice.

When he got to her hut he imitated her mother's voice perfectly:

Tselane my child,
Tselane my child,
Open the door, my child,
Open the door, my child;
I've brought you bread to eat,
Tselane, my child.

Tselane, who had pressed her ear against the door to listen, had two hearts. Her good heart told her that it wasn't her mother's voice and her bad heart told her that it was. After she had thought for a while she replied,

Vocabulary

implement (im′ plə mənt) *n.* tool, instrument, or utensil used to carry out tasks

issue (ish′ o͞o) *v.* to come forth; to emerge

"If you are my mother, you will sing to me again."

Limo replied in a soft voice, "Yes, my child, I will sing." Then he licked his ugly lips with his huge red tongue as though he already had his prey in the bag. He sang in an even sweeter and softer voice:

Tselane my child,
Tselane my child,
Open the door, my child,
Open the door, my child;
I've brought you bread to eat,
Tselane, my child.

She pressed her ear closer to the door. She was sure it was her mother's voice; and though she had two hearts and her good heart was beating fast, she replied tenderly:

I hear you my mother,
I hear you my mother.

Then Limo heard her turn the key in the door and prepared to grab hold of her as soon as the door opened. When he felt sure she had unlocked it, he gave it a violent push, knocking down the poor girl inside. When she saw who it was she fainted with fright. He picked her up and put her into his hunting sack, locked the door and went back to his cave.

His timid and kind-hearted wife could always tell when Limo had caught a human being because his face looked even more sour and cruel than usual. He hated to share human flesh with her. So when he got home in the evening he was humorless and moody and spoke harshly to his wife, his red eyes glowering at her like a lion. Cautiously she asked, "What animal have you caught today?"

His reply was harsh and full of meaning: "Nothing, just a lean buck!"

She pretended to be excited and asked him, "And when do we eat it?"

"When I've rested," was the cross reply. He put the wriggling sack into his special room and immediately went to sleep. He had instructed his wife to light the fire in the special room and to boil the water in the huge pot early next morning.

When Limo was sound asleep his wife crept to the sack to find out what was in it. When she put her ear to it she heard the faint sound of a girl's voice saying, "Oh mother, dear mother, come to my rescue; save me from the cruel giant. Oh my mother dear, if my life is saved I shall always obey your wise advice." Tselane then started to sob bitterly, her whole body trembling with sorrow and terror. Limo's wife was touched and moved by the child's bitter weeping, so she opened the sack and let her out. As there was no time to speak, she hurriedly hid the girl in one of the huge unused pots and told her to be very quiet. She then put a heavy lid over it. For the time being Tselane was safe, but Limo's wife did not know how to get her away from the cave, or what she would say if Limo discovered that Tselane had disappeared in the morning. She was very agitated and ran on tiptoe between the special room and Limo's bedroom, wringing her hands and racking her brain for a plan before he woke up. She just couldn't think of anything. Her motherly tears began to flow down her cheeks. She was not sorry for herself. She was worried about what would happen to Tselane when her husband woke up.

When morning was about to break, the wretched woman got up from where she had fallen asleep. Her head was aching and she was trembling with fear. The fire had to be lit and the water boiled for Limo to cook his 'lean buck.' As the cocks began to crow she went to the door of the cave to bring in the logs for the fire. Now near the entrance to the cave was a large tree on which

Vocabulary

glower (glou′ ər) *v.* to look or stare with sullen annoyance or anger were numerous bee hives and wasps' and hornets' nests. Suddenly an idea struck her when she saw the tree, and she exclaimed excitedly, "I have it!"

She ran back with the pile of logs and lit the fire to boil the water. Dawn was rapidly approaching and Limo was turning restlessly on his bed. This made his wife work feverishly to get her plan ready. When the fire had caught, she snatched up the empty sack and ran to the tree. With great skill she raked the sleepy bees and wasps and hornets into the sack with her hands. She then rolled away a big stone at the foot of the tree and also swept the many fat scorpions, with their poisonous stings, into the sack. She tied it as it was and put it back in the place where Limo had left it the night before. She had just put the sack down when she heard him yawn like a roaring lion and lick his lips with relish. While he rubbed his blood-red eyes he yelled at her to put the sack near the boiling pot. When he was ready he went into the special room and bolted the door, closing the holes in the walls with stones to prevent his quarry from escaping. The sun was up. The cattle and sheep were already grazing. Even the young herdboys were out, chanting their hunting songs, their tiny spears poised for action:

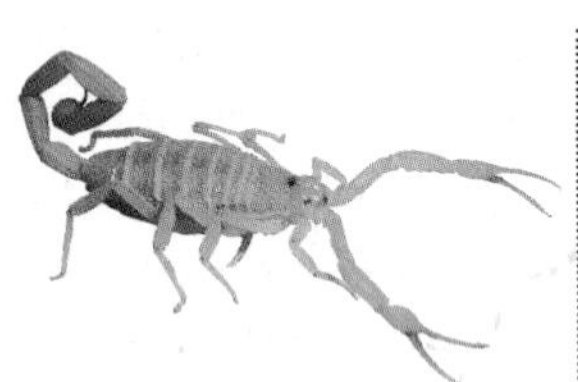

Did You Know?
A *scorpion* is a member of the spider family with an elongated body and a narrow tail with a stinger at the tip.

You're fat field mouse,
You're delicious field mouse.

Tselane's mother, meanwhile, had tossed restlessly the whole night. Her head was full of ugly dreams about snakes and lions. She was outside her daughter's hut at the first streaks of dawn. This was about the same time that Limo woke from his sleep. She began to sing her song with a trembling voice. There was no reply. She repeated the song again and again, each time singing louder and louder, with tears of anguish streaming down her cheeks. But still there was no reply. Then terror-stricken, she beat the door with her hands and with stones, shouting and screaming, "Tselane my child, open the door! Tselane my child, wake up and eat your bread!" And still there was no answer except the hollow echo from the empty hut. In despair she sat on the doorstep with her head in her hands and wept bitterly, for she had seen the big footprints and realized that Limo had taken her only daughter. She sat there for a great while and wept a long, long time.

When Limo was sure the door and the holes in the walls were secure, he lifted the sack onto his back. A scorpion stung him. Thinking that it was Tselane who had bitten him, he put the sack down and scratched his back while he smiled to himself, "Well, the last kicks of a dying animal are always vicious. Kick as much as you like, die you shall die!" He swung the sack onto his back again. This time a bee and a wasp and a hornet stung him and he let the sack fall to the ground with a curse. And he could curse, that man! The stings itched like scabies,[2] forcing him to scratch his back violently as he pranced about the room like a wild horse. His wife had her ear pressed to the door. She did not see his pranks, yet she smiled with satisfaction as she imagined what he was suffering. She thought with pleasure, "Aha,

2. *Scabies* (skā′ bēz) is a disease causing itching sores.

Vocabulary
quarry (kwôr′ ē) *n.* something that is sought or pursued; prey

the one who eats last also enjoys his food!" Had he not always been unkind to her? Well, now he would soon be face to face with his equals.

The last three stings had been particularly painful. Although Limo was a strong and cruel man he was not going to take chances with this girl with the stinging teeth. He approached the sack very carefully. He wanted to open it so that it would be ready for him to dump the contents into the boiling cauldron quickly.

Did You Know?
A *cauldron* is a large round kettle that is usually made of iron and sits on three or four small legs.

The bees, wasps and hornets were buzzing angrily now. Limo thought this buzzing was that of a person weeping. It made him feel braver. He carefully loosened the opening of the sack, ready to tip his 'lean buck' into the pot. But alas, poor fellow, this was not to be! As soon as the sack was open, a buzzing swarm of bees and wasps and hornets flew out and immediately attacked him. He was completely stunned and stood there for a moment wondering what had happened.

Hundreds of scorpions had also crawled out of the fallen sack. Their piercing, poisonous stings roused him from his state of helplessness. The wild creatures had covered his entire body. He tried frantically to scrape them off. Suddenly he realized that his wife had tricked him. He forgot about Tselane and rushed off to find her. But who can think of killing when he is fighting against bees and wasps and hornets and scorpions? His only thought now was to save himself. Because his wife was not cruel she did not mock him. He screamed and hit the door with his fists and butted the walls with his head and kicked them with his large feet. His wife was busy all this time trying to think of how to save Tselane. Limo fought so furiously that the door soon flew open and he dashed out, howling with pain. The bees and wasps and hornets flew out after their victim.

The deadly scorpions had not been idle either. Near the cave there was a deep sunken lake. As he ran towards it, the distance between him and the bees and wasps increased. But once you have disturbed a hornets' nest you have to face the results. Although he moved much faster than they did and his running feet stirred up a cloud of dust behind him, still they followed. When he plunged into the water the mad bees and wasps caught up with him again. He was forced to put his head under the water to escape the dreadful stings. His screams and howls filled the whole valley. Tselane's mother heard his drowning cries from the hut where she was still sitting weeping. That is how the cruel, bad giant died.

When Limo's wife was absolutely certain that he was dead, she took the heavy lid off the pot and let Tselane out. Tselane fell on her knees sobbing and thanked Limo's wife and asked her to go to the hut with her. The poor woman, who had always wanted to lead a good life, went with Tselane. They found Tselane's sad mother at the hut. When she saw her daughter she wept again—this time with joy. After Limo's wife had told the story of her husband's death, they all went off to find their old friends to tell them the good news.

There was much rejoicing and many people returned to live in the valley. They invited Limo's wife to live with them. Ever since, Lekhalong La 'Mantsopa has been a happy, safe and prosperous place.

And that is the end of the story!

Responding to Literature

Personal Response

How did you react to the death of Limo the giant? Share your response with a classmate.

Analyzing Literature

Recall

1. How is Limo described in the tale?
2. Why do people decide to move away from the valley?
3. What is the arrangement that Tselane makes with her mother that allows her to stay?
4. How does Limo get Tselane to let him inside her hut?
5. How does Limo's wife help Tselane?

Interpret

6. What details suggest the degree of fear that Limo inspires in the residents of the valley?
7. How is Limo's behavior changed by the departure of the residents of the valley?
8. **Folktales** often suggest the values that are important to a people or a community (see **Literary Terms Handbook,** page R5). What values does Tselane represent?
9. When Limo sings to Tselane, she is described as having "two hearts." How do you interpret this phrase?
10. What do you think are the reasons that motivate Limo's wife to help Tselane?

Evaluate and Connect

11. In the Reading Focus on page 42, you were asked to discuss how giants are portrayed in myths and legends. Is the portrayal of Limo typical? Why or why not?
12. What role does trickery play in "Tselane and the Giant"?
13. **Conflict** is a struggle between two opposing forces in the plot of a story (see **Literary Terms Handbook,** page R2). Describe two conflicts in "Tselane and the Giant."
14. What contemporary social issue does the story remind you of?
15. Why do you think stories about giants have developed in so many different cultures?

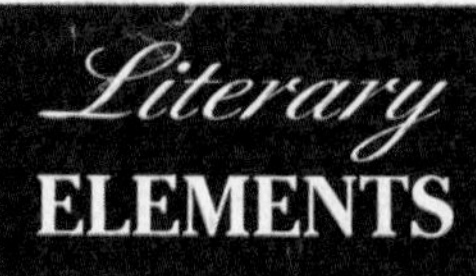

Setting

Setting is the time and place in which the events of a literary work occur. The elements of setting may include geographical location, historical period, season of the year, time of day, and the beliefs and customs of a society. Setting can help establish the mood of a story. It can also influence the way characters think and behave. For example, young lovers who wish to get married may be less concerned about their parents' approval in a contemporary story than in a story set during the Middle Ages. Some stories are closely tied to a particular setting. In other stories the setting plays a less important role; the story remains the same even if the setting changes.

1. What is the setting of "Tselane and the Giant"?
2. What role does the setting play in this story?

- See **Literary Terms Handbook,** p. R11.

Literature and Writing

Writing About Literature

Analyzing Plot An important literary element in folktales is the **plot** (see page R9). Write an analysis of the plot of "Tselane and the Giant." Discuss which events are part of the story's exposition, rising action, climax, and falling action. Do you think the plot is organized effectively? Explain.

Creative Writing

A Wife's Burden In "Tselane and the Giant," we are told how Limo's wife responds to his cruelty. With a partner, create an advice column about her situation. One of you will write a letter from the wife describing Limo's behavior. The other will write a response from the columnist.

Extending Your Response

Literature Groups

Extreme Solution The happy ending of "Tselane and the Giant" follows a gruesome death scene. Do you think that the action Limo's wife took against the giant was justified? Could she have saved Tselane any other way? Discuss these questions in your group. When you are finished, share your conclusions with the class.

Interdisciplinary Activity

Art: Gigantic Vision The narrator of "Tselane and the Giant" provides a vivid description of Limo. Create artwork based on this description. You might portray the fearsome giant in a painting, drawing, sculpture, puppet, or collage. Show your finished artwork to the class and explain which details from the story inspired it.

Learning for Life

News Report In a small group, create a television news report about Limo's drowning. The reporter should begin by explaining the facts he or she has uncovered. Then show interviews with people who witnessed the incident and valley residents who can offer opinions about Limo. Have a news anchor ask the reporter follow-up questions. Videotape the report or present it "live" to the class.

Reading Further

You might wish to read the following stories:

"A Sunrise on the Veld," by Doris Lessing and "Johannesburg, Johannesburg," by Nathaniel Nakasa from *Stories from Central & Southern Africa,* edited by Paul A. Scanlon.

Save your work for your portfolio.

VOCABULARY • Analogies

Analogies are comparisons based on relationships between words. Some analogies are based on antonyms, words whose meanings are opposite.

sorrow : joy :: pride : humility

To finish an analogy, decide on the relationship of the first two words. Then apply that relationship to the second set of words. *Sorrow* is an antonym of *joy*; *pride* is an antonym of *humility*.

- For more on analogies, see **Communications Skills Handbook,** p. R77.

PRACTICE Choose the pair that best completes each analogy.

1. danger : safety ::
   a. poetry : rhyme
   b. cruelty : hurt
   c. surprise : joy
   d. sorrow : joy
   e. justice : judge

2. friendship : enmity ::
   a. success : wealth
   b. family : worry
   c. autobiography : confessions
   d. fast : slow
   e. dance : rhythm

Before You Read

Swahili Love Poetry

Reading Focus

What phrases and sayings do you associate with romantic love?

Share Ideas Brainstorm with a partner to come up with a list of phrases and sayings.

Setting a Purpose Read the following poems to see what some early Swahili-speaking poets had to say about love.

Building Background

The Swahili Language

Swahili is an African language that has been significantly influenced by Arabic. It contains many Arabic words, including *swahili,* which means "of the coast." The language developed over centuries through contact between Arab traders and Africans. Many people living on the east coast of Africa use Swahili as their mother tongue. For millions of others in East Africa, it is an important second language. Swahili was traditionally written in Arabic script, but most modern writers have adopted the Roman alphabet.

Swahili Poetry

Poetry has flourished among the Swahili since at least the seventeenth century. Newspapers published for Swahili-speaking readers today usually print a page of poetry in each issue. Swahili poets use sophisticated verse forms, with patterns of rhyme that are difficult to reproduce in translation. Perhaps because of the influence of Islamic literature, much Swahili writing is devoted to religious themes. However, the Swahili also write about secular topics such as love and current events, and women have played an important role both in creating and preserving Swahili poetry.

Swahili love poems come in the form of songs, which can either be recited or sung. At weddings and on other festive occasions, groups of musicians perform them with music from a variety of instruments. The songs are composed orally and passed along from generation to generation before being copied down. This process can lead to several variations of the same song. Some love poems are over a century old. Newer poems often incorporate phrases and even whole stanzas from older poems.

Danger Love, 1990. Zephania Tshuma (Zimbabwe). Painted wood, height: 42 cm. The Pigozzi Collection, Geneva.

Swahili Love Poetry

Translated by
Ali Ahmed Jahadhmy

Courtship, 1994. Abdim Dr No (Somalia). Oil on canvas. Private collection.

Sudden Moods

I send you my greetings,
may they reach you where you are,
these are my words,
keep them in your heart.
Love weighs on me,
listen to my word.

My love, you went away from me,
you went back to where you came from.
I remember how it used to be,
your mildness and kindness.
From dusk to dawn I cry,
my heart has nothing to hold on to.
Suddenly you have pulled away from me
the beauty of your shapely body.
When I sleep I dream
of your caresses and smiles.
I am close to regretting
even making friends with you.

I do not feel ashamed
to follow you wherever you are.
Illness tortures me,
the medicine for it is your appearance.
By God, I do not find it hard
to suffer for your sake.

Love Does Not Know Secrets

Love knows no secrets,
when it is hidden it will be discovered.
Love has no choice;
when it seizes a man,
he will confess everything,
everything that was not done.

Love has no pity,
even an old man may be put to shame,
love does not return
to a Thing it desires.
When it pursues a man,
he turns mad.

Love humbles a man,
his body becomes emaciated;
when a friend of ours is humiliated
it is not fair to laugh at him.
A man does not have the stamina
to put love aside.

Love never agrees
to share (a man's attention) with anything;
If you irritate love,
you melt away at once.
Love is a disease,
a malignant incurable disease.

Tears of Love

Tears of love
trickle down my face,
I do not eat enough
and it pleases me not.
My beloved
has deserted me.

She has deserted me,
my darling, comrades!
The forest and the savannah
a sob in my throat.
I am distraught
for I do not see her.

I do not see her,
I do not know where she is,
she gives me sorrow,
and regret.
I sing with all my voice
so that she may know where I am.

Responding to Literature

Personal Response

What statements in these poems made the biggest impression on you? Write your response in your journal.

Analyzing Literature

Recall

1. How has the absence of the loved one affected the speaker of "Sudden Moods"?
2. What hope does the speaker express in "Sudden Moods"?
3. Describe the pattern that "Love Does Not Know Secrets" follows.
4. Whom is the speaker addressing in "Tears of Love"?
5. What reason does the speaker of "Tears of Love" offer for singing the poem?

Interpret

6. Is the speaker of "Sudden Moods" angry with the loved one? Support your answer with evidence from the poem.
7. Do you think that the speaker of "Sudden Moods" would like to forget the beloved? Why or why not?
8. How do you interpret lines 9–10 of "Love Does Not Know Secrets"?
9. Does "Love Does Not Know Secrets" express sympathy for lovers? Explain.
10. How do you interpret lines 9–10 of "Tears of Love"?

Evaluate and Connect

11. Compare and contrast the speakers of "Sudden Moods" and "Love Does Not Know Secrets."
12. In both "Sudden Moods" and "Love Does Not Know Secrets," disease is used as a **metaphor** for love (see page R7). Is it an effective metaphor? What qualities do love and disease have in common?
13. In your opinion, which of these poems presents the most negative view of love? Why?
14. Do you think that these poems could only have come from the Swahili culture? Why or why not?
15. Compared with other love poems, what was most surprising about these? Explain.

Literary Criticism

Commenting on "Love Does Not Know Secrets," scholar Jan Knappert observes that among the Swahili, "love is an evil spirit, a *shetani,* sent by God to tempt us. . . . [A person] of strong character could theoretically resist love and put it down, but only a very few iron minds have that capacity." Is there any evidence in the poem that love is an evil spirit sent by God and, except for a "few iron minds," impossible to resist? Discuss your answer with a small group.

Literary ELEMENTS

Speaker

The **speaker** of a poem is the voice that talks to the reader or to the person whom the poem addresses. In some poems, the speaker is a disembodied voice. In other poems, the speaker has a distinct identity, like a character in a story. One should never assume that the speaker and the poet are identical. The speaker may differ from the poet in age, race, or gender, or may express emotions and beliefs that the poet does not share. For example, an old poet who is happily married may use a young, anguished speaker in a love poem simply to follow the conventions of love poetry.

1. In which of the Swahili love poems is the speaker a disembodied voice?
2. In which of the poems does the speaker have a distinct identity? What do you know about this speaker?

- See **Literary Terms Handbook,** p. R11.

Literature and Writing

Writing About Literature

Comparing and Contrasting Compare and contrast one of the Swahili poems with a love poem from another historical period or region of the world. You might focus on literary elements such as imagery, rhythm, and figurative language, or on the thoughts about love expressed.

Creative Writing

Poem Write a brief poem in response to one of the Swahili poems. Decide whether you want to express your personal reaction or create a fictional speaker. Include some of the phrases you wrote for the Reading Focus on page 52.

Extending Your Response

Literature Groups

Romance Reconsidered All three poems describe the anguish that can result from love. Do you think the Swahili poets wanted to warn people against falling in love? Is the anguish they describe part of what makes love a powerful emotion? Discuss these questions in your group. Then share your conclusions with the class.

Interdisciplinary Activity

Music: Love Lyrics Which popular songs do these Swahili love poems remind you of? With a partner, make a list of songs that express similar feelings. Bring in a recording of a song to play for the class. Explain what it has in common with one of the Swahili poems.

Performing

Reading Aloud In a small group, perform a round-robin reading of the three Swahili poems. Before you begin, decide which stanzas or passages each student should read. Think about how you can use your voice and gestures to give the reading greater emotional impact.

Reading Further

If you liked these poems, you might enjoy the following: "Silence Makes Mighty Noise" by Muyaka bin Haji al-Ghassaniy and "Love Is Sweetness, Elated" by Kaluta Amri Abedi, from *Searching for My Brother: Poems from the Kiswahili,* translated by Jan Feidel and Ibrahim Noor Shariff.

Save your work for your portfolio.

VOCABULARY • Analogies

Analogies are comparisons based on relationships between words and ideas. Some analogies are based on degree of intensity.

respond : retort :: avoid : shun

To finish an analogy, decide on the relationship of the first two words. Then apply that relationship to the second set.

- For more on analogies, see **Communications Skills Handbook,** p. R77.

PRACTICE Choose the pair that best completes each analogy.

1. annoyance : anger ::
   a. cry : tears
   b. work : toil
   c. touch : texture
   d. toll : fee
   e. unhappiness : glee
2. arrogance : self-assurance ::
   a. love : hate
   b. sorrow : hatred
   c. benefit : advantage
   d. recklessness : courage
   e. disgust : disdain

MEDIA connection

Web Site

Why might Swahili speakers use words such as *baiskeli* for "bicycle," *mashine* for "machine," and *penseli* for "pencil"? Look for the answers to these and all of your questions about this language at the Web site below.

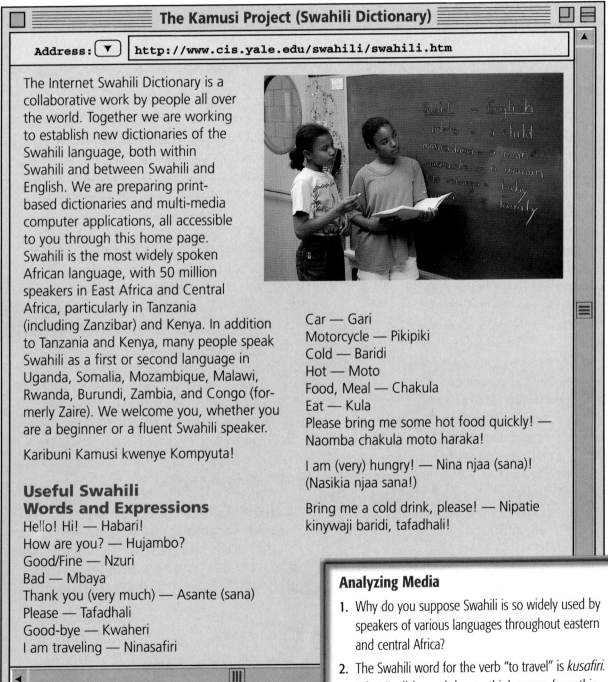

The Kamusi Project (Swahili Dictionary)

Address: http://www.cis.yale.edu/swahili/swahili.htm

The Internet Swahili Dictionary is a collaborative work by people all over the world. Together we are working to establish new dictionaries of the Swahili language, both within Swahili and between Swahili and English. We are preparing print-based dictionaries and multi-media computer applications, all accessible to you through this home page. Swahili is the most widely spoken African language, with 50 million speakers in East Africa and Central Africa, particularly in Tanzania (including Zanzibar) and Kenya. In addition to Tanzania and Kenya, many people speak Swahili as a first or second language in Uganda, Somalia, Mozambique, Malawi, Rwanda, Burundi, Zambia, and Congo (formerly Zaire). We welcome you, whether you are a beginner or a fluent Swahili speaker.

Karibuni Kamusi kwenye Kompyuta!

Useful Swahili Words and Expressions

Hello! Hi! — Habari!
How are you? — Hujambo?
Good/Fine — Nzuri
Bad — Mbaya
Thank you (very much) — Asante (sana)
Please — Tafadhali
Good-bye — Kwaheri
I am traveling — Ninasafiri
Car — Gari
Motorcycle — Pikipiki
Cold — Baridi
Hot — Moto
Food, Meal — Chakula
Eat — Kula
Please bring me some hot food quickly! — Naomba chakula moto haraka!

I am (very) hungry! — Nina njaa (sana)! (Nasikia njaa sana!)

Bring me a cold drink, please! — Nipatie kinywaji baridi, tafadhali!

Analyzing Media

1. Why do you suppose Swahili is so widely used by speakers of various languages throughout eastern and central Africa?
2. The Swahili word for the verb "to travel" is *kusafiri.* What English word do you think comes from this verb? (Hint: *ku* is a prefix.)

Before You Read

Anansi's Fishing Expedition

Reading Focus

Baseball fans cheer when one of the players on their team steals a base. What other forms of trickery are commonly admired? What forms of trickery do people generally disapprove of?

Share Ideas Discuss your response in a small group.

Setting a Purpose Read this story for an amusing look at trickery.

Building Background

The Ashanti

"Anansi's Fishing Expedition" is set in an Ashanti village. The Ashanti are a West African people who live in central Ghana and neighboring areas of Togo and the Ivory Coast. Most of them are farmers, although they are also known for their fine carvings and goldwork. Their traditional religion involves the worship of ancestor spirits and a supreme god named Nyame as well as minor deities. Over the centuries, the Ashanti have developed a rich body of folklore.

During the seventeenth and eighteenth centuries, the Ashanti united their villages into a powerful state led by a paramount chief, or supreme ruler. His throne, the Golden Stool, became a sacred symbol of Ashanti unity. At a time when women in most other parts of the world were excluded from the political process, Ashanti noblewomen played a role in choosing leaders. The Ashanti trace their ancestry through the mother's side of the family.

Asante Goldweight. 18th–19th century, Ghana.

Tricky Tales

Every folklore tradition has its own trickster figures. Some of them are human, such as the clever rabbis in Jewish tales and the Mexican trickster Quevedo, who is based on legends about a seventeenth-century Spanish poet. Other tricksters come in animal form. Tricksters may be portrayed as heroes, fools, or cunning predators, but they all share a disregard for accepted standards of behavior. Why are they so popular? Scholars have offered various explanations. Tricksters often expose our illusions about life. They also remind us of the rules that allow people to live together in peace. But most important, trickster tales are a lot of fun.

One of the more famous tricksters is Anansi, who appears in many West African tales. During the years of the slave trade, he migrated to the Caribbean and North America, where he became known as Anancy or Nancy. Brer Rabbit, a trickster in African American folklore, may have also originated from an African trickster.

Reading Further

You might enjoy reading the following stories: "The Tale of the Enchanted Yam," "The Wise Man Takes a Wise Wife," and "Why Hippo Wears No Coat" from *West African Folktales,* translated by Jack Berry.

Vocabulary Preview

hack (hak) *v.* to use heavy blows to cut or chop in an irregular or unskillful manner; p. 60

hoist (hoist) *v.* to raise or pull up; p. 60

indignantly (in dig′ nənt lē) *adv.* quality of being filled with a dignified anger; aroused by unfair or mean actions or comments; p. 61

Anansi's Fishing Expedition

Translated by Harold Courlander and George Herzog

IN THE COUNTRY OF ASHANTI, not far from the edge of the great West African forest, there was a man named Anansi, who was known to all the people for miles around. Anansi was not a great hunter, or a great worker, or a great warrior. His specialty was being clever. He liked to outwit people. He liked to live well, and to have other people do things for him. But because all the people of the country knew about Anansi and had had trouble with him he had to keep thinking of new ways to get something for nothing.

One day Anansi was sitting in the village when a man named Osansa came along.

The Niger River at sunset.

"I have an idea," Anansi said. "Why don't we go and set fish traps together? Then we shall sell the fish and be quite rich."

But Osansa knew Anansi's reputation very well, and so he said:

"No, I have as much food as I can eat or sell. I am rich enough. Why don't you set your fish traps by yourself?"

"Ha! Fish alone? Then I'd have to do all the work!" Anansi said. "What I need is a fool for a partner."

Osansa went away, and after a while another man named Anene came along.

"I have an idea," Anansi said. "Why don't the two of us go and set fish traps together? Then we shall sell the fish and be quite rich."

Anene knew Anansi very well too, but he seemed to listen thoughtfully.

"That sounds like a fine idea," he said. "Two people can catch more fish than one. Yes, I'll do it."

The news went rapidly around the village that Anansi and Anene were going on a fishing expedition together. Osansa met Anene in the market and said:

"We hear you are going to trap fish with Anansi. Don't you know he is trying to make a fool of you? He has told everyone that he needs a fool to go fishing with him. He wants someone to set the fish traps and do all the work, while he gets all the money for the fish."

"Don't worry, friend Osansa, I won't be Anansi's fool," Anene said.

Early the next morning Anansi and Anene went into the woods to cut palm branches to make their fish traps.

Anansi was busy thinking how he could make Anene do most of the work. But when they came to the place where the palm trees grew, Anene said to Anansi:

"Give me the knife, Anansi. I shall cut the branches for the traps. We are partners. We share everything. My part of the work will be to cut branches, your part of the work will be to get tired for me."

"Just a minute, let me think," Anansi said. "Why should I be the one to get tired?"

"Well, when there's work to be done someone must get tired," Anene said. "That's the way it is. So if I cut the branches the least you can do is to get tired for me."

"Hah, you take me for a fool?" Anansi said. "Give me the knife. I shall cut the branches and *you* get tired for *me!*"

So Anansi took the knife and began cutting the branches from the trees. Every time he chopped, Anene grunted. Anene sat down in the shade and groaned from weariness, while Anansi chopped and hacked and sweated. Finally the wood for the fish traps was cut. Anansi tied it up into a big bundle. Anene got up from the ground holding his back and moaning.

"Anansi, let me carry the bundle of wood now, and you can get tired for me," Anene said.

"Oh, no, my friend Anene," Anansi said, "I am not that simple-minded. I'll carry the wood myself, and you can take the weariness for me."

So he hoisted the bundle to the top of his head and the two of them started back to the village. Anene groaned all the way.

"Oh, oh!" he moaned. "Take it easy, Anansi! Oh, oh!"

When they came to the village Anene said:

"Let me make the fish traps, Anansi, and you just sit down and get tired for me."

"Oh, no," Anansi said. "You just keep on as you are." And he made the fish traps while

Vocabulary

hack (hak) *v.* to use heavy blows to cut or chop in an irregular or unskillful manner

hoist (hoist) *v.* to raise or pull up

Anene lay on his back in the shade with his eyes closed, moaning and groaning.

And while he was making the traps, working in the heat with perspiration running down his face and chest, Anansi looked at Anene lying there taking all his weariness and sore muscles for him, and he shook his head and clucked his tongue.

"Anene thinks he is intelligent," he said to himself. "Yet look at him moaning and groaning there, practically dying from weariness!"

When the fish traps were done Anene climbed to his feet and said, "Anansi, my friend, now let me carry the fish traps to the water, and you can get tired for me."

"Oh, no," Anansi said. "You just come along and do your share. I'll do the carrying, you do the getting-tired."

So they went down to the water, Anansi carrying and Anene moaning. When they arrived, Anene said to Anansi:

"Now wait a minute, Anansi, we ought to think things over here. There are sharks in this water. Someone is apt to get hurt. So let me go in and set the traps, and should a shark bite me, then you can die for me."

"Wah!" Anansi howled. "Listen to that! What do you take me for? I'll go in the water and set the traps myself, and if I am bitten, then *you* can die for *me!*" So he took the fish traps out into the water and set them, and then the two of them went back to the village.

The next morning when they went down to inspect the traps they found just four fish. Anene spoke first.

"Anansi, there are only four fish here. You take them. Tomorrow there will probably be more, and then I'll take my turn."

"Now, what do you take me for?" Anansi said indignantly. "Do you think I am simple-minded?

Kukujumuku, 1992. John Goba (Sierra Leone). Painted wood and porcupine quills, height: 130 cm. The Pigozzi Collection, Geneva.

Viewing the sculpture: **How could the form of this sculpture suggest Anene's manipulation of Anansi in the story?**

Oh, no, Anene, you take the four fish and I'll take my turn tomorrow."

So Anene took the four fish and carried them to town and sold them.

Next day when they came down to the fish traps, Anene said:

"Look, there are only eight fish here. I'm glad it's your turn, because tomorrow there doubtless will be more."

"Just a minute," Anansi said. "You want me to take today's fish so that tomorrow you get a

Vocabulary

indignantly (in dig′ nənt lē) *adv.* **with dignified anger; aroused by unfair actions or comments**

bigger catch? Oh no, these are all yours, partner, tomorrow I'll take my share."

So Anene took the eight fish and carried them to town and sold them.

Next day when they came to look in the traps they found sixteen fish.

"Anansi," Anene said, "take the sixteen fish. Little ones, too. I'll take my turn tomorrow."

"Of course you'll take your turn tomorrow, it's my turn today," Anansi said. He stopped to think. "Well, now, you are trying to make a fool out of me again! You want me to take these sixteen miserable little fish so that you can get the big catch tomorrow, don't you? Well, it's a good thing I'm alert! You take the sixteen today and I'll take the big catch tomorrow!"

So Anene carried the sixteen fish to the market and sold them.

Next day they came to the traps and took the fish out. But by this time the traps had rotted in the water.

"Well, it's certainly your turn today," Anene said. "And I'm very glad of that. Look, the fish traps are rotten and worn out. We can't use them any more. I'll tell you what—you take the fish to town and sell them, and I'll take the rotten fish traps and sell them. The fish traps will bring an excellent price. What a wonderful idea!"

"Hm," Anansi said. "Just a moment, don't be in such a hurry. I'll take the fish traps and sell them myself. If there's such a good price to be had, why shouldn't I get it instead of you? Oh, no, *you* take the fish, my friend."

Anansi hoisted the rotten fish traps up on his head and started off for town. Anene followed him, carrying the fish. When they arrived in the town Anene sold his fish in the market, while Anansi walked back and forth singing loudly:

"I am selling rotten fish traps! I am selling wonderful rotten fish traps!"

But no one wanted rotten fish traps, and the townspeople were angry that Anansi thought they were so stupid they would buy them. All day long Anansi wandered through the town singing:

"Get your rotten fish traps here! I am selling wonderful rotten fish traps!"

Finally the head man of the town heard about the affair. He too became very angry, and he sent messengers for Anansi. When they brought Anansi to him he asked indignantly:

"What do you think you are doing, anyway? What kind of nonsense is this you are trying to put over the people of the town?"

"I'm selling rotten fish traps," Anansi said, "very excellent rotten fish traps."

"Now what do you take us for?" the chief of the town said. "Do you think we are ignorant people? Your friend Anene came and sold good fish, which the people want, but you come trying to sell something that isn't good for anything and just smell the town up with your rotten fish traps. It's an outrage. You insult us."

The head man turned to the townspeople who stood near by, listening.

"Take him away and whip him," he said.

The men took Anansi out to the town gate and beat him with sticks. Anansi shouted and yelled and made a great noise. When at last they turned him loose, Anene said to him:

"Anansi, this ought to be a lesson to you. You wanted a fool to go fishing with you, but you didn't have to look so hard to find one. You were a fool yourself."

Anansi nodded his head.

"Yes," he said thoughtfully, rubbing his back and his legs where they had beat him. And he looked reproachfully at Anene. "But what kind of partner are you? At least you could have taken the pain while I took the beating."

Responding to Literature

Personal Response

What went through your mind as you finished reading this story? Jot down your thoughts in your journal.

Analyzing Literature

Recall and Interpret

1. Why does Anansi want someone to set fish traps with him? What adjectives would you use to describe Anansi?
2. How do people in the village respond to Anansi's proposal? Do they agree or disagree about Anansi?
3. What suggestion does Anene make about dividing up the work? Why does Anansi respond as he does?
4. What offer does Anene make about the fish they catch? Why does Anansi keep refusing Anene's offer?
5. What happens when Anansi tries to sell rotten fish traps in town? Why do the townspeople react this way?

Evaluate and Connect

6. Do you think Anansi has learned his lesson by the end of the story? Why or why not?
7. **Irony** is a contrast between what is expected and what actually exists or occurs. Describe an example of irony in this tale.
8. What strategy does Anene use to make a fool out of Anansi?
9. According to your response to the Reading Focus on page 58, how would you classify Anansi's trickery? Explain.
10. What characters in literature or the movies does Anansi remind you of? What qualities do they have in common?

Literary ELEMENTS

Humor

The main purpose of **humor** is to entertain people, although it can also be an important tool of persuasion. There are three basic types of humor. **Humor of situation** develops from the plot of a literary work, which may contain exaggerated or unexpected events. **Humor of character** uses exaggerated personalities to make us laugh at the flaws of human nature. **Humor of language** may include wordplay, verbal irony, exaggeration, or sarcasm.

1. Which of the three basic types of humor appear in "Anansi's Fishing Expedition"?
2. Which passage or event in the tale did you find the most humorous? Why?

- See **Literary Terms Handbook,** p. R6.

Extending Your Response

Creative Writing

Modern Trickery Imagine that Anansi came to your community. Write an advertisement in which he announces a great business opportunity for someone who is willing to be his partner. Read your advertisement aloud to a small group and explain how Anansi would try to take advantage of people who respond to it.

Listening and Speaking

The Anansi Verdict Role-play a trial to see whether Anansi should be banished from the village for his deceptive practices. First decide which students will be the judge, defense lawyer, prosecutor, defendant, witnesses, and jury members. The jury should consider whether Anansi serves any beneficial role that might balance the harm he does to his victims.

Save your work for your portfolio.

NIGERIA, Traditional

Before You Read

Edju and the Two Friends

Reading Focus

Think of a time when you quarreled with a friend.

Quickwrite What led to the quarrel? Was one person responsible, or did it result from a misunderstanding? Jot down your thoughts in your journal.

Setting a Purpose Read the following tale to see how a trickster interferes with a close friendship.

Building Background

Edju the Trickster-God

Edju (also spelled Eshu) is one of the most important gods of the Yoruba people of Nigeria. Religious officials take good care of his shrines, and communities honor him with annual festivals that last seventeen days. At first glance he hardly seems to deserve such respect. Edju stirs up all kinds of trouble. He tricks his victims into offending other gods and then helps the gods take their vengeance. Sometimes he even kills people by crushing them under walls or trees. Neither gods nor humans are safe from his antics. Yet the Yoruba see Edju as both a creative and destructive force. He is like a devastating storm that leads people to build stronger homes. By creating chaos, Edju makes it possible for society to renew itself.

Yoruba bowl.

The Yoruba call on Edju to carry messages and sacrifices to the gods. Artists often portray him in motion to suggest his restless energy. He walks around with a pipe, a whistle, or a thumb in his mouth. Sometimes he appears as an ugly old man, sometimes as a beautiful child. His symbolic color is black. At festivals, dancers whirl around to express his playful, defiant nature.

Yoruba Society and Religion

The Yoruba people live mainly in the southwestern part of Nigeria. In the past they formed many independent kingdoms consisting of a town or city surrounded by farmland. Traditionally, women control the marketplaces, while men work as farmers, craftsmen, or traders. Yoruba craftsmen are among the most skilled in Africa.

Some Yoruba have become Christians or Muslims. Others practice the traditional Yoruba religion, which includes about four hundred gods and spirits and a supreme creator named Olorun. Like the gods of Greek mythology, Yoruba gods are deeply involved in the affairs of humans. They behave much like humans, making mistakes and sometimes acting unjustly.

Reading Further

If you like this folktale, you might enjoy the following:

Trickster Tales: Forty Folk Stories from Around the World, edited by Josepha Sherman.

The African Mask, by Janet E. Rupert.

Vocabulary Preview

nape (nāp) *n.* the back of the neck; p. 66

toil (toil) *n.* fatiguing work or effort; p. 66

retort (ri tort′) *v.* to reply in kind, especially with anger or with a witty or insulting response; p. 66

assailant (ə sā′ lənt) *n.* attacker; p. 66

dissension (di sen′ shən) *n.* disagreement; discord; p. 66

Edju and the Two Friends

Translated by Paul Radin

Ayo, 1990. Agbagli Kossi (Togo). Painted wood, height: 107 cm. The Pigozzi Collection, Geneva.

ONCE UPON A TIME, Olorun[1] first created Enja, or mortal man, and, after that, Edju, the god. Once there were a pair of friends. When they went out they were always dressed alike. Everyone said, "These two men are the best of friends." Edju saw them and said, "These men are very dear to each other. I will make them differ and that will be a fine beginning for a very big Idja [lawsuit]." The fields of these friends adjoined. A path ran between and separated them. Edju used to walk on it of a morning and then wore a "filla" or black cap.

1. **According to Yoruba belief, *Olorun* is the original and supreme sky god who created hundreds of other lesser gods.**

Now, when Edju wanted to start this quarrel, he made himself a cap of green, black, red, and white cloth, which showed a different color from whatever side it was looked at. He put it on one morning on his walk abroad. Then he took his tobacco pipe and put it, not, as usual, in his mouth, but at the nape of his neck, as if he were smoking at the back of his head. And then he took his staff as usual, but, this time, carried it upside down, that is to say, so that it hung, not over his breast in front, but over his shoulder behind. Both the friends were at work in their fields. They looked up for a second. Edju called out, "Good morning!" They gave him the same and went on with their toil.

Then they went home together. One said to the other, "The old man (Edju) went the opposite road through the fields today. I noticed that by his pipe and his stick." The other said, "You're wrong. He went the same way as usual, I saw it by the way his feet were going." The first said, "It's a lie; I saw his pipe and his staff much too plainly; and, besides, he had on a white instead of a black cap." The second one retorted, "You must be blind or asleep; his cap was red." His friend said, "Then you must already have had some palm-wine this morning, if you could see neither the color of his cap, nor the way he was walking." The other one answered him, "I haven't even seen a drop this morning, but you must be crazed." The other man said, "You are making up lies to annoy me." Then the other one said, "Liar yourself! And not for the first time by a good deal." One of them drew his knife and went for the other who got a wound. He also drew his knife and cut his assailant. They both ran away bleeding to the town. The folk saw them and said, "Both these friends have been attacked. There will be war." One of them said, "No, this liar is no friend of mine." And the other one, "Don't believe a single word of his. When he opens his mouth, the lies swarm from it."

Meanwhile, Edju had gone to the King of the town. He said to the King, "Just ask the two friends what is the matter with them! They have cut each other's heads about with knives and are bleeding!" The King said, "What, the two friends, who always wear clothes alike have been quarreling? Let them be summoned!" So it was done. The King asked them, "You are both in sad case. What made you fall out?" They both said, "We could not agree as to what it was that went through our fields this morning." Then the King asked, "How many people went along your footpath?" "It was a man who goes the same way every day. Today he went in another direction, wearing a white cap instead of a black one," said one of the friends. "He lies," shouted the other; "the old man had on a red cap and walked along in the usual direction!" Then the King asked, "Who knows this old man?" Edju said, "It is I. These two fellows quarreled because I so willed it." Edju pulled out his cap and said, "I put on this cap, red on one side, white on the other, green in front, and black behind. I stuck my pipe in my nape. So my steps went one way while I was looking another. The two friends couldn't help quarreling. I made them do it. Sowing dissension is my chief delight."

Vocabulary

nape (nāp) *n.* the back of the neck
toil (toil) *n.* fatiguing work or effort
retort (ri tort′) *v.* to reply in kind, especially with anger or with a witty or insulting response
assailant (ə sā′ lənt) *n.* attacker
dissension (di sen′ shən) *n.* disagreement or discord

Responding to Literature

Personal Response

Did you find this story humorous? Explain why or why not to a classmate.

Analyzing Literature

Recall and Interpret

1. What does Edju decide to do to the two friends? Why does he choose them as his victims?
2. What routine has Edju followed up until now? How and why does he alter this routine?
3. What happens when Edju walks past the friends? How does Edju's behavior set off a chain of events?
4. What suggestion does Edju make to the king? Why do you think he makes this suggestion?

Evaluate and Connect

5. What do you predict will happen to Edju after his confession?
6. In your opinion, does the tale portray Edju as evil or merely mischievous? Use evidence from the tale to support your answer.
7. Do you think that the two farmers really were good friends before the quarrel, or was their friendship superficial? Explain.
8. Think of your response to the Reading Focus on page 64. How was your quarrel like that of the two friends in the story?

Literary Criticism

Robert D. Pelton writes that the two friends "are bound by habit. It is the past that holds them, not the present. Finally, their quarrel reveals all sorts of suppressed animosity. . . . The friendship was held together by custom, not by mutual awareness. . . . Thus Edju has only to draw attention to the real boundary between them to shatter their false peace." In a brief paragraph, discuss Pelton's ideas, citing details from the tale for support.

Literary ELEMENTS

Dramatic Irony

Irony is a conflict between reality and appearance or expectations. **Dramatic irony** occurs when the reader or audience knows something that a character does not know. Writers sometimes use this technique for comic effect, encouraging us to laugh at a character's mistakes. Dramatic irony can also generate suspense about when the character will find out the truth.

1. What is the dramatic irony of "Edju and the Two Friends"?
2. Do you think that this dramatic irony is used for comic effect, to create suspense, or for some other purpose? Explain.

- See **Literary Terms Handbook,** p. R6.

Extending Your Response

Personal Writing

Excuses, Excuses The Yoruba traditionally blame Edju when they experience trouble in their lives. When you have a problem, do you ever blame some force that is beyond your control? Why do you think people find comfort in such explanations? Write one or two paragraphs in response to these questions.

Performing

Puppet Theater With a small group, perform a puppet show based on "Edju and the Two Friends." First write a script and create a puppet for each of the characters. Make sure that your Edju puppet fits the description of him in the tale. You might invite students from other classes to watch your performance.

Save your work for your portfolio.

Word Processing: Using Advanced Features

Today's word processing software makes it easy to correct mistakes and add, replace, or move words, sentences, or entire paragraphs. However, these programs can do much more. They help in all stages of the writing process–prewriting, drafting, revising, editing, presenting–even allowing you to print out a publication-quality document. Following are a few features that can help you in the writing process.

Multi-Windows

Most word processing programs allow users to work with more than one window open at a time. If you have a separate document for your prewriting notes, you can keep it open while you're writing the first draft.

1. Open your notes document and adjust the size of that document's window so that it fills only half of your monitor's screen.
2. Next, open a second document for your draft and adjust its window so that it fits the other half of the screen.

With both documents open, you can consult your notes as you draft. You can even cut and paste words and phrases from your notes into your draft.

Technology Tip

Save your work often. One inescapable fact about working with a computer is that some day–when you least expect it–your computer will crash. It happens to everyone sooner or later. A crash, a brief power surge, or a kicked power cord can erase hours of your work unless you have saved recently.

Tracking Revisions

Good writing is a matter of revising until you are satisfied. You may find it convenient to keep track of the revisions you have made. Some word processing programs allow you to do so. Use your Help option or check with your teacher or lab instructor to find out if you have this feature and, if so, whether it works any differently from the following procedure.

1. After you have finished a first draft, and with the document open, pull down the **Tools** menu to **Track Changes.** Select **Highlight Changes** in the submenu that appears.
2. A dialogue box will pop up. (A dialogue box is a small window that usually asks you to make choices by clicking on buttons or typing into text boxes.) Click in the boxes labeled **Track changes while editing** and **Highlight changes on screen.** A checkmark will appear in each box.
3. Close the dialogue box and return to your document. From this point on, the computer will mark and highlight any changes made in your draft document. Words you delete will have lines through them. Words you add will be underlined.
4. When you have finished editing your document, pull down the **Tools** menu to **Track Changes** again. This time, select **Accept or Reject Changes** from the submenu. A new dialogue box will appear, giving you the choice of accepting all the changes, rejecting all the changes, or looking at your changes one at a time for acceptance or rejection.

Tracking revisions is also useful in the peer-review step of the writing process. You can see the revisions your reviewer has suggested, evaluate them, and choose either to accept or reject them.

EXAMPLE OF TRACK-CHANGES FEATURE

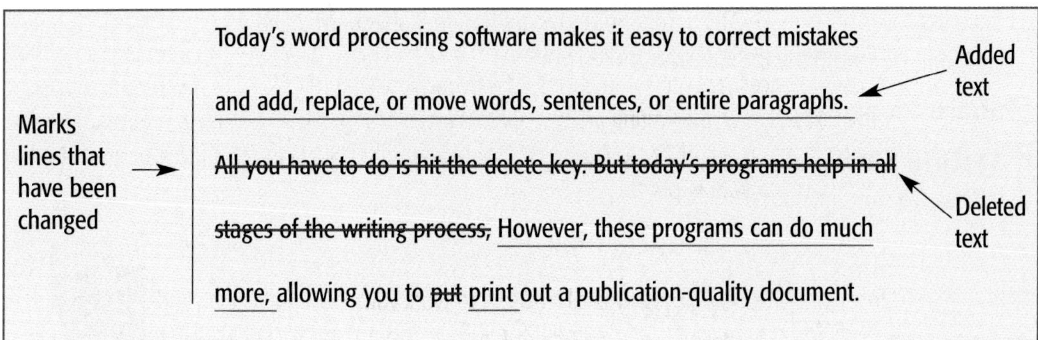
Today's word processing software makes it easy to correct mistakes
and add, replace, or move words, sentences, or entire paragraphs.
All you have to do is hit the delete key. But today's programs help in all
stages of the writing process, However, these programs can do much
more, allowing you to put print out a publication-quality document.
Marks lines that have been changed
Added text
Deleted text

Styles

Your word processing software offers style features you can use to make your final paper attractive. Experiment with styles to see what they look like. Start with an existing document, such as an old report that you have on an electronic file.

1. Pull down the **Format** menu to **Style Gallery.** A menu of available styles will appear. You may also see a reduced image of your current document. The styles available will include such types as letter, memo, report, and résumé. Each type may also be available in different styles–for example, professional, elegant, and contemporary.
2. Select one of the styles for a report and click **OK.** Your document will change to that style, with new fonts (typefaces) for the basic text and the various headings you may have in your document. Try some of the other styles to see how they affect your document's appearance. Be sure to use a typeface and size that is easily readable and that is appropriate for the document you are creating.
3. You don't have to stop there. Suppose, for example, you don't like the style and size of the title. Simply select it and use the font and font size windows on the format toolbar to change it. You can change any aspect of the program's set style to suit your own preferences.

TECHNOLOGY TIP

Back up your files regularly. Keep a second copy of every important document somewhere other than on the computer's hard drive–a floppy disk will do. Be sure to update this back-up copy whenever you change the document. Then, if you have a problem with your hard drive, you'll still have a current copy of your work.

ACTIVITIES

1. Use the features described in this Technology Skills lesson to complete your Writing Workshop assignment.
2. Use the Help feature of your word processing software as you experiment with other advanced features in your menus. In your journal or learning log, keep a list of the new skills you master.

Before You Read

The Story of the Dress that Sang

Reading Focus

Have you ever been tricked by someone? How did you feel afterwards? Did you try to get even with the person who tricked you?

Share Ideas Discuss your experience with the class.

Setting a Purpose Read this story to see how the victim of a trickster gets his revenge.

Building Background

The Original Spiderman

Anansi is the most prominent trickster figure of the Ashanti people of West Africa. He is constantly trying to outwit people, animals, and even gods. All stories are supposedly owned by Anansi, who used trickery to obtain them from Nyame, the supreme Ashanti deity.

Most tales portray Anansi as greedy and amoral, although he is sometimes admired for his victories over much stronger opponents. Despite his cunning, he often fails to achieve his goals and winds up being punished. Thus his great cleverness is shown to be a kind of stupidity.

There are many stories that tell how Anansi came to acquire the shape and characteristics of a spider. African storytellers also use Anansi to explain the origin of natural phenomena and various aspects of human life. For example, Anansi is blamed for the greed and debt that plague humanity.

The West African Environment

West Africa, where tales of Anansi and other tricksters are told, can be divided into two main geographical areas. Along the coast, and extending inland for at least a hundred miles, the landscape is dominated by tropical rain forest. To the north is the savanna, a parklike region of short grass and isolated groups of trees. These two environments have produced different cultural and economic patterns.

In the north, where travel is relatively easy and horses can be used for transportation, large kingdoms and empires developed. Although crops could be raised in some areas, herding and trade were the foundations of the economy.

Travel in the forest region is much more difficult. Here single villages often stand on their own as political units, and agriculture is the dominant economic activity. The rain forest soil can support crops for only a few years; then it must renew itself.

These two regions have been interdependent in many ways. Rain forest farmers exchange agricultural produce for goods produced or imported by savanna herders. Traders, bringing goods and news from the outside world, are always welcomed by both groups.

The Messenger, 1991. Agbagli Kossi (Togo). Painted wood, height: 64 cm. The Pigozzi Collection, Geneva.

Vocabulary Preview

compound (kom′ pound) *n.* a fenced or walled-in area containing a group of buildings; p. 71

vex (veks) *v.* to annoy; p. 71

granary (grā′ nər ē) *n.* storehouse; p. 73

Literature and Writing

Writing About Literature

Comparing and Contrasting Write several paragraphs in which you compare and contrast "The Story of the Dress that Sang" with a folktale from another region of the world. Try to find a folktale that is either a trickster tale or an escape tale for your comparison.

Creative Writing

Explaining Animal Characteristics "The Story of the Dress that Sang" explains why spiders seem to avoid being seen by humans. Write a brief tale that explains one characteristic of another animal. For example, you might explain why turtles hide in their shells.

Extending Your Response

Literature Groups

Trickster Mania In many parts of the world, tricksters such as Anansi are the most popular subjects of folktales. In your group, discuss why these deceitful and even dangerous characters are entertaining. Then create a list of contemporary books and movies with characters who resemble Anansi. Share your list with the class.

Interdisciplinary Activity

Art: Cover Illustration Imagine that you have been hired to create a cover illustration for "The Story of the Dress that Sang." Before you start working on your illustration, decide whether you want to portray an event or character in the tale or create an abstract design. Explain to a classmate which passage or element of the tale inspired your artwork.

Learning for Life

Persuasive Memo Write a memo to your school librarian in which you offer your opinion about whether "The Story of the Dress that Sang" should be included in the library collection. Discuss the tale's literary merits and the values that it can teach students. Indicate an age range for which the tale is suitable.

Reading Further

If you enjoyed this story, you might like the following collection:

The Hat-Shaking Dance and Other Ashanti Tales from Ghana, by Harold Courlander and Albert Kofi Prempeh.

Save your work for your portfolio.

VOCABULARY • Analogies

Analogies are comparisons based on relationships between words. Some analogies are based on antonym variants–words not exactly opposites, but whose meanings are opposed.

venture : safe :: tackle : easy

Venture can mean "to attempt something that is not safe," and *tackle* can mean "to attempt something that is not easy."

- For more on analogies, see **Communications Skills Handbook,** p. R77.

PRACTICE Choose the word that best completes each analogy. All are based on antonym variants.

1. generous : selfishness :: trivial :
   a. order b. importance c. kindness
2. honest : wiliness :: indifferent :
   a. confusion b. concern c. anger
3. calm : exasperation :: crude :
   a. wisdom b. refinement c. sense
4. forgiving : grudge :: forgetful :
   a. misdeed b. compassion c. memory

THE ARCTIC, Traditional

Before You Read

Magic Words

Reading Focus

What thoughts come to your mind when you hear the word *magic?*

Quickwrite Jot down your response in your journal.

Setting a Purpose Read the following poem to learn about Eskimo beliefs regarding words and magic.

Building Background

The Power of Words

"Magic Words" is an Eskimo poem based on myths about the distant past. The title refers to magical formulas traditionally used to cure illness, end storms, and lure prey to hunters. These "magic words" or "magic songs" are considered part of a person's wealth. To be effective, they must be performed properly–either sung slowly or spoken in a soft voice. The performer must have complete faith in the power of words.

Not all Eskimo oral literature has such a serious purpose. Many songs and tales are performed for entertainment or to instruct children. Some stories are prized for their ability to put listeners to sleep during the long winter nights. Of a really good sleep story, the performer might claim that no listener has ever heard its ending.

Eskimo building igloo.

Life in the Arctic

The Eskimo, also known as Inuit, inhabit the Arctic regions of North America and parts of Greenland and northeast Siberia. They developed a way of life that was superbly adapted to their harsh environment. Because they could not grow vegetables on the frozen Arctic land, they depended on fishing and hunting for food. Nearly every part of the animals they killed served some purpose.

The Eskimo traditionally have great reverence for nature. According to the Eskimo religion, all living things and parts of nature have spirits or souls. It is important for hunters to show respect for their prey, since an offended animal spirit might interfere with future hunts. The Eskimo also believe that words and names carry great power. For example, there is an old custom that forbids travelers from speaking the name of a river or mountain until it is safely crossed, to avoid offending its spirit.

During the twentieth century, the Eskimo were greatly influenced by contact with modern society. Many Eskimo have given up the traditional way of life to work in towns and cities.

Reading Further

If you would like to read more about Eskimo life and culture, you might enjoy the following:

Poetry: from *I Breathe a New Song: Poems of the Eskimo,* edited by Richard Lewis, "Magic Prayer," "The Kayak Paddler's Joy at the Weather," "Lullaby," and "Hunger."

Magic Words

Translated by Edward Field

In the very earliest time,
when both people and animals lived on earth,
a person could become an animal if he wanted to
and an animal could become a human being.
Sometimes they were people
and sometimes animals
and there was no difference.
All spoke the same language.
That was the time when words were like magic.
The human mind had mysterious powers.
A word spoken by chance
might have strange consequences.
It would suddenly come alive
and what people wanted to happen could
happen—
all you had to do was say it.
Nobody could explain this:
That's the way it was.

Responding to Literature

Personal Response

What ideas in this poem did you find most thought-provoking? Share your response with the class.

Analyzing Literature

Recall and Interpret

1. According to the poem, what were people and animals able to do in the very earliest time?
2. How was language once different from the way it is now?
3. What "strange consequences" could have come from speaking a word?
4. How does the speaker of the poem explain the power that words once had?

Evaluate and Connect

5. Do you think that the ending of "Magic Words" is effective? Why or why not?
6. **Tone** is the attitude that a speaker takes toward a subject (see page R12). How would you describe the tone of "Magic Words"?
7. In the Reading Focus on page 76, you indicated what you think of when you hear the word *magic.* Compare your thoughts with the statements in "Magic Words."
8. What other literary works have you read that portray communication between human beings and animals?

Literary Criticism

"Traditional Inuit poetry," writes scholar Penny Petrone, "was intense and direct. In a society where there were no luxuries, it is not surprising that the poetic imagination was straightforward and sparse. . . . The power of the emotion is isolated in a few words, in sharp and vivid images." Do you think this statement applies to "Magic Words"? Why or why not? Explain your answers in a brief paragraph analyzing specific examples of diction and imagery.

Literary ELEMENTS

Myth

A **myth** is an anonymous, traditional story that was once widely believed to be true. Myths, which are closely related to religion, often involve the exploits of gods and heroes. Many myths explain some aspect of human society or the natural world, such as the origin of a custom or the changing of the seasons. In Eskimo oral literature, myths are set in a time when the world had not yet reached its present form.

1. How is the world portrayed in "Magic Words" different from the world in its present form?
2. Does "Magic Words" refer to anything supernatural? Explain.

- See **Literary Terms Handbook,** p. R8.

Extending Your Response

Writing About Literature

Comparing Myths Find a myth from another culture that deals with communication or relations between humans and animals. Compare that myth with the myth told in "Magic Words." You might discuss how each myth portrays the past or analyze the literary techniques that are used in these versions of the myths.

Interdisciplinary Activity

Art: Eskimo Sculpture The Eskimo often portray mythological subjects in their artwork. Bring in a photograph of an Eskimo carving, sculpture, or mask. In a small group, discuss the myths that are associated with the artwork. Think about how the artwork is related to the beliefs expressed in "Magic Words."

Save your work for your portfolio.

COMPARING *selections*

The Story of the Dress that Sang and Magic Words

COMPARE **RESPONSES**

Discuss In a small group, compare your responses to "The Story of the Dress that Sang" and "Magic Words." Use the following questions to guide your discussion:

- Which work expresses beliefs that are closer to your own?
- Which work do you think requires more background knowledge to be understood and appreciated?
- Which work did you find more interesting? Give examples from the work to support your response.

COMPARE **EXPERIENCES**

Write Write a paragraph comparing the experiences of people and animals in these two works. You might consider discussing issues such as the following:

- How harmonious are the relations between people and animals?
- What is explained in each work? What element of the experience is left unexplained?
- What moral lessons does the narrator or speaker intend to communicate through the experiences related?
- What tone does the narrator or speaker use in describing the experiences?

COMPARE **CULTURES**

Investigate "The Story of the Dress that Sang" and "Magic Words" come from traditional cultures that developed in very different parts of the world. With a partner, find out more information about the cultures of the Ashanti (or another ethnic group from West Africa) and the Eskimo. Compare religious beliefs, artistic expressions, literary traditions, and beliefs about the origin of the world and the development of humans and animals.

The Art of Translation

The Storyteller as Translator

Among the Mandingo of West Africa, the *Sundiata*—the epic of Mali—is a story that lives, grows, and changes. It's a part of people's lives. From childhood on, they experience the story through the dynamic performances of a *griot,* a storyteller-musician who chants or sings the verses to music and acts out dramatic parts. Griots perform the *Sundiata* at ceremonies and festivals in villages and towns throughout West Africa. Oral versions of the story can be traced back to the thirteenth century; however, it wasn't until the twentieth century that they were captured in writing. As a result, there are hundreds of variations of the *Sundiata*—as many versions as there are griots. Such variety of interpretation in retelling is a kind of translation.

> *"My guitar, for me, is like a book. Once I start playing, I am inspired and everything comes into my mind."*

Improvising an Epic

Each time an audience experiences a performance of the *Sundiata,* it's a little different. The griot takes the basic story and fits it to the situation and the mood of the audience. The griot may make up a song that praises the host or patron—or even add an ancestor of the patron as a character in an episode. A griot may modernize the epic by referring to contemporary weapons, clothing, or historical figures. The epic may be used to explain a village custom. If the audience is enjoying a battle scene, the griot may draw out the scene, making it last longer. If the audience gets bored, the griot may condense a scene. The griot constantly adapts to the audience, who not only clap and sing, but also interject questions and comments.

In essence, the griot translates the *Sundiata* from a basic story to a specific art form with each performance. As a result, there are innumerable versions of the story. The version you will read was told by the griot Djeli Mamoudou Kouyaté to the historian D. T. Niane, who

adapted it into prose. Notice how the story of Sundiata's first attempt to walk differs from this version by the griot Bamba Suso:

When he had grasped the rods, they both broke.
They said, "How will Sunjata [Sundiata] get up?"
He himself said to them, "Call my mother;
When a child has fallen down, it is his mother
who picks him up."
When his mother came,
He laid his hand upon his mother's shoulder,
And he arose and stood up.

Becoming a Living Library

Griots have been called "living libraries" because they store in their minds the history, stories, songs, and traditions of their people. They pass on this library from one generation to the next by reciting epics and other stories.

What does it take to build up a library in your mind? A griot is both born to the role and trained for it. The Mandingo have occupational castes, or classes, and to become a griot, a person must be born into the griot caste. But not every child of a griot becomes a storyteller. Only the ones who show special talent become apprenticed to a master griot within their clan or extended family.

Apprentices learn to repair, build, and play musical instruments, such as the guitar and drums. They study the tunes, rhythms, and words for all the stories in the repertoire of their master. As they practice storytelling, the master griot coaches them on how to use their voices and incorporate movements and gestures into their performances. Eventually, the apprentice pulls all this training together into the performance of an epic. But a typical griot spends fifty years becoming a master.

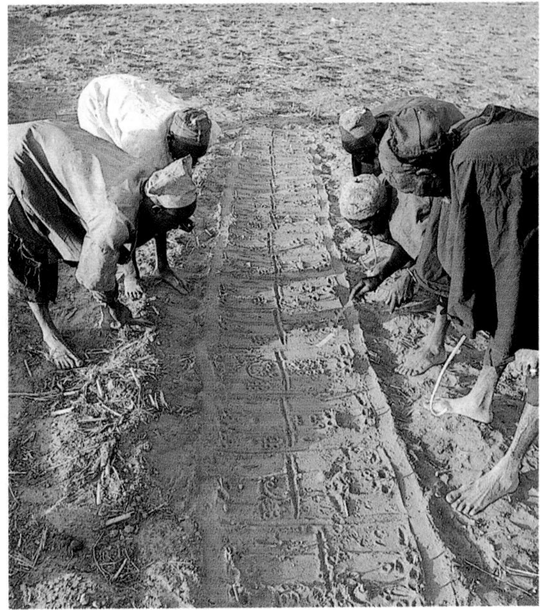

Viewing the photographs: Griots are found among a number of the peoples of West Africa. Among the Dogon people, as shown in these photographs, the griots draw a grid in the sand and leave it overnight. Foxes run across the grid during the night, and the next day, the griot interprets the tracks and tells the future of the Dogon people. He also relates his people's history.

Music is as important to the griot as words. When asked how he remembered all the lines in a long epic, Djeli Baba Sissoko replied that it was his guitar who remembered: "My guitar, for me, is like a book. Once I start playing, I am inspired and everything comes into my mind." This reliance on music is so great that a griot typically cannot recite the words of an epic without playing the rhythm that accompanies it.

Griots are proud of their knowledge, skill, and art. Djeli Mamoudou Kouyaté, who related the version of the *Sundiata* episode that you will read, claimed that the "warmth of the human voice" was superior to books, which cannot speak.

RESPOND

1. Do you agree with Kouyaté's statement, which implies that it is better to hear a story told than to read it in a book? Why or why not?
2. What aspects of a griot's performance do you bring to a story when you read it? What aspects do you lack in reading?

Before You Read

from *Sundiata*

Reading Focus

Think of some heroes whom you admire. What qualities make them heroic?

Share Ideas Share your response with the class.

Setting a Purpose Read the following episode to see how a boy shows the first signs of his heroic nature.

Building Background

The *Sundiata*

"[W]e are the memory of mankind; by the spoken word we bring to life the deeds and exploits of kings for younger generations."

—from the griot's introduction to the *Sundiata*

The *Sundiata* (so͞on dyä′ tə) is the national epic of the Mandingo people, who live in present-day Mali and parts of the coastal region of West Africa. It celebrates the founding of the ancient Mali empire. Although a king named Sundiata really did play an important role in establishing Mali as a powerful state, the *Sundiata* is not a historical account of his rule. In the epic he appears as a mythical hero, endowed with superhuman strength and other qualities that allow him to overcome great obstacles.

For over five centuries, oral poets known as griots (grē′ ōz) have performed the *Sundiata.* Griots were employed by kings and other leaders to recite their nation's legendary history. Since they did not work from a written text, they could alter the story to suit the occasion and the audience. This process led to the development of many different versions of the *Sundiata.* The episode you will read comes from a version told to the historian D. T. Niane, who adapted it into prose. The *Sundiata* continues to be recited today by Mandingo griots. Their performances, which can last several hours, are enlivened by musical accompaniment, dramatic gestures, and frequent interjections from the audience, suggesting agreement and enthusiasm.

Ancient Mali

Sundiata came to power around 1235, when he freed Mali from the control of a neighboring kingdom. Soon afterward he moved the capital to Niani, located on the Niger River. Enriched by profits from the gold trade, Niani became an important commercial center. Sundiata continued to expand the empire until his death in 1255. Under his successors, the empire flourished during the fourteenth century.

List of Characters

Mari Djata (also called Sundiata and Sogolon Djata): hero of the epic
Sogolon Kedjou: Mari Djata's mother
Sassouma: the queen mother
Balla Fasséké: Mari Djata's griot
Farakourou: master smith and soothsayer
Sogolon Djamarou: Mari Djata's sister

Queen Mother (Iye Oba) Commemorative Head. 19th century, Benin Kingdom. Brass, height: 53.3 cm. Detroit Institute of Arts.

Vocabulary Preview

derisively (di rī′ siv lē) *adv.* using ridicule or scorn to show contempt; p. 83
blandly (bland′ lē) *adv.* quietly; without concern; p. 84
affront (ə frunt′) *n.* a deliberate insult; p. 84
discreetly (dis krēt′ lē) *adv.* unnoticeably; p. 84
heedless (hēd′ lis) *adj.* inconsiderate, thoughtless; p. 84

from Sundiata
from The Lion's Awakening

Retold by D. T. Niane
Translated by G. D. Pickett

Even before he was born, Sundiata was destined for greatness. Acting on the instructions of a soothsayer, his father, the King of Mali, marries a hideous, hunchbacked woman named Sogolon. As foretold, the couple has a son. It seems, however, that the boy is unlikely to become a great leader as has been predicted. At the age of seven Sundiata is still unable to walk. He and his ugly mother are the object of cruel jokes and jealous abuse by the old king's first wife.

Sogolon Kedjou and her children lived on the queen mother's leftovers, but she kept a little garden in the open ground behind the village. It was there that she passed her brightest moments looking after her onions and gnougous.[1] One day she happened to be short of condiments and went to the queen mother to beg a little baobab[2] leaf.

"Look you," said the malicious Sassouma, "I have a calabash[3] full. Help yourself, you poor woman. As for me, my son knew how to walk at seven and it was he who went and picked these baobab leaves. Take them then, since your son is unequal to mine." Then she laughed derisively with that fierce laughter which cuts through your flesh and penetrates right to the bone.

1. *Gnougous* (noo′ gooz′) is a vegetable similar to spinach.
2. A *baobab* (bā′ ə bab′) is a tropical tree of the silk-cotton family. Its edible fruit resembles a gourd, and its bark can be used for making paper, cloth, and rope.
3. A *calabash* is a gourd whose hard shell is used as a utensil, such as a bottle or a dipper.

Vocabulary
derisively (di rī′ siv lē) *adv.* with ridicule or scorn

Sogolon Kedjou was dumbfounded. She had never imagined that hate could be so strong in a human being. With a lump in her throat she left Sassouma's. Outside her hut Mari Djata, sitting on his useless legs, was blandly eating out of a calabash. Unable to contain herself any longer, Sogolon burst into sobs and seizing a piece of wood, hit her son.

"Oh son of misfortune, will you never walk? Through your fault I have just suffered the greatest affront of my life! What have I done, God, for you to punish me in this way?"

Mari Djata seized the piece of wood and, looking at his mother, said, "Mother, what's the matter?"

"Shut up, nothing can ever wash me clean of this insult."

"But what then?"

"Sassouma has just humiliated me over a matter of a baobab leaf. At your age her own son could walk and used to bring his mother baobab leaves."

"Cheer up, Mother, cheer up."

"No. It's too much. I can't."

"Very well then, I am going to walk today," said Mari Djata. "Go and tell my father's smiths to make me the heaviest possible iron rod. Mother, do you want just the leaves of the baobab or would you rather I brought you the whole tree?"

"Ah, my son, to wipe out this insult I want the tree and its roots at my feet outside my hut."

Balla Fasséké, who was present, ran to the master smith, Farakourou, to order an iron rod.

Sogolon had sat down in front of her hut. She was weeping softly and holding her head between her two hands. Mari Djata went calmly back to his calabash of rice and began eating again as if nothing had happened. From time to time he looked up discreetly at his mother who was murmuring in a low voice, "I want the whole tree, in front of my hut, the whole tree."

All of a sudden a voice burst into laughter behind the hut. It was the wicked Sassouma telling one of her serving women about the scene of humiliation and she was laughing loudly so that Sogolon could hear. Sogolon fled into the hut and hid her face under the blankets so as not to have before her eyes this heedless boy, who was more preoccupied with eating than with anything else. With her head buried in the bedclothes Sogolon wept and her body shook violently. Her daughter, Sogolon Djamarou, had come and sat down beside her and she said, "Mother, Mother, don't cry. Why are you crying?"

Mari Djata had finished eating and, dragging himself along on his legs, he came and sat under the wall of the hut for the sun was scorching. What was he thinking about? He alone knew.

The royal forges were situated outside the walls and over a hundred smiths worked there. The bows, spears, arrows and shields of Niani's warriors came from there. When Balla Fasséké came to order the iron rod, Farakourou said to him, "The great day has arrived then?"

"Yes. Today is a day like any other, but it will see what no other day has seen."

The master of the forges, Farakourou, was the son of the old Nounfaïri, and he was a soothsayer like his father. In his

Figure. c. 14th–16th century, Region of Segou, Mali. Terra-cotta, height: 44.3 cm. Barbier-Mueller Museum, Geneva.

Vocabulary

blandly (bland′ lē) *adv.* quietly; without concern
affront (ə frunt′) *n.* a deliberate insult
discreetly (dis krēt′ lē) *adv.* unobtrusively, unnoticeably
heedless (hēd′ lis) *adj.* inconsiderate, thoughtless

workshops there was an enormous iron bar wrought by his father Nounfaïri. Everybody wondered what this bar was destined to be used for. Farakourou called six of his apprentices and told them to carry the iron bar to Sogolon's house.

When the smiths put the gigantic iron bar down in front of the hut the noise was so frightening that Sogolon, who was lying down, jumped up with a start. Then Balla Fasséké, son of Gnankouman Doua, spoke.

"Here is the great day, Mari Djata. I am speaking to you, Maghan, son of Sogolon. The waters of the Niger can efface the stain from the body, but they cannot wipe out an insult. Arise, young lion, roar, and may the bush know that from henceforth it has a master."

The apprentice smiths were still there, Sogolon had come out and everyone was watching Mari Djata. He crept on all fours and came to the iron bar. Supporting himself on his knees and one hand, with the other hand he picked up the iron bar without any effort and stood it up vertically. Now he was resting on nothing but his knees and held the bar with both his hands. A deathly silence had gripped all those present. Sogolon Djata closed his eyes, held tight, the muscles in his arms tensed. With a violent jerk he threw his weight on to it and his knees left the ground. Sogolon Kedjou was all eyes and watched her son's legs which were trembling as though from an electric shock. Djata was sweating and the sweat ran from his brow. In a great effort he straightened up and was on his feet at one go—but the great bar of iron was twisted and had taken the form of a bow!

Then Balla Fasséké sang out the "Hymn to the Bow," striking up with his powerful voice:

"Take your bow, Simbon,
Take your bow and let us go.
Take your bow, Sogolon Djata."

When Sogolon saw her son standing she stood dumb for a moment, then suddenly she sang these words of thanks to God who had given her son the use of his legs:

"Oh day, what a beautiful day,
Oh day, day of joy;
Allah Almighty, you never created a finer day.
So my son is going to walk!"

Standing in the position of a soldier at ease, Sogolon Djata, supported by his enormous rod, was sweating great beads of sweat. Balla Fasséké's song had alerted the whole palace and people came running from all over to see what had happened, and each stood bewildered before Sogolon's son. The queen mother had rushed there and when she saw Mari Djata standing up she trembled from head to foot. After recovering his breath Sogolon's son dropped the bar and the crowd stood to one side. His first steps were those of a giant. Balla Fasséké fell into step and pointing his finger at Djata, he cried:

"Room, room, make room!
The lion has walked;
Hide antelopes,
Get out of his way."

Behind Niani there was a young baobab tree and it was there that the children of the town came to pick leaves for their mothers. With all his might the son of Sogolon tore up the tree and put it on his shoulders and went back to his mother. He threw the tree in front of the hut and said, "Mother, here are some baobab leaves for you. From henceforth it will be outside your hut that the women of Niani will come to stock up."

Sogolon Djata walked. From that day forward the queen mother had no more peace of mind.

Responding to Literature

Personal Response

In your journal, describe your feelings about the main characters.

Analyzing Literature

Recall and Interpret

1. How does Sassouma (the queen mother) respond to Sogolon Kedjou's request for some baobab leaves? Why?
2. What does Mari Djata declare when he learns about his mother's encounter with Sassouma? What word would you use to describe his attitude on this occasion?
3. Why does Balla Fasséké go to the royal forges? How do he and the master smith seem to feel about Mari Djata?
4. Describe how Mari Djata stands up. Why do you think Sassouma trembles when she sees him in this position?
5. What action does Mari Djata perform for his mother? How do you interpret the last statement he makes in this episode?

Evaluate and Connect

6. In your opinion, was Sogolon's reaction to the treatment she received from Sassouma justified? Why or why not?
7. **Motivation** is the reason behind a character's actions (see page R8). What, do you think, motivates Mari Djata's actions in this episode?
8. A **symbol** is an object or action that stands for something else in addition to itself (see page R12). What does Mari Djata's act of standing up symbolize in this episode?
9. In the Reading Focus on page 82, you were asked to discuss heroes' qualities. Which of those qualities does Mari Djata display?
10. Which literary character does Mari Djata most remind you of? Explain.

Literary ELEMENTS

Epic

An **epic** is a long narrative poem about a larger-than-life hero who embodies the values of his or her people. Many earlier epics, including the *Sundiata,* were composed orally and preserved by storytellers before being written down. Such oral epics may be developed in different versions as they are passed along from generation to generation. Literary epics, such as Virgil's *Aeneid,* are composed as written texts, although they are modeled on oral epic poetry.

1. Based on this episode of the *Sundiata,* what values do you think were important to the ancient Mandingo people?
2. Which details make Mari Djata a larger-than-life figure?

- See **Literary Terms Handbook,** p. R3.

Extending Your Response

Creative Writing

Diary Entry Sassouma, the queen mother, is distressed by Mari Djata's sudden ability to walk. Write a **diary entry** in which she describes her feelings about this momentous occasion. Explain why she has lost her peace of mind, and indicate what regrets, if any, she has about her treatment of Mari Djata's mother.

Literary Groups

Shaky Starts Not all heroes seem destined for glory in their youth. Like Mari Djata, many are slow to reveal their abilities. In your group, make a list of heroes who have had shaky starts in life. Discuss how stories about their early years may have influenced your impression of them. Share your conclusions with the class.

Save your work for your portfolio.

Vo•cab•u•lar•y Skills

Multiple Meanings of Words

A word's definition does not necessarily always remain the same. Instead, the meaning depends on the agreement of the people using the word. The verb *doubt,* for example, once meant "to be fearful or suspicious of." Today, *to doubt* usually means "to be uncertain in opinion or belief." A word may also have more than one meaning. *Air* is a word that has acquired many meanings. The *air* we breathe is certainly not the *air* referred to by radio or television broadcasters. *Air,* in fact, has more than ten different definitions. For another example, read the following sentence:

> Although Claudia had tears in her eyes, everyone knew her sadness was only an act, and she was not truly sorry.

If you were to look up the word *act* in the dictionary, you might discover the following definitions:

act *n.* **1.** a thing done; a deed; **2.** the formal product of a legislative body; **3.** an affected display or behavior; **4.** one of the main divisions of a dramatic or theatrical work; **5.** a short performance by one or more entertainers *v.i;* **6.** to do something

In this example, the third definition is the correct one. The rest of the sentence provides the information you need to understand which is the correct meaning.

EXERCISE

Read each of the sentences below. On your paper, write the letter of the best definition for the underlined word.

1. To reach the right answer, it is first necessary to eliminate all the wrong ones.
   a. being in accordance with what is morally just
   b. correct
   c. opposite from the left
2. I was five years old when I was first cast into boarding school and removed from the comforts of life at home.
   a. to throw forth or discard
   b. to arrange or assign parts
   c. to shape by molding
3. I look carefully and adjust the position of my hand before I shoot the marble from between my fingers.
   a. to photograph or film
   b. to detonate or explode
   c. to project or impel

LISTENING, SPEAKING, and VIEWING

Effective Listening Strategies

In "Tselane and the Giant," Tselane listens carefully at the door of her hut to determine whether the singing voice belongs to the cruel giant Limo or to her mother. Although listening effectively is not always the life-or-death matter it is for Tselane, the skill is an important one in a world where so much information is delivered as sound waves. How would you describe your listening skills? Are they excellent, very good, or merely adequate? If you think they could use improvement, try these strategies for becoming a more effective listener.

- **Listen actively:** Focus your attention on the speaker. Work to understand and analyze the messages you hear. One way to make sure that you're listening actively is to take notes in an informal outline form. As you write, jot down the main ideas of the message, leaving room after each main idea to fill in the details. Ask questions, if possible, to clarify what you think you have heard.
- **Listen critically:** Instead of simply accepting everything you hear, evaluate the message. For example, when listening to political candidates' speeches, remember that you're hearing a mix of fact and opinion. Similarly, commercial advertisements cleverly blend emotional appeal, celebrity endorsement, and fact. Learn to separate fact from opinion, emotional appeal, and celebrity endorsement. Then, evaluate any facts by asking yourself whether they can be interpreted in more than one way. Try to determine what facts, if any, have been omitted.
- **Listen with your eyes:** As you watch speakers, gather clues about their opinions and feelings. Facial expressions and body gestures–such as hand or arm gestures–are clues to a speaker's feelings and can signal important ideas. Nervous habits, such as pacing before or while speaking, are an indication that the speaker is not comfortable with the subject. On the other hand, a speaker who is obviously at ease will inspire confidence in what is said.

ACTIVITIES

1. Working in a small group, listen to and watch a political speech on television or videotape. During the speech, take notes on the speaker's purpose. In addition, note the main ideas presented. After the speech, use your notes to write a summary of what you heard. Compare your summary with those of the rest of your group. What ideas or information did you miss as you listened? Compile your ideas into one summary that explains the speech's purpose and tells whether, in the group's opionion, the speaker accomplished the purpose.
2. Divide a sheet of paper into two columns. Label the left-hand column "facts" and the right-hand column "nonfacts." Then watch five television commercials. For each commercial, list the facts and nonfacts. Under the "nonfacts" heading, include such things as opinions, emotional appeals, and paid celebrity endorsements. Under "facts" list conclusions from scientific studies and tests.

Responding to Literature

Personal Response

On the basis of this account, do you think you would have enjoyed living in Benin? Explain why or why not to a classmate.

Analyzing Literature

Recall and Interpret

1. What luxuries were available in Benin? What luxuries that existed in the eighteenth century were not available in Benin?
2. Describe the eating habits of people in Benin. What "refinements in cookery" might Equiano be referring to in his discussion of food?
3. What kind of houses did people live in? Why did some families have more houses than others?
4. What crops were grown in Benin? What difficulties did people face while farming?
5. What were the religious beliefs of people in Benin? How did their beliefs affect their lives?

Evaluate and Connect

6. **Imagery** is language that appeals to the senses (see **Literary Terms Handbook,** page R6). Which images in this description did you find most memorable?
7. What examples does Equiano offer of cooperation among families in Benin?
8. How were families in Benin different from a typical family in your community?
9. Which aspect of life in Benin would you have liked Equiano to explain more clearly or in greater detail? Why?
10. Which details in this account remind you of the customs and activities you listed in the Reading Focus on page 89?

Literary ELEMENTS

Author's Purpose

Authors write with a **purpose** in mind—a reason or reasons for creating a literary work. Authors might wish to inform, persuade, narrate, describe, explore ideas, entertain, or move readers. Most complex works have several purposes, although one purpose may be dominant. For example, a book about rain forests may be written not only to inform readers but also to persuade them to support environmental efforts. When analyzing an author's purpose, one should first identify his or her intended audience.

1. What do you think was Equiano's main purpose in writing "Life in Benin"?
2. What other purpose or purposes might Equiano have had when he wrote the selection?

- See **Literary Terms Handbook,** p. R1.

Extending Your Response

Creative Writing

A Traveler's Viewpoint Imagine that you are a traveler from another continent who visits Benin during the eighteenth century. Write a brief letter in which you describe your impression of Benin to a friend or relative back home. In the letter, include details and information from "Life in Benin."

Interdisciplinary Activity

Art: Images of Benin Create an artwork based on one of Equiano's descriptions in "Life in Benin." For example, you might draw the clothing that he describes or make a diorama that shows how houses were designed. Lend your artwork to a classroom display about Benin's culture.

Save your work for your portfolio.

Writing Workshop

Narrative Writing: Autobiographical Incident

Written thousands of years ago, the poem "The Immortality of Writers" expresses a belief still held today: Written documents survive long after the person who wrote them is gone. Because they want their life experiences to be recorded for the ages, many authors write autobiographies–the stories of their own lives. **In this workshop, you will write about an autobiographical incident, with the intention of preserving the memory of an event that was meaningful to you.**

- As you write your autobiographical incident, refer to **Writing Handbook,** pp. R58–R63.

EVALUATION RUBRIC

By the time you complete this Writing Workshop, you will have

- recounted an event or incident from your life that was significant to you
- presented events in a clear order using first-person point of view
- used details, dialogue, and description to bring your story to life
- presented an autobiographical incident that is free of errors in grammar, usage, and mechanics

The Writing Process

PREWRITING

PREWRITING TIP

Look through your scrapbooks, notebooks, and journals. Note which of your past experiences you would be most interested in writing about.

Explore ideas

Your autobiographical narrative will probably be most interesting if you write about an incident that has some larger meaning. You can find a meaningful incident to write about in one of two ways. You can either begin by brainstorming a list of incidents that seem interesting, vivid, or humorous to you and think about their meanings later. Or you can consider the meaning first, by asking yourself the following questions:

- Have you ever been in the position of having to make a difficult moral or ethical choice, as Limo's wife does in "Tselane and the Giant"?
- Have you ever done something extraordinary, as Mari Djata does in the episode from the *Sundiata*?
- Have you ever used your wits to better your condition, as the Chameleon does in "The Story of the Dress that Sang"?
- Have you ever let someone come between you and someone close to you, as the friends do in "Edju and the Two Friends"?

Consider your purpose

Your narrative should tell the story of the incident as well as show your readers how and why the incident was significant to you.

Consider your audience

Remember that your narrative will speak for you when you aren't there to speak for yourself. How can you make sure that your readers get an accurate picture of the real you? How can you help them understand the incident as you understood it?

Make a plan

You have two basic options for narrating an autobiographical incident. You can begin at the beginning, or you can start with the most important part and use flashbacks–leaps back to an earlier time–to fill in the necessary background.

An event organizer like the one below can help you relate your autobiographical incident in the most effective order. First, write the events as they occur to you, using a separate block for each scene. Then number them in the order you will write about them. While you should try to break down your incident into as many scenes as possible, don't worry if you don't fill all of the boxes.

After you have planned the basic order of your events, start gathering details that will make the incident seem real to a reader. Ask yourself the following questions about each event and then jot down your responses in the appropriate block.

- What happened?
- When, where, how, and why did the event happen?
- Who was involved?
- What did you see and hear?
- What did you think or feel?

STUDENT MODEL

One day, when I was forgetting my lines, I started to cry. I was on stage. The girl playing Aunt Spiker was impatient with me. I felt my face get red. I wanted to quit.	**3.**
I kept forgetting my lines and speaking too softly. I felt like the only one in my class who couldn't say my lines loud enough. "Louder, Lauren!" my teacher, Mrs. Wu, shouted.	**2.**
I told my mother what had happened. She gave me some advice. We were at home, in the kitchen. She told me to pretend the audience was just a bunch of chickens.	**4.**
I was chosen for a part in *James and the Giant Peach.* It was in second grade. I was going to play the part of Aunt Sponge. She had many lines. "I'm too shy for this part," I thought.	**1.**
After the play, everyone congratulated me. I felt successful. My family hugged me. Mrs. Wu shook my hand. I heard "Great job!" all around me.	**7.**
I looked at the audience. I thought of the audience as chickens, as my mother told me to. I said the line perfectly. I felt more comfortable. I began to have fun.	**6.**
On the performance night, I was late for my entrance, and then I missed a line. I felt like the silence, which only really lasted a second, lasted forever. Aunt Spiker whispered the line.	**5.**

Complete Student Model on p. R108.

DRAFTING

DRAFTING TIP

Don't try to get your wording perfect, just try to get words down. Turn your editor's eye off. You can turn it back on when you revise.

Tell the story

Just because an incident really happened doesn't mean it can't be told as interestingly as fiction. Add drama to your narrative by searching your memory for the bits of dialogue, details of setting, and emotional nuances that will make your incident come to life for your reader.

Write your draft

Use your plan to help organize your draft but remember that it is only a guide, not a set of orders. If you find as you're writing that another organizational strategy might be more effective, go ahead and change your plan.

STUDENT MODEL

I stood up on the vast stage, embarrassed by the sound of my own voice. It sounded much too loud to me. I couldn't believe it when Mrs. Wu told me to speak up. My hands and face suddenly felt hot. Tears welled up and I wished I were anywhere else but in an uncomfortable costume on display in front of my whole class.

Complete Student Model on p. R108.

REVISING

REVISING TIP

If you're using flashbacks, make sure that the transitions in time are clearly indicated.

Take another look

Put your draft aside for a while. Then reread it and revise it to make the written version as vivid as your memory. Use the **Rubric for Revising** to guide you as you revise.

Read your narrative aloud

Find someone to listen while you read your work aloud. Go through the **Rubric for Revising** with your listener and decide what revisions you need to make.

STUDENT MODEL

Of course, ~~what also helped was that~~ I did ^finally, memorize ^all my lines. ^On the night of the performance, My mother whispered her advice to me right before I went on stage. ^and that helped too. I walked onto ~~that~~ stage feeling ^pretty confident.

Complete Student Model on p. R108.

RUBRIC FOR REVISING

Your revised narrative should have

- ☑ a clear order of events, with transitions leading from one to the next
- ☑ an explanation of the incident's importance
- ☑ dialogue that brings scenes to life
- ☑ vivid details and descriptions
- ☑ any background information necessary for the reader to understand the story

Your revised narrative should be free of

- ☑ details or descriptions that distract from the flow of the narrative
- ☑ passages not written from a first-person point of view

EDITING/PROOFREADING

When you are satisfied with the content of your autobiographical narrative, edit a copy of your work to find and correct errors in grammar, usage, mechanics, and spelling.

PROOFREADING TIP

Use the **Proofreading Checklist** on the inside back cover to help you mark errors that you find.

Grammar Hint

A plural pronoun must have a plural antecedent, and a singular pronoun needs a singular antecedent.

INCORRECT: *Each of us learned our lines.*

CORRECT: *All of us learned our lines.*

CORRECT: *Each of us learned his or her lines.*

STUDENT MODEL

After that, I didn't miss another entrance or line, and I even started to feel comfortable. At one point I looked around. I realized everybody ~~were~~ was having fun, and that included me.

Complete Student Model on p. R108.

Complete Student Model

For a complete version of the model developed in this workshop, refer to **Writing Workshop Models**, p. R108.

PUBLISHING/PRESENTING

You and your classmates might create an anthology of autobiographical incidents and add the volume to the school library, or you may want to take turns reading your narratives to each other. To reach a larger audience, you could submit a recording of your work to a local public radio station that accepts contributions from listeners.

PRESENTING TIP

If you're using a computer, use a page layout program to make the text look like a magazine article.

Reflecting

How did writing about an autobiographical incident stir old memories? How did it inspire new thoughts? In your journal, jot down how you might react to this narrative if you read it twenty years from now. Then read your work once more. Note one thing that you did particularly well and one thing that you want to improve in your next piece of writing.

Save your work for your portfolio.

Continuity and Change

The story of contemporary Africa combines continuity and rapid change. In all parts of the continent, most people live as they have for centuries—in small villages, growing their own food. Village storytellers relate the history and legends of their ancestors to each successive generation. People entertain themselves and celebrate the events of the year with music and dance.

At the same time, profound changes are occurring. More and more young people leave their villages in search of work in cities or other countries. In some countries, people are still struggling for a voice in their own government. In others, democratic governments try to cope with national and international economic problems. Radio, television, and movies compete with traditional music and storytelling. Despite the diversity of traditional African societies, the people of the continent share a common challenge: to preserve their heritage while adapting to the modern world.

Traditional wall painting in Mauritania.

Marketplace, Madagascar.

Africa

1806 Cape Town comes under British rule

1816–1828 Shaka establishes Zulu kingdom

1822 Liberia founded by former enslaved people from the United States

1830 France invades Algeria

1835 Boers begin Great Trek

1800 — **1825** — **1850**

World

1807 Britain abolishes slave trade

1812 Brothers Grimm publish their fairy tales

1822 Brazil proclaims independence from Portugal

1840s Potato famine strikes Ireland

1844 Samuel F. B. Morse sends the first message by telegram

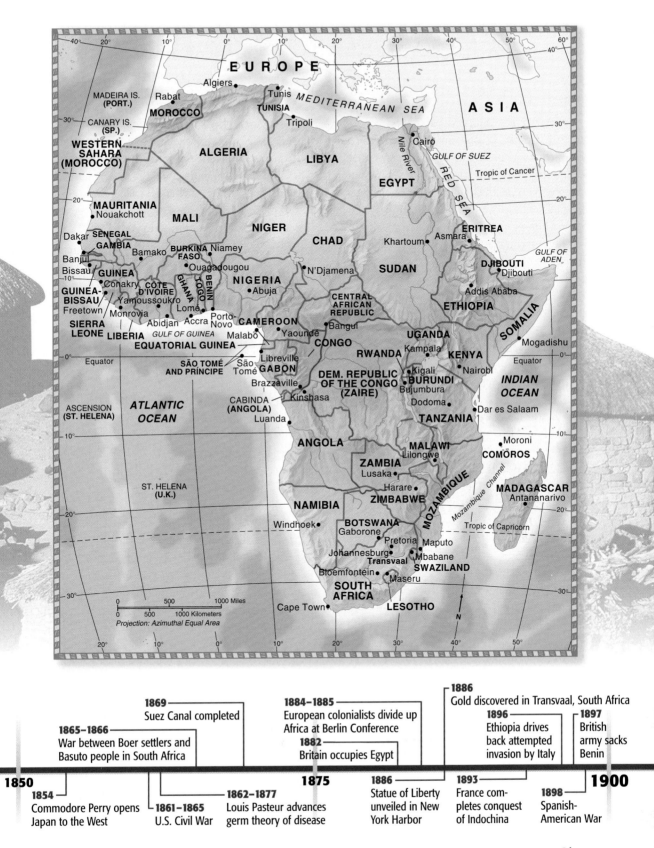

EUROPE
ASIA
MEDITERRANEAN SEA
Algiers
Rabat
Tunis
TUNISIA
Tripoli
MADEIRA IS. (PORT.)
CANARY IS. (SP.)
MOROCCO
WESTERN SAHARA (MOROCCO)
ALGERIA
LIBYA
EGYPT
Cairo
Nile River
GULF OF SUEZ
RED SEA
Tropic of Cancer
MAURITANIA
Nouakchott
MALI
NIGER
CHAD
SUDAN
Khartoum
Asmara
ERITREA
GULF OF ADEN
DJIBOUTI
Djibouti
Addis Ababa
ETHIOPIA
SOMALIA
Mogadishu
Dakar
SENEGAL
GAMBIA
Banjul
Bissau
GUINEA-BISSAU
GUINEA
Conakry
Freetown
SIERRA LEONE
Monrovia
LIBERIA
Bamako
BURKINA FASO
Ouagadougou
Niamey
CÔTE D'IVOIRE
Yamoussoukro
Abidjan
GHANA
Accra
TOGO
Lomé
BENIN
Porto-Novo
NIGERIA
Abuja
N'Djamena
GULF OF GUINEA
CAMEROON
Yaoundé
Malabo
EQUATORIAL GUINEA
SÃO TOMÉ AND PRÍNCIPE
São Tomé
Libreville
GABON
CENTRAL AFRICAN REPUBLIC
Bangui
CONGO
Brazzaville
Kinshasa
DEM. REPUBLIC OF THE CONGO (ZAIRE)
CABINDA (ANGOLA)
Luanda
ANGOLA
UGANDA
Kampala
RWANDA
Kigali
BURUNDI
Bujumbura
KENYA
Nairobi
Equator
INDIAN OCEAN
Dodoma
Dar es Salaam
TANZANIA
ASCENSION (ST. HELENA)
ATLANTIC OCEAN
ST. HELENA (U.K.)
MALAWI
Lilongwe
ZAMBIA
Lusaka
Moroni
COMOROS
Harare
ZIMBABWE
MOZAMBIQUE
Mozambique Channel
MADAGASCAR
Antananarivo
NAMIBIA
Windhoek
BOTSWANA
Gaborone
Pretoria
Maputo
Johannesburg
Transvaal
Mbabane
SWAZILAND
Tropic of Capricorn
Bloemfontein
Maseru
SOUTH AFRICA
LESOTHO
Cape Town
0 500 1000 Miles
0 500 1000 Kilometers
Projection: Azimuthal Equal Area
N

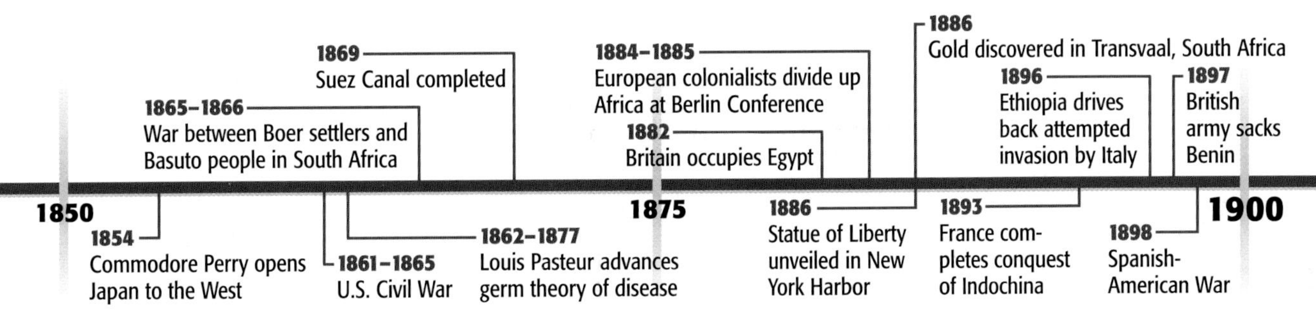

The Road to Self-Rule

Foreign Rule

For centuries, people from other parts of the world had contact only with the coastal areas of Africa. Knowing nothing of the vast continent's interior, they depended on local merchants, who traded resources—including gold, copper, ivory, leather, timber, and even slaves—for imported goods.

The first European colonies in Africa grew from naval stations and trading posts. By the late nineteenth century, the entire continent had been divided into colonies. The age of colonialism lasted only a hundred years, yet it had a profound and traumatic effect on the continent.

The European countries' reasons for establishing colonies included setting up sources of goods and establishing markets for European manufactured goods. Sometimes, a European power would set up a colony simply to keep its rivals out.

Some colonial powers treated their African territories harshly, taking as much from them as possible and giving little back. Others did bring benefits to the local people, building schools, roads, and hospitals. But all of the European countries kept the power firmly in their own hands.

Thonga Colonial Figure. c. 1900, Mozambique. Private collection.

Independence

Resistance to foreign rule began as soon as the colonies were established. By the late 1940s, most colonies had strong independence movements. During the '50s and '60s, most of Africa regained its independence. Sometimes this was achieved peacefully, as in Chad and Uganda; other times it came only after years of war, as in Algeria and Mozambique.

But problems remained. Africans had mostly been kept out of government and had little experience administrating it. Only few people had any higher education or technical training. The economic structures of the former colonies did not meet the needs of the local inhabitants. In addition, former colonial powers often supported dictatorial governments, not democracies.

Nigerian senator.

Village Life

South of the Sahara, most Africans still live in rural areas. Typically, an extended family, consisting of three to five generations, live together in separate one-room huts that enclose a central courtyard. Women do most of the agricultural work, carry water, and gather firewood. Men may be absent from the village for long periods of time tending to herds or working as migrant laborers.

Africa

- **1910** British colonists and Dutch (Afrikaner) settlers form Union of South Africa
- **1922** Egypt declares independence from Britain
- **1935** Italy invades Ethiopia
- **1941** Haile Selassie regains throne in Ethiopia
- **1948** Apartheid established in South Africa

1900 — **1925** — **1950**

World

- **1903** Wright brothers make first powered flight
- **1914** U.S. opens Panama Canal
- **1914–1918** World War I
- **1929** Stock market crash leads to start of Great Depression
- **1939–1945** World War II
- **1949** Communists assume rule of China

What People Believe

Christianity and Islam

Along with the European colonialism of the nineteenth century came a wave of European and American Christian missionary activity in Africa. Most colonial governments supported this activity to some extent. Independent African Christian churches were founded by people who felt that the European churches were not entirely relevant to their lives. Christianity spread rapidly throughout the continent. Islam remained the dominant religion in northern Africa; in recent years, conversion from the older African beliefs to Islam has increased.

Priest of the ancient Ethiopian Coptic church.

Zulu *songoma,* or medicine woman.

Traditional Beliefs

Millions of people in Africa remain loyal to the continent's traditional beliefs. They believe in a supreme being who created the universe and in other deities who watch over the natural world. Ancestors and traditional tribal heroes are often revered. Adherence to traditional beliefs is not confined to the countryside; many people in Africa's largest cities follow these beliefs as well.

Active Reading Strategies

Reading the Time Line

1. How many years passed from the time Cape Town came under British rule to the British occupation of Egypt?
2. What occurred one hundred years after Brazil declared its independence?

1950

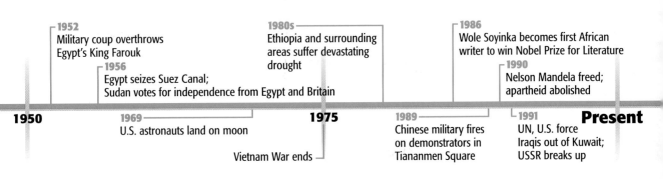

- **1952** Military coup overthrows Egypt's King Farouk
- **1956** Egypt seizes Suez Canal; Sudan votes for independence from Egypt and Britain
- **1969** U.S. astronauts land on moon

1975

- Vietnam War ends
- **1980s** Ethiopia and surrounding areas suffer devastating drought
- **1986** Wole Soyinka becomes first African writer to win Nobel Prize for Literature
- **1989** Chinese military fires on demonstrators in Tiananmen Square
- **1990** Nelson Mandela freed; apartheid abolished
- **1991** UN, U.S. force Iraqis out of Kuwait; USSR breaks up

Present

Arts and Entertainment

Tradition and Innovation

Art reflects its society, and contemporary African art often reflects both traditional forms and new developments. For example, hand-printed West African textiles might now contain a political slogan or an image of a national leader. And, although pottery might still be decorated in traditional forms, it might also now be glazed to appeal to the foreign buyer. The pace of these changes is not the same throughout the continent, and many traditional arts continue to thrive.

African music has responded to change by combining elements of the old and the new. In Algeria, traditional Arab-influenced songs are accompanied by synthesizers and digital drums. In South Africa, choirs combining Zulu and Christian church choral styles provided anthems for the liberation struggle there. Throughout the continent, musicians have maintained the traditional role of social commentator and critic.

African musicians have also experimented freely. Many play music from the folk tradition—such as Shona *mbira* (bēr′ ä) melodies from Zimbabwe—on electric guitars. Others have worked with musicians from other cultures. For example, Kora players from Mali have recorded with Spanish guitar players and Arab percussionists to produce music that blends a variety of traditions.

Kora player, Gambia.

The band *Les Têtes Brulées,* Cameroon.

Critical Thinking

Connecting Cultures

1. In a small group, discuss the traditional role of the musician in Africa as a social commentator or critic. How might musicians help in times of great change and in struggles for freedom?
2. In what ways do musicians in the United States act as social commentators and critics? Discuss your answers in a small group.

Paintings and *Prints*

During the past fifty years, African artists have begun to produce more and more paintings and prints. The subject matter of these works ranges from traditional folktales and everyday life to contemporary politics and the struggle against colonialism. Although painting on canvas is a relatively recent art, two-dimensional art does have a long history in Africa. The tradition can be observed in ancient rock-paintings, on the painted walls of contemporary South African mud villages, and in traditional ritual body and face painting.

Traditional Ndebele village, South Africa.

Art in Context

Traditionally, many forms of African art were intended to be seen only when in use. For example, masks were meant to be seen bobbing and weaving in motion, made mysterious by shadow or torchlight. In many cases, masks are still used in this way. However, as the rest of the world gained an appreciation for African art, museums, galleries, and shops around the world began collecting, displaying, and selling it. Artists have begun to produce masks and other traditional objects as works of art in themselves, rather than for their functional role.

Determined Woman. Colleen Madamombe (Zimbabwe, b. 1964). Opalstone, height: 27.5 in. Private collection.

Language and Literature

Egyptian school.

Written Languages

Until the 1900s, few of the more than 1,000 African languages had a written form. Today most African languages are written using either the Roman alphabet or Arabic script.

Writers in Africa must choose what language to write in. This is not a simple decision, for most contemporary writers were educated in the language of their former colonial rulers, usually English or French. And in most African countries, many different languages are spoken.

Today, most well-known African writers choose to write in Arabic or in a European language that caters to an international as well as a pan-African audience. Recently, some writers have begun publishing first in their own languages, then translating the work for a larger audience.

Oral and Written Literature

Today African literature is a mixture of oral and written traditions. Some traditional oral forms, such as praise poems extolling the virtues of deities and heroes, are now used to list the positive qualities of a favored candidate in political campaigns. The influence of oral tradition can also be found in contemporary literature. Some writers draw upon the rich store of oral trickster tales and animal fables for their work. Other writers deal with modern-day subjects but use the rhythm and repetition found in oral tales.

influences

Africans who were carried to North and South America as enslaved people took many aspects of their culture with them. In time, these customs profoundly affected the culture of their new homes. African religious ideas, music, and agricultural products traveled with the enslaved people. For example, though no one knows the origin of the word *jazz,* everyone agrees that the music evolved from African musical traditions and from the experiences of African Americans.

Words from African languages have also traveled to the Americas. These include the following:

- *goober* for peanut
- *gumbo* for a type of stew
- *marimba* for xylophone

Bookseller, Cairo.

The Role of the Writer

Much of the literature written in Africa during the colonial period arose from writers' discontent with imperialism. The writer's role as social critic continued into postindependence days, when this role was not always welcome. One South African poet, Dennis Brutus, calls the writer the voice of society, someone who celebrates when society does its job well or speaks harshly when society does its job badly. "He is always at the wedding to express the community's joy. . . . He is always at the funeral to express their sorrow."

The tension between tradition and modernism is among the most powerful themes in contemporary African literature. The Nigerian writer Chinua Achebe addresses this theme when he writes movingly about Ibo village life. Achebe tries to show the good and the bad that existed in the past and also exists in the present. "Our past was not one technicolor idyll," he has said.

Many African writers have been forced to spend long periods of time in exile because of their criticism of authoritarian governments. Wole Soyinka, who in 1986 became the first African to be awarded the Nobel Prize for Literature, spent four years in exile after being charged with treason by the military government of Nigeria. In South Africa, white writers such as Nadine Gordimer, as well as many black wriers, voiced strong opposition to the former policy of apartheid.

Critical Thinking

Modern Africa

1. With a partner, use the time line's brief history of Africa from 1800 until present day (pages 98–101) to make a list of major issues that Africans have dealt with in the last 200 years.
2. Discuss with a partner how Africa's major historical developments may have influenced some of the topics and themes of the continent's literature.

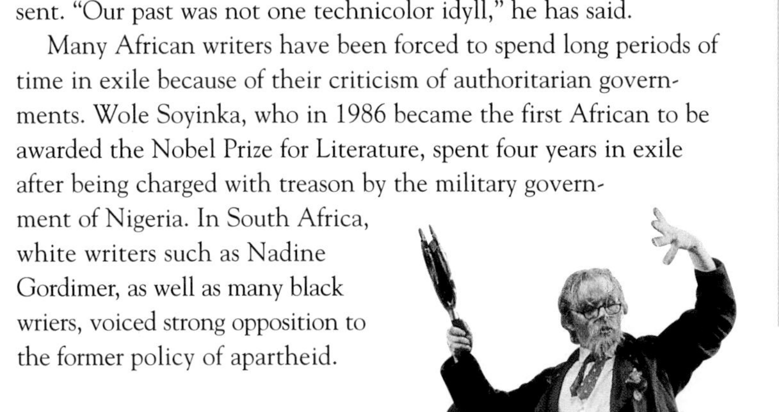

Scene from *The Road*, by Wole Soyinka.

Before You Read

Half a Day

Meet Naguib Mahfouz

"If the urge to write should ever leave me, I want that day to be my last."

When Naguib Mahfouz (nä zhēb′ mä fo͞oz′) was growing up, the novel held only a minor place in Arabic literature. Mahfouz loved books, however, so he learned his craft by reading European authors. After studying philosophy at the University of Cairo, Mahfouz took a civil service job and wrote fiction in his spare time. He skillfully adapted Western literary techniques to portray the society and culture of Egypt. Although Mahfouz writes about local subjects, the universal significance of his work is widely recognized. In 1988 he became the first Arabic writer to win the Nobel Prize for Literature.

Mahfouz's most famous work is *The Cairo Trilogy*. In these three novels, Mahfouz explores the modern transformation of Egypt by focusing on several generations of a Cairo family. Many younger Arabic writers have been influenced by the realistic style of the trilogy.

Naguib Mahfouz was born in 1911.

Reading Focus

Think about your first day in a new school. What worries did you have before you arrived? How did your classmates and teachers treat you?

Journal Writing Write for a few minutes in your journal in response to these questions.

Setting a Purpose Read how the narrator recalls his experiences at school.

Building Background

The Time and Place

Cairo, the capital of Egypt, is located mainly on the eastern bank of the Nile River. The older sections contain medieval mosques, monuments, and other historic architecture. These buildings stand in sharp contrast to the high-rises that dominate the city's modern downtown area. Over a thousand years old, Cairo grew rapidly during the twentieth century; this growth has led to overcrowding and pollution. Mahfouz imaginatively portrays how the city has changed in "Half a Day."

Education in Egypt

In 1923 Egypt passed a law providing free education for children from seven to twelve years old. Since then, successive governments have increasingly emphasized education as a priority. Notably, women—who were once virtually excluded from higher education—now make up nearly a third of the country's university students. The center of the country's educational system is al-Azhar University, which has been a center of learning for nearly a thousand years.

Vocabulary Preview

unmarred (un märd′) *adj.* unspoiled; p. 108
throng (thrông) *n.* crowding together of many persons; p. 110
avail (ə vāl′) *n.* use or advantage; p. 110
horde (hôrd) *n.* teeming crowd or throng; p. 110
refuse (ref′ ūs) *n.* trash, garbage; p. 110
conjurer (kon′ jər ər) *n.* individual who practices magic; magician, juggler, snake charmer; p. 110

Half a Day

Naguib Mahfouz

Translated by Denys Johnson-Davies

I PROCEEDED ALONGSIDE MY FATHER, clutching his right hand, running to keep up with the long strides he was taking. All my clothes were new: the black shoes, the green school uniform, and the red tarboosh. My delight in my new clothes, however, was not altogether unmarred, for this was no feast day but the day on which I was to be cast into school for the first time.

Did You Know?
A *tarboosh* is a brimlesss red hat worn by some Muslims.

My mother stood at the window watching our progress, and I would turn toward her from time to time, as though appealing for help. We walked along a street lined with gardens; on both sides were extensive fields planted with crops, prickly pears, henna trees, and a few date palms.

"Why school?" I challenged my father openly. "I shall never do anything to annoy you."

"I'm not punishing you," he said, laughing. "School's not a punishment. It's the factory that makes useful men out of boys. Don't you want to be like your father and brothers?"

I was not convinced. I did not believe there was really any good to be had in tearing me away from the intimacy of my home and throwing me into this building that stood at the end of the road like some huge, high-walled fortress, exceedingly stern and grim.

When we arrived at the gate we could see the courtyard, vast and crammed full of boys and girls. "Go in by yourself," said my father, "and join them. Put a smile on your face and be a good example to others."

I hesitated and clung to his hand, but he gently pushed me from him. "Be a man," he said. "Today you truly begin life. You will find me waiting for you when it's time to leave."

I took a few steps, then stopped and looked but saw nothing. Then the faces of boys and girls came into view. I did not know a single one of them, and none of them knew me. I felt I was a stranger who had lost his way. But glances of curiosity were directed toward me, and one boy approached and asked, "Who brought you?"

"My father," I whispered.

"My father's dead," he said quite simply.

I did not know what to say. The gate was closed, letting out a pitiable screech. Some of the children burst into tears. The bell rang. A lady came along, followed by a group of men. The men began sorting us into ranks. We were formed into an intricate pattern in the great courtyard surrounded on three sides by high buildings of several floors; from each floor we were overlooked by a long balcony roofed in wood.

"This is your new home," said the woman. "Here too there are mothers and fathers. Here there is everything that is enjoyable and beneficial to knowledge and religion. Dry your tears and face life joyfully."

We submitted to the facts, and this submission brought a sort of contentment. Living beings were drawn to other living beings, and from the first moments my heart made friends with such boys as were to be my friends and fell in love with such girls as I was to be in love with, so that it seemed my misgivings had had no basis. I had never imagined school would have this rich variety. We played all sorts of different games: swings, the vaulting horse, ball games. In the music room we chanted our first songs. We also had our first introduction to language. We saw a globe of the Earth, which revolved and showed the various continents and countries. We started learning the

Vocabulary
unmarred (un märd′) *adj.* unspoiled

numbers. The story of the Creator of the universe was read to us, we were told of His present world and of His Hereafter, and we heard examples of what He said. We ate delicious food, took a little nap, and woke up to go on with friendship and love, play and learning.

As our path revealed itself to us, however, we did not find it as totally sweet and unclouded as we had presumed. Dust-laden winds and unexpected accidents came about suddenly, so we had to be watchful, at the ready, and very patient. It was not all a matter of playing and fooling around. Rivalries could bring about pain and hatred or give rise to fighting. And while the lady would sometimes smile, she would often scowl and scold. Even more frequently she would resort to physical punishment.

In addition, the time for changing one's mind was over and gone and there was no question of ever returning to the paradise of home. Nothing lay ahead of us but exertion, struggle, and perseverance. Those who were able took advantage of the opportunities for success and happiness that presented themselves amid the worries.

Journey to the Unknown #1, 1981. Acha Debela (Ethiopia). Acrylic on canvas, 30 x 40 in. University of Maryland, University College.

Viewing the painting: What emotions does this painting stir in you? Do you feel similar emotions while reading the story?

Half a Day

The bell rang announcing the passing of the day and the end of work. The throngs of children rushed toward the gate, which was opened again. I bade farewell to friends and sweethearts and passed through the gate. I peered around but found no trace of my father, who had promised to be there. I stepped aside to wait. When I had waited for a long time without avail, I decided to return home on my own. After I had taken a few steps, a middle-aged man passed by, and I realized at once that I knew him. He came toward me, smiling, and shook me by the hand, saying, "It's a long time since we last met—how are you?"

With a nod of my head, I agreed with him and in turn asked, "And you, how are you?"

"As you can see, not all that good, the Almighty be praised!"

Again he shook me by the hand and went off. I proceeded a few steps, then came to a startled halt. Good Lord! Where was the street lined with gardens? Where had it disappeared to? When did all these vehicles invade it? And when did all these hordes of humanity come to rest upon its surface? How did these hills of refuse come to cover its sides? And where were the fields that bordered it? High buildings had taken over, the street surged with children, and disturbing noises shook the air. At various points stood conjurers showing off their tricks and making snakes appear from baskets. Then there was a band announcing the opening of a circus, with clowns and weight lifters walking in front. A line of trucks carrying central security troops crawled majestically by. The siren of a fire engine shrieked, and it was not clear how the vehicle would cleave its way to reach the blazing fire. A battle raged between a taxi driver and his passenger, while the passenger's wife called out for help and no one answered. Good God! I was in a daze. My head spun. I almost went crazy. How could all this have happened in half a day, between early morning and sunset? I would find the answer at home with my father. But where was my home? I could see only tall buildings and hordes of people. I hastened on to the crossroads between the gardens and Abu Khoda. I had to cross Abu Khoda to reach my house, but the stream of cars would not let up. The fire engine's siren was shrieking at full pitch as it moved at a snail's pace, and I said to myself, "Let the fire take its pleasure in what it consumes." Extremely irritated, I wondered when I would be able to cross. I stood there a long time, until the young lad employed at the ironing shop on the corner came up to me. He stretched out his arm and said gallantly, "Grandpa, let me take you across."

Vocabulary

throng (thrông) *n.* crowding together of many persons
avail (ə vāl′) *n.* use or advantage
horde (hôrd) *n.* teeming crowd or throng
refuse (ref′ ūs) *n.* trash, garbage
conjurer (kon′ jər ər) *n.* individual who practices magic; magician, juggler, snake charmer

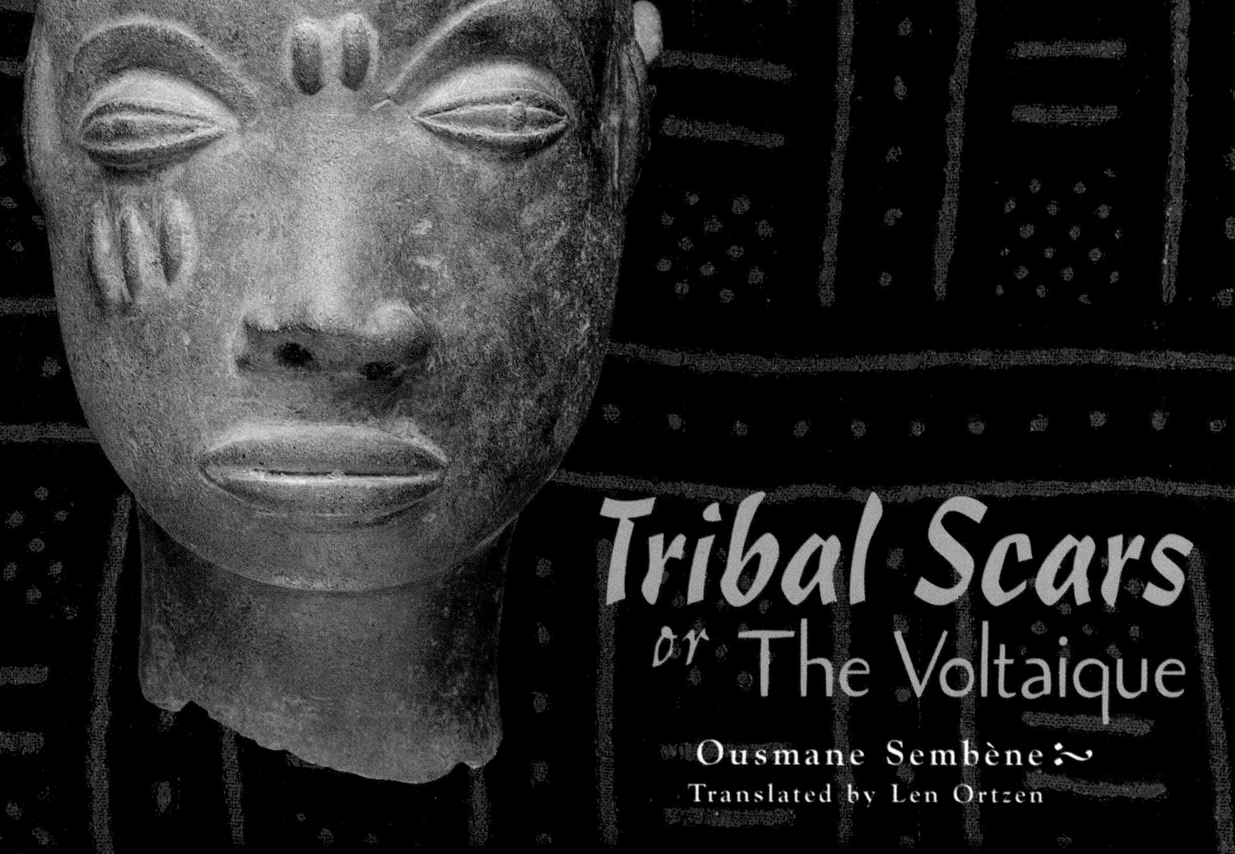

Tribal Scars
or The Voltaique

Ousmane Sembène
Translated by Len Ortzen

In the evenings we all go to Mane's place, where we drink mint tea and discuss all sorts of subjects, even though we know very little about them. But recently we neglected the major problems such as the ex-Belgian Congo, the trouble in the Mali Federation, the Algerian War and the next UNO meeting—even women, a subject which normally takes up about a quarter of our time. The reason was that Saer, who is usually so stolid and serious, had raised the question, "Why do we have tribal scars?"

Vocabulary
stolid (stol′ id) *adj.* having or expressing little or no sensibility; unemotional

(I should add that Saer is half Voltaique, half Senegalese; but he has no tribal scars.)

Although not all of us have such scars on our faces, I have never heard such an impassioned discussion, such a torrent of words, in all the time we have been meeting together at Mane's. To hear us, anyone would have thought that the future of the whole continent of Africa was at stake. Every evening for weeks the most fantastic and unexpected explanations were put forward. Some of us went to neighboring villages and even farther afield to consult the elders and the griots,[1] who are known as the "encyclopedias" of the region, in an endeavor to plumb the depths of this mystery, which seemed buried in the distant past.

Saer was able to prove that all the explanations were wrong.

Someone said vehemently that "it was a mark of nobility"; another that "it was a sign of bondage." A third declared that "It was decorative—there was a tribe which would not accept a man or a woman unless they had these distinctive marks on the face and body." One joker told us with a straight face that: "Once upon a time, a rich African chief sent his son to be educated in Europe. The chief's son was a child when he went away, and when he returned he was a man. So he was educated, an intellectual, let us say. He looked down on the tribal traditions and customs. His father was annoyed by this, and wondered how to bring him back into the royal fold. He consulted his chief counselor. And one morning, out on the square and in front of the people, the son's face was marked with cuts."

No one believed that story, and the teller was reluctantly obliged to abandon it.

Someone else said: "I went to the French Institute and hunted around in books, but found nothing. However, I learned that the wives of the gentlemen in high places are having these marks removed from their faces; they go to Europe to consult beauticians. For the new rules for African beauty disdain the old standards of the country; the women are becoming Americanized. . . . And as the trend develops, tribal scars lose their meaning and importance and are bound to disappear."

We talked about their diversity, too; about the variety even within one tribe. Cuts were made on the body as well as on the face. This led someone to ask: "If these tribal scars were signs of nobility, or of high or low caste, why aren't they ever seen in the Americas?"

"Ah, we're getting somewhere at last!" exclaimed Saer, who obviously knew the right answer to his original question, or thought he did.

"Tell us then. We give up," we all cried.

"All right," said Saer. He waited while the man on duty brought in glasses of hot tea and passed them round. The room became filled with the aroma of mint.

"So we've got around to the Americas," Saer began. "Now, none of the authoritative writers on slavery and the slave trade has ever mentioned tribal scars, so far as I know. In South America, where fetishism[2] and witchcraft as practiced by slaves still survive to this day, no tribal scars have ever been seen. Neither do Negroes living in the Caribbean have them, nor in Haiti, Cuba, the Dominican Republic nor anywhere else. So we come back to Black Africa before the slave trade, to the time of the old Ghana Empire, the Mali and Gao Empires, and the cities and kingdoms of the Hausa, Bournou, Benin, Mossi and so on. Now, not one of the travelers who visited those places and wrote about them mentions this practice of tribal scars. So where did it originate?"

By now everyone had stopped sipping hot tea; they were all listening attentively.

"If we study the history of the slave trade objectively we find that the dealers sought blacks who were strong and healthy and without

1. *Griots* (grē′ ōz) are storytellers of western Africa.

2. *Fetishism* is a belief that an object possesses magical power to protect or help its owner.

blemish. We find too, among other things, that in the markets here in Africa and on arrival overseas the slave was inspected, weighed and evaluated like an animal. No one was inclined to buy merchandise which had any blemish or imperfection, apart from a small mark which was the stamp of the slave trader; but nothing else was tolerated on the body of the beast. For there was also the preparation of the slave for the auction market; he was washed and polished—whitened, as they said then—which raised the price. How, then, did these scars originate?"

We could find no answer. His historical survey had deepened the mystery for us.

"Go on, Saer, you tell us," we said, more eager than ever to hear his story of the origin of tribal scars.

And this is what he told us:

The slave ship *African* had been anchored in the bay for days, waiting for a full load before sailing for the Slave States. There were already more than fifty black men and thirty Negro women down in the hold. The captain's agents were scouring the country for supplies. On this particular day only a few of the crew were on board; with the captain and the doctor, they were all in the latter's cabin. Their conversation could be heard on deck.

Amoo bent lower and glanced back at the men who were following him. He was a strong, vigorous man with rippling muscles, fit for any manual work. He gripped his ax firmly in one hand and felt his long cutlass[3] with the other, then crept stealthily forward. More armed men dropped lithely over the bulwarks, one after the other. Momutu, their leader, wearing a broad-brimmed hat, a blue uniform with red facings, and high black boots, signaled with his musket[4] to surround the galley. The ship's cooper[5] had appeared from nowhere and tried to escape by jumping into the sea. But the blacks who had remained in the canoes seized him and speared him to death.

Fighting had broken out aboard the *African*. One of the crew tried to get to close quarters with the leading attackers and was struck down. The captain and the remaining men shut themselves in the doctor's cabin. Momutu and his band, armed with muskets and cutlasses, besieged the cabin, firing at it now and again. Meanwhile the vessel was being looted. As the shots rang out, the attackers increased in number; canoes left the shore, glided across the water to the *African*, and returned laden with goods.

Momutu called his lieutenants to him—four big fellows armed to the teeth. "Start freeing the prisoners and get them out of the hold."

"What about him?" asked his second-in-command, nodding towards Amoo who was standing near the hatchway.

"We'll see about him later," replied Momutu. "He's looking for his daughter. Get the hold open—and don't give any arms to the local men. Take the lot!"

The air was heavy with the smell of powder and sweat. Amoo was already battering away at the hatch covers,[6] and eventually they were broken open with axes and a ram.

Down in the stinking hold the men lay chained together by their ankles. As soon as they had heard the firing they had begun shouting partly with joy, partly from fright.

3. A *cutlass* is a large knife or machete.

4. A *musket* is a large-caliber gun.

5. A *ship's cooper* made and repaired wooden casks and tubs.

6. *Hatch covers* are covers placed on the small openings of a ship.

Vocabulary

lithely (līth′ lē) *adv.* with flexibility and grace; easily; athletically

bulwark (bool′ wərk) *n.* the side of a ship above the upper deck

galley (gal′ ē) *n.* the kitchen and cooking apparatus, especially of a ship or airplane

From between decks, where the women were, came terrified cries. Among all this din, Amoo could make out his daughter's voice. Sweat pouring from him, he hacked at the panels with all his strength.

"Hey, brother, over here!" a man called to him. "You're in a hurry to find your daughter?"

"Yes," he answered, his eyes glittering with impatience.

After many hours of hard work the hold was wide open and Momutu's men had brought up the captives and lined them up on deck, where the ship's cargo for barter[7] had been gathered together: barrels of spirits, boxes of knives, crates containing glassware, silks, parasols[8] and cloth. Amoo had found his daughter, Iome, and the two were standing a little apart from the rest. Amoo knew very well that Momutu had rescued the captives only in order to sell them again. It was he who had lured the *African*'s captain into the bay.

"Now we're going ashore," Momutu told them. "I warn you that you are my prisoners. If anyone tries to escape or to kill himself, I'll take the man next in the line and cut him to pieces."

The sun was sinking towards the horizon and the bay had become a silvery, shimmering sheet of water; the line of trees along the shore stood out darkly. Momutu's men began to put the booty into canoes and take it ashore. Momutu, as undisputed leader, directed operations and gave orders. Some of his men still stood on guard outside the cabin, reminding those inside of their presence by discharging their muskets at the door every few minutes. When the ship had been cleared, Momutu lit a long fuse that ran to two kegs of gunpowder. The captain, finding that all was quiet, started to make his way up top; as he reached the deck, a ball from a musket hit him full in the chest. The last canoes pulled away from the ship, and when they were halfway to the shore the explosions began; then the *African* blew up and sank.

By the time everything had been taken ashore it was quite dark. The prisoners were herded together and a guard set over them, although their hands and feet were still tied. Throughout the night their whisperings and sobs could be heard, punctuated now and then by the sharp crack of a whip. Some distance away, Momutu and his aides were reckoning up their haul, drinking quantities of spirits under the starry sky as they found how well they had done for themselves.

Momutu sent for Amoo to join them.

"You'll have a drink with us, won't you?" said Momutu when Amoo approached with his sleeping daughter on his back (but they only appeared as dim shadows).

"I must be going. I live a long way off and the coast isn't a safe place now. I've been working for you for two months," said Amoo, refusing a drink.

"Is it true that you killed your wife rather than let her be taken prisoner by slave traders?" asked one of the men, reeking of alcohol.

"Ahan!"

"And you've risked your life more than once to save your daughter?"

"She's my daughter! I've seen all my family sold into slavery one after another, and taken away into the unknown. I've grown up with fear, fleeing with my tribe so as not to be made a slave. In my tribe there are no slaves, we're all equal."

"That's because you don't live on the coast," put in a man, which made Momutu roar with laughter. "Go on, have a drink! You're a great fighter. I saw how you cut down that sailor. You're good with an ax."

"Stay with me. You're tough and you know what you want," said Momutu, passing the keg of spirits to him. Amoo politely declined a drink. "This is our work," Momutu went on. "We scour the grasslands, take prisoners and sell them to the whites. Some captains know

7. The term *barter* means the exchange of one item for another or trading goods without using money.

8. *Parasols* are lightweight umbrellas used to shade a person from the sun.

me, but I entice others to this bay and some of my men lure the crew off the ship. Then we loot the ship and get the prisoners back again. We kill any whites left on board. It's easy work, and we win all round. I've given you back your daughter. She's a fine piece and worth several iron bars."

(Until the seventeenth century on the west coast of Africa slaves were paid for with strings of cowries[9] as well as with cheap goods; later, iron bars took the place of cowries. It is known that elsewhere in other markets iron bars have always been the medium of exchange.)

"It's true that I've killed men," said Amoo, "but never to take prisoners and sell them as slaves. That's your work, but it isn't mine. I want to get back to my village."

"He's an odd fellow. He thinks of nothing but his village, his wife and his daughter."

Amoo could only see the whites of their eyes. He knew that these men would not think twice of seizing himself and his daughter and selling them to the first slave trader encountered. He was not made in their evil mold.

"I wanted to set off tonight."

"No," snapped Momutu. The alcohol was beginning to take effect, but he controlled himself and softened his voice. "We'll be in another fight soon. Some of my men have gone with the remaining whites to collect prisoners. We must capture them. Then you'll be free to go."

"I'm going to get her to lie down and have some sleep. She's had a bad time," said Amoo, moving away with his daughter.

"Has she had something to eat?"

"We've both eaten well. I'll be awake early."

The two disappeared into the night; but a shadowy figure followed them.

"He's a fine, strong fellow. Worth four kegs."

"More than that," added another. "He'd fetch several iron bars and some other stuff as well."

9. *Cowries* are the small, brightly colored, glossy shells of a marine animal that were used as money and as ornaments.

Slave House in Goreé, 1975. Mafaly Sene (Senegal). Oil on hardboard, 122 x 82 cm. Collection of the Government of Senegal.

Viewing the painting: How does the composition of this painting relate to its meaning?

"Don't rush it! After the fight tomorrow we'll seize him and his daughter too. She's worth a good bit. We mustn't let them get away. There aren't many of that kind to be found along the coast now."

A soothing coolness was coming in from the sea. Night pressed close, under a starry sky. Now and then a scream of pain rose sharply, followed by another crack of the whip. Amoo had settled down with Iome some distance away from the others. His eyes were alert, though his face looked sleepy. During the dozen fights he had taken part in to redeem his daughter, Momutu had been able to judge his qualities, his great strength and supple body. Three times three moons ago, slave hunters had raided Amoo's village and carried off all the able-bodied people. He had escaped their clutches because that day he had been out in the bush. His mother-in-law, who had been spurned because of her elephantiasis,[10] had told him the whole story.

When he had recovered his daughter from the slave ship, his tears had flowed freely. Firmly holding the girl's wrist and clutching the blood-stained ax in his other hand, his heart had beat fast. Iome, who was nine or ten years old, had wept too.

He had tried to soothe away her fears. "We're going back to the village. You mustn't cry, but you must do what I tell you. Do you understand?"

"Yes, father."

"Don't cry any more. It's all over now! I'm here with you."

And there in the cradle of the night, Iome lay asleep with her head on her father's thigh. Amoo unslung his ax and placed it close at hand. Sitting with his back against a tree, his whole attention was concentrated on the immediate surroundings. At the slightest rustle, his hand went out to grasp his weapon. He dozed a little from time to time.

Even before a wan gleam had lighted the east, Momutu roused his men. Some of them were ordered to take the prisoners and the loot to a safe place. Amoo and Iome kept out of the way. The girl had deep-set eyes and was tall for her age; her hair was parted in the middle and drawn into two plaits which hung down to her shoulders. She clung to her father's side; she had seen her former companions from the slave ship, and although she may not have known the fate in store for them, the sound of the whips left her in no doubt as to their present state.

"They'll wait for us farther on," said Momutu, coming across to Amoo. "We mustn't let ourselves be surprised by the whites' scouting party. Why are you keeping your child with you? You could have left her with one of my men."

"I'd rather keep her with me. She's very frightened," answered Amoo, watching the prisoners and escort moving off.

"She's a beautiful girl."

"Yes."

"As beautiful as her mother?"

"Not quite."

Momutu turned away and got the rest of his men, about thirty, on the move. They marched in single column. Momutu was well known among slave traders, and none of them trusted him. He had previously acted as an agent for some of the traders, then had become a "master of language" (interpreter), moving between the forts and camps where the captured Negroes were held.

They marched all that morning, with Amoo and his daughter following in the rear. When Iome was tired, her father carried her on his back. He was well aware that a watch was being kept on him. The men ahead of him were coarse, sorry-looking creatures; they looked ridiculous, trailing their long muskets. They began to leave the grasslands behind and soon were among tall trees where flocks of vultures perched. No one spoke. All that could be heard was the chattering of birds and now and again a distant, echoing howling. Then they reached the forest, humid and hostile, and Momutu called a halt; he dispersed his men and told them to rest.

"Are you tired, brother?" one of them asked Amoo. "And what about her?"

Iome raised her thick-lashed eyes towards the man, then looked at her father.

"She's a bit tired," said Amoo, looking round for a resting place. He saw a fallen trunk at the foot of a tree and took Iome to it. The man set to keep watch on them remained a little distance away.

Momutu had a few sweet potatoes distributed to the men, and when this meager meal was over he went to see Amoo.

"How's your daughter?"

10. *Elephantiasis* (el′ ə fan tī′ ə sis) is a disease in which a person's tissues or limbs enlarge or thicken.

"She's asleep," said Amoo, who was carving a doll out of a piece of wood.

"She's a strong girl," said Momutu, sitting down beside him and taking off his broad-brimmed hat. His big black boots were all muddy. "We'll have a rest and wait for them here. They're bound to come this way."

Amoo was more and more on his guard. He nodded, but kept his eyes on Iome in between working at the piece of wood, which was gradually taking shape.

"After that you'll be free to go. Do you really want to go back to your village?"

"Yes."

"But you haven't anybody left there," said Momutu, and without waiting for Amoo to reply went on, "I once had a village, too, on the edge of a forest. My mother and father lived there, many relatives—a whole clan! We had meat to eat and sometimes fish. But over the years, the village declined. There was no end to lamentations. Ever since I was born I'd heard nothing but screams, seen mad flights into the bush or the forest. You go into the forest, and you die from some disease; you stay in the open, and you're captured to be sold into slavery. What was I to do? Well, I made my choice. I'd rather be with the hunters than the hunted."

Amoo, too, knew that such was life. You were never safe, never sure of seeing the next day dawn. But what he did not understand was the use made of the men and women who were taken away. It was said that the whites used their skins for making boots.

They talked for a long time, or rather Momutu talked without stopping. He boasted of his exploits and his drinking bouts. As Amoo listened, he became more and more puzzled about Momutu's character. He was like some petty warlord, wielding power by force and constraint. Eventually, after what seemed a very long time to Amoo, a man came to warn the chief that the whites were approaching. Momutu gave his orders—kill them all, and hold their prisoners. In an instant the forest fell silent; only the neutral voice of the wind could be heard.

The long file of black prisoners came into view, led by four Europeans each armed with two pistols and a culverin.[11] The prisoners, men and women, were joined together by a wooden yoke bolted round the neck and attached to the man in front and the one behind. Three more Europeans brought up the rear, and a fourth, probably ill, was being carried in a litter[12] by four natives.

A sudden burst of firing from up in the trees echoed long and far. This was followed by screams and confused fighting. Amoo took advantage to fell the man guarding him and, taking his daughter by the hand, slipped away into the forest.

They crossed streams and rivers, penetrating ever deeper into the forest but heading always to the southeast. Amoo's knife and ax had never been so useful as during this time. They traveled chiefly at night, never in broad daylight, avoiding all human contact.

Three weeks later they arrived at the village—about thirty huts huddled together between the bush and the source of a river. There were few inhabitants about at that hour of the day; besides, having been frequently drained of its virile members, the village was sparsely populated. When Amoo and Iome reached the threshold of his mother-in-law's hut, the old woman limped out and her cries drew other people, many of them feeble. They were terrified at first, but stood uttering exclamations of joy and

11. A *culverin* (kul′ vər in) is an old-fashioned firearm, much like a musket.

12. A *litter,* or stretcher, is a device used for carrying a sick or injured person.

Vocabulary

lamentation (lam′ ən tā′ shən) *n.* act of mourning, crying, or wailing surprise when they saw Amoo and Iome. Tears and questions mingled as they crowded round. Iome's grandmother gathered her up and took her into the hut like a most precious possession, and the girl replied to her questions between floods of tears.

The elders sent for Amoo to have a talk and tell them of his adventures.

"All my life, and since before my father's life," said one of the oldest present, "the whole country has lived in the fear of being captured and sold to the whites. The whites are barbarians."

"Will it ever end?" queried another. "I have seen all my children carried off, and I can't remember how many times we have moved the village. We can't go any farther into the forest . . . there are the wild beasts, diseases . . ."

"I'd rather face wild beasts than slave hunters," said a third man. "Five or six rains ago, we felt safe here. But we aren't any longer. There's a slave camp only three-and-a-half days' march from the village."

They fell silent; their wrinkled, worn and worried faces bore the mark of their epoch. They discussed the necessity to move once again. Some were in favor, others pointed out the danger of living in the heart of the forest without water, the lack of strong men, and the family graves that would have to be abandoned. The patriarch, who had the flat head and thick neck of a degenerate, proposed that they should spend the winter where they were but send a group to seek another suitable site. It would be sheer madness to leave without having first

Vocabulary
query (kwēr′ ē) *v.* to ask, especially with a desire for authoritative information

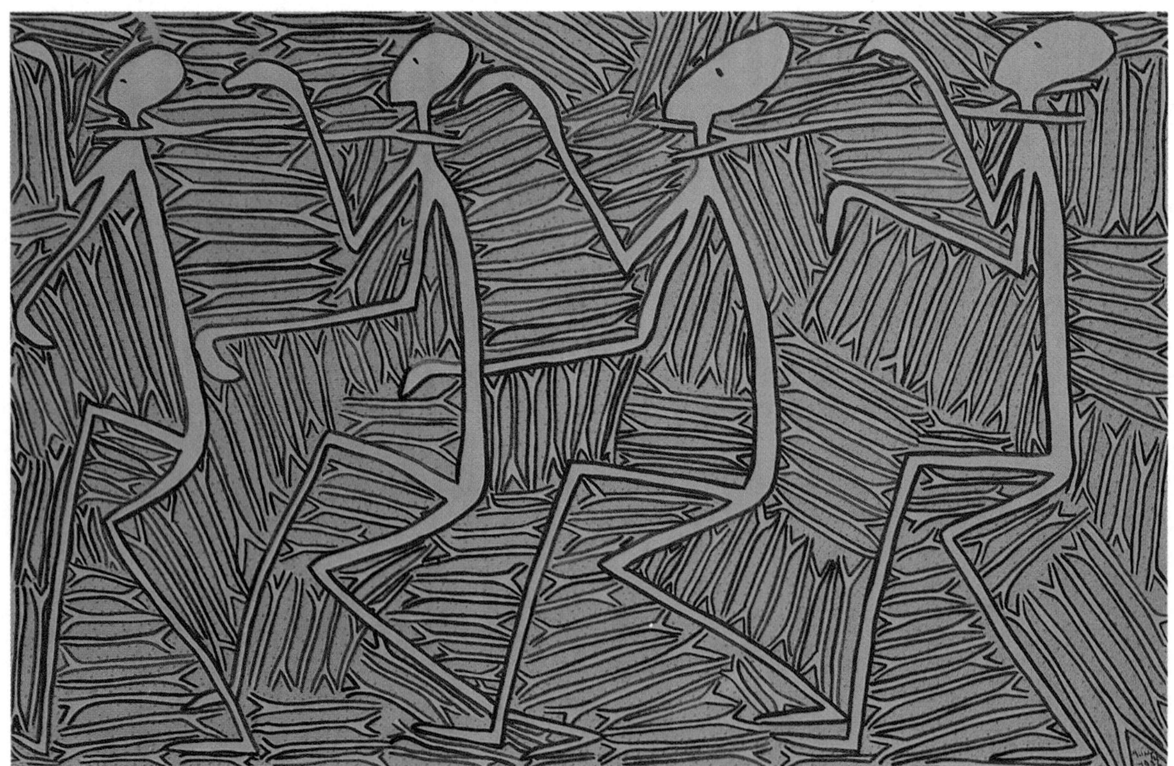

Slaves Yoked Together, 1973. Mode Muntu (Zaire). Gouache on paper, 31 x 48 cm. Collection of Bogumil Jewsiewicki.
Viewing the painting: Describe the slaves in the painting. How are they like or unlike the slaves in the story?

Writing Skills

Writing Effective Introductions

Just as you want to put your best self forward when you meet someone for the first time, you also want to introduce your writing in a way that will grab readers' attention and present your topic well. The most effective way to do this will depend on what you are writing. If you're writing a short story, for example, you may want to use a strategy similar to the one that Ousmane Sembène does in the beginning of "Tribal Scars *or* The Voltaique," which is reprinted below.

> **In the evenings we all go to Mane's place, where we drink mint tea and discuss all sorts of subjects, even though we know very little about them. But recently we neglected the major problems such as the ex-Belgian Congo, the trouble in the Mali Federation, the Algerian War and the next UNO meeting—even women, a subject which normally takes up about a quarter of our time. The reason was that Saer, who is usually so stolid and serious, had raised the question, "Why do we have tribal scars?"**

Sembène begins by using a single, strong detail to set the scene: "We all go to Mane's place, where we drink mint tea." He also gives a tantalizing glimpse of where the story will lead by having Saer ask, "Why do we have tribal scars?" If their curiosity is raised, readers are likely to read on.

The following suggestions may help you write effective introductions for other types of writing:

- In personal writing, you may want to start out with an interesting anecdote or opinion, so that the reader gets to know you right away.
- In descriptive writing, consider beginning by describing an especially important or evocative detail. That will help your reader grasp the tone of your description.
- In expository writing–writing that explains and informs–it is especially important to state the purpose of your writing in a thesis statement. Stating the purpose in your introduction lets the reader know what to expect.
- In persuasive writing, you may want to begin by asking a question or presenting a scenario that's likely to arouse your reader's sympathy. Then state your position.

EXERCISES

1. Search through newspapers, magazines, and this book to find at least three examples of strong introductions. Explain what strategy each writer has used to create an effective introduction.
2. Using one of the four strategies described, write the introduction to a detailed description of your home, your neighborhood, or your favorite place.

NIGERIA, 1965

Before You Read

The Voter

Meet Chinua Achebe

"The worst thing that can happen to any people is the loss of their dignity and self-respect. The writer's duty is to help them regain it. . . ."

Chinua Achebe (chēn′ wä ä chā′ bā) grew up in an Ibo (also spelled Igbo) village in eastern Nigeria. The son of Christian missionary teachers, he became fascinated by his own people's traditional beliefs and customs. He feels that he grew up during a fortunate time, saying, "[I]t was easy, especially if you lived in a village, to see, if not in whole, at least in part, these old ways of life. I was particularly interested in listening to the way old people talked. . . ." Achebe often describes Ibo customs in his fiction.

Achebe attracted international recognition with his first novel, *Things Fall Apart* (1958), the story of a traditional Ibo community that disintegrates after the arrival of European missionaries. In later novels, Achebe portrays Nigerian society during colonial times and following independence. Achebe has also published volumes of short stories, essays, and children's fiction.

Chinua Achebe was born in 1930.

Reading Focus

What motivates people to vote in elections?

Share Ideas Discuss this question with a classmate. Consider your own experiences, such as voting in class elections.

Setting a Purpose Read about how one man behaves during an election.

Five-naira bill from the Central Bank of Nigeria.

Building Background

Nigeria After Independence

Nigeria became an independent nation in 1960. Nigeria's efforts to establish a democratic system have been hampered by corruption among some politicians. Lingering traditional hostilities between ethnic groups with different languages, religions, and culture patterns have also posed a serious obstacle to establishing a stable democracy. After episodes of violence and a full-scale civil war, Nigeria at the end of the twentieth century came under the rule of military regimes, which continued to encounter resistance from democracy activists in Nigeria and in other African countries. Achebe's story "The Voter" takes place in an Ibo village shortly after independence.

Research

Use the library or the Internet to learn more about Nigeria's government since independence. As you read "The Voter," think about ways a knowledge of Nigeria's history might help you understand the story better.

The VOTER

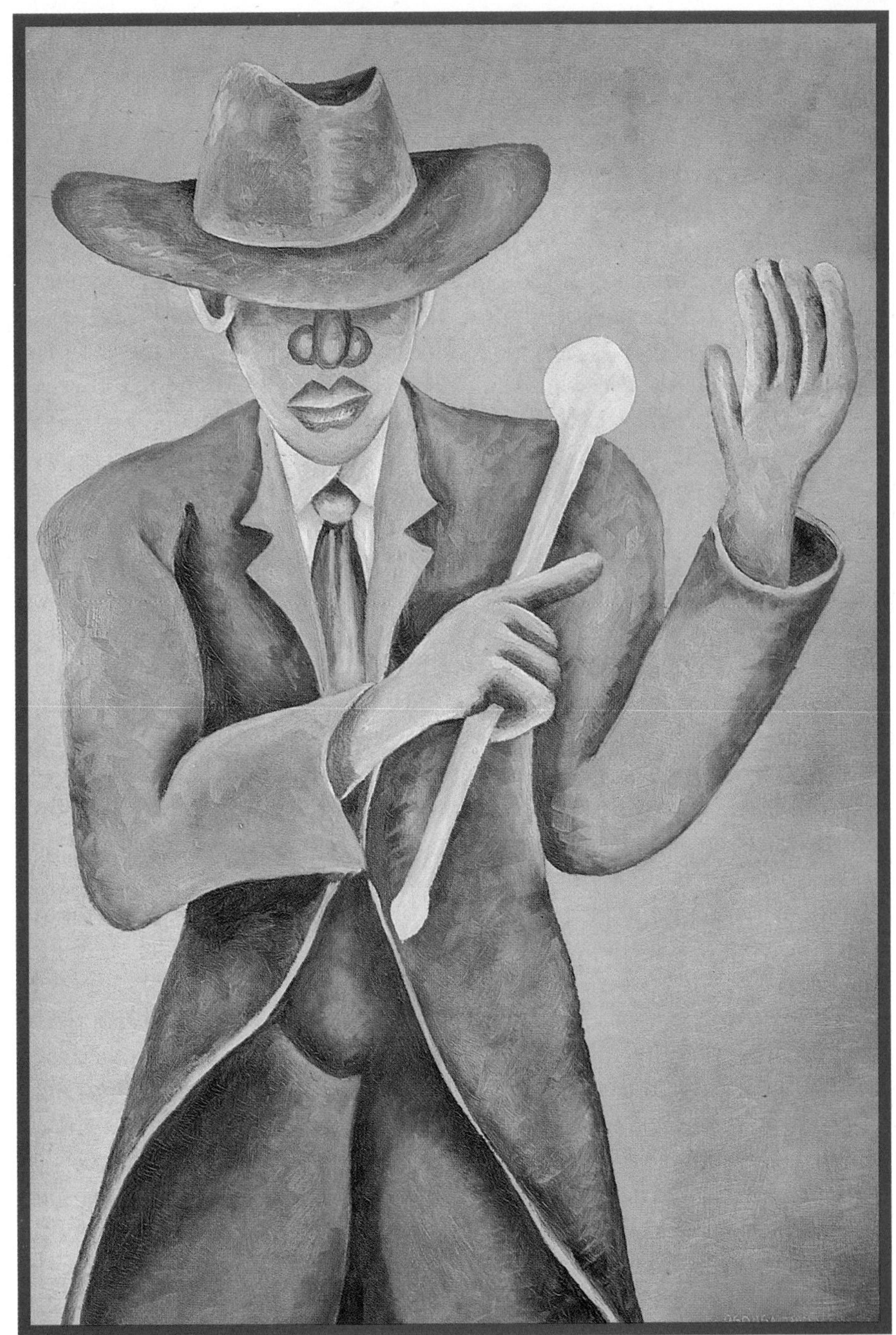

Election Time, 20th century. Tom Ogonga (Kenya). Oil on paper. Collection of the artist.

Chinua Achebe

RUFUS OKEKE—ROOF FOR SHORT—WAS A VERY POPULAR MAN in his village. Although the villagers did not explain it in so many words Roof's popularity was a measure of their gratitude to an energetic young man who, unlike most of his fellows nowadays had not abandoned the village in order to seek work, any work, in the towns.

And Roof was not a village lout either. Everyone knew how he had spent two years as a bicycle repairer's apprentice in Port Harcourt, and had given up of his own free will a bright future to return to his people and guide them in these difficult times. Not that Umuofia needed a lot of guidance. The village already belonged *en masse* to the People's Alliance Party, and its most illustrious son, Chief the Honorable Marcus Ibe, was Minister of Culture in the outgoing government (which was pretty certain to be the incoming one as well). Nobody doubted that the Honorable Minister would be elected in his constituency. Opposition to him was like the proverbial fly trying to move a dunghill. It would have been ridiculous enough without coming, as it did now, from a complete nonentity.

As was to be expected Roof was in the service of the Honorable Minister for the coming elections. He had become a real expert in election campaigning at all levels—village, local government or national. He could tell the mood and temper of the electorate at any given time. For instance he had warned the Minister months ago about the radical change that had come into the thinking of Umuofia since the last national election.

The villagers had had five years in which to see how quickly and plentifully politics brought wealth, chieftaincy titles, doctorate degrees and other honors some of which, like the last, had still to be explained satisfactorily to them; for in their naïveté they still expected a doctor to be able to heal the sick. Anyhow, these honors and benefits had come so readily to the man to whom they had given their votes free of charge five years ago that they were now ready to try it a different way.

Their point was that only the other day Marcus Ibe was a not too successful mission school teacher. Then politics had come to their village and he had wisely joined up, some said just in time to avoid imminent dismissal arising from a female teacher's pregnancy. Today he was Chief the Honorable; he had two long cars and had just built himself the biggest house anyone had seen in these parts. But let it be said that none of these successes had gone to Marcus's head as well they might. He remained devoted to his people. Whenever he could he left the good things of the capital and returned to his village which had neither running water nor electricity, although he had lately installed a private plant to supply electricity to his new house. He knew the source of his good fortune, unlike the little bird who ate and drank and went out to challenge his personal spirit. Marcus had christened his new house "Umuofia Mansions" in honor of his village, and he had slaughtered five bulls and countless goats to entertain the people on the day it was opened by the Archbishop.

Everyone was full of praise for him. One old man said: "Our son is a good man; he is not like the mortar which as soon as food comes its way turns its back on the ground." But when the feasting was over, the villagers told themselves that they had underrated the power of the ballot paper before and should not do so again. Chief the Honorable Marcus Ibe was not unprepared. He had drawn five months' salary in advance, changed a few hundred pounds into shining shillings and armed his campaign boys with eloquent little jute bags. In the day he made his speeches; at night his stalwarts conducted their whispering campaign. Roof was the most trusted of these campaigners.

"We have a Minister from our village, one of our own sons," he said to a group of elders in the house of Ogbuefi Ezenwa, a man of high traditional title. "What greater honor can a village have? Do you ever stop to ask yourselves why we should be singled out for this honor? I will tell you; it is because we are favored by the leaders of PAP. Whether or not we cast our paper for Marcus, PAP will continue to rule. Think of the pipe-borne water they have promised us . . ."

Besides Roof and his assistant there were five elders in the room. An old hurricane lamp with a cracked, sooty, glass chimney gave out yellowish light in their midst. The elders sat on very low stools. On the floor, directly in front of each of them, lay two shilling pieces. Outside beyond the fastened door, the moon kept a straight face.

"We believe every word you say to be true," said Ezenwa. "We shall, every one of us, drop his paper for Marcus. Who would leave an ozo feast and go to a poor ritual meal? Tell Marcus he has our papers, and our wives' papers too. But what we do say is that two shillings is shameful." He brought the lamp close and tilted it at the money before him as if to make sure he had not mistaken its value. "Yes, two shillings is too shameful. If Marcus were a poor man—which our ancestors forbid—I should be the first to give him my paper free, as I did before. But today Marcus is a great man and does his things like a great man. We did not ask him for money yesterday; we shall not ask him tomorrow. But today is our day; we have climbed the iroko tree today and would be foolish not to take down all the firewood we need."

Roof had to agree. He had lately been taking down a lot of firewood himself. Only yesterday he had asked Marcus for one of his many rich robes—and had got it. Last Sunday Marcus's wife (the teacher that nearly got him in trouble) had objected (like the woman she was) when Roof pulled out his fifth bottle of beer from the refrigerator; she was roundly and publicly rebuked by her husband. To cap it all Roof had won a land case recently because, among other things, he had been chauffeur-driven to the disputed site. So he understood the elders about the firewood.

"All right," he said in English and then reverted to Ibo. "Let us not quarrel about small things." He stood up, adjusted his robes and plunged his hand once more into the bag. Then he bent down like a priest distributing the host and gave one shilling more to every man; only he did not put it into their palms but on the floor in front of them. The men, who had so far not deigned to touch the things, looked at the floor and shook their heads. Roof got up again and gave each man another shilling.

"I am through," he said with a defiance that was no less effective for being transparently faked. The elders too knew how far to go without losing decorum. So when Roof added: "Go cast your paper for the enemy if you like!" they quickly calmed him down with a suitable speech from each of them. By the time the last man had spoken it was possible, without great loss of dignity, to pick up the things from the floor . . .

The enemy Roof had referred to was the Progressive Organization Party (POP) which had been formed by the tribes down the coast to save themselves, as the founders of the party proclaimed, from "total political, cultural, social and religious annihilation." Although it was clear the party had no chance here it had plunged, with typical foolishness, into a straight fight with PAP, providing cars and loudspeakers to a few local rascals and thugs to go around and make a lot of noise. No one knew for certain how much money POP had let loose in Umuofia but it was said to be very considerable. Their local campaigners would end up very rich, no doubt.

Up to last night everything had been "moving according to plan," as Roof would have put it. Then he had received a strange visit from the leader of the POP campaign team. Although he and Roof were well-known to each other, and might even be called friends, his visit was cold and business-like. No words were wasted. He placed five pounds on the floor before Roof and said, "We want your vote." Roof got up from his chair, went to the outside door, closed it carefully and returned to his chair. The brief exercise gave him enough time to weigh the proposition. As he spoke his eyes never left the red notes on the floor. He seemed to be mesmerized by the picture of the cocoa farmer harvesting his crops.

Self-Elevated One, 1991. Meek Gichugu (Kenya). Oil on canvas, 27 x 38 cm. Collection of Marc Van Rampelberg.
Viewing the painting: How does the entangled image in this painting reflect the politics depicted in "The Voter"?

"You know I work for Marcus," he said feebly. "It will be very bad . . ."

"Marcus will not be there when you put in your paper. We have plenty of work to do tonight; are you taking this or not?"

"It will not be heard outside this room?" asked Roof.

"We are after votes not gossip."

"All right," said Roof in English.

The man nudged his companion and he brought forward an object covered with a red cloth and proceeded to remove the cover. It was a fearsome little affair contained in a clay pot with feathers stuck into it.

"The *iyi* comes from Mbanta. You know what that means. Swear that you will vote for Maduka. If you fail to do so, this *iyi* take note."

Roof's heart nearly flew out when he saw the *iyi;* indeed he knew the fame of Mbanta in these things. But he was a man of quick decision. What could a single vote cast in secret for Maduka take away from Marcus's certain victory? Nothing.

"I will cast my paper for Maduka; if not this *iyi* take note."

"Das all," said the man as he rose with his companion who had covered up the object again and was taking it back to their car.

"You know he has no chance against Marcus," said Roof at the door.

"It is enough that he gets a few votes now; next time he will get more. People will hear that he gives out pounds, not shillings, and they will listen."

Election morning. The great day every five years when the people exercise power. Weather-beaten posters on walls of houses, tree trunks and telegraph poles. The few that were still whole called out their message to those who could read. Vote for the People's Alliance Party! Vote for the Progressive Organization Party! Vote for PAP! Vote for POP! The posters that were torn called out as much of the message as they could.

As usual Chief the Honorable Marcus Ibe was doing things in grand style. He had hired a highlife band from Umuru and stationed it at such a distance from the voting booths as just managed to be lawful. Many villagers danced to the music, their ballot papers held aloft, before proceeding to the booths. Chief the Honorable Marcus Ibe sat in the "owner's corner" of his enormous green car and smiled and nodded. One enlightened villager came up to the car, shook hands with the great man and said in advance, "Congrats!" This immediately set the pattern. Hundreds of admirers shook Marcus's hand and said "Corngrass!"

Roof and the other organizers were prancing up and down, giving last minute advice to the voters and pouring with sweat.

"Do not forget," he said again to a group of illiterate women who seemed ready to burst with enthusiasm and good humor, "our sign is the motor car . . ."

"Like the one Marcus is sitting inside."

"Thank you, mother," said Roof. "It is the same car. The box with the car shown on its body is the box for you. Don't look at the other with the man's head: it is for those whose heads are not correct."

This was greeted with loud laughter. Roof cast a quick and busy-like glance towards the Minister and received a smile of appreciation.

"Vote for the car," he shouted, all the veins in his neck standing out. "Vote for the car and you will ride in it!"

"Or if we don't, our children will," piped the same sharp, old girl.

The band struck up a new number: "Why walk when you can ride . . ."

In spite of his apparent calm and confidence Chief the Honorable Marcus was a relentless stickler for detail. He knew he would win what the newspapers called "a landslide victory" but he did not wish, even so, to throw away a single vote. So as soon as the first rush of voters was over he promptly asked his campaign boys to go one at a time and put in their ballot papers.

"Roof, you had better go first," he said.

Roof's spirits fell; but he let no one see it. All morning he had masked his deep worry with a surface exertion which was unusual even for him. Now he dashed off in his springy fashion towards the booths. A policeman at the entrance searched him for illegal ballot papers and passed him. Then the electoral officer explained to him about the two boxes. By this time the spring had gone clean out of his walk. He sidled in and was confronted by the car and the head. He brought out his ballot paper from his pocket and looked at it. How could he betray Marcus even in secret? He resolved to go back to the other man and return his five pounds . . . Five pounds! He knew at once it was impossible. He had sworn on that *iyi*. The notes were red; the cocoa farmer busy at work.

At this point he heard the muffled voice of the policeman asking the electoral officer what the man was doing inside. "Abi na pickin im de born?"

Quick as lightning a thought leapt into Roof's mind. He folded the paper, tore it in two along the crease and put one half in each box. He took the precaution of putting the first half into Maduka's box and confirming the action verbally: "I vote for Maduka."

They marked his thumb with indelible purple ink to prevent his return, and he went out of the booth as jauntily as he had gone in.

Responding to Literature

Personal Response

How did you react to the characters in the story? Why do you think you reacted to them in that way? In your journal, write a few paragraphs describing and explaining your reactions.

Analyzing Literature

Recall and Interpret

1. Why is Roof popular in his village? What can you infer about the village from the narrator's explanation of his popularity?
2. How has Marcus Ibe's life changed since becoming Minister of Culture? What do the villagers think of him?
3. Why do the village elders reject Roof's first bribe offer? What does their rejection reveal about their attitude toward the elections?
4. Why does the leader of the opposition party offer Roof a bribe? Do you think that Roof believes he is betraying Marcus Ibe when he accepts the bribe? Explain.
5. What is the decision that Roof makes in the voting booth? What do you think will be the result of Roof's vote?

Evaluate and Connect

6. In the Reading Focus on page 128, you were asked to discuss what motivates people to vote in elections. Apart from offering them bribes, in what ways does Roof try to motivate the villagers to vote for his candidate, Marcus Ibe?
7. A **theme** is a central message or idea about life that is implied or stated in a literary work (see **Literary Terms Handbook,** page R12). What theme is implied in "The Voter"?
8. In addition to making sure voters do not bring illegal ballot papers into the voting booth, what other steps could officials take to ensure the fairness of the election?
9. A **symbol** is an object or action that stands for something else in addition to itself (see **Literary Terms Handbook,** page R12). What does Roof's torn ballot paper symbolize?
10. Do you think that the problems Achebe describes in the Nigerian political system also occur in other countries? Explain.

Literary Criticism

"The Voter," argues C. L. Innes, "is told from the point of view of a narrator sympathetic to [Roof] . . . Except perhaps for Roof's energy and lack of malice (he is just doing his job), there are no redeeming features in this election campaign." Do you agree with Innes's reading of the story? Why or why not? Discuss your answers with a partner and present your group's conclusions to the entire class.

Literary ELEMENTS

Motivation

Motivation is the reason or reasons behind a character's actions. A character's motivation may be stated directly, or the reader may have to infer motivation from details in the story. Many characters are motivated by a combination of factors. For example, a woman might risk her life to save a drowning child not only because she wants to help the child, but also because she feels guilty about not having helped someone in the past.

1. What important factors motivated Marcus Ibe to go into politics?
2. What do you think motivates Roof's decision in the voting booth?

- See **Literary Terms Handbook,** p. R8.

As I still marveled at the beauty of this young woman, Podho told me, 'Out of all the women in this land, we have chosen this one. Let her offer herself as a sacrifice to the lake monster! And on that day, the rain will come down in torrents. Let everyone stay at home on that day, lest he be carried away by the floods.'"

Outside there was a strange stillness, except for the thirsty birds that sang lazily on the dying trees. The blinding mid-day heat had forced the people to retire to their huts. Not far away from the chief's hut, two guards were snoring away quietly. Labong'o removed his crown and the large eagle-head that hung loosely on his shoulders. He left the hut, and instead of asking Nyabog'o the messenger to beat the drum, he went straight and beat it himself. In no time the whole household had assembled under the siala tree where he usually addressed them. He told Oganda to wait a while in her grandmother's hut.

When Labong'o stood to address his household, his voice was hoarse and the tears choked him. He started to speak, but words refused to leave his lips. His wives and sons knew there was great danger. Perhaps their enemies had declared war on them. Labong'o's eyes were red, and they could see he had been weeping. At last he told them. "One whom we love and treasure must be taken away from us. Oganda is to die." Labong'o's voice was so faint, that he could not hear it himself. But he continued, "The ancestors have chosen her to be offered as a sacrifice to the lake monster in order that we may have rain."

They were completely stunned. As a confused murmur broke out, Oganda's mother fainted and was carried off to her own hut. But the other people rejoiced. They danced around singing and chanting, "Oganda is the lucky one to die for the people. If it is to save the people, let Oganda go."

In her grandmother's hut Oganda wondered what the whole family were discussing about her that she could not hear. Her grandmother's hut was well away from the chief's court and, much as she strained her ears, she could not hear what was said. "It must be marriage," she concluded. It was an accepted custom for the family to discuss their daughter's future marriage behind her back. A faint smile played on Oganda's lips as she thought of the several young men who swallowed saliva at the mere mention of her name.

There was Kech, the son of a neighboring clan elder. Kech was very handsome. He had sweet, meek eyes and a roaring laughter. He would make a wonderful father, Oganda thought. But they would not be a good match. Kech was a bit too short to be her husband. It would humiliate her to have to look down at Kech each time she spoke to him. Then she thought of Dimo, the tall young man who had already distinguished himself as a brave warrior and an outstanding wrestler. Dimo adored Oganda, but Oganda thought he would make a cruel husband, always quarreling and ready to fight. No, she did not like him. Oganda fingered the glittering chain on her waist as she thought of Osinda. A long time ago when she was quite young Osinda had given her that chain, and instead of wearing it around her neck several times, she wore it round her waist where it could stay permanently. She heard her heart pounding so loudly as she thought of him. She whispered, "Let it be you they are discussing, Osinda, the lovely one. Come now and take me away . . ."

The lean figure in the doorway startled Oganda, who was rapt in thought about the man she loved. "You have frightened me, Grandma," said Oganda laughing. "Tell me, is it my marriage you are discussing? You can take it from me that I won't marry any of them."

Vocabulary

torrent (tôr′ ənt) *n.* enormous outpouring of rainwater

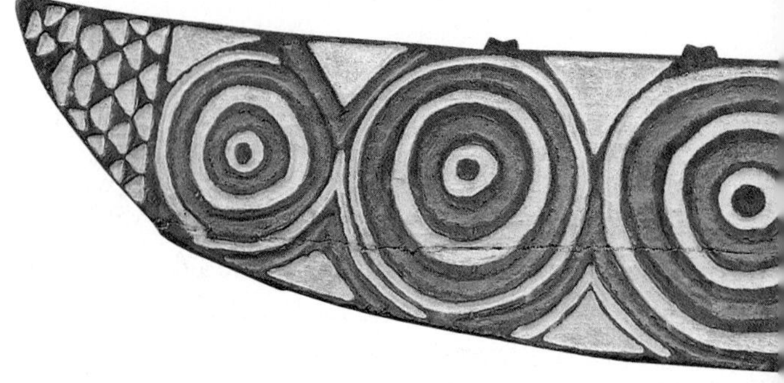

A smile played on her lips again. She was coaxing the old lady to tell her quickly, to tell her they were pleased with Osinda.

In the open space outside the excited relatives were dancing and singing. They were coming to the hut now, each carrying a gift to put at Oganda's feet. As their singing got nearer Oganda was able to hear what they were saying: "If it is to save the people, if it is to give us rain, let Oganda go. Let Oganda die for her people, and for her ancestors." Was she mad to think that they were singing about her? How could she die? She found the lean figure of her grandmother barring the door. She could not get out. The look on her grandmother's face warned her that there was danger around the corner. "Mother, it is not marriage then?" Oganda asked urgently. She suddenly felt panicky like a mouse cornered by a hungry cat. Forgetting that there was only one door in the hut Oganda fought desperately to find another exit. She must fight for her life. But there was none.

She closed her eyes, leapt like a wild tiger through the door, knocking her grandmother flat to the ground. There outside in mourning garments Labong'o stood motionless, his hands folded at the back. He held his daughter's hand and led her away from the excited crowd to the little red-painted hut where her mother was resting. Here he broke the news officially to his daughter.

For a long time the three souls who loved one another dearly sat in darkness. It was no good speaking. And even if they tried, the words could not have come out. In the past they had been like three cooking stones, sharing their burdens. Taking Oganda away from them would leave two useless stones which would not hold a cooking-pot.

News that the beautiful daughter of the chief was to be sacrificed to give the people rain spread across the country like wind. At sunset the chief's village was full of relatives and friends who had come to congratulate Oganda. Many more were on their way coming, carrying their gifts. They would dance till morning to keep her company. And in the morning they would prepare her a big farewell feast. All these relatives thought it a great honor to be selected by the spirits to die, in order that the society may live. "Oganda's name will always remain a living name among us," they boasted.

But was it maternal love that prevented Minya from rejoicing with the other women? Was it the memory of the agony and pain of childbirth that made her feel so sorrowful? Or was it the deep warmth and understanding that passes between a suckling babe and her mother that made Oganda part of her life, her flesh? Of course it was an honor, a great honor, for her daughter to be chosen to die for the country. But what could she gain once her daughter was blown away by the wind? There were so many other women in the land, why choose her daughter, her only child! Had human life any meaning at all—other women had houses full of children while she, Minya, had to lose her only child!

In the cloudless sky the moon shone brightly, and the numerous stars glittered with a bewitching beauty. The dancers of all age-groups assembled to dance before Oganda, who sat close to her mother, sobbing quietly. All these years she had been with her people she thought she understood them. But now she discovered that she was a stranger among them. If they loved her as they had always professed why were they not making

Vocabulary
coax (kōks) *v.* to persuade by means of gentle urging or flattery

Bobo Butterfly Mask. Early 20th century, Bwa people, Burkina Faso. Pigment on wood, width: 245.1 cm. Collection of Thomas G. B. Wheelock.

Viewing the mask: What might this mask represent to its wearer? What do natural creatures and events represent to the characters in the story?

any attempt to save her? Did her people really understand what it felt like to die young? Unable to restrain her emotions any longer, she sobbed loudly as her age-group got up to dance. They were young and beautiful and very soon they would marry and have their own children. They would have husbands to love and little huts for themselves. They would have reached maturity. Oganda touched the chain around her waist as she thought of Osinda. She wished Osinda was there too, among her friends. "Perhaps he is ill," she thought gravely. The chain comforted Oganda—she would die with it around her waist and wear it in the underground world.

In the morning a big feast was prepared for Oganda. The women prepared many different tasty dishes so that she could pick and choose. "People don't eat after death," they said. Delicious though the food looked, Oganda touched none of it. Let the happy people eat. She contented herself with sips of water from a little calabash.

The time for her departure was drawing near, and each minute was precious. It was a day's journey to the lake. She was to walk all night, passing through the great forest. But nothing could touch her, not even the denizens of the forest. She was already anointed with sacred oil. From the time Oganda received the sad news she had expected Osinda to appear any moment. But he was not there. A relative told her that Osinda was away on a private visit. Oganda realized that she would never see her beloved again.

In the afternoon the whole village stood at the gate to say good-bye and to see her for the last time. Her mother wept on her neck for a long time. The great chief in a mourning skin came to the gate barefooted, and mingled with the people—a simple father in grief. He took off his wrist bracelet and put it on his daughter's wrist saying, "You will always live among us. The spirit of our forefathers is with you."

Tongue-tied and unbelieving Oganda stood there before the people. She had nothing to say. She looked at her home once more. She could hear her heart beating so painfully within her. All her childhood plans were coming to an end. She felt like a flower nipped in the bud never to enjoy the morning dew again. She looked at her weeping mother, and whispered, "Whenever you want to see me, always look at the sunset. I will be there."

Oganda turned southwards to start her trek to the lake. Her parents, relatives, friends and admirers stood at the gate and watched her go.

Her beautiful slender figure grew smaller and smaller till she mingled with the thin dry trees in the forest. As Oganda walked the lonely path that wound its way in the wilderness, she sang a song, and her own voice kept her company.

Vocabulary

denizen (den′ ə zən) *n.* inhabitant

The ancestors have said Oganda must die
The daughter of the chief must be sacrificed,
When the lake monster feeds on my flesh.
The people will have rain.
Yes, the rain will come down in torrents.
And the floods will wash away the sandy beaches
When the daughter of the chief dies in the lake.
My age-group has consented
My parents have consented
So have my friends and relatives.
Let Oganda die to give us rain.
My age-group are young and ripe,
Ripe for womanhood and motherhood
But Oganda must die young,
Oganda must sleep with the ancestors.
Yes, rain will come down in torrents.

The red rays of the setting sun embraced Oganda, and she looked like a burning candle in the wilderness.

The people who came to hear her sad song were touched by her beauty. But they all said the same thing: "If it is to save the people, if it is to give us rain, then be not afraid. Your name will forever live among us."

At midnight Oganda was tired and weary. She could walk no more. She sat under a big tree, and having sipped water from her calabash, she rested her head on the tree trunk and slept.

When Oganda woke up in the morning the sun was high in the sky. After walking for many hours, she reached the *tong'*, a strip of land that separated the inhabited part of the country from the sacred place *(kar lamo)*. No layman could enter this place and come out alive—only those who had direct contact with the spirits and the Almighty were allowed to enter this holy of holies. But Oganda had to pass through this sacred land on her way to the lake, which she had to reach at sunset.

A large crowd gathered to see her for the last time. Her voice was now hoarse and painful, but there was no need to worry any more. Soon she would not have to sing. The crowd looked at Oganda sympathetically, mumbling words she could not hear. But none of them pleaded for life. As Oganda opened the gate, a child, a young child, broke loose from the crowd, and ran towards her. The child took a small earring from her sweaty hands and gave it to Oganda saying, "When you reach the world of the dead, give this earring to my sister. She died last week. She forgot this ring." Oganda, taken aback by the strange request, took the little ring, and handed her precious water and food to the child. She did not need them now. Oganda did not know whether to laugh or cry. She had heard mourners sending their love to their sweethearts, long dead, but this idea of sending gifts was new to her.

Oganda held her breath as she crossed the barrier to enter the sacred land. She looked appealingly at the crowd, but there was no response. Their minds were too preoccupied with their own survival. Rain was the precious medicine they were longing for, and the sooner Oganda could get to her destination the better.

A strange feeling possessed Oganda as she picked her way in the sacred land. There were strange noises that often startled her, and her first reaction was to take to her heels. But she remembered that she had to fulfill the wish of her people. She was exhausted, but the path was still winding. Then suddenly the path ended on sandy land. The water had retreated miles away from the shore leaving a wide stretch of sand. Beyond this was the vast expanse of water.

Oganda felt afraid. She wanted to picture the size and shape of the monster, but fear would not let her. The society did not talk about it, nor did the crying children who were silenced by the mention of its name. The sun was still up, but it was no longer hot. For a long time Oganda walked ankle-deep in the sand. She was exhausted and longed desperately for her calabash of water. As she moved on, she had a strange feeling that something

was following her. Was it the monster? Her hair stood erect, and a cold paralyzing feeling ran along her spine. She looked behind, sideways and in front, but there was nothing, except a cloud of dust.

Oganda pulled up and hurried but the feeling did not leave her, and her whole body became saturated with perspiration.

The sun was going down fast and the lake shore seemed to move along with it.

Oganda started to run. She must be at the lake before sunset. As she ran she heard a noise from behind. She looked back sharply, and something resembling a moving bush was frantically running after her. It was about to catch up with her.

Oganda ran with all her strength. She was now determined to throw herself into the water even before sunset. She did not look back, but the creature was upon her. She made an effort to cry out, as in a nightmare, but she could not hear her own voice. The creature caught up with Oganda. In the utter confusion, as Oganda came face to face with the unidentified creature, a strong hand grabbed her. But she fell flat on the sand and fainted.

When the lake breeze brought her back to consciousness, a man was bending over her. ". . . . . !" Oganda opened her mouth to speak, but she had lost her voice. She swallowed a mouthful of water poured into her mouth by the stranger.

"Osinda, Osinda! Please let me die. Let me run, the sun is going down. Let me die, let them have rain." Osinda fondled the glittering chain around Oganda's waist and wiped the tears from her face.

"We must escape quickly to the unknown land," Osinda said urgently. "We must run away from the wrath of the ancestors and the retaliation of the monster."

"But the curse is upon me, Osinda, I am no good to you any more. And moreover the eyes of the ancestors will follow us everywhere and bad luck will befall us. Nor can we escape from the monster."

Oganda broke loose, afraid to escape, but Osinda grabbed her hands again.

"Listen to me, Oganda! Listen! Here are two coats!" He then covered the whole of Oganda's body, except her eyes, with a leafy attire made from the twigs of *Bwombwe*. "These will protect us from the eyes of the ancestors and the wrath of the monster. Now let us run out of here." He held Oganda's hand and they ran from the sacred land, avoiding the path that Oganda had followed.

The bush was thick, and the long grass entangled their feet as they ran. Halfway through the sacred land they stopped and looked back. The sun was almost touching the surface of the water. They were frightened. They continued to run, now faster, to avoid the sinking sun.

"Have faith, Oganda—that thing will not reach us."

When they reached the barrier and looked behind them trembling, only a tip of the sun could be seen above the water's surface.

"It is gone! It is gone!" Oganda wept, hiding her face in her hands.

"Weep not, daughter of the chief. Let us run, let us escape."

There was a bright lightning. They looked up, frightened. Above them black furious clouds started to gather. They began to run. Then the thunder roared, and the rain came down in torrents.

Vocabulary

retaliation (ri tal′ ē ā′ shən) *n.* revenge

Responding to Literature

Personal Response

Were you surprised by the outcome of the story? Describe your reaction in your journal.

Analyzing Literature

Recall

1. According to the medicine man's prophecy, what is the only way to end the drought in Oganda's village?
2. As she waits in her grandmother's hut, what does Oganda assume her father is discussing with the villagers?
3. How do the villagers react when Labong'o tells them about the prophecy?
4. How does Oganda react when she realizes what is planned for her?
5. What happens to Oganda when she approaches the lake?

Interpret

6. Why does Labong'o decide to obey the prophecy?
7. **Dramatic irony** occurs when the reader knows something important that a character does not know (see page R6). What is ironic about the scene in which Oganda waits in her grandmother's hut?
8. Why does Oganda feel like a stranger among her people during the feast held in her honor?
9. Do you think that Oganda's feelings about what is planned for her change as the story unfolds? Explain.
10. Do you think that the prophecy has been fulfilled by the end of the story? Why or why not?

Evaluate and Connect

11. An **internal conflict** is a struggle within a character (see page R2). Describe an internal conflict in "The Rain Came."
12. A **symbol** is an object or action that stands for something else in addition to itself (see page R12). What does the brass chain around Oganda's waist symbolize?
13. What view of Luo traditions does "The Rain Came" offer the reader? Explain.
14. What kinds of sacrifices do people today make for the good of their communities?
15. How does Oganda's planned sacrifice compare with your thoughts about sacrifice in the Reading Focus on page 136?

Literary Criticism

According to Brenda F. Berrian, "women [in Ogot's stories] sacrifice themselves to maintain family harmony; they rarely oppose their men. Preservation of the family is more important to them . . . However, the wronged woman always has Ogot's sympathy." Do you think this statement applies to the women in "The Rain Came"? Explain your answer in a brief paragraph.

Literary ELEMENTS

Suspense

Suspense is the tension or excitement that a reader feels about what will happen next in a story. Writers often create suspense by raising questions in the reader's mind about the outcome of a conflict. In some stories, the actual outcome might not be in question, but the writer can create suspense about when it will happen. For example, readers of a story might already know that the protagonist's husband has been killed in battle, but they might feel tension anticipating when the protagonist will learn the news. Suspense helps keep readers interested in a story and is especially important in the plots of adventure or mystery stories.

1. What suspense did you feel early on in "The Rain Came"?
2. What is suspenseful about the conclusion of the story?

- See **Literary Terms Handbook,** p. R12.

Literature and Writing

Writing About Literature

Review Write a review of "The Rain Came," describing the story's strengths and weaknesses and discussing its main theme. Include a brief plot summary. Answer questions such as the following: Are the characters interesting and believable? How effectively did Ogot organize the plot? Why might Ogot have chosen to tell this story? Use quotes from the story and references to specific scenes to support your analysis.

Personal Writing

Family Sacrifice Write one or two paragraphs about a personal sacrifice that was made in your family or in the family of someone you know. What was sacrificed? Who benefited from the sacrifice? Do you think that the sacrifice was necessary, or could the situation have been resolved differently? What lesson did you learn from this experience?

Extending Your Response

Literature Groups

A Leader's Burden In a small group, discuss the graphic organizers that you created for the Reading Focus on page 136. Then consider whether your own feelings about sacrifice support Labong'o's decision in the story. What sacrifices do you think a community should expect from its leaders? When you are finished, share your conclusions with other groups.

Interdisciplinary Activity

Music: Oganda's Song As she walks toward the lake where she must sacrifice herself, Oganda sings a song about her fate. Write lyrics for a new version of the song, taking into account the story's surprise ending. You may follow the style of the song in Ogot's story, or you may choose a new style for your version.

Listening and Speaking

Role-play The ending of "The Rain Came" is bittersweet, since Oganda must remain away from her family. With a partner, role-play an encounter between Oganda and Labong'o many years after the events portrayed in the story. How would Oganda explain her decision to disobey her father's orders? Would Labong'o feel guilty for not trying to save her as Osinda did?

Save your work for your portfolio.

VOCABULARY • Analogies

Some analogies are based on degrees of intensity. For example, at the end of this story, rain comes down in torrents. Would the ending have had the same impact if the rain came down in a slow drizzle? The difference between a torrent and a drizzle is one of degree.

torrent : drizzle :: tornado : breeze

To complete an analogy, decide on the relationship of the first two words. Then apply that relationship to the second set of words.

PRACTICE Choose the pair that best completes each analogy.

1. glow : blaze ::
   a. green : red
   b. walk : talk
   c. mutter : shout
   d. close : shut
   e. repeat : amplify
2. creek : river ::
   a. valley : mountain
   b. cloud : sun
   c. ant : elephant
   d. pond : lake
   e. cliff : precipice

NIGERIA, 1967

Before You Read

Civilian and Soldier

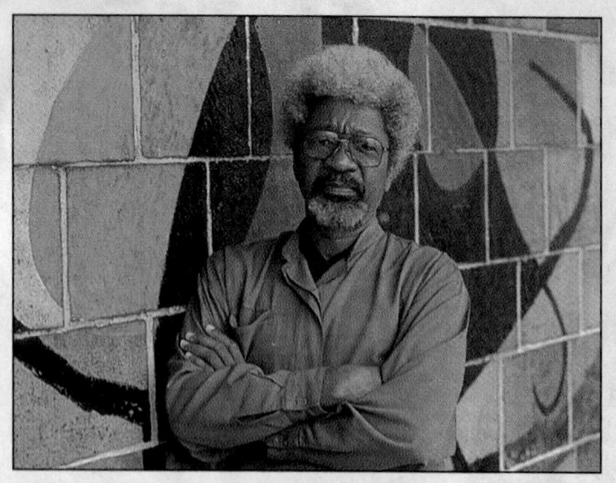

Meet Wole Soyinka

"I have one abiding religion—human liberty."

Wole Soyinka (wō′ lā shoi än′ kä) once remarked that if he had a choice, he would devote all of his energy to literature instead of getting involved in social issues. Yet he never hesitates to speak out against injustice and corruption in his homeland of Nigeria. He believes that African artists should serve as the conscience of their society. Over the years, Soyinka has been imprisoned and forced to live in exile because he insists on fulfilling this role.

Soyinka is known primarily for his plays, although he has also published poetry, novels, essays, and memoirs. Soyinka spent vacations in his father's birthplace, a community that followed traditional Yoruba ways. After finishing high school, he studied literature and theater in England. He returned to Nigeria in 1960 and quickly gained prominence as a playwright, director, and college lecturer. In 1986 he became the first African to win the Nobel Prize for Literature.

Wole Soyinka was born in 1934.

Reading Focus

"[M]y writing grows more and more preoccupied with the theme of the oppressive boot, the irrelevance of the color of the foot that wears it, and the struggle for individuality."

Share Ideas In a small group, discuss this statement by Wole Soyinka. What sort of poetry would you expect him to write?

Setting a Purpose As you read "Civilian and Soldier," think about who is speaking and who is being addressed.

Building Background

Nigeria's Civil War

Since gaining independence from Britain in 1960, Nigeria has experienced ethnic and religious conflict. Thousands of Ibo living in the North were massacred in 1966 during a military revolt against the civilian government. Many Ibo fled to their traditional homeland in the eastern region. In 1967, after the Ibo declared this region the Independent Republic of Biafra, Nigeria plunged into civil war.

"Civilian and Soldier" belongs to a group of six poems that Soyinka wrote during the buildup to the war. He published them in *Idanre and Other Poems* (1967). In the summer of 1967, Soyinka met with Ibo rebels in an attempt to restore peace. This failed effort led to his arrest. For over two years the government held him in prison without a trial, often keeping him in solitary confinement. While in prison, Soyinka wrote several works, including prison notes that he published as *The Man Died.*

Makonde figure of European man with gun and lunch box, Congo River Basin.

The Prisoner Who Wore Glasses

Bessie Head

Scarcely a breath of wind disturbed the stillness of the day and the long rows of cabbages were bright green in the sunlight. Large white clouds drifted slowly across the deep blue sky. Now and then they obscured the sun and caused a chill on the backs of the prisoners who had to work all day long in the cabbage field. This trick the clouds were playing with the sun eventually caused one of the prisoners who wore glasses to stop work, straighten up and peer shortsightedly at them. He was a thin little fellow with a hollowed out chest and comic knobbly knees. He also had a lot of fanciful ideas because he smiled at the clouds.

"Perhaps they want me to send a message to the children," he thought, tenderly, noting that the clouds were drifting in the direction of his home some hundred miles away. But before he could frame the message, the warder in charge of his work span shouted: "Hey, what do you think you're doing, Brille?"

The prisoner swung round, blinking rapidly, yet at the same time sizing up the enemy. He was a new warder, named Jacobus Stephanus Hannetjie. His eyes were the color of the sky but they were frightening. A simple, primitive, brutal soul gazed out of them. The prisoner bent down quickly and a message was quietly passed down the line: "We're in for trouble this time, comrades."

"Why?" rippled back up the line.

"Because he's not human," the reply rippled down and yet only the crunching of the spades as they turned over the earth disturbed the stillness.

This particular work span was known as Span One. It was composed of ten men and they were all political prisoners.

They were grouped together for convenience as it was one of the prison regulations that no black warder should be in charge of a political prisoner lest this prisoner convert him to his view. It never seemed to occur to the authorities that this very reasoning was the strength of Span One and a clue to the strange terror they aroused in the warders. As political prisoners they were unlike the other prisoners in the sense that they felt no guilt nor were they outcasts of society. All guilty men instinctively cower, which was why it was the kind of prison where men got knocked out cold with a blow at the back of the head from an iron bar. Up until the arrival of Warder Hannetjie, no warder had dared beat any member of Span One and no warder had lasted more than a week with them. The battle was entirely psychological. Span One was assertive and it was beyond the scope of white warders to handle assertive black men. Thus, Span One had got out of control. They were the best thieves and liars in the camp. They lived all day on raw cabbages. They chatted and smoked tobacco. And since they moved, thought and acted as one, they had perfected every technique of group concealment.

Trouble began that very day between Span One and Warder Hannetjie. It was because of the shortsightedness of Brille. That was the nickname he was given in prison and is the Afrikaans word for someone who wears glasses. Brille could never judge the approach of the prison gates and on several occasions he had munched on cabbages and dropped them almost

---

Vocabulary

knobbly (nob′ lē) *adj.* shaped like a knob

warder (wôr′ dər) *n.* a prison guard

at the feet of the warder and all previous warders had overlooked this. Not so Warder Hannetjie.

"Who dropped that cabbage?" he thundered.

Brille stepped out of line.

"I did," he said meekly.

"All right," said Hannetjie. "The whole Span goes three meals off."

"But I told you I did it," Brille protested.

The blood rushed to Warder Hannetjie's face.

"Look 'ere," he said. "I don't take orders from a kaffir.[1] I don't know what kind of kaffir you think you are. Why don't you say Baas.[2] I'm your Baas. Why don't you say Baas, hey?"

Brille blinked his eyes rapidly but by contrast his voice was strangely calm.

"I'm twenty years older than you," he said. It was the first thing that came to mind but the comrades seemed to think it a huge joke. A titter swept up the line. The next thing Warder Hannetjie whipped out a knobkerrie and gave Brille several blows about the head. What surprised his comrades was the speed with which Brille had removed his glasses or else they would have been smashed to pieces on the ground.

Did You Know?
A *knobkerrie* is a short, wooden club with a heavy round knob at one end. South African aborigines used this weapon in close attack or threw it as a missile.

That evening in the cell Brille was very apologetic.

"I'm sorry, comrades," he said. "I've put you into a hell of a mess."

"Never mind, brother," they said. "What happens to one of us, happens to all."

"I'll try to make up for it, comrades," he said. "I'll steal something so that you don't go hungry."

Privately, Brille was very philosophical about his head wounds. It was the first time an act of violence had been perpetrated against him but he had long been a witness of extreme, almost unbelievable human brutality. He had twelve children and his mind traveled back that evening through the sixteen years of bedlam in which he had lived. It had all happened in a small drab little three-bedroomed house in a small drab little street in the Eastern Cape, and the children kept coming year after year because neither he nor Martha ever managed the contraceptives the right way, and a teacher's salary never allowed moving to a bigger house, and he was always taking exams to improve his salary only to have it all eaten up by hungry mouths. Everything was pretty horrible, especially the way the children fought. They'd get hold of each other's heads and give them a good bashing against the wall. Martha gave up somewhere along the line so they worked out a thing between them. The bashings, biting and blood were to operate in full swing until he came home. He was to be the bogeyman[3] and when it worked he never failed to have a sense of godhead at the way in which his presence could change savages into fairly reasonable human beings.

Yet somehow it was this chaos and mismanagement at the center of his life that drove him into politics. It was really an ordered beautiful world with just a few basic slogans to learn along with the rights of mankind. At one stage,

1. Usually used disparagingly, *kaffir* (kaf′ ər) is a term for a black South African.
2. *Baas* is a form of address meaning "master" or "boss."

3. A *bogeyman* is a terrifying or dreaded person.

Vocabulary
titter (ti′ tər) *n.* a laugh; a snicker
bedlam (bed′ ləm) *n.* a state of uproar or confusion
bashing (bash′ ing) *n.* a forceful blow

Colonie Belge (Belgian Colony), early 1970s. Tshibumba Kanda Matulu (Zaire). Collection of V. Bol.

Viewing the painting: What do you learn about the relationships among the people in this painting? How does the figure in the foreground remind you of Hannetjie?

before things became very bad, there were conferences to attend, all very far away from home.

"Let's face it," he thought ruefully. "I'm only learning right now what it means to be a politician. All this while I've been running away from Martha and the kids."

And the pain in his head brought a hard lump to his throat. That was what the children did to each other daily and Martha wasn't managing and if Warder Hannetjie had not interrupted him that morning he would have sent the following message: "Be good comrades, my children. Cooperate, then life will run smoothly."

The next day Warder Hannetjie caught this old man of twelve children stealing grapes from the farm shed. They were an enormous quantity of grapes in a ten gallon tin and for this misdeed the old man spent a week in the isolation cell. In fact, Span One as a whole was in constant trouble. Warder Hannetjie seemed to have eyes at the back of his head. He uncovered the trick about the cabbages, how they were split in two with the spade and immediately covered with earth and then unearthed again and eaten with split-second timing. He found out how tobacco smoke was beaten into the ground and he found out how conversations were whispered down the wind.

For about two weeks Span One lived in acute misery. The cabbages, tobacco and conversations had been the pivot of jail life to them. Then one evening they noticed that their good old comrade who wore the glasses was looking rather pleased with himself. He pulled out a four ounce packet of tobacco by way of explanation and the comrades fell upon it with great greed. Brille merely smiled. After all, he was the father of many children. But when the last shred had disappeared, it occurred to the comrades that they ought to be puzzled. Someone said: "I say, brother. We're watched like hawks these days. Where did you get the tobacco?"

"Hannetjie gave it to me," said Brille.

There was a long silence. Into it dropped a quiet bombshell.

"I saw Hannetjie in the shed today," and the failing eyesight blinked rapidly. "I caught him in the act of stealing five bags of fertilizer and he bribed me to keep my mouth shut."

Vocabulary

pivot (piv′ ət) *n.* a person, thing, or factor having a central role, function, or effect

There was another long silence.

"Prison is an evil life," Brille continued, apparently discussing some irrelevant matter. "It makes a man contemplate all kinds of evil deeds."

He held out his hand and closed it.

"You know, comrades," he said. "I've got Hannetjie. I'll betray him tomorrow."

Everyone began talking at once.

"Forget it, brother. You'll get shot."

Brille laughed.

"I won't," he said. "That is what I mean about evil. I am a father of children and I saw today that Hannetjie is just a child and stupidly truthful. I'm going to punish him severely because we need a good warder."

The following day, with Brille as witness, Hannetjie confessed to the theft of the fertilizer and was fined a large sum of money. From then on Span One did very much as they pleased while Warder Hannetjie stood by and said nothing. But it was Brille who carried this to extremes. One day, at the close of work Warder Hannetjie said: "Brille, pick up my jacket and carry it back to the camp."

"But nothing in the regulations says I'm your servant, Hannetjie," Brille replied coolly.

"I've told you not to call me Hannetjie. You must say Baas," but Warder Hannetjie's voice lacked conviction. In turn, Brille squinted up at him.

"I'll tell you something about this Baas business, Hannetjie," he said. "One of these days we are going to run the country. You are going to clean my car. Now, I have a fifteen year old son and I'd die of shame if you had to tell him that I ever called you Baas."

Warder Hannetjie went red in the face and picked up his coat.

On another occasion Brille was seen to be walking about the prison yard, openly smoking tobacco. On being taken before the prison commander he claimed to have received the tobacco from Warder Hannetjie. Throughout the tirade from his chief, Warder Hannetjie failed to defend himself but his nerve broke completely. He called Brille to one side.

"Brille," he said. "This thing between you and me must end. You may not know it but I have a wife and children and you're driving me to suicide."

"Why don't you like your own medicine, Hannetjie?" Brille asked quietly.

"I can give you anything you want," Warder Hannetjie said in desperation.

"It's not only me but the whole of Span One," said Brille, cunningly. "The whole of Span One wants something from you."

Warder Hannetjie brightened with relief.

"I think I can manage if it's tobacco you want," he said.

Brille looked at him, for the first time struck with pity, and guilt.

He wondered if he had carried the whole business too far. The man was really a child.

"It's not tobacco we want, but you," he said. "We want you on our side. We want a good warder, because without a good warder we won't be able to manage the long stretch ahead."

Warder Hannetjie interpreted this request in his own fashion and his interpretation of what was good and human often left the prisoners of Span One speechless with surprise. He had a way of slipping off his revolver and picking up a spade and digging alongside Span One. He had a way of producing unheard of luxuries like boiled eggs from his farm nearby and things like cigarettes, and Span One responded nobly and got the reputation of being the best work span in the camp. And it wasn't only take from their side. They were awfully good at stealing certain commodities like fertilizer which were needed on the farm of Warder Hannetjie.

Responding to Literature

Personal Response

What new ideas or insights did you gain from reading this story? Discuss your response with a classmate.

Analyzing Literature

Recall

1. How were political prisoners treated differently from other prisoners before Warder Hannetjie's arrival at the camp?
2. Why is Brille singled out for abuse by Warder Hannetjie?
3. What violence had Brille witnessed at home before he became a prisoner?
4. How does Brille gain control over Warder Hannetjie?
5. What deal do the prisoners of Span One strike with Warder Hannetjie?

Interpret

6. Why were the warders intimidated by the political prisoners?
7. What incidents early in the story provide clues about Brille's personality?
8. How does Brille's memory of his family give him insight into Warder Hannetjie's character?
9. **Irony** is a contrast between what is expected and what actually exists or occurs (see page R6). What is ironic about Brille's eyesight?
10. Early in the story, Brille says that Warder Hannetjie is not human. Do you think he changes his mind by the end of the story? Explain.

Evaluate and Connect

11. Did you find the story believable? Why or why not?
12. **Foreshadowing** occurs when a writer provides hints about what will happen in a story (see page R5). How is Brille's transformation of Warder Hannetjie into a "good warder" foreshadowed earlier in the story?
13. In the Reading Focus on page 150, you were asked to list heroic qualities. Which of these qualities does Brille display in the story?
14. Do you think that the story expresses optimism or pessimism about the future of South Africa? Explain.
15. What acts of cooperation in your community or in the world does the story remind you of?

Literary Criticism

Greta D. Little makes the following observation about Head's short story collection *Tales of Tenderness and Power:* "Although Head claims no interest in politics, her fears about the misuse of power and her implicit humanistic teachings are much in evidence." In your opinion, does "The Prisoner Who Wore Glasses" explore political issues? What humanistic teachings does the story contain? Explain your answers in a brief essay, analyzing details from the story for support.

Literary ELEMENTS

Characters

Literary characters can be classified as round or flat characters, depending on how they are developed in a story. A **round character** displays a variety of personality traits, as opposed to a **flat character,** whose personality is dominated by a single trait. Usually the protagonist of a story is a round character. Characters can also be distinguished as either dynamic or static. A **dynamic character** changes significantly in a story. A **static character** undergoes little if any change.

1. Is Brille a round or flat character? What trait or traits does he display?
2. Would you classify Warder Hannetjie as a static or a dynamic character? Explain.

- See **Literary Terms Handbook,** p. R2.

Literature and Writing

Writing About Literature

Theme What central message or idea about life is implied in "The Prisoner Who Wore Glasses"? Write a statement of the story's theme. Then explain how this theme is developed in the story. In your explanation, discuss the author's use of literary elements such as setting, plot, and characterization to develop the theme.

Creative Writing

Letter to Loved Ones Imagine that you are either Brille or Warder Hannetjie. Write a letter to your family describing the events of the story from your point of view. Explain to them what you have learned in the prison camp. You might also discuss how this lesson will affect your relationship with the family.

Extending Your Response

Literature Groups

Friends or Allies? Warder Hannetjie and the prisoners learn the value of cooperation by the end of the story. Do you think that they come to like and trust one another, or do they remain adversaries who cooperate only because it is in their interest? Discuss this question in your group. When you are finished, share your conclusions with the class.

Learning for Life

Report on Prison Life Imagine that you and a classmate have been sent to Brille's prison camp to report on the treatment of political prisoners. Decide whether you will arrive at the camp before or after Hannetjie becomes a "good warder." Make a list of the conditions you would observe at the camp. Then write your report using details from the story.

Internet Connection

Cyber–South Africa Use an Internet search engine to find Web sites about South Africa. You might look for general information about the country and its people, or you might try to find out what social and political conditions are like after apartheid. Share the results with the class.

Reading Further

You might enjoy the following short stories by Bessie Head:

"Snowball," from *Tales of Tenderness and Power.*

"The Deep River: A Story of Ancient Tribal Migration," from *The Collector of Treasure and other Botswana Village Tales.*

Save your work for your portfolio.

VOCABULARY • Etymologies

The **etymology** of a word is its linguistic history. Etymologies trace a word's development from the earliest recorded occurrence in its language of origin to its current meaning and usage. For example, in this story, the word *bedlam* was defined as a state of uproar or confusion. The word *bedlam* comes from *Bedlam,* the popular name for the Hospital of Saint Mary of Bethlehem, London, an insane asylum founded in 1522. Now that you know the etymology of *bedlam,* reread the sentence in which it appears in the story.

PRACTICE Using a collegiate dictionary, look up the etymologies of the following words.

1. geometry
2. maverick
3. gerrymandering
4. chauvinism
5. nihilistic

Mji Ni Watu Bila Watu Si Mji Na Sisi Hapa Tulipo Ni Watu Kama Wewe (A Town Is Composed of People. Without People It Is No Longer a Town. We Are Here as People Just Like You.), 1992. Georges Lilanga Di Nyama (Tanzania). Acrylic on plywood, 242 x 122 cm. The Pigozzi Collection, Geneva.

Viewing the painting: How does this painting illustrate its title?

many humiliations, and he had not resisted. Was there any need? But his soul and all the vigor of his manhood had rebelled and bled with rage and bitterness.

One day these wazungu[6] would go!

One day his people would be free! Then, then—he did not know what he would do. However, he bitterly assured himself no one would ever flout his manhood again.

He mounted the hill and then stopped. The whole plain lay below. The new village was before him—rows and rows of compact mud huts, crouching on the plain under the fast-vanishing sun. Dark blue smoke curled upward from various huts, to form a dark mist that hovered over the village. Beyond, the deep, blood-red sinking sun sent out fingerlike streaks of light that thinned outward and mingled with the gray mist shrouding the distant hills.

In the village, he moved from street to street, meeting new faces. He inquired. He found his home. He stopped at the entrance to the yard and breathed hard and full. This was the moment of his return home. His father sat huddled up on a three-legged stool. He was now very aged and Kamau pitied the old man. But he had been spared—yes, spared to see his son's return—

"Father!"

The old man did not answer. He just looked at Kamau with strange vacant eyes. Kamau was impatient. He felt annoyed and irritated. Did he not see him? Would he behave like the women Kamau had met by the river?

In the street, naked and half-naked children were playing, throwing dust at one another. The sun had already set and it looked as if there would be moonlight.

"Father, don't you remember me?" Hope was sinking in him. He felt tired. Then he saw his father suddenly start and tremble like a leaf. He saw him stare with unbelieving eyes. Fear was discernible in those eyes. His mother came, and his brothers too. They crowded around him. His aged mother clung to him and sobbed hard.

"I knew my son would come. I knew he was not dead."

6. A *wazungu* (wä zo͞o′ ngo͞o) is a white person.

"Why, who told you I was dead?"

"That Karanja, son of Njogu."

And then Kamau understood. He understood his trembling father. He understood the women at the river. But one thing puzzled him: he had never been in the same detention camp with Karanja. Anyway he had come back. He wanted now to see Muthoni. Why had she not come out? He wanted to shout, "I have come, Muthoni; I am here." He looked around. His mother understood him. She quickly darted a glance at her man and then simply said:

"Muthoni went away."

Kamau felt something cold settle in his stomach. He looked at the village huts and the dullness of the land. He wanted to ask many questions but he dared not. He could not yet believe that Muthoni had gone. But he knew by the look of the women at the river, by the look of his parents, that she was gone.

"She was a good daughter to us," his mother was explaining. "She waited for you and patiently bore all the ills of the land. Then Karanja came and said that you were dead. Your father believed him. She believed him too and keened for a month. Karanja constantly paid us visits. He was of your Rika,[7] you know. Then she got a child. We could have kept her. But where is the land? Where is the food? Ever since land consolidation, our last security was taken away. We let Karanja go with her. Other women have done worse—gone to town. Only the infirm and the old have been left here."

He was not listening; the coldness in his stomach slowly changed to bitterness. He felt bitter against all, all the people including his father and mother. They had betrayed him. They had leagued against him, and Karanja had always been his rival. Five years was admittedly not a short time. But why did she go? Why did they allow her to go? He wanted to speak. Yes, speak and denounce everything—the women by the river, the village and the people who dwelled there. But he could not. This bitter thing was choking him.

"You—you gave my own away?" he whispered.

"Listen, child, child . . ."

The big yellow moon dominated the horizon. He hurried away bitter and blind, and only stopped when he came to the Honia River.

And standing at the bank, he saw not the river, but his hopes dashed on the ground instead. The river moved swiftly, making ceaseless monotonous murmurs. In the forest the crickets and other insects kept up an incessant buzz. And above, the moon shone bright. He tried to remove his coat, and the small bundle he had held on to so firmly fell. It rolled down the bank and before Kamau knew what was happening, it was floating swiftly down the river. For a time he was shocked and wanted to retrieve it. What would he show his—Oh, had he forgotten so soon? His wife had gone. And the little things that had so strangely reminded him of her and that he had guarded all those years, had gone! He did not know why, but somehow he felt relieved. Thoughts of drowning himself dispersed. He began to put on his coat, murmuring to himself, "Why should she have waited for me? Why should all the changes have waited for my return?"

7. *Rika* (rē kä′) is Swahili for age group or generation.

Vocabulary

keen (kēn) *v.* to lament or mourn loudly

Responding to Literature

Personal Response

What went through your mind as you finished reading the story? Share your thoughts with the class.

Analyzing Literature

Recall and Interpret

1. Why has Kamau been away from his village? How would you describe his feelings as he approaches the village?
2. What happens when Kamau meets a group of women at the river? What did Kamau expect to happen?
3. What does Kamau learn from the women? How does this news affect him?
4. What does Kamau find out when he reaches his parents' hut? Why do you think that Karanja has spread false information about him?
5. What does Kamau intend to do when he rushes from his parents' hut? Why do you think he changes his mind after losing the bundle?

Evaluate and Connect

6. What impression do you have of Kamau? Write two adjectives to describe him.
7. A **symbol** is an object or action that stands for something else in addition to itself (see page R12). What does Kamau's bundle symbolize?
8. What details in the story suggest why Kamau and other Kikuyu men revolted against the colonial rulers?
9. Do you think that Kamau will remain in the village with his parents? Why or why not?
10. If you wanted to set this story in the present day, in what country would you place it? Explain your choice.

Literary ELEMENTS

Personification

When writers give human characteristics to an animal, object, or idea, they are using a figure of speech known as **personification.** For example, a tree might be described as mournful, or sleep might be called miserly by someone who has stayed awake all night. Many common phrases, such as "winter is cruel" and "love is blind," are examples of personification. Writers often use personification to suggest the feelings of human characters in a story.

1. What examples of personification can you find in the first two paragraphs of "The Return"?
2. What does Ngugi's use of personification tell the reader about the emotions of Kamau?

- See **Literary Terms Handbook,** p. R9.

Extending Your Response

Creative Writing

Dialogue In the story, Kamau is denied his long-awaited reunion with Muthoni. Suppose their paths should cross at a later time. How might Muthoni feel when she finds out that Kamau is still alive? Do you think that Kamau would try to resume their relationship? Portray their meeting in a dialogue. Try to keep the characters consistent with what you know about them from the story.

Learning for Life

Interview In the Reading Focus on page 158, you described how you felt when you returned to a place after a long absence. Interview a friend or relative about a similar experience of returning. Ask questions such as the following: What expectations did you have? What surprised you the most? Read excerpts from the interview to the class.

Save your work for your portfolio.

SOUTH AFRICA, 1973

Before You Read

My Country

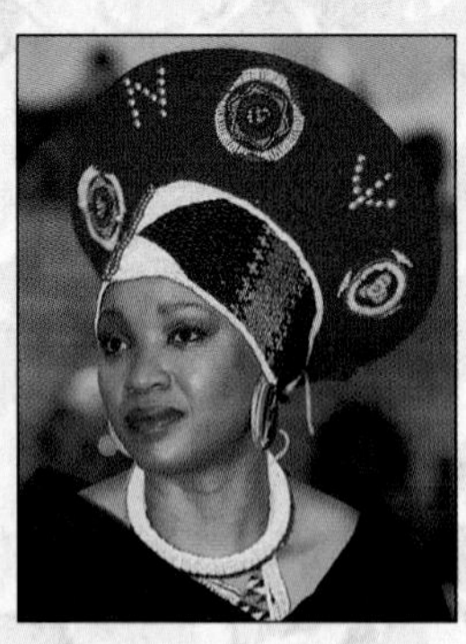

Meet Zindziswa Mandela

"I have suffered like every black child has, so I have a certain duty and role to play in my own society—independent of my being Mandela's daughter."

Zindziswa (zind′ zē swä′) Mandela's parents named her in honor of a renowned South African poet. Their choice turned out to be prophetic. As a young girl, "Zindzi" began writing poetry. Mandela is the daughter of Nelson and Winnie Mandela. When she was four, the South African government imprisoned her father for opposing apartheid (ə pär′ tīd).

At age seven, Mandela traveled with an older sister to the neighboring country of Swaziland to attend boarding school, where she was encouraged to write poems. While visiting South Africa when she was fifteen, she saw her father for the first time in prison. She says that she felt nervous approaching him because Nelson Mandela "was more a great figure than a father. . . . The warders were breathing down our necks all the time but he put me at my ease at once—recalling little incidents from the time when I was a baby."

Zindziswa Mandela was born in 1960.

Reading Focus

Think of someone you have read about who suffered because of his or her beliefs. How do you think this person found the strength to carry on?

Share Ideas Discuss your response with a classmate.

Setting a Purpose Read to discover the speaker's feelings about her country and family.

Building Background

Nelson and Winnie Mandela

Nelson Mandela spent over a quarter century in prison for his opposition to apartheid. In 1944, when he was a twenty-six-year-old lawyer, he joined a black liberation group called the African National Congress. He soon became one of the group's leaders. Mandela was arrested in 1962, and two years later he was sentenced to life in prison on charges of sabotage and treason. At his trial he said, "I have cherished the ideal of a democratic and free society in which all persons live together in harmony and with equal opportunities." Since his release in 1990 and his election as president in 1994, he has worked to make this ideal a reality.

In 1958 Nelson Mandela married Winnie Madikizela. While her husband was in prison, she continued his work against apartheid. She was imprisoned in 1969, and from 1977 to 1985 she was banished to a remote South African town. She later served in the postapartheid government as a deputy minister. The Mandelas' marriage did not survive the years of sacrifice. They separated in 1992.

"Nkosi Sikelel' iAfrika"

One symbol of the change that has taken place in South Africa is the country's new national anthem. It was written in 1897 by a Methodist mission school teacher, Enoch Sontonga, a member of the Xhosa people. In 1912 it was sung at the end of the first meeting of the African National Congress, and it became the anthem of the anticolonial, and later antiapartheid, movement. In 1994 the song was given equal status with the old national anthem; and soon after, the two were combined to provide a new, united anthem for the new South Africa.

Nelson Mandela, 1990. Cheïk Ledy (Zaire). Acrylic on canvas, 90 x 146 cm. The Pigozzi Collection, Geneva.

My Country

For Mandela

Zindziswa Mandela

I stand by the gate
School's out
Smoke fills the location
Tears come to my eyes

I wipe them away
I walk into the kitchen
To see my mother's
Black hard-washing hands
A forceful smile from
A tired face

We sit and have supper
I pick up a picture of
My father and look
My mother turns away
Tries to hide
My father left my mother
In his arms
He is roughly separated
From her

The van pulls away
Mother watches bravely enough
I as a child do
Not understand

My heart aches
How I long to see my father
At least to hold his hand
And comfort him
Or at least to tell him
He'll be back some day

Responding to Literature

Personal Response

What lines from the poem did you find most moving? Share your response with the class.

Analyzing Literature

Recall and Interpret

1. Why does the speaker's mother turn away from the picture of her husband? What does this action suggest about her?
2. What happened to the speaker's father? How did the speaker react to this event at the time?
3. How do you interpret the following lines?
   "My father left my mother / In his arms"

Evaluate and Connect

4. **Tone** is the attitude that a writer or speaker takes toward a subject (see **Literary Terms Handbook,** page R12). How would you describe the speaker's tone in "My Country"? What lines in the poem support your answer?
5. In the Reading Focus on page 164, you were asked to discuss how a person found the strength to suffer for his or her beliefs. Whose suffering is Mandela describing in her poem? What is the source of their strength?
6. **Style** is a writer's distinctive manner of expression–not *what* is said but *how* it is said (see **Literary Terms Handbook,** page R12). Style can include word choice and length and arrangement of sentences, as well as the use of figurative language and imagery. How would you describe the style of "My Country"?

Literary ELEMENTS

Free Verse

Free verse is poetry that does not follow a regular meter or rhyme scheme. Although poets who write free verse ignore traditional rules, they can use techniques such as repetition and alliteration to create patterns in their poems. Free-verse poems often follow the rhythms of ordinary speech. Many poets in the twentieth century have chosen to write in free verse.

1. Mandela left out all punctuation in "My Country." Does the lack of punctuation make the poem hard for you to follow? Explain your response.
2. Provide an example of a line break in the poem that emphasizes a particular word or image.

- See **Literary Terms Handbook,** p. R5.

Extending Your Response

Creative Writing

Wish You Were Here Think of a time when you missed someone very much. Write a poem about this experience of separation. In your poem, describe why you were separated from the person you missed, and indicate how old you were at the time. Use images to convey your emotions to the reader.

Interdisciplinary Activity

Music: Songs of Resistance The contemporary music of South Africa is a blend of traditional forms and modern influences. South African music helped bring the world's attention to the struggle against apartheid. In the audio-visual section of your library, look for recordings by South African musicians during the apartheid (1948–1994) era. Try to find a song that reminds you of Mandela's poem.

Save your work for your portfolio.

COMPARING selections

THE RETURN and My Country

COMPARE RESPONSES

Discuss Both "The Return" and "My Country" portray personal losses that result from a political struggle. In a small group, compare your responses to these works.

- Which work did you find more moving?
- Which work gave you a better sense of what the families of political prisoners must endure?
- Which work offers a more forceful condemnation of a political system?
- Do you think Ngugi's story and Mandela's poem would convince you to support a revolutionary struggle or not? Give reasons for your response.

Nelson Mandela, 1990 (detail).

COMPARE EXPERIENCES

Write Write a paragraph comparing how the protagonist of "The Return" and the speaker of "My Country" face the sacrifices that are thrust upon them. In your paragraph, you might consider discussing issues such as the following:

- Which one seems more devastated by the experience? Which seems more hopeful? How is that hope expressed?
- Which one has a better understanding of why the experience occurred? In what way is age a factor in that understanding?

COMPARE POLITICAL DEVELOPMENTS

Investigate With a partner, investigate recent political developments in Kenya (the setting of "The Return") and South Africa (the setting of "My Country"). You might consult history books, newspaper indexes, and the Internet for information. Which country has made more progress toward achieving a just political system? What might account for this progress? How do you think the protagonist of "The Return" and the speaker of "My Country" would feel about the changes that have occurred in their countries? Prepare a report and present it to the class.

MEDIA connection

Editorial Cartoons

Although the main purpose of a cartoon is to make you laugh, often the subject is of a serious, sometimes life-threatening nature.

Stuart Carlson

...AND HAVE YOU SEEN HOW THEY PROCESS HAMBURGER? DISGUSTING!! PERSONALLY, I'D NEVER TOUCH BEEF AGAIN! YOU'RE WELCOME, NO PROBLEM!
E. COLI POISON HOTLINE

Tom Toles

STERILITY MONITOR
Clean Room
AUTHORIZED PERSONNEL ONLY
TEMPERATURE REGULATION CENTER
Burger Flipping: soon to be one of the highest paying jobs.
TOLES
NEXT: Hamburger Maintenance Organizations TO CONTROL COSTS

Stuart Carlson

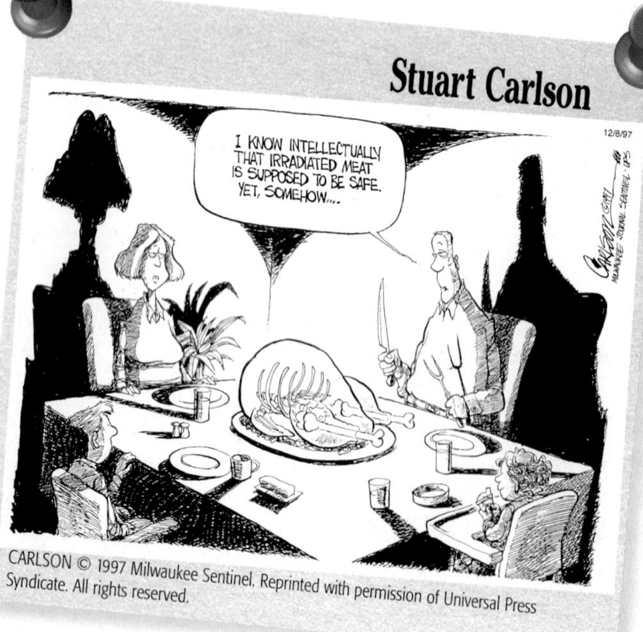
I KNOW INTELLECTUALLY THAT IRRADIATED MEAT IS SUPPOSED TO BE SAFE. YET, SOMEHOW....
12/8/97

Analyzing Media

1. What is the message of each of these cartoons? How effective do you think the cartoon format is for presenting these messages?
2. Have you ever thought about what happens to your food before it reaches you as a consumer? Explain.

Before You Read

Bones

KENYA, 1968

Meet Sadru Kassam

"[W]ith the Free Travelling Theatre, performance in the open air would give birth to a huge 'cast' of three hundred, four hundred, and more people because all the villagers used to join in. . . ."

—*Mĩcere Gĩthae Mũgo, Kenyan playwright and poet*

Sadru Kassam (sä dro͞o′ kä säm′) was born in Mombasa, Kenya's second largest city. He has made his living as a high school teacher. While studying English at Makerere University in Uganda, he became involved with the Free Travelling Theatre, which was formed by professors and students to bring theater to rural villages and towns. It was an important testing ground for new African drama.

Kassam originally wrote "Bones" in Swahili, Kenya's official language. He performed the lead role of the Butcher with exaggerated comic gestures. According to one of the founders of the Free Travelling Theatre, the play was "unfailingly a tumultuous success." Audiences from different cultures identified with the social problems that Kassam satirized in his play.

Sadru Kassam was born in 1941.

Reading Focus

Are you confident that the food you eat is fresh and safe?

Share Ideas Share your response with the class. Discuss measures that individuals and government can take to promote food safety.

Setting a Purpose Read to discover what goes on at a local butcher shop.

Building Background

One Theater, Many Languages

Africa has a great tradition of public entertainers–not only the griots of West Africa, but also tellers of epic tales throughout the continent. This tradition of the single entertainer still continues, but it has been joined by modern group theater. This new form has been well received, but its performers have encountered problems.

In Kenya, as in most African countries, a number of languages are spoken. Yet the Free Travelling Theatre and companies influenced by it were popular nationwide. The actors had to learn to perform in several languages, including Runyoro, Luganda, English, and Swahili. But they also had to learn to perform the plays in ways that would help make the meaning clear to speakers of other languages. They had to adapt their timing and their performing style to different audience reactions–for example, in some cultures it is considered rude to laugh in public, which sometimes made it difficult when the actors were performing a comedy.

Vocabulary Preview

frock (frok) n. a woman's dress; p. 172

endorse (en dôrs′) *v.* to inscribe with one's signature to show approval; p. 172

pester (pes′ tər) *v.* to harass or annoy with petty irritations; p. 172

whitewash (hwīt′ wôsh) *v.* to apply a mixture of lime and water for whitening a surface; p. 173

fumble (fum′ bəl) *v.* to grope or handle clumsily; p. 174

nib (nib) *n.* pen point; p. 174

BONES

Sadru Kassam
Translated by the Author

CHARACTERS

THE BUTCHER

DONGO: a health inspector

KANUBHAI: a Hindu trader

A WOMAN } customers
A GIRL }

SCENE: *A butcher's shop. A sign reads: "SALEH BIN AWADH, The Big Butcher, P. O. MAJI MOTO, Coast Region." On one wall is a painting of a bull, and on another a picture of the* BUTCHER *slaughtering another bull. There are notices reading: "FRASH MEAT" and "WEL-COME."*

NOTE: *It is intended that each scene shall open with an extended mime by the* BUTCHER*, which can be developed from the outlines in the stage directions.*

The pieces of art in this selection are painted panels from a butcher shop in Nairobi, Kenya.

SCENE 1

[The shop is tolerably clean and tidy. The BUTCHER *wears an almost white coat and his hair is combed. He sings as he arranges his meat to conceal its shortcomings. A joint tumbles to the ground: he looks to see if anyone is around, then picks it up and brushes it before replacing it, clean side upwards. He spits and scratches himself vigorously. He starts dividing some meat into smaller sections with a large knife, swinging the blade dangerously. At length he cuts himself, shrieks, prances around, tends his bleeding finger, wipes the blood off on a piece of meat and sucks the wound. The* WOMAN *is heard singing as she approaches. She enters, wearing a khanga.]*[1]

WOMAN. Eee, banakuba![2] How are you?

BUTCHER. Me? Very well, mama, very well. You want meat?

WOMAN. Yes, banakuba, I want meat. How's your meat? Is it good?

BUTCHER. Very good, mama. Good and fresh. Can't you see me in the picture there slaughtering a bull?

WOMAN. From what part will you give me?

BUTCHER. Any part you want, mama. Whatever you ask for, I'm here to serve you.

[He sharpens his knife on his file.]

WOMAN. I want some of that. I hope it's fresh.

BUTCHER. Completely fresh, mama: numberi[3] one. How much do you want?

WOMAN. Aaaah! A shilling's worth only—unless you want to give me more on credit.

BUTCHER. No, no, no, not today.

[The BUTCHER *cuts a small piece from the meat the* WOMAN *has chosen, and then begins to cut larger pieces from another joint.]*

1. A *khanga* (KHän′ gä) is a loincloth worn by women in East Africa. Khangas are usually decorated and are often inscribed with slogans or proverbs.
2. *Eee, banakuba* (ē bä nä ko͞o′ bä) is a Swahili slang term of respect meaning "hey, big man."
3. *Numberi* (no͞om bā′ rē) means number.

WOMAN. A-a-a-a, I want off that only.

BUTCHER. Yes, but you want good and fresh meat, isn't it? This is very good. See . . . excellent! Numberi one! I tell you.

WOMAN. *[Violently.]* I *don't* want it.

BUTCHER. O.K. . . . your wish. Was it this one you wanted?

WOMAN. That's it. Now you know it.

[He puts some meat on the scales, and is about to add several bones.]

WOMAN. What's that you're doing there? I didn't ask for stones. I don't want them. Remove them at once.

BUTCHER. Mama, they aren't stones. They are very good bones with plenty of meat on them. See . . . excellent! Grade one!

WOMAN. And what am I to do with bones? I'm not a dog.

[He finishes weighing the meat and wraps it. The WOMAN *takes out a small pouch and offers money which she draws back as the* BUTCHER *tries to snatch it, so that he pitches across his counter before she gives it to him.]*

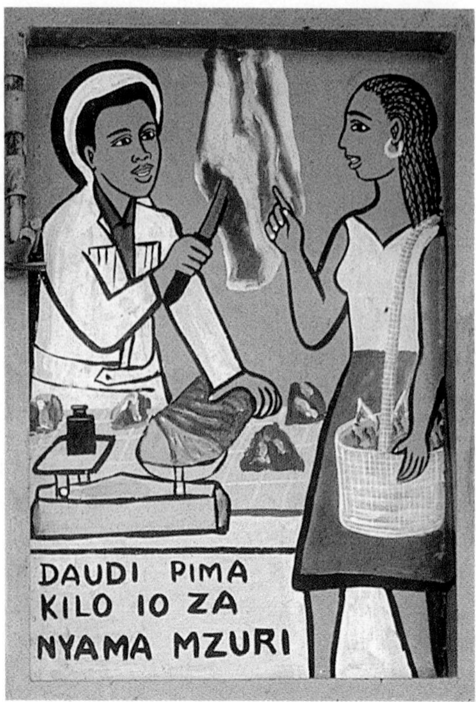

BUTCHER. Here it is, mama, your meat.

WOMAN. And here's your money . . . unless you don't want it.

BUTCHER. Eh, why not? Thank you, mama, thank you very much. God help you.

WOMAN. O.K., banakuba, good-bye.

[A GIRL enters, dressed in a dirty, tattered frock and carrying a kikapu.][4]

GIRL. Get me half a pound of meat, please. Nice—like you!

[As the WOMAN is going out she bumps into DONGO as he enters.]

DONGO. Good morning, mama.

WOMAN. Good morning, brother.

DONGO. What's the quarrel with the butcher?

WOMAN. Aaaa, nothing.

DONGO. Weren't you complaining of ill-treatment? I heard you shouting.

WOMAN. No, no, no. I was just joking with him. That butcher is a very nice man, you know.

DONGO. I see. O.K. Good-bye.

WOMAN. Good-bye. [*Exit.*]

GIRL. Give me very good meat, and no bones, please.

BUTCHER. No, no, no. No bones. Just a little one for your father.

GIRL. No. My father has no teeth.

BUTCHER. Oh, I see. [*DONGO has been clearing his throat loudly to attract the BUTCHER's attention.*] Dongo, Mr. Dongo! Just come over here, please. I'm delighted to see you. How are you?

DONGO. Excellent, thank you. And you?

BUTCHER. Aaaa, not well at all, because you know you still haven't endorsed my trading license. Please do it just now. Only a week is left before the closing date.

[DONGO stands as if ready to receive a gift. He looks away, pauses, then looks back at his hand as if surprised to see it empty.]

DONGO. Your trading license? Hasn't anyone taught you how to get it? [*The BUTCHER shakes his head.*] Just look at your shop! [*DONGO sweeps a pile of scraps from the counter onto the floor.*] See, the whole floor is littered with scraps and bones. When did you last sweep it? [*DONGO wipes his hands, now covered in blood from the meat, on the BUTCHER's apron.*] And why is your apron so dirty? Where is your file? [*DONGO takes the file and breaks it in two.*] Why is it broken? [*He runs his hands through the BUTCHER's hair, ruffling it.*] And why have you not combed your hair? Who made you a big butcher? Look, you must get things in order before pestering me to endorse your license. Do you understand that?

4. A *kikapu* (kē kä′ po͞o) is a basket.

Vocabulary

frock (frok) *n.* a woman's dress
endorse (en dôrs′) *v.* to inscribe with one's signature to show approval
pester (pes′ tər) *v.* to harass or annoy with petty irritations

BUTCHER. I . . . I . . . I'm sorry. I didn't know about these things. If . . . if you return next week, I promise everything will be in order. But please, I must have the license endorsed by next Monday.

DONGO. That's your business. I'm warning you, if everything is not ready by next week, you won't get your license, is that clear?

BUTCHER. Yes, yes. Everything will be in order next week. I promise.

DONGO. Your business. [*Exit.*]

GIRL. Come on, where's my meat?

Did You Know?
A *dhoti* (thō′ tē) is a loincloth worn by Hindu men.

BUTCHER. Oh, dear, yes. I'm sorry. I won't be a minute. Here it is. [*She exits. The BUTCHER surveys his shop in despair.*] What's to be done? And that girl, she didn't pay me. Which way did she go? Too late: she's made off. [*Enter KANUBHAI, a Hindu trader, in dhoti and cap. He holds his nose in disgust as he passes the BUTCHER's shop.*] Kanubhai! Oh, Kanubhai! Just come over here please, quick.

KANUBHAI. Come near your stinking meat? No, no, no, never!

BUTCHER. Ah, this old man! [*He comes from his shop and crosses to KANUBHAI.*] Kanubhai, please help me. You know that health inspector, he's refusing to endorse my trading license. I whitewashed my shop and I bought a new apron, but still he comes and asks me why my shop's dirty, and why my hair is not stylishly done, and what not. What am I to do?

KANUBHAI. That man! I know him. He's a dog. He's hungry.

BUTCHER. Hungry?

KANUBHAI. Yes, hungry. He wants some bones. [*He pretends to snarl.*]

BUTCHER. Bones?

KANUBHAI. Yes, bones. You still don't understand? [*He takes out some coins, jingles them, and pretends to eat them, snarling as he does so.*] He wants bones, bones!

BUTCHER. Oh, bones, bones! Yes, I see, he wants some bones.

[*As KANUBHAI exits, the BUTCHER leaps joyfully into the air, claps his hands, and returns purposefully to his shop.*]

Scene 2

[*The same scene a week later. The floor is littered with rubbish. The BUTCHER's apron is filthy. Rusty knives and broken implements lie around.*]

ANNOUNCER. The same scene. One week later.

[*The BUTCHER stretches, yawns, scratches himself, spits on the floor, kicks at the rubbish. Enter DONGO; he coughs. The BUTCHER works at his counter, pretending not to have seen DONGO, who strolls with exaggerated casualness up to the shop. The BUTCHER looks up, pretending surprise.*]

BUTCHER. Oh, Dongo! Good morning. How are you?

DONGO. Mmm! Not so well.

BUTCHER. Not well? I'm very sorry. Anyway, I hope you've come to endorse my license.

DONGO. Endorse your license? Just like that? With such a dirty shop?

Vocabulary
whitewash (hwīt′ wôsh) *v.* to apply a mixture of lime and water for whitening a surface

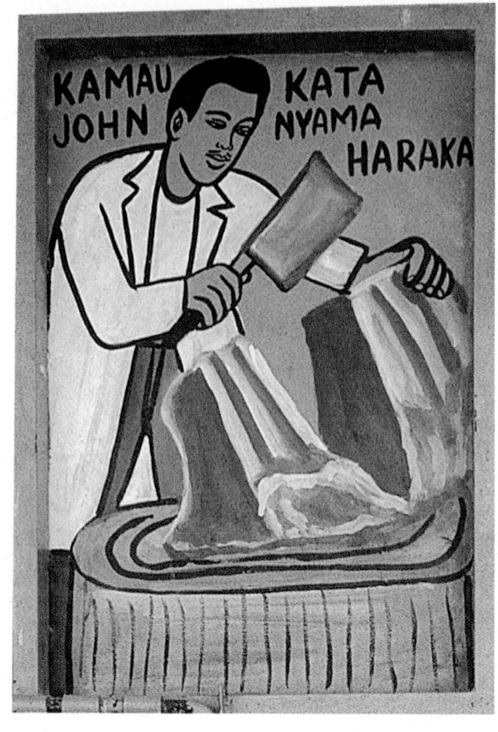

BUTCHER. Oh, by the way, Mr. Dongo, I almost forgot: I have something for you. I thought you might like a few bones to take home.

[*The* BUTCHER *hands* DONGO *a small package.*]

DONGO. Bones? Bones? What should I want with bones? [*As he fumbles with the package, a couple of coins fall out. He chases after them, and then slips the package in his pocket.*] Oh, bones, bones! That's very thoughtful of you. They will come in very handy. [*He smiles broadly.*] Mr. Awadh, your shop looks really clean today. See, no cobwebs, a clean scale, a new broom, a dustbin outside. It's the way we want it. Don't you worry about your hair. Come on, give me those forms. [*The* BUTCHER *hands him the forms.* DONGO *takes out a pen, goes to sign, but finds the nib is broken.*] Just lend me your pen, please. Something's gone wrong with mine.

BUTCHER. Certainly, certainly. I'm at your service.

[*The* BUTCHER *hands over his pen, which* DONGO *examines admiringly.*]

DONGO. Eh, you've bought a new pen. [*He finishes signing and slips the pen into his own pocket.*] Well that's done. Now you'll be all right. O.K., Mr. Awadh, kwaheri.[5]

BUTCHER. Thank you. Kwaheri, kwaheri.

DONGO. Kwaheri.

BUTCHER. Kwaheri.

[DONGO *goes out and then returns for his hat, which he had put on the counter while signing.*]

DONGO. Ah, my hat, there it is. Kwaheri, kwaheri.

BUTCHER. Kwaheri. [DONGO *goes out. The* BUTCHER *returns to his work. Enter the* WOMAN. *She surveys the shop, screws up her face, holds her nose, and walks past with her head in the air.*] Hello, mama! Good morning. [*She eyes him sourly.*] Aren't you coming to buy meat today?

WOMAN. Just look at your shop! And at yourself! Dirty and stinking! I'm not going to buy meat from you anymore. I'm going to the next butcher, to a cleaner shop. [*Exit.*]

BUTCHER. But mama, mama, I have my license. Listen. [*He reads.*] "Certified clean and fit to sell meat for human consumption." Mama! Mama!

Curtain.

5. *Kwaheri* (kwä hā′ rē) is Swahili for "good-bye."

Vocabulary

fumble (fum′ bəl) *v.* to grope or handle clumsily
nib (nib) *n.* pen point

Responding to Literature

Personal Response

What memories did this story stimulate in you? Write your response in your journal.

Analyzing Literature

Recall and Interpret

1. How do the children pass the time together? What do these activities reveal about them?
2. How would you describe the relationship between Rami and the narrator before Rami tells his story?
3. What happened to Rami's house in Bethlehem? Why do you think he tells this story to the narrator?
4. How does the narrator react to Rami's story? Why do you think the narrator reacts this way?
5. Why does the narrator draw pictures of the house? What does the last sentence of the story suggest about the narrator's feelings?

Evaluate and Connect

6. Do you think that the narrator is a boy or a girl? Explain.
7. What factors create conflict between Rami and the narrator?
8. A **symbol** is an object or action that stands for something else in addition to itself (see page R12). What symbols appear in the story?
9. How would you explain the author's shift from present to past tense in the story?
10. In the Reading Focus on page 176, you were asked to discuss how you drifted apart from a friend in the past. Why is it sometimes difficult to maintain a close friendship?

Literary ELEMENTS

Description

Description is writing that creates a clear image of a feeling, an action, or a scene in the reader's mind. Good descriptive writing appeals to the senses through imagery. In the following sentence, Osman uses visual imagery to describe Rami's appearance:

> Your almond-shaped eyes, wide in silent distress yet tearless, gave off a brownish flash.

The use of figurative language and precise verbs, adjectives, and adverbs can also help make a description vivid.

1. Which description in "A House for Us" is important to the story's plot?
2. In Osman's description of the marble game, which words picture the children's movements?

- See **Literary Terms Handbook,** p. R3.

Extending Your Response

Creative Writing

Advice Column Imagine that you are either Rami or the narrator. Write a letter to an advice columnist about your troubled friendship. Explain the conflict between you and your friend, referring to specific details from the story. Then trade letters with a classmate and write a response to your partner's letter.

Interdisciplinary Activity

Social Studies: Middle East Conflict Osman's story shows how the Arab-Israeli conflict affects people who do not even live on the West Bank. At the library, do research to find out what efforts are currently under way to resolve this conflict. Discuss whether you think a family such as Rami's would now be able to live in peace in Bethlehem.

Save your work for your portfolio.

Grammar Link

Avoiding Sentence Fragments

A fragment is an incomplete part of something. You might overhear a fragment of a conversation or sweep up the fragments of a broken flower pot. A **sentence fragment** is a word or group of words that is only part of a sentence.

Problem 1 Lacks either a subject or a verb (or both)
Travel together to the land of marvels. [lacks a subject]
From that one open window, a single eye. [lacks a verb]

Solution Add the missing subject and/or verb.
Children and adults travel together to the land of marvels.
From that one open window, a single eye gazed out.

Problem 2 Subordinate clauses that have been mistaken for a complete sentence (although they have a subject and a verb, subordinate clauses do not express a complete thought and cannot stand alone as a sentence)
That the patterns in the weaving were becoming blurred.

Solution A Join the subordinate clause to a main clause.
The elderly artisan found that the patterns in the weaving were becoming blurred.

Solution B Remove the subordinating conjunction at the beginning of the clause.
The patterns in the weaving were becoming blurred.

People often use sentence fragments in conversation. The fragment "Got to run" lacks a subject. It could mean that the speaker has to go or that the listener should hurry, but it is unlikely to be misunderstood because the listener understands the context. In writing, however, a fragment that leaves out important information can be confusing.

- For more about sentence fragments, see **Language Handbook**, pp. R14–R15.

EXERCISES

1. **Proofreading:** Use the strategies presented above to correct the sentence fragments in this paragraph.

> **Rami came to visit the narrator. Divided up the colored crystal marbles, the color of the sea and the color of the plants. They always fight over the lustrous, silvery marble. In the late afternoon. They open books, lots of them, bright with pictures. Rami says, "In Bethlehem there's a house. That belongs to us." Rami has to go home. Because his mother is calling him.**

2. Revise a piece of your own writing using these strategies to eliminate sentence fragments.

Before You Read

All That You Have Given Me, Africa

Reading Focus

What images come to mind when you think of Africa?

Share Ideas Discuss this question in a small group, and create a word web to show your impressions of Africa.

Setting a Purpose Read to discover the images of Africa used in the poem.

Building Background

The Negritude Movement

"All That You Have Given Me, Africa" clearly shows the influence that the Negritude movement has had on Anoma Kanié. A group of French-speaking African and Caribbean intellectuals started this literary movement in the 1930s as a response to French colonial policies of assimilating Africans into European culture. The intellectuals used the term *Negritude* to suggest a common heritage shared by all black people. Rejecting the notion of Europe's superiority, Negritude writers emphasized that Africa already had a vibrant culture of its own. The leading figure of the Negritude movement was Léopold Sédar Senghor (page 24), a poet who became the first president of Senegal in 1960.

In the late 1950s, some African intellectuals began to criticize the Negritude movement for its idealized view of Africa. Writers such as Wole Soyinka and Chinua Achebe preferred to explore both the good and bad aspects of traditional African society. Although it eventually fell out of fashion, the Negritude movement was an important influence in the development of modern African literature.

The Ivory Coast

The Ivory Coast (officially Côte d'Ivoire) covers an area of 123,847 square miles—somewhat larger than Illinois and Iowa combined. Sixteen major languages are spoken by its 13 million people, and nearly sixty others are spoken by 100,000 speakers or fewer. The largest ethnic group, the Baule, number approximately 2,200,000. One of the most difficult questions facing a writer there is what language to write in. Just as in East Africa—where many writers use Swahili, as it is widely known and not identified with a specific ethnic group—many Ivoirean writers use French, their country's official language, to reach a wider audience both within the Ivory Coast and worldwide. This poem by Anoma Kanié was first published as "Tout ce que tu m'as donné, Afrique."

Reading Further

If you like this poem, you might enjoy the following poems by other African writers:

"Yet Still," by Rashidah Ismaili; "Rain at Noon-time," by Molara Ogundipe; and "I Will Still Sing," by Amelia Blossom Pegram from *The Heinemann Book of African Women's Poetry,* edited by Stella and Frank Chipasula.

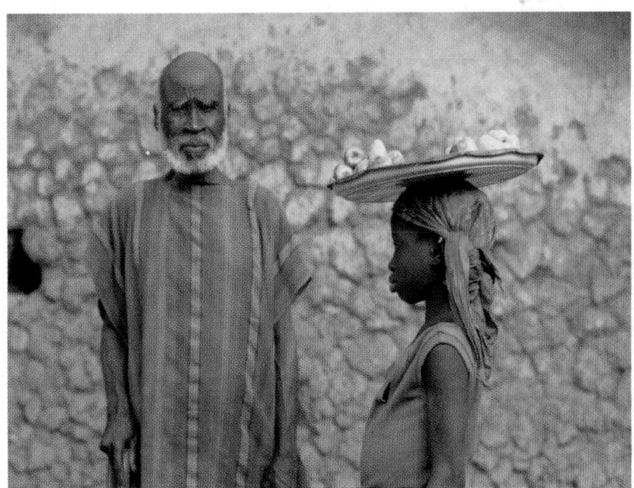

Kohrogo region, Ivory Coast.

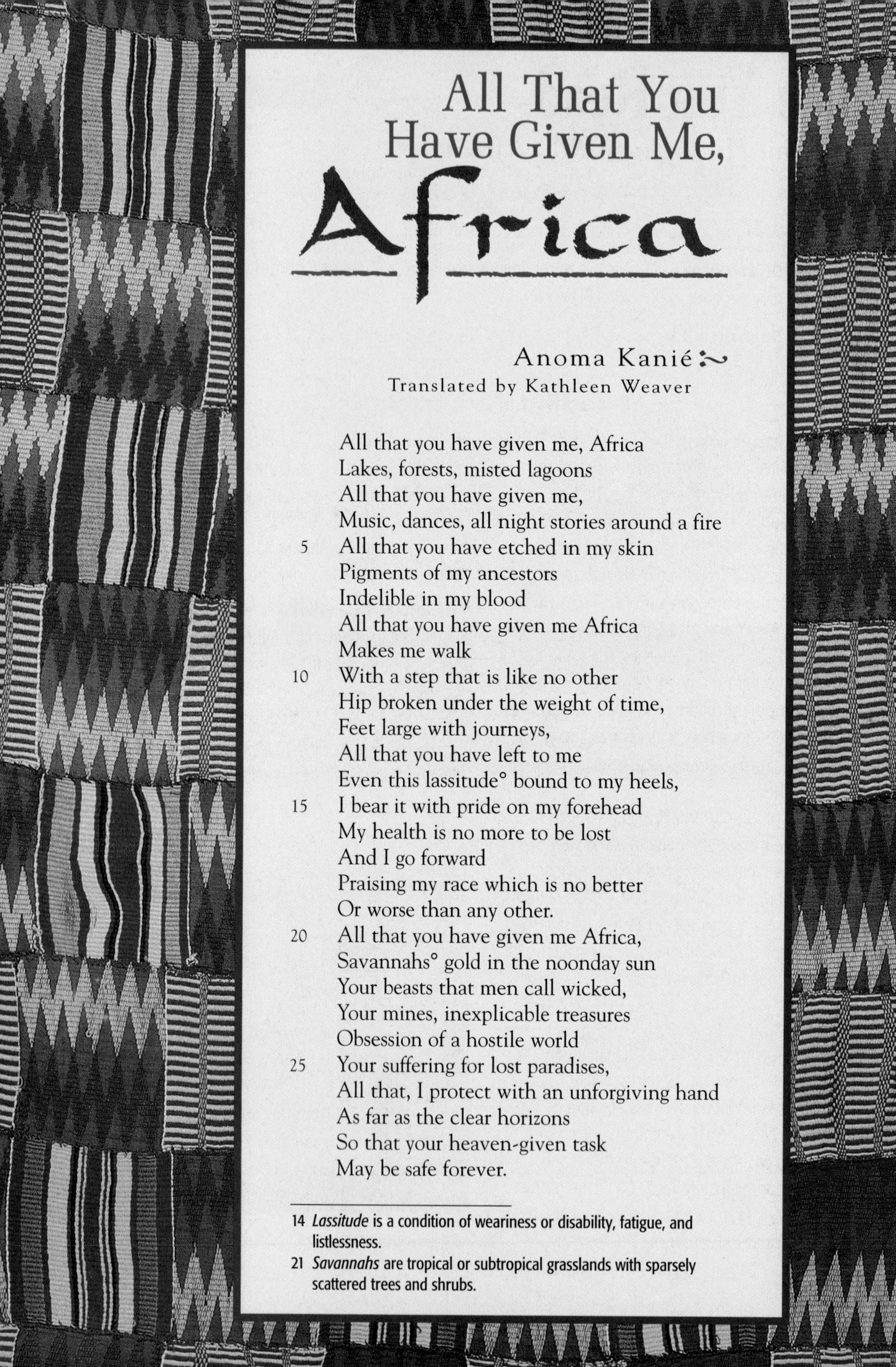

All That You Have Given Me, Africa

Anoma Kanié

Translated by Kathleen Weaver

All that you have given me, Africa
Lakes, forests, misted lagoons
All that you have given me,
Music, dances, all night stories around a fire
All that you have etched in my skin
Pigments of my ancestors
Indelible in my blood
All that you have given me Africa
Makes me walk
With a step that is like no other
Hip broken under the weight of time,
Feet large with journeys,
All that you have left to me
Even this lassitude° bound to my heels,
I bear it with pride on my forehead
My health is no more to be lost
And I go forward
Praising my race which is no better
Or worse than any other.
All that you have given me Africa,
Savannahs° gold in the noonday sun
Your beasts that men call wicked,
Your mines, inexplicable treasures
Obsession of a hostile world
Your suffering for lost paradises,
All that, I protect with an unforgiving hand
As far as the clear horizons
So that your heaven-given task
May be safe forever.

---

14 *Lassitude* is a condition of weariness or disability, fatigue, and listlessness.

21 *Savannahs* are tropical or subtropical grasslands with sparsely scattered trees and shrubs.

Responding to Literature

Personal Response

Which images from this poem linger in your mind? Share your response with the class.

Analyzing Literature

Recall and Interpret

1. What has Africa given the speaker in the first seven lines of the poem?
2. According to lines 8–15, what effect have the gifts from Africa had on the speaker? How does the speaker feel about this effect?
3. An **allusion** is a reference to a well-known person, place, or event from history, literature, or religion (see **Literary Terms Handbook,** page R1). What event do you think the speaker is alluding to in line 24–"Obsession of a hostile world"?
4. What responsibility does the speaker declare in the last four lines of the poem?

Evaluate and Connect

5. How would you describe the speaker's attitude toward Africa?
6. The speaker says that "my race . . . is no better / Or worse than any other." Why might the poet include such a statement in this poem?
7. In the Reading Focus on page 181, you were asked to discuss your impressions of Africa. How do your impressions compare with those of the poet?
8. Compare Kanié's poem with another selection in this unit. What similarities and differences do you see in the authors' portrayal of their homelands?

Parallelism

Poets often use repetition to create a sense of unity, to stress an idea, or to create a rhythmic effect. One form of repetition is **parallelism**–the repetition of phrases that have the same grammatical structure. The following lines from "The Immortality of Writers" (page 39) provide an example of parallelism:

> Better is a book than a well-built
> house,
> Than tomb-chapels in the West;
> Better than a solid mansion,
> Than a stela in the temple!

1. Describe the parallelism in lines 1–8 of Kanié's poem.
2. Find another example of parallelism in the poem. Why might Kanié have chosen to create this pattern?

- See **Literary Terms Handbook,** p. R9.

Extending Your Response

Creative Writing

Praise Poem In "All That You Have Given Me, Africa," Anoma Kanié praises Africa's rich heritage. Think of some ways in which your life has been shaped by living in a particular community, nation, or region. Then write a poem in praise of this heritage. Use imagery to give your readers a vivid impression of the place you are writing about.

Performing

Multimedia Performance With a small group, perform a reading of Kanié's poem accompanied by music, dance, or some kind of visual art. Practice reading the poem aloud with the accompaniment you have chosen. Then present your multimedia performance to the class. Invite questions from the audience and respond to them.

Save your work for your portfolio.

SOUTH AFRICA, 1989

Before You Read

from *Kaffir Boy in America*

Meet Mark Mathabane

"There was a time when I thought that if life meant unending suffering and pain, there was no use living. . . . What kept me going was my discovery of books."

Mark Mathabane (mot′ ə bän′ ē) grew up in a black township near Johannesburg, South Africa, where he lived in a tiny, crumbling shack. His mother worked as a washerwoman to raise enough money for him to attend school. An excellent student and promising tennis player, Mathabane managed to win a college scholarship that brought him to the United States.

After graduating, he decided to write about his childhood. His autobiography, *Kaffir Boy* (*kaffir* is a derogatory South African term for blacks) became a best-seller when it was published in 1986. According to Mathabane, the book allowed him to free himself from negative feelings: "I was finally able to fully accept who I was and where I came from. In short, I wrote to heal myself as well as inform others."

Mark Mathabane was born in 1960.

Reading Focus

Think of a journey you took to a place where you had never been before. What expectations did you have about this place? What surprises did you find there?

Journal Record your response in your journal.

Setting a Purpose Read about the author's expectations as he travels to a new place.

Building Background

Mathabane's Escape from Apartheid

When he was thirteen, Mark Mathabane received an old tennis racket from his grandmother's employer. He taught himself how to play tennis and started competing in tournaments. At about this time, the American tennis star Arthur Ashe visited South Africa. Ashe's pride and outspoken condemnation of apartheid (ə pär′ tīd) greatly impressed Mathabane, who said later that Ashe "was the first free black man I had ever seen." Mathabane dreamed of using his tennis skills to leave South Africa. His dream came true when Stan Smith, an American player, helped him get a tennis scholarship at Limestone College in South Carolina. He wrote about his college experiences in *Kaffir Boy in America,* his second autobiographical work. In his 1994 book, *African Women: Three Generations,* he discusses the struggles of black South African women under apartheid through the lives of his grandmother, his mother, and his sister.

Vocabulary Preview

ruse (rōōz) *n.* trick; p. 186
queue (kū) *n.* waiting line; p. 187
irate (ī rāt′) *adj.* hot-tempered or angry; p. 188
lanky (lang′ kē) *adj.* ungracefully tall and thin; p. 188
virulent (vir′ yə lənt) *adj.* exceptionally severe and malicious; p. 189
ubiquitous (ū bik′ wə təs) *adj.* existing or being everywhere at the same time; p. 189

from Kaffir Boy in America

Mark Mathabane

Township Scene, 1972. James Salang (South Africa). Pastel on paper, 58 x 64 cm. De Beers Centenary Art Gallery, University of Fort Hare, South Africa.

I Leave South Africa

The plane landed at Atlanta's International Airport the afternoon of September 17, 1978. I double-checked the name and description of Dr. Killion's friend who was to meet me. Shortly after the plane came to a standstill at the gate, and I was stashing Dr. Killion's letter into my totebag, I felt a tap on my shoulder, and turning met the steady and unsettling gaze of the Black Muslim.

"Are you from Africa?" he asked as he offered to help me with my luggage.

"Yes." I wondered how he could tell.

"A student?"

"Yes." We were aboard a jumbo jet, almost at the back of it. From the throng in front it was clear that it would be some time before we disembarked, so we fell into conversation. He asked if it was my first time in the United States and I replied that it was. He spoke in a thick American accent.

"Glad to meet you, brother," he said. We shook hands. "My name is Nkwame."

"I'm Mark," I said, somewhat intimidated by his aspect.

"Mark is not African," he said coolly. "What's your African name, brother?"

"Johannes."

"That isn't an African name either."

I was startled by this. How did he know I had an African name? I hardly used it myself because it was an unwritten rule among black youths raised in the ghettos to deny their tribal identity and affiliation, and that denial applied especially to names. But I didn't want to offend this persistent stranger, so I gave it to him. "Thanyani."

"What does it stand for?"

How did he know that my name stood for something? I wondered in amazement. My worst fears were confirmed. Black Americans did indeed possess the sophistication to see through any ruse an African puts up. Then and there I decided to tell nothing but the truth.

"The wise one," I said, and quickly added, "but the interpretation is not meant to be taken literally, sir."

We were now headed out of the plane. He carried my tennis rackets.

"The wise one, heh," he mused. "You Africans sure have a way with names. You know," he went on with great warmth, "one of my nephews is named after a famous African chief. Of the Mandingo tribe, I believe. Ever since I saw 'Roots'[1] I have always wanted to know where my homeland is."

I found this statement baffling for I thought that as an American his homeland was America. I did not know about "Roots."

"Which black college in Atlanta will you be attending, Thanyani?" he asked. "You will be attending a black college, I hope?"

Black colleges? I stared at him. My mind conjured up images of the dismal tribal schools I hated and had left behind in the ghetto. My God, did such schools exist in America?

"No, sir," I stammered. "I won't be attending school in Atlanta. I'm headed for Limestone College in South Carolina."

"Is Limestone a black college?"

"No, sir," I said hastily.

"What a pity," he sighed. "You would be better off at a black college."

I continued staring at him.

He went on. "At a black college," he said with emphasis, "you can meet with your true brothers and sisters. There's so much you can teach them about the true Africa and the struggles of our people over there. And they have a lot to teach you about being black in America. And, you know, there are lots of black colleges in the South."

I nearly fainted at this revelation. Black schools in America? Was I hearing things or what? I almost blurted out that I had attended black schools all my life and wanted to have nothing to do with them. But instead I said, "Limestone College is supposed to be a good college, too, sir. It's integrated."

"That don't mean nothing," he snapped. "Integrated schools are the worst places for black folks. I thought you Africans would have enough brains to know that this integration business in America is a fraud. It ain't good for the black mind and culture. Integration, integration," he railed. "What good has integration done the black man? We've simply become more dependent on the white devil and forgotten how to do things for ourselves. Also, no matter how integrated we become, white folks won't accept us as equals. So why should we break our backs trying to mix with them, heh? To them we will always be niggers."

1. *Roots* refers to the televised miniseries that first aired in 1977 and was based on Alex Haley's novel *Roots.* The story begins in Gambia, West Africa.

Vocabulary

ruse (ro͞oz) *n.* trick

I was shaken by his outburst. I longed to be gone from him, especially since he had drawn me aside in the corridor leading toward customs. The Black Muslim must have realized that I was a complete stranger to him, that his bitter tone terrified and confused me, for he quickly recollected himself and smiled.

"Well, good luck in your studies, brother," he said handing me my rackets. "By the way, where in Africa did you say you were from? Nigeria?"

"No. South Africa."

"South what!" he said.

"South Africa," I repeated. "That place with all those terrible race problems. Where black people have no rights and are being murdered every day."

I expected my statement to shock him; instead he calmly said, "You will find a lot of South Africa in this country, brother. Keep your eyes wide open all the time. Never let down your guard or you're dead. And while you're up there in South Carolina, watch out for the Ku Klux Klan.[2] That's their home. And don't you ever believe that integration nonsense."

He left. I wondered what he meant by his warning. I stumbled my way to customs. There was a long queue and when my turn came the white, somber-faced immigration official, with cropped reddish-brown hair, seemed transformed into an Afrikaner[3] bureaucrat. I almost screamed. He demanded my passport. After inspecting it, he asked to see my plane ticket. I handed it to him.

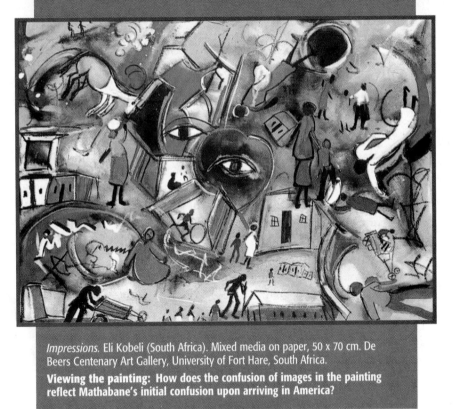

Impressions. Eli Kobeli (South Africa). Mixed media on paper, 50 x 70 cm. De Beers Centenary Art Gallery, University of Fort Hare, South Africa.

Viewing the painting: How does the confusion of images in the painting reflect Mathabane's initial confusion upon arriving in America?

"It's a one-way ticket," he said.

"Yes, sir. I couldn't afford a return ticket," I answered, wondering what could be wrong.

"Under the student visa regulations you're required to have a return ticket," he said icily. "Otherwise how will you get back home? You intend returning home after your studies, don't you?"

"Yes, sir."

"Then you ought to have a return ticket."

I remained silent.

"Do you have relatives or a guardian in America?"

I speedily handed him a letter from Stan Smith, along with several completed immigration forms indicating that he had pledged to be my legal guardian for the duration of my stay in the States. The immigration official inspected the documents, then left his cubicle and went to

2. The *Ku Klux Klan* is a white racist secret society.
3. An *Afrikaner* is a descendant of people from the Netherlands who settled in South Africa in the seventeenth century.

Vocabulary
queue (kū) *n.* waiting line

consult his superior. I trembled at the thought that I might be denied entry into the United States. But the one-way ticket, which created the impression that I was coming to America for good, was hardly my fault. Having had no money to purchase a ticket of my own, I had depended on the charity of white friends, and I was in no position to insist that they buy me a return ticket. The immigration official came back. He stamped my passport and welcomed me to the United States. I almost fell on my knees and kissed the hallowed ground.

"Welcome to America, Mark," a tall, lean-faced white man greeted me as I came out of customs. It was Dr. Waller.

His kind voice and smiling face, as he introduced himself and asked me if I had a good flight, raised my spirits. As we walked toward the baggage claim area I stared at everything about me with childlike wonder. I scarcely believed I had finally set foot in *the* America. I felt the difference between South Africa and America instantly. The air seemed pervaded with freedom and hope and opportunity. Every object seemed brighter, newer, more modern, fresher, the people appeared better dressed, more intelligent, richer, warmer, happier, and full of energy—despite the profound impersonality of the place.

"I would like to use the lavatory," I told Dr. Waller.

"There should be one over there." He pointed to a sign ahead which read RESTROOMS. "I'll wait for you at the newsstand over there."

When I reached the restroom I found it had the sign MEN in black and white on it. Just before I entered I instinctively scoured the walls to see if I had missed the other more important sign: BLACKS ONLY or WHITES ONLY, but there was none. I hesitated before entering: this freedom was too new, too strange, too unreal, and called for the utmost caution. Despite what I believed about America, there still lingered in the recesses of my mind the terror I had suffered in South Africa when I had inadvertently disobeyed the racial etiquette, like that time in Pretoria[4] when I mistakenly boarded a white bus, and Granny had to grovel before the irate redneck driver, emphatically declare that it was an insanity "not of the normal kind" which had made me commit such a crime, and to appease him proceeded to wipe, with her lovely tribal dress, the steps where I had trod. In such moments of doubt such traumas made me mistrust my instincts. I saw a lanky black American with a mammoth Afro[5] enter and I followed. I relieved myself next to a white man and he didn't die.

The black American washed his hands and began combing his Afro. I gazed at his hair with wonder. In South Africa blacks adored Afros and often incurred great expense cultivating that curious hairdo, in imitation of black Americans. Those who succeeded in giving their naturally crinkly, nappy, and matted hair, which they loathed, that buoyant "American" look were showered with praise and considered handsome and "glamorous," as were those who successfully gave it the permanent wave or jerry-curl, and bleached their faces white with special creams which affected the pigmentation.

I remember how Uncle Pietrus, on my father's side, a tall, athletic, handsome man who earned slave wages, was never without creams such as Ambi to bleach his face, and regularly wore a meticulously combed Afro greased with Brylcreem. Many in the neighborhood considered him the paragon of manly beauty, and women were swept away by his "American" looks.

4. *Pretoria* is the administrative capital of South Africa.
5. An *Afro* is a hairstyle of tight curls in a full, evenly rounded shape popular in the United States during the 1960s and 1970s.

Vocabulary

irate (ī rāt′) *adj.* hot-tempered or angry
lanky (lāng′ kē) *adj.* ungracefully tall and thin

From time to time he proudly told me stories of how, in the center of Johannesburg,[6] whites who encountered black men and women with bleached faces, Afros, or straightened hair, and clad in the latest fashion from America, often mistook them for black Americans and treated them as honorary whites. A reasonable American accent made the masquerade almost foolproof. So for many blacks there were these incentives to resemble black Americans, to adopt their mannerisms and lifestyles. And the so-called Coloreds (mixed race), with their naturally lighter skin and straightened hair, not only frequently took advantage of this deception but often passed for whites. But they were rarely secure in their false identity. And in their desperation to elude discovery and humiliation at being subjected to fraudulent race-determining tests like the pencil test (where the authorities run a pencil through one's hair: if the pencil slides smoothly through, one gets classified white; if it gets tangled, that's "positive" proof of being black), they often adopted racist attitudes toward blacks more virulent than those of the most racist whites.

I had sense enough to disdain the practice of whitening one's skin. I considered it pathetic and demeaning to blacks. As for the companies which manufactured these popular creams, they are insidiously catering to a demand created by over three hundred years of white oppression and domination. During that traumatic time the black man's culture and values were decimated in the name of civilization, and the white man's culture and values, trumpeted as superior, became the standards of intelligence, excellence, and beauty.

I left the bathroom and rejoined Dr. Waller at the newsstand. I found him reading a magazine.

"There's so much to read here," I said, running my eyes over the newspapers, magazines, and books. Interestingly, almost all had white faces on the cover, just as in South Africa.

"Yes," replied Dr. Waller.

I was shocked to see pornography magazines, which are banned in South Africa, prominently displayed. The puritan and Calvinistic religion of the Afrikaners sought to purge South African society of "influences of the devil" and "materials subversive to the state and public morals" by routinely banning and censoring not only books by writers who challenged the status quo, but also publications like *Playboy*.

"So many black people fly in America," I said.

"A plane is like a car to many Americans," said Dr. Waller.

"To many of my people cars are what planes are to Americans."

At the baggage-claim area I saw black and white people constantly rubbing shoulders, animatedly talking to one another, and no one seemed to mind. There were no ubiquitous armed policemen.

"There truly is no apartheid[7] here," I said to myself. "This is indeed the Promised Land."

I felt so happy and relieved that for the first time the tension that went with being black in South Africa left me. I became a new person.

6. *Johannesburg* is the largest city in the Republic of South Africa.

7. *Apartheid* (ə pär′ tīd) was a system, in force for nearly fifty years, that imposed social and economic disabilities on the non-European majority in South Africa. It was finally abolished in 1990.

Vocabulary

virulent (vir′ yə lənt) *adj.* exceptionally severe and malicious

ubiquitous (ū bik′ wə təs) *adj.* existing or being everywhere at the same time

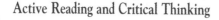

Responding to Literature

Personal Response

What impression of Mark did you get from reading this selection? Share your response with the class.

Analyzing Literature

Recall

1. How does Mark react when the Black Muslim insists on learning his African name?
2. What does the Black Muslim suggest about choosing a college?
3. What causes Mark to hesitate before entering the men's restroom?
4. What does Mark recall about his uncle while he is in the restroom?
5. What leads Mark to call the United States the "Promised Land"?

Interpret

6. Do you think that Mark wants to start a conversation with the Black Muslim? Why or why not?
7. Why do you think Mark is "terrified and confused" by the Black Muslim's remarks about education?
8. What does Mark's concern about entering the restroom suggest about his life in South Africa?
9. **Irony** is a contrast between what is expected and what actually exists or occurs (see page R6). What is ironic about the behavior of Mark's uncle?
10. What sights and experiences at the airport detract from Mark's generally positive impression of the United States?

Evaluate and Connect

11. How would you compare Mark's and the Black Muslim's attitudes toward Africa?
12. Do you think that Mark has formed a realistic impression of the United States at the airport? Why or why not?
13. Mark Mathabane arrived in the United States in 1978. Do you think his experience would have been different if he had arrived several decades earlier? Explain.
14. In the Reading Focus on page 184, you were asked to describe your expectations about arriving at a new place. How does this experience help you understand Mark's feelings when he arrives in the United States?
15. What do you predict will happen to Mark in his new school?

Literary ELEMENTS

Autobiography

An **autobiography** is the story of a person's life written by that person. Since autobiographies generally stress the author's personal views, they are often not as objective as other forms of nonfiction, such as history books. With the purpose of the autobiography in mind, the author selects the events to write about. Some autobiographies cover the subject's entire life, presenting a general self-portrait. Others focus on a particular experience or the author's relationship with another person. For example, Elie Weisel's *Night* (page 1001) is an account of the author's struggle to survive in a Nazi concentration camp.

1. Why might Mathabane have chosen to describe at length his encounter with the Black Muslim?
2. Identify a passage in the selection in which Mathabane presents his views directly to the reader, as opposed to portraying the thoughts he had as a young man.

- See **Literary Terms Handbook,** p. R1.

Literature and Writing

Writing About Literature

Analyzing Narrative Summarize the incidents in this selection from *Kaffir Boy in America.* Then write a paragraph analyzing how Mathabane portrays his arrival. Do you think that he could have organized his material more effectively? Which incidents would you have liked him to cover in greater detail? Which people would you like to hear more or less about?

Creative Writing

Another View Imagine that you are one of the people Mathabane portrays in this selection, such as the Black Muslim or Dr. Waller. Write an account of Mark's arrival from that person's point of view. Although your impression of this event may differ greatly from Mark's, make sure that the details in your account are consistent with those in the selection.

Extending Your Response

Literature Groups

Reading the Author's Mind Do you think that Mathabane has distanced himself from his youth, or does he continue to hold most of the views he had when he arrived in the United States? Discuss this question in your group, using evidence from the selection to support your opinion. Present your group's conclusions to the class.

Interdisciplinary Activity

Art: Scenes from an Airport Mark's feelings about the United States are influenced by the crowds and sights at the airport. Draw a picture of one of the scenes that Mathabane describes in the selection. Share your picture with a classmate, explaining why you chose to draw that particular scene.

Internet Activity

Black Colleges Mark's opinion of black colleges is based on his experiences of segregated schools in South Africa. Use an Internet search engine to find out more about black colleges in the United States. Type in keywords such as "black colleges," "United Negro College Fund," or the name of a particular school. Discuss your findings with the class.

Save your work for your portfolio.

VOCABULARY • Connotation and Denotation

Because many writers want to evoke a particular emotion through words, the emotional meaning of a word is as important as its literal meaning. The literal definition of a word is its **denotation.** You can find a word's denotation in the dictionary. Some words convey feelings and thoughts that you do not always find in a dictionary. The emotional meaning of a word is its **connotation.** For example, the word *snicker* literally means "to laugh in a suppressed manner." The word *chuckle* has the same denotation, but a different connotation. If someone told a story about something you did, would you rather the listener chuckled or snickered?

PRACTICE Using a dictionary, look up the denotation of each of the following words, and then write what you think its connotation is.

1. lanky
2. henchman
3. glitter
4. ostentatious

Writing Workshop

Descriptive Writing: Travel Article

How can you get a sense of what Africa is like without ever leaving your hometown? You can read. The best travel writing makes us feel that we are in the place being described. It helps us see scenery, hear street sounds, smell aromas, and taste food in restaurants that are miles away from where we sit turning pages. **In this workshop, you will write a travel article that uses descriptive techniques that enable your readers to experience a place as if they had visited it with you.**

- As you write your travel article, refer to **Writing Handbook,** pp. R58–R63.

EVALUATION RUBRIC

By the time you complete this Writing Workshop, you will have

- **demonstrated an awareness of your audience—in this case, readers who are not familiar with the place that you are writing about**
- **used details in your description that appeal to all five senses**
- **organized the details in a logical, effective order**
- **presented a travel article that is free of errors in grammar, usage, and mechanics**

The Writing Process

PREWRITING

PREWRITING TIP

Use your daydreams to find a place to write about. If you could be somewhere else, where would you like to be?

Explore ideas

To get yourself started, jot down a list of places that you

- would like to visit
- have already visited
- have read about
- would like to introduce others to

Go over your list. Which of the places can you picture in your mind most vividly? Which of them would you most like to spend time thinking about? Which of them could you make most interesting to others? Write about that place.

Choose an audience

Who will your intended audience be? What would they most want to know about it? Why do you think they should visit? Remember, they are probably not familiar with the place you're writing about. You have to make it come alive in their minds.

Consider your purpose

First and foremost, you must help your audience experience the place you are describing. You may also want to express your opinions of that place or on an issue related to it.

Collect details

A sensory web is a good way to gather details for a travel article. Write the name of the place at the center. List the five senses—sight, hearing, smell, touch, taste—in the circles around it. Then jot notes for each of the senses, circle them, and link them to their appropriate senses.

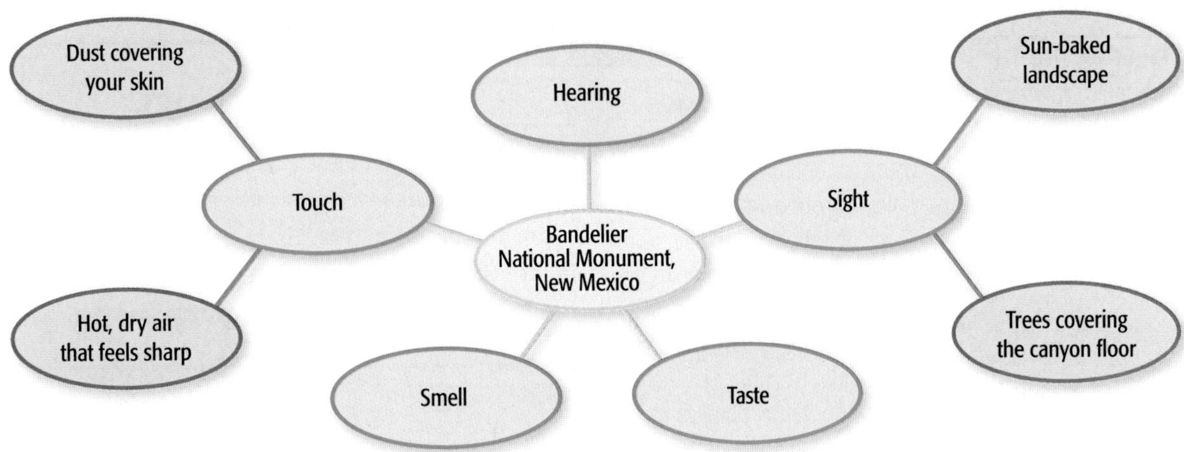

Make a plan

This chart explains several ways to present the information in a travel article.

		STUDENT MODEL
Order of importance	Grab the audience's attention with the most important detail first. Then fill in the background.	Some of the most interesting and inviting trails anywhere in the country can be found only thirteen miles from Los Alamos in the sun-scorched countryside of New Mexico.
Sequence of events	You can tell the story of your visit to the place, describing things as you come to them.	I followed a dusty path with the cliffs at my side. As I climbed, I gazed out at the beautiful cottonwood and box elders that covered the canyon floor below.
Spatial order	You can describe the place as a camera would record it. You can start with a wide-angle shot and then zoom in on the important details. You can pan as a camera would, sweeping from one side of the scene to the other.	A hike through Bandelier National Monument provides a series of dramatic views. All around are the 10,000-foot peaks of the Jemez Mountains. In the distance stands a centuries-old pueblo. Below is the amazing sight of multistory dwellings built into the sides of canyon cliffs—America's first apartment houses.

Complete Student Model on p. R110.

DRAFTING

DRAFTING TIP

Use topic sentences to give each paragraph a clear focus.

Use prepositional phrases

Before you begin drafting, close your eyes and picture yourself walking around your location. Touch objects, smell the air, turn corners. Then start writing. As you create word pictures of the place you're describing, remember that your reader has not been there. Use prepositional phrases to show the reader where details are located.

STUDENT MODEL

The drama of Bandelier comes from walking quietly through the awesome remains of these ancient people's lives. There are dwellings built into the sides of the cliffs and scooped out of the soft volcanic rock at the base of the canyon.

Complete Student Model on p. R110.

Write your draft

If you get stuck, refer to your sensory web to see what details you are leaving out. Follow the plan you've chosen, but remember that you can reorganize later.

REVISING

REVISING TIP

Look for places where vivid verbs or more specific adjectives can strengthen your description.

Evaluate your work

Let your draft sit for a while. Then read it, looking for places where your description is less than clear. Use the **Rubric for Revising** to guide you as you revise.

Have a writing conference

Read your travel article aloud to a writing partner. (Keep the copy to yourself, though–it's probably not ready for a reader yet.) Use the **Rubric for Revising** to guide a discussion with your partner about improvements you might make.

STUDENT MODEL

After a while, you will catch your first views of Tyuonyi. It is a ^circular two-story^ pueblo built in the 1200s^, which might have housed one hundred people^.

Complete Student Model on p. R110.

RUBRIC FOR REVISING

Your revised travel article should have

- ☑ an attention-getting opening
- ☑ a clear awareness of your audience and purpose
- ☑ interesting factual information about your topic
- ☑ details that appeal to all five senses
- ☑ vivid language that brings your descriptions to life
- ☑ a logical and effective organization

Your revised travel article should be free of

- ☑ paragraphs that lack topic sentences
- ☑ irrelevant details that may distract readers from the main idea

EDITING/PROOFREADING

Revise your travel article until you are sure that it will give your reader a strong impression of the place. Then use the **Proofreading Checklist** on the inside back cover to edit it carefully for errors in grammar, usage, mechanics, and spelling.

PROOFREADING TIP

Use a geographical dictionary, maps, or official information on your location to double-check that you have spelled all place names correctly.

Grammar Hint

Make sure that each pronoun refers clearly to a single antecedent.

VAGUE: *When approaching Bandelier National Monument, they feel as if they are entering another time and place.*

CLEAR: *When visitors approach Bandelier National Monument, they feel as if they are entering another time and place.*

- For more about pronoun agreement, see **Language Handbook,** pp. R19–R21.

STUDENT MODEL

```
In 1880 when Adolph Bandalier, who was a selftaught
anthopologist, saw the ruins of these dwelings for the
first time, he said this is the grandest thing I ever saw.
```

Complete Student Model on p. R110.

Complete Student Model

For a complete version of the model developed in this workshop, refer to **Writing Workshop Models**, p. R110.

PUBLISHING/PRESENTING

You may want to submit your article to a travel magazine or other periodical. A community newspaper may like the idea of a local resident's impressions of a distant spot, or a newspaper in a distant spot may be interested in your insider's view of your own hometown. In addition, many sites on the World Wide Web are devoted to travelers' impressions of the places they've visited. Post your article on your own or someone else's Web site.

PRESENTING TIP

Illustrate an oral presentation with slides or photographs.

TECHNOLOGY TIP

If you have software that can create page layouts, format your article as it would appear in a magazine, complete with a headline and photograph.

Reflecting

Think about how you would change your article if you revised it one more time. What effect would changing the organization have on the article? Then take a few minutes to read the article for pleasure, as if someone else had written it.

Save your work for your portfolio.

Unit Assessment

Personal Response

1. Which selections in Unit One expressed ideas about life that are familiar to you? What are the ideas? In what ways are they familiar? Which of them did you find most relevant to your own life? What elements in these selections helped you to bridge any gaps of time and culture?
2. Which of the selections in this unit did you find the most moving or inspiring?
3. What did you learn about the relationship between actual events and the literature about them?
4. What suggestions would you make to someone who is interested in learning about the literature and culture of Africa?

Analyzing Literature

Compare and Contrast The literature of Africa takes many different forms, including lyric poetry, short stories, folktales, and nonfiction. Write several paragraphs in which you compare and contrast a few of these forms, exploring at least one of the following elements in detail:

- subject matter
- literary elements
- theme
- language
- form

Refer to at least two of the selections you have read in the unit to support your opinion. You might conclude your analysis by stating which of the selections was your favorite and why you feel that way.

Evaluate and Set Goals

Evaluate

1. What was your strongest contribution to group activities as you worked through this unit?
2. What was the most challenging task presented in this unit?
   - How did you approach this task?
   - W hat was the result?
3. How would you assess your work in this unit, using the following scale? Give at least two reasons for your assessment.
   4 = outstanding 3 = good 2 = fair 1 = weak

Set Goals

1. Choose a goal to work toward while reading Unit Two. It could involve reading, writing, speaking, researching, or working in a group.
2. Discuss your goal with your teacher.
3. List two or three steps that you will take to achieve your goal.
4. Plan checkpoints at which you will stop and assess your progress toward that goal.

BUILD YOUR PORTFOLIO

Select Look over the writing that you did in this unit and select two pieces to include in your portfolio. Use the following questions to help you choose the most significant pieces:

- Which piece do you consider your best?
- Which challenged you the most?
- Which piece was the most fun to write?
- Which one led you to new discoveries about yourself or your world as you wrote?

Reflect Write some notes to accompany the pieces you chose for your portfolio. Use the following questions as a guide:

- What did you learn from the process of writing each piece?
- What are the overall strengths and weaknesses of each piece of writing?
- How might you revise each piece to make it stronger?

Reading on Your Own

If you have enjoyed the literature in this unit, you might also be interested in the following books.

Things Fall Apart
by Chinua Achebe In his first novel, Achebe tells the story of a thriving traditional Ibo community and the problems that develop with the arrival of British missionaries. Achebe's Ibo protagonist, Okonkwo, is a proud man whose ruin epitomizes the destruction of an entire culture.

Cry, the Beloved Country
by Alan Paton Paton narrates the moving story of two families in South Africa, one black and one white, that are brought together by the loss of their sons and the injustice of apartheid. The reader empathizes with both the Zulu priest, Stephen Kumalo, and his white counterpart, James Jarvis.

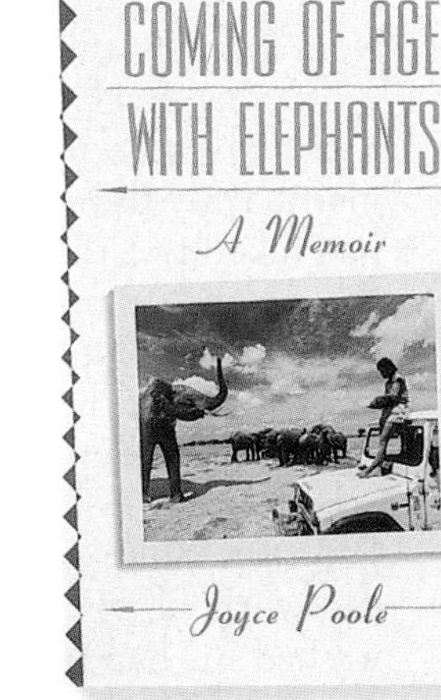

Coming of Age with Elephants: A Memoir
by Joyce Poole Poole lives among the endangered African elephants of Kenya's Amboseli National Park, where she discovers and explores the intricacies of elephant life, while suffering the loneliness and discrimination of an ambitious white woman living in Kenya. Poole was raised in Kenya and is versed in several cultures–American, Masai, and elephant. Her American culture is evident in her independence and ambition, the Masai taught her how to live in the bush, and the elephants made her aware of their intelligence.

Waiting for the Rain
by Sheila Gordon Frikkie, a white boy destined to inherit his uncle's land, and Tengo, who works the land Frikkie will one day own, develop a close friendship as children. The boys meet again when they are grown and apartheid is crumbling, revealing new obstacles in their relationship. Tengo has committed his life to change, and Frikkie is dedicated to preserving life as it has always been.

California English–Language Arts

Reading and Analyzing Test Questions

The passage below is followed by six questions based on its content. Select the best answer and write the corresponding letter on your paper.

PROSE FICTION: This passage is adapted from the novel *Things Fall Apart* by Chinua Achebe (©1959 by Chinua Achebe.)

Okonkwo was well known throughout the nine villages and even beyond. His fame rested on solid personal achievements. As a young man of eighteen he had brought honor to his village by throwing Amalinze the Cat. Amalinze was the great wrestler who for seven years was unbeaten, from Umuofia to Mbaino. He was called the Cat because his back would never touch the earth. It was this man that Okonkwo threw in a fight which the old men agreed was one of the fiercest since the founder of their town engaged a spirit of the wild for seven days and seven nights.

The drums beat and the flutes sang and the spectators held their breath. Amalinze was a wily craftsman, but Okonkwo was as slippery as a fish in water. Every nerve and every muscle stood out on their arms, on their backs and their thighs, and one almost heard them stretching to breaking point. In the end Okonkwo threw the Cat.

That was many years ago, twenty years or more, and during this time Okonkwo's fame had grown like a bush-fire in the harmattan. He was tall and huge, and his bushy eyebrows and wide nose gave him a very severe look. He breathed heavily, and it was said that, when he slept, his wives and children in their houses could hear him breathe. When he walked, his heels hardly touched the ground and he seemed to walk on springs, as if he was going to pounce on somebody. And he did pounce on people quite often. He had a slight stammer and whenever he was angry and could not get his words out quickly enough, he would use his fists. He had no patience with unsuccessful men. He had had no patience with his father.

Unoka, for that was his father's name, had died ten years ago. In his day he was lazy and improvident and was quite incapable of thinking about tomorrow. If any money came his way, and it seldom did, he immediately bought gourds of palm-wine, called round his neighbors and made merry. He always said that whenever he saw a dead man's mouth he saw the folly of not eating what one had in one's lifetime. Unoka was, of course, a debtor, and he owed every neighbor some money, from a few cowries to quite substantial amounts.

When Unoka died he had taken no title at all and he was heavily in debt. Any wonder then that his son Okonkwo was ashamed of him? Fortunately, among these people a man was judged according to his worth and not according to the worth of his father. Okonkwo was clearly cut out for great things. He was still young but he had won fame as the greatest wrestler in the nine villages. He was a wealthy farmer and had two barns full of yams, and had just married his third wife. To crown it all he had taken two titles and had shown incredible prowess in two inter-tribal wars. And so although Okonkwo was still young, he was already one of the greatest men of his time. Age was respected among his people, but achievement was revered. As the elders said, if a child washed his hands he could eat with kings. Okonkwo had clearly washed his hands and so he ate with kings and elders.

1. According to the passage, Okonkwo had
   A. a slight speech problem
   B. a limp in his left leg
   C. a beard
   D. many children

2. It is implied in the passage that, at the time the story was written, Okonkwo was
   F. younger than 18 years old
   G. about 18 years old
   H. about 28 years old
   J. over 38 years old

3. The passage implies that Okonkwo viewed his father as being
   A. aggressive and warlike
   B. compassionate and caring
   C. firm but loving
   D. carefree and lazy

4. As it is used on line 67, the word *prowess* most nearly means
   F. patience
   G. skill
   H. indifference
   J. concern

5. It is implied in the fifth paragraph (lines 57–60) that the members of Okonkwo's tribe judged each other primarily on the basis of
   A. wealth
   B. accomplishments
   C. the social status of their parents
   D. cleanliness

6. When the narrator states that whenever Umoka "saw a dead man's mouth he saw the folly of not eating what one had in one's lifetime," (lines 48–50) he means that Umoka
   F. was usually hungry
   G. was afraid of dead bodies
   H. did not like to save for the future
   J. thought that wars should be avoided

STOP

Sappho with Homer and Other Arcadian Figures in a Landscape, 1824. Charles Nicholas Rafael Lafond (France). Oil on canvas, 65.4 x 81.3 cm. Private collection.

UNIT TWO

Ancient Greece and Rome

1500 B.C.–A.D. 476

μνάcεcθαί τινα φαίμι καί
ἕτερον ἀμμέων

I think that someone will remember us in another time.

—Sappho

The Land and Its People

Greece is a land of islands, mountains, and peninsulas. Rocky hilltops separate parts of the territory from each other and make the soil difficult to farm. White limestone cliffs drop off into the blue and ever-present sea. Most parts of Greece are within fifty miles of salt water, and this rugged, maritime landscape has affected Greece's history from its beginning. The rough terrain meant that settlements were isolated and self-sufficient. The access to the sea encouraged trade and provided access to other cultures. Eventually, organized city-states such as Athens and Sparta emerged. Although they were fiercely independent, these communities shared a common language, religion, and social organization.

The area's challenging landscape was matched by its history. Early centuries were marked by waves of destructive invasions. Later, the Greeks were always conscious of their mighty and often hostile neighbor, the vast Persian Empire.

History and geography combined to form the Greek character. More than the earlier civilizations in Egypt and Mesopotamia, Greek civilization was interested in the individual human being. Their art, history, and philosophy focused on the human body and mind.

Marble relief of woman, c. 4th century B.C.

Warriors in horse-drawn chariot, 6th century B.C.

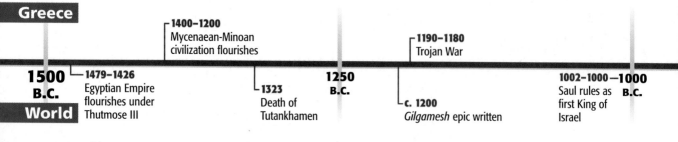

Greece

1400–1200 Mycenaean-Minoan civilization flourishes

1190–1180 Trojan War

1500 B.C.

1250 B.C.

1000 B.C.

World

1479–1426 Egyptian Empire flourishes under Thutmose III

1323 Death of Tutankhamen

c. 1200 *Gilgamesh* epic written

1002–1000 Saul rules as first King of Israel

BALKAN MOUNTAINS
RHODOPE MOUNTAINS
PINDOS MOUNTAINS
Lake Scutari
Lake Ohrid
Lake Prespa
Macedonia
PERSIAN EMPIRE
Thrace
BLACK SEA
Bosporus
SEA OF MARMARA
Dardanelles
Troy
Mt. Ida
Mt. Olympus
Larissa
Mt. Pelion
GREECE
Phthia
LESBOS
Lydia
Sardis
Ionia
Mt. Parnassus
Delphi
Thebes
AEGEAN SEA
SAMOS
Athens
Piraeus
Patras
IONIAN SEA
Olympia
Mycenae
Corinth
Argos
Laconia
Sparta
RHODES
MEDITERRANEAN SEA
Mt. Dicte
CRETE
N
20°
40°
30°
0 100 200 Miles
0 100 200 Kilometers
Projection: Azimuthal Equal Area

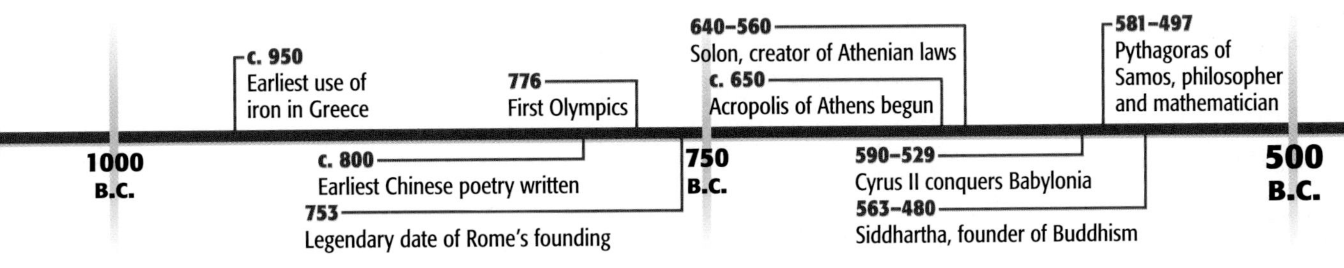

How People Lived

Vase painting of couple fishing, c. 480 B.C.

In Athens

Over the centuries, Athens grew from a small city-state into the center of one of the most successful, sophisticated, and cultured societies in the history of the world. By the fifth century B.C., history's first democratic government had taken hold there.

Free men spent much of their life in public outdoor spaces, discussing philosophy and politics. Wealth from the nearby silver mines, from other cities paying tribute, and from trade allowed citizens ample time to pursue learning.

However, while citizens enjoyed freedom and opportunity, most people who lived in Athens were not citizens. Scholars estimate that at least 40 percent of the Athenian population were enslaved. Although enslaved people could often buy their freedom, they could never gain full rights as citizens. Free women could not participate openly in politics and were expected to spend their time at home.

In Sparta

While Athens was known for its democratic government and flourishing culture, Sparta was known for its military strength. The Spartan government believed that the lives of its citizens should be totally devoted to the military. For this reason, young boys were taken away from their parents and housed in dormitories while they underwent physical training. Girls were trained in all-female groups. From the age of twenty until the age of sixty, boys and men belonged to the army and were supposed to eat in barracks. Although men were allowed to marry, only after age thirty could they live with their wives.

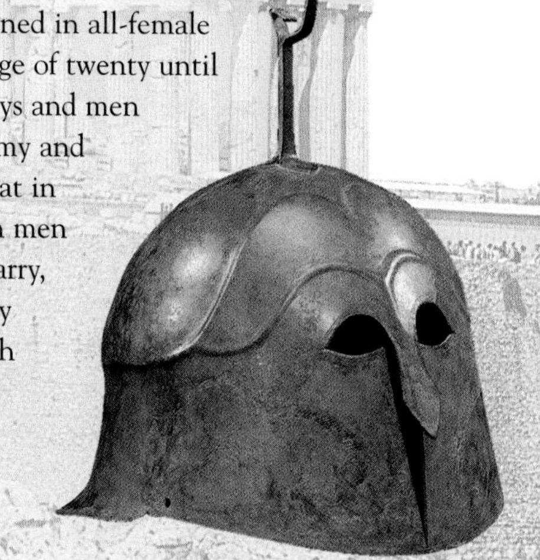

Bronze helmet, 5th century B.C.

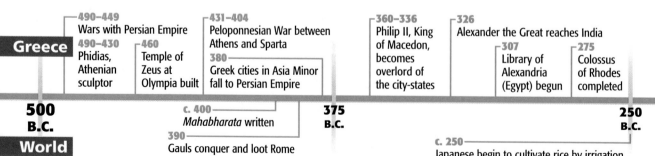

Greece

- **490–449** Wars with Persian Empire
- **490–430** Phidias, Athenian sculptor
- **460** Temple of Zeus at Olympia built
- **431–404** Peloponnesian War between Athens and Sparta
- **380** Greek cities in Asia Minor fall to Persian Empire
- **360–336** Philip II, King of Macedon, becomes overlord of the city-states
- **326** Alexander the Great reaches India
- **307** Library of Alexandria (Egypt) begun
- **275** Colossus of Rhodes completed

500 B.C. — **375 B.C.** — **250 B.C.**

World

- **c. 400** *Mahabharata* written
- **390** Gauls conquer and loot Rome
- **c. 250** Japanese begin to cultivate rice by irrigation

Traditions and Beliefs

Gold coin showing Helios, God of the Sun.

Family of Deities

Different as they were, the Greek city-states all believed in the same family of deities—gods and goddesses in human form who behaved like people with superhuman powers. The Greeks erected temples in honor of these deities and sacrificed animals to them. The twelve major gods and goddesses were believed to often gather on Mount Olympus, a real mountain located roughly in the center of Greece. Known as the Olympians, they include

- Zeus, the chief god, ruler of the sky and the weather
- Pluto, the brother of Zeus and the god of the underworld
- Athena, Zeus's favorite daughter, goddess of wisdom
- Apollo, the son of Zeus and the god of light, health, and poetry
- Artemis, the twin sister of Apollo, goddess of the hunt and the moon

Human Philosophers

Not all Greeks were content to attribute life's occurrences to the whims of the deities. The Greek emphasis on the human experience gave rise to systematic questioning and observation of the world at large. As a result, the Greeks made great advances in science, philosophy, and medicine. Greek thinkers included

- Hippocrates (hi pok′ rə tēz), who trained doctors to look into the causes of disease
- Aristotle (ar′ is tot′ əl), who systematized the study of science
- Socrates (sok′ rə tēz), who questioned all assumptions in search of the truth
- Herodotus (hə rod′ ə təs), who established the idea that history could be studied as a collection of true facts, rather than a series of legends

Active Reading Strategies

Reading the Time Line

1. How old was mathematician and philosopher Pythagoras when Siddhartha, founder of Buddhism, was born?
2. About how many years before the composition of the earliest Chinese poetry was the epic *Gilgamesh* written?

Athenian philosophers, 1508. Raphael.

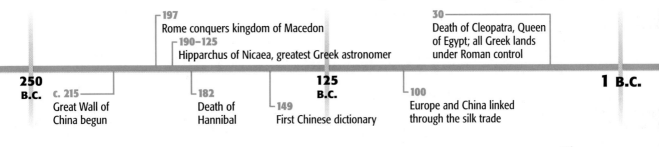

250 B.C.
- c. 215 Great Wall of China begun
- 197 Rome conquers kingdom of Macedon
- 190–125 Hipparchus of Nicaea, greatest Greek astronomer
- 182 Death of Hannibal
- 149 First Chinese dictionary

125 B.C.
- 100 Europe and China linked through the silk trade
- 30 Death of Cleopatra, Queen of Egypt; all Greek lands under Roman control

1 B.C.

Arts and Entertainment

Painted vase, c. 320 B.C.

Sculpture

Greek sculptors usually chose the human figure as their subject. They used symmetry, harmony, and proportion to create a new kind of beauty in a search for the ideal. Initially, they borrowed ideas from the Egyptians, as can be seen in the early Kouros figures—sculptures of the male form often used to decorate temples. These sculptures showed figures posed in rigid positions with their weight balanced equally on both legs. However, the Greeks soon became interested in capturing natural human movement. They studied anatomy to get a better sense of how muscles and bones work together, and their realistic sculptures of people in motion reflected this new knowledge. Although we think of Greek statues as bright white, the color of marble, they were actually painted in lifelike colors, adding to their realism. Even deities were sometimes represented this way. Other religious art laid less emphasis on realism. The great sculptor Phidias, for example, created a 40-foot-high gold and ivory statue of Athena for the Parthenon.

Painting

Greek vases or other vessels were often decorated with paintings that showed scenes from mythology, war, or everyday life. Greek painters started off by trying to capture an idealized beauty—a fixed, generic sense of human perfection. However, they gained an interest in showing human individuality. They began exploring people's feelings and communicated these emotions through facial expressions and postures. Vase paintings were either red on black outlines or black on red. Although few examples have survived, we know Greek painters also did full color paintings, often on walls. Again, realism was stressed. In one legend, a Greek artist proved his skill by painting a bunch of grapes so realistically that birds swooped down to try to eat them.

Ariadne sleeping, c. 200 B.C.

Architecture

Although Greek people lived in humble houses, they constructed magnificent public buildings. Each city-state had an acropolis, or a fortified area at the highest point in their city, where temples were built. The Acropolis of Athens, remains of which still stand, was considered to be the grandest of them all. It includes the Parthenon, a temple to Athena that has come to symbolize classical Greek architecture. Millions of tourists, art historians, and archeologists have climbed the steep rock outcropping to view the white marble building, which glows with a gold light against the sky. By using mathematical principles and critical observation to organize the Parthenon's columns and other elements, the architects achieved a perfection that builders since have sought to duplicate. The Athenian Acropolis contains examples of the three main styles, or "orders," of Greek architecture:

A temple on the Acropolis, Athens.

- The Doric order, which is plain, simple, and regal, came into wide use before the Ionic order did. The Parthenon uses the Doric order.
- The Ionic order, which was more delicate, complex, and ornate, came into wide use about one hundred years after the Doric order.
- The Corinthian order was the most elaborate and latest style. It featured decorations of leaves and scrolls.

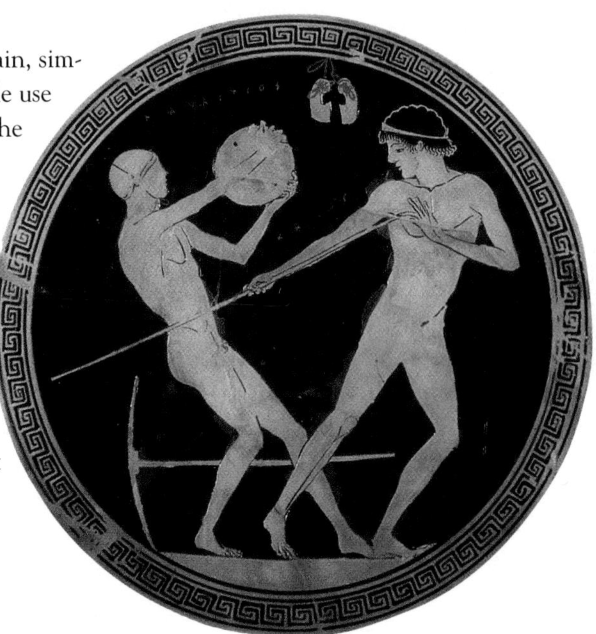

Athletes, 4th century B.C.

The Olympics

Athleticism, as a way of measuring human achievement, was highly valued in Greece, and the best athletes trained for years in order to participate in the Olympic games, the premier competition of the time. Held every four years in the Greek city of Olympia, the games weren't simply sporting events. They were elaborate festivals that focused on religion, poetry, and music as well as on sports.

The first Olympics featured only one event—a foot race across the distance of the stadium. In later years more races were added, along with the discus throw, the javelin throw, boxing, wrestling, and other events. Only men could compete in the Olympics, and usually only wealthy men had the time to train, practice, and travel to Olympia. Winners became even wealthier. While there were no official cash prizes, cities often rewarded their champions with large sums.

Critical Thinking

Connecting Cultures

1. The Olympic games originated in ancient Greece. What is their significance in our current society? Discuss your answer with a small group of classmates.
2. In a small group, discuss ways in which the modern Olympics differ from the Olympics of ancient Greece. How would you explain the differences?

Language and Literature

Written Language

The earliest Greek writing systems were lost and forgotten during the age of invasions. During the city-state periods, the Greeks adapted an alphabet from the Phoenicians, seafaring merchants who lived in what is today Israel and Lebanon. Different forms of the alphabet were developed for carving inscriptions on stone and for writing in ink on papyrus or parchment.

Α Β Γ Δ Ε Ζ
Η Θ Ι Κ Λ Μ
Ν Ξ Ο Π Ρ Σ
Τ Υ Φ Χ Ψ Ω

Greek alphabet.

Poetry for Different Purposes

Homer's epic poems, set in the legendary "Heroic Age" and retelling stories of war and adventure, were passed on orally for hundreds of years. In the Classical Period, Homer's epics were finally written down in the form we are familiar with today. In the written form, they were used in schools to teach Greek students the values of loyalty, bravery, and pride.

Later poets wrote odes, praising local heroes such as Olympic winners. Last came lyric poetry—dealing with the concerns of individuals and everyday life. For example, the poet Sappho wrote about love and her conflicting emotions. The poet Hesiod wrote of rural life and the changing seasons of the farmer's year.

Mosaic of Odysseus, A.D. 200–400.

influences

The following English words are just a few of the many that take their meaning from people or places of ancient Greece.

- **Draconian,** which means "severe or cruel," refers to the harsh laws enacted by the Athenian lawgiver Draco.
- The **Hippocratic oath** is the vow of ethics usually taken by people about to enter the medical profession. It is named after the Greek doctor Hippocrates.
- The **Pythagorean theorem** states that the square of the hypotenuse of a right triangle is equal to the sum of the square of the other two sides. It takes its name from the Greek mathematician Pythagoras.
- **Laconic,** which means "using few words," refers to Laconia, the region around Sparta, and to the fact that Spartans were encouraged to use short, direct comments rather than to study oratory as in other Greek states.

Reproductions of Greek masks.

Drama

One of the great Greek achievements was tragic and comic drama. At first, these plays were simple retellings of familiar stories, but slowly playwrights began adding characters.

Tragedies were performed at religious festivals and often explored the relationship between humans and the gods. In the process, they asked important questions about life.

Comedies sometimes retold legends and sometimes were set in the contemporary world. They also commented on the human condition, but in a humorous and satirical way. The plays were so insightful and complex that they continue to be relevant today. They have had great impact on the Western literary tradition.

Critical Thinking

Ancient Greece

1. In a small group, discuss the main themes of Greek poetry. How did these themes reflect Greek society and values?
2. In a small group, discuss the main themes of Greek drama. How did these themes reflect Greek society and values?

Theater on the Acropolis, A.D. 161.

Before You Read

from the *Iliad*

Meet Homer

"We can say nothing but what hath been said. Our poets steal from Homer."

—*Robert Burton*

The poet Homer is traditionally given credit for Greece's two great epics, the *Iliad* and the *Odyssey*. We know almost nothing about Homer, except that he probably lived in Ionia, in what is now western Turkey. Ancient writers often mention his blindness, but this legend probably arose from a desire to portray Homer as a wise man, for the Greeks associated blindness with inner vision.

Scholars have long debated whether one individual created the *Iliad* and the *Odyssey*. Some have argued that each epic developed over an extended period, with many poets contributing toward the final version. Today most experts believe that Homer composed at least one, if not both, of the poems.

The poems attributed to Homer show a thorough understanding of traditional storytelling techniques. Homer used these techniques to create poetry of unprecedented length and complexity.

Homer probably lived in the eighth century B.C.

Reading Focus

Imagine that you are fighting in a war and your commander, out of jealousy, takes back an honor you have received. How would you respond?

Journal Write about your feelings in your journal and what you might say to the commander.

Setting a Purpose As you read, think about how the main characters respond to different situations.

Building Background

The *Iliad*

The *Iliad* opens *in medias res,* or "in the middle of things," during the tenth year of the Trojan War. This war, which began in the early twelfth century B.C., was fought because Paris, a Trojan prince, abducted Helen, the queen of Sparta in Greece. For nine years the Greeks attacked Troy, and for nine years the Trojans successfully resisted them. At the beginning of the *Iliad*–from the word *Ilion,* another name for Troy–a bitter quarrel has erupted between Agamemnon, leader of the Greeks, and Achilles, their greatest warrior. Achilles abandons the battlefield. The Greeks suffer heavy losses, and at times they are nearly defeated. After refusing Agamemnon's apology, Achilles allows his best friend Patroclus to join the fighting. Patroclus is then killed by Hector, the chief defender of Troy, at which point Achilles turns his rage from Agamemnon to Hector. The final battle between Achilles and Hector seals Troy's fate, although the poem ends before the city is won by the Greeks.

A brief outline cannot suggest the richness of this epic poem, which runs nearly sixteen thousand lines. Although most of the action in the *Iliad* occurs within a few days, Homer includes much of Greek and Trojan history as background for the battles. The *Iliad* is set in a mythic era when gods intervened directly in human affairs and even fought in some of the battles. Events in the war are therefore shown from the Trojan, Greek, and divine points of view. Beyond its exciting story, the *Iliad* offers a fascinating exploration of the ancient Greek religion and Greek ideals of heroism and honor. In ancient Greece, the outcome of fighting is less important than how characters behave when they are tested in the face of death.

The *Iliad*'s Epic Style

For centuries prior to Homer, Greek poets improvised songs without benefit of writing. Homer relied on this oral tradition not only for stories but also for many literary techniques that he used in the *Iliad.* He probably created the poem orally, dictating it later to a scribe.

The *Iliad* contains many formulaic, or fixed, expressions which made it easy to remember the poem when it was sung. Most noticeable are the epithets, which were almost like nicknames, such as "the swift runner Achilles." Epithets allowed Homer to fit names into any part of a verse without disrupting the metrical pattern and made it easy to finish off a verse that otherwise would have been too short. In addition to epithets, Homer repeated phrases and groups of verses to express similar ideas in different contexts. These techniques were developed by oral poets to help them improvise as they sang.

The *Iliad* was written in dactylic hexameter–six "feet" (groups) of syllables stressed ´˘˘ (e.g. "wonderful")–the style traditional for heroic verse. Since Greek verse forms are based on the sound of each syllable in a word, while English verses are based on the stresses in each word, translators have come up with many different ways of translating Homer's work into English. Robert Fagles, who translated the episodes you will read, generally uses a six-beat line to approximate Homer's verse, sometimes varying to five or seven beats.

Homer opens the *Iliad* with a traditional invocation, or plea, to the goddess of poetry for inspiration. The poem then follows the epic tradition of *in medias res* by plunging the reader into the middle of the action. Homer could begin in this manner without confusing his listeners because they were already familiar with the legend of Troy.

Judgement of Paris, 15th century. Verona da Cecchino (Italy). Oil on canvas. Museo Nazionale del Bargello, Florence.

Viewing the painting: Eris, the goddess of strife, started a rivalry among the goddesses Hera, Athena, and Aphrodite. They appointed Paris, who had been living as a shepherd, to judge their beauty. After being bribed by Aphrodite with the promise of Helen, Paris awarded Aphrodite the prize. During the resulting Trojan War, Athena sided with the Greeks, Aphrodite with the Trojans, and Hera interfered with both sides. Why do you think the painting shows several different scenes? Can you identify what is happening in each?

MAJOR CHARACTERS IN THE ILIAD

GREEKS

ACHAEANS (ə kē′ ənz): another name for the Greeks, also called ARGIVES and DANAANS (dan′ ē ənz)

ACHILLES (ə kil′ ēz): greatest Greek warrior; invincible in battle but doomed to an early death; son of Peleus and the sea goddess Thetis (thē′ tis)

AGAMEMNON (ag′ ə mem′ non): also called Atrides (ə trī′ dēz) or son of Atreus; king of Mycenae and leader of the Greek armies; his wife is CLYTEMNESTRA (klī′ tem nes′ trə)

CALCHAS (kal′ chəs): seer or prophet who counsels the Greeks

HELEN: wife of Menelaus; her abduction by Paris started the Trojan War

MENELAUS (men′ əl ā′ əs): Agamemnon's brother and Helen's husband

MYRMIDONS (mur′ mə donz′): Greek soldiers commanded by Achilles

NESTOR (nes′ tər): oldest of the Greek leaders and a respected counselor

ODYSSEUS (ō dis′ ē əs): the lord of Ithaca, known for his cleverness

PATROCLUS (pə trō′ kləs): friend of Achilles

TROJANS

ANDROMACHE (an drom′ ə kē): Hector's wife

ASTYANAX (as tī′ ə naks′): infant son of Hector and Andromache

BRISEIS (bri sē′ is): captured girl given to Achilles as a war prize

CHRYSEIS (krī sē′ is): captured girl given to Agamemnon as a war prize

CHRYSES (krī′ sēz): priest of Apollo; father of Chryseis

DARDANIANS: another name for the Trojans

DEIPHOBUS (dē′ ə pho′ bəs): son of Priam, brother of Paris

HECTOR: son of Priam and Hecuba; leader of the Trojan forces

HECUBA (hek′ yə bə): queen of Troy

PARIS: son of Priam and Hecuba; abductor of Helen

PRIAM (prī′ əm): king of Troy

GODS AND GODDESSES

APHRODITE (af′ rə dī′ tē): goddess of love; sides with the Trojans

APOLLO (ə pol′ ō): also called Phoebus, Phoebus Apollo, and the Archer; god of prophecy, music, healing, and poetry; sides with the Trojans

ATHENA (ə thē′ nə): also called Pallas or Pallas Athena; goddess of wisdom, the practical arts, and warfare; sides with the Greeks

HERA (her′ ə): wife of Zeus; sides with the Greeks

ZEUS (zo͞os): also called the son of Cronus; most powerful of the gods

But the lord of men Agamemnon shot back,
"*Desert*, by all means—if the spirit drives you home!
I will never beg you to stay, not on *my* account.
Never—others will take my side and do me honor,
Zeus above all, whose wisdom rules the world.
You—I hate you most of all the warlords
loved by the gods. Always dear to your heart,
strife, yes, and battles, the bloody grind of war.
What if you are a great soldier? That's just a gift of god.
Go home with your ships and comrades, lord it over
your Myrmidons!°
You *are* nothing to me—you and your overweening° anger!
But let this be my warning on your way:
since Apollo insists on taking my Chryseis,
I'll send her back in my own ships with *my* crew.
But I, I will be there in person at your tents
to take Briseis in all her beauty, your own prize—
so you can learn just how much greater I am than you
and the next man up may shrink from matching words
with me,
from hoping to rival Agamemnon strength for strength!"

212 Myrmidons: warriors who followed Achilles to Troy.

213 overweening: arrogant; presumptuous; overstepping proper bounds.

He broke off and anguish gripped Achilles.
The heart in his rugged chest was pounding, torn . . .
Should he draw the long sharp sword slung at his hip,
thrust through the ranks° and kill Agamemnon now?—
or check his rage and beat his fury down?
As his racing spirit veered back and forth,
just as he drew his huge blade from its sheath,
down from the vaulting heavens swept Athena,
the white-armed goddess Hera sped her down:
Hera loved both men and cared for both alike.
Rearing behind him Pallas seized his fiery hair—
only Achilles saw her, none of the other fighters—
struck with wonder he spun around, he knew her at once,
Pallas Athena! the terrible blazing of those eyes,
and his winged words went flying: "Why, why now?
Child of Zeus with the shield of thunder,° why come now?
To witness the outrage Agamemnon just committed?
I tell you this, and so help me it's the truth—
he'll soon pay for his arrogance with his life!"

225 thrust through the ranks: push past Agamemnon's bodyguards.

237 shield of thunder: Zeus is the god of thunder and lightning. He often hurled thunderbolts as an expression of his anger.

Her gray eyes clear, the goddess Athena answered,
"Down from the skies I come to check your rage
if only you will yield.

The white-armed goddess Hera sped me down:
she loves you both, she cares for you both alike.
Stop this fighting, now. Don't lay hand to sword.
Lash him with threats of the price that he will face.°
And I tell you this—and I *know* it is the truth—
one day glittering gifts will lie before you,
three times over to pay for all his outrage.
Hold back now. Obey us both."
So she urged
and the swift runner complied at once: "I must—
when the two of you hand down commands, Goddess,
a man submits though his heart breaks with fury.
Better for him by far. If a man obeys the gods
they're quick to hear his prayers."
And with that
Achilles stayed his burly hand on the silver hilt
and slid the huge blade back in its sheath.
He would not fight the orders of Athena.
Soaring home to Olympus, she rejoined the gods
aloft in the halls of Zeus whose shield is thunder.

But Achilles rounded on Agamemnon once again,
lashing out at him, not relaxing his anger for a moment:
"Staggering drunk, with your dog's eyes, your fawn's heart!°
Never once did you arm with the troops and go to battle
or risk an ambush packed with Achaea's picked men—
you lack the courage, you can see death coming.
Safer by far, you find, to foray° all through camp,
commandeering the prize of any man who speaks against you.
King who devours his people! Worthless husks, the men you rule—
if not, Atrides, this outrage would have been your last.
I tell you this, and I swear a mighty oath upon it . . .
by this, this scepter,° look,
that never again will put forth crown and branches,
now it's left its stump on the mountain ridge forever,
nor will it sprout new green again, now the brazen° ax
has stripped its bark and leaves,° and now the sons of Achaea
pass it back and forth as they hand their judgments down,
upholding the honored customs whenever Zeus commands—
This scepter will be the mighty force behind my oath:
someday, I swear, a yearning for Achilles will strike
Achaea's sons and all your armies! But then, Atrides,
harrowed° as you will be, *nothing* you do can save you—
not when your hordes of fighters drop and die,

247 **Lash him with threats of the price that he will face:** Warn Agamemnon that his arrogance will cost him your support and that Achilles and the Myrmidons will withdraw from the war.

264 **your dog's eyes, your fawn's heart:** expressions meant to suggest that Agamemnon is a coward.

268 **foray:** to plunder.

273 **scepter** (sep′ tər): a staff borne by a ruler as an emblem or symbol of authority.

274–277 **that never again . . . stripped its bark and leaves:** having been cut and carved from a living tree, the staff is dead wood.

276 **brazen:** Here, the adjective has a double meaning: figuratively–bold, defiant; literally–the blade of the ax may have been made from brass.

283 **harrowed:** under constant attack.

cut down by the hands of man-killing Hector! Then—
then you will tear your heart out, desperate, raging
that you disgraced the best of the Achaeans!"
                    Down on the ground
he dashed the scepter studded bright with golden nails,
then took his seat again. The son of Atreus smoldered,
glaring across at him, but Nestor rose between them,
the man of winning words, the clear speaker of Pylos . . .
Sweeter than honey from his tongue the voice flowed on
    and on.
Two generations of mortal men he had seen go down by now,
those who were born and bred with him in the old days,
in Pylos' holy realm, and now he ruled the third.
He pleaded with both kings, with clear good will,
"No more—or enormous sorrow comes to all Achaea!
How they would exult, Priam and Priam's sons
and all the Trojans. Oh they'd leap for joy
to hear the two of you battling on this way,
you who excel us all, first in Achaean councils,
first in the ways of war.
            Stop. Please.
Listen to Nestor. You are both younger than I,
and in my time I struck up with better men than you,
even you, but never once did they make light of me.
I've never seen such men, I never will again . . .
men like Pirithous, Dryas, that fine captain,
Caeneus and Exadius, and Polyphemus, royal prince,
and Theseus,° Aegeus' boy, a match for the immortals.°
They were the strongest mortals ever bred on earth,
the strongest, and they fought against the strongest too,
shaggy Centaurs,° wild brutes of the mountains—
they hacked them down, terrible, deadly work.
And I was in their ranks, fresh out of Pylos,
far away from home—they enlisted me themselves
and I fought on my own, a free lance,° single-handed.
And none of the men who walk the earth these days
could battle with those fighters, none, but they,
they took to heart my counsels, marked my words.
So now you listen too. Yielding is far better . . .
Don't seize the girl, Agamemnon, powerful as you are—
leave her, just as the sons of Achaea gave her,
his prize from the very first.°
And you, Achilles, never hope to fight it out
with your king, pitting force against his force:
no one can match the honors dealt a king, you know,

307–309 **Pirithous . . . Theseus:** The individuals named are all heroes of Nestor's generation.

309 **Aegeus' boy, a match for the immortals:** Theseus of Athens is the hero of many adventure tales.

312 **Centaurs:** a race of savage creatures fabled to be half man and half horse who lived in the mountains of Greece.

316 **free lance:** a roving soldier available for hire; one who acts independently without allegiance to a single authority.

322–323 **leave her . . . his prize from the very first:** Let her remain with Achilles since the Greek army agreed that she should be his reward for valor in battle.

a sceptered king to whom great Zeus gives glory.°
Strong as you are—a goddess was your mother—
he has more power because he rules more men.
Atrides, end your anger—look, it's Nestor!
I beg you, cool your fury against Achilles.
Here the man stands over all Achaea's armies,
our rugged bulwark° braced for shocks of war."

But King Agamemnon answered him in haste.
"True, old man—all you say is fit and proper—
but this soldier wants to tower over the armies,
he wants to rule over all, to lord it over all,
give out orders to every man in sight. Well,
there's one, I trust, who will never yield to *him*!
What if the everlasting gods have made a spearman of him?
Have they entitled him to hurl abuse at *me*?"

"Yes!"—blazing Achilles broke in quickly—
"What a worthless, burnt-out coward I'd be called
if I would submit to you and all your orders,
whatever you blurt out. Fling them at others,
don't give me commands!
Never again, *I* trust, will Achilles yield to *you*.
And I tell you this—take it to heart, I warn you—
my hands will never do battle for that girl,
neither with you, King, nor any man alive.
You Achaeans gave her, now you've snatched her back.
But all the rest I possess beside my fast black ship—
not one bit of it can you seize against my will, Atrides.
Come, try it! So the men can see, that instant,
your black blood gush and spurt around my spear!"

Once the two had fought it out with words,
battling face-to-face, both sprang to their feet
and broke up the muster° beside the Argive squadrons.
Achilles strode off to his trim ships and shelters,
back to his friend Patroclus and their comrades.
Agamemnon had a vessel hauled down to the sea,
he picked out twenty oarsmen to man her locks,
put aboard the cattle for sacrifice to the god
and led Chryseis in all her beauty amidships.°
Versatile Odysseus took the helm as captain.
All embarked,
the party launched out on the sea's foaming lanes
while the son of Atreus told his troops to wash,

326–327 **no one can match . . . great Zeus gives glory:** No one has the right to defy a king who rules by the will of the gods.

333 **bulwark** (bool′ wərk): a solid wall-like structure raised for defense; a strong support or protection. Here, it refers to Achilles' position of strength among the Greek army.

358 **muster:** here, an assembly, specifically a formal military gathering.

364 **amidships:** midway between the bow and the stern; most stable part of the ship, and, therefore, the location of the best living quarters.

to purify themselves from the filth of plague.
They scoured it off, threw scourings in the surf
and sacrificed to Apollo full-grown bulls and goats
along the beaten shore of the fallow barren sea
and savory smoke went swirling up the skies.

So the men were engaged throughout the camp.
But King Agamemnon would not stop the quarrel,
the first threat he hurled against Achilles.
He called Talthybius and Eurybates briskly,
his two heralds, ready, willing aides:
"Go to Achilles' lodge. Take Briseis at once,
his beauty Briseis by the hand and bring her here.
But if he will not surrender her, I'll go myself,
I'll seize her myself, with an army at my back—
and all the worse for him!"
He sent them off
with the strict order ringing in their ears.
Against their will the two men made their way
along the breaking surf of the barren salt sea
and reached the Myrmidon shelters and their ships.
They found him beside his lodge and black hull,
seated grimly—and Achilles took no joy
when he saw the two approaching.
They were afraid, they held the king in awe
and stood there, silent. Not a word to Achilles,
not a question. But he sensed it all in his heart,
their fear, their charge,° and broke the silence for them:
"Welcome, couriers!° Good heralds of Zeus and men,
here, come closer. You have done nothing to me.
You are not to blame. No one but Agamemnon—
he is the one who sent you for Briseis.
Go, Patroclus, Prince, bring out the girl
and hand her to them so they can take her back.
But let them both bear witness to my loss . . .
in the face of blissful gods and mortal men,
in the face of that unbending, ruthless king—
if the day should come when the armies need *me*
to save their ranks from ignominious,° stark defeat.
The man is raving—with all the murderous fury in his heart.
He lacks the sense to see a day behind, a day ahead,
and safeguard the Achaeans battling by the ships."

Patroclus obeyed his great friend's command.
He led Briseis in all her beauty from the lodge

Achilles and Ajax Playing Dice Game. Exekias, Ancient Greece. Black-figured amphora. Museo Gregoriano Estrusco, Rome.

Viewing the art: Why do you think the artist might have chosen to depict Achilles and Ajax in the midst of a game? Why are they in armor with their spears in hand?

393 **their charge:** the instructions they had been given; their orders or mission.

394 **couriers:** a member of the armed forces whose duties include carrying mail, information, or supplies.

404 **ignominious** (ig′ nə min′ ē əs): marked or characterized by disgrace or shame.

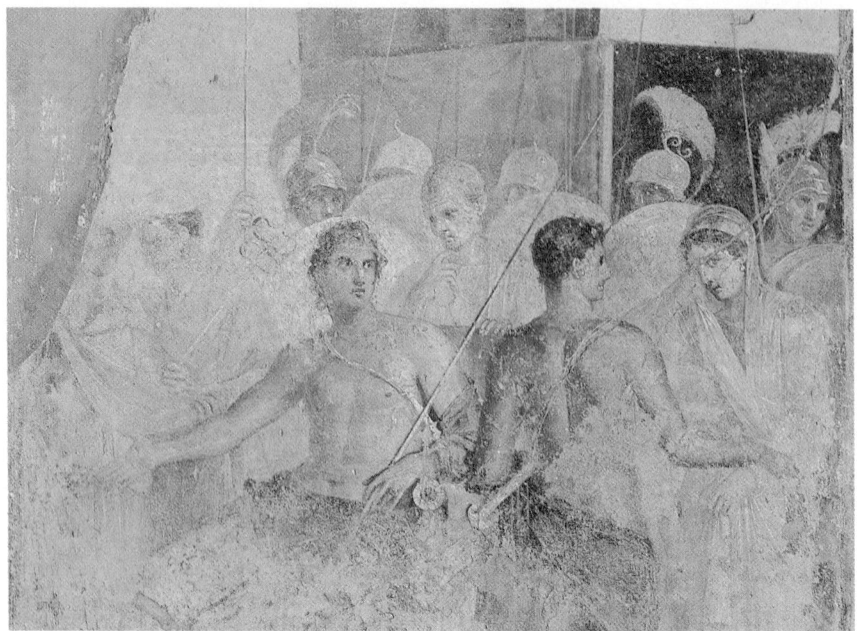

The Surrender of Briseis (detail). c. A.D. 63–79, Ancient Rome. Wall painting from the House of the Tragic Poet, Pompeii. National Museum, Naples, Italy.

Viewing the art: How do you interpret Achilles' expression in this painting? How does the incompleteness of the picture affect your interpretation of the scene?

and handed her over to the men to take away.
And the two walked back along the Argive ships
while she trailed on behind, reluctant, every step.
But Achilles wept, and slipping away from his companions,
far apart, sat down on the beach of the heaving gray sea
and scanned the endless ocean. Reaching out his arms,
again and again he prayed to his dear mother: "Mother!
You gave me life, short as that life will be,°
so at least Olympian Zeus, thundering up on high,
should give me honor—but now he gives me nothing.
Atreus' son Agamemnon, for all his far-flung kingdoms—
the man disgraces me, seizes and keeps my prize,
he tears her away himself!"
So he wept and prayed
and his noble mother heard him, seated near her father,
the Old Man of the Sea° in the salt green depths.
Suddenly up she rose from the churning surf
like mist and settling down beside him as he wept,
stroked Achilles gently, whispering his name, "My child—
why in tears? What sorrow has touched your heart?
Tell me, please. Don't harbor it deep inside you.
We must share it all."
And now from his depths
the proud runner groaned: "You know, you know,
why labor through it all? You know it all so well . . .

417 short as that life will be: The Fates, goddesses who determine human affairs, prophesied that Achilles would die in the war if he joined the expedition against Troy.

424 the Old Man of the Sea: Nereus, a sea god.

We raided Thebe once, Eetion's° sacred citadel,
we ravaged° the place, hauled all the plunder here
and the armies passed it round, share and share alike,
and they chose the beauty Chryseis for Agamemnon.
But soon her father, the holy priest of Apollo
the distant deadly Archer, Chryses approached
the fast trim ships of the Argives armed in bronze
to win his daughter back, bringing a priceless ransom
and bearing high in hand, wound on a golden staff,
the wreaths of the god who strikes from worlds away.°
He begged the whole Achaean army but most of all
the two supreme commanders, Atreus' two sons,
and all ranks of Achaeans cried out their assent,
'Respect the priest, accept the shining ransom!'
But it brought no joy to the heart of Agamemnon,
our high and mighty king dismissed the priest
with a brutal order ringing in his ears.
And shattered with anger, the old man withdrew
but Apollo heard his prayer—he loved him, deeply—
he loosed his shaft° at the Argives, withering plague,
and now the troops began to drop and die in droves,
the arrows of god went showering left and right,
whipping through the Achaeans' vast encampment.
But the old seer who knew the cause full well
revealed the will of the archer god Apollo.
And I was the first, mother, I urged them all,
'Appease the god at once!' That's when the fury
gripped the son of Atreus. Agamemnon leapt to his feet
and hurled his threat—his threat's been driven home.
One girl, Chryseis, the fiery-eyed Achaeans
ferry out in a fast trim ship to Chryse Island,
laden with presents for the god. The other girl,
just now the heralds came and led her away from camp,
Briseus' daughter, the prize the armies gave me.
But you, mother, if you have any power at all,
protect your son! Go to Olympus, plead with Zeus,
if you ever warmed his heart with a word or any action . . .

Time and again I heard your claims in father's halls,
boasting how you and you alone of all the immortals
rescued Zeus, the lord of the dark storm cloud,
from ignominious, stark defeat . . .
That day the Olympians tried to chain him down,
Hera, Poseidon lord of the sea, and Pallas Athena—
you rushed to Zeus, dear Goddess, broke those chains,

433 **Eetion:** king of Thebes, slain by Achilles.

434 **ravaged:** devastated destructively and violently.

442 **the god who strikes from worlds away:** Apollo, god of archery, whose arrows are deadly.

452 **loosed his shaft:** shot his arrow.

quickly ordered the hundred-hander° to steep Olympus,
that monster whom the immortals call Briareus
but every mortal calls the Sea-god's son, Aegaeon,
though he's stronger than his father. Down he sat,
flanking Cronus' son,° gargantuan in the glory of it all,
and the blessed gods were struck with terror then,
they stopped shackling Zeus.
Remind him of that,
now, go and sit beside him, grasp his knees . . .
persuade him, somehow, to help the Trojan cause,
to pin the Achaeans back against their ships,
trap them round the bay and mow them down.
So all can reap the benefits of their king—
so even mighty Atrides can see how mad he was
to disgrace Achilles, the best of the Achaeans!"

And Thetis answered, bursting into tears,
"O my son, my sorrow, why did I ever bear you?
All I bore was doom . . .°
Would to god you could linger by your ships
without a grief in the world, without a torment!
Doomed to a short life, you have so little time.
And not only short, now, but filled with heartbreak too,
more than all other men alive—doomed twice over.
Ah to a cruel fate I bore you in our halls!
Still, I shall go to Olympus crowned with snow
and repeat your prayer to Zeus who loves the lightning.
Perhaps he will be persuaded.
But you, my child,
stay here by the fast ships, rage on at the Achaeans,
just keep clear of every foray° in the fighting.
Only yesterday Zeus went off to the Ocean River°
to feast with the Aethiopians,° loyal, lordly men,
and all the gods went with him. But in twelve days
the Father returns to Olympus. Then, for your sake,
up I go to the bronze floor, the royal house of Zeus—
I'll grasp his knees, I think I'll win him over."
With that vow
his mother went away and left him there, alone,
his heart inflamed for the sashed and lovely girl
they'd wrenched away from him against his will. . . .

477 **hundred-hander:** Briareus, a monster with one hundred hands who warred with the gods until he was banished to the infernal regions.

481 **Cronus' son:** Zeus.

493 **All I bore was doom:** a reference to the fact that Achilles' life is to be short and unhappy.

504 **foray:** in this use, a raid or sudden attack.

505 **the Ocean River:** The Greeks believed that the oceans of the world were one body of water that surrounded the earth.

506 **Aethiopians:** to the ancient Greeks, residents of Aethiopia (Ethiopia), the lands in Africa south of Egypt and close to the Ocean River.

Responding to Literature

Personal Response

In your journal, describe your thoughts as you finished this episode.

Analyzing Literature

Recall and Interpret

1. Why has a plague struck the Greek camp? Why is the prophet Calchas reluctant to explain the cause of the plague?
2. On what condition will Agamemnon give back Chryseis? Why does Achilles take offense at this condition?
3. How does Agamemnon intend to punish Achilles for arguing with him? Why does Achilles accept this punishment?
4. Who tries to act as mediator in the dispute between Achilles and Agamemnon? Why does his attempt fail?
5. How does Achilles intend to get even with Agamemnon for seizing Briseis? Why does he turn to his mother for help?

Evaluate and Connect

6. In your opinion, when did the quarrel between Agamemnon and Achilles actually begin? Explain your response.
7. Based on what you have read in Book I, how would you characterize the Greek gods and their relationship with humans?
8. In the Reading Focus on page 210, you described how you would respond if a commander took back an honor you had received. How does Achilles behave in this episode? Do you approve? Explain.
9. **Internal conflict** is a struggle within a character (see page R2). Describe an internal conflict in Book I of the *Iliad.*
10. Groups sometimes fail to achieve their goals because members fight among themselves. What are some causes of friction within a group?

Literary Criticism

Michael Grant sums up the character of Achilles as follows: "Savage, sulky, and vindictive, at times, but also the most handsome, eloquent, courteous, generous, wise, and cultured of all the heroes . . . . He is by turns lustful for imperishable fame, valorous in battle, and furiously sensitive to insults." Which of these traits does Achilles display in the selection? Explain your answer in a brief paragraph.

Literary ELEMENTS

Epic Hero

An **epic hero** is a larger-than-life figure whose adventures are portrayed in an epic poem. A person of extraordinary ability and courage, the hero embodies the ideals of his or her culture. Most epics focus on the exploits of one central hero, although both Achilles and Hector can be considered the heroes of the *Iliad.* The poem also portrays other figures of heroic stature, including Odysseus, the resourceful hero of Homer's *Odyssey.*

1. In what ways is Achilles a larger-than-life figure?
2. Most of Homer's characters have both strengths and weaknesses. Does Homer show Achilles as entirely admirable? Explain.

- See **Literary Terms Handbook,** p. R4.

Extending Your Response

Creative Writing

From the Sidelines Imagine that you are a witness to the quarrel between Achilles and Agamemnon. Write a brief account of the quarrel from that point of view. Suggest a peaceful solution.

Literature Groups

Taking Sides Who is more at fault–Achilles or Agamemnon? Discuss this question in your group. Consider what the poem tells about Greek social values. Hold a vote in your group and share the results.

Save your work for your portfolio.

from the ILIAD

BOOK XXII
THE DEATH OF HECTOR

The Fury of Achilles. Charles-Antoine Coypel (France, 1694–1752). Hermitage, St. Petersburg, Russia. Do you think this is an apt title for this painting? Why?

Achilles and the Myrmidons, his followers, withdraw from the war after Agamemnon seizes Briseis. In their absence, the battle turns in favor of Troy. Led by Hector, greatest of the Trojan warriors, the Trojan army drives the Greeks back to the edge of the sea.

Patroclus, Achilles' best friend, cannot sit by and watch the slaughter of their comrades. With Achilles' blessing, Patroclus leads the Myrmidons into combat, turning the battle in favor of the Greeks. However, near the walls of Troy, Patroclus is slain by Hector.

The death of his friend sends Achilles into a murderous rage. He returns to the battlefield in search of Hector. So frightening is he in his rage that the Trojan army flees into the city. Hector, alone, stands before the gates awaiting his rival.

So all through Troy the men who had fled like panicked fawns
were wiping off their sweat, drinking away their thirst,
leaning along the city's massive ramparts now
while Achaean troops, sloping shields to shoulders,
closed against the walls. But there stood Hector,
shackled fast by his deadly fate,° holding his ground,
exposed in front of Troy and the Scaean Gates.°
And now Apollo turned to taunt Achilles:
"Why are you chasing *me?*° Why waste your speed?—
son of Peleus, you a mortal and I a deathless god.
You still don't know that I am immortal, do you?—
straining to catch me in your fury! Have you forgotten?
There's a war to fight with the Trojans you stampeded,
look, they're packed inside their city walls, but you,
you've slipped away out here. You can't kill *me*—
I can never die—it's not my fate!"
Enraged at that,
Achilles shouted in mid-stride, "You've blocked my way,
you distant, deadly Archer, deadliest god of all—
you made me swerve away from the rampart there.
Else what a mighty Trojan army had gnawed the dust
before they could ever straggle through their gates!
Now you've robbed me of great glory, saved their lives
with all your deathless ease. Nothing for you to fear,
no punishment to come. Oh I'd pay you back
if I only had the power at my command!"

No more words—he dashed toward the city,
heart racing for some great exploit, rushing on
like a champion stallion drawing a chariot full tilt,
sweeping across the plain in easy, tearing strides—
so Achilles hurtled on, driving legs and knees.

And old King Priam was first to see him coming,
surging over the plain, blazing like the star
that rears at harvest,° flaming up in its brilliance,—
far outshining the countless stars in the night sky,
that star they call Orion's° Dog—brightest of all
but a fatal sign emblazoned on the heavens,
it brings such killing fever down on wretched men.
So the bronze flared on his chest as on he raced—
and the old man moaned, flinging both hands high,
beating his head and groaning deep he called,
begging his dear son who stood before the gates,
unshakable, furious to fight Achilles to the death.

6 by his deadly fate: Hector had told his wife, Andromache, that he knew in his heart that he would die in the war and Troy would fall.

7 Scaean (skē′ ən) Gates: one of the main gates in the wall around Troy.

9 "Why are you chasing *me?*": Apollo had disguised himself as a Trojan leader, tempting Achilles into pursuing him. This gave the Trojan army time to flee.

32–33 the star that rears at harvest: Sirius, the dog star, which first appears in the fall and was thought to bring disease.

35 Orion: a mighty hunter who was placed among the stars as a constellation by Artemis, goddess of the hunt.

The old man cried, pitifully, hands reaching out to him,
"Oh Hector! Don't just stand there, don't, dear child,
waiting that man's attack—alone, cut off from friends!
You'll meet your doom at once, beaten down by Achilles,
so much stronger than you—that hard, headlong man.
Oh if only the gods loved him as much as I do . . .°
dogs and vultures would eat his fallen corpse at once!—
with what a load of misery lifted from my spirit.
That man who robbed me of many sons, brave boys,
cutting them down or selling them off as slaves,
shipped to islands half the world away . . .
Even now there are two, Lycaon and Polydorus°—
I cannot find them among the soldiers crowding Troy,
those sons Laothoë° bore me, Laothoë queen of women.
But if they are still alive in the enemy's camp,
then we'll ransom them back with bronze and gold.
We have hoards inside the walls, the rich dowry
old and famous Altes presented with his daughter.
But if they're dead already, gone to the House of Death,
what grief to their mother's heart and mine—we gave them life.
For the rest of Troy, though, just a moment's grief
unless you too are battered down by Achilles.
Back, come back! Inside the walls, my boy!
Rescue the men of Troy and the Trojan women—
don't hand the great glory to Peleus' son,
bereft° of your own sweet life yourself.
Pity me too!—
still in my senses, true, but a harrowed, broken man
marked out by doom—past the threshold of old age . . .
and Father Zeus will waste me with a hideous fate,
and after I've lived to look on so much horror!
My sons laid low,° my daughters dragged away
and the treasure-chambers looted, helpless babies
hurled to the earth in the red barbarity of war . . .
my sons' wives hauled off by the Argives' bloody hands!
And I, I last of all—the dogs before my doors
will eat me raw, once some enemy brings me down
with his sharp bronze sword or spits° me with a spear,
wrenching the life out of my body, yes, the very dogs
I bred in my own halls to share my table, guard my gates—
mad, rabid at heart° they'll lap their master's blood
and loll before my doors.
Ah for a young man
all looks fine and noble if he goes down in war,
hacked to pieces under a slashing bronze blade—

48 **if only the gods loved him as much as I do:** an example of irony–the real meaning of the statement is the opposite of the surface meaning. Priam then explains his hatred for Achilles.

54 **Lycaon and Polydorus:** sons of Priam slain by Achilles in battle.

56 **Laothoë:** one of Priam's wives; daughter of Altes, a wealthy king.

68 **bereft:** deprived or robbed.

73 **laid low:** slain.

79 **spits:** here, pierces with something pointed; impales.

82 **rabid at heart:** extremely violent; exhibiting the behavior of an animal suffering from rabies.

he lies there dead . . . but whatever death lays bare,
all wounds are marks of glory. When an old man's killed
and the dogs go at the gray head and the gray beard
and mutilate the genitals—that is the cruelest sight
in all our wretched lives!"
So the old man groaned
and seizing his gray hair tore it out by the roots
but he could not shake the fixed resolve of Hector.
And his mother wailed now, standing beside Priam,
weeping freely, loosing her robes with one hand
and holding out her bare breast with the other,
her words pouring forth in a flight of grief and tears:
"Hector, my child! Look—have some respect for *this!*
Pity your mother too, if I ever gave you the breast
to soothe your troubles, remember it now, dear boy—
beat back that savage man from safe inside the walls!
Don't go forth, a champion pitted against him—
merciless, brutal man. If he kills you now,
how can I ever mourn you on your deathbed?—
dear branch in bloom, dear child I brought to birth!—
Neither I nor your wife, that warm, generous woman . . .
Now far beyond our reach, now by the Argive ships
the rushing dogs will tear you, bolt your flesh!"

So they wept, the two of them crying out
to their dear son, both pleading time and again
but they could not shake the fixed resolve of Hector.
No, he waited Achilles, coming on, gigantic in power.
As a snake in the hills, guarding his hole, awaits a man—
bloated with poison, deadly hatred seething inside him,
glances flashing fire as he coils round his lair . . .
so Hector, nursing his quenchless fury, gave no ground,
leaning his burnished shield against a jutting wall,
but harried still, he probed his own brave heart:
"No way out. If I slip inside the gates and walls,
Polydamas° will be first to heap disgrace on me—
he was the one who urged me to lead our Trojans
back to Ilium° just last night, the disastrous night
Achilles rose in arms like a god. But did I give way?
Not at all. And how much better it would have been!
Now my army's ruined, thanks to my own reckless pride,
I would die of shame to face the men of Troy
and the Trojan women trailing their long robes . . .
Someone less of a man than I will say, 'Our Hector—

119 Polydamas: a cautious Trojan leader; a rival who often opposes Hector's military strategy.

121 Ilium: another name for the city of Troy.

staking all on his own strength, he destroyed his army!'
So they will mutter. So now, better by far for me
to stand up to Achilles, kill him, come home alive
or die at his hands in glory out before the walls.
But wait—what if I put down my studded shield
and heavy helmet, prop my spear on the rampart
and go forth, just as I am, to meet Achilles,
noble Prince Achilles . . .
why, I could promise to give back Helen, yes,
and all her treasures with her, all those riches
Paris once hauled home to Troy in the hollow ships—
and they were the cause of all our endless fighting—
Yes, yes, return it all to the sons of Atreus now
to haul away, and then, at the same time, divide
the rest with all the Argives, all the city holds,
and then I'd take an oath for the Trojan royal council
that we will hide nothing! Share and share alike the hoards
our handsome citadel stores within its depths and—
Why debate, my friend? Why thrash things out?
I must not go and implore him. He'll show no mercy,
no respect for me, my rights—he'll cut me down
straight off—stripped of defenses like a woman
once I have loosed the armor off my body.
No way to parley° with that man—not now—
not from behind some oak or rock to whisper,
like a boy and a young girl, lovers' secrets
a boy and girl might whisper to each other . . .
Better to clash in battle, now, at once—
see which fighter Zeus awards the glory!"
So he wavered,
waiting there, but Achilles was closing on him now
like the god of war, the fighter's helmet flashing,
over his right shoulder shaking the Pelian ash spear,°
that terror, and the bronze around his body° flared
like a raging fire or the rising, blazing sun.
Hector looked up, saw him, started to tremble,
nerve gone, he could hold his ground no longer,
he left the gates behind and away he fled in fear—
and Achilles went for him, fast, sure of his speed
as the wild mountain hawk, the quickest thing on wings,
launching smoothly, swooping down on a cringing dove
and the dove flits out from under, the hawk screaming
over the quarry, plunging over and over, his fury
driving him down to beak and tear his kill—
so Achilles flew at him, breakneck on in fury

Helen of Troy. Dante Gabriel Rossetti (Great Britain, 1828–1882).

Viewing the painting: What impression of Helen do you get from this painting?

151 parley: to discuss terms.

159 Pelian ash spear: Achilles' spear was carved from an ash tree on Mount Pelion. Chiron, wisest of the Centaurs, gave it to him and taught him to use it.

160 the bronze around his body: his armor.

with Hector fleeing along the walls of Troy,
fast as his legs would go. On and on they raced,
passing the lookout point, passing the wild fig tree
tossed by the wind, always out from under the ramparts
down the wagon trail they careered° until they reached
the clear running springs where whirling Scamander°
rises up from its double wellsprings bubbling strong—
and one runs hot and the steam goes up around it,
drifting thick as if fire burned at its core
but the other even in summer gushes cold
as hail or freezing snow or water chilled to ice . . .
And here, close to the springs, lie washing-pools
scooped out in the hollow rocks and broad and smooth
where the wives of Troy and all their lovely daughters
would wash their glistening robes in the old days,
the days of peace before the sons of Achaea came . . .
Past these they raced, one escaping, one in pursuit
and the one who fled was great but the one pursuing
greater, even greater—their pace mounting in speed
since both men strove, not for a sacrificial beast
or oxhide trophy, prizes runners fight for, no,
they raced for the life of Hector breaker of horses.°
Like powerful stallions sweeping round the post for trophies,
galloping full stretch with some fine prize at stake,
a tripod, say, or woman offered up at funeral games
for some brave hero fallen—so the two of them
whirled three times around the city of Priam,
sprinting at top speed while all the gods gazed down,
and the father of men and gods broke forth among them now:
"Unbearable—a man I love, hunted round his own city walls
and right before my eyes. My heart grieves for Hector.
Hector who burned so many oxen in my honor, rich cuts,
now on the rugged crests of Ida, now on Ilium's heights.°
But now, look, brilliant Achilles courses him round
the city of Priam in all his savage, lethal speed.
Come, you immortals, think this through. Decide.
Either we pluck the man from death and save his life
or strike him down at last, here at Achilles' hands—
for all his fighting heart."
But immortal Athena,
her gray eyes wide, protested strongly: "Father!
Lord of the lightning, king of the black cloud,
what are you saying? A man, a mere mortal,
his doom sealed long ago?° You'd set him free

176 **careered:** went at top speed, especially in a headlong manner.

177 **Scamander** (skə man′ dər): chief river near the city of Troy.

193 **breaker of horses:** Hector was famed for his ability to tame horses.

203–204 **Hector who burned . . . heights:** Hector sacrificed oxen to Zeus on Mount Ida, overlooking Troy.

214 **his doom sealed long ago:** his fate: all humans are mortal and doomed to die from birth.

from all the pains of death?
Do as you please—
but none of the deathless gods will ever praise you."

And Zeus who marshals the thunderheads replied,
"Courage, Athena, third-born of the gods, dear child.
Nothing I said was meant in earnest, trust me,
I mean you all the good will in the world. Go.
Do as your own impulse bids you. Hold back no more."

So he launched Athena already poised for action—
down the goddess swept from Olympus' craggy peaks.

And swift Achilles kept on coursing Hector, nonstop
as a hound in the mountains starts a fawn from its lair,
hunting him down the gorges, down the narrow glens
and the fawn goes to ground,° hiding deep in brush
but the hound comes racing fast, nosing him out
until he lands his kill. So Hector could never throw
Achilles off his trail, the swift racer Achilles—
time and again he'd make a dash for the Dardan Gates,
trying to rush beneath the rock-built ramparts, hoping
men on the heights might save him, somehow, raining spears
but time and again Achilles would intercept him quickly,
heading him off, forcing him out across the plain
and always sprinting along the city side himself—
endless as in a dream . . .
when a man can't catch another fleeing on ahead
and he can never escape nor his rival overtake him—
so the one could never run the other down in his speed
nor the other spring away. And how could Hector have fled
the fates of death so long? How unless one last time,
one final time Apollo had swept in close beside him,
driving strength in his legs and knees to race the wind?
And brilliant Achilles shook his head at the armies,
never letting them hurl their sharp spears at Hector—
someone might snatch the glory, Achilles come in second.
But once they reached the springs for the fourth time,
then Father Zeus held out his sacred golden scales:
in them he placed two fates of death that lays men low—
one for Achilles, one for Hector breaker of horses—
and gripping the beam mid-haft° the Father raised it high
and down went Hector's day of doom, dragging him down
to the strong House of Death—and god Apollo left him.°
Athena rushed to Achilles, her bright eyes gleaming,

227 **goes to ground:** tries to avoid notice by remaining motionless.

249–254 **Zeus held out . . . Apollo left him:** Fate determined that Hector would lose this battle. Apollo, realizing that further help was futile, returned to Olympus.
252 **gripping the beam mid-haft:** holding the scales impartially so as not to favor one side or the other.

standing shoulder-to-shoulder, winging orders now:
"At last our hopes run high, my brilliant Achilles—
Father Zeus must love you—
we'll sweep great glory back to Achaea's fleet,
we'll kill this Hector, mad as he is for battle!
No way for him to escape us now, no longer—
not even if Phoebus the distant deadly Archer
goes through torments, pleading for Hector's life,
groveling over and over before our storming Father Zeus.
But you, you hold your ground and catch your breath
while I run Hector down and persuade the man
to fight you face-to-face."
So Athena commanded
and he obeyed, rejoicing at heart—Achilles stopped,
leaning against his ashen spearshaft barbed in bronze.
And Athena left him there, caught up with Hector at once,

Statue of Athena, the goddess of war.

Viewing the sculpture: How does the sculptor create a feeling of intensity in the subject? Does Athena seem powerful to you? Explain.

and taking the build and vibrant voice of Deiphobus
stood shoulder-to-shoulder with him, winging orders:
"Dear brother, how brutally swift Achilles hunts you—
coursing you round the city of Priam in all his lethal speed!
Come, let us stand our ground together—beat him back."

"Deiphobus!"—Hector, his helmet flashing, called out
to her—
"dearest of all my brothers, all these warring years,
of all the sons that Priam and Hecuba produced!
Now I'm determined to praise you all the more,
you who dared—seeing me in these straits—
to venture out from the walls, all for *my* sake,
while the others stay inside and cling to safety."

The goddess answered quickly, her eyes blazing,
"True, dear brother—how your father and mother both
implored me, time and again, clutching my knees,
and the comrades round me begging me to stay!
Such was the fear that broke them, man for man,
but the heart within me broke with grief for you.
Now headlong on and fight! No letup, no lance spared!
So now, now we'll *see* if Achilles kills us both
and hauls our bloody armor back to the beaked ships
or *he* goes down in pain beneath your spear."

Athena luring him on with all her immortal cunning—
and now, at last, as the two came closing for the kill
it was tall Hector, helmet flashing, who led off:
"No more running from you in fear, Achilles!
Not as before. Three times I fled around
the great city of Priam—I lacked courage then
to stand your onslaught. Now my spirit stirs me
to meet you face-to-face. Now kill or be killed!
Come, we'll swear to the gods, the highest witnesses—
the gods will oversee our binding pacts. I swear
I will never mutilate you—merciless as you are—
if Zeus allows me to last it out and tear your life away.
But once I've stripped your glorious armor, Achilles,
I will give your body back to your loyal comrades.
Swear you'll do the same."
A swift dark glance
and the headstrong runner answered, "Hector, stop!
You unforgivable, you . . . don't talk to me of pacts.
There are no binding oaths between men and lions—

Hector Killed by Achilles, (detail) c. 1635. Peter Paul Rubens (Flanders). Oil on canvas (design for tapestry). Musée des Beaux-Arts, Pau, France.

Viewing the painting: Who is hovering overhead in this painting? What role does she seem to be playing? Explain.

wolves and lambs can enjoy no meeting of the minds—
they are all bent on hating each other to the death.
So with you and me. No love between us. No truce
till one or the other falls and gluts with blood
Ares° who hacks at men behind his rawhide shield.
Come, call up whatever courage you can muster.
Life or death—now prove yourself a spearman,
a daring man of war! No more escape for you—
Athena will kill you with my spear in just a moment.
Now you'll pay at a stroke for all my comrades' grief,
all you killed in the fury of your spear!"
With that,
shaft poised, he hurled and his spear's long shadow flew
but seeing it coming glorious Hector ducked away,
crouching down, watching the bronze tip fly past
and stab the earth—but Athena snatched it up
and passed it back to Achilles
and Hector the gallant captain never saw her.°
He sounded out a challenge to Peleus' princely son:
"You missed, look—the great godlike Achilles!
So you knew nothing at all from Zeus about my death—
and yet how sure you were! All bluff,° cunning° with words,
that's all you are—trying to make me fear you,
lose my nerve, forget my fighting strength.
Well, you'll never plant your lance in my back
as I flee *you* in fear—plunge it through my chest
as I come charging in, if a god gives you the chance!
But now it's for you to dodge *my* brazen spear—
I wish you'd bury it in your body to the hilt.
How much lighter the war would be for Trojans then
if you, their greatest scourge, were dead and gone!"

Shaft poised,° he hurled and his spear's long shadow flew
and it struck Achilles' shield—a dead-center hit—
but off and away it glanced and Hector seethed,
his hurtling spear, his whole arm's power poured
in a wasted shot. He stood there, cast down . . .
he had no spear in reserve. So Hector shouted out
to Deiphobus bearing his white shield—with a ringing shout
he called for a heavy lance—
but the man was nowhere near him,
vanished°—
yes and Hector knew the truth in his heart
and the fighter cried aloud, "My time has come!
At last the gods have called me down to death.

314–315 **gluts with blood Ares:** spills so much blood that even Ares, the god of war, becomes nauseated.

325–327 **Athena . . . never saw her:** The deities can hide their presence and their movements from certain people.

330–331 **you knew nothing . . . All bluff:** You were lying when you said the gods were on your side.

331 **cunning:** here, wily; tricky.

341 **Shaft poised:** the long handle of the spear held in the proper position for throwing it.

348 **the man . . . vanished:** Athena had cast off her disguise as his brother and deserted him.

I thought he was at my side, the hero Deiphobus—
he's safe inside the walls, Athena's tricked me blind.
And now death, grim death is looming up beside me,
no longer far away. No way to escape it now. This,
this was their pleasure after all, sealed long ago—
Zeus and the son of Zeus, the distant deadly Archer—
though often before now they rushed to my defense.
So now I meet my doom. Well let me die—
but not without struggle, not without glory, no,
in some great clash of arms that even men to come
will hear of down the years!"
And on that resolve
he drew the whetted° sword that hung at his side,
tempered,° massive, and gathering all his force
he swooped like a soaring eagle
launching down from the dark clouds to earth
to snatch some helpless lamb or trembling hare.
So Hector swooped now, swinging his whetted sword
and Achilles charged too, bursting with rage, barbaric,°
guarding his chest with the well-wrought° blazoned° shield,
head tossing his gleaming helmet, four horns strong
and the golden plumes shook that the god of fire°
drove in bristling thick along its ridge.
Bright as that star amid the stars in the night sky,
star of the evening, brightest star that rides the heavens,
so fire flared from the sharp point of the spear Achilles
brandished high in his right hand, bent on Hector's death,
scanning his splendid body—where to pierce it best?
The rest of his flesh seemed all encased in armor,
burnished, brazen—*Achilles'* armor that Hector stripped
from strong Patroclus when he killed him—true,
but one spot lay exposed,
where collarbones lift the neckbone off the shoulders,°
the open throat, where the end of life comes quickest—*there*
as Hector charged in fury brilliant Achilles drove his spear
and the point went stabbing clean through the tender neck
but the heavy bronze weapon failed to slash the windpipe—
Hector could still gasp out some words, some last reply . . .
he crashed in the dust—
godlike Achilles gloried over him:
"Hector—surely you thought when you stripped Patroclus' armor
that you, you would be safe! Never a fear of me—
far from the fighting as I was—you fool!
Left behind there, down by the beaked ships
his great avenger waited, a greater man by far—

363 **whetted:** sharpened.

364 **tempered:** hardened by reheating and cooling in oil; strengthened.

369 **barbaric:** This word choice is ironic because barbaric originally meant anyone not belonging to one's cultural group, which to a Greek would be a non-Greek.

370 **well-wrought:** fashioned with great effort and artistry. **blazoned:** in this use, adorned with ornate symbolic inscriptions and artwork.

372 **god of fire:** Hephaestus (hi fes′ təs), son of Zeus, god of fire and metalworking (blacksmithing). At Thetis's request, he had made armor for Achilles.

378–383 **scanning . . . off the shoulders:** Since the armor had once been his own, Achilles knew where to look for its one vulnerable spot.

that man was I, and I smashed your strength! And you—
the dogs and birds will maul you, shame your corpse
while Achaeans bury my dear friend in glory!"

Struggling for breath, Hector, his helmet flashing,
said, "I beg you, beg you by your life, your parents—
don't let the dogs devour me by the Argive ships!
Wait, take the princely ransom of bronze and gold,
the gifts my father and noble mother will give you—
but give my body to friends to carry home again,
so Trojan men and Trojan women can do me honor
with fitting rites of fire° once I am dead."

405 fitting rites of fire: proper religious funeral services that included cremation of the body.

Staring grimly, the proud runner Achilles answered,
"Beg no more, you fawning dog—begging me by my parents!
Would to god my rage, my fury would drive me now
to hack your flesh away and eat you raw—
such agonies you have caused me! Ransom?
No man alive could keep the dog-packs off you,
not if they haul in ten, twenty times that ransom
and pile it here before me and promise fortunes more—
no, not even if Dardan Priam should offer to weigh out
your bulk in gold! Not even then will your noble mother
lay you on your deathbed, mourn the son she bore . . .
The dogs and birds will rend you—blood and bone!"

At the point of death, Hector, his helmet flashing,
said, "I know you well—I see my fate before me.
Never a chance that I could win you over . . .
Iron inside your chest, that heart of yours.
But now beware, or my curse will draw god's wrath
upon your head, that day when Paris and lord Apollo—
for all your fighting heart—destroy you at the Scaean Gates!"°

422–424 beware . . . Scaean Gates: Hector predicts the place and circumstances of Achilles' own death.

Death cut him short. The end closed in around him.
Flying free of his limbs
his soul went winging down to the House of Death,
wailing his fate, leaving his manhood far behind,
his young and supple strength. But brilliant Achilles
taunted Hector's body, dead as he was, "Die, die!
For my own death, I'll meet it freely—whenever Zeus
and the other deathless gods would like to bring it on!"

With that he wrenched his bronze spear from the corpse,
laid it aside and ripped the bloody armor off the back.

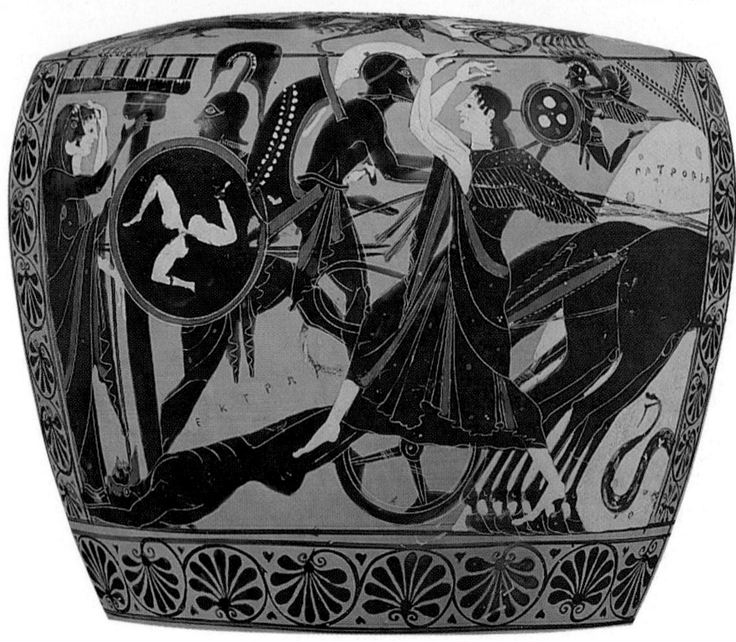

Achilles Dragging the Body of Hector (detail). c. 520–510 B.C., attributed to The Anitope Group, Ancient Greece. Black-figured vase, height: 56 cm, diameter: 33 cm. Museum of Fine Arts, Boston.

Viewing the painting: Several scenes from the *Iliad* are combined on this vase painting. How does the artist's decision to compress the action into one frame affect your reaction to the scene? What is your response to Achilles' treatment of Hector's body?

And the other sons of Achaea, running up around him,
crowded closer, all of them gazing wonder-struck
at the build and marvelous, lithe beauty of Hector.
And not a man came forward who did not stab his body,
glancing toward a comrade, laughing: "Ah, look here—
how much softer he is to handle now, this Hector,
than when he gutted our ships with roaring fire!"

Standing over him, so they'd gloat and stab his body.
But once he had stripped the corpse the proud runner Achilles
took his stand in the midst of all the Argive troops
and urged them on with a flight of winging orders:
"Friends—lords of the Argives, O my captains!
Now that the gods have let me kill this man
who caused us agonies, loss on crushing loss—
more than the rest of all their men combined—
come, let us ring their walls in armor, test them,
see what recourse the Trojans still may have in mind.
Will they abandon the city heights with this man fallen?
Or brace for a last, dying stand though Hector's gone?
But wait—what am I saying? Why this deep debate?
Down by the ships a body lies unwept, unburied—
Patroclus . . . I will never forget him,
not as long as I'm still among the living
and my springing knees will lift and drive me on.
Though the dead forget° their dead in the House of Death,
I will remember, even there, my dear companion.
Now,
come, you sons of Achaea, raise a song of triumph!

459 the dead forget: a mental state oblivious to emotions, such as love or sorrow, was a characteristic of the dead in Greek mythology.

Down to the ships we march and bear this corpse on high—
we have won ourselves great glory. We have brought
magnificent Hector down, that man the Trojans
glorified in their city like a god!"
                                                  So he triumphed
and now he was bent on outrage, on shaming noble Hector.
Piercing the tendons,° ankle to heel behind both feet,
he knotted straps of rawhide through them both,
lashed them to his chariot, left the head to drag
and mounting the car, hoisting the famous arms aboard,
he whipped his team to a run and breakneck on they flew,
holding nothing back. And a thick cloud of dust rose up
from the man they dragged, his dark hair swirling round
that head so handsome once, all tumbled low in the dust—
since Zeus had given him over to his enemies now
to be defiled in the land of his own fathers.

So his whole head was dragged down in the dust.
And now his mother began to tear her hair . . .
she flung her shining veil to the ground and raised
a high, shattering scream, looking down at her son.
Pitifully his loving father groaned and round the king
his people cried with grief and wailing seized the city—
for all the world as if all Troy were torched and smoldering
down from the looming brows of the citadel to her roots.
Priam's people could hardly hold the old man back,
frantic, mad to go rushing out the Dardan Gates.
He begged them all, groveling in the filth,
crying out to them, calling each man by name,
"Let go, my friends! Much as you care for me,
let me hurry out of the city, make my way,
all on my own, to Achaea's waiting ships!
I must implore that terrible, violent man . . .
Perhaps—who knows?—he may respect my age,
may pity an old man. He has a father too,
as old as I am—Peleus sired him once,
Peleus reared him to be the scourge of Troy
but most of all to me—he made my life a hell.
So many sons he slaughtered, just coming into bloom . . .
but grieving for all the rest, one breaks my heart the most
and stabbing grief for him will take me down to Death—
my Hector—would to god he had perished in my arms!
Then his mother who bore him—oh so doomed,
she and I could glut ourselves with grief."

467 Piercing the tendons: ironic, because a wound in the tendon of the heel, his only vulnerable spot, will kill Achilles.

So the voice of the king rang out in tears,
the citizens wailed in answer, and noble Hecuba
led the wives of Troy in a throbbing chant of sorrow:
"O my child—my desolation! How can I go on living?
What agonies must I suffer now, now *you* are dead and gone?
You were my pride throughout the city night and day—
a blessing to us all, the men and women of Troy:
throughout the city they saluted you like a god.
You, you were their greatest glory while you lived—
now death and fate have seized you, dragged you down!"

Her voice rang out in tears, but the wife of Hector
had not heard a thing. No messenger brought the truth
of how her husband made his stand outside the gates.
She was weaving at her loom, deep in the high halls,
working flowered braiding into a dark red folding robe.
And she called her well-kempt women through the house
to set a large three-legged cauldron over the fire
so Hector could have his steaming hot bath
when he came home from battle—poor woman,
she never dreamed how far he was from bathing,
struck down at Achilles' hands by blazing-eyed Athena.
But she heard the groans and wails of grief from the rampart now
and her body shook, her shuttle° dropped to the ground,
she called out to her lovely waiting women, "Quickly—
two of you follow me—I must see what's happened.
That cry—that was Hector's honored mother I heard!
My heart's pounding, leaping up in my throat,
the knees beneath me paralyzed—Oh I know it . . .
something terrible's coming down on Priam's children.
Pray god the news will never reach my ears!
Yes but I dread it so—what if great Achilles
has cut my Hector off from the city, daring Hector,
and driven him out across the plain, and all alone?—
He may have put an end to that fatal headstrong pride
that always seized my Hector—never hanging back
with the main force of men, always charging ahead,
giving ground to no man in his fury!"

So she cried,
dashing out of the royal halls like a madwoman,
her heart racing hard, her women close behind her.
But once she reached the tower where soldiers massed
she stopped on the rampart, looked down and saw it all—
saw him dragged before the city, stallions galloping,
dragging Hector back to Achaea's beaked warships—

526 shuttle: a device used in weaving for passing thread through the loom.

ruthless work. The world went black as night
before her eyes, she fainted, falling backward,
gasping away her life breath . . .
She flung to the winds her glittering headdress,
the cap and the coronet,° braided band and veil,
all the regalia° golden Aphrodite gave her once,
the day that Hector, helmet aflash in sunlight,
led her home to Troy from her father's house
with countless wedding gifts to win her heart.
But crowding round her now her husband's sisters
and brothers' wives supported her in their midst,
and she, terrified, stunned to the point of death,
struggling for breath now and coming back to life,
burst out in grief among the Trojan women: "O Hector—
I am destroyed! Both born to the same fate after all!
You, you at Troy in the halls of King Priam—
I at Thebes, under the timberline of Placos,°
Eetion's° house . . . He raised me as a child,
that man of doom, his daughter just as doomed—
would to god he'd never fathered *me!*
Now you go down
to the House of Death, the dark depths of the earth,
and leave me here to waste away in grief, a widow
lost in the royal halls—and the boy only a baby,
the son we bore together, you and I so doomed.
Hector, what help are you to him, now you are dead?—
what help is he to you? Think, even if he escapes
the wrenching horrors of war against the Argives,
pain and labor will plague him all his days to come.
Strangers will mark his lands off, stealing his estates.

551 **coronet:** a small crown.

552 **regalia** (ri gā′ lē ə): emblems or symbols indicating royalty.

563 **Placos:** mountain which dominates the landscape near Thebes.

564 **Eetion:** Andromache's father, king of Thebes, killed by Achilles during the sacking of that city.

The Siege of Troy I: The Death of Hector, c. 1490 (detail). Biagio di Antonio (Italy). Oil on panel, 47 x 161 cm.

Viewing the painting: Which incident related to Hector's death is shown in this painting? How is this incident portrayed differently in the *Iliad*?

The day that orphans a youngster cuts him off from friends.
And he hangs his head low, humiliated in every way . . .
his cheeks stained with tears, and pressed by hunger
the boy goes up to his father's old companions,
tugging at one man's cloak, another's tunic,
and some will pity him, true,
and one will give him a little cup to drink,
enough to wet his lips, not quench his thirst.
But then some bully with both his parents living
beats him from the banquet, fists and abuses flying:
'You, get out—you've got no father feasting with us here!'
And the boy, sobbing, trails home to his widowed mother . . .
Astyanax!
And years ago, propped on his father's knee,
he would only eat the marrow, the richest cuts of lamb,
and when sleep came on him and he had quit his play,
cradled warm in his nurse's arms he'd drowse off,
snug in a soft bed, his heart brimmed with joy.
Now what suffering, now he's lost his father—
Astyanax!
The Lord of the City, so the Trojans called him,
because it was you, Hector, you and you alone
who shielded the gates and the long walls of Troy.
But now by the beaked ships, far from your parents,
glistening worms will wriggle through your flesh,
once the dogs have had their fill of your naked corpse—
though we have such stores of clothing laid up in the halls,
fine things, a joy to the eye, the work of women's hands.
Now, by god, I'll burn them all, blazing to the skies!
No use to you now, they'll never shroud your body—
but they will be your glory
burned by the Trojan men and women in your honor!"

Her voice rang out in tears and the women wailed in answer.

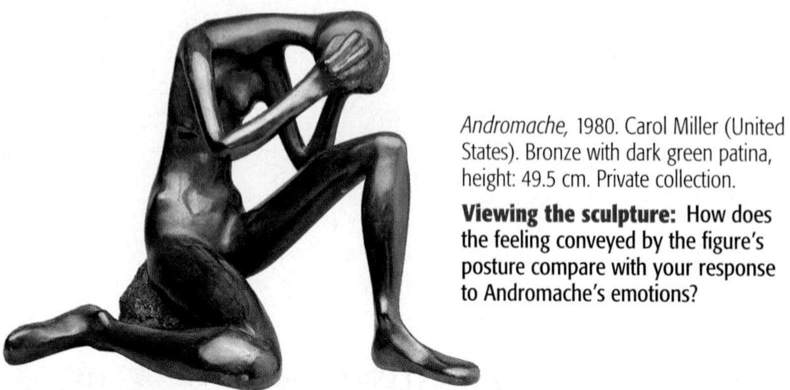

Andromache, 1980. Carol Miller (United States). Bronze with dark green patina, height: 49.5 cm. Private collection.

Viewing the sculpture: How does the feeling conveyed by the figure's posture compare with your response to Andromache's emotions?

Responding to Literature

Personal Response

How do you feel about what happens to Hector? Share your reaction with your classmates.

Analyzing Literature

Recall

1. Why do Hector's mother and father plead with him to come inside the gates of Troy?
2. What happens when Achilles approaches Hector at the gates?
3. How does Athena help Achilles in his attack on Hector?
4. What request does Hector make after he is defeated by Achilles?
5. How does Hector's wife, Andromache, learn about his death?

Interpret

6. Why does Hector refuse to come inside the gates for protection?
7. In your opinion, does Hector behave like a coward when Achilles approaches him for battle? Why or why not?
8. What adjective would you use to describe Hector's response when he realizes that the gods are acting against him?
9. What motivates Achilles to deny Hector's final request?
10. A **symbol** is an object or action that stands for something else in addition to itself (see page R12). What object or action is a symbol for Andromache's mourning of Hector?

Evaluate and Connect

11. Why might Homer have chosen to include a long chase scene in this episode?
12. Which character do you admire more, Achilles or Hector? Give details from the text to explain your answer.
13. What does this episode suggest to you about Greek beliefs about death?
14. The Greeks and Trojans closely follow the exploits of their heroes. What figures in today's society attract similar attention from ordinary citizens?
15. Think of a time when you mourned the death of a public figure. What effect did his or her death have on you? How did you express your grief?

Epic Simile

A **simile** is a comparison of two things that are basically unlike but share some quality. The comparison is indicated by the word *like* or *as.* An **epic simile** is a longer and more elaborate simile. Homer uses the following epic simile in lines 165–170 of Book XXII to describe how Achilles chases after Hector:

and Achilles went for him, fast, sure of his speed
as the wild mountain hawk, the quickest thing on wings,
launching smoothly, swooping down on a cringing dove
and the dove flits out from under, the hawk screaming
over the quarry, plunging over and over, his fury
driving him down to beak and tear his kill–

Many writers who created epics after Homer followed his practice of using epic similes.

1. Find another example of an epic simile in Book XXII. Identify the elements that the simile compares.
2. How does your experience of reading an epic simile differ from reading a simile in a narrative work?

- See **Literary Terms Handbook,** pp. R4, R11.

Literature and Writing

Writing About Literature

Analyze a Character Write a character analysis of Achilles, Agamemnon, or Hector. Describe what is revealed about the character through his own words and actions and the words of others. Consider the narrator's direct statements about the character, including the epithets that accompany the character's name.

Personal Writing

Make Yourself Epic Epic similes describe the actions of larger-than-life figures. Write a paragraph with an epic simile to describe one of your own actions. You might portray yourself behaving heroically, or describe an activity such as washing dishes. Before beginning, consider the quality that you would like the simile to express.

Extending Your Response

Literature Groups

Analyzing Heroism Achilles and Hector both understand that they cannot escape their individual fates no matter how hard they fight. If the outcome of their final battle is controlled by the gods, are these characters truly heroic? Discuss this issue in your group. Use details from the poem to support your views. When you are finished, share your conclusions with the class.

Learning for Life

Creating Storyboards Suppose you have been asked to create a film about the battle between Achilles and Hector. In a small group, draw a sequence of storyboards that shows important moments in Book XXII of the *Iliad.* Under each picture, write a quotation from the poem, either dialogue or a description.

Performing

Reciting Poetry Choose a passage of fifty to one hundred lines from the *Iliad* for your group to read aloud. Go over the passage with the group to clarify any unfamiliar words or phrases. Then assign at least ten lines to each person. Practice reading aloud individually and together before presenting your reading to the class. Vary your pitch, volume, and speed to reflect the mood of the passage.

Reading Further

If you enjoyed reading these passages from the *Iliad,* the following account might also be of interest to you:

"The Hellenistic Age," Chapter 8, from *The Ancient Greeks,* by M. I. Finley.

Save your work for your portfolio.

VOCABULARY • Roots

A **root** is the part of a word that contains its basic meaning. We often form a number of different words from roots by adding prefixes, suffixes, and even other roots. Many English roots come from classical Greek and Latin. For example, the words *fraternal* and *fraternity* both come from the Latin root *frater* meaning "brother." Each word also contains a suffix, *-al* and *-ity,* that creates a new word from the root.

PRACTICE Form a familiar word by adding a prefix, suffix, or new root to each classical Greek root. The meaning of the root is in parentheses.

1. bio (life)
2. geo (earth)
3. graph (write)
4. photo (light)
5. tele (distant)
6. thermo (heat)

Web Site

The influence of the gods and goddesses of ancient Greece continues even today. The interactive Web site featured below is modeled after the famous Greek seers and oracles. Here's *your* chance to ask the oracle.

Ask the Oracle

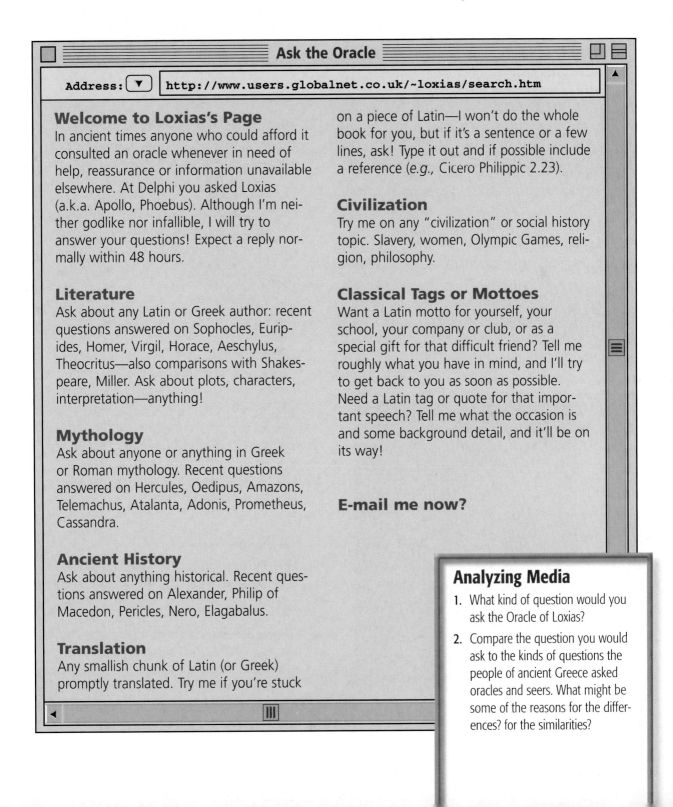

Address: http://www.users.globalnet.co.uk/~loxias/search.htm

Welcome to Loxias's Page

In ancient times anyone who could afford it consulted an oracle whenever in need of help, reassurance or information unavailable elsewhere. At Delphi you asked Loxias (a.k.a. Apollo, Phoebus). Although I'm neither godlike nor infallible, I will try to answer your questions! Expect a reply normally within 48 hours.

Literature

Ask about any Latin or Greek author: recent questions answered on Sophocles, Euripides, Homer, Virgil, Horace, Aeschylus, Theocritus—also comparisons with Shakespeare, Miller. Ask about plots, characters, interpretation—anything!

Mythology

Ask about anyone or anything in Greek or Roman mythology. Recent questions answered on Hercules, Oedipus, Amazons, Telemachus, Atalanta, Adonis, Prometheus, Cassandra.

Ancient History

Ask about anything historical. Recent questions answered on Alexander, Philip of Macedon, Pericles, Nero, Elagabalus.

Translation

Any smallish chunk of Latin (or Greek) promptly translated. Try me if you're stuck on a piece of Latin—I won't do the whole book for you, but if it's a sentence or a few lines, ask! Type it out and if possible include a reference (*e.g.,* Cicero Philippic 2.23).

Civilization

Try me on any "civilization" or social history topic. Slavery, women, Olympic Games, religion, philosophy.

Classical Tags or Mottoes

Want a Latin motto for yourself, your school, your company or club, or as a special gift for that difficult friend? Tell me roughly what you have in mind, and I'll try to get back to you as soon as possible. Need a Latin tag or quote for that important speech? Tell me what the occasion is and some background detail, and it'll be on its way!

E-mail me now?

Analyzing Media

1. What kind of question would you ask the Oracle of Loxias?
2. Compare the question you would ask to the kinds of questions the people of ancient Greece asked oracles and seers. What might be some of the reasons for the differences? for the similarities?

The Art of Translation

Homer Through the Ages

Homer is one of the most widely translated authors in history. Today the *Iliad* appears in many different languages and literary forms. In English, since the first complete translation of Homer was made by George Chapman in 1611, almost every generation has seen a new translation of the *Iliad* and the *Odyssey*.

Agamemnon, King of Mycenae, 12th-century Europe.

The Challenges of Translating

Why do translators feel the need to create these new translations and what purpose do they serve? Before trying to answer this question, it is necessary to consider some of the difficulties that arise when attempting to translate a piece of literature.

- A word might have the same meaning (denotation) in another language, but not the same associations and feelings (connotation).
- Idiomatic expressions–such as "he's pulling your leg"–are unique to their original language, and their meanings have little to do with the literal meaning of the words.
- Sentence structure and grammar vary from one language to another.
- Every translator will have a different idea of the author's meaning and intentions.

Add to these challenges the changes that the English language has undergone over time and the change in writing styles and taste of a given period, and you can begin to get a sense of the many possible ways in which a translator would interpret the ancient works of Homer for readers of their day.

Achilles Recognized Among the Daughters of King Lycomedes, c. 1750. Pompeo Girolamo Batoni, Italy.

Translating Homer

When describing the process of translating Homer, the British poet Matthew Arnold noted that a good translator must try to capture the key elements of Homer's work: fast-paced reading, plainness and directness of expression and idea, and a highly noble style. Throughout the ages, translators have emphasized each of these qualities to differing degrees based on their own interests and the interests of their audiences.

Literal Translation

Sing, O Goddess (Muse), (the) destroying anger
of Achilles, son of Peleus which placed innumerable woes
to the Achaeans but (and) prematurely-sent many brave
souls of heroes to Hades and made them prey
to dogs and to all birds of prey.

Chapman's Translation, 1611

Achilles' baneful wrath resound, O Goddess, that imposed
Infinite sorrows on the Greeks, and many brave souls losed
From breasts heroic; sent them far to that invisible cave
That no light comforts; and their limbs to dogs and vultures gave.

Lattimore's Translation, 1951

Sing goddess, the anger of Peleus' son Achilleus
and its devastation, which put pains thousandfold upon the Achaians
hurled in their multitudes to the house of Hades strong souls
of heroes, but gave their bodies to be the delicate feasting
of dogs, of all birds.

A word-for-word, or literal, translation gives the reader a sense of Homer's directness—his use of just a few words to establish that the poem is about human weakness and tragedy. But the awkwardness of the translation fails to capture Homer's spirit, noble style, and powerful images. George Chapman chose to render Homer's noble style in rhyming couplets, the most elevated poetic form of his own day. But changing styles, and the evolution of the language, make Chapman's version somewhat difficult for modern readers. Today, straightforward translations that read as if the works were originally written in English are in favor. Modern translators like Richmond Lattimore and, more recently, Robert Fagles have replaced the long similes used by Homer with quick, direct phrases.

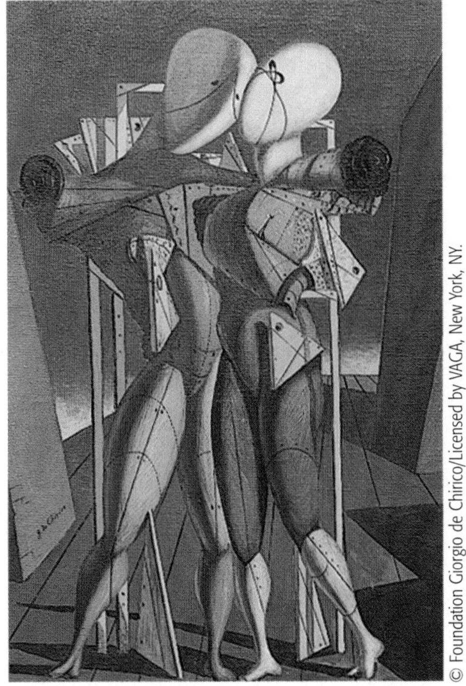

Hector and Andromache, 1924. Giorgio de Chirico (Italy).

RESPOND

1. Robert Fagles translated the selections of the *Iliad* presented in this book. Compare his translation of the opening passage with the translations in this feature.
2. **Viewing the art:** Just as changes in writing style and taste have given rise to different translations of Homer, changes in artistic style and taste have given rise to different visual interpretations of Homer's work. Look back over the images in the *Iliad* selection, as well as those on these pages, and think about how the artists interpreted Homer's work. Share your insights with the class.

GREECE, c. 600–500 B.C.

Before You Read

The Dog and the Wolf

Meet Aesop

"Do not count your chickens before they are hatched."

Aesop (ē′ sop) supposedly was a Greek slave famous for telling fables. If he did exist, he certainly was not an author in the usual sense, but a teller of stories from many sources.

Aesop's fables express values that were held widely among ancient Greeks. Orators often quoted the fables in political speeches to make a point or support an argument. The fables were also appreciated simply for their entertainment value. While in prison awaiting execution, the philosopher Socrates amused himself by setting fables into verse. Today, these homespun tales continue to delight and instruct people of all ages. They are frequently parodied in cartoons and television commercials. Many common phrases can be traced to Aesop, including "sour grapes," "wolf in sheep's clothing," "familiarity breeds contempt," and "killing the goose that laid the golden egg."

Aesop is said to have lived in Greece in the sixth century B.C.

Reading Focus

Think about what the word *freedom* means to you.

Quickwrite Write a paragraph expressing your personal views about freedom. You might offer a definition of freedom or describe how one form of freedom can conflict with another form.

Setting a Purpose Read to discover some canine views of freedom.

Building Background

Aesop's Fables

Aesop's fables were first collected in the fourth century B.C. by the Athenian politician Demetrius of Phalerum. Countless versions in prose and verse have been published since then. The earliest surviving collection is a Latin verse adaptation by Phaedrus, who lived in the first century A.D. Several famous collections were produced during the Middle Ages. Many critics believe that the fables reached their highest form in the verse adaptations of Jean de la Fontaine, a seventeenth-century French poet. La Fontaine used fables to satirize French politics and society. From the nineteenth century on, Aesop's fables have been regarded essentially as children's literature. Yet they influenced J. R. R. Tolkien, George Orwell, James Thurber, and other modern writers whose work is aimed primarily at adults.

Fables Around the World

Fables are popular in many different cultures. In Western literature, fables are generally modeled on the Greek tales associated with Aesop. In Eastern literature, fables are traced back to the Indian fable tradition, which may be as old as the Greek tradition. Fables were originally used in India to teach Buddhist principles. As Buddhism spread, fables began to appear in other parts of Asia. Indian fables also influenced Arabic and Jewish literature.

Vocabulary Preview

gaunt (gônt) *adj.* excessively thin, as from suffering; p. 251
chafe (chāf) *v.* to make sore or irritate by constant rubbing; p. 251

The Dog and the Wolf

Aesop

Retold by Joseph Jacobs

A gaunt Wolf was almost dead with hunger when he happened to meet a Housedog who was passing by. "Ah, Cousin," said the Dog, "I knew how it would be; your irregular life will soon be the ruin of you. Why do you not work steadily as I do, and get your food regularly given to you?"

"I would have no objection," said the Wolf, "if I could only get a place."

"I will easily arrange that for you," said the Dog; "come with me to my master and you shall share my work."

So the Wolf and the Dog went towards the town together. On the way there the Wolf noticed that the hair on a certain part of the Dog's neck was very much worn away, so he asked him how that had come about.

"Oh, it is nothing," said the Dog. "That is only the place where the collar is put on at night to keep me chained up; it chafes a bit, but one soon gets used to it."

"Is that all?" said the Wolf. "Then good-bye to you, Master Dog."

"Better starve free than be a fat slave."

Vocabulary

gaunt (gônt) *adj.* excessively thin, as from suffering

chafe (chāf) *v.* to make sore or irritate by constant rubbing

Responding to Literature

Personal Response

A moral is the lesson a fable teaches. Do you agree with the moral of this fable? Why or why not?

Analyzing Literature

Recall and Interpret

1. What does the Dog suggest to the Wolf when they meet? What do you think prompts this suggestion?
2. How does the Wolf respond to the Dog's suggestion?
3. What offer does the Dog make to the Wolf?
4. What causes the Wolf to change its mind at the end? Why does the Wolf react this way?

Evaluate and Connect

5. Why might Aesop have chosen a dog and a wolf as characters in this fable?
6. In the Reading Focus on page 250 you expressed your thoughts about freedom. In your opinion, which of the characters in the fable has more freedom? has a better life? Explain.
7. **Internal conflict** is a mental or emotional struggle within a character (see page R2). Identify an example of internal conflict in this fable.
8. Have you ever had to choose between following your personal beliefs and following the path to success? How did you decide?

Literary Criticism

Scholar Mary Ellen Snodgrass states that the collection of Aesop's fables "lampoons the standard human failings of pride, arrogance, greed, and folly." Which of these failings does "The Dog and the Wolf" lampoon? Explain your answer in a brief paragraph. Use details from the fable to support your answer.

Literary ELEMENTS

Fable

A **fable** is a brief story that teaches a lesson. Most fables feature animal characters that act and speak like human beings. Plants, objects, natural forces, humans, and gods may also appear as characters. The lesson of a fable is dramatized through dialogue and the interaction of characters. Usually the moral is stated directly at the end. Although fables are written to teach proper behavior, the memorable ones tell a good, often humorous, story as well.

1. What are some ways in which a fable differs from a short story?
2. Restate the moral of "The Dog and the Wolf" in your own words.

- See **Literary Terms Handbook**, p. R4.

Extending Your Response

Creative Writing

Fable Write a fable that illustrates one of the following morals or a moral of your own choice:

- If at first you don't succeed, try, try again.
- Beauty is in the eye of the beholder.
- All that glitters is not gold.

In your fable, dramatize the moral through dialogue and the interaction of animal characters. Keep your fable brief, and try to make it entertaining.

Performing

Act like an Animal Create a performance of "The Dog and the Wolf" or another fable. Use gestures or simple costumes to suggest the animal qualities of your character. Before performing the fable, rehearse with your partner or group.

Save your work for your portfolio.

Before You Read

The Oak and the Reed

FRANCE, c. 1668–1678

Meet Jean de la Fontaine

"Long works frighten me. Far from exhausting a subject, one must only take its flower."

In seventeenth-century France, fables were considered a minor literary form, not worth the attention of sophisticated readers. Jean de la Fontaine (zhän də lä fon tān′) challenged this notion. Of all genres, only the fable allowed him to make full use of his dazzling variety of literary techniques.

La Fontaine briefly studied theology and law, but found his true calling as a poet. He had difficulty supporting himself and relied mainly on the help of wealthy patrons in Paris. A charming and witty conversationalist, La Fontaine was popular in the literary salons of Paris. Although some members of France's literary establishment disliked him because of his unconventional views, at age sixty-two La Fontaine was finally elected to the prestigious French Academy. His *Fables* have become classics of French literature.

La Fontaine was born in 1621 and died in 1695.

Reading Focus

Chart It! List your strengths and weaknesses in a chart like the one below. With a partner, discuss how you might turn some of your weaknesses into strengths.

Strengths	Weaknesses

Setting a Purpose As you read the fable, think about the strengths and weaknesses of the characters.

Building Background

La Fontaine's Fables

Jean de la Fontaine published his fables in three collections over a twenty-five-year period. Most of them are adaptations of stories from Phaedrus and others who wrote in the tradition of Aesop. He also borrowed fables from the Indian writer Bidpai. Although La Fontaine depended on earlier writers for material, his manner of telling fables was highly original. He enhanced the dramatic impact of these brief tales through subtle characterization and rich imagery. Within a single fable, he could shift from epic to tragic to comic styles.

La Fontaine used stories about non-human characters to point out human weaknesses. Yet he did not want this educational purpose to detract from the "gaiety" of his poems: "I call gaiety not that which arouses laughter, but a certain charm, an agreeable air that one can give to all sorts of subjects, even the most serious." Often the morals of La Fontaine's fables are suggested rather than stated, allowing readers to draw their own conclusions.

The Oak and the Reed

Jean de la Fontaine
Translated by James Michie

One day the oak said to the reed:
"You have good cause indeed
To accuse Nature of being unkind.
To you a wren° must seem
An intolerable burden, and the least puff of wind
That chances to wrinkle the face of the stream
Forces your head low; whereas I,
Huge as a Caucasian peak,° defy
Not only the sun's glare, but the worst the weather can do.
What seems a breeze to me is a gale for you.
Had you been born in the lee° of my leaf-sheltered ground,
You would have suffered less, I should have kept you warm;
But you reeds are usually found
On the moist borders of the kingdom of the storm.
It strikes me that to you Nature has been unfair."
"Your pity," the plant replied, "springs from a kind heart.
But please don't be anxious on my part.
Your fear of the winds ought to be greater than mine.
I bend, but I never break. You, till now, have been able to bear
Their fearful buffets° without flexing your spine.
But let us wait and see." Even as he spoke,
From the horizon's nethermost gloom
The worst storm the north had ever bred in its womb
        Furiously awoke.
The tree stood firm, the reed began to bend.
The wind redoubled° its efforts to blow—
        So much so
        That in the end
It uprooted the one that had touched the sky with its head,
But whose feet reached to the region of the dead.

---

4 A *wren* is a very small European bird.

8 *Caucasian peak* refers to the Caucasus mountains, which lie between Russia, Turkey, and Iran, and contain the highest mountains in Europe.

11 The *lee* is the side (as of a tree) that is sheltered from the wind.

20 *Buffets* (buf′ əts) means "blows."

26 *Redoubled* means "intensified."

The Great Piece of Turf (detail). Albrecht Dürer (Germany, 1471–1528). Albertina Graphic Collection, Vienna.

Responding to Literature

Personal Response

How do you feel about the characters in this fable? Discuss your response with a classmate.

Analyzing Literature

Recall and Interpret

1. Why does the oak pity the reed? What adjective would you use to describe the oak?
2. How would the oak have liked to help the reed? In your opinion, why does the oak express this wish?
3. Summarize the reed's response to the oak. Do you think the reed is offended by the oak's comments? Explain.
4. What happens to the oak during the storm? Which character proves to be stronger in the end?

Evaluate and Connect

5. **Tone** is the attitude–such as serious, light-hearted, or ironic–that a writer takes toward a subject (see page R12). Do you think la Fontaine's tone in this fable is consistent, or does it change during the narrative? Explain your response.
6. **Hyperbole** (hī pur′ bə lē) is a figure of speech in which exaggeration is used for emphasis or comic effect (see page R6). Identify an example of hyperbole in "The Oak and the Reed."
7. What did you find humorous in this fable? What other humorous fables have you read or heard, and why were they funny to you?
8. Think of a time when you were overconfident about yourself. How did you learn that you were mistaken in your judgment?

Literary ELEMENTS

Rhyme

Words **rhyme** when their accented vowels and all the letters that follow sound the same. For example, the word *borrow* rhymes with *tomorrow,* and *sincere* rhymes with *fear.* Rhyme can add to the pleasure of reading poetry and can also help link lines in a poem together. When rhyme occurs at the ends of lines, it is called **end rhyme.** Literary scholars use letters to indicate a poem's **rhyme scheme,** or pattern of end rhyme, by assigning the same letter to rhyming words (for example, *aabbcc* or *ababcdcd*).

1. What is the rhyme scheme of "The Oak and the Reed"?
2. Why do you think La Fontaine varies the pattern of end rhyme in the fable?

- See **Literary Terms Handbook,** p. R10.

Extending Your Response

Personal Writing

Strength and Weakness In the Reading Focus on page 253, you listed some of your strengths and weaknesses. Write a description of an experience that illustrates one of those strengths or weaknesses. Do you think that your strength could leave you vulnerable in certain situations, or that your weakness could possibly be helpful? Explain.

Literature Groups

Moralizing "The Oak and the Reed" does not end with a moral statement, but a moral can be inferred. Would you prefer the author to state the moral directly, or do you like to figure it out on your own? Discuss this question in your group. Agree on a moral for "The Oak and the Reed" and present it to the class.

Save your work for your portfolio.

COMPARING *selections*

The Dog and the Wolf and *The Oak and the Reed*

COMPARE **STYLES**

Write a paragraph comparing the styles of "The Dog and the Wolf" and "The Oak and the Reed." Use examples from the fables to support your analysis. You might wish to focus on one or more of the following elements:

- imagery
- tone
- setting
- dialogue

COMPARE **RESPONSES**

Aesop's fables began as oral tales. Their simplicity made them easy for people to remember. La Fontaine wrote longer fables for a highly sophisticated audience, more accustomed to literary devices. In your group, compare your responses to the work of these two fable writers. Discuss the following questions, giving reasons for your choices:

1. Which fable did you find more entertaining?
2. Which fable is better at teaching a moral?
3. Which fable offers a more complex view of human behavior?

The Great Piece of Turf. Albrecht Dürer (1471–1528).

COMPARE **CHARACTERS**

With a partner, compare the characters in "The Dog and the Wolf" with those in "The Oak and the Reed." Which characters seem more human to you, Aesop's animals or la Fontaine's plants? Which characters are more fully developed? What lines in the fable influenced your answer? What plant characters might Aesop have used to teach the moral of "The Dog and the Wolf"? What animals might La Fontaine have substituted for the plants in "The Oak and the Reed"?

Before You Read

GREECE, c. 600 B.C.

Lyric Poems

Meet Sappho

"Some say there are nine Muses: but they're wrong. / Look at Sappho of Lesbos; she makes ten." —*Plato*

The poet Sappho (sa′ fō) lived on Lesbos, a Greek island off the coast of what is now Turkey. She was born into a prominent family and addressed family members in many of her poems. Lesbos produced a number of famous lyric poets, but Sappho was recognized as the greatest. Some scholars believe that she was in charge of a school that trained young women in the arts.

After her death, Sappho became famous throughout the Mediterranean world. Greek and Roman writers imitated her poems, and she was honored with public statues. Unfortunately, very little of her work survives. Yet Sappho continues to influence writers. Her poetry provides a rare glimpse of ancient Greece from a woman's perspective.

Sappho was born around 630 B.C. and died around 570 B.C.

Reading Further

Sappho: A Garland, translated by Jim Powell, is a book of the surviving poems and fragments by Sappho.

Reading Focus

Think about experiences in your life that might be the subject of a poem.

Freewrite Write about one of the experiences, without planning ahead or worrying whether your language is "poetic." After you have finished, consider how you might create a poem out of your writing.

Setting a Purpose As you read, notice what Sappho's poetry tells you about how she feels about her life.

Building Background

Sappho's Poetry

Greek lyric poets usually performed their work only in private for friends and invited guests. They often sang or chanted their poetry, accompanying themselves on the harp-like "lyra." Sappho herself frequently used a verse form that came to be called after her, the "sapphic stanza" of four lines–three long and one shorter. Sappho wrote in a style that was closer to everyday speech than to the more literary established style of her time. Like most Greek lyric poetry, her work deals with personal feelings–love, anger, sorrow, and joy.

We do not know how Sappho's poems were first published. Long after her death, Greek scholars collected her poetry in nine volumes. Nearly all of this work was lost during the early Middle Ages. Only one complete poem and about a hundred fragments were preserved as quotations in the works of other writers. Additional fragments have been discovered on archeological digs in the twentieth century. For example, one fragment appeared on a strip of papyrus removed from a mummified crocodile.

Lyric Poems

Sappho

Translated by Jim Powell

Most Beautiful of All the Stars

Most beautiful of all the stars
O Hesperus, bringing everything
the bright dawn scattered:
you bring the sheep, you bring the goat,
you bring the child back to her mother.

Sappho (detail). Gustave Moreau (France, 1826–1898). Watercolor, 18.4 x 12.4 cm. Victoria & Albert Museum, London. How does this image of Sappho match the one you get from her poems?

In My Eyes He Matches the Gods

In my eyes he matches the gods, that man who
sits there facing you—any man whatever—
listening from closeby to the sweetness of your
voice as you talk, the

sweetness of your laughter: yes, that—
I swear it—
sets the heart to shaking inside my
breast, since
once I look at you for a moment, I can't
speak any longer,

but my tongue breaks down, and then
all at once a
subtle fire races inside my skin, my
eyes can't see a thing and a whirring whistle
thrums at my hearing,

cold sweat covers me and a trembling takes
ahold of me all over: I'm greener than the
grass is and appear to myself to be little
short of dying.

Some Say Thronging Cavalry

Some say thronging cavalry, some say foot soldiers,
others call a fleet the most beautiful of
sights the dark earth offers, but I say it's whatever you love best.

And it's easy to make this understood by
everyone, for she who surpassed all human
kind in beauty, Helen,° abandoning her
husband—that best of

men—went sailing off to the shores of Troy and
never spent a thought on her child or loving
parents: when the goddess seduced her wits and
left her to wander,

she forgot them all, she could not remember
anything but longing, and lightly straying
aside, lost her way. But that reminds me
now: Anactória,

she's not here, and I'd rather see her lovely
step, her sparkling glance and her face than gaze on
all the troops in Lydia° in their chariots and
glittering armor.

7 Helen of Troy (see page 212).

19 Lydia: a wealthy kingdom in Asia Minor in the fifth century B.C.

For My Mother Said

for my mother said

that when she was a girl if you
bound the locks of your hair in back,
gathered there in a circlet of plaited purple,°

that was truly a fine adornment,
but for blondes with hair yellower
than a torch it is better to fasten it

with fresh garlands of flowers in bloom,
and more recently there were headbands
decorated in Sardis,° elaborately

embroidered . . .

4 a circlet of plaited purple: a circular ornament of woven or braided strands made from purple material.

10 Sardis: capital of Lydia.

Responding to Literature

Personal Response

What memories do these poems stir up in you? Write your response in your journal.

Analyzing Literature

Recall and Interpret

1. Why does the speaker praise Hesperus, the evening star, in "Most Beautiful of All the Stars"?
2. Summarize the first stanza of "In My Eyes He Matches the Gods."
3. List the emotions described by the speaker of "In My Eyes He Matches the Gods."
4. In "Some Say Thronging Cavalry," do you think that the speaker is sympathetic toward Helen or critical of her? Explain.
5. Do you think that the speaker of "My Mother Said" is a child or an adult? What led you to make this assumption?

Evaluate and Connect

6. You know that the **speaker** of a poem is the voice that talks to the reader (see page R11). Do you think that all of these poems have the same speaker, or different speakers? Explain your answer.
7. How would you describe the subject matter of Sappho's poems? Why do you think Sappho chose to write about these subjects?
8. Almost all of Sappho's surviving poems are fragments. Which of the poems that you read seems most incomplete to you? Explain why.
9. In "Some Say Thronging Cavalry," the speaker says that whatever one loves best is the most beautiful of sights. Do you agree? Explain.
10. What writer does Sappho most remind you of? Why?

Literary ELEMENTS

Imagery

Imagery is language that appeals to the senses. Because people usually rely on sight more than the other senses, much imagery is visual. The following lines from "Some Say Thronging Cavalry" are rich in visual imagery:

I'd rather see her lovely / step, her sparkling glance and her face than gaze on / all the troops in Lydia in their chariots and / glittering armor.

Imagery can also help readers hear sounds, feel textures, smell aromas, and taste foods.

1. What do the images in "For My Mother Said" describe?
2. Identify three images in "For My Mother Said" that suggest the speaker's emotions.

- See **Literary Terms Handbook,** p. R6.

Extending Your Response

Creative Writing

Write a Poem Use material from the Reading Focus on page 257 to create a poem. Think first about which images you might use from your earlier writing. Trade poems with a classmate and provide feedback on his or her work.

Interdisciplinary Activity

Art: Images of Women Find photographs of Greek art that portrays women. Bring to class a photocopy that you think would make a good illustration for one of Sappho's poems.

Save your work for your portfolio.

Literature FOCUS

Greek Drama

Myths and Festivals Greek drama is one of the oldest forms of drama we know. In ancient Greece, plays grew out of religion and myths. From the sixth century B.C., religious festivals featured a chorus, or group of actors, that danced and sang hymns to Dionysus, the god of wine and fertility.

In about 534 B.C., the lyric poet Thespis introduced the use of a single actor, separate from the chorus. As drama evolved, the chorus voiced the attitudes and values of society while the actor delivered speeches, answered the chorus, and performed the story. With these changes, drama (from the Greek word for *doing,* rather than *telling*) was born, and actors today are still called thespians.

Drama grew to become a vital part of life in Athens. The festival of Dionysus, the most important Greek religious festival, introduced a drama competition. The four greatest writers of Greek drama—Aeschylus (525–456 B.C.), Sophocles (496–406 B.C.), Euripides (480–406 B.C.), and Aristophanes (448–385 B.C.)—presented their plays at these festivals. Greek dramas appealed to the audience because they focused on the myths and legends that were known and loved by Athenians. Favorite subjects included the Trojan War and such legendary figures as Oedipus, Agamemnon, and the Greek gods and goddesses.

Greek Tragedies and Comedies Greek tragedies examined the consequences of an individual's actions, the relationship of people to the gods, and the role that fate plays in everyday life. Central to Greek tragedy is the fall of a great man or woman—the **tragic hero,** whose fate is brought about by a flaw within his or her character. Comedies offered some relief from the sobering tragedies. They delighted and outraged Athenian audiences with bawdy satires that mischievously mocked politicians, famous cultural figures, and even the gods themselves.

Costumes and Masks Every role in ancient Greek theater was performed by male actors. The plays were usually directed by the playwright himself, who sometimes acted as well. In order to be seen by audiences in huge theaters seating thousands, actors wore high boots and large, padded costumes. They also wore masks made of linen or leather, attached to wooden frames. The mouths of the masks acted as megaphones to amplify the actors' voices in the large theaters. Aside from displaying basic expressions such as fear, joy, and surprise, the masks were essential for indicating whether the male actor was playing a man, woman, or child.

Mask sketch for *Oedipus Rex.*

Plays served several important functions in ancient Greece. Performances entertained and delighted thousands of people, but they also served a more serious didactic function. Audiences were challenged by the playwrights to consider the moral and ethical dilemmas that the characters confronted and to reflect upon such issues in their own lives.

ACTIVITY

As you read the following Greek tragedy, *Oedipus the King,* think about how you would stage the play if you were a director during Sophocles' time. Then consider how you might stage it if you were a director today. Keep a list of your "ancient" and "modern" ideas. Compare and contrast them. Share your ideas with the class.

GREECE, c. 450 B.C.

Before You Read

Oedipus the King

Meet Sophocles

"Of all the ills afflicting men the worst is lack of judgment."

Sophocles (sof′ ə klēz′) lived in the fifth century B.C., a time of spectacular cultural and political achievement in Athens. Few writers have ever been as warmly embraced by their fellow citizens. At twenty-eight he won a prestigious drama competition held annually to honor the god Dionysus, and he continued to write plays and win prizes well into his eighties. Sophocles also held important public positions. Contemporaries described him as handsome and witty, with an easy-going charm that made him very popular.

Although Sophocles avoided personal misfortune, his insight into human suffering was profound. Focusing on the fates of individual characters, he explored complex issues such as the struggle for self-knowledge and the conflict between personal and social values. Only seven of his 123 plays survive intact. *Oedipus the King* is often singled out as the finest play of the classical period.

Sophocles was born around 496 B.C. and died in 406 B.C.

Reading Focus

What is the most surprising thing you have ever learned about yourself?

Survey It! Pose this question to six of your classmates. After you have finished the survey, present your findings to the class.

Setting a Purpose As you read, think about what the characters come to learn about themselves.

Building Background

Oedipus and the Sphinx

Sophocles expected his audience to be familiar with the mythical background of his play. According to ancient legend, when Oedipus arrived at Thebes he found the city oppressed by the Sphinx, a winged creature with a lion's body and a woman's head. This monster stationed herself on a rock and demanded an answer to the following riddle: What walks on four legs in the morning, on two at noon, and on three in the evening? The Thebans offered the throne and the hand of Jocasta, their widowed queen, to anyone who could solve the riddle. Many took up this challenge and were thrown to their deaths when they failed. Finally Oedipus came along and told the Sphinx that the answer was man, who crawls as a baby, stands on two legs in maturity, and walks supported by a stick in old age. Upon hearing this answer the Sphinx killed herself, and Oedipus claimed his reward. The play opens *in medias res,* or "in the middle of things." Oedipus has ruled the city successfully for many years and has fathered four children with Jocasta.

Oedipus and the Sphinx. 5th century B.C., Ancient Greece. Red-figured kylix. Museo Gregoriano Etrusco, Rome.

Pictograph #4, 1943. Adolph Gottlieb (United States). Oil on canvas, 35¼ x 22⅞ in. Adolph and Esther Gottlieb Foundation. Licensed by VAGA, New York.

Oedipus the King

Sophocles

Translated by Robert Fagles

Oedipus the King

CHARACTERS

OEDIPUS: king of Thebes

A PRIEST: of Zeus

CREON: brother of Jocasta

A CHORUS:° of Theban citizens and their **LEADER**

TIRESIAS: a blind prophet

JOCASTA: the queen, wife of Oedipus

A MESSENGER: from Corinth

A SHEPHERD

A MESSENGER: from inside the palace

ANTIGONE, ISMENE: daughters of Oedipus and Jocasta

GUARDS AND ATTENDANTS

PRIESTS OF THEBES

Chorus: a group of characters, usually singers, who comment on the action of the play.

TIME AND SCENE: *The royal house of Thebes. Double doors dominate the façade; a stone altar stands at the center of the stage.*

Many years have passed since OEDIPUS solved the riddle of the Sphinx and ascended the throne of Thebes, and now a plague has struck the city. A procession of PRIESTS enters; suppliants,° broken and despondent, they carry branches wound in wool° and lay them on the altar.

The doors open. GUARDS assemble. OEDIPUS comes forward, majestic but for a telltale limp, and slowly views the condition of his people.

suppliants: people humbly asking a monarch to grant a request.
branches wound in wool: symbolic goodwill offerings to the gods.

OEDIPUS. Oh my children, the new blood of ancient Thebes,
why are you here? Huddling at my altar,
praying before me, your branches wound in wool.
Our city reeks with the smoke of burning incense,
rings with cries for the Healer° and wailing for the dead.
I thought it wrong, my children, to hear the truth
from others, messengers. Here I am myself—
you all know me, the world knows my fame:
I am Oedipus.

5 the Healer: Apollo, god of sunlight, healing, prophecy, and archery.

[*Helping a PRIEST to his feet.*]

Speak up, old man. Your years,
your dignity—you should speak for the others.
Why here and kneeling, what preys upon you° so?
Some sudden fear? some strong desire?
You can trust me; I am ready to help,
I'll do anything. I would be blind to misery
not to pity my people kneeling at my feet.

11 preys upon you: troubles your mind.

PRIEST. Oh Oedipus, king of the land, our greatest power!
You see us before you, men of all ages
clinging to your altars. Here are boys,
still too weak to fly from the nest,
and here the old, bowed down with the years,
the holy ones—a priest of Zeus° myself—and here
the picked, unmarried men, the young hope of Thebes.
And all the rest, your great family gathers now,
branches wreathed, massing in the squares,
kneeling before the two temples of queen Athena°
or the river-shrine where the embers glow and die
and Apollo sees the future in the ashes.°
Our city—
look around you, see with your own eyes—
our ship pitches wildly, cannot lift her head
from the depths, the red waves of death . . .
Thebes is dying. A blight° on the fresh crops
and the rich pastures, cattle sicken and die,
and the women die in labor, children stillborn,
and the plague, the fiery god of fever hurls down
on the city, his lightning slashing through us—
raging plague in all its vengeance, devastating
the house of Cadmus!° And Black Death luxuriates°
in the raw, wailing miseries of Thebes.

Now we pray to you. You cannot equal the gods,
your children know that, bending at your altar.
But we do rate you first of men,
both in the common crises of our lives
and face-to-face encounters with the gods.
You freed us from the Sphinx;° you came to Thebes
and cut us loose from the bloody tribute we had paid
that harsh, brutal singer. We taught you nothing,
no skill, no extra knowledge, still you triumphed.
A god was with you, so they say, and we believe it—
you lifted up our lives.
So now again,
Oedipus, king, we bend to you, your power—
we implore you, all of us on our knees:
find us strength, rescue! Perhaps you've heard
the voice of a god or something from other men,
Oedipus . . . what do you know?
The man of experience—you see it every day—
his plans will work in a crisis, his first of all.

21 **Zeus:** the chief Greek god.

25 **Athena:** also Pallas Athena, goddess of wisdom and the arts and sciences.

26–27 **river-shrine . . . in the ashes:** a nearby shrine where Apollo's priests read the future in the ashes left by burnt offerings.

31 **blight:** a disease that kills plants.

37 **house of Cadmus:** Thebes; Cadmus founded the city. **luxuriates:** indulges in pleasure; grows abundantly.

44 **freed us from the Sphinx:** When the young Oedipus solved the Sphinx's riddle, the monster plunged to her death.

Act now—we beg you, best of men, raise up our city!
Act, defend yourself, your former glory!
Your country calls you savior now
for your zeal, your action years ago.
Never let us remember of your reign:
you helped us stand, only to fall once more.
Oh raise up our city, set us on our feet.
The omens were good that day you brought us joy—
be the same man today!
Rule our land, you know you have the power,
but rule a land of the living, not a wasteland.
Ship and towered city are nothing, stripped of men
alive within it, living all as one.

OEDIPUS. My children,
I pity you. I see—how could I fail to see
what longings bring you here? Well I know
you are sick to death, all of you,
but sick as you are, not one is sick as I.
Your pain strikes each of you alone, each
in the confines of himself, no other. But my spirit
grieves for the city, for myself and all of you.
I wasn't asleep, dreaming. You haven't wakened me—
I've wept through the nights, you must know that,
groping, laboring over many paths of thought.
After a painful search I found one cure:
I acted at once. I sent Creon,
my wife's own brother, to Delphi°—

82 **Delphi:** site of a shrine to Apollo; Delphi was the most famous oracle in ancient Greece.

Aegeus Consulting the Delphic Oracle. Ancient Greece. Athenian red-figured vase. Staatliche Museen, Berlin.

Viewing the painting: What do you think the artist might have intended by placing the pillar between the two figures?

Apollo the Prophet's oracle°—to learn
what I might do or say to save our city.

Today's the day. When I count the days gone by
it torments me . . . what is he doing?
Strange, he's late, he's gone too long.
But once he returns, then, then I'll be a traitor
if I do not do all the god makes clear.

PRIEST. Timely words. The men over there
are signaling—Creon's just arriving.

OEDIPUS. [*Sighting* CREON, *then turning to the altar.*] Lord Apollo,
let him come with a lucky word of rescue,
shining like his eyes!

PRIEST. Welcome news, I think—he's crowned, look,
and the laurel wreath is bright with berries.°

OEDIPUS. We'll soon see. He's close enough to hear—

[*Enter* CREON *from the side; his face is shaded with a wreath.*]

Creon, prince, my kinsman, what do you bring us?
What message from the god?

CREON. Good news.
I tell you even the hardest things to bear,
if they should turn out well, all would be well.

OEDIPUS. Of course, but what were the god's *words?*° There's no hope
and nothing to fear in what you've said so far.

CREON. If you want my report in the presence of these . . .

[*Pointing to the* PRIESTS *while drawing* OEDIPUS *toward the palace.*]

I'm ready now, or we might go inside.

OEDIPUS. Speak out,
speak to us all. I grieve for these, my people,
far more than I fear for my own life.

CREON. Very well,
I will tell you what I heard from the god.
Apollo commands us—he was quite clear—
"Drive the corruption from the land,
don't harbor° it any longer, past all cure,
don't nurse it in your soil—root it out!"

OEDIPUS. How can we cleanse ourselves—what rites?°
What's the source of the trouble?

83 **oracle:** a shrine at which questions might be answered about the hidden past or the future; the term *oracle* can also refer to the answer itself or to the priestess who gives the answer.

94–95 **crowned . . . with berries:** A crown of laurel was given as a prize for victory or excellence.

101 **the god's *words:*** Apollo; it was believed that the god spoke through the voice of the priestess at the oracle.

110 **harbor:** to give shelter; to conceal.

112 **rites:** religious ceremonies; symbolic acts often required to atone for a wrongdoing.

CREON. Banish the man, or pay back blood with blood.
Murder sets the plague-storm on the city.

OEDIPUS. Whose murder?
Whose fate does Apollo bring to light?

CREON. Our leader,
my lord, was once a man named Laius,°
before you came and put us straight on course.

OEDIPUS. I know—
or so I've heard. I never saw the man myself.

CREON. Well, he was killed, and Apollo commands us now—
he could not be more clear,
"Pay the killers back—whoever is responsible."

OEDIPUS. Where on earth are they? Where to find it now,
the trail of the ancient guilt so hard to trace?

CREON. "Here in Thebes," he said.
Whatever is sought for can be caught, you know,
whatever is neglected slips away.

OEDIPUS. But where,
in the palace, the fields or foreign soil,
where did Laius meet his bloody death?

CREON. He went to consult an oracle, he said,
and he set out and never came home again.

OEDIPUS. No messenger, no fellow-traveler saw what happened?
Someone to cross-examine?

CREON. No,
they were all killed but one. He escaped,
terrified, he could tell us nothing clearly,
nothing of what he saw—just one thing.

OEDIPUS. What's that?
One thing could hold the key to it all,
a small beginning give us grounds for hope.

CREON. He said thieves attacked them—a whole band,
not single-handed, cut King Laius down.

OEDIPUS. A thief,
so daring, so wild, he'd kill a king? Impossible,
unless conspirators paid him off in Thebes.

CREON. We suspected as much. But with Laius dead
no leader appeared to help us in our troubles.

117 Laius: the king who immediately preceded Oedipus; first husband of Jocasta.

OEDIPUS. Trouble? Your *king* was murdered—royal blood!
What stopped you from tracking down the killer
then and there?

CREON. The singing, riddling Sphinx.
She . . . persuaded us to let the mystery go
and concentrate on what lay at our feet.

OEDIPUS. No,
I'll start again—I'll bring it all to light myself!
Apollo is right, and so are you, Creon,
to turn our attention back to the murdered man.
Now you have *me* to fight for you, you'll see:
I am the land's avenger by all rights°
and Apollo's champion° too.
But not to assist some distant kinsman, no,
for my own sake I'll rid us of this corruption.
Whoever killed the king may decide to kill me too,
with the same violent hand—by avenging Laius
I defend myself.

[*To the* PRIESTS.]

Quickly, my children.
Up from the steps, take up your branches now.

[*To the* GUARDS.]

One of you summon the city here before us,
tell them I'll do everything. God help us,
we will see our triumph—or our fall.

[OEDIPUS *and* CREON *enter the palace, followed by the* GUARDS.]

PRIEST. Rise, my sons. The kindness we came for
Oedipus volunteers himself.
Apollo has sent his word, his oracle—
Come down, Apollo, save us, stop the plague.

[*The* PRIESTS *rise, remove their branches and exit to the side.*]

[*Enter a* CHORUS, *the citizens of Thebes, who have not heard the news that* CREON *brings. They march around the altar, chanting.*]

CHORUS. Zeus!
Great welcome voice of Zeus,° what do you bring?
What word from the gold vaults of Delphi
comes to brilliant Thebes? I'm racked with terror—
terror shakes my heart
and I cry your wild cries, Apollo, Healer of Delos°
I worship you in dread . . . what now, what is your price?

154 land's avenger by all rights: As king, Oedipus has the authority to punish crimes.

155 champion: one who defends a worthy person or a just cause.

169 voice of Zeus: Apollo, as the god of prophecy, spoke for his father, Zeus.

173 Delos: island birthplace of Apollo and a famous center of his worship.

The Chariot of Apollo. Odilon Redon (France, 1840–1916). Pastel on paper, 91 x 77 cm. Louvre Museum, Paris.

Viewing the painting: Look at the details in this painting. How do they express Apollo's powers and stature?

some new sacrifice? some ancient rite from the past
come round again each spring?—
        what will you bring to birth?°
Tell me, child of golden Hope
    warm voice that never dies!

You are the first I call, daughter of Zeus
deathless Athena—I call your sister Artemis,°
heart of the market place enthroned in glory,
                      guardian of our earth—
I call Apollo, Archer° astride the thunderheads° of heaven—
O triple shield against death,° shine before me now!
If ever, once in the past, you stopped some ruin
launched against our walls
        you hurled the flame of pain
far, far from Thebes—you gods
    come now, come down once more!
                                    No, no
the miseries numberless, grief on grief, no end—
too much to bear, we are all dying
O my people . . .
   Thebes like a great army dying
and there is no sword of thought° to save us, no
and the fruits of our famous earth, they will not ripen
no and the women cannot scream their pangs to birth—
screams for the Healer, children dead in the womb°
          and life on life goes down
                           you can watch them go
   like seabirds winging west,° outracing the day's fire
down the horizon,° irresistibly
          streaking on to the shores of Evening
                                          Death
so many deaths, numberless deaths on deaths, no end—
Thebes is dying, look, her children
stripped of pity . . .
   generations strewn on the ground
unburied, unwept, the dead spreading death
and the young wives and gray-haired mothers with them
cling to the altars, trailing in from all over the city—
Thebes, city of death, one long cortege°
          and the suffering rises
                     wails for mercy rise
    and the wild hymn for the Healer blazes out
clashing with our sobs our cries of mourning—

174–177 worship you in dread . . . bring to birth: They fear what sacrifice the gods will demand from them to end the plague.

181 Artemis: goddess of the hunt and of the moon.

184 Archer: Apollo was sometimes referred to as "the distant deadly Archer," whose arrows caused disease or death. **astride the thunderheads:** riding atop storm clouds.

185 triple shield against death: Athena, Artemis, and Apollo.

195 sword of thought: keen insight.

197–198 women . . . womb: The plague in Thebes causes not only the earth not to bring forth fruit, but affects Theban women as well, for their infants are stillborn.

201 winging west: The west, where the sun sets, was thought to be where the dead resided.

201–202 outracing . . . horizon: moving faster than the setting sun.

211 cortege: funeral procession.

O golden daughter of god,° send rescue
radiant as the kindness in your eyes!
Drive him back!—the fever, the god of death
that raging god of war
not armored in bronze, not shielded now, he burns me,
battle cries in the onslaught burning on°—
O rout him from our borders!
Sail him, blast him out to the Sea-queen's chamber
the black Atlantic gulfs°
or the northern harbor, death to all
where the Thracian surf° comes crashing.
Now what the night spares he comes by day and kills—
the god of death.

O lord of the stormcloud,
you who twirl the lightning, Zeus, Father,
thunder Death to nothing!

Apollo, lord of the light, I beg you—
whip your longbow's golden cord
showering arrows on our enemies—shafts of power
champions strong before us rushing on!

Artemis, Huntress,
torches flaring over the eastern ridges—
ride Death down in pain!

God of the headdress gleaming gold, I cry to you—
your name and ours are one, Dionysus°—
come with your face aflame with wine
your raving women's cries°
your army on the march! Come with the lightning
come with torches blazing, eyes ablaze with glory!
Burn that god of death that all gods hate!

[*OEDIPUS enters from the palace to address the CHORUS, as if addressing the entire city of Thebes.*]

OEDIPUS. You pray to the gods? Let me grant your prayers.
Come, listen to me—do what the plague demands:
you'll find relief and lift your head from the depths.

I will speak out now as a stranger to the story,
a stranger to the crime. If I'd been present then,
there would have been no mystery, no long hunt
without a clue in hand. So now, counted

216 **golden daughter of god:** Athena.

218–221 **the fever . . . burning on:** The plague is compared to a battle raging inside the body.

223–24 **blast him . . . Atlantic gulfs:** send winds to carry the plague westward to the Atlantic Ocean.

226 **Thracian surf:** Thrace was a region northeast of Thebes.

239 **your name . . . Dionysus:** Thebes was the first city to celebrate the rites of Dionysus, god of wine and vegetation. His father was Zeus, and his mother was a Theban woman.

241 **raving women's cries:** The Maenads, female attendants, helped Dionysus punish enemies.

a native Theban years after the murder,
to all of Thebes I make this proclamation:
if any one of you knows who murdered Laius,
the son of Labdacus, I order him to reveal
the whole truth to me. Nothing to fear,
even if he must denounce himself,
let him speak up
and so escape the brunt of the charge—
he will suffer no unbearable punishment,
nothing worse than exile, totally unharmed.

[OEDIPUS *pauses, waiting for a reply.*]

Next,
if anyone knows the murderer is a stranger,
a man from alien soil, come, speak up.
I will give him a handsome reward, and lay up
gratitude in my heart for him besides.

[*Silence again, no reply.*]

But if you keep silent, if anyone panicking,
trying to shield himself or friend or kin,
rejects my offer, then hear what I will do.
I order you, every citizen of the state
where I hold throne and power: banish this man—
whoever he may be—never shelter him, never
speak a word to him, never make him partner
to your prayers, your victims burned to the gods.
Never let the holy water touch his hands.
Drive him out, each of you, from every home.
He is the plague, the heart of our corruption,
as Apollo's oracle has revealed to me
just now. So I honor my obligations:
I fight for the god and for the murdered man.

Now my curse on the murderer. Whoever he is,
a lone man unknown in his crime
or one among many, let that man drag out
his life in agony, step by painful step—
I curse myself as well . . . if by any chance
he proves to be an intimate of our house,
here at my hearth, with my full knowledge,
may the curse I just called down on him strike me!

These are your orders: perform them to the last.
I command you, for my sake, for Apollo's, for this country
blasted root and branch by the angry heavens.

Sphinx and the Elders of Thebes. c. 490–470 B.C., Haimon Painter, Ancient Greece. Athenian black-figured lekythos, height: 16.2 cm. Freud Museum, London.

Viewing the art: This exquisitely painted lekythos also had a practical purpose. What do you think that might have been? Explain.

Even if god had never urged you on to act,
how could you leave the crime uncleansed so long?
A man so noble—your king, brought down in blood—
you should have searched. But I am the king now,
I hold the throne that he held then, possess his bed
and a wife who shares our seed . . . why, our seed
might be the same, children born of the same mother
might have created blood-bonds between us
if his hope of offspring hadn't met disaster°—
but fate swooped at his head and cut him short.
So I will fight for him as if he were my father,
stop at nothing, search the world
to lay my hands on the man who shed his blood,
the son of Labdacus descended of Polydorus,
Cadmus of old and Agenor,° founder of the line:
their power and mine are one.
Oh dear gods,
my curse on those who disobey these orders!
Let no crops grow out of the earth for them—
shrivel their women,° kill their sons,
burn them to nothing in this plague
that hits us now, or something even worse.
But you, loyal men of Thebes who approve my actions,
may our champion, Justice, may all the gods
be with us, fight beside us to the end!

296–299 our seed . . . disaster: If Laius had fathered children before his death, Oedipus would be their stepfather.

305 Agenor: father of Cadmus.

309 shrivel their women: keep them from bearing any more children and carrying on the family line.

Oedipus Replying to the Sphinx, 1930–1931. Glyn Philpot (Great Britain). Bronze, height: 84 cm. Tate Gallery, London.

Viewing the sculpture: What do you think the figure's hand gestures and facial expression suggest about Oedipus?

LEADER. In the grip of your curse, my king, I swear
I'm not the murderer, cannot point him out.
As for the search, Apollo pressed it on us—
he should name the killer.

OEDIPUS. Quite right,
but to force the gods to act against their will—
no man has the power.

LEADER. Then if I might mention
the next best thing . . .

OEDIPUS. The third best too—
don't hold back, say it.

LEADER. I still believe . . .
Lord Tiresias sees with the eyes of Lord Apollo.°
Anyone searching for the truth, my king,
might learn it from the prophet, clear as day.

OEDIPUS. I've not been slow with that. On Creon's cue
I sent the escorts, twice, within the hour.
I'm surprised he isn't here.

LEADER. We need him—
without him we have nothing but old, useless rumors.

OEDIPUS. Which rumors? I'll search out every word.

LEADER. Laius was killed, they say, by certain travelers.

OEDIPUS. I know—but no one can find the murderer.

LEADER. If the man has a trace of fear in him
he won't stay silent long,
not with your curses ringing in his ears.

OEDIPUS. He didn't flinch at murder,
he'll never flinch at words.

[*Enter* TIRESIAS, *the blind prophet, led by a boy with escorts in attendance. He remains at a distance.*]

LEADER. Here is the one who will convict him, look,
they bring him on at last, the seer, the man of god.
The truth lives inside him, him alone.°

OEDIPUS. O Tiresias,
master of all the mysteries of our life,
all you teach and all you dare not tell,
signs in the heavens, signs that walk the earth!°
Blind as you are, you can feel all the more
what sickness haunts our city. You, my lord,
are the one shield, the one savior we can find.

323 **sees with the eyes of Lord Apollo:** knows information hidden from other mortals.

339 **The truth lives . . . alone:** Only the seer Tiresias can reveal what happened so long ago.

343 **signs . . . the earth:** the will of the gods as shown in the movement of celestial bodies and in animal behavior.

We asked Apollo—perhaps the messengers
haven't told you—he sent his answer back:
"Relief from the plague can only come one way.
Uncover the murderers of Laius,
put them to death or drive them into exile."
So I beg you, grudge us nothing now, no voice,
no message plucked from the birds,° the embers
or the other mantic° ways within your grasp.°
Rescue yourself, your city, rescue me—
rescue everything infected by the dead.
We are in your hands. For a man to help others
with all his gifts and native strength:
that is the noblest work.

TIRESIAS. How terrible—to see the truth
when the truth is only pain to him who sees!
I knew it well, but I put it from my mind,
else I never would have come.

OEDIPUS. What's this? Why so grim, so dire?

TIRESIAS. Just send me home. You bear your burdens,
I'll bear mine. It's better that way,
please believe me.

OEDIPUS. Strange response . . . unlawful,
unfriendly too to the state that bred and raised you;
you're withholding the word of god.

TIRESIAS. I fail to see
that your own words are so well-timed.
I'd rather not have the same thing said of me . . .

OEDIPUS. For the love of god, don't turn away,
not if you know something. We beg you,
all of us on our knees.

TIRESIAS. None of you knows—
and I will never reveal my dreadful secrets,
not to say your own.

OEDIPUS. What? You know and you won't tell?
You're bent on betraying us, destroying Thebes?

TIRESIAS. I'd rather not cause pain for you or me.
So why this . . . useless interrogation?
You'll get nothing from me.

OEDIPUS. Nothing! You,
you scum of the earth, you'd enrage a heart of stone!
You won't talk? Nothing moves you?
Out with it, once and for all!

352–354 **grudge us nothing . . . within your grasp:** do not hold back any of your power to help us.

353 **message plucked from the birds:** mystery revealed by studying internal organs of dead birds or the flight of living ones.

354 **mantic:** relating to divination, the discovery or interpretation of divine will.

TIRESIAS. You criticize my temper . . .° unaware
of the one *you* live with, you revile° me.

OEDIPUS. Who could restrain his anger hearing you?
What outrage—you spurn the city!

TIRESIAS. What will come will come.
Even if I shroud it all in silence.

OEDIPUS. What will come? You're bound to *tell* me that.

TIRESIAS. I'll say no more. Do as you like, build your anger
to whatever pitch you please, rage your worst—

OEDIPUS. Oh I'll let loose, I have such fury in me—
now I see it all. You helped hatch the plot,
you did the work, yes, short of killing him
with your own hands—and given eyes° I'd say
you did the killing single-handed!

TIRESIAS. Is that so!
I charge you, then, submit to that decree
you just laid down: from this day onward
speak to no one, not these citizens, not myself.
You are the curse, the corruption of the land!

OEDIPUS. You, shameless—
aren't you appalled to start up such a story?
You think you can get away with this?

TIRESIAS. I have already.
The truth with all its power lives inside me.

OEDIPUS. Who primed you° for this? Not your prophet's
trade.

TIRESIAS. You did, you forced me, twisted it out of me.

OEDIPUS. What? Say it again—I'll understand it better.

TIRESIAS. Didn't you understand, just now?
Or are you tempting me to talk?

OEDIPUS. No, I can't say I grasped your meaning.
Out with it, again!

TIRESIAS. I say you are the murderer you hunt.

OEDIPUS. That obscenity, twice—by god, you'll pay.

TIRESIAS. Shall I say more, so you can really rage?

OEDIPUS. Much as you want. Your words are nothing—
futile.

TIRESIAS. You cannot imagine . . . I tell you,
you and your loved ones live together in infamy,
you cannot see how far you've gone in guilt.

384 temper: Here, *temper* refers to character; the qualities that determine how a person behaves.

385 revile: abuse verbally.

396 and given eyes: (ironic) if I had knowledge of the past.

406 primed you: instructed you beforehand in what to say.

OEDIPUS. You think you can keep this up and never suffer?

TIRESIAS. Indeed, if the truth has any power.

OEDIPUS. It does
but not for you, old man. You've lost your power,
stone-blind, stone-deaf—senses, eyes blind as stone!

TIRESIAS. I pity you, flinging at me the very insults
each man here will fling at you so soon.

OEDIPUS. Blind,
lost in the night, endless night that nursed you!
You can't hurt me or anyone else who sees the light—
you can never touch me.

TIRESIAS. True, it is not your fate
to fall at my hands. Apollo is quite enough,
and he will take some pains to work this out.

OEDIPUS. Creon! Is this conspiracy his or yours?

TIRESIAS. Creon is not your downfall, no, you are your own.

OEDIPUS. O power—
wealth and empire, skill outstripping skill
in the heady° rivalries of life,
what envy lurks inside you!° Just for this,
the crown the city gave me—I never sought it,
they laid it in my hands—for this alone, Creon,
the soul of trust, my loyal friend from the start
steals against me . . . so hungry to overthrow me
he sets this wizard on me, this scheming quack,
this fortune-teller peddling lies, eyes peeled
for his own profit—seer blind in his craft!

433–435 O power . . . lurks inside you: competition for power leads to jealousy.

434 heady: intoxicating; dizzying.

Come here, you pious fraud. Tell me,
when did you ever prove yourself a prophet?
When the Sphinx, that chanting Fury° kept her
deathwatch here,
why silent then, not a word to set our people free?
There was a riddle, not for some passer-by to solve—
it cried out for a prophet. Where were you?
Did you rise to the crisis? Not a word,
you and your birds, your gods—nothing.
No, but I came by, Oedipus the ignorant,
I stopped the Sphinx! With no help from the birds,
the flight of my own intelligence hit the mark.

445 Fury: The Furies were three avenging spirits who punished crimes that were beyond the reach of human justice. This reference is used loosely by Oedipus; the Sphinx was not one of the Furies.

And this is the man you'd try to overthrow?

Tiresias, 1946. Mark Rothko (United States). Oil on canvas, 79⅞ x 46¼ in. Collection of Christopher Rothko.

Viewing the painting: Which shapes in the painting suggest the form of a human being? How do they reflect the character of Tiresias in the play?

You think you'll stand by Creon when he's king?
You and the great mastermind—
you'll pay in tears, I promise you, for this,
this witch-hunt.° If you didn't look so senile
the lash° would teach you what your scheming means!

LEADER. I would suggest his words were spoken in anger,
Oedipus . . . yours too, and it isn't what we need.
The best solution to the oracle, the riddle°
posed by god—we should look for that.

TIRESIAS. You are the king no doubt, but in one respect,
at least, I am your equal: the right to reply.
I claim that privilege too.
I am not your slave. I serve Apollo.
I don't need Creon to speak for me in public.
So,
you mock my blindness? Let me tell you this.
You with your precious eyes,
you're blind to the corruption of your life,
to the house° you live in, those you live with—
who *are* your parents? Do you know? All unknowing
you are the scourge of your own flesh and blood,
the dead below the earth and the living here above,
and the double lash of your mother and your father's curse
will whip you from this land one day, their footfall
treading you down in terror,° darkness shrouding°
your eyes that now can see the light!
Soon, soon
you'll scream aloud—what haven won't reverberate?°
What rock of Cithaeron° won't scream back in echo?
That day you learn the truth about your marriage,
the wedding-march that sang you into your halls,
the lusty voyage home to the fatal harbor!°
And a load of other horrors you'd never dream
will level you with yourself and all your children.

There. Now smear us with insults—Creon, myself
and every word I've said. No man will ever
be rooted from the earth as brutally as you.

OEDIPUS. Enough! Such filth from him? Insufferable°—
what, still alive? Get out—
faster, back where you came from—vanish!

TIRESIAS. I'd never have come if you hadn't called me here.

458 witch-hunt: false accusation; search for evidence that does not exist.

459 lash: whip.

462 solution to the . . . riddle: The precise meaning of an oracle was often vague or ambiguous (open to different interpretations).

472 house: in this use, a family including ancestors, descendants, and close relatives.

477–478 footfall . . . in terror: memory of what occurred will haunt you.

478 shrouding: covering; ironic, because a shroud is also used to cover the dead.

480 you'll scream . . . reverberate: you will find no escape from the horror.

481 Cithaeron: a remote mountain range.

484 lusty voyage . . . harbor: refers to the consummation of Oedipus' marriage to Jocasta.

490 Insufferable: unbearable; intolerable.

OEDIPUS. If I thought you'd blurt out such absurdities,
you'd have died waiting before I'd had you summoned.

TIRESIAS. Absurd, am I? To you, not to your parents:
the ones who bore you found me sane enough.

OEDIPUS. Parents—who? Wait . . . who is my father?

TIRESIAS. This day will bring your birth and your destruction.

OEDIPUS. Riddles—all you can say are riddles, murk and darkness.

TIRESIAS. Ah, but aren't you the best man alive at solving riddles?

OEDIPUS. Mock me for that, go on, and you'll reveal my greatness.

TIRESIAS. Your great good fortune, true, it was your ruin.

OEDIPUS. Not if I saved the city—what do I care?

The Oracle. George Edward Robertson (Great Britain, b. 1864). Oil on canvas, 145.5 x 250.2 cm. Private collection.

Viewing the painting: Which figure in this painting do you think has come, like Creon, to request a prophecy from the oracle? How can you tell?

TIRESIAS. Well then, I'll be going.

[*To his* ATTENDANT.]

Take me home, boy.

OEDIPUS. Yes, take him away. You're a nuisance here.
Out of the way, the irritation's gone.

[*Turning his back on* TIRESIAS, *moving toward the palace*.]

TIRESIAS. I will go,
once I have said what I came here to say.
I'll never shrink from the anger in your eyes—
you can't destroy me. Listen to me closely:
the man you've sought so long, proclaiming,
cursing up and down, the murderer of Laius—
he is here. A stranger,°
you may think, who lives among you,
he soon will be revealed a native Theban
but he will take no joy in the revelation.
Blind who now has eyes, beggar who now is rich,
he will grope his way toward a foreign soil,
a stick tapping before him step by step.

[OEDIPUS *enters the palace*.]

Revealed at last, brother and father both
to the children he embraces, to his mother
son and husband both—he sowed the loins
his father sowed,° he spilled his father's blood!

Go in and reflect on that, solve that.
And if you find I've lied
from this day onward call the prophet blind.

[TIRESIAS *and the* BOY *exit to the side*.]

CHORUS. Who—
who is the man the voice of god denounces
resounding out of the rocky gorge of Delphi?
The horror too dark to tell,
whose ruthless bloody hands have done the work?
His time has come to fly
to outrace the stallions of the storm
his feet a streak of speed—
Cased in armor, Apollo son of the Father°
lunges on him, lightning-bolts afire!
And the grim unerring Furies
closing for the kill.

513 **stranger:** in its original sense, a stranger was a foreigner or a person in another's house as a guest or as an intruder.

522–523 **sowed the loins . . . sowed:** had children with the same woman with whom his father had children.

534 **the Father:** Zeus.

Look,
the word of god has just come blazing
flashing off Parnassus'° snowy heights!
That man who left no trace—
after him, hunt him down with all our strength!
Now under bristling timber
up through rocks and caves he stalks
like the wild mountain bull—
cut off from men, each step an agony, frenzied, racing blind
but he cannot outrace the dread voices of Delphi
ringing out of the heart of Earth,°
the dark wings° beating around him shrieking doom
the doom that never dies, the terror—
The skilled prophet scans the birds and shatters me with terror!
I can't accept him, can't deny him, don't know what to say,
I'm lost, and the wings of dark foreboding beating—
I cannot see what's come, what's still to come . . .
and what could breed a blood feud between
Laius' house and the son of Polybus?°
I know of nothing, not in the past and not now,
no charge to bring against our king, no cause
to attack his fame that rings throughout Thebes—
not without proof—not for the ghost of Laius,
not to avenge a murder gone without a trace.

Zeus and Apollo know, they know, the great masters
of all the dark and depth of human life.
But whether a mere man can know the truth,
whether a seer can fathom° more than I—
there is no test, no certain proof
though matching skill for skill
a man can outstrip a rival. No, not till I see
these charges proved will I side with his accusers.
We saw him then, when the she-hawk° swept against him,
saw with our own eyes his skill, his brilliant triumph—
there was the test—he was the joy of Thebes!°
Never will I convict my king, never in my heart.

539 Parnassus: twin-peaked mountain near Delphi, sacred to Apollo and Dionysus.

547 the heart of Earth: a sacred, egg-shaped stone in the temple at Delphi was said to mark the center of the earth.

548 dark wings: The Furies are often depicted as winged monsters.

555 son of Polybus: Oedipus; Polybus was the king of Corinth who raised Oedipus.

563–571 whether a mere man . . . joy of Thebes: They will not believe that the hero who saved Thebes can be guilty without positive proof.

564 fathom: here, understand a mysterious or complex matter.

569 she-hawk: the Sphinx.

Responding to Literature

Personal Response

What did you find most surprising in this section of the play? Explain.

Analyzing Literature

Recall and Interpret

1. Why do the Theban citizens come to Oedipus at the beginning of the play? How would you describe Oedipus' response to them?
2. According to Apollo's oracle, why has the plague hit Thebes? What does this explanation suggest about ancient Greek beliefs?
3. Who is Tiresias? Why has Oedipus summoned him?
4. What accusation does Tiresias make against Oedipus? How do you interpret his statement that Oedipus is "blind"?
5. How does Oedipus react to Tiresias's accusation? What might this suggest about his character?

Evaluate and Connect

6. How would you describe the **mood** of the play (see page R7)? What speeches help establish this mood?
7. How might a modern leader respond to the plea of the Theban citizens at the beginning of the play?
8. In your opinion, does Oedipus propose a just punishment for the murderer of Laius? Explain.
9. In what ways does *Oedipus the King* resemble a mystery story?
10. Do you think it is always better to know the truth, no matter what the consequences? Explain.

Literary ELEMENTS

Chorus

In ancient Greek drama, the **chorus** was a group of performers who danced and sang together between scenes. They performed on a circular platform between the audience and the stage. Usually their songs comment on the action that has just occurred. The chorus served as a bridge between actors and audience, expressing traditional social and religious views that many in the audience would have shared.

1. Who, do you think, is represented by the chorus in *Oedipus the King*?
2. How do the lines of the chorus differ from other speeches in the play?
3. How does Sophocles involve the chorus in the play's action?

- See **Literary Terms Handbook**, p. R2.

Extending Your Response

Creative Writing

Letter from a Troubled City Imagine that you are traveling through ancient Greece. When you arrive in Thebes, you find the city in turmoil because of the plague. Describe this crisis in a letter to a friend or relative. Express your opinion of the Theban citizens and their leaders. Make sure to base your description on information in the play.

Literature Groups

Rounding Up Suspects Tiresias makes a surprising accusation when he is brought before Oedipus. Do you think that Oedipus is a likely suspect in the murder case? How did you react to Oedipus' charge that Tiresias and Creon have plotted against him? Discuss these accusations in your group. Support your opinions with evidence from the play.

Save your work for your portfolio.

JOCASTA. There were five in the party, a herald among them,
and a single wagon carrying Laius.

OEDIPUS. Ai—
now I can see it all, clear as day.
Who told you all this at the time, Jocasta?

JOCASTA. A servant who reached home, the lone survivor.

OEDIPUS. So, could he still be in the palace—even now?

JOCASTA. No indeed. Soon as he returned from the scene
and saw you on the throne with Laius dead and gone,
he knelt and clutched my hand, pleading with me
to send him into the hinterlands,° to pasture,
far as possible, out of sight of Thebes.
I sent him away. Slave though he was,
he'd earned that favor—and much more.

OEDIPUS. Can we bring him back, quickly?

JOCASTA. Easily. Why do you want him so?

OEDIPUS. I'm afraid,
Jocasta, I have said too much already.
That man—I've got to see him.

JOCASTA. Then he'll come.
But even I have a right, I'd like to think,
to know what's torturing you, my lord.

OEDIPUS. And so you shall—I can hold nothing back from you,
now I've reached this pitch of dark foreboding.
Who means more to me than you? Tell me,
whom would I turn toward but you
as I go through all this?

My father was Polybus, king of Corinth.
My mother, a Dorian,° Merope. And I was held
the prince of the realm among the people there,
till something struck me out of nowhere,
something strange . . . worth remarking perhaps,
hardly worth the anxiety I gave it.
Some man at a banquet who had drunk too much
shouted out—he was far gone, mind you—
that I am not my father's son. Fighting words!
I barely restrained myself that day
but early the next I went to mother and father,
questioned them closely, and they were enraged
at the accusation and the fool who let it fly.

837 **hinterlands:** remote regions lying inland from the coast.

853 **Dorian:** one of four cultural groups that occupied ancient Greece; the Dorians founded the city of Corinth.

So as for my parents I was satisfied,
but still this thing kept gnawing at me,
the slander° spread—I had to make my move.
And so,
unknown to mother and father I set out for Delphi,
and the god Apollo spurned me, sent me away
denied the facts I came for,
but first he flashed before my eyes a future
great with pain, terror, disaster—I can hear him cry,
"You are fated to couple with° your mother, you will bring
a breed of children into the light no man can bear to see—
you will kill your father, the one who gave you life!"
I heard all that and ran. I abandoned Corinth,
from that day on I gauged its landfall only
by the stars,° running, always running
toward some place where I would never see
the shame of all those oracles come true.
And as I fled I reached that very spot
where the great king, you say, met his death.
Now, Jocasta, I will tell you all.
Making my way toward this triple crossroad
I began to see a herald, then a brace° of colts
drawing a wagon, and mounted on the bench . . . a man,
just as you've described him, coming face-to-face,
and the one in the lead and the old man himself
were about to thrust me off the road—brute force—
and the one shouldering me aside, the driver,
I strike him in anger!—and the old man, watching me
coming up along his wheels—he brings down
his prod, two prongs straight at my head!
I paid him back with interest!
Short work, by god—with one blow of the staff
in this right hand I knock him out of his high seat,
roll him out of the wagon, sprawling headlong—
I killed them all—every mother's son!

Oh, but if there is any blood-tie
between Laius and this stranger . . .
what man alive more miserable than I?
More hated by the gods? *I* am the man
no alien, no citizen welcomes to his house,
law forbids it—not a word to me in public,
driven out of every hearth° and home.

867 slander: false speech meant to damage another's reputation.

873 couple with: marry.

877–878 gauged . . . the stars: never went near Corinth.

885 brace: matched pair.

905 hearth: fireplace; in ancient Greece, the most important part of the home.

And all these curses I—no one but I
brought down these piling° curses on myself!
And you, his wife, I've touched your body with these,
the hands that killed your husband cover you with blood.

Wasn't I born for torment? Look me in the eyes!
I am abomination°—heart and soul!
I must be exiled, and even in exile
never see my parents, never set foot
on native earth° again. Else I'm doomed
to couple with my mother and cut my father down . . .
Polybus who reared me, gave me life.
But why, why?
Wouldn't a man of judgment say—and wouldn't he be
right—
some savage power has brought this down upon my head?

Oh no, not that, you pure and awesome° gods,
never let me see that day! Let me slip
from the world of men, vanish without a trace
before I see myself stained with such corruption,
stained to the heart.

LEADER. My lord, you fill our hearts with fear.
But at least until you question the witness,
do take hope.

OEDIPUS. Exactly. He is my last hope—
I am waiting for the shepherd. He is crucial.°

JOCASTA. And once he appears, what then? Why so urgent?

907 **piling:** mounting.

911 **abomination:** something disgusting or loathsome; wickedness.

913–914 **set foot . . . native earth:** return to Corinth.

919 **awesome:** in this use, deserving of fear and worship.

927 **crucial:** essential; decisive.

Oedipus Kills Laius on Chariot. 3rd century A.D., Ancient Rome. Marble relief from a sarcophagus. Vatican Museums, Vatican City.

Viewing the relief: What does this scene tell you about Laius' murder? Do you see anything that might foreshadow a future event?

OEDIPUS. I'll tell you. If it turns out that his story
matches yours, I've escaped the worst.

JOCASTA. What did I say? What struck you so?

OEDIPUS. You said *thieves*—
he told you a whole band of them murdered Laius.
So, if he still holds to the same number,
I cannot be the killer. One can't equal many.
But if he refers to one man, one alone,
clearly the scales° come down on me:°
I am guilty.

JOCASTA. Impossible. Trust me,
I told you precisely what he said,
and he can't retract° it now;
the whole city heard it, not just I.
And even if he should vary his first report
by one man more or less, still, my lord,
he could never make the murder of Laius
truly fit the prophecy. Apollo was explicit:
my son was doomed to kill my husband . . . my son,
poor defenseless thing, he never had a chance
to kill his father. They destroyed him first.

So much for prophecy. It's neither here nor there.
From this day on, I wouldn't look right or left.

OEDIPUS. True, true. Still, that shepherd,
someone fetch him—now!

JOCASTA. I'll send at once. But do let's go inside.
I'd never displease you, least of all in this.

[*OEDIPUS and JOCASTA enter the palace.*]

CHORUS. Destiny° guide me always
Destiny find me filled with reverence
pure in word and deed.
Great laws tower above us, reared on high
born for the brilliant vault of heaven—
Olympian° Sky their only father,
nothing mortal, no man gave them birth,
their memory deathless, never lost in sleep:
within them lives a mighty god, the god does not grow old.°

Pride° breeds the tyrant
violent pride, gorging, crammed to bursting
with all that is overripe and rich with ruin—

936 scales: an instrument of measurement made from two trays of equal weight on either side of a balanced center beam. **scales come down on me:** the weight of the evidence is against me.

939 retract: take back or deny.

954 Destiny: refers to a future that has been determined in advance and the outcome of which is inevitable.

957–962 Great laws . . . grow old: The gods have decreed certain unchanging laws that cannot be disobeyed.

959 Olympian: of or relating to Olympus, the highest mountain in Greece and home of the gods.

963 Pride: here, the Greek concept of *hubris;* pride that goes beyond acceptable limits and brings on divine punishment.

clawing up to the heights, headlong pride
crashes down the abyss—sheer doom!
No footing helps, all foothold lost and gone.°
But the healthy strife° that makes the city strong—
I pray that god will never end that wrestling:
god, my champion, I will never let you go.

But if any man comes striding, high and mighty
in all he says and does,
no fear of justice, no reverence
for the temples of the gods—
let a rough doom tear him down,
repay his pride, breakneck, ruinous pride!
If he cannot reap his profits fairly
cannot restrain himself from outrage—
mad, laying hands on the holy things untouchable!

Can such a man, so desperate, still boast
he can save his life from the flashing bolts of god?
If all such violence goes with honor now
why join the sacred dance?°

Never again will I go reverent to Delphi,
the inviolate° heart of Earth
or Apollo's ancient oracle at Abae
or Olympia° of the fires—
unless these prophecies all come true
for all mankind to point toward in wonder.
King of kings, if you deserve your titles
Zeus, remember, never forget!
You and your deathless, everlasting reign.

They are dying, the old oracles sent to Laius,
now our masters strike them off the rolls.°
Nowhere Apollo's golden glory now—
the gods, the gods go down.

966–968 **clawing up . . . lost and gone:** Hubris can make the mighty overreach and bring about their own doom.

969 **strife:** competition.

983–984 **If all such . . . why join the sacred dance:** If actions such as these go unpunished, why should anyone show reverence for the gods?

986 **inviolate:** pure.

987–988 **Abae or Olympia:** other famous shrines.

995 **rolls:** official records.

Responding to Literature

Personal Response

Has your opinion of Oedipus changed since reading this section of the play? Share your feelings about him with your classmates.

Analyzing Literature

Recall and Interpret

1. Why is Creon upset at the beginning of this section? Why might the leader of the chorus respond as he does to Creon's questions?
2. How is the argument between Oedipus and Creon interrupted? In your opinion, why does Oedipus decide to release Creon?
3. What reason does Jocasta offer for not believing Tiresias? Why does her speech fail to calm Oedipus?
4. Why did Oedipus leave his home in Corinth? What happened on his way to Thebes?
5. Why is Oedipus eager to question the man who witnessed Laius' murder?

Evaluate and Connect

6. In the argument between Oedipus and Creon, which character makes a stronger case? Why?
7. The term **rising action** refers to the part of a plot where complications develop (see page R9). What is the most significant complication in this section of the play?
8. In their song at the end of this section, the chorus says that "Pride breeds the tyrant." Do you think that Oedipus has shown excessive pride? Explain.
9. From your reading of the play, why do you think prophecy was important in ancient Greek religion?
10. Think of a modern political leader who was accused of committing a crime. What steps were taken to investigate the leader?

Literary **ELEMENTS**

Tragedy

A **tragedy** is a play in which the main character is brought to ruin or suffers a great sorrow. In **Greek tragedy,** the main character is a person of dignified or heroic stature. He or she may be a victim of outside forces, but usually the character's downfall is at least partly caused by a flaw or error in judgment. According to the Greek philosopher Aristotle, the purpose of tragedy is to arouse pity (through identification with the main character) and fear (through dread at the possibility of sharing the main character's tragic flaw) in the audience as the main character's terrible fate unfolds.

1. How does knowing that the play is a tragedy influence your expectations about the play?
2. What might encourage you to feel sympathy or admiration for Oedipus?

- See **Literary Terms Handbook,** p. R12.

Extending Your Response

Writing About Literature

Conflict Write an analysis of two conflicts that develop in this section of the play. Explain whether each conflict is **internal** or **external** (see page R2). Offer predictions about how the conflicts you discuss will be resolved.

Interdisciplinary Activity

Art: Making Faces As you have read, Greek actors wore masks while performing, allowing their voices to be amplified and their characters to be recognized easily. Create a mask for a character in *Oedipus the King.*

Save your work for your portfolio.

So for years I've given Corinth a wide berth,
and it's been my good fortune too. But still,
to see one's parents and look into their eyes
is the greatest joy I know.

MESSENGER. You're afraid of that?
That kept you out of Corinth?

OEDIPUS. My *father*, old man—
so I wouldn't kill my father.

MESSENGER. So that's it.
Well then, seeing I came with such good will, my king,
why don't I rid you of that old worry now?

OEDIPUS. What a rich reward you'd have for that.

MESSENGER. What do you think I came for, majesty?
So you'd come home and I'd be better off.

OEDIPUS. Never, I will never go near my parents.

MESSENGER. My boy, it's clear, you don't know what you're doing.

OEDIPUS. What do you mean, old man? For god's sake, explain.

MESSENGER. If you ran from *them*, always dodging home . . .

OEDIPUS. Always, terrified Apollo's oracle might come true—

MESSENGER. And you'd be covered with guilt, from both your parents.

OEDIPUS. That's right, old man, that fear is always with me.

MESSENGER. Don't you know? You've really nothing to fear.

OEDIPUS. But why? If I'm their son—Merope, Polybus?

MESSENGER. Polybus was nothing to you, that's why, not in blood.

OEDIPUS. What are you saying—Polybus was not my father?

MESSENGER. No more than I am. He and I are equals.

OEDIPUS. My father—
how can my father equal nothing? You're nothing to me!

MESSENGER. Neither was he, no more your father than I am.

OEDIPUS. Then why did he call me his son?

MESSENGER. You were a gift,
years ago—know for a fact he took you
from my hands.

OEDIPUS. No, from another's hands?
Then how could he love me so? He loved me, deeply . . .

MESSENGER. True, and his early years without a child
made him love you all the more.

OEDIPUS. And you, did you . . .
buy me? find me by accident?

MESSENGER. I stumbled on you,
down the woody flanks of Mount Cithaeron.

OEDIPUS. So close,
what were you doing here, just passing through?

MESSENGER. Watching over my flocks, grazing them on the slopes.

OEDIPUS. A herdsman, were you? A vagabond, scraping for wages?

MESSENGER. Your savior too, my son, in your worst hour.

OEDIPUS. Oh—
when you picked me up, was I in pain? What exactly?

MESSENGER. Your ankles . . . they tell the story. Look at them.

OEDIPUS. Why remind me of that, that old affliction?

MESSENGER. Your ankles were pinned together; I set you free.

OEDIPUS. That dreadful mark—I've had it from the cradle.

MESSENGER. And you got your name from that misfortune too,
the name's still with you.°

1135–1136 you got your name . . . still with you: One meaning of the word *Oedipus* is "swollen foot."

OEDIPUS. Dear god, who did it?—
mother? father? Tell me.

MESSENGER. I don't know.
The one who gave you to me, he'd know more.

OEDIPUS. What? You took me from someone else?
You didn't find me yourself?

MESSENGER. No sir,
another shepherd passed you on to me.

OEDIPUS. Who? Do you know? Describe him.

MESSENGER. He called himself a servant of . . .
if I remember rightly—Laius.

[JOCASTA *turns sharply.*]

OEDIPUS. The king of the land who ruled here long ago?

MESSENGER. That's the one. That herdsman was *his* man.

OEDIPUS. Is he still alive? Can I see him?

MESSENGER. They'd know best, the people of these parts.

[*OEDIPUS and the MESSENGER turn to the CHORUS.*]

OEDIPUS. Does anyone know that herdsman,
the one he mentioned? Anyone seen him
in the fields, in town? Out with it!
The time has come to reveal this once for all.

LEADER. I think he's the very shepherd you wanted to see,
a moment ago. But the queen, Jocasta,
she's the one to say.

OEDIPUS. Jocasta,
you remember the man we just sent for?
Is *that* the one he means?

JOCASTA. That man . . .
why ask? Old shepherd, talk, empty nonsense,
don't give it another thought, don't even think—

OEDIPUS. What—give up now, with a clue like this?
Fail to solve the mystery of my birth?
Not for all the world!

JOCASTA. Stop—in the name of god,
if you love your own life, call off this search!
My suffering is enough.

OEDIPUS. Courage!
Even if my mother turns out to be a slave,
and I a slave, three generations back,
you would not seem common.

JOCASTA. Oh no,
listen to me, I beg you, don't do this.

OEDIPUS. Listen to you? No more. I must know it all,
see the truth at last.

JOCASTA. No, please—
for your sake—I want the best for you!

OEDIPUS. Your best is more than I can bear.°

1171 Your best . . . I can bear: Not knowing the truth is unbearable.

JOCASTA. You're doomed—
may you never fathom who you are!

OEDIPUS. [*To a SERVANT.*] Hurry, fetch me the herdsman,
now!
Leave her to glory in her royal birth.

JOCASTA. Aieeeeee—
man of agony—
that is the only name I have for you,
that, no other—ever, ever, ever!

[Flinging through the palace doors. A long, tense silence follows.]

LEADER. Where's she gone, Oedipus?
Rushing off, such wild grief . . .
I'm afraid that from this silence
something monstrous may come bursting forth.

OEDIPUS. Let it burst! Whatever will, whatever must!
I must know my birth, no matter how common
it may be—must see my origins face-to-face.
She perhaps, she with her woman's pride
may well be mortified by my birth,
but I, I count myself the son of Chance,
the great goddess, giver of all good things—
I'll never see myself disgraced. She is my mother!°
And the moons have marked me out, my blood-brothers,
one moon on the wane, the next moon great with power.°
That is my blood, my nature—I will never betray it,
never fail to search and learn my birth!

CHORUS. Yes—if I am a true prophet
if I can grasp the truth,
by the boundless skies of Olympus,°
at the full moon of tomorrow, Mount Cithaeron
you will know how Oedipus glories in you—
you, his birthplace, nurse, his mountain-mother!
And we will sing you, dancing out your praise—
you lift our monarch's heart!
Apollo, Apollo, god of the wild cry
may our dancing please you!
Oedipus—
son, dear child, who bore you?
Who of the nymphs° who seem to live forever
mated with Pan,° the mountain-striding Father?
Who was your mother? who, some bride of Apollo
the god who loves the pastures spreading toward the sun?
Or was it Hermes,° king of the lightning ridges?
Or Dionysus, lord of frenzy, lord of the barren peaks—
did he seize you in his hands, dearest of all his lucky
finds?—
found by the nymphs, their warm eyes dancing, gift
to the lord who loves them dancing out his joy!°

1188–1190 I count myself . . . She is my mother: Oedipus believes that he has always had good fortune and therefore has nothing to fear.

1191–1192 the moons . . . great with power: What has seemed to be misfortune has always led to triumph.

1197 by . . . Olympus: by all that is holy.

1205–1214 who bore you . . . dancing out his joy: In mythology, mysterious children often turn out to be the offspring of gods. The Chorus imagines this might be the case with Oedipus.

1206 nymphs: minor female deities who lived in forests, on hills, or in rivers.

1207 Pan: god of fields, forests, and herdsmen, who often was involved romantically with woodland nymphs.

1210 Hermes: god of science, travelers, and vagabonds; pictured with winged helmet and sandals, he was the messenger of the gods.

Jocasta in scene from the 1997 Stratford production of *Oedipus Rex.*

Viewing the play: What do the expressions and gestures of the actors tell you about the scene? Which part of the play do you think is being presented?

[*OEDIPUS strains to see a figure coming from the distance. Attended by PALACE GUARDS, an old SHEPHERD enters slowly, reluctant to approach the king.*]

OEDIPUS. I never met the man, my friends . . . still,
if I had to guess, I'd say that's the shepherd,
the very one we've looked for all along.
Brothers in old age, two of a kind,
he and our guest here. At any rate
the ones who bring him in are my own men,
I recognize them.

[*Turning to the LEADER.*]

But you know more than I,
you should, you've seen the man before.

LEADER. I know him, definitely. One of Laius' men,
a trusty shepherd, if there ever was one.

OEDIPUS. You, I ask you first, stranger,
you from Corinth—is this the one you mean?

MESSENGER. You're looking at him. He's your man.

OEDIPUS. [*To the SHEPHERD.*] You, old man, come over here—
look at me. Answer all my questions.

Did you ever serve King Laius?

SHEPHERD. So I did . . .
a slave, not bought on the block though,
born and reared in the palace.

OEDIPUS. Your duties, your kind of work?

SHEPHERD. Herding the flocks, the better part of my life.

OEDIPUS. Where, mostly? Where did you do your grazing?

SHEPHERD. Well,
Cithaeron sometimes, or the foothills round about.

OEDIPUS. This man—you know him? ever see him there?

SHEPHERD. [*Confused, glancing from the* MESSENGER *to the King.*] Doing what?—what man do you mean?

OEDIPUS. [*Pointing to the* MESSENGER.] This one here—ever have dealings with him?

SHEPHERD. Not so I could say, but give me a chance,
my memory's bad . . .

MESSENGER. No wonder he doesn't know me, master.
But let me refresh his memory for him.
I'm sure he recalls old times we had
on the slopes of Mount Cithaeron;
he and I, grazing our flocks, he with two
and I with one—we both struck up together,
three whole seasons, six months at a stretch
from spring to the rising of Arcturus° in the fall,
then with winter coming on I'd drive my herds
to my own pens, and back he'd go with his
to Laius' folds.°

[*To the* SHEPHERD.]

Now that's how it was,
wasn't it—yes or no?

SHEPHERD. Yes, I suppose . . .
it's all so long ago.

MESSENGER. Come, tell me,
you gave me a child back then, a boy, remember?
A little fellow to rear, my very own.

SHEPHERD. What? Why rake up that again?

MESSENGER. Look, here he is, my fine old friend—
the same man who was just a baby then.

SHEPHERD. Damn you, shut your mouth—quiet!

1249 Arcturus: a star in the northern sky; its rising, or reappearance, in mid-September signaled the end of summer.

1252 folds: enclosure or pen for livestock.

And then—
but how she died is more than I can say. Suddenly
Oedipus burst in, screaming, he stunned us so
we couldn't watch her agony to the end,
our eyes were fixed on him. Circling
like a maddened beast, stalking, here, there,
crying out to us—
Give him a sword! His wife,
no wife, his mother, where can he find the mother earth
that cropped two crops at once, himself and all his children?
He was raging—one of the dark powers pointing the way,
none of us mortals crowding around him, no,
with a great shattering cry—someone, something leading him on—
he hurled at the twin doors and bending the bolts back
out of their sockets, crashed through the chamber.
And there we saw the woman hanging by the neck,
cradled high in a woven noose, spinning,
swinging back and forth. And when he saw her,
giving a low, wrenching sob that broke our hearts,
slipping the halter° from her throat, he eased her down,
in a slow embrace he laid her down, poor thing . . .
then, what came next, what horror we beheld!

He rips off her brooches, the long gold pins
holding her robes—and lifting them high,
looking straight up into the points,
he digs them down the sockets of his eyes, crying, "You,
you'll see no more the pain I suffered, all the pain I caused!
Too long you looked on the ones you never should have seen,°
blind to the ones you longed to see, to know!° Blind
from this hour on! Blind in the darkness—blind!"
His voice like a dirge, rising, over and over
raising the pins, raking them down his eyes.
And at each stroke blood spurts from the roots,
splashing his beard, a swirl of it, nerves and clots—
black hail of blood pulsing, gushing down.

These are the griefs that burst upon them both,
coupling man and woman. The joy they had so lately,
the fortune of their old ancestral house
was deep joy indeed. Now, in this one day,

1399 halter: rope or strap.

1407 the ones you never should have seen: Laius as his victim and Jocasta as his wife.

1408 the ones you longed . . . to know: Laius and Jocasta as his parents.

wailing, madness and doom, death, disgrace,
all the griefs in the world that you can name,
all are theirs forever.

LEADER. Oh poor man, the misery—
has he any rest from pain now?

[*A voice within, in torment.*]

MESSENGER. He's shouting,
"Loose the bolts, someone, show me to all of Thebes!
My father's murderer, my mother's—"
No, I can't repeat it, it's unholy.
Now he'll tear himself from his native earth,°
not linger, curse the house with his own curse.
But he needs strength, and a guide to lead him on.
This is sickness more than he can bear.

[*The palace doors open.*]

Look,
he'll show you himself. The great doors are opening—
you are about to see a sight, a horror
even his mortal enemy would pity.

[*Enter* OEDIPUS, *blinded, led by a boy. He stands at the palace steps, as if surveying his people once again.*]

CHORUS. O the terror—
the suffering, for all the world to see,
the worst terror that ever met my eyes.
What madness swept over you? What god,
what dark power leapt beyond all bounds,
beyond belief, to crush your wretched life?—
godforsaken, cursed by the gods!
I pity you but I can't bear to look.
I've much to ask, so much to learn,
so much fascinates my eyes,
but you . . . I shudder at the sight.

OEDIPUS. Oh, Ohh—
the agony! I am agony—
where am I going? where on earth?
where does all this agony hurl me?
where's my voice?—
winging, swept away on a dark tide—
My destiny, my dark power, what a leap you made!

CHORUS. To the depths of terror, too dark to hear, to see.

OEDIPUS. Dark, horror of darkness
my darkness, drowning, swirling around me

1426 tear . . . his native earth: leave Thebes.

crashing wave on wave—unspeakable, irresistible
headwind, fatal harbor! Oh again,
the misery, all at once, over and over
the stabbing daggers, stab of memory
raking me insane.

CHORUS. No wonder you suffer
twice over, the pain of your wounds,
the lasting grief of pain.

OEDIPUS. Dear friend, still here?
Standing by me, still with a care for me,
the blind man? Such compassion,
loyal to the last. Oh it's you,
I know you're here, dark as it is
I'd know you anywhere, your voice—
it's yours, clearly yours.

CHORUS. Dreadful, what you've done . . .
how could you bear it, gouging out your eyes?
What superhuman power drove you on?

OEDIPUS. Apollo, friends, Apollo—
he ordained my agonies—these, my pains on pains!
But the hand that struck my eyes was mine,
mine alone—no one else—
I did it all myself!
What good were eyes to me?
Nothing I could see could bring me joy.

CHORUS. No, no, exactly as you say.

OEDIPUS. What can I ever see?
What love, what call of the heart
can touch my ears with joy? Nothing, friends.
Take me away, far, far from Thebes,
quickly, cast me away, my friends—
this great murderous ruin, this man cursed to heaven,
the man the deathless gods hate most of all!

CHORUS. Pitiful, you suffer so, you understand so much . . .
I wish you'd never known.

OEDIPUS. Die, die—
whoever he was that day in the wilds
who cut my ankles free of the ruthless pins,
he pulled me clear of death, he saved my life
for this, this kindness—
Curse him, kill him!

If I'd died then, I'd never have dragged myself,
my loved ones through such hell.

CHORUS. Oh if only . . . would to god.

OEDIPUS. I'd never have come to this,
my father's murderer—never been branded
mother's husband, all men see me now! Now,
loathed by the gods, son of the mother I defiled
coupling in my father's bed, spawning lives in the loins
that spawned my wretched life. What grief can crown this grief?
It's mine alone, my destiny—I am Oedipus!

CHORUS. How can I say you've chosen for the best?
Better to die than be alive and blind.

OEDIPUS. What I did was best—don't lecture me,
no more advice. I, with *my* eyes,
how could I look my father in the eyes
when I go down to death? Or mother, so abused . . .
I have done such things to the two of them,
crimes too huge for hanging.

Oedipus, from the 1997 Stratford production of *Oedipus Rex.*

Viewing the play: How does this image depict Oedipus' state at the end of the play?

Worse yet,
the sight of my children, born as they were born,
how could I long to look into their eyes?
No, not with these eyes of mine, never.
Not this city either, her high towers,
the sacred glittering images of her gods—
I am misery! I, her best son, reared
as no other son of Thebes was ever reared,
I've stripped myself, I gave the command myself.°
All men must cast away the great blasphemer,°
the curse now brought to light by the gods,
the son of Laius—I, my father's son!

Now I've exposed my guilt, horrendous guilt,
could I train a level glance on you,° my countrymen?
Impossible! No, if I could just block off my ears,
the springs° of hearing, I would stop at nothing—
I'd wall up my loathsome body like a prison,
blind to the sound of life, not just the sight.
Oblivion—what a blessing . . .
for the mind to dwell a world away from pain.

O Cithaeron, why did you give me shelter?
Why didn't you take me, crush my life out on the spot?
I'd never have revealed my birth to all mankind.

O Polybus, Corinth, the old house of my fathers,
so I believed—what a handsome prince you raised—
under the skin, what sickness to the core.
Look at me! Born of outrage, outrage to the core.

O triple roads—it all comes back, the secret,
dark ravine, and the oaks closing in
where the three roads join . . .
You drank my father's blood, my own blood
spilled by my own hands—you still remember me?
What things you saw me do? Then I came here
and did them all once more!
Marriages! O marriage,
you gave me birth, and once you brought me into the
world
you brought my sperm rising back, springing to light
fathers, brothers, sons—one murderous breed—
brides, wives, mothers. The blackest things
a man can do, I have done them all!

1512 **I've stripped . . . command myself:** Oedipus issued the proclamation that decreed the murderer's punishment.

1513 **blasphemer:** one who has shown contempt for something sacred.

1517 **train a level glance on you:** look you in the eye.

1519 **springs:** here, source.

No more—
it's wrong to name what's wrong to do. Quickly,
for the love of god, hide me somewhere,
kill me, hurl me into the sea
where you can never look on me again.

[*Beckoning to the* CHORUS *as they shrink away.*]

Closer,
it's all right. Touch the man of sorrow.
Do. Don't be afraid. My troubles are mine
and I am the only man alive who can sustain° them.

[*Enter* CREON *from the palace, attended by palace* GUARDS.]

LEADER. Put your requests to Creon. Here he is,
just when we need him. He'll have a plan, he'll act.
Now that he's the sole defense of the country
in your place.

OEDIPUS. Oh no, what can I say to him?
How can I ever hope to win his trust?
I wronged him so, just now, in every way.
You must see that—I was so wrong, so wrong.

CREON. I haven't come to mock you, Oedipus,
or to criticize your former failings.

[*Turning to the* GUARDS.]

You there,
have you lost all respect for human feeling?
At least revere the Sun, the holy fire
that keeps us all alive. Never expose a thing
of guilt and holy dread so great it appalls
the earth, the rain from heaven, the light of day!
Get him into the halls—quickly as you can.
Piety° demands no less. Kindred alone
should see a kinsman's shame. This is obscene.

OEDIPUS. Please, in god's name . . . you wipe my fears away,
coming so generously° to me, the worst of men.
Do one thing more, for your sake, not mine.

CREON. What do you want? Why so insistent?

OEDIPUS. Drive me out of the land at once, far from sight,
where I can never hear a human voice.

CREON. I'd have done that already, I promise you.
First I wanted the god to clarify my duties.

OEDIPUS. The god? His command was clear, every word:

1549 sustain: here, suffer; Oedipus is suggesting that his troubles are not contagious and cannot be transmitted to others by touch.

1565 Piety: loyalty to natural or fundamental obligations, often used with respect to religious devotion.

1568 coming so generously: Creon's kindness goes beyond what Oedipus has any right to expect.

death for the father-killer, the curse—
he said destroy me!

CREON. So he did. Still, in such a crisis
it's better to ask precisely what to do.

OEDIPUS. You'd ask the oracle about a man like me?°

CREON. By all means. And this time, I assume,
even you will obey the god's decrees.

OEDIPUS. I will,
I will. And you, I command you—I beg you . . .
the woman inside, bury her as you see fit.
It's the only decent thing,
to give your own the last rites. As for me,
never condemn the city of my fathers
to house my body, not while I'm alive, no,
let me live on the mountains, on Cithaeron,
my favorite haunt, I have made it famous.
Mother and father marked out that rock
to be my everlasting tomb—buried alive.
Let me die there, where they tried to kill me.

Oh but this I know: no sickness can destroy me,
nothing can. I would never have been saved
from death—I have been saved
for something great and terrible, something strange.
Well let my destiny come and take me on its way!

About my children, Creon, the boys at least,
don't burden yourself. They're men;°
wherever they go, they'll find the means to live.
But my two daughters, my poor helpless girls,
clustering at our table, never without me
hovering near them . . . whatever I touched,
they always had their share. Take care of them,
I beg you. Wait, better—permit me, would you?
Just to touch them with my hands and take
our fill of tears. Please . . . my king.
Grant it, with all your noble heart.
If I could hold them, just once, I'd think
I had them with me, like the early days
when I could see their eyes.

[ANTIGONE and ISMENE, two small children, are led in from the palace by a nurse.]

1580 ask the oracle . . . me: refers to the practice of consulting oracles only for matters of utmost importance. Oedipus now thinks he is unworthy; ironic, because the oracle has already played a large role in Oedipus' life.

1600 They're men: refers to the boys' gender and the opportunities open to males in ancient Greek society; it is not a reference to their age.

What's that?
O god! Do I really hear you sobbing?—
my two children. Creon, you've pitied me?
Sent me my darling girls, my own flesh and blood!
Am I right?

CREON. Yes, it's my doing.
I know the joy they gave you all these years,
the joy you must feel now.

OEDIPUS. Bless you, Creon!
May god watch over you for this kindness,
better than he ever guarded me.
Children, where are you?
Here, come quickly—

[*Groping for* ANTIGONE *and* ISMENE, *who approach their father cautiously, then embrace him.*]

Come to these hands of mine,
your brother's hands, your own father's hands°
that served his once bright eyes so well—
that made them blind. Seeing nothing, children,
knowing nothing, I became your father,
I fathered you in the soil that gave me life.

How I weep for you—I cannot see you now . . .
just thinking of all your days to come, the bitterness,
the life that rough mankind will thrust upon you.
Where are the public gatherings you can join,
the banquets of the clans? Home you'll come,
in tears, cut off from the sight of it all,
the brilliant rites unfinished.
And when you reach perfection, ripe for marriage,
who will he be, my dear ones? Risking all
to shoulder the curse that weighs down my parents,
yes and you too—that wounds us all together.
What more misery could you want?
Your father killed his father, sowed his mother,
one, one and the selfsame womb sprang you—
he cropped the very roots of his existence.°

Such disgrace, and you must bear it all!
Who will marry you then? Not a man on earth.
Your doom is clear: you'll wither away to nothing,
single, without a child.

[*Turning to* CREON.]

1622 your brother's . . . father's hands: because Oedipus married his mother and had children with her, these children are both sisters and daughters to him.

1641 cropped . . . existence: fathered children by his own mother.

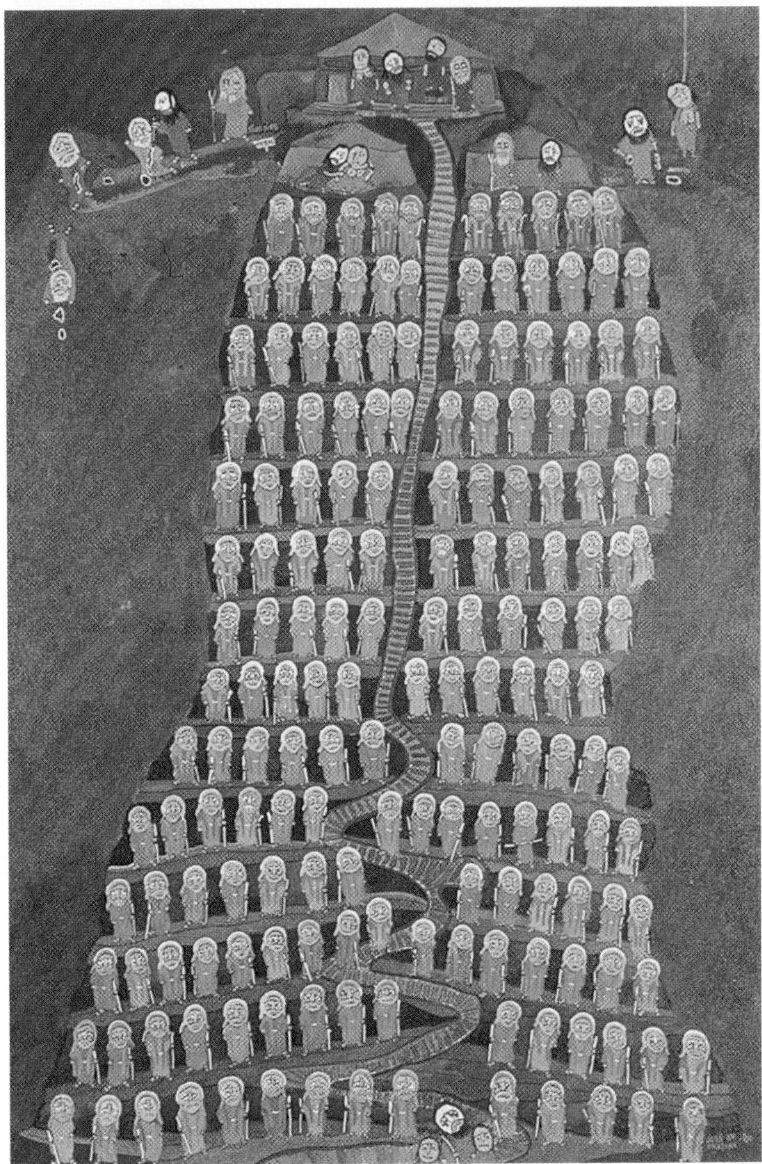

Oedipus Rex. Jose de Freitas (Brazil, b. 1935). Fundaccao Nacional de Arte, Brazil.

Viewing the painting: What elements from the tragedy has the artist included in this scene?

Oh Creon,
you are the only father they have now . . .
we who brought them into the world
are gone, both gone at a stroke—
Don't let them go begging, abandoned,
women without men. Your own flesh and blood!
Never bring them down to the level of my pains.
Pity them. Look at them, so young, so vulnerable,
shorn of everything—you're their only hope.
Promise me, noble Creon, touch my hand.

[*Reaching toward* CREON, *who draws back.*]

You, little ones, if you were old enough
to understand, there is much I'd tell you.
Now, as it is, I'd have you say a prayer.

Pray for life, my children,
live where you are free to grow and season.°
Pray god you find a better life than mine,
the father who begot you.

CREON. Enough.
You've wept enough. Into the palace now.

OEDIPUS. I must, but I find it very hard.

CREON. Time is the great healer, you will see.

OEDIPUS. I am going—you know on what condition?

CREON. Tell me. I'm listening.

OEDIPUS. Drive me out of Thebes, in exile.

CREON. Not I. Only the gods can give you that.

OEDIPUS. Surely the gods hate me so much—

CREON. You'll get your wish at once.

OEDIPUS. You consent?

CREON. I try to say what I mean; it's my habit.

OEDIPUS. Then take me away. It's time.

CREON. Come along, let go of the children.

OEDIPUS. No—
don't take them away from me, not now! No no no!

[*Clutching his daughters as the* GUARDS *wrench them loose and take them through the palace doors.*]

CREON. Still the king, the master of all things?
No more: here your power ends.
None of your power follows you through life.

[*Exit* OEDIPUS *and* CREON *to the palace. The* CHORUS *comes forward to address the audience directly.*]

CHORUS. People of Thebes, my countrymen, look on
Oedipus.
He solved the famous riddle with his brilliance,
he rose to power, a man beyond all power.
Who could behold his greatness without envy?
Now what a black sea of terror has overwhelmed him.
Now as we keep our watch° and wait the final day,°
count no man happy till he dies, free of pain at last.°

[*Exit in procession.*]

1659 **season:** mature; age properly.

1683 **watch:** period of time during which a person is employed to protect someone or something. **keep . . . final day:** try to live our lives in keeping with honor and duty.

1684 **count no man . . . at last:** Do not call any man happy until he dies, because up until that point his fate is unknown and no one can predict what the future holds in store.

Responding to Literature

Personal Response

What went through your mind as you finished reading this play? Record your reactions in your journal.

Analyzing Literature

Recall

1. At the beginning of this section, a messenger arrives in Thebes. What news does he bring?
2. What does the messenger tell Oedipus about his birth?
3. What does Oedipus learn from the shepherd who gave him to the messenger when he was an infant?
4. How does Oedipus explain his decision to blind himself?
5. What additional punishment does Oedipus ask for?

Interpret

6. Why does the message from Corinth make Jocasta happy?
7. After the messenger tells Oedipus about his birth, what is the worst outcome that Oedipus foresees?
8. Why does Jocasta try to prevent Oedipus from questioning the shepherd?
9. Why, do you think, does Oedipus ask for a sword after finding out that Jocasta is his mother?
10. How do you interpret the final speech of the chorus?

Evaluate and Connect

11. In a dramatic work, the **climax** is the point of greatest interest or emotional intensity (see **Literary Terms Handbook,** page R2). What is the climax of *Oedipus the King*?
12. Do you think that Oedipus should have figured out the truth about his past sooner than he does? Why or why not?
13. In your opinion, should Oedipus be banished from Thebes? Explain your answer.
14. What do you predict will happen in Thebes after Oedipus' fall from power?
15. Think of a real-life tragic event that you have read about or witnessed. Compare your reaction to this event with your feelings as you finished reading *Oedipus the King.*

Literary ELEMENTS

Dramatic Irony

Dramatic irony occurs when the reader or audience knows something important that a character does not know. This technique can add to the enjoyment of a literary work, much as one might enjoy knowing a secret in real life. Sophocles is considered a master of dramatic irony, which he used to great effect in *Oedipus the King.* Since most ancient Greeks were familiar with the story of Oedipus, they would have known from the outset that Oedipus killed Laius and married his mother. Many of Oedipus' statements in the play carry a meaning unknown to him but understood by the audience. The dramatic irony results in a contrast between Oedipus' intended meaning and the audience's interpretation of his words.

1. What are two examples of dramatic irony in *Oedipus the King*?
2. How would having prior knowledge of Oedipus' story affect your reading of the play?

- See **Literary Terms Handbook,** p. R6.

Literature and Writing

Writing About Literature

Review Write a review of *Oedipus the King,* describing the play's strengths and weaknesses and discussing its major themes. Include a brief plot summary. Answer questions such as the following: How effectively did Sophocles organize the plot? Why might Sophocles have chosen to tell this story? Use quotes from the play and references to specific scenes to support your analysis.

Personal Writing

Give Advice In the Reading Focus on page 262, you were asked to recall the most surprising thing you ever learned about yourself. Based on that experience, what advice would you offer Oedipus as he uncovers the truth about himself? In your journal, describe how Oedipus responds to the secrets of his past. Then offer suggestions to help him cope with this terrible knowledge.

Extending Your Response

Literature Groups

Placing Blame Is Oedipus at all responsible for his actions? Could he have avoided his fate? Discuss this issue, using evidence from the play to support your opinion. Summarize the conclusions and present them to the class.

Performing

Act It Out In readers theater, the actors read from the text instead of memorizing their lines. Choose a scene, or part of one to perform with a partner or small group. Discuss ways of delivering the dialogue. If you perform a choral song, you may wish to choreograph dance movements to accompany it.

Interdisciplinary Activity

Music: Create a Soundtrack Music is used in films and performances to draw the audience into the story. Music can increase feelings of suspense, fear, happiness, or anger. Select appropriate background music for two episodes of *Oedipus the King.* Bring in recordings to play for the class, and explain your choices.

Reading Further

If you found *Oedipus the King* interesting, the following Greek tragedies might also interest you:

The Orestia, by Aeschylus, three haunting plays about the family of Agamemnon, leader of the Greeks at Troy.

Save your work for your portfolio.

VOCABULARY • Analogies

Analogies are comparisons based on relationships between words and ideas. In some analogies, the words in each pair are synonyms.

primal : fundamental :: trivial : insignificant

PRACTICE To construct an analogy, identify the relationship of the first two words. Then apply that relationship to the second set of words.

- For more about analogies, see **Communications Skills Handbook,** p. R77.

Choose the word that best completes each analogy.

1. wonderful : amazing :: solemn :
   a. marvelous b. somber c. awesome
2. praiseworthy : commendable :: execrable :
   a. detestable b. mediocre c. agreeable
3. condemn : reproach :: praise :
   a. censure b. ignore c. congratulate

The Oedipus Complex

In Sophocles' play *Oedipus the King*, the Delphic oracle's warning proves true, and Oedipus finally realizes the horror of who he has become—the murderer of his own father, Laius, and the husband of his own mother, Jocasta. In anguish, Oedipus cries out, "What grief can crown this grief?"

Based on a Greek folk tale, the myth of Oedipus is one of the classic themes of literature. Over the centuries, writers as diverse as Homer, Sophocles, Seneca, William Shakespeare, Jean Cocteau, Frank O'Conner, and Tennessee Williams have explored and echoed this tragic theme. It was the Austrian psychiatrist, Sigmund Freud, however, who in 1910 drew upon the myth of Oedipus to describe his theory concerning the role of sexuality in the development of the human personality. Freud used the label "Oedipus complex" to describe the unconscious or hidden feelings of desire a child experiences toward a parent of the opposite sex. According to Freud's theory, these feelings of desire toward one parent are paired with feelings of rivalry toward the other parent. Freud wrote, "It is the fate of all of us [men], perhaps, to direct our first sexual impulse toward our mother and our first hatred . . . against our father."

Etching of Sigmund Freud, 1914 (detail). Max Pollack (Austria). Freud Museum, London.

Freud was aware that Sophocles' Oedipus the King had a strong impact on both ancient and modern audiences. Apparently he assumed that the play confirmed his hypothesis that the harboring of oedipal feelings was a universal phenomenon. One of the central questions raised by the myth is that if King Oedipus—one of the wisest men in the Greek empire—does not truly know who he is, how can any of us expect to know who we are? Sophocles made Oedipus' dilemma extreme—he actually does murder his father and marry his mother. But for us, the dilemmas are more subtle, more hidden. A large part of who we are is made up of how we feel. Yet, according to Freud, many of these feelings remain beyond our grasp in our unconscious mind. In the myth, Oedipus is unable to witness the horror of his own fate so he blinds himself. Similarly, according to Freud's Oedipus complex theory, we try to ignore our feelings of anxiety by repressing our wishes in the unconscious, and becoming "blind" to them.

Activity

Describe a situation from a television show or movie in which the main character's feelings about a friend or relative cause the character to worry or feel anxious. Write about how the character resolves the conflict: by choosing "blindness" (pretending there is no problem) or by confronting the problem with his or her "eyes open" and addressing the issue. Then write about whether you think the character made the right decision.

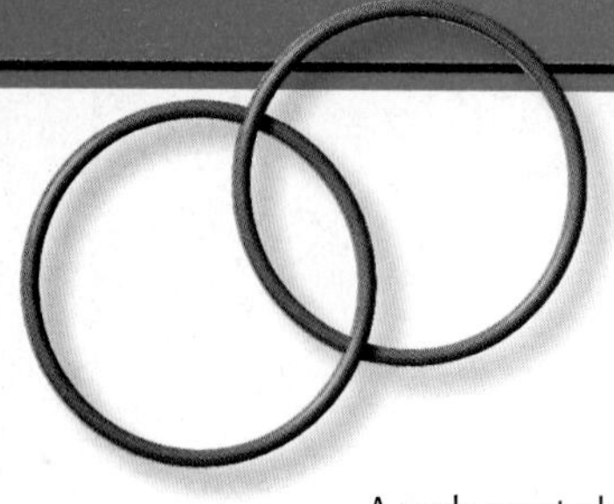

Grammar Link

Subject-Verb Agreement

A verb must always agree with its subject in person and number. Sometimes it is easy to mistake a word in an intervening prepositional phrase for the subject of that sentence. The subject of a sentence, however, never appears in a prepositional phrase. Also, don't be confused by an inverted sentence–a sentence in which the subject follows the verb. Many inverted sentences begin with a prepositional phrase. Finally, when a collective noun is used as a subject, use a singular verb unless the individuals forming the group are to be emphasized.

Problem 1 An intervening prepositional phrase
What word from Delphi's gold vaults come to brilliant Thebes?
The verb agrees with the object of the preposition, *vaults.*

Solution Make the verb agree with the subject word, which is not the object of a preposition.
What word from Delphi's gold vaults comes to brilliant Thebes?

Problem 2 An inverted sentence
Through the wide palace doors come an old shepherd.
The verb agrees with the noun *doors,* instead of the subject, *shepherd.*

Solution Look for the subject after the verb, and make the verb agree with the singular subject, *shepherd.*
Through the wide palace doors comes an old shepherd.

Problem 3 Collective nouns
The audience always applaud the performance of Oedipus the King.
The verb does not agree with the collective noun as it is used in the sentence.

Solution If the collective noun refers to a group as a whole, use a singular verb.
The audience always applauds the performance of Oedipus the King.

- For more on subject-verb agreement, see **Language Handbook,** p. R17.

ACTIVITIES

1. Rewrite the following paragraph, correcting all problems of agreement between subjects and verbs.

> **Of all the playwrights of ancient Greece, at the top of the list stand Sophocles. The tragedies of Sophocles is known the world over. The most famous of his more than a hundred plays are *Oedipus the King*. In addition to being a brilliant dramatist, Sophocles played an active role in daily life in Athens. He was known and loved by his fellow citizens.**

2. Review a draft of your writing and correct problems of agreement.

Before You Read

from the *Apology*

Meet Plato

"Plato is philosophy, and philosophy, Plato." —*Ralph Waldo Emerson*

Plato (plā′ tō) came from a distinguished family in Athens and was groomed for a political career. He put that life aside to follow the philosopher Socrates. Many of the basic concepts of Western philosophy go back to Plato. A brilliant literary stylist and profound thinker, Plato has inspired writers for two thousand years.

Almost all of Plato's surviving writings are dialogues, in which he uses the techniques of drama to express philosophical ideas. Socrates is usually the central figure: for example, in the *Crito*, a friend tries to help Socrates escape from prison. In the later dialogues, Plato often uses Socrates to voice his own ideas. The early dialogues portray the historical Socrates to a greater extent, although Plato probably refined the ideas that Socrates expresses. Regardless of who said what, both men were committed to using reason in a relentless search for truth.

Plato was born around 428 B.C. and died around 347 B.C.

Reading Focus

Who is the wisest person you have ever known?

Discuss With a partner, discuss why you believe that certain people are wise. Then work together to create a definition of wisdom.

Setting a Purpose As you read, note whether Socrates behaves in accordance with your idea of wisdom.

Building Background

The Trial of Socrates

Socrates (470–399 B.C.) claimed that a divine voice led him to challenge the statements of people who considered themselves wise. For him, being wise meant recognizing that he was ignorant. His probing questions and nontraditional approach eventually got him into trouble with the authorities. During a period of political turmoil, some leaders blamed Socrates for undermining Athenian patriotism. At the age of seventy, he was charged with religious irreverence and corrupting the youth of Athens. His accusers asked for the death penalty.

The *Apology* is a collection of speeches that Socrates made in his defense. It opens with Socrates brilliantly denying the charges against him. After he is voted guilty by a narrow margin, the jury asks him to propose an alternative punishment. He suggests that Athens reward him with a pension for his services as a gadfly, or pest. This response, and indeed his entire defense, shows that Socrates was more concerned with justifying his life than preserving it. The speech included in this volume follows the jury's decision to sentence Socrates to death.

Vocabulary Preview

detractor (di trak′ tər) *n.* one who speaks ill of someone or something; p. 328

reproach (ri prōch′) *v.* to express disappointment for conduct that is blameworthy; p. 328

acquittal (ə kwit′ əl) *n.* setting free from a criminal charge by verdict, sentence, or other legal process; p. 328

censure (sen′ shər) *v.* to find fault with and criticize; p. 330

faculty (fak′ əl tē) *n.* an inherent or natural ability; p. 330

intimation (in′ ti mā′ shən) *n.* an indirect suggestion; p. 330

from the Apology

from the Dialogues

Plato

Translated by Benjamin Jowett

NOT MUCH TIME WILL BE GAINED, O Athenians, in return for the evil name which you will get from the detractors of the city, who will say that you killed Socrates, a wise man; for they will call me wise, even although I am not wise, when they want to reproach you. If you had waited a little while, your desire would have been fulfilled in the course of nature. For I am far advanced in years, as you may perceive, and not far from death. I am speaking now not to all of you, but only to those who have condemned me to death. And I have another thing to say to them: You think that I was convicted because I had no words of the sort which would have procured my acquittal—I mean, if I had thought fit to leave nothing undone or unsaid.

As used here, an *apology* is a formal explanation for actions or beliefs.

Vocabulary

detractor (di trak′ tər) *n.* one who speaks ill of someone or something
reproach (ri prōch′) *v.* to express disappointment for conduct that is blameworthy
acquittal (ə kwit′ əl) *n.* setting free from a criminal charge by verdict, sentence, or other legal process

Literature and Writing

Writing About Literature

Comparing Characters Socrates was a figure in history, yet he also functions as a literary character in Plato's dialogues. Compare Socrates in the *Apology* with another character you have read about who faces death. Describe how each character confronts his or her fate. How are the traits of each character revealed? Which character do you find more admirable? Explain.

Personal Writing

Apology The word *apology* here means "a formal defense or justification." In Plato's dialogue, Socrates defends his values and his practice of questioning Athenians about their beliefs. Write a speech in which you defend or justify one of your own values, beliefs, or actions. Before you write, consider the type of audience you would like to persuade with your speech.

Extending Your Response

Literature Groups

Fighting Words Socrates says that he was condemned to death merely for asking questions. Do you think that a government is ever justified in punishing people for what they say? What limits, if any, would you place on freedom of speech? Debate these questions in your group. When you are finished, summarize your conclusions and present them to the class.

Interdisciplinary Activity

Art: Capturing the Scene Create a painting, drawing, sculpture, or diorama based on the *Apology.* You might choose a moment when Socrates is speaking, or you might want to illustrate an idea he expresses in his speech, such as his theory about death. When you are finished, present your artwork to the class. Invite questions from other students.

Learning for Life

Interview Imagine that you are given an opportunity to interview Socrates after his trial. Write a list of questions for the interview. You might ask him to clarify some of the ideas in his speech, or you might question him regarding the trial itself. Trade your list with a partner, and answer each other's questions as you think Socrates might have.

Reading Further

If you are interested in learning more about Athens or the trial of Socrates, the following books might be helpful:

The Trial of Socrates, by I. F. Stone, how the trial of Socrates occurred in Athens, the birthplace of democracy.

"From the Peloponnesian War to Alexander the Great" from *Ancient Greece*, by Thomas R. Martin.

Save your work for your portfolio.

VOCABULARY • Prefixes

Many words are formed by combining different prefixes with the same root. The basic meaning of the root stays the same, but the prefix gives the word its particular meaning. The verb *detract* contains the prefix *de-,* meaning "from," and the Latin root *tractus,* meaning "to draw or pull." *Detract* means "to draw (or take) away from"; hence the meaning, "to take away from a person's reputation."

PRACTICE Identify the prefixes used below. Then write a definition for each verb. Finally, write a sentence using each word.

attract	contract	distract
protract	retract	subtract
decline	incline	recline

Writing Workshop

Creative Writing: A Dramatic Scene

When it is performed, drama shows what a written narrative tells. However, while the author of a story addresses the audience directly, the author of a dramatic scene writes instructions for all the actors and the director who will bring the story to life for the audience. In a script, the entire narrative must be told through action and dialogue. **In this workshop, you will adapt a fable or other short narrative into a dramatic scene or play.**

- As you plan and compose your dramatic scene, refer to **Writing Handbook**, pp. R58–R63.

EVALUATION RUBRIC

By the time you complete this Writing Workshop, you will have

- written a scene with rising action, climax, and resolution
- used dialogue, action, and setting to develop characters, introduce a conflict, and move the plot along
- used stage directions to support and develop your scene
- presented a scene that is free of errors in grammar, usage, and mechanics

The Writing Process

PREWRITING

PREWRITING TIPS

Think in terms of characters on stage, speaking the dialogue you write.

Remember that character and conflict are the keys to a scene's success.

Explore ideas

The selections in this part offer many possibilities for dramatic adaptations. You may wish to base your scene on one of them or choose another work to adapt. To get started, consider basing a scene on one of these ideas:

- characters opposed to each other, like Achilles and Agamemnon in the *Iliad*
- characters testing one another to see who is better or stronger
- a character struggling to live up to the expectations of others
- two characters trying to overcome something that keeps them apart
- a character struggling with a difficult or frightening memory

Choose an audience

If your audience doesn't know the story on which your scene is based, they may need background information. Before the action begins, you could have a character speak directly to the audience, or have two characters discuss background events.

Consider your purpose

Your purpose is to translate a story that was meant to be read into one that will be performed for an audience. Cut the work down to its essentials. Use scenery and dialogue to express thoughts and descriptions.

Make a plan

Once you have a story or idea that you like, ask yourself these questions about the basic story elements and how to translate them into dramatic elements. Take notes on your answers, and use the notes as a guide when you plan your scene.

STUDENT MODEL

Plot	What is the problem or conflict? How can you establish it through dialogue and action? How is the conflict resolved? How can you show the resolution through dialogue and action?	Urban lifestyle vs. rural lifestyle. City Mouse visits Country Mouse for a simple, hearty lunch. Then City Mouse invites Country Mouse back to the city to dine. They sit down to an elegant dinner but keep getting interrupted—by a dog, a cat, maybe servants. They never even get to finish eating!
Characters	Who are the main characters? What are they like? How can you show their characteristics through action and dialogue? Which minor characters do you really need? (In a brief scene, you won't be able to develop many.)	City Mouse and Country Mouse. City Mouse is elegant and condescending. Country Mouse is simple and kind. Make Country Mouse eager to please and City Mouse snobbish and superior acting. At first it will seem as though City Mouse has a better life. Need a few other nonspeaking characters—a dog, a cat, etc.
Setting	What is essential to the action? What will create atmosphere?	Country cottage; city palace. Open with tape of birds chirping. Close with offstage screech of cat, bark of dog, and clatter of dishes.

Complete Student Model on p. R111.

Use this graphic to help you shape your scene. Begin by identifying the climax. Plan to make the rest of the action build to that point. When you have identified the climax, decide what events you really need to include to move from the beginning to the climax. You should have enough action to develop the characters and make the climax meaningful to the audience. However, if you include too many events, the audience may anticipate the climax or simply get bored.

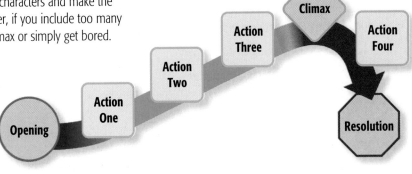

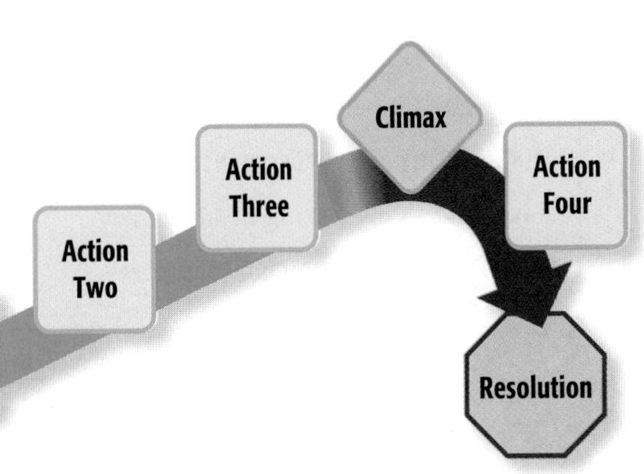

DRAFTING

DRAFTING TIP

Start by writing some dialogue.

Draft the heart of the scene first

In every dramatic scene, one event is more important than any other. This event is the heart of the scene. Usually it is the climax, but not always. Find the heart of your scene. Draft that part of the scene first, and build the rest of the scene around it.

Write your draft

Refer to your plan as you write to make sure that your scene is structured with rising action, a climax, and a resolution. If you get stuck in one spot, move on to another.

STUDENT MODEL

A cat enters the room.

COUNTRY MOUSE (running to the mouse hole): Lucinda, help! Help!

CITY MOUSE: Don't be such a scaredy-mouse. We just have to wait until she leaves. Then we can proceed with our delicious gourmet dinner.

COUNTRY MOUSE (shaken): Is it really worth it to live in fear like this, just to have these luxuries?

Complete Student Model on p. R111.

REVISING

REVISING TIP

Read your scene out loud to yourself as you revise it.

Test the audience reaction

Rehearse your scene by reading it to a friend, keeping the written copy to yourself. Notice your friend's response and make notes for improvements. Then, using the **Rubric for Revising** to guide you, make revisions to your draft.

STUDENT MODEL

All is well, as you can see.
COUNTRY MOUSE: I love this country life.
quiet

CITY MOUSE: Do you?
I would miss the city.

COUNTRY MOUSE: Oh, Lucinda. You're so different from me.
I'm glad I left the city years ago.

Really,
CITY MOUSE: I suppose you're right, my dear. I do so love living in this palace.

Well, everything I need is right here.
COUNTRY MOUSE: I'm content here.

Complete Student Model on p. R111.

RUBRIC FOR REVISING

Your revised dramatic scene should have

- ☑ a clearly established setting
- ☑ a plot that introduces a conflict and has rising tension, a climax, and a resolution
- ☑ dialogue that creates dramatic tension and develops character
- ☑ stage directions to help actors bring your story to life
- ☑ any background information necessary to understand your scene

Your revised dramatic scene should be free of

- ☑ extra characters that may make the scene confusing to readers

EDITING/PROOFREADING

When you are satisfied with your scene's content, edit it carefully to correct errors in grammar, usage, mechanics, and spelling. Use the **Proofreading Checklist** as a guide.

Grammar Hint

Incorrect pronoun shifts occur when a writer or speaker uses a pronoun in one person and then switches to a pronoun in another person. Replace the incorrect pronoun with a pronoun that agrees with it.

INCORRECT: *If one enjoys the finer things in life, you should live in a city.*

CORRECT: *If you enjoy the finer things in life, you should live in a city.*

PROOFREADING CHECKLIST

- ☑ Correct pronoun shifts.
- ☑ Make subjects and verbs agree.
- ☑ Check your use of commas, semicolons, and other punctuation marks.
- ☑ Check the capitalization of names and place names.
- ☑ Check the spelling of words.

STUDENT MODEL

COUNTRY MOUSE: Oh, I've never seen anything quit like this.

CITY MOUSE: Really? I eat like this evry day. Here, try this french bread.

COUNTRY MOUSE: Ummm . . . good.

CITY MOUSE: Don't forget the fresh chive salad, ether. One must get your vitamins!

Complete Student Model on p. R111.

Complete Student Model

For a complete version of the model developed in this workshop, refer to **Writing Workshop Models**, p. R111.

PUBLISHING/PRESENTING

The best way to present a dramatic scene is to perform it. Find actors to play the roles. Present the scene live, or videotape it and add the videotape to the school library. With your classmates, hold a theater festival or film festival and present all of your scenes.

PRESENTING TIP

If you plan a performance, find appropriate music.

Reflecting

Look back at your script-writing experience. What was the most enjoyable part? What did you learn as a writer? In what ways did the original story change during the translation to a script? What was "lost in translation"? What was gained?

Save your work for your portfolio.

The Land and Its People

Although only a small farming town in the beginning, Rome had great natural advantages. The seven hills on which it was built offered protection from its more powerful neighbors. Its position fifteen miles up the Tiber River offered easy access to the sea, and its position at the crossing of several trade routes brought foreign goods and ideas.

In the rugged hills and fertile valleys, Romans found the right mixture of natural resources:

- *clay for making pottery, tiles, and brick*
- *iron and copper for making weapons and tools*
- *trees for fueling fireplaces and the workshops of metalsmiths*
- *land that was fertile and well-watered for growing food*

As Rome expanded, Romans improved the lands they gained. They paved roads, constructed great aqueducts to carry water, built cities, encouraged trade, and applied the rule of law.

Etruscan terra-cotta figure.

The Italian Alps.

Active Reading Strategies

Reading the Time Line

1. Coins were first used in Southwest Asia about 650 B.C. How many years later did the first Roman coins appear?
2. How large was Rome's territory at the time of the emergence of Nok culture in western Africa?

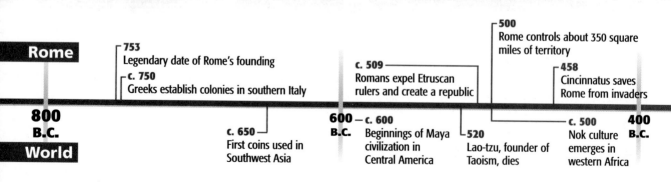

Rome

- **753** Legendary date of Rome's founding
- **c. 750** Greeks establish colonies in southern Italy
- **c. 509** Romans expel Etruscan rulers and create a republic
- **500** Rome controls about 350 square miles of territory
- **458** Cincinnatus saves Rome from invaders

800 B.C. — **600 B.C.** — **400 B.C.**

World

- **c. 650** First coins used in Southwest Asia
- **c. 600** Beginnings of Maya civilization in Central America
- **520** Lao-tzu, founder of Taoism, dies
- **c. 500** Nok culture emerges in western Africa

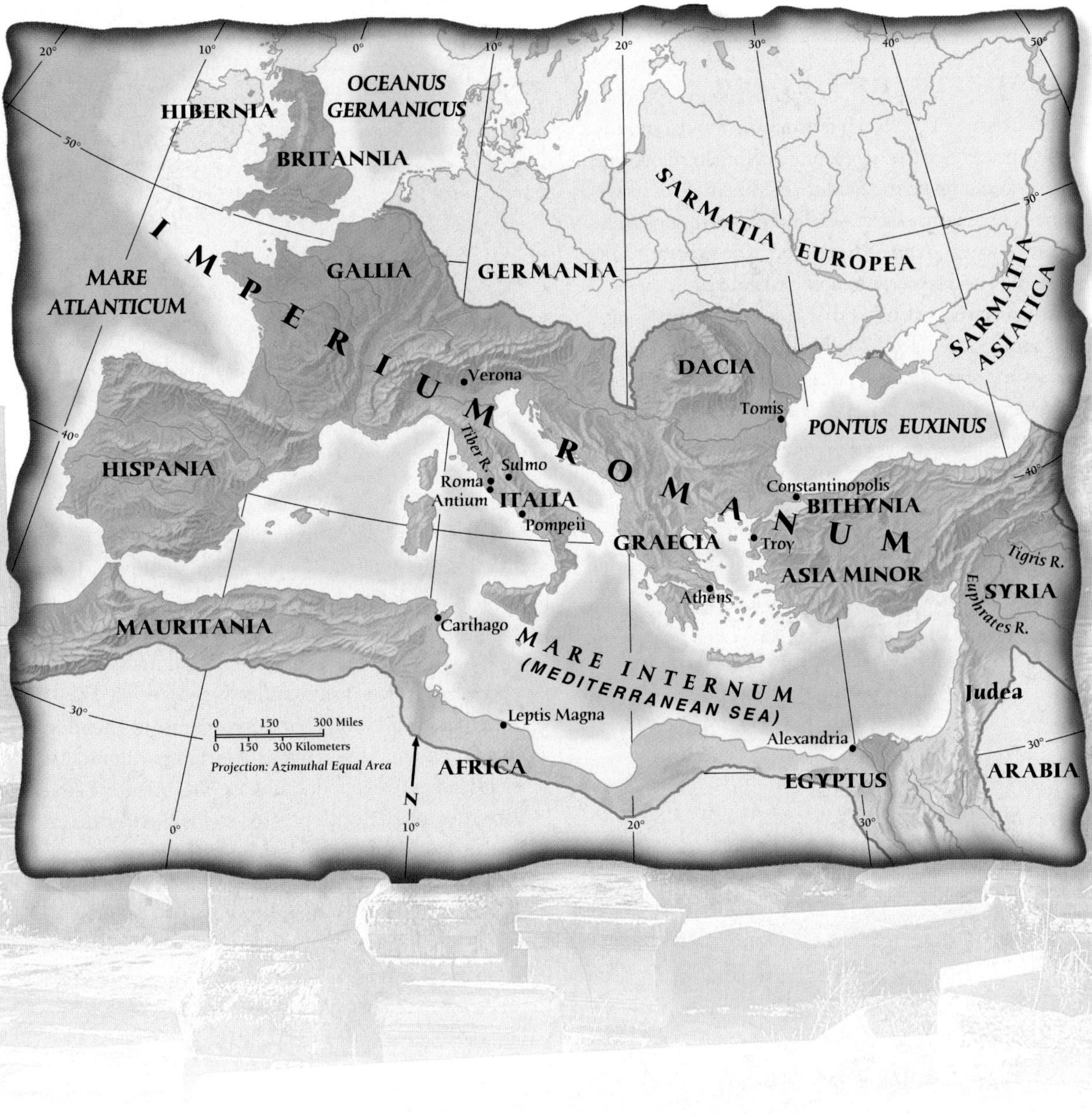

OCEANUS
GERMANICUS
HIBERNIA
BRITANNIA
IMPERIUM ROMANUM
MARE
ATLANTICUM
GALLIA
GERMANIA
SARMATIA EUROPEA
SARMATIA
ASIATICA
DACIA
Verona
Tomis
PONTUS EUXINUS
HISPANIA
Tiber R.
Sulmo
Roma
Antium
ITALIA
Pompeii
Constantinopolis
BITHYNIA
GRAECIA
Troy
ASIA MINOR
Tigris R.
SYRIA
Euphrates R.
Athens
MAURITANIA
Carthago
MARE INTERNUM
(MEDITERRANEAN SEA)
Judea
Leptis Magna
Alexandria
0 150 300 Miles
0 150 300 Kilometers
Projection: Azimuthal Equal Area
AFRICA
EGYPTUS
ARABIA
N

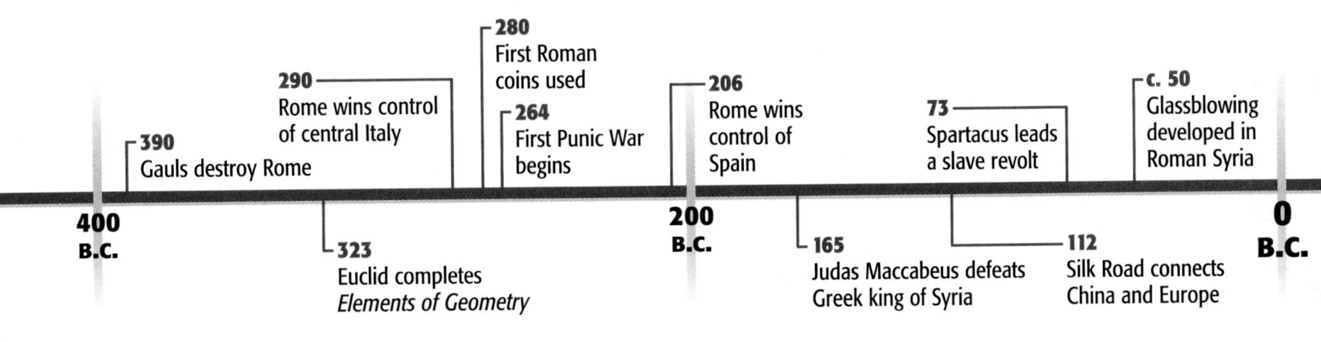
390
Gauls destroy Rome
290
Rome wins control of central Italy
280
First Roman coins used
264
First Punic War begins
206
Rome wins control of Spain
73
Spartacus leads a slave revolt
c. 50
Glassblowing developed in Roman Syria
400 B.C.
323
Euclid completes *Elements of Geometry*
200 B.C.
165
Judas Maccabeus defeats Greek king of Syria
112
Silk Road connects China and Europe
0 B.C.

Life in Society

Prosperity and Peace

The backbone of the Roman economy was agriculture. Ninety percent of the people under Roman rule farmed. They raised most of the food to feed themselves as well as the people in the cities. The Roman diet consisted mostly of wheat, prepared as porridge or as bread, a few vegetables, and sometimes pork or lamb.

Romans were open to other cultures. In particular, they admired the intellectual achievements of the Greeks and spread Greek culture throughout their lands. However, unlike the Greeks, who tightly restricted citizenship, Romans allowed men of any social or ethnic background to become citizens. Similarly, they treated all cultural groups under their rule equally. Everyone shared in the glories of Rome. One result of this openness was the *Pax Romana*, a remarkable era of peace within the Roman sphere that lasted from 31 B.C. to A.D. 180.

Mosaic of grape harvest, 4th century A.D.

Roman soldiers, 2nd century A.D.

The People of Pompeii

On August 24 A.D. 79, on the southeast coast of Italy, a volcano erupted, spewing poisonous gases, hot lava, stone, and ash. Up to sixty feet of volcanic debris rained down on nearby towns—including the summer resort of Pompeii—stopping life in its tracks. For centuries, these towns lay buried. When serious excavations finally began in the 1700s, archaeologists uncovered market stalls still stocked with nuts, fruits, and loaves of bread. They saw horse hoof prints and chariot wheel ruts indented in the cities' roads, and the remains of pet dogs straining at their leashes. They found homes with brightly colored floor tiles, plaster walls painted to look like brick, and bronze couches decorated with ivory. On some buildings, they found political endorsements etched on walls. For example, "The petty thieves support Vatia for the aedileship." (Whether a supporter or an opponent of Vatia wrote this is unknown.) Today, tourists can walk the streets of excavated Pompeii and get a sense of how life was lived in Italy nearly 2,000 years ago.

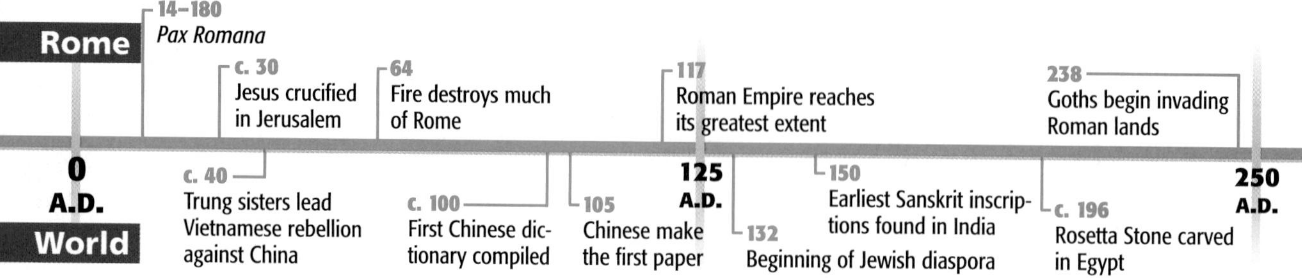
Rome
14–180
Pax Romana
c. 30
Jesus crucified in Jerusalem
64
Fire destroys much of Rome
117
Roman Empire reaches its greatest extent
238
Goths begin invading Roman lands
0 A.D.
125 A.D.
250 A.D.
World
c. 40
Trung sisters lead Vietnamese rebellion against China
c. 100
First Chinese dictionary compiled
105
Chinese make the first paper
132
Beginning of Jewish diaspora
150
Earliest Sanskrit inscriptions found in India
c. 196
Rosetta Stone carved in Egypt

Traditions and Beliefs

The Time of Many Gods

Like the Greeks, the Romans believed in many gods. When they encountered other peoples, they simply assumed that the gods those people worshipped were the same ones, under different names. For example, they took the Greek Zeus, mightiest of the gods and lord of the weather, to be the same as their own Jupiter, who also ruled over the weather and the other gods. Roman poets wrote often of the Greek gods and their doings. Still, the gods the Roman people cherished most were not the mighty and unpredictable Olympians, but the guardian spirits who watched over each household. The most sacred temple in Rome was that of Vesta, goddess of the hearth, or home fireplace.

Artemis, Goddess of Hunting, 2nd century B.C.

Detail of a mosaic showing Jesus' miracle of the loaves and the fishes.

The Coming of Christianity

The Romans cared little what deities a person worshipped, or how. What was important was to show reverence and respect to some god. Ironically, early Christians were often prosecuted for atheism, since they denied the existence of the old gods. They were also accused of disloyalty, as they refused to make sacrifices to the well-being of the empire.

Eventually, Christians gained respect for their work in feeding the poor and tending the sick. And the virtues they emphasized—piety, hard work, courage—were those the Romans had always most admired. By the time the emperor Constantine the Great legalized the Christian religion, it had already become the most widespread religion in the empire.

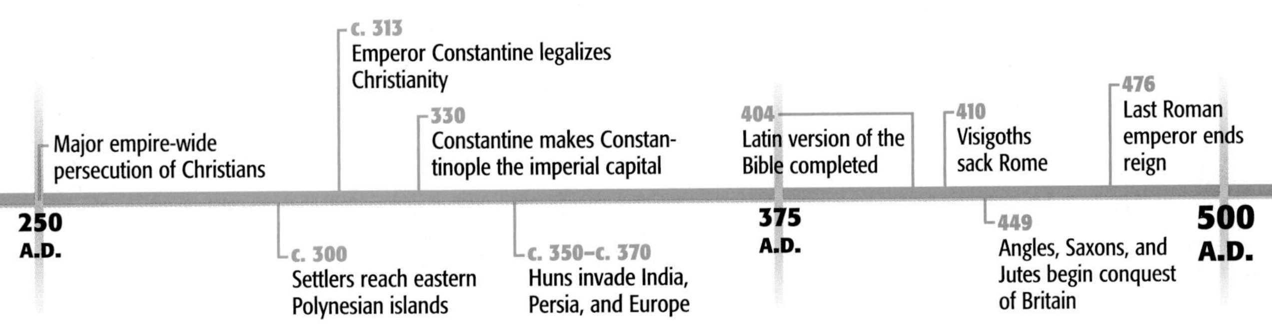
250 A.D.
Major empire-wide persecution of Christians
c. 300
Settlers reach eastern Polynesian islands
c. 313
Emperor Constantine legalizes Christianity
330
Constantine makes Constantinople the imperial capital
c. 350–c. 370
Huns invade India, Persia, and Europe
375 A.D.
404
Latin version of the Bible completed
410
Visigoths sack Rome
449
Angles, Saxons, and Jutes begin conquest of Britain
476
Last Roman emperor ends reign
500 A.D.

Arts and Entertainment

Etruscan wall painting of a cithara player.

Visual Arts

Roman art was heavily influenced by that of Greece. Many artists were Greeks themselves, or trained in Greece. There was some difference in emphasis, however: where Greek art had stressed ideal forms, the Romans were more interested in realism.

The Roman government was a major patron of the arts, and many original Roman statues were portraits of generals, senators, and emperors. Wealthy Romans were also patrons of the arts. Their homes had central courtyards for light and air, and few outside windows, so they hired artists to paint frescoes on the big, unbroken walls. To make a fresco, artists painted directly on a thin wet layer of plaster. These paintings, which include cityscapes, scenes of gardens, and scenes of everyday life, are often painted to appear as if they were viewed from a window. Today, the surviving paintings provide a window back in time, helping us to see the kinds of clothes, architecture, and activities common to the Roman Empire.

Critical Thinking

Connecting Cultures

1. What does Roman art tell us about daily life in Roman times? Write your answer in a short essay.
2. Will today's art help future generations understand our daily lives? Write a short essay explaining your ideas.

Architecture

Above all, the Romans were builders. Theaters, temples, and public buildings sprang up all along the roads they built, from the rainy lowlands of Scotland to the arid deserts of Iraq. The city of Rome itself became the most magnificent anyone had ever seen; even today, after centuries of decay and destruction, its ruins are one of the wonders of the world.

The styles of architecture were largely those that had originated in Greece, but the Romans made great advances in building techniques. Compared with the Greeks, they used rounded forms, such as arches, vaults, and domes more frequently. In addition, they invented cement, built the first apartment houses in Eurasia, and piped hot air under bathing rooms to keep them warm.

Artist's impression of the Roman forum.

Public Activities

The fact that Rome's grandest buildings include bathhouses, arenas, and amphitheaters shows how important bathing and entertainment were to the social life of Romans. Many people visited the public baths every day, not only to use the hot and cold baths but also to use the gymnasiums, libraries, gardens, and other recreational spaces that bathhouses were often equipped with. Up to 3,000 people at a time might visit these massive structures, which were lavishly decorated with gold and marble.

Romans of all economic groups also attended the many public entertainments sponsored by the government. Not only did acting troupes wander the streets and perform comedies and tragedies in small theaters, but huge sporting events took place in venues that held more people than some of today's sports arenas do. The largest Roman arena was the Circus Maximus, which seated about 150,000 people. Spectators would come to watch chariot races in which two or four horses would pull chariots around the track at breathtaking speeds. Other entertainment was more violent. On holidays, crowds piled into amphitheaters like the Colosseum to watch gladitorial combats (the "games"). Such contests originated among the Etruscans as sacred rituals, but they came to be considered entertainment. Many educated Romans condemned the games, but they appealed greatly to the huge crowds that thronged to the city from all parts of the empire and beyond.

Marble bust of the Empress Faustina Minor, c. A.D. 175.

Relief sculpture of a chariot race.

Language and Literature

Roman milestone inscription.

Fresco from Pompeii showing a woman writing.

The Influence of Latin

The speech of the city of Rome became the official language of the empire. Latin became the everyday speech, as well, for many different peoples. Even when the empire was only a memory, Latin continued, both in its pure form as the language of church and state, and in the changing forms in which people spoke it among themselves. Eventually, the spoken forms evolved enough to form new languages, such as Italian, French, Spanish, and Portuguese.

The influence of the Roman alphabet was also strong. The Romans started from the alphabets already in use around the Mediterranean, including Greek and Phoenician, and changed them to meet their needs. The alphabet they developed is still used, thousands of years later, for writing languages all over the world.

Poets and Poetry

In literature, as in other areas, the Romans learned from the Greeks. They used the poetic forms the Greeks had established: the epic, the ode of praise, and the lyric. Often they took Greek myths as their subject matter, offering their own interpretations. For example, when the Roman poet Virgil wrote an epic poem based on Rome's history, he looked to the *Iliad* and the *Odyssey* for inspiration. When Ovid wrote the *Metamorphoses*, he took Greek mythology as his subject.

Besides producing great work in the Greek tradition, Roman poets developed forms of their own. Notable among these are the satires of Horace and others: poems that commented humorously on the attitudes and behavior of the times. Whether Roman poets were using original forms or following Greek models, the best of them had such skill with language and form that their works are still appreciated today.

influences

Many English words have a connection to the Latin language, and some English words are Latin in their entirety. For example, in our solar system, every planet but our own is named after a Roman deity.

- Mercury is named after the Roman messenger god
- Venus is named after the Roman goddess of love
- Mars is named after the Roman god of war
- Jupiter is named after the chief Roman god
- Saturn is named after the Roman god of agriculture
- Uranus is the Roman name for the Greek god of the sky
- Neptune is the name of the Roman god of the sea
- Pluto is named after the Roman god of the underworld

Great Speakers

Although literacy was widespread throughout the empire, most literature was intended to be heard, not read. The printing press had not yet been invented, so writing could not be easily reproduced and disseminated. Romans relied on the power of the spoken word to express their ideas, especially in government forums. Speakers, or orators, used carefully crafted, refined Latin, and the best communicators could gain fame and fortune. For example, Cicero, one of the greatest orators in history, rose to the highest office in the Roman Republic. After he gave his speeches, written copies of it were made and circulated.

> O CATILINE,
> FINISH AS YOU BEGAN;
> LEAVE THE CITY,
> THE GATES ARE OPEN;
> YOU MAY NO LONGER
> WALK AMONG US—
> I WILL NOT BEAR IT,
> I WILL NOT SUFFER IT,
> I WILL NOT PERMIT IT.
>
> —*CICERO*

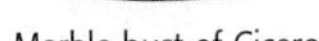

Marble bust of Cicero.

Cicero denouncing Catiline in the Roman Senate.

Critical Thinking

Ancient Rome

1. How would you describe the fundamental values of the Romans? Discuss your ideas in a small group.
2. Can you think of any contradictions between the Romans' stated values and their activities. Discuss your ideas in a small group.

Web Site

The Romans left monuments throughout the Mediterranean world. At this Web site an architecture student tells how he used a computer to reconstruct an image of the Roman baths in the African city of Leptis Magna.

The Hadrianic Baths: A Computer Reconstruction by Bill Rattenbury

Address: http://archpropplan.auckland.ac.nz

Although not the largest of Roman baths, the Hadrianic Baths are a grand complex of buildings with varied and interesting internal volumes.

Materials

The baths were the first buildings in the city to be built largely in marble. Several types of marble have been described by authors, including pink marble columns surrounding the swimming bath and black granite columns around the frigidarium plunge baths. Another marble mentioned as being used in the city was green.

Sculpture

The baths were filled with a large amount of statues. Images of Bacchus and Hercules, who were patron deities for the city of Leptis Magna, are of particular importance though the full pantheon of gods appear to have been represented.

Computer Modeling

The process of the computer reconstruction is important as it will affect the style of the resulting graphics:

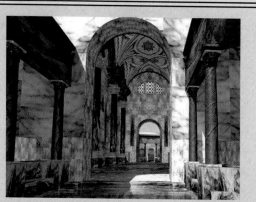

A plan of the baths was "scanned" into the computer. This formed a "bitmark" picture of black and white dots. This picture was then traced to form a plan composed of shapes, which could be transferred to the modeling program and re-scaled to the final size. Each wall had to be drawn and then given thickness, columns revolved as if on a lathe, and all parts then moved into their final position. Complex shapes like the pools, Corinthian column capitals, and vaults had to be made up of a number of separate pieces.

Computer Rendering

The program was then left to generate each final image, with textures and shadows. This is a lengthy and complex process. The amount of time varies depending on: the type of rendering ("quicktracing" shows textures and basic lighting, "raytracing" adds shadows and reflections); the complexity of the model; the size of the image; the number of light sources the computer has to allow for.

Analyzing Media

1. What kinds of decoration were used in the baths?
2. What are some factors governing the amount of time it takes to generate a computer image?

Before You Read

Poems of Catullus

Meet Catullus

"It is difficult suddenly to give up a long-cherished love."

The fluid style of Catullus's (kə tul′ əs) poems gives the impression that he simply poured his thoughts and feelings onto the writing tablet. He wrote about love affairs, described playful encounters with friends, repeated gossip, and viciously mocked those who aroused his disapproval, including Julius Caesar (a family friend). Yet he also helped to bring about a new sophistication to Latin poetry.

Catullus came from a wealthy family in the northern Italian city of Verona. Encouraged by one of his brothers, Catullus began writing poetry at an early age. He spent much of his adult life in Rome, although he traveled to Asia Minor to serve on the Roman governor's staff. Catullus died at the age of thirty, but his work influenced many important Latin poets, including Virgil, Horace, and Ovid.

Catullus was born around 84 B.C. and died around 54 B.C.

Reading Focus

Do you know someone who inspires mixed feelings in you?

Journal Writing Write for a few minutes in your journal about this person. Provide specific examples of the person's behavior to help explain your feelings.

Setting a Purpose As you read, notice what the speaker reveals about his feelings.

Building Background

Lesbia

Catullus's best-known poems are about a woman he calls "Lesbia." This pseudonym pays homage to the Greek poet Sappho of Lesbos (see page 257), whose verse had a great influence on him. The real "Lesbia" was probably Clodia, sister of the notorious political gangster Clodius. The speaker describes moments of happiness with her, but in most of the poems he expresses anguish over her behavior and wishes that he could overcome his obsessive love. Their relationship inspired some of the finest lyric poetry of the ancient world.

Catullus's Literary Circle

Catullus belonged to a literary circle known as the Neoterics. Members of this group scorned poets who blindly followed tradition. They encouraged innovation in subject matter as well as technique. The Neoterics especially admired the Greek poets of Alexandria for their sophistication and craftsmanship. Catullus captured the playful spirit of this movement in a poem addressed to Calvus, a fellow Neoteric. The poem joyfully describes a day when the two poets spent hours together improvising love verses.

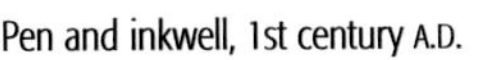

Pen and inkwell, 1st century A.D.

Poems of Catullus

Translated by Carl Sesar

My woman says there's nobody she'd rather marry
than me, not even Jupiter° himself if he asked her.
She says, but what a woman says to a hungry lover
you might as well scribble in wind and swift water.

My mind's sunk so low, Lesbia, because of you,
wrecked itself on your account so bad already,
I couldn't like you if you were the best of women,
or stop loving you, no matter what you do.

I hate her and I love her. Don't ask me why.
It's the way I feel, that's all, and it hurts.

2 *Jupiter,* also called Jove, is the chief Roman god. He is the god of light, the sky, and the weather. In Greek mythology, he is known as Zeus.

Neaera Reading a Letter from Catullus, 1894. Henry J. Hudson (Great Britain). Oil on canvas, 155.5 x 104.5 cm. Bradford City Art Gallery & Museum, England.

Viewing the painting: What are some of the details the artist uses to indicate that his subject is from antiquity?

Responding to Literature

Personal Response

What emotions did these poems stir in you? In your journal, describe how you reacted to the feelings that Catullus expresses in them.

Analyzing Literature

Recall and Interpret

1. How do you interpret Catullus's image of scribbling "in wind and swift water" in the first poem?
2. An **internal conflict** is a struggle within a character. What internal conflict does the speaker describe in the second poem?
3. **Tone** is the attitude that a writer takes toward a subject (see **Literary Terms Handbook,** page R12). What does the tone of the third poem reveal about this speaker's attitude toward his subject?

Evaluate and Connect

4. What attitude does the speaker in these poems appear to have toward women?
5. In the Reading Focus on page 347, you wrote about someone who inspires mixed feelings in you. How do the views of the speakers in these poems compare with yours?
6. How would you describe Catullus's style and use of poetic techniques?
7. Can you think of another character in literature who, like Catullus, had conflicting emotions about someone? How did that character resolve the conflict?

Literary Criticism

"Through his short poems," writes scholar Michael Grant, "[Catallus] became the founder of a new form in Latin literature, the light, witty, brief piece of poetry that occupied a place between serious epic and tragedy on the one hand and humorous satire and comedy on the other." Do you think Grant's comment on the form of Catallus's short poems applies to the poems on page 348? Write a few paragraphs explaining your answer. Analyze specific details for support.

Literary ELEMENTS

Speaker

The **speaker** of a poem is the voice that talks to the reader or to the person addressed by the poem. Although some poets seem to speak in their own voice, the reader should never assume that the speaker is identical to the poet. Poets often create characters to speak for them; such speakers may differ from the poet in age, race, or gender. A speaker may also express concerns and emotions that the poet may or may not share.

1. Do you think that all three of these poems by Catullus have the same speaker? Why or why not?
2. What adjectives would you use to describe the speaker or speakers of these poems?

- See **Literary Terms Handbook,** p. R11.

Extending Your Response

Creative Writing

A Poetic Response Write a poem in response to one of the poems by Catullus in this selection. If you wish, you may speak in your own voice, or you may use Lesbia as the speaker of your poem. When you are finished, read the poem aloud to the class. Explain why you decided to use a particular speaker in your poem.

Interdisciplinary Activity

Music: Song Lyrics Like many contemporary songwriters, Catullus speaks in a direct and passionate voice. Find a song that reminds you of a poem by Catullus. Play a recording of the song for the class, and explain what the song's lyrics and Catullus's poem have in common.

Save your work for your portfolio.

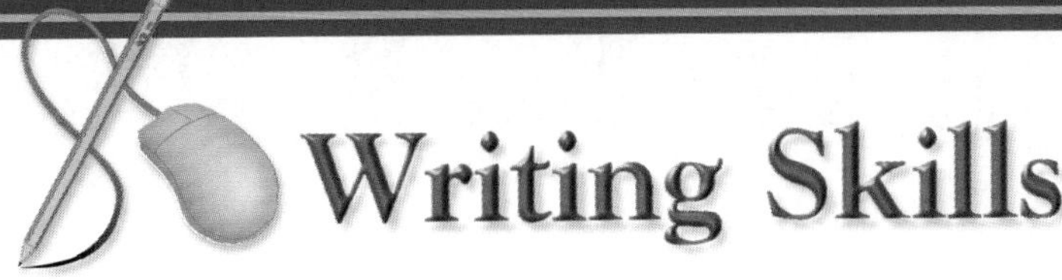

Writing Skills

Organizing Details

Catullus was a master at selecting details for his poetry that mirrored his emotional state:

> **My mind's sunk so low, Lesbia, because of you,**
> **wrecked itself on your account so bad already**

Good writers know that effective writing depends on the thoughtful use of details. A few well-placed details can vividly depict a person, a place, a scene, an object, or an emotion. Details are used in all kinds of writing, from poetry to news articles. The most effective use of any type of detail requires careful and clear organization. Details are usually arranged in one of four different patterns: spatial order, order of importance, order of impression, and chronological order.

Spatial Order	presents details according to their location, such as near to far, front to back, left to right, top to bottom, clockwise, counterclockwise and so on
Order of Importance	presents details from least important to most important, or vice versa
Order of Impression	presents details in the order a narrator or a character perceives them
Chronological Order	presents details in the order in which they occur. Often used to describe a process or tell about a series of events, this pattern of organization shows time relationships and often uses transitional words, such as *first, next,* and *finally*

Depending upon your purpose, patterns of organization may be combined. For example, you may choose to combine spatial order, order of impression, and chronological order when describing a specific event.

ACTIVITIES

1. Write a brief description of a particular place using spatial organization or order of impression.
2. Choose an event you would like to write about. Make a list of vivid details you wish to include in your description of the event. Then arrange those details using one of the four patterns of organization.
3. How does Catullus describe his feelings for Lesbia in his poetry? Based on the poems, give your own description of what sort of relationship Catullus and Lesbia have.

Before You Read

Better to Live, Licinius

Meet Horace

"Seize the day, put no trust in the morrow!"

Horace knew from experience that life can take sudden turns. The son of a freed slave, he managed to acquire an excellent education in Rome and Athens. When he was twenty-three, he helped command a legion against the forces of Octavian and Mark Antony in the civil war that followed Julius Caesar's assassination. Horace's side was roundly defeated. He fled home, only to discover that his father's property had been confiscated. The future must have appeared bleak. However, in a few years his poetry caught the attention of Maecenas, an important literary patron. Eventually Octavian (who later became the emperor Augustus Caesar) also befriended Horace. With the emperor's support, Horace became Rome's leading poet.

The lessons that Horace drew from these experiences survive in his poetry. His graceful writing set a standard that poets have long striven to reach.

Horace was born in 65 B.C. and died in 8 B.C.

Reading Focus

If you were asked to give advice to a contemporary politician, what would you say?

Dicuss In a small group, choose a politician and come up with some words of wisdom for him or her. Consider how you might express this advice in a poem.

Setting a Purpose As you read, think about the times you have either offered or been given advice.

Building Background

Avoiding Extremes

Horace often praised "golden moderation," or the "golden mean," in his poems. Although this phrase includes the Latin word *mediocritas,* Horace was certainly not promoting mediocrity. Along with many other Romans, he believed in an ethical formula developed by the Greek philosopher Aristotle. According to Aristotle, virtue lies midway between two extreme forms of behavior. For example, courage is between cowardice and rashness, and generosity is between stinginess and extravagance. Similarly, at this time in ancient India, the Buddha advised following the middle path between self-indulgence and self-renunciation.

A Fall from Favor

The ode "Better to Live, Licinius" is probably addressed to the brother-in-law of Maecenas, Horace's patron. Aulus Terentius Varra Murena (formerly known as Licinius Murena) rose to the consulship, Rome's highest official position, in 23 B.C. The Emperor Augustus soon had him removed from office because of his outspoken political views. Murena was put to death the following year for allegedly conspiring against Augustus.

Augustus, first Emperor of Rome.

By the Roman Well, 19th century. Eduardo Forti (Italy). Oil on canvas.

Viewing the painting: What do the expressions of the people in the painting suggest about their relationships with one another?

At Last It's Come

Sulpicia
Translated by Mary Maxwell

At last it's come, and to be said to hide this kind of love
would shame me more than rumors that I'd laid it bare.
Won over by the pleading of my Muse,° Cytherea
delivered him to me. She placed him in my arms.
Venus has fulfilled what she promised: Let my joys be told
by one who is said to have no joy of her own.
I would hate to keep what I've written under seal where none
could read me sooner than my lover, for pleasure
Likes a little infamy;° discretion is nothing but a tedious pose.
Let it be known I have found a fitting partner.

3 A *Muse* is any one of nine sister goddesses in Greek mythology who preside over and inspire song, poetry, and the arts and sciences. A muse in the general use of the term is a source of inspiration.

9 *Infamy* means disgrace.

Responding to Literature

Personal Response

Which lines in this poem made the strongest impression on you? Why? Write your response in your journal and then discuss it with a classmate.

Analyzing Literature

Recall and Interpret

1. In your opinion, why does the speaker say that she would be ashamed to hide her love affair?
2. What promise has Venus, or Cytherea, fulfilled for the speaker?
3. Why might the speaker suggest that a joyless woman tell the story of her love affair?
4. How do you interpret the speaker's remark that "pleasure / Likes a little infamy"?

Evaluate and Connect

5. The **speaker** of a poem is the voice that talks to the reader (see **Literary Terms Handbook,** page R11). What adjective would you use to describe the speaker of Sulpicia's poem? Support your answer with details from the poem.
6. In the Reading Focus on page 356, you described secret loves in literature. Although the speaker of "At Last It's Come" boasts about her feelings, she does not reveal her lover's name. What might be the reason for this secrecy?
7. In your opinion, how well does Sulpicia portray the emotions of someone who has fallen in love? Explain.
8. Do you think the speaker is young, middle-aged, or old? What leads you to this opinion?

Literary ELEMENTS

Lyric Poetry

In **lyric poetry,** the speaker expresses personal thoughts and feelings. Lyric poems are usually brief and songlike and can take the form of an ode, an elegy, or a sonnet. The term *lyric* comes from *lyre,* a stringed instrument that Greek poets such as Sappho used to accompany their singing. By Sulpicia's time, however, most poets no longer sang their lyrics to the accompaniment of music.

1. What personal thoughts and feelings does the speaker of Sulpicia's poem express?
2. In what ways does the poem resemble the lyrics of a song?

- See **Literary Terms Handbook,** p. R7.

Extending Your Response

Creative Writing

Letter to a Friend Imagine that you are a friend of the speaker in Sulpicia's poem. Write a letter to the speaker in response to the poem. In your letter, describe your reaction to her love affair and offer advice. Do you think it is always better to reveal one's love than to hide it? What concerns might you have regarding the speaker's relationship?

Literature Groups

Think About Gender The pronouns in the poem indicate that the speaker is a woman. Does the speaker's gender make any difference to your understanding of the poem? Could the poem also describe the emotions of a man? Discuss these questions in your group, using evidence from the poem to support your opinion. When you are finished, share your group's conclusions with the class.

Save your work for your portfolio.

Before You Read

ROME, c. A.D. 8

The Story of Pyramus and Thisbe from the *Metamorphoses*

Meet Ovid

"The heavens and all below them, earth and her creatures, / All change, and we, part of creation, also / Must suffer change."

Ovid (ov′ id) came from a well-off family in the small town of Sulmo. His father sent him to Rome to be educated, expecting that he would become a public official. As a teenager, Ovid began reading his verses in public. He held some minor government positions in his twenties, but he soon gave up politics and devoted himself to literature. His imaginative storytelling and witty, elegant style brought him early success.

Love was Ovid's favorite theme, whether he wrote about mythological subjects or Roman society. His greatest work, the *Metamorphoses*, portrays the passions of people and gods in many stories brilliantly woven together. Shortly before it was published, Ovid's life took a disastrous turn. In A.D. 8, Emperor Augustus exiled him to Tomis (Constantza in modern Romania), a bleak outpost where he spent the rest of his life.

Ovid was born in 43 B.C. and died around A.D. 17.

Reading Focus

Think of a time when you incorrectly assumed something on the basis of appearances.

Share Ideas Determine why the appearances were misleading. Recall the consequences that resulted from your assumption. Consider how you might have avoided your mistake. Then share your experience with a partner.

Setting a Purpose Read to learn about the effects of mistaken assumptions.

Building Background

The Time and Place

"The Story of Pyramus and Thisbe" is set in ancient Babylon—the "brick-walled city" mentioned in the first line of the poem—located between the Tigris and Euphrates Rivers in what is now Iraq. According to legend, Babylon, the capital of ancient Babylonia, was built by Semiramis, the daughter of a goddess, and the wife of King Ninus. Assuming the throne after her husband's death, Semiramis built many monuments and cities. Archaeologists believe that these legends grew from the accomplishments of the historical queen, Sammu-ramat.

Myths and Metamorphoses

In the *Metamorphoses,* which runs nearly twelve thousand lines, Ovid links together stories adapted from Greek and Roman mythology. The stories are arranged in chronological order, from the creation of the universe to the founding of the Roman empire. Each one involves some sort of metamorphosis, or transformation—usually a person turning into an animal, plant, mineral, or body of water. Although Ovid generally uses a playful tone in the *Metamorphoses,* the stories can be quite moving. His real focus is on the characters' emotions, which he portrays with compassion and insight.

Although he based the work largely on Greek myths, Ovid enriched them with his own imagination. For example Fama, goddess of rumor, is barely mentioned in the Greek myths; Ovid depicts her living on a mountaintop, in a palace with walls of echoing brass. Often Ovid's versions of Greek myths are those that have survived in art and literature.

Pyramus and Thisbe, 1472.Lucas Cranach the Elder (Saxony). Oil on canvas. Neue Residenz, Bamberg, Germany.

Viewing the painting: Describe the emotions expressed by the characters in this painting.

The Story of Pyramus and Thisbe

from the *Metamorphoses*

Ovid

Translated by Rolfe Humphries

Next door to each other, in the brick-walled city
Built by Semiramis, lived a boy and girl,
Pyramus, a most handsome fellow, Thisbe,
Loveliest of all those Eastern° girls. Their nearness
Made them acquainted, and love grew, in time,
So that they would have married, but their parents
Forbade it. But their parents could not keep them
From being in love: their nods and gestures showed it—
You know how fire suppressed burns all the fiercer.
There was a chink° in the wall between the houses,
A flaw the careless builder had never noticed,
Nor anyone else, for many years, detected,
But the lovers found it—love is a finder, always—
Used it to talk through, and the loving whispers
Went back and forth in safety. They would stand–
One on each side, listening for each other,
Happy if each could hear the other's breathing,
And then they would scold the wall: 'You envious barrier,
Why get in our way? Would it be too much to ask you
To open wide for an embrace, or even
Permit us room to kiss in? Still, we are grateful,
We owe you something, we admit; at least
You let us talk together.' But their talking
Was futile, rather; and when evening came
They would say *Good-night!* and give the good-night kisses
That never reached the other.

"The next morning
Came, and the fires of night burnt out, and sunshine
Dried the night frost, and Pyramus and Thisbe
Met at the usual place, and first, in whispers,
Complained, and came—high time!—to a decision.
That night, when all was quiet, they would fool
Their guardians, or try to, come outdoors,
Run away from home, and even leave the city.
And, not to miss each other, as they wandered
In the wide fields, where should they meet? At Ninus'
Tomb,° they supposed, was best; there was a tree there,

---

4 The Roman empire extended from the Atlantic Ocean on the west to the eastern rim of the Mediterranean Sea. To ancient Romans, people who lived in southwest Asia were *Eastern.*

10 A *chink* is a small slit or opening in a wall.

35–36 Ninus was an Assyrian king and the husband of Semiramis (sə mir′ ə mis). He founded the Assyrian capital, Nineveh. After his death, Semiramis erected a temple on the outskirts of Babylon–*Ninus' tomb.*

A mulberry-tree,° loaded with snow-white berries,
Near a cool spring. The plan was good, the daylight
Was very slow in going, but at last
The sun went down into the waves,° as always,
And the night rose, as always, from those waters.

And Thisbe opened her door, so sly, so cunning,
There was no creaking of the hinge, and no one
Saw her go through the darkness, and she came,
Veiled, to the tomb of Ninus, sat there waiting
Under the shadow of the mulberry-tree.
Love made her bold. But suddenly, here came something!—
A lioness, her jaws a crimson froth
With the blood of cows, fresh-slain, came there for water,
And far off through the moonlight Thisbe saw her
And ran, all scared, to hide herself in a cave,
And dropped her veil as she ran. The lioness,
Having quenched her thirst, came back to the woods, and saw
The girl's light veil, and mangled it and mouthed it
With bloody jaws. Pyramus, coming there
Too late, saw tracks in the dust, turned pale, and paler
Seeing the bloody veil. 'One night,' he cried,
'Will kill two lovers, and one of them, most surely,
Deserved a longer life. It is all my fault,
I am the murderer, poor girl; I told you
To come here in the night, to all this terror,
And was not here before you, to protect you.
Come, tear my flesh, devour my guilty body,
Come, lions, all of you, whose lairs lie hidden
Under this rock! I am acting like a coward,
Praying for death.' He lifts the veil and takes it
Into the shadow of their tree; he kisses
The veil he knows so well, his tears run down
Into its folds: 'Drink my blood too!' he cries,
And draws his sword, and plunges it into his body,
And, dying, draws it out, warm from the wound.
As he lay there on the ground, the spouting blood
Leaped high, just as a pipe sends water spurting

---

37 *Mulberry* trees are Asian trees cultivated as ornamental trees and for their sweet, edible fruits.

40 *The sun went down into the waves* refers to the horizon on which the sun appears to set. Babylon was located between the Tigris and Euphrates Rivers.

Through a small hissing opening, when broken
With a flaw in the lead,° and all the air is sprinkled.
The fruit of the tree, from that red spray, turned crimson,
And the roots, soaked with the blood, dyed all the berries
The same dark hue.
"Thisbe came out of hiding,
Still frightened, but a little fearful, also,
To disappoint her lover. She kept looking
Not only with her eyes, but all her heart,
Eager to tell him of those terrible dangers,
About her own escape. She recognized
The place, the shape of the tree, but there was something
Strange or peculiar in the berries' color.
Could this be right? And then she saw a quiver
Of limbs on bloody ground, and started backward,

75 *A flaw in the lead* compares the way water issues from a broken pipe to how blood spurts from a wound.

Night and Sleep. Evelyn De Morgan (Great Britain, 1855–1919). Oil on canvas. De Morgan Foundation, London.

Viewing the painting: What is the mood of this painting? What part of this story does it reflect?

Paler than boxwood,° shivering, as water
Stirs when a little breeze ruffles the surface.
It was not long before she knew her lover,
And tore her hair, and beat her innocent bosom
With her little fists, embraced the well-loved body,
Filling the wounds with tears, and kissed the lips
Cold in his dying. 'O my Pyramus,'
She wept, 'What evil fortune takes you from me?
Pyramus, answer me! Your dearest Thisbe
Is calling you. Pyramus, listen! Lift your head!'
He heard the name of Thisbe, and he lifted
His eyes, with the weight of death heavy upon them,
And saw her face, and closed his eyes.
"And Thisbe
Saw her own veil, and saw the ivory scabbard°
With no sword in it, and understood. 'Poor boy,'
She said, 'So, it was your own hand,
Your love, that took your life away. I too
Have a brave hand for this one thing, I too
Have love enough, and this will give me strength
For the last wound. I will follow you in death,
Be called the cause and comrade of your dying.
Death was the only one could keep you from me,
Death shall not keep you from me. Wretched parents
Of Pyramus and Thisbe, listen to us,
Listen to both our prayers, do not begrudge us,
Whom death has joined, lying at last together
In the same tomb. And you, O tree, now shading
The body of one, and very soon to shadow
The bodies of two, keep in remembrance always
The sign of our death, the dark and mournful color.'
She spoke, and fitting the sword-point at her breast,
Fell forward on the blade, still warm and reeking
With her lover's blood. Her prayers touched the gods,
And touched her parents, for the mulberry fruit
Still reddens at its ripeness, and the ashes
Rest in a common urn."°

---

88 *Boxwood* is a shrub used for hedges and borders.

101 A *scabbard* is a sheath for a sword or dagger.

123 An *urn* is a vessel, typically an ornamental vase on a pedestal. Urns are often used for preserving the ashes of the dead after cremation.

Responding to Literature

Personal Response

Were you surprised by the outcome of this story? How do you think it could have been avoided? Share your thoughts with the class.

Analyzing Literature

Recall and Interpret

1. Why must Pyramus and Thisbe talk through a wall? What does the narrator suggest with the remark, "You know how fire suppressed burns all the fiercer"?
2. What decision do Pyramus and Thisbe make? The narrator says of Thisbe that "Love made her bold." What is your interpretation of this comment?
3. Why does Thisbe run off after she arrives at the tomb of Ninus?
4. What does Pyramus believe happened to Thisbe at the tomb? Why does Pyramus blame himself for Thisbe's "death"?
5. How does Thisbe finally end her separation from Pyramus?

Evaluate and Connect

6. **Myths** often explain some aspect of nature (see **Literary Terms Handbook,** page R8). In what way does the end of the poem function as a myth?
7. In your opinion, what factors led to the deaths of Pyramus and Thisbe?
8. In the Reading Focus on page 359, you described an assumption that you made in the past. Identify an assumption in "The Story of Pyramus and Thisbe" that has tragic consequences. What leads the character to make this incorrect assumption?
9. Which story, play, or film most reminds you of "The Story of Pyramus and Thisbe"? What do these works have in common?
10. What does Ovid's poem suggest to you about love? Explain, citing details from the poem for support.

Literary ELEMENTS

Narrative Poetry

Poetry that tells a story is called **narrative poetry.** Like a prose story, a narrative poem has characters and a plot that centers on a conflict. Some poems, such as verse fables, portray a single episode, but narrative poems can be as complex as prose stories. Epic poems, such as the *Iliad* and the *Aeneid,* are long works that portray the actions of gods and heroes. Although the *Metamorphoses* is not an epic, it retells many Greek and Roman myths and epics.

1. What is the main conflict in "The Story of Pyramus and Thisbe"?
2. You know that a lyric poem is a brief, songlike poem expressing personal thoughts and feelings. How would you compare the experience of reading a lyric poem with that of reading a narrative poem?

- See **Literary Terms Handbook,** p. R8.

Extending Your Response

Writing About Literature

Evaluating an Author's Technique Select a passage from the poem that you found especially dramatic. Write a paragraph analyzing how Ovid made that passage effective. You may wish to discuss images, asides by the narrator, or use of dialogue.

Literature Groups

Modernizing a Story If you were updating the story of Pyramus and Thisbe, what elements would you change? In your group, brainstorm ideas for a contemporary version of the story. Present your final suggestions to the class.

Save your work for your portfolio.

Reading & Thinking Skills

Identifying Chronological Order

In "The Story of Pyramus and Thisbe," Ovid narrates a series of events that end tragically for the two young lovers. To explain the relationship between these events and to clarify for the reader the order in which they happen, Ovid arranges the events chronologically. **Chronological order** is an organizational strategy that records events in the order in which they happen. Because it is straightforward, chronological order is the most obvious and workable way of arranging material in a narrative.

Transitional words and phrases such as *first, later that day, the next morning,* and *yesterday* alert readers to the order of events in time and to the relationship in time between one event and another. In "The Story of Pyramus and Thisbe," the use of chronological order serves two purposes: to relate the events in the order in which they happened, and to show that particular consequences resulted *because* of the order of the events.

Read the following excerpt from Ovid's story. Notice how the transitional phrases (in italics) clarify the chronological order of events and details.

> "*The next morning*
> *Came,* and the fires of night burnt out, and sunshine
> Dried the night frost, and Pyramus and Thisbe
> Met at the usual place, *and first,* in whispers,
> Complained, and came—high time!—to a decision.
> *That night, when all was quiet,* they would fool
> Their guardians, or try to, come outdoors,
> Run away from home, and even leave the city."

- For more about chronological order, see **Reading Handbook,** p. R86.

ACTIVITIES

1. List the transitional words and phrases used in Ovid's story to organize the events and details in chronological order. Expand your list by adding as many other transitional words and expressions as you can think of.
2. Create a flowchart to illustrate the chronological order of key events in "The Story of Pyramus and Thisbe."
3. How does the sequence of events in the story dramatically affect the outcome?

Before You Read

from the *Aeneid*

ROME, 30–19 B.C.

Meet Virgil

"For you [Virgil] are my true master and first author, / the sole maker from whom I drew the breath / of that sweet style whose measures have brought me honor." —Dante, *Inferno*

Virgil was a shy man who grew up on a farm in northern Italy. He loved the countryside, which was unfortunately ravaged by civil wars. When Augustus Caesar took control of Rome after defeating his rivals, Virgil looked forward to an era of peace and stability, and he expressed his support for Augustus in the *Aeneid*. Although this epic celebrates Rome's long tradition of military conquest, Virgil did not overlook the tragic side of warfare. He continually reminds his audience that heroic deeds come at a terrible cost in human suffering.

Virgil began writing the *Aeneid* at age forty. Eleven years later he finished a draft of it, but he died shortly thereafter. The *Aeneid* secured Virgil's reputation as the greatest of Latin poets. Later, he had an especially strong influence on such poets as Dante and Milton, who used the *Aeneid* as a model for their religious epics.

Virgil was born in 70 B.C. and died in 19 B.C.

Reading Focus

Think about heroic acts you have witnessed or read about.

Chart It! In a chart such as the one below, write down the names of people whom you consider to be heroic. Then briefly explain why each one is heroic.

Hero	Explanation

Setting a Purpose As you read, think about the ways in which Aeneas might be considered a hero.

Building Background

The Aeneid

The *Aeneid* tells the story of Aeneas, son of the goddess Venus and a mortal father named Anchises. Virgil based the structure and style of the poem on Homer's epics. He also borrowed episodes and characters from his Greek predecessor, but he shaped this material to express distinctly Roman values such as piety, duty, and self-denial.

The poem begins after the fall of Troy. Aeneas and his Trojan followers have wandered around the Mediterranean for years in search of a new homeland. Fierce winds force them to land their ships in Carthage, a North African city ruled by Queen Dido. Aeneas and Dido soon fall in love, but the gods command Aeneas to continue his journey. As her lover sails away, a forlorn Dido commits suicide. Aeneas finally reaches Italy, where he must defeat the native inhabitants before he can establish a settlement. His descendants are destined to build Rome and spread their civilization through conquest.

Research

Use the library or the Internet to learn more about Augustus Caesar and his leadership of Rome. Then as you read this excerpt from the *Aeneid,* think about questions such as the following: Why did Virgil believe that Augustus would bring peace and stability to Rome? In what ways does this selection show Virgil's support for Augustus?

from the AENEID

Book II: THE FALL OF TROY

Virgil
Translated by Robert Fitzgerald

Aeneas Telling Dido About the Troubles of Troy, 1815. Pierre-Narcisse Gúerin (France, 1774–1833). Oil on canvas, 292 x 390 cm. Louvre Museum, Paris.

Viewing the painting: How do you think Dido and her companions are reacting to Aeneas's story in this painting? Why do you get this impression?

The following episode appears in Book II of the *Aeneid.* At a feast held in his honor, Aeneas reluctantly agrees to tell Queen Dido the story of Troy's destruction. In the tenth year of the Trojan War, the Greeks built a large wooden horse, which they claimed was an offering to ensure their safe passage home. After hiding warriors inside the horse's belly, the Greek forces pretended to sail away. Some Trojans wanted to bring the horse into their city, but others urged caution. The debate was interrupted by a captured Greek named Sinon, whose lies convinced the Trojans to drag the horse inside. Under cover of darkness, the hidden Greeks dropped out of the horse and opened Troy's gates to their fellow warriors. Aeneas was asleep at the time, dreaming that the dead Trojan hero Hector told him to take his household gods and abandon the city. He awoke to the sound of battle.

While I dreamed,
The turmoil rose, with anguish, in the city.
More and more, although Anchises'° house
Lay in seclusion, muffled among trees,
The din at the grim onset grew; and now
I shook off sleep, I climbed to the roof top
To cup my ears and listen. And the sound
Was like the sound a grassfire makes in grain,
Whipped by a Southwind, or a torrent foaming
Out of a mountainside to strew° in ruin
Fields, happy crops, the yield of plowing teams,
Or woodlands borne off in the flood; in wonder
The shepherd listens on a rocky peak.
I knew then what our trust had won for us,
Knew the Danaan° fraud: Deïphobus'°
Great house in flames, already caving in
Under the overpowering god of fire;°
Ucalegon's already caught nearby;
The glare lighting the straits beyond Sigeum;°
The cries of men, the wild calls of the trumpets.

To arm was my first maddened impulse—not
That anyone had a fighting chance in arms;
Only I burned to gather up some force
For combat, and to man some high redoubt.°
So fury drove me, and it came to me
That meeting death was beautiful in arms.

3 **Anchises** (an kī′ sēz): father of Aeneas; king of Dardania and ally of Priam (king of Troy).

10 **strew:** here, flood.

15 **Danaan** (dan′ ē ən): Greek. **Deïphobus** (dē′ ə phō′ bəs): a son of Priam who married Helen after the death of Paris in the war.

17 **god of fire:** Vulcan, especially associated with destructive fires and volcanoes; he favored the Greeks.

19 **Sigeum** (si jē′ əm): a promontory, or rock jutting out into the water, near Troy.

24 **redoubt:** fortified place.

Then here, eluding the Achaean spears,
Came Panthus, Othrys' son, priest of Apollo,°
Carrying holy things, our conquered gods,
And pulling a small grandchild along: he ran
Despairing to my doorway.
'Where's the crux,°
Panthus,' I said. 'What strongpoint shall we hold?'

Before I could say more, he groaned and answered:
'The last day for Dardania° has come,
The hour not to be fought off any longer.
Trojans we have been; Ilium° has been;
The glory of the Teucrians° is no more;
Black Jupiter° has passed it on to Argos.°
Greeks are the masters in our burning city.
Tall as a cliff, set in the heart of town,
Their horse pours out armed men. The conqueror,
Gloating Sinon, brews new conflagrations.
Troops hold the gates—as many thousand men
As ever came from great Mycenae;° others
Block the lanes with crossed spears; glittering
In a combat line, swordblades are drawn for slaughter.
Even the first guards at the gates can barely
Offer battle, or blindly make a stand.' . . .

The desperate odds doubled their fighting spirit:
From that time on, like predatory wolves
In fog and darkness, when a savage hunger
Drives them blindly on, and cubs in lairs
Lie waiting with dry famished jaws—just so
Through arrow flights and enemies we ran
Toward our sure death, straight for the city's heart,
Cavernous black night over and around us.
Who can describe the havoc of that night
Or tell the deaths, or tally wounds with tears?°
The ancient city falls, after dominion
Many long years. In windrows° on the streets,
In homes, on solemn porches of the gods,°
Dead bodies lie. And not alone the Trojans
Pay the price with their heart's blood; at times
Manhood returns to fire even the conquered
And Danaan conquerors fall. Grief everywhere,
Everywhere terror, and all shapes of death. . . .

28 **Apollo:** god of sunlight, healing, prophecy, archery, music, and poetry. He favored the Trojans.

31 **crux:** focal point or most important moment of the battle.

34 **Dardania:** a region in the Trojan lands.

36 **Ilium** (il′ ē əm): Troy.

37 **Teucrians** (to͞o′ krē ənz): descendants of Teucer (a former king of Troy); Trojans.

38 **Jupiter:** The chief god and god of the sky and the weather; he favored Troy but knew it could not be saved. **Argos:** a Greek city and the general name for the kingdom of Agamemnon who is the leader of the Greek armies.

44 **Mycenae** (mī sē′ nē): capital of the kingdom ruled by Agamemnon.

58 **tally wounds with tears:** use tears to count the number of wounds.

60 **windrows:** long raised rows, usually of hay that has been raked together; here, the windrows are made of dead Trojans.

61 **porches of the gods:** temple steps.

Mistaken for Greeks, Aeneas and his companions are able to destroy a Greek faction. Then, encouraged by their victory, they try a new strategy. The Trojan men disguise themselves in Greek armor and continue fighting.

When gods are contrary
They stand by no one. Here before us came
Cassandra, Priam's virgin daughter, dragged
By her long hair out of Minerva's° shrine,
Lifting her brilliant eyes in vain to heaven—
Her eyes alone, as her white hands were bound.
Coroebus,° infuriated, could not bear it,
But plunged into the midst to find his death.
We all went after him, our swords at play,
But here, here first, from the temple gable's height,
We met a hail of missiles from our friends,
Pitiful execution,° by their error,
Who thought us Greek from our Greek plumes and shields.
Then with a groan of anger, seeing the virgin
Wrested° from them, Danaans from all sides
Rallied and attacked us: fiery Ajax,°
Atreus' sons,° Dolopians° in a mass—
As, when a cyclone breaks, conflicting winds
Will come together, Westwind, Southwind, Eastwind
Riding high out of the Dawnland; forests
Bend and roar, and raging all in spume
Nereus° with his trident° churns the deep.
Then some whom we had taken by surprise
Under cover of night throughout the city
And driven off, came back again: they knew
Our shields and arms for liars now, our speech
Alien to their own. . . .°

Mars° gone berserk, Danaans
In a rush to scale the roof; the gate besieged
By a tortoise shell of overlapping shields.
Ladders clung to the wall, and men strove upward
Before the very doorposts, on the rungs,
Left hand putting the shield up, and the right
Reaching for the cornice.° The defenders
Wrenched out upperworks and rooftiles: these
For missiles, as they saw the end, preparing
To fight back even on the edge of death.
And gilded beams, ancestral ornaments,

Cassandra, 1898. Evelyn De Morgan (Great Britain). Oil on canvas, 97.7 x 48.2 cm. De Morgan Foundation Collection at Cragside, Northumberland.

Viewing the painting: What does Cassandra's gesture in this painting suggest about her state of mind?

70 **Minerva** (mi nur′ və): goddess of wisdom and the arts and sciences.

73 **Coroebus** (kər ō′ ə bəs): Trojan ally who loves Cassandra.

78 **Pitiful execution:** Trojans attack Aeneas and his followers because they were dressed like Greeks.

81 **Wrested:** taken by force.

82 **Ajax:** Ajax the Lesser, a great warrior in the Greek army.

83 **Atreus' sons:** Agamemnon and Menelaus. **Dolopians:** inhabitants of a kingdom ruled by Achilles' father.

88 **Nereus** (nēr′ ē əs): a sea god; the old man of the sea. **trident:** three-pronged spear carried by a sea god.

92–93 **Our shields . . . alien to their own:** the Greek armor that we wear as a disguise no longer fools the Greeks.

94 **Mars:** god of war.

100 **cornice** (kôr′ nis): molding that projects along the top of a wall.

They rolled down on the heads below. In hall
Others with swords drawn held the entrance way,
Packed there, waiting. Now we plucked up heart
To help the royal house, to give our men
A respite,° and to add our strength to theirs,
Though all were beaten. And we had for entrance
A rear door, secret, giving on a passage
Between the palace halls; in other days
Andromachë,° poor lady, often used it,
Going alone to see her husband's parents°
Or taking Astyanax° to his grandfather.
I climbed high on the roof, where hopeless men
Were picking up and throwing futile missiles.
Here was a tower like a promontory
Rising toward the stars above the roof:
All Troy, the Danaan ships, the Achaean camp,
Were visible from this. Now close beside it
With crowbars, where the flooring made loose joints,
We pried it from its bed and pushed it over.
Down with a rending crash in sudden ruin
Wide over the Danaan lines it fell;
But fresh troops moved up, and the rain of stones
With every kind of missile never ceased.

Just at the outer doors of the vestibule
Sprang Pyrrhus,° all in bronze and glittering,
As a serpent, hidden swollen underground
By a cold winter, writhes into the light,
On vile grass fed, his old skin cast away,
Renewed and glossy, rolling slippery coils,
With lifted underbelly rearing sunward
And triple tongue a-flicker. Close beside him
Giant Periphas and Automedon,
His armor-bearer, once Achilles' driver,
Besieged the place with all the young of Scyros,°
Hurling their torches at the palace roof.
Pyrrhus shouldering forward with an axe
Broke down the stony threshold, forced apart
Hinges and brazen° doorjambs, and chopped through
One panel of the door, splitting the oak,
To make a window, a great breach. And there
Before their eyes the inner halls lay open,
The courts of Priam and the ancient kings,
With men-at-arms ranked in the vestibule.
From the interior came sounds of weeping,

109 respite (res′ pit): temporary rest or relief.

113 Andromachë (an drom′ ə kē): the wife of Hector, Troy's greatest hero, who was killed by Achilles.

114 her husband's parents: Priam and Hecuba, the king and queen of Troy.

115 Astyanax (as tī′ ə naks): young son of Hector and Andromachë.

129 Pyrrhus (pi′ rəs): the son of Achilles.

138 Scyros (skī′ rəs): island in the Aegean Sea off Greece, birthplace of Pyrrhus.

142 brazen: made of brass.

Pitiful commotion, wails of women
High-pitched, rising in the formal chambers
To ring against the silent golden stars;
And, through the palace, mothers wild with fright
Ran to and fro or clung to doors and kissed them.
Pyrrhus with his father's brawn stormed on,
No bolts or bars or men availed to stop him:
Under his battering the double doors
Were torn out of their sockets and fell inward.
Sheer force cleared the way: the Greeks broke through
Into the vestibule, cut down the guards,
And made the wide hall seethe with men-at-arms—
A tumult greater than when dikes are burst
And a foaming river, swirling out in flood,
Whelms° every parapet° and races on
Through fields and over all the lowland plains,
Bearing off pens and cattle. I myself
Saw Neoptolemus° furious with blood
In the entrance way, and saw the two Atridae;°
Hecuba I saw, and her hundred daughters,
Priam before the altars, with his blood
Drenching the fires that he himself had blessed.
Those fifty bridal chambers, hope of a line°
So flourishing; those doorways high and proud,
Adorned with takings of barbaric gold,°
Were all brought low: fire had them, or the Greeks.

What was the fate of Priam, you may ask.
Seeing his city captive, seeing his own
Royal portals rent° apart, his enemies
In the inner rooms, the old man uselessly
Put on his shoulders, shaking with old age,
Armor unused for years, belted a sword on,
And made for the massed enemy to die.
Under the open sky in a central court
Stood a big altar; near it, a laurel tree
Of great age, leaning over, in deep shade
Embowered the Penatës.° At this altar
Hecuba and her daughters, like white doves
Blown down in a black storm, clung together,
Enfolding holy images in their arms.
Now, seeing Priam in a young man's gear,
She called out:
'My poor husband, what mad thought
Drove you to buckle on these weapons?

163 **Whelms:** engulfs completely usually with a disastrous effect; overwhelms. **parapet:** wall or protective barrier.

166 **Neoptolemus** (nē op tôl′ ə məs′): another name for Pyrrhus.

167 **Atridae** (ə trī′ dē): sons of Atreus; refers to Agamemnon and Menelaus.

171 **line:** descendants; royal line that rules continuously for generations.

173 **barbaric gold:** gold taken from defeated peoples; barbaric originally meant anyone not from one's own culture.

177 **portals rent:** palace doors torn apart.

185 **Embowered the Penatës** (pə nā′ tēz): sheltered statues of the Penatës, gods who protected homes.

Where are you trying to go? The time is past
For help like this, for this kind of defending,
Even if my own Hector could be here.
Come to me now: the altar will protect us,°
Or else you'll die with us.'
She drew him close,
Heavy with years, and made a place for him
To rest on the consecrated° stone.
Now see
Politës, one of Priam's sons, escaped
From Pyrrhus' butchery and on the run
Through enemies and spears, down colonnades,
Through empty courtyards, wounded. Close behind
Comes Pyrrhus burning for the death stroke: has him,
Catches him now, and lunges with the spear.
The boy has reached his parents, and before them
Goes down, pouring out his life with blood.
Now Priam, in the very midst of death,
Would neither hold his peace nor spare his anger.

'For what you've done, for what you've dared,' he said,
'If there is care in heaven for atrocity,
May the gods render fitting thanks, reward you
As you deserve. You forced me to look on
At the destruction of my son: defiled
A father's eyes with death. That great Achilles
You claim to be the son of—and you lie—
Was not like you to Priam, his enemy;
To me who threw myself upon his mercy
He showed compunction, gave me back for burial
The bloodless corpse of Hector, and returned me
To my own realm.'
The old man threw his spear
With feeble impact; blocked by the ringing bronze,
It hung there harmless from the jutting boss.°
Then Pyrrhus answered:
'You'll report the news
To Pelidës,° my father; don't forget
My sad behavior, the degeneracy
Of Neoptolemus. Now die.'
With this,
To the altar step itself he dragged him trembling,
Slipping in the pooled blood of his son,
And took him by the hair with his left hand.
The sword flashed in his right; up to the hilt

195 altar will protect us: it would be an offense to the gods to shed human blood on the altar.

198 consecrated: made sacred by means of a religious ceremony.

222 boss: raised ornament; embossment.

223–224 report . . . To Pelidës: tell my father when you reach the House of the Dead.

224 Pelidës (pē′ li dēz): the son of Peleus, Achilles.

He thrust it in his body.
That was the end
Of Priam's age, the doom that took him off,
With Troy in flames before his eyes, his towers
Headlong fallen—he that in other days
Had ruled in pride so many lands and peoples,
The power of Asia.
On the distant shore
The vast trunk headless lies without a name.°

237 vast trunk . . . name: Priam's headless body now lies on the shore unburied and without any identifying marker.

Aeneas and His Father Fleeing Troy, c. 1635. Simon Vouet (France). Oil on canvas, 140.3 x 110 cm. San Diego Museum of Art, CA.

Viewing the painting: What does this painting suggest about the relationship between Aeneas and his father?

For the first time that night, inhuman shuddering
Took me, head to foot. I stood unmanned,°
And my dear father's image came to mind
As our king, just his age, mortally wounded,
Gasped his life away before my eyes.
Creusa° came to mind, too, left alone;
The house plundered; danger to little Iulus.°
I looked around to take stock of my men,
But all had left me, utterly played out,
Giving their beaten bodies to the fire
Or plunging from the roof.
It came to this,
That I stood there alone. And then I saw
Lurking beyond the doorsill of the Vesta,°
In hiding, silent, in that place reserved,
The daughter of Tyndareus.° Glare of fires
Lighted my steps this way and that, my eyes
Glancing over the whole scene, everywhere.
That woman, terrified of the Trojans' hate
For the city overthrown, terrified too
Of Danaan vengeance, her abandoned husband's
Anger after years—Helen, that Fury°
Both to her own homeland and Troy,° had gone
To earth, a hated thing, before the altars.
Now fires blazed up in my own spirit—
A passion to avenge my fallen town
And punish Helen's whorishness.
'Shall this one
Look untouched on Sparta and Mycenae°
After her triumph, going like a queen,
And see her home and husband, kin and children,
With Trojan girls for escort, Phrygian° slaves?
Must Priam perish by the sword for this?
Troy burn, for this? Dardania's littoral°
Be soaked in blood, so many times, for this?
Not by my leave.° I know
No glory comes of punishing a woman,
The feat can bring no honor. Still, I'll be
Approved for snuffing out a monstrous life,
For a just sentence carried out. My heart
Will teem with joy in this avenging fire,
And the ashes of my kin will be appeased.'°

So ran my thoughts. I turned wildly upon her,
But at that moment, clear, before my eyes—

239 **unmanned:** my courage gone.

243 **Creusa** (krē ū′ sə): wife of Aeneas; Priam's daughter.

244 **Iulus** (ū′ ləs): son of Aeneas and Creusa; also called Ascanius.

250 **Vesta:** here, a temple to Vesta, goddess of the hearth and household activities.

252 **daughter of Tyndareus** (tin der′ ē əs): Helen.

258 **Fury:** the Furies were avenging goddesses who punished criminals or sinners beyond the reach of human justice.

258–259 **Fury . . . and Troy:** the cause of the madness and suffering on both sides.

264 **Look . . . Mycenae:** Aeneas is outraged that Helen will return unpunished to the cities of Menelaus and Agamemnon.

267 **Phrygian** (frij′ ē ən): people from a region near Troy.

269 **littoral** (lit′ ər əl): seashore.

271 **by my leave:** with my permission.

277 **appeased:** soothed; pacified by an offering.

Never before so clear—in a pure light
Stepping before me, radiant through the night,
My loving mother° came: immortal, tall,
And lovely as the lords of heaven know her.
Catching me by the hand, she held me back,
Then with her rose-red mouth reproved° me:
'Son,

Why let such suffering goad° you on to fury
Past control? Where is your thoughtfulness
For me, for us? Will you not first revisit
The place you left your father, worn and old,
Or find out if your wife, Creusa, lives,
And the young boy, Ascanius—all these
Cut off by Greek troops foraging° everywhere?
Had I not cared for them, fire would by now
Have taken them, their blood glutted° the sword.
You must not hold the woman of Laconia,°
That hated face, the cause of this,° nor Paris.
The harsh will of the gods it is, the gods,
That overthrows the splendor of this place
And brings Troy from her height into the dust.
Look over there: I'll tear away the cloud
That curtains you, and films your mortal sight,
The fog around you.—Have no fear of doing
Your mother's will, or balk at obeying her.—
Look: where you see high masonry thrown down,
Stone torn from stone, with billowing smoke and dust,
Neptune° is shaking from their beds the walls
That his great trident pried up, undermining,
Toppling the whole city down. And look:
Juno° in all her savagery holds
The Scaean Gates,° and raging in steel armor
Calls her allied army from the ships.
Up on the citadel—turn, look—Pallas Tritonia°
Couched in a stormcloud, lightening, with her Gorgon!°
The Father himself empowers the Danaans,
Urges assaulting gods on the defenders.
Away, child; put an end to toiling so.
I shall be near, to see you safely home.'

She hid herself in the deep gloom of night,
And now the dire forms appeared to me
Of great immortals, enemies of Troy.
I knew the end then: Ilium was going down
In fire, the Troy of Neptune going down,

282 **My loving mother:** Venus, goddess of love and beauty.

285 **reproved:** rebuked; scolded.

286 **goad:** arouse; incite; encourage to take action.

292 **foraging:** literally, searching for food; figuratively, looting, plundering.

294 **glutted:** excessively covered; overwhelmed; drenched.

295 **Laconia:** Sparta, Greek city-state ruled by Menelaus; here, it refers to Helen.

296 **That hated face, the cause of this:** refers to Helen, whose beauty was the reason for which Paris abducted her and the war began.

306 **Neptune:** chief sea god; he favored the Greeks.

309 **Juno:** chief goddess and protector of marriage; wife of Jupiter, she favored the Greeks.

310 **Scaean Gates** (skē′ ən): a set of gates in the wall around Troy.

312 **Pallas Tritonia:** the goddess Athena, who was born near Lake Tritonus.

313 **Gorgon:** any of three monsters with huge teeth, sharp claws, and snakes for hair.

As in high mountains when the countrymen
Have notched an ancient ash, then make their axes
Ring with might and main, chopping away
To fell the tree—ever on the point of falling,
Shaken through all its foliage, and the treetop
Nodding; bit by bit the strokes prevail
Until it gives a final groan at last
And crashes down in ruin from the height.

Now I descended where the goddess guided,
Clear of the flames, and clear of enemies,
For both retired; so gained my father's door,
My ancient home. I looked for him at once,
My first wish being to help him to the mountains;
But with Troy gone he set his face against it,
Not to prolong his life, or suffer exile.

'The rest of you, all in your prime,' he said,
'Make your escape; you are still hale and strong.
If heaven's lords had wished me a longer span
They would have saved this home for me. I call it
More than enough that once before I saw

Procession of the Trojan Horse into Troy. Giovanni Battista Tiepolo (Italy, 1696–1770). Oil on canvas, 38.8 x 66.7 cm. National Gallery, London.

Viewing the painting: How would you describe the crowd's reaction to the Trojan horse in this painting?

My city taken and wrecked, and went on living.
Here is my death bed, here. Take leave of me.
Depart now. I'll find death with my sword arm.
The enemy will oblige; they'll come for spoils.
Burial can be dispensed with. All these years
I've lingered in my impotence, at odds
With heaven, since the Father of gods and men
Breathed high winds of thunderbolt upon me
And touched me with his fire.'°
He spoke on
In the same vein, inflexible. The rest of us,
Creusa and Ascanius and the servants,
Begged him in tears not to pull down with him
Our lives as well, adding his own dead weight
To the fates' pressure. But he would not budge,
He held to his resolve and to his chair.
I felt swept off again to fight, in misery
Longing for death. What choices now were open,
What chance had I?
'Did you suppose, my father,
That I could tear myself away and leave you?
Unthinkable; how could a father say it?
Now if it please the powers above that nothing
Stand of this great city; if your heart
Is set on adding your own death and ours
To that of Troy, the door's wide open for it:
Pyrrhus will be here, splashed with Priam's blood;
He kills the son before his father's eyes,
The father at the altars.
My dear mother,
Was it for this, through spears and fire, you brought me,
To see the enemy deep in my house,
To see my son, Ascanius, my father,
And near them both, Creusa,
Butchered in one another's blood? My gear,
Men, bring my gear. The last light calls the conquered.
Give me back to the Greeks. Let me take up
The combat once again. We shall not all
Die this day unavenged.'
I buckled on
Swordbelt and blade and slid my left forearm
Into the shield strap, turning to go out,
But at the door Creusa hugged my knees,°
Then held up little Iulus to his father.

350–351 **Breathed . . . fire:** Jupiter made Anchises blind for revealing that Venus was the mother of Aeneas.

381 **hugged my knees:** kneeled before; a gesture that accompanies a request or plea.

'If you are going out to die, take us
To face the whole thing with you. If experience
Leads you to put some hope in weaponry
Such as you now take, guard your own house here.
When you have gone, to whom is Iulus left?
Your father? Wife?—one called that long ago.'

She went on, and her wailing filled the house,
But then a sudden portent° came, a marvel:
Amid his parents' hands and their sad faces
A point on Iulus' head seemed to cast light,
A tongue of flame that touched but did not burn him,
Licking his fine hair, playing round his temples. . . .

Now indeed
My father, overcome, addressed the gods,
And rose in worship of the blessed star.

'Now, now, no more delay. I'll follow you.
Where you conduct me, there I'll be.
Gods of my fathers,
Preserve this house, preserve my grandson. Yours
This portent was. Troy's life is in your power.
I yield. I go as your companion, son.'
Then he was still. We heard the blazing town
Crackle more loudly, felt the scorching heat.

'Then come, dear father. Arms around my neck:
I'll take you on my shoulders, no great weight.
Whatever happens, both will face one danger,
Find one safety. Iulus will come with me,
My wife at a good interval behind.
Servants, give your attention to what I say.
At the gate inland there's a funeral mound
And an old shrine of Ceres° the Bereft;°
Near it an ancient cypress, kept alive
For many years by our fathers' piety.°
By various routes we'll come to that one place.
Father, carry our hearthgods, our Penatës.
It would be wrong for me to handle them—
Just come from such hard fighting, bloody work—
Until I wash myself in running water.'°

When I had said this, over my breadth of shoulder
And bent neck, I spread out a lion skin

390 portent: a sign; an omen.

412 Ceres: goddess of agriculture. **Ceres the Bereft:** Pluto, god of the underworld, carried Proserpina (prō sur′ pə nə), Ceres' daughter, to the underworld to be his wife. By Jupiter's compromise, Proserpina spends six months (winter) in the underworld. During these months Ceres mourns her daughter's absence, and the land lies fallow or uncultivated.

414 piety: devotion.

419 wash myself . . . water: perform a purification ritual.

For tawny cloak and stooped to take his weight.
Then little Iulus put his hand in mine
And came with shorter steps beside his father.
My wife fell in behind. Through shadowed places
On we went, and I, lately unmoved
By any spears thrown, any squads of Greeks,
Felt terror now at every eddy of wind,
Alarm at every sound, alert and worried
Alike for my companion and my burden.
I had got near the gate, and now I thought
We had made it all the way, when suddenly
A noise of running feet came near at hand,
And peering through the gloom ahead, my father
Cried out:
'Run, boy; here they come; I see
Flame light on shields, bronze shining.'
I took fright,
And some unfriendly power, I know not what,
Stole all my addled wits—for as I turned
Aside from the known way, entering a maze
Of pathless places on the run—
Alas,
Creusa, taken from us by grim fate, did she
Linger, or stray, or sink in weariness?
There is no telling. Never would she be
Restored to us. Never did I look back
Or think to look for her, lost as she was,
Until we reached the funeral mound and shrine
Of venerable Ceres. Here at last
All came together, but she was not there;
She alone failed her friends, her child, her husband.
Out of my mind, whom did I not accuse,
What man or god? What crueller loss had I
Beheld, that night the city fell? Ascanius,
My father, and the Teucrian Penates,
I left in my friends' charge, and hid them well
In a hollow valley.
I turned back alone
Into the city, cinching my bright harness.°
Nothing for it but to run the risks
Again, go back again, comb all of Troy,
And put my life in danger as before:
First by the town wall, then the gate, all gloom,
Through which I had come out—and so on backward,
Tracing my own footsteps through the night;

456 cinching my bright harness: putting on or tightening the swordbelt.

And everywhere my heart misgave me: even
Stillness had its terror. Then to our house,
Thinking she might, just might, have wandered there.
Danaans had got in and filled the place,
And at that instant fire they had set,
Consuming it, went roofward in a blast;
Flames leaped and seethed in heat to the night sky.
I pressed on, to see Priam's hall and tower.
In the bare colonnades of Juno's shrine
Two chosen guards, Phoenix° and hard Ulysses,
Kept watch over the plunder. Piled up here
Were treasures of old Troy from every quarter,
Torn out of burning temples: altar tables,
Robes, and golden bowls. Drawn up around them,
Boys and frightened mothers stood in line.
I even dared to call out in the night;
I filled the streets with calling; in my grief
Time after time I groaned and called Creusa,
Frantic, in endless quest from door to door.
Then to my vision her sad wraith° appeared—
Creusa's ghost, larger than life, before me.
Chilled to the marrow, I could feel the hair
On my head rise, the voice clot in my throat;
But she spoke out to ease me of my fear:

'What's to be gained by giving way to grief
So madly, my sweet husband? Nothing here
Has come to pass except as heaven willed.
You may not take Creusa with you now;
It was not so ordained, nor does the lord
Of high Olympus° give you leave. For you
Long exile waits, and long sea miles to plough.
You shall make landfall on Hesperia°
Where Lydian Tiber° flows, with gentle pace,
Between rich farmlands, and the years will bear
Glad peace, a kingdom, and a queen for you.
Dismiss these tears for your beloved Creusa.
I shall not see the proud homelands of Myrmidons
Or of Dolopians, or go to serve
Greek ladies, Dardan lady that I am
And daughter-in-law of Venus the divine.
No: the great mother of the gods detains me
Here on these shores. Farewell now; cherish still
Your son and mine.'

472 **Phoenix** (fē′ niks): a Greek leader, he had been Achilles' tutor.

482 **wraith** (rāth): ghost.

491–492 **lord Of high Olympus:** Jupiter; Mount Olympus, the highest mountain in Greece, was the home of the gods.

494 **Hesperia** (he sper′ ē ə): land to the west where the sun sets, known as the "land of the evening"; Italy, the peninsula on which Rome is located.

495 **Tiber** (tī′ bər): Italian river that flows through Rome: at that time, controlled by Etruscans, who may have come to Italy from Lydia (li′ dē ə), in Asia Minor.

Aeneas Carrying His Father Anchises from the Blazing City of Troy. Daniel Van Heil (Flanders, 1604–1662). Oil on copper, 18.2 x 25.4 cm. Private collection.

Viewing the painting: What impression is created by the color and lighting in this painting?

With this she left me weeping,
Wishing that I could say so many things,
And faded on the tenuous air. Three times
I tried to put my arms around her neck,
Three times enfolded nothing, as the wraith
Slipped through my fingers, bodiless as wind,
Or like a flitting dream.
So in the end
As night waned I rejoined my company.
And there to my astonishment I found
New refugees in a great crowd: men and women
Gathered for exile, young—pitiful people
Coming from every quarter, minds made up,
With their belongings, for whatever lands
I'd lead them to by sea.
The morning star
Now rose on Ida's ridges,° bringing day.
Greeks had secured the city gates. No help
Or hope of help existed.
So I resigned myself, picked up my father,
And turned my face toward the mountain range."

519 Ida's ridges: Ida was a mountain near Troy.

Responding to Literature

Personal Response

What passage in this episode did you find most exciting? Explain why the passage made such an impression on you.

Analyzing Literature

Recall

1. What strategy do Aeneas and his followers adopt when they fight the Greek invaders?
2. What are the circumstances of Priam's death?
3. After he watches Priam die, Aeneas comes across Helen. Why does he want to kill her?
4. Why does Aeneas prepare to continue fighting the Greeks after he arrives home?
5. How does Aeneas become separated from his wife?

Interpret

6. Even as he prepares to attack the Greeks, Aeneas realizes that he does not have "a fighting chance in arms" (line 22). In your opinion, what motivates him to fight?
7. What does Aeneas emphasize about Priam's death?
8. Why does Venus reveal the hidden actions of the gods to her son Aeneas?
9. How would you characterize Aeneas's attitude toward his father?
10. What impression do you have of Aeneas's relationship with his wife?

Evaluate and Connect

11. In the Reading Focus on page 367, you listed several people whom you consider to be heroes. Compare one of them with Aeneas.
12. An **epic hero** represents the ideals of a society (see pages R3–R4). What ideals does Aeneas represent?
13. To what extent are the human characters in the *Aeneid* responsible for their actions, and to what extent are they controlled by the gods?
14. Compare Aeneas's actions in this episode with the actions of Pyrrhus. Is one character more admirable than the other? Why or why not?
15. Virgil portrays the suffering and chaos that results from Troy's destruction. What modern event does this remind you of? Why?

Literary Criticism

Scholar Michael Grant makes the following statement about the *Aeneid*: "Victory . . . is no longer seen as a triumphant, Homeric affair; Virgil knows all too well the weariness, frustration, and harrowing pathos that fighting and winning wars involve . . . He saw the true victory, it appears, not so much in military conquest as in the human spirit's conquest of itself." Do you agree that Virgil portrays victory differently from Homer (see pages 213–244) and believes it lies in the "human spirit's conquest of itself"? Write a brief comparison-and-contrast essay explaining your answer.

Literary ELEMENTS

Imagery

Imagery is language that appeals to the senses. Because people usually rely on sight more than the other senses, most imagery is visual. In the following passage from the *Aeneid* (lines 140–144), visual images help us form a mental picture of the destruction of Priam's palace:

Pyrrhus shouldering forward with
an axe
Broke down the stony threshold,
forced apart
Hinges and brazen doorjambs,
and chopped through
One panel of the door, splitting
the oak,
To make a window, a great breach.

Imagery can also help readers hear sounds, feel textures, smell aromas, and taste foods.

1. What images from the *Aeneid* were the most memorable for you? Explain why.
2. Find an example of a nonvisual image in the *Aeneid*. Which sense does it appeal to?

- See **Literary Terms Handbook,** p. R6.

Literature and Writing

Writing About Literature

Plot Summary Imagine that you are going to make a film about Aeneas's experiences during the destruction of Troy. With a partner, write a summary of the events that Virgil portrays in this episode. Then determine whether each event is part of the exposition, rising action, climax, or falling action. What sort of events would you add to make a film script?

Creative Writing

Another Perspective Virgil tells the story of Troy's fall from Aeneas's perspective. Write a brief account of the city's destruction from the perspective of Hecuba, Anchises, Pyrrhus, Helen, or another character mentioned in the selection.

Extending Your Response

Literature Groups

A Hero's Dilemma Just prior to this episode, Aeneas awakens and realizes that the Greek warriors have entered Troy. Should he fight to defend the city or go home immediately? Discuss this in your group and share your conclusions with another group.

Interdisciplinary Activity

Social Studies: Digging Up Troy In 1871 archaeologists began to uncover the ruins of Troy. Conduct research at the library to find out what scholars have learned about this ancient city. Share your notes with a partner, and compare the historical Troy with the legendary city portrayed in the *Aeneid.* How does archaeological information shed light on Virgil's descriptions?

Performing

Choral Reading In a small group, practice a section of the *Aeneid* to read aloud to the class. Discuss how you can use your voices to make the reading more dramatic. Choose one member of the group to guide the reading with hand gestures.

Reading Further

If you are interested in finding out more about the background of the *Aeneid,* the following books might be helpful:

In Search of the Trojan War, by Michael Wood, a discussion of the excavation of Troy and Greek daily life.

Roman Myths, by Jane F. Gardner, an introduction to Roman religion and myths about the founding of Rome.

Save your work for your portfolio.

VOCABULARY • Synonyms

Mark Twain said that the difference between the right word and the "almost right word" is like the difference between lightning and a lightning bug. He meant that synonyms are not necessarily interchangeable.

For example, *reprove* means "to criticize with the kindly intent to correct a fault." *Rebuke* suggests a sharp or stern reproof, whereas *reprimand* implies a severe, formal, often public or official rebuke.

PRACTICE Consult a dictionary or thesaurus to learn the precise differences that distinguish each of the following synonyms. Write the meaning of each word, and then write a sentence that illustrates its exact meaning.

appease	pacify
conciliate	placate
mollify	propitiate

GREECE, 1900

Before You Read

The Trojans

Meet Constantine Cavafy

"I could never write a novel or a play, but I hear inside me a hundred and twenty-five voices telling me that I could write history."

When Constantine Cavafy (kä vä′ fē) was sixteen, his mother enrolled him in business school, hoping he would become a merchant like his father. Instead, the school's director inspired in Cavafy a love for classical literature and history. Soon he began to write poems, many of them set in the ancient Mediterranean world. He had a gift for writing about the distant past in a personal way, as if he were describing friends and neighbors.

Cavafy was born of Greek parents in Alexandria, Egypt. A harsh critic of his own work, Cavafy destroyed all but four or five of the dozens of poems he wrote each year. He published only two slim volumes during his lifetime. Other poems appeared in literary magazines, but his work remained fairly obscure until after his death. Today Cavafy is widely considered to be the finest modern Greek poet.

Cavafy was born in 1863 and died in 1933.

Reading Focus

When reading about historical conflicts, are you generally more interested in learning about those who were victorious or those who were defeated?

Journal Writing Write a brief response to this question in your journal. Give examples from historical fiction, nonfiction, or poetry that you have enjoyed.

Setting a Purpose As you read the poem, think about who is victorious and who is defeated.

Building Background

Cavafy's Poetry

Cavafy wrote stirring poems about life in modern Alexandria. He also set many poems in ancient Greece and Rome, often portraying people caught up in momentous events. Whether contemporary or historical, his poetry offers the same distinctive voice and style. The English poet W. H. Auden once commented, "I have read translations of Cavafy made by many different hands, but every one of them was immediately recognizable as a poem by Cavafy; nobody else could possibly have written it." Cavafy almost never used metaphors or similes. Despite the absence of figurative language, his descriptions are quite vivid. One aspect of his writing that often gets lost in translation is his innovative approach to language. His ability to blend formal and colloquial styles of Greek in his poetry has been widely praised by scholars.

The island of Santorini, Greece.

THE TROJANS

Constantine Cavafy
Translated by Rae Dalven

Our efforts are the efforts of the unfortunate;
our efforts are like those of the Trojans.
We succeed somewhat; we regain confidence
somewhat; and we start once more
to have courage and high hopes.

But something always happens and stops us.
Achilles in the trench emerges before us
and with loud cries dismays us.—

Our efforts are like those of the Trojans.
We think that with resolution and daring,
we will alter the downdrag of destiny,
and we stand outside ready for battle.

But when the great crisis comes,
our daring and our resolution vanish;
our soul is agitated, paralyzed;
and we run all around the walls
seeking to save ourselves in flight.

However, our fall is certain. Above,
on the walls, the dirge has already begun.
The memories and the feelings of our own days weep.
Priam and Hecuba weep bitterly for us.

A Scene from the Trojan War. Antonio Rafaelle Calliano (Italy, 1785–1824). Oil on canvas, 75 x 135.6 cm.

Viewing the painting: What in this painting suggests the chaos and violence of war? How does it remind you of the poem above?

Responding to Literature

Personal Response

What feelings did you experience while reading this poem? Share your response with a classmate.

Analyzing Literature

Recall and Interpret

1. How would you summarize the poem's first two stanzas?
2. What does the speaker suggest with the statement "our efforts are like those of the Trojans"?
3. What false hope does the speaker describe in the third stanza?
4. In the last stanza, the speaker says that "our fall is certain." Explain what you think this statement refers to.

Evaluate and Connect

5. "The Trojans" is written in the first-person plural (we) instead of the more common first-person singular (I). How does the use of a plural subject influence your experience of the poem?
6. **Mood** is the overall feeling or atmosphere of a literary work (see page R7). What adjective would you use to describe the mood of "The Trojans"?
7. Do you think that actions are without value if they end in failure? Why or why not?
8. In the Reading Focus on page 386, you were asked to discuss whether you are generally more interested in those who were victorious or those who were defeated in a historical conflict. What new insights or ideas about defeat did Cavafy's poem give you?

Literary ELEMENTS

Allusion

An **allusion** is a reference to a well-known person, place, or event from history, literature, or religion. Allusions enrich our reading experience by adding another dimension of meaning. In "The Trojans," Cavafy alludes to events and images from Virgil's *Aeneid* and Homer's *Iliad.* Through these allusions, Cavafy encourages us to compare our own experiences to those of the legendary Trojans.

1. In the second stanza, the speaker alludes to the Greek hero Achilles. What does this image of Achilles suggest to you?
2. What do you think Cavafy is suggesting with his allusion to Priam and Hecuba in the last line of "The Trojans"?

- See **Literary Terms Handbook,** p. R1.

Extending Your Response

Personal Writing

Describing Fear In "The Trojans," the speaker refers to one's soul becoming paralyzed from fear. Think of a time when fear held you back from taking action. Write a paragraph about this experience, describing your thoughts and any physical symptoms you felt at the time. Include any techniques you used to help you overcome the fear.

Literature Groups

Discussing Fate What does "The Trojans" suggest about fate or destiny? Do you think Cavafy presents this idea seriously, or could his remarks about human behavior be ironic? Discuss these questions in your group. Refer to specific lines in the poem to support your opinion. When you are finished, present your conclusions to the class.

Save your work for your portfolio.

COMPARING *selections*

from the AENEID and THE TROJANS

COMPARE **STYLES**

Virgil and Cavafy had distinctive literary styles. Write a paragraph comparing the styles of "The Fall of Troy" and "The Trojans." Use examples from the poems to support your analysis. You might wish to focus on one or more of the following elements:

- imagery
- tone
- metaphors and similes
- rhythm
- repetition
- alliteration and assonance

COMPARE **RESPONSES**

In "The Fall of Troy," Virgil focuses on the specific actions of one hero during the destruction of Troy. Cavafy offers a more abstract view of the same event, describing the general behavior of the Trojans. Discuss the following questions in your group:

1. Which approach did you find more interesting?
2. Which poem do you think offers a more realistic view of human behavior? How does the time period in which the works were written influence the attitude of the author?

Procession of the Trojan Horse into Troy (detail).

COMPARE **EXPERIENCES**

Both poems portray how the Trojans responded to an attack on their city. Research a recent event similar to the destruction of Troy to find out how people today react when their city is threatened. You might begin by searching the Internet to learn the names of some cities that have been under attack (try using the keyword "siege"). When you are finished, compare your findings with Virgil's and Cavafy's portrayals of the Trojans. Share your findings with other students in your group.

Technology Skills

Spreadsheet: Estimating Expenses

If traveling is one of your dreams, spreadsheet software can help you compare options and estimate how much money you would need to take the trip of a lifetime.

Consider Your Choices

Make a chart with four columns as follows. Leave plenty of space to fill in information. (If you create your chart on the computer with word processing software, it will grow by itself as you add information.)

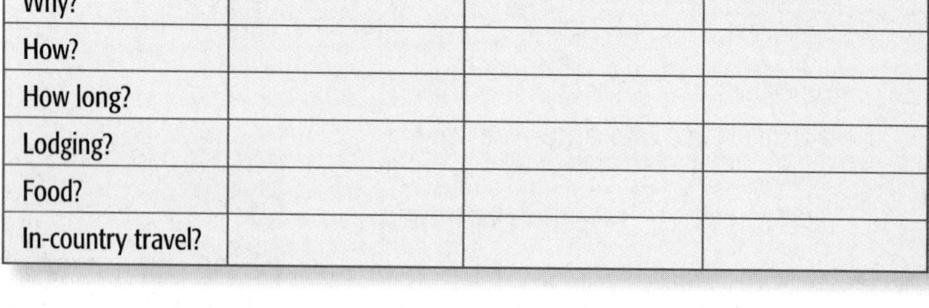

My Three Travel Destinations			
	Country No. 1	Country No. 2	Country No. 3
Why?			
How?			
How long?			
Lodging?			
Food?			
In-country travel?			

In each column, brainstorm answers to the following questions. Each of them will have economic consequences.

Why? Why do you want to go to the countries you've named? Do you want to see the sights? experience the culture? visit with people? find relatives abroad? Write down as many possible responses as possible.

How? How might you get where you want to go? Flying may not be the only option. If you can spare the time, other means of transportation–ship, train, or bus–may be less expensive.

How long? Would you like to stay for a week or two? A month? A year?

Lodging? Will you stay with friends or family? At a hotel? In a youth hostel? At a campground?

Food? Will you pack energy bars, or do you plan to eat in restaurants? Do you want to sample the local cuisine, or will you head for the nearest fast-food hamburger-and-fries place?

In-country travel Will you get around the country by backpack? Bike? Car? Trains and buses?

Searching on the Internet

1. Log on to the Internet and search for travel sites. Gather as much financial information as possible relating to the options you've listed. For instance, how much money would you need for a round-trip plane ticket to Peru? How much does it cost to spend a night in a youth hostel in Paris? Are there special train passes for tourists? Add information about costs to your chart.

2. Visit the Web sites of a few on-line travel agents. Find out if they have any information geared specifically toward young travelers. If the information is not on-line, E-mail them and ask them to forward it to you.
3. To learn about travel advisories for your destination, go to the State Department's travel warnings site: (http://travel.state.gov/travel_warnings.html).
4. Add any other important new information to your chart.

Reviewing Spreadsheet Tools

Take a few minutes to review the major functions of spreadsheets. If you have trouble at any time in this activity, use the program's Help function or consult with your teacher, the lab instructor, or a classmate who knows the program.

Estimating Your Travel Costs

1. Go back through your chart of travel destinations and look at the options you've listed for each destination.
2. Using your spreadsheet program, open a new worksheet. List your preferred travel options and add your estimates of the sums needed for travel to each of your destination countries.
3. Have the software program compute totals for each option. Your completed worksheet might look something like this:

	A	B	C	D
1	**Item**	**Mexico**	**South Africa**	**Japan**
2	Air travel	$ 380.00	$ 1,180.00	$ 860.00
3	In-country travel	$ 100.00	$ 125.00	$ 150.00
4	Lodging	$ 150.00	$ 175.00	$ 420.00
5	Food	$ 140.00	$ 170.00	$ 250.00
6	Other expenses	$ 150.00	$ 150.00	$ 200.00
7				
8	Totals	$ 920.00	$ 1,800.00	$ 1,880.00

ACTIVITIES

1. Experiment with the different charts and chart styles available on your spreadsheet software. What are the advantages and disadvantages of each style?
2. Compare your estimated expenses to advertised travel "specials" on the Internet. What items do these "specials" include? Can you save money by traveling with a group? Do you get a better deal if you plan your travel yourself? What advantages might there be to using a travel agent?

Before You Read

The Burning of Rome from the *Annals*

Meet Tacitus

"It seems to me a historian's foremost duty to ensure that merit is recorded, and to confront evil deeds and words with the fear of posterity's denunciations."

Although he was a successful politician and lawyer, Tacitus (tas′i təs) is best known as the historian of the early Roman Empire. Tacitus wrote his histories during a turbulent time in Rome, when the democratic rule of the republic was replaced by the absolute rule of the Roman emperor. Having experienced emperors who abused their power, Tacitus found himself confronting their evil deeds more than singing their praises in his histories.

Born into a wealthy family, Tacitus rose to political prominence during Emperor Domitian's reign (A.D. 81–96). He saw many fellow senators destroyed by this tyrannical emperor, which no doubt influenced his view of imperialism. Despite his pessimism, Tacitus rose to the position of governor of Asia, Rome's most important province.

Tacitus was born c. A.D. 56 and died c. 120.

Reading Focus

Think of a disastrous event that occurred recently. What effect did it have on you?

Share Ideas Create a brief questionnaire for your classmates to find out how they reacted to the event. Then compare their responses with your own perceptions.

Setting a Purpose Read this selection to discover how the author describes a disastrous event.

Building Background

Nero

Nero (A.D. 37–68) was one of Rome's most criticized emperors. He came to power when he was sixteen through the influence of his mother, Agrippina. Early in his reign he enacted a number of wise and humane laws. But after some years in power he began to act strangely. The senate turned against him, and eventually he killed himself to avoid being deposed and executed.

A Great Conflagration

While much of Rome burned to the ground in A.D. 64, Nero was at a villa thirty-five miles away. Nevertheless, many Romans suspected that he had set the fire to clear space for one of his grandiose construction projects. His rebuilding plans helped fuel this rumor; had it been completed, his new palace would have covered a third of the city. Tacitus portrays the fire and its political consequences as vividly as an eyewitness, although in fact he relied on sources such as public records and accounts by earlier historians.

Vocabulary Preview

demolition (dem′ ə lish′ ən) *n.* act of tearing down or breaking to pieces; destruction; p. 394

precipitous (pri sip′ ə təs) *adj.* having very steep sides; p. 395

appease (ə pēz′) *v.* to make peace with through concessions; p. 396

munificence (mū nif′ ə sens) *n.* great generosity; p. 396

sinister (sin′ is tər) *adj.* singularly evil; menacing; p. 396

depraved (di prāvd′) *adj.* marked by evil; p. 396

from the *Annals*: The Burning of Rome

Tacitus

Translated by Michael Grant

NOW STARTED THE MOST TERRIBLE and destructive fire which Rome had ever experienced. It began in the Circus,[1] where it adjoins the hills. Breaking out in shops selling inflammable goods, and fanned by the wind, the conflagration instantly grew and swept the whole length of the Circus. There were no walled mansions or temples, or any other obstructions which could arrest it. First, the fire swept violently over the level spaces. Then it climbed the hills—but returned to ravage the lower ground again. It outstripped every countermeasure. The ancient city's narrow winding streets and irregular blocks encouraged its progress.

1. Originally, a *circus* was a large arena enclosed by tiers of seats and used for sports or spectacles. Ancient Rome had several. Tacitus may be referring to the Circus Maximus, the oldest such structure, which was located between the Palatine and Aventine hills.

Terrified, shrieking women, helpless old and young, people intent on their own safety, people unselfishly supporting invalids or waiting for them, fugitives and lingerers alike—all heightened the confusion. When people looked back, menacing flames sprang up before them or outflanked them. When they escaped to a neighboring quarter, the fire followed—even districts believed remote proved to be involved. Finally, with no idea where or what to flee, they crowded on to the country roads, or lay in the fields. Some who had lost everything—even their food for the day—could have escaped, but preferred to die. So did others, who had failed to rescue their loved ones. Nobody dared fight the flames. Attempts to do so were prevented by menacing gangs. Torches, too, were openly thrown in, by men crying that they acted under orders. Perhaps they had received orders. Or they may just have wanted to plunder unhampered.

Nero was at Antium.[2] He only returned to the city when the fire was approaching the mansion he had built to link the Gardens of Maecenas to the Palatine. The flames could not be prevented from overwhelming the whole of the Palatine, including his palace. Nevertheless, for the relief of the homeless, fugitive masses he threw open the Field of Mars,[3] including Agrippa's public buildings, and even his own Gardens. Nero also constructed emergency accommodation for the destitute multitude. Food was brought from Ostia and neighboring towns, and the price of corn was cut. Yet these measures, for all their popular character, earned no gratitude. For a rumor had spread that, while the city was burning, Nero had gone to his private stage and, comparing modern calamities with ancient, had sung of the destruction of Troy.[4]

By the sixth day enormous demolitions had confronted the raging flames with bare ground and open sky, and the fire was finally stamped out. But before panic had subsided, or hope revived, flames broke out again in the more open regions of the city. Here there were fewer casualties; but the destruction of temples and pleasure arcades was even worse. This new conflagration caused additional ill feeling because it started on Tigellinus'[5] estate. For people believed that Nero was ambitious to found a new city to be called after himself.

Of Rome's fourteen districts only four remained intact. Three were leveled to the ground. The other seven were reduced to a few scorched and mangled ruins. To count the mansions, blocks, and temples destroyed would be difficult. They included shrines of remote antiquity, the precious spoils of countless victories, Greek artistic masterpieces, and authentic records of old Roman genius. All the splendor of the rebuilt city did not prevent the older generation from remembering these irreplaceable objects. It was noted that the fire had started on July 19th, the day on which the Senonian Gauls[6] had captured and burned the city.

But Nero profited by his country's ruin to build a new palace. Its wonders were not so much customary and commonplace luxuries like gold and jewels, but lawns and lakes and faked rusticity—woods here, open spaces and

2. *Antium* (now Anzio) is an ancient coastal city about thirty miles south of Rome. It was Nero's birthplace.
3. The *Field of Mars* was a grassy area used for athletic and military events honoring Mars, the Roman god of war.

4. *Troy* was an ancient city of Asia Minor. Its destruction by the Greeks is told in the *Aeneid,* an epic poem by Virgil.
5. *Tigellinus* was a close adviser and friend of Nero.
6. The *Gauls* were Celtic-speaking peoples who lived in modern-day northern Italy, France, and Germany. The *Senonian Gauls* captured and burned Rome in 390 B.C.

Vocabulary

demolition (dem′ ə lish′ ən) *n.* act of tearing down or breaking to pieces; destruction

However, as you know, you can increase the drama by beginning ***in medias res***—by plunging the reader "into the middle of things." This technique gets the reader into the action quickly. After the dramatic beginning, flash back in time and fill in any necessary background. See page 351 for suggestions on how to organize details.

Sketch an event organizer like the one below to help you organize the details effectively. Write the details of your account in the blocks in any order. Then number them in the order you'll write about them. Remember that you can start your account in the middle and then go back to the beginning. You can also introduce flashbacks at any point in your account.

STUDENT MODEL

7 butterflies alight on tourists' arms and heads–including my own!	4 an army of people hike the last quarter of a mile to the sanctuary	5 we pass merchants selling butterfly souvenirs, tamales and empanadas, fried meat, ice cold drinks
6 I see a few monarchs in the air above me; suddenly, a vast sea of orange	8 through my binoculars: trees covered, every square inch, with monarchs–as many as 10,000 on each tree?	9 I think: all these monarchs are as beautiful as a million diamonds
1 while visiting Grandma in Mexico, we take a trip to Agangueo, the monarch butterfly sanctuary	2 Grandma tells us that the butterflies fly as many as 1800 miles to Agangueo from North America every winter	3 riding up the mountainside in a flatbed truck

Add details

For each event, jot down notes about the following:

- What happened?
- When, where, how, and why did it happen?
- Who was involved?
- What did witnesses see, smell, hear, taste and feel?

DRAFTING

DRAFTING TIP

Try to include all your details in your draft. Do not feel that you have to cut anything at this stage.

Draft details

Give your account the immediacy of an eyewitness report, as Tacitus did in conveying the frenzy of the crowd. Be as detailed as you can, but don't stretch the facts. Remember that Tacitus reports Nero's singing as a rumor, not as a fact.

Write your draft

Follow your plan, but don't let it interfere with the flow of your drafting. If you have some events out of order, you can always move them into place later.

STUDENT MODEL

By the time we had climbed a few feet higher, we began to see a vast sea of orange. Butterflies blanketed entire trees, and branches drooped under the combined weight of these delicate creatures.

Complete Student Model on p. R113.

REVISING

REVISING TIPS

Be sure to use transitions to help the reader follow the narrative.

Use specific words, not general ones, to create a vivid impression.

Take another look

Give yourself some distance from your draft by setting it aside for a while. Then use the **Rubric for Revising** to guide you as you revise it.

Read your narrative aloud

Now try reading your nonfiction narrative to an audience. Keep the written copy to yourself for now. Then go through the **Rubric for Revising** with your listener.

RUBRIC FOR REVISING

Your revised eyewitness account should have

- ☑ information about the who, what, when, where, and whys of the event
- ☑ a logical organization
- ☑ transitions to show sequence
- ☑ striking, memorable details
- ☑ active verbs and adverbs to depict action
- ☑ words and images that appeal to all five senses

Your revised eyewitness account should be free of

- ☑ vague or overused verbs, adverbs, and adjectives

STUDENT MODEL

The last part of the ~~walk~~ climb took us through an congested area of stands busy where merchants were selling butterfly souvenirs, ~~cooking~~ frying fragrant meats, making spicy tamales and empanadas, and selling ice cold, green and pink drinks.

Complete Student Model on p. R113.

EDITING/PROOFREADING

When you are satisfied with your narrative, proofread it slowly and carefully for errors in grammar, usage, mechanics, and spelling. Check for only one kind of error at a time.

Grammar Hint

Your reader may be puzzled if you use a relative pronoun—such as *which* or *who*—that does not refer clearly to an antecedent. Revise your pronouns to make the meaning clear.

VAGUE: *The ride went up a rural road to the sanctuary, which was exhausting but exciting.*

CLEAR: *It was exhausting but exciting to ride up a rural road to the sanctuary.*

- For more about pronouns, see Language Handbook, pp. R19–R22.

EDITING CHECKLIST

- Make every pronoun refer clearly to its antecedent.
- Check your punctuation marks, especially any with quotation marks.
- Be sure that subjects and verbs agree.
- Fix run-on sentences and fragments.
- Check the meanings of words.
- Check the spellings of words.

STUDENT MODEL

If I had too guess how many monachs I saw in just one day, I wuold say milions. I would guess though I do not know this that some trees held tenthousand or more.

Complete Student Model on p. R113.

Complete Student Model

For a complete version of the model developed in this workshop, refer to **Writing Workshop Models**, p. R113.

PUBLISHING/PRESENTING

For a student audience, you could read your account, or you could exchange accounts with other writers. For a larger audience, think about special-interest groups that might be interested in your topic. For example, if your account includes local color—events or information from a particular part of the country—a regional magazine may be interested.

PRESENTING TIP

Graphics may help your readers follow the events.

Reflecting

No eyewitness account can include everything that happened. How complete is your account? What is missing from it? In your journal, list some aspect of your writing that you did particularly well and something that you want to improve in your next assignment.

Save your work for your portfolio.

Unit Assessment

Personal Response

1. Most of the selections in Unit 2 were written about two thousand years ago. Which of them did you find most relevant to your own life? What elements in these selections helped you to bridge any gaps of time and culture?
2. Which of the selections in this unit did you find the most moving or inspiring?
3. What suggestions would you make to someone who is interested in learning about the literature and culture of ancient Greece and Rome?

Analyzing Literature

Compare and Contrast The Greeks and Romans wrote in a variety of forms. Write several paragraphs in which you compare and contrast two forms. Explore at least one of the following elements in detail:

- theme
- literary elements
- form
- language

Refer to at least two of the selections you have read in the unit to support your opinion. You might conclude your analysis by stating which of the selections was your favorite and why you feel that way.

Evaluate and Set Goals

Evaluate

1. What was your strongest contribution to group activities as you worked through this unit?
2. What was your most challenging task in this unit?
   - How did you approach this task?
   - What was the result?
3. How would you assess your work in this unit, using the following scale? Give at least two reasons for your assessment.
   4 = outstanding **3** = good **2** = fair **1** = weak

Set Goals

1. Choose a goal to work toward during the next week. It could involve reading, writing, speaking, researching, or working in a group.
2. Discuss your goal with your teacher and, if you wish, with a partner.
3. Jot down three or four steps that you will take to achieve your goal.
4. Decide at which points in the next unit you will stop and assess your progress toward that goal.
5. Record your goal and the checkpoints you have decided on. Refer to them periodically to check your progress.

 Build Your Portfolio

Select Review the writing that you did in this unit and choose two pieces to include in your portfolio. Use the following questions to help you choose:

- Which piece are you most satisfied with?
- Which piece did you find the most challenging?
- Which piece of writing led you to new discoveries as you wrote?

Reflect Write some notes to accompany the pieces you selected. Use the following questions to guide you:

- What did you learn from the process of writing each one?
- What are the strengths of the piece? the weaknesses?
- How might those strengths help in your future writing?
- How might you overcome the weaknesses?

Reading on Your Own

If you have enjoyed the literature in this unit, you might also be interested in the following books.

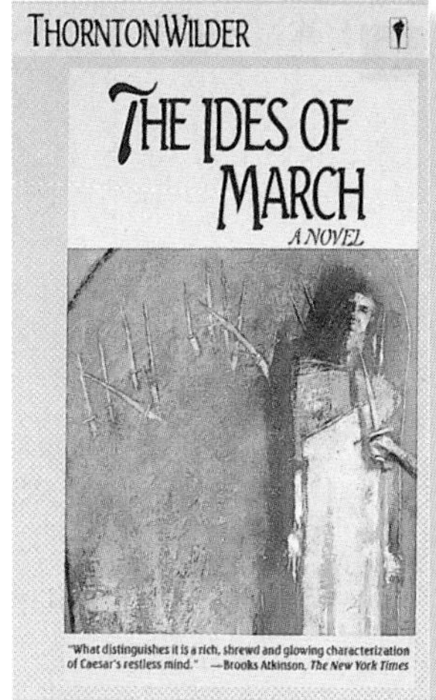

The Ides of March
by Thornton Wilder
In the form of letters exchanged by Julius Caesar and friends, including Cleopatra and Catullus, Wilder reveals the escalating drama of the months leading up to the assassination of ancient Rome's leader. Because of the letter format, Wilder is able to show an event from a variety of perspectives and also to include philosophical obervations.

Mythology
by Edith Hamilton
In an engaging introduction to the myths and legends of ancient Greece and Rome, Hamilton narrates stories of gods and heroes. Hamilton discusses the major heroes of Western mythology in great detail.

The Frogs
by Aristophanes In one of Aristophanes' funniest comedies, the god Dionysus must decide who is the greatest poet, Aeschylus or Euripedes, both of whom dwell in Hades. The lucky winner will return from the depths of hell to guide Athens to its former glory. This play is often found in a volume with three other comedies by Aristophanes: *The Clouds*, *The Birds*, and *Lysistrata*.

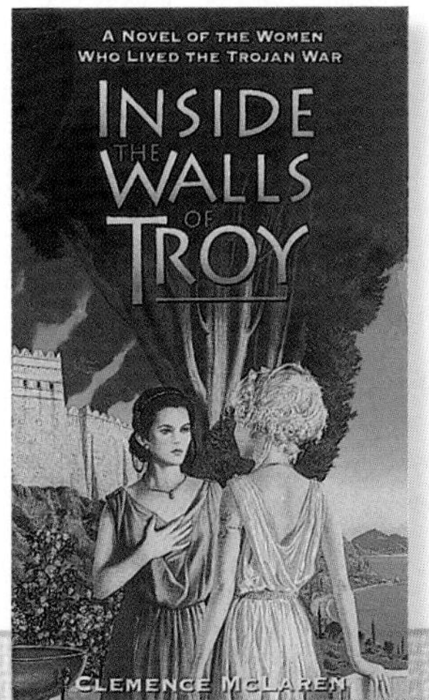

Inside the Walls of Troy
by Clemence McLaren In a refreshing twist, McLaren describes the Trojan War from the viewpoint of two extraordinary women, the breathtakingly beautiful Helen and the doomed prophetess Cassandra. The women of Troy, whose lot is to care for the injured and view the fighting from a distance, receive little attention from the classical writers. This interesting, modern perspective remedies that omission.

Standardized Test Practice

Directions: The following sentences test your knowledge of grammar, usage, diction (choice of words), and idiom.

Some sentences are correct.
No sentence contains more than one error.

You will find that the error, if there is one, is underlined and lettered. Elements of the sentence that are not underlined will not be changed. In choosing answers, follow the requirements of standard written English.

If there is an error, select the one underlined part that must be changed to make the sentence correct. Write the corresponding letter on your paper.

If there is no error, select answer E.

1. The motorcycles attracted (A) a group of onlookers, for (B) it (C) looked unlike anything the spectators had ever seen (D) before. No Error (E)

2. If one has an interest (A) in studying (B) the works of (C) Camus, you might (D) begin by reading *The Stranger*. No Error (E)

3. For many years, both physicists (A) as well as chemists have been trying (B) to duplicate (C) the results recorded (D) by Pons and Fleischmann. No Error (E)

4. Some of (A) the most beautiful places on earth are (B) in secluded areas where there are scarcely no (C) towns in sight (D). No Error (E)

5. Many people have heard of (A) the Universal Declaration of Human Rights, but not until today (B) has (C) the origins of this document been so widely (D) understood. No Error (E)

6. Regardless of how (A) frequent (B) planes are flown, they require (C) timely inspections to insure (D) that they are safe. No Error (E)

7. A nurse at the local blood bank claims that (A) a curiously low (B) percentage of their (C) donations comes from its annual (D) holiday blood drive. No Error (E)

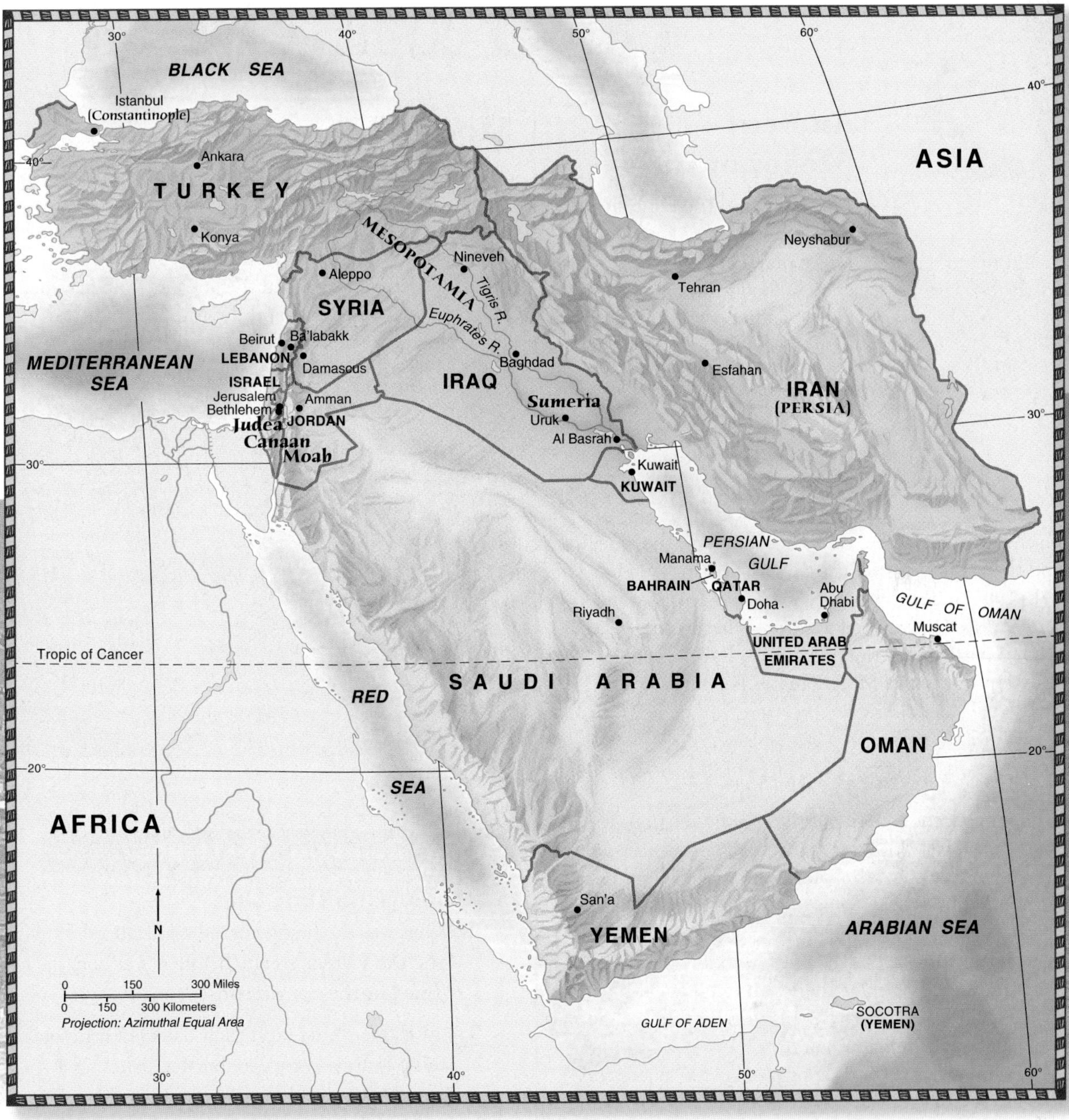

BLACK SEA
Istanbul (Constantinople)
Ankara
TURKEY
Konya
MESOPOTAMIA
Nineveh
Tigris R.
Euphrates R.
Aleppo
SYRIA
Beirut
Ba'labakk
LEBANON
Damascus
MEDITERRANEAN SEA
ISRAEL
Jerusalem
Bethlehem
Amman
JORDAN
Judea
Canaan
Moab
IRAQ
Baghdad
Sumeria
Uruk
Al Basrah
Kuwait
KUWAIT
ASIA
Neyshabur
Tehran
Esfahan
IRAN (PERSIA)
PERSIAN GULF
Manama
BAHRAIN
QATAR
Doha
Abu Dhabi
GULF OF OMAN
Muscat
Riyadh
UNITED ARAB EMIRATES
Tropic of Cancer
SAUDI ARABIA
RED SEA
OMAN
AFRICA
San'a
YEMEN
ARABIAN SEA
GULF OF ADEN
SOCOTRA (YEMEN)
0 150 300 Miles
0 150 300 Kilometers
Projection: Azimuthal Equal Area
N
30° 40° 50° 60°
40° 30° 20°

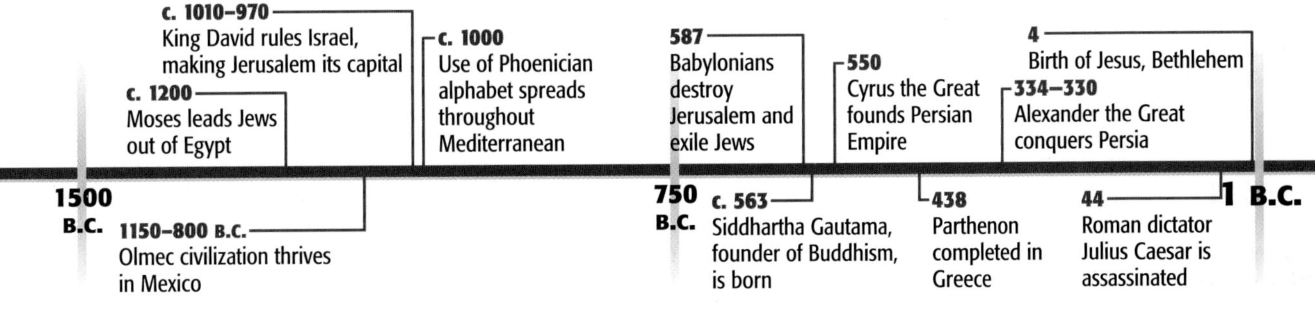
c. 1010–970
King David rules Israel, making Jerusalem its capital
c. 1200
Moses leads Jews out of Egypt
c. 1000
Use of Phoenician alphabet spreads throughout Mediterranean
587
Babylonians destroy Jerusalem and exile Jews
550
Cyrus the Great founds Persian Empire
4
Birth of Jesus, Bethlehem
334–330
Alexander the Great conquers Persia
1500 B.C.
1150–800 B.C.
Olmec civilization thrives in Mexico
750 B.C.
c. 563
Siddhartha Gautama, founder of Buddhism, is born
438
Parthenon completed in Greece
44
Roman dictator Julius Caesar is assassinated
1 B.C.

How People Live

Decorative detail on a Sumerian harp, c. 2450 B.C.

Ancient Mesopotamia

The Tigris and the Euphrates river waters allowed ancient Mesopotamian farmers to grow enough food for themselves and for specialized workers, such as kings, priests, craft workers, government workers, and scholars. Because of this, some people had enough time to pursue new knowledge. Mesopotamian inventions included the sixty-minute hour, the concept of place value in number notation, the plow, the wheel, and the sailboat, as well as the first writing system.

In time, independent city-states of Mesopotamia formed into larger kingdoms, ruled first by the Sumerians, then by the Akkadians, Babylonians, Assyrians, Persians, Macedonians, Parthians, and finally by Islamic Arabs.

The Islamic World

Muhammad, the founder of the Islamic religion, was born in the city of Mecca in the Arabian Peninsula. He taught that ties of religion were greater than ties of nationality or even of kinship. After Muhammad's death in A.D. 632, his followers spread the new religion from Spain to India. Although Jews and Christians were allowed to practice their own religions, the teachings of Muhammad became the basis for political and social as well as religious law.

Several dynasties of Caliphs (Arabic for "Successors") ruled after Muhammad. Later the region was dominated by the Turkish and Persian empires.

Modern Times

After World War I, the Arabic provinces of the Turkish Empire came under British and French administration. By the late 1940s all these areas had gained their independence. In the former Turkish province of Palestine, Jewish settlers reestablished the ancient state of Israel. Relations between Israel and the Muslim countries have often been strained. The region has also been troubled by strife among the Muslim states.

Loading dock, Kuwait.

Active Reading Strategies

Reading the Time Line

1. What was the first recorded civilization? How long was it in existence before it was conquered by the Babylonians?
2. List these events (and their dates) chronologically: Jesus is born; Siddhartha Gautama is born; Muhammad begins preaching; Moses leads the Jews out of Egypt.

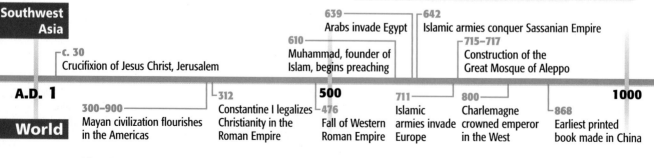

Southwest Asia

- c. 30 Crucifixion of Jesus Christ, Jerusalem
- 610 Muhammad, founder of Islam, begins preaching
- 639 Arabs invade Egypt
- 642 Islamic armies conquer Sassanian Empire
- 715–717 Construction of the Great Mosque of Aleppo

A.D. 1 — 500 — 1000

World

- 300–900 Mayan civilization flourishes in the Americas
- 312 Constantine I legalizes Christianity in the Roman Empire
- 476 Fall of Western Roman Empire
- 711 Islamic armies invade Europe
- 800 Charlemagne crowned emperor in the West
- 868 Earliest printed book made in China

Traditions and Beliefs

People of the Book

Judaism, Christianity, and Islam all have their roots in Southwest Asia, and share many ideas.

- They all believe in a single God.
- They all respect common patriarchs such as Abraham, who first led followers from Mesopotamia to what became known as Palestine.
- They all follow a divinely revealed scripture. The Jews follow the Tanakh, which includes the Old Testament of the Bible; the Christians follow the Bible; and the Muslims follow the Qur'an.

Islam recognizes the intellectual kinship of these three religions by referring to their followers as "people of the Book."

Muhammad ascending into heaven. Persian miniature.

The Mystic Tradition

Another common trait these religions share is *mysticism*, the attempt to go beyond the traditional outward forms of religion in search of the true meaning of the divine plan. In Islam, Sufism is the best-known mystical tradition. The Kabbalists, and the later Hasidim, represent the Jewish tradition. In Christianity, many different movements have appeared, some dating back to the earliest days of the Church.

Dome of the Rock, Jerusalem, enshrines an area sacred to Muslims, Jews, and Christians.

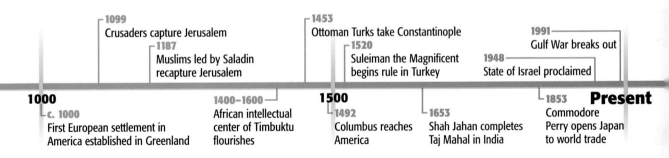

1000

- c. 1000 — First European settlement in America established in Greenland
- 1099 — Crusaders capture Jerusalem
- 1187 — Muslims led by Saladin recapture Jerusalem
- 1400–1600 — African intellectual center of Timbuktu flourishes
- 1453 — Ottoman Turks take Constantinople

1500

- 1492 — Columbus reaches America
- 1520 — Suleiman the Magnificent begins rule in Turkey
- 1653 — Shah Jahan completes Taj Mahal in India
- 1853 — Commodore Perry opens Japan to world trade
- 1948 — State of Israel proclaimed
- 1991 — Gulf War breaks out

Present

Arts and Entertainment

Islamic Art

Despite wide regional variety, arts created in Islamic countries share many characteristics, including the following:

- Many Islamic artists will not represent humans or animals in their art, believing that only God can create life or the illusion of life. However, Iran developed its own tradition, the Persian miniature. This miniature painting was usually done to illustrate works of literature. Sometimes borrowing from Chinese or European artistic traditions, Persian artists used rich, jewel-like colors to paint elaborate pictures showing scenes from epics and poems. (See page 417.)
- In the absence of representation, elaborate arabesques, floral motifs, and geometric patterns take on special importance.
- Three-dimensional sculpture is rare. The major arts are painting and architecture.
- Arts and crafts, such as pottery, metalwork, and carpet weaving, are much appreciated and given high status.

Ceramic tiles, c. 1570. Turkey.

Turkish Ceramic Ware

Many buildings of the Ottoman period in Turkey are adorned with magnificent colored tiles. Some of the earliest were influenced by blue and white Chinese patterns, imported through Persia. By the 1550s, tiles were produced in a range of colors. The designs—often executed by experts from Persia—influenced, in their turn, designers in western Europe.

Religious Architecture

Many of the most beautiful buildings in the region are of religious inspiration. Although many buildings were destroyed by Mongol invaders in the thirteenth century, cities such as Aleppo in Syria, Isfahan in Iran, and Istanbul in Turkey contain magnificent mosques. There are also beautiful Christian churches, notably in Istanbul. And many great temples of the ancient world, such as Baalbek in Lebanon, survive near the western coastal region.

Madar-i-Shah Mosque. c. 1620. Isfahan, Iran.

Critical Thinking

Connecting Cultures

1. Many buildings in Southwest Asia have great religious significance. In a group, discuss what might inspire architecture in the United States today. How does our architecture represent our values?
2. What buildings do you find beautiful or interesting? List reasons why.

Islamic Music

As in the visual arts, traditional Islamic music differs from region to region but shares these common features:

- an emphasis on the voice as the primary instrument
- a single melodic line, with little or no harmonization
- complex rhythms
- improvisation
- the use of microtones (intervals that fall between Western half-notes)
- aural transmission from teacher to student

Short- and long-necked lutes, dulcimers, fiddles, reed instruments, trumpets, flutes, drums, and cymbals are some of the instruments used to create the music of Southwest Asia.

Dervish dancer, Turkey.

Dance

In pre-Islamic days, dance was strongly connected with songs and religious ceremonies. In Islam, however, dance is not considered appropriate religious expression. Instead, it is relegated to royal courts and popular festivals. The one exception is the tradition of dervish dancing practiced by Sufi mystics. For seven centuries, this dance has been kept alive by the order of Mevlevi (or Mawlawi) dervishes founded by the great Sufi poet Rumi in the thirteenth century. The dervishes, who wear robes and tall conical hats, begin their dance standing in a circle. Each dervish then moves from east to west, with one hand pointed palm up to the sky and the other hand down, whirling faster and faster. They say the goal of their whirling dance is to put themselves into a trance to experience mystical union with God.

چون ابر درآمدیم، وچون باد شدیم

I came in like a cloud, and I left like a wind.

—*Rumi*

Language and Literature

Cuneiform Writing

The first writing to appear in Mesopotamia—possibly in the world—probably took the form of pictographs. As part of a record-keeping system, merchants used reeds to press these symbols onto wet clay. By 2500 B.C., scribes had started using a series of wedge-shaped symbols (*cuneiform* means "wedge-shaped"). Archaeologists have discovered thousands of clay tablets that record trade transactions, kingdoms, omens, prophecies, and epics. Eventually, cuneiform writing evolved into a script that formed the basis for the alphabetic systems used today.

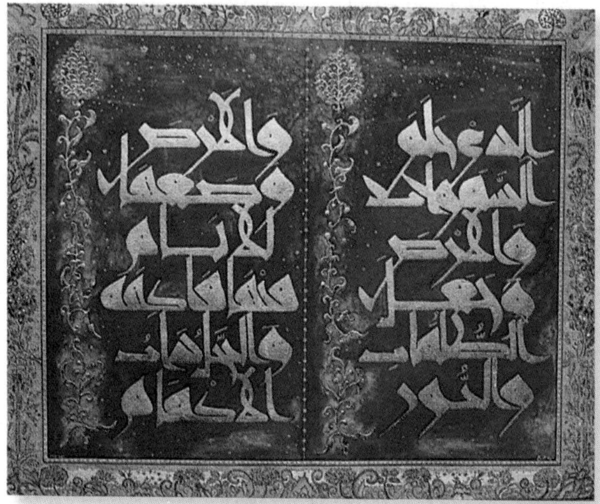

The Creation II, 1993. Khairat al-Saleh (Syria). Gouache, gold leaf, and gold ink on paper, 46 x 70 cm. Collection of the artist.

Calligraphy

As in East Asia, calligraphy is highly valued. Verses from the Qur'an written in Arabic script embellish all the visual arts. Verses are cut into stone buildings, painted onto pottery, and etched or inlaid on metalwork. Two styles of calligraphy dominate. Kufic script, bold and angular, was used primarily from 800 to 1100. Since then the more flowing nakshi script has been commonly used.

Languages

The earliest written language of the region was Sumerian, which is not known to be related to any other language. As the Semitic peoples gained power thoughout the region, languages such as Akkadian, Arabic, Aramaic, and Hebrew became important. The Arabic language spread throughout the region with the coming of Islam. Many Muslims believe that the Qur'an can be fully understood only when read in Arabic. The Arabic script came to be widely used and was adapted for use in writing other languages.

Many languages are spoken in the region today. Among the most important are Arabic, Armenian, Hebrew, Kurdish, Persian, and Turkish.

influences

When foods and clothing move from one culture to another, the terms for the borrowed items also move. Words that have entered English through Southwest Asian languages include the following:

- kabob (from Persian *kabab*), cubes of meat or vegetables cooked on a skewer
- pilaf, pilau (from Persian *pilau*), cooked rice, usually with meat and vegetables
- café (from Turkish *kahve*), a coffee house
- caftan (from Persian *qaftan*), a loose, ankle-length garment
- hallelujah (from Hebrew "praise [ye] the Lord"), expression of praise, joy, or thanks

Zodiac constellations Virgo & Libra. 14th-century Persian miniature.

Poetry and Prose

Both Arabic and Persian literature have strong poetic traditions dating back to pre-Islamic times. For centuries only poetry written in these classical traditions was accepted as real literature. More recently, free verse and prose fiction have gained respect. Turkish literature, at first based strongly on Arabic and Persian models, has developed a tradition of its own incorporating European influences. Israel has produced a number of noted writers, most often working in the European tradition, both in the revived Hebrew language and in Yiddish, the old German-Jewish language.

Critical Thinking

Southwest Asia

1. With a partner, discuss Mesopotamia's earliest system of writing. Why do you think it took the form of pictographs? What developments in an early culture might have spurred the need for a system of writing?
2. In a group discussion, compare and contrast the literature of the major groups living in Southwest Asia.

Classical Persian Poetry

During the classical period, poetry was preferred over all other literary forms. The outstanding Persian poet was Firdawsi, who pulled together existing Persian myth and history in his tenth-century epic *Shah-nameh*. In short, rhyming couplets, Firdawsi told the story of Persia from the time of its mythical kings through the invasions of Alexander the Great and conquest by the Arabs. The *Shah-nameh* became the inspiration for many masterpieces of Persian miniature painting.

Islamic manuscript with case.

MESOPOTAMIA, c. 2500 B.C.

Before You Read

from the *Epic of Gilgamesh*

Reading Focus

Heroes in myth and legend often go on long, dangerous journeys. What kinds of quests do they undertake?

Discuss As a class, discuss legendary heroes you have read about in literature or seen in movies. For what were these heroes searching? What obstacles did they have to overcome to complete their quests?

Setting a Purpose Read to discover the difficult quest that Gilgamesh undertakes.

Building Background

The History of the *Epic of Gilgamesh*

The *Epic of Gilgamesh* is the greatest surviving literary work of ancient Mesopotamia (located in what is now Iraq). Mesopotamia was home to a series of important ancient cultures, including the Sumerian, the Babylonian, and the Assyrian. These cultures played a role in the development and preservation of this epic.

As we know it today, the *Epic of Gilgamesh* is a series of separate tales that describe the exploits of the hero Gilgamesh. Although the epic projects Gilagamesh into the realm of myth, he was an actual person who ruled the ancient Sumerian city of Uruk around the year 2700 B.C. Historians believe that Sumerian storytellers began to convey tales of Gilgamesh's adventures and accomplishments soon after his death. These stories may not have been written down, however, for nearly a thousand years. Sometime between 2000 and 1600 B.C., the tales were recorded in Akkadian, the language of the Babylonian Empire, which succeeded the Sumerian civilization. Later, a narrative describing a great flood was added to the cycle of Gilgamesh tales. By the seventh century B.C., the Assyrians dominated the region, and their emperor, Ashurbanipal, had the tales recorded on clay tablets and deposited in the library of his palace at Nineveh. Lost for nearly 2,500 years, tablets from the library were unearthed in the mid-1800s by a young English amateur archaeologist named Austen Henry Layard. His discovery brought to light one of the oldest and most important epics in all world literature. Since then, many other tablets and fragments belonging to the Gilgamesh epic have been discovered.

Sumerian Civilization

Judging from the different languages in which tales of the *Epic of Gilgamesh* have been found, it is likely that the epic developed over many centuries. It has its roots, however, in one of the first Mesopotamian civilizations known to us. The Sumerians, believed to have settled in Mesopotamia as early as 3500 B.C., developed a sophisticated culture.

The basic Sumerian political structure was the city-state, which consisted of a large town and its surrounding lands. Each of these towns had its own ruler and was protected by a thick wall built to discourage invaders.

Perhaps the greatest achievement of the Sumerians was their invention of one of the earliest known forms of writing—"cuneiform" (kū nē′ ə fôrm′)—writing with a reed pen on clay tablets.

Despite their many achievements, the Sumerians held a pessimistic world view. Exposed to the dangers of flood, drought, and warfare, the Sumerians seem to have believed that earthly life was fleeting and fraught with peril. But unlike many other ancient cultures, they held no consoling vision of possible salvation or happiness after death. The *Epic of Gilgamesh,* for example, paints a bleak picture of mortal destiny in the afterlife.

Summary of the Epic

The selection that follows was pieced together from Babylonian and Assyrian tablets that recorded a similar episode in the adventures of Gilgamesh. Prior to this episode, a narrator describes Gilgamesh as two-thirds divine and one-third mortal—the handsome and mighty, but tyrannical, king of Uruk. Gilgamesh's subjects beseech the gods to end his oppression, and the gods answer by sending an enormously strong man named Enkidu to conquer Gilgamesh. The two men fight, but Gilgamesh wins (in some versions of the story). The men, however, develop a close friendship that diverts Gilgamesh's attention from his subjects. The people are thus released from the burden of his oppressive policies.

In search of fame and glory, Gilgamesh and Enkidu undertake a dangerous quest to cut down a cedar tree in the sacred forest, which is guarded by a monster named Humbaba. They succeed, and when they return to Uruk, they receive a hero's welcome. But again they incur the wrath of the gods, who send an ominous dream as a warning.

The *Epic of Gilgamesh* and Oral Tradition

Although the Sumerians possessed a system of writing, oral tradition—the transmission of songs, tales, or myths from one generation to the next by word of mouth—shaped the *Epic of Gilgamesh* at many stages of its development.

The influence of oral tradition is evident in some features of the epic's style. Passages of narrative and dialogue are sometimes repeated, as in Homer's *Iliad.* Like Homer's epics, the *Epic of Gilgamesh* employs elaborate forms of greeting, as well as epithets, or adjectives to describe the characters. For example, Shamash, the sun-god, is called "glorious," and Utnapishtim is "the faraway (one)."

The *Epic of Gilgamesh* and World Literature

Although the *Epic of Gilgamesh* was lost for thousands of years, its importance in literary history can hardly be overstated. As the world's earliest surviving work of fiction, it gives a fascinating insight into the evolution of storytelling. Adventures and journeys like those of Gilgamesh are the basis for books and movies even now, and the questions Gilgamesh ponders—the role of destiny, the meaning of existence—are still basic human questions.

Reading Further

To read about other legendary heroes, try these books:

The *Odyssey,* by Homer, the adventures of Odysseus.

Hercules: The Complete Myths of a Legendary Hero, by George Moroz, the twelve labors of Hercules.

The Once and Future King, by T. H. White, the legend of King Arthur and his Knights of the Round Table.

Stele Depicting Gilgamesh. 9th century, Syrio-Hittite. Private collection.

Vocabulary Preview

incantation (in′ kan tā′ shən) *n.* use of spells or verbal charms as part of a magic ritual; p. 422

ominous (om′ ə nəs) *adj.* foreboding or foreshadowing evil; p. 422

firmament (fur′ mə ment) *n.* the sky; p. 427

clamor (klam′ ər) *n.* noisy shouting; p. 427

libation (lī bā′ shən) *n.* a liquid used in ceremonial drinking; p. 428

sluice (slo͞os) *n.* floodgate; p. 431

PROPER NAMES IN THE EPIC

CHARACTERS

ANU (ā′ no͞o): Primeval father of the gods who had an important temple in Gilgamesh's city Uruk

ANUNNAKI (ä no͞o nä′ kē): Judges of the dead in the underworld

BELIT-SHERI (bel′ ēt sher′ ē): Scribe of the gods of the underworld

EA (ā′ ä): God of the waters and of wisdom; usually a friend to humans, whom he helped to create

ENKIDU (en′ kē do͞o): Created to be the challenger and then the companion of Gilgamesh; originally lived with the beasts of the forest as a wild or natural man

ENLIL (en lil′): God of earth and wind, agent of Anu; carries out the supreme god's orders

ENNUGI (en′ oog ē): God of irrigation and canals

ERESHKIGAL (er esh′ kə gäl): Queen of the underworld

GILGAMESH (gil′ gə mesh′): King of Uruk and the hero of the epic; son of the goddess Ninsun and the mortal King Lugulbanda; named in a Sumerian list of kings as the fifth monarch after the flood

HUMBABA (hum bä′ bə): Evil monster who guards the cedar forest; slain by Gilgamesh and Enkidu

IRKALLA (ir kä′ lə): Another name for Ereshkigal

ISHTAR (ish′ tär): Goddess of love, fertility, and war, as well as patron of the city of Uruk, where she had an important temple; falls in love with Gilgamesh but is spurned by him

MAMMETUN (mä′ mə tən): Goddess of destinies

NINURTA (nə ner′ tə): God of wells; also a war god and a herald

PUZUR-AMURRI (po͞o′ zo͞or ä′ mo͞o rē): Utnapishtim's steersman

SAMUQAN (säm′ o͞o kän): God of cattle

SHAMASH (shä′ mäsh): God of the sun; also a judge and law-giver

SIDURI (sə do͞o′ rē): Winemaker for the gods

SIN (sēn): God of the moon

URSHANABI (er′ shə nä bē): Ferryman across the waters of death

UTNAPISHTIM (o͞ot nə pēsh′ təm): Survivor of the flood, he narrates the story of the deluge to Gilgamesh and is the only mortal to be given eternal life by the gods

Gate Guardian in the Form of a Lion. c. 1800 B.C., Sumeria.

PLACES

DILMUN (dil′ mən): The place of Paradise, where Utnapishtim is taken to live forever

MASHU (mä′ sho͞o): Twin-peaked mountain that guards the rising and setting sun

NISIR (ni zēr′): The "mountain of salvation," where Utnapishtim's boat comes aground after the flood

SHURRUPAK (shə ro͞o′ pək): City of Utnapishtim before the flood, it was located on the banks of the Euphrates River

URUK (o͞o′rook): City of Gilgamesh

The Death of Enkidu

from the Epic of Gilgamesh

Translated by
N. K. Sandars

. . . As Enkidu slept alone in his sickness, in bitterness of spirit he poured out his heart to his friend. "It was I who cut down the cedar, I who leveled the forest, I who slew Humbaba and now see what has become of me. Listen, my friend, this is the dream I dreamed last night. The heavens roared, and earth rumbled back an answer; between them stood I before an awful being, the somber-faced man-bird; he had directed on me his purpose. His was a vampire face, his foot was a lion's foot, his hand was an eagle's talon.[1] He fell on me and his claws were in my hair, he held me fast and I smothered; then he transformed me so that my arms became wings covered with feathers. He turned his stare towards me, and he led me away to the palace of Irkalla, the Queen of Darkness, to the house from which none who enters ever returns, down the road from which there is no coming back.

1. A *talon* is a bird's claw.

"There is the house whose people sit in darkness; dust is their food and clay their meat. They are clothed like birds with wings for covering, they see no light, they sit in darkness. I entered the house of dust and I saw the kings of the earth, their crowns put away forever; rulers and princes, all those who once wore kingly crowns and ruled the world in the days of old. They who had stood in the place of the gods like Anu and Enlil, stood now like servants to fetch baked meats in the house of dust, to carry cooked meat and cold water from the water skin.[2] In the house of dust which I entered were high priests and acolytes,[3] priests of the incantation and of ecstasy; there were servers of the temple, and there was Etana, that king of Kish whom the eagle carried to heaven in the days of old. I saw also Samuqan, god of cattle, and there was Ereshkigal the Queen of the Underworld; and Belit-Sheri squatted in front of her, she who is recorder of the gods and keeps the book of death. She held a tablet from which she read. She raised her head, she saw me and spoke: 'Who has brought this one here?' Then I awoke like a man drained of blood who wanders alone in a waste of rushes; like one whom the bailiff has seized and his heart pounds with terror."

Gilgamesh had peeled off his clothes, he listened to his words and wept quick tears, Gilgamesh listened and his tears flowed. He opened his mouth and spoke to Enkidu: "Who is there in strong-walled Uruk who has wisdom like this? Strange things have been spoken, why does your heart speak strangely? The dream was marvelous but the terror was great; we must treasure the dream whatever the terror; for the dream has shown that misery comes at last to the healthy man, the end of life is sorrow." And Gilgamesh lamented, "Now I will pray to the great gods, for my friend had an ominous dream."

This day on which Enkidu dreamed came to an end and he lay stricken with sickness. One whole day he lay on his bed and his suffering increased. He said to Gilgamesh, the friend on whose account he had left the wilderness, "Once I ran for you, for the water of life, and I now have nothing." A second day he lay on his bed and Gilgamesh watched over him but the sickness increased. A third day he lay on his bed, he called out to Gilgamesh, rousing him up. Now he was weak and his eyes were blind with weeping. Ten days he lay and his suffering increased, eleven and twelve days he lay on his bed of pain. Then he called to Gilgamesh, "My friend, the great goddess cursed me and I must die in shame. I shall not die like a man fallen in battle; I feared to fall, but happy is the man who falls in the battle, for I must die in shame." And Gilgamesh wept over Enkidu. . . .

The Search for Everlasting Life

Bitterly Gilgamesh wept for his friend Enkidu; he wandered over the wilderness as a hunter, he roamed over the plains; in his bitterness he cried, "How can I rest, how can I be at peace? Despair is in my heart. What my brother is now, that shall I be when I am dead. Because I am afraid of death I will go as best I can to find Utnapishtim whom they call the Faraway, for he has entered the assembly of the gods." So Gilgamesh traveled over the wilderness, he wandered over the grasslands, a long journey, in search of Utnapishtim, whom the gods took after the deluge; and they set him to live in the

2. A *water skin* is a water container made of animal hide.

3. An *acolyte* (ak′ ə līt) is a priest's or minister's assistant.

Vocabulary

incantation (in′ kan tā′ shən) *n.* use of spells or verbal charms as part of a magic ritual

ominous (om′ ə nəs) *adj.* foreboding or foreshadowing evil land of Dilmun, in the garden of the sun; and to him alone of men they gave everlasting life.

At night when he came to the mountain passes Gilgamesh prayed: "In these mountain passes long ago I saw lions, I was afraid and I lifted my eyes to the moon; I prayed and my prayers went up to the gods, so now, O moon god Sin, protect me." When he had prayed he lay down to sleep, until he was woken from out of a dream. He saw the lions round him glorying in life; then he took his axe in his hand, he drew his sword from his belt, and he fell upon them like an arrow from the string, and struck and destroyed and scattered them.

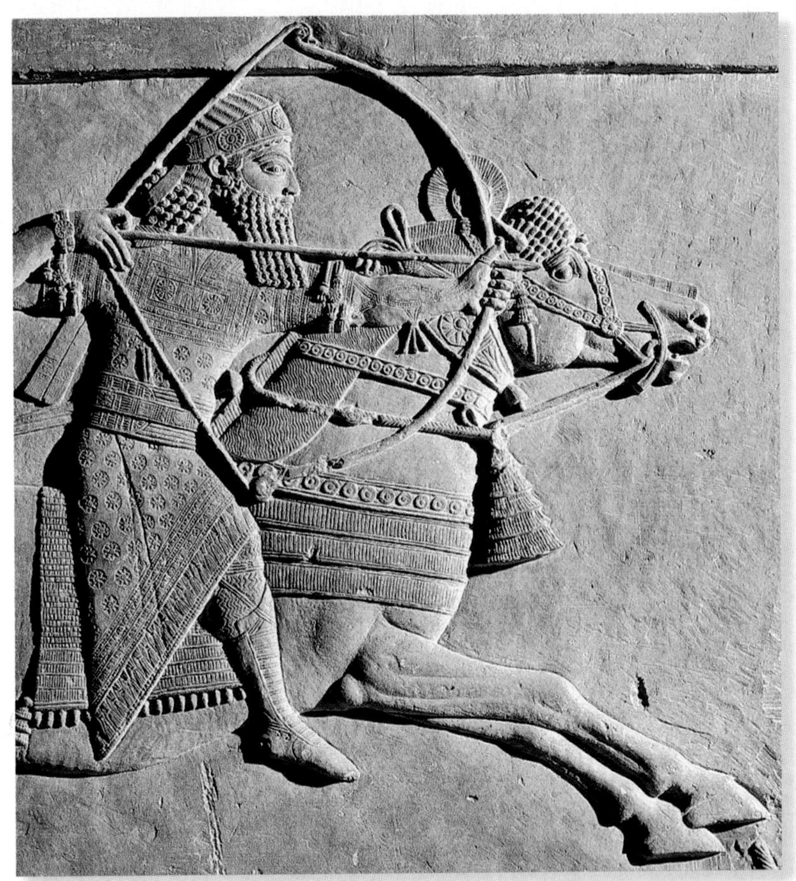

Ashurbanipal on a Horse, Hunting Lion. c. 668–627 B.C., Sumeria. Relief from the North Palace at Nineveh.

Viewing the relief: What do you think the man on the horse is like, based on his expression and his posture? In what ways might he remind you of Gilgamesh?

So at length Gilgamesh came to Mashu, the great mountains about which he had heard many things, which guard the rising and the setting sun. Its twin peaks are as high as the wall of heaven and its paps reach down to the underworld. At its gate the Scorpions stand guard, half man and half dragon; their glory is terrifying, their stare strikes death into men, their shimmering halo sweeps the mountains that guard the rising sun. When Gilgamesh saw them he shielded his eyes for the length of a moment only; then he took courage and approached. When they saw him so undismayed the Man-Scorpion called to his mate, "This one who comes to us now is flesh of the gods." The mate of the Man-Scorpion answered, "Two-thirds is god but one-third is man."

Then he called to the man Gilgamesh, he called to the child of the gods: "Why have you come so great a journey; for what have you traveled so far, crossing the dangerous waters; tell me the reason for your coming?" Gilgamesh answered, "For Enkidu; I loved him dearly, together we endured all kinds of hardships; on his account I have come, for the common lot of man has taken him. I have wept for him day and night, I would not give up his body for burial, I thought my friend would come back because of my weeping. Since he went, my life is nothing; that is why I have traveled here in search of Utnapishtim my father; for men say he has entered the assembly of the gods, and has found everlasting life. I have a desire to question him concerning the living and the dead." The Man-Scorpion opened his mouth and said, speaking to Gilgamesh, "No man born of woman has done what you have asked, no mortal man has gone into the mountain; the length of it is twelve leagues of darkness; in it there is no light, but the heart is oppressed with darkness. From the rising of the sun to the setting of the sun there is no light." Gilgamesh said, "Although I should go in sorrow and in pain, with sighing and with weeping, still I must go. Open the gate of the mountain." And the Man-Scorpion said, "Go, Gilgamesh, I permit you to pass through the mountain of Mashu and through the high ranges; may your feet carry you safely home. The gate of the mountain is open." . . .

Gilgamesh crosses to the other side of Mashu. There he steps into an amazing place.

There was the garden of the gods; all round him stood bushes bearing gems. Seeing it he went down at once, for there was fruit of carnelian[4] with the vine hanging from it, beautiful to look at; lapis lazuli leaves hung thick with fruit, sweet to see. For thorns and thistles there were hematite and rare stones, agate, and pearls from out of the sea. While Gilgamesh walked in the garden by the edge of the sea Shamash saw him, and he saw that he was dressed in the skins of animals and ate their flesh. He was distressed, and he spoke and said, "No mortal man has gone this way before, nor will, as long as the winds drive over the sea." And to Gilgamesh he said, "You will never find the life for which you are searching." Gilgamesh said to glorious Shamash, "Now that I have toiled and strayed so far over the wilderness, am I to sleep, and let the earth cover my head forever? Let my eyes see the sun until they are dazzled with looking. Although I am no better than a dead man, still let me see the light of the sun."

Did You Know?
Lapis lazuli (lap′is laz′ə lē) is an azure blue or violet-blue semiprecious stone used in carvings and jewelry.

Beside the sea she lives, the woman of the vine, the maker of wine; Siduri sits in the garden at the edge of the sea, with the golden bowl and the golden vats that the gods gave her. She is covered with a veil; and where she sits she sees Gilgamesh coming towards her, wearing skins, the flesh of the gods in his body, but despair in his heart, and his face like the face of one who has made a long journey. She looked, and as she scanned the distance she said in her own heart, "Surely this is some felon; where is he going now?" And she barred her gate against him with the crossbar and shot home the bolt. But Gilgamesh, hearing the sound of the bolt, threw up his head and lodged his foot in the gate; he called to her, "Young woman, maker of wine, why do you bolt your door; what did you see that made you bar your gate? I will break in your door and burst in your gate, for I am Gilgamesh who seized and killed the Bull of Heaven, I killed the watchman of the cedar forest, I overthrew Humbaba who lived in the forest, and I killed the lions in the passes of the mountain."

Then Siduri said to him, "If you are that Gilgamesh who seized and killed the Bull of Heaven, who killed the watchman of the cedar forest, who overthrew Humbaba that lived in the forest, and killed the lions in the passes of the mountain, why are your cheeks so starved and why is your face so drawn? Why is despair in your heart and your face like the face of one who has made a long journey? Yes, why is your face burned from heat and cold, and why do you come here wandering over the pastures in search of the wind?"

Gilgamesh answered her, "And why should not my cheeks be starved and my face drawn? Despair is in my heart and my face is the face of one who has made a long journey, it was burned with heat and with cold. Why should I not wander over the pastures in search of the wind? My friend, my younger brother, he who

4. *Carnelian* is a red or reddish-orange semiprecious stone often set in jewelry.

hunted the wild ass of the wilderness and the panther of the plains, my friend, my younger brother who seized and killed the Bull of Heaven and overthrew Humbaba in the cedar forest, my friend who was very dear to me and who endured dangers beside me, Enkidu my brother, whom I loved, the end of mortality has overtaken him. I wept for him seven days and nights till the worm fastened on him. Because of my brother I am afraid of death, because of my brother I stray through the wilderness and cannot rest. But now, young woman, maker of wine, since I have seen your face do not let me see the face of death which I dread so much."

She answered, "Gilgamesh, where are you hurrying to? You will never find that life for which you are looking. When the gods created man they allotted to him death, but life they retained in their own keeping. As for you, Gilgamesh, fill your belly with good things; day and night, night and day, dance and be merry, feast and rejoice. Let your clothes be fresh, bathe yourself in water, cherish the little child that holds your hand, and make your wife happy in your embrace; for this too is the lot of man."

But Gilgamesh said to Siduri, the young woman, "How can I be silent, how can I rest, when Enkidu whom I love is dust, and I too shall die and be laid in the earth. You live by the seashore and look into the heart of it; young woman, tell me now, which is the way to Utnapishtim, the son of Ubara-Tutu? What directions are there for the passage; give me, oh, give me directions. I will cross the Ocean if it is possible; if it is not I will wander still farther in the wilderness." The wine-maker said to him, "Gilgamesh, there is no crossing the Ocean; whoever has come, since the days of old, has not been able to pass that sea. The Sun in his glory crosses the Ocean, but who beside Shamash has ever crossed it? The place and the passage are difficult, and the waters of death are deep which flow between. Gilgamesh, how will you cross the Ocean? When you come to the waters of death what will you do? But Gilgamesh, down in the woods you will find Urshanabi, the ferryman of Utnapishtim; with him are the holy things, the things of stone. He is fashioning the serpent prow of the boat. Look at him well, and if it is possible, perhaps you will cross the waters with him. . . ."

But Gilgamesh smashes some of the sacred stones and then builds his own boat. Urshanabi is his guide across the ocean.

So Urshanabi the ferryman brought Gilgamesh to Utnapishtim, whom they call the Faraway, who lives in Dilmun at the place of the sun's transit, eastward of the mountain. To him alone of men the gods had given everlasting life.

Now Utnapishtim, where he lay at ease, looked into the distance and he said in his heart, musing to himself, "Why does the boat sail here without tackle and mast; why are the sacred stones destroyed, and why does the master not sail the boat? That man who comes is none of mine; where I look I see a man whose body is covered with skins of beasts. Who is this who walks up the shore behind Urshanabi, for surely he is no man of mine?" So Utnapishtim looked at him and said, "What is your name, you who come here wearing the skins of beasts, with your cheeks starved and your face drawn? Where are you hurrying to now? For what reason have you made this great journey, crossing the seas whose passage is difficult? Tell me the reason for your coming."

He replied, "Gilgamesh is my name. I am from Uruk, from the house of Anu." Then Utnapishtim said to him, "If you are Gilgamesh, why are your cheeks so starved and your face drawn? Why is despair in your heart and your face like the face of one who has made a long journey? Yes, why is your face burned with heat and cold; and why do you come here, wandering over the wilderness in search of the wind?" . . .

Nile Mosaic (detail). Late 2nd century B.C. Museo Archeologico Prenestino, Palestrina, Italy.
Viewing the mosaic: Do you imagine Gilgamesh's boat to look anything like this one?

Again Gilgamesh said, speaking to Utnapishtim, "It is to see Utnapishtim whom we call the Faraway that I have come this journey. For this I have wandered over the world, I have crossed many difficult ranges, I have crossed the seas, I have wearied myself with traveling; my joints are aching, and I have lost acquaintance with sleep which is sweet. My clothes were worn out before I came to the house of Siduri. I have killed the bear and hyena, the lion and panther, the tiger, the stag[5] and the ibex,[6] all sorts of wild game and the small creatures of the pastures. I ate their flesh and I wore their skins; and that was how I came to the gate of the young woman, the maker of wine, who barred her gate of pitch[7] and bitumen[8] against me. But from her I had news of the journey; so then I came to Urshanabi the ferryman, and with him I crossed over the waters of death. Oh, father Utnapishtim, you who have entered the assembly of the gods, I wish to question you concerning the living and the dead, how shall I find the life for which I am searching?"

Utnapishtim said, "There is no permanence. Do we build a house to stand forever, do we seal a contract to hold for all time? Do brothers divide an inheritance to keep forever, does the flood time of rivers endure? It is only the nymph[9] of the dragonfly who sheds her larva and sees the sun in his glory. From the days of old there is no permanence. The sleeping and the dead, how alike they are, they are like a painted death. What is there between the master and the servant when both have fulfilled their doom? When the Anunnaki, the judges, come together, and Mammetun the mother of destinies, together they decree the fates of men. Life and death they allot but the day of death they do not disclose."

Then Gilgamesh said to Utnapishtim the Faraway, "I look at you now, Utnapishtim, and your appearance is no different from mine; there is nothing strange in your features. I thought I should find you like a hero prepared for battle, but you lie here taking your ease on your back. Tell me truly, how was it that you came to enter the company of the gods and to possess everlasting life?" Utnapishtim said to Gilgamesh, "I will reveal to you a mystery, I will tell you a secret of the gods."

5. A *stag* is a full-grown male deer.
6. An *ibex* (ī′ bex) is a wild mountain goat with curving horns that is native to Europe, Asia, and northern Africa.
7. *Pitch* is resin from pine trees.
8. *Bitumen* (bī to͞o′ mən) is a type of coal.

9. Here, a *nymph* (nimf) is an insect in the larval state that has not completely metamorphosed.

The Story of the Flood

"You know the city Shurrupak, it stands on the banks of Euphrates?[10] That city grew old and the gods that were in it were old. There was Anu, lord of the firmament, their father, and warrior Enlil their counselor, Ninurta the helper, and Ennugi watcher over canals; and with them also was Ea. In those days the world teemed, the people multiplied, the world bellowed like a wild bull, and the great god was aroused by the clamor. Enlil heard the clamor and he said to the gods in council, 'The uproar of mankind is intolerable and sleep is no longer possible by reason of the babel.' So the gods agreed to exterminate mankind. Enlil did this, but Ea because of his oath warned me in a dream. He whispered their words to my house of reeds, 'Reed-house, reed-house! Wall, O wall, hearken reed-house, wall reflect; O man of Shurrupak, son of Ubara-Tutu; tear down your house and build a boat, abandon possessions and look for life, despise worldly goods and save your soul alive. Tear down your house, I say, and build a boat. These are the measurements of the bark as you shall build her: let her beam equal her length, let her deck be roofed like the vault that covers the abyss; then take up into the boat the seed of all living creatures.'

"When I had understood I said to my lord, 'Behold, what you have commanded I will honor and perform, but how shall I answer the people, the city, the elders?' Then Ea opened his mouth and said to me, his servant, 'Tell them this: I have learned that Enlil is wrathful against me, I dare no longer walk in his land nor live in his city; I will go down to the Gulf to dwell with Ea my lord. But on you he will rain down abundance, rare fish and shy wildfowl, a rich harvest-tide. In the evening the rider of the storm will bring you wheat in torrents.'

"In the first light of dawn all my household gathered round me, the children brought pitch and the men whatever was necessary. On the fifth day I laid the keel[11] and the ribs, then I made fast the planking. The ground-space was one acre, each side of the deck measured one hundred and twenty cubits,[12] making a square. I built six decks below, seven in all, I divided them into nine sections with bulkheads between. I drove in wedges where needed, I saw to the punt-poles,[13] and laid in supplies. The carriers brought oil in baskets, I poured pitch into the furnace and asphalt and oil; more oil was consumed in caulking, and more again the master of the boat took into his stores. I slaughtered bullocks for the people and every day I killed sheep. I gave the shipwrights wine to drink as though it were river water, raw wine and red wine and oil and white wine. There was feasting then as there is at the time of the New Year's festival; I myself anointed my head. On the seventh day the boat was complete.

Did You Know?
The *ribs* of a ship run perpendicular from the keel upwards to the deck.

10. The *Euphrates* (ū frā′ tēz) River flows in southwestern Asia.

11. The *keel* is the chief structural part of a boat; it extends longitudinally along the bottom.
12. A *cubit* is an ancient unit of measure based on the length of the forearm from the elbow to the tip of the middle finger. It usually equals about eighteen inches.
13. *Punt-poles* are used to move a ship forward, by pushing against the bottom in shallow water.

Vocabulary
firmament (fur′ mə ment) *n.* the sky
clamor (klam′ ər) *n.* noisy shouting

"Then was the launching full of difficulty; there was shifting of ballast[14] above and below till two thirds was submerged. I loaded into her all that I had of gold and of living things, my family, my kin, the beast of the field both wild and tame, and all the craftsmen. I sent them on board, for the time that Shamash had ordained was already fulfilled when he said, 'In the evening, when the rider of the storm sends down the destroying rain, enter the boat and batten her down.'[15] The time was fulfilled, the evening came, the rider of the storm sent down the rain. I looked out at the weather and it was terrible, so I too boarded the boat and battened her down. All was now complete, the battening and the caulking; so I handed the tiller to Puzur-Amurri the steersman, with the navigation and the care of the whole boat.

"With the first light of dawn a black cloud came from the horizon; it thundered within where Adad, lord of the storm was riding. In front over hill and plain Shullat and Hanish, heralds of the storm, led on. Then the gods of the abyss rose up; Nergal pulled out the dams of the nether[16] waters, Ninurta the warlord threw down the dikes, and the seven judges of hell, the Annunaki, raised their torches, lighting the land with their livid flame. A stupor of despair went up to heaven when the god of the storm turned daylight to darkness, when he smashed the land like a cup. One whole day the tempest raged, gathering fury as it went, it poured over the people like the tides of battle; a man could not see his brother nor the people be seen from heaven. Even the gods were terrified at the flood, they fled to the highest heaven, the firmament of Anu; they crouched against the walls, cowering like curs.[17] Then Ishtar the sweet-voiced Queen of Heaven cried out like a woman in travail: 'Alas the days of old are turned to dust because I commanded evil; why did I command this evil in the council of all the gods? I commanded wars to destroy the people, but are they not my people, for I brought them forth? Now like the spawn of fish they float in the ocean.' The great gods of heaven and hell wept, they covered their mouths.

"For six days and six nights the winds blew, torrent and tempest and flood overwhelmed the world, tempest and flood raged together like warring hosts. When the seventh day dawned the storm from the south subsided, the sea grew calm, the flood was stilled; I looked at the face of the world and there was silence, all mankind was turned to clay. The surface of the sea stretched as flat as a rooftop; I opened a hatch and the light fell on my face. Then I bowed low, I sat down and I wept, the tears streamed down my face, for on every side was the waste of water. I looked for land in vain, but fourteen leagues distant there appeared a mountain, and there the boat grounded; on the mountain of Nisir the boat held fast, she held fast and did not budge. One day she held, and a second day on the mountain of Nisir she held fast and did not budge. A third day, and a fourth day she held fast on the mountain and did not budge; a fifth day and a sixth day she held fast on the mountain. When the seventh day dawned I loosed a dove and let her go. She flew away, but finding no resting place she returned. Then I loosed a swallow, and she flew away but finding no resting place she returned. I loosed a raven, she saw that the waters had retreated, she ate, she flew around, she cawed, and she did not come back. Then I threw everything open to the four winds, I made a sacrifice and poured out a libation on

14. *Ballast* (bal′ əst) is a weighty material installed in a ship to maintain stability.

15. The nautical term *batten her down* means "to place tarpaulins over the hatches of the ship in preparation for bad weather."

16. *Nether* means "low" or "deep."

17. A *cur* is a bad-tempered dog or mongrel.

Vocabulary

libation (lī bā′ shən) *n.* a liquid used in ceremonial drinking the mountain top. Seven and again seven cauldrons I set up on their stands, I heaped up wood and cane and cedar and myrtle. When the gods smelled the sweet savor, they gathered like flies over the sacrifice. Then, at last, Ishtar also came, she lifted her necklace with the jewels of heaven that once Anu had made to please her. 'O you gods here present, by the lapis lazuli round my neck I shall remember these days as I remember the jewels of my throat; these last days I shall not forget. Let all the gods gather round the sacrifice, except Enlil. He shall not approach this offering, for without reflection he brought the flood; he consigned my people to destruction.'

Did You Know?
Myrtle is a common evergreen shrub with shiny leaves, fragrant white or pink flowers, and black berries.

"When Enlil had come, when he saw the boat, he was wroth and swelled with anger at the gods, the host of heaven, 'Has any of these mortals escaped? Not one was to have survived the destruction.' Then the god of the wells and canals Ninurta opened his mouth and said to the warrior Enlil, 'Who is there of the gods that can devise without Ea? It is Ea alone who knows all things.' Then Ea opened his mouth and spoke to warrior Enlil, 'Wisest of gods, hero Enlil, how could you so senselessly bring down the flood?

Lay upon the sinner his sin,
Lay upon the transgressor his transgression,
Punish him a little when he breaks loose,
Do not drive him too hard or he perishes;
Would that a lion had ravaged mankind
Rather than the flood,
Would that a wolf had ravaged mankind
Rather than the flood,
Would that famine had wasted the world
Rather than the flood,
Would that pestilence had wasted mankind
Rather than the flood.

It was not I that revealed the secret of the gods; the wise man learned it in a dream. Now take your counsel what shall be done with him.'

"Then Enlil went up into the boat, he took me by the hand and my wife and made us enter the boat and kneel down on either side, he standing between us. He touched our foreheads to bless us saying, 'In time past Utnapishtim was a mortal man; henceforth he and his wife shall live in the distance at the mouth of the rivers.' Thus it was that the gods took me and placed me here to live in the distance, at the mouth of the rivers."

The Return

Utnapishtim said, "As for you, Gilgamesh, who will assemble the gods for your sake, so that you may find that life for which you are searching? But if you wish, come and put it to the test: only prevail against sleep for six days and seven nights." But while Gilgamesh sat there resting on his haunches, a mist of sleep like soft wool teased from the fleece drifted over him, and Utnapishtim said to his wife, "Look at him now, the strong man who would have everlasting life, even now the mists of sleep are drifting over him." His wife replied, "Touch the man to wake him, so that he may return to his own land in peace, going back through the gate by which he came." Utnapishtim said to his wife, "All men are deceivers, even you he will attempt to deceive; therefore bake loaves of bread, each day one loaf, and put it beside his head; and make a mark on the wall to number the days he has slept."

So she baked loaves of bread, each day one loaf, and put it beside his head, and she marked on the wall the days that he slept; and there came a day when the first loaf was hard, the second loaf was like leather, the third was soggy, the crust of the fourth had mold, the fifth was mildewed, the sixth was fresh, and the seventh was still on the embers. Then Utnapishtim touched him and he woke. Gilgamesh said to Utnapishtim the Faraway, "I hardly slept when you touched and roused me." But Utnapishtim said, "Count these loaves and learn how many days you slept, for your first is hard, your second like leather, your third is soggy, the crust of your fourth has mold, your fifth is mildewed, your sixth is fresh and your seventh was still over the glowing embers when I touched and woke you." Gilgamesh said, "What shall I do, O Utnapishtim, where shall I go? Already the thief in the night has hold of my limbs, death inhabits my room; wherever my foot rests, there I find death."

Then Utnapishtim spoke to Urshanabi the ferryman: "Woe to you Urshanabi, now and forevermore you have become hateful to this harborage; it is not for you, nor for you are the crossings of this sea. Go now, banished from the shore. But this man before whom you walked, bringing him here, whose body is covered with foulness and the grace of whose limbs has been spoiled by wild skins, take him to the washing place. There he shall wash his long hair clean as snow in the water, he shall throw off his skins and let the sea carry them away, and the beauty of his body shall be shown, the fillet[18] on his forehead shall be renewed, and he shall be given clothes to cover his nakedness. Till he reaches his own city and his journey is accomplished, these clothes will show no sign of age, they will wear like a new garment." So Urshanabi took Gilgamesh and led him to the washing place, he washed his long hair as clean as snow in the water, he threw off his skins, which the sea carried away, and showed the beauty of his body. He renewed the fillet on his forehead, and to cover his nakedness gave him clothes which would show no sign of age, but would wear like a new garment till he reached his own city, and his journey was accomplished.

18. A *fillet* is a narrow strip of ornamental material worn in the hair or, in this case, across the forehead.

A God Killing a Fiery Cyclops. 1800 B.C., Sumeria. Terra-cotta relief from Khafaje. Iraq Museum, Baghdad.

Viewing the relief: Does this scene remind you of any scenes in movies you have seen? In what ways does it suggest a scene from the story of Gilgamesh?

Then Gilgamesh and Urshanabi launched the boat onto the water and boarded it, and they made ready to sail away; but the wife of Utnapishtim the Faraway said to him, "Gilgamesh came here wearied out, he is worn out; what will you give him to carry him back to his own country?" So Utnapishtim spoke, and Gilgamesh took a pole and brought the boat in to the bank. "Gilgamesh, you came here a man wearied out, you have worn yourself out; what shall I give you to carry you back to your own country? Gilgamesh, I shall reveal a secret thing, it is a mystery of the gods that I am telling you. There is a plant that grows under the water, it has a prickle like a thorn, like a rose; it will wound your hands, but if you succeed in taking it, then your hands will hold that which restores his lost youth to a man."

When Gilgamesh heard this he opened the sluices so that a sweet-water current might carry him out to the deepest channel; he tied heavy stones to his feet and they dragged him down to the water bed. There he saw the plant growing; although it pricked him he took it in his hands; then he cut the heavy stones from his feet, and the sea carried him and threw him onto the shore. Gilgamesh said to Urshanabi the ferryman, "Come here, and see this marvelous plant. By its virtue a man may win back all his former strength. I will take it to Uruk of the strong walls; there I will give it to the old men to eat. Its name shall be 'The Old Men Are Young Again'; and at last I shall eat it myself and have back all my lost youth." So Gilgamesh returned by the gate through which he had come, Gilgamesh and Urshanabi went together. They traveled their twenty leagues and then they broke their fast; after thirty leagues they stopped for the night.

Gilgamesh saw a well of cool water and he went down and bathed; but deep in the pool there was lying a serpent, and the serpent sensed the sweetness of the flower. It rose out of the water and snatched it away, and immediately it sloughed its skin and returned to the well. Then Gilgamesh sat down and wept, the tears ran down his face, and he took the hand of Urshanabi; "O Urshanabi, was it for this that I toiled with my hands, is it for this I have wrung out my heart's blood? For myself I have gained nothing; not I, but the beast of the earth has joy of it now. Already the stream has carried it twenty leagues back to the channels where I found it. I found a sign and now I have lost it. Let us leave the boat on the bank and go."

After twenty leagues they broke their fast, after thirty leagues they stopped for the night; in three days they had walked as much as a journey of a month and fifteen days. When the journey was accomplished they arrived at Uruk, the strong-walled city. Gilgamesh spoke to him, to Urshanabi the ferryman, "Urshanabi, climb up onto the wall of Uruk, inspect its foundation terrace, and examine well the brickwork; see if it is not of burned bricks; and did not the seven wise men lay these foundations? One third of the whole is city, one third is garden, and one third is field, with the precinct of the goddess Ishtar. These parts and the precinct are all Uruk."

This too was the work of Gilgamesh, the king, who knew the countries of the world. He was wise, he saw mysteries and knew secret things, he brought us a tale of the days before the flood. He went a long journey, was weary, worn out with labor, and returning engraved on a stone the whole story.

Vocabulary
sluice (slo͞os) *n.* floodgate

Responding to Literature

Personal Response

How did you expect Gilgamesh's quest to turn out? Did the ending meet your expectations? Explain.

Analyzing Literature

Recall

1. Where does Enkidu travel in his dream?
2. Which three characters try to persuade Gilgamesh to give up his journey? What argument does each present?
3. Why did the gods want to destroy humankind? How did Utnapishtim escape death?
4. Why does Utnapishtim challenge Gilgamesh to undergo a test?
5. What secret does Utnapishtim reveal to Gilgamesh as a parting gift?

Interpret

6. How does Enkidu's dream **foreshadow,** or provide clues to, his fate?
7. In your opinion, why does Gilgamesh refuse to give up his journey to find Utnapishtim?
8. What human qualities do the gods display in the flood narrative?
9. What might sleep **symbolize,** or represent, in Utnapishtim's challenge to Gilgamesh? What might the ability to stay awake represent?
10. **Irony** is a contrast between what is expected and what actually happens. What is ironic about the outcome of Utnapishtim's gift to Gilgamesh?

Evaluate and Connect

11. What, if anything, did Gilgamesh gain from his quest? Would you call it a success or a failure? Explain.
12. What is the **theme,** or main idea, of this selection?
13. Although the epic is fictional, it contains many realistic details. What are some of these details, and what do they add to the story?
14. In what ways does Gilgamesh's quest parallel those you discussed during the Reading Focus on page 418? Based on these parallels, what conclusions might you draw about heroes and their quests?
15. In your view, is the story of Gilgamesh's quest still relevant to people today? Explain.

Literary Criticism

According to one critic, the story of the flood illustrates that the gods are inscrutable, or unknowable. The flood, for example, "happens simply because the gods want it to happen. Similarly, at the end of the story, equally inscrutable is the gentle grace of the high god Enlil's decision to grant immortality to the flood's survivors." Do you agree with this critic's opinion? Why or why not? Write a brief paragraph explaining your answers.

Literary ELEMENTS

Legendary and Mythical Heroes

Legendary heroes are idealized figures, sometimes based on real people, who embody qualities admired by the cultural group to which they belong. The adventures and accomplishments of these heroes are preserved in legends or tales that are handed down from generation to generation. Over the years, storytellers embellish and exaggerate these exploits. Legendary heroes sometimes evolve into **mythical heroes,** or supernatural beings. Gilgamesh, for example, was eventually deified by the Sumerians as a god of the underworld.

1. Based on the portrayal of Gilgamesh, what qualities would you say the Sumerians admired in their leaders?
2. Virtually all cultures have legendary heroes. What are some qualities heroes might represent? Is it important to have heroes?

- See **Literary Terms Handbook,** p. R7.

Literature and Writing

Writing About Literature

Analyzing Mood Enkidu's dream sets the **mood** for the rest of the tale. How would you describe this mood? What descriptive words and phrases establish it? In a few paragraphs, summarize the dream, define the mood, and explain which descriptions help create it.

Creative Writing

Dear MGM You are a producer who wants to persuade a film studio to make a movie of the *Epic of Gilgamesh.* Write a one-page letter explaining why it would make a good movie, what type of audience would enjoy the movie, and which actors might play major roles.

Extending Your Response

Literature Groups

Man and Superman At what points in the epic does Gilgamesh seem superhuman? How do his human traits help define his character? Discuss these questions in a group, and share your answers with the class.

Interdisciplinary Activity

Science: The Discovery of the Tablets How did Austen Henry Layard find the *Epic of Gilgamesh*? What difficulties did he overcome to uncover and preserve the tablets? Where are the tablets today? Use an encyclopedia, a book about the epic, or the Internet to find answers to these questions. Then, present a brief oral report to the class.

Cuneiform tablet chronicling the great flood.

Save your work for your portfolio.

Skill Minilesson

VOCABULARY • Analogies

Analogies are comparisons based on relationships between words and ideas. Sometimes analogies are based on synonyms, or words that have almost the same meaning and that are the same part of speech. Study the example that follows:

ominous : foreboding :: auspicious : fortunate

To finish an analogy based on synonyms, determine the relationship between the first two words. Then apply that relationship to the second pair.

PRACTICE Choose the pair that best completes *each* analogy.

1. flower : blossom ::
   a. myrtle : flower
   b. cur : mongrel
   c. noisy : clamor
   d. affable : friendship
   e. lion : tiger
2. disdain : contempt ::
   a. chagrin : blush
   b. laud : criticize
   c. implausible : disbelief
   d. ardor : passion
   e. enmity : irritation

• For more on analogies, see **Communications Skills Handbook,** p. R77.

Literature FOCUS

Sacred Texts

Sacred texts are writings that are revered as holy or are closely linked to religion or religious ritual. These texts, sometimes called scriptures, are often regarded as divine revelations, directly communicated from God to human beings on specific occasions. Some sacred texts are said to have been divinely inspired. Some are the records of oral teachings or sermons of a religion's founder or teacher. Many originated in the oral tradition. Through reciting, chanting, and singing, the oral dimension of sacred texts remains an important part of many religions today, often featured in daily or weekly rituals.

Sacred texts are not a characteristic of all religions. Ancient Greek and Roman religions, which viewed divinities as personal forces, lacked sacred texts in the sense of widely shared "holy books," although myths and legends surrounding individual cults were told and retold with reverence, and many such stories were eventually written down.

Some sacred texts include the following:

The Bible In at least five of the major religions of the modern world, sacred texts compiled many centuries ago continue to play a vital role. For example, the Bible (from Greek *biblia*, meaning "books") is said to be the most widely read book in the world. Originally written in Hebrew, Aramaic, and Greek over a period of more than a thousand years, all or part of the books of the Bible have been translated into more than 1,500 languages. Judaism regards the first five books of the Bible as a repository of the law, rituals, and history of Israel. These books (called the Torah, which is the Hebrew word for "law"), together with the books of the prophets and other writings, make up the Tanakh, or Hebrew Bible.

Since Christianity originated in Judaism, Christians also consider the first part of the Bible, or Old Testament, a sacred text. In addition, Christian sacred texts include books on the life, death, and teachings of Christianity's central figure, Jesus Christ. These books, which include the four gospels, the Epistles of Paul and other disciples, and the Book of Revelation, are called the New Testament, the second half of the Christian Bible.

The Qur'an The Qur'an (kô rän′) is the holy book of Islam. Muslims believe its contents to be the actual words of the deity Allah as they were revealed to the prophet Muhammad in the years A.D. 610–632. The word *Qur'an* (also spelled Koran) is Arabic for "recitation" or "oral reading." The written text of the Qur'an was standardized within thirty years after Muhammad's death (see page 449). Today the Qur'an is the world's most ideologically influential text.

The Vedas Hinduism has no single founder and acknowledges a number of deities. Nevertheless, most Hindus accept the Vedas (from Sanskrit for "knowledge") as a sacred text endowed with special authority. The Vedas are four ancient collections of hymns and verses, the oldest of which is the Rig Veda, dating from 1500–1000 B.C. (see page 497).

Buddhist Texts Buddhism has a large body of sacred texts, consisting of hundreds of works that have been transmitted both orally and in written form. The sacred texts of Buddhism include philosophical treatises, manuals of ritual, biographies, and histories. Central to these works is the doctrine, or *dharma*, of Buddha, the founder and teacher of Buddhism. The oral teachings and sermons of Buddha were written down by monks and nuns after their teacher's death.

Before You Read

from the *Tanakh*

Reading Focus

Human beings always seem to have had a need to tell or listen to stories. What are some of the first stories you remember hearing?

List It! Brainstorm a list of these stories and note what their purposes seem to be. Then exchange lists and compare ideas with a classmate.

Setting a Purpose Read to discover some of the oldest stories of civilization.

Building Background

The Flood Story

The Hebrew account of Noah and the flood may preserve the memory of a great deluge in Southwest Asia. If the flood narrative in the *Epic of Gilgamesh* refers to the same event, the flood probably occurred hundreds of years before the Book of Genesis was written down. Certain details in the story show that the authors of the Torah—the first five books of the Tanakh (tä näkh′), or Old Testament—who relied on oral tradition, combined at least two accounts of the flood in the Genesis narrative. In one account, Noah is ordered to take one pair of every living species into the ark, while in another he is commanded to take seven pairs of one category of animal and one pair of another. The duration of the flood is said to have been both forty days and one hundred and fifty days. Despite these contradictions, the fundamental outlines of the story are clear.

Torah Mantle. c. 1870, Eastern Europe. Velvet, embroidered with beads and metallic thread. Jewish Museum, New York.

Although God punishes human beings for their wickedness, his love for humanity is great. He saves Noah, his family, and a pair of every kind of creature.

The Book of Ruth

The Book of Ruth, which is among the briefest books in the Tanakh, has been called one of the first short stories. As you will discover, it has all the elements of a good story: a vivid setting, convincing characters who seem drawn from real life, and a suspenseful plot that revolves around a conflict. From the point of view of the Israelites, the central character, Ruth, is an outsider. She comes from Moab, a neighboring kingdom whose worship of idols was condemned by the Hebrews. Furthermore, Ruth is a childless widow with no property rights and, as a result, is in urgent need of shelter and protection.

Vocabulary Preview

covenant (kuv′ ə nənt) *n.* a formal, solemn, and binding agreement; p. 437

debar (di bär′) *v.* to shut out or exclude from doing something; p. 442

glean (glēn) *v.* to pick up or gather grain left on the field after the reaping; p. 443

prostrate (pros′ trāt) *v.* to throw oneself face downward on the ground as a gesture of humility or submission; p. 443

winnow (win′ ō) *v.* to separate the grain from the chaff; p. 444

stealthily (stelth′ ə lē) *adv.* slowly and secretly; p. 444

Genesis 6–9:

The Flood

from the Tanakh

Chapter 6

When men began to increase on earth and daughters were born to them, the divine beings saw how beautiful the daughters of men were and took wives from among those that pleased them.—The Lord said, "My breath shall not abide in man forever, since he too is flesh; let the days allowed him be one hundred and twenty years."—It was then, and later too, that the Nephilim[1] appeared on earth—when the divine beings cohabited with the daughters of men, who bore them offspring. They were the heroes of old, the men of renown.

The Lord saw how great was man's wickedness on earth, and how every plan devised by his mind was nothing but evil all the time. And the Lord regretted that He had made man on earth, and His heart was saddened. The Lord said, "I will blot out from the earth the men whom I created—men together with beasts, creeping things, and birds of the sky; for I regret that I made them." But Noah found favor with the Lord.

This is the line of Noah.—Noah was a righteous man; he was blameless in his age; Noah walked with God.—Noah begot three sons: Shem, Ham, and Japheth.

The earth became corrupt before God; the earth was filled with lawlessness. When God saw how corrupt the earth was, for all flesh had corrupted its ways on earth, God said to Noah, "I have decided to put an end to all flesh, for the earth is filled with lawlessness because of them: I am about to destroy them with the earth. Make yourself an ark of gopher wood; make it an ark with compartments, and cover it inside and out with pitch.[2] This is how you shall make it: the length of the ark shall be three hundred cubits,[3] its width fifty cubits, and its height thirty cubits. Make an opening for daylight in the ark, and terminate it within a cubit of the top. Put the entrance to the ark in its side; make it with bottom, second, and third decks.

1. ***Nephilim*** **(nef′ ə lim′) is a biblical race of demigods or giants.**

2. ***Pitch*** **is a black, tar-like substance that was used as a waterproofing compound.**

3. **A *cubit* equals about eighteen inches.**

The Animals Entering Noah's Ark, 1650. Adriaen Van Nieulandt (Netherlands). Oil on canvas, 130 x 165 cm. Private collection.

Viewing the painting: What words would you use to capture the mood of this scene? Is this how you imagine Noah and the animals boarding the ark? Explain.

"For My part, I am about to bring the Flood—waters upon the earth—to destroy all flesh under the sky in which there is breath of life; everything on earth shall perish. But I will establish My covenant with you, and you shall enter the ark, with your sons, your wife, and your sons' wives. And of all that lives, of all flesh, you shall take two of each into the ark to keep alive with you; they shall be male and female. From birds of every kind, cattle of every kind, every kind of creeping thing on earth, two of each shall come to you to stay alive. For your part, take of everything that is eaten and store it away, to serve as food for you and for them." Noah did so; just as God commanded him, so he did.

Chapter 7

Then the Lord said to Noah, "Go into the ark, with all your household, for you alone have I found righteous before Me in this generation. Of every clean animal you shall take seven pairs, males and their mates, and of every animal that is not clean, two, a male and its mate; of the birds of the sky also, seven pairs, male and female, to keep seed alive upon all the earth. For in seven days' time I will make it rain upon the earth, forty days and forty nights, and I will blot out from the earth all existence that I created." And Noah did just as the Lord commanded him.

Noah was six hundred years old when the Flood came, waters upon the earth. Noah, with his sons, his wife, and his sons' wives, went into the ark because of the waters of the Flood. Of the clean animals, of the animals that are not clean, of the birds, and of everything that creeps on the ground, two of each, male and female, came to Noah into the ark, as God had commanded Noah. And on the seventh day the waters of the Flood came upon the earth.

In the six hundredth year of Noah's life, in the second month, on the seventeenth day of the month, on that day

Vocabulary

covenant (kuv′ ə nənt) *n.* a formal, solemn, and binding agreement

All the fountains of the great deep burst apart,
And the floodgates of the sky broke open.

(The rain fell on the earth forty days and forty nights.) That same day Noah and Noah's sons, Shem, Ham, and Japheth, went into the ark, with Noah's wife and the three wives of his sons—they and all beasts of every kind, all cattle of every kind, all creatures of every kind that creep on the earth, and all birds of every kind, every bird, every winged thing. They came to Noah into the ark, two each of all flesh in which there was breath of life. Thus they that entered comprised male and female of all flesh, as God had commanded him. And the Lord shut him in.

The Flood continued forty days on the earth, and the waters increased and raised the ark so that it rose above the earth. The waters swelled and increased greatly upon the earth, and the ark drifted upon the waters. When the waters had swelled much more upon the earth, all the highest mountains everywhere under the sky were covered. Fifteen cubits higher did the waters swell, as the mountains were covered. And all flesh that stirred on earth perished—birds, cattle, beasts, and all the things that swarmed upon the earth, and all mankind. All in whose nostrils was the merest breath of life, all that was on dry land, died. All existence on earth was blotted out—man, cattle, creeping things, and birds of the sky; they were blotted out from the earth. Only Noah was left, and those with him in the ark.

Chapter 8

And when the waters had swelled on the earth one hundred and fifty days, God remembered Noah and all the beasts and all the cattle that were with him in the ark, and God caused a wind to blow across the earth, and the waters subsided. The fountains of the deep and the floodgates of the sky were stopped up, and the rain from the sky was held back; the waters then receded steadily from the earth. At the end of one hundred and fifty days the waters diminished, so that in the seventh month, on the seventeenth day of the month, the ark came to rest on the mountains of Ararat. The waters went on diminishing until the tenth month; in the tenth month, on the first of the month, the tops of the mountains became visible.

Noah Releasing the White Dove (detail). 13th century, Italy. Mosaic. San Marco, Venice.

Viewing the mosaic: What might Noah's thoughts have been as he released the dove?

At the end of forty days, Noah opened the window of the ark that he had made and sent out the raven; it went to and fro until the waters had dried up from the earth. Then he sent out the dove to see whether the waters had decreased from the surface of the ground. But the dove could not find a resting place for its foot, and returned to him to the ark, for there was water over all the earth. So putting out his hand, he took it into the ark with him. He waited another seven days, and again sent out the dove from the ark. The dove came back to him toward evening, and there in its bill was a plucked-off olive leaf! Then Noah knew that the waters had decreased on the earth. He waited still another seven days and sent the dove forth; and it did not return to him any more.

In the six hundred and first year, in the first month, on the first of the month, the waters began to dry from the earth; and when Noah removed the covering of the ark, he saw that the surface of the ground was drying. And in the second month, on the twenty-seventh day of the month, the earth was dry.

God spoke to Noah, saying, "Come out of the ark, together with your wife, your sons, and your sons' wives. Bring out with you every living thing of all flesh that is with you: birds, animals, and everything that creeps on earth; and let them swarm on the earth and be fertile and increase on earth." So Noah came out, together with his sons, his wife, and his sons' wives. Every animal, every creeping thing, and every bird, everything that stirs on earth came out of the ark by families.

Then Noah built an altar to the Lord and, taking of every clean animal and of every clean bird, he offered burnt offerings on the altar. The Lord smelled the pleasing odor, and the Lord said to Himself: "Never again will I doom the earth because of man, since the devisings of man's mind are evil from his youth; nor will I ever again destroy every living being, as I have done.

> So long as the earth endures,
> Seedtime and harvest,
> Cold and heat,
> Summer and winter,
> Day and night
> Shall not cease."

Chapter 9

God blessed Noah and his sons, and said to them, "Be fertile and increase, and fill the earth. The fear and the dread of you shall be upon all the beasts of the earth and upon all the birds of the sky—everything with which the earth is astir—and upon all the fish of the sea; they are given into your hand. Every creature that lives shall be yours to eat; as with the green grasses, I give you all these. You must not, however, eat flesh with its life-blood in it. But for your own life-blood I will require a reckoning: I will require it of every beast; of man, too, will I require a reckoning for human life, of every man for that of his fellow man!

> Whoever sheds the blood of man,
> By man shall his blood be shed;
> For in His image
> Did God make man.

Be fertile, then, and increase; abound on the earth and increase on it."

And God said to Noah and to his sons with him, "I now establish My covenant with you and your offspring to come, and with every living thing that is with you—birds, cattle, and every wild beast as well—all that have come out of the ark, every living thing on earth. I will maintain My covenant with you: never again shall all flesh be cut off by the waters of a flood, and never again shall there be a flood to destroy the earth."

God further said, "This is the sign that I set for the covenant between Me and you, and every living creature with you, for all ages to come. I have set My bow in the clouds, and it shall serve as a sign of the covenant between Me and the earth. When I bring clouds over the earth, and the bow appears in the clouds, I will remember My covenant between Me and you and every living creature among all flesh, so that the waters shall never again become a flood to destroy all flesh. When the bow is in the clouds, I will see it and remember the everlasting covenant between God and all living creatures, all flesh that is on earth. That," God said to Noah, "shall be the sign of the covenant that I have established between Me and all flesh that is on earth."

Responding to Literature

Personal Response

If you could talk to Noah, what questions would you like to ask him? Write your questions in your journal.

Analyzing Literature

Recall and Interpret

1. Why does God decide to destroy humankind? For what reason is Noah spared?
2. What test does Noah devise to determine whether the waters have receded?
3. What does Noah build after leaving the ark? What does this action suggest about his character?
4. What does God promise in the covenant he makes with Noah after the flood?

Evaluate and Connect

5. In your opinion, what is the **theme,** or main idea, of the flood story?
6. What ideas or feelings do you associate with rainbows? In your view, is the rainbow an effective **symbol,** or representation, of God's covenant? (See **Literary Terms Handbook,** page R12.) Explain.
7. In your opinion, do parts of the story seem pieced together or contradictory at times? Give evidence from the selection. How do these inconsistencies affect the story?
8. Review your response to the Reading Focus on page 435. Did you list any purposes that might apply to the story of the flood? Would you add any purposes to your list after reading the story? Explain your answer, citing details from the story for support.

Literary **ELEMENTS**

Comparative Literature

Comparative literature is the study of literatures of different cultures in order to examine the relationships between them.

Scholars of comparative literature have long been intrigued by the parallels between the flood story in Genesis and in the *Epic of Gilgamesh.* Some think that the Sumerian story influenced the Hebrew. Others hypothesize that both works were derived from a common source. Neither theory has been substantiated.

1. What similarities can you find between the flood story in Genesis and in *Gilgamesh,* on page 427?
2. In what significant ways do the two stories differ? What do these differences suggest about the religious beliefs of the two cultures?

- See **Literary Terms Handbook,** p. R2.

Extending Your Response

Creative Writing

Noah's Journal What was life like on the ark? How did Noah and his family pass the time and take care of the animals? Imagine that you are Noah, and write a series of journal entries in which you describe everyday life on the ark. Use your imagination to "fill in the blanks," but remain true to Noah's character and style of speech.

Interdisciplinary Activity

Math: Calculating Size According to Genesis, the ark was 300 cubits by 50 cubits by 30 cubits. If a cubit equals 18 inches, how many feet long, wide, and high was the ark? How does the size of the ark compare with the size of today's ocean liners? (Assume that the average ocean liner is about 900 feet long.)

Save your work for your portfolio.

Ruth Parting From Naomi, 1803. William Blake (Great Britain). Wash, pencil, colored chalk on paper, 34.2 x 31.4 cm. Southampton City Art Gallery, Hampshire, UK.

The Book of Ruth

from the Tanakh

Chapter 1

In the days when the chieftains ruled, there was a famine in the land; and a man of Bethlehem in Judah, with his wife and two sons, went to reside in the country of Moab. The man's name was Elimelech, his wife's name was Naomi,[1] and his two sons were named Mahlon and Chilion—Ephrathites of Bethlehem in Judah. They came to the country of Moab and remained there.

Elimelech, Naomi's husband, died; and she was left with her two sons. They married Moabite women, one named Orpah and the other Ruth, and they lived there about ten years. Then those two—Mahlon and Chilion—also died; so the woman was left without her two sons and without her husband.

She started out with her daughters-in-law to return from the country of Moab; for in the country of Moab she had heard that the Lord had taken note of His people and given them food. Accompanied by her two daughters-in-law, she left the place where she had been living; and they set out on the road back to the land of Judah.

But Naomi said to her two daughters-in-law, "Turn back, each of you to her mother's house. May the Lord deal kindly with you, as you have dealt with the dead and with me! May the Lord grant that each of you find security in the house of a husband!" And she kissed them farewell. They broke into weeping and said to her, "No, we will return with you to your people."

But Naomi replied, "Turn back, my daughters! Why should you go with me? Have I any more sons in my body who might be husbands for you? Turn back, my daughters, for I am too old to be married. Even if I thought there was hope for me, even if I were married tonight and I also bore sons, should you wait for them to grow up? Should you on their account debar yourselves from marriage? Oh no, my daughters! My lot is far more bitter than yours, for the hand of the Lord has struck out against me."

They broke into weeping again, and Orpah kissed her mother-in-law farewell. But Ruth clung to her. So she said, "See, your sister-in-law has returned to her people and her gods. Go follow your sister-in-law." But Ruth replied, "Do not urge me to leave you, to turn back and not follow you. For wherever you go, I will go; wherever you lodge, I will lodge; your people shall be my people, and your God my God. Where you die, I will die, and there I will be buried. Thus and more may the Lord do to me if anything but death parts me from you." When [Naomi] saw how determined she was to go with her, she ceased to argue with her; and the two went on until they reached Bethlehem.

When they arrived in Bethlehem, the whole city buzzed with excitement over them. The women said, "Can this be Naomi?" "Do not call me Naomi," she replied. "Call me Mara,[2] for Shaddai[3] has made my lot very bitter. I went away full, and the Lord has brought me back empty. How can you call me Naomi, when the Lord has dealt harshly with me, when Shaddai has brought misfortune upon me!"

Thus Naomi returned from the country of Moab; she returned with her daughter-in-law Ruth the Moabite. They arrived in Bethlehem at the beginning of the barley harvest.

Chapter 2

Now Naomi had a kinsman on her husband's side, a man of substance, of the family of Elimelech, whose name was Boaz.[4]

1. In Hebrew, *Naomi* means beautiful, pleasant, or delightful.

2. *Mara* means "bitter."
3. *Shaddai* (shə dī′) is another name for God.
4. In Hebrew, the name *Boaz* (bō′ az) is associated with the word for strength. *Boaz* is also the name of a pillar in a great temple built by Solomon, the son and successor of King David.

Vocabulary

debar (di bär′) *v.* to shut out or exclude from doing something

Ruth the Moabite said to Naomi, "I would like to go to the fields and glean among the ears of grain, behind someone who may show me kindness." "Yes, daughter, go," she replied; and off she went. She came and gleaned in a field, behind the reapers; and, as luck would have it, it was the piece of land belonging to Boaz, who was of Elimelech's family.

Presently Boaz arrived from Bethlehem. He greeted the reapers, "The Lord be with you!" And they responded, "The Lord bless you!" Boaz said to the servant who was in charge of the reapers, "Whose girl is that?" The servant in charge of the reapers replied, "She is a Moabite girl who came back with Naomi from the country of Moab. She said, 'Please let me glean and gather among the sheaves behind the reapers.' She has been on her feet ever since she came this morning. She has rested but little in the hut."

Boaz said to Ruth, "Listen to me, daughter. Don't go to glean in another field. Don't go elsewhere, but stay here close to my girls. Keep your eyes on the field they are reaping, and follow them. I have ordered the men not to molest you. And when you are thirsty, go to the jars and drink some of [the water] that the men have drawn."

She prostrated herself with her face to the ground, and said to him, "Why are you so kind as to single me out, when I am a foreigner?"

Boaz said in reply, "I have been told of all that you did for your mother-in-law after the death of your husband, how you left your father and mother and the land of your birth and came to a people you had not known before. May the Lord reward your deeds. May you have a full recompense from the Lord, the God of Israel, under whose wings you have sought refuge!"

She answered, "You are most kind, my lord, to comfort me and to speak gently to your maidservant—though I am not so much as one of your maidservants."

At mealtime, Boaz said to her, "Come over here and partake of the meal, and dip your morsel in the vinegar." So she sat down beside the reapers. He handed her roasted grain, and she ate her fill and had some left over.

When she got up again to glean, Boaz gave orders to his workers, "You are not only to let her glean among the sheaves, without interference, but you must also pull some [stalks] out of the heaps and leave them for her to glean, and not scold her."

She gleaned in the field until evening. Then she beat out what she had gleaned—it was about an *ephah*[5] of barley—and carried it back with her to the town. When her mother-in-law saw what she had gleaned, and when she also took out and gave her what she had left over after eating her fill, her mother-in-law asked her, "Where did you glean today? Where did you work? Blessed be he who took such generous notice of you!" So she told her mother-in-law whom she had worked with, saying, "The name of the man with whom I worked today is Boaz."

Naomi said to her daughter-in-law, "Blessed be he of the Lord, who has not failed in His kindness to the living or to the dead! For," Naomi explained to her daughter-in-law, "the man is related to us; he is one of our redeeming kinsmen." Ruth the Moabite said, "He even told me, 'Stay close by my workers until all my harvest is finished.'" And Naomi answered her daughter-in-law Ruth, "It is best, daughter, that you go out with his girls, and not be annoyed in some other field." So she stayed close to the maidservants of Boaz, and gleaned until the barley harvest and the wheat

5. An *ephah* (ē′ fə) is an ancient Hebrew unit of measure that equals a little more than a bushel.

Vocabulary

glean (glēn) *v.* to pick up or gather grain left on the field after the reaping

prostrate (pros′ trāt) *v.* to throw oneself face downward on the ground as a gesture of humility or submission

Ruth Returning from Gleaning. Samuel Palmer (Great Britain, 1805–1881). Pen and ink wash with white heightening. Victoria & Albert Museum, London.

Viewing the drawing: How does this artist depict Ruth? Is this similar to the way she is depicted in the Tanakh?

harvest were finished. Then she stayed at home with her mother-in-law.

Chapter 3

Naomi, her mother-in-law, said to her, "Daughter, I must seek a home for you, where you may be happy. Now there is our kinsman Boaz, whose girls you were close to. He will be winnowing barley on the threshing floor tonight. So bathe, anoint yourself, dress up, and go down to the threshing floor. But do not disclose yourself to the man until he has finished eating and drinking. When he lies down, note the place where he lies down, and go over and uncover his feet and lie down. He will tell you what you are to do." She replied, "I will do everything you tell me."

She went down to the threshing floor and did just as her mother-in-law had instructed her. Boaz ate and drank, and in a cheerful mood went to lie down beside the grainpile. Then she went over stealthily and uncovered his feet and lay down. In the middle of the night, the man gave a start and pulled back—there was a woman lying at his feet!

"Who are you?" he asked. And she replied, "I am your handmaid Ruth. Spread your robe over your handmaid, for you are a redeeming kinsman."

He exclaimed, "Be blessed of the Lord, daughter! Your latest deed of loyalty is greater than the first, in that you have not turned to younger men, whether poor or rich. And now, daughter, have no fear. I will do in your behalf whatever you ask, for all the elders of my town know what a fine woman you are. But while it is true I am a redeeming kinsman, there is another redeemer closer than I. Stay for the night. Then in the morning, if he will act as a redeemer, good! let him redeem. But if he does not want to act as redeemer for you, I will do so myself, as the Lord lives! Lie down until morning."

So she lay at his feet until dawn. She rose before one person could distinguish another, for he thought, "Let it not be known that the woman came to the threshing floor." And he

Vocabulary

winnow (win′ ō) *v.* to separate the grain from the chaff
stealthily (stelth′ ə lē) *adv.* slowly and secretly

said, "Hold out the shawl you are wearing." She held it while he measured out six measures of barley, and he put it on her back.

When she got back to the town, she came to her mother-in-law, who asked, "How is it with you, daughter?" She told her all that the man had done for her; and she added, "He gave me these six measures of barley, saying to me, 'Do not go back to your mother-in-law empty-handed.'" And Naomi said, "Stay here, daughter, till you learn how the matter turns out. For the man will not rest, but will settle the matter today."

Chapter 4

Meanwhile, Boaz had gone to the gate and sat down there. And now the redeemer whom Boaz had mentioned passed by. He called, "Come over and sit down here, So-and-so!" And he came over and sat down. Then [Boaz] took ten elders of the town and said, "Be seated here"; and they sat down.

He said to the redeemer, "Naomi, now returned from the country of Moab, must sell the piece of land which belonged to our kinsman Elimelech. I thought I should disclose the matter to you and say: Acquire it in the presence of those seated here and in the presence of the elders of my people. If you are willing to redeem it, redeem! But if you will not redeem, tell me, that I may know. For there is no one to redeem but you, and I come after you." "I am willing to redeem it," he replied. Boaz continued, "When you acquire the property from Naomi and from Ruth the Moabite, you must also acquire the wife of the deceased, so as to perpetuate the name of the deceased upon his estate." The redeemer replied, "Then I cannot redeem it for myself, lest I impair my own estate. You take over my right of redemption, for I am unable to exercise it."

Now this was formerly done in Israel in cases of redemption or exchange: to validate any transaction, one man would take off his sandal and hand it to the other. Such was the practice in Israel. So when the redeemer said to Boaz, "Acquire for yourself," he drew off his sandal. And Boaz said to the elders and to the rest of the people, "You are witnesses today that I am acquiring from Naomi all that belonged to Elimelech and all that belonged to Chilion and Mahlon. I am also acquiring Ruth the Moabite, the wife of Mahlon, as my wife, so as to perpetuate the name of the deceased upon his estate, that the name of the deceased may not disappear from among his kinsmen and from the gate of his home town. You are witnesses today."

All the people at the gate and the elders answered, "We are. May the Lord make the woman who is coming into your house like Rachel and Leah, both of whom built up the House of Israel! Prosper in Ephrathah and perpetuate your name in Bethlehem! And may your house be like the house of Perez whom Tamar bore to Judah—through the offspring which the Lord will give you by this young woman."

So Boaz married Ruth; she became his wife, and he cohabited with her. The Lord let her conceive, and she bore a son. And the women said to Naomi, "Blessed be the Lord, who has not withheld a redeemer from you today! May his name be perpetuated in Israel! He will renew your life and sustain your old age; for he is born of your daughter-in-law, who loves you and is better to you than seven sons."

Naomi took the child and held it to her bosom. She became its foster mother, and the women neighbors gave him a name, saying, "A son is born to Naomi!" They named him Obed; he was the father of Jesse, father of David.

This is the line of Perez: Perez begot Hezron, Hezron begot Ram, Ram begot Amminadab, Amminadab begot Nahshon, Nahshon begot Salmon, Salmon begot Boaz, Boaz begot Obed, Obed begot Jesse, and Jesse begot David.

Responding to Literature

Personal Response

Which character do you like best or most admire? Why? Write your answers in your journal.

Analyzing Literature

Recall

1. What is the tragedy that befalls Naomi and her daughters-in-law in Moab?
2. Why does Naomi want her daughters-in-law to remain in Moab?
3. How does Boaz treat Ruth when he first meets her?
4. What happens to the property owned by Naomi's husband?
5. What happens to Ruth at the end of the story? What happens to Naomi?

Interpret

6. Why do you think Naomi asks people to call her *Mara* after tragedy befalls her family?
7. What might Ruth's refusal to remain in Moab suggest about her relationship with Naomi?
8. What do you think Boaz's treatment of Ruth suggests about his character?
9. In your opinion, why does Boaz remind the redeemer of the particulars of Bethlehem's property laws?
10. How does Naomi's attitude toward God change during the course of the story?

Evaluate and Connect

11. The story ends with the lineage of King David. How might this ending help illuminate the purpose of the story? Does this purpose reflect a purpose you listed in the Reading Focus on page 435? Explain.
12. In your opinion, what is the **theme,** or main idea, of the story? (See **Literary Terms Handbook,** page R12.) Support your opinion with evidence from the selection.
13. How does dialogue help develop the main characters in the Book of Ruth?
14. In what ways might Boaz's name **symbolize,** or represent, his character?
15. How would you describe the status of women in ancient Hebrew culture? Compare that status with your view of the status of women in Western culture today.

Literary ELEMENTS

Historical Context

Historical context refers to the time and place in which a literary work was written, including the traditions, customs, beliefs, and values of that time and place. The Book of Ruth springs from an agricultural society, in which the success of the crops meant the difference between survival or famine and death. This agricultural society was highly patriarchal, and decisions affecting marriage and property ownership were made almost exclusively by men.

1. In what ways might the story change if its historical context were different?
2. How might the setting of this story at harvest time–spring in ancient Israel–be appropriate for the narrative as a whole?
3. Given the patriarchal nature of society in ancient Israel, what, do you think, is unusual in the way Obed, the son of Ruth and Boaz, acquires his name?

- See **Literary Terms Handbook,** p. R5.

Literature and Writing

Writing About Literature

Analyzing Conflict Like all good stories, the Book of Ruth contains both internal and external **conflicts,** or struggles. In a few paragraphs, identify the major conflicts in the story, what causes these conflicts, and how these conflicts are resolved.

Creative Writing

The Book of Boaz Little information is given about Boaz's motivations, thoughts, or feelings. Rewrite the story from his point of view. Include Boaz's thoughts about Naomi's return from Moab, and what rights he thinks Naomi's other kinsmen have to her property.

Extending Your Response

Literature Groups

In a Word If you could describe Ruth in only one word, what would that word be? Together with your group, analyze Ruth's character by carefully examining what she says and how she behaves. Then choose a word that sums up her most outstanding character traits. Share your choice and the reasons behind it with the class.

Learning for Life

Interview Naomi is an interesting character who reveals a number of different sides to her personality. Sometimes it is up to readers to draw conclusions about her motives. What questions would you like to ask Naomi about her actions in the story? Draw up a list.

Listening and Speaking

Storytelling Imagine that you are an ancient storyteller and that your classmates are villagers who have never heard the story of Ruth. Relate the story in your own words, using appropriate facial expressions, gestures, or actions to emphasize important points. Be sure to express the emotions of the characters in your tone of voice. If you want, involve classmates in the story by asking rhetorical questions as you tell the tale.

Internet Connection

Surfing for Civilization What was everyday life like in Ruth's time? What did people eat? wear? do for a living? What kinds of entertainment did they enjoy? Use the Internet to answer these questions. Then share your findings in a brief oral report to the class.

Reading Further

To read about other biblical heroines, try these stories from the Old Testament:

Chapters 4 and 5 of the Book of Judges tell the story of Deborah.

The Book of Esther tells the story of Queen Esther.

Save your work for your portfolio.

Skill Minilesson

VOCABULARY • Technical Vocabulary

To describe actions or objects associated with a particular field, writers may use use technical, or specialized, vocabulary. For example, in a story about caves, you might encounter words such as *spelunking* and *stalagmite.* The Book of Ruth contains several technical terms associated with farming.

PRACTICE Find each of the following words in the story. Use a dictionary to look up the meaning of the words; then write a paragraph using each of these specialized terms.

glean — thresh
sheaves — reaper
winnow

ARABIA, C. A.D. 610–632

Before You Read

from the *Qur'an*

Reading Focus

What does the word *compassion* mean to you?

Journal In your journal, jot down your definition of the word and a few specific examples of compassionate behavior.

Setting a Purpose Read to discover the role of compassion in the doctrines of Islam.

Building Background

The Qur'an

The Qur'an is the holy book of Islam, and for Muslims the Qur'an is the sacred word of Allah, the name for God in Arabic. The Arabic word *Islam* means "submission to the will of Allah," and the word *Qur'an* means "recitation or reading aloud."

According to Muslim belief, the Qur'an was revealed directly by Allah to the prophet Muhammad (A.D. 570–632). Muhammad was born into a merchant family in the city of Mecca (also spelled Makkah) in Arabia and was orphaned when he was about six years old. Around the year 610, he began to experience visions in a hillside cave where he went to meditate at night. The divine message that he received called upon him to preach a new religion, marked by devotion to a single deity, by upright and pious conduct, and by submission to the will of Allah. Muhammad's preaching inspired controversy, and he was forced to flee to the city of Medina in the year 622. Eight years later, the prophet and his followers victoriously reentered Mecca. In the century after Muhammad's death in 632, Islam spread rapidly, and the Islamic Empire expanded to include Persia to the east and much of North Africa and Spain to the west.

The five "pillars of Islam" are the fundamental doctrines underlying Muslim religious belief and practice. These doctrines are acknowledging Allah as the only God, praying five times a day, fasting from dawn to dusk during the holy month of Ramadan, giving alms to the poor, and making a pilgrimage to Mecca once in a lifetime, if the believer has the means.

Did You Know?

About twenty years after the prophet Muhammad's death, the Qur'an was written down in a standard text. The book consists of 114 chapters; in Arabic, each chapter is called a *sura.* Except for the brief opening *sura*—"The Exordium" (or introduction)—these chapters are arranged approximately according to length, beginning with the longer ones.

Muslims show their respect for the Qur'an in many ways. The art of calligraphy, for example, has been used for many centuries to decorate manuscripts of the Qur'an. Because the words of the Qur'an are believed to be literally the utterance of Allah, every Muslim, whatever his or her native language or cultural background, uses the Arabic text for recitation in formal worship.

Celebration of the End of Ramadan, from *The Maqamat (The Meetings).* 13th century, Persia. Illustration by Hariri from a literary text. Bibliothèque Nationale, Paris.

from the Qur'an

Translated by N. J. Dawood

The Exordium

In the Name of Allah,
the Compassionate, the Merciful

Praise be to Allah, Lord of the Creation,
The Compassionate, the Merciful,
King of the Last Judgement!
You alone we worship, and to You alone
we pray for help.
Guide us to the straight path,
The path of those whom You have favored,
Not of those who have incurred Your wrath,
Nor of those who have gone astray.

Daylight

In the Name of Allah,
the Compassionate, the Merciful

By the light of day, and by the fall of night, your Lord has not forsaken you, nor does He abhor you.
The life to come holds a richer prize for you than this present life. You shall be gratified with what your Lord will give you.
Did He not find you an orphan and give you shelter?
Did He not find you in error and guide you?
Did He not find you poor and enrich you?
Therefore do not wrong the orphan, nor chide away the beggar. But proclaim the goodness of your Lord.

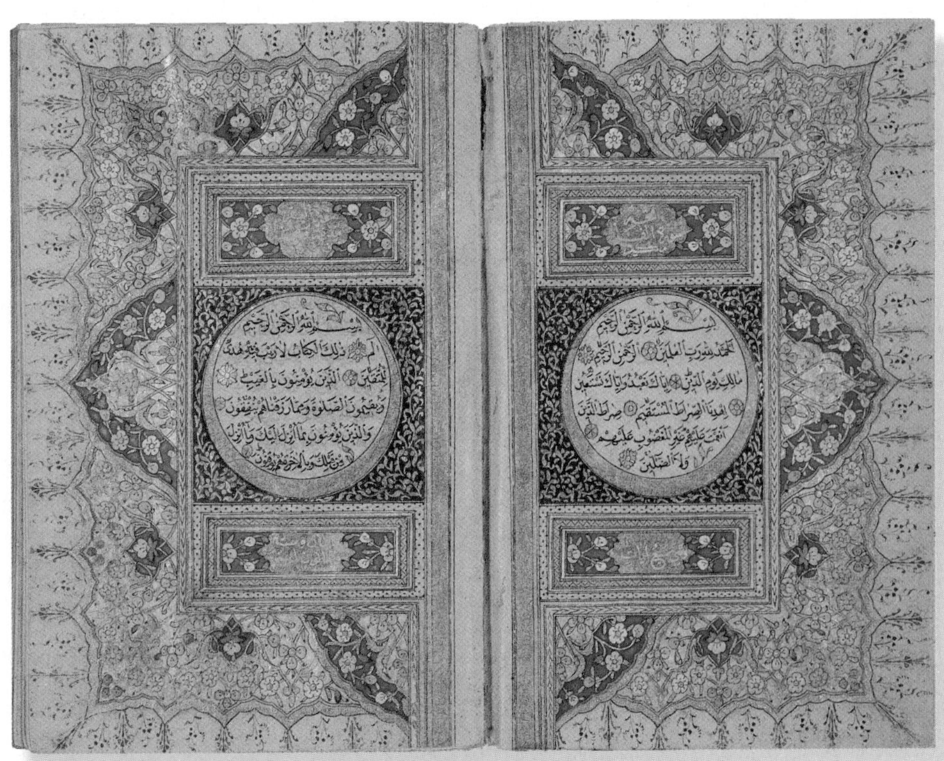

Page from the Qur'an. 17th century, Turkey. Musée Condé, Chantilly, France.
Viewing the art: How do you think the person who decorated these pages felt about the text?

Responding to Literature

Personal Response

What insights into Islam have you gained by reading the selections?

Analyzing Literature

Recall and Interpret

1. In the first three lines of "The Exordium," how does the speaker describe Allah?
2. What does the speaker ask Allah to do for the worshippers?
3. Where does the path mentioned in line 6 of "The Exordium" lead? What does the straightness of the path **symbolize,** or represent?
4. What promise does the speaker in "Daylight" extend to those whom he addresses in lines 3–5?
5. How does the use of rhetorical questions in lines 6–8 affect your reading of the selection?
6. According to "Daylight," how has Allah helped humankind? How will Allah help the faithful in the future?

Evaluate and Connect

7. What kind of **tone,** or attitude toward the subject matter, does "The Exordium" set for the book as a whole?
8. Did reading "Daylight" change your response to the Reading Focus on page 448? How?

Literary Criticism

Mahmoud M. Ayoub makes the following statement about the Qur'an: "In its written form, the Qur'an has set the standard for Arabic language and literature as the proper and indeed the highest expression of literary Arabic." What literary devices contribute to the power and beauty of N. J. Dawood's translation of the Qur'an? Write a brief essay analyzing the literary devices found in this selection.

Literary ELEMENTS

Antithesis

Antithesis (an ti′ thə sis) is the balanced contrast of two phrases or ideas, as in lines 6–9 of "The Exordium":

> Guide us to the straight path,
> The path of those whom You have favored,
> Not of those who have incurred Your wrath,
> Nor of those who have gone astray.

Through the use of antithesis, authors help emphasize important ideas.

1. What ideas in "The Exordium" are emphasized through the use of antithesis?
2. In what lines of "Daylight" is antithesis used?

- See **Literary Terms Handbook,** p. R1.

Extending Your Response

Writing About Literature

Analyzing Theme How would you state the main message, or **theme,** of "Daylight"? What words and phrases develop this theme? In a few paragraphs, state the theme of the chapter in your own words and explain how this theme is developed.

Interdisciplinary Activity

Social Studies: Ramadan What is the significance of Ramadan to followers of Islam? When does Ramadan take place, and what rituals do Muslims observe? Use an encyclopedia or the Internet to answer these questions; then present a brief oral report on your findings to the class.

Save your work for your portfolio.

LISTENING, SPEAKING, and VIEWING

Storytelling

In the frame story of *The Thousand and One Nights,* the sultana Scheherazade is such a masterful storyteller that she not only saves her own life from her cruel husband's threat of death, but she teaches her husband about humanity and the doctrines of Islam. A storyteller brings a tale to life by making the telling of a story into a performance. One of Scheherazade's techniques was to stop each night's story just before the climax, leaving her husband in suspense, hungry for the next night's chapter. Most likely, you will never be in the position of having to tell a story to save your life. Nevertheless, good storytelling is a skill you may find helpful in other situations. The following guidelines can help you prepare and tell a story.

Practicing the Story

- Become familiar enough with your story that you remember all the important details in the correct order. Remember, you won't *read* the story, you'll *tell* it. So don't memorize the story word for word; just be sure that you know all the events and the order in which they occur.
- Practice telling your story in front of a mirror. Speak clearly and distinctly. Vary the pitch and tone of your voice to convey excitement, surprise, and other emotions. Let your voice rise and fall naturally and get louder and softer in accordance with the events or emotions taking place in the story.
- If you wish, add sound effects or music to enhance your performance. You can make your own sound effects using your voice, your hands, or simple tools, or you can tape appropriate instrumental music as a background.
- Use gestures and facial expressions to emphasize parts of your story.
- Ask a friend or family member to watch your performance and give you tips on ways to make it more effective. Revise your performance upon the basis of the feedback you received and your own impressions of your performance.

Telling the Story

- Before you begin, take a deep breath and relax.
- Prepare your audience to listen to your story. If necessary, set the scene by telling where and when the story takes place, and what it is about.
- Enjoy your performance! Your listeners are likely to share your level of enthusiasm if it is genuine.

ACTIVITIES

1. Research storytelling on the Internet. Prepare a report on the kinds of information resources that are available. Include information on well-known storytellers who may be performing in your area.
2. Search through books of folktales and myths to find one you would like to tell, or choose one of the stories in this book. Use the suggestions given in this lesson to prepare and practice your performance.

Before You Read

from *The Thousand and One Nights*

Reading Focus

For thousands of years, people have enjoyed adventure tales about seafarers. The stories of Odysseus, Gulliver, and Captain Nemo are well-known examples.

Chart It! With a partner, recall a sea adventure story that you have read. On a chart, list the characters, the dangers faced, and the ways the characters escaped danger.

Setting a Purpose Read to discover the adventures Sindbad faces.

Building Background

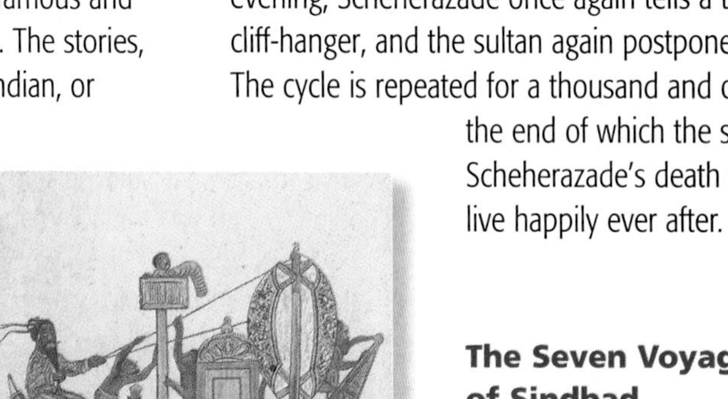

The History of the Tales

The Thousand and One Nights, also known as *The Arabian Nights,* is one of the world's most famous and beloved collections of legends and folktales. The stories, most of which are believed to be Persian, Indian, or Arabian in origin, probably evolved over many centuries of storytelling before they were written down. The earliest known collection was Persian; this collection was translated into Arabic during the 800s.

During the early 1700s, Antoine Galland's twelve-volume French translation introduced Europeans to the tales.

Arab trading ship.

Stories Within a Story

The stories in *The Thousand and One Nights* are loosely tied together by a frame story. The frame story features a woman named Scheherazade (shə her′ ə zäd′), who has been condemned to die by her husband Shahriyar (shä′ rē yär′), a cruel sultan. The night before she is to die, she tells him a fascinating tale, cleverly leaving it unfinished. The sultan, burning with curiosity, postpones her execution for thirty-six hours so that she can tell him how the story ends. The following evening, Scheherazade once again tells a tale ending in a cliff-hanger, and the sultan again postpones her death. The cycle is repeated for a thousand and one nights, at the end of which the sultan lifts Scheherazade's death sentence. They live happily ever after.

The Seven Voyages of Sindbad

One of the best-known series of tales in *The Thousand and One Nights* recounts the adventures of Sindbad the Sailor. The first tale opens in the city of Baghdad (the modern capital of Iraq). In Sindbad's time, Baghdad was a thriving city whose merchants traded with kingdoms in many parts of the ancient world. To set out on a trading expedition, sailors traveled down the Tigris River from Baghdad to Basra, a port near where the Tigris and Euphrates Rivers meet and flow into the Persian Gulf, a body of water east of the Arabian Peninsula.

Vocabulary Preview

thicket (thik′ it) *n.* dense growth of shrubbery or small trees; p. 453

prodigy (prod′ ə jē) *n.* extraordinary person, thing, or deed; p. 454

tumult (to͞o′ məlt) *n.* noisy confusion; p. 456

impale (im pāl′) *v.* to pierce with a pointed object; p. 457

boon (bo͞on) *adj.* convivial or sociable; p. 457

hundred men could shelter from the sun. It is from these trees that the aromatic substance known as camphor[4] is extracted. The trunks are hollowed out, and the sap oozes drop by drop into vessels which are placed beneath, soon curdling into a crystal gum.

In that island I saw a gigantic beast called the karkadan, or rhinoceros, which grazes in the fields like a cow or buffalo. Taller than a camel, it has a single horn in the middle of its forehead, and upon this horn Nature has carved the likeness of a man. The karkadan attacks the elephant and, impaling it upon its horn, carries it aloft from place to place until its victim dies. Before long, however, the elephant's fat melts in the heat of the sun and, dripping down into the karkadan's eyes, puts out its sight, so that the beast blunders helplessly along and finally drops dead. Then the roc swoops down upon both animals and carries them off to its nest in the high mountains. I also saw many strange breeds of buffalo in that island.

I sold a part of my diamonds for a large sum and exchanged more for a vast quantity of merchandise. Then we set sail and, trading from port to port and from island to island, at length arrived safely in Basrah. After a few days' sojourn there I set out upstream to Baghdad, the City of Peace.

Loaded with precious goods and the finest of my diamonds, I hastened to my old street and, entering my own house, rejoiced to see my friends and kinsfolk. I gave them gold and presents, and distributed alms[5] among the poor of the city.

I soon forgot the perils and hardships of my travels and took again to sumptuous living. I ate well, dressed well, and kept open house for innumerable gallants and boon companions.

From far and near men came to hear me speak of my adventures and to learn the news of foreign lands from me. All were astounded at the dangers I had escaped and wished me joy of my return. Such was my second voyage.

Tomorrow, my friends, if Allah wills, I shall relate to you the extraordinary tale of my third voyage.

The famous mariner ended. The guests marvelled at his story.

When the evening feast was over, Sindbad the Sailor gave Sindbad the Porter a hundred pieces of gold, which he took with thanks and many blessings, and departed, lost in wonderment at all he had heard.

4. *Camphor* is used in lotions and medicines.

5. *Alms* are money or food given to aid the poor.

Vocabulary

impale (im pāl′) *v.* to pierce with a pointed object

boon (bo͞on) *adj.* convivial or sociable

Responding to Literature

Personal Response

Which parts of the story did you find the most entertaining? Why?

Analyzing Literature

Recall and Interpret

1. Why does Sindbad long to visit distant cities and islands?
2. Briefly describe the roc and its egg. How do Sindbad's descriptions help create a sense of **suspense?** (See **Literary Terms Handbook,** page R12.)
3. How does Sindbad escape from the roc's island? What does his plan of escape suggest about his **character?** (See **Literary Terms Handbook,** page R2.)
4. How do merchants obtain diamonds from the valley where Sindbad next lands? How does this method help Sindbad escape?
5. What does Sindbad do with his riches when he first returns home? Why might he take these actions?

Evaluate and Connect

6. **Hyperbole** is exaggeration or overstatement for effect. What are some examples of this technique in the story? (See **Literary Terms Handbook,** page R6.)
7. Does Sindbad fit your definition of a hero? Explain.
8. What conclusions might you draw about the religious beliefs of the storytellers who shaped the tale? about Persian attitudes toward travel and trade in Sindbad's day?
9. Think of the adventure story you recalled for the Reading Focus on page 452. In what ways is Sindbad's tale similar? What do these similarities suggest about sea tales?
10. What aspects of the story might account for its enduring popularity?

Literary **ELEMENTS**

Verisimilitude

Storytellers, no matter how fantastic their tales, strive to create **verisimilitude** (ver′ ə si mil′ ə to͞od′), or the illusion of reality, to make their stories believable. In fantasy tales, verisimilitude is often achieved by presenting detailed "eyewitness" descriptions, such as those offered by Sindbad; by combining fact with fiction, as in Sindbad's description of the rhinoceros; or by comparing the fantastic to the familiar.

1. At what points does Sindbad's story seem grounded in fact? How is this effect achieved?
2. To what does Sindbad compare the roc's egg? How might the comparison help listeners picture the egg?

- See **Literary Terms Handbook,** p. R13.

Extending Your Response

Creative Writing

Once Upon a Time Imagine that a group of family members or friends has asked you to tell an entertaining story. Using one of your own journeys or experiences, write a short adventure story in the style of Sindbad. In your story, interweave realistic details with exaggerated, fantastic elements in a way that you think will entertain your audience. Then share your story with others.

Listening and Speaking

Sindbad, the Movie The adventures of Sindbad (also spelled "Sinbad") have been made into movies and animated cartoons. Find one of these versions and take notes on its presentation of Sindbad's adventures on the roc's island. Is the video presentation similar to or different from what you expected after reading the story? How so? Write a brief review, and present it to your class.

Save your work for your portfolio.

INTERDISCIPLINARY MUSIC CONNECTION

Scheherazade, Op. 35

Where do composers get their inspiration? Sometimes they get it from literature or literary characters, including those of cultures other than their own. In the nineteenth century, many European artists and musicians were turning to Southwest Asia for ideas. One composer took the most famous set of stories from the region and turned it into a piece of music that is now known and loved throughout the world.

Nikolai Rimsky-Korsakov

The symphonic suite *Scheherazade* was written in 1888 by the Russian composer Nikolai Rimsky-Korsakov, who was inspired by the collection of Persian legends and folktales, *The Thousand and One Nights*. The suite is made up of four movements:

I. The Sea and Sinbad's Ship
II. The Story of the Kalender Prince
III. The Young Prince and the Young Princess
IV. Festival at Baghdad, The Sea, The Ship Goes to Pieces on a Rock Surmounted by a Bronze Warrior, and Conclusion.

Just as in *The Thousand and One Nights*, Scheherazade's ongoing narrative connects the otherwise individual tales; in *Scheherazade*, the eloquent sound of the solo violin—which represents Scheherazade's voice—unites the four movements. In the first and fourth movements, the sound of the thundering, full orchestra assumes the role of the cruel sultan.

Rimsky-Korsakov attended the Naval Academy at St. Petersburg, and when he left there, he embarked on a three-year cruise. During the cruise, he completed his first symphony. After he left the navy, Nikolai taught himself music theory, becoming so expert that he in turn taught such famous pupils as Sergei Prokofief and Igor Stravinski.

Since Rimsky-Korsakov was a naval officer who loved the sea, perhaps it is not surprising that he masterfully conveyed in music the sound of crashing waves and the feeling of calm, bright waters. The Russian pianist and composer Sergei Rachmaninoff described Rimsky-Korsakov's "sound-painting" this way: "When there is a snowstorm, the flakes seem to dance and drift from the woodwinds and the sound holes of the violins; when the sun is high, all the instruments shine with an almost fiery glare; when there is water, the waves ripple and dance audibly through the orchestra. . . ."

In composing *Scheherazade*, Rimsky-Korsakov hoped "that the hearer . . . should carry away the impression that it is beyond doubt an Oriental narrative of some numerous and varied fairy-tale wonders. . . ."

Activity

There are many different recordings of Rimsky-Korsakov's *Scheherazade*. Find and listen to one of these recordings. Analyze the four movements for their musical interpretation of narrative elements, such as setting, character, and plot.

PERSIA, c. 1100

Before You Read

from the *Rubáiyát*

Meet Omar Khayyám

"[The *Rubáiyát* (roo′ bī ät′) warns] us of the danger of Greatness, the instability of Fortune, and while advocating Charity to all Men, recommending us to be too intimate with none."

—*Edward FitzGerald*

Ironically, Omar Khayyám (KHĪ yam′), the best-known Persian poet in the Western world, was known during his own lifetime as a mathematician, not as a poet. Though the details of Khayyám's life are sketchy, scholars believe he was born in 1048 in Nishapur (now Iran's Neyshabur), the intellectual capital of Islam at that time. While in his twenties, he wrote a scholarly work on algebra that brought him to the attention of Sultan Malik-shah, who asked him to join a learned group that was reforming the calendar.

Khayyám's verse was not known in the West until the mid-1800s, when copies were found in Oxford University's Bodleian library. Edward FitzGerald translated them into English, publishing them under the title *The Rubáiyát of Omar Khayyám*.

Khayyám was born in 1048 and died in 1122.

Reading Focus

Some people believe that we should make the most of each moment because we may never get another chance to enjoy ourselves. What do you think?

Journal List some of your thoughts on your philosophy of life in your journal.

Setting a Purpose Read to discover Omar Khayyám's philosophy of life.

Building Background

Khayyám's Poetic Form

Khayyám wrote in a verse form known as the *ruba'i,* which was popular in Persia during medieval times. The *ruba'i* is a four-line stanza that expresses a single, complete thought. Typically, the first two lines of the stanza introduce a problem or situation, the third line creates tension or surprise, and the fourth line offers a resolution, sometimes with an unexpected slant or twist. In effect, each *ruba'i* is an **epigram**—a concise, quotable statement of the poet's philosophy of life or feelings about an aspect of human experience.

FitzGerald's Translation

FitzGerald, whose translation of the *Rubáiyát* is the best-known version in English, changed the order of Khayyám's stanzas. He arranged them so that they appear to be an account of a single day in the poet's life. It is probable, however, that the stanzas were written on many different occasions and were meant to be independent of one another.

Farhad Carrying Shirin and Her Horse, from *Kushraw u Shirin.* 17th-century Persian miniature. Victoria & Albert Museum, London.

A Dancing Girl with a Tambourine. 19th century. Qajar school (Persia). Oil on canvas, 85 x 50 cm. Private collection.

Viewing the painting: Imagine the kind of music this girl might play or dance to. How would you describe the musical qualities of the *Rubáiyát*?

from the Rubáiyát

Omar Khayyám

Translated by Edward FitzGerald

I

Awake! for Morning in the Bowl of Night°
Has flung the Stone° that puts the Stars to Flight:
   And Lo! the Hunter of the East has caught
The Sultán's Turret° in a Noose of Light.

VII

Come, fill the Cup, and in the Fire of Spring
The Winter Garment of Repentance fling:
   The Bird of Time has but a little way
To fly—and Lo! the Bird is on the Wing.

XII

"How sweet is mortal Sovranty!"°—think some:
Others—"How blest the Paradise to come!"
   Ah, take the Cash in hand and waive the Rest;
Oh, the brave Music of a *distant* Drum!

XIII

Look to the Rose that blows about us—"Lo,
Laughing," she says, "into the World I blow:
   At once the silken Tassel of my Purse
Tear, and its Treasure on the Garden throw."

I, 1 The *Bowl of Night* refers to the night sky.

I, 2 The *Stone* refers to the rising sun.

I, 4 A *Turret* is a small, often ornamental, tower projecting from a larger structure.

XII, 1 *Sovranty* (spelled *sovereignty* in Standard English) means "freedom from external control."

XVII

They say the Lion and the Lizard keep
The Courts where Jamshýd° glory'd and drank deep;
   And Bahrám,° that great Hunter—the Wild Ass
Stamps o'er his Head, and he lies fast asleep.

XXVII

Myself when young did eagerly frequent
Doctor and Saint, and heard great Argument
   About it and about: but evermore
Came out by the same Door as in I went.

Courtier from the Court of Shah Abbas. 18th century, Persia. Private collection.

Viewing the painting: How would you describe the mood of this couple, based on their expressions? Is this mood reflected in the selection?

XXVIII

With them the Seed of Wisdom did I sow,
And with my own hand labor'd it to grow:
   And this was all the Harvest that I reap'd—
"I came like Water, and like Wind I go."

LXVIII

We are no other than a moving row
Of Magic Shadow-shapes that come and go
   Round with the Sun-illumined Lantern held
In Midnight by the Master of the Show.

LXIX

But helpless Pieces of the Game He plays
Upon this Checker-board of Nights and Days;
   Hither and thither moves, and checks, and slays,
And one by one back in the Closet lays.

LXXI

And much as Wine has play'd the Infidel,
And robb'd me of my Robe of Honor—well,
   I often wonder what the Vintners° buy
One half so precious as the Goods they sell.

XCIX

Ah, Love! could you and I with Him conspire
To grasp this sorry Scheme of Things entire,
   Would not we shatter it to bits—and then
Re-mold it nearer to the Heart's Desire!

XVII, 2 In Persian mythology, *Jamshýd* was a king of celestial beings condemned to live as a mortal being.

XVII, 3 *Bahrám,* a legendary king, was killed while hunting an ass.

LXXI, 3 *Vintners* sell wine and liquor.

Responding to Literature

Personal Response

What images linger in your mind after reading the verses?

Analyzing Literature

Recall and Interpret

1. What time of day is **personified,** or given human characteristics, in stanza I? (See **Literary Terms Handbook,** page R9.)
2. In stanza VII, what does the speaker urge readers to do? What reason does the speaker give?
3. What is the **theme,** or overall message, of stanza XVII? What **images** develop this theme? (See **Literary Terms Handbook,** pages R12, R6.)
4. What personal experiences does the speaker refer to in stanzas XXVII and XXVIII? What was the outcome of these experiences?
5. A **metaphor** links one thing with another seemingly very different thing. What metaphors does the speaker use for human beings in stanzas LXVIII and LXIX? (See **Literary Terms Handbook,** page R7.)

Evaluate and Connect

6. Critics have said that the love of life displayed in the *Rubáiyát* is driven by the knowledge of death. In your opinion, is this view accurate? Explain.
7. How might Khayyám answer the question in the Reading Focus on page 460? How does this response compare with yours?
8. In your opinion, is there an audience for the *Rubáiyát* in the United States today? On what do you base your opinion? Explain.

Literary Criticism

Critic Ralph L. Woods writes that FitzGerald "found in [Khayyám] a temperament akin to his own: a lover of beauty, a sentimental recollection of past glories and delights, and a sad recognition that all pleasures quickly end." With a small group, discuss how the verses in the selection show signs of this temperament. Cite specific examples from the verses for support.

Literary ELEMENTS

Rhyme Scheme

Stanzas are often structured around a particular **rhyme scheme,** or regular pattern of rhyme. Rhyme schemes are analyzed by assigning a different letter of the alphabet to each rhyme, beginning with the letter *a,* as in the following example from the *Rubáiyát:*

Awake! for Morning in the Bowl
of Night *a*
Has flung the Stone that puts
the Stars to Flight: *a*
And Lo! the Hunter of
the East has caught *b*
The Sultan's Turret in a Noose
of Light. *a*

1. What is the rhyme scheme of most of Khayyám's *Rubáiyát*?
2. Do you think the poems would be more or less effective if all the lines rhymed? Explain.

- See **Literary Terms Handbook,** p. R10.

Extending Your Response

Listening and Speaking

Multimedia Performance With a small group of classmates, select appropriate background music and lighting for the *Rubáiyát* and practice reading a verse aloud with expression. Then present your oral interpretation of the verse to your class.

Literature and Writing

Analyzing Tone What **tone,** or attitude, does the speaker in the *Rubáiyát* display toward life? In a few paragraphs, state and defend your view by referring to specific lines of the poem.

Save your work for your portfolio.

Web Site

Much of Southwest Asia is a desert or semi-desert. For thousands of years, the camel has been used in the region. From the Web site below, find out what the camel's role is today.

The A–Z of Camels

Address: http://www.arab.net/camels/welcome.html

Domesticated thousands of years ago, the camel went on to become the desert dweller's primary source of transport. In technologically advanced Saudi Arabia, camels are valued more as thoroughbred racing animals and sentimental images of the past than as the mainstay of transportation. But in many parts of Africa and Asia today, camels still pull plows, turn waterwheels and transport people and goods to market.

Body Temperature

Camels do not pant, and they perspire very little. The camel has a unique body thermostat. It can raise its body temperature tolerance level as much as 6°C before perspiring, thereby conserving body fluids and avoiding unnecessary water loss. No other mammal can do this.

Ears

A camel's ears are lined with fur to filter out sand and dust blowing into the ear canal.

Eyes

A camel's eyes are protected by a double row of long curly eyelashes that also help keep out sand and dust, while thick and bushy eyebrows shield the eyes from the desert sun.

Feet

Camels have broad, flat, leathery pads with two toes on each foot. When the camel places its foot on the ground the pads spread, preventing the foot from sinking into the sand.

Food

A camel can go five to seven days with little or no food and water, and can lose a quarter of its body weight without impairing its normal functions. These days, camels rely on humans for their preferred food of dates, grass, and grains, but a working camel traveling across an area where food is scarce can survive on whatever it can find—bones, seeds, dried leaves, or even its owner's tent!

Nose

A camel's nasal passages are protected by large muscular nostrils that can be opened and closed at will. When a camel twitches its nose, it is cooling the incoming air.

Water

Although camels can withstand severe dehydration, a large animal can drink as much as 100 liters (21 gallons) in ten minutes. Such an amount would kill another land mammal, but the camel's unique metabolism enables the animal to store the water in its bloodstream.

Analyzing Media

1. Explain how camels' ability to survive in hot, dry regions makes them useful to humans.
2. Would you like to cross a desert by camel, or would you prefer to go by truck? Explain.

Before You Read

PERSIA, c. 1250

The Counsels of the Bird from *The Masnavi*

Meet Rumi

"Know that your body nurtures the spirit, helps it grow, and gives it wrong advice."

Legend has it that, as a child, Jalal al Din Rumi (ro͞o′ mē) was marked for greatness by the Persian poet Attar, who proclaimed that the boy would someday be a great leader. Whether or not this legend is true, Rumi did go on to become a revered spiritual leader and a brilliant poet.

Born in 1207 in Balkh (now a district of Afghanistan), Rumi fled his hometown when the armies of Genghis Khan invaded the area. After settling in Konya (in what is now Turkey), Rumi met a Sufi mystic named Shams al Din Tabrizi. Their friendship played a pivotal role in Rumi's life. Inspired by Tabrizi's religious teachings, Rumi founded the Mevlevi order of Sufis and began to express his own beliefs in verse. His best-known work is *The Masnavi*, a long collection of verse fables, anecdotes, and meditations. Rumi died at the age of sixty-six, but his *Masnavi* lives on. Many people around the world regard it as a source of wisdom and guidance.

Rumi was born in 1207 and died in 1273.

Reading Focus

What does the saying "A bird in the hand is worth two in the bush" mean to you?

Journal Do you agree with the saying? Jot down your thoughts in your journal.

Setting a Purpose Read to discover one man's experience with a bird in the hand.

Building Background

Sufism

Rumi was deeply influenced by Sufism, an Islamic movement that first developed during the seventh century among Muslims who disapproved of their rulers' lack of piety. Early Sufis encouraged Muslims to obey the Qur'an's dictates to fear Allah and live in anticipation of Judgment Day. The eighth-century saint Rabia of Bara believed that people should strive to attain a spiritual union with Allah, and her teachings added mystical overtones to Sufism. Early on, many Muslims criticized the more mystical aspects of Sufism on the grounds that they contradicted the Islamic principle of Allah's "otherness." Gradually, however, the mysticism of Sufism became more acceptable to the Muslim world.

Rumi's Mevlevi

Rumi's religious order, the Mevlevi, departed from Islamic custom by including dance in its rituals. Nicknamed the "whirling dervishes" for their whirling dance and vow of poverty (*dervish* is Persian for "beggar"), the Mevlevis preached religious tolerance, humility, equality, and charity.

Calligraphic illustration, 1995. Es. Rouya.

The Counsels of the Bird

from The Masnavi

Rumi

Translated by E. H. Winfield

Bird on a Branch and a Butterfly. Persian miniature. Free Library of Philadelphia.

A man captured a bird by wiles and snares;
The bird said to him, "O noble sir,
In your time you have eaten many oxen and sheep,
And likewise sacrificed many camels;
You have never become satisfied with their meat,
So you will not be satisfied with my flesh.
Let me go, that I may give you three counsels,
Whence you will see whether I am wise or foolish.
The first of my counsels shall be given on your wrist,
The second on your well-plastered roof,
And the third I will give you from the top of a tree.
On hearing all three you will deem yourself happy.
As regards the counsel on your wrist, 'tis this,—
'Believe not foolish assertions of any one!'"
When he had spoken this counsel on his wrist, he flew
Up to the top of the roof, entirely free.
Then he said, "Do not grieve for what is past;
When a thing is done, vex not yourself about it."
He continued, "Hidden inside this body of mine
Is a precious pearl, ten drachms° in weight.
That jewel of right belonged to you,
Wealth for yourself and prosperity for your children.
You have lost it, as it was not fated you should get it,
That pearl whose like can nowhere be found."
Thereupon the man, like a woman in her travail,°
Gave vent to lamentations and weeping.
The bird said to him, "Did I not counsel you, saying,
'Beware of grieving over what is past and gone?'
When 'tis past and gone, why sorrow for it?
Either you understood not my counsel or are deaf.
The second counsel I gave you was this, namely,
'Be not misguided enough to believe foolish assertions.'
O fool, altogether I do not weigh three drachms,
How can a pearl of ten drachms be within me?"
The man recovered himself and said, "Well then,
Tell me now your third good counsel!"
The bird replied, "You have made a fine use of the others,
That I should waste my third counsel upon you!
To give counsel to a sleepy ignoramus
Is to sow seeds upon salt land.
Torn garments of folly and ignorance cannot be patched.
O counselors, waste not the seed of counsel on them!"

---

20 A *drachm* is about half an ounce.

25 A *woman in her travail* refers to a woman in labor.

Responding to Literature

Personal Response

Were you surprised by the ending of the story? Explain why or why not.

Analyzing Literature

Recall and Interpret

1. What does the bird promise to give the man in exchange for its freedom?
2. What advice does the bird give when it is on the man's wrist? on the rooftop?
3. How does the man react to the loss of the pearl? What does this reaction suggest about the man's **character?** (See **Literary Terms Handbook,** page R2.)
4. What is the bird's final piece of advice? How does the bird manage to give advice and withhold it at the same time?

Evaluate and Connect

5. **Irony** is a contrast between what happens and what is expected to happen. In what way is the beginning of the story ironic? What irony do you see in the conclusion?
6. What is the **theme,** or main idea, of the story? (See **Literary Terms Handbook,** page R12.)
7. What might the **purpose** of the story be?
8. How might the man in the story answer the Reading Focus question on page 465? How does this answer compare with yours?

Literary Criticism

Jonathan Star and Shahram Shiva observe in the introduction to their translation of Rumi's verse: "Nothing with Rumi can be taken literally: one must always be aware of the meaning behind the meaning, and the veils behind the veils." In what ways in "The Counsels of the Bird" do meanings hide behind meanings? Explain your answer in a paragraph, using details from the poem for support.

Literary ELEMENTS

Maxim

A **maxim** is a concise, memorable statement of advice, for example, the three counsels of the bird in Rumi's story. Also known as sayings, adages, aphorisms, and proverbs, these brief statements are at their most memorable when they express a generally acknowledged truth with wit, fresh imagery, and penetrating insight.

1. Reread the maxims in lines 14, 17–18, and 39–41. In your opinion, are these maxims effectively stated? Why or why not?
2. Restate the third counsel of the bird (lines 39–41) in your own words. What, if anything, is lost "in interpretation"? Explain.

- See **Literary Terms Handbook,** p. R7.

Extending Your Response

Personal Writing

A Lesson in Life What lessons can be learned from "The Counsels of the Bird"? In a few paragraphs, describe a time when you or someone you know might have benefited from one of the bird's maxims. Begin by quoting and explaining the maxim; then describe the situation to which it applies.

Internet Connection

Surfing for Sayings How do Rumi's maxims compare with those of other cultures and times? Using the Internet, find maxims from different periods and regions of the world. For example, you might research the sayings of the Chinese philosopher Confucius (551–479 B.C.), the biblical book of Proverbs, the oral traditions of Africa, or the French writer François de La Rochefoucauld (1613–1680). Sum up your findings in an oral report to your class.

Save your work for your portfolio.

Before You Read

The Sound of Birds at Noon

ISRAEL, 1974

Meet Dahlia Ravikovitch

"I tell you, even rocks crack, and not because of age."

Teacher, author, peace activist—all these titles can be used to describe Dahlia Ravikovitch (rə vē kō′ vich). She is probably best known, however, for her award-winning poetry.

Ravikovitch was born in Israel in a suburb of Tel Aviv in 1936. After studying at the Hebrew University of Jerusalem, she taught school. Eventually, she found her true calling when she began to write. She has published fiction, children's books, and several collections of poems, including *The Love of an Orange* and *The Window*.

Ravikovitch is also a grass-roots activist for peace in Southwest Asia, where tensions between Israel and Arab nations have sometimes erupted into war. Explaining that "everyone wants peace, but everyone thinks someone else should bring it," she has tried to establish dialogue by such simple actions as arranging for a Palestinian Boy Scout troop to spend a day visiting with Israeli teenagers.

Dahlia Ravikovitch was born in 1936.

Reading Focus

What qualities do you associate with birds?

List It! Make a list of at least three qualities, ideas, or things that you associate with birds.

Setting a Purpose Read to discover how Ravikovitch characterizes birds.

Building Background

The Time and Place

Much of Ravikovitch's poetry is informed by the conflicts within and around her homeland. In her antiwar poems, Ravikovitch vividly conveys the suffering of those who have been victims of acts of violence. In her more personal poems, such as "The Sound of Birds at Noon," the tensions between nations play a less prominent, but still unmistakable, role.

Ravikovitch's Style

Ravikovitch is known for writing intensely lyrical poems that reach their emotional peak in an **epiphany,** or sudden, unexpected moment of insight. Composing her poems in Hebrew, she prefers simple, everyday words and a relaxed, conversational tone. The translation that follows preserves these elements of her style.

Garden of Birds, 1983. Suad al-Attar (Iraq). Oil on canvas, 14 x 18 in. Collection of the artist.

The Sound of Birds at Noon

Dahlia Ravikovitch

Translated by Chana Bloch and Ariel Bloch

This chirping
is not in the least malicious.
They sing without giving us a thought
and they are as many
as the seed of Abraham.°
They have a life of their own,
they fly without thinking.
Some are rare, some common,
but every wing is grace.
Their hearts aren't heavy
even when they peck at a worm.
Perhaps they're light-headed.
The heavens were given to them
to rule over day and night
and when they touch a branch,
the branch too is theirs.
This chirping is entirely free of malice.
Over the years
it even seems to have
a note of compassion.

---

5 *The seed of Abraham* refers to Genesis 22:17, in which God promises that Abraham's descendants will be "as numerous as the stars in the sky and the grains of sand on the seashore."

Responding to Literature

Personal Response

What images in the poem did you find the most striking or memorable? In your journal, jot down these images and write a few lines explaining why each one had such a strong effect on you.

Analyzing Literature

Recall and Interpret

1. In lines 1–2, in what way does the speaker characterize the song of the birds?
2. What two things are compared in lines 4–5? What impression does this **simile** create?
3. In lines 6–11, what qualities of birds impress the speaker?
4. How does line 17 echo lines 1–2? In your opinion, what effect does this echo produce?

Evaluate and Connect

5. Why might the poet have chosen to refer to the birds as "they" throughout the poem?
6. In your view, is the **allusion,** or reference, to Abraham in line 5 effective? Why or why not?
7. In your opinion, which lines of the poem might be viewed as **epiphanies,** or moments of sudden insight? Support your answer with details from the poem.
8. After reading the poem, are there any qualities that you would like to add to the list you made for the Reading Focus on page 469? Why or why not?

Literary ELEMENTS

Enjambment

Enjambment is the breaking of a sentence from one line of a poem to another, as in lines 1–2 of "The Sound of Birds at Noon." Enjambment enables poets to mimic the natural rhythms of speech, breaking lines where people might normally pause in conversation while still maintaining unity of thought.

1. What other lines in the poem are enjambed?
2. How do the line breaks in the poem help establish a conversational tone?

- See **Literary Terms Handbook,** p. R3.

Extending Your Response

Learning for Life

Proposing Solutions Ravikovitch has found small but effective ways to lessen troubling problems in her part of the world. What might you do to make your school or community a better place? With a partner, discuss a problem that your school or community currently faces. Then think of ways that you and your classmates might help solve the problem. Decide which solutions are the most practical and likely to succeed, and present them to your class. At the end of your presentation, discuss your solutions with the class and encourage constructive criticism.

Creative Writing

Describing Using Ravikovitch's poem and your own observations as starting points, write a description of an insect, bird, fish, or other animal. In your writing, focus on distinctive characteristics or qualities of your subject. Use imagery, factual details, and comparisons to make your description as vivid as possible.

Save your work for your portfolio.

COMPARING selections

The Counsels of the Bird and The Sound of Birds at Noon

COMPARE **STYLES**

Discuss How does Rumi's style compare with Ravikovitch's? With a small group of students, compare and contrast the styles of the two poets by answering the following questions:

1. Does the poet use similes? If so, in what lines?
2. Does the poet use metaphors? If so, in what lines?
3. Does the poet use imagery? If so, in what lines?
4. Does the poet use learned or unfamiliar words? If so, in what lines? In which poem are the words less familiar? What accounts for this?
5. Does the poet use rhyme? If so, do the rhymes follow a pattern?
6. Does the poet use repetition? If so, in what lines?

Which poet's style do you prefer? Why?

COMPARE **CHARACTERIZATIONS**

Write How would you describe the bird in Rumi's poem? the birds in Ravikovitch's poem? In a few paragraphs, compare and contrast the two poets' characterizations of birds, explaining which characterization you prefer and why.

COMPARE **CULTURES**

Investigate How do the fables of other cultures characterize birds? Using the Internet or the library, find examples of fables in which birds play a prominent role. To begin, you might look up Aesop's "The Fox and the Crow" (also known as "The Raven and the Fox") or Ambrose Bierce's "The Man and the Bird." List the qualities associated with the bird in each fable; then compare them to the qualities of the bird in Rumi's poem. What characteristics, if any, do the birds share?

Before You Read

IRAQ, 1957

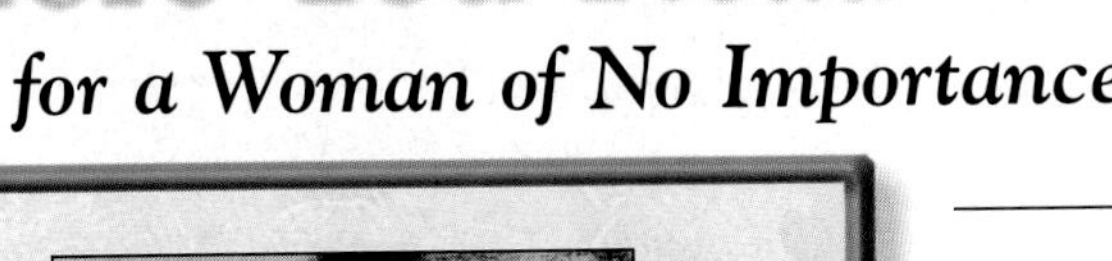

Elegy for a Woman of No Importance

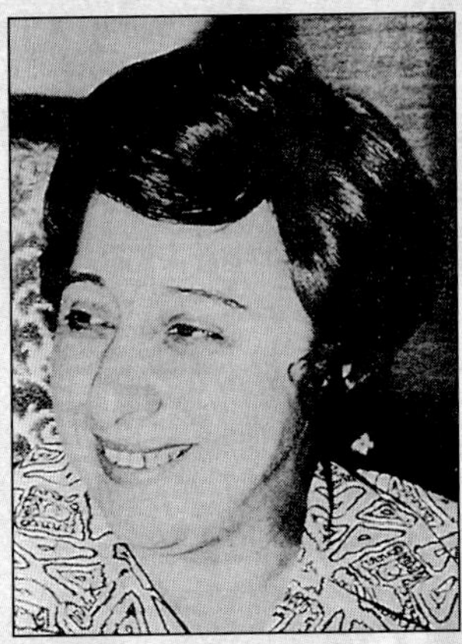

Meet Nāzik al-Malā'ikah

Writing poetry is a family tradition for Nāzik al-Malā'ikah (nä′ zēk äl′ mäl i′ KHä). Both her father and grandfather are known as distinguished poets in their native Iraq.

Born in Baghdad, Iraq's capital city, al-Malā'ikah studied Arabic literature at Baghdad University. She then traveled to the United States and earned an advanced degree in comparative literature at Princeton University. When she returned to Iraq, she accepted a position at Baghdad University, where she taught for many years.

Known as a leading proponent of the Arabic free-verse movement, which introduced modern poetic forms and informal diction to Arabic poetry, al-Malā'ikah has written literary criticism as well as poetry. Her verse collections include *Lover of the Night*, *Splinters and Ashes*, *The Bottom of the Waves*, and *The Moon Tree*. Currently, al-Malā'ikah lives in Kuwait, a Persian Gulf state that borders Iraq.

Nāzik al-Malā'ikah was born in 1923.

Reading Focus

Christian missionary Mother Theresa, who worked to help the poverty-stricken and sick in Calcutta, India, once said that "loneliness and the feeling of being unwanted is the most terrible poverty." Do you agree?

Journal Jot down your opinion in your journal, explaining why you feel as you do.

Setting a Purpose Read to discover a poet's portrayal of a woman's lonely death.

Building Background

Muslim Women

Most of Iraq's population is Muslim. Traditionally, the identity of women in Muslim cultures has been shaped by family, husband, and home. Although the roles of Muslim women are in transition, with many women achieving a greater degree of autonomy and independence than in the past, an unmarried or widowed woman is still considered to be adrift in most Muslim cultures.

The Elegy

Named for an ancient Greek metrical form, the **elegy** has been one of poetry's most enduring forms. This is not surprising, as its theme—human mortality and its emotional consequences—is a universal one. Poets in all times and cultures have written elegies. Although elegies originally dealt with famous people or events, many—like al-Malā'ikah's elegy, which follows—deal with people who are obscure or little-known.

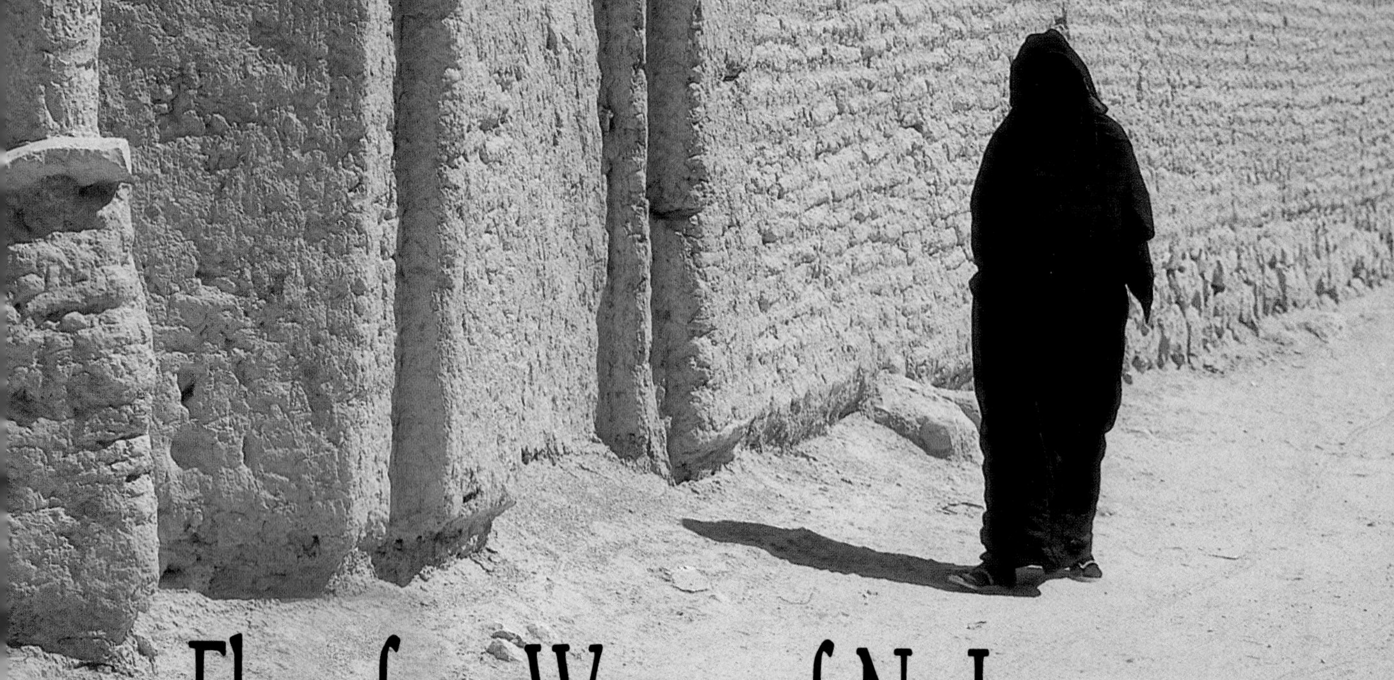

Elegy for a Woman of No Importance

Nāzik al-Malā'ikah

Translated by Chris Knipp and Mohammad Sadiq

When she died no face turned pale, no lips trembled
doors heard no retelling of her death
no curtains opened to air the room of grief
no eyes followed the coffin to the end of the road—
only, hovering in the memory, a vague form
passing in the lane

The scrap of news stumbled in the alleyways
its whisper, finding no shelter,
lodged obscurely in an unseen corner.
The moon murmured sadly.

Night, unconcerned, gave way to morning
light came with the milk cart and the call to fasting
with the hungry mewing of a cat of rags and bones
the shrill cries of vendors in the bitter streets
the squabbling of small boys throwing stones
dirty water spilling along the gutters
smells on the wind
which played about the rooftops
playing in deep forgetfulness
playing alone

Responding to Literature

Personal Response

How did you feel about the woman's death after reading the poem? What words or images made you feel this way? Express your thoughts in a few paragraphs in your journal.

Analyzing Literature

Recall and Interpret

1. According to lines 1–5, how did the woman's neighborhood react to her death?
2. What is the "scrap of news" the speaker refers to in lines 6–8? What do these lines suggest about the woman's status in the neighborhood?
3. How does the author convey a sense of the loneliness in the woman's life? What images of loneliness does she use in the poem?
4. Based on lines 11–15, how would you describe the **setting** of the poem?
5. What do the last two lines of the poem suggest about the woman's life? about her death?

Evaluate and Connect

6. Why might the poet have chosen not to name the woman or present the details of her life?
7. In your opinion, would the poet agree that the woman was "of no importance"? Explain.
8. After reading the poem, would you change your response to the Reading Focus on page 473? Why or why not? Support your answer with details from the poem.

Literary ELEMENTS

Personification

Poets often write of inanimate objects and other things as if they were capable of human feeling or actions, as in "the sun smiled" or "the clouds wept." This device is called **personification**—the attribution of human qualities or thoughts to an animal, object, or idea. In this poem, personification is used to reinforce the indifference with which news of the woman's death is received.

1. What examples of personification can you find in this poem?
2. How do they reinforce the ideas of solitude and indifference?

- See **Literary Terms Handbook,** p. R9.

Extending Your Response

Listening and Speaking

Giving a Report In some countries, the custom has developed of honoring an unidentified wartime casualty as a way of paying tribute to all those people—named and anonymous—who have died in the nation's service. Using encyclopedias or the Internet, find out more about the Tomb of the Unknowns in the United States, France, England, or other countries. Then present your findings in a brief oral report to your class.

Creative Writing

Writing an Elegy Think about a loss that you have experienced that would be a fitting subject for an elegy. Think about images that would be effective for expressing this loss and creating an appropriate mood. Write your elegy and share it with others if you care to.

Save your work for your portfolio.

Grammar Link

Pronoun and Antecedent Agreement

Pronouns can make your writing much smoother if you use them correctly. A **pronoun** takes the place of a noun or another pronoun. An **antecedent** is the word that is being replaced. In order for your writing to be clear, each pronoun must agree with its antecedent in number, gender, and person.

Problem 1 A singular antecedent that can be either male or female
A poet may express deep, personal feelings about controversial topics in his poetry.

Solution A Traditionally, a masculine pronoun is used when the gender of the antecedent is not known or may be either masculine or feminine. This usage excludes females. Reword the sentence to use *he or she, him or her,* and so on.
A poet may express deep, personal feelings in his or her poetry.

Solution B Reword the sentence so that both the antecedent and pronoun are plural.
Poets may express deep, personal feelings in their poetry.

Problem 2 A singular indefinite pronoun as an antecedent
Neither poet used rhyme in their poems.

Solution A *Neither, either, each, one, another, any,* and *every* are singular; they therefore require singular pronouns.
Neither poet used rhyme in his or her poem.

Solution B Reword the sentence to avoid the singular pronoun.
Both poets avoided rhyme in their poems.

Problem 3 Two possible antecedents for a pronoun
Max gave Ernesto a book by his favorite poet.

Solution Replace the pronoun with the correct noun.
Max gave Ernesto a book by Ernesto's favorite poet.

- For more about pronouns and antecedents, see **Language Handbook,** p. R19.

EXERCISE

Revise each sentence to correct problems in pronoun use.

1. Poets often give readers a glimpse into their souls.
2. A poet may write about such a personal subject that they do not want their work published.
3. If readers dislike a poet's poems, should they be considered worthless?
4. Each poet who wrote about war dealt with its destruction in their own way.
5. One poet credits their writing career to their love for reading poetry.

Before You Read

The Diameter of the Bomb

Meet Yehuda Amichai

"My personal history has coincided with a larger history. For me it's always been one and the same."

Author Yehuda Amichai (ye hœʹ dä ä mēʹ KHĪ) often wrote about the history, natural beauty, and political concerns of Israel, a nation for which he fought during the 1940s. Born in Germany to Orthodox Jewish parents, Amichai moved to Palestine with his family in 1936 when he was eleven years old. During World War II, he served with the British army (Palestine was under British rule at that time). He then joined underground forces fighting for the creation of a Jewish state. This goal was achieved on May 14, 1948, when Israel proclaimed its independence.

Considered to have been Israel's leading poet, Amichai published several collections of verse, including *Love Poems* and *Poems of Jerusalem*. He also wrote fiction, including the novel *Not of This Time, Not of This Place* and the collection *The World Is a Room and Other Short Stories*. All these works are available in English translation.

Yehuda Amichai was born in 1924 and died in 2000.

Reading Focus

Some people think reporters should report only facts of a story and let people decide for themselves how they would feel about the reported event. Do you agree?

Share Ideas Discuss your response to this issue in a small group.

Setting a Purpose Read to discover a poet's point of view about the effects of a bombing.

Building Background

Terrorism

Terrorism, as we use the term today, means the use of violence against non-military targets with no advance warning. As such, it dates back to the late nineteenth century, when dissident groups–especially in Tsarist Russia–were denied any peaceful means of working toward their goals. These terrorists directed their attacks at government representatives. More recently terrorists have regarded any unarmed civilians as fair game. It is doubtful that terrorist activities have ever caused a significant or lasting change in any government's policies.

Although terrorist acts have been committed all over the world, including the United States, terrorism has played an especially prominent role in the politics of Southwest Asia. Besides such acts as airplane hijacking, terrorism includes the random bombings of nonmilitary targets. Such acts, as Amichai shows in "The Diameter of the Bomb," often result in emotional and physical devastation.

The Diameter of the Bomb

Yehuda Amichai
Translated by Chana Bloch and Stephen Mitchell

The diameter of the bomb was thirty centimeters
and the diameter of its effective range about seven meters,
with four dead and eleven wounded.
And around these, in a larger circle
of pain and time, two hospitals are scattered
and one graveyard. But the young woman
who was buried in the city she came from,
at a distance of more than a hundred kilometers,
enlarges the circle considerably,
and the solitary man mourning her death
at the distant shores of a country far across the sea
includes the entire world in the circle.
And I won't even mention the crying of orphans
that reaches up to the throne of God and
beyond, making
a circle with no end and no God.

Sabbath at the Kibbutz, 1949. Yohanan Simon (Israel). Oil on canvas. Tel Aviv Museum of Art.

Viewing the painting: What qualities does the painting share with the poem? How does this painting differ from the poem in mood and content?

Responding to Literature

Personal Response

Based on the title, what did you expect the poem to be about? Did the poem meet your expectations? Explain your answer in a few paragraphs in your journal.

Analyzing Literature

Recall and Interpret

1. What specific facts about the bombing does the poems speaker present in lines 1–3?
2. In lines 4–5, to what might the "larger circle of pain and time" refer?
3. How does the circle grow in lines 5–12?
4. Who and what are included in the circle by the end of the poem? How do lines 13–16 provide an emotional **climax** to the poem? (See **Literary Terms Handbook,** page R2.)

Evaluate and Connect

5. The speaker's attitude toward the subject gradually shifts from emotional detachment to strong emotional involvement. In your view, is this shift in **tone** effective? Explain.
6. **Irony** is a pointed difference between appearance and reality. What is ironic about the title of the poem? about the phrase "effective range of the bomb"?
7. The poem is unified by the image of ever-widening circles. In your opinion, is this image an appropriate one for the subject matter? Why or why not?
8. How might the speaker in the poem answer the Reading Focus questions on page 477? How are these answers different from or similar to yours?

Literary ELEMENTS

Theme

The **theme** of a literary work is the main idea that the work conveys about life or human experience. In some works, the theme is directly stated by a character or the speaker. In other works, such as "The Diameter of the Bomb," the theme is implied, or indirectly revealed through imagery, conflict, and the speaker's or characters' responses to conflict.

1. What **internal conflict,** or psychological suffering, do the people in the poem experience? What **external conflict,** or force, causes this suffering?
2. How does the speaker feel about the people's suffering? Based on the speaker's attitude, how would you state the theme of the poem?

- See **Literary Terms Handbook,** p. R12.

Extending Your Response

Creative Writing

Facts and Feelings Use the facts in "The Diameter of the Bomb" to write a news account of the explosion. Fill in the gaps by using your imagination; then provide your readers with a narrative of events that includes the reactions of bystanders that you "interview." When you are finished, exchange papers with a partner and offer each other ideas on your writing.

Literature Groups

Just the Facts? Think about a recent news event in which your group was (or might have been) involved. To help other people understand what it was like, would you prefer to simply tell the facts of what happened, or to tell how you felt? Discuss this question in your group and report your findings to the class.

Save your work for your portfolio.

Reading & Thinking Skills

Identifying Cause and Effect

Suppose that your basketball team has an out-of-town game on a school night. By the time you get home and go to bed, it's quite late. The next day at school, you feel so tired that you doze off in class. The basketball game is the cause of your not getting enough sleep. Your dozing off in class is an effect of getting home late from the basketball game. Your dozing off in class may be the cause of your missing an assignment. When one event causes another one to happen, a **cause-and-effect relationship** exists.

Writers often describe events in terms of cause-and-effect relationships. Identifying these relationships helps you understand events more fully.

To identify causes and effects, think about the following:

- *Why* something happened is its cause.
- *What* happened as a result of something is its effect.
- Words and phrases such as *because, as a result,* and *consequently* often signal cause-and-effect relationships.

In written accounts of events, just as in real life, a single cause may have several effects, and one effect may have multiple causes. In its turn, an effect may become the cause of one or more other effects. As you look for causes and effects, be aware that the causal relationship is often subtle and multilayered.

"The Diameter of the Bomb" comments on an ever-widening circle of effects–like the ripples in a pool of water when a stone is dropped into it.

- The bomb itself measures thirty centimeters around.
- The "effective range" of the bomb is seven meters.
- The emotional effect of the bomb spreads from the point where it landed all the way out to "the throne of God."

• For more about identifying cause and effect, see **Reading Handbook,** p. R86.

ACTIVITY

Reread "The Diameter of the Bomb." Then rewrite the poem in prose. Explain the way the effect of the bomb keeps expanding. Finish by giving your own opinion as to what the bomb's most important effect is.

Before You Read

Butterflies

SAUDI ARABIA, 1988

Meet Fawziyya Abu Khalid

**"The girls of Arabia will soon grow to full stature
They will look about and say:
'She has passed by this road.'"**

Fawziyya Abu Khalid (fô zē′ yä ä bo͞o′ KHä′ lēd) published her first collection of verse when she was only eighteen years old. This remarkable accomplishment is especially notable for a young woman raised in Saudi Arabia during the 1950s and 1960s. At that time, relatively few Saudi girls were educated. Then, as now, girls and boys were raised in strict separation, and the first Saudi girls' school did not open until 1956, the year after she was born.

After university studies in sociology in the United States, Abu Khalid returned to Saudi Arabia. There she began teaching at the girls' college of King Saud University in Riyadh, the city where she was born. She has also continued to write poetry. Her second collection, *Secret Reading in the History of Arab Silence*, appeared in 1985. Her poetry often celebrates the strength, wisdom, and capabilities of the women of Saudi Arabia.

"Butterflies" and other poems by Abu Khalid appear in English translation in *The Literature of Modern Arabia* (1988), a landmark collection of works by nearly a hundred writers from the Arabian Peninsula.

Fawziyya Abu Khalid was born in 1955.

Reading Focus

What images, feelings, or thoughts do you associate with butterflies?

Web It! With a classmate, record your associations on a word web similar to the one pictured.

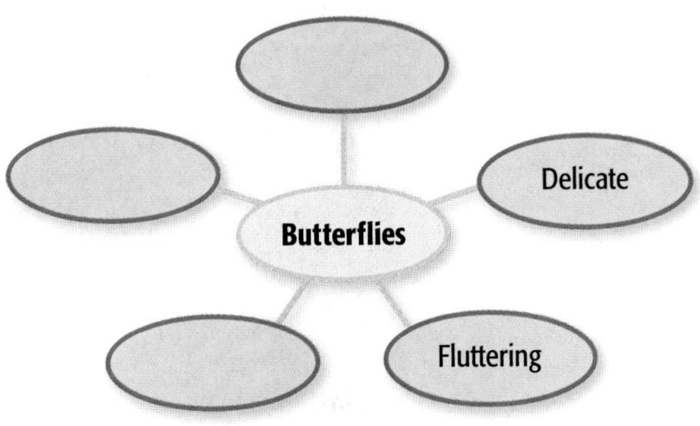

Setting a Purpose Read to discover the images the speaker associates with butterflies.

Building Background

The Bedouins

In her poem "Butterflies," Abu Khalid refers to the Bedouins—Arabic-speaking nomads of Southwest Asia and North Africa. The name comes from the Arabic *badawi*, meaning "desert dweller." Until quite recently, the Bedouin way of life remained much the same as it had for a thousand years.

During the hot, dry months, the scattered elements of the Bedouin clans would form larger groups, congregating at the edge of desert areas around water sources. During the cooler months, they would migrate in small groups into the desert on horseback or camelback with their herds of animals. The modernization of the Arab world has led to changes among the Bedouins, some of whom have adopted a more settled way of life.

Relationship, early 1970s. Abd al-Wahab Morsi (Egypt). Oil on canvas, 110 x 80 cm. National Museum of Modern Art, Cairo.

Butterflies

Fawziyya Abu Khalid

When you abandoned me,
I didn't need an elegy
because you had planted
a flight of butterflies in my heart
whose path I follow
like a bedouin who knows
how to perfectly trace the footsteps
   of his truant mare.

EDITING/PROOFREADING

Are you satisfied with the content of your reflective essay? If so, it's time to edit and proofread your essay carefully for errors in grammar, usage, mechanics, and spelling.

Grammar Hint

Use the same verb tense when you describe events that occur at the same time.

INCORRECT: *Gilgamesh mourned Enkidu and reflects on his own mortality.*

CORRECT: *Gilgamesh mourns Enkidu and reflects on his own mortality.*

- For more on verb tense, see **Language Handbook**, p. R44.

PROOFREADING TIP

Use the **Proofreading Checklist** on the inside back cover of this book to help you mark errors that you find.

TECHNOLOGY TIP

Each time an unfamiliar title or name comes up during spell-check, make sure the spelling is correct before clicking on "ignore."

STUDENT MODEL

From the very begining, when Enkidu relates his dream, there seemed to be far to many details and strange names to take in. As I went over it again however I start to understand the feelings and ideas convayed in these tales.

Complete Student Model on p. R114.

Complete Student Model

For a complete version of the model developed in this workshop, refer to **Writing Workshop Models**, p. R114.

PUBLISHING/PRESENTING

Consider sharing your essay with classmates who wrote about the same selection that you did. Then discuss why you may have had different responses to the literature and in what ways your responses are similar. What did you learn about the selection while writing the essay?

PRESENTING TIP

Give your essay a title that includes both the title of your selection and the change in your response.

Reflecting

More than two thousand years ago, the Greek writer Dionysius Longinus wrote that a piece of writing "is truly great only if it can stand up to repeated examination." That's still true today. Why? What is it about great writing that makes it worth reading more than once?

Read your essay one last time, reflecting upon its strengths and weaknesses. Plan to build on the strengths and correct the weaknesses in your next piece of writing.

Save your work for your portfolio.

The Land and Its People

South Central Asia is one of the most diverse regions on Earth. The area is often referred to as a subcontinent for its size and importance. Geographically, it stretches from the snow-capped Himalayas to tropical islands, passing both deserts and fertile river valleys along the way. Climatically, periods of intense heat are followed by drenching monsoon rains. Today the area is home to one-fifth of the world's population, living in the modern countries of Afghanistan, Bangladesh, Bhutan, India, Nepal, Pakistan, and Sri Lanka.

South Central Asia is also an area of great cultural wealth and diversity. The world's oldest continuous civilization had its beginnings there some 4,500 years ago. The rich agricultural lands and mineral resources of India have long attracted invaders, from the Indo-European tribes 3,500 years ago to the British who left in 1947. All of them made their own contributions to the area's civilization. From this diversity has come an understanding of the value of tolerance. Rulers as different as the Buddhist emperor Ashoka and the Mongol conqueror Akbar recognized the importance of showing respect for the beliefs of others.

Traditional dancer, Orissa.

Boy selling spices at Udaipur market.

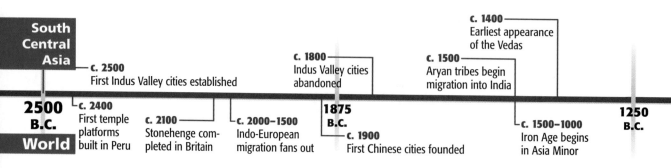

South Central Asia

- **c. 2500** First Indus Valley cities established
- **c. 1800** Indus Valley cities abandoned
- **c. 1500** Aryan tribes begin migration into India
- **c. 1400** Earliest appearance of the Vedas

2500 B.C. — **1875 B.C.** — **1250 B.C.**

World

- **c. 2400** First temple platforms built in Peru
- **c. 2100** Stonehenge completed in Britain
- **c. 2000–1500** Indo-European migration fans out
- **c. 1900** First Chinese cities founded
- **c. 1500–1000** Iron Age begins in Asia Minor

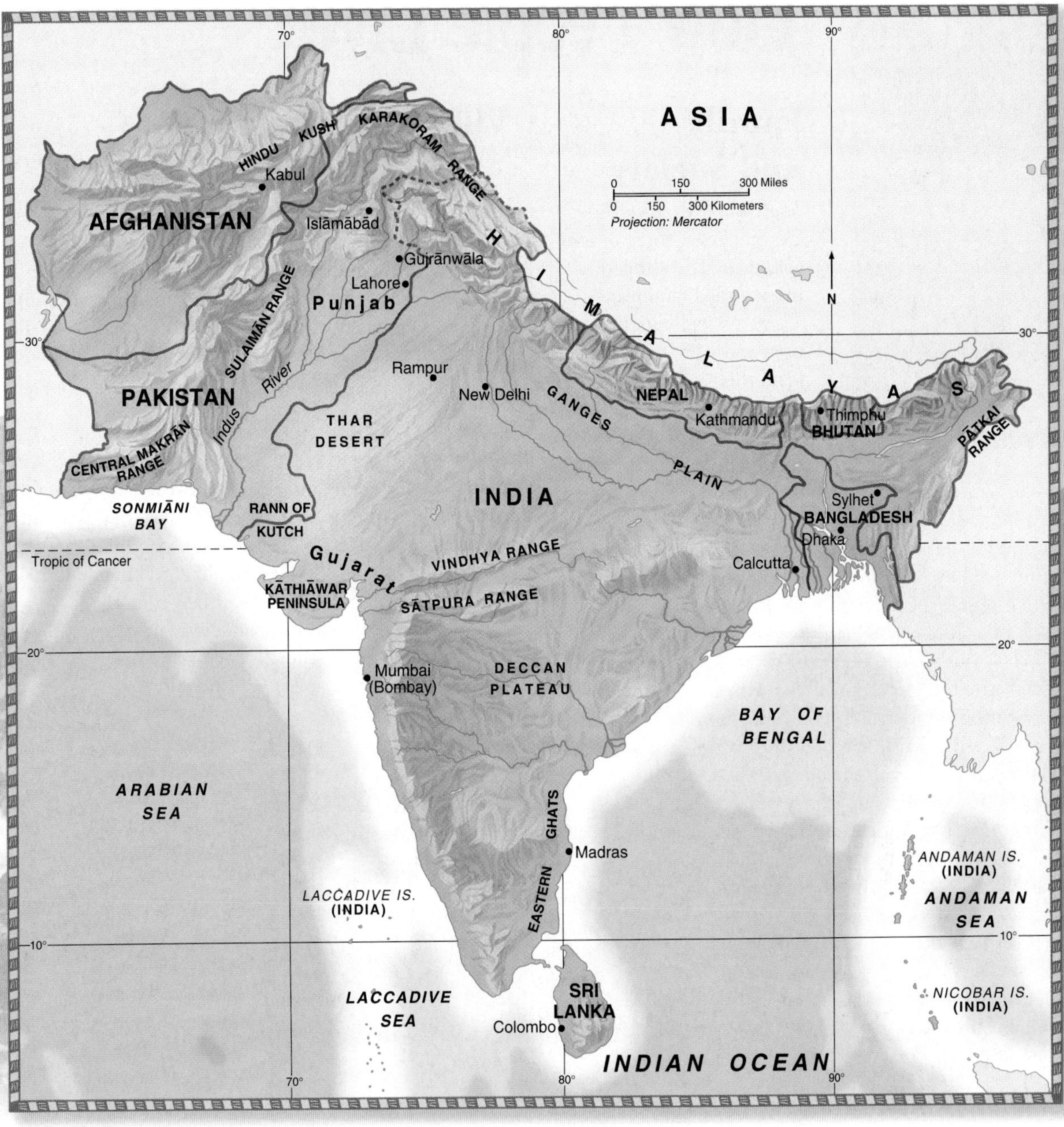

ASIA

0 150 300 Miles
0 150 300 Kilometers
Projection: Mercator

N

70° 80° 90°
30° 20° 10°

HINDU KUSH
KARAKORAM RANGE
HIMALAYAS
Kabul
AFGHANISTAN
Islāmābād
Gujrānwāla
Lahore
Punjab
SULAIMĀN RANGE
Indus River
PAKISTAN
CENTRAL MAKRĀN RANGE
SONMIĀNI BAY
Rampur
New Delhi
THAR DESERT
GANGES PLAIN
NEPAL
Kathmandu
Thimphu
BHUTAN
PĀTKAI RANGE
Sylhet
BANGLADESH
Dhaka
INDIA
RANN OF KUTCH
Tropic of Cancer
Gujarat
VINDHYA RANGE
Calcutta
KĀTHIĀWAR PENINSULA
SĀTPURA RANGE
Mumbai (Bombay)
DECCAN PLATEAU
BAY OF BENGAL
ARABIAN SEA
EASTERN GHATS
Madras
ANDAMAN IS. (INDIA)
ANDAMAN SEA
LACCADIVE IS. (INDIA)
LACCADIVE SEA
SRI LANKA
Colombo
NICOBAR IS. (INDIA)
INDIAN OCEAN

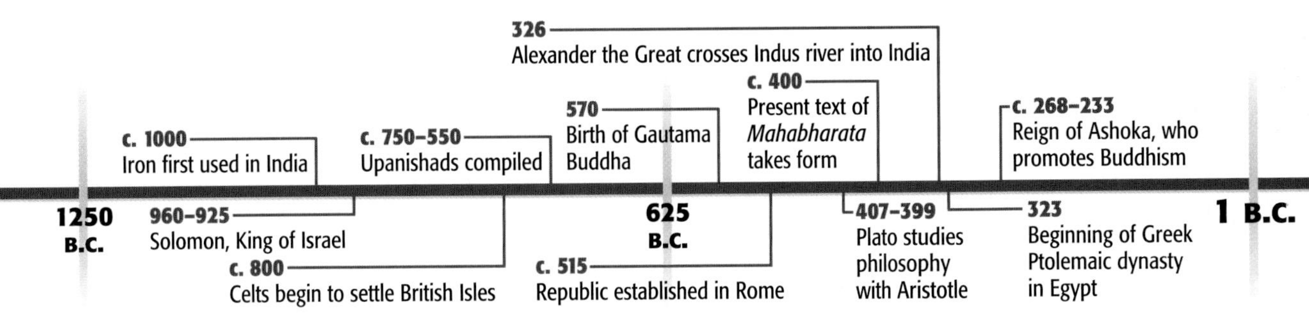
326 Alexander the Great crosses Indus river into India
c. 400 Present text of *Mahabharata* takes form
570 Birth of Gautama Buddha
c. 268–233 Reign of Ashoka, who promotes Buddhism
c. 1000 Iron first used in India
c. 750–550 Upanishads compiled
1250 B.C.
960–925 Solomon, King of Israel
c. 800 Celts begin to settle British Isles
625 B.C.
c. 515 Republic established in Rome
407–399 Plato studies philosophy with Aristotle
323 Beginning of Greek Ptolemaic dynasty in Egypt
1 B.C.

How People Live

Family and Society

Traditionally in South Central Asia, three or four generations live together in extended families. These typically include a man and wife; their sons (and their wives); any unmarried daughters; and the children of their sons. In Sri Lanka and in some urban centers today, the nuclear family—consisting of a man and wife and their unmarried children—is more the rule. Muslims and others who live in areas influenced by Muslim rule commonly observe *purdah*, which requires women to wear veils when in the presence of non-family members.

The Hindu caste system of India is a hierarchical social structure determined by birth. In former times, occupation, residence, friends, and marriage partners were determined by the caste into which one was born. Major caste divisions include priests, soldiers, merchants, farmers, and the lowest caste, "untouchables." The degrading aspects of the caste system were ruled illegal when India achieved independence, and more upward social mobility exists now than ever before. However, the caste system does still continue, affecting non-Hindus as well as Hindus.

Village Life

Most of the region's people live in villages and farm or herd animals. Families of the same caste tend to live near one another, with the lowest castes at the fringes of the villages. In former days, families created alliances with families of other castes and traded specialized services, such as carpentry, barbering, or officiating at religious rites. These hereditary alliances could be traced back over many generations.

Modern Times

During their century of rule, the British created a modern infrastructure in South Central Asia, building railroads, a court system, hospitals, and schools, although they also exploited India economically. The modern Indian independence movement began in 1885, and in 1947, the empire became two independent nations: India, officially secular with a Hindu majority, and Pakistan, officially Muslim.

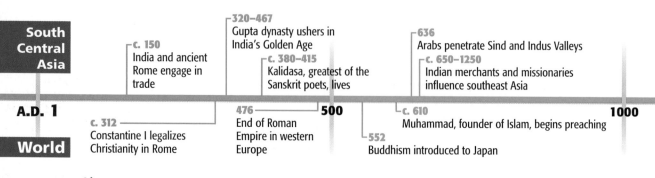

South Central Asia

- **c. 150** India and ancient Rome engage in trade
- **320–467** Gupta dynasty ushers in India's Golden Age
- **c. 380–415** Kalidasa, greatest of the Sanskrit poets, lives
- **636** Arabs penetrate Sind and Indus Valleys
- **c. 650–1250** Indian merchants and missionaries influence southeast Asia

A.D. 1 — **500** — **1000**

World

- **c. 312** Constantine I legalizes Christianity in Rome
- **476** End of Roman Empire in western Europe
- **552** Buddhism introduced to Japan
- **c. 610** Muhammad, founder of Islam, begins preaching

What People Believe

Bodhisattva (Buddhist), 4th century A.D. Pakistan.

A Variety of Beliefs

Religion dominates all aspects of life in the area, though the faiths themselves differ. In India, Hindus make up some 80 percent of the population; Muslims account for some 10 percent. Other religions have either originated or established themselves in India throughout history. They include Jainism, dating back to the sixth century B.C., and Sikhism, founded in the fifteenth century A.D. There is a small but influential community of Parsis, followers of the ancient religion of the Persian empire, who fled from the Muslim invaders of their land. The first Christians in India arrived in the south by sea during the first century A.D. Most of the people of Afghanistan, Pakistan, and Bangladesh are Muslim, while those in Nepal practice a form of Hinduism highly influenced by Buddhism. Although India was the birthplace of Buddhism, Sri Lanka and Bhutan are the only Buddhist countries in the area today.

Hinduism

Although many gods are worshipped within Hinduism, they are usually considered to be the many forms of a single uiversal divine spirit. The most important forms are the three gods Brahma, the creator; Vishnu, the preserver; and Shiva, the destroyer. The Hindu deities are often represented symbolically; for example, Ganesh, god of wisdom, is shown as having the head of an elephant. Common to all forms of Hinduism is a desire to break through what is believed to be a cycle of rebirths and to unite the individual soul with the universal spirit. Most worship is conducted at family shrines and small local temples, though pilgrimages to major temples and participation in festivals devoted to particular deities or mythological events are very popular.

Mahadeo (Hindu deity), 1852–1860. Nepal.

Active Reading Strategies

Reading the Time Line

1. How many years after the birth of Gautama Buddha was Buddhism introduced in Japan?
2. List these events in chronological order, citing the year for each: the Taj Mahal is completed; the Mughal Empire is established; the U.S. declares its independence; Sepoys revolt in India.

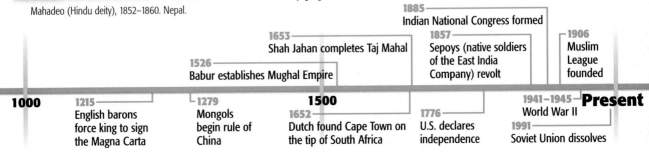

1000

- 1215 English barons force king to sign the Magna Carta
- 1279 Mongols begin rule of China
- 1526 Babur establishes Mughal Empire

1500

- 1652 Dutch found Cape Town on the tip of South Africa
- 1653 Shah Jahan completes Taj Mahal
- 1776 U.S. declares independence
- 1857 Sepoys (native soldiers of the East India Company) revolt
- 1885 Indian National Congress formed
- 1906 Muslim League founded
- 1941–1945 World War II
- 1991 Soviet Union dissolves

Present

Arts and Entertainment

Indian musician, Jaipur.

The Arts

Arts throughout South Central Asia are similar in many ways. Many of the differences that do exist reflect the influence of different religions, since much of the art is religiously based.

- Most sculpture is Hindu or Buddhist and is used to adorn temples.
- Some Muslims disapprove of representational art, but Mughal paintings—often book illustrations—are among the world's masterpieces.
- Music is highly developed among both Muslims and Hindus, and both regard song as the highest form of music.

Although the area has its own distinctive styles, its artists have been open to influences from outside—from Greek sculpture to Arabic calligraphy.

The Golden Temple, Amritsar, India.

Music

In classical times, music was performed in courts and in temples. It is now usually performed in concert halls and at festivals. The two classical traditions, Northern and Southern, share many common characteristics. These include the following:

- Each composition has a particular musical shape, called a *raga*, which consists of a series of scale intervals.
- Each part of a composition has its own time measure, called a *tala*.
- Improvisation, stressing melody rather than harmony, is emphasized.
- Ensembles of three to six instruments might include variations of plucked or bowed string instruments, drums, and wind and reed instruments.
- Drone instruments repeat a single note or series of notes over and over to provide the basic background.

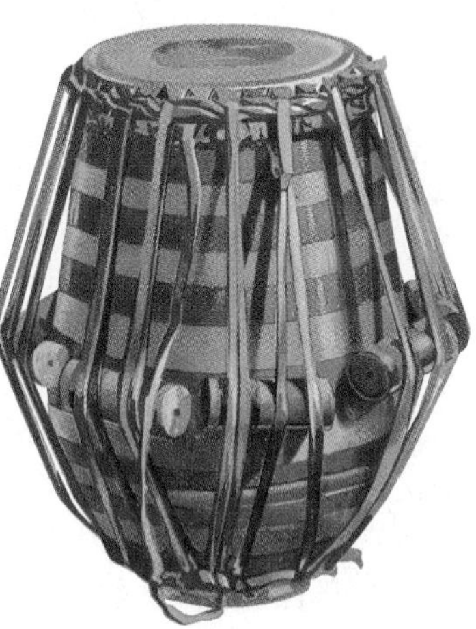

Tan tan (Indian drum).

Dance

Dance is especially important in Hindu culture. The continuity of dance forms can be seen by comparing the sculptures of dancers on ancient monuments with contemporary stage performances. Modern dancers and their teachers still consult a 2,000-year-old text, the *Natya-sastra,* for information on style and gestures.

Classical dance acts out religious stories and mythological episodes using elaborate hand and body gestures.

Folk dance is also an important part of Hindu religious festivals, occasionally lasting late into the night. In both the folk and classical traditions, musicians and dancers maintain close communication with one another, reacting to changes in one another's rhythms. Audiences respond to the familiar stories by counting out the rhythms and by shouting their approval.

Indian folk dancer, Rajasthan.

Critical Thinking

Connecting Cultures

1. In a small group, make a list of instruments and sounds that are typical of the music that we listen to in the United States today.
2. In a small group, discuss how the sound of our music in the West might differ from that of music in South Central Asia.

Language and Literature

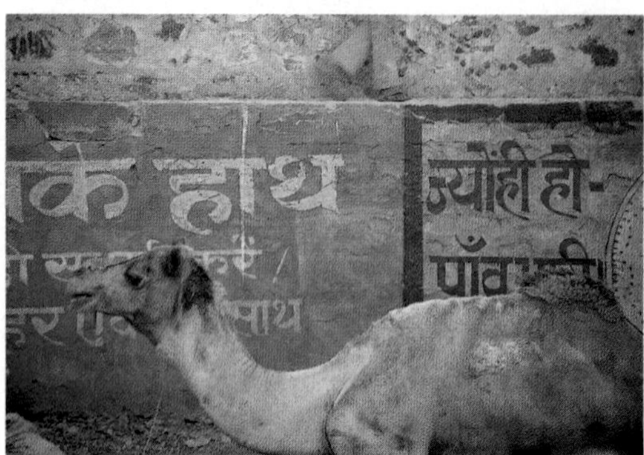

Camel with Hindi signage.

The Languages of a Subcontinent

More than twenty major languages are spoken in South Central Asia, along with hundreds of other languages and dialects. Sanskrit, an ancient Indo-European language, was the dominant language until about A.D. 1000 and is the language of Hindu sacred literature. The official national language of India (Hindi) and that of Pakistan (Urdu) are both descended from Sanskrit. Hindi uses the ancient Devanagari alphabet and has a vocabulary largely derived from Sanskrit; Urdu is written in Arabic-style script, and its vocabulary contains many words of Persian derivation.

The languages commonly spoken in South India—including Telugu, Tamil, Kannada, and Malayalam—belong to the non-Indo-European Dravidian language family and have their own scripts. All these languages have thriving, well-established literatures, often dating back more than a thousand years. English, introduced into India by the British during their rule, is also widely used, particularly between South Central Asians of different linguistic backgrounds.

Indian miniature with Sanskrit text.

influences

In the 1960s, many people traveled to India in search of spiritual knowledge. Many words from Indian languages describing food, clothing, musical instruments, and religious beliefs entered English usage then, as well as during earlier periods. These words include the following:

- bungalow (from Hindi *bangla*, "house in the Bengal style"), a single-story house usually surrounded by a verandah
- cot (from Hindi *khat*, "bedstead"), a light bed, often collapsible
- guru (from Hindi and Sanskrit *guru*, "heavy, weighty, venerable"), a personal religious teacher and spiritual guide
- karma (from Sanskrit *karman*, "work"), a person's destiny, determined by one's good or bad deeds
- shampoo (from Hindi *capo*, "to press, knead"), to massage the hair or head with soap and water
- yoga (from Sanskrit *yoga*, "yoking, union"), a discipline by which a person prepares for the union of his or her individual self with the universal spirit

Classical Literature

The earliest South Central Asian literature—the Vedas, the *Mahabharata* (mə hä′ bär′ ə tə), and the *Ramayana*—was first composed and transmitted orally and later written down. The *Mahabharata* tells of a war between two sets of cousins. The god Krishna assists the winning side, the Pandavas (pän dä′ väs), and the passage in which Lord Krishna instructs a Pandava warrior on moral behavior, called the *Bhagavad Gita* (bä′ gə väd′ gē′ tə), is the most famous poem in all Indian literature. The second great epic, the *Ramayana,* relates the story of the god-king Rama, whose wife is abducted by a demon but then is rescued with the help of monkey and bear armies. The *Ramayana* continues to inspire paintings, dance, and theater performances in India and throughout Southeast Asia.

An increased emphasis on spirituality within Hinduism in the thirteenth to seventeenth centuries inspired many fine poets such as Tulsidas, who translated the *Ramayana* into Hindi; the blind poet Surdas; and the Rajput princess, Mirabai. The mystic poet Kabir was a Muslim weaver by birth who sought to combine the spiritual elements of Islam and Hinduism. His verse is still widely quoted today.

Muslim poets wrote lyrics—some mystical, some romantic—in Urdu. Among these poets were Nazir Akbarabadi, who wrote of everyday life using nonclassical verse forms, and Bahadur Shah Zafar, the last Mughal emperor.

Modern Literature

Poetry was the major literary form until the British introduced new genres such as the novel and the short story. Prem Chand, who wrote novels and short stories of country life in both Urdu and Hindi, and Rabindranath Tagore, who won the Nobel Prize for Literature in 1913, were among the first to explore the new forms. Tagore wrote most of his work in Bengali, which he then often translated into English himself. Hindi and Urdu are the most widely read languages of the area, but all the other languages—some spoken by millions of people—have their own literature. English offers a world-wide audience. It is not identified with a specific ethnic group, and several major writers, such as R. K. Narayan, write in English.

Movie marquee, New Delhi.

Critical Thinking

South Central Asia

1. Why might the great language diversity of South Central Asia lead some writers to use the English language? Discuss your answers in a small group.
2. What are the benefits of writing in English for a South Central Asian writer? What are the disadvantages? With your group, list the pros and cons.

INDIA, c. 1400 B.C.

Before You Read

Creation Hymn from the *Rig Veda*

Reading Focus

What stories about the creation of the world are you familiar with?

Share Ideas In a small group, share the stories and theories about creation that you know.

Setting a Purpose Read to discover ancient, timeless Hindu ideas about creation.

Building Background

The Vedas

The Vedas are the oldest sacred writings of Hinduism, a religion that originated in India. These scriptures are older than those of any other major world religion. Composed in Sanskrit beginning about 1500 to 1200 B.C., they consist of four collections of hymns or verses. The term *veda* means "knowledge." Hindus believe the Vedas contain eternal truths that were divinely revealed to ancient seers or prophets. Hindus revere these scriptures as *shruti,* which literally means "that which is heard." The term refers both to the way the texts were acquired and to the way they were passed on to future generations. Memorized and recited orally, the Vedas formed the basis for ancient religious rituals in India.

The Rig Veda

The Rig Veda, which means "knowledge in verse," is the oldest and most important of the four Vedas. It contains over one thousand verse hymns. Although the text of this collection runs as long as the *Iliad* and the *Odyssey* together, the Rig Veda was orally recited and passed on from generation to generation for more than three thousand years. Priests known as *Brahmans* (also spelled brahmins) preserved the text during this long time span by using special memorization techniques, including group chanting. The Rig Veda is a classic of world literature as well as an invaluable source of historical information about early Indian religious and social development.

Vishnu, Seated on the Serpent Sesha, Holding a Shell, Mace, Disc, and Lotus. Early 20th century, India. Ivory. Freud Museum, London.

Vedism

Vedism was the religion of the Aryans who entered India from central Asia about 1500 B.C. The religion involved elaborate sacrifices to a number of gods, among them the fire god Agni and the warrior god Indra. The hymns of the Rig Veda were composed for these sacrificial ceremonies, which were led by Brahmans. Hinduism, the predominant religion in India today, gradually evolved from Vedism, and Hindu priests still recite Vedic verses as part of religious rituals and ceremonies.

Hymns

The word *hymn* comes from the Greek *hymnos,* meaning "song of praise," and it has kept close to this original meaning, especially in a Christian context. The earliest known hymns were written by the Sumerians and praise the ancient gods of Mesopotamia. The ancient Egyptians and the Greeks and Romans also sang songs of praise to their deities. The term is also applied to a section of a longer religious poem that describes a particular event, like the Creation Hymn in this selection and in the selection from the Mayan Popol Vuh (page 1041).

from the Rig Veda

Translated by
Wendy Doniger O'Flaherty

Indra. 7th–8th century, Balawaste, India. Wall painting. National Museum of India, New Delhi. Indra is a major god in Indian mythology.

Viewing the art: What qualities might you associate with Indra, based on this painting?

Creation Hymn (Nāsadīya)

1 There was neither non-existence nor existence then;
there was neither the realm of space nor the sky
which is beyond. What stirred? Where? In whose
protection? Was there water, bottomlessly deep?

2 There was neither death nor immortality then. There
was no distinguishing sign of night nor of day. That
one breathed, windless, by its own impulse. Other
than that there was nothing beyond.

3 Darkness was hidden by darkness in the beginning;
with no distinguishing sign, all this was water. The
life force that was covered with emptiness, that one
arose through the power of heat.

4 Desire came upon that one in the beginning; that
was the first seed of mind. Poets seeking in their
heart with wisdom found the bond of existence in
non-existence.

5 Their cord was extended across. Was there below?
Was there above? There were seed-placers; there were
powers. There was impulse beneath; there was giving-
forth above.
6 Who really knows? Who will here proclaim it?
Whence was it produced? Whence is this creation?
The gods came afterwards, with the creation of this
universe. Who then knows whence it has arisen?
7 Whence this creation has arisen—perhaps it formed
itself, or perhaps it did not—the one who looks down
on it, in the highest heaven, only he knows—or
perhaps he does not know.

Vishnu Sleeping Between the Two Periods of Cosmic Evolution. 17th century, Rajasthan, India. Painting on paper, 24 x 30 cm. National Gallery, Prague, Czech Republic.

Viewing the painting: Why is the composition of this painting important? What does it tell you about Vishnu?

Responding to Literature

Personal Response

What images or phrases in this hymn do you find most striking or puzzling? Share and discuss your choices with a partner.

Analyzing Literature

Recall and Interpret

1. How does the speaker describe the conditions before creation?
2. Who or what might the speaker be referring to in the sentence "That one breathed, windless, by its own impulse"?
3. What does the speaker suggest might be the source or sources of creation?
4. How does the speaker describe the relationship of the gods to creation? What does this imply about the gods?
5. What conclusions does the speaker draw about creation?

Evaluate and Connect

6. What is your opinion of the speaker's conclusions about creation? Explain the reasons for your opinion.
7. A **paradox** is a statement that seems contradictory but may reveal an unexpected truth (see page R9). Identify a paradox in this hymn and explain it in your own words.
8. In the Reading Focus on page 496, you discussed familiar creation stories and theories. Compare one of them with this creation hymn.
9. Why does this hymn pose so many unanswered questions?
10. This hymn was composed thousands of years ago. Do you find it relevant today? Explain your answer.

Literary ELEMENTS

Connotation

Connotation refers to the unspoken or unwritten meanings associated with a word beyond its dictionary definition, or *denotation.* In the "Creation Hymn," for example, a number of words and phrases in stanzas four and five are associated with fertility and growth, including "seed," "seed-placers," "impulse beneath," and "giving-forth above." Paying attention to the connotations of words is often helpful in understanding literature that deals with abstract concepts.

1. Create a word web listing the associations you have with the word *poet.*
2. Why might "poets" be mentioned in stanza four of this hymn in connection with creation?

- See **Literary Terms Handbook,** p. R2.

Extending Your Response

Interdisciplinary Activity

Social Studies: Vedic Religion The Vedic religion involved the worship of many gods who were linked to various elements of nature and the ritual sacrifices that were made to these gods. Use reference sources in the library to find out more about the Vedic deities and rituals. Summarize your findings in a brief written report.

Performing

Choral Reading The Vedic hymns were originally composed to be recited, chanted, or sung aloud. Working with a small group, prepare a choral reading of the "Creation Hymn." During your group rehearsal, try to capture the spirit and mood of the hymn. Present your reading to your classmates.

Save your work for your portfolio.

INDIA, c. 400 B.C.–A.D. 400

Before You Read

Hundred Questions from the *Mahabharata*

Reading Focus

Suppose you wanted to test a person's wisdom and character. What questions would you pose?

List Questions With a small group, brainstorm a list of questions you might ask for this test.

Setting a Purpose Read to see what kinds of questions are used to test the wisdom and character of the hero in this ancient Indian epic.

Building Background

The *Mahabharata*

The *Mahabharata* (mə hä′ bär′ ə tə) is a classic epic poem of ancient India. The title is a Sanskrit word meaning "great story of the Bharata dynasty." The *Mahabharata* tells about a feud between two related families–the Pandavas (pän dä′ väs) and the Kauravas (kôr ä′ vəs)–who live in northern India and are descendants of King Bharata. In the story, the five Pandava brothers lose their kingdom and all their wealth to the Kauravas, their cousins, and are exiled for twelve years in the forest. After completing their long exile, they battle to regain their kingdom. Although they win the battle, the destruction is so great that their victory is hollow.

Interwoven with this main story in the *Mahabharata* are other myths and legends as well as discussions of religion and other subjects. One part of the epic, the *Bhagavad Gita* (bä′ gə väd′ gē′ tə), is one of the most important religious texts of Hinduism. However, Hindus value all of the *Mahabharata* for its religious teachings. The central focus of the epic is the Hindu concept of *dharma* (där′ mə), which is a code of conduct or a person's duty in life. Hindus believe that people preserve the natural order of the universe by fulfilling their responsibilities according to their station in life.

Hindu tradition holds that a wise man named Vyasa dictated the Sanskrit verses of the *Mahabharata* to the god of wisdom, Ganesha, who wrote them down. Many scholars, however, consider the epic to be a collection of writings by different authors, compiled in its present form about A.D. 400.

"Hundred Questions" is an episode from Book 2 of the *Mahabharata.* This episode takes place when the Pandava brothers have nearly completed their twelve-year exile in the forest. The account you will read is from a simplified prose version of the epic by the Indian author R. K. Narayan.

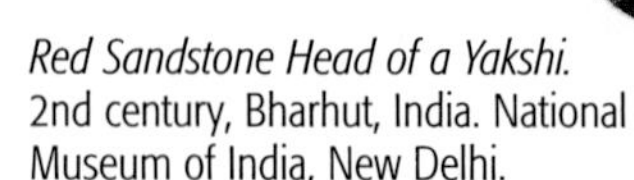
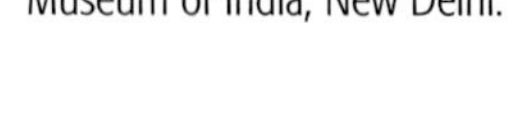

Red Sandstone Head of a Yakshi. 2nd century, Bharhut, India. National Museum of India, New Delhi.

Vocabulary Preview

austerity (ôs ter′ ə tē) *n.* a spiritual, morally strict act; p. 502

poignancy (poin′ yən sē) *n.* the quality of painfully affecting one's feelings; p. 503

inordinate (in ôr′ də nit) *adj.* excessive; p. 503

fatuous (fa′cho͞o əs) *adj.* silly, foolish; p. 504

avarice (av′ ər is) *n.* greed; p. 505

"Who is the friend of one about to die?"

"The charity done in one's lifetime."

"Who is that friend you could count as God given?"

"A wife."

"What is one's highest duty?"

"To refrain from injury."

To another series of questions on renunciation, Yudhistira gave the answers: "Pride, if renounced, makes one agreeable; anger, if renounced, brings no regret; desire, if renounced, will make one rich; avarice, if renounced, brings one happiness. True tranquility is of the heart. . . . Mercy may be defined as wishing happiness to all creatures. . . . Ignorance is not knowing one's duties. . . . Wickedness consists in speaking ill of others."

"Who is a true brahmin? By birth or study or conduct?"

"Not by birth, but by knowledge of the scriptures and right conduct. A brahmin born to the caste,[8] even if he has mastered the Vedas,[9] must be viewed as of the lowest caste if his heart is impure."

There were a hundred or more questions in all. Yudhistira felt faint from thirst, grief, and suspense, and could only whisper his replies. Finally, the yaksha asked, "Answer four more questions, and you may find your brothers—at least one of them—revived. . . . Who is really happy?"

"One who has scanty means but is free from debt; he is truly a happy man."

"What is the greatest wonder?"

"Day after day and hour after hour, people die and corpses are carried along, yet the onlookers never realize that they are also to die one day, but think they will live for ever. This is the greatest wonder of the world."

"What is the Path?"

"The Path is what the great ones have trod. When one looks for it, one will not find it by study of scriptures or arguments, which are contradictory and conflicting."

At the end of these answers, the yaksha said, "From among these brothers of yours, you may choose one to revive."

Yudhistira said, "If I have only a single choice, let my young brother, Nakula, rise."

The yaksha said, "He is after all your stepbrother. I'd have thought you'd want Arjuna or Bhima, who must be dear to you."

"Yes, they are," replied Yudhistira. "But I have had two mothers. If only two in our family are to survive, let both the mothers have one of their sons alive. Let Nakula also live, in fairness to the memory of my other mother Madri."

The yaksha said, "You have indeed pleased me with your humility and the judiciousness of your answers. Now let all your brothers rise up and join you."

The yaksha thereafter revived all his brothers and also conferred on Yudhistira the following boon: "Wherever you may go henceforth, with your brothers and wife, you will have the blessing of being unrecognized." The yaksha was none other than Yama, the God of Justice, and father of Yudhistira, who had come to test Yudhistira's strength of mind and also to bless him with the power to remain incognito—a special boon in view of the conditions laid down for the last year of exile.

8. *Caste* here means "a position of social rank or prestige."
9. The *Vedas*—sacred Hindu writings—are believed to contain eternal truths that have been divinely revealed.

Vocabulary
avarice (av′ ər is) *n.* greed

Responding to Literature

Personal Response

What questions would you like to ask Yudhistira?

Analyzing Literature

Recall

1. What does the brahmin ask the Pandavas to do?
2. Summarize what happens to the first four Pandava brothers at the pond.
3. What happens to Yudhistira at the pond?
4. What choice does the yaksha pose to Yudhistira at the end? What decision does Yudhistira make?
5. How does the yaksha reward Yudhistira?

Interpret

6. In your opinion, what does Yudhistira's reaction to the brahmin's request reveal about Yudhistira's character?
7. How would you characterize the way that the four younger Pandava brothers act at the pond?
8. What kinds of questions does the yaksha pose to Yudhistira? How would you characterize Yudhistira's answers?
9. What does Yudhistira's decision to revive his step-brother reveal about his character? Support your answer with details from the selection.
10. Why is the yaksha pleased with Yudhistira?

Evaluate and Connect

11. In this episode, how does Yudhistira differ from his brothers? Support your answer with details from the selection.
12. For the Reading Focus on page 500, you brainstormed a list of questions that you would use to test a person's wisdom and character. How are your questions similar to the yaksha's? How are they different?
13. An **epic** reflects the values of the culture in which it originates (see **Literary Terms Handbook**, page R3). What values are promoted in this episode of the *Mahabharata*?
14. What do you think is the most important question the yaksha poses to Yudhistira? Give reasons for your opinion.
15. What kinds of tests of character does modern life pose? Describe a situation from your own experience that tested your character.

Literary Criticism

"The *Mahabharata,*" suggests critic E. Washburn Hopkins, "may be viewed as a rich store of philosphical and religious lore as well as a tale . . . The chief interest of the religious lore," Hopkins adds, "lies in the insistence upon the loving devotion of the worshipper and the saving grace of the supreme spirit." Do you agree that this episode has both a moral and narrative dimension? How are the religious ideas expressed? Answer in a one-page essay, citing specific passages for support.

Literary ELEMENTS

Epic Hero

An **epic hero** is a legendary, larger-than-life figure whose adventures form the core of an epic poem. The epic hero personifies a society's ideals of courage and nobility. In this episode from the *Mahabharata,* Yudhistira embodies the virtues that people in ancient Indian society aspired to.

1. In many epics, such as *Gilgamesh* and the *Iliad,* heroes demonstrate great physical strength and endurance. How is Yudhistira different from these heroes?
2. Skim through "Hundred Questions" again. Make a list of Yudhistira's virtues based on his actions and on his answers to the yaksha's questions.

- See **Literary Terms Handbook,** p. R3.

Literature and Writing

Writing About Literature

Analyzing Theme What is the main message or lesson of this episode from the *Mahabharata*? What do you learn from Yudhistira's actions and answers? In a paragraph, state the central theme of "Hundred Questions" and explain how the theme is demonstrated in the story.

Personal Writing

Original Answers In your journal, write your own answers to the following questions that the yaksha posed to Yudhistira: What is important for those who seek prosperity? What is one's highest duty? Who is really happy? What is the greatest wonder?

Extending Your Response

Literature Groups

Explaining Riddles Many of the questions that the yaksha poses to Yudhistira are riddles. The answers to some of these riddles are puzzling. Make a list of the riddles and discuss the meaning of the answers in your group. Share your explanations with the rest of the class.

Learning for Life

Code of Conduct Yudhistira follows the dharma of his caste, which is the caste of rulers and warriors. Write a dharma, or code of conduct, for yourself as a student. What is a student's main duty? What responsibilities do students have to their teachers? to their fellow students? to themselves?

Internet Connection

Investigate Hinduism Search the Internet for information on Hinduism and choose one aspect to investigate in detail, such as Hindu divinities, sacred writings, or the concepts of karma or dharma. Choose a way to present your findings, such as in a poster, brochure, or a written or oral report.

Save your work for your portfolio.

VOCABULARY • Analogies

Analogies are comparisons based on relationships between words and ideas. Some analogies are based on function relationships.

guard : protect :: teacher : instruct

A function of a *guard* is to *protect;* a *teacher instructs.*

To finish an analogy, decide on the relationship of the first two words. Then apply that relationship to the second set of words.

PRACTICE Choose the word that best completes each analogy.

1. comedy : entertain :: medicine :
   a. doctor b. science c. heal
2. soap : clean :: lightbulb :
   a. change b. illuminate c. idea
3. house : shelter :: bus :
   a. car b. drive c. transportation
4. library : information :: cafeteria :
   a. food b. trays c. diners
5. information : knowledge :: food :
   a. drink b. dinner c. energy

- For more about analogies, see **Communications Skills Handbook,** p. R77.

The Art of Translation

The *Mahabharata* as Shadow Play

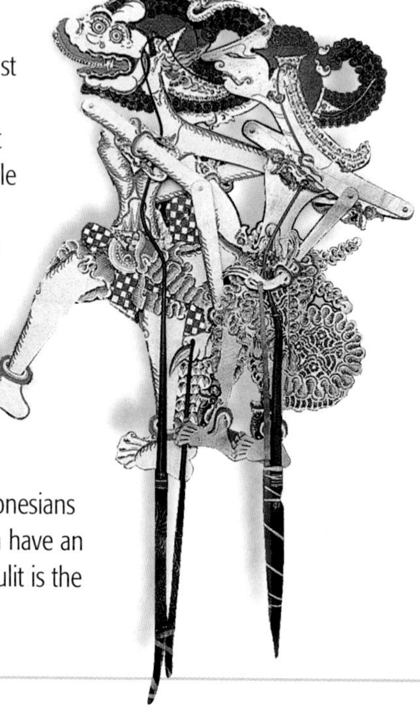

In a village home in Indonesia at midnight, a few dozen people sit before a long screen lit from behind, watching vibrant shadow images of Arjuna and his brothers as they fight a bloody battle against the Kauravas. These Indonesian villagers know the story of the *Mahabharata* well, even though most of them do not know Sanskrit and have never read this Indian epic. They've learned the popular tale from watching *wayang kulit*–Indonesian shadow puppet plays.

Like many other classic works of literature, the *Mahabharata* has been retold in other languages and translated into different media, such as film. Translating a written story into other media, such as plays, dance, or film, can greatly increase the audience that the work reaches. Many people, for example, may experience the drama *Romeo and Juliet* as a ballet or the memoir *Out of Africa* as a movie.

Watching shadow puppet plays is one of the main ways that Indonesians experience the stories of the *Mahabharata.* The people of Indonesia have an especially strong tradition in the performing arts, of which wayang kulit is the most prestigious.

Staging a Shadow Play

Staging a shadow theater performance of the *Mahabharata* is no simple task. A performance may last for eight or nine hours, beginning at around nine in the evening and continuing until dawn. The performance may take place in the home of a wealthy sponsor in a rural village, where shadow plays often are commissioned for weddings and other special occasions, or it may be presented in a city auditorium.

No matter where the play takes place, the key figure in the performance is the *dalang,* a skilled artist who functions as a storyteller, puppeteer, singer, sound effects technician, and director. Sitting cross-legged on the floor for the entire performance, the dalang works with a large wooden chest of leather puppets, intricately carved and painted to indicate not only a particular character or character type but also that character's personality. The puppets are animated by sticks–one for the body and one for each arm.

The puppet chest doubles as a sound effects box. The dalang strikes the wood, or a small bronze plate on the chest, with two wooden hammers, making sounds that set a rhythm or punctuate moments in the drama. The dalang holds one hammer between the toes of the right foot and the other in the left hand. Accompanying the dalang are singers and an orchestra that includes gongs, bronze bar instruments, and drums.

Bringing a Story to Life

Besides manipulating the puppets and creating sound effects, the dalang brings the stories of the *Mahabharata* to life for the audience through narration, dialogue, and singing. The dalang speaks all the parts and interprets the characters by giving them distinctive voices and ways of moving. Arjuna, for example, is portrayed as a refined character who speaks in a high voice and moves fluidly, while Bhima bounds across the screen. In battle scenes, Bhima strikes opponents with a big club and Arjuna shoots his bow. Female characters, like Draupadi, the wife of the Pandava brothers, take small, dainty steps. The dalang also imitates the chatter of monkeys, the grunts of pigs, and the neighing of horses. Birds are made to swoop down, and monkeys take graceful leaps.

Although parts of every shadow play are standardized, much of the dalang's work involves improvisation. Working without a script, the dalang makes up dialogue to fill out stories, weaves subplots into the main story, and injects jokes and slapstick into the stories.

Music is played throughout the performance. In cuing the orchestra, the dalang chooses from a repertoire of over a hundred musical selections that fit certain types of scenes, characters, or other elements of the drama. The dalang also displays his musical skill by singing lines of classical poetry or songs.

Through the magic of shadow puppet theater, enjoyed by both adults and children, the story and characters of the *Mahabharata* have become part of the common culture of Indonesians. In everyday life, people often refer to characters from the *Mahabharata.* An Indonesian might say another person is "like Bhima"—that is, honest, brave, and strong. Or a person might be said to be "like Arjuna," refined and attractive to women.

Viewing the photographs: Some viewers of the shadow theater like to sit behind the screen, where they can watch the dalang as he brings the puppets to life. A larger (and more enthusiastic) group sits on the other side, where they can watch images like the one shown above.

RESPOND

1. In what ways would the experience of watching a shadow puppet performance of the *Mahabharata* differ from the experience of reading the story?
2. Which experience do you think you would prefer? Why?

INDIA, c. 200 B.C.

Before You Read

The Lion-Makers from the *Panchatantra*

Reading Focus

What stories have you read or heard that teach practical lessons about life?

Quickwrite In your journal, list the titles of some of these stories, such as the Aesop fable "The Tortoise and the Hare." Next to each title, write a sentence or two that sums up the lesson to be learned.

Setting a Purpose Read to discover the life lesson in the story "The Lion-Makers."

Building Background

The *Panchatantra*

The *Panchatantra* (pun′ chə tän′ trə) is a collection of ancient Indian fables or stories that contain lessons about living wisely. The Sanskrit *Pancha-tantra* means "Five Chapters," which describes the way the collection is arranged. Each of the five chapters in the collection contains a variety of stories told within a single "frame" story. This story tells of a king who asks a learned Brahman, or Hindu priest, to educate his three foolish sons. The Brahman, named Vishnusharman (vish′ nōō shär′ mən), teaches the boys with stories that are instructive as well as entertaining. Featuring verse proverbs that are easily memorized, the *Panchatantra* is intended as a *niti-shastra* (ni′ tē shä′ strə), or a "textbook on the wise conduct of life."

The fables of the *Panchatantra* were first collected and written down around 200 B.C., though many of the stories had already been part of the oral tradition for much longer. Over time, the fables spread through Asia and Europe, inspiring storytellers in many lands. Relatives of some of the tales can be found in *The Thousand and One Nights* (see page 453) and in Aesop's fables (see page 251).

Warriors Fighting a Lion-Griffin. 5th century, Gupta Dynasty, India. Stone relief. Samath Museum, Uttar Pradesh, India.

Vocabulary Preview

scholarship (skol′ ər ship′) *n.* academic achievement or knowledge; p. 511

attainment (ə tān′ mənt) *n.* an accomplishment; p. 511

dullard (dul′ ərd) *n.* a stupid or unimaginative person; p. 512

nullity (nul′ ə tē) *n.* a mere nothing; insignificance; p. 512

from the Panchatantra

Translated by Arthur W. Ryder

Indeed, there is wisdom in the saying:

Scholarship is less than sense;
Therefore seek intelligence:
Senseless scholars in their pride
Made a lion; then they died.

"How was that?" asked the wheel-bearer. And the gold-finder told the story of

The Lion-Makers

In a certain town were four Brahmans who lived in friendship. Three of them had reached the far shore of all scholarship, but lacked sense. The other found scholarship distasteful; he had nothing but sense.

One day they met for consultation. "What is the use of attainments," said they, "if one does not travel, win the favor of kings, and acquire money? Whatever we do, let us all travel."

Vocabulary
scholarship (skol′ ər ship′) *n.* academic achievement or knowledge
attainment (ə tān′ mənt) *n.* an accomplishment

Prince Salim Surprised by Lion While Hunting. c. 1595, Mughal India. Miniature. Private collection.
Viewing the painting: Compare the mood of this painting with the mood of the fable.

But when they had gone a little way, the eldest of them said: "One of us, the fourth, is a dullard, having nothing but sense. Now nobody gains the favorable attention of kings by simple sense without scholarship. Therefore we will not share our earnings with him. Let him turn back and go home."

Then the second said: "My intelligent friend, you lack scholarship. Please go home." But the third said: "No, no. This is no way to behave. For we have played together since we were little boys. Come along, my noble friend. You shall have a share of the money we earn."

With this agreement they continued their journey, and in a forest they found the bones of a dead lion. Thereupon one of them said: "A good opportunity to test the ripeness of our scholarship. Here lies some kind of creature, dead. Let us bring it to life by means of the scholarship we have honestly won."

Then the first said: "I know how to assemble the skeleton." The second said: "I can supply skin, flesh, and blood." The third said: "I can give it life."

So the first assembled the skeleton, the second provided skin, flesh, and blood. But while the third was intent on giving the breath of life, the man of sense advised against it, remarking: "This is a lion. If you bring him to life, he will kill every one of us."

"You simpleton!" said the other, "it is not I who will reduce scholarship to a nullity." "In that case," came the reply, "wait a moment, while I climb this convenient tree."

When this had been done, the lion was brought to life, rose up, and killed all three. But the man of sense, after the lion had gone elsewhere, climbed down and went home.

"And that is why I say:
Scholarship is less than sense, . . .
and the rest of it."

Vocabulary
dullard (dul′ ərd) *n.* a stupid or unimaginative person
nullity (nul′ ə tē) *n.* a mere nothing; insignificance

Responding to Literature

Personal Response

What is your initial reaction to this story?

Analyzing Literature

Recall and Interpret

1. How does the fourth Brahman differ from the other three?
2. What do the four Brahmans seek on their travels?
3. Why do the first two Brahmans want to exclude the fourth from their travels?
4. What do the Brahmans discover in the forest, and what do the first three decide to do? Why does the fourth Brahman disagree with their plan?
5. Describe the end of the story and the lesson suggested by it.

Evaluate and Connect

6. Do you think the three Brahmans are most handicapped by their education, their lack of common sense, or their pride? Explain your answer.
7. Do you agree or disagree with the lesson of this story? Why?
8. A **fable** is a brief story told to teach a lesson (see page R4). How is "The Lion-Makers" like or unlike other fables you know?
9. Describe a contemporary situation in which the lesson of this story might apply.
10. Describe a book or movie that teaches a similar lesson.

Literary Criticism

According to one critic, the "*Panchatantra* belongs in part to a class of works known as . . . *arthashastra* ('science of polity'), which involves . . . practical and shrewd knowledge." In a few paragraphs, explain what practical knowledge "The Lion-Makers" offers. Give specific evidence to support your view.

Literary ELEMENTS

Moral

A **moral** is a practical lesson about right and wrong conduct, often in an instructive story such as a fable or parable. A moral is the equivalent of a theme, or main idea. In a fable, the moral is dramatized through narration. In some fables, the writer states the moral explicitly; in others, the reader must infer the moral from what happens in the story.

1. Is the moral of "The Lion-Makers" explicitly stated? If so, where and how?
2. State the moral of "The Lion-Makers" in your own words.

- See **Literary Terms Handbook,** p. R8.

Extending Your Response

Interdisciplinary Activity

Zoology: Asiatic Lion When the *Panchatantra* stories were first collected in India about two thousand years ago, Asiatic lions were common on the subcontinent. Today, only a small population of about three hundred Asiatic lions remains, living in the Gir forest of Gujarat, in western India. Use library resources and the Internet to investigate the prospects for the survival of these lions and summarize your findings in an oral report.

Creative Writing

Retelling a Fable Review the list of stories and lessons you made for the Reading Focus on page 510. Choose a story and write your own version of it. Feel free to invent details to make the tale as entertaining as possible. At the end, state the story's moral. After rehearsing your fable, read it aloud to the class.

Save your work for your portfolio.

Technology Skills

Internet: Researching World Cultures

Cultures and traditions vary from community to community, region to region, country to country. The literature of a community reflects its beliefs, its traditions, and its uniqueness. In essence, the literature of a culture offers a word-picture of its people.

You might want to know more about those aspects of culture that interest you–that connect in some way with your own life. For instance, you might want to know how young people live in a particular culture or what daily life is like in that culture. You may be interested in a culture's food preferences, clothing styles, entertainment, music, or other art forms.

Decide What You Want

Look through your World Literature textbook and select a region that interests you. In your journal, write the name of the region you wish to research and explain why you chose that particular place. Brainstorm the kinds of cultural traditions you wish to explore. If you find yourself getting stuck, think about the kinds of things you enjoy in your own culture. For example, if you like holidays, you may wish to explore how other cultures celebrate their festivals and national observances. Generate a list of four or five customs or traditions to explore.

TECHNOLOGY TIP

Tools for searching the Internet include search engines and directories. Search engines look for keywords you provide; directories arrange sites into a hierarchy of topics and subtopics. In reality, the distinction between the two tools is somewhat blurred. Many search engines include a directory, and most directories include a keyword search feature. Usually, it's best to start with a directory when your topic is general (for example, astronomy) and a search engine when you are looking for a very specific topic (for example, black holes).

About Languages

English is the major language of the Internet, but as you connect to sites in other countries, you will encounter other languages from time to time. If you use Alta Vista as your search engine, it will allow you to get a translation into English. Look for the underlined word *Translation* at the end of the site description. In some cases, a site will offer a choice of languages, usually at or near the top of its home page. Some sites, however, will be available only to those who know the language of the people who created it.

If you are fluent in one or more languages other than English, you may want to seek out sites that use another language. Also, if you are studying another language, sites in a country that uses that language will give you an interesting opportunity for practice.

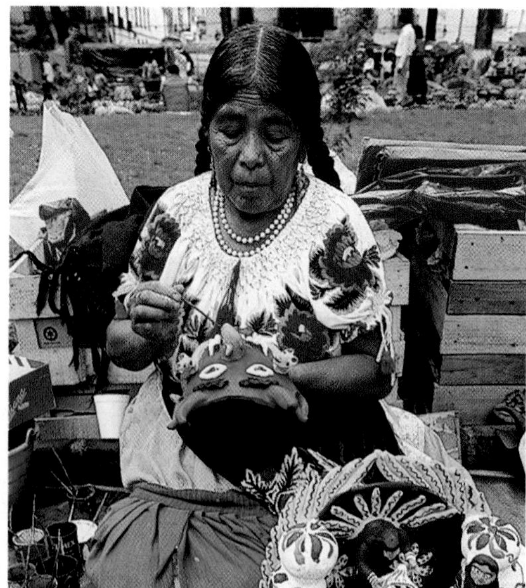

Woman making ceramic figures. Morelia, Mexico.

Take a Virtual Tour

1. Conduct an Internet search for information about your topic. You can begin with the site *www.yahoo.com/regional/countries,* which will bring up a list of countries around the world. Clicking on any major country's name will lead to a list of subtopics, including *Society and Culture.* You could also try a search using a country's name and *"official site"* or *"cultural traditions"* as keywords. You may still have to sift through a number of sites before you find the information you want. On the other hand, you may come across information that will encourage you to refine or change the nature of your inquiry. In either case, be sure to allow enough time to do adequate and satisfying research on your chosen area.

2. Record the URL (Net address) of each site you find useful and jot down or print out what you learn about the topic you are researching. Remember: You should have a URL for every fact you discover. That way, others who wish to learn more can benefit from your research. Take notes and document your research. (See pages R64–R69 of Writing Handbook.)

3. Download text, pictures, music, graphs, maps, or other items of interest. Check with the lab instructor about where your files should be saved.

4. Organize your research and compose a report on the cultural traditions of the country or region you toured on the Internet. Compare them with the traditions in your culture.

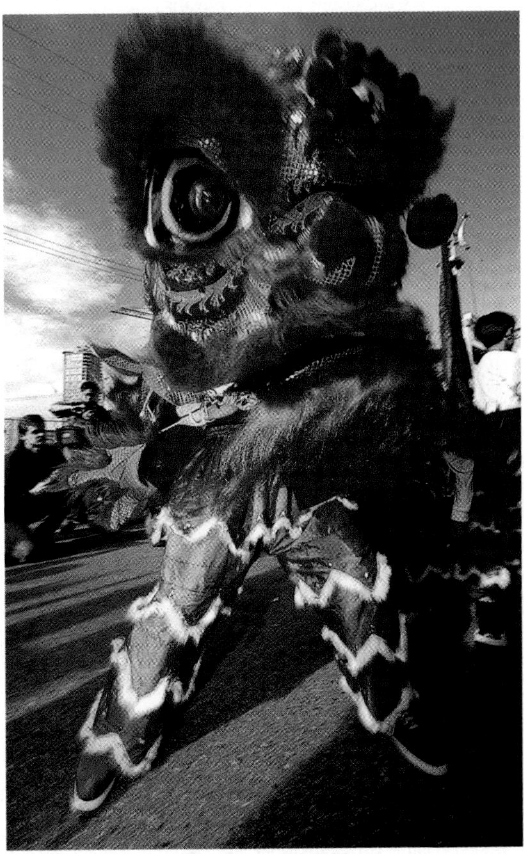

Dragon mask at Chinese New Year celebration.

ACTIVITIES

1. Share your presentation with your class, using both factual information and visual aids that you have obtained in the course of your research.

2. With your classmates, volunteer to present your cultural research to a local elementary school class, a community center, a nursing home, or a senior center. Adapt your report as necessary to suit your audience. Practice and time your presentation so that it can be completed within the expected time frame.

INDIA, 1892

Before You Read

The Kabuliwallah

Meet Rabindranath Tagore

"Every child comes with the message that God is not yet discouraged of man."

Rabindranath Tagore (rə bēn′ drə nät tə gôr′) was born in Calcutta, India, into an upper-caste Hindu family with strong religious and artistic traditions. "Our home was permeated with the spirit of creation," Tagore wrote. Besides writing poetry, short stories, novels, plays, and essays, Tagore also composed songs—and when he was nearly seventy years old, he became a painter. Considered by many to be the greatest creative writer of modern India, he introduced new literary forms and styles into Bengali literature. (Bengal is a region in eastern India and Bangladesh; Bengali is the language spoken there.) In 1913 Tagore became the first Asian writer to be awarded the Nobel Prize for Literature.

In the 1890s, Tagore managed his family's country estate, an experience that aroused his sympathy for the poor living in India's villages. He wrote many of his best short stories, including *The Kabuliwallah*, during this period.

Tagore was born in 1861 and died in 1941.

Reading Focus

Have you ever known someone who easily develops a rapport with young children?

List It! Think about the qualities that enable this person to communicate and bond with young children. In your journal, make a list of the person's traits.

Setting a Purpose Read about an unusual character who develops a rapport with a young child.

Building Background

Kabuliwallahs in Calcutta

A *Kabuliwallah* (kə bo͞o′ lē wä′ lä) is a peddler from Kabul, the capital of Afghanistan. Kabul is more than a thousand miles northwest of Calcutta, India, where this story takes place. In the late 1800s, peddlers from Kabul were common on the streets of Calcutta. They sold fruits and nuts, carrying them in huge bags on their shoulders. As outsiders, the Kabuliwallahs were often viewed with fear or disdain.

A Tireless Artist

Rabindranath Tagore worked all his life for a world where, as he wrote in his Nobel Prize–winning *Gitanjali,* "the mind is without fear and the head is held high." For some artists, this prize, which brought Tagore's work to the attention of the world, might have been the culmination of a career. Yet Tagore–already fifty-two when he received the award–continued to experiment. With international recognition, he lectured around the world, speaking of India's spiritual traditions and urging independence for his country. When he passed away, at the age of eighty, he might well have claimed to have lived a life, in his own words, "where tireless striving stretches its arms toward perfection."

Vocabulary Preview

vex (veks) *v.* to annoy or agitate; p. 517
demur (di mur′) *n.* hesitation or objection; p. 519
formidable (for′ mi də bəl) *adj.* tending to inspire awe, wonder, or fear; p. 520
arid (ar′ id) *adj.* excessively dry; p. 520
fettered (fe′ tərd) *adj.* chained; p. 521

The Kabuliwallah

Rabindranath Tagore
Translated by Sister Nivedita

Bhuleshwar 2, 1978. Anjolie Ela Menon (India). Mixed media. Private collection.

My five years' old daughter Mini cannot live without chattering. I really believe that in all her life she has not wasted a minute in silence. Her mother is often vexed at this, and would stop her prattle, but I would not. To see Mini quiet is unnatural, and I cannot bear it long. And so my own talk with her is always lively.

Vocabulary
vex (veks) *v.* to annoy or agitate

One morning, for instance, when I was in the midst of the seventeenth chapter of my new novel, my little Mini stole into the room, and putting her hand into mine, said: "Father! Ramdayal the door-keeper calls a crow a krow! He doesn't know anything, does he?"

Before I could explain to her the differences of language in this world, she was embarked on the full tide of another subject. "What do you think, Father? Bhola says there is an elephant in the clouds, blowing water out of his trunk, and that is why it rains!"

And then, darting off anew, while I sat still making ready some reply to this last saying, "Father! what relation is Mother to you?"

"My dear little sister in the law!" I murmured involuntarily to myself, but with a grave face contrived to answer: "Go and play with Bhola, Mini! I am busy!"

The window of my room overlooks the road. The child had seated herself at my feet near my table, and was playing softly, drumming on her knees. I was hard at work on my seventeenth chapter, where Protrap Singh, the hero, had just caught Kanchanlata, the heroine, in his arms, and was about to escape with her by the third story window of the castle, when all of a sudden Mini left her play, and ran to the window, crying, "A Kabuliwallah! a Kabuliwallah!" Sure enough in the street below was a Kabuliwallah, passing slowly along. He wore the loose soiled clothing of his people, with a tall turban; there was a bag on his back, and he carried boxes of grapes in his hand.

I cannot tell what were my daughter's feelings at the sight of this man, but she began to call him loudly. "Ah!" I thought, "he will come in, and my seventeenth chapter will never be finished!" At which exact moment the Kabuliwallah turned, and looked up at the child. When she saw this, overcome by terror, she fled to her mother's protection, and disappeared. She had a blind belief that inside the bag, which the big man carried, there were perhaps two or three other children like herself. The peddler meanwhile entered my doorway, and greeted me with a smiling face.

So precarious was the position of my hero and my heroine, that my first impulse was to stop and buy something, since the man had been called. I made some small purchases, and a conversation began about Abdurrahman, the Russians, the English, and the Frontier Policy.[1]

As he was about to leave, he asked: "And where is the little girl, sir?"

And I, thinking that Mini must get rid of her false fear, had her brought out.

She stood by my chair, and looked at the Kabuliwallah and his bag. He offered her nuts and raisins, but she would not be tempted, and only clung the closer to me, with all her doubts increased.

This was their first meeting.

One morning, however, not many days later, as I was leaving the house, I was startled to find Mini, seated on a bench near the door, laughing and talking, with the great Kabuliwallah at her feet. In all her life, it appeared, my small daughter had never found so patient a listener, save her father. And already the corner of her little *sari* was stuffed with almonds and raisins, the gift of her visitor. "Why did you give her those?" I said, and taking out an eight-anna bit,[2] I

Did You Know?
A *sari* is a garment worn by women of southern Asia. It is made from several yards of lightweight cloth draped so that one end forms a skirt and the other a shoulder or head covering.

1. This discussion refers to political issues between India and Afghanistan.
2. An *eight-anna bit* is a small coin, worth half a rupee.

"For them, it's not a sin."

"Who told you this nonsense?"

"I just know it."

"I read. I must be sinning."

"For city women, it's no sin. It is for village women."

We both laughed at this remark. She had not learned to question all that she was told to believe. I thought that if she found peace in her convictions, who was I to question them?

Her body redeemed her dark complexion, an intense sense of ecstasy always radiating from it, a resilient sweetness. They say a woman's body is like a lump of dough, some women have the looseness of underkneaded dough while others have the clinging plasticity of leavened dough. Rarely does a woman have a body that can be equated to rightly kneaded dough, a baker's pride. Angoori's body belonged to this category, her rippling muscles impregnated with the metallic resilience of a coiled spring. I felt her face, arms, breasts, legs with my eyes and experienced a profound languor. I thought of Prabhati: old, short, loose-jawed, a man whose stature and angularity would be the death of Euclid.[3] Suddenly a funny idea struck me: Angoori was the dough covered by Prabhati. He was her napkin, not her taster. I felt a laugh welling up inside me, but I checked it for fear that Angoori would sense what I was laughing about. I asked her how marriages are arranged where she came from.

"A girl, when she's five or six, adores someone's feet. He is the husband."

"How does she know it?"

"Her father takes money and flowers and puts them at his feet."

"That's the father adoring, not the girl."

"He does it for the girl. So it's the girl herself."

"But the girl has never seen him before!"

"Yes, girls don't see."

"Not a single girl ever sees her future husband!"

"No . . . ," she hesitated. After a long, pensive pause, she added, "Those in love . . . they see them."

"Do girls in your village have love affairs?"

"A few."

"Those in love, they don't sin?" I remembered her observation regarding education for women.

"They don't. See, what happens is that a man makes the girl eat the weed and then she starts loving him."

"Which weed?"

"The wild one."

"Doesn't the girl know that she has been given the weed?"

"No, he gives it to her in a *paan*.[4] After that, nothing satisfies her but to be with him, her man. I know. I've seen it with my own eyes."

"Whom did you see?"

"A friend; she was older than me."

"And what happened?"

"She went crazy. Ran away with him to the city."

"How do you know it was because of the weed?"

"What else could it be? Why would she leave her parents. He brought her many things from the city: clothes, trinkets, sweets."

"Where does this weed come in?"

"In the sweets: otherwise how could she love him?"

3. *Euclid* was a Greek mathematician credited with developing geometry.

4. *Paan* is the Hindi word for "betel," a type of palm tree whose seeds and leaves are chewed as a mild stimulant.

Vocabulary

resilience (ri zil′ yens) *n.* ability to recover or adjust easily

languor (lang′ gər) *n.* weakness or weariness of body or mind

pensive (pen′ siv) *adj.* sadly or dreamily thoughtful

"Love can come in other ways. No other way here?"

"No other way. What her parents hated was that she was that way."

"Have you seen the weed?"

"No, they bring it from a far country. My mother warned me not to take *paan* or sweets from anyone. Men put the weed in them."

"You were very wise. How come your friend ate it?"

"To make herself suffer," she said sternly. The next moment her face clouded, perhaps in remembering her friend. "Crazy. She went crazy, the poor thing," she said sadly. "Never combed her hair, singing all night. . . ."

"What did she sing?"

"I don't know. They all sing when they eat the weed. Cry too."

The conversation was becoming a little too much to take, so I retired.

I found her sitting under the *neem* tree one day in a profoundly abstracted mood. Usually one could hear Angoori coming to the well; her ankle-bells would announce her approach. They were silent that day.

"What's the matter, Angoori?"

She gave me a blank look and then, recovering a little, said, "Teach me reading, *bibi*."

"What has happened?"

"Teach me to write my name."

"Why do you want to write? To write letters? To whom?"

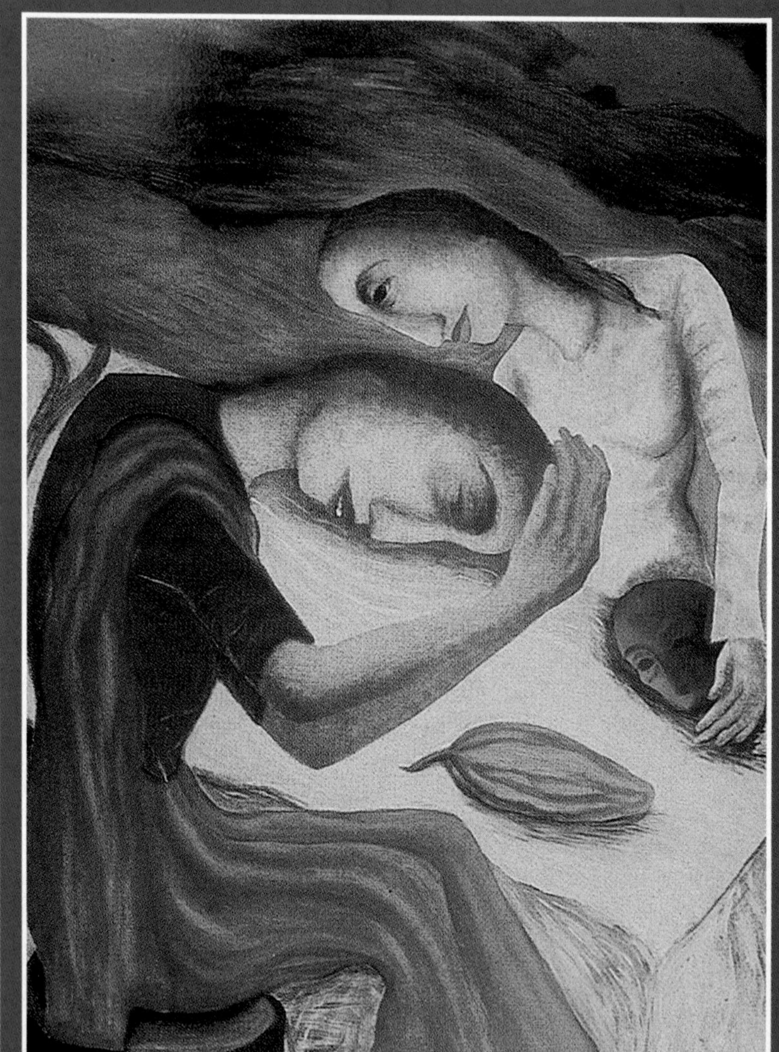

Untitled II, 1997. Lalitha Lajmi (India). 48 x 36 in. Private collection.
Viewing the painting: What type of relationship do you think exists between the people in the painting? In what ways might the relationship be similar to one of the relationships in the story?

Vocabulary
abstracted (ab strak′ tid) *adj.* preoccupied; absent-minded

She did not answer, but was once again lost in her thoughts.

"Won't you be sinning?" I asked, trying to draw her out of her mood. She would not respond. I went in for an afternoon nap. When I came out again in the evening, she was still there singing sadly to herself. When she heard me approaching, she turned around and stopped abruptly. She sat with hunched shoulders because of the chill in the evening breeze.

"You sing well, Angoori." I watched her great effort to turn back the tears and spread a pale smile across her lips.

"I don't know singing."

"But you do, Angoori!"

"This was the. . . ."

"The song your friend used to sing." I completed the sentence for her.

"I heard it from her."

"Sing it for me."

She started to recite the words. "Oh, it's just about the time of year for change. Four months winter, four months summer, four months rain! . . ."

"Not like that. Sing it for me," I asked. She wouldn't, but continued with the words:

Four months of winter reign in my heart;
My heart shivers, O my love.
Four months of summer, wind shimmers
in the sun.
Four months come the rains; clouds tremble
in the sky.

"Angoori!" I said loudly. She looked as if in a trance, as if she had eaten the weed. I felt like shaking her by the shoulders. Instead, I took her by the shoulders and asked if she had been eating regularly. She had not; she cooked for herself only, since Prabhati ate at his master's. "Did you cook today?" I asked.

"Not yet."

"Did you have tea in the morning?"

"Tea? No milk today."

"Why no milk today?"

"I didn't get any. Ram Tara. . . ."

"Fetches the milk for you?" I added. She nodded.

Ram Tara was the night watchman. Before Angoori married Prabhati, Ram Tara used to get a cup of tea at our place at the end of his watch before retiring on his cot near the well. After Angoori's arrival, he made his tea at Prabhati's. He, Angoori, and Prabhati would all have tea together sitting around the fire. Three days ago Ram Tara went to his village for a visit.

"You haven't had tea for three days?" I asked. She nodded again. "And you haven't eaten, I suppose?" She did not speak. Apparently, if she had been eating, it was as good as not eating at all.

I remembered Ram Tara: good-looking, quick-limbed, full of jokes. He had a way of talking with smiles trembling faintly at the corner of his lips.

"Angoori?"

"Yes, *bibi*."

"Could it be the weed?"

Tears flowed down her face in two rivulets, gathering into two tiny puddles at the corners of her mouth.

"Curse on me!" she started in a voice trembling with tears, "I never took sweets from him . . . not a betel even . . . but tea. . . ." She could not finish. Her words were drowned in a fast stream of tears.

Vocabulary
rivulet (riv′ yə lət) *n.* a small stream

Responding to Literature

Personal Response

What is your reaction to Angoori's predicament? Share your reaction with your classmates.

Analyzing Literature

Recall

1. Describe Angoori, her husband, and the circumstances of their marriage.
2. What are Angoori's views about reading?
3. What is the weed, and what happens to Angoori's friend when she eats it?
4. How does Angoori's behavior change?
5. How do the narrator and Angoori account for the change?

Interpret

6. Why does the narrator call Angoori a new bride "in a different way"?
7. From Angoori's comments about reading, what can you infer about her upbringing?
8. Is the weed real? What does the story imply about it and women's romantic feelings?
9. **Foreshadowing** is the use of clues by the author to prepare readers for events that will happen in a story (see **Literary Terms Handbook,** page R5). How does Angoori's singing foreshadow the outcome of the story?
10. What is Angoori's predicament at the end of the story?

Evaluate and Connect

11. What purpose might the story of the weed serve in raising daughters?
12. From the clues given in the story, what do you suppose is the narrator's life situation?
13. Like Angoori, your life is affected by the traditions of your culture. If you could change one custom of your society, what would it be? Explain why you would make that change.
14. For the Reading Focus on page 526, you made a list of the pros and cons of arranged marriages. After reading this story, how would your list change?
15. Angoori and the narrator differ in their attitudes toward literacy. How important do you think it is for a person to be able to read? What changes might the abilty to read make in a person's life?

Literary ELEMENTS

Conflict

Conflict is a struggle between two opposing forces in the plot of a story. An **external conflict** exists when a character struggles against an outside force, such as another person or the rules of society. An **internal conflict** occurs within the mind of a character who is torn between opposing feelings or goals. In many stories, the characters experience both external and internal conflicts.

1. How does Angoori's request to the narrator to teach her to read and write hint at a conflict?
2. Is Angoori's conflict external, internal, or both? Explain.

- See **Literary Terms Handbook,** p. R2.

Pratiksha (The Wait), 1994. Satish Parashar (India). Watercolor on paper, 14 x 10 in. Private collection.

Literature and Writing

Writing About Literature

Analyzing Mood In a brief essay, compare and contrast the mood at the beginning of the story with the mood at the conclusion. What does the change in mood reflect? Describe how Pritam uses sensory images to help create different moods in different parts of the story.

Personal Writing

Conflict Resolution Put yourself in Angoori's place and imagine how you would feel and react. How would you resolve the conflict you feel? In your journal, describe the options you have and tell how you would act. Then explain why you would choose such a course of action.

Extending Your Response

Literature Groups

Think About Marriage Vows Even a person who marries for love could one day be in a predicament like Angoori's. Suppose a married person falls in love with someone else. Should the person honor his or her marriage vows? Discuss these questions in your group and come to a consensus. Share your conclusion and reasons with the rest of the class.

Learning for Life

Comparing Traditions Weddings are often conducted in traditional ways even when other aspects of a culture are more internationalized. Conduct research to compare wedding traditions that are still observed today in South Central Asia with those that take place in another culture, such as East Asia or Europe.

Listening and Speaking

Dramatic Reading With a partner, stage a dramatic reading of "The Weed" for your class. One student could take the part of the narrator, and the other, Angoori. Consider adding sound effects to accompany your reading, such as jingling bracelets and Indian music.

Reading Further

If you enjoyed reading this story you might also enjoy the following:

Village India, by Stephen P. Huyler, an illustrated book that examines the ways of life in different regions of rural India.

Save your work for your portfolio.

VOCABULARY • Analogies

In some analogies, the relationship between the words is based on the degree of a condition or quality.

rivulet : river :: knoll : mountain

A rivulet and a river, for example, are both streams of water, but a *river* is larger than a *rivulet.* A knoll and a mountain are both land elevations, but a *mountain* is much higher than a *knoll.*

- For more about analogies, see **Communications Skills Handbook,** p. R77.

PRACTICE Choose the pair of words that best completes each of the following analogies.

1. tired : exhausted ::
   a. evil : naughty
   b. chipper : perky
   c. tire : automobile
   d. happy : ecstatic
   e. humiliated : embarrassed
2. misfortune : tragedy ::
   a. laughter : comedy
   b. accident : disaster
   c. yawn : boredom
   d. love : affection
   e. disappointment : satisfaction

FRANCE, c. 1160

Before You Read

The Lark

Meet Bernart de Ventadorn

"Bernart was honored and esteemed by all good people, and his songs were honored and beloved."

—*Anonymous*

Bernart de Ventadorn (ber nart′ də vähn′ tə dorn′) was a French troubadour—a poet-musician—who lived in the 1100s. Little is known for certain about his life. However, the legends about him read like a fairy tale. According to these legends, Bernart was the son of servants who worked in the castle of Ventadorn. He grew up to be a handsome, charming poet-singer who entertained the Viscount of Ventadorn and his young beautiful wife with his songs. Bernart and the Viscount's wife fell in love, and they tried to keep their relationship secret. When the Viscount finally learned of their love, he banished Bernart, who then became the troubadour of the Duchess of Normandy. The Duchess soon fell in love with Bernart also, but she eventually married the King of England. Heartbroken, Bernart spent the last years of his life in a monastery.

Bernart de Ventadorn lived from approximately 1140 to 1195.

Reading Focus

Why do you think that unrequited love, or love that is not returned, is such a popular subject in poetry and song?

Share Ideas With your classmates, brainstorm a list of contemporary songs that focus on this subject. Jot down the titles and list your favorite lines from the lyrics.

Setting a Purpose Read to see how a poet of the 1100s describes the experience of unrequited love.

Building Background

Troubadour Poetry

In the 1100s and 1200s, poet-musicians called troubadours entertained audiences at the courts of lords and ladies in southern France. They composed their poems in Provençal, the language of the region. One of the most common forms of troubadour poetry was the *canso d'amor,* or love song. This type of poem, idealizing romantic love, consists of five or more stanzas of verse and ends with a short stanza called an *envoy.*

Bernart de Ventadorn's *cansos* were greatly admired in his time. Forty-five of these *cansos* survive today, and scholars regard them as some of the best poetry written in Provençal. "The Lark" is a prime example of a *canso d'amor.* This translation of the poem by Ezra Pound, a well-known modern American poet, focuses on the first two of the original eight stanzas.

Troubadour from a French illuminated manuscript.

The Lark

Bernart de Ventadorn
Translated by Ezra Pound

Lark Ascending, 20th century. Osmund Caine (Great Britain). Oil on canvas. Private collection.

Viewing the painting: How important are the lark and the landscape in this painting, both separately and in relation to each other? Explain.

When I see the lark a-moving
For joy his wings against the sunlight,
Who forgets himself and lets himself fall
For the sweetness which goes into his heart;
Ai! what great envy comes unto me for him whom I see so rejoicing!
I marvel that my heart melts not for desiring.
Alas! I thought I knew so much
Of Love, and I know so little of it, for I cannot
Hold myself from loving
Her from whom I shall never have anything toward.
She hath all my heart from me, and she hath from me all my wit
And myself and all that is mine.
And when she took it from me she left me naught
Save desiring and a yearning heart.

Responding to Literature

Personal Response

What do you like or dislike about this poem? Why? Write your thoughts in your journal.

Analyzing Literature

Recall and Interpret

1. How does the speaker characterize the lark?
2. What is the speaker's reaction to seeing the lark? Why does the speaker react this way?
3. What is the speaker's emotional state in the poem and what seems to have caused it?
4. **Mood** is the emotional quality created by a literary work–the overall feeling that the piece creates for readers (see page R7). What is the overall mood of this poem?

Evaluate and Connect

5. In your opinion, which are the most powerful lines in this poem? Explain.
6. For the Reading Focus on page 534, you listed song titles and lyrics that describe the experience of unrequited love. In what ways are they similar to or different from the lines in this poem that you think are most powerful?
7. What do you learn about the speaker and his beloved in this poem? Explain how you learn about them. Support your answer with details from the poem.
8. What other characters in literature or film can you recall who experience feelings like those of the speaker? Explain.

Literary **ELEMENTS**

Implied Metaphor

An **implied metaphor** is a metaphor in which the similarities or differences between two things are suggested or hinted at, but not directly stated. Simply by juxtaposing two things in a literary work, a writer may create an implied metaphor. "The Lark" gains much of its power from its implied metaphor.

1. Explain the implied metaphor in "The Lark."
2. Explain why this implied metaphor is effective.

- See **Literary Terms Handbook,** p. R7.

Extending Your Response

Personal Writing

Giving Advice Many people experience unrequited love at some time in their lives. How does it make them feel? How do they get over it? Pretend that you are an advice columnist. In your journal, offer advice to the speaker in this poem on how to deal with his feelings of emptiness and longing.

Interdisciplinary Activity

Music: Setting a Poem to Music There are CDs available of the music that accompanied troubadour poetry, including that of Bernart de Ventadorn. Listen to a recording of this music. Notice how the music supports the mood of the poetry. Then compose or select music to accompany "The Lark." Read or sing the poem with the music you've chosen for the class.

Save your work for your portfolio.

COMPARING selections

The Weed and The Lark

COMPARE **EXPERIENCES**

Write Both "The Weed" and "The Lark" focus on the experience of romantic love that cannot be satisfied. However, the situations presented in the two works are different from one another. Write a paragraph comparing the experience of Angoori in "The Weed" with that of the speaker in "The Lark." Consider the following questions in your comparison.

- How is Angoori's situation similar to or different from that of the speaker in "The Lark"? For example, is Angoori's love unrequited, as the speaker's is in "The Lark"? How do you know?
- How is Angoori's emotional state at the end of the story similar to that of the speaker in "The Lark"?
- How might Angoori react to the feelings expressed in "The Lark"?

Paper Boat (detail).

COMPARE **MOODS**

Discuss Despite the difference in genre, "The Weed" and "The Lark" have certain similarities in mood. Think about the mood of each work and how it changes. Discuss the following questions in your group.

1. How is the mood at the beginning of "The Weed" similar to the mood in the first part of "The Lark"? How is this mood conveyed in each work?
2. How is the mood at the end of the "The Weed" similar to the mood at the end of "The Lark"? How is this mood conveyed in each work?

COMPARE **CUSTOMS**

Research Modern India and medieval Europe are far apart in time and distance. Does this difference in time and distance apply to culture as well? Using the Internet and library resources, investigate the two cultures' ideas about romantic love. Then imagine a historical time warp in which a modern Indian woman converses with a medieval troubadour about their notions on love. Work with a partner to create and stage the conversation for the class.

INDIA, 1985

Before You Read

Like the Sun

Meet R. K. Narayan

"For human beings the greatest source of strength lies in each other's presence."

Born into the brahmin caste (the highest class) in Madras in South India, R. K. Narayan (nä rä′ yan) was educated in English schools, which he hated. Still, he became fond of the English language, in which he wrote. He called English "a very adaptable language . . . [that can] take on the tint of any country."

After a brief period of teaching early in his life, Narayan decided to devote himself full-time to writing. He relied on newspaper and magazine work to earn a living as he wrote novels. Just as his writing career was taking off, Narayan lost his wife to typhoid, after only six years of marriage. Her death left him in a depression and with a young daughter to raise alone. For a time Narayan thought he would never write again. His largely autobiographical novel *The English Teacher* describes this turning point in his life. Since then, Narayan has become one of the best-known and most highly acclaimed writers of India.

R. K. Narayan was born in 1906 and died in 2001.

Reading Focus

How truthful are you with people? Do you always say exactly what you think or feel?

Journal On a scale of one to ten, what ranking would you give yourself for honesty? In your journal, record your ranking and explain why and when you are or are not completely honest.

Setting a Purpose Read to discover what happens when one character in this short story tells other people the truth.

Building Background

Indian Music

India has an ancient and varied musical tradition. In the classical music of India, which is featured in "Like the Sun," a melody pattern called a *raga* provides the framework for creating a piece of music. The word *raga* is derived from a Sanskrit word meaning "to color" or "to tinge with emotion." In a raga, the precise sequence of notes is not fixed. In order to create a mood, the musician improvises, following certain basic musical rules. Thus, the performer actually becomes a composer.

Traditionally, a musical performance takes place in a private home before an audience of knowledgeable music enthusiasts. A solo vocalist is often accompanied by a drummer and violinist, as in "Like the Sun," and the performance may last an hour or more.

Vocabulary Preview

culinary (kə′ lə ner′ ē) *adj.* related to the kitchen or cooking; p. 539

shirk (shurk) *v.* to evade or avoid one's duty; p. 539

ingratiating (in grā′ shē āt′ ing) *adj.* deliberately intending to win another's favor; p. 540

stupefied (sto͞o′ pə fīd′) *adj.* groggy or insensible; p. 540

increment (ing′ krə mənt) *n.* something gained or added in a series, usually at regular intervals; p. 541

scrutinize (skro͞ot′ ən īz) *v.* to examine with close attention to detail; p. 541

Like the Sun

R. K. Narayan

TRUTH, SEKHAR REFLECTED, IS LIKE the sun. I suppose no human being can ever look it straight in the face without blinking or being dazed. He realized that, morning till night, the essence of human relationships consisted in tempering truth so that it might not shock. This day he set apart as a unique day—at least one day in the year we must give and take absolute Truth whatever may happen. Otherwise life is not worth living. The day ahead seemed to him full of possibilities. He told no one of his experiment. It was a quiet resolve, a secret pact between him and eternity.

The very first test came while his wife served him his morning meal. He showed hesitation over a tidbit, which she had thought was her culinary masterpiece. She asked, "Why, isn't it good?" At other times he would have said, considering her feelings in the matter, "I feel full-up, that's all." But today he said, "It isn't good. I'm unable to swallow it." He saw her wince and said to himself, Can't be helped. Truth is like the sun.

His next trial was in the common room[1] when one of his colleagues came up and said, "Did you hear of the death of so and so? Don't you think it a pity?" "No," Sekhar answered. "He was such a fine man—" the other began. But Sekhar cut him short with: "Far from it. He always struck me as a mean and selfish brute."

During the last period when he was teaching geography for Third Form A, Sekhar received a note from the headmaster: "Please see me before you go home." Sekhar said to himself: It must be about these horrible test papers. A hundred papers in the boys' scrawls; he had shirked this work for weeks, feeling all the time as if a sword were hanging over his head.

1. The *common room* is the teacher's lounge.

Vocabulary

culinary (kə′ lə ner′ ē) *adj.* related to the kitchen or cooking

shirk (shurk) *v.* to evade or avoid one's duty

The bell rang and the boys burst out of the class.

Sekhar paused for a moment outside the headmaster's room to button up his coat; that was another subject the headmaster always sermonized about.

He stepped in with a very polite "Good evening, sir."

The headmaster looked up at him in a very friendly manner and asked, "Are you free this evening?"

Sekhar replied, "Just some outing which I have promised the children at home—"

"Well, you can take them out another day. Come home with me now."

"Oh . . . yes, sir, certainly . . ." And then he added timidly, "Anything special, sir?"

"Yes," replied the headmaster, smiling to himself . . . "You didn't know my weakness for music?"

"Oh, yes, sir . . ."

"I've been learning and practicing secretly, and now I want you to hear me this evening. I've engaged a drummer and a violinist to accompany me—this is the first time I'm doing it full-dress and I want your opinion. I know it will be valuable."

Sekhar's taste in music was well known. He was one of the most dreaded music critics in the town. But he never anticipated his musical inclinations would lead him to this trial. . . . "Rather a surprise for you, isn't it?" asked the headmaster. "I've spent a fortune on it behind closed doors. . . ." They started for the headmaster's house. "God hasn't given me a child, but at least let him not deny me the consolation of music," the headmaster said, pathetically, as they walked. He incessantly chattered about music: how he began one day out of sheer boredom; how his teacher at first laughed at him, and then gave him hope; how his ambition in life was to forget himself in music.

At home the headmaster proved very ingratiating. He sat Sekhar on a red silk carpet, set before him several dishes of delicacies, and fussed over him as if he were a son-in-law of the house. He even said, "Well, you must listen with a free mind. Don't worry about these test papers." He added half humorously, "I will give you a week's time."

"Make it ten days, sir," Sekhar pleaded.

"All right, granted," the headmaster said generously. Sekhar felt really relieved now—he would attack them at the rate of ten a day and get rid of the nuisance.

The headmaster lighted incense sticks. "Just to create the right atmosphere," he explained. A drummer and a violinist, already seated on a Rangoon mat, were waiting for him. The headmaster sat down between them like a professional at a concert, cleared his throat, and began an alapana,[2] and paused to ask, "Isn't it good Kalyani?"[3] Sekhar pretended not to have heard the question. The headmaster went on to sing a full song composed by Thyagaraja[4] and followed it with two more. All the time the headmaster was singing, Sekhar went on commenting within himself, *He croaks like a dozen frogs. He is bellowing like a buffalo. Now he sounds like loose window shutters in a storm.*

The incense sticks burnt low. Sekhar's head throbbed with the medley of sounds that had assailed his eardrums for a couple of hours now. He felt half stupefied. The headmaster had gone nearly hoarse, when he paused to ask, "Shall

2. An *alapana* is a musical improvisation.
3. *Kalyani* means "music."
4. *Thyagaraja* (thyä′ gä rä zhä) was an Indian composer (1767–1847) known for his devotional songs.

Vocabulary

ingratiating (in grā′ shē āt′ ing) *adj.* deliberately intending to win another's favor
stupefied (stōō′ pə fīd′) *adj.* groggy or insensible

Sitar Player. M. F. Hussain (India, b. 1915). Collection of the artist.

I go on?" Sekhar replied, "Please don't, sir, I think this will do. . . ." The headmaster looked stunned. His face was beaded with perspiration. Sekhar felt the greatest pity for him. But he felt he could not help it. No judge delivering a sentence felt more pained and helpless. Sekhar noticed that the headmaster's wife peeped in from the kitchen, with eager curiosity. The drummer and the violinist put away their burdens with an air of relief. The headmaster removed his spectacles, mopped his brow, and asked, "Now, come out with your opinion."

"Can't I give it tomorrow, sir?" Sekhar asked tentatively.

"No. I want it immediately—your frank opinion. Was it good?"

"No, sir . . ." Sekhar replied.

"Oh! . . . Is there any use continuing my lessons?"

"Absolutely none, sir . . ." Sekhar said with his voice trembling. He felt very unhappy that he could not speak more soothingly. Truth, he reflected, required as much strength to give as to receive.

All the way home he felt worried. He felt that his official life was not going to be smooth sailing hereafter. There were questions of increment and confirmation and so on, all depending upon the headmaster's goodwill. All kinds of worries seemed to be in store for him. . . . Did not Harischandra[5] lose his throne, wife, child, because he would speak nothing less than the absolute Truth whatever happened?

At home his wife served him with a sullen face. He knew she was still angry with him for his remark of the morning. Two casualties for today, Sekhar said to himself. If I practice it for a week, I don't think I shall have a single friend left.

He received a call from the headmaster in his classroom next day. He went up apprehensively.

"Your suggestion was useful. I have paid off the music master. No one would tell me the truth about my music all these days. Why such antics at my age! Thank you. By the way, what about those test papers?"

"You gave me ten days, sir, for correcting them."

"Oh, I've reconsidered it. I must positively have them here tomorrow. . . ." A hundred papers in a day! That meant all night's sitting up! "Give me a couple of days, sir . . ."

"No. I must have them tomorrow morning. And remember, every paper must be thoroughly scrutinized."

"Yes, sir," Sekhar said, feeling that sitting up all night with a hundred test papers was a small price to pay for the luxury of practicing Truth.

5. *Harischandra* (ha′ rē shän′ drä) was a king who sacrificed his kingdom for the *Sat Panth*, or the Path of Truth.

Vocabulary

increment (ing′ krə mənt) *n.* something gained or added in a series, usually at regular intervals

scrutinize (skroot′ ən īz) *v.* to examine with close attention to detail

Responding to Literature

Personal Response

How did you react to the end of the story? Write your answer in your journal.

Analyzing Literature

Recall and Interpret

1. What does Sekhar think is the essence of human relationships? On the basis of that belief, what does he decide to do for one day?
2. What does Sekhar tell his wife about her "culinary masterpiece"? How does she react?
3. Why is music so important to the headmaster?
4. Summarize the events that occur at the headmaster's house.
5. How do you think the headmaster feels about Sekhar's judgment of his musical ability? Explain your answer with details from the story.

Evaluate and Connect

6. How would you characterize the headmaster? Do you feel sorry for him? Why or why not?
7. **Tone** is the attitude a writer takes toward the audience, subject, or characters of a work (see **Literary Terms Handbook,** page R12). How would you describe the tone of this story?
8. What is your opinion of Sekhar's experiment? Give reasons for your opinion.
9. Is honesty really a "luxury," as the last paragraph of this story implies? Explain your answer.
10. Imagine that everybody in the world always told the truth. What would daily life be like?

Literary Criticism

"Narayan's [vision]," writes Charles R. Larson, "has been predominantly comic, reflecting with humor the struggle of the individual consciousness to find peace within the framework of public life." Do you think this story is predominately comic? How does the narrator reconcile his private and his public self? Explain your answer in a brief essay. Refer to specific passages for support.

Literary ELEMENTS

Analogy

An **analogy** is a comparison made between two things to show how one is like the other. Analogies often explain something unfamiliar or abstract by comparing it to something familiar or concrete. In "Like the Sun," the first paragraph draws an analogy between truth and the sun. The title of the story highlights this analogy.

1. How do the second and third sentences in the first paragraph of the story develop the analogy between truth and the sun?
2. How does the story "prove" the correctness of Sekhar's analogy?
3. Imagine that you are planning to develop this analogy for a story of your own. In what other ways might truth be compared to the sun?

- See **Literary Terms Handbook,** p. R1.

Extending Your Response

Creative Writing

Truth and Consequences Review the journal entry you made for the Reading Focus on page 538, in which you rated your own level of honesty. Think about situations in which you "temper" the truth. Use one of these situations as the basis of a short story in which the main character decides to conduct an experiment like Sekhar's, being honest for a day.

Interdisciplinary Activity

Music: A Review Listen to a recording of Indian music and write a review. Begin by identifying the type of music, the composer, the performer(s), and the instruments. Then describe the music and give your reactions to it.

Save your work for your portfolio.

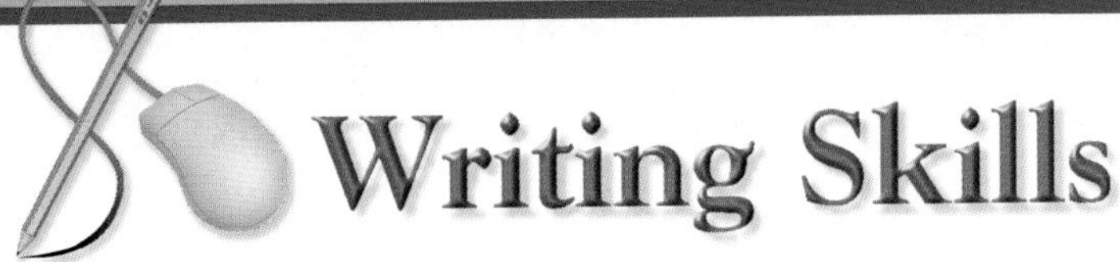

Using Topic Sentences and Supporting Details

In the opening sentence of "Like the Sun," author R. K. Narayan directly states the main idea of his story: Truth is like the sun. On many levels, the story proceeds to explore, illustrate, and support its main idea with a variety of details. Within the story, individual paragraphs express main ideas that are supported with details, dialogue, events, and examples. The effect of this careful structure is a coherent, unified story. Each paragraph in an effective piece of writing–whether narrative, expository, descriptive, persuasive, or personal–expresses one main idea supported by details.

Read the following paragraph from "Like the Sun."

> **The very first test came while his wife served him his morning meal. He showed hesitation over a tidbit, which she had thought was her culinary masterpiece. She asked, "Why, isn't it good?" At other times he would have said, considering her feelings in the matter, "I feel full-up, that's all." But today he said, "It isn't good. I'm unable to swallow it." He saw her wince and said to himself, Can't be helped. Truth is like the sun.**

The **main idea,** or focus, of a paragraph is often presented in a direct statement–that is, in a **topic sentence.** The other sentences in the paragraph supply details that prove, clarify, or expand the main idea. In the excerpt above, the first sentence states the main idea: Sekhar's first test came at breakfast. Each of the following sentences supports the main idea with details and dialogue that prove it. The excerpt ends with a restatement of the story's main idea.

Although a topic sentence often appears at the beginning of a paragraph, it can appear anywhere in a paragraph. Where you place your topic sentence depends on the effect you want to achieve.

- Begin a paragraph with a topic sentence if you want to let the reader know what is to come. You may find this arrangement effective in expository writing.
- End a paragraph with a topic sentence if you want to summarize the main idea and reinforce the reader's understanding of the main idea. This arrangement of topic sentence and supporting ideas is often used in persuasive writing.

ACTIVITY

Write a paragraph in which you describe someone performing an ordinary task, such as walking a dog, eating an ice cream cone, or reading the newspaper. How does he or she go about it? What personal characteristics are revealed by his or her actions? State your main idea in a topic sentence and be sure that the other sentences in the paragraph support the main idea.

INDIA, 1951

Before You Read

By Any Other Name

Meet Santha Rama Rau

"Really, in the end, the only thing that can make you a writer is the person that you are, the intensity of your feeling, the honesty of your vision, the unsentimental acknowledgment of the endless interest of the life around and within you."

Santha Rama Rau (sän′ tä rä′ mä rou) was born in Madras, India. Her father was a high-ranking government official, and because of his work, the family traveled extensively. Rau attended schools in India, England, and the United States. Shortly after graduating from Wellesley College in Massachusetts, she published the autobiography *Home to India* (1945), which became a best-seller. She subsequently published other books of autobiography, travel writing, and fiction.

Rau frequently writes about interactions among people of different cultures. Noting that "a formidable screen of fantasy and half-truths has grown up between India and the Western world," Rau has worked to open the doors to cultural understanding.

Santha Rama Rau was born in 1923.

Reading Focus

How important is your name to you? How do you feel when people mispronounce or misspell your name?

Discuss With your classmates, briefly discuss how you feel about your own name and why.

Setting a Purpose Read about the author's experience at a school where her name is taken away from her.

Building Background

Education in British India

The events in "By Any Other Name" take place during the late 1920s, when India was a British colony. During their rule of India, the British introduced Western education into the country, primarily in the cities and towns and among people in the higher Indian castes (hereditary social classes). The British goal was to create a Western-educated class of Indians, fluent in English, who could help interpret British policies to the rest of the population. Many Western-educated Indians became government administrators, political leaders, and professionals, both before and after India won its independence in 1947.

Reading Further

You might enjoy the following:

This Is India by Santha Rama Rau, an account of the cultures of India.

Gifts of Passage by Santha Rama Rau, a collection of mostly autobiographical stories.

Vocabulary Preview

provincial (prə vin′ shəl) *adj.* relating to or coming from a province; lacking sophistication and refinement; p. 546

insular (in′ sə lər) *adj.* characteristic of island people; especially, reflecting a narrow, isolated viewpoint; p. 546

wizened (wiz′ ənd) *adj.* dry, shrunken, and wrinkled as a result of aging; p. 548

sedately (si dāt′ lē) *adv.* quietly; seriously; p. 548

tepid (tep′ id) *adj.* moderately warm; lukewarm; p. 548

peevishness (pē′ vish nəs) *n.* fretful temperament or mood marked by ill temper; p. 549

Udaipur Girl. N. S. Bendre (India, b. 1910). Collection of the artist.

By Any Other Name

Santha Rama Rau

At the Anglo-Indian day school in Zorinabad to which my sister and I were sent when she was eight and I was five and a half, they changed our names. On the first day of school, a hot, windless morning of a north Indian September, we stood in the headmistress's[1] study and she said, "Now you're the new girls. What are your names?"

My sister answered for us. "I am Premila, and she"—nodding in my direction—"is Santha."

The headmistress had been in India, I suppose, fifteen years or so, but she still smiled her helpless inability to cope with Indian names. Her rimless half-glasses glittered, and the precarious bun on the top of her head trembled as she shook her head. "Oh, my dears, those are much too hard for me. Suppose we give you pretty English names. Wouldn't that be more jolly? Let's see, now—Pamela for you, I think." She shrugged in a baffled way at my sister. "That's as close as I can get. And for *you*," she said to me, "how about Cynthia? Isn't that nice?"

My sister was always less easily intimidated than I was, and while she kept a stubborn silence, I said, "Thank you," in a very tiny voice.

1. A *headmistress* is a woman who directs a school, usually a private school.

We had been sent to that school because my father, among his responsibilities as an officer of the civil service, had a tour of duty to perform in the villages around that steamy little provincial town, where he had his headquarters at that time. He used to make his shorter inspection tours on horseback, and a week before, in the stale heat of a typically postmonsoon day,[2] we had waved good-bye to him and a little procession—an assistant, a secretary, two bearers,[3] and the man to look after the bedding rolls and luggage. They rode away through our large garden, still bright green from the rains, and we turned back into the twilight of the house and the sound of fans whispering in every room.

Up to then, my mother had refused to send Premila to school in the British-run establishments of that time, because, she used to say, "you can bury a dog's tail for seven years and it still comes out curly, and you can take a Britisher away from his home for a lifetime and he still remains insular." The examinations and degrees from entirely Indian schools were not, in those days, considered valid. In my case, the question had never come up, and probably never would have come up if Mother's extraordinary good health had not broken down. For the first time in my life, she was not able to continue the lessons she had been giving us every morning. So our Hindi books were put away, the stories of the Lord Krishna[4] as a little boy were left in midair, and we were sent to the Anglo-Indian school.

That first day at school is still, when I think of it, a remarkable one. At that age, if one's name is changed, one develops a curious form of dual personality. I remember having a certain detached and disbelieving concern in the actions of "Cynthia," but certainly no responsibility. Accordingly, I followed the thin, erect back of the headmistress down the veranda to my classroom feeling, at most, a passing interest in what was going to happen to me in this strange, new atmosphere of School.

The building was Indian in design, with wide verandas opening onto a central courtyard, but Indian verandas are usually whitewashed, with stone floors. These, in the tradition of British schools, were painted dark brown and had matting on the floors. It gave a feeling of extra intensity to the heat.

I suppose there were about a dozen Indian children in the school—which contained perhaps forty children in all—and four of them were in my class. They were all sitting at the back of the room, and I went to join them. I sat next to a small, solemn girl who didn't smile at me. She had long, glossy-black braids and wore a cotton dress, but she still kept on her Indian jewelry—a gold chain around her neck, thin gold bracelets, and tiny ruby studs in her ears. Like most Indian children, she had a rim of black kohl[5] around her eyes. The cotton dress should have looked strange, but all I could think of was that I should ask my mother if I couldn't wear a dress to school, too, instead of my Indian clothes.

I can't remember too much about the proceedings in class that day, except for the

2. A *postmonsoon day* is a day that occurs just after a monsoon, or heavy rainfall.

3. *Bearers* are porters who carry the equipment and supplies for a journey.

4. *Lord Krishna* is an incarnation of the Hindu god Vishnu.

5. *Kohl* is a cosmetic that women in Southwest and South Central Asia use to darken the edges of their eyelids.

Vocabulary

provincial (prə vin′ shəl) *adj.* relating to or coming from a province; lacking in urban sophistication and refinement

insular (in′ sə lər) *adj.* characteristic of an island people; especially, reflecting a narrow, isolated viewpoint

A View of the Nile Above Aswan (detail). Edward Lear (Great Britain, 1812–1888). Private collection.

The WAGON

Khalida Asghar

Translated by Muhammad Umar Memon

IN A RUSH TO GET BACK TO THE CITY, I quickly crossed the dirt road and walked onto the Ravi bridge, looking indifferently at the blazing edge of the sun steadily falling into the marsh. I had a queer feeling, as though I saw something. I spun around. There they were, three of them, leaning over the bridge's guard rails and gazing straight into the sunset. Their deathly concentration made me look at the sunset myself, but I found nothing extraordinary in the scene; so I looked back at them instead. Their faces, although not at all similar, still looked curiously alike.

Their outfits suggested that they were well-to-do villagers, and their dust-coated shoes that they had trudged for miles just to watch the sun as it set over the marshes of the receding Ravi. Impervious to the traffic on the bridge, they went on staring at the marshes which were turning a dull, deep red in the sun's last glow.

I edged closer to them. The sun had gone down completely; only a dark red stripe remained on the far horizon. Suddenly the three looked at each other, lowered their heads, and silently walked away, toward the villages outside the city. For some time I stood watching their tired figures recede into the distance. Soon the night sounds coming to life in the city reminded me that it was getting late and I'd better rush home. I quickened my pace and walked on under the blue haze of the night sky, pierced here and there by the blinking lights of the city ahead.

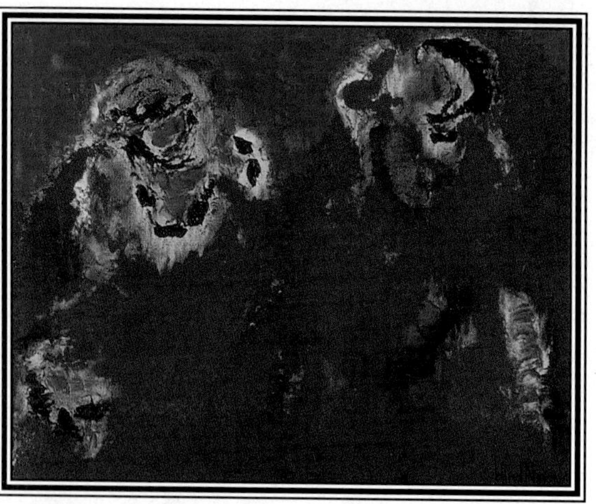

The Couple, 1984. Hind Nasser (Jordan). Oil on canvas, 90 x 100 cm. Collection of the Mango Family.

Viewing the painting: How does color affect your response to this painting? How does color affect the characters in the story?

The next evening when I reached the bridge, the sunset was a few minutes away. I suddenly recalled the three men and stopped to watch the sunset even though I knew Munna would be waiting on the front porch for sweets and Zakiya, my wife, would be ready for us to go to the movies. I couldn't budge. An inexorable force seemed to have tied me to the ground. Through almost all the previous night I'd wondered what it was about the marsh and the sunset that had engrossed those strange men so entirely.

And then, just as the blazing orange disc of the sun tumbled into the marsh, I saw the three walk up the road. They were coming from villages outside the city limits. They wore identical clothes and resembled each other in their height and gait. Again they walked up to the bridge, stood at the same spot they had the previous evening and peered into the sunset with their flaming eyes filled with a dull sadness. I watched them and wondered why, despite their diverse features, they looked so much alike. One of them, who was very old, had a long, bushy snow-white beard. The second, somewhat lighter in complexion than the other, had a face that shone like gold in the orange glow of sunset. His hair hung down to his shoulders like a fringe, and he had a scar on his forehead. The third was dark and snub-nosed.

The sun sank all the way into the marsh. As on the previous day, the men glanced at each other, let their heads drop and, without exchanging a word, went their way.

That evening I felt terribly ill at ease. In a way I regretted not asking them about their utter fascination with the sunset. What could they be looking for in the sun's fading light?—I wondered. I told Zakiya about the strange threesome. She just laughed and said, "Must be peasants, on their way to the city to have a good time."

An air of strangeness surrounded these men. Zakiya, of course, could not have known it:

Vocabulary

impervious (im pur′ vē əs) *adj.* not easily affected or disturbed
inexorable (i nek′ sər ə bəl) *adj.* relentless; unyielding

one really had to look at them to feel the weird aura.[1]

The next day I waited impatiently for the evening. I walked to the bridge, expecting them to show up. And they did, just as the daylight ebbed away. They leaned over the bridge and watched the sun go down, indifferent to the sound of traffic. Their absorption in the scene made it impossible to talk to them. I waited until the sun had gone down completely and the men had started to return. This would be the time to ask them what it was they expected to find in the vanishing sun and the marshes of the receding river.

When the sun had sunk all the way, the men gave one another a sad, mute look, lowered their heads and started off. But, instead of returning to the village, they took the road to the city. Their shoes were covered with dust and their feet moved on rhythmically together.

I gathered my faltering courage and asked them, "Brothers! what village do you come from?"

The man with the snub nose turned around and stared at me for a while. Then the three exchanged glances, but none of them bothered to answer my question.

"What do you see over there . . . on the bridge?" I asked. The mystery about the three men was beginning to weigh heavily upon me now. I felt as though molten lead had seeped into my legs—indeed into my whole body, and that it was only a matter of time before I'd crumble to the ground reeling from a spell of dizziness.

Again they did not answer. I shouted at them in a choking voice, "Why are you always staring at the sunset?"

No answer.

We reached the heavily congested city road. The evening sounds grew closer. It was late October, and the air felt pleasantly cool. The sweet scent of jasmine wafted in, borne by the breeze. As we passed the octroi post,[2] the old man with snow-white hair suddenly spoke, "Didn't you see? Has nobody in the city seen . . . ?"

"Seen what?"

"When the sun sets, when it goes down all the way . . . ?" asked the hoary old man, rearranging his mantle[3] over his shoulders.

"When the sun goes down all the way?" I repeated. "What about it? That happens every day!"

I said that very quickly, afraid that the slightest pause might force them back into their impenetrable silence.

"We knew that, we knew it would be that way. That's why we came. That other village, there, too . . ." He pointed toward the east and lowered his head.

"From there we come . . ." said the snub-nosed man.

"From where?" I asked, growing impatient. "Please tell me clearly."

The third man peered back at me over his shoulder. The scar on his forehead suddenly seemed deeper than before. He said, "We didn't notice, nor, I believe, did you. Perhaps nobody did. Because, as you say, the sun rises and sets every day. Why bother to look? And we didn't, when day after day, there, over there," he pointed in the direction of the east, "the sky became blood-red and so bright it blazed like fire even at nightfall. We just failed to notice . . ." He stopped abruptly, as if choking over his words. "And now this redness," he resumed after a pause, "it keeps spreading from place to place. I'd never seen such a phenomenon before. Nor my elders. Nor, I believe, did

1. An *aura* is a distinctive character or atmosphere surrounding a person or thing.

2. An *octroi* is a local customs tax, payable on goods moved within a country; it would be collected at an *octroi post.*

3. A *mantle* is a loose, sleeveless garment.

Vocabulary

hoary (hôr′ ē) *adj.* extremely old or ancient

they hear their elders mention anything quite like that ever happening."

Meanwhile the darkness had deepened. All I could see of my companions were their white flowing robes; their faces became visible only when they came directly under the pale, dim light of the lampposts. I turned around to look at the stretch of sky over the distant Ravi. I was stunned: it was glowing red despite the darkness.

"You are right," I said, to hide my puzzlement, "we really did fail to notice that." Then I asked, "Where are you going?"

"To the city, of course. What would be the point of arriving there *afterwards?*"

A sudden impulse made me want to stay with them, or to take them home with me. But abruptly, they headed off on another road, and I remembered I was expected home soon. Munna would be waiting on the front porch for his daily sweets and Zakiya must be feeling irritated by my delay.

The next day I stopped at the bridge to watch the sunset. I was hoping to see those three men. The sun went down completely, but they didn't appear. I waited impatiently for them to show up. Soon, however, I was entranced by the sunset's last magical glow.

The entire sky seemed covered with a sheet soaked in blood, and it scared me that I was standing all alone underneath it. I felt an uncanny presence directly behind me. I spun around. There was nobody. All the same, I felt sure there was someone—standing behind my back, within me, or perhaps, somewhere near.

Vehicles, of all shapes and sizes, rumbled along in the light of the street lamps. Way back in the east, a stretch of evening sky still blazed like a winding sheet of fire, radiating heat and light far into the closing darkness. I was alarmed and scurried home. Hastily I told Zakiya all I'd seen. But she laughed off the whole thing. I took her up to the balcony and showed her the red and its infernal bright glow against the dark night sky. That sobered her up a little. She thought for a while, then remarked, "We're going to have a storm any minute—I'm sure."

The next day in the office, as I worked, bent over my files, I heard Mujibullah ask Hafiz Ahmad, "Say, did you see how the sky glows at sunset these days? Even after it gets dark? Amazing, isn't it?"

All at once I felt I was standing alone and defenseless under that bloodsheet of a sky. I was frightened. Small drops of sweat formed on my forehead. As the evening edged closer, a strange restlessness took hold of me. The receding Ravi, the bridge, the night sky and the sun frightened me; I wanted to walk clear out of them. And yet, I also felt irresistibly drawn toward them.

I wanted to tell my colleagues about the three peasants who in spite of their distinctly individual faces somehow looked alike; about how they had come to the city accompanying this strange redness, had drawn my attention to it, and then dropped out of sight; and about how I'd searched in vain for them everywhere. But I couldn't. Mujibullah and Hafiz Ahmad, my office-mates, had each borrowed about twenty rupees from me some time ago, which they conveniently forgot to return, and, into the bargain, had stopped talking to me ever since.

On my way home when I entered the bridge, a strange fear made me walk briskly, look away from the sun, and try to concentrate instead on the street before me. But the blood-red evening kept coming right along. I could feel its presence everywhere. A flock of evening birds flew overhead in a "V" formation. Like the birds, I too was returning home. Home—yes, but no longer my haven against the outside world; for the flame-colored evening came pouring in from its windows, doors, even through its walls of solid masonry.

I now wandered late in the streets, looking for the three peasants. I wanted to ask them where that red came from. What was to follow? Why did they leave the last settlement? What shape was it in? But I couldn't find them anywhere. Nobody seemed to care.

A few days later I saw some men pointing up to the unusual red color of the evening. Before long, the whole city was talking about it. I hadn't told a soul except Zakiya. How they had found out about it was a puzzle to me. Those three peasants must be in the city—I concluded. They have got to be.

The red of evening had now become the talk of the town.

Chaudhri Sahib, who owns a small bookshop in Mozang Plaza, was an old acquaintance of mine. People got together at his shop for a friendly chat every evening. Often, so did I. But for some time now, since my first encounter with those mantle-wrapped oracular figures, I had been too preoccupied with my own thoughts to go there. No matter where I went, home or outside, I felt restless. At home, an inexorable urge drove me outdoors; outdoors, an equally strong urge sent me scrambling back home, where I felt comparatively safer. I became very confused about where I wanted to be. I began to feel heavy and listless.

All the same, I did go back to the bookshop once again that evening. Most of the regulars had already gathered. Chaudhri Sahib asked, "What do you think about it, fellows? Is it all due to the atomic explosions as they say? The rumor also has it that pretty soon the earth's cold regions will turn hot and the hot ones cold and the cycle of seasons will also be upset."

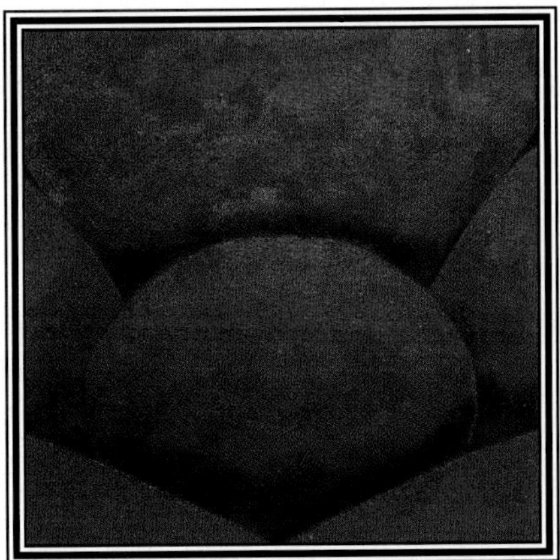

Scheherezade 101/no. 27. Rabbia Sukkarieh (Lebanon, b. 1953). Oil on canvas, 15 x 15 in. Collection of artist.

Viewing the painting: The story contains an abundance of sensory detail. How does this painting appeal to your senses?

I wanted to tell them about my encounter with the three villagers but felt too shy to talk before so many people. Just then a pungent smell, the likes of which I'd never smelled before, wafted in from God knows where. My heart sank and a strange, sweet sort of pain stabbed my body. I felt nauseous, unable to decide whether it was a stench, a pungent aroma, or even a wave of bittersweet pain. I threw the newspaper down and got up to leave.

"What's the matter?" asked Chaudhri Sahib.

"I must go. God knows what sort of smell that is."

"Smell? What smell?" Chaudhri Sahib sniffed the air.

I didn't care to reply and walked away. That offensive smell, the terrifying wave of pain, followed me all the way home. It made me giddy. I thought I might fall any minute. My condition frightened Zakiya, who asked, "What's the matter—you look so pale?"

"I'm all right. God knows what that smell is," I said, wiping sweat off my brow, although it was the month of November.

Zakiya also sniffed the air, then said, "Must be coming from the house of Hakim Sahib. Heaven knows what strange herb concoctions they keep making day and night. Or else it's from burnt food. I burnt some today accidentally."

"But it seems to be everywhere . . . in every street and lane . . . throughout the city."

Vocabulary

pungent (pun′ jənt) *adj.* having a sharp or stinging quality, especially affecting the sense of taste or smell

"Why, of course. The season's changed. It must be the smell of winter flowers," she said inattentively, and became absorbed in her knitting.

With great trepidation I again sniffed the air, but couldn't decide whether the sickening odor still lingered on or had subsided. Perhaps it had subsided. The thought relieved me a bit. But there was no escape from its memory, which remained fresh in my mind, like the itching that continues for some time even after the wound has healed. The very thought that it might return gave me the chills.

Conflict. Laila Shahzada (Pakistan). Oil on canvas, 108 x 68.5 cm. Collection of the Jordan National Gallery.

Viewing the painting: Describe the figure in the painting. How might this figure reflect the state of mind of someone from the story?

By next morning I'd forgotten all about that rotten, suffocating smell. In the office, I found a mountain of files waiting for me. But Mujibullah and Hafiz Ahmad went on noisily discussing some movie. I couldn't concentrate on the work and felt irritated. So I decided to take a break. I called our office boy and sent him to the cafeteria for a cup of tea. Meanwhile I pulled out a pack of cigarettes from my pocket and lit up.

Just then I felt a cracking blow on my head, as if I had fallen off a cliff and landed on my head, which fused everything before my eyes in a swirling blue and yellow streak. It took my numbed senses some time to realize that I was being assaulted once again by the same pain, the same terrible stench. It kept coming at me in waves, and it was impossible to know its source. I found myself frantically shutting every single window in the office, while both Mujibullah and Hafiz Ahmad gawked at me uncomprehendingly.

"Let the sun in! Why are you slamming the windows?" asked Hafiz Ahmad.

"The stench . . . the stench! My God, it's unbearable! Don't you smell it?"

Both of them raised their noses to the air and sniffed. Then Hafiz Ahmad remarked. "That's right. What sort of stench . . . or fragrance is that? It makes my heart sink."

Soon, many people were talking about the stink-waves which came in quick succession and then receded, only to renew their assault a little while later. At sundown they became especially unbearable.

Within a few weeks the stinking odor had become so oppressive that I often found it difficult to breathe. People's faces, usually quite lively and fresh, now looked drained and wilted.

Many complained of constant palpitation and headaches. The doctors cashed in. Intellectuals hypothesized that it must be due to nuclear blasts, which were producing strange effects throughout the world, including this foul odor in our city, which attacked people's nerves and left them in a mess. People scrambled to buy tranquilizers, which sold out instantly. Not that the supply was inadequate, but a sudden frenzy to stock up and horde had seized people. Even sleeping pills fetched the price of rare diamonds.

I found both tranquilizers and sleeping pills useless. The stench cut sharper than a sword and penetrated the body like a laser. The only way to guard against it was to get used to it—I thought; and people would do well to remember that. But I was too depressed to tell them myself. Within a few weeks, however, they themselves came to live with the stench.

Just the same, the stench struck terror in the city. People were loath to admit it, but they could not have looked more tense: their faces contorted from the fear of some terrible thing happening at any moment. Nor was their fear unreasonable, as a subsequent event showed a few weeks later.

On a cold mid-December evening, I was returning home from Chaudhri Sahib's. The street was full of traffic and jostling crowds. The stores glittered with bright lights, and people went about their business as usual. Every now and then a stench-wave swept in, made me giddy, and receded. I would freeze in my stride the instant it assailed me and would start moving again as soon as it had subsided. It was the same with others. An outsider would surely have wondered why we suddenly froze, closed our eyes, stopped breathing, then took a deep breath and got started again. But that was our custom now.

That December evening I'd just walked onto the bridge when I felt as if a lance had hit me on the head. My head whirled and my legs buckled. Reeling, I clung on to a lamppost and tried to support my head with my hands. There was no lance, nor was there a hand to wield it. It was that smell—that same rotten smell—I realized with terror. In fact, it seemed that the source of the oppressive stench had suddenly moved very close to me, between my shoulder blades, near my back, immediately behind me—so close that it was impossible to think of it as apart from me.

It was then that my eyes fell on the strange carriage, rambling along in front of me. It was an oversized wagon pulled by a pair of scrawny white oxen with leather blinders over their eyes and thick ropes strung through their steaming nostrils. A wooden cage sat atop the base of the wagon, its interior hidden behind black curtains—or were they just swaying walls of darkness?

Two men, sitting outside the cage enclosure in the front of the wagon, drove the two emaciated, blindfolded animals. I couldn't make out their faces, partly because of the darkness, but partly also because they were buried in folds of cloth thrown loosely around them. Their heads drooped forward and they seemed to have dozed off, overcome by fatigue and sleep.

Behind them the interior of the curtained wagon swelled with darkness and from the heart of that darkness shot out the nauseating stench which cut sharper than a sword . . . Before I knew it, the wagon had creaked past me, flooding my senses with its cargo of stink. My head swirled. I jumped off the main road onto the dirt sidewalk . . . and vomited.

I had no idea whether the people in the city had also seen the eerie wagon. If they had, what must have they endured? I had the hardest time getting home after what I had seen. Once inside the house, I ran to my bed and

Vocabulary
palpitation (pal′ pə tā′ shən) *n.* a rapid heartbeat

threw myself on it. Zakiya kept asking me what had happened, but a blind terror sealed my lips.

A few days later a small news item appeared in the local papers. It railed against the local Municipal Office for allowing garbage carts to pass through busy streets in the evening. Not only did muck-wagons pollute the air, they also hurt the fine olfactory sense of the citizenry.

I took a whole week off from work. During those seven days, though hardly fit to go out and observe first-hand the plight of the city, I was nonetheless kept posted of developments by local newspapers. Groups of concerned citizens demanded that the municipal authorities keep the city clear of the muck-wagons or, if that was impossible, assign them routes along less busy streets.

On the seventh day I ventured out. A change was already visible. Wrecked by insomnia and exhaustion, people strained themselves to appear carefree and cheerful, but managed only to look painfully silly. Suddenly I recalled that in the morning I had myself looked no different in the mirror.

About this time, the number of entertainment programs and movies shot up as never before. People swarmed to box offices—often hours before a show—where they formed long lines and patiently waited to be let in, and then filed out from the entertainment still looking pale and ridiculous.

In the office, no matter how hard I tried, I couldn't concentrate on work. Intermittently, the image of the muck-wagon lumbering down the streets flashed across my mind. Was it really one of those municipal dump-carts? No. It couldn't be. Municipal dump-carts never looked like that eerie wagon, with its sleepy drivers, a pair of blindfolded bony oxen, black curtains and the outrageously nauseating smell. What on earth could give off such an odd smell—at once fragrant and foul!

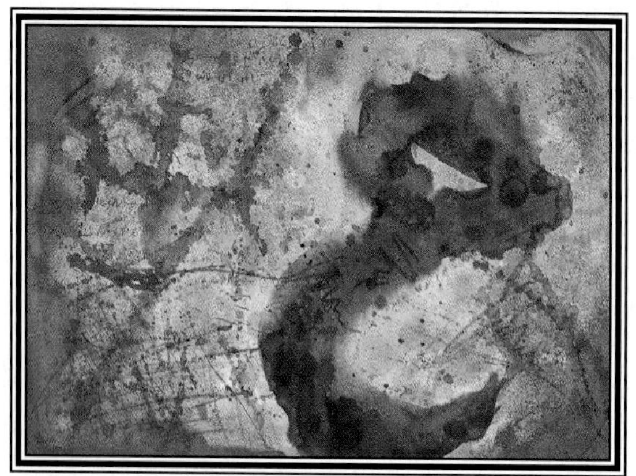

Karbala–Al-Hussein. Princess Wijdan Ali (Jordan). 35.4 x 75 cm. The International Museum of 20th Century Arts, Laguna Beach, CA.

Viewing the painting: How would you describe the colors in this painting? What feelings from the story do these colors suggest to you?

An insane desire suddenly overwhelmed me: to rush up to the wagon, lift up those swaying curtains, and peek inside. I must discover the source of the stench!

Coming to the bridge my feet involuntarily slowed down. There was still some time before sunset and the waves of the pain-filled odor came faster and stronger. I leaned over the bridge, an unknown fear slowly rising in my throat. The bottomless swamp, its arms ominously outstretched, seemed to be dragging me down toward it. I was afraid I might jump into the swamp, sink with the sun and become buried forever in that sprawling sheet of blood.

I became aware of something approaching me—or was I myself drawing closer to something? . . . Something awaited by all men—those before and those after us. My whole body felt as though it was turning into a piece of granite, with no escape from the bridge, the miasma, the sun, for now they all seemed inseparable from

Vocabulary

miasma (mī az′ mə) *n.* a heavy vaporous emanation or atmosphere my being. Helplessly, I looked around myself and almost dropped dead.

The three men were coming towards me from the direction of the countryside. As before, they were wrapped in their flowing white robes and walked with their amazingly identical gait. I kept staring at them with glassy eyes until they walked right up to me and stopped. The hoary old man was crying, and his snow-white beard was drenched in tears. The other two couldn't look up; their eyes were lowered mournfully, their teeth clenched and their faces withered by a deathly pallor.

"Where were you hiding all these days?" I said between gasps and stammers. "I searched for you everywhere. Tell me, please, what's happening to the city?"

"We were waiting. Trying to hold ourselves back. We had tied ourselves with ropes. Here, look!" They spread their arms before me and bared their shoulders and backs, revealing the deep marks of the rope.

"We did not want to come . . ." the old man said, drowned out by a fit of sobs.

"But there was no choice . . ." the second man said. Before he had finished, he doubled over. His companions also doubled over, as if unable to control a sudden surge of pain. The same wave of pain-filled stench stabbed the air about us, cutting us into halves, flooding our senses, as it scrambled past us.

"There! Look!" said the old man, pointing in the direction of the distant villages and turning deathly pale.

In the distance, I saw the wagon come up the road from behind a cloud of dust. The drowsing coachmen had wrapped their faces because of their nearness to the cutting stench.

A cold shiver ran through my spine. The eyes of the three men suddenly became dull. They were approaching their end—perhaps.

The wagon rumbled close—the stench from it draining the blood from our bodies—and then passed us. Its sinister, jet-black curtains, fluttering in the gentle breeze, appeared, oddly enough, entirely motionless.

The three men ran after the wagon, caught up to it and lifted the curtains. A split second later, a nonhuman scream burst from their gaping mouths. They spun around and bolted toward the distant fields.

"What was it? What did you see?" I asked, running after them. But they did not reply and kept running madly. Their eyes had frozen in a glazed stare.

I followed them until we had left the city several miles behind us, then grabbed the old man's robe and implored, "Tell me! Please tell me!"

He turned his deathly gaze and threw open his mouth. His tongue had got stuck to his palate.

All three had become dumb.

My head whirled, and I collapsed. The three men continued to run, soon disappearing in the distance behind a spiraling cloud of dust. Slowly the dust settled and I returned home.

For months now I have searched in vain for those men. They have vanished without a trace. And the wagon . . . from that fateful evening, it too has changed its route. It no longer passes through the city. After crossing the bridge, it now descends onto the dirt trail leading to villages in the countryside.

The cityfolk are no longer bothered by the slashing stench. They have become immune to it and think it has died, like an old, forgotten tale.

But it continues to torment my body, and day and night a voice keeps telling me, "Now, your turn! Now you shall *see!*"

And this evening I find myself on the bridge, waiting for the wagon . . . waiting.

Responding to Literature

Personal Response

How did you feel as you read about the mysterious occurrences? Explain.

Analyzing Literature

Recall

1. As the story opens, whom does the narrator see on the Ravi bridge? What are these individuals doing?
2. What change in the sky has occurred?
3. Describe the strange odor that troubles the narrator.
4. How does Zakiya react to the mysterious phenomena? How do the people in the city react?
5. Describe the first appearance of the wagon.

Interpret

6. What **atmosphere,** or emotional climate, is established at the beginning of the story? (See **Literary Terms Handbook,** page R1.) How is this atmosphere established?
7. The narrator seems overwrought with fear. What evidence indicates that he is not hallucinating?
8. To what do the people attribute the strange odor? Do you agree with them? Why or why not?
9. What do the people's reactions to the phenomena suggest about human nature?
10. What might the wagon contain? What makes you think so? Explain your answer with details from the story.

Evaluate and Connect

11. By the end of the story, the three villagers have vanished. What might their disappearance **symbolize,** or represent? (See **Literary Terms Handbook,** page R12.)
12. Why might the author have chosen not to reveal the actual cause of the phenomena? In your opinion, would the story be better if she had? Explain.
13. In your view, is the ending of "The Wagon" effective? Why or why not?
14. In what ways is "The Wagon" similar to the thrillers you discussed during the Reading Focus on page 552? In what ways is it different? Explain your answer, citing details from the story for support.
15. What **theme,** or message, does the story convey to you? (See **Literary Terms Handbook,** page R12.) Do you think this theme is still relevant today? Explain.

Suspense

Suspense refers to the tension readers feel as the events of a mysterious or frightening story unfold. When the outcome of a story is uncertain, suspense resides in wondering what will happen next and to whom it will happen. For stories in which the outcome is certain, suspense resides in wondering when the anticipated event will occur.

To feel suspense, readers must care about what happens to the characters in a story. For this reason, the main character of a thriller is often an "everyman" or "everywoman" with whom readers can easily identify.

1. What questions did *you* have while reading "The Wagon"? How did these questions help create a sense of suspense?
2. How does the **first-person narrator** add to the suspense of the story? In your opinion, is he an "everyman"—an ordinary person?

- See **Literary Terms Handbook,** pp. R8 and R12.

Literature and Writing

Writing About Literature

Analyzing a Thriller Walter Thompson, critic, once observed that "horror resides in the transformation of what we know best; in the intimate and comfortable details of our lives made suddenly threatening." How might this analysis apply to "The Wagon"? In a few paragraphs, explain what Thompson's statement means, what transformations the narrator's world undergoes, and why these transformations seem so threatening.

Creative Writing

"The Wagon" II "The Wagon" has an open ending. What do you think might happen after the story ends? Will the narrator see the wagon again? Will the people in the town change their attitude? Will the actual cause of the phenomena be discovered? Write a brief sequel to the story in which you answer these questions. Use your imagination, but remain true to the overall framework and atmosphere of the story.

Extending Your Response

Literature Groups

Sense Appeal "The Wagon" is rich with sensory detail. Which images did you find the most striking? What do these images contribute to the story? With a small group, skim the story to find examples of vivid imagery; then classify them on a chart similar to the one below. Share your chart and your analysis with other groups.

sight	sound	taste	touch	smell

Interdisciplinary Activity

Science: Nuclear Winter Chaudhri Sahib, the bookseller in the story, suggests that nuclear explosions might cause radical changes in the weather. Is he right? Using an encyclopedia, a science book, or the Internet, investigate the possible effects of a nuclear explosion on the atmosphere and report back to your class.

Internet Connection

Investigate an Accident In December 1984, the city of Bhopal in central India was the scene of the worst industrial accident in history. A toxic gas leak from an insecticide plant killed about 2,500 people and seriously injured tens of thousands more. Use the Internet to research the accident and its aftermath; then share your findings in a brief oral report to your class.

Save your work for your portfolio.

Skill Minilesson

VOCABULARY • Connotation and Denotation

Authors choose language carefully, considering both the **denotations,** or literal definitions of words, as well as their **connotations,** or emotional associations. This story contains many words with unpleasant connotations, such as *miasma, concoction,* and *pungent.* The negative connotations of these words help establish an ominous mood that is full of foreboding.

PRACTICE Using a dictionary, look up the denotation of each of the following words. Use each word in a sentence that indicates its connotation.

ennui	permeated	wan	weary
fiasco	trudging	wasted	yearned

JAPAN, 1967

Before You Read

River Light

Meet Yasushi Inoue

"Inoue is a strong, poetic writer, whom we need to know far better."

—*Francis King, literary critic*

After years of writing for newspapers, Yasushi Inoue (yä s o͞o′ shē ē nō′ ē ə) decided to return to his first love, writing fiction. The first works he submitted for publication—*The Bullfight* and *The Hunting Gun*—earned him the Akutagawa Prize, a prestigious literary award. At the age of forty-three, Inoue began a new career that would span four decades.

Inoue was born in Ishikari on Hokkaido, the northernmost island of Japan. He planned to be a doctor, like his father, but when his application to medical school was rejected, he changed his major to literature and began to write. His books in English translation include *Shirobamba: A Childhood in Old Japan*, *Lou-lan and Other Stories*, and *Chronicle of My Mother*. In 1976 the Japanese government honored Inoue, who had become one of Japan's most popular authors, with the Order of Culture, the nation's highest literary award.

Inoue was born in 1907 and died in 1991.

Reading Focus

Many people look back on their childhood with nostalgia. If you could recapture a specific moment from your childhood, what would it be?

Quickwrite Write for a few minutes about a special moment from your childhood and the feelings it evokes in you.

Setting a Purpose Read to discover a man's vivid memory of a moment from his childhood.

Building Background

Kyoto Bridge by Moonlight, from the series *100 Views of Edo,* 1857. Andō Hiroshige (Japan). Color woodblock print. British Library, London.

Inoue's Prose Poem

Inoue's "River Light" is a **prose poem,** a usually short, descriptive prose work that contains such poetic elements as imagery, symbolism, rhythm, and repetition. Like carefully composed photographs, prose poems usually focus on a single situation or scene and seek to create a single overall **mood** or emotional impression.

"River Light" focuses on a scene from Inoue's childhood. As a boy, Inoue lived with his grandparents in a tiny rural village on the Izu Peninsula. As was usual in the Japanese countryside at the time, he washed his hands before meals and bathed in a nearby river.

Directions: The following sentences test your knowledge of grammar, usage, diction (choice of words), and idiom.

Some sentences are correct.
No sentence contains more than one error.

You will find that the error, if there is one, is underlined and lettered. Elements of the sentence that are not underlined will not be changed. In choosing answers, follow the requirements of standard written English.

If there is an error, select the one underlined part that must be changed to make the sentence correct. Write the corresponding letter on your paper.

If there is no error, select answer E.

1. The fruit that Mark and Mindy picked (A) for their father (B) was less (C) expensive and much more colorful than the grocery store. (D) No Error (E)

2. As a result of her extensive injuries, (A) the skier was told (B) that she would have to remain in (C) the hospital for an indefinable (D) period of time. No Error (E)

3. The untested herbal supplements taken by (A) some athletes to increase performance may be (B) hazardous to (C) their (D) health. No Error (E)

4. While (A) searching in the attic, Jimmy found an old photograph of (B) the poor but (C) well-dressed ancestor who (D) had brought his parents to America. No Error (E)

5. The budget committee's report included (A) a proposal where (B) each of the departments was to reduce (C) its (D) spending. No Error (E)

6. Health researchers have discovered that the chance of survival is substantially (A) increased when (B) a doctor detected (C) the disease in its early stages. (D) No Error (E)

7. There has never been much contact (A) between James and I, (B) even though there are (C) several projects to which (D) we each contribute. No Error (E)

STOP

Autumn Maple with Poem Slips, c. 1675 (detail). Edo Period. Tosa Mitsuoki (Japan). Six-fold screen, ink, colors, gold leaf, and powdered silk. 142.5 x 293.2 cm. The Art Institute of Chicago.

UNIT FOUR

East Asia and the Pacific

2000 B.C.–Present

E pala ma'a, 'ae le pala 'upu.

Stones rot, but words last forever.

—Samoan proverb

The Land and Its People

East Asia stretches from the windswept plains of Mongolia and the rugged mountains of Tibet, through the rich agricultural lands of eastern China, across the Yellow Sea to the mountainous peninsula of Korea, and then across the Sea of Japan to the island country of Japan. The diverse countries in the region have been bound together for centuries by culture and history.

China is one of the world's largest countries. The most fertile land is found in the eastern third of the country, where the great majority of its people live. One of the world's oldest civilizations developed there. Chinese culture had a great influence on the art, philosophy, and technology of the entire region.

For thousands of years, the people of Korea lived mainly by farming. Today, South Korea in particular is one of Asia's most technologically developed countries.

Japan, one of the most densely populated countries in the world, consists of four large islands and numerous smaller ones. During the first half of the twentieth century, the Japanese government was dominated by the military. Today, with a democratic government, Japan is the most prosperous country in Asia.

Shinjuko, Tokyo, Japan.

Terraced fields, Guangxi, China.

Active Reading Strategies

Reading the Time Line

1. How many years after David became king of Israel did Jimmu Tenno become Japan's first emperor?
2. How many years separate the birth of Chinese philosopher Confucius and the assassination of Roman dictator Julius Caesar?

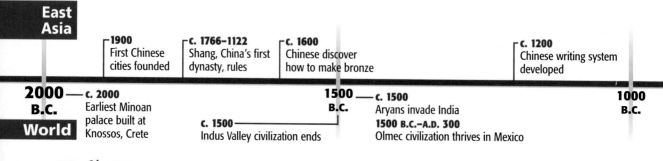

East Asia

- **1900** First Chinese cities founded
- **c. 1766–1122** Shang, China's first dynasty, rules
- **c. 1600** Chinese discover how to make bronze
- **c. 1200** Chinese writing system developed

2000 B.C. — **1500 B.C.** — **1000 B.C.**

World

- **c. 2000** Earliest Minoan palace built at Knossos, Crete
- **c. 1500** Indus Valley civilization ends
- **c. 1500** Aryans invade India
- **1500 B.C.–A.D. 300** Olmec civilization thrives in Mexico

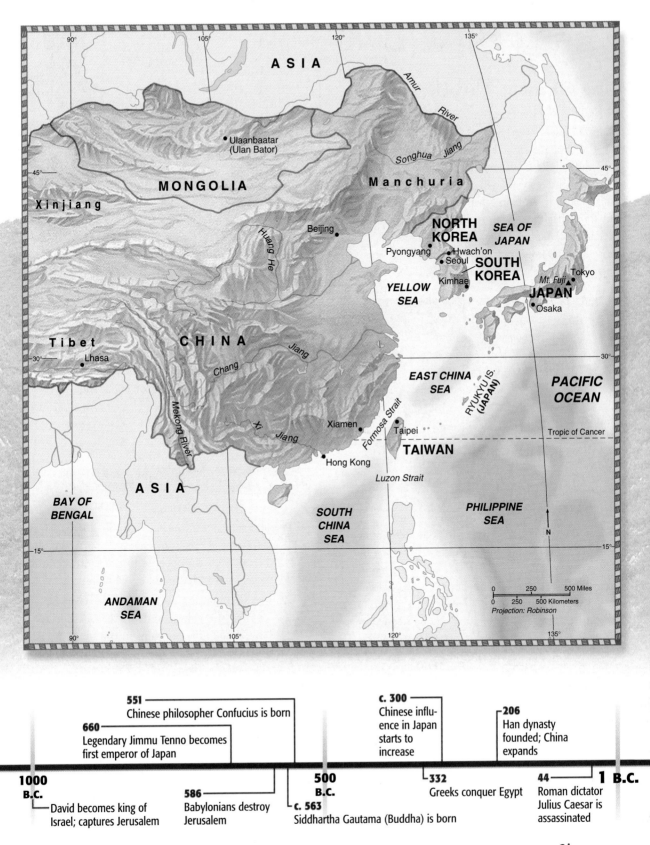

ASIA
MONGOLIA
Ulaanbaatar (Ulan Bator)
Xinjiang
Manchuria
Amur River
Songhua Jiang
Beijing
Huang He
NORTH KOREA
Pyongyang
Hwach'on
Seoul
SOUTH KOREA
Kimhae
SEA OF JAPAN
YELLOW SEA
JAPAN
Tokyo
Mt. Fuji
Osaka
Tibet
Lhasa
CHINA
Chang Jiang
EAST CHINA SEA
RYUKYU IS. (JAPAN)
PACIFIC OCEAN
Mekong River
Xi Jiang
Xiamen
Formosa Strait
Taipei
TAIWAN
Tropic of Cancer
Hong Kong
Luzon Strait
ASIA
BAY OF BENGAL
SOUTH CHINA SEA
PHILIPPINE SEA
ANDAMAN SEA
N
0 250 500 Miles
0 250 500 Kilometers
Projection: Robinson
90° 105° 120° 135° 45° 30° 15°

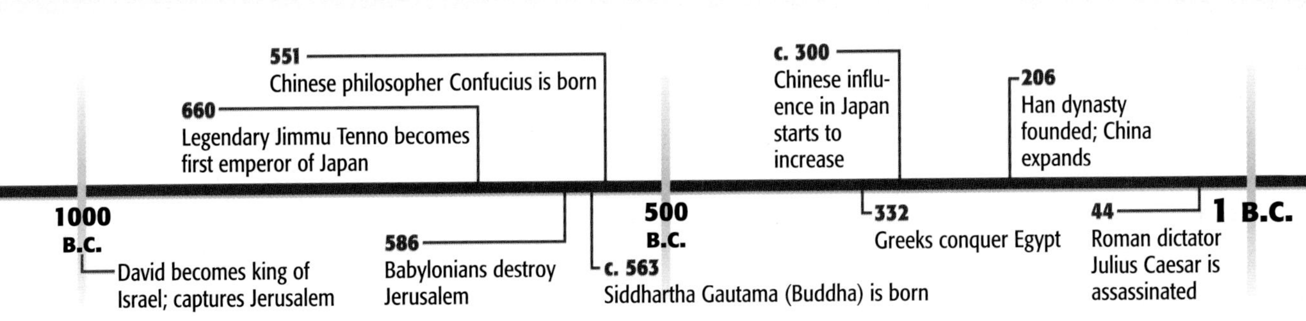

c. 300 Chinese influence in Japan starts to increase
206 Han dynasty founded; China expands

How People Live

The Chinese Family

The family was the most important social unit in classical Chinese society. Several generations lived together in large extended families. Chinese values, especially under Confucian influence, stressed respect for elders and ancestors. In early days only the upper class played any role in government, but in later days any family that could afford to do so sent one of their members to the university. After an education, if one passed the all-important civil-service exams, one could begin a career as a government official.

Family meal, mid-autumn festival, China.

Medieval Japan

During the eleventh to thirteenth centuries, Japan developed a feudal system that in many ways resembled the system in medieval Europe. Powerful lords were granted large territories that they governed as long as they accepted the authority of the central government. They were supported by military retainers called samurai. Samurai lived according to a strict code of honor and behavior, the Bushido ("The Way of the Warrior"). The daughters and wives of samurai were held to the same strict code of courage and honor as the warriors; and they managed family affairs when the samurai were off at war. Peasants had few rights but were usually allowed to govern themselves as long as they paid their taxes.

Martial arts student with naginata, traditional samurai weapon.

Modern Times

During the twentieth century, China, Korea, and Japan have undergone massive social, political, and technological changes. All three countries have become more industrialized. In China the ruling Communists have initiated many changes. They have discouraged the practice of religion and attempted to control population growth. During the 1950s and 1960s, they organized agricultural and industrial collectives, which were required to meet state production schedules.

Critical Thinking

Connecting Cultures

1. The tradition of respect for the elderly is fundamental in Chinese society. In a paragraph, discuss ways that people in the United States today view older members of society.
2. In a small group, discuss the following: Do we treat the elderly with sufficient respect? How do family structures in the United States today reflect our values concerning older family members?

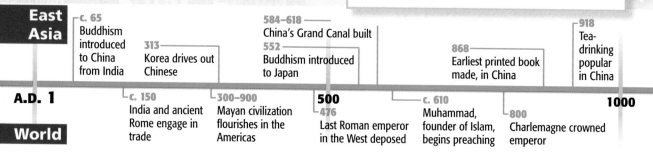

East Asia

- **c. 65** Buddhism introduced to China from India
- **313** Korea drives out Chinese
- **584–618** China's Grand Canal built
- **552** Buddhism introduced to Japan
- **868** Earliest printed book made, in China
- **918** Tea-drinking popular in China

A.D. 1 — **500** — **1000**

World

- **c. 150** India and ancient Rome engage in trade
- **300–900** Mayan civilization flourishes in the Americas
- **476** Last Roman emperor in the West deposed
- **c. 610** Muhammad, founder of Islam, begins preaching
- **800** Charlemagne crowned emperor

What People Believe

Ancient Beliefs

Underlying the philosophical traditions of all the East Asian countries are the ancient traditional beliefs of the people, including reverence for ancestors and belief in a number of gods and spirits. Buddhism, throughout the region, as well as Taoism in China and Shinto (or Shintoism) in Japan, have absorbed many of these traditional beliefs.

Confucianism, Taoism, and Buddhism

Followers of Confucianism and Taoism (tou′ iz′ əm), systems that originated in China in the sixth century B.C., differ on the individual's duty in the world. Confucius taught the importance of behaving properly in accordance with tradition, emphasizing order in human relationships. Confucianism became the backbone of the Chinese civil service and was also influential in Korea and Japan. Taoists emphasized the need to follow the natural order of things.

The teachings of the Buddha arrived in China by the first century A.D., carried by Indian merchants. Buddhism became widespread in China. The fundamental Buddhist principle is that a person should try to live a pure and upright life. From China, Buddhism spread to Korea and Japan. Zen Buddhism, probably the most widely known form in the West, was developed in Japan from the Chinese ch'an school.

Confucian shrine, On' Yang, South Korea.

Other Beliefs

Christianity came to China in the seventh century, but it never made great inroads there. Islam has been more successful and is well established in the vast western province of Xinjiang. Christianity was introduced to Korea in the seventeenth century and survived to become a major belief there today. In Japan, Shinto, based on traditional beliefs, remains an important part of everyday life.

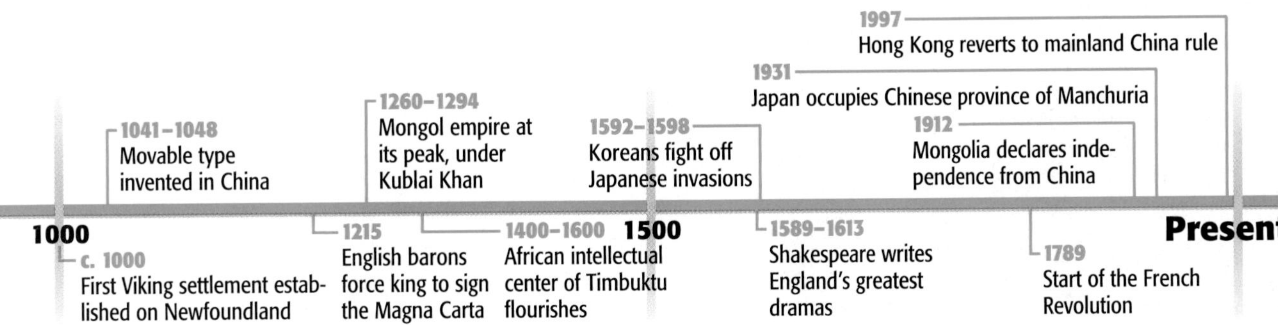

1000
c. 1000
First Viking settlement established on Newfoundland
1041–1048
Movable type invented in China
1215
English barons force king to sign the Magna Carta
1260–1294
Mongol empire at its peak, under Kublai Khan
1400–1600
African intellectual center of Timbuktu flourishes
1500
1589–1613
Shakespeare writes England's greatest dramas
1592–1598
Koreans fight off Japanese invasions
1789
Start of the French Revolution
1912
Mongolia declares independence from China
1931
Japan occupies Chinese province of Manchuria
1997
Hong Kong reverts to mainland China rule
Present

Arts and Entertainment

Korean Ceramics

Pottery and ceramics were perfected in all three East Asian countries. Korea's strength lay in the production of serene, natural pottery of simple beauty. In the eleventh to thirteenth centuries, Korea learned the Chinese techniques of producing high-fired porcelains and used them to create porcelain with a distinctive green glaze, called celadon (se′ lə dän). This work was appreciated by the Japanese, who copied Korean styles, and by the Chinese, who called Korean celadon ware "one of the ten best things in the world."

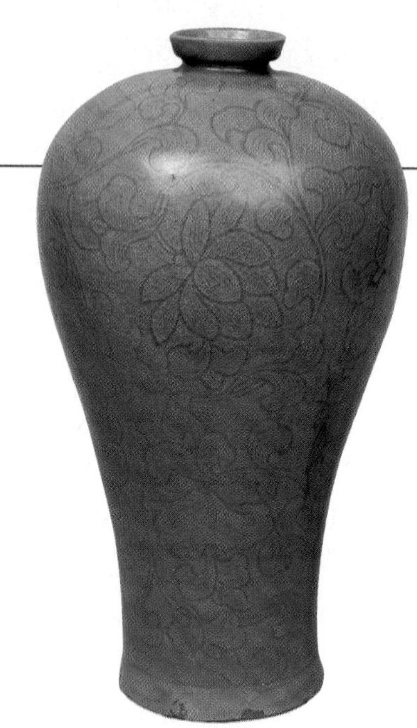

Korean celadon, Koyo Period (12th century).

Puppet Theater

Puppet theater is an important part of the East Asian tradition. Although children may enjoy some of the presentations, most puppet plays are intended for an adult audience.

In China, several types of puppet theater can be found. One of the liveliest uses glove puppets. This simple form is used to present all sorts of plays, from retellings of old folktales to versions of Peking Opera performances. Productions today often use dry ice, laser lighting, and other modern effects.

In Korea, *Kkoktukaksi* (kok too̅′ käk sē) puppet plays have been performed for hundreds of years. The basic story is always the same but leaves plenty of room for the performers to improvise a satirical commentary on current affairs. These plays are still performed by theaters that travel around the countryside.

Japanese *bunraku* (bən rä′ ko̅o̅) puppets act out traditional plays that date back to the late seventeenth century. These lifelike three-foot-high puppets are treated almost as miniature actors. In fact, the Kabuki acting style was influenced by the movements and gestures of *bunraku* puppets.

Japanese bunraku puppeteer.

East Asian Theater

Although there are actually many styles of opera in China, the best-known style of theater is referred to in the West as "Peking Opera," because it is associated with the capital, Peking (or Beijing). Chinese opera tells traditional stories using a variety of theatrical effects, including dancing, singing, and acrobatics, all performed in colorful costumes and makeup. The most popular operas retell stories from hundreds of years ago, although attempts have been made to produce operas with modern subjects.

Japan has two highly stylized forms of theater, Noh and Kabuki. The 600-year-old Noh dance-drama was developed for the nobility and the samurai. Performers do not act out the stories as actors do in other styles, but suggest them with references to scenes and stories with which the audience is expected to be familiar. Kabuki originated around A.D. 1600 as theater for the common people. The heroes of Kabuki plays were often people of the lower classes who resisted oppression by the samurai class. Kabuki actors perform on a stage that has passageways projecting into the audience on the left and right, which means that the actors can virtually encircle the audience. Kabuki programs sometimes continue from morning to night, prompting a continuous coming and going of the audience. Performers and the audience interact constantly. Sometimes performers stop and address the crowd directly. Occasionally, members of the audience break into the performance to praise a favorite scene or to call out the name of a favorite performer.

The Peking Opera.

Language and Literature

Korean calligraphy based on a Chinese character meaning "etiquette" or "proper behavior."

The Art of Writing

One of the unifying forces of East Asian civilization is the Chinese writing system. Most of the world's other systems focus on indicating the sound of a word. Chinese writing, however, emphasizes symbols that indicate the meaning of a word. This system makes it possible to read Chinese without actually being able to speak it; you simply need to be able to recognize the symbols. Problems do arise, however, when writing Chinese words in an alphabetic system, because the written characters do not indicate any specific pronunciation. For example, the capital of China, long spelled as Peking, is now written as Beijing.

Both the Koreans and the Japanese used the Chinese system when they first began to write their languages, which are completely different from Chinese. Chinese characters are still the basis of written Japanese, although additional characters have been developed to make the meanings clearer. Korea invented a system of its own in 1443 but still uses a number of Chinese characters.

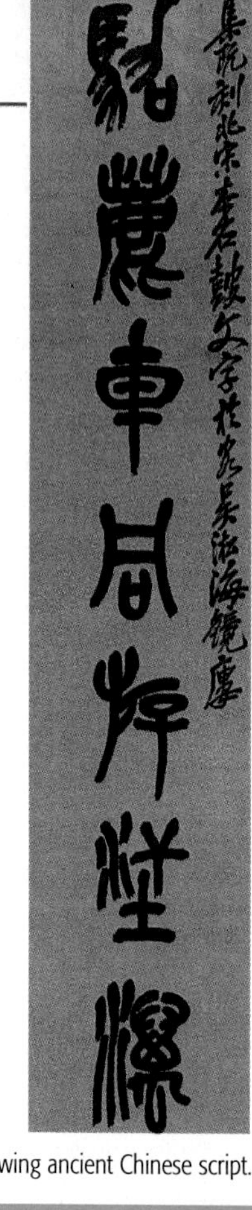

Calligraphy showing ancient Chinese script.

East Asian Languages

Over a billion people speak Chinese, more than speak any other language on Earth. Several different but closely related languages, called dialects, make up the Chinese language group. The most widely known is Mandarin, spoken by over 70 percent of all Chinese and taught throughout the country. More than a hundred minority languages are also spoken in China. Some, like Tibetan, have millions of speakers and their own literary history. Others, with only a few thousand speakers, had no written form until recently. Mandarin is the official language of the Chinese Nationalist government on Taiwan. Chinese, like a number of other languages in the area, is a "tonal" language. In such languages, the meaning of a word is indicated by the tone in which it is spoken.

Other countries in the area have more uniform language groups: more than 90 percent of the people in Mongolia speak Mongol, and in Japan and Korea nearly everyone speaks the national language. Some scholars believe that these three languages, which are not tonal, are distantly related.

influences

In recent years, with the growing interest in East Asian culture, a number of words from the region have entered the English language, joining older words such as "tea" (from the Chinese *t'e*).

- futon (Japanese), a thin mattress placed on the floor for sleeping, and folded and stored during the day
- kimono (Japanese *kimono*, "clothes"), a loose wraparound robe with wide sleeves and a broad sash
- honcho (Japanese *hancho*, "squadron leader"), leader, person in charge
- lama (Tibetan *bla-ma*, "superior one"), a Buddhist priest or monk

Witter Bynner

My hair had hardly covered my forehead.
I was picking flowers, playing by my door,
When you, my lover, on a bamboo horse,
Came trotting in circles and throwing green plums.
We lived near together on a lane in Ch'ang-kan,
Both of us young and happy-hearted.

Wai-lim Yip

My hair barely covered my forehead.
I played in front of the gate, plucking flowers,
You came riding on a bamboo-horse
And around the bed we played with green plums.
We were then living in Ch'ang-kan.
Two small people, no hate nor suspicion.

Florence Ayscough and Amy Lowell

When the hair of your Unworthy One first began to
cover her forehead.
She picked flowers and played in front of the door.
Then you, my Lover, came riding a bamboo horse.
We ran round and round the bed, and tossed about
the sweetmeats of green plums.
We both lived in the village of Ch'ang Kan.
We were both very young, and knew neither
jealousy nor suspicion.

Untitled, 18th century. Lam Qua (China).

Viewing the painting: In this painting the artist has used a number of techniques from the European painting tradition. In particular, the use of perspective to show the distance between objects in the room, and the use of shadows to indicate rounded shapes, are techniques not used in traditional Chinese art.

RESPOND

Compare Pound's translation of the opening lines from Li Po's poem with the versions in this feature.

1. Which translation is most like Pound's? How is Pound's version unique?
2. What poetic devices does Pound use to lend a musical quality to his translation?
3. **Viewing the painting:** Look at the painting on this page and think about how it suggests a mood. Although it is a Chinese work, it is not painted in the traditional Chinese style, as the painting on page 605 is. Rather, it is painted in a style that suggests a strong European influence. In what ways can you compare this painting to "The River Merchant's Wife: A Letter"?

CHINA, c. 757

Before You Read

Jade Flower Palace

Meet Tu Fu

"I will not rest until my verses astound and awe people."

Although many people regard Tu Fu (to͞o′ fo͞o′) as China's greatest poet, his work was virtually ignored during his lifetime. Nor did Tu Fu enjoy success in other areas of life. He never achieved his lifelong goal of serving the emperor, since he was unable to pass the required civil service exam.

Disappointed in his ambitions, Tu Fu turned his attention to poetry. A tireless perfectionist, he rewrote his poems again and again. The result was technically brilliant and innovative poems that both vividly describe Tu Fu's own personal experiences and critique current social problems.

During his later years, Tu Fu experienced bitter poverty. His children died of starvation. Despite his personal suffering, he never lost his compassion for others. He wrote, "Considering what bitter things happened to me, ordinary people must be truly in dire straits."

Tu Fu was born in 712 and died in 770.

Reading Focus

Have you ever passed an abandoned building and thought: "Who lived there? Why was it built? How did it become abandoned?"

Share Ideas With a partner, discuss any abandoned buildings you have seen and the emotions, thoughts, or questions these places brought to mind.

Setting a Purpose Read to find out how one poet responds to the sight of an abandoned place.

Building Background

The Careless Court

In many of his poems, Tu Fu criticizes the incompetence and conspicuous wealth of the imperial court. In 755 a civil war broke out in China due to power struggles among the wealthy aristocrats of the court. As a result, many Chinese died. In his poetry, Tu Fu describes the sufferings of the common people in the face of this war, and condemns those responsible for their suffering. In other poems, he satirizes courtiers' preoccupation with luxury and prestige.

A Tale of Two Poets

Li Po (see page 599) and Tu Fu, two of the most celebrated poets in Chinese history, were born only eleven years apart, and they became close friends. At the time of their first meeting, Tu Fu was about thirty and was just beginning to establish his reputation. Li Po was already famous for the beauty of his poetry and for his unconventional ways. The older poet had a profound influence on Tu Fu. Li Po encouraged Tu Fu to study Taoism and to question his lifelong devotion to Confucian ideals. For a time the poets traveled together, then separated, never to meet again. Despite his admiration for Li Po, Tu Fu ultimately returned to his Confucian principles.

Reading Further

If you enjoy reading "Jade Flower Palace," you might also like to read the following poetry:

Poems by Tu Fu in *The Charcoal Burner and Other Poems,* translated by Henry H. Hart.

Li Po and Tu Fu, translated by Arthur Cooper.

Blue and Green Landscapes. Li Qing (China, d. 1853). Ink and color on paper, 10 x 11 in. Private collection.

Jade Flower Palace

Tu Fu

Translated by Kenneth Rexroth

The stream swirls. The wind moans in
The pines. Gray rats scurry over
Broken tiles. What prince, long ago,
Built this palace, standing in
Ruins beside the cliffs? There are
Green ghost fires in the black rooms.
The shattered pavements are all
Washed away. Ten thousand organ
Pipes whistle and roar. The storm
Scatters the red autumn leaves.
His dancing girls are yellow dust.
Their painted cheeks have crumbled
Away. His gold chariots
And courtiers are gone. Only
A stone horse is left of his
Glory. I sit on the grass and
Start a poem, but the pathos of
It overcomes me. The future
Slips imperceptibly away.
Who can say what the years will bring?

Responding to Literature

Personal Response

After reading lines 1–19, how did you respond to the question at the end of the poem?

Analyzing Literature

Recall and Interpret

1. What images are included in the first three lines of the poem? What overall **mood**, or feeling, do these images create (see page R7)?
2. How is the condition of the palace described in lines 3–8? What can you infer about the reasons for its present state?
3. What has happened to the prince's dancing girls, gold chariots, and courtiers? How would you characterize the prince's manner of living, based on lines 11–16?
4. How does the speaker feel at the end of this poem? How might his vision of the palace be related to his inability to start a poem?

Evaluate and Connect

5. Tu Fu wrote many poems criticizing imperial opulence and power. Do you think this is one of them? Use examples from the poem to support your answer.
6. Refer to your answer to the Reading Focus on page 604. How are your thoughts and feelings similar to or different from those of the speaker?
7. In this poem, the speaker describes feeling a sense of pathos, or compassion, when confronted with the abandoned palace. What other sights might cause a person to experience this emotion?
8. In this poem, Tu Fu uses images from nature to convey the overall mood. Name three images from nature that you might include to create a poem with a similar mood. Explain your choices.

Literary ELEMENTS

Imagery

The term **imagery** refers to words or phrases that appeal to one or more of the five senses. Writers use such language to convey how things look, taste, feel, sound, and smell. An innovative and dynamic poet, Tu Fu was known for his striking imagery and for combining images in surprising ways. In "Jade Flower Palace," Tu Fu uses imagery that helps readers both visualize and experience a palace in a state of ruins.

1. Which images in the poem appeal to your sense of hearing? How do these images contribute to the impact and meaning of the poem?
2. How do you interpret the image of "green ghost fires"? How might it relate to the rest of the poem?

- See **Literary Terms Handbook,** p. R6.

Extending Your Response

Literature Groups

Discuss In your group, try to identify the main theme, or message, of "Jade Flower Palace." Do you think, for instance, this poem is chiefly about the ravaging effects of time on a building? Or is it about the nature of time itself, or some other topic? Use evidence from the poem to support your opinions. When you are finished, share your conclusions with the class.

Creative Writing

Express Yourself Write a poem that captures your reaction to seeing a building you mentioned in the Focus Activity on page 604. In your poem, try to use images from nature as well as other sensory images to convey the emotions this building evoked in you.

Save your work for your portfolio.

Travel Writing

In this article from *Outside* magazine, travel writer Tim Cahill tells of his trip to Mongolia as part of a scientific expedition.

from A Good Hair Week in Mongolia

by Tim Cahill—*Outside*, April 1996

Mongolian nomadic tradition emphasizes hospitality: when travelers meet, they exchange food, such as yogurt, and gifts. Cahill's party has run out of gifts to offer the two riders who appear in the distance, bearing yogurt. The most polite thing they can do is make a run for it . . .

The riders were coming toward us at a stiff trot. They were at least two miles back and about 1,000 feet above us. Each man held something in his right hand. I could plainly see the glint of metal.

"They carrying?" one of the Americans asked.

"Yeah," I said, "both of them."

Bayaraa Sanjaasuren, our translator, conveyed the information to the Mongolian wranglers. This was serious: we had yogurt riders on our tail.

"Tchoo," half a dozen men shouted at once.

"Tchoo" is the Mongolian equivalent of "giddyup." Mongolian horses respond smartly to "tchoo," no matter who says it. Guy next to you says "tchoo," you're off at a gallop. We were riding 12 abreast because Mongols do not ride in single file. A defeated army, they say, rides in single file. And now, with the dreaded yogurt riders in pursuit, our little party sounded like the whole first grade trying to imitate a locomotive.

"Tchoo, tchoo . . ."

"Tchoo, tchoo, tchoo . . ."

Significantly, there is no Mongolian word for "whoa."

We'd been riding eight to 12 hours a day, every day, for a week, and I was fairly comfortable in the old Russian cavalry saddle I'd been given.

"Tchoo," I said, and stood up a bit in the saddle so my horse could stretch into a gallop.

The ground we were approaching, however, was humped up in marshy tussocks characteristic of soil that is permanently frozen a few feet below the surface. We were only at about 48 degrees north—the latitude of Seattle—but cold fronts originating in Siberia flow down the great Yenisey River, northern Asia's Amazon, and funnel into Mongolia. Nowhere else in the hemisphere does permafrost extend so far south.

Trees cannot grow in permafrost, and here, in the shadow of the mountain called Otgon Tenger, with bare hills rising to 10,000 feet on all sides, we were sitting ducks. We could run, but we couldn't hide. There were no fences, no trees, no telephone poles, no buildings, no cattle or livestock of any kind. It was just us: 11 men and one woman, along with several packhorses and a string of remounts, all of us dwarfed under the immense vault of the sky.

Analyzing Media

1. Why do you think it would be more polite to run away than to meet the riders?
2. What would you have done in this situation? Explain.

JAPAN, c. 850–1150

Before You Read

Tanka

Meet Four Japanese Poets

“[P]oetry, without effort, moves heaven and earth, . . . smooths the relations of men and women, and calms the hearts of fierce warriors.”

—Tsurayuki (from the preface to the *Kokinshū*)

One of the most important anthologies of Japanese verse is the *Kokinshū* (kō kēn′ sho͞o), a collection gathered around A.D. 905 for Japan’s emperor. Ki no Tsurayuki (kē nō tso͞o rä yo͞o′ kē), an official in the imperial court and a celebrated poet, critic, and diarist, was largely responsible for compiling this anthology. His opinions about poetry helped define Japanese verse for years to come.

Two prominent Kokinshū women poets were the novelist Lady Ise (ē sä′) and Ono no Komachi (ō′ nō′ nō kō mä′ chē). Komachi was a legendary figure, both for her poetry and for her beauty. According to legend, she was often cruel to others, but she herself suffered as well, as time diminished her beauty.

The twelfth-century poet Saigyō (sä′ ē gyō) was a guardian of the imperial palace who renounced court life to become a Buddhist monk. He traveled throughout Japan, often living in the mountains as a recluse. His poems reflect his devotion to Buddhism and to nature.

Ki no Tsurayuki was born c. 872 and died c. 945.

Lady Ise was born c. 875 and died c. 938.

Ono no Komachi was born c. 833 and died c. 857.

Saigyō was born in 1118 and died in 1190.

Reading Focus

Recall a time when you were struck by a thought, sensation, or emotion that you didn’t want to forget.

Quickwrite What did you do when it happened? Did you jot it down, call a friend, or write a poem? Describe the moment and how you tried to capture it.

Setting a Purpose Read to find out how four poets capture specific moments in time.

Building Background

Tanka Poetry

The four poems presented here are examples of the **tanka** (page R12), an unrhymed Japanese verse form that consists of five lines. The first and third lines have five syllables each; the other lines have seven syllables each. From the eighth century until the sixteenth century, the tanka was the dominant form in Japanese poetry. Poets viewed the tanka as ideal for capturing a fleeting emotion or experience. As the poet Ishikawa Takuboku wrote, “Although a sensation may last only a second, it is a second that will never return again. I refuse to let such moments slip by.”

Two frequent themes in tanka are the splendors of nature and the passage of time. Poets wrote about the changing seasons both to reflect upon nature’s beauty and to express sorrow about the passage of time.

Ono no Komachi

Poetry was often combined with painting on Japanese screens. Folding screens with panels were common in aristocratic mansions and the imperial palace. Screens could contain scenes from nature, sometimes with different scenes on each panel, and other times with one large scene unfolding across several panels. Often, poems were inscribed on the screen to complement the art; many Kokinshū poems were used this way.

Tanka

Translated by Geoffrey Bownas and Anthony Thwaite

Flowering Plants and Fruits of the Four Seasons. Watanabe Shiko (Japan, 1683–1755). One of a pair of six-panel screens, ink, colors, and gold on paper, 154.5 x 352 cm. Asian Art Museum of San Francisco.

When I Went to Visit

Ki no Tsurayuki

When I went to visit
The girl I love so much,
That winter night
The river blew so cold
That the plovers° were crying.

5 *Plovers* are a kind of shore bird.

Forsaking the Mists

Lady Ise

Forsaking the mists
That rise in the spring,
Wild geese fly off.
They have learned to live
In a land without flowers.

Was It That I Went to Sleep

Ono no Komachi

Was it that I went to sleep
Thinking of him,
That he came in my dreams?
Had I known it a dream
I should not have wakened.

Trailing on the Wind

Saigyō

Trailing on the wind,
The smoke from Mount Fuji°
Melts into the sky.
So too my thoughts—
Unknown their resting place.

2 *Mount Fuji,* the highest peak in Japan, was an active volcano in Saigyō's time.

Responding to Literature

Personal Response

Which images or lines in these poems did you find most appealing?

Analyzing Literature

Recall and Interpret

1. Who is the speaker visiting in Tsurayuki's poem? How might lines 1–2 relate to the last three lines of the poem?
2. What might the speaker of "Forsaking the Mists" mean by the words the geese "have learned to live / In a land without flowers"?
3. In Komachi's poem, what does the speaker wish she had not done? Why?
4. In Saigyō's poem, to what are the speakers' thoughts compared? What might he be implying about his state of mind?

Evaluate and Connect

5. Which of the poems do you think best conveys a personal feeling or emotion? Explain.
6. Have you, like the speaker in Komachi's poem, ever had a dream that seemed especially real? Explain.
7. Recall your answer to the Reading Focus on page 608. What images from nature could you use to help convey the thought or feeling that you had?
8. What, in your opinion, are the benefits and limitations of the tanka form? Explain.

Mood

Mood is the emotional quality that a piece of writing conveys. To express mood, writers use such devices as powerful imagery, evocative word choice, and vivid description. Japanese poets, for example, use images that stir the reader's power of association and then juxtapose those images in startling ways. In doing so, they often create powerful emotional responses in the reader.

1. What emotions are evoked by the imagery in Tsurayuki's poem? How do the images he includes contribute to these emotions?
2. What mood does the imagery in Saigyō's tanka create?

- See **Literary Terms Handbook,** p. R7.

Extending Your Response

Creative Writing

Renga Rounds **Renga** (see page R10), or linked verse, was a group poetry activity that evolved from the tanka. One poet wrote the first three lines of a tanka and a second poet completed the poem. A third poet then composed the first three lines in the next tanka of the renga, based on the previous poem. There are usually five tanka in a renga. Work with a small group to create your own renga.

Internet Connection

Japan Yesterday and Today A wealth of information about both classical and contemporary Japanese culture is available on the Internet–from modern art exhibitions to E-texts of tenth-century tanka. Choose one facet of Japan that you are curious about, and go on a Web hunt to see what information you can discover.

Save your work for your portfolio.

Literature FOCUS

Journals and Diaries

Journal Keeping

Have you ever kept, or do you still keep, a journal? In a journal or diary, you try to make faithful entries at the end of each day, at your writing desks or keyboards, noting in details—large and small—what you observed or experienced that day. A journal is also a place to record your thoughts and feelings about your life and experiences. In some ways, you are writing to yourself, focusing your thoughts in a quiet, private moment. You would probably gasp at the thought of someone *else* reading your private observations. And yet, you feel compelled to read the journals and diaries of such people as Samuel Pepys, James Boswell, Dorothy Wordsworth, Anton Chekhov, or Anne Frank.

Journals and diaries are two important types of nonfiction that provide information about actual people, places, events, things, and ideas. Reading these writings can give you an understanding of what life must have been like during the time the writer lived. Detailed entries provide an engaging source of material—factual, opinionated, insightful, sometimes witty, sometimes ordinary—about daily life during a particular time. For example, from Chekhov's May 5, 1896, journal entry, you learn that during the opening of a school in Talezh, "The sexton Ivan Nicolayevitch brought my portrait, which he has painted from a photograph. In the evening V. N. S. brought his friend N. He is director of the Foreign department . . . editor of a magazine . . . and doctor of medicine. He gives the impression of being an unusually stupid person and a reptile." In a later entry, you see firsthand Chekhov's keen eye for human character and behavior. He writes: "In fine weather N. walks in galoshes, and carries an umbrella, so as not to die of sunstroke."

The Pillow Book In this unit you will read excerpts from *The Pillow Book of Sei Shōnagon*, one of the most insightful and detailed journals ever written. Sei Shōnagon, the author of *The Pillow Book*, served as a lady-in-waiting at the Court of the Japanese empress during the late tenth century. Sei Shōnagon filled her journal with observations and opinions on subjects as diverse as wind instruments, the correct behavior for lovers, and why oxen should have very small foreheads. She also wrote lists, such as "Surprising and Distressing Things" and "Times When One Should Be on One's Guard." While *The Pillow Book* provides little information about Sei Shōnagon herself, it is a rich source of information about tenth-century imperial life, as can be seen in the excerpt "The Cat Who Lived in the Palace."

The Pillow Book also includes observations about human behavior that, ten centuries later, remain universal: "One is in a hurry to leave, but one's visitor keeps chattering away" or "Someone has torn up a letter and thrown it away. Picking up the pieces, one finds that many of them can be fitted together."

By reading journals and diaries, you can learn about individual life experiences in times past. In the details of daily life, you also rediscover the bond that joins people across cultures as well as centuries—our humanity.

Untitled. Suzuki Harunobu (Japan, 1705–1772). Pillar print, 26¾ x 4½ in. The Newark Museum, NJ.

Before You Read

from *The Pillow Book*

Meet Sei Shōnagon

"When I first went into waiting at Her Majesty's Court, so many different things embarrassed me that . . . I was always on the verge of tears."

Sei Shōnagon (sā′ ē shō′ nä gōn′) was born into a family known for its literary talent. As a young woman, she became lady-in-waiting to Japan's Empress Sadako. At first, Shōnagon feared she would be unable to perform her duties and stood in awe of the other ladies-in-waiting. These fears were not based on mere nervousness on Sei Shōnagon's part. In her time, the wealthy Fujiwara family were the real rulers of Japan, and the imperial court's function was purely symbolic. Under the circumstances, ceremony and ritual were of the highest importance; a mistake in their performance could mean the end of a career. Soon she overcame her embarrassment and became a highly regarded member of court.

The Pillow Book is Sei Shōnagon's personal diary that includes her impressions of court life during the nearly ten years she spent in imperial service in tenth-century Japan. It is made up of anecdotes, poems, and lists of her likes and dislikes. Throughout *The Pillow Book*, Shōnagon applies wit and perception, bringing a thousand-year-old world to life for us.

Sei Shōnagon was born in 966 and died c. 1013.

Reading Focus

Everyone has particular likes and dislikes. What are some of yours?

List It! Write five things other people do that you find annoying or enjoyable.

Setting a Purpose Read to discover the things that one author likes and dislikes.

Building Background

The Time and Place

For centuries, Japan was dominated by the culture of China. By the late ninth century, however, a distinctively Japanese culture began to emerge, triggered in part by the development of a Japanese script.

Interestingly, the most important early literature written in Japanese was by women, including Sei Shōnagon, Ono no Komachi, and Murasaki Shikibu, author of the novel *The Tale of Genji.* Japanese men were slower to adopt *kana*, the Japanese script, for literature.

Japanese women took advantage of the evolving script to write in original, new forms. Sei Shōnagon's "lists," for example, have no predecessors in either Chinese or Japanese literature.

Vocabulary Preview

gesticulate (jes tik′ yə lāt′) *v.* to make gestures, especially when speaking; p. 614

inquisitive (in kwiz′ ə tiv) *adj.* curious about the affairs of others; p. 614

trivial (triv′ ē əl) *adj.* commonplace; of little importance; p. 614

chastise (chas tīz′) *v.* to punish, reprimand, or discipline severely; p. 616

banish (ban′ ish) *v.* to drive away or remove by authority; p. 616

reproach (ri prōch′) *v.* to charge with blame or fault for a wrongdoing; p. 616

from The Pillow Book

Girl with a Mirror, c. 1790. Kitagawa Utamaro (Japan). Color woodblock print. British Library, London.

Sei Shōnagon
Translated by Ivan Morris

Hateful Things

One is in a hurry to leave, but one's visitor keeps chattering away. If it is someone of no importance, one can get rid of him by saying, "You must tell me all about it next time"; but, should it be the sort of visitor whose presence commands one's best behavior, the situation is hateful indeed.

One finds that a hair has got caught in the stone on which one is rubbing one's inkstick, or again that gravel is lodged in the inkstick, making a nasty, grating sound.

Someone has suddenly fallen ill and one summons the exorcist.[1] Since he is not at home, one has to send messengers to look for him. After one has had a long fretful wait, the exorcist finally arrives, and with a sigh of relief one asks him to start his incantations.[2] But perhaps he has been exorcizing too many evil spirits recently; for hardly has he installed himself and begun praying when his voice becomes drowsy. Oh, how hateful!

1. An *exorcist* is someone who expels evil spirits.
2. *Incantations* are verbal charms spoken or sung as part of a ritual of magic.

A man who has nothing in particular to recommend him discusses all sorts of subjects at random as though he knew everything.

An elderly person warms the palms of his hands over a brazier[3] and stretches out the wrinkles. No young man would dream of behaving in such a fashion; old people can really be quite shameless. I have seen some dreary old creatures actually resting their feet on the brazier and rubbing them against the edge while they speak. These are the kind of people who in visiting someone's house first use their fans to wipe away the dust from the mat and, when they finally sit on it, cannot stay still but are forever spreading out the front of their hunting costume or even tucking it up under their knees. One might suppose that such behavior was restricted to people of humble station; but I have observed it in quite well-bred people, including a Senior Secretary of the Fifth Rank in the Ministry of Ceremonial and a former Governor of Suruga.

I hate the sight of men in their cups[4] who shout, poke their fingers in their mouths, stroke their beards, and pass on the wine to their neighbors with great cries of "Have some more! Drink up!" They tremble, shake their heads, twist their faces, and gesticulate like children who are singing, "We're off to see the Governor." I have seen really well-bred people behave like this and I find it most distasteful.

To envy others and to complain about one's own lot; to speak badly about people; to be inquisitive about the most trivial matters and to resent and abuse people for not telling one, or, if one does manage to worm out some facts, to inform everyone in the most detailed fashion as if one had known all from the beginning—oh, how hateful!

3. A *brazier* (brā′ zhər) is a pan that holds burning coals.

4. The phrase *in their cups* means they have had too much to drink.

One is just about to be told some interesting piece of news when a baby starts crying.

A flight of crows circle about with loud caws.

One has gone to bed and is about to doze off when a mosquito appears, announcing himself in a reedy voice. One can actually feel the wind made by his wings and, slight though it is, one finds it hateful in the extreme.

A carriage passes with a nasty, creaking noise. Annoying to think that the passengers may not even be aware of this! If I am traveling in someone's carriage and I hear it creaking, I dislike not only the noise but also the owner of the carriage.

One is in the middle of a story when someone butts in and tries to show that he is the only clever person in the room. Such a person is hateful, and so, indeed, is anyone, child or adult, who tries to push himself forward.

One is telling a story about old times when someone breaks in with a little detail that he happens to know, implying that one's own version is inaccurate—disgusting behavior!

Very hateful is a mouse that scurries all over the place.

Some children have called at one's house. One makes a great fuss of them and gives them toys to play with. The children become accustomed to this treatment and start to come regularly, forcing their way into one's inner rooms and scattering one's furnishings and possessions. Hateful!

A certain gentleman whom one does not want to see visits one at home or in the Palace, and one pretends to be asleep. But a maid comes to tell one and shakes one awake, with a look on her face that says, "What a sleepyhead!" Very hateful.

A newcomer pushes ahead of the other members in a group; with a knowing look,

Vocabulary

gesticulate (jes tik′ yə lāt′) *v.* to make gestures, especially when speaking
inquisitive (in kwiz′ ə tiv) *adj.* curious about the affairs of others
trivial (triv′ ē əl) *adj.* commonplace; of little importance

this person starts laying down the law and forcing advice upon everyone—most hateful.

In Spring It Is the Dawn

In spring it is the dawn that is most beautiful. As the light creeps over the hills, their outlines are dyed a faint red and wisps of purplish cloud trail over them.

In summer the nights. Not only when the moon shines, but on dark nights too, as the fireflies flit to and fro, and even when it rains, how beautiful it is!

In autumn the evenings, when the glittering sun sinks close to the edge of the hills and the crows fly back to their nests in threes and fours and twos; more charming still is a file of wild geese, like specks in the distant sky. When the sun has set, one's heart is moved by the sound of the wind and the hum of the insects.

Untitled, from the series *100 Views of Edo,* 1857. Andō Hiroshige (Japan). Color woodblock print. Private collection.

Viewing the print: Describe the composition in this print. How does it remind you of the way the narrator sees the world?

In winter the early mornings. It is beautiful indeed when snow has fallen during the night, but splendid too when the ground is white with frost; or even when there is no snow or frost, but it is simply very cold and the attendants hurry from room to room stirring up the fires and bringing charcoal, how well this fits the season's mood! But as noon approaches and the cold wears off, no one bothers to keep the braziers alight, and soon nothing remains but piles of white ashes.

The Cat Who Lived in the Palace

The cat who lived in the Palace had been awarded the headdress of nobility and was called Lady Myōbu. She was a very pretty cat, and His Majesty saw to it that she was treated with the greatest care.

One day she wandered on to the veranda, and Lady Uma, the nurse in charge of her, called out, "Oh, you naughty thing! Please come inside at once." But the cat paid no attention and went on basking sleepily in the sun. Intending to give her a scare, the nurse called for the dog, Okinamaro.

"Okinamaro, where are you?" she cried. "Come here and bite Lady Myōbu!" The foolish

Okinamaro, believing that the nurse was in earnest, rushed at the cat, who, startled and terrified, ran behind the blind in the Imperial Dining Room, where the Emperor happened to be sitting. Greatly surprised, His Majesty picked up the cat and held her in his arms. He summoned his gentlemen-in-waiting. When Tadataka, the Chamberlain,[5] appeared, His Majesty ordered that Okinamaro be chastised and banished to Dog Island. The attendants all started to chase the dog amid great confusion. His Majesty also reproached Lady Uma. "We shall have to find a new nurse for our cat," he told her. "I no longer feel I can count on you to look after her." Lady Uma bowed; thereafter she no longer appeared in the Emperor's presence.

The Imperial Guards quickly succeeded in catching Okinamaro and drove him out of the Palace grounds. Poor dog! He used to swagger about so happily. Recently, on the third day of the Third Month, when the Controller First Secretary paraded him through the Palace grounds, Okinamaro was adorned with garlands of willow leaves, peach blossoms on his head, and cherry blossoms round his body. How could the dog have imagined that this would be his fate? We all felt sorry for him. "When Her Majesty was having her meals," recalled one of the ladies-in-waiting, "Okinamaro always used to be in attendance and sit opposite us. How I miss him!"

It was about noon, a few days after Okinamaro's banishment, that we heard a dog howling fearfully. How could any dog possibly cry so long? All the other dogs rushed out in excitement to see what was happening. Meanwhile a woman who served as a cleaner in the Palace latrines ran up to us. "It's terrible," she said. "Two of the Chamberlains are flogging a dog. They'll surely kill him. He's being punished for having come back after he was banished. It's Tadataka and Sanefusa who are beating him." Obviously the victim was Okinamaro. I was absolutely wretched and sent a servant to ask the men to stop; but just then the howling ceased. "He's dead," one of the servants informed me. "They've thrown his body outside the gate."

That evening, while we were sitting in the Palace bemoaning Okinamaro's fate, a wretched-looking dog walked in; he was trembling all over, and his body was fearfully swollen.

"Oh dear," said one of the ladies-in-waiting. "Can this be Okinamaro? We haven't seen any other dog like him recently, have we?"

We called to him by name, but the dog did not respond. Some of us insisted that it was Okinamaro, others that it was not. "Please send for Lady Ukon," said the Empress, hearing our discussion. "She will certainly be able to tell." We immediately went to Ukon's room and told her she was wanted on an urgent matter.

"Is this Okinamaro?" the Empress asked her, pointing to the dog.

"Well," said Ukon, "it certainly looks like him, but I cannot believe that this loathsome creature is really our Okinamaro. When I called Okinamaro, he always used to come to me, wagging his tail. But this dog does not react at all. No, it cannot be the same one. And besides, wasn't Okinamaro beaten to death and his body thrown away? How could any dog be alive after being flogged by two strong men?" Hearing this, Her Majesty was very unhappy.

When it got dark, we gave the dog something to eat; but he refused it, and we finally decided that this could not be Okinamaro.

On the following morning I went to attend the Empress while her hair was being dressed

5. A *chamberlain* is the chief officer in the emperor's household.

Vocabulary

chastise (chas tīz′) *v.* to punish, reprimand, or discipline severely
banish (ban′ ish) *v.* to drive away or remove by authority
reproach (ri prōch′) *v.* to charge with blame or fault for a wrongdoing

and she was performing her ablutions.[6] I was holding up the mirror for her when the dog we had seen on the previous evening slunk into the room and crouched next to one of the pillars. "Poor Okinamaro!" I said. "He had such a dreadful beating yesterday. How sad to think he is dead! I wonder what body he has been born into this time. Oh, how he must have suffered!"

At that moment the dog lying by the pillar started to shake and tremble, and shed a flood of tears. It was astounding. So this really was Okinamaro! On the previous night it was to avoid betraying himself that he had refused to answer to his name. We were immensely moved and pleased. "Well, well, Okinamaro!" I said, putting down the mirror. The dog stretched himself flat on the floor and yelped loudly, so that the Empress beamed with delight. All the ladies gathered round, and Her Majesty summoned Lady Ukon. When the Empress explained what had happened, everyone talked and laughed with great excitement.

The news reached His Majesty, and he too came to the Empress's room. "It's amazing," he said with a smile. "To think that even a dog has such deep feelings!" When the Emperor's ladies-in-waiting heard the story, they too came along in a great crowd. "Okinamaro!" we called, and this time the dog rose and limped about the room with his swollen face. "He must have a meal prepared for him," I said. "Yes," said the Empress, laughing happily, "now that Okinamaro has finally told us who he is."

The Chamberlain, Tadataka, was informed, and he hurried along from the Table Room. "Is it really true?" he asked. "Please let me see for myself." I sent a maid to him with the following reply: "Alas, I am afraid that this is not the same dog after all." "Well," answered Tadataka, "whatever you say, I shall sooner or later have occasion to see the animal. You won't be able to hide him from me indefinitely."

6. The phrase *performing her ablutions* means that she was bathing.

Before long, Okinamaro was granted an Imperial pardon and returned to his former happy state. Yet even now, when I remember how he whimpered and trembled in response to our sympathy, it strikes me as a strange and moving scene; when people talk to me about it, I start crying myself.

Embarrassing Things

While entertaining a visitor, one hears some servants chatting without any restraint in one of the back rooms. It is embarrassing to know that one's visitor can overhear. But how to stop them?

A man whom one loves gets drunk and keeps repeating himself.

To have spoken about someone not knowing that he could overhear. This is embarrassing even if it be a servant or some other completely insignificant person.

To hear one's servants making merry. This is equally annoying if one is on a journey and staying in cramped quarters or at home and hears the servants in a neighboring room.

Parents, convinced that their ugly child is adorable, pet him and repeat the things he has said, imitating his voice.

An ignoramus who in the presence of some learned person puts on a knowing air and converses about men of old.

A man recites his own poems (not especially good ones) and tells one about the praise they have received—most embarrassing.

Lying awake at night, one says something to one's companion, who simply goes on sleeping.

In the presence of a skilled musician, someone plays a zither just for his own pleasure and without tuning it.

Did You Know?
A *zither* is a stringed instrument that is placed horizontally and is plucked with the fingers.

A son-in-law who has long since stopped visiting his wife runs into his father-in-law in a public place.

Pleasing Things

Finding a large number of tales that one has not read before. Or acquiring the second volume of a tale whose first volume one has enjoyed. But often it is a disappointment.

Someone has torn up a letter and thrown it away. Picking up the pieces, one finds that many of them can be fitted together.

One has had an upsetting dream and wonders what it can mean. In great anxiety one consults a dream-interpreter, who informs one that it has no special significance.

A person of quality is holding forth about something in the past or about a recent event that is being widely discussed. Several people are gathered round him, but it is oneself that he keeps looking at as he talks.

A person who is very dear to one has fallen ill. One is miserably worried about him even if he lives in the capital and far more so if he is in some remote part of the country. What a pleasure to be told that he has recovered!

I am most pleased when I hear someone I love being praised or being mentioned approvingly by an important person.

A poem that someone has composed for a special occasion or written to another person in reply is widely praised and copied by people in their notebooks. Though this is something that has never yet happened to me, I can imagine how pleasing it must be.

A person with whom one is not especially intimate refers to an old poem or story that is unfamiliar. Then one hears it being mentioned by someone else and one has the pleasure of recognizing it. Still later, when one comes across it in a book, one thinks, "Ah, this is it!" and feels delighted with the person who first brought it up.

I feel very pleased when I have acquired some Michinoku paper, or some white, decorated paper, or even plain paper if it is nice and white.

A person in whose company one feels awkward asks one to supply the opening or closing line of a poem. If one happens to recall it, one is very pleased. Yet often on such occasions one completely forgets something that one would normally know.

I look for an object that I need at once, and I find it. Or again, there is a book that I must see immediately; I turn everything upside down, and there it is. What a joy!

When one is competing in an object match (it does not matter what kind), how can one help being pleased at winning?

I greatly enjoy taking in someone who is pleased with himself and who has a self-confident look, especially if he is a man. It is amusing to observe him as he alertly waits for my next repartee;[7] but it is also interesting if he tries to put me off my guard by adopting an air of calm indifference as if there were not a thought in his head.

I realize that it is very sinful of me, but I cannot help being pleased when someone I dislike has a bad experience.

It is a great pleasure when the ornamental comb that one has ordered turns out to be pretty.

I am more pleased when something nice happens to a person I love than when it happens to myself.

Entering the Empress's room and finding that ladies-in-waiting are crowded round her in a tight group, I go next to a pillar which is some distance from where she is sitting. What a delight it is when Her Majesty summons me to her side so that all the others have to make way!

7. *Repartee* is an interchange of witty remarks.

Untitled. Utagawa Kunisada (Japan, 1786–1864). Color woodblock print. Private collection.

Viewing the print: How is the woman in the painting like the narrator?

Responding to Literature

Personal Response

What is your overall impression of Sei Shōnagon? Do you find her a likable person? Explain.

Analyzing Literature

Recall

1. Name four or five of the things that Shōnagon finds hateful.
2. Which parts of the day does Shōnagon prefer in each of the four seasons? Why?
3. Summarize what happens to Okinamaro after he rushes at the royal cat.
4. What kinds of behavior does Shōnagon find embarrassing in pretentious people?
5. What pleasing things does Shōnagon mention that relate to either the act of writing or reading?

Interpret

6. How would you characterize Shōnagon's personality, based on her list of hateful things?
7. What can you infer about Shōnagon's relationship to nature from reading "In Spring It Is the Dawn"?
8. What, in your opinion, does "The Cat Who Lived in the Palace" reveal about court life?
9. What do "Embarrassing Things" and the other sections reveal about Shōnagon's attitude toward children and people of lower rank?
10. How important do you think reading and writing are to Shōnagon? Explain.

Evaluate and Connect

11. Choose an item from Shōnagon's lists that you think displays her best qualities and one that displays her worst. Explain your choices.
12. Which part of the day do you prefer in each of the four seasons? Why?
13. Compare the list you made for the Reading Focus on page 612 with Shōnagon's list of "Hateful Things." Does your list share any similar items? Explain.
14. Do you feel that Shōnagon is completely honest in her diary? Support your answer with details from the selection.
15. Describe a situation from your own experience that fits one of the categories in Shōnagon's lists.

Literary Criticism

Translator Ivan Morris comments that *The Pillow Book* "reveals a complicated, intelligent, well-informed woman who was quick, impatient, keenly observant of detail, high-sprited, witty, emulative, sensitive to the charms and beauties of the world and to the pathos of things, yet intolerant and callous about people whom she regarded as her social or intellectual inferiors." What evidence of these qualities can you find in the selection you have read? Write an analysis of the selection, exploring the characteristics that Shōnagon reveals about herself through her writing.

Literary ELEMENTS

Author's Purpose

Author's purpose refers to the author's reasons for creating a literary work. These may include a desire to entertain readers, to inform or explain, or to express feelings, impressions, and opinions. Usually, diarists keep journals for self-expression. Shōnagon, however, may have had a different purpose in mind, since she knew that the impressions she recorded would be circulated among her peers in the court.

1. In your opinion, what was Shōnagon's main purpose for keeping a journal? Explain.
2. Shōnagon's rival, Murasaki Shikibu, felt that Shōnagon's purpose in writing was to shock people and to draw attention to herself. Do you agree with her opinion? Explain.

- See **Literary Terms Handbook,** p. R1.

Literature and Writing

Writing About Literature

Analyzing Organization *The Pillow Book* is organized very differently from a standard daily-entry diary. Write several paragraphs describing your reaction to Shōnagon's use of lists. How effective do you find it? Do you think Shōnagon's impressions of imperial life would have been more interesting written as a chronological account?

Personal Writing

Writing an Anecdote An **anecdote** (page R1) is a brief account of something that happened in a person's life. It can be told in a few sentences, or require a page or more. An effective anecdote provides insight into the characters or events being described. Choose an event from your own life, and write a brief anecdote that tells the tale.

Extending Your Response

Literature Groups

Personality Profile How do you picture Sei Shōnagon, based upon your readings from her diary? What are her dominant personality traits? Working with your group, see if you can agree upon five words or phrases that capture the essence of Shōnagon's personality.

Performing

Pillow Book Theater In your group, create skits that illustrate situations in Shōnagon's lists. Choose a section, and discuss how to present it, rehearse, and perform it for your class.

Interdisciplinary Activity

Social Studies Japan's history is marked by periods in which foreign cultures (such as those of China and Europe) held great influence, and periods in which the country rejected foreign influences. Find out more about the major influences of other cultures on Japan and the time periods in which they occurred. Display your findings graphically, with a time line or a map.

Reading Further

If you enjoyed reading *The Pillow Book,* you might enjoy the following memoirs:

Ake: The Years of Childhood, by Wole Soyinka, in which the Nobel Prize–winning author provides a rich picture of life in colonial Nigeria.

Murasaki Shikibu: Her Diary and Poetic Memoirs, translated by Richard Bowring.

Save your work for your portfolio.

VOCABULARY • Connotation and Denotation

The denotation of a word is its literal meaning. Its connotation is the positive or negative meaning the reader associates with the word. For example, the denotation of the word *overhear* is to hear accidentally; the word does not have any negative implications. The word *eavesdrop,* however, meaning to listen secretly, evokes a negative response.

PRACTICE With each pair, indicate which word has the more positive connotation and which has the more negative one.

1. curious–nosy
2. trivial–minor
3. resign–quit
4. challenging–stressful
5. crowded–busy

Write a sentence for each pair of words, showing their connotations.

1. hoard–save
2. cabin–shack
3. funny–ridiculous
4. confident–pushy
5. slim–skinny

JAPAN, Traditional

Before You Read

Green Willow

Reading Focus

Fulfilling a duty or doing what you want—everyone faces this conflict at various times in life. How do you resolve such conflicts?

Discuss In a small group, brainstorm a list of situations that involve a conflict between responsibility and personal desire. Discuss the ways in which you have resolved such conflicts in the past.

Setting a Purpose Read a Japanese folktale to learn about a warrior who must choose between carrying out a responsibility and doing what he desires.

Building Background

A Samurai's Duty

The main character in "Green Willow" is a samurai, a member of the warrior class in medieval Japan. In the 1100s, a system called *feudalism* began to develop in Japan. Under this system, the samurai protected the estates of large landowners, or feudal lords. Like the knights of medieval Europe, the samurai pledged loyalty to their lords and lived by a strict code of ethics. Besides the development of military skills, the code emphasized such virtues as courage, honor, frugality, and self-discipline. Above all, the samurai were expected to remain loyal and fulfill their duty to their lords. Samurai were taught to value obedience more than their own lives. Feudalism lasted into the 1800s in Japan, much longer than it lasted in Europe.

Scene from Chushingura, 1862. Meirindo Kakujujo (Japan). Woodcut, diptych, 36 x 24.5 cm (each). Spencer Museum of Art, The University of Kansas.

Buddhism in Japan

Long before feudalism developed in Japan, Buddhism had become an important part of the country's culture. It became the official state religion in Japan in the A.D. 700s. Buddhism is based on the teachings of Siddhartha Gautama (si där′ tə gau′ tə mä), known as the Buddha, or the Enlightened One. Among other things, Buddhism stresses the importance of trying to achieve spiritual peace, living in harmony with nature and the world, and leading one's life responsibly. Some Buddhist priests live in temples or monasteries; others live as hermits or wandering pilgrims.

Vocabulary Preview

instinctively (in stingk′ tiv lē) *adv.* naturally or unconsciously; p. 624

renounce (ri nouns′) *v.* to give up, to abandon; p. 625

disciple (di sī′ pəl) *n.* one who accepts or assists in spreading the teachings of another; p. 625

meditate (med′ ə tāt′) *v.* to quietly focus one's thoughts; p. 625

pilgrimage (pil′ grə mij) *n.* a journey taken by a disciple; p. 625

Green Willow

Retold by Rafe Martin

Once there lived a young samurai named Tomotada.

Though he had been trained for war and was skilled in handling the bow, spear, and sword, he spent much of his time tending the trees of the palace grounds. Tomotada loved all green, growing things. But he greatly loved trees.

One day Tomotada was entrusted with an important mission. He was to carry a message scroll from his lord to the lord whose castle lay beyond the mountains. It was a great honor.

It was early autumn, the day bright and clear, when he rode out of the palace gates. The golden willow leaves waved in the breeze as if in farewell.

Hanrei and Seishi. Kiyohara Yukinobu (Japan, 1643–1682). Hanging scroll, ink and colors on silk, 71.8 x 32.3 cm. Museum of Fine Arts, Boston.

Tomotada rode all through that day. As he approached the mountains, the sky grew black. Lightning flashed, a cold wind blew, and a heavy rain was soon pelting down. Tomotada rode on, urging his horse forward along the slippery trails. Night was fast approaching. A fall on those mountain passes could easily mean death. Up ahead Tomotada saw a gleam of light. It vanished, then shone again. Heading toward it, he came to a small hut. Near the hut, by the banks of a stream, stood three willow trees. Two of the willows were old, heavy-limbed, and grew close together. The third willow was young, graceful, and slender. Willow branches tossed by the wind had hidden and then revealed the light shining through a crack in the hut's shuttered window.

Soaked and chilled, Tomotada tied his horse's reins to a willow and knocked at the door. It opened. "Come in, young sir," said the old man who stood in the doorway. "Come in out of the storm. Green Willow will see to your horse." Tomotada turned and saw a cloaked figure leading his horse to shelter. He stepped inside.

A hot bath took the chill from his bones. Dressed in dry clothes, Tomotada sat down to a steaming meal prepared by the old man's wife. The door opened and a cold, wet wind blew in.

"My daughter," said his host, "Green Willow." Shyly the figure removed the wet cloak. Tomotada's heart skipped. The girl was beautiful, graceful as her namesake, the willow. Tomotada forgot his dinner. He forgot his mission. He could think only of Green Willow.

Late into the night Tomotada sat and talked with the old couple and with Green Willow. Green Willow's voice seemed as soft and sweet as the rustling of willow leaves to Tomotada. The turn of her neck, the lifting of her hands and arms were as graceful, as beautiful to him as the swaying of a young willow in a spring breeze.

At last Tomotada lay down to sleep. Outside, the wind moving through the leaves of the willow trees made a gentle music. Words for that music rose in his mind: "Green Willow. My wife will be Green Willow."

Alas for Tomotada, the next day dawned fair and clear. He would not be able to remain. Once more his mission called. With a heavy heart Tomotada watched as Green Willow led his horse from the stable. He saw the tears in her eyes. He knew then that he could never leave her. "I will be back," he said, "as soon as my duty is fulfilled." He mounted his horse and rode away.

All that day worry gnawed at his heart. Shouldn't he have asked for Green Willow's hand in marriage before he had left? Would he still find her there when he returned? Such thoughts gave him no peace.

As darkness fell he came to an abandoned temple. Wearily he dismounted. As he entered the temple, he heard a movement in the darkness. Instinctively drawing his sword, he called out, "Who is there? Show yourself or I strike." A figure rose from the shadows. "Green Willow!" And so it was. He sheathed his sword and held her close. How she had ever found him in that lonely spot, how she had arrived there before him—such thoughts he did not think. No. He had his Green Willow.

Tomotada could not leave Green Willow again. They set off along the roads together, little caring where those roads might lead. In time they came to a city where Tomotada's lord was unknown. They married and, with the money and jewels Tomotada carried sewn into the lining of his robe, they built a house near a stream. "Someday," he said, "I shall return to my lord and ask for his forgiveness. But not yet. No. I cannot leave yet."

Tomotada and Green Willow created a garden of many trees and flowers. Green Willow's love of trees and of green, growing things was as great as, if not greater than, Tomotada's own.

Vocabulary

instinctively (in stingk′ tiv lē) *adv.* naturally or unconsciously

They planted cherry trees and peach trees, pines and firs. And such flowers! Great blossomed peonies and chrysanthemums and tall irises all grew in profusion. And by the stream, there were willows. Tomotada and Green Willow were happy.

One summer's night Tomotada and Green Willow sat in their garden. Water splashed in the little stream nearby. Leaves rustled on the evening breeze. The perfume of many flowers scented the air. Suddenly Green Willow cried out in pain, "My tree! My tree!"

"What is it?" Tomotada asked urgently.

Perspiration stood on Green Willow's brow. "My tree!" she cried again. "My tree. Don't let them! Not now! Oh, but they are cutting, cutting. The pain! They are cutting my tree! Oh, dear Tomotada, husband," she said feverishly, "I am sorry that I took you from your duty. But I loved you. I shall always love you. Farewell."

"What are you saying?" he cried. "You are here with me. All is well. What . . . !" But before he could finish, Green Willow was gone! In his arms he held not a woman but a bunch of long, slender, golden willow leaves.

In his heart Tomotada knew the truth. But it was a truth that even he found hard to accept. He renounced the world, gave away all his possessions, and became a wandering monk, a disciple of the compassionate Buddha. Often he slept in the open fields beneath the stars or meditated alone in the mountains with only wild animals, rocks, and trees as companions. He prayed for all living things—animals, plants, and trees.

One day he found himself standing beside a familiar stream. It was, he realized with a start, the place where the hut had been when he had first met Green Willow. There were no traces of the hut at all. But three cutoff stumps remained standing there—all that was left of two old willows and a young one.

Putting his hands together, palm to palm, Tomotada sank to his knees and recited a prayer for the dead before the willow stumps.

Foolish man, he thought to himself, *what would people think to see you praying over willow stumps?*

Then hands still palm to palm, he once again chanted the words that bring peace to those gone beyond this earthly life.

Tomotada's pilgrimage was over. He built a hut on the spot, and there he remained. In the spring he discovered a green shoot growing from the stump of the young willow. Tomotada tended the shoot. It grew into a graceful sapling, which put forth slender leaves that rustled and whispered in the breeze. At night the music those leaves made moved through his dreams. "Green Willow," a voice sang to that music, "Green Willow."

The tree grew taller and more beautiful with each passing year.

At last Tomotada's life came to an end. A seed drifted down from the tree to rest where his bones had joined the earth. In time a new shoot came forth. The shoot grew and grew until it too was a sturdy tree. The trunks of the two willows grew together. The branches intertwined. Down under the earth the roots found each other in the darkness and embraced.

When the wind moves, rustling the leaves of those trees, it is as if they speak. "Tomotada," one tree seems to whisper, like a dreamer turning in sleep.

And the other seems to murmur as if in tender reply, "Green Willow, Green Willow."

Vocabulary

renounce (ri nouns′) *v.* to give up, to abandon
disciple (di sī′ pəl) *n.* one who accepts or assists in spreading the teachings of another
meditate (med′ ə tāt′) *v.* to quietly focus one's thoughts
pilgrimage (pil′ grə mij) *n.* a journey taken by a disciple

Responding to Literature

Personal Response

What do you think of the ending of the story? Share your reaction with your classmates.

Analyzing Literature

Recall and Interpret

1. How do Tomotada and Green Willow meet? Why is Tomotada attracted to Green Willow?
2. **Internal conflict** is a struggle that takes place within the mind of a character (see page R2). Describe the internal conflict that Tomotada faces. How does he resolve it?
3. Describe Tomotada and Green Willow's married life. Why does Green Willow disappear?
4. After Green Willow disappears, what does Tomotada do for the rest of his life?
5. At the end of the story, what do the intertwined branches and roots of the two willows represent?

Evaluate and Connect

6. What message about people and nature does "Green Willow" express?
7. Does Tomotada fit your image of a samurai? Explain your answer.
8. For the Reading Focus on page 622, you discussed how you have resolved conflicts between responsibility and personal desire. What decision would you make if you were in Tomotada's place? Why?
9. What insights into Japanese culture do you gain from this story?
10. What other folktale or story does "Green Willow" remind you of? Share the tale with your classmates.

Japanese earthenware vase, late 19th century.

Literary ELEMENTS

Foreshadowing

Foreshadowing is the use of clues by the author to prepare readers for events that will happen in a story. Much like eerie background music in a horror film, foreshadowing helps build suspense and draws the reader into a tale. The folktale "Green Willow" contains a number of instances of foreshadowing. For example, at the beginning of the story, the author emphasizes Tomotada's love of trees and says that the willow trees "waved in the breeze as if in farewell" as Tomotada rode off to deliver the scroll. These references to Tomotada's relationship with trees foreshadow what will happen later. Likewise, the stormy weather into which Tomotada rides suggests that something ominous will follow.

1. What early clues suggest that the lives of the willow trees outside the hut are entwined with those of the hut's occupants?
2. Were you surprised by the manner of Green Willow's death? Why or why not?

- See **Literary Terms Handbook**, p. R5.

Literature and Writing

Writing About Literature

Dear Tomotada Write a letter to Tomotada, consoling him for the loss of Green Willow. Remind him of the happiness he enjoyed and what might be his fate after death. Support your statements with details from the story.

Creative Writing

Apology to the Master In "Green Willow," Tomotada breaks his vow of loyalty to his lord by not fulfilling his duty. He hopes, however, to return one day to his lord and beg his forgiveness. Imagine that this day has arrived. Write a speech in which Tomotada explains to his lord why he failed to carry out his responsibility.

Extending Your Response

Literature Groups

A Fateful Decision In your group, discuss the consequences of Tomotada's decision to abandon his mission and go away with Green Willow. What were the results? What happened to Green Willow and her parents because of it? How were Tomotada and Green Willow ultimately reunited? If you were in Tomotada's place, would you have made the same decision? After your discussion, present your conclusions to the class.

Performing

Choices, Choices In your group, decide on a modern-day situation in which a choice similar to Tomotada's must be made. Collaborate on a skit that presents the alternatives, the choice, and the consequences of the decision. Identify the characters involved, and decide on dialogue. Practice the skit; then present it to the class.

Interdisciplinary Activity

Social Studies: Buddhism and Japanese Culture Buddhism has influenced the development of many aspects of Japanese culture, including landscape gardening, flower arranging, the tea ceremony, and painting and sculpture. Investigate the Buddhist influence on one of these aspects of Japanese culture, and prepare a visual and oral presentation to share with the class.

Save your work for your portfolio.

VOCABULARY • Diminutive Suffixes

As an adjective, "diminutive" means "small." As a noun, a diminutive is a suffix that makes the word it is attached to smaller. For example, the word *rosette* refers to an ornament usually made of ribbon shaped to resemble a small rose.

PRACTICE Use a dictionary to discover the meaning of each of the words below. Then write an original sentence using the word.

1. rivulet
2. floweret
3. coronet
4. kitchenette
5. eaglet
6. islet
7. piglet
8. statuette

MEDIA connection

Web Site

The ancient Chinese sport of dragon boat racing has spread around the globe; it is now one of the most popular sports in the world. The boats, 30 to 100 feet long, are paddled by male, female, and mixed teams.

Awakening the Dragon

Address: http://www.alvin.org/dragon/history.htm

The tragic tale of Ch'u Yuan further integrated the dragon boat races into the lives of the Chinese.

Ch'u Yuan was a poet and a minister and counselor to the king of Ch'u—truly a great patriot. He feared for the future of his kingdom, and to do the best for his country, he gave advice to the king. The advice was not accepted and he was exiled. Ch'u Yuan, in desperation and sorrow, threw himself into the Mi Lo River.

The people of Ch'u loved Ch'u Yuan. They grieved over his death and spent much time trying to scare the fish and water dragons away from Ch'u Yuan's body by rowing around the river in their fishing boats, splashing their oars, and beating their drums. And to ensure that Ch'u Yuan never went hungry, they wrapped rice in leaves and threw them into the river. Rice cakes are still eaten today as part of the dragon boat festival celebration.

To experience a dragon boat race—either watching or participating—is a thrill in itself and can be enjoyed by everyone.

You'll watch as long, multicolored boats, with frightening dragons' heads, long tails, and scaly bodies, splash through the water. You'll see men, women, and children grunt and sweat as they push themselves faster and faster to be the first to the finish line. You'll hear the crowds screaming and cheering for their favorite team, while the drummers pound on their drums and yell at the paddlers. The event is not intended to be quiet and peaceful but loud and exciting—a celebration.

The race has come to symbolize both man's struggle against nature and his fight against dangerous enemies.

Analyzing Media

1. Why do you think dragon boat racing might be popular around the world?
2. Would you rather watch or paddle in a dragon boat race? Explain.

Before You Read

Two Lies

Reading Focus

In *The Taming of the Shrew,* Shakespeare wrote, "There's small choice in rotten apples." What does this statement mean to you?

Journal Have you ever been in a no-win situation in which you were faced with two bad choices? In your journal, describe the situation and explain how you made a decision.

Setting a Purpose Read this Korean folktale about a man who puts himself into a no-win situation.

Building Background

Chosŏn Dynasty in Korea

The folktale "Two Lies" dates from the period of the Chosŏn or Yi (yē) dynasty in Korea. During this period, which lasted from 1392 to 1910, the country was ruled by kings from the Yi family, who established a government based on Confucianism. This ethical system originated with the Chinese philosopher Confucius. Confucianism aimed to bring order and harmony to society by establishing principles for moral conduct by individuals and government.

The Chosŏn king deliberated with a state council in establishing government policies. These policies were then executed by separate ministries. The country was divided into eight provinces, each headed by a governor appointed by the central government.

Most high-level officials in the Chosŏn government belonged to a hereditary upper class called the *yangban,* whose members studied Confucianism and took civil service examinations to qualify for public offices. Besides controlling the government, the *yangban* also owned most of the land in the country. Thus, they formed a wealthy, powerful class.

In the story "Two Lies," the Minister holds a high-level office in the central government and so would be a member of the *yangban.*

Reading Further

If you enjoy reading "Two Lies," you might also enjoy the following folktale collections:

Korean Folk-Tales, published by Oxford University Press.

Tales of a Korean Grandmother, by Frances Carpenter.

Dong-ja (Altar Attendants). 18th century, Yi Dynasty, Korea. Pair of polychromed wood figures, height: 20 in. Brooklyn Museum, New York.

Two Lies

Told by An Zŏng-Og

Translated by Zŏng In-Sŏb

Portrait of Chief Minister Mun Suk-kong, 19th century. Artist unknown (Korea). Brooklyn Museum, New York.

Once there was a Minister who was so fond of being told lies that he announced, "Any man who can tell me two lies that I find interesting shall marry my only daughter." So all the leading liars in the eight provinces came to his house. But with all the stories they told he was never satisfied, and refused to give his daughter to any of them.

One day, however, a young man came and said, "It will be very hot in summer, you know. So you should go out now and dig a great pit under the main street of Seoul.[1] Then when the hot weather comes you can sell it and make your fortune."

"That's a wonderful lie," answered the Minister as usual. "And the next?"

The young man took an old document from his pocket. "This is a bond of debt amounting to one hundred thousand *yang*[2] which your late father borrowed from me before he died. I have come to demand payment."

Now the Minister was in a quandary.[3] "If I say it's a lie," he said to himself, "I must give him my daughter. But if I say it is not a lie, I must pay all that money." In the end he had to say, "It's a lie," and the young man married his daughter.

---

1. *Seoul* (sōl) was the capital of the Kingdom of Korea; since 1948, it has been the capital of the Republic of South Korea.
2. A *yang* is a unit of Korean currency.
3. A *quandary* is a state of uncertainty or a predicament.

Responding to Literature

Personal Response

What is your opinion of the second lie the young man tells?

Analyzing Literature

Recall and Interpret

1. What announcement does the Minister make?
2. What is the first lie the young man tells? How does the Minister react to it?
3. How does the young man get the better of the Minister with his second lie?
4. Why might the Minister hesitate to give his daughter in marriage to the young man? What is the Minister's final decision?

Evaluate and Connect

5. In your opinion, does the Minister deserve to be in this predicament? Explain.
6. What does the Minister's decision suggest about the values he considers important?
7. For the Reading Focus on page 629, you wrote about a time when you were faced with two equally bad choices. How does the decision you made reflect your values?
8. If you were in the Minister's situation, what decision would you make? Why? In your own words, tell what the implied **moral** (page R8) of the story is.

Literary **ELEMENTS**

Fable

A **fable** is a very brief folktale told to teach a lesson. In some fables, such as those of Aesop, the lesson or moral is stated explicitly. In other fables, the reader must infer the lesson based on what happens in the story. "Two Lies" is an example of a fable in which the lesson must be inferred. Different readers might easily discover different lessons in this story.

1. What lesson or lessons do you infer from this fable?
2. In this fable, what makes a lie "interesting"?
3. What elements of this fable remind you of other fables or folktales that you have read or heard?

- See **Literary Terms Handbook,** p. R4.

Extending Your Response

Creative Writing

A Tall Tale Imagine that you are one of the "leading liars in the eight provinces." Write a lie that demonstrates this talent. Have a competition with your classmates to see who can come up with the tallest of tall tales. You may have one student play the part of the *yangban* in the story, and decide who has told the "best" lie.

Interdisciplinary Activity

Science: Zoology The Korean tiger is one of that country's national symbols. Yet today this animal has almost disappeared from the peninsula. Use the library and the Internet to research the history of the Korean tiger and its status today. You may wish to write a report, or to make a collage of tiger images from photographs and Korean art.

Save your work for your portfolio.

Before You Read

The Damask Drum

Meet Seami Motokiyo

"The actor who has not a good play at his disposal is like an army without weapons."

In 1374 a single performance may have changed the course of Japanese theater, when the shogun, or governor, Ashikaga Yoshimitsu (ä shē kä′ gä yō shē mē′ tz o͞o) went to see a theater company. He was so impressed by two of the actors that he became the company's greatest supporter. Under his patronage, the company turned Noh (also spelled Nō) theater, a type of theater that combines drama, music, and dance, into one of Japan's classic art forms.

The younger actor, Seami (also spelled Zeami) Motokiyo (zā ä′ mē mō tō kē′ yō), was only eleven at the time of the performance. The older actor was Seami's father, Kan'ami, who was a brilliant playwright and the head of the theater company. When Seami reached adulthood, he expanded upon his father's innovations, writing new plays and establishing guidelines on how Noh plays should be written and performed.

Today Seami Motokiyo is considered one of Japan's greatest playwrights. His influence on the Noh drama is as strong as it ever was: of the approximately 250 Noh plays that are still performed today, nearly sixty were written by Seami.

Seami Motokiyo was born in 1363 and died in 1443.

Reading Focus

Think about a time in your life when you behaved badly toward someone.

Quickwrite Spend two or three minutes quickwriting to describe what happened and any lessons you learned from the experience.

Setting a Purpose Read to find out what happens to one character as a result of her bad behavior toward someone else.

Building Background

Japanese Noh Drama

Japanese Noh plays have changed little since they developed their permanent form in the fourteenth century. A Noh play combines music, dancing, and acting, and differs greatly from Western theatrical performances. The stage on which the Noh play is performed contains few props. The actors, in contrast, wear elaborate costumes and masks. A typical play has only three or four roles, all performed by men. The main character may appear in human form, as a ghost, or both. A secondary character generally introduces the play. Other characters may include a narrator and children or friends of the lead characters. Music is supplied by a flute player and three drummers. There is also a chorus, usually of eight people, which narrates and helps to explain the story as it happens.

Most action in a Noh play is symbolic. For example, a character may take only a few steps to indicate he is on a long journey. Years of training are required to master the techniques of Noh. Although all professional performers are men, both men and women study and perform as amateurs.

A traditional Noh performance lasts most of a day, and consists of five Noh dramas. Between the dramas come short farcical plays (four in all) called *kyōgen.* These brief comedies, performed without masks and in ordinary dress, relieve the tension of the serious and formal noh plays.

The Damask Drum

Seami Motokiyo

Translated by Arthur Waley

CHARACTERS

A COURTIER[1]

AN OLD GARDENER

THE PRINCESS

THE GARDENER'S GHOST

CHORUS

COURTIER. I am a courtier at the Palace of Kinomaru in the country of Chikuzen. You must know that in this place there is a famous pond called the Laurel Pond, where the royal ones often take their walks; so it happened that one day the old man who sweeps the garden here caught sight of the Princess. And from that time he has loved her with a love that gives his heart no rest.

Someone told her of this, and she said, "Love's equal realm[2] knows no divisions," and in her pity she said, "By that pond there stands a laurel tree, and on its branches there hangs a drum. Let him beat the drum, and if the sound is heard in the Palace, he shall see my face again."

I must tell him of this.

1. A *courtier* is someone in attendance at a royal court.

2. A *realm* is a kingdom or a country.

Listen, old Gardener! The worshipful lady has heard of your love and sends you this message: "Go and beat the drum that hangs on the tree by the pond, and if the sound is heard in the Palace, you shall see my face again." Go quickly now and beat the drum!

GARDENER. With trembling I receive her words. I will go and beat the drum.

COURTIER. Look, here is the drum she spoke of. Make haste and beat it! [*He leaves the* GARDENER *standing by the tree and seats himself at the foot of the "Waki's pillar."*][3]

GARDENER. They talk of the moon tree, the laurel that grows in the Garden of the Moon. . . . But for me there is but one true tree, this laurel by the lake. Oh, may the drum that hangs on its branches give forth a mighty note, a music to bind up my bursting heart.

Listen! the evening bell to help me chimes;
But then tolls in
A heavy tale of day linked onto day,

CHORUS. [*Speaking for the* GARDENER.] And hope stretched out from dusk to dusk.
But now, a watchman of the hours, I beat
The longed-for stroke.

GARDENER. I was old, I shunned the daylight,
I was gaunt[4] as an aged crane;
And upon all that misery
Suddenly a sorrow was heaped,
The new sorrow of love.
The days had left their marks,
Coming and coming, like waves that beat on a sandy shore . . .

CHORUS. Oh, with a thunder of white waves
The echo of the drum shall roll.

GARDENER. The afterworld draws near me,
Yet even now I wake not
From this autumn of love that closes
In sadness the sequence of my years.

CHORUS. And slow as the autumn dew
Tears gather in my eyes, to fall
Scattered like dewdrops from a shaken flower
On my coarse-woven dress.
See here the marks, imprint of tangled love,
That all the world will read.

GARDENER. I said "I will forget,"

CHORUS. And got worse torment so
Than by remembrance. But all in this world
Is as the horse of the aged man of the land of Sai;
And as a white colt flashes
Past a gap in the hedge, even so our days pass.
And though the time be come,
Yet can none know the road that he at last must tread,
Goal of his dewdrop life.
All this I knew; yet knowing,
Was blind with folly.[5]

GARDENER. "Wake, wake," he cries,—

CHORUS. The watchman of the hours,—
"Wake from the sleep of dawn!"
And batters on the drum.
For if its sound be heard, soon shall he see
Her face, the damask[6] of her dress . . .
Aye, damask! He does not know
That on a damask drum he beats,
Beats with all the strength of his hands, his aged hands,
But hears no sound.
"Am I grown deaf?" he cries, and listens, listens:
Rain on the windows, lapping of waves on the pool—
Both these he hears, and silent only
The drum, strange damask drum.

3. The *"Waki's pillar"* is an area at the front of the Noh stage.
4. *Gaunt* means "extremely thin."
5. *Folly* means "tragically foolish conduct."
6. *Damask* is a firm, lustrous fabric. By asking the gardener to make sound from a damask drum, the princess has given him an impossible task.

Gion Kaji, from *The Stories of Wise Women,* early 18th century. Kaji Kuniyoshi (Japan). Woodblock print, 15 x 10 in. Museum of Fine Arts, Springfield, MA.

Viewing the print: In what ways might this woman remind you of the princess?

Oh, will it never sound?
I thought to beat the sorrow from my heart,
Wake music in a damask drum; an echo of love
From the voiceless fabric of pride!

GARDENER. Longed for as the moon that hides
In the obstinate clouds of a rainy night
Is the sound of the watchman's drum,
To roll the darkness from my heart.

CHORUS. I beat the drum. The days pass and the hours.
It was yesterday, and it is today.

GARDENER. But she for whom I wait

CHORUS. Comes not even in dream. At dawn and dusk

GARDENER. No drum sounds.

CHORUS. She has not come. Is it not sung that those
Whom love has joined
Not even the God of Thunder can divide?
Of lovers, I alone
Am guideless, comfortless.
Then weary of himself and calling her to witness of his woe,
"Why should I endure," he cried,
"Such life as this?" and in the waters of the pond
He cast himself and died.

[*GARDENER leaves the stage.*]

[*Enter the PRINCESS.*]

COURTIER. I would speak with you, madam.

The drum made no sound, and the aged Gardener in despair has flung himself into the pond by the laurel tree, and died. The soul of such a one may cling to you and do you injury. Go out and look upon him.

PRINCESS. [*Speaking wildly, already possessed by the GARDENER's angry ghost, which speaks through her.*]

Listen, people, listen!
In the noise of the beating waves
I hear the rolling of a drum.
Oh, joyful sound, oh joyful!
The music of a drum.

COURTIER. Strange, strange!
This lady speaks as one
By fantasy possessed.
What is amiss, what ails her?

PRINCESS. Truly, by fantasy I am possessed.
Can a damask drum give sound?
When I bade[7] him beat what could not ring,
Then tottered first my wits.

COURTIER. She spoke, and on the face of the evening pool
A wave stirred.

PRINCESS. And out of the wave

COURTIER. A voice spoke.

[*The voice of the GARDENER is heard; as he gradually advances along the hashigakari*[8] *it is seen that he wears a "demon mask," leans on a staff, and carries the "demon mallet" at his girdle.*]

GARDENER'S GHOST. I was driftwood in the pool, but the waves of bitterness

CHORUS. Have washed me back to the shore.

GARDENER'S GHOST. Anger clings to my heart,
Clings even now when neither wrath nor weeping
Are aught[9] but folly.

CHORUS. One thought consumes me,
The anger of lust denied
Covers me like darkness.
I am become a demon dwelling
In the hell of my dark thoughts,
Storm cloud of my desires.

GARDENER'S GHOST. "Though the waters parch[10] in the fields
Though the brooks run dry,
Never shall the place be shown

7. *Bade,* the past tense of *bid,* means "commanded."
8. The *hashigakari* is an area at the back of the Noh stage.
9. *Aught* means "anything."
10. Here, *parch* refers to being scorched or dried up in the heat.

Of the spring that feeds my heart."
So I had resolved. Oh, why so cruelly
Set they me to win
Voice from a voiceless drum,
Spending my heart in vain?
And I spent my heart on the glimpse of a moon that slipped
Through the boughs of an autumn tree.

CHORUS. This damask drum that hangs on the laurel tree

GARDENER'S GHOST. Will it sound, will it sound?

[*He seizes the* PRINCESS *and drags her towards the drum.*]

Try! Strike it!

CHORUS. "Strike!" he cries;
"The quick beat, the battle charge!
Loud, loud! Strike, strike," he rails,
And brandishing his demon stick
Gives her no rest.
"Oh, woe!" the lady weeps,
"No sound, no sound. Oh, misery!" she wails.
And he, at the mallet stroke, "Repent, repent!"
Such torments in the world of night
Abōrasetsu, chief of demons, wields,
Who on the Wheel of Fire
Sears sinful flesh and shatters bones to dust.
Not less her torture now!
"Oh, agony!" she cries, "What have I done,
By what dire seed this harvest sown?"

GARDENER'S GHOST. Clear stands the cause before you.

CHORUS. Clear stands the cause before my eyes;
I know it now.
By the pool's white waters, upon the laurel's bough
The drum was hung.

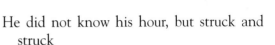

Noh Dancer. Netsuke, Edo Period, Japan. Ceramic. The Lowe Art Museum, The University of Miami, FL.

Viewing the ceramic: What is this figure doing? At what point in the play might such a character appear?

He did not know his hour, but struck and struck
Till all the will had ebbed[11] from his heart's core;
Then leapt into the lake and died.
And while his body rocked
Like driftwood on the waves,
His soul, an angry ghost,
Possessed the lady's wits, haunted her heart with woe.
The mallet lashed, as these waves lash the shore,
Lash on the ice of the eastern shore.
The wind passes; the rain falls
On the Red Lotus, the Lesser and the Greater.
The hair stands up on my head.
"The fish that leaps the falls
To a fell[12] snake is turned,"
I have learned to know them;
Such, such are the demons of the World of Night.
"O hateful lady, hateful!" he cried, and sank again
Into the whirlpool of desire.

11. Here, *ebbed* means "gone out" or "left."
12. *Fell* means "evil."

Responding to Literature

Personal Response

Were you surprised by the outcome of the play? Explain why or why not. Write your answer in your journal.

Analyzing Literature

Recall

1. What is the "new sorrow" that is "heaped" upon the gardener?
2. Describe the task that the princess gives the gardener.
3. Why does the gardener's character leave the stage, and in what form does he reappear?
4. What emotions does the gardener express when he reappears on the stage in a new form?
5. What is the princess forced to do at the end of the play?

Interpret

6. How does the princess respond when she hears about the gardener's love for her?
7. Why is the gardener's task impossible? Why, in your opinion, does the princess give him this task?
8. What danger does the gardener pose to the princess when he reappears on the stage?
9. At the end of the play, what reasons does the gardener give for his inability to find peace?
10. In your opinion, what lessons does the princess learn from her actions? Use details from the play to support your answer.

Evaluate and Connect

11. What is your opinion of the characters of the gardener and the princess?
12. Refer to the Reading Focus on page 632. Were the lessons you learned from your experience similar to or different from those learned by the princess? Explain.
13. What aspect of the play's structure did you find most interesting? Explain.
14. What movie or television drama that you have seen has a **theme** (see **Literary Terms Handbook,** page R12) that is similar to that of *The Damask Drum*? Explain.
15. How would you describe the language used in *The Damask Drum*? How might it contribute to the impact of the play?

Dramatic Convention

An unrealistic device that a playwright uses to present a story on stage and that the audience accepts as realistic is a **dramatic convention.** Because Noh drama emphasizes symbolism over realism, it contains many dramatic conventions. Audiences at Noh plays accept, for example, the convention of male actors playing female roles. They also accept unrealistic shifts in time.

1. What unrealistic shifts in time can you find in *The Damask Drum*? What purpose do such shifts serve, in your opinion?
2. Find another example of the use of a dramatic convention in this play. Why might Seami have chosen to use such a convention?

- See **Literary Terms Handbook,** p. R3.

Noh robe, 17th century. Japan.

Literature and Writing

Writing About Literature

Drama Critic Is *The Damask Drum* your first experience of Noh drama? Try describing the experience to others in a review that provides a description of the characters, a plot summary, background on Noh theater, and your own opinions. Present your review to a small group of classmates and invite constructive comments.

Creative Writing

Create Dialogue Seami tells the story of the gardener's love for the princess from the gardener's perspective. How might the princess herself feel? Write a brief dialogue in which the princess tells the courtier her side of the story and he responds. Before you begin writing, think about the reasons why the princess might not want to become involved with the gardener.

Extending Your Response

Literature Groups

Discuss the Question Discuss the following question: Is the princess solely responsible for the gardener's death, or does Seami suggest that the gardener played a part in his own troubles? Have each person present his or her opinion, using details from *The Damask Drum* for support. Share your conclusions with the class.

Internet Connection

Conduct Research Do a Web search to learn more about Noh drama. Available online resources include photos of the Noh stage and its performers, examples of Noh masks and costumes, video clips from Noh performances, and e-texts of Noh plays.

Performing

Choral Reading In your group, practice a section of *The Damask Drum* to read aloud to the class. You might pause at certain places, change the pace of your reading, read passages in a high or low voice, or stress particular words. Then perform your reading before the class.

Reading Further

If you enjoyed reading *The Damask Drum,* you may also enjoy the following:

The Classic Noh Theatre of Japan by Ezra Pound and Ernest Fenollosa.

The Nō Plays of Japan, by Arthur Waley.

Save your work for your portfolio.

VOCABULARY • Etymology

The **etymology** of a word is its history. In a dictionary, the language from which a word comes is usually given in abbreviations. For example, *ME* stands for "Middle English," *L* for "Latin," and *Gk* for "Greek."

etymology (et′ ə mol′ ə jē) *n.* [ME *ethimologie,* fr. L *etymologia,* fr. Gk, fr. *etymon* "true meaning" + *-logia* "explanation or study" -logy] **1:** the history of a word

PRACTICE Use a dictionary to find the origins of the words listed. Then answer the questions that follow.

chorus brandish champion
pretty lady

1. From how many earlier languages does the word *brandish* come?
2. From which original language does the word *chorus* derive?
3. Which word came from medieval Latin?
4. Which word originally meant "tricky"?
5. Which word meant "kneader of bread"?

JAPAN, c. 1660–1820

Before You Read

Haiku

Meet Matsuo Bashō

"Don't follow in the footsteps of the old poets, seek what they sought."

Matsuo Bashō (mä′ tso͞o′ ō bä′ shō) is known as Japan's master of the haiku. As a young man, he served a samurai until this man's death left him free to concentrate on poetry. His style—influenced by Chinese poetry and Zen Buddhism—revitalized the haiku form. Bashō's poetry reflects his passion for nature.

Bashō was born in 1644 and died in 1694.

Meet Yosa Buson

Yosa Buson (yō sä′ bo͞o sōn′) is considered the haiku's second-greatest master. Buson studied painting and poetry in Edo (now Tokyo). Though he became an accomplished painter, Buson is best known for his poetry, which displays a fascination with color and visual detail.

Buson was born in 1716 and died in 1783.

Meet Kobayashi Issa

The life of Kobayashi Issa (kō bä yä′ shē ē′ sä) was marked by tragedy. He lost his mother at age two and later, his wife and children. The pain from these losses is reflected in his poems.

Issa was born in 1763 and died in 1827.

Reading Focus

What do you think of when you stare at the moon? when it's raining?

Word Web Make a word web with "moon" at the center. List all the words or ideas that come into your mind when you see the moon.

Setting a Purpose Read to discover three poets' insights that connect to aspects of the natural world.

Building Background

The Development of the Haiku

The haiku (hī′ ko͞o′) is a Japanese poetry form consisting of seventeen syllables arranged in three lines. The first and third lines have five syllables each, and the middle line has seven. The haiku developed from a type of poetry called the **renga** (see page R10). To create a renga, one poet would write the first three lines of a tanka (the first and third lines have five syllables each; the other lines have seven syllables each), and a second poet would complete the tanka. Another poet would then begin the next tanka, or link, in the renga. In the hands of Bashō and his contemporaries, the first three lines, or *hokku* (ho′ ko͞o′), of the renga became an independent verse form that was eventually known as the haiku.

Because they are so short, haiku rely heavily on the power of suggestion. Comparisons are implied rather than stated outright. Words in a haiku are chosen for the associations they create in the reader's mind. Traditional haiku were written to strict guidelines; poems were thought incomplete without a *kigo* (kē′ gō)–a season word or image. For example, haiku readers understood that "frogs" or "cherry blossoms" suggested spring; "evening showers," summer; and "snowfall," the winter season.

Reading Further

If you enjoy reading haiku, you might also enjoy the following:

"Bashō," from *The Essential Haiku: Versions of Bashō, Buson, and Issa,* edited and translated by Robert Hass.

An Introduction to Haiku: An Anthology of Poems and Poets from Bashō to Shiki, by Harold G. Henderson.

Young Woman in a Summer Shower, 1765. Suzuki Harunobu (Japan). Woodblock print, 28.6 x 22 cm. Art Institute of Chicago.

Haiku

Yosa Buson

Translated by Geoffrey Bownas
and Anthony Thwaite

Spring rain:
Telling a tale as they go,
Straw cape, umbrella.

Spring rain:
Soaking on the roof
A child's rag ball.

Matsuo Bashō

Translated by
Harold G. Henderson

Poverty's child—
    he starts to grind the rice,
        and gazes at the moon.

The sun's way:
    hollyhocks turn toward it
        through all the rain of May.

Kobayashi Issa

Translated by Geoffrey Bownas
and Anthony Thwaite

The world of dew is
A world of dew . . . and yet,
And yet . . .

Melting snow:
And on the village
Fall the children.

View of Mt. Fuji, from the painted scroll of *Twelve Views of Mt. Fuji.* Katsushika Hokusai (Japan, 1760–1849). Color woodblock print. Chester Beatty Library and Gallery of Oriental Art, Dublin, Ireland.

Viewing the print: How would you describe the moods of the prints in this selection? How are they comparable to the way haiku conveys a mood?

Responding to Literature

Personal Response

Which of the six poems do you like the best? Why? Share your opinion with a partner.

Analyzing Literature

Recall and Interpret

1. What might cause "poverty's child" to gaze at the moon in Bashō's first poem?
2. Where do the hollyhocks turn in Bashō's second poem? What, in your opinion, is the significance of their action?
3. What images in Buson's poems follow the words "Spring rain"? What moods or emotions do you think these images suggest?
4. What might "a world of dew" represent or symbolize in Issa's first haiku? Explain your answer.

Evaluate and Connect

5. Consider the last line of Issa's second poem. Do you find it surprising? Explain.
6. Think about your answer to the Reading Focus on page 640. How does your response to the moon compare with the response of the child in Bashō's poem?
7. **Connotations** (see page R2) are all the associations that a word brings to mind, beyond its dictionary definition. Describe all the connotations that words in one of the haiku have for you.
8. What is your response to the haiku form? Do you find the form puzzling or enjoyable? Explain.

Literary ELEMENTS

Implied Comparison

An **implied comparison** is a comparison made between two or more images that is suggested rather than directly stated. The implied comparison is conveyed by connecting the two images in a new or unexpected way, rather than by indicating that one image *is* the other (metaphor) or is *like* the other (simile). Classical haiku poets preferred the implied comparison to metaphors and similes, and used this device to convey powerful emotions in their poems.

1. To what image does Issa link melting snow in his haiku?
2. What do you feel is the point of this implied comparison?

- See **Literary Terms Handbook,** p. R6.

Extending Your Response

Creative Writing

Signals of the Seasons Words that suggest "fall" to a resident of Japan might not suggest that season to a resident of Maine or Hawaii. What suggests fall to you? The color of the leaves? The crispness of the air? Halloween masks? Create your own list of local *kigo,* or season words, for each of the four seasons. Then write four haiku using the words or phrases on your list.

Listening and Speaking

Hearing Haiku Hearing a poem read aloud can provide a different experience from reading it silently, particularly with haiku, which rely on connotation and association for their power. With a partner, take turns reading the haiku aloud. Discuss any new insights or feelings you experience after hearing the poems spoken.

Save your work for your portfolio.

CHINA, 1935

Before You Read

The Long March

Meet Mao Tse-tung

"A revolution is not a dinner party."

Born the son of a peasant, Mao Tse-tung (mau′ dzə′ doong′; also spelled Mao Zedong) led the revolution that made China a Communist country. Mao spent nearly thirty years building up the Communist Party and fighting a civil war before he gained control of China in 1949. He then sought to mold Chinese society into his concept of an ideal Communist state. He redistributed land and began a program for rapid economic development called the Great Leap Forward. The program was designed to increase agricultural and industrial production; instead it ruined the economy. To maintain revolutionary ideals and to silence opponents, Mao initiated the Cultural Revolution. Those who opposed Mao's ideas were publicly humiliated, jailed, or executed, and youth groups called the Red Guards destroyed temples and burned books with the intention of eradicating all old ideas and customs. Writers and artists were pressured to celebrate communism, as Mao himself did in both poetry and prose.

Mao Tse-tung was born in 1893 and died in 1976.

Reading Focus

Recall a time when you or someone you've read about suffered hardships or made sacrifices in order to achieve a goal.

Quickwrite Which aspect of the experience stands out in your mind, the difficulty of the struggle or the feeling of satisfaction with the accomplishment? Write a few lines describing how you look back upon the experience.

Setting a Purpose Read to discover how a famous leader of the twentieth century portrays his memories of an arduous undertaking.

Building Background

The Long March

During the 1930s and 1940s in China, Communist and Nationalist forces fought for control of the country. In 1934, the Nationalists encircled the Communist base in southeastern China. The Communist Red Army broke through weak points in the Nationalist lines and began a westward retreat that came to be known as the Long March. Three months after it began, Mao Tse-tung took command of the march. Under repeated attack, the Communists marched 6,000 miles from southeast to northwest China, crossing eighteen mountain ranges and twenty-four rivers. About 100,000 people started on the march; only about 8,000 made it to the end a year later. Many froze or starved to death; others died from wounds, exhaustion, or disease.

Despite the great losses, the Long March was a victory for the Communists and for Mao. Many young Chinese were inspired to join the Communist Party. Mao emerged as the undisputed party leader.

The Little Red Book: the Thoughts of Chairman Mao Tse-Tung, c. 1950s. Artist unknown (China). Colored lithograph. Private collection.

Before You Read

The Jay

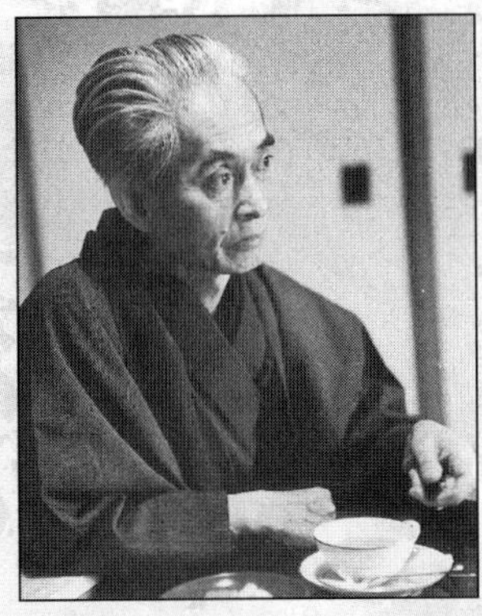

Meet Yasunari Kawabata

"Many writers in their youth write poetry; I, instead of poetry, wrote the palm-of-the-hand stories . . . the poetic spirit of my young days lives on in them."

Yasunari Kawabata (kä wä bä′ tä), the first Japanese writer to win the Nobel Prize for Literature, was born in Osaka. His parents, grandmother, and sister all had died by the time he was ten years old.

Not surprisingly, loneliness, death, and unobtainable love are recurring themes in Kawabata's work, including the novels *Snow Country* and *The Sound of the Mountain*.

Although his novels brought him the most acclaim during his lifetime, throughout his career Kawabata wrote many short stories. He called these vignettes of life "palm-of-the-hand stories" for their small size. Critics have compared the stories to haiku because they convey striking observations in a few words.

Yasunari Kawabata was born in 1899 and died in 1972.

Reading Focus

In your opinion, what long-term effects can divorce have on families?

Share Ideas With your classmates, discuss the effects of divorce on family members. Jot down your thoughts on a piece of paper.

Setting a Purpose Read about a young Japanese woman whose family life has been changed by divorce.

Building Background

Arranged Marriages in Japan

In "The Jay," which is set in the 1940s in Japan, a young woman's father finds a marriage partner for her. In Japan, as in many Asian countries, marriages were traditionally arranged by parents. Marriage was viewed as an institution that served to satisfy family—rather than individual—needs, and love was not considered a requirement. In this system, the wife devoted herself to caring for her husband's family under the firm direction of the mother-in-law. Since the 1920s, the traditional arranged marriage has gradually become less common in Japanese culture. Today, some young people find their own mates, though many others still rely on family help. Commonly, families arrange a first meeting between a prospective couple, but young people are not pressured to marry against their wishes.

Vocabulary Preview

furtively (fur′ tiv lē) *adv.* in a secretive manner; p. 652
deficiency (di fish′ ən sē) *n.* a shortage or lack of something essential; p. 653
intransigence (in tran′ sə jəns) *n.* the state of being uncompromising; p. 654
assiduously (ə sij′ o͞o əs lē) *adv.* attentively or busily; p. 655
plaintively (plān′ tiv lē) *adv.* in a manner expressing suffering or woe; p. 655

The Jay

Yasunari Kawabata

Translated by Lane Dunlop and J. Martin Holman

Since daybreak, the jay had been singing noisily.

When they'd slid open the rain shutters, it had flown up before their eyes from a lower branch of the pine, but it seemed to have come back. During breakfast, there was the sound of whirring wings.

"That bird's a nuisance." The younger brother started to get to his feet.

"It's all right. It's all right." The grandmother stopped him. "It's looking for its child. Apparently the chick fell out of the nest yesterday. It was flying around until late in the evening. Doesn't she know where it is? But what a good mother. This morning she came right back to look."

"Grandmother understands well," Yoshiko said.

Her grandmother's eyes were bad. Aside from a bout with nephritis[1] about ten years ago, she had never been ill in her life. But, because of her cataracts,[2] which she'd had since girlhood, she could only see dimly out of her left eye. One had to hand her the rice bowl and the chopsticks. Although she could grope her way around the familiar interior of the house, she could not go into the garden by herself.

Sometimes, standing or sitting in front of the sliding-glass door, she would spread out her hands, fanning out her fingers against the sunlight that came through the glass, and gaze out. She was concentrating all the life that was left to her into that many-angled gaze.

At such times, Yoshiko was frightened by her grandmother. Though she wanted to call out to her from behind, she would furtively steal away.

This nearly blind grandmother, simply from having heard the jay's voice, spoke as if she had seen everything. Yoshiko was filled with wonder.

When, clearing away the breakfast things, Yoshiko went into the kitchen, the jay was singing from the roof of the neighbor's house.

1. *Nephritis* is an acute or chronic inflammation of the kidneys.
2. *Cataracts* are a clouding of the lens of the eyes.

Vocabulary

furtively (fur′ tiv lē) *adv.* in a secretive manner

Kōbō Daishi (Kūkai) *as a Child,* 14th century. Artist unknown (Japan). Hanging scroll, ink and color on silk, 86.7 x 48.9 cm. Art Institute of Chicago.

In the back garden, there was a chestnut tree and two or three persimmon trees. When she looked at the trees, she saw that a light rain was falling. It was the sort of rain that you could not tell was falling unless you saw it against the dense foliage.

The jay, shifting its perch to the chestnut tree, then flying low and skimming the ground, returned again to its branch, singing all the while.

The mother bird could not fly away. Was it because her chick was somewhere around there?

Worrying about it, Yoshiko went to her room. She had to get herself ready before the morning was over.

In the afternoon, her father and mother were coming with the mother of Yoshiko's fiancé.

Sitting at her mirror, Yoshiko glanced at the white stars under her fingernails. It was said that, when stars came out under your nails, it was a sign that you would receive something, but Yoshiko remembered having read in the newspaper that it meant a deficiency of vitamin C or something. The job of putting on her makeup went fairly pleasantly. Her eyebrows and lips all became unbearably winsome. Her kimono,[3] too, went on easily.

3. A *kimono* is a long robe with wide sleeves and a broad sash, traditionally worn in Japan.

Vocabulary

deficiency (di fish′ ən sē) *n.* a shortage or lack of something essential

She'd thought of waiting for her mother to come and help with her clothes, but it was better to dress by herself, she decided.

Her father lived away from them. This was her second mother.

When her father had divorced her first mother, Yoshiko had been four and her younger brother two. The reasons given for the divorce were that her mother went around dressed in flashy clothes and spent money wildly, but Yoshiko sensed dimly that it was more than that, that the real cause lay deeper down.

Her brother, as a child, had come across a photograph of their mother and shown it to their father. The father hadn't said anything but, with a face of terrible anger, had suddenly torn the photograph to bits.

When Yoshiko was thirteen, she had welcomed the new mother to the house. Later, Yoshiko had come to think that her father had endured his loneliness for ten years for her sake. The second mother was a good person. A peaceful home life continued.

When the younger brother, entering upper school, began living away from home in a dormitory, his attitude toward his stepmother changed noticeably.

"Elder sister, I've met our mother. She's married and lives in Azabu. She's really beautiful. She was happy to see me."

Hearing this suddenly, Yoshiko could not say a word. Her face paled, and she began to tremble.

From the next room, her stepmother came in and sat down.

"It's a good thing, a good thing. It's not bad to meet your own mother. It's only natural. I've known for some time that this day would come. I don't think anything particular of it."

But the strength seemed to have gone out of her stepmother's body. To Yoshiko, her emaciated stepmother seemed pathetically frail and small.

Her brother abruptly got up and left. Yoshiko felt like smacking him.

"Yoshiko, don't say anything to him. Speaking to him will only make that boy go bad." Her stepmother spoke in a low voice.

Tears came to Yoshiko's eyes.

Her father summoned her brother back home from the dormitory. Although Yoshiko had thought that would settle the matter, her father had then gone off to live elsewhere with her stepmother.

It had frightened Yoshiko. It was as if she had been crushed by the power of masculine indignation and resentment. Did their father dislike even them because of their tie to their first mother? It seemed to her that her brother, who'd gotten to his feet so abruptly, had inherited the frightening male intransigence of his father.

And yet it also seemed to Yoshiko that she could now understand her father's sadness and pain during those ten years between his divorce and remarriage.

And so, when her father, who had moved away from her, came back bringing a marriage proposal, Yoshiko had been surprised.

"I've caused you a great deal of trouble. I told the young man's mother that you're a girl with these circumstances and that, rather than treating you like a bride,[4] she should try to bring back the happy days of your childhood."

When her father said this kind of thing to her, Yoshiko wept.

If Yoshiko married, there would be no woman's hand to take care of her brother and grandmother. It had been decided that the two households would become one. With that, Yoshiko had made up her mind. She had

4. *". . . rather than treating you like a bride"* refers to the fact that brides in arranged marriages are traditionally treated harshly by the husband's mother.

Vocabulary

intransigence (in tran′ sə jəns) *n.* the state of being uncompromising dreaded marriage on her father's account, but, when it came down to the actual talks, it was not that dreadful after all.

When her preparations were completed, Yoshiko went to her grandmother's room.

"Grandmother, can you see the red in this kimono?"

"I can faintly make out some red over there. Which is it, now?" Pulling Yoshiko to her, the grandmother put her eyes close to the kimono and the sash.

"I've already forgotten your face, Yoshiko. I wish I could see what you look like now."

Yoshiko stifled a desire to giggle. She rested her hand lightly on her grandmother's head.

Wanting to go out and meet her father and the others, Yoshiko was unable just to sit there, vaguely waiting. She went out into the garden. She held out her hand, palm upward, but the rain was so fine that it didn't wet the palm. Gathering up the skirts of her kimono, Yoshiko assiduously searched among the little trees and in the bear-grass bamboo thicket. And there, in the tall grass under the bush clover, was the baby bird.

Her heart beating fast, Yoshiko crept nearer. The baby jay, drawing its head into its neck feathers, did not stir. It was easy to take it up into her hand. It seemed to have lost its energy. Yoshiko looked around her, but the mother bird was nowhere in sight.

Running into the house, Yoshiko called out, "Grandmother! I've found the baby bird. I have it in my hand. It's very weak."

"Oh, is that so? Try giving it some water."

Her grandmother was calm.

When she ladled some water into a rice bowl and dipped the baby jay's beak in it, it drank, its little throat swelling out in an appealing way. Then—had it recovered?—it sang out, "Ki-ki-ki, Ki-ki-ki . . ."

The mother bird, evidently hearing its cry, came flying. Perching on the telephone wire, it sang. The baby bird, struggling in Yoshiko's hand, sang out again, "Ki-ki-ki . . ."

"Ah, how good that she came! Give it back to its mother, quick," her grandmother said.

Yoshiko went back out into the garden. The mother bird flew up from the telephone wire but kept her distance, looking fixedly toward Yoshiko from the top of a cherry tree.

As if to show her the baby jay in her palm, Yoshiko raised her hand, then quietly placed the chick on the ground.

As Yoshiko watched from behind the glass door, the mother bird, guided by the voice of its child singing plaintively and looking up at the sky, gradually came closer. When she'd come down to the low branch of a nearby pine, the chick flapped its wings, trying to fly up to her. Stumbling forward in its efforts, falling all over itself, it kept singing.

Still the mother bird cautiously held off from hopping down to the ground.

Soon, however, it flew in a straight line to the side of its child. The chick's joy was boundless. Turning and turning its head, its outspread wings trembling, it made up to its mother. Evidently the mother had brought it something to eat.

Yoshiko wished that her father and stepmother would come soon. She would like to show them this, she thought.

Vocabulary

assiduously (ə sij′ o͞o əs lē) *adv.* attentively or busily

plaintively (plān′ tiv lē) *adv.* in a manner expressing suffering or woe

Responding to Literature

Personal Response

What questions linger in your mind after reading this story? Jot them down on a piece of paper.

Analyzing Literature

Recall

1. What reason does the grandmother give for the jay's noisy singing at the beginning of the story?
2. Describe Yoshiko's family history.
3. How does Yoshiko's stepmother react to her stepson's meeting with his biological mother?
4. What meeting is Yoshiko preparing for? What is the reason for the meeting?
5. What happens with Yoshiko and the jays at the end of the story?

Interpret

6. What does the jay's reaction to the loss of its chick suggest about the maternal bond in animals?
7. What effect does her father's leaving have on Yoshiko?
8. How does the stepmother's reaction to the boy's meeting with his mother differ from the father's reaction? Why might their reactions differ?
9. How does Yoshiko seem to feel about her impending marriage?
10. Why does Yoshiko want to show the jays to her father and stepmother?

Evaluate and Connect

11. If you were Yoshiko or the brother in this story, would you want to find your mother? Why or why not?
12. Do you think the father is right or wrong to prohibit contact between the children and their mother? Why?
13. Yoshiko guesses that there is a deeper cause for her parents' divorce than the reasons her father gives. From clues in the story, what might be the cause?
14. An **implied comparison** is one in which the similarities or differences between two things are suggested, but not directly stated (see page R6). What implied comparison is made in this story?
15. For the Reading Focus on page 651, you listed some effects of divorce on family members. What are the effects of her parents' divorce on Yoshiko, and how do these effects compare with those you listed?

Literary Criticism

One critic sums up Kawabata's fiction as follows: "There are no clear-cut good or evil forces in [it]. He leaves matters unresolved, and his endings are ambiguous. Kawabata's fiction relies on his readers and their imagination to decide the fate of his characters." Write a brief essay in response to this criticism. Consider the following questions: How would you describe the conflict in "The Jay"? Do you think the ending of the story is ambiguous? What do you think will happen to the narrator?

Literary ELEMENTS

Conflict

Conflict is the struggle that lies at the center of the plot in a story. In a story that has a standard plot structure, the central conflict reaches a climax and is resolved at the end. "The Jay," however, like many of Kawabata's stories, does not follow this typical plot development. Instead, the story portrays a slice of family life and suggests several conflicts that are left unresolved or only partially resolved–just as in real life, many conflicts are never completely resolved.

1. What conflicts exist between Yoshiko and the men in this story? Are any of these conflicts resolved? Explain your answer.
2. How would you characterize the relationships between Yoshiko and the women in the story? How do these relationships compare with those Yoshiko has with the men in her family?
3. How do the characters in this story tend to deal with their feelings? Give specific examples. What effect does this have on the resolution or lack of resolution of conflicts?

- See **Literary Terms Handbook**, p. R2.

Literature and Writing

Writing About Literature

Analyzing Tone How would you describe the tone—the attitude taken by the author toward the subject—in "The Jay"? How is that tone conveyed, both by what is said and what is left unsaid? In a brief paragraph, identify the tone of the story, and describe how it is conveyed.

Creative Writing

Yoshiko's Diary In "The Jay," Yoshiko's personal thoughts about her separation from her mother are never directly expressed. Imagine the thoughts and feelings Yoshiko might harbor about her mother and her absence. In Yoshiko's words, write a diary entry in which you express her thoughts and feelings.

Extending Your Response

Literature Groups

Lingering Questions Think of a question that remains unanswered in your mind after reading and discussing this story. Make a list of your group's questions, and take turns discussing possible answers. Use details from the story to support your answers. Share a summary of your discussion with the rest of the class.

Interdisciplinary Activity

Biology: Maternal Instinct Work with a partner to investigate the ways in which different species of animals display maternal instinct, as the jay does in this story. You might compare and contrast the behavior of two species, or choose one type of behavior common to several species. Prepare a visual presentation of your findings, such as a poster, brochure, or bulletin-board display.

Performing

The Grandmother's Tale Although the grandmother in the story is nearly blind, she seems to know everything that goes on around her. How might she have viewed the family events described in the story? Create a brief dramatic monologue that provides her view of these events. Practice your monologue and perform it for the class.

Reading Further

If you enjoyed "The Jay," you might also enjoy these stories by Kawabata:

"The Grasshopper and the Bell Cricket," "A Sunny Place," and "Umbrella," in *Palm-of-the-Hand Stories.*

Save your work for your portfolio.

VOCABULARY • Greek Roots

A **root** is a word, or part of a word, to which prefixes and/or suffixes are added to form new words. A root may be a word that can stand alone, such as *graph,* or it may be a word part, such as *hydr* in *hydrant.* Many roots come from Greek.

PRACTICE Study the meanings of the roots listed and give two other examples of words that have the same root. Then write a sentence using each of your example words.

Greek Root	Meaning	Example
graphein	to write	autograph
hydros	water	hydrant
pathos	feeling	pathetically
polis	city-state	politics
thermē	heat	thermometer

KOREA, 1964

Before You Read

Song of Peace

Meet Hwang Tonggyu

"What happens if you pull down beams and supports? / A host of opinions greet the leaning skeleton house."

Hwang Tonggyu (hwäng ton′ gyū) grew up in a literary environment—his father, Hwang Sunwŏn (hwäng sun′ wōn), was one of Korea's leading novelists. At Seoul National University in South Korea, Hwang Tonggyu concentrated on English literature, graduating in 1961 with a degree in that subject. That same year, Hwang published his first collection of poems, *One Fine Day*. Since then, he has written several books of poetry and a collection of critical essays.

In Korea, a country with a long history of poetic achievement, there is always the question of whether to follow tradition or to experiment with Western styles. Hwang has written that he is trying to steer between the two. Similarly, he tries to strike a balance between writing poetry for its own sake and writing poetry that deals with contemporary issues.

Hwang Tonggyu was born in 1938.

Reading Focus

What do you think it might be like to live in a divided country with a military presence and the threat of civil war always in the background?

Share Ideas Jot down some responses to this question. Then share your opinions with a partner.

Setting a Purpose Read to discover one author's feelings about war and peace.

Building Background

Twentieth-Century Korean Poetry

The development of modern Korean poetry dates back to the late nineteenth century, when Korea began to open up to the world after centuries of isolation. During this period, Korean poets began to experiment with poetic forms and styles found in newly translated Western poems.

Early twentieth-century poetry reflects both Koreans' interest in experimentation and their growing feelings of nationalism. Following nearly a decade of Japanese rule, Koreans rose up against their oppressors in 1919. The rebellion failed, however, and Japan continued to rule Korea until 1945, intensifying its censorship of Korean writers in the 1930s. Following the liberation of 1945, Korean writers were once again able to express themselves freely. Some returned to traditional forms, while others were wildly experimental. In the aftermath of the Korean War (1950–1953), many poets began to express concern for the fate of their country. The evils of war, the division of Korea into South and North Korea, and the effect of rapid industrialization on a formerly agricultural society are some of the themes they have explored.

Reading Further

If you liked "Song of Peace," you might also enjoy the following poetry:

Modern Korean Poetry, translated by Jaihiun Kim.

Poetry from *Modern Korean Literature: An Anthology,* edited by Peter H. Lee.

Song of Peace

Hwang Tonggyu
Translated by Peter H. Lee

I'm told
We are a puny race.
Doors locked even in daytime,
Bathing our eyes with Trust Drops,°
We read essays, hugging the stove.

Dragging the anguish of no place to hide
Like a common soldier,
Travel the country from Kimhae° to Hwach'ŏn,°
Winter fatigues hanging on you,
A canteen flapping at your side,
Wherever you turn, barbed wire;
Wherever you turn, checkpoints.
I do not understand this love,
This smothering jealous love.

I spread my gloved hands, palms up.
Snow falling for some time now,
A snow colder than snow.

---

4 *Trust Drops* is the brand name of a Korean eyedrop.
8 *Kimhae* (kim hā′) is located in the southeastern part of South Korea. *Hwach'ŏn* (hwä′ chōn) is located far to the north, near the border of North Korea.

Responding to Literature

Personal Response

What image does the poem leave in your mind? Draw a sketch of the image that you see.

Analyzing Literature

Recall and Interpret

1. Summarize the activities of the "we" in the first stanza. According to stanza 1, how does the speaker characterize this group of people referred to as "we"?
2. What **extended simile** is included in stanza 2 (see **Literary Terms Handbook,** page R11)? For what reasons might Hwang have chosen to include this simile?
3. In stanza 2, what does the speaker claim you find "wherever you turn"? To what might "this smothering jealous love" refer?
4. How might the image of "snow colder than snow" relate to the rest of the poem?

Evaluate and Connect

5. What does "Song of Peace" suggest to you about war?
6. Recall your response to the Reading Focus on page 658. How do your feelings compare with those the speaker expresses in the poem? Give specific details.
7. Think of another poem, story, or song about peace. Compare and contrast it with this poem.
8. A **paradox** is a statement that at first seems self-contradictory, but that may be true, either literally or figuratively. (See **Literary Terms Handbook,** page R9.) Compared with the subject of the poem, how is the title paradoxical?

Literary ELEMENTS

Exaggeration

Exaggeration is an overstatement of an idea. Writers may use this technique to emphasize an idea or to heighten its emotional impact. In "Song of Peace," Hwang uses exaggeration to emphasize the immense impact of war and division on his country.

1. What example of exaggeration can you find in stanza 1? How does it add to the overall effect of the poem?
2. Find another example of exaggeration in "Song of Peace" and explain why Hwang might have chosen to use it.

- See **Literary Terms Handbook,** p. R4.

Extending Your Response

Personal Writing

Striking Images Hwang's poem is rich in imagery that evokes a mood–images like "hugging the stove," "barbed wire," and "canteen flapping." Write two or three paragraphs describing your response to the imagery in the poem. What did it make you think about? How did it make you feel?

Learning for Life

Korean Itinerary Work in a group to research South Korea's geography, history, and cultural heritage. Then plan and create an itinerary for a five-day trip to the country. Include descriptions of the sites your group plans to visit, a map that shows these sites, and the order in which you will visit them.

Save your work for your portfolio.

Writing Skills

Creating Emphasis

When presenting information–whether in a work of fiction, like a story, or in nonfiction, like an investigative report–you want to **emphasize,** or draw attention to, your most important details and ideas. Read the epigraph below from "The Nonrevolutionaries" to see how the writer uses the opening quotation to make a strong point about revolution. Notice the use of repetition to create emphasis.

> ***Revolution, counterrevolution, nonrevolution.***
>
> ***The revolutionaries are executed by the counterrevolutionaries and the counterrevolutionaries by the revolutionaries.***
>
> ***The nonrevolutionaries are sometimes taken for revolutionaries and executed by the counterrevolutionaries, sometimes taken for counterrevolutionaries and executed by the revolutionaries, and sometimes executed by either the revolutionaries or the counter-revolutionaries for no apparent reason at all.***

The circular repetition of the words *revolutionaries, counter revolutionaries,* and *nonrevolutionaries* not only creates a dizzying effect but also emphasizes the pointless violence of this cycle.

In addition to repetition, you might also try some of these strategies for creating emphasis in your writing:

- Use short, simple, direct sentences.
- Use alliteration–that is, draw attention to important ideas by using words that begin with the same consonant sound.
- Use parallel construction, so that phrases or sentences with similar functions also have similar grammatical structure.
- Use inverted sentence order, placing the verb before the subject.

It would be counterproductive to try to use all of these strategies in one piece of writing. For each different piece of writing, choose only those strategies that work best for your particular purpose and audience.

ACTIVITY

Identify an issue or a topic that you believe in strongly and would like to investigate. Then write a paragraph summarizing why you believe this is an important topic to explore. Ask a partner to read your paragraph and tell you which of your ideas comes across most strongly. If these ideas aren't the ones that are most important to you, take another look at how you emphasized your ideas. Then revise the paragraph. Exchange papers again with your partner and offer each other feedback on the effectiveness of the emphasis used.

KOREA, 1961

Before You Read

The Nonrevolutionaries

Meet Yu-Wol Chong-Nyon

"More than fifty years after the Korean people were divided, the two halves regard each other as an enemy and keep threatening to turn each other into a sea of flames. . . ."

—*Hwang Jang Yop, a North Korean government official who defected to the South in 1997*

Little is known about Yu-Wol Chong-Nyon (yū wôl chông nyôn). Her pen name, Yu-Wol Chong-Nyon, means "Month-of-June-Youth." This name is a reference to the young generation who grew up during and after the Korean civil war during the early 1950s. In the story "The Nonrevolutionaries," the author captures the confusion of the civil war period and the anguish of a people split in two.

Reading Focus

"Confusion, indecision, fear: these are my weapons." So said the German dictator Adolf Hitler, who ordered the slaughter of millions of people. In your mind, span the globe and your knowledge of history to think of other places and times in which leaders have used the weapons of "confusion, indecision, and fear" to carry out atrocities.

List It! Make a list of the times and places that come to mind.

Setting a Purpose Read about a young Korean woman's experience of a reign of fear and terror in her country.

Building Background

The Division of Korea

Since the 1950s, no single fact of life has so dominated Korean fiction as the division of the country into North and South, a by-product of World War II. Since 1910 the Japanese had occupied Korea, but Japanese control over the country ended with Japan's defeat in World War II. Northern Korea was occupied by Soviet troops, while the South was occupied by American troops. Each side supported its own government, and these governments quickly became rivals. What was initially considered a temporary solution became a permanent division. A communist government eventually took power in the North, and a democratic one in the South. In June 1950, North Korean troops invaded the South. A three-year war ensued, which ended with the country once again divided. The dividing line–the thirty-eighth parallel–has become a symbol of Korea's suffering.

Vocabulary Preview

counterrevolutionary (koun′ tər rev′ ə lo͞o′ shə ner′ ē) *n.* a person actively opposed to a government established by a revolution; p. 664

boorishness (boor′ ish nəs) *n.* rudeness and insensitivity; p. 664

primordial (prī môr′ dē əl) *adj.* ancient, from the beginning of time; p. 666

reactionary (rē ak′ shə ner′ ē) *adj.* supporting a return to a previous form of government; p. 666

malevolently (mə lev′ ə lənt lē′) *adv.* in an intentionally harmful manner; p. 666

sabotage (sab′ ə tazh′) *v.* to cause damage for political reasons; p. 666

harangue (hə rang′) *v.* to make an angry, ranting speech; p. 667

THE NONREVOLUTIONARIES

Yu-Wol Chong-Nyon
Translated by the author and Daniel L. Milton

Revolution, counterrevolution, nonrevolution.

The revolutionaries are executed by the counterrevolutionaries and the counterrevolutionaries by the revolutionaries.

The nonrevolutionaries are sometimes taken for revolutionaries and executed by the counterrevolutionaries, sometimes taken for counterrevolutionaries and executed by the revolutionaries, and sometimes executed by either the revolutionaries or the counterrevolutionaries for no apparent reason at all.

—*Lu Hsun (1881–1936)*
Translated from Chinese by Chi-chen Wang

Cursed be the men of the East. Cursed be the men of the West. Cursed be those who have left my beloved homeland bleeding and torn.

They banged on the doors. They hammered at the walls. Out! *Out!* Everybody out! Everybody to the playfield.

With fear and with trembling we all got up, we got up out of our blankets into the chilly dawn. My father and my mother, my sisters and my brother. Out. *Out.* The shouting and the hammering continued. Out to the playfield.

"What about Ok-Sun?" my mother said to my father, pointing to me. "They don't know she's here. Maybe she should hide?"

"No, no," said my father. "They'll surely find her."

"But why? If we keep her hidden in the back, no one will see her."

"They will, they will. They're breaking in without warning. Only the night before they broke into twelve houses in our district. In the middle of the night, at two and three in the morning. They banged at the doors and pushed their way in, stamped into the houses with their boots on and dragged the men away."

"With their boots on!" My mother was silent for a moment, shocked at this revelation of incredible boorishness. The poorest rag-picker, the most unlearned peasant, would never dream of entering another's home without removing his footwear.

But she returned to the argument. "I'm sure we can hide her safely—"

"No! No!" my father again protested. "Too dangerous. Better she go with all of us."

"But— "

But there was no time to argue. Out! *Out!* The shouting and the banging went on. They were still there, rounding up every man, woman, and child. Out I went, too, with my sisters and brother, my father and mother, out to the playfield.

I had returned home only a month ago. My year's scholarship had ended, and I was coming back to bring the wisdom of the West to my "underdeveloped" homeland. The boat had arrived at Seoul a day earlier than expected, but late at night. When I had reached home after midnight, none of the neighbors had seen me come. My father, glad as he and all the family were to see me, had said, "Enough. We'll go to bed and talk in the morning. She must be tired."

Vocabulary

counterrevolutionary (koun′ tər rev′ ə lo͞o′ shə ner′ ē) *n.* a person actively opposed to a government established by a revolution

boorishness (boor′ ish nəs) *n.* rudeness and insensitivity

Clean Out the Filth!, c. 1974. Shi Qiren and Chen Guo (China). Oils. Private collection.

Viewing the painting: What is happening in this painting? Do you think the artists meant it to be taken seriously? Explain.

Tired I was, tired of the long, long voyage, still ill adjusted to the many-houred change in time, so tired that I developed a fever of exhaustion that night. It was as though I had been holding it in until I could get back to my own bed before letting it go. For weeks I lay there sick.

It was at the beginning of my illness that the armies suddenly and without warning swarmed down from the north, blasting their way through my homeland, leaving us overnight under a strange regime,[1] ruled by men of our own nation, but men warped and twisted by their training in a foreign land, by the rule of an oppressive hand, of cruel and unfeeling heart and mind.

In a faraway country on the other side of the globe, the President of the United States, the Prime Minister of His Majesty's Government,[2] and the chairman of the Supreme Soviet,[3] accompanied by their Chiefs of Staff and other experts on human welfare, had met. The map had glistened brightly before them with its greens and reds and yellows and blues. The fate of the world was decided. Here a cut, there a snip, and here a line. "For purposes of military convenience," the history books say, my beloved homeland was cut in two. Our minds and hearts, our families and lives were cut into shreds.

My beloved homeland! Will your rice and your wine ever taste the same again? Will your flutes and your harps ever sound the same again?

We were at the playfield once more. The playfield of so many mixed memories, now to be the site of the most sharply etched memory of

1. A *regime* (rə zhēm′) is a government.

2. *His Majesty's Government* refers to Great Britain, which has a monarch (at that time a king) as ceremonial head of government.
3. *Supreme Soviet* refers to the former communist government of Russia.

them all. The playfield where with the girls of my class I had spent so many happy hours of childhood and adolescence. The playfield which had been built during the days of our Japanese lords, the days when here as everywhere in Korea we were taught to speak and to write and to think only in a foreign tongue, when a phrase spoken in our mother tongue in a public place brought a slap on the face from the lords or their Korean vassals.[4] The playfield where my father with all the other fathers had had to go so often to prostrate himself before the Shinto[5] shrines. The playfield where our masters revealed a change of heart to us, where they suddenly called us brothers, members of the same race, fruit of the same cultural heritage, and "invited" our young men to join their armies to fight for the glory of our "common primordial ancestors." Then we knew that the war was truly going badly for them, that their men were dying.

EVERYONE FELT THE
ALIEN PRESENCE
CLOSE TO HIS
SKIN. . . .

The playfield! We waited in the chilly dawn for our new lords to guide us. We were there by the thousand, fathers and mothers, children and elders. I saw many neighbors I hadn't seen for well over a year, but they were too preoccupied to be surprised at my sudden reappearance. We waited in the chilly dawn for our new lords to guide us.

They came. They came with their heavy boots and their heavy rifles. They came dragging twelve men behind them. Twelve men we all knew. Twelve men we had grown up with.

The men with the boots and the rifles distributed themselves among the crowd. A hundred men or more. A man here, a man there. Everyone felt the alien presence close to his skin, everyone felt the gnawing cancer digging into his soul.

Their leader climbed up on the platform and slowly turned his eyes over us, at the sea of faces all around him. A signal, and one of the twelve men was set up next to him, one of the twelve men we knew. He was a clerk in our municipal office, a man as inoffensive as he was inefficient, a man who did his insignificant work as well as his limited abilities permitted him, a man whose main interest in his job consisted in receiving his pay regularly and going home to his family at the end of each day.

I had noticed his wife and children in the crowd.

"Comrades!" bellowed the leader. "Behold a traitor to the people. As you all know, the man you see before you has for years held in his hands the lives and well-being of all the people of this community. It is he who handles the rationing records, he who can decide how much rice you are to receive and when you are to get it. Comrades, an investigation of his records has revealed gross mismanagement of the rationing system of our community. When this treacherous criminal was directed to mend his ways, he offered nothing but resistance and reactionary proposals. For ten days now he has deliberately and malevolently sabotaged every effort on our

4. *Vassals* are people who serve a feudal lord.

5. *Shinto,* the traditional religion of Japan, was imposed on Korea while it was a Japanese colony.

Vocabulary

primordial (prī môr′ dē əl) *adj.* ancient, from the beginning of time
reactionary (rē ak′ shə ner′ ē) *adj.* supporting a return to a previous form of government
malevolently (mə lev′ ə lənt lē′) *adv.* in an intentionally harmful manner
sabotage (sab′ ə tazh′) *v.* to cause damage for political reasons

part to establish the system of food distribution in this community on a rational and an honest basis. Comrades," he cried out again to the crowd, "what shall we do with this traitor?"

"Kill him!" The hundred men who had distributed themselves among the crowd had raised their fists and roared out this response with a single voice: *"Kill him!"*

The leader on the platform nodded in approval. "Thank you, comrades. That is indeed the only proper treatment for traitors."

He took his heavy pistol out of its holster, held it against the man's temple, and pulled the trigger. The clerk slumped to the boards of the platform. The crowd gasped.

"Death to traitors!" roared the hundred men. The man's blood trickled through the cracks between the boards and stained the soil of the playfield.

Another man was hoisted up onto the platform to take his place.

"Comrades," again cried the leader, "behold a traitor to the people. . . ."

An excited murmur went through the crowd as we recognized the man. I heard my brother whisper to my father, "Daddy! Isn't he the leader of the Communists?"

"Yes!"

"Then why?"

"Three kinds—Communists who've been in South Korea all the time; those trained in Russia and China; those trained in North Korea since the partition. They're fighting among themselves already."

The leader had finished his charges. Again he cried to the crowd; "Comrades, what shall we do with this traitor?"

"Kill him!" the hundred shouted as before.

But this time the leader looked displeased. "Comrades, I ask you what to do with a traitor and there is hardly any response! Comrades, think it over well. Take your time and reflect on the matter. I will ask once again a minute from now."

The hundred men glared at us, swung around in their places, and looked us each in the eye in turn. "I wonder if there could be any traitors here among us," they said for all to hear.

Then again the leader turned to the crowd. "Comrades," he bellowed once more, "What shall we do with this traitor to the people?"

"Kill him!" roared the hundred.

"Kill him!" we cried with our lips.

The leader looked pleased. He again unholstered his pistol, pressed it to the man's head, and his blood joined that of the other, dripping down to the soil of the playfield.

Ten more times did the leader harangue us. Ten more times did we shudder as we cried aloud with our lips, *"Kill him!"* Ten more times did the blood of a Korean stain the soil of Korea.

We watched and we trembled as the chilly dawn unfolded into the chilly day.

My beloved homeland!
Will your rice and your wine
ever taste the same again?
Will your flutes and your harps
ever sound the same again?

Cursed be the men of the East.
Cursed be the men of the West.
Cursed be those
who have left my beloved homeland
bleeding and torn.

Vocabulary

harangue (hə rang′) *v.* to make an angry, ranting speech

Responding to Literature

Personal Response

What is your reaction to the tactics of the Communists in this story? Share your reaction in class.

Analyzing Literature

Recall

1. Who does the narrator curse at the beginning and end of the story?
2. Who invades the narrator's homeland?
3. What does the leader of the Communists do after rounding up the people on the playfield?
4. What do the hundred soldiers do?
5. How do the people react to the leader's question: "What shall we do with this traitor to the people?"

Interpret

6. What is the reason for the narrator's curse at the beginning and end of the story?
7. How does the narrator characterize the invaders?
8. Why do you suppose the Communist leader carries out his actions publicly?
9. What purpose do you think the hundred soldiers serve?
10. Why do the people react as they do to the leader's question about what to do with each "traitor"?

Evaluate and Connect

11. What is your judgment of the conduct of the people? Give reasons for your views.
12. If you had been one of the people in the crowd, how do you think you would have reacted? Why?
13. For the Reading Focus on page 662, you listed several places and times in which ruthless leaders have used the weapons of "confusion, indecision, fear." Which of those weapons are used in the situation portrayed in this story? Describe how.
14. **Repetition** is the recurrence of words, phrases, or lines in a piece of writing (see page R10). Identify an example of the use of repetition in this story. What effect does the repetition have?
15. Based on what the story tells you, do you think the narrator is justified in blaming other countries for the suffering in her homeland? Explain your answer.

Epigraph

An **epigraph** is a quotation that occurs at the beginning of a literary work and highlights a theme. "The Nonrevolutionaries" begins with a quotation from Lu Hsun, one of the greatest Chinese writers of the twentieth century. The epigraph both explains the title of the story and alludes to one of the story's themes.

1. Reread the epigraph to this story. In the story, who are the revolutionaries, the counterrevolutionaries, and the nonrevolutionaries? Which of the three groups is the main focus of this story? Give reasons for your answer.
2. How does the epigraph reflect what happens in the story?
3. To what theme of the story does the epigraph allude?

- See **Literary Terms Handbook**, p. R4.

Before You Read

Assembly Line

Meet Shu Ting

"[Ting's] poems search the emotional life for signs of what lies beneath and beyond the self."

—*J. D. McClatchy, editor*

Shu Ting (**shōō′ ting′**) is one of the most celebrated Chinese poets of her generation. Her bold and sensitive poems have twice earned her China's National Poetry Award, as well as popular acclaim.

Shu Ting was born a few years after the Communist takeover of China. When she was a child, her father was labeled a "nonconformist" by Communist authorities and was banished to the countryside. In 1969 Shu Ting was also sent to a small village. Three years later she returned to the city of Xiamen (**shä′ men**), where she has worked in various factories.

Despite the events of her past, Shu Ting chose to ignore the Communists' call for nonsubjective literature by composing highly personal poems charged with strong emotions. In so doing, she has been linked with a like-minded group of poets known as the Misty Poets. Unlike many Misty Poets, however, Shu Ting did not leave China during the 1989 crackdown on pro-democracy protests.

Shu Ting was born in 1952.

Reading Focus

Throughout the ages, writers have expressed their view of work. Henry Wadsworth Longfellow, for instance, wrote "Taste the joy / That springs from labor," while Alfred, Lord Tennyson stated "Ah, why should life / all labour be?" With which quote do you agree more?

Quickwrite Spend two or three minutes quickwriting to explore your response to this question.

Setting a Purpose Read to learn one writer's view of an assembly line.

Building Background

The Assembly Line

The assembly line system dates back to the nineteenth century. A pioneer of the modern assembly line was Henry Ford, who introduced the system to his automobile factory in 1913. Since workers could stand in one place and concentrate on a single task, factories were able to produce more cars faster. The time required to assemble an automobile chassis dropped from twelve hours to just ninety-three minutes. Assembly line production quickly spread throughout industry despite the arguments of some who believed that this type of labor dehumanized workers.

Reading Further

If you find "Assembly Line" interesting, you might like to read the following poetry:

A Splintered Mirror, translated by Donald Finkel, a collection of poems by Shu Ting, Bei Dao, and others.

Assembly Line

Shu Ting
Translated by Carolyn Kizer

In time's assembly line
Night presses against night.
We come off the factory night-shift
In line as we march towards home.
Over our heads in a row
The assembly line of stars
Stretches across the sky.
Beside us, little trees
Stand numb in assembly lines.

The stars must be exhausted
After thousands of years
Of journeys which never change.
The little trees are all sick,
Choked on smog and monotony,
Stripped of their color and shape.
It's not hard to feel for them;
We share the same tempo and rhythm.

Yes, I'm numb to my own existence
As if, like the trees and stars
—perhaps just out of habit
—perhaps just out of sorrow,
I'm unable to show concern
For my own manufactured fate.

Responding to Literature

Personal Response

How did you feel after reading this poem? Explain.

Analyzing Literature

Recall and Interpret

1. What words does the speaker use to describe the movements of the workers as they leave the factory? What do these words suggest about the workers' lives?
2. Which images from nature are described in terms of an assembly line? Why might the speaker see nature in these terms?
3. What sensations does the speaker ascribe to the stars and trees? What might the speaker mean by saying "we share the same tempo and rhythm"?
4. What reasons does the speaker give for being numb to his or her own existence? What is the speaker saying about his or her life in this poem? Explain.

Evaluate and Connect

5. How does the speaker extend the ideal of an assembly line beyond factory walls?
6. Ting repeats the phrase "assembly line" twice in the first stanza. How does this use of **repetition** reinforce the meaning of the poem (see page R10)?
7. Do you think the feelings expressed in "Assembly Line" apply only to people living in China, or are they universal? Explain.
8. Have you ever experienced any of the emotions described in "Assembly Line"? Explain.

Literary ELEMENTS

Personification

Personification is the attribution of human qualities or thoughts to an animal, object, or idea. Poets use this device to highlight an idea, to create striking descriptions, and to give readers a fresh view of commonplace things. In "Assembly Line," Shu Ting uses personification when she writes of little trees that "stand numb in assembly lines." In so doing, she emphasizes the dehumanizing nature of factory work.

1. What examples of personification can you find in the poem?
2. How does Ting describe the trees in lines 13–15? What does line 15 suggest about what happens to a person in a factory setting?

- See **Literary Terms Handbook,** p. R9.

Extending Your Response

Interdisciplinary Activity

Music: On the Job Pop music has long used the experience of work for musical material. Songs such as "Summertime Blues," "Working in a Coalmine," and "Factory" express feelings about being on the job or use work as a metaphor for other aspects of experience. Make a list of three work songs. With your classmates, listen to the songs on your list and discuss the ideas expressed in each.

Personal Writing

What Is Work? Refer to your response to the Reading Focus on page 673. Then write a brief composition describing what you think of work. Do you see work, for instance, as something that can enrich your life? Or do you view work as a "necessary evil"?

Save your work for your portfolio.

Writing Workshop

Expository Writing: Feature Story

Whether the subject is a celebrity's life, an interesting local event, or a new trend in the art world, newspaper and magazine articles often take the form of feature stories. Feature stories are meant to provide interesting background information on topics of general interest. They are often found in the "Arts" or "Lifestyle" sections of a newspaper. **In this workshop, you will write a feature story on some aspect of East Asian culture.**

- As you write your feature story, refer to **Writing Handbook,** pp. R58–R69.

EVALUATION RUBRIC

By the time you complete this Writing Workshop, you will have

- **written an opening that grabs readers' attention**
- **organized your research in a careful, effective manner**
- **answered *who, what, where, when,* and *why* questions**
- **developed your story through anecdotes, quotes, examples, and description**
- **presented a feature story that is free of errors in grammar, usage, and mechanics**

The Writing Process

PREWRITING

PREWRITING TIP

Although a feature story, unlike a research report, does not require a formal bibliography, it is still a good idea to keep track of your sources.

Explore ideas

In order to identify an aspect of East Asian culture that you want to know more about, review the selections in the first part of Unit Four. Note which selections interest you most and jot down the questions these works raise. For example:

- "The Jay": What are family relationships like in Japan? How have they changed in recent years, and how have they remained the same?
- "Green Willow": What role does nature play in Japanese art and literature?
- The Damask Drum: What does a Noh play look like? Are there any groups near you that perform Noh plays?

Choose an audience

Feature stories are usually written for a general audience. Most people in the audience will not know much about the topic, so you will have to provide background for them. If you are writing with the intention of submitting your story to a particular newspaper or magazine—perhaps a school publication—study that journal's style and adjust your approach accordingly.

Consider your purpose

You want to convey information to your readers, but you also want to entertain them. Highlight aspects of the topic that will keep readers interested while they are being informed.

Refine your topic

Using library books, Internet sources, and other reference tools, acquaint yourself with your topic. As you do so, you may find that you want to change the focus of your story. In particular, you may want to narrow your topic so that you aren't trying to cover too much information in your feature story. For example:

- The topic "Family relations in Japan" can be narrowed to "Marriage patterns in modern Japan."
- The topic "Nature in the art and literature of Japan" can be narrowed to "Nature paintings in Japan."

Collect the facts

The main questions to ask when writing any kind of report are *Who? What? When? Where? How?* and *Why?* List the questions you have about your topic and search a variety of sources until you can jot down the answers. Make notes about any vivid, interesting, or amusing pieces of information that you come across while researching your topic. Be sure to allow a reasonable amount of time for research because you probably won't find all of the information that you need at once.

Make a plan

After you have investigated your topic, you must decide how to organize your findings and what to emphasize. Will you begin with the most interesting or important detail and place the more minor points towards the end of your story? Or will you make yourself a subject in the story that you tell and organize your report chronologically, beginning with the start of your search?

In either case, an organizer like the one at the right can help you put the details of your report into an effective order. Fill the boxes with the experiences or facts you want to include. Then number the boxes according to the order in which you want their contents to appear.

- For more information on creating emphasis, see **Writing Skills,** p. 661.

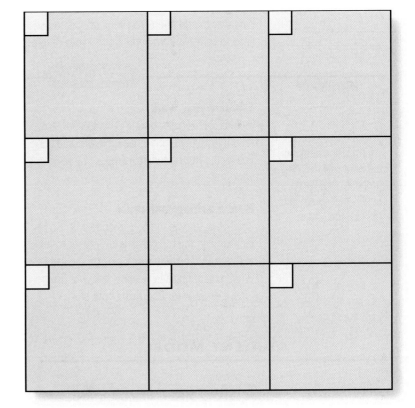

DRAFTING

DRAFTING TIP

As you draft your feature story, keep your readers in mind. Anticipate questions that they might ask and make sure that your text provides information to answer those questions.

Keep the reader reading

Formulate an opening paragraph that will "hook" your audience. In addition to presenting the topic of your story, the opening should contain an intriguing, interesting, or exciting piece of information. To keep the story lively throughout, use examples, descriptions, and explanations.

Write your draft

As you draft, follow your plan, but don't be afraid to alter it if needed. Similarly, refer to your notes, but if you find holes in your information or explanations, hit the books again for the answers.

STUDENT MODEL

> I'm not a coffee drinker. In fact, I prefer tea. Perhaps this is why I was intrigued when I read about the Japanese tea ceremony. Still, there's a lot more to this action that slipping bags into teacups, pouring in some boiling water, and drinking this hot beverage. In fact, nowhere else in the world is tea drunk in quite this way.

Complete Student Model on p. R116.

Use graphics to convey information

One way to add interest to your story is to use illustrations, photographs, maps, diagrams, or time lines to convey information. Some types of information are easier to show than tell.

REVISING

REVISING TIP

Did you write your draft on a computer? If so, print the story and do your revision work on the hard copy. You will probably spot weaknesses that you might miss on the screen.

Evaluate your work

To find confusing or boring parts in your story, read it from the point of view of your audience. Follow the **Rubric for Revising** as you revise your draft.

Have a writing conference

Read your story aloud to someone who isn't familiar with the topic. Ask your listener to look at the **Rubric for Revising** as he or she listens. When you're finished reading, ask your listener for suggestions for improving your story.

RUBRIC FOR REVISING

Your revised feature story should have

- ☑ an opening paragraph that engages the reader
- ☑ details arranged to highlight most important and interesting points
- ☑ a clear overall organizational pattern
- ☑ background information to meet the reading needs of a general audience
- ☑ various kinds of elaboration, such as anecdotes, quotes, and examples
- ☑ a conclusion with a final insight or summary statement

Your revised feature story should be free of

- ☑ irrelevant details that might distract your audience
- ☑ short, choppy sentences that make your writing sound monotonous
- ☑ errors in grammar, usage, and mechanics

STUDENT MODEL

> The tea ceremony ~~is based on~~ also incorporates the ideas ~~about~~ of purity, harmony, and ~~simpleness~~ elegant simplicity. It is ~~beautiful and peaceful~~ an art form and a kind of meditation.

Complete Student Model on p. R116.

EDITING/PROOFREADING

Revise your story until it is both interesting and informative. Then edit it for errors in grammar, usage, mechanics, and spelling.

Grammar Hint

Adjective clauses are a great way to give your readers background information. Be sure to set off nonrestrictive adjective clauses with commas.

INCORRECT: *The tea ceremony takes place in the teahouse which is located in the garden.*

CORRECT: *The tea ceremony takes place in the teahouse, which is located in the garden.*

- For more on adjective clauses, see **Language Handbook**, pp. R26–R27.

PROOFREADING TIP

Use the **Proofreading Checklist** on the inside back cover of this book to help you mark errors that you find.

STUDENT MODEL

The guests are first showed into a waiting room. Just before recieving his guests, the host clean his hands, and mouth. Then the host leads the guests to the tearoom. The main guest who has been chosen by the others enters first.

Complete Student Model on p. R116.

Complete Student Model

For a complete version of the student model developed in this workshop, refer to **Writing Workshop Models**, p. R116.

PUBLISHING/PRESENTING

You might submit your story to the school newspaper or a local magazine. Study the publication first to learn what types of articles it prints. Then write to the editor, briefly summarizing the story and asking whether he or she would be interested in considering it for publication.

PRESENTING TIP

If you give your report orally, ask listeners to save their questions for the end.

Reflecting

Now that your story is finished, read it to see what it can teach you as a writer. To help yourself see your work through fresh eyes, think about adapting it for a much younger audience. Then think about adapting it for presentation as a television documentary.

Save your work for your portfolio.

The Land and Its People

Divided by mountains, jungles, and oceans, the nations of this region are still linked in many ways. The earliest settlers arrived from the north and west thousands of years ago, traveling down through Indochina to eventually spread as far east as Polynesia.

From the second century A.D.*, a succession of great kingdoms arose—the Champa kingdom in Vietnam, Angkor kingdom in Cambodia, Pagan kingdom in Myanmar, Srivijaya kingdom in Indonesia. Even in ruins, their magnificent temples and palaces are among the world's treasures. But rivalries between kingdoms led to their decline. Much of the region was under colonial control for parts of the nineteenth and twentieth centuries, but all the nations of the region are now independent.*

To the east and south lie the vast arid island continent of Australia; the smaller more humid islands of New Zealand; and the thousands of islands that stretch across the Pacific Ocean. The majority of the inhabitants of Australia and New Zealand are descendants of European settlers. The Pacific islands, now almost all grouped into independent republics, are still inhabited by descendants of the peoples who came there from Southeast Asia centuries ago.

Buddha overgrown with forest, Thailand.

Kangaroos, Kinchega National Park, Australia.

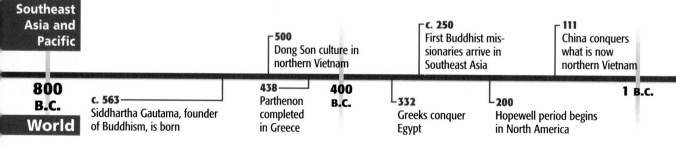

Southeast Asia and Pacific

- **500** Dong Son culture in northern Vietnam
- **c. 250** First Buddhist missionaries arrive in Southeast Asia
- **111** China conquers what is now northern Vietnam

800 B.C. — **400 B.C.** — **1 B.C.**

World

- **c. 563** Siddhartha Gautama, founder of Buddhism, is born
- **438** Parthenon completed in Greece
- **332** Greeks conquer Egypt
- **200** Hopewell period begins in North America

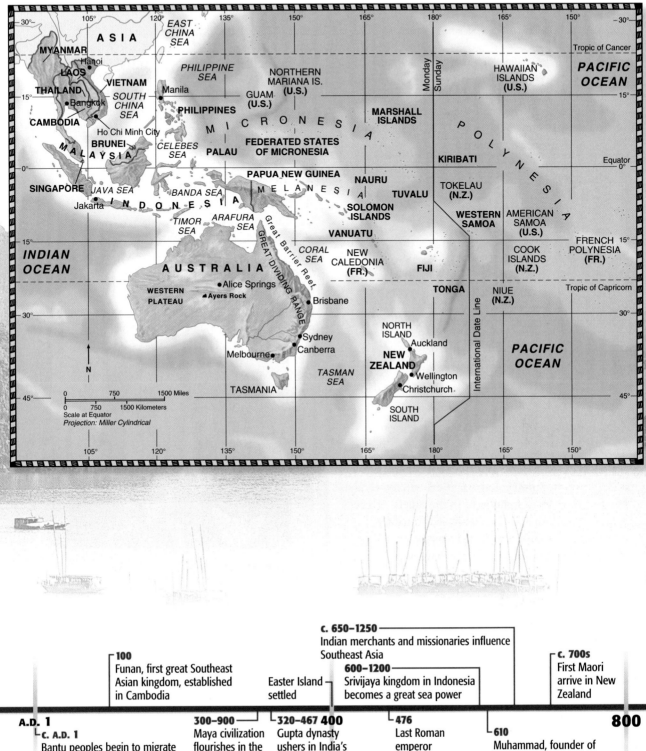

ASIA
EAST CHINA SEA
MYANMAR
Hanoi
LAOS
VIETNAM
THAILAND
Bangkok
SOUTH CHINA SEA
CAMBODIA
Ho Chi Minh City
Manila
PHILIPPINE SEA
PHILIPPINES
NORTHERN MARIANA IS. (U.S.)
GUAM (U.S.)
Monday
Sunday
HAWAIIAN ISLANDS (U.S.)
Tropic of Cancer
PACIFIC OCEAN
MARSHALL ISLANDS
MICRONESIA
POLYNESIA
BRUNEI
MALAYSIA
CELEBES SEA
PALAU
FEDERATED STATES OF MICRONESIA
KIRIBATI
Equator
SINGAPORE
JAVA SEA
Jakarta
INDONESIA
BANDA SEA
PAPUA NEW GUINEA
MELANESIA
NAURU
TUVALU
TOKELAU (N.Z.)
SOLOMON ISLANDS
WESTERN SAMOA
AMERICAN SAMOA (U.S.)
TIMOR SEA
ARAFURA SEA
Great Barrier Reef
VANUATU
FRENCH POLYNESIA (FR.)
INDIAN OCEAN
AUSTRALIA
GREAT DIVIDING RANGE
CORAL SEA
NEW CALEDONIA (FR.)
FIJI
COOK ISLANDS (N.Z.)
Alice Springs
WESTERN PLATEAU
Ayers Rock
TONGA
NIUE (N.Z.)
Tropic of Capricorn
Brisbane
NORTH ISLAND
Sydney
Canberra
Auckland
Melbourne
NEW ZEALAND
International Date Line
PACIFIC OCEAN
TASMAN SEA
Wellington
Christchurch
TASMANIA
SOUTH ISLAND
N
0 750 1500 Miles
0 750 1500 Kilometers
Scale at Equator
Projection: Miller Cylindrical
105° 120° 135° 150° 165° 180° 165° 150°
30° 15° 0° 15° 30° 45°

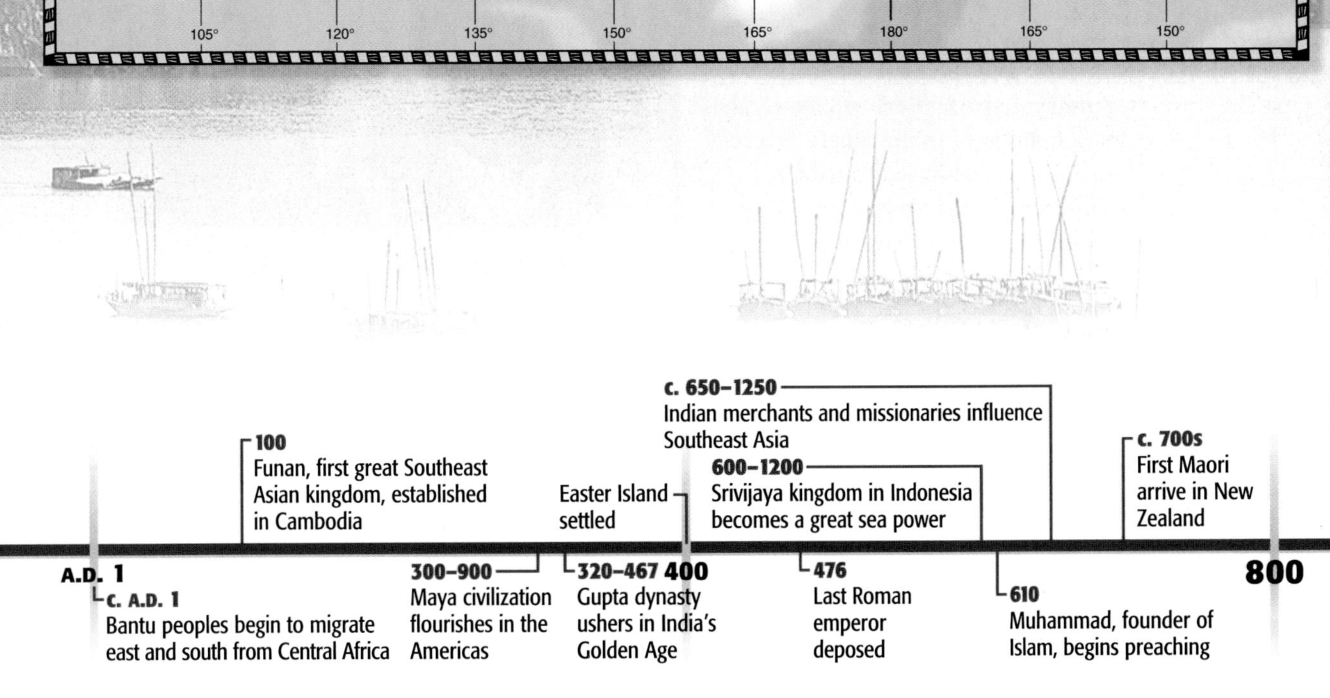

c. 650–1250 Indian merchants and missionaries influence Southeast Asia

100 Funan, first great Southeast Asian kingdom, established in Cambodia

Easter Island settled

600–1200 Srivijaya kingdom in Indonesia becomes a great sea power

c. 700s First Maori arrive in New Zealand

A.D. 1

c. A.D. 1 Bantu peoples begin to migrate east and south from Central Africa

300–900 Maya civilization flourishes in the Americas

320–467 Gupta dynasty ushers in India's Golden Age

400

476 Last Roman emperor deposed

610 Muhammad, founder of Islam, begins preaching

800

How People Live

In the Villages

Most Southeast Asians live in small villages and grow their own food on small, sometimes terraced, plots. Houses in the countryside are often built on poles above the ground to prevent them from flooding during the rainy season and to provide shelter under the houses for domesticated animals.

Houseboats on Halong Bay, Vietnam.

Fields and Forests

Much of the region is excellent for agriculture. Rice has always been a staple crop, both for use at home and for export. Another important export crop is rubber, first introduced from Brazil in the nineteenth century. Although their soil is usually not suited for agriculture, the great forests of the region are a valuable—and sometimes threatened—natural resource.

In the Cities

Cities continue to play an important role in the region's evolving history. Cities like Pagan, founded in 849 in Myanmar, and Ayutthaya, founded in Thailand in 1350, were political, cultural, and religious centers all at once. World-famous trade centers, like Singapore and Bangkok, are also found there.

In Australia and New Zealand

Most of the people are of European ancestry. They speak English and attend Christian churches. The Aboriginals in Australia and the Maori in New Zealand constitute a minority. Australia is dry and thinly populated. Most people live in the cities on the coast. Only about thirteen percent live in the interior—called the *bush* or the *outback*.

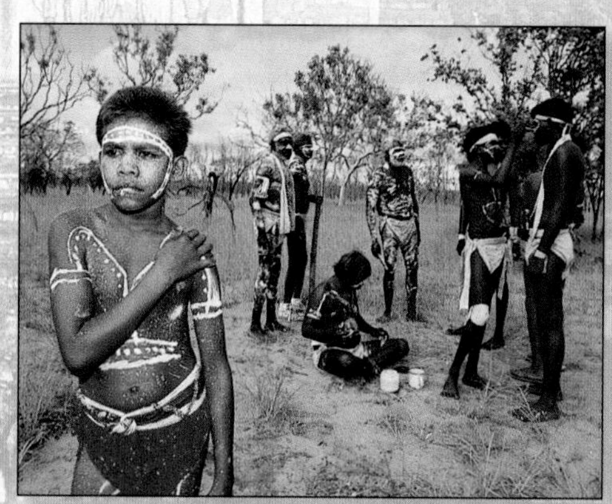

Aboriginal boy and tribal elders, western Australia.

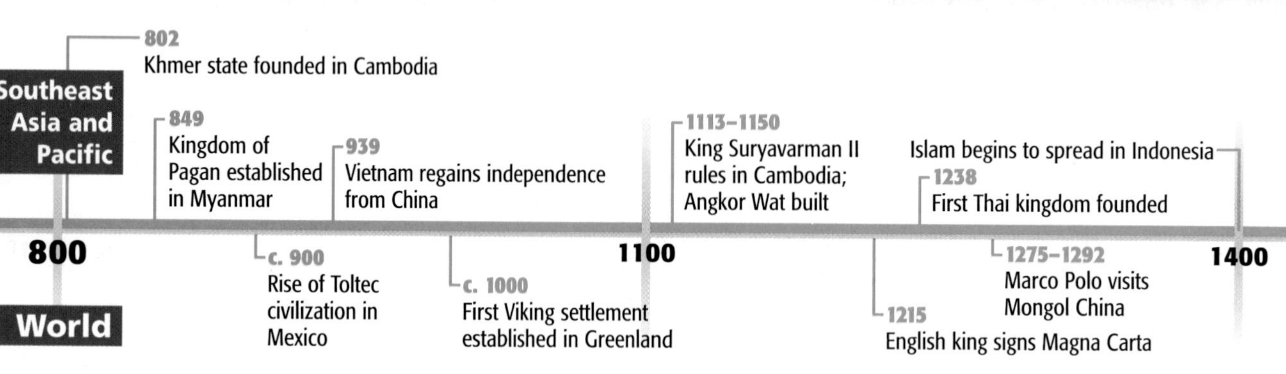
Southeast Asia and Pacific
802
Khmer state founded in Cambodia
849
Kingdom of Pagan established in Myanmar
939
Vietnam regains independence from China
1113–1150
King Suryavarman II rules in Cambodia; Angkor Wat built
Islam begins to spread in Indonesia
1238
First Thai kingdom founded
800
1100
1400
World
c. 900
Rise of Toltec civilization in Mexico
c. 1000
First Viking settlement established in Greenland
1215
English king signs Magna Carta
1275–1292
Marco Polo visits Mongol China

What People Believe

Religions and Cultures

The religious beliefs of Southeast Asians and Pacific Islanders often combine many layers of cultural influences. The oldest beliefs are animistic, requiring the performance of ceremonies and rituals to communicate with deities, nature spirits, and ancestors. Later, Indian missionaries and merchants carried both Buddhist and Hindu traditions as far east as Indonesia. In Myanmar, Thailand, Laos, and Cambodia, most people practice a variety of Buddhism that is in many ways close to the Buddha's original teachings. In Vietnam, the influence of Confucian thought has been strong.

In the thirteenth century, Arab traders played a large part in converting Malaysia and most of Indonesia to Islam. Today, only the people of Bali retain a form of Hinduism, but Indian traditions are still very much in evidence throughout Indonesian music, dance, theater, and textile arts. Christianity, introduced by European missionaries, is widespread in the Philippines and the Pacific Islands.

Church in Bora Bora, French Polynesia.

Young Buddhist monk, Sukhothai, Thailand.

Southeast Asian Buddhism

Southeast Asian Buddhism differs from the type of Buddhism practiced in Korea, China, and Japan. Its rituals are simpler, and it does not have as large a pantheon of gods and goddesses.

Southeast Asian Buddhists believe that everyone is capable of achieving *nirvana,* the highest spiritual state, in a single lifetime, through meditation and monasticism. It is traditional for men to spend at least a few months during their lifetime as monks—meditating, reciting sacred texts, and begging for food. The temple or monastery is the social and religious center of the village.

Active Reading Strategies

Reading the Time Line

1. List the following Southeast Asian kingdoms (and the year in which each was founded or established) in chronological order: first Thai kingdom; kingdom of Pagan in Myanmar; Funan.
2. How many years after the beginning of the French Revolution did France first take control of Indochina?

1400

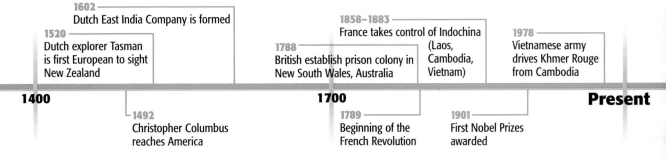

1492 Christopher Columbus reaches America

1520 Dutch explorer Tasman is first European to sight New Zealand

1602 Dutch East India Company is formed

1700

1788 British establish prison colony in New South Wales, Australia

1789 Beginning of the French Revolution

1858–1883 France takes control of Indochina (Laos, Cambodia, Vietnam)

1901 First Nobel Prizes awarded

1978 Vietnamese army drives Khmer Rouge from Cambodia

Present

Arts and Entertainment

Architecture

Borobodur in Java and Angkor Wat in Cambodia rank among the world's greatest architectural monuments. Borobodur, built about A.D. 800, is both a Buddhist temple and an exposition in stone of the Buddhist faith. As pilgrims circle the five terraces, they symbolically move from the material world towards spiritual enlightenment—shown as an only partially visible figure of the Buddha. The twelfth-century Hindu temple, Angkor Wat,is the crowning achievement of the temple-building Khmers. Angkor Wat, which covers 495 acres, was conceived as an image of the sacred mountain that was believed to be the source of all creation. It was also built as a royal tomb; it is the resting place of King Suryavarman II, who was king while the temple was built.

Angkor Thom temple, Cambodia.

Art of the Pacific Islands

The kind of art produced in the islands often depends on what resources are available. In New Zealand, which is larger than the rest of the islands put together, materials are abundant; great carved wooden gateways and intricate jade sculptures are found there. In eastern Polynesia, art has ranged from the monumental stone effigies of Easter Island to the magnificent feather capes and headdresses of Hawaii. And on the small islands throughout the Pacific, where raw materials are few, artists and craftspeople concentrate on making everyday objects as simple and elegant as possible. Art has always played a major role in maintaining the culture and identity of the people.

Carvings from New Guinea.

Performing Arts

Southeast Asian theater combines music, song, dance, drama, mime, and narrative. The performers often wear masks or have heavily painted faces, and they wear rich, gold-decorated textiles. Tales from the two Indian epics, the *Mahabharata* and the *Ramayana*, are popular even in non-Hindu countries; the classical tales are often interwoven with local legends and histories.

Although each nation has its own individual style, classical dance characteristics include the following:

- dancers perform close to the ground
- they use extensive, controlled arm and hand gestures
- dancers maintain a composed face
- tempos of the dances are slow, except for the vigorous battle scenes

Legong dancers, Bali.

Gong Orchestras

The use of gong orchestras is a characteristic common to most Southeast Asian music. The gongs differ in material, number, size, the way they are played, and the sounds they produce. In Java and Bali, *gamelan* orchestras are found; these use an array of different types of gongs and may also include wooden instruments, such as xylophones with bamboo resonators. In Thailand, Laos, and Cambodia, families of instruments—gongs, xylophones, reeds, and drums—play different parts of the music. In Myanmar, a row of tuned drums is used. In Malaysia, parts of Indonesia, and the Philippines, heavy suspended and horizontally laid gongs produce a deep, booming sound. The gong orchestras are used to accompany dance dramas, masked and shadow dramas, and religious and social ceremonies.

Critical Thinking

Connecting Cultures

1. In what ways do Southeast Asian music and drama differ from Western music and drama? Discuss your ideas in a small group.

2. In a small group, discuss how audiences in the United States might respond to the performing arts of Southeast Asia.

Language and Literature

Chinatown, Bangkok, Thailand.

Many languages are spoken in Southeast Asia, reflecting the diversity of peoples in the region. Each country has a national language, however, spoken by the majority of the population: Burmese in Myanmar, Lao in Laos, Khmer in Cambodia, Thai in Thailand, and Vietnamese in Vietnam. The first four use alphabets of their own, developed from ancient Indian writing. Vietnam, after using Chinese-influenced characters for centuries, now uses a modified Roman alphabet introduced by French missionaries. Most of these languages are **tonal;** that is, the tone in which a word is spoken helps determine its meaning.

A New Language for a New Nation

Indonesia is a vast country made up of thousands of islands, where approximately 600 languages are spoken. When it regained independence after World War II, language could have been a major problem for the new country. Javanese is spoken by the largest number of people, but it was felt that a language that was not identified with any one group would be more acceptable. Fortunately, a decision had already been made. In 1928 members of the independence movement agreed on a compromise: Malay was widely used throughout the islands for communication between speakers of different languages, and a version of Malay was decided upon as the national language. Today, as *Bahasa Indonesia,* "the language of Indonesia," it is taught and understood throughout the country.

influences

Words from Southeast Asia and the Pacific have entered the English language along with the animals, foods, clothing, actions, and arts they signify. Following are some of these terms:

- batik (Malay, from Javanese, "painted"), a method of hand-printing textiles
- dingo (native Australian name), a wild dog of Australia
- gong (Malay and Java, imitative of its sound), a bronze plate that gives a resonant sound when struck
- taboo (Tonga, *tabu*), forbidden
- koala (native Australian name), a marsupial native to Australia that feeds on eucalyptus leaves
- sarong (Malay *kain sarong*, from *kain*, "cloth," and *sarong*, "sheath"), a loose skirt made from a single long piece of cloth worn wrapped around the body

Southeast Asian Literature

The diverse contributions to Southeast Asian literature—indigenous oral traditions; cultural influences from India, China, and Arabia; new forms introduced by colonial rulers—are all visible today, though each country has developed its own distinct mix. A consistent theme in contemporary literature is the struggle of the writer to express a personal identity in the midst of social and political change.

During the age of Southeast Asia's great empires, writers were honored and patronized by the kings. However, only a few copies of their manuscripts were made; the oral tradition still dominated. Poetry, religious writings, and history were favored.

Today's writers include Pramoedya Ananta Toer of Indonesia and democracy activist Aung San Suu Kyi of Myanmar, winner of the Nobel Peace Prize.

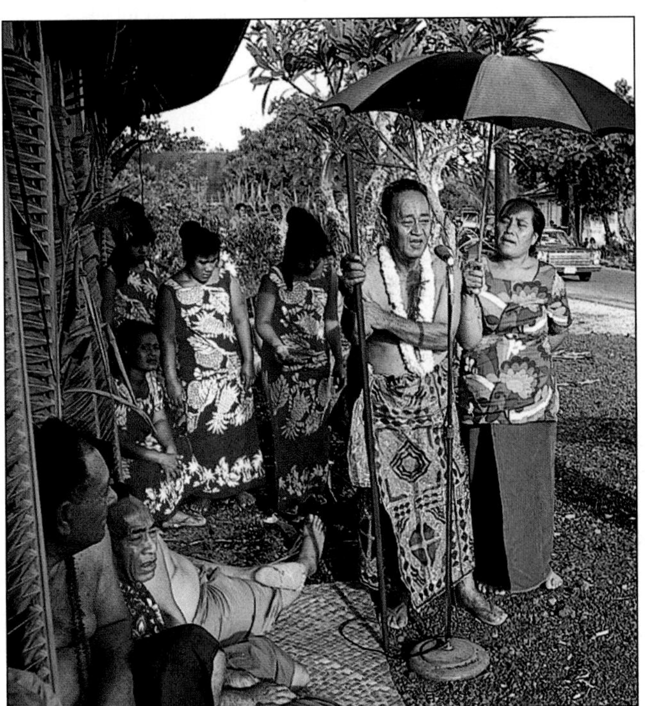

"Talking Chief," Samoa.

Ned Kelly, 1946. Sidney Nolan (Australia). Enamel on composition board, 90.8 x 121.5 cm. National Gallery of Australia, Canberra.

Australian and New Zealand Literature

The earliest published writing from Australia often conveyed a sense of homesickness for the British Isles; many were "convict novels," written by or about persons sent to the prison colonies there. Australian outlaws (the "bushrangers") such as Ned Kelly were popular subjects for folktales and songs. Later novelists examined the Australian national character. Among them was Patrick White, who was awarded the Nobel Prize for Literature in 1973. New Zealand literature established an international reputation due to the fame of such writers as Katherine Mansfield and Janet Frame. Since the late 1940s, more indigenous people—the Aborigines in Australia and the Maori in New Zealand—have been writing, usually in English. One of the best known is the poet Hone Tuwhare, who also writes in the Maori language.

Critical Thinking

Southeast Asia and the Pacific

1. There are many island countries in Southeast Asia and the Pacific. In a group, discuss possible cultural effects of living on an island.
2. Write an essay on the impact geography may have had on the art and literature of these various island countries.

VIETNAM, c. 1430

Before You Read

The Bamboo Hut

Meet Nguyen Trai

"Better conquer hearts than citadels."

Nguyen Trai (no͞o yin′ trī) led a life full enough for several people. He was a soldier, politician, historian, geographer, scholar, and poet, and he excelled in each of those endeavors.

When Nguyen Trai was twenty-seven, Vietnam was invaded by China. He joined the Vietnamese resistance forces and fought the Chinese invaders. His skill as a military strategist helped his people to achieve a decisive victory that restored Vietnamese independence. When the war was over, he wrote a poetic account of it, titled the *Proclamation of Victory over the Chinese*.

After the war, he was instrumental in rebuilding his war-torn homeland. Later in life, he retired to the village where he had been born to spend the rest of his days as a scholar and poet. He produced the first major geography of Vietnam, and he pioneered writing poetry in Vietnamese, rather than Chinese as had been the custom.

Nguyen Trai was born in 1380 and died in 1442.

Reading Focus

Do you sometimes like to get away from the world and be alone with your thoughts? Where do you go when you feel that way?

Freewrite Jot down your impressions of the ideal place to get away from the world. It might be an actual place or one that exists only in your imagination.

Setting a Purpose Read about the place where a Vietnamese poet goes to be alone.

Building Background

Execution of Nguyen Trai

After fighting to free the land he loved from foreign domination, Nguyen Trai retired to a simple life in the country. Still, he served as an advisor to the king, and some members of the court were jealous of his influence. Accused of planning to kill the king, Nguyen Trai was executed along with all of his family. Today, he is honored as a hero in Vietnam.

The Rise of Vietnamese Literature

Throughout its early history, Vietnam was strongly influenced by Chinese culture, including its language and literature. Until the end of the 1200s, all Vietnamese literature was written in Chinese. In 1282 a written form of the Vietnamese language called *chu nom* (choo′ nôm′), based on Chinese characters, was developed, and its use gradually became widespread.

When the Chinese invaded Vietnam in the early 1400s, they destroyed books and works of art in an attempt to wipe out Vietnamese culture. After the occupation ended, the entire culture had to be rebuilt. At the forefront of this effort, Nguyen Trai wrote much of his poetry in *chu nom,* helping to create a national literature in simple, direct language that all the people could understand.

The Bamboo Hut

Nguyen Trai
Translated by Nguyen Ngoc Bich
with Burton Raffel and W. S. Merwin

Plum Blossoms, 1972. Guan Tianying (Bonnie Kwan Huo) (China). Watercolor, 37.5 x 15 cm. Private collection.

A bamboo hut and a plum tree bower°—
That's where I spend my days, far from the world's talk.
For meals, only some pickled cabbage,
But I've never cared for the life of damask° and silk.
There's a pool of water for watching the moon,
And land to plough into flower beds.
Sometimes I feel inspired on snowy nights—
That's when I write my best poems, and sing.

---

1 A *bower* (bou′ ər) is a shelter (as in a garden) made with tree boughs.

4 *Damask* (dam′ əsk) is a rich, patterned fabric.

Responding to Literature

Personal Response

Can you identify with the feelings in this poem? Why or why not?

Analyzing Literature

Recall and Interpret

1. Where does the speaker spend his days?
2. What does the speaker like about this place?
3. What does the speaker mean by "the life of damask and silk"?
4. The **theme** of a literary work is its main idea or message (see page R12). What do you think is the theme of this poem?
5. Do you think the poet is the speaker in this poem? Why or why not?

Evaluate and Connect

6. Do you agree with the speaker's ideas about what makes a happy life? Why or why not?
7. Do you think that most Americans would choose "a bamboo hut and a plum tree bower" over "the life of damask and silk"? Explain. Which would you choose? Why?
8. What circumstances would be the modern-day equivalents of a bamboo hut? of a life of damask and silk?
9. Why do some people prefer to spend their days "far from the world's talk"?
10. The speaker says he writes his best poems on snowy nights. When or where do you feel most creative? Why?

Literary ELEMENTS

Imagery

In a literary work, **images** are the word pictures that help evoke an emotional response. In creating images, writers use sensory details or descriptions that appeal to one or more of the five senses.

1. Create a two-column chart. In one column, list images from the poem that depict the speaker's life. In the other, write your reaction to each image.
2. This poem manages to make appealing what many Americans would consider a life of poverty. How does the poem achieve this feat?

- See **Literary Terms Handbook,** p. R6.

Extending Your Response

Creative Writing

The Perfect Spot For the Reading Focus on page 688, you jotted down notes about your ideal spot "far from the world's talk." Use those notes as the basis of a poem modeled on "The Bamboo Hut." Use sensory details that capture the kind of life you would lead in your ideal spot. Share your poem with your classmates by reading it aloud or posting it on a bulletin board.

Interdisciplinary Activity

Art: Illustration Create an illustration that evokes the theme or the mood of "The Bamboo Hut," using any medium or style you choose. For example, you might paint a picture that represents the setting realistically, or one that captures the mood in an abstract style; or you might create a collage of images inspired by the poem.

Save your work for your portfolio.

Travel Writing

Some of the world's great long-distance train rides are to be found in Australia. This excerpt from Simon Rowe's *Riding the Ghan* describes one.

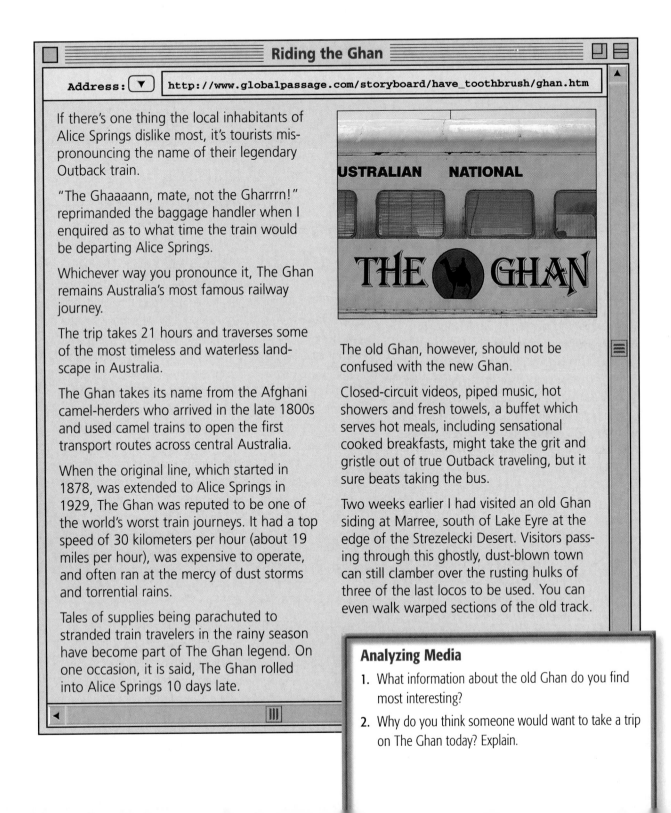

Riding the Ghan

Address: http://www.globalpassage.com/storyboard/have_toothbrush/ghan.htm

If there's one thing the local inhabitants of Alice Springs dislike most, it's tourists mispronouncing the name of their legendary Outback train.

"The Ghaaaann, mate, not the Gharrrn!" reprimanded the baggage handler when I enquired as to what time the train would be departing Alice Springs.

Whichever way you pronounce it, The Ghan remains Australia's most famous railway journey.

The trip takes 21 hours and traverses some of the most timeless and waterless landscape in Australia.

The Ghan takes its name from the Afghani camel-herders who arrived in the late 1800s and used camel trains to open the first transport routes across central Australia.

When the original line, which started in 1878, was extended to Alice Springs in 1929, The Ghan was reputed to be one of the world's worst train journeys. It had a top speed of 30 kilometers per hour (about 19 miles per hour), was expensive to operate, and often ran at the mercy of dust storms and torrential rains.

Tales of supplies being parachuted to stranded train travelers in the rainy season have become part of The Ghan legend. On one occasion, it is said, The Ghan rolled into Alice Springs 10 days late.

The old Ghan, however, should not be confused with the new Ghan.

Closed-circuit videos, piped music, hot showers and fresh towels, a buffet which serves hot meals, including sensational cooked breakfasts, might take the grit and gristle out of true Outback traveling, but it sure beats taking the bus.

Two weeks earlier I had visited an old Ghan siding at Marree, south of Lake Eyre at the edge of the Strezelecki Desert. Visitors passing through this ghostly, dust-blown town can still clamber over the rusting hulks of three of the last locos to be used. You can even walk warped sections of the old track.

Analyzing Media

1. What information about the old Ghan do you find most interesting?
2. Why do you think someone would want to take a trip on The Ghan today? Explain.

AUSTRALIA, 1892

Before You Read

The Drover's Wife

Meet Henry Lawson

"Death is about the only cheerful thing in the bush."

Henry Lawson had a difficult life both as a child and as an adult. At nine, he began to go deaf, and at fourteen, he quit school to work with his father in construction. Lawson eventually became a journalist and published poetry and stories in the *Bulletin*, the most important Australian literary journal of the time. In 1892 his first long trip through the bush country, on foot and in the middle of a terrible drought, gave him a bleak view of bush life and provided material for more stories. After he married and began a family, Lawson grew increasingly bitter over his inability to earn a living by writing. In 1900 he wrote in a letter, "I am wasting my work, wasting my life, spoiling the reputation I have gained, and wearing out my brains and heart here in Australia." His marriage failed, and Lawson spent time in prison and mental hospitals. But his writings remained popular, and he was honored with a state funeral when he died.

Lawson was born in 1867 and died in 1922.

Reading Focus

In his book *Walden,* Henry David Thoreau said, "We can never have enough of Nature." When you hear the word *nature* or *wilderness,* what do you picture in your mind? What associations do you have with these words?

Map It! Create a word map listing your mental associations with nature or wilderness.

Setting a Purpose Read to see how the main character in this story experiences and responds to the Australian wilderness.

Building Background

The Australian Bush

In Australia the term *bush* refers to unsettled land, whether desert, scrubland, grassland, or jungle. Except along the coast, much of Australia consists of flat, dry land where few people live. Beginning in the 1860s, free parcels of rural land, called *selections,* were distributed to small farmers. However, the climate and soil conditions in the bush made most family farms unprofitable. Squatters—those who ran large sheep-grazing operations—generally prospered.

Since the 1890s, many Australian authors have written about life in the bush, helping to make it an integral part of Australia's national identity. Ideas about the bush and the people who live there vary widely. Some writers portray it as a hostile environment that defeats the haggard men and women who struggle to survive there. Others depict bush characters as rugged, self-reliant individuals who accept the demands of bush life and fall under the spell of its haunting beauty and isolation. "The Drover's Wife" is a famous story of life in the Australian bush that has inspired both a painting and a movie.

Vocabulary Preview

gaunt (gônt) *adj.* excessively thin and angular; p. 694
provisions (prō vizh′ ənz) *n.* food supplies; p. 695
besiege (bi sēj′) *v.* to surround with hostile forces; p. 697
cringing (krinj′ ing) *adj.* shrinking back, as if in fear; p. 697
monotony (mə nä′ tə nē) *n.* sameness leading to boredom; lack of variety; p. 697

The Drover's Wife

Henry Lawson

Betty Bon Cordillo, Australia (detail). David Dridon (Australia, 20th century). Private collection. What types of life do you think could survive in this kind of country?

The two-roomed house is built of round timber, slabs, and stringy bark, and floored with split slabs. A big bark kitchen standing at one end is larger than the house itself, verandah included.

Bush all around—bush with no horizon, for the country is flat. No ranges in the distance. The bush consists of stunted, rotten native apple trees. No undergrowth. Nothing to relieve the eye save the darker green of a few sheoaks[1] which are sighing above the narrow, almost waterless creek. Nineteen miles to the nearest sign of civilization—a shanty on the main road.

1. *Sheoaks* (shē′ ōks) are Australian hardwood trees.

The drover, an ex-squatter, is away with sheep. His wife and children are left here alone.

Four ragged, dried-up-looking children are playing about the house. Suddenly one of them yells: "Snake! Mother, here's a snake!"

The gaunt, sun-browned bushwoman dashes from the kitchen, snatches her baby from the ground, holds it on her left hip, and reaches for a stick.

"Where is it?"

"Here! gone into the wood-heap!" yells the eldest boy—a sharp-faced, excited urchin[2] of eleven. "Stop there, mother! I'll have him. Stand back! I'll have the beggar!"

"Tommy, come here, or you'll be bit. Come here at once when I tell you, you little wretch!"

The youngster comes reluctantly, carrying a stick bigger than himself. Then he yells, triumphantly:

"There it goes—under the house!" and darts away with club uplifted. At the same time the big, black, yellow-eyed dog-of-all-breeds, who has shown the wildest interest in the proceedings, breaks his chain and rushes after that snake. He is a moment late, however, and his nose reaches the crack in the slabs just as the end of its tail disappears. Almost at the same moment the boy's club comes down and skins the aforesaid nose. Alligator takes small notice of this, and proceeds to undermine the building; but he is subdued after a struggle and chained up. They cannot afford to lose him.

The drover's wife makes the children stand together near the doghouse while she watches for the snake. She gets two small dishes of milk and sets them down near the wall to tempt it to come out; but an hour goes by and it does not show itself.

It is near sunset, and a thunderstorm is coming. The children must be brought inside. She will not take them into the house, for she knows the snake is there, and may at any moment come up through the cracks in the rough slab floor; so she carries several armfuls of firewood into the kitchen, and then takes the children there. The kitchen has no floor—or, rather, an earthen one—called a "ground floor" in this part of the bush. There is a large, roughly made table in the center of the place. She brings the children in, and makes them get on this table. They are two boys and two girls—mere babies. She gives them some supper, and then, before it gets dark, she goes into the house, and snatches up some pillows and bedclothes—expecting to see or lay her hand on the snake any minute. She makes a bed on the kitchen table for the children, and sits down beside it to watch all night.

She has an eye on the corner, and a green sapling club laid in readiness on the dresser by her side, together with her sewing basket and a copy of the *Young Ladies' Journal.* She has brought the dog into the room.

Tommy turns in, under protest, but says he'll lie awake all night and smash that blinded snake.

His mother asks him how many times she has told him not to swear.

He has his club with him under the bedclothes, and Jacky protests:

"Mummy! Tommy's skinnin' me alive wif his club. Make him take it out."

Tommy: "Shet up, you little—! D'yer want to be bit with the snake?"

Jacky shuts up.

"If yer bit," says Tommy, after a pause, "you'll swell up, an' smell,

2. An *urchin* is a mischievous child.

Vocabulary
gaunt (gônt) *adj.* excessively thin and angular

an' turn red an' green an' blue all over till yer bust. Won't he, mother?"

"Now then, don't frighten the child. Go to sleep," she says.

The two younger children go to sleep, and now and then Jacky complains of being "skeezed." More room is made for him. Presently Tommy says: "Mother! listen to them little 'possums. I'd like to screw their blanky necks."

And Jacky protests drowsily:

"But they don't hurt us, the little blanks!"

Mother: "There, I told you you'd teach Jacky to swear." But the remark makes her smile. Jacky goes to sleep.

Presently Tommy asks:

"Mother! Do you think they'll ever extricate[3] the kangaroo?"

"Lord! How am I to know, child? Go to sleep."

"Will you wake me if the snake comes out?"

"Yes. Go to sleep."

3. To *extricate* something is to get it out of a troublesome situation. Tommy probably means "exterminate."

Pedda Podda Snake, 1796. English School. Engraving. R.S.A., London.

Near midnight. The children are all asleep and she sits there still, sewing and reading by turns. From time to time she glances round the floor and wall-plate, and whenever she hears a noise she reaches for the stick. The thunderstorm comes on, and the wind, rushing through the cracks in the slab wall, threatens to blow out her candle. She places it on a sheltered part of the dresser and fixes up a newspaper to protect it. At every flash of lightning, the cracks between the slabs gleam like polished silver. The thunder rolls, and the rain comes down in torrents.

Alligator lies at full length on the floor, with his eyes turned towards the partition. She knows by this that the snake is there. There are large cracks in that wall opening under the floor of the dwelling-house.

She is not a coward, but recent events have shaken her nerves. A little son of her brother-in-law was lately bitten by a snake, and died. Besides, she has not heard from her husband for six months, and is anxious about him.

He was a drover, and started squatting here when they were married. The drought of 18— ruined him. He had to sacrifice the remnant of his flock and go droving again. He intends to move his family into the nearest town when he comes back, and, in the meantime, his brother, who keeps a shanty on the main road, comes over about once a month with provisions. The wife has still a couple of cows, one horse, and a few sheep. The brother-in-law kills one of the sheep occasionally, gives her what she needs of it, and takes the rest in return for other provisions.

She is used to being left alone. She once lived like this for eighteen months. As a girl she built the usual castles in the air; but all her

Vocabulary

provisions (prə vizh′ ənz) *n.* food supplies

girlish hopes and aspirations have long been dead. She finds all the excitement and recreation she needs in the *Young Ladies' Journal*, and, Heaven help her! takes a pleasure in the fashion plates.

Her husband is an Australian, and so is she. He is careless, but a good enough husband. If he had the means he would take her to the city and keep her there like a princess. They are used to being apart, or at least she is. "No use fretting," she says. He may forget sometimes that he is married; but if he has a good check when he comes back he will give most of it to her. When he had money he took her to the city several times—hired a railway sleeping compartment, and put up at the best hotels. He also bought her a buggy, but they had to sacrifice that along with the rest.

The last two children were born in the bush—one while her husband was bringing a drunken doctor, by force, to attend to her. She was alone on this occasion, and very weak. She had been ill with a fever. She prayed to God to send her assistance. God sent Black Mary. . . . Or, at least, God sent "King Jimmy" first, and he sent Black Mary. He put his black face round the door-post, took in the situation at a glance, and said cheerfully: "All right, Missis—I bring my old woman, she down alonga creek."

One of her children died while she was here alone. She rode nineteen miles for assistance, carrying the dead child.

It must be near one or two o'clock. The fire is burning low. Alligator lies with his head resting on his paws, and watches the wall. He is not a very beautiful dog to look at, and the light shows numerous old wounds where the hair will not grow. He is afraid of nothing on the face of the earth or under it. He will tackle a bullock as readily as he will tackle a flea. He hates all other dogs—except kangaroo-dogs—and has a marked dislike to friends or relations of the family. They seldom call, however. He sometimes makes friends with strangers. He hates snakes and has killed many, but he will be bitten some day and die; most snake-dogs end that way.

Now and then the bushwoman lays down her work and watches, and listens, and thinks. She thinks of things in her own life, for there is little else to think about.

The rain will make the grass grow, and this reminds her how she fought a bush fire once while her husband was away. The grass was long, and very dry, and the fire threatened to burn her out. She put on an old pair of her husband's trousers and beat out the flames with a green bough, till great drops of sooty perspiration stood out on her forehead and ran in streaks down her blackened arms. The sight of his mother in trousers greatly amused Tommy, who worked like a little hero by her side, but the terrified baby howled lustily for his "mummy." The fire would have mastered her but for four excited bushmen who arrived in the nick of time. It was a mixed-up affair all round; when she went to take up the baby he screamed and struggled convulsively. . . ;[4] and Alligator, trusting more to the child's sense than his own instinct, charged furiously, and (being old and slightly deaf) did not in his excitement at first recognize his mistress's voice, but continued to hang on to the moleskins until choked off by Tommy with a saddle-strap. The dog's sorrow for his blunder, and his anxiety to let it be known that it was all a mistake, was as evident as his ragged tail and a twelve-inch grin could make it. It was a glorious time for the boys; a day to look back to, and talk about, and laugh over for many years.

She thinks how she fought a flood during her husband's absence. She stood for hours in the drenching downpour, and dug an overflow gutter to save the dam across the creek. But she could not save it. There are things that a bushwoman cannot do. Next morning the dam was

4. *Convulsively* means "having the quality of spasms or violent upheavals."

broken, and her heart was nearly broken too, for she thought how her husband would feel when he came home and saw the result of years of labor swept away. She cried then.

She also fought the *pleuro-pneumonia*—dosed and bled the few remaining cattle, and wept again when her two best cows died.

Again, she fought a mad bullock that besieged the house for a day. She made bullets and fired at him through cracks in the slabs with an old shotgun. He was dead in the morning. She skinned him and got seventeen-and-six for the hide.

She also fights the crows and eagles that have designs on her chickens. Her plan of campaign is very original. The children cry "Crows, mother!" and she rushes out and aims a broomstick at the birds as though it were a gun, and says "Bung!" The crows leave in a hurry; they are cunning, but a woman's cunning is greater.

Occasionally a bushman in the horrors, or a villainous-looking sundowner, comes and nearly scares the life out of her. She generally tells the suspicious-looking stranger that her husband and two sons are at work below the dam, or over at the yard, for he always cunningly enquires for the boss.

Only last week a gallows-faced swagman[5]—having satisfied himself that there were no men on the place—threw his swag down on the verandah,[6] and demanded tucker.[7] She gave him something to eat; then he expressed his intention of staying for the night. It was sundown then. She got a batten[8] from the sofa, loosened the dog, and confronted the stranger, holding the batten in one hand and the dog's collar with the other. "Now you go!" she said. He looked at her and at the dog, said "All right, mum," in a cringing tone, and left. She was a determined-looking woman, and Alligator's yellow eyes glared unpleasantly—besides, the dog's chawing-up apparatus greatly resembled that of the reptile he was named after.

She has few pleasures to think of as she sits here alone by the fire, on guard against a snake. All days are much the same to her, but on Sunday afternoon she dresses herself, tidies the children, smartens up baby, and goes for a lonely walk along the bush-track, pushing an old perambulator in front of her. She does this every Sunday. She takes as much care to make herself and the children look smart as she would if she were going to do the block in the city. There is nothing to see, however, and not a soul to meet. You might walk for twenty miles along this track without being able to fix a point in your mind, unless you are a bushman. This is because of the everlasting, maddening sameness of the stunted trees—that monotony which makes a man long to break away and travel as far as trains can go, and sail as far as ships can sail—and further.

Did You Know?
A *perambulator* (pər am′ byə lā′ tər) is a baby carriage.

But this bushwoman is used to the loneliness of it. As a girl-wife she hated it, but now she would feel strange away from it.

She is glad when her husband returns, but she does not gush or make a fuss about it. She

5. *Swagman* is Australian slang for *drifter,* one who carries a pack (a *swag*) of personal belongings.
6. A *verandah* is an open porch, usually roofed.
7. *Tucker* is Australian slang for *food.*
8. A *batten* is a piece of lumber.

Vocabulary

besiege (bi sēj′) *v.* to surround with hostile forces
cringing (krinj′ ing) *adj.* shrinking back, as if in fear
monotony (mə nä′ tə nē) *n.* sameness leading to boredom; lack of variety

gets him something good to eat, and tidies up the children.

She seems contented with her lot. She loves her children, but has no time to show it. She seems harsh to them. Her surroundings are not favorable to the development of the "womanly" or sentimental side of nature.

It must be near morning now; but the clock is in the dwelling-house. Her candle is nearly done; she forgot that she was out of candles. Some more wood must be got to keep the fire up, and so she shuts the dog inside and hurries round to the wood-heap. The rain has cleared off. She seizes a stick, pulls it out, and—crash! the whole pile collapses.

Yesterday she bargained with a stray black-fellow to bring her some wood, and while he was at work she went in search of a missing cow. She was absent an hour or so, and the native black made good use of his time. On her return she was so astonished to see a good heap of wood by the chimney, that she gave him an extra fig of tobacco, and praised him for not being lazy. He thanked her, and left with head erect and chest

Landscape with Tent. Duncan McGregor Whyte (Australia, 1866–1953). Whitford & Hughes, London.
Viewing the painting: Describe the painting. What do you think living in such a place would be like?

Children Dancing. Sir George Russell Drysdale (Australia, 1912–1981). Oil on canvas. Private collection.

The Doll's House

Katherine Mansfield

When dear old Mrs. Hay went back to town after staying with the Burnells she sent the children a doll's house. It was so big that the carter and Pat carried it into the courtyard, and there it stayed, propped up on two wooden boxes beside the feed room door. No harm could come to it: it was summer. And perhaps the smell of paint would have gone off by the time it had to be taken in. For, really, the smell of paint coming from that doll's house ("Sweet of old Mrs. Hay, of course; most sweet and generous!")—but the smell of paint was quite enough to make anyone seriously ill, in Aunt Beryl's opinion. Even before the sacking was taken off. And when it was . . .

There stood the Doll's house, a dark, oily, spinach green, picked out with bright yellow. Its two solid little chimneys, glued on to the roof, were painted red and white, and the door, gleaming with yellow varnish, was like a little slab of toffee. Four windows, real windows, were divided into panes by a broad streak of green. There was actually a tiny porch, too, painted yellow, with big lumps of congealed paint hanging along the edge.

But perfect, perfect little house! Who could possibly mind the smell. It was part of the joy, part of the newness.

"Open it quickly, someone!"

The hook at the side was stuck fast. Pat pried it open with his penknife, and the whole house front swung back, and—there you were, gazing at one and the same moment into the drawing room and dining room, the kitchen and two bedrooms. That is the way for a house to open! Why don't all houses open like that? How much more exciting than peering through the slit of a door into a mean little hall with a hatstand and two umbrellas! That is—isn't it?—what you long to know about a house when you put your hand on the knocker. Perhaps it is the way God opens houses at the dead of night when He is taking a quiet turn with an angel . . .

It was too marvelous; it was too much for them.

"O-oh!" The Burnell children sounded as though they were in despair. It was too marvelous; it was too much for them. They had never seen anything like it in their lives. All the rooms were papered. There were pictures on the walls, painted on the paper, with gold frames complete. Red carpet covered all the floors except the kitchen; red plush chairs in the drawing room, green in the dining room; tables, beds with real bedclothes, a cradle, a stove, a dresser with tiny plates and one big jug. But what Kezia liked more than anything, what she liked frightfully, was the lamp. It stood in the middle of the dining room table, an exquisite little amber lamp with a white globe. It was even filled all ready for lighting, though, of course, you couldn't light it. But there was something inside that looked like oil and moved when you shook it.

The father and mother dolls, who sprawled very stiff as though they had fainted in the drawing room, and their two little children asleep upstairs, were really too big for the doll's house. They didn't look as though they belonged. But the lamp was perfect. It seemed to smile at Kezia, to say, "I live here." The lamp was real.

The Burnell children could hardly walk to school fast enough the next morning. They burned to tell everybody, to describe, to—well—to boast about their doll's house before the school-bell rang.

"I'm to tell," said Isabel, "because I'm the eldest. And you two can join in after. But I'm to tell first."

There was nothing to answer. Isabel was bossy, but she was always right, and Lottie and Kezia knew too well the powers that went with being eldest. They brushed through the thick buttercups at the road edge and said nothing.

"And I'm to choose who's to come and see it first. Mother said I might."

For it had been arranged that while the doll's house stood in the courtyard they might ask the girls at school, two at a time, to come and look. Not to stay to tea, of course, or to come traipsing[1] through the house. But just to stand quietly

1. *Traipsing* means "walking around idly or aimlessly."

Vocabulary

congealed (kən jēld′) *adj.* thickened; changed from a liquid to a solid state

Did You Know?
Palings are the stakes or pickets that make a fence.

in the courtyard while Isabel pointed out the beauties, and Lottie and Kezia looked pleased . . .

But hurry as they might, by the time they had reached the tarred palings of the boys' playground the bell had begun to jangle. They only just had time to whip off their hats and fall into line before the roll was called. Never mind. Isabel tried to make up for it by looking very important and mysterious and by whispering behind her hand to the girls near her, "Got something to tell you at playtime."

Playtime came and Isabel was surrounded. The girls of her class nearly fought to put their arms round her, to walk away with her, to beam flatteringly, to be her special friend. She held quite a court under the huge pine trees at the side of the playground. Nudging, giggling together, the little girls pressed up close. And the only two who stayed outside the ring were the two who were always outside, the little Kelveys. They knew better than to come anywhere near the Burnells.

For the fact was, the school the Burnell children went to was not at all the kind of place their parents would have chosen if there had been any choice. But there was none. It was the only school for miles. And the consequence was all the children of the neighborhood, the Judge's little girls, the doctor's daughters, the storekeeper's children, the milkman's, were forced to mix together. Not to speak of there being an equal number of rude, rough little boys as well. But the line had to be drawn somewhere. It was drawn at the Kelveys. Many of the children, including the Burnells, were not allowed even to speak to them. They walked past the Kelveys with their heads in the air, and as they set the fashion in all matters of behavior, the Kelveys were shunned by everybody. Even the teacher had a special voice for them, and a special smile for the other children when Lil Kelvey came up to her desk with a bunch of dreadfully common-looking flowers.

They were the daughters of a spry, hard-working little washerwoman, who went about from house to house by the day. This was awful enough. But where was Mr. Kelvey? Nobody knew for certain. But everybody said he was in prison. So they were the daughters of a washerwoman and a jailbird. Very nice company for other people's children! And they looked it. Why Mrs. Kelvey made them so conspicuous was hard to understand. The truth was they were dressed in "bits" given to her by the people for whom she worked. Lil, for instance, who was a stout, plain child, with big freckles, came to school in a dress made from a green art-serge tablecloth of the Burnells', with red plush sleeves from the Logans' curtains. Her hat, perched on top of her high forehead, was a grown-up woman's hat, once the property of Miss Lecky, the postmistress. It was turned up at the back and trimmed with a large scarlet quill. What a little guy she looked! It was impossible not to laugh. And her little sister, our Else, wore a long white dress, rather like a nightgown, and a pair of little boy's boots. But whatever our Else wore she would have looked strange. She was a tiny wishbone of a child, with cropped hair and enormous solemn eyes—a little white owl. Nobody had ever seen her smile; she scarcely ever spoke. She went through life holding on to Lil, with a piece of Lil's skirt screwed up in her hand. Where Lil went, our Else followed. In the playground, on the road going to and from school, there was Lil marching in front and our Else holding on behind. Only when she wanted anything, or when she was out of breath, our Else gave Lil a tug, a twitch, and Lil stopped and turned round. The Kelveys never failed to understand each other.

Now they hovered at the edge; you couldn't stop them listening. When the little girls turned round and sneered, Lil, as usual, gave her silly, shamefaced smile, but our Else only looked.

And Isabel's voice, so very proud, went on telling. The carpet made a great sensation, but so did the beds with real bedclothes, and the stove with an oven door.

When she finished Kezia broke in. "You've forgotten the lamp, Isabel."

"Oh, yes," said Isabel, "and there's a teeny little lamp, all made of yellow glass, with a white globe that stands on the dining room table. You couldn't tell it from a real one."

"The lamp's best of all," cried Kezia. She thought Isabel wasn't making half enough of the little lamp. But nobody paid any attention. Isabel was choosing the two who were to come back with them that afternoon and see it. She chose Emmie Cole and Lena Logan. But when the others knew they were all to have a chance, they couldn't be nice enough to Isabel. One by one they put their arms round Isabel's waist and walked her off. They had something to whisper to her, a secret. "Isabel's *my* friend."

Only the little Kelveys moved away forgotten; there was nothing more for them to hear.

Days passed, and as more children saw the doll's house, the fame of it spread. It became the one subject, the rage. The one question was, "Have you seen Burnells' doll's house? Oh, ain't it lovely!" "Haven't you seen it? Oh, I say!"

Even the dinner hour was given up to talking about it. The little girls sat under the pines eating their thick mutton sandwiches and big slabs of johnny cake[2] spread with butter. While always, as near as they could get, sat the

Suffragette's House. Tirzah Ravilious (née Garwood) (Great Britain, 1908–1951). Oil on canvas. Private collection.

Viewing the painting: How does this painting, with its careful placement of the dancers around the little house, remind you of the story?

2. A *johnny cake* is a flat, crisp cake made of cornmeal.

Vocabulary

hover (huv′ ər) *v.* to linger or remain nearby

Kelveys, our Else holding on to Lil, listening too, while they chewed their jam sandwiches out of a newspaper soaked with large red blobs.

"Mother," said Kezia, "can't I ask the Kelveys just once?"

"Certainly not, Kezia."

"But why not?"

"Run away, Kezia; you know quite well why not."

At last everybody had seen it except them. On that day the subject rather flagged. It was the dinner hour. The children stood together under the pine trees, and suddenly, as they looked at the Kelveys eating out of their paper, always by themselves, always listening, they wanted to be horrid to them. Emmie Cole started the whisper.

"Lil Kelvey's going to be a servant when she grows up."

"O-oh, how awful!" said Isabel Burnell, and she made eyes at Emmie.

Emmie swallowed in a very meaning way and nodded to Isabel as she'd seen her mother do on those occasions.

"It's true—it's true—it's true," she said.

Then Lena Logan's little eyes snapped. "Shall I ask her?" she whispered.

"Bet you don't," said Jessie May.

"Pooh, I'm not frightened," said Lena. Suddenly she gave a little squeal and danced in front of the other girls. "Watch! Watch me! Watch me now!" said Lena. And sliding, gliding, dragging one foot, giggling behind her hand, Lena went over to the Kelveys.

Lil looked up from her dinner. She wrapped the rest quickly away. Our Else stopped chewing. What was coming now?

"Is it true you're going to be a servant when you grow up, Lil Kelvey?" shrilled Lena.

Dead silence. But instead of answering, Lil only gave her silly, shamefaced smile. She didn't seem to mind the question at all. What a sell for Lena! The girls began to titter.

Lena couldn't stand that. She put her hands on her hips; she shot forward. "Yah, yer father's in prison!" she hissed, spitefully.

This was such a marvelous thing to have said that the little girls rushed away in a body, deeply, deeply excited, wild with joy. Someone found a long rope, and they began skipping. And never did they skip so high, run in and out so fast, or do such daring things as on that morning.

In the afternoon Pat called for the Burnell children with the buggy and they drove home. There were visitors. Isabel and Lottie, who liked visitors, went upstairs to change their pinafores. But Kezia thieved out at the back. Nobody was about; she began to swing on the big white gates of the courtyard. Presently, looking along the road, she saw two little dots. They grew bigger, they were coming towards her. Now she could see that one was in front and one close behind. Now she could see that they were the Kelveys. Kezia stopped swinging. She slipped off the gate as if she was going to run away. Then she hesitated. The Kelveys came nearer, and beside them walked their shadows, very long, stretching right across the road with their heads in the buttercups. Kezia clambered back on the gate; she had made up her mind; she swung out.

"Hullo," she said to the passing Kelveys.

They were so astounded that they stopped. Lil gave her silly smile. Our Else stared.

"You can come and see our doll's house if you want to," said Kezia, and she dragged one toe on the ground. But at that Lil turned red and shook her head quickly.

"Why not?" asked Kezia.

Lil gasped, then she said, "Your ma told our ma you wasn't to speak to us."

Vocabulary

flag (flag) *v.* to decline in interest or attention

titter (ti′ tər) *v.* to laugh nervously

"Oh, well," said Kezia. She didn't know what to reply. "It doesn't matter. You can come and see our doll's house all the same. Come on. Nobody's looking."

But Lil shook her head still harder.

"Don't you want to?" asked Kezia.

Suddenly there was a twitch, a tug at Lil's skirt. She turned round. Our Else was looking at her with big, imploring eyes; she was frowning; she wanted to go. For a moment Lil looked at our Else very doubtfully. But then our Else twitched her skirt again. She started forward. Kezia led the way. Like two little stray cats they followed across the courtyard to where the doll's house stood.

Like two little stray cats they followed across the courtyard . . .

"There it is," said Kezia.

There was a pause. Lil breathed loudly, almost snorted; our Else was still as stone.

"I'll open it for you," said Kezia kindly. She undid the hook and they looked inside.

"There's the drawing room and the dining room, and that's the—"

"Kezia!"

Oh, what a start they gave!

"Kezia!"

It was Aunt Beryl's voice. They turned round. At the back door stood Aunt Beryl, staring as if she couldn't believe what she saw.

"How dare you ask the little Kelveys into the courtyard?" said her cold, furious voice. "You know as well as I do, you're not allowed to talk to them. Run away, children, run away at once. And don't come back again," said Aunt Beryl. And she stepped into the yard and shooed them out as if they were chickens.

"Off you go immediately!" she called, cold and proud.

They did not need telling twice. Burning with shame, shrinking together, Lil huddling along like her mother, our Else dazed, somehow they crossed the big courtyard and squeezed through the white gate.

"Wicked, disobedient little girl!" said Aunt Beryl bitterly to Kezia, and she slammed the doll's house to.

The afternoon had been awful. A letter had come from Willie Brent, a terrifying, threatening letter, saying if she did not meet him that evening in Pulman's Bush, he'd come to the front door and ask the reason why! But now that she had frightened those little rats of Kelveys and given Kezia a good scolding, her heart felt lighter. That ghastly pressure was gone. She went back to the house humming.

When the Kelveys were well out of sight of Burnells', they sat down to rest on a big red drainpipe by the side of the road. Lil's cheeks were still burning; she took off the hat with the quill and held it on her knee. Dreamily they looked over the hay paddocks, past the creek, to the group of wattles[3] where Logan's cows stood waiting to be milked. What were their thoughts?

Presently our Else nudged up close to her sister. But now she had forgotten the cross lady. She put out a finger and stroked her sister's quill; she smiled her rare smile.

"I seen the little lamp," she said, softly.

Then both were silent once more.

3. *Wattles* are branches or poles woven together to make walls.

Vocabulary

imploring (im plôr′ ing) *adj.* begging, or beseeching

Responding to Literature

Personal Response

What is your reaction to the way the Kelvey girls are treated? In your journal, write a few paragraphs to explain your reaction.

Analyzing Literature

Recall

1. Describe the doll's house that the Burnell children receive. Where do they have to keep it? Why must they keep it there?
2. Under what conditions are the girls' school friends allowed to see the doll's house?
3. What rule must the Burnell girls obey regarding the Kelvey sisters? Why?
4. Describe Aunt Beryl's behavior toward Kezia and the Kelveys.
5. What does the usually silent Else tell her sister at the end of the story?

Interpret

6. What do the Burnell children think of their new doll's house? What does Kezia like best about it? Why?
7. Why do the Burnells set such strict conditions for the viewing of the doll's house?
8. What effect do adult prejudices have on the children? Give examples.
9. How is Kezia different from the rest of her family? Support your answer with details from the story.
10. What is significant about Else's statement at the end of the story?

Evaluate and Connect

11. The **theme,** or main idea, of a story can often be expressed as a general statement (see **Literary Terms Handbook,** page R12). How would you express the theme of this story?
12. What do you think Kezia will be like when she grows up? Why?
13. If you were Lil or Else, how might you deal with the way the other children at school treat you? Why would you deal with the situation in that way?
14. Do people tend to socialize primarily with others of their own social class? Why?
15. For the Reading Focus on page 702, you wrote about your own experience of social class. Compare the impact of social class in your community with its impact in the society depicted in this story.

Literary Criticism

Scholar Claire Tomalin calls "The Doll's House" a "study of the cruelty of petty snobbery taught to children by their families." Which characters in the story display a superior attitude toward others? How are the children influenced by their families? Write a paragraph or two in response, citing specific details from the story as support.

Literary ELEMENTS

Symbol

A **symbol** is an object, person, place, or experience that also stands for something else, often an abstract quality or idea. For example, a red heart is a common symbol for love; a dove is a common symbol for peace. In this short story, the doll's house might be thought of as representing the Burnell household. Like the doll's house, the Burnell's house is a "display" home–more for show than for living in. The Burnell children, for example, are not allowed to invite their school friends into the house. The father and mother dolls in the doll's house are described as being "very stiff," much like the adults in the Burnell household.

1. Why does Kezia value the little lamp? Why does Else value the lamp?
2. What abstract qualities or values might the little lamp symbolize?

- See **Literary Terms Handbook,** p. R12.

Literature and Writing

Writing About Literature

Analyzing Tone The term **tone** refers to the attitude that an author takes toward his or her subject. Write a brief composition comparing the author's attitudes toward two of the characters in "The Doll's House," such as Kezia, Lena Logan, Aunt Beryl, or the Kelvey sisters. Give examples of words the author uses to describe the characters, and tell what tone the words convey.

Personal Writing

Effects of Social Class In "The Doll's House," Lena Logan taunts Lil Kelvey about growing up to be a servant. Think about the effects of social class on one's opportunities in life. How does social class limit or expand one's opportunities? Is it possible to overcome such limitations? How? Jot down your thoughts in your journal.

Extending Your Response

Literature Groups

Critic's Corner One critic has suggested that in writing "The Doll's House," Katherine Mansfield expressed the "mixed emotions of pleasure and guilt generated by her family's privilege." In your group, discuss examples of how these mixed emotions are conveyed in the story. Do you agree with the critic's opinion? Share your examples and conclusions with the rest of the class.

Performing

A Contemporary Skit What sort of gifts make a strong impression on children today? Work with a partner to develop a short skit that presents a modern-day version of "The Doll's House" set in your community. Ask for volunteers to perform the skit with you for the rest of the class.

Interdisciplinary Connection

Geography: New Zealand Many Americans know little about New Zealand. Use the Internet and library resources to investigate the history, culture, and geography of the country. Prepare a report on one aspect of your research.

Reading Further

If you enjoyed reading "The Doll's House," you might also enjoy the following story by Katherine Mansfield, which can be found in *Undiscovered Country,* edited by Ian A. Gordon:

"The Little Girl," a story about young Kezia and her relationship with her father.

Save your work for your portfolio.

VOCABULARY • Homographs

Homographs are words that are spelled alike but have different meanings and sometimes different pronunciations. In this sentence from the story, look for the homograph, "On that day the subject rather flagged." In the sentence, *flagged* is a verb, meaning "declined in interest or attention." Another verb usage of *flag* is to signal, as one flags a cab. *Flag* is also a noun referring to a nation's symbol or a signaling device. *Flags* are also attached to some musical notes.

PRACTICE Find at least two meanings for the homographs listed below. Then write a paragraph using as many of the homographs with as many different meanings as you can.

1. bow
2. redress
3. overall
4. affect
5. reject
6. discount
7. remark
8. discharge
9. convert
10. progress

Vo•cab•u•lar•y Skills

Analyzing Words

When you come across an unfamiliar word in your reading, you can use many kinds of clues to determine its meaning. Some clues, called "context clues," occur outside the word itself, in the sentence or paragraph in which the word appears. For example, read the following sentence from "Stay Alive, My Son."

> For another quarter of an hour, he continued his harangue, his voice growing louder and louder.

Clues within this sentence, such as references to the length of time and increasing loudness of his voice, help to determine the meaning of the word *harangue*—a long, vehement speech or a scolding.

Other sentences may provide no context clues for the meaning of an unfamiliar word, but the word itself will provide clues.

> Thay, you are a counterrevolutionary, but fortunately for you, you are a good worker.

Notice that the word *counterrevolutionary* contains the base word *revolution,* which is familiar. In addition, the prefix *counter-,* meaning "against," is familiar from such words as *counterclockwise* and *counterintelligence.* Therefore, as you might guess, someone who is a counterrevolutionary is against a revolution.

Even if a word does not have a base word that you know, it may contain one or more word parts that are familiar from other words. For example, look at *denounce* in this sentence: "I will denounce you." If you think about *announce* and *deny,* you should realize that *denounce* has something to do with accusing or condemning.

Although analyzing an unfamiliar word is not entirely a substitute for looking it up in a dictionary, there are two reasons to try to do it. First, you may be able to get a good idea of what the word means. Second, when you break a word into pieces and put it back together, you notice its parts and its relationship to other words, and that can help you remember its meaning.

EXERCISE

Analyze the underlined words, using whatever clues they contain to help you determine meaning. Try to match each one to its meaning in the list lettered *a* to *j*.

1. to subsist on rations
2. tetracycline, an antibiotic
3. their malevolent presence
4. his rapid ascendancy
5. phrases of condemnation
6. a contributory factor
7. a thermal spring
8. the two comrades' collusion
9. his demented state
10. their exhibitionism

a. hot
b. rise
c. insane
d. additional
e. wishing harm
f. severe disapproval
g. live
h. tendency to show off
i. substance that destroys life
j. secret agreement

Before You Read

Autumn Night from the *Prison Diary*

Meet Ho Chi Minh

"Vietnam is not only a country of poets, but Vietnam itself perhaps is a human poem."

—Tran Van Dinh, *Of Quiet Courage*

Ho Chi Minh's (hō chē min) original name was Nguyen Sinh Cung. As a Vietnamese Communist leader, he adopted the name Ho Chi Minh, which means "He Who Enlightens." He traveled to Europe in his twenties, working as a waiter, among other jobs. He rose from these humble beginnings to become an important Communist leader. With the motto "nothing is as dear to the heart of the Vietnamese as independence and liberation," he led the movement to gain independence for Vietnam. He founded the Communist party in Vietnam, and he served as president of North Vietnam from 1945 to 1969. Saigon was renamed Ho Chi Minh City after the Communist conquest of South Vietnam in 1975.

As a writer, Ho Chi Minh is best known for the *Prison Diary*, which contains the poems he wrote while in prison in China during World War II.

Ho Chi Minh was born in 1890 and died in 1969.

Reading Focus

If you were confined to an empty room for a day, with only a pen and paper, what do you think you would write?

Journal In your journal, jot down a few notes about the subjects you might focus on.

Setting a Purpose Read to discover how an imprisoned political leader turned his thoughts into poetry.

Building Background

A Country of Poets

In Vietnam, people in all walks of life–from farmers to soldiers to politicians–write poems. So it is not unusual that Ho Chi Minh, a Communist revolutionary and later the president of North Vietnam, should have written poetry. Even children in Vietnam create poems that are published.

Poetry, which can be preserved in memory, survived wars and invasions when art in other forms was lost or destroyed. This is one reason for its importance to the Vietnamese. In fact, the greatest eras for the creation of Vietnamese poetry came in the late thirteenth and early nineteenth centuries, during and after invasions from China. Poetry has come to be both an art form and a symbol of Vietnam's national identity.

Ho Chi Minh's Imprisonment

During World War II, the Japanese invaded French-ruled Vietnam. In 1942 Ho Chi Minh went to China to seek support from the government of Chiang Kai-shek for a common battle against the Japanese. But as a non-Communist leader who had fought against Communists in his own country, Chiang Kai-shek did not trust Ho Chi Minh and had him arrested. After more than a year, Ho's friends finally negotiated his release. Ho Chi Minh later assisted the Allies in the war against the Japanese.

Reading Further

If you enjoy reading "Autumn Night," you might also like the following poetry:

"Three Bullets" and "Worried Over the Days Past," from *Mountain River: Vietnamese Poetry from the Wars, 1948–1993,* edited by Kevin Bowen.

from the Prison Diary

Autumn Night

Ho Chi Minh

Translated by Aileen Palmer

A Testimony, 1974. Bu'u Chi (Vietnam). Mixed media artist's book. Collection of the artist.

In front of the gate, the guard stands with his rifle.
Above, untidy clouds are carrying away the moon.
The bedbugs are swarming round like army tanks on maneuvers,°
While the mosquitoes form squadrons, attacking like fighter planes.
My heart travels a thousand *li*° toward my native land.
My dream intertwines with sadness like a skein° of a thousand threads.
Innocent, I have now endured a whole year in prison.
Using my tears for ink, I turn my thoughts into verses.

---

3 Here, *maneuvers* are simulated battles to help soldiers practice for combat.

5 A *li* is a Chinese unit of distance (one *li* equals about one-third mile).

6 A *skein* (skān) is a loosely coiled length of thread or yarn wound on a reel.

Responding to Literature

Personal Response

What is your initial reaction to this poem? Record your reaction in your journal.

Analyzing Literature

Recall and Interpret

1. The **speaker** is the voice of a poem (see page R11). In some poems, the speaker is the poet; in others, it may be a fictional person, an animal, or even an object. Who is the speaker in this poem? What makes you think this?
2. What does the speaker say is happening to the moon? How might that description relate to what happened to Ho Chi Minh?
3. What does the speaker say the bedbugs and the mosquitoes are doing? How might the insects' activities relate to what was happening in Vietnam while Ho Chi Minh was in prison?
4. How does the speaker feel about his imprisonment? What does he do to endure his time in prison?

Evaluate and Connect

5. What do you most like or dislike about this poem? Explain why.
6. For the Reading Focus on page 712, you noted what you would probably write about if you were confined to an empty room for a day. In what ways does this poem influence your thoughts about the things you might focus on? Explain.
7. What impressions of Ho Chi Minh do you gain from reading this poem?
8. What other world leaders do you know who are or were writers? With your classmates, discuss why political leaders might also be poets.

Literary ELEMENTS

Figures of Speech

A **figure of speech** is a specific device or kind of figurative language, such as simile, metaphor, or personification. "Autumn Night" contains a number of striking figures of speech in just eight lines of poetry. For example, the phrase "untidy clouds are carrying away the moon" is an example of personification. "The bedbugs are swarming round like army tanks on maneuvers" is a simile. The word *like* is used to compare the bedbugs to tanks.

1. Identify and explain the effectiveness of another example of personification in the poem.
2. Identify and explain the effectiveness of two other similes in the poem.

- See **Literary Terms Handbook,** p. R4.

Extending Your Response

Interdisciplinary Activity

Social Studies: Vietnam Today Vietnam is a country that has known long periods of conflict. Use the Internet and other sources to find out what life is like today for the Vietnamese people. What legacies of the Vietnam War (1954–1975) still haunt them? How is the country recovering? Share your findings in an oral, visual, or written report.

Learning for Life

Interviewing Ho Chi Minh Imagine that you are a journalist and have been assigned the task of interviewing Ho Chi Minh after his release from prison in China. Prepare a list of interview questions. Then work with a partner to make up responses, researching Ho Chi Minh's life, if necessary. Role-play the interview for your classmates.

Save your work for your portfolio.

Before You Read

Pulse of the Land

PHILIPPINES, 1952

Meet Hermel A. Nuyda

"Above all, the burden of the writer has been . . . to startle into image the Philippine presence, beyond all question of human worth."

—Leonard Casper, *New Writing from the Philippines*

Hermel A. Nuyda (har′ mel nōō ē′ dä) grew up near Mayon Volcano on the island of Luzon in the Philippines, the setting of "Pulse of the Land." He left his home for Manila, the capital city, where he taught social studies for six years. Then he combined writing with a legal and political career. Nuyda's father had served in congress, and Nuyda followed in his father's footsteps, pursuing a career in the government. He became an assistant in the Philippine Senate and helped draft a variety of laws, including those regulating trade between the United States and the Philippines.

Hermel A. Nuyda was born in 1919.

Reading Focus

Imagine that you are a tourist from a distant country visiting the United States for the first time. Think about your neighborhood from the point of view of that tourist. What would you want to photograph to show the people back home?

Share Ideas In small groups, discuss what aspects of your locale would seem odd, picturesque, beautiful, or quaint enough for a tourist to photograph.

Setting a Purpose As you read, notice the details of the setting of this story from the Philippines.

Building Background

Time and Place

"Pulse of the Land" is set on Luzon, the largest of the islands that make up the Philippines. Mountain ranges and volcanoes, some of which are still active, dominate the landscape. Mayon Volcano in southeastern Luzon has erupted more than thirty times since 1616, when records began to be kept. This volcano is famous for its almost perfect cone shape.

The events in "Pulse of the Land" take place in the early years of Philippine independence, after over 300 years as a Spanish colony and almost 50 years as a possession of the United States. During that period of time, most Filipinos lived in rural areas. In the decades since the war, however, many Filipinos have moved to Manila and other cities.

Vocabulary Preview

populace (pop′ yə ləs) *n.* the inhabitants of a place; p. 716
reverie (re′ və rē) *n.* the condition of being lost in thought; p. 717
trek (trek) *n.* a slow and difficult journey; p. 720
immutable (i mū′ tə bəl) *adj.* unchanging; p. 720
sentinel (sen′ tə nəl) *n.* a person standing guard or keeping watch; p. 720

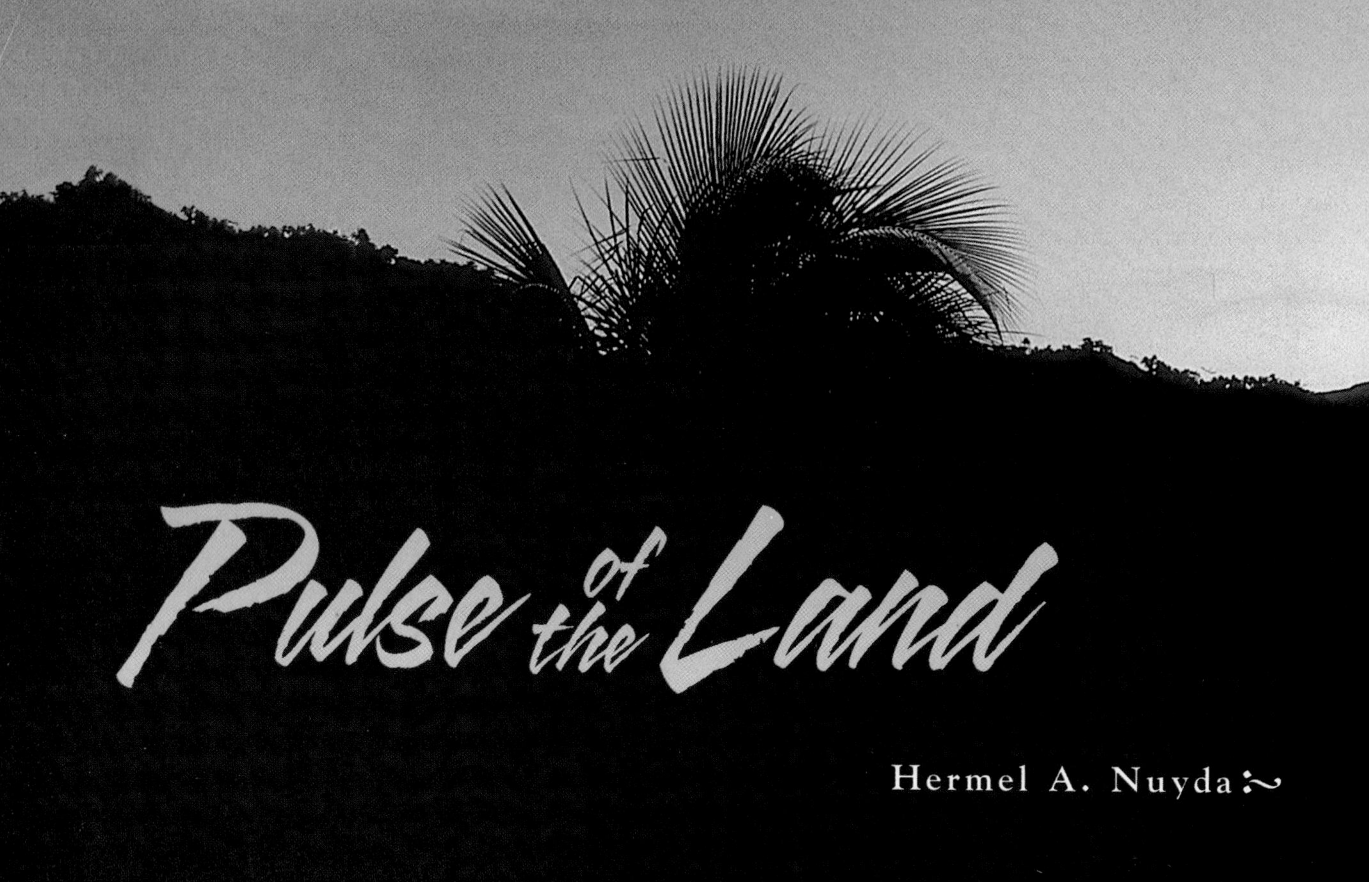

Pulse of the Land

Hermel A. Nuyda

THE AMERICAN WAS THIRSTY; VERY THIRSTY. The water jug had been emptied of its contents a mile back and, but for the assurance of his guide that they would find water in one of the huts scattered about the vicinity, he would have turned back and called it a day.

"You mean to tell me people actually live on this volcano?" he said, wiping the sweat off his forehead with the back of his hand. Although the morning was still early, already the sun had reddened his lean face, and his shirt was wet with sweat.

"Yes," the guide informed him. "People have been living on it for years." The guide was a short fellow and for every step the American took he took two. But there was power in his arms and legs, and he could speak English.

"But I understand this is an active volcano," the American said. "What happens to the people when it erupts?"

"That happens very seldom," the guide said, "and when it does they seek refuge in safer places. Then they come back after the eruption is over."

"Isn't that something!" the American said. "Well, tell me—how do they go about making a living?"

"They plant in the daytime," the guide explained, "and make charcoal at night. It is their fires you see at the foot of the mountain after dark."

The American shook his head. "What an odd way to live," he said.

"Have you stayed long in the country?" the guide asked in turn.

"Three months," the American answered. "Manila." This reminded him of the book he was writing about the country, of Manila and its populace. He smiled to himself. As he walked he thought of the pictures he had taken; the

Vocabulary

populace (pop′ yə ləs) *n.* the inhabitants of a place

biting wit of the captions he had given them. That one about the market place, for instance: "*Native wares of all kinds, and one hundred odors for every one hundred yards.*" Or that one about the street scene: "*And we can talk about the gals, and the smells, and the cartellas, and the smells, and the caribou carts, and the smells.*" His was going to be some travel book! It was going to turn the country inside out, and the essence of it he would unfold by a few lines on the cover: "*If all the negatives I've shot in Manila were laid end to end, they would serve no lawful purpose. But, printed here, they'll serve to remind you that East is East and West is West, and I'll take North Overshoe, Nebraska.*" He would be denounced; he could not help that. He had decided to tell the truth. "*Confused—not a trace of individuality—sadly wanting in sincerity and in clarity of purpose—a flax seed caught in the meeting of the winds—*" Such was his impression of the twenty-two million. Perhaps they would hate him for it, but it would not be his fault.

"Are you staying longer in the country?" the guide's voice broke into his reverie.

"Stay longer here?" he repeated. "No, no, I've stayed long enough. In fact I should be on my way back to the States, you know, but the fame of your Mayon Volcano altered my plans. I had to see the cone[1] for myself."

The barking of dogs meant that they had come upon a dwelling. That meant water too.

When they reached the clearing where a hut squatted on the dry earth, two lean dogs bared their fangs at them so that they had to stop on the trail until a small boy (he could not have been more than eight years old) backed off slowly toward the hut, staring at them as he did, with timidity and fright.

1. *Cone* refers to the shape of the volcano.

Vocabulary

reverie (re′ və rē) *n.* the condition of being lost in thought

When the American grinned, the boy smiled back; and his hands inched their way to cover his front which was uncovered from the waist down. The boy stood thus for several seconds: shoulders hunched, arms straight across the belly, and the hands slipped in between the thin dark legs. Then he ran up the low steps of the hut and almost immediately came down again, this time followed by a young girl dressed in a red chemise, a little taller than he was and, by her looks, no doubt his sister.

Did You Know?
A *chemise* (shə mēz′) is a loose dress that hangs straight from the shoulders.

The girl stared at the American in very much the same manner as did her brother a moment before: shy, withdrawing. She had long stringy hair, and her smile was pleasant; she kept biting at her fingers as she looked at the strangers.

As the two children stood by their squalid hut—the boy awkwardly shielding his nakedness with his hands, and the girl, giggling, biting her fingers, the long stringy hair rubbing against her scant red garment—the American thought they made such splendid subjects for a candid shot! Without their knowing it, he took their picture. The caption flashed in his mind: "*The Slops*[2] *of* Mt. *Mayon.*"

The American told the guide to see if there was water in the house and if they could be spared some. The guide talked to the children in the dialect.

"May we have some water?" he inquired.

The small girl nodded and said: "I will get some." She hurried up into the hut.

The two men walked to a bamboo bench. As the American straddled the bench, the little boy edged near him. The American laughed and said: "Hello, boy, what's your name?" The boy shook his head and, covering his cheeks with his two hands, ran up into the hut. He disappeared for a brief spell. Then slowly his head stuck out in the doorway, his big black eyes looking at the American excitedly. "Well, how do you like that!" the American exclaimed.

"They have not seen an American before," the guide explained.

"They're cute," the American observed as he looked at the little boy's face, at the same time peering into the interior of the hut which was almost bare except for a frail-looking bamboo stool, a crudely-fashioned weaving loom, a mat rolled up and laid against a corner, and a calendar with the picture of a saint nailed on the bamboo wall.

The girl came out with a black earthen bowl filled with water.

At first she made signs of giving it to the American, but on second thought, she turned to the guide and gave him the bowl instead. The guide handed the bowl to the American who took it, gave it a careful look, and before raising it to his lips, asked: "Think it's safe?"

"They drink it," the guide said.

The American saw the boy and girl watching him with great interest. They were smiling at him as if their not doing so would offend him and make him decide not to drink the water. "Oh, well," he said, and raised the bowl to his lips.

The American gargled with his first gulp. He gargled with the second and the third. He gargled with half the contents of the bowl, the water he spat out forming a dark splotch on the dry earth. The next half he drank. The water was cool, sweetish, with a queer but pleasant smell. He liked it. He smiled at the girl and asked for more by holding up an index finger and nodding his head at the same time. The girl understood and returned his nod gleefully. She went into the hut once more, the boy running after her. "How white he is," she said, looking

2. *Slops* are cheap, ready-made garments.

back as if to make sure the strangers had not decided to leave. "And big. How big!" exclaimed the boy.

The American drank half of the next bowl of water. The rest he offered to the guide. When the latter had finished drinking, the small boy suddenly jumped down the low steps and grabbed the bowl from him. Then with great excitement the boy faced the American, holding up his little index finger, his head nodding up and down, trying to ask if the tall white man wanted one more.

The American grinned and nodded back.

Proudly the boy went up the steps, laughing at his sister and sticking out the tip of his tongue at her as he passed by. When he came back, he walked very carefully, holding the bowl is if he were carrying the world in his hands. He pursed his lips, gave his sister a triumphant wink and, trembling, raised the bowl to the big white man.

For the third time the American took the black earthen bowl. But this time he did not drink. He stepped out into the yard and poured the water over his head, his face. After he finished he threw the rest of the water on the ground. Then he gave the bowl to the boy and sat on the bench once more.

"How come," he asked the guide, "these kids are alone in such a wild place?"

"They are used to it," the guide answered. "Their folks must be somewhere near, planting or looking for greens to eat." And to the girl, "Where are your parents?"

"In the *camote*[3] patch," the girl replied. Then she walked straight to a jackfruit tree by the edge of the clearing, from which an empty bomb shell was hung. From the foot of the tree she took an iron rod with which she struck the shell five times. It made a sound clear as a church bell.

"That's one of our shells," the American observed. "How on earth did it ever get here?"

"Many of those were dropped on the towns," the guide explained, "before your soldiers came."

3. A *camote* is a sweet potato.

Shortly after the last impact of metal against metal, a woman's voice came from way back of the clearing. A little later an old woman rushed into view. A strip of cloth was tied around her head and in her right hand was clutched a bolo smudged with fresh soil. When she saw the two men seated on the bench, she stopped and stared at them, her face tense and drawn. It was only after the children had talked to her that the tension on her face disappeared. She approached the two men and nodded politely to them.

Did You Know?
A *bolo* is a long, heavy, single-edged knife of Philippine origin.

"We came to ask for water," the guide said.

"We have water," the old woman answered and addressed the girl: "Go get the men water."

"They already have given us enough," the guide said.

"Are you sure? You must excuse these children if they have been rude. They are young and do not know much. Perhaps they did not even ask you to come up into the house?"

"That is all right," the guide assured her. "We are only resting for a while."

"I am glad it is all right. They are my grandchildren, you know, and there is only me to teach them what is right. Their father and mother died two years ago."

"The children have been good," the guide said.

The old woman looked at the American, and when she saw that he was looking at her, listening to her talk, she tried in the least noticeable way she could to rub the earth off her hands with her faded skirt. Then to the guide she said: "Where are you bound for?"

"He wants to go up the volcano," the guide replied, looking at the American.

"Why should he want to do that?" the woman asked. "There are no people living there."

"He is a visitor to our land," the guide explained. "And he wants to take pictures."

"Oh," the woman said. "Well, tell him that we are very sorry it is only water we can give. But if he can wait, I can fry some *camotes* in a short time."

"What's she saying?" the American interrupted, conscious that he was the subject of their conversation.

"She says she is sorry the children did not ask you to come up into the house, and she is ashamed she can only offer water. But if you care to wait she could fry sweet potatoes."

"Oh no," the American objected, shaking his head. "Tell her not to do that. And thank her for me."

The guide conveyed the American's words.

"Well then," the woman said, "you must take some water with you. It is hot and you will be thirsty on the way." Then she picked up the empty water jug. "Is this for water?" she asked. The guide nodded. Without speaking further the woman went into the hut, taking each rung very slowly and with the same leading foot. She was gone for only a short time.

"Here," she said when she came back to the doorway. "It is full." The guide took the water jug.

The American stood up and thrust his hand into his pocket for some loose change, but as he did so, the woman shook her head and frowned. The American withdrew his hand slowly from the pocket and smiled his thanks instead, after which he bowed to her, nodded to the children, and walked out of the clearing. He looked back once and saw the three of them still looking at him; their lean dogs lapping the dark splotch formed by the water he had spat on the earth.

How far they had walked the American could not exactly tell. The guide said they had covered two miles from the hut. To him it seemed much more. But he did not care. The feeling inside him as he stood on the huge rock was well worth the cuts on his arms, the long uphill trek, the descent into the steep ravines and the arduous walk over their beds of rock and sand, the blistering heat of the noonday sun.

From where he stood, the peak of the volcano, although it had lost the smoothness of its contours, loomed before him like a tower in the sky: powerful in its ruggedness, immutable in its lordship over the land below—a sentinel keeping vigil over the brown and green of the plains, the blue of the distant mountain ranges, and the dull gray of the sea beyond them.

He breathed deeply of the cool air, feeling as big as the vastness of it all. Then he took his camera and set to work. He shot as many negatives from as many angles as suited his critical eye. Then he walked to where the guide was resting and said: "Nature has been most generous to your country. You should take pride in the beauty of your land."

"It is high noon," the guide remarked casually. "It is bad to let hunger pass."

They ate in silence.

Half an hour later the American decided it was time to go back.

"If you do not mind walking up a little more," the guide suggested, "there is a better way back."

"Lead on," the American said. "You're the guide."

They walked uphill for several minutes along the edge of a deep ravine until they came upon a trail that led to its bottom. This they followed. The trees were bigger and their

Vocabulary

trek (trek) *n.* a slow and difficult journey
immutable (i mū′ tə bəl) *adj.* unchanging
sentinel (sen′ tə nəl) *n.* a person standing guard or keeping watch

foliage greener than those at the foot of the mountain. Around them they could hear the soft cooing of wild doves.

When they got to the bottom of the ravine, the American saw a group of people huddled on the other side of the ravine where the opposite cliff cast its shade. He could make out an old man sitting on a stone, some women squatting on the sand, and several children grouped in a circle playing with pebbles. Propped against the cliff, some pillowed on stones, were long bamboo tubes.

"What are all these people doing here?" the American asked the guide, wondering. "And what are the bamboos for?"

"The people are waiting for their turns," the guide explained. "The tubes are for fetching water."

"Water?" said the American, surprised. "How on earth could they get water from such a dry place? I don't see any sign of it anywhere."

"This place is called 'Tagdo.' In English it means 'drops.' It is the only place where folks for miles around can find water to drink. But go ahead," the guide suggested, "and take a look for yourself."

The American decided to do that. Curiously he walked toward the people who stared at him as he passed, smiled past them and looked for the source of the water.

What he saw startled him.

In the hard rock which was the base of the cliff was a very small well about six inches deep and a foot across. It was not a spring. Water did not come from under it but flowed into it over an inch-wide strip of banana leaf which was so arranged as to receive the weak flow of a very tiny stream formed by little drops of moisture. They came from the moss clinging to the rock and to the protruding roots of trees growing alongside the cliff. The American watched the tiny stream trickle over the banana leaf and flow into the well. He watched for a long time; saw the old man scoop the water up carefully with a coconut shell and pour it into his bamboo tube.

The American stood there, just watching, forgetting for the moment who he was, why he was there. "Twenty minutes," he said aloud to himself. "It would take twenty minutes to fill the well and four wells-full to fill the tube." Slowly he took his gaze off the well, and facing about, saw the people were watching him, smiling politely at him.

As he stared at them, searching into their brown faces for what he did not know, a small boy naked from the waist down broke out from the group of children and in a streak was at the well holding the coconut shell in his hand and twiddling the index finger of the other, his head nodding up and down, up and down. The American stared at him. He stared good and hard, and felt the blood creeping up his back, his shoulders, his face. Never before had he felt such dryness in his throat. There was no mistaking that ever-ready smile, those big black eyes, the eager nodding of the familiar head.

The American's white hand slowly found its way to the boy's hunched shoulder and, forgetting that the boy could not understand his language, blurted: "You mean you walk all that distance and get your water here too?"

Surprisingly the boy understood. He gave his biggest smile and nodded, his eyes gleaming with elation as he glanced about at the women, at his little friends, for his having been recognized and talked to by this tall white man. Then he pointed to a long-haired girl in red chemise hugging a bamboo tube twice her own length and smiling with her fingertips in her mouth.

As the American silently watched the scene before him, the guide approached him and softly asked: "Would you like to take a picture?"

Responding to Literature

Personal Response

What were your reactions to the story? Discuss them with a partner.

Analyzing Literature

Recall

1. Why did the American come to the Philippines, and how long has he been in the country?
2. What are the American's opinions of the Filipino people?
3. What request does the American make of the Filipinos at the hut? How do the boy, the girl, and the grandmother react to the request?
4. What does the American do with the water that the family gives him?
5. What does the American find out at Tagdo about the family's water?

Interpret

6. What is surprising about the amount of time the American has spent in the Philippines, given what his plans are?
7. For the Reading Focus on page 715, you listed places visitors might want to photograph. How does what the American photographs compare with them?
8. What does the reaction of the Filipino family to the American's request reveal about their values and customs?
9. What does the American's behavior with the water reveal about him?
10. What does the American realize at Tagdo, and how does the realization make him feel? How do you know?

Evaluate and Connect

11. Do you think this experience will change the American's views on Filipino culture? Why or why not?
12. In life, a **stereotype** is a mental image of a group of people based on a collection of traits supposedly shared by members of a group. What stereotypes of Filipinos does the American have?
13. In literature, a **stereotype** is a character who is portrayed not as an individual but as a collection of traits and mannerisms supposedly shared by members of a group. In what ways has Nuyda made the American into a stereotype?
14. From what you have read or heard, does this story reflect the way in which some people in other countries view Americans?
15. What examples of cultural insensitivity have you witnessed? Share examples with your classmates.

Setting

The **setting** is the time and place in which the events of a story occur. The setting is a crucial element of "Pulse of the Land." From descriptions of the setting, readers gain information not only about the physical features of a country but also about the way people live there. For example, the description of the sparse furnishings of the hut reveals the people's poverty and lack of material possessions.

1. What impressions of the land and climate of the Philippines do you gain from the story?
2. What impressions of the culture of the people living near Mayon Volcano did you get from Nuyda's descriptions?
3. How is the title "Pulse of the Land" related to the setting and theme of the story?

- See **Literary Terms Handbook,** p. R11.

Literature and Writing

Writing About Literature

Examining Characterization None of the characters in "Pulse of the Land" have names. What reason might the author have had for not naming the characters? What effect does his decision have? Write a paragraph in which you answer these questions.

Creative Writing

Photo Captions Imagine that the American produces a travel brochure on Mayon Volcano after he returns to the United States. Based on details in the story, make a list of the photographs in the brochure and write one- to three-sentence captions for each one.

Extending Your Response

Literature Groups

Cultural Sensitivity Guidelines How might this story affect the way you act if you travel abroad? Discuss your response to this question in your group. Then work together to make up cultural sensitivity guidelines for anyone traveling abroad. Compare your guidelines with those of other groups.

Internet Connection

Mayon Volcano Today Search the Internet for information about Mayon Volcano as a tourist attraction today. Compare the impressions you gain of the volcano today with your previous impressions from reading the story.

Listening and Speaking

Role-Playing Suppose that the American from "Pulse of the Land" has come to your community to conduct research for a travel book like the one he originally intended to write about Manila. He wants to meet and interview people in the community. With a partner, role-play an interview for the class.

Reading Further

If you enjoyed reading "Pulse of the Land," you might also enjoy the following short stories:

"A Night in the Hills," by Paz Marquez-Benitez, and "Writer in War," by Francesco Arcellana, from *Philippine Writing,* edited by T. D. Agcaoili.

"Scent of Apples" and "Immigration Blues," from *Scent of Apples,* by Bienvenido N. Santos.

Save your work for your portfolio.

T'Boli woman, Mindanao, Philippines.

Skill Minilesson

VOCABULARY • Roots

A **root** is a word or word part to which prefixes and/or suffixes are added to form new words.

PRACTICE For each root given below, list another example of a word having the same root. Then write a sentence using each example word.

Root	Meaning	Example
pop-	people	populace
leg-, lig-, -lect	talk, read	dialect
dict-	say, speak	predict
port-	carry	transport

Before You Read

A Handful of Dates

Meet Tayeb Salih

"[Writing] came by mere chance. . . . It was not an ambition. But sometimes a man discovers basic things which he should have done earlier, though he may discover these things by chance."

Tayeb Salih (tä′ yeb sä′ li) grew up in a rural village in the northern part of the Sudan, but his adult life took him far from home. Although he has worked in London and Paris, in his fiction he often returns to the rural Sudanese villages he knew as a boy.

Salih initially planned to pursue a career in agriculture and teaching. At Khartoum University, however, he became interested in broadcasting. He went to England, where he became director of Arabic drama programming for the British Broadcasting Corporation. In 1953, while living in London, he began writing. Salih has said, "Had I been in the Sudan, perhaps I wouldn't have become a writer, because the society's values were against writing at that time." His novel *Season of Migration to the North* has been called a masterpiece of African literature.

Tayeb Salih was born in 1929.

Reading Focus

Suppose that two sports teams are so mismatched that one is winning by a huge margin late in the game. Should the coach of the stronger team continue to pile up points, or send in weaker players to avoid humiliating the other team?

Share Ideas With a partner, discuss how you would handle the situation if you were the coach.

Setting a Purpose Read about a mismatch of abilities in this African short story.

Building Background

The Sudan and the Nile River

"A Handful of Dates" is set in a farming village along the Nile River in the northern part of the Sudan. Located in northeast Africa, the Sudan has historically been a cultural crossroads. (See map, page 99.) A major division exists between the northern and the southern parts of the Sudan. In the northern and central two-thirds of the country, most of the people are Muslims who speak Arabic. In the south live a number of groups of people who speak African languages and practice traditional African religions or Christianity. Throughout the country, the population is concentrated along the Nile River, and agriculture is the most important economic activity.

Reading Further

If you enjoy reading "A Handful of Dates," you might also enjoy this story:

"The Doum Tree of Wad Hamid" in *The Wedding of Zein and Other Stories* by Tayeb Salih, translated by Denys Johnson-Davies, a short story about life in a rural village in the Sudan.

Vocabulary Preview

lilting (lil′ ting) *adj.* characterized by a rhythmical flow or cadence; p. 726

indolent (in′ də lənt) *adj.* lazy; p. 726

surfeited (sur′ fi tid) *adj.* having overindulged, as with food; p. 728

braying (brā′ ing) *n.* the loud, harsh cry of a donkey; p. 728

From *Aqaba Series,* 1994. Ali Jabri (Jordan). Acrylic on boat-wood, 70 x 90 cm. Collection of Sehnaoui Family, Beirut, Lebanon.

A Handful of Dates

Tayeb Salih
Translated by Denys Johnson-Davies

I must have been very young at the time. While I don't remember exactly how old I was, I do remember that when people saw me with my grandfather they would pat me on the head and give my cheek a pinch—things they didn't do to my grandfather. The strange thing was that I never used to go out with my father, rather it was my grandfather who would take me with him wherever he went, except for the mornings when I would go to the mosque[1] to learn the Koran.[2] The mosque, the river and the fields—these were the landmarks in our life. While most of the children of my age grumbled at having to go to the mosque to learn the Koran, I used to love it.

1. A *mosque* (mosk) is a building used for public worship by Muslims.
2. The *Qur'an* or *Koran* is the Muslim book of sacred writings.

The reason was, no doubt, that I was quick at learning by heart and the Sheikh[3] always asked me to stand up and recite the *Chapter of the Merciful* whenever we had visitors, who would pat me on my head and cheek just as people did when they saw me with my grandfather.

Yes, I used to love the mosque, and I loved the river too. Directly we finished our Koran reading in the morning I would throw down my wooden slate and dart off, quick as a genie,[4] to my mother, hurriedly swallow down my breakfast, and run off for a plunge in the river. When tired of swimming about I would sit on the bank and gaze at the strip of water that wound away eastwards and hid behind a thick wood of acacia trees. I loved to give rein to my imagination and picture to myself a tribe of giants living behind that wood, a people tall and thin with white beards and sharp noses, like my grandfather. Before my grandfather ever replied to my many questions he would rub the tip of his nose with his forefinger; as for his beard, it was soft and luxuriant and as white as cotton-wool—never in my life have I seen anything of a purer whiteness or greater beauty. My grandfather must also have been extremely tall, for I never saw anyone in the whole area address him without having to look up at him, nor did I see him enter a house without having to bend so low that I was put in mind of the way the river wound round behind the wood of acacia trees. I loved him and would imagine myself, when I grew to be a man, tall and slender like him, walking along with great strides.

I believe I was his favorite grandchild: no wonder, for my cousins were a stupid bunch and I—so they say—was an intelligent child. I used to know when my grandfather wanted me to laugh, when to be silent; also I would remember the times for his prayers and would bring him his prayer-rug and fill the ewer for his ablutions[5] without his having to ask me. When he had nothing else to do he enjoyed listening to me reciting to him from the Koran in a lilting voice, and I could tell from his face that he was moved.

Did You Know?
A *ewer* (ū′ ər) is a vase-shaped pitcher or jug.

One day I asked him about our neighbor Masood. I said to my grandfather: "I fancy you don't like our neighbor Masood?"

To which he answered, having rubbed the tip of his nose: "He's an indolent man and I don't like such people."

I said to him: "What's an indolent man?"

My grandfather lowered his head for a moment, then looking across at the wide expanse of field, he said: "Do you see it stretching out from the edge of the desert up to the Nile bank? A hundred *feddans*.[6] Do you see all those date palms? And those trees—*sant*, acacia, and *sayal*? All this fell into Masood's lap, was inherited by him from his father."

Taking advantage of the silence that had descended upon my grandfather, I turned my gaze from him to the vast area defined by his words. "I don't care," I told myself, "who owns those date palms, those trees or this black,

3. A *sheikh* (shēk) is a Muslim religious leader.
4. A *genie* is a supernatural spirit, according to Arabian legends, that often takes human form.
5. *Ablutions* (ə bloo͞′ shənz) refer to cleansing of the body as part of a religious rite.
6. *Feddans* (fə dänz′) are Egyptian units of area equal to 1.038 acres.

Vocabulary
lilting (lil′ ting) *adj.* characterized by a rhythmical flow or cadence
indolent (in′ də lənt) *adj.* lazy

cracked earth—all I know is that it's the arena for my dreams and my playground."

My grandfather then continued: "Yes, my boy, forty years ago all this belonged to Masood—two-thirds of it is now mine."

This was news to me for I had imagined that the land had belonged to my grandfather ever since God's Creation.

"I didn't own a single feddan when I first set foot in this village. Masood was then the owner of all these riches. The position has changed now, though, and I think that before Allah[7] calls me to Him I shall have bought the remaining third as well."

I do not know why it was I felt fear at my grandfather's words—and pity for our neighbor Masood. How I wished my grandfather wouldn't do what he'd said! I remembered Masood's singing, his beautiful voice and powerful laugh that resembled the gurgling of water. My grandfather never used to laugh.

I asked my grandfather why Masood had sold his land.

"Women," and from the way my grandfather pronounced the word I felt that "women" was something terrible. "Masood, my boy, was a much-married man. Each time he married he sold me a feddan or two." I made the quick calculation that Masood must have married some ninety women. Then I remembered his three wives, his shabby appearance, his lame donkey and its dilapidated saddle, his *galabia* with the torn sleeves. I had all but rid my mind of the thoughts that jostled in it when I saw the man approaching us, and my grandfather and I exchanged glances.

Did You Know?
A *galabia* (gə lä′ bē ə) is a long, loose garment with full sleeves and a hood.

"We'll be harvesting the dates today," said Masood. "Don't you want to be there?"

I felt, though, that he did not really want my grandfather to attend. My grandfather, however, jumped to his feet and I saw that his eyes sparkled momentarily with an intense brightness. He pulled me by the hand and we went off to the harvesting of Masood's dates.

Someone brought my grandfather a stool covered with an ox-hide, while I remained standing. There was a vast number of people there, but though I knew them all, I found myself for some reason, watching Masood: aloof from that great gathering of people he stood as though it were no concern of his, despite the fact that the date palms to be harvested were his own. Sometimes his attention would be caught by the sound of a huge clump of dates crashing down from on high. Once he shouted up at the boy perched on the very summit of the date palm who had begun hacking at a clump with his long, sharp sickle: "Be careful you don't cut the heart of the palm."

No one paid any attention to what he said and the boy seated at the very summit of the date palm continued, quickly and energetically, to work away at the branch with his sickle till the clump of dates began to drop like something descending from the heavens.

I, however, had begun to think about Masood's phrase "the heart of the palm." I pictured the palm tree as something with feeling, something possessed of a heart that throbbed. I remembered Masood's remark to me when he had once seen me playing about with the branch of a young palm tree: "Palm trees, my boy, like humans, experience joy and suffering." And I had felt an inward and unreasoned embarrassment.

When I again looked at the expanse of ground stretching before me I saw my young companions swarming like ants around the

7. *Allah* is the name of the Supreme Being of Islam, the religious faith of Muslims.

trunks of the palm trees, gathering up dates and eating most of them. The dates were collected into high mounds. I saw people coming along and weighing them into measuring bins and pouring them into sacks, of which I counted thirty. The crowd of people broke up, except for Hussein the merchant, Mousa the owner of the field next to ours on the east, and two men I'd never seen before.

I heard a low whistling sound and saw that my grandfather had fallen asleep. Then I noticed that Masood had not changed his stance, except that he had placed a stalk in his mouth and was munching at it like someone surfeited with food who doesn't know what to do with the mouthful he still has.

Suddenly my grandfather woke up, jumped to his feet and walked towards the sacks of dates. He was followed by Hussein the merchant, Mousa the owner of the field next to ours, and the two strangers. I glanced at Masood and saw that he was making his way towards us with extreme slowness, like a man who wants to retreat but whose feet insist on going forward. They formed a circle round the sacks of dates and began examining them, some taking a date or two to eat. My grandfather gave me a fistful, which I began munching. I saw Masood filling the palms of both hands with dates and bringing them up close to his nose, then returning them.

Then I saw them dividing up the sacks between them. Hussein the merchant took ten; each of the strangers took five. Mousa the owner of the field next to ours on the eastern side took five, and my grandfather took five. Understanding nothing, I looked at Masood and saw that his eyes were darting about to left and right like two mice that have lost their way home.

"You're still fifty pounds in debt to me," said my grandfather to Masood. "We'll talk about it later."

Hussein called his assistants and they brought along donkeys, the two strangers produced camels, and the sacks of dates were loaded on to them. One of the donkeys let out a braying which set the camels frothing at the mouth and complaining noisily. I felt myself drawing close to Masood, felt my hand stretch out towards him as though I wanted to touch the hem of his garment. I heard him make a noise in his throat like the rasping of a lamb being slaughtered. For some unknown reason, I experienced a sharp sensation of pain in my chest.

I ran off into the distance. Hearing my grandfather call after me, I hesitated a little, then continued on my way. I felt at that moment that I hated him. Quickening my pace, it was as though I carried within me a secret I wanted to rid myself of. I reached the river bank near the bend it made behind the wood of acacia trees. Then, without knowing why, I put my finger into my throat and spewed up the dates I'd eaten.

Vocabulary

surfeited (sur′ fi tid) *adj.* having overindulged, as with food
braying (brā′ ing) *n.* the loud, harsh cry of a donkey

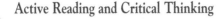

Responding to Literature

Personal Response

At the end of the story, how did you feel toward the grandfather? toward Masood? Share your responses with a partner.

Analyzing Literature

Recall and Interpret

1. At the beginning of the story, how does the boy view his grandfather?
2. What reason does the grandfather give for not liking Masood? According to him, why does he own so much of Masood's land?
3. What does the boy like about Masood?
4. Why are Masood's dates divided up after they are harvested? What do the grandfather's parting words to Masood imply?
5. How and why do the boy's feelings for his grandfather change?

Evaluate and Connect

6. For the Reading Focus on page 724, you discussed how you would coach a game between two widely mismatched teams. How does that situation relate to what happens in this story?
7. If you were in the grandfather's position, how would you handle Masood's debt? Why?
8. What qualities make Masood a good person but a bad businessman? Does Masood get what he deserves? Explain.
9. At the beginning of the story, the boy recalls reciting to his grandfather and others from the *Chapter of the Merciful.* What is the significance of that recollection to the theme of the story?
10. A **symbol** is an object, person, place, or experience that stands for something else in addition to itself (see **Literary Terms Handbook,** page R12). Identify two examples of symbols in the story and explain what they mean.

Literary ELEMENTS

Narrator

The **narrator** is the person who tells a story from a particular point of view. A **first-person narrator** tells the story as he or she experiences it, using the pronoun *I.* A **third-person narrator,** on the other hand, tells the story from outside. In some cases, the third-person narrator is **limited** to revealing the thoughts and feelings of only one character; in other cases, the narrator is all-knowing, or **omniscient.**

1. What kind of narrator tells the story in "A Handful of Dates"?
2. "A Handful of Dates" portrays a child's developing awareness of a major flaw in a beloved adult. How does the choice of narrator affect the story?
3. How might a reader's experience change with a different kind of narrator?

- See **Literary Terms Handbook,** p. R8.

Extending Your Response

Writing About Literature

Contrasting Characters Think about the grandfather and Masood as businesspeople and as human beings. Who is the shrewder businessperson? Who is more kind? more generous? Write two paragraphs in which you evaluate the differences between the two characters.

Performing

From the Heart of the Palm Imagine you are Masood as he walks home after the end of the story. Prepare and perform a **soliloquy,** a speech by a character alone on stage, in which you reveal Masood's inner feelings.

Save your work for your portfolio.

COMPARING *selections*

Pulse of the Land and A Handful of Dates

COMPARE **NARRATORS**

Discuss "Pulse of the Land" and "A Handful of Dates" are short stories that have different kinds of narrators. In your group, identify the kind of narrator telling each story and discuss the following questions:

1. How does the choice of narrator affect the reader's feelings toward the main character?
2. How does the choice of narrator fit the theme and the author's purpose in each story?
3. How would the impact of each story be affected if the kind of narrator were changed?

COMPARE **SETTINGS**

Diagram In both stories, the setting plays an important role. Use a Venn diagram, like the one at the right, to list the similarities and differences in the settings of the two stories. Then write one or two paragraphs comparing the settings. You might wish to focus on one or more of the following elements:

- the role of the setting in the plot
- how the setting affects the mood
- how the setting relates to the title and to the theme

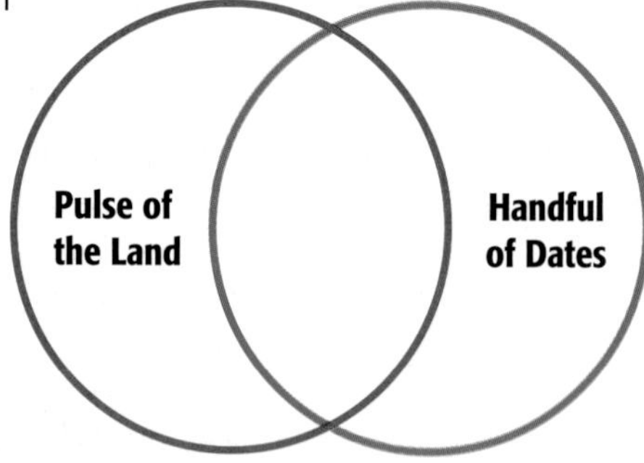

COMPARE **EXPERIENCES**

Write Both the American in "The Pulse of the Land" and the boy in "A Handful of Dates" experience an **epiphany,** a sudden realization of the meaning or essence of something. Make a few notes on the epiphany that each character experienced. Then think of when you may have experienced such a feeling. Share the story of your experience with a partner. Then write one or two paragraphs in which you compare and contrast the epiphanies that occurred in the stories with your own experience.

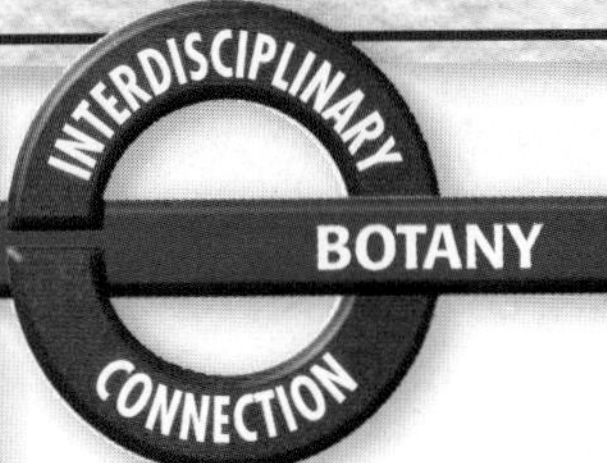

The Palm Tree

In Tayeb Salih's story "A Handful of Dates," the phrase "heart of the palm" stays in the young narrator's mind and causes him to imagine the palm tree as having a throbbing heart, as if it were human. An ancient species of palm native to the Middle East, the date palm has been grown for its fruit since 6000 B.C.

Throughout the tropics and subtropics, there are 2,600 known species of palm. A few of the most economically important of the species of palms include the date, sugar, cohune, palmyra, coconut, and carnauba palm, and the cabbage palmetto.

The **date palm,** which has been prized as a source of food and wealth since antiquity, may bear as much as 550 pounds of dates each year for 100 years. Dates are a chief food item in parts of Africa, Iran, and Arabia. In addition to dates, the date palm provides timber from its trunk, crating material from its leaf midribs, fuel from its leaf bases, rope from the stalks, and stock feed from its seeds.

The **sugar palm** grows in Malaysia. Sugar is processed from its sap. From its pith, a starch called sago is made; its leaves produce a moisture-resistant fiber. The **cohune palm,** which grows in Central America, produces an oil in its seeds that is used in soap. The **palmyra palm** of tropical Asia yields edible fruits and seeds and produces a fiber used to make brooms, hats, and mats. Now widely grown in tropical coastal areas, the **coconut palm** originated in Malaysia. The meat of the coconut is eaten raw or shredded and dried, and its milk is a delicious beverage. Other coconut palm products include timber from the trunk and vinegar from the flower buds. The leaves of the **carnauba palm,** which grows in tropical South America, produce a wax that is used in candles, polishes, and varnishes. It is also used by bookbinders to polish the edges of books after gilding. In the southeastern United States and the West Indies, the **cabbage palmetto** is grown for the shade provided by its fan-shaped leaves.

Activities

1. Palm trees are a valuable source of food and products in many different tropical regions of the world. In order to produce many of these materials, however, the palm trees must be cut down. Find out what methods are used to plant, harvest, and maintain the trees as a resource.
2. Using information in this Connection as a starting point, find out more about the economic importance of one particular species of palm. Present your information to the class. In your presentation, you might include a chart of products made from the species of palm.

AUSTRALIA, c. 1980s

Before You Read

Full Moon Rhyme, *Rainforest*, and *River Bend*

Meet Judith Wright

"I know it dark against the stars, the high lean country / Full of old stories that still go walking in my sleep."

Judith Wright is one of Australia's most celebrated poets. Her family has lived in Australia since the 1820s, and her lifelong quest to describe the beauty and history of the land has earned her numerous literary awards and the devotion of the public.

Wright's connection to the natural world was formed during her childhood on a ranch in the mountains of New South Wales. She was sent away to boarding school when she was twelve, and did not return for ten years. As an adult, Wright has fought to protect Australian land and wildlife and to promote the rights of the Aborigines, Australia's earliest inhabitants.

In beautifully crafted, lyrical poems, Wright presents a world in which humans and nature are bonded together. Of the Australian countryside, she once wrote: "It is haunted. We owe it repentance and such amends as we can make."

Judith Wright was born in 1915.

Reading Focus

To what aspects of the natural world do you think people are particularly connected? Why?

List It! Make a list of the animals, plants, and other elements of nature to which you feel particularly drawn, and below each item, explain why.

Setting a Purpose Read to find out one poet's views of the ways in which humans, animals, and plants are interconnected.

Building Background

The Environment

Before the arrival of Europeans in the late eighteenth century, the Aborigines lived off the land without adversely affecting it. But since then, much of the land has been cleared to sell timber and provide farm land. In Wright's native state of New South Wales, the forest that once covered a third of the land now covers only 10 percent, which environmentalists like Wright are fighting to preserve. Though the destruction harmed the animal population, the country is still rich in wildlife. In New South Wales, visitors can see such uniquely Australian animals as koalas, kangaroos, wallabies, bandicoots, and wombats.

The Aborigines

Australia's earliest inhabitants arrived from Southeast Asia thousands of years ago. They lived a very simple life, with few material possessions. The British settlers, with their own totally different culture and values, had no interest in trying to understand the Aborigines. War and disease killed many Aborigines; the survivors were treated as second-class citizens at best. At one point, it was even thought they would die out. However, the second half of the twentieth century saw a recovery in their numbers and the removal of a number of unjust laws.

Reading Further

You might also enjoy the following poems by Judith Wright: "Bora Ring," "Bullocky," and "South of My Days," from *New Land, New Language: An Anthology of Australian Verse*, edited by Judith Wright.

Municipal Gum

Oodgeroo Noonuccal
(Kath Walker)

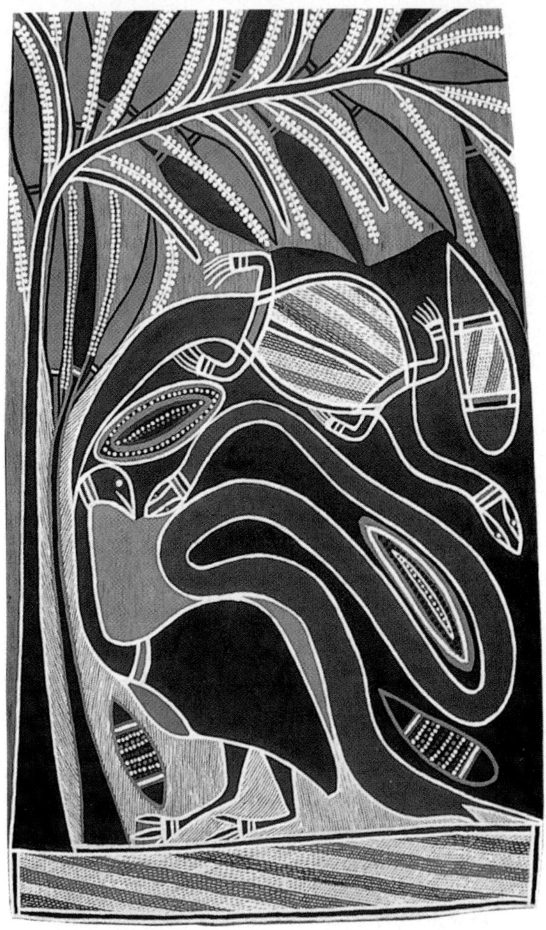

The Tree of Life and His Totems. David Malangi (Australia, 20th century). Bark painting. Arnhem Land, Northern Territory, Australia.

Viewing the painting: How is this tree similar to the "Municipal Gum" of the poem? How is it different?

Gumtree in the city street,
Hard bitumen° around your feet,
Rather you should be
In the cool world of leafy forest halls
And wild bird calls.
Here you seem to me
Like that poor cart-horse
Castrated,° broken, a thing wronged,
Strapped and buckled, its hell prolonged,
Whose hung head and listless mien° express
Its hopelessness.
Municipal gum, it is dolorous°
To see you thus
Set in your black grass of bitumen—
O fellow citizen,
What have they done to us?

Oodgeroo of the tribe Noonuccal

Municipal means "belonging to a city."

2 *Bitumen* (bī to͞o′ mən) can mean "tar" or "asphalt."

8 *Castrated* means "impotent" or "lacking in vitality."

10 *Mien* (mēn) is a person's manner or appearance.

12 Anything *dolorous* (dō′ lər əs) expresses sadness or causes pain.

Clouds on the Sea

Ruth Dallas

I walk among men with tall bones,
With shoes of leather, and pink faces;
I meet no man holding a begging bowl;
All have their dwelling places.

In my country
Every child is taught to read and write,
Every child has shoes and a warm coat,
Every child must eat his dinner,
No one must grow any thinner;
It is considered remarkable and not nice
To meet bed-bugs or lice.
Oh we live like the rich
With music at the touch of a switch,
Light in the middle of the night,
Water in the house as if from a spring.
Hot, if you wish, or cold, anything
For the comfort of the flesh,
In my country. Fragment
Of new skin at the edge of the world's ulcer.

For the question
That troubled you as you watched the reapers
And a poor woman following,
Gleaning the ears on the ground,
Why should I have grain and this woman none?
No satisfactory answer has been found.

Central Otago, 1940. Rita Angus (New Zealand). Oil on board. 13¾ x 21½ in. Auckland Art Gallery Toi o Tamaki, New Zealand.

Viewing the painting: Describe the mood of this painting. In what ways is it comparable to the mood of the poem?

Responding to Literature

Personal Response

Which lines from these poems did you find the most memorable?

Analyzing Literature

Recall and Interpret

1. What contrast does the speaker in "Municipal Gum" draw between the life of a city gum tree and that of a gum tree in the forest? How does the speaker describe the state of the cart-horse? What might the gum tree and cart-horse represent?
2. How do you interpret the ending of Oodgeroo's poem?
3. Describe the appearance of the men in lines 1–2 of Dallas's poem. Based on this description, what can you infer about their identity?
4. In "Clouds on the Sea," summarize what the adults and children of New Zealand have. How do you interpret the line "Fragment / Of new skin at the edge of the world's ulcer"?
5. What is the question that troubles the speaker in the final stanza of "Clouds on the Sea"? How might this question relate to the **theme** (see page R12), or central message, of the poem?

Evaluate and Connect

6. Based on "Municipal Gum," what can you infer about the speaker's relationship with, and attitude toward, the natural world?
7. Refer to the Reading Focus on page 736. How do the things you thought of compare with the examples presented in these two poems?
8. **Tone** is the attitude that a writer takes toward his or her subject. How would you describe the tone used by Dallas in "Clouds on the Sea"?
9. Are the thoughts of the writers and the situations they describe relevant only to Australia and New Zealand, or do they apply to any of your own experiences?

Literary ELEMENTS

End Rhyme

Rhyme is the repetition of sound in the syllables at the end of lines that appear close to each other in a poem. With **end rhyme,** the rhymes occur at the ends of lines. Poets use rhyme to create rhythm, to stress particular ideas, and/or to amuse their audiences. The rhymes in "Clouds on the Sea," for instance, function to amuse the audience and to lend the poem a musical quality.

1. What two end-rhyme adjectives describe the condition of the cart-horse in "Municipal Gum"? What idea might the poet be trying to express through this end rhyme?
2. How does the end rhyme in "Municipal Gum" add to the overall effect of the poem?

- See **Literary Terms Handbook,** p. R3.

Extending Your Response

Creative Writing

Good and Bad Using your response to the Reading Focus on page 736, write a poem in which you contrast good and bad things about living in a modern city. As you write your poem, try to use some poetic techniques, such as **alliteration, end rhyme,** and **imagery** (see pages R1, R3, and R6).

Literature Groups

Choosing Titles Why, do you think, did the poets choose to title their poems "Municipal Gum" and "Clouds on the Sea"? How might the title of each poem relate to its content? Discuss these questions in your group. Then, present the results of your discussion to the class.

Save your work for your portfolio.

Before You Read

Thoughts of Hanoi

Meet Nguyen Thi Vinh

"How many families are weeping under this same moon?"

—Huyen Quang Ly Dao Tai (1254–1334)

For much of her life, Nguyen Thi Vinh (no͞o yin′ tī vin′) has lived in the presence of war. In 1930, when Nguyen was just six, the people of northwestern Vietnam, near her home in Hanoi, staged an unsuccessful revolt against French colonial forces. Ten years later, Japanese troops invaded Vietnam and controlled the country until 1945. Then, from 1946 to 1954, the Viet Minh, led by Communist general Vo Nguyen Giap, fought a bloody war for independence from France.

Following the Indochina War, Nguyen moved to Saigon in South Vietnam to escape the Communists in the north. A few years later she watched as conflict between South Vietnamese Communist rebels and the South Vietnamese government turned friends into bitter enemies. Though Nguyen remained in South Vietnam following the Communist takeover in 1975, she eventually emigrated to Norway.

Nguyen Thi Vinh was born in 1924.

Reading Focus

Imagine living in a country that has been split in two by a civil war. Travel between the two areas is forbidden, and your best friend or closest relative lives in the other area. How would you feel?

Quickwrite Write a note to this friend or relative in which you describe your feelings about being separated and your hopes for the future.

Setting a Purpose Read to find out how one character feels about being separated from the land and people he loves.

Building Background

A Divided Nation

In 1954 when Nguyen Thi Vinh was thirty, Vietnam was divided into two countries. That year Vietnamese forces overthrew the French after nearly one hundred years of colonial rule and forced an international conference on the fate of Vietnam. The conference, held in Geneva, called for the temporary division of Vietnam along the 17th parallel. Ho Chi Minh's Communist government would rule North Vietnam, and a democratic government would rule South Vietnam.

For 300 days after the Geneva Conference, people were allowed to pass freely from one zone to the other. Nguyen was among the hundreds of thousands who left North Vietnam. Others, who were sympathetic to the goals of Ho Chi Minh's Communist government, moved from South to North Vietnam. This migration sometimes divided families and ended friendships and business associations. People who had grown up together and been close throughout their lives now found themselves on different sides of what Nguyen calls "a frontier of hatred." Some were even forced to confront loved ones in battle when supporters of the Communist regime in the north began waging a guerrilla war against the South Vietnamese government.

Ham Rong Bridge, 1970. Vu Giang Huong (Vietnam).

Thoughts of Hanoi

Nguyen Thi Vinh

Translated by Nguyen Ngoc Bich
with Burton Raffel and W. S. Merwin

The night is deep and chill
as in early autumn. Pitchblack,
it thickens after each lightning flash.
I dream of Hanoi:°
Co-ngu° Road
ten years of separation
the way back sliced by a frontier of hatred.
I want to bury the past
to burn the future
still I yearn
still I fear
those endless nights
waiting for dawn.

---

4 *Hanoi* (ha noi′) is the capital city of Vietnam, located in the northern part of the country.

5 *Co-ngu* (kô′ əng)

Brother,
how is Hang Dao° now?
How is Ngoc Son° temple?
Do the trains still run
each day from Hanoi
to the neighboring towns?
To Bac-ninh,° Cam-giang,° Yen-bai,°
the small villages, islands
of brown thatch in a lush green sea?
The girls
bright eyes
ruddy cheeks
four-piece dresses
raven-bill scarves
sowing harvesting
spinning weaving
all year round,
the boys
ploughing
transplanting
in the fields
in their shops
running across
the meadow at evening
to fly kites
and sing alternating songs.

Stainless blue sky,
jubilant voices of children
stumbling through the alphabet,
village graybeards strolling to the temple,
grandmothers basking in twilight sun,
chewing betel leaves°
while the children run—

Brother,
how is all that now?
Or is it obsolete?
Are you like me,
reliving the past,
imagining the future?
Do you count me as a friend
or am I the enemy in your eyes?
Brother, I am afraid
that one day I'll be with the
March-North Army°
meeting you on your way to the South.
I might be the one to shoot you then
or you me
but please
not with hatred.

For don't you remember how it was,
you and I in school together,
plotting our lives together?
Those roots go deep!

Brother, we are men,
conscious of more
than material needs.
How can this happen to us
my friend
my foe?

---

15 *Hang Dao* (häɴ dou)
16 *Ngoc Son* (nyok′ sun)
20 *Bac-ninh* (bäk′ nēn); *Cam-giang* (käm′ yē äɴ); *Yen-bai* (yin′ bī)

45 *Betel* (bē′ təl) *leaves,* from a type of pepper tree, are a mild stimulant; the habit of chewing them, although diminishing, is still widespread in Southeast Asia.
56 The *March-North Army* is a reference to the South Vietnamese army at the time of the Vietnam War.

Responding to Literature

Personal Response

What did you find yourself thinking about when you read the final lines of the poem? How would you answer that question if you were the speaker's friend?

Analyzing Literature

Recall and Interpret

1. How long has the speaker been away from Hanoi? What has sliced the way back to this city, according to line 7? How might line 7 relate to the speaker's desire to "bury the past" and "burn the future"?
2. What questions about Hanoi does the speaker ask the person addressed as "Brother"? What scenes from his past does the speaker recall?
3. In lines 50–64, what does the speaker wonder about Brother? What emotion does the speaker fear?
4. What final question does the speaker ask Brother? What can you infer about the speaker's thoughts and feelings about the war?

Evaluate and Connect

5. Nguyen begins "Thoughts of Hanoi" with an **image** (see page R6), or word picture, of a dark, lightning-filled sky. What, in your opinion, might this image represent?
6. In this poem, Nguyen expresses great affection for her native land. What place that you have lived in or visited are you particularly attached to? For what reasons?
7. What situations do you know of, from news reports or personal experience, in which people who were once friends became enemies? In your opinion, how could such a change of feelings have been prevented?
8. What picture does this poem give you of Vietnam as a country?

Literary ELEMENTS

Flashback

A **flashback** is an interruption in the plot of a literary work to relate a scene from an earlier time. A writer may use this device in order to give the reader background information, or to create tension or contrast. In "Thoughts of Hanoi," Nguyen uses this device when she presents a picture of Hanoi and its surrounding area before the war.

1. For what reasons might Nguyen have wanted to paint such a picture?
2. How does the **tone** of this flashback differ from the tone of the rest of the poem (see page R12)?

- See **Literary Terms Handbook,** p. R5.

Extending Your Response

Creative Writing

A Letter to the Speaker In the Reading Focus on page 740, you wrote a note to a friend separated from you by civil war. Using that note for inspiration, write a letter to the speaker in "Thoughts of Hanoi" in which you answer the question posed at the end of the poem.

Internet Connection

A Virtual Visit to Hanoi Hanoi was founded nearly a thousand years ago by Emperor Ly Thai To. The Temple of Literature there is Vietnam's oldest university, dating back to the year 1070. Search the Internet to find out more about this city. Share your findings with the class.

Save your work for your portfolio.

Multimedia: Creating a Presentation

If you have completed the Technology Skills lesson on pages 514–515, you have already done research on another culture via the Internet. (If you have not done so, see those pages and complete the research before going on.) Now it's time for you to share what you've learned in a more ambitious presentation.

What Is Multimedia?

As a presenter, you want to capture and hold the attention of your audience. An excellent way to do that is to engage as many of their senses as you can. A multimedia presentation makes that possible. In such a presentation, you can use not only the written word but also sounds (speech, music, sound effects) and images (photos, artwork, graphs, maps, movies). Multimedia software allows you to combine these various media into an elegant presentation.

Here are three possible ways to put together a multimedia presentation.

TECHNOLOGY TIP

There are many Internet sources for photos, sound clips, and movies. To download a picture you find on a Web site, right-click on it (click and hold on the Mac) and select **Save picture as....** In the dialogue box that appears, you can change the name of the file if you wish and select the place on your hard drive where you want to save the file. Be advised that movie clips are very large and may take some time to download, especially if your modem is slow. Check with your lab instructor to find out whether you have software that will enable you to use movies and sound clips.

METHOD	HARDWARE/SOFTWARE NEEDED	DESCRIPTION OF PRESENTATION
Noncomputer presentation	Camera, slide projector or overhead projector, screen, tape recorder	Use 35mm slides or overhead transparencies for the visuals (text and images). Display appropriate colorful posters. Use a tape recorder for narration, music, or other sounds.
Hypertext presentation	Computer with HyperStudio, Hypercard, or other hypertext software *Also useful:* microphone, digital camera	Use a hypertext program to combine text, graphic images, and sound on a series of "cards" that make up a stack that can be shown in sequence on a computer monitor.
Slide-show presentation	Computer with PowerPoint, Persuasion, or other presentation software *Also useful:* microphone, digital camera	Use presentation software to create a group of "slides" that make up a computer-based slide show combining text, graphic images, and sound.

Create a Presentation

1. Examine the information you gathered from the Internet in the previous Technology Skills lesson. Supplement that research with print sources, such as books and magazines. Remember to document both your Internet and print sources. (See page R68 of Writing Handbook.)
2. Think about what illustrations or sounds could augment your text. Decide how you can best combine words, images, and sounds into an effective presentation. If you did not acquire appropriate images and sound files earlier, do so now.

3. Create an outline or storyboard that shows the text, images, and sounds of each segment.

STORYBOARD: FILM IN JAPAN			
Segment	**Text**	**Sounds**	**Images**
1	Title: Film in Japan A Multimedia Presentation by Peter Salinas	koto music	Background design
2	Until about the 1950s, few Americans were aware that Japan had a film industry. In fact, the Japanese were making films in the early 1900s.	none	Photo from Japanese silent movie

4. Begin with a title slide.
5. Add slides to complete your report. Keep text information succinct—four or five lines per segment. Where appropriate, use a few numbered or bulleted lists to emphasize the information you want to communicate. Try to supplement each segment with an eye-catching graphic that adds visual support to your main point. Add sound files as appropriate.
6. Save your work often.
7. Keep your presentation relatively brief, about five to ten minutes.
8. At the end of your presentation, include one or more segments as needed to credit the sources you used.
9. Go through your completed presentation several times, looking for ways you can improve it. Ask a family member or a friend for feedback. After final revisions are made, show your presentation to your class.

Seven Samurai (1954), probably Akira Kurosawa's most influential film, was remade in Hollywood as a western, *The Magnificent Seven,* which later became a TV series. This scene is from the film's celebrated battle in the rain.

ACTIVITIES

1. Work with a small group to combine your multimedia presentations into one that takes a broader look at world cultures. Be sure to edit it so that it doesn't look like three or four individual presentations run together.
2. Upload your group's multimedia presentation to your school's Intranet or to the project section of your school's Internet site.
3. Contribute an electronic copy of your presentation to the school library for others to check out.

Before You Read

from *When Heaven and Earth Changed Places*

Meet Le Ly Hayslip

"For most of us [the Vietnam War] was a fight for independence—like the American Revolution."

When Le Ly Hayslip (lā lē hā′ slip) was twelve, the Vietnam War came to Ky La, her native village in central Vietnam. Soon, it was overrun, both by South Vietnamese communist rebels known as Viet Cong, and by soldiers fighting for the South Vietnamese government.

At thirteen, Hayslip joined the Viet Cong's children's troop. "For my next three years," wrote Hayslip, "I loved, labored, and fought steadfastly for the Viet Cong against American and South Vietnamese soldiers." She and other village children were taught that the Viet Cong would free South Vietnam from oppression.

During the war, Hayslip was imprisoned and tortured by South Vietnamese soldiers. Then the Viet Cong sentenced her to death, falsely believing she had betrayed them. Finally, Hayslip escaped to the United States, where she found peace and a new life.

Le Ly Hayslip was born in 1949.

Reading Focus

Who among your family members and friends has had the greatest impact on your life?

List It! Make a list of the ways in which this person's actions, personality, and advice have influenced you.

Setting a Purpose Read to find out how one author was influenced by the example and advice of her father.

Building Background

The Vietnam War

In 1954 a diplomatic conference held in Geneva, Switzerland, resulted in the division of Vietnam into two countries, North Vietnam and South Vietnam. By the late 1950s, the South Vietnamese government was losing popular support; the communist Viet Cong rebels were trying to overthrow it, with the help of the North Vietnamese.

The United States assisted the South Vietnamese government by sending troops, gradually becoming more and more involved. The North Vietnamese responded by sending troops south, and the war escalated. Eventually, America's leaders decided to end their country's involvement in the war, and in 1973 a cease-fire agreement was signed. But fighting between north and south continued, and in 1975, the North Vietnamese took over South Vietnam and reunited the two countries under a communist government.

Vocabulary Preview

diligent (dil′ ə jənt) *adj.* characterized by steady, earnest, and energetic effort; p. 747

empathy (em′ pə thē) *n.* an understanding and entering into the feelings and experiences of another person; p. 747

abstain (ab stān′) *v.* to refrain with an effort of self-denial from a practice or action; p. 748

defect (di fekt′) *v.* to desert one group or political entity for another; p. 752

avenge (ə venj′) *v.* to take revenge for a wrong by punishing the wrongdoer; p. 752

from

When Heaven and Earth Changed Places

from *Fathers and Daughters*

Le Ly Hayslip

Giong, 1982. Tran Khanh Chuong (Vietnam). Plastercut on black rice paper, 16 x 16 in. Collection of the artist.

After my brother Bon went North, I began to pay more attention to my father.

He was built solidly—big-boned—for a Vietnamese man, which meant he probably had well-fed, noble ancestors. People said he had the body of a natural-born warrior. He was a year younger and an inch shorter than my mother, but just as good-looking. His face was round, like a Khmer or Thai,[1] and his complexion was brown as soy[2] from working all his life in the sun. He was very easygoing about everything and seldom in a hurry. Seldom, too, did he say no to a request—from his children or his neighbors. Although he took everything in stride, he was a hard and diligent worker. Even on holidays, he was always mending things or tending to our house and animals. He would not wait to be asked for help if he saw someone in trouble. Similarly, he always said what he thought, although he knew, like most honest men, when to keep silent. Because of his honesty, his empathy, and his openness to people, he understood life deeply. Perhaps that is why he was so easygoing. Only a half-trained mechanic thinks everything needs fixing.

---

1. A *Khmer* (kə mer′) is a native of Cambodia; a *Thai* (tī) is a native of Thailand.
2. *Soy* is a salty, dark brown sauce made from fermented soybeans.

Vocabulary

diligent (dil′ ə jənt) *adj.* characterized by steady, earnest, and energetic effort

empathy (em′ pə thē) *n.* understanding and entering into the feelings and experiences of another person

He loved to smoke cigars and grew a little tobacco in our yard. My mother always wanted him to sell it, but there was hardly ever enough to take to market. I think for her it was the principle of the thing: smoking cigars was like burning money. Naturally, she had a song for such gentle vices—her own habit of chewing betel nuts included:

> Get rid of your tobacco,
> And you will get a water buffalo.
> Give away your betel,
> And you will get more paddy land.[3]

Despite her own good advice, she never abstained from chewing betel, nor my father from smoking cigars. They were rare luxuries that life and the war allowed them.

My father also liked rice wine, which we made; and enjoyed an occasional beer, which he purchased when there was nothing else we needed. After he'd had a few sips, he would tell jokes and happy stories and the village kids would flock around. Because I was his youngest daughter, I was entitled to listen from his knee—the place of honor. Sometimes he would sing funny songs about whoever threatened the village and we would feel better. For example, when the French or Moroccan[4] soldiers were near, he would sing:

> There are many kinds of vegetables,
> Why do you like spinach?
> There are many kinds of wealth,
> Why do you use Minh money?
> There are many kinds of people,
> Why do you love terrorists?

We laughed because these were all the things the French told us about the Viet Minh[5] fighters whom we favored in the war. Years later, when the Viet Cong were near, he would sing:

> There are many kinds of vegetables,
> Why do you like spinach?
> There are many kinds of money,
> Why do you use Yankee dollars?
> There are many kinds of people,
> Why do you disobey your ancestors?

This was funny because the words were taken from the speeches the North Vietnamese cadres delivered to shame us for helping the Republic. He used to have a song for when the Viet Minh were near too, which asked in the same way, "Why do you use francs?"[6] and "Why do you love French traitors?" Because he sang these songs with a comical voice, my mother never appreciated them. She couldn't see the absurdity of our situation as clearly as we children. To her, war and real life were different. To us, they were all the same.

Even as a parent, my father was more lenient than our mother, and we sometimes ran to him for help when she was angry. Most of the time, it didn't work and he would lovingly rub our heads as we were dragged off to be spanked. The village saying went: "A naughty child learns more from a whipping stick than a sweet stick." We children were never quite sure about that, but agreed the whipping stick was an eloquent teacher. When he absolutely had to punish us himself, he didn't waste time. Wordlessly,

3. *Paddy land* is wet land in which rice is grown.
4. *Moroccan* soldiers served in the French army at that time, as Morocco was ruled by France.
5. The *Viet Minh* (vē et′ min) were Vietnamese guerrillas, both communists and non-communists, who fought the French after World War II.
6. *Francs* are French units of currency. Vietnam was a French colony from the late 1800s to 1954.

Vocabulary
abstain (ab stān′) *v.* to refrain with an effort of self-denial from a practice or action

he would find a long, supple bamboo stick and let us have it behind our thighs. It stung, but he could have whipped us harder. I think seeing the pain in his face hurt more than receiving his halfhearted blows. Because of that, we seldom did anything to merit a father's spanking—the highest penalty in our family. Violence in any form offended him. For this reason, I think, he grew old before his time.

One of the few times my father ever touched my mother in a way not consistent with love was during one of the yearly floods, when people came to our village for safety from the lower ground. We sheltered many in our house, which was nothing more than a two-room hut with woven mats for a floor. I came home one day in winter rain to see refugees and Republican soldiers[7] milling around outside. They did not know I lived there so I had to elbow my way inside. It was nearly supper time and I knew my mother would be fixing as much food as we could spare.

In the part of the house we used as our kitchen, I discovered my mother crying. She and my father had gotten into an argument outside a few minutes before. He had assured the refugees he would find something to eat for everyone and she insisted there would not be enough for her children if everyone was fed. He repeated his order to her, this time loud enough for all to hear. Naturally, he thought this would end the argument. She persisted in contradicting him, so he had slapped her.

This show of male power—we called it *do danh vo*[8]—was usual behavior for Vietnamese husbands but unusual for my father. My mother could be as strict as she wished with his children and he would seldom interfere. Now, I discovered there were limits even to his great patience. I saw the glowing red mark on her cheek and asked if she was crying because it hurt. She said no. She said she was crying because her action had caused my father to lose face in front of strangers. She promised that if I ever did what she had done to a husband, I would have both cheeks glowing: one from his blow and one from hers.

Once, when I was the only child at home, my mother went to Danang[9] to visit Uncle Nhu, and my father had to take care of me. I woke up from my nap in the empty house and cried for my mother. My father came in from the yard and reassured me, but I was still cranky and continued crying. Finally, he gave me a rice cookie to shut me up. Needless to say, this was a tactic my mother never used.

The next afternoon I woke up and although I was not feeling cranky, I thought a rice cookie might be nice. I cried a fake cry and my father came running in.

"What's this?" he asked, making a worried face. "Little Bay Ly[10] doesn't want a cookie?"

I was confused again.

"Look under your pillow," he said with a smile.

I twisted around and saw that, while I was sleeping, he had placed a rice cookie under my pillow. We both laughed and he picked me up like a sack of rice and carried me outside while I gobbled the cookie.

In the yard, he plunked me down under a tree and told me some stories. After that, he got some scraps of wood and showed me how to make things: a doorstop for my mother and a toy duck for me. This was unheard of—a father doing these things with a child that was not a son! Where my mother would instruct me on cooking and cleaning and tell stories about brides, my father showed me the mystery of hammers and explained the customs of our people.

His knowledge of the Vietnamese went back to the Chinese Wars[11] in ancient times. I learned how one of my distant ancestors, a woman

7. *Republican soldiers* refers to the army of South Vietnam.

8. *Do danh vo* (dō dän vō)

9. *Danang* (dä nän′) is a city and port in Vietnam.

10. *Bay Ly* (bī lē) was the author's nickname as a child.

11. *Chinese Wars* refers to the Chinese invasions of Vietnam in ancient and medieval times.

Village Named Khoa, 1990. Hoàng Nam Thái (Vietnam). Gouache on paper, 5½ x 7 in. Collection of the artist.

named Phung Thi Chinh,[12] led Vietnamese fighters against the Han.[13] In one battle, even though she was pregnant and surrounded by Chinese, she delivered the baby, tied it to her back, and cut her way to safety wielding a sword in each hand. I was amazed at this warrior's bravery and impressed that I was her descendant. Even more, I was amazed and impressed by my father's pride in her accomplishments (she was, after all, a humble female), and his belief that I was worthy of her example. "*Con phai theo got chan co ta*"[14] (Follow in her footsteps), he said. Only later would I learn what he truly meant.

Never again did I cry after my nap. Phung Thi women were too strong for that. Besides, I was my father's daughter and we had many things to do together.

On the eve of my mother's return, my father cooked a feast of roast duck. When we sat down to eat it, I felt guilty and my feelings showed on my face. He asked why I acted so sad.

"You've killed one of mother's ducks," I said. "One of the fat kind she sells at the market. She says the money buys gold which she saves for her daughters' weddings. Without gold for a dowry[15]—*con o gia*[16]—I will be an old maid!"

My father looked suitably concerned, then brightened and said, "Well, Bay Ly, if you can't get married, you will just have to live at home forever with me!"

I clapped my hands at the happy prospect.

My father cut into the rich, juicy bird and said, "Even so, we won't tell your mother about the duck, okay?"

I giggled and swore myself to secrecy.

The next day, I took some water out to him in the fields. My mother was due home any time and I used every opportunity to step outside and watch for her. My father stopped working, drank gratefully, then took my hand and led me to the top of a nearby hill. It had a good view of the village and the land beyond it, almost to the ocean. I thought he was going to show me my mother coming back, but he had something else in mind.

He said, "Bay Ly, you see all this here? This is the Vietnam we have been talking about. You understand that a country is more than a lot of dirt, rivers, and forests, don't you?"

I said, "Yes, I understand." After all, we had learned in school that one's country is as sacred as a father's grave.

"Good. You know, some of these lands are battlefields where your brothers and cousins are fighting. They may never come back. Even your

12. ***Phung Thi Chinh*** (fung tī zhēn)
13. ***Han*** (hän) refers to the Chinese soldiers who occupied Vietnam from 206 B.C. to A.D. 221.
14. ***Con phai theo got chan co ta*** (kôn fī tā′ o gôt zhen kō tä)
15. A *dowry* is the money, goods, or estate that a woman brings to her husband in marriage.
16. ***Con o gia*** (kôn ə zä)

sisters have all left home in search of a better life. You are the only one left in my house. If the enemy comes back, you must be both a daughter and a son. I told you how the Chinese used to rule our land. People in this village had to risk their lives diving in the ocean just to find pearls for the Chinese emperor's gown. They had to risk tigers and snakes in the jungle just to find herbs for his table. Their payment for this hardship was a bowl of rice and another day of life. That is why Le Loi,[17] Gia Long,[18] the Trung Sisters, and Phung Thi Chinh fought so hard to expel the Chinese. When the French came, it was the same old story. Your mother and I were taken to Danang to build a runway for their airplanes. We labored from sunup to sundown and well after dark. If we stopped to rest or have a smoke, a Moroccan would come up and whip our behinds. Our reward was a bowl of rice and another day of life. Freedom is never a gift, Bay Ly. It must be won and won again. Do you understand?"

I said that I did.

"Good." He moved his finger from the patchwork of brown dikes, silver water, and rippling stalks to our house at the edge of the village. "This land here belongs to me. Do you know how I got it?"

I thought a moment, trying to remember my mother's stories, then said honestly, "I can't remember."

He squeezed me lovingly. "I got it from your mother."

"What? That can't be true!" I said. Everyone in the family knew my mother was poor and my father's family was wealthy. Her parents were dead and she had to work like a slave for her mother-in-law to prove herself worthy. Such women don't have land to give away!

"It's true." My father's smile widened. "When I was a young man, my parents needed someone to look after their lands. They had to be very careful about who they chose as wives for their three sons. In the village, your mother had a reputation as the hardest worker of all. She raised herself and her brothers without parents. At the same time, I noticed a beautiful woman working in the fields. When my mother said she was going to talk to the matchmaker[19] about this hard-working village girl she'd heard about, my heart sank. I was too attracted to this mysterious tall woman I had seen in the rice paddies. You can imagine my surprise when I found out the girl my mother heard about and the woman I admired were the same.

"Well, we were married and my mother tested your mother severely. She not only had to cook and clean and know everything about children, but she had to be able to manage several farms and know when and how to take the extra produce to the market. Of course, she was testing her other daughters-in-law as well. When my parents died, they divided their several farms among their sons, but you know what? They gave your mother and me the biggest share because they knew we would take care of it best. That's why I say the land came from her, because it did."

I suddenly missed my mother very much and looked down the road to the south, hoping to see her. My father noticed my sad expression.

"Hey." He poked me in the ribs. "Are you getting hungry for lunch?"

"No. I want to learn how to take care of the farm. What happens if the soldiers come back? What did you and Mother do when the soldiers came?"

My father squatted on the dusty hilltop and wiped the sweat from his forehead. "The first thing I did was to tell myself that it was my duty to survive—to take care of my family and my farm. That is a tricky job in wartime. It's as hard as being a soldier. The Moroccans were very savage. One day the rumor passed that they were coming to destroy the village. You may

17. *Le Loi* (lā lī)

18. *Gia Long* (zä long)

19. A *matchmaker* is someone who is hired to arrange marriages.

remember the night I sent you and your brothers and sisters away with your mother to Danang."

"You didn't go with us!" My voice still held the horror of the night I thought I had lost my father.

"Right! I stayed near the village—right on this hill—to keep an eye on the enemy and on our house. If they really wanted to destroy the village, I would save some of our things so that we could start over. Sure enough, that was their plan.

"The real problem was to keep things safe and avoid being captured. Their patrols were everywhere. Sometimes I went so deep in the forest that I worried about getting lost, but all I had to do was follow the smoke from the burning huts and I could find my way back.

"Once, I was trapped between two patrols that had camped on both sides of a river. I had to wait in the water for two days before one of them moved on. When I got out, my skin was shriveled like an old melon. I was so cold I could hardly move. From the waist down, my body was black with leeches.[20] But it was worth all the pain. When your mother came back, we still had some furniture and tools to cultivate the earth. Many people lost everything. Yes, we were very lucky."

My father put his arms around me. "My brother Huong[21]—your uncle Huong—had three sons and four daughters. Of his four daughters, only one is still alive. Of his three sons, two went north to Hanoi and one went south to Saigon.[22] Huong's house is very empty. My other brother, your uncle Luc, had only two sons. One went north to Hanoi, the other was killed in the fields. His daughter is deaf and dumb. No wonder he has taken to drink, eh? Who does he have to sing in his house and tend his shrine when he is gone? My sister Lien[23] had three daughters and four sons. Three of the four sons went to Hanoi and the fourth went to Saigon to find his fortune. The girls all tend their in-laws and mourn slain husbands. Who will care for Lien when she is too feeble to care for herself? Finally, my baby sister Nhien[24] lost her husband to French bombers. Of her two sons, one went to Hanoi and the other joined the Republic, then defected, then was murdered in his house. Nobody knows which side killed him. It doesn't really matter."

My father drew me out to arm's length and looked me squarely in the eye. "Now, Bay Ly, do you understand what your job is?"

I squared my shoulders and put on a soldier's face. "My job is to avenge my family. To protect my farm by killing the enemy. I must become a woman warrior like Phung Thi Chinh!"

My father laughed and pulled me close. "No, little peach blossom. Your job is to stay alive—to keep an eye on things and keep the village safe. To find a husband and have babies and tell the story of what you've seen to your children and anyone else who'll listen. Most of all, it is to live in peace and tend the shrine of our ancestors. Do these things well, Bay Ly, and you will be worth more than any soldier who ever took up a sword."

20. *Leeches* are bloodsucking parasitic worms that live in salt water, fresh water, and moist soil.

21. *Huong* (hōōng)

22. *Saigon* (sī gon′)

23. *Lien* (lē′ ən)

24. *Nhien* (nən)

Vocabulary

defect (di fekt′) *v.* to desert one group or political entity for another

avenge (ə venj′) *v.* to take revenge for a wrong by punishing the wrongdoer

Responding to Literature

Personal Response

How did you react to Hayslip's father

Analyzing Literature

Recall

1. Describe the appearance and personality of Hayslip's father.
2. What groups of people are alluded to in the "funny songs" that Hayslip's father sings?
3. Describe the relationships Hayslip has with her parents. Describe her parents' relationship with each other.
4. How does Hayslip's father say he came to acquire his land?
5. How does Hayslip define her job at the end of the selection? How does her father define it?

Interpret

6. How would you describe Hayslip's attitude toward her father?
7. What purpose do the funny tunes sung by Hayslip's father serve, in your opinion?
8. Based on this selection, what can you infer about traditional Vietnamese family roles and traditional Vietnamese values? What can you tell about the mother's and father's attitudes toward these roles and values?
9. For what reasons might Hayslip's father have told her the story of how he acquired his land?
10. Why might Hayslip's father have defined her job as he did?

Evaluate and Connect

11. Hayslip's father tells her that freedom must be won again and again. Do you agree with his opinion? Explain.
12. Do you think that Hayslip's father would have treated her in the same manner if one of his sons had remained at home? Explain, using details from the selection.
13. What insights do you think Hayslip gained from her father's stories? What insights did you gain?
14. To inspire Hayslip, her father tells her the story of a brave female ancestor. What stories in your family history have inspired you?
15. If you had been in Hayslip's place, how might you have reacted to the father's final words?

Literary Criticism

David K. Shipler makes the following statement about *When Heaven and Earth Changed Places:* "Lucidly, sometimes even lyrically, Ms. Hayslip paints an intensely intimate portrait that begins with the war's corruption of family and community life in her village of Ky La." In a brief essay, explain how the war affects family and community life in Ky La. Do you agree that Hayslip's writing is lucid and lyrical? Support your opinions with evidence from the selection.

Literary ELEMENTS

Autobiography

An **autobiography** is a type of nonfiction in which a writer gives an account of his or her own life. It may not entirely reflect reality, since the writer may have forgotten certain events or wish to hide certain facts. However, the person who can "read between the lines" and make inferences about the writer's motives can gain a great deal of insight into a person from an autobiography.

1. How does Hayslip present herself as a young girl? Do you think that she presents herself clearly and understandably?
2. What details are included in this autobiography that would probably not be possible to include in a biography?

- See **Literary Terms Handbook,** p. R1.

Literature and Writing

Writing About Literature

Summary Write a one-page summary of this selection. In your summary, describe the most important incidents in the selection and the people involved in each. In one paragraph, present the **themes,** or central ideas, of the selection. Remember that the theme of a particular work is the writer's thoughts and feelings about the subject.

Creative Writing

Autobiographical Sketch Using the Reading Focus on page 746 for inspiration, write two or three paragraphs in which you describe the person you mentioned and present a story or piece of advice he or she told you. Then, discuss the ways in which this story or piece of advice has influenced you.

Extending Your Response

Literature Groups

Debating Roles for Bay Ly At the end of the selection, Bay Ly and her father have different ideas about how she should respond to the situation in her homeland. Divide your group in half. One side will take Bay Ly's side of the issue; the other will take her father's. Debate the issue, and close by summarizing the arguments for the whole class.

Interdisciplinary Activity

World History: Vietnamese History Vietnam has suffered through many wars against foreign invaders over the course of two thousand years. Use the library or the Internet to research the history of these struggles and what the country is like today.

Performing

Our Town, Ky La In his play *Our Town,* the American playwright Thornton Wilder presented a series of vignettes of small-town life linked together by an onstage narrator. In your group, choose a section of this selection to dramatize, and select one member of the group to act as the narrator. When you have finished practicing your vignette, perform it before the class.

Save your work for your portfolio.

VOCABULARY • Homographs

A homograph is a word that is spelled the same as another word but that differs in meaning and pronunciation. In a dictionary, homographs have separate entries with superscripts, such as [1] or [2].

wind[1] (wind) *n.* a natural movement of air

wind[2] (wīnd) *v.* to wrap around

PRACTICE Choose the correct definition of each word in bold type.

1. The farmer brought his **produce** to market.
   a. to make or yield
   b. fruits and vegetables
2. Each convention **delegate** wore a name badge.
   a. representative
   b. appoint
3. Magicians **entrance** their audiences with tricks.
   a. amaze
   b. doorway
4. You can **contract** pneumonia from a virus.
   a. binding agreement
   b. catch
5. We caught two **bass** for dinner.
   a. fish with spiny fins
   b. male singer with deep voice

LISTENING, SPEAKING, and VIEWING

Interviewing

Le Ly Hayslip, the author of "When Heaven and Earth Changed Places," grew up in Vietnam and spent her adult life in the United States. After reading the selection, what questions would you want to ask Hayslip about her life, her family, and her experiences growing up? How would you go about setting up an interview? How would you decide what questions to ask?

Preparing for an Interview

Preparation is the key to a successful interview. Follow these steps:

- Request an interview, explain your purpose, and make an appointment.
- Research the background of the person you will be interviewing and the topic you will be discussing.
- Write interview questions that relate directly to your topic and purpose. Review your questions to make sure they are clear and tightly focused.

Conducting an Interview

You've done the necessary preparation; now it's time to conduct your interview. Keep these tips in mind:

- Arrive on time. Be polite, friendly, and businesslike.
- Request permission to tape the interview before you begin.
- Ask a question and listen to the answer. Don't interrupt.
- Ask appropriate follow-up questions.

Writing Up an Interview

After the interview, transcribe your recording or review your notes. Then decide how you will present the information you have gathered. Consider these options:

- Put your interview questions and answers in a script format, with the text of each speech indented after the name of the speaker, or use the letters *Q* and *A* as labels.
- Incorporate the information from the interview into a report.
- When using exact quotations in a report or article, be sure to get your interviewee's approval on their accuracy.

ACTIVITIES

1. Learn from the professionals by reading newspaper and magazine interviews or by watching or listening to interviews on television and radio. Analyze the techniques used by each interviewer. Share your observations with the class.
2. Practice and polish your own skills by conducting an interview. You might interview someone to fulfill a class assignment or to learn about a topic that interests you. Follow the steps described in this feature as you prepare, conduct, and write up your interview.

Before You Read

from *Stay Alive, My Son*

Meet Pin Yathay

"Through our suffering, I want . . . my readers to see how fine-sounding ideals of justice and equality can be perverted by fanatics to create brutal oppression. . . ."

Pin Yathay (pin yä′ tī) was an engineer in Cambodia's Ministry of Public Works. In April 1975, the communist guerrillas known as the Khmer Rouge (kə mer′ ro͞ozh) took control of Phnom Penh (pə näm′ pen′), the capital of Cambodia. At first, Pin Yathay welcomed them. He hoped the Khmer Rouge would restore order to his nation. His hopes were soon dashed.

Claiming a U.S. bombing of Phnom Penh was imminent, the Khmer Rouge ordered people to evacuate the capital with the assurance they could soon return. Few, however, did. Most were sent to live in rural labor camps.

Deprived of food, many people died of malnutrition and disease; others were killed. It is estimated that three million died. Pin Yathay himself lost seventeen members of his family.

Pin Yathay was born around 1953.

Reading Focus

Think about people you know or have read about who were treated unjustly. What happened? Who was involved? How did the people feel about their mistreatment?

Journal Spend three or four minutes responding to these questions in your journal.

Setting a Purpose Read to learn about a period in Cambodian history when people's rights were ignored.

Building Background

The Khmer Rouge

From 1970 to 1975, Cambodia was ruled by an army general named Lon Nol, who had seized power from the previous ruler, Prince Sihanouk, in a *coup* (ko͞o)—a sudden, violent overthrow of the government. In 1975 the Khmer Rouge overthrew Lon Nol's regime with the support of the North Vietnamese and the exiled Prince Sihanouk. They fought in the name of the country's poorest peasants.

In 1976 a Khmer Rouge leader named Pol Pot became prime minister of Cambodia. Under his leadership, the country's entire population was forced to live and work as peasants in rural camps. Those who disobeyed orders or behaved in a "counter-revolutionary" way were killed. From 1975 to 1979, the Khmer Rouge murdered two to three million people.

Vocabulary Preview

frantically (fran′ tik lē) *adv.* in a manner marked by fast and nervous activity; p. 759

prelude (prel′ ūd) *n.* an event preceding and preparing for a more important matter; p. 759

accomplice (ə kom′ plis) *n.* a participant in a crime or wrong-doing; p. 760

plausible (plô′ zə bəl) *adj.* appearing worthy of belief; p. 760

taint (tānt) *v.* to contaminate morally; to corrupt; p. 761

impassive (im pas′ iv) *adj.* giving no sign of feeling or emotion; p. 761

Boys in the Field, 1991. Monirith Chhea (Cambodia). Oil on canvas, 58 x 48 in. Collection of the artist.

Viewing the painting: What kind of work are these boys doing? What kind of work do you picture Yathay doing?

from Stay Alive, My Son
Feeding the Fire of Enmity

Pin Yathay with John Man

For the first couple of months in Leach[1]—November and December 1976—we survived as we had in Veal Vong,[2] by supplementing our rations buying rice on the black market,[3] with the occasional addition of sugar, fruit and fish. Though our hoard of spare clothing and jewelry inherited from my family was running low, I still had dollars, and these were valued in Leach. A hundred dollars bought fifteen cans of rice (a hundred-dollar bill being once again the basic unit of currency).

1. *Leach* (lē′ ich)
2. *Veal Vong* (vil vong)
3. The *black market* is illegal trade in goods and foods.

My job was clearing trees, along with a hundred other men. Our first assignment involved a scheme that was typical of the way the Khmer Rouge[4] did things. We were marched off to a rice field in which grew a scattering of fruit trees and bushes. It looked like a perfectly serviceable rice field to me, perhaps better than most because it supported the fruit trees as well, mostly rather fine mangoes and tamarinds.

Our leader, Comrade Run, explained our task with obvious pride. Apparently, at harvest time the place was infested with sparrows that gorged themselves on the rice. The sparrows nested in the fruit trees. Eager to display true revolutionary initiative, to apply the sacred spirit of self-sufficiency that Angkar[5] demanded, Comrade Run planned an assault on the sparrows. How? By destroying their nests. And how again? By cutting down the fruit trees. While people were dying of hunger a mile away, we were out chopping down fruit trees. The damage wrought by the sparrows was nothing compared to the damage we did to Leach's fruit harvest.

After that notable objective was achieved, we were turned loose on the forest to make new clearings. We were divided into ten groups. I belonged to a group of twelve who were considered the best workers and thus designated Group No. 1. In the morning, we walked in columns to the work site. At noon, there was an hour's break for lunch, then we returned to work until six p.m. At night, when the moon shone, we worked up until ten or eleven p.m. We would return to the village every tenth day to rest, but also to attend a political meeting.

There was, however, another unofficial side to our lives. Out in our forest camp, I and two others hung our hammocks a little apart from the rest, in the hope of having some peace, away from constant supervision. Sometimes, when our comrades and our group leader were fast asleep, we would sneak away two at a time to go back to the village. The third always stayed in his hammock to tell any snooping Khmer Rouge that the other two had gone into the forest to relieve themselves. On these trips, I would pass through a number of Leach's other subsidiary camps, each one a collection of eight foot by ten foot bamboo huts, thatched with palm leaves and raised on stilts. It was on these occasions I was able to continue making exchanges. I would make a deal on the way in with a broker—as in Veal Vong, the brokers were well-known to the New People[6]—go home to see Any,[7] collect clothing, jewelry, or dollars, and pick up the extra cans of rice on my way back. Any was the focus of this activity. Seeing her and talking with her was my only pleasure, my only strength. We were life itself to each other, each other's only hope.

We were forbidden to have extra food, but we managed. Though not allowed to cook rice, we could boil water, so when we saw our group leader, Run, coming, we would snatch up a water can, and put it on the fire, whipping away any rice that was cooking and hiding it in the bushes. Thus, whenever it was my turn to go back to the village, I could take cooked rice to Any, returning to the forest camp before dawn, so that on waking up no one noticed my absence.

One rest day, I decided to stay in my hut rather than go to the political meeting. It was foolhardy, but all I had to do was remain out of sight until I heard the gong, which rang to call the children to eat—an hour or so before the adults' meal—and also signified the end of the meeting. Then it would take the men about an hour to get back to camp. It would be easy for me to drift back in time for the communal meal.

4. *Khmer Rouge* (kə mer′ ro͞ozh)
5. According to the author, *Angkar* (āng′ kär), represents "the faceless all-pervading authority" of the new government.
6. The *New People* refers to former urban dwellers like Pin Yathay.
7. *Any* is the author's wife.

Seven Women in the Field, 1990. Monirith Chhea (Cambodia). Oil on canvas, 58 x 64 in. Collection of the artist.

Viewing the painting: How does the artist use different shapes to create a mood in this painting? How is this mood present in the selection?

When I left, I took with me in my scarf one can's worth of newly bought raw rice which I intended to cook that evening. At the campsite, however, I found to my surprise that everyone had eaten. Apparently, the meeting had been shorter than usual and my workmates had returned and eaten early. For a moment I was taken aback, thinking I was about to go hungry, until I saw that they had kept some rice aside for me. I was touched—in those harsh conditions, it was more than I would have expected. Eager for food, I unthinkingly put my scarf containing the rice into the nearest hammock and sat down to eat about twenty yards away.

Just then, the owner of the hammock, a friend of mine called Chorn, came back, went to lie down, and sat right on the bundle of rice. He jumped up in surprise, and prodded the scarf. His jaw dropped. "Rice!" he said, in an appalled voice. Possessing extra rice was a major offense, and here was a whole bundle of it in his hammock. In panic, he held the scarf up and shouted, "But it's not mine! This rice doesn't belong to me! Who left rice in my hammock?"

You would have thought he was holding a bomb. I flapped my hand and mouthed frantically at him to attract his attention. Too late—the camp chief, the boss of the whole operation, was already on his way across to us. Seeing him, Chorn protested even more loudly: "It's not my rice! It's not my rice!" He kept repeating the words over and over, as if they were some sort of incantation.

"Whose is it then?" the chief asked. "And whose scarf is it? You're sure they're not yours?"

"No! I found them under me when I lay in my hammock."

The chief turned to the rest of us. "Whose rice is this?" he asked, his gaze wandering from one to another.

Everyone knew the scarf was mine. Sooner or later the truth would come out.

I stood up. "Comrade, the rice is mine."

Then Run, my immediate supervisor, the group leader, whose responsibility it was to deal with the situation, stepped forward. It would, in normal circumstances, have been the prelude to my death. Fortunately, however, Run and I were not complete strangers.

Two weeks before I had seen Run sitting in front of his house, looking utterly crushed. When I asked him what the matter was, he said, "It's my wife, Thay. She's very sick. She's in such pain she sometimes screams for relief."

"Have you no medicine for her?" I asked.

"I've tried our medicines, but they're not effective," he said. He was obviously a very worried man, for he had tried everything

Vocabulary

frantically (fran′ tik lē) *adv.* in a manner marked by fast and nervous activity

prelude (prel′ ūd) *n.* an event preceding and preparing for a more important matter available to a Khmer Rouge. At once, I saw there was a chance here to get some extra rations, for I knew someone who could obtain some tetracyclin, an antibiotic.[8] There were doctors among the New People who still did what they could for us. They brought their medicines into the black market, as others provided food, clothing, jewelry, or watches. One tablet of tetracyclin was worth a can of rice. I would ask two cans—one for me, one for my supplier. But I had to proceed cautiously.

"Comrade, have you tried foreign medicine?" It was a harmless way to suggest the idea. If he disapproved of foreign medicine, I wouldn't be trapped. But he leaped at it.

"Comrade, do you happen to have any? Do you know where to get any?"

"Not me," I said innocently, placing my hand on my heart. "I don't want to be mixed up in anything illegal. I have never seen any foreign medicines, but I've heard about them in the camp."

He couldn't care less about my guilt or innocence. He just wanted his wife to be free of the pain. "Try to do something for me, Thay! My wife cries all the time. I don't know what to do. I'm desperate."

I said I would do my best.

The next day, having done precisely nothing, I told him that, despite the risks involved, I had contacted a man who had two tablets of tetracyclin. Not, of course, that I could guarantee a complete cure . . .

"How can I get them?"

"The man wants two cans' worth of rice for one tablet. I can arrange that for you."

"Come back tomorrow. I'll find the rice. Don't let me down."

So we became accomplices. I found him the tablets, and he gave me the rice. The two of us shared a secret. If one of us betrayed his promise, in the eyes of the authorities we would both be guilty.

Now here was Run, bombarding me with questions as he had to in the presence of the camp leader and a whole crowd of others. "The rice is yours? Where did it come from? Why did you leave the rice in your comrade's hammock? Do you want to eat more than others? You're a counterrevolutionary, is that it?"

I was on a knife-edge. Run had the power of life and death over me, and nobody would have reproached him for having me killed. He had reason enough—theft and black-marketeering were capital offenses.[9] Moreover, I knew he had another reason to show himself as an intransigent leader—by having me killed, he could get rid of a witness to his own crime. "Who sold you the rice?" he shouted. "You must denounce the person who sold it to you!"

I certainly didn't want to do that. The only thing I could do was make up something plausible and then somehow turn the conversation to my advantage. "A soldier," I said. "I exchanged a pair of trousers for it with a soldier who was passing on his bicycle." No, I had no idea of his name. I had never seen him before. "Anyway, comrade, the rice was not for me."

Run was taken aback. "I don't understand. Why did you bring the rice here then?"

"I was going to trade it to find *medicine for my wife*," I said, looking him in the eye.

There was the briefest of pauses.

"She's getting worse," I went on. "Angkar's medicines have not cured her. I have to find some tablets. You know how it is."

8. An *antibiotic* is a medicine derived from a microorganism that inhibits or kills another microorganism.

9. *Capital offenses* are crimes punishable by death.

Vocabulary

accomplice (ə kom′ plis) *n.* a participant in a crime or wrongdoing

plausible (plô′ zə bəl) *adj.* appearing worthy of belief

I could see that he did.

"But why did you bring the rice to the worksite?"

"I told you: I thought perhaps one of us had medicine."

"Who then?"

"Oh! I didn't have anybody special in mind, comrade. I—"

At this point, the camp leader interrupted. "This is a serious crime, comrades! Comrade Run, it is up to you to decide how to punish Comrade Thay."

Run tied my elbows behind my back, and led me away. From their terrified expressions, it was obvious my friends thought I was going to my death.

Run pushed me towards his hammock, away from the others, and told me to squat down in front of him. He sat back and began to lecture me. I would have expected nothing less, and lowered my head, playing my role as the ritual phrases of condemnation poured over me. "Thay, you are a counterrevolutionary . . . you participated in exchanges . . . you don't know how to get rid of individualist leanings . . . you taint our group . . . you've been in reeducation for more than a year and a half, yet you have remained a counterrevolutionary . . ." and on and on for an hour or more.

It occurred to me as he talked that he seemed to be so taken up with the need to show himself as strong that he was in danger of forgetting the favor I'd done him. If he went on like that, he would leave himself no other course but to have me cudgeled to death in the forest or sent off to a reeducation camp. I thought I'd better take action.

As he drew breath, I said in a low voice, "Comrade, remember your sick wife. Remember my efforts to help you. If you hurt me, I will denounce you." I looked up at him, so there could be no doubt about my seriousness. "If I die, you die."

His eyes widened, and the color drained from his face, and I knew I had a chance.

In a second or two, he resumed the look of an austere and inflexible leader, his face impassive. For another quarter of an hour, he continued his harangue, his voice growing louder and louder. It became clear to me that he was putting on a show for everyone to hear, especially the camp leader. I began to relax, wondering how he could retract his accusations without loss of face.

"Thay, you are a counterrevolutionary, but fortunately for you, you are a good worker." Then he began to praise me, still talking in a loud voice—"I have noticed you are the first to wake in the mornings and that you are the best worker," and on and on he went about how I gave everything I had to my work. It was such an astonishing performance that I could hardly believe our undeclared conspiracy would not be discovered. Never had the most assiduous Khmer Rouge, the most perfect revolutionary, been garlanded with such praise. An hour before I was criminal scum; now Comrade Run found it hard to do justice to my merits. And he concluded: "As a result, this time—and only this time—I will ask the chief to give you a warning so that you can cleanse yourself. It will be a serious warning, Thay. The next time, you will become fertilizer on our rice fields."

After that, it only remained for the camp leader to give me a brief, formal warning—"Don't do it again! Next time, you'll be fertilizer"—and I was saved.

Vocabulary

taint (tānt) *v.* to contaminate morally; to corrupt

impassive (im pas′ iv) *adj.* giving no sign of feeling or emotion

Responding to Literature

Personal Response

In the Reading Focus on page 756, you wrote about someone who was treated unjustly. How does this selection compare with that experience? Explain.

Analyzing Literature

Recall and Interpret

1. Why do the Khmer Rouge want to eliminate the sparrows? What is their plan for destroying the birds? Why is Pin Yathay critical of the Khmer Rouge's plan?
2. What is Yathay's work after the sparrows are eliminated? Where is this work done? What are the living quarters for the workers like?
3. What item does Yathay hide in his scarf and why? How do Chorn and the Khmer Rouge react when they discover this item? Based on this incident, what can you infer about the Khmer Rouge's treatment of the people in its camps?
4. What favor did Yathay do for Comrade Run? For what reasons might Comrade Run have wanted to keep this favor a secret?
5. Summarize what Comrade Run says to Yathay in response to his crime. How does Yathay use the favor he has done for Comrade Run to his advantage?

Evaluate and Connect

6. **Tone** is the attitude a writer takes toward his or her subject (see **Literary Terms Handbook,** page R12). Based on the tone of this selection, what conclusions can you draw about Pin Yathay's feelings toward the Khmer Rouge?
7. An **author's purpose** is his or her reasons for writing a particular work. (See **Literary Terms Handbook,** page R1.) In your opinion, what was Yathay's purpose for writing *Stay Alive, My Son*? Explain the reasons for your thinking.
8. If you had been in Yathay's place, would you have helped Comrade Run get medicine for his wife? Explain your reasons.
9. If you were Comrade Run, what would you have done about the narrator's law breaking?
10. Can you think of any situations in world history similar to those Yathay describes?

Protagonist and Antagonist

The plots of classical Greek tragedies were built around *agons,* or conflicts. The characters who were opposed to one another in an *agon* were the *agonistes,* the combatants. The main combatant was called the **protagonist.** The opposing character was called the **antagonist.** Often a protagonist had more than one antagonist. Today the protagonist is the main character in a work of literature, and the antagonist is the opposing character.

1. Who is the protagonist of this selection?
2. Who is the main antagonist? With what other antagonists must the protagonist contend?

- See **Literary Terms Handbook,** pp. R10 and R1.

Stone relief of Aspara, Angkor Wat, Cambodia.

Literature and Writing

Creative Writing

Dialogue With a partner, create a dialogue that might have taken place between Yathay and Comrade Run if they had been out of earshot of the Khmer Rouge. Pass a sheet of paper back and forth, with each person writing either Yathay's or Comrade Run's lines. When you have finished, peform your dialogue in front of the class.

Personal Writing

You Are There Pretend that you are a member of the same work group as Thay. You are secretly keeping a diary of your experiences. Write several days' entries in your diary. Describe the events surrounding the discovery of the rice in the hammock. Include your feelings about your situation and your hopes and fears for the future. Share your diary entries with other members of your class.

Extending Your Response

Performing

Secret Meeting With a small group, plan a dramatization of a meeting between Thay and his wife Any. Make up dialogue in which they exchange black market items and relate the experiences they have had since their last meeting. Plan the tone of voice in which each character speaks. Choose students to play the parts of Thay and Any and to narrate the setting. Rehearse the dramatization and present it to the class as a radio play.

Interdisciplinary Activity

History: Cambodia After Pol Pot Conduct research at the library to discover what has happened in Cambodia since the Khmer Rouge were driven from power in 1979. Find out who leads the country, its current system of government, and what conditions are like there now. Present your findings to the class.

Literature Groups

Comrades in Crime Thay and Comrade Run shared a guilty secret about the antibiotics. In what ways were the two men alike? In what ways were they different? In your group, discuss the way in which the two men compare and contrast with one another. Consider their relationship with their wives, their loyalty to the government, their concern for others. Choose one member of your group to summarize your discussion for the class.

Save your work for your portfolio.

VOCABULARY • Antonyms

Antonyms are words with opposite or nearly opposite meanings. Knowing antonyms can help extend your vocabulary. For example, knowing that *unusual* is an antonym for *customary* can help you add words such as *atypical* and *unprecedented,* synonyms for *unusual,* to your vocabulary.

PRACTICE Choose the word that is most nearly opposite in meaning to the word given in bold. Write a definition for the word that you have chosen. Consult a dictionary or thesaurus if you like.

1. **finite**
   a. limited b. boundless c. restricted
2. **audacity**
   a. timidity b. insolence c. presumption
3. **obscured**
   a. ambiguous b. clarified c. diminished
4. **oblique**
   a. slanting b. straightforward c. vague
5. **potency**
   a. capacity b. tenacity c. infirmity

MEDIA connection

Web Site

By far the biggest part of the Pacific region's area consists of ocean. The OCEAN98 Web site was created in 1998, the year of the Ocean, to heighten awareness of this vast and vital space that surrounds all of us.

Ocean Facts

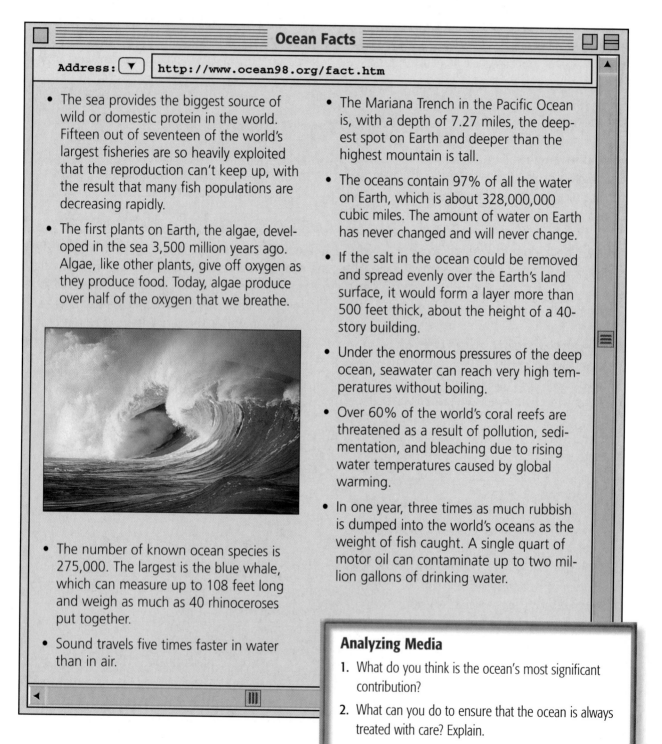

Address: http://www.ocean98.org/fact.htm

- The sea provides the biggest source of wild or domestic protein in the world. Fifteen out of seventeen of the world's largest fisheries are so heavily exploited that the reproduction can't keep up, with the result that many fish populations are decreasing rapidly.
- The first plants on Earth, the algae, developed in the sea 3,500 million years ago. Algae, like other plants, give off oxygen as they produce food. Today, algae produce over half of the oxygen that we breathe.

- The number of known ocean species is 275,000. The largest is the blue whale, which can measure up to 108 feet long and weigh as much as 40 rhinoceroses put together.
- Sound travels five times faster in water than in air.
- The Mariana Trench in the Pacific Ocean is, with a depth of 7.27 miles, the deepest spot on Earth and deeper than the highest mountain is tall.
- The oceans contain 97% of all the water on Earth, which is about 328,000,000 cubic miles. The amount of water on Earth has never changed and will never change.
- If the salt in the ocean could be removed and spread evenly over the Earth's land surface, it would form a layer more than 500 feet thick, about the height of a 40-story building.
- Under the enormous pressures of the deep ocean, seawater can reach very high temperatures without boiling.
- Over 60% of the world's coral reefs are threatened as a result of pollution, sedimentation, and bleaching due to rising water temperatures caused by global warming.
- In one year, three times as much rubbish is dumped into the world's oceans as the weight of fish caught. A single quart of motor oil can contaminate up to two million gallons of drinking water.

Analyzing Media

1. What do you think is the ocean's most significant contribution?
2. What can you do to ensure that the ocean is always treated with care? Explain.

Before You Read

Taaroa, Moana, Islands, and *Island*

Meet Three Poets of the Pacific Islands

"Our oral literatures . . . are astounding collections of mythologies, genealogies, poetry, stories, songs, chants, and incantations." —*Wendt*

Since the 1960s, the Pacific Islands have experienced a blossoming of literature by native peoples. The person most responsible for this is Albert Wendt (photograph above) from the republic of Western Samoa, an editor and champion of indigenous writing. In his own work, Wendt blends Polynesian oral and European literary traditions to portray islanders and their way of life.

Through his verse and his work as an anthropologist, Kauraka Kauraka from the Cook Islands has studied and brought attention to his people's rich oral traditions. Nicholas Hasluck, son of a governor-general of Australia, has written a number of novels exploring the reality and the European myths of the Pacific Islands. This theme is also present in his collection of poems, *On the Edge*.

Wendt was born in 1939. Kauraka was born in 1951. Hasluck was born in 1942.

Reading Focus

What do you think of when you hear the words *island* and *ocean?*

Word Webs Make two word webs, one with the word *island* at its center and the other with the word *ocean.* Around each word, indicate all the thoughts and feelings that it evokes.

Setting a Purpose Read to discover different writers' impressions of islands and the Pacific Ocean.

Building Background

The Pacific Islands

The Pacific island nations (not counting New Zealand and Papua New Guinea) occupy some 34,000 square miles of land spread over millions of square miles of ocean. Their inhabitants came from Asia, by way of Indochina and Indonesia, thousands of years ago. Geographers divide the area into three parts: Melanesia and Micronesia in the west, and Polynesia to the east.

The more than 10,000 islands fall into two general types. Islands produced by volcanic action are generally mountainous and covered with rain forest. Islands that grew from coral reefs are usually smaller; often they are only a few feet above sea level, with sparse vegetation and limited fresh water.

The Pacific Islanders are among the world's greatest navigators, finding their way across the sea by the stars, the sun, and even the shape of the waves. In spite of the great distances between the islands, language, society, and beliefs are remarkably consistent among them.

Literature: Tradition and Innovation

At the heart of indigenous writing, states Wendt, are "the techniques of oral storytelling . . . and indigenous philosophies and visions." Many of the stories arising from this rich oral tradition date back hundreds of years. Today, they are being used and revised to explore the present.

Most modern Oceanic literature is written in English. In part, this is to enable the writers to speak to a larger audience. In part it also shows the confidence writers feel in their use of the language to express themselves and their culture. The language is often used in distinctive ways, to reflect the influence of traditional Oceanic spoken literature.

Taaroa

Tahitian Traditional Poem

English version by Ulli Beier

He was there—Taaroa was his name.
Around him void:
no earth no sky
no sea no people.
Taaroa calls—there is no echo.
In his loneliness he changes himself into the world.
These entangled roots are Taaroa.
These rocks are Taaroa.
Taaroa: sand of the sea.
Taaroa: clarity.°
Taaroa: seed.
Taaroa: ground.
Taaroa the eternal
the powerful
creator of the world
the large sacred world
the world
which is only the shell.
Taaroa is the life inside it.

---

10 *Clarity* means "clearness."

Post with Human Head. 20th century, Admiralty Islands. Polychrome wood, height: 58¾ in. The Newark Museum, NJ.

Viewing the sculpture: Which of the poems does this sculpture best illustrate? Explain.

Moana

Kauraka Kauraka

Name of the Great Ocean
the dark blue sea
the mysterious
Moana-Nui-o-Kiva°
Moana-Vai-a-Vare°
mysterious ocean
Moana our daughter
graceful rider through space
from Havaiki°
today you have earned
the keys to enter
the four rooms
of the mysterious
ocean of life
many will call upon
your name for guidance
for interpretation
of these mysteries
Moana our sister
you were born and raised
in the mysterious ocean
we look to you for understanding
of the fish we eat
the waves that destroy us
the waves that create new lands
for us
Moana our daughter
Moana our sister
Moana our mother

Seashells on the Seashore. Brian Kere (Solomon Islands, b. 1960). Mixed media, 90 x 64 cm. The International Museum of 20th Century Arts, Laguna Beach, CA.

Viewing the art: How do the fluctuating designs reflect the content in these poems?

4–5 Lines 4 and 5 refer to the Pacific Ocean.

9 *Havaiki* (hä vä ē′ kē) is the legendary homeland of the Maori. Cook Islanders are considered a branch of the Maori people.

Islands

Nicholas Hasluck

Islands which have
never existed
have made their way
onto maps nevertheless.

And having done so
have held their place,
quite respectably,
sometimes for centuries.

Voyages of undiscovery, deep
into the charted wastes,
were then required
to move them off.

The Auroras, for instance.
Beneath Cape Horn.
Sighted first in 1762
and confirmed by
Captain Manuel de Oyarvido
thirty years later.

But since the voyage of
someone whose name
escapes me, on a date
I can't quite remember—
they are now known
not to exist.

Cartographers°—hands high
in the frail rigging of
latitudes and longitudes—
wiped them out, reluctantly.

25 *Cartographers* are mapmakers.

And so, some mariners
who pushed beyond the pale,°
forfeit the names they left
in lonely seas.

Remember them
Respect their enterprise.
It takes a certain
kind of boldness
to have seen such
islands first of all.

In the mind's atlas,
footnotes, like broken rules,
are not without importance.

Who found America?
Those canny° trawlers,
absent for months,
fishing the depths,
must have been somewhere
with their sealed lips.

30 *Beyond the pale* means "past the limits or boundaries."

43 *Canny* means "clever."

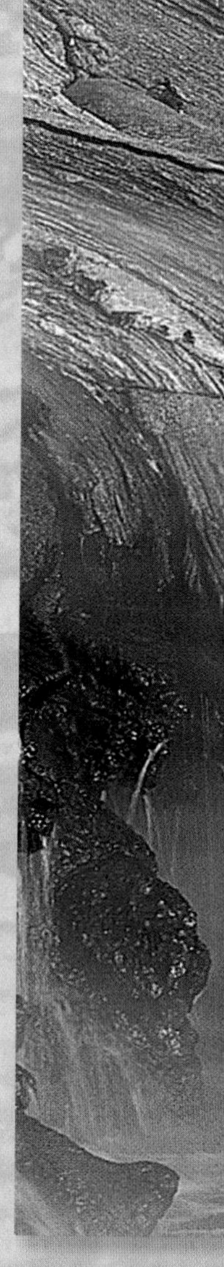

Island

Albert Wendt ~

This island was a frail tremor snared
in stingray seas dark with threat of storm.
The tremor was strong enough
to give us birth.

Lava flow, Hawaii Volcanoes National Park, Hawaii.

Responding to Literature

Personal Response

What feelings did you experience while reading these poems? How do they compare with the feelings you indicated in the Reading Focus on page 765?

Analyzing Literature

Recall

1. According to the first poem, who is Taaroa and where can he be found?
2. The **speaker** (see page R11) of a poem is the voice that talks to the reader. What do the speaker of the second poem and the people look to Moana for?
3. According to the third poem, what islands have made their way onto maps?
4. What does the poet say it takes to see an imaginary island?
5. In the fourth poem, what does the speaker say the island once was?

Interpret

6. How would you characterize Taaroa and his relationship to the world?
7. How would you describe the relationship between the people, and Moana, the Pacific Ocean?
8. What, in your opinion, is the speaker's attitude toward the mariners who made the "voyages of undiscovery"?
9. What do you think the speaker in "Islands" means by saying "In the mind's atlas, footnotes are not without importance"?
10. Why might the speaker of "Island" describe "this island" this particular way?

Evaluate and Connect

11. What aspects of the Taaroa myth do you admire? Why?
12. What adjectives would you use to describe the speaker of Kauraka's poem?
13. Do Taaroa and Moana represent the same thing? Explain.
14. What new insights into exploration and discovery did Hasluck's poem give you?
15. What example of **alliteration** (see page R1) can you find in Wendt's poem? How, in your opinion, does it add to the overall effect of the poem?

Literary ELEMENTS

Myths

Myths are traditional, usually anonymous, stories that explain the creation of the world and its inhabitants, the mysteries of nature, or an aspect of human behavior. Typically, a myth involves a god, goddess, hero, or heroine, and it reflects the culture from which it sprang.

1. In what ways do the Taaroa and Moana myths reflect the culture in which they were created?
2. In what ways might the fourth poem, "Island," fit the definition of a myth?

- See **Literary Terms Handbook,** p. R8.

Colossal standing sculpture, Easter Island.

Literature and Writing

Writing About Literature

Characterization In many myths, gods, goddesses, and other superhuman beings are given human qualities. Write an essay in which you describe the personalities of Taaroa, Moana, or the mariners mentioned in Hasluck's poem. First, analyze the thoughts and actions of the character. Then tell what personality traits are revealed through these thoughts and behaviors. Use details from the poem to support your conclusions.

Creative Writing

Myth Making Write a myth in which you explain the origins of the universe, an aspect of nature, or a social custom through the actions of a god, goddess, or other superhuman being. In your myth, try to include details that reflect your own cultural heritage and to incorporate the poetic techniques and styles used in the first three poems in this selection. When you are finished, share your myth with the class.

Extending Your Response

Literature Groups

Find the Theme In your group, discuss the following question: What is the central **theme,** or message, of Hasluck's poem "Islands"? To help you pinpoint the theme, first analyze the poem's **tone** (see page R12) and its **characterization** (see page R2) of mariners and cartographers. Then discuss what idea about islands and their discovery Hasluck is trying to convey. Share the results of your discussion with the class.

Interdisciplinary Activity

History: Pacific Island Explorers Conduct research at the library to find out about European exploration of the Pacific Islands during the sixteenth, seventeenth, and eighteenth centuries. Focus on one particular period or explorer. If you like, share your findings with the class.

Performing

Recite a Poem In a small group, practice either "Taaroa" or "Moana" to read before the class. You might emphasize certain words, reading particular lines in a high or low voice, or pause at specific places. Then take turns reading sections of the poem before the class.

Save your work for your portfolio.

VOCABULARY • Analogies

Some analogies are based on synonyms. Synonyms are words that have the same meaning and are always the same part of speech.

clarity : clearness :: obscurity : darkness

Clarity and *clearness* mean the same thing, just as *obscurity* and *darkness* do. To complete an analogy, decide on the relationship between the first two terms. Apply that relationship to the second set of words.

- For more about analogies, see **Communications Skills Handbook,** p. R77.

PRACTICE Complete each analogy.

1. mariner : sailor ::
   a. horse : mammal
   b. strained : wit
   c. teacher : classroom
   d. physician : doctor
   e. powerful : weak
2. dexterity : coordination ::
   a. courage : bravery
   b. poet : sonnet
   c. trite : new
   d. chair : furniture
   e. virus : cold

Writing Workshop

Business Writing: Letter of Application

According to an old saying, "Opportunity knocks but once." More often, it doesn't knock at all. Most people who get great opportunities don't wait for them to come knocking. They go out and find them!

One way to open up opportunities is to write letters of application to organizations or businesses that can help you reach your goals. How would you like to travel to another country? **In this workshop, you will choose a country you would like to visit and write a letter of application to a student exchange organization.**

- As you write your letter of application, refer to **Writing Handbook,** pp. R58–R69.

EVALUATION RUBRIC

By the time you complete this Writing Workshop, you will have

- introduced yourself and stated your goal
- provided examples to develop your argument
- used effective language to make a case for yourself
- summarized why your qualifications are noteworthy
- presented a letter of application that is free of errors in grammar, usage, and mechanics

The Writing Process

PREWRITING

PREWRITING TIP

Do your homework. Investigate the organization you are going to write to and find out what they are looking for in an applicant.

Explore ideas

Many organizations sponsor student exchange programs. Get information from language club sponsors, resource center staff, academic advisors, and counselors to identify programs geared to high school students and direct your letter of application to one of the sponsoring organizations. To get started, jot down answers to these questions.

- To what country would you like to travel? Why? Have any of the stories you have read made you curious about another country or culture?
- What qualities do you have that would make you a good exchange student?
- What reasons can you offer to convince an organization to accept you as an exchange student?

Think about your purpose

In a letter of application, your purpose is to persuade your reader to choose you over other applicants. To do that, you need to clearly state what your goal is, describe your qualifications, and prove why you are a superior candidate.

Consider your audience

Your audience consists of educated adults who will be reading many letters from many applicants. Anything *positive* that makes your application stand out from the crowd will help your cause. On the other hand, anything negative, even a single misspelling, may hurt your chances.

Make a plan

You can write an effective letter of application in as few as three paragraphs. Your letter needs only an introduction, body, and conclusion. Use your prewriting notes to plan your letter.

		STUDENT MODEL
Introduction	Who are you? Where do you want to travel? Why do you want to go there?	Sophomore at West Racine High School, West Racine, Wiconsin. Want to participate in a student exchange program with a Spanish school. Studied Spanish language and culture since seventh grade; interested in Spain since fifth grade.
Body	What are your qualifications? Why are you better qualified than other applicants?	Have good grades in Spanish, am responsible, get along with all kinds of people, have traveled to another Spanish-speaking country.
Conclusion	What makes your application stand out?	Have had a prior positive experience traveling to a Spanish-speaking country.

Complete Student Model on p. R117.

Use this graphic to help you visualize the structure of your letter of application.

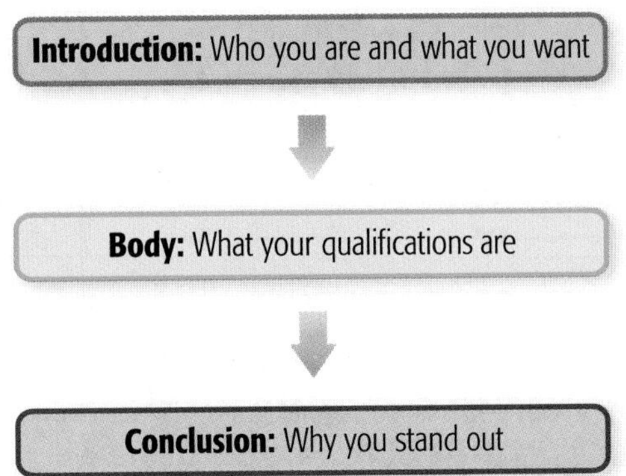

DRAFTING

DRAFTING TIP

Word your letter as if you were trying to convince a teacher or a parent. Be honest, confident, and persuasive.

TECHNOLOGY TIP

Some word processing programs will automatically format a business letter for you.

Follow the conventions of a business letter

Your letter of application should follow the standard format of a business letter. It should have your return address, the date, an inside address, a salutation, the text of the letter, a complimentary close, your signature, and your printed name.

Sell your product

A letter of application is like an advertisement. The product you are trying to sell is yourself. To do that, show interest and enthusiasm. You also might use the following techniques:

- focus on your best points
- show how the audience will benefit from choosing you
- show how you compare with others

Write your draft

As you write your draft, refer to your plan to make sure you are covering all the important points.

STUDENT MODEL

I believe several experiences have prepared me for your program. First, I have already visited a foreign country. When our junior high school sponsored a trip to Venezuela, I was one of the first to sign up. Although some students became homesick or in some way frightened on this trip, I never did.

Complete Student Model on p. R117.

REVISING

REVISING TIP

To strengthen the impression you make, think about your word choice. Use specific nouns and active verbs.

Take another look

Put your letter away for a while. Then reread it to find its weak spots and strengthen them. Use the **Rubric for Revising** to guide you as you work.

Read your letter aloud

Read the letter out loud to an adult and use your listener's responses to help you revise.

STUDENT MODEL

For the past year, I have been going to the language lab ~~four times a week~~ almost every day during study or after school in order to ~~learn to have a conversation better~~ improve my conversational skills. My current teacher, Miss Nunez, ~~has told~~ tells me I am ~~getting a lot better~~ showing great improvement.

Complete Student Model on p. R117.

RUBRIC FOR REVISING

Your revised application letter should have

- ☑ a clear sense of your audience
- ☑ an opening that clearly establishes who you are and why you're writing
- ☑ supporting paragraphs that convincingly describe your qualifications
- ☑ transitions that make logical connections between ideas and paragraphs
- ☑ a conclusion that restates why you are an outstanding applicant

Your revised application letter should be free of

- ☑ vague or unneccessary words
- ☑ statements aboout yourself that are exaggerated or misleading

EDITING/PROOFREADING

Revise your letter until your message comes through the way you want it to. Then edit your letter to correct any errors.

PROOFREADING TIP

Use the **Proofreading Checklist** on the inside back cover of this book to help you mark errors that you can find.

Grammar Hint

A comma alone is not enough to join two clauses as a single sentence. Either make the clauses separate sentences, join them with a semicolon, or add a conjunction.

INCORRECT: *I can't promise that I will be the best exchange student ever, I do know that I'll try as hard as possible.*

CORRECT: *I can't promise that I will be the best exchange student ever, but I do know that I'll try as hard as possible.*

STUDENT MODEL

~~So anyhow~~ In closing, let me say that I think I can a^d^just to this experience, ben^e^fit from it, and get along with others^,^ including my host family. ~~Plus~~ I ^also^ believe that I have the skills that ~~might~~ will enable me to succeed ^both academically and^ socially.

Complete Student Model on p. R117.

Complete Student Model

For a complete version of the model developed in this workshop, refer to **Writing Workshop Models,** p. R117.

PUBLISHING/PRESENTING

Pool your letter with the letters of your classmates. Then form a "selection committee" to review all the letters and to choose the one or two best applicants based on their letters.

PRESENTING TIP

Remember that a flaw in your letter may work against you. Make a neat, error-free final copy of your letter.

Reflecting

People compete for many things throughout life–for a place in college or in a training program, for scholarships or other financial aid, for jobs, or for promotions. What has writing this letter taught you about making yourself more likely to succeed in such competitions? Read your letter again. How might you use some of the persuasive techniques in future writing?

Save your work for your portfolio.

Unit Assessment

Personal Response

1. Which selections in Unit 4 did you enjoy the most? Which selections did you not care for? Explain your responses and what elements of the selections helped create your responses.
2. Which of the selections in this unit did you find the most moving or inspiring? Which seemed closest to your own experiences and ideas?
3. What did you learn about the relationship between different cultures and the literature written about them? What elements in these selections helped you to bridge any gaps of time and culture?
4. What suggestions would you make to someone who is interested in learning about the literature and culture of East Asia and the Pacific?

Analyzing Literature

The literature of East Asia and the Pacific takes many different forms, including sacred text, short stories, folk-tales, and poetry. Write several paragraphs in which you select one of these forms and explore at least one of the following elements in detail:

- literary elements
- language
- subject matter
- theme
- form

Refer to at least two of the selections you have read in the unit to support your opinion. You might conclude your analysis by stating which of the selections was your favorite and why.

Evaluate and Set Goals

Evaluate

1. Make a list of three things you contributed to the class as you worked through this unit.
2. What aspect of this unit was the most challenging for you?
   - How did you approach this task?
   - What was the result?
3. How would you assess your work in this unit, using the following scale? Give at least two reasons for your assessment.
   4 = outstanding **3** = good **2** = fair **1** = weak

Set Goals

1. Set a goal to work toward while reading Unit 5. Try to focus on improving a skill area, such as listening and speaking or critical thinking.
2. Discuss your goal with your teacher.
3. Write down steps that you will take to achieve your goal.
4. Plan checkpoints at which you will stop and assess your progress toward that goal.

Build Your Portfolio

Select Look over the writing that you did in this unit and select two pieces to include in your portfolio. Use the following questions to help you choose:

- Which piece was the most fun to write?
- Which piece challenged you the most?
- Which one led you to new discoveries as you wrote?
- Which of the pieces do you consider more complete and satisfactory?

Reflect Include some explanatory notes with the portfolio pieces you chose. Use these questions as a guide:

- What did you learn from the process of writing each one?
- What are the strengths and weaknesses of the piece?
- How might you revise the piece to make it stronger?

Reading on Your Own

If you have enjoyed the literature in this unit, you might also be interested in the following books.

Kon-Tiki

by Thor Heyerdahl

According to the author, sailors on reed rafts from South America found and populated Polynesia. Six men risked their lives in their own handmade raft to prove this theory, in a true tale of adventure. On their two-thousand-mile journey, the men tried to duplicate the experience of the original travelers, even depending on the sea for much of their food supply.

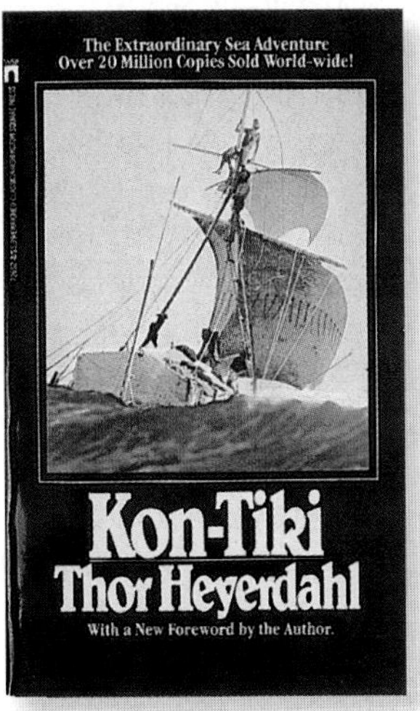

A Healing Family

by Kenzaburo Oe Although doctors urge Oe and his wife to let their baby die when he is born disabled, Oe refuses. In this inspiring story, the Nobel Prize–winning novelist explores his life raising a special-needs child. Despite the fact that Hikari, Oe's son, suffered from autism and near-blindness, he has become an accomplished composer of classical music.

Talking to High Monks in the Snow: An Asian-American Odyssey

by Lydia Yuri Minatoya In her memoirs, a Japanese American professor tries to reconcile her American childhood with her Asian heritage. Her mother's life had been governed by a feudal code under which females were silent and yielding. This code influenced much of Minatoya's girlhood. However, she also absorbed American traits of choice and hope. Struggling with cultural differences, including the role of women in society, she travels to Asia and back again to search for answers.

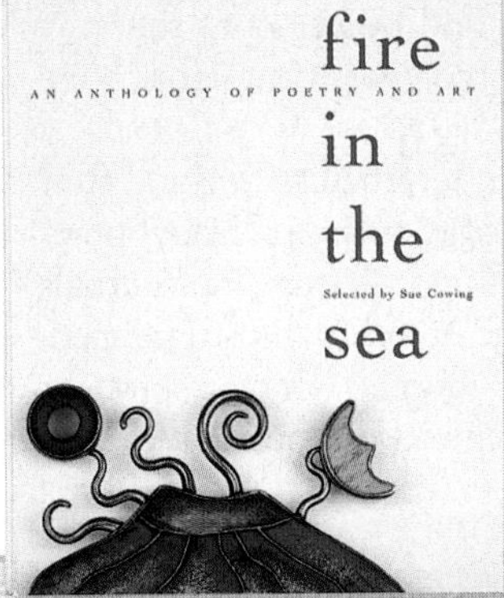

Fire in the Sea: An Anthology of Poetry and Art

edited by Sue Cowing Cowing has gathered writers and artists from New Guinea, Fiji, Samoa, Hawaii, and other Pacific islands in this highly visual celebration of poetry. Of the more than 150 poems, most were written in English. A few are translations from the original. Works of art from the Honolulu Academy of Arts are included.

California English–Language Arts

Reading and Analyzing Test Questions

The passage below is followed by six questions based on the content. Select the best answer and write the corresponding letter on your paper.

LIFE SCIENCE: This passage is from *Biology: Life on Earth* by Gerald Audesirk and Teresa Audesirk (©1986, Macmillan Publishing Co NY)

Like many modern students, Charles Darwin only excelled in those subjects that intrigued him. Although his father was a physician, Darwin wasn't interested in medicine and he couldn't stand the sight of surgery. Instead he eventually obtained a degree in theology from Cambridge, although this too was of minor interest to him. What he really liked to do was to tramp over the hills, observing plants and animals, collecting new specimens, scrutinizing their structures, and then categorizing them. As he later put it, "I was a born naturalist." Fortunately for Darwin (and for the development of biology), some of his professors at Cambridge had similar interests, notably the botanist Jon Henslow. In fact, their companionship in the field became so constant that Darwin was sometimes called "the man who walks with Henslow."

In 1831, when Darwin was 22 years old, the British government sent Her Majesty's Ship *Beagle* on an expedition along the coast of South America. As was common on such expeditions, the *Beagle* carried along a naturalist to observe and collect geological and biological specimens encountered along the route, and thanks both to Henslow's encouragement of his natural studies and to Henslow's recommendation to the captain, Robert FitzRoy, Darwin was offered the position. (When they first met, though, FitzRoy almost rejected Darwin for the post on account of the shape of Darwin's nose. Apparently FitzRoy believed that personality could be predicted by the shape of the facial features, and Darwin's nose failed to measure up, as it were. Later, Darwin opined that FitzRoy was "afterwards well satisfied that my nose had spoken falsely.")

The *Beagle* sailed to South America, making numerous stops along the coast and visiting the now-famous Galapagos Islands. Along the way, Darwin observed the fauna and flora of the tropics, and was stunned by the diversity of indigenous species. He discovered a snake with rudimentary hind limbs, calling it "the passage by which Nature joins the lizards to the snakes." Another snake he found vibrated its tail like the rattlesnake, though it had no rattles and made no noise. He saw penguins whose wings looked like paddles and who seemed almost to fly through the water. It made Darwin wonder what the purpose behind these makeshift arrangements could be. To Darwin, it didn't make sense that an omniscient Creator would have created each animal in such odd, improbable forms.

Perhaps the most significant stopover of the voyage was the month spent on the Galapagos Islands. Here Darwin found huge tortoises (*galapagos* in Spanish). And on islands where tortoises lived, prickly pears grew high above the reach of the voracious and tough-mouthed tortoises. On islands without tortoises, prickly pear cactus grew in the common style, with succulent though spiny pads spread out over the ground. Darwin also discovered several varieties of mockingbirds and finches, and as with the tortoises, on different islands there were subtly different forms of these birds. Unfortunately, Darwin "was not aware of these facts [about the finches] till [his] collection was nearly completed," and so he did not bring a systematically labeled collection back to England with him. Regardless, the diversity of tortoises and birds "haunted" him for years afterward, and he began to seriously consider how such diversity might have occurred.

In 1836, Darwin returned to England after five years on the *Beagle*. He was already somewhat famous, based upon letters and journals he'd forwarded home on other ships. The specimens and further journals Darwin brought back with him enhanced his fame, and to all outward appearances he'd settled down to be one of the foremost naturalists of his day. However, he was still troubled by the problem of the origin of species. For over 20 years, Darwin continued collecting evidence that might provide insight into its solution. When he finally published *On the Origin of Species* in 1859, the evidence he presented was overwhelming. Although its full impact would not be realized for decades, Darwin's theory of evolution by natural selection would become a unifying concept for virtually all of biology.

1. According to the passage, the prickly pears grew in an unusual fashion on those islands where

   A. there were finches and mockingbirds
   B. there were tortoises
   C. the climate was particularly dry
   D. the winters were unusually cold

2. It seems reasonable to infer from the passage that the Galapagos Islands took their name from

   F. an English ship captain
   G. a Spanish monarch
   H. an animal common to the islands
   J. one of the plants that Darwin studied

3. According to the information provided in the passage, a *naturalist* is most accurately defined as someone who

   A. takes long walks in the hills
   B. studies penguins and tortoises
   C. classifies organisms according to their form
   D. attempts to establish a person's personality based on his facial features

4. As it is used in line 44, the word *indigenous* most nearly means

   F. native
   G. deadly
   H. unlikely
   J. colorful

5. It can be reasonably inferred from the passage that the British government

   A. admired the work of John Henslow
   B. encouraged naturalistic research
   C. disagreed with Darwin's findings
   D. sent many expeditions to South America

6. According to the passage, what "haunted" (line 75) Darwin most after his voyage was his

   F. inability to understand the varieties of animals he had seen during his voyage
   G. lack of a complete collection of finches
   H. difficulties in sleeping aboard the ship
   J. disagreement with the captain of the *Beagle*

My Love For Freedom, 1990. Ali Miruku (Albania). Oil on canvas. Collection of the artist.

UNIT FIVE

Europe

A.D. 400–Present

quel est ce chemin qui nous sépare
à travers lequel je tends la main de ma pensée

what is this road that separates us
across which I hold out the hand of my thoughts

—Tristan Tzara

The Land and Its People

On a map, Europe is little more than a peninsula on the northwest corner of Asia. A band of fertile plains stretches through the heart of this peninsula, from the coasts of the Atlantic Ocean and the North Sea eastward into Russia. The region to the north of this band is rugged and chilly. The region to the south runs along the coasts of the Mediterranean and Black Seas. Its mild, sunny climate includes enough rain to grow a variety of fruits, vegetables, and grains. This region provided the setting for the classical Greek and Roman civilizations.

When the Roman Empire fell apart in the 400s, few people in Europe thought of themselves as Europeans. The diversity of their languages, religious beliefs, and ways of life overshadowed any common cultural traits. By the year 1000, though, this had changed. In the legacy of Greek philosophy, the Latin language and, most importantly, the Christian religion, Europeans started to notice their similarities. By 1800 this relatively small region—only one-fifteenth of the land surface of the earth—had developed amazing technological innovations, impressive military power, and enormous wealth.

Harold crowned King of England, 1066. From the Bayeux Tapestry.

Peasants harvesting hay. From *The Book of Hours,* late 15th century.

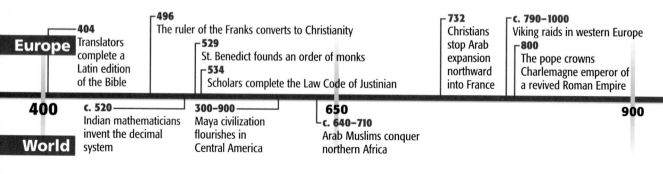

Europe

- **404** Translators complete a Latin edition of the Bible
- **496** The ruler of the Franks converts to Christianity
- **529** St. Benedict founds an order of monks
- **534** Scholars complete the Law Code of Justinian
- **732** Christians stop Arab expansion northward into France
- **c. 790–1000** Viking raids in western Europe
- **800** The pope crowns Charlemagne emperor of a revived Roman Empire

400 — **650** — **900**

World

- **c. 520** Indian mathematicians invent the decimal system
- **300–900** Maya civilization flourishes in Central America
- **c. 640–710** Arab Muslims conquer northern Africa

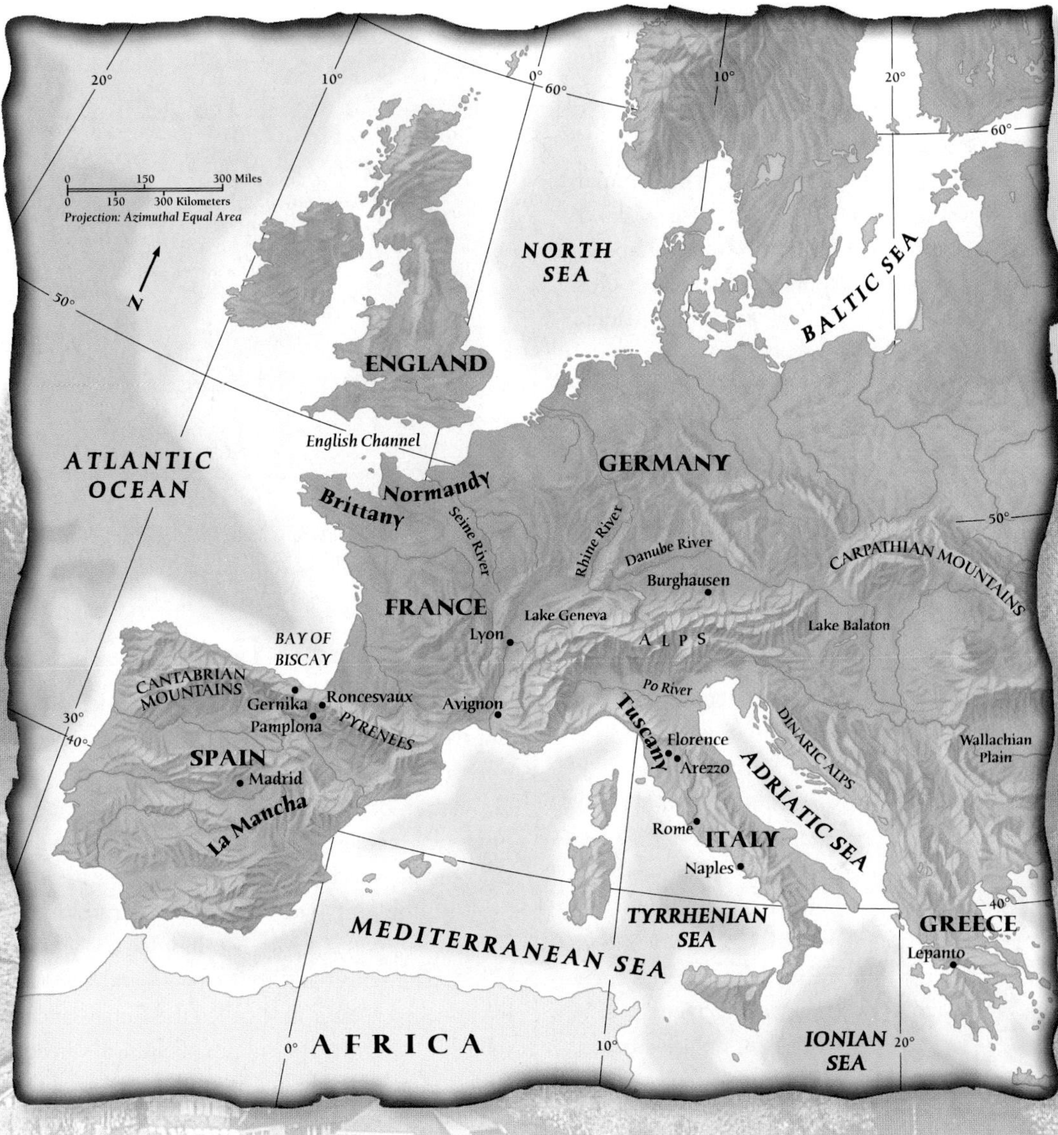

20° 10° 0° 60° 10° 20° 60°
0 150 300 Miles
0 150 300 Kilometers
Projection: Azimuthal Equal Area
N
50°
NORTH SEA
BALTIC SEA
ENGLAND
English Channel
ATLANTIC OCEAN
GERMANY
Normandy
Brittany
Seine River
Rhine River
Danube River
CARPATHIAN MOUNTAINS
50°
Burghausen
FRANCE
Lake Geneva
Lake Balaton
Lyon
ALPS
BAY OF BISCAY
CANTABRIAN MOUNTAINS
Gernika
Roncesvaux
Pamplona
PYRENEES
Avignon
Po River
Tuscany
DINARIC ALPS
30°
40°
Florence
Arezzo
Wallachian Plain
SPAIN
Madrid
La Mancha
ADRIATIC SEA
Rome
ITALY
Naples
40°
TYRRHENIAN SEA
GREECE
MEDITERRANEAN SEA
Lepanto
0° AFRICA
10°
IONIAN SEA
20°

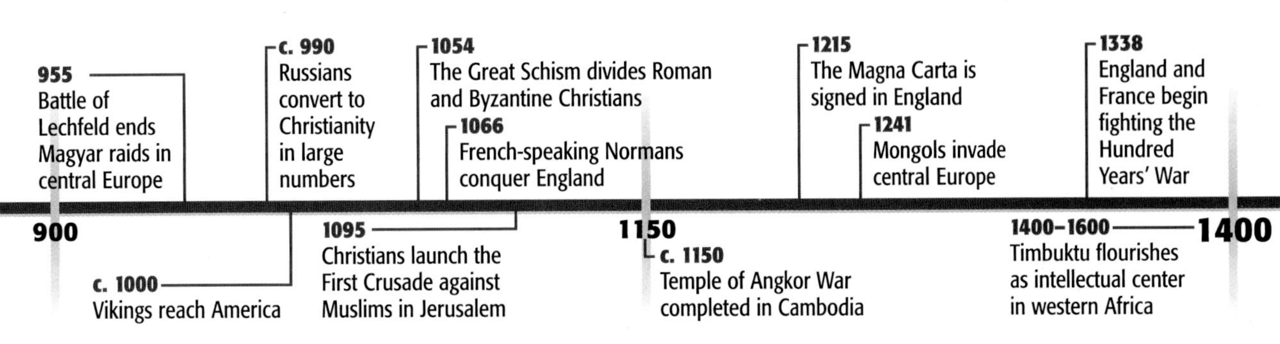
955
Battle of Lechfeld ends Magyar raids in central Europe
c. 990
Russians convert to Christianity in large numbers
1054
The Great Schism divides Roman and Byzantine Christians
1066
French-speaking Normans conquer England
1215
The Magna Carta is signed in England
1241
Mongols invade central Europe
1338
England and France begin fighting the Hundred Years' War
900
1150
1400
c. 1000
Vikings reach America
1095
Christians launch the First Crusade against Muslims in Jerusalem
c. 1150
Temple of Angkor War completed in Cambodia
1400–1600
Timbuktu flourishes as intellectual center in western Africa

Life in Society

Feudal Life

For hundreds of years after the fall of the Roman Empire, most Europeans were peasants, living in small villages and working year after year on strips of land controlled by nobles. The Christian church shaped every aspect of their lives. It taught them about God, helped them in times of need, educated their leaders, and provided unchanging rituals that gave life its structure.

While religion was powerful, government was not. Marauders, including some from far-away places in Scandinavia and central Asia, constantly threatened. To protect themselves and their peasants, nobles worked out a complex set of agreements. A powerful noble would grant portions of land, sometimes called a *feudum*, to those with less power. In exchange for the land, a lesser noble pledged his loyalty and military service. Through these arrangements, called feudalism, nobles created armed forces to provide some security for people in their homes.

Suit of armor, c. 1550.

The Wedding Banquet, c. 1540 (detail). Pieter Brueghel the Elder (Flanders).

Change and Growth

Around the year 1000, attacks by invaders from outside Europe began to decrease, and trade expanded. Use of a new style of plow boosted food production, and the population began growing. Cities revived, and the use of money increased. Village life became more linked to the outside world.

With these changes came a new spirit of inquiry, one bolstered by contact with Muslim, Jewish, and Byzantine Christian intellectuals. In the 1300s and 1400s, Europe experienced what is now called the Renaissance—a rebirth in studying the culture of classical Greece and Rome. Art, literature, music, and the study of the natural world flourished. Cities, trade, money, and science were transforming Europe into a modern region.

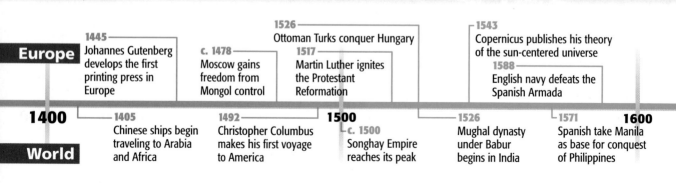

Europe

- **1445** Johannes Gutenberg develops the first printing press in Europe
- **c. 1478** Moscow gains freedom from Mongol control
- **1517** Martin Luther ignites the Protestant Reformation
- **1526** Ottoman Turks conquer Hungary
- **1543** Copernicus publishes his theory of the sun-centered universe
- **1588** English navy defeats the Spanish Armada

1400 — **1500** — **1600**

World

- **1405** Chinese ships begin traveling to Arabia and Africa
- **1492** Christopher Columbus makes his first voyage to America
- **c. 1500** Songhay Empire reaches its peak
- **1526** Mughal dynasty under Babur begins in India
- **1571** Spanish take Manila as base for conquest of Philippines

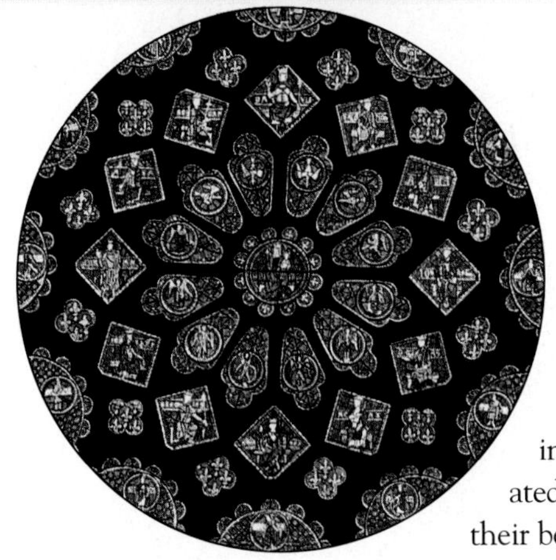

Rose window, Chartres Cathedral, France.

What People Believed

Rivals to Christianity

Christianity existed alongside several other belief systems in Europe. Many Christians maintained their traditional trust in spirits, spells, and omens. People might keep a lock of hair from a deceased ancestor to bring them good luck or interpret the flight of an owl as a sign of events to come. Such beliefs were tolerated as long as they remained on the level of folklore. Jews were often persecuted for their beliefs, especially in times of crisis, although popes frequently condemned such acts. Islam, introduced by the Moorish conquerors of Spain and the Turkish conquerors of the Balkans, left few followers in Europe when those empires retreated.

Splits in Christianity

Between the 1000s and the 1500s, European Christianity split into three broad groups:

- Orthodox Christians, strongest in Greece and Russia, followed the patriarch in Byzantium
- Catholics, strongest in Italy and France, followed the pope in Rome
- Protestants, strongest in Germany and Scandinavia, followed leaders such as Martin Luther and John Calvin

Active Reading Strategies

Reading the Time Line

1. Between what years did the Maya civilization flourish in Central America? How many years later did the Vikings reach America?
2. What year did Russians begin building St. Petersburg? About how many years before that did Moscow gain freedom from Mongol control?

Rise of Science

Inspired by classical Greece and Rome, European scholars after the 1300s focused increasingly on how this world works rather than on religious questions. People began to challenge long-accepted beliefs. The brilliant scholar Desiderius Erasmus edited and clarified the Greek text of the New Testament. Polish astronomer Nicholaus Copernicus analyzed data on the movements of the planets. In 1543 he shocked other Christian scholars with his theory that the sun—not the earth—was the center of the universe. Such claims shook the hold of tradition on the minds of people.

Erasmus

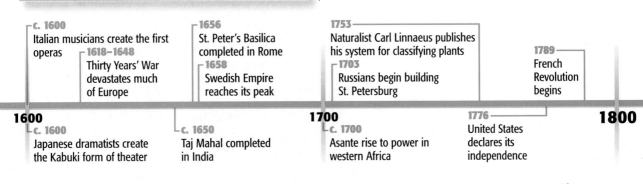

Time line: 1600 – 1700 – 1800

- c. 1600 Italian musicians create the first operas
- c. 1600 Japanese dramatists create the Kabuki form of theater
- 1618–1648 Thirty Years' War devastates much of Europe
- c. 1650 Taj Mahal completed in India
- 1656 St. Peter's Basilica completed in Rome
- 1658 Swedish Empire reaches its peak
- c. 1700 Asante rise to power in western Africa
- 1703 Russians begin building St. Petersburg
- 1753 Naturalist Carl Linnaeus publishes his system for classifying plants
- 1776 United States declares its independence
- 1789 French Revolution begins

Arts and Entertainment

Portrait of a lady writing, c. 1510.

Visual Arts

Prior to the Renaissance of the 1300s, painting was a minor art in Europe. Painters created colorful but flat two-dimensional images, usually biblical and other religious scenes. With the Renaissance, though, painters began to paint more secular scenes, often showing classical heroes or gods. More importantly, artists in Italy in the early 1400s revolutionized painting by figuring out how to show perspective. They learned to arrange images on a flat surface to provide a sense of depth, thus making their paintings more realistic and powerful. In the following centuries, artists such as Raphael, Rembrandt van Rijn, and Diego Velázquez created masterpieces that remain among the greatest achievements of European culture.

Like other artists, sculptors revived classical themes during and after the Renaissance. Beginning in the 1300s, Donatello, Michelangelo, and others created magnificent works that glorified the human form and portrayed human emotions.

Religious Architecture

Most of the greatest architectural achievements of this period were religious buildings. Romanesque architecture, dominant from 1000 to about 1150, emphasized rounded forms and arches. Large buildings in this style needed massive walls to support their weight. Builders of the Gothic period, which followed, developed pointed arches and other techniques that allowed them to use thinner walls, often featuring magnificent stained glass windows. Buildings in both styles were adorned with carvings inside and out, usually illustrating Bible stories.

Many people consider the buildings of the Renaissance to be the crowning achievement of all European architecture. Architects of this period (which spread throughout the continent from Italy beginning in the 1400s) combined Romanesque ideas and Gothic technology with Roman and ancient Greek models. Churches and other buildings in the Renaissance style often included Doric or Corinthian columns and other ancient elements in their decoration.

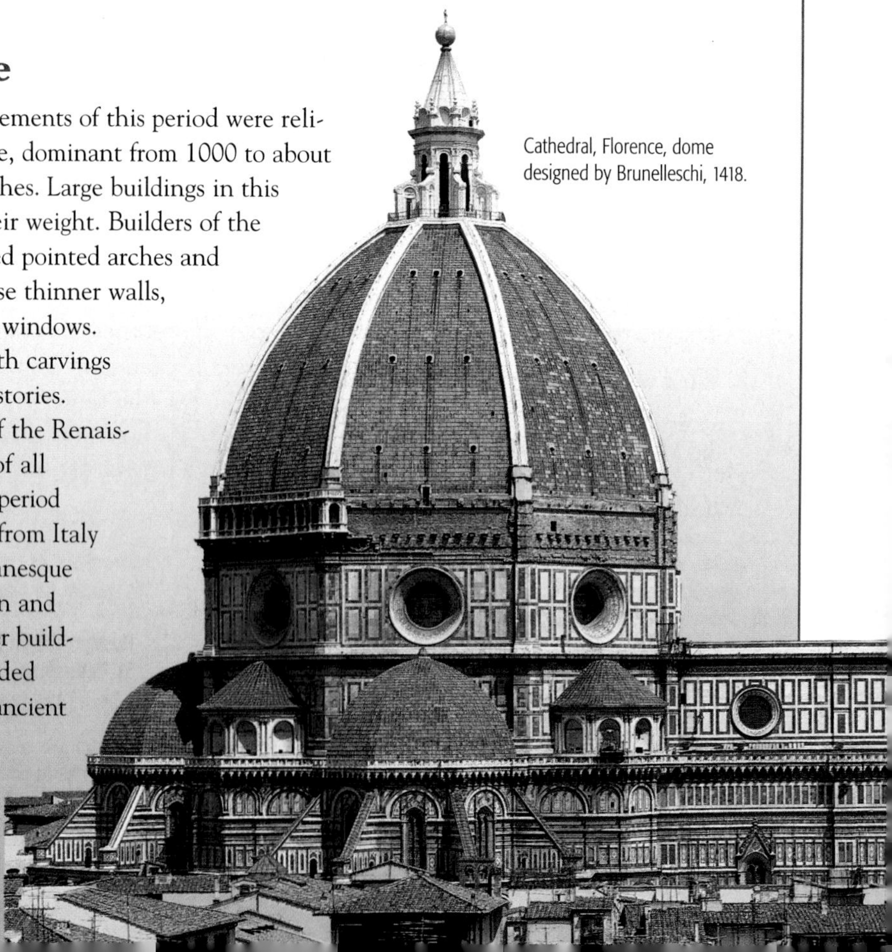

Cathedral, Florence, dome designed by Brunelleschi, 1418.

Music

Between 500 and 1800, European music became increasingly varied, complex, and secular. In the first part of this period, Gregorian chant was the leading style of European music. Chants were religious music, often sung by monks. Performers sang in unison or with simple harmonies. They used few instruments. Composers remained anonymous, and tunes evolved from one performance to the next. Over the following centuries, people became more accepting of a wider range of harmonies, as well as other changes:

- By the 1200s, minstrels traveling from one noble's court to another sang about love, politics, and other secular themes.
- By the 1300s, musicians played instruments such as the lute independently, rather than solely to accompany singing.
- By the 1500s, individual composers such as the Italian Giovanni Palestrina were becoming known.

After 1600 the pace of change quickened. New technology meant new instruments. For example, the modern piano was developed in the early 1700s. Composers experimented with new harmonies, rhythms, and forms. Both religiously inspired music and secular music flourished. The compositions of the 1700s, from Johann Sebastian Bach's intricate tunes to the operas and symphonies of Wolfgang Amadeus Mozart, remain staples of performances today.

Italian lira, 1511.

Ceremony in Renaissance costume, Siena.

Contests

In Europe in the 800s, nobles enjoyed horse racing, hunting, and jousting tournaments. Jousts were intended to encourage the skills needed in warfare. Though these competitions were not supposed to result in deaths, knights sometimes literally lost their heads in jousting matches. As foot soldiers armed with bows (and later guns) replaced mounted knights, tournaments became occasions for the display of costly armor and costumes.

The masses were banned from jousting. But they developed their own recreations. Some emphasized individual strength—wrestling, boxing, and weightlifting. Others were communal games, including an early form of soccer. Matches often became all-village events in which everyone joined in. Goals might be miles apart, in the centers of competing villages.

Critical Thinking

Connecting Cultures

1. Europeans in the Middle Ages played a variety of sports. What sports do we play today? List some important skills and values that our sports emphasize.
2. Make an oral presentation to the class comparing and contrasting sports today to those of the Middle Ages, including a discussion of the values emphasized by sports of each period.

Language and Literature

Writing About People

The first writers of early Europe were trained by the Christian church, and they usually wrote about Christianity. They produced lives of the saints, collections of sermons, poems in praise of moral behavior, and other religiously oriented works. But from the beginning, they also treated other topics. History, accounts of travel, and studies of plants and animals were produced. Many years passed, however, before works that were simply intended to be entertaining, rather than useful, were considered worthy of being written down.

July, from the *Tres Riches Heures du Duc de Berry.* c. 1400, Flanders.

Epic poems were among the earliest works to be recorded. Many of them had serious as well as entertaining content. The *Song of Roland*, for example, might inspire courage in its listeners, as well as serious discussion of Roland's tactics and leadership.

Lyric poetry was next to be written down, notably the love poems of the French *troubadours*. Their work influenced poets in other countries, such as the German *minnesingers*. In particular they influenced Italian poets; the combined influence of the troubadours and the poets of ancient Greece and Rome is apparent in the work of Petrarch and other poets of the Italian Renaissance.

Prose fiction was the last form to be recorded, but it was to become the most popular. From anecdotes and animal fables influenced by ancient sources to the artistically crafted short stories of Boccaccio and the beginnings of the novel (like *Don Quixote*, with its insight into human nature and character), fiction was to become Europe's dominant literary form.

influences

Although it is classified as a Germanic language, many of the most common words in English come from Romance languages. In particular, French, the language of the Norman invaders in 1066, left a lasting mark on English. Among the words that came into English from Old French in the Middle Ages are

- beef (from *buef*)
- river (from *rivere*)
- pork (from *porc*)
- poem (from *poeme*)
- forest (from *forest*)
- story (from *estorie*)
- mountain (from *montaigne*)

grasps that olifant that he will never lose,
strikes on the helm° beset with gems in gold,
shatters the steel, and the head, and the bones,
sent his two eyes flying out of his head,
dumped him over stretched out at his feet dead;
and said: "You nobody! how could you dare
lay hands on me—rightly or wrongly: how?
Who'll hear of this and not call you a fool?
Ah! the bell-mouth of the olifant is smashed,
the crystal and the gold fallen away."

123 **helm:** helmet.

Charlemagne in His Coronation Robes, 16th century. Dutch School after Albrecht Dürer. Oil on canvas, 213 x 113 cm. Kunsthistorisches Museum, Vienna.

Viewing the painting: This painting was done hundreds of years after Charlemagne's time. How has the artist tried to give a sense of the emperor's personality?

173

Roland the Count strikes down on a dark rock,
and the rock breaks, breaks more than I can tell,
and the blade grates, but Durendal will not break,
the sword leaped up, rebounded toward the sky.
The Count, when he sees that sword will not be broken,
softly, in his own presence, speaks the lament:
"Ah Durendal, beautiful, and most sacred,
the holy relics in this golden pommel!
Saint Peter's tooth and blood of Saint Basile,
a lock of hair of my lord Saint Denis,
and a fragment of blessed Mary's robe:
your power must not fall to the pagans,
you must be served by Christian warriors.
May no coward ever come to hold you!
It was with you I conquered those great lands
that Charles has in his keeping, whose beard is white,
the Emperor's lands, that make him rich and strong."

176

Count Roland lay stretched out beneath a pine;
he turned his face toward the land of Spain,
began to remember many things now:
how many lands, brave man, he had conquered;
and he remembered: sweet France, the men of his line,
remembered Charles, his lord, who fostered him:°
cannot keep, remembering, from weeping, sighing;
but would not be unmindful of himself:
he confesses his sins, prays God for mercy:
"Loyal Father, you who never failed us,
who resurrected Saint Lazarus from the dead,

154 **Charles . . . him:** Roland was brought up in the household of Charlemagne, his uncle.

Death of Roland During the Battle in the Valley of Roncesvalles, from *Les Grandes Chroniques des Rois de France.* 15th century, attributed to Jean Fouquet. French illuminated manuscript. Bibliothèque Nationale, Paris.

Viewing the painting: Does the scene here match your image of the death of Roland? Why or why not?

and saved your servant Daniel° from the lions:
now save the soul of me from every peril
for the sins I committed while I still lived."
Then he held out his right glove to his Lord:
Saint Gabriel took the glove from his hand.
He held his head bowed down upon his arm,
he is gone, his two hands joined, to his end.
Then God sent him his angel Cherubin
and Saint Michael, angel of the sea's Peril;
and with these two there came Saint Gabriel:°
they bear Count Roland's soul to Paradise.

160 Daniel: According to the Bible, Daniel was thrown into a den of lions as punishment for praying to God rather than to King Darius of Babylon. God kept the lions from harming Daniel.

164–169 Cherubin . . . Gabriel: The poet here depicts the cherubim—a group of angels whose function is to praise God—as Cherubin, a single angel. St. Michael the Archangel is the patron saint of sailors. The archangel Gabriel served as God's messenger.

Responding to Literature

Personal Response

Review the notes you made for the Reading Focus on page 790. In your opinion, is Roland a good example of a leader? Why or why not?

Analyzing Literature

Recall

1. What lines in the first stanza **foreshadow** the outcome of the battle?
2. What causes the quarrel between Roland and Oliver in stanzas 130–132? What reasoning does Turpin use to resolve it?
3. How does Ganelon try to mislead Charles in stanza 134?
4. In stanzas 170 and 173, what does Roland struggle to do before he dies?
5. In stanza 176, what does Roland pray for?

Interpret

6. **Hyperbole** is deliberate exaggeration for effect. How does the poet use this device in the opening stanza?
7. Why do you think that Roland rejected Oliver's advice to sound the olifant until it was too late?
8. Does Ganelon's criticism of Roland contain a grain of truth? Explain.
9. A **symbol** is a person, place, or thing that stands for something else in addition to itself (see page R12). How does Roland's sword, Durendal, function as a symbol?
10. When Roland is dying (stanzas 173 and 176), does he express any guilt or remorse for his arrogance? How do you think the poet wants us to regard Roland in these stanzas?

Evalute and Connect

11. Identify two examples of **repetition** in this selection and then comment on how effective you think this device is.
12. What is your opinion of the way in which the historical facts are altered in this poem? What are some reasons that could justify the author's use of poetic license?
13. If these events had taken place in modern times, do you think Roland would be celebrated as a hero? Why or why not?
14. On the basis of this excerpt, do you think the *Song of Roland* could be adapted successfully as a film? Why or why not?
15. Roland dies from sounding the horn to call for help, not from a wound suffered in battle. What do you think the poet means to imply?

Literary Criticism

"The narrative [of the *Song of Roland*] is as dull as that of the babbling Norman chroniclers," argues H. A. Taine. While Homer uses "grand abounding similes, . . . here we have facts, always facts, nothing but facts." Compare this selection to the excerpt from the *Iliad* on pages 213-226. Do you agree that the *Iliad* is more poetic? Answer in a brief essay, supporting your ideas with quotations from both texts.

Literary ELEMENTS

Epic

An **epic** is a long narrative poem that tells the story of a hero's adventures. Typical characteristics of the medieval epic are long formal speeches, supernatural elements, battle descriptions, and repetition of key words or phrases. Like the *Iliad,* the *Song of Roland* has an uncertain authorship; it stems from an oral tradition that combines history with myth and embodies the cultural values of the society in which the epic is composed.

1. List three character traits that qualify Roland as an epic hero.
2. Many epics include supernatural elements. The great storm and Durendal, the unbreakable sword, are examples. How effective do you think these elements are?

- See **Literary Terms Handbook,** p. R3.

Literature and Writing

Writing About Literature

Comparing Characters In a few paragraphs, compare and contrast Roland's and Oliver's concepts of what makes a good leader, taking into account Oliver's criticisms of Roland in stanza 131. Whose point of view do you find more convincing? Why? Answer these questions in your work, citing specific references from the selection.

Creative Writing

Narrating a Sequel How do you think Charlemagne will react when he finds out that Roland, Oliver, and their troops have died in battle? How will he punish Ganelon? Write an imaginative sequel to the story. Try to be faithful to the style and tone of these episodes from the epic. Then read your sequel to the class.

Extending Your Response

Literature Groups

Evaluating Roland's Code of Honor In your group, discuss how Roland's actions in the poem are the result of his concept of honor. How does his idea of honor compare with those of your group? Choose a spokesperson to defend Roland and a spokesperson to criticize him. Report both points of view to the rest of the class.

Learning for Life

Identifying Mediation Skills In stanza 132, Archbishop Turpin is a successful mediator between Roland and Oliver. What mediation skills does Turpin display? Make a list of the skills and character traits that you think would be important in mediating a quarrel in everyday life today.

Performing

Enacting an Episode Choose one of the episodes from the selection that you find especially dramatic and appealing. Together with a partner, rehearse speeches, gestures, and movements for a dramatic re-enactment of the scene you have chosen. Then perform your scene for the class.

Save your work for your portfolio.

VOCABULARY • Analogies

Analogies are comparisons based on relationships between words and ideas. Some analogies are based on definition.

haven : safety :: food : nourishment

A *haven* is by definition a place that provides *safety* as *food* provides *nourishment.*

PRACTICE Choose the word that best completes each analogy.

- For more on analogies, see **Communications Skills Handbook,** p. R77.

1. profanity : irreverence :: prayer :
   a. blasphemy
   b. answer
   c. piety
2. carpenter : build :: farmer :
   a. raze
   b. grow
   c. compose
3. illogic : fallacy :: bargain :
   a. discount
   b. reason
   c. indulge

Vo•cab•u•lar•y Skills

Homophones

The word *homophone* comes from the Greek *homos,* meaning "same," and *phone,* meaning "sound." Homophones are words that sound the same even though they differ in spelling, meaning, and origin. Take a look at this brief list of homophones:

board	bored	would	wood
sum	some	two	too
creek	creak	wear	ware
hear	here	write	right

Homophones may have very different meanings and are not interchangeable. For example, you convey a totally different meaning if you write "The *knight* fell suddenly" than if you write "The *night* fell suddenly." Also, using homophones such as *profit* instead of *prophet,* or *marshal* instead of *martial,* can give readers the impression that you are unaware of the difference in meaning or that you are careless.

If you use an incorrect homophone in your writing, don't expect your computer to help you fix it. Computer software that checks spelling as well as grammar can be helpful. However, since a computer can't discern the meaning you intend, it can't tell you that you have used *rain* when you should have used *reign,* because both of these words are spelled correctly. If you are unsure about which spelling to use for a word, refer to a dictionary, where you can compare the spelling with the appropriate meaning.

By carefully proofreading your work, you will eliminate any mistakes with homophones. Also, thinking about the meaning of each homophone will help you to use it correctly.

EXERCISE

If the underlined word is correct, write *Correct.* If it is a homophone for the correct word, write the correct word.

The bravest feet attempted by Roland and the other nights occurs when they are ambushed by four hundred thousand Saracens. Roland's close friend, Oliver, begs Roland to sound his horn to recall the mane body of the army. Roland refuses, crushing Oliver's hope to lesson their losses.

Finally, when only sixty of there twenty thousand men are still alive, Roland sounds his ivory horn. On the third blow, Roland's horn cracks and the vanes in Roland's neck burst. It is too late to save anyone, and Roland and Oliver dye as well.

When Charlemagne and his army arrive, they find everyone dead. To avenge their dead friends, Charlemagne and his army defeat the Saracens. Ganelon, whose duel loyalties led to the disaster, paid for the betrayal with his life.

FRANCE, c. 1200

Before You Read

Bisclavret: The Lay of the Werewolf

Meet Marie de France

"He to whom God has granted wisdom and eloquence in speech ought not to hide these gifts in silence, but gladly to make use of them."

Marie de France is considered one of the finest poets of her century. Although little is known for certain about her life, she was well educated and is thought to have been of aristocratic, perhaps noble, birth. She appears to have spent many years in England, and some historians speculate that she was the half-sister of Henry II, who ruled from 1154 to 1189.

Marie is best known for her *lais*, short narrative poems written in rhyming couplets. In these "lays," whose subjects range from love to adventure, Marie presents keenly observed pictures of western European court life in the twelfth century, including descriptions of the speech and behavior of the men and women of the nobility. A major theme appearing in these narratives is that of characters trapped in a hostile world from which they attempt to escape by seeking ideal love.

Marie de France lived in the late twelfth century.

Reading Focus

Have you ever known or read about a person who had a hidden or secret side to his or her personality?

Journal Write a brief entry in your journal about how you might react if you discovered someone's hidden personality trait.

Setting a Purpose Read to observe how various people react to surprising discoveries.

Building Background

Did You Know?

In folklore, a werewolf is a human being who turns into a wolf at times and devours animals or people. Legends about werewolves were common in European folklore. Medieval bandits and outlaws sometimes exploited the superstition by wearing wolfskins over their armor. The werewolf tradition became extremely popular in twentieth-century horror films, which also made extensive use of stories about vampires. The two traditions are related, since werewolves were thought to turn into vampires after death.

Courtly Love Tradition

In the Middle Ages in Europe, women were generally regarded as inferior to men, but the "courtly love" tradition idealized women. The lover, smitten by the beauty and virtue of his lady, worshipped her from afar, often without seriously expecting a relationship to develop. Marie de France wrote within this tradition, but she gave it a new twist by portraying women characters possessing their own individual personalities, frailties, and desires.

Aldebrande de Florence, Medical Treatise: the Heart. 14th century, French illuminated manuscript. Bibliotecha d'Ajuda, Lisbon, Portugal.

Bisclavret

The Lay of the Werewolf

Marie de France
Translated by Robert Hanning
and Joan Ferrante

Knight in Blue Tunic on Green Horse, from *Capodilista Codex.* Italian illuminated manuscript. Biblioteca Civica, Padua, Italy.

Since I am undertaking to compose *lais*,
I don't want to forget Bisclavret;°
In Breton,° the *lai*'s name is *Bisclavret*—
the Normans° call it *Garwaf [The Werewolf]*.
In the old days, people used to say—
and it often actually happened—
that some men turned into werewolves
and lived in the woods.
A werewolf is a savage beast;
while his fury is on him
he eats men, does much harm,
goes deep in the forest to live.
But that's enough of this for now:
I want to tell you about the Bisclavret.

In Brittany there lived a nobleman
whom I've heard marvelously praised;
a fine, handsome knight
who behaved nobly.
He was close to his lord,
and loved by all his neighbors.

---

2 ***Bisclavret*** (bēs′ klä vrā′)

3–4 ***Breton*** (bre′ tən) **was the language spoken by the people of Brittany in northwest France. The *Normans* lived just west of Brittany.**

He had an estimable wife,
one of lovely appearance;
he loved her and she him,
but one thing was very vexing to her:
during the week he would be missing
for three whole days, and she didn't know
what happened to him or where he went.
Nor did any of his men know anything about it.
One day he returned home
happy and delighted;
she asked him about it.
"My lord," she said, "and dear love,
I'd very much like to ask you one thing—
if I dared;
but I'm so afraid of your anger
that nothing frightens me more."
When he heard that, he embraced her,
drew her to him and kissed her.
"My lady," he said, "go ahead and ask!
There's nothing you could want to know,
that, if I knew the answer, I wouldn't tell you."
"By God," she replied, "now I'm cured!
My lord, on the days when you go away from me
I'm in such a state—
so sad at heart,
so afraid I'll lose you—
that if I don't get quick relief
I could die of this very soon.
Please, tell me where you go,
where you have been staying.
I think you must have a lover,
and if that's so, you're doing wrong."
"My dear," he said, "have mercy on me, for God's sake!
Harm will come to me if I tell you about this,
because I'd lose your love
and even my very self."
When the lady heard this
she didn't take it lightly;
she kept asking him,
coaxed and flattered him so much,
that he finally told her what happened to him—
he hid nothing from her.
"My dear, I become a werewolf:
I go off into the great forest,
in the thickest part of the woods,

and I live on the prey I hunt down."
When he had told her everything,
she asked further
whether he undressed or kept his clothes on [when he became a werewolf].
"Wife," he replied, "I go stark naked."
"Tell me, then, for God's sake, where your clothes are."
"That I won't tell you;
for if I were to lose them,
and then be discovered,
I'd stay a werewolf forever.
I'd be helpless
until I got them back.
That's why I don't want their hiding place to be known."
"My lord," the lady answered,
"I love you more than all the world;
you mustn't hide anything from me
or fear me in any way:
that doesn't seem like love to me.
What wrong have I done? For what sin of mine
do you mistrust me about anything?
Do the right thing and tell me!"
She harassed and bedeviled him so,°
that he had no choice but to tell her.
"Lady," he said, "near the woods,
beside the road that I use to get there,
there's an old chapel
that has often done me good service;
under a bush there is a big stone,
hollowed out inside;
I hide my clothes right there
until I'm ready to come home."
The lady heard this wonder
and turned scarlet from fear;
she was terrified of the whole adventure.
Over and over she considered
how she might get rid of him;
she never wanted to sleep with him again.
There was a knight of that region
who had loved her for a long time,
who begged for her love,
and dedicated himself to serving her.
She'd never loved him at all,
nor pledged her love to him,

87 She exhausted him by her persistent questioning.

but now she sent a messenger for him,
and told him her intention.
"My dear," she said, "cheer up!
I shall now grant you without delay
what you have suffered for;
you'll meet with no more refusals—
I offer you my love and my body;
make me your mistress!"
He thanked her graciously
and accepted her promise,
and she bound him to her by an oath.
Then she told him
how her husband went away and what happened to him;
she also taught him the precise path
her husband took into the forest,
and then she sent the knight to get her husband's clothes.
So Bisclavret was betrayed,
ruined by his own wife.
Since people knew he was often away from home
they all thought
this time he'd gone away forever.
They searched for him and made inquiries
but could never find him,
so they had to let matters stand.
The wife later married the other knight,
who had loved her for so long.
A whole year passed
until one day the king went hunting;
he headed right for the forest
where Bisclavret was.
When the hounds were unleashed,
they ran across Bisclavret;
the hunters and the dogs
chased him all day,
until they were just about to take him
and tear him apart,
at which point he saw the king
and ran to him, pleading for mercy.
He took hold of the king's stirrup,
kissed his leg and his foot.
The king saw this and was terrified;
he called his companions.
"My lords," he said, "come quickly!
Look at this marvel—
this beast is humbling itself to me.

Wolf-Beast, from *December: Book of Hours.* 15th century, Workshop of the Bedford Master. French illuminated manuscript. The Huntington Library, San Marino, CA.

Viewing the painting: Is this how you imagine Bisclavret under the spell? Why or why not?

It has the mind of a man, and it's begging me for mercy!
Chase the dogs away,
and make sure no one strikes it.
This beast is rational—he has a mind.
Hurry up: let's get out of here.
I'll extend my peace to the creature;°
indeed, I'll hunt no more today!"
Thereupon the king turned away.
Bisclavret followed him;
he stayed close to the king, and wouldn't go away;
he'd no intention of leaving him.
The king led him to his castle;
he was delighted with this turn of events,
for he'd never seen anything like it.
He considered the beast a great wonder
and held him very dear.
He commanded all his followers,
for the sake of their love for him, to guard Bisclavret well,
and under no circumstances to do him harm;
none of them should strike him;
rather, he should be well fed and watered.°
They willingly guarded the creature;
every day he went to sleep
among the knights, near the king.
Everyone was fond of him;
he was so noble and well behaved
that he never wished to do anything wrong.
Regardless of where the king might go,
Bisclavret never wanted to be separated from him;
he always accompanied the king.
The king became very much aware that the creature loved him.
Now listen to what happened next.
The king held a court;
to help him celebrate his feast
and to serve him as handsomely° as possible,
he summoned all the barons°
who held fiefs° from him.
Among the knights who went,
and all dressed up in his best attire,

---

159 The king offers the creature his royal protection.

174 Here, *watered* means that Bisclavret was given water to drink.

188 Here, *handsomely* means "abundantly" or "richly."

189–190 Under the feudal system of medieval Europe, a king granted parcels of land *(fiefs)* to nobles *(barons)*. In return, the nobles pledged to support and serve the king.

was the one who had married Bisclavret's wife.
He neither knew nor suspected
that he would find Bisclavret so close by.
As soon as he came to the palace
Bisclavret saw him,
ran toward him at full speed,
sank his teeth into him, and started to drag him down.
He would have done him great damage
if the king hadn't called him off,
and threatened him with a stick.
Twice that day he tried to bite the knight.
Everyone was extremely surprised,
since the beast had never acted that way
toward any other man he had seen.
All over the palace people said
that he wouldn't act that way without a reason:
that somehow or other, the knight had mistreated Bisclavret,
and now he wanted his revenge.
And so the matter rested
until the feast was over
and until the barons took their leave of the king
and started home.
The very first to leave,
to the best of my knowledge,
was the knight whom Bisclavret had attacked.
It's no wonder the creature hated him.
Not long afterward,
as the story leads me to believe,
the king, who was so wise and noble,
went back to the forest
where he had found Bisclavret,
and the creature went with him.
That night, when he finished hunting,
he sought lodging out in the countryside.
The wife of Bisclavret heard about it,
dressed herself elegantly,
and went the next day to speak with the king,
bringing rich presents for him.
When Bisclavret saw her coming,
no one could hold him back;
he ran toward her in a rage.
Now listen to how well he avenged himself!
He tore the nose off her face.
What worse thing could he have done to her?
Now men closed in on him from all sides;

they were about to tear him apart,
when a wise man said to the king,
"My lord, listen to me!
This beast has stayed with you,
and there's not one of us
who hasn't watched him closely,
hasn't traveled with him often.
He's never touched anyone,
or shown any wickedness,
except to this woman.
By the faith that I owe you,
he has some grudge against her,
and against her husband as well.
This is the wife of the knight
whom you used to like so much,
and who's been missing for so long—
we don't know what became of him.
Why not put this woman to torture°
and see if she'll tell you
why the beast hates her?
Make her tell what she knows!
We've seen many strange things
happen in Brittany!"
The king took his advice;
he detained the knight.
At the same time he took the wife
and subjected her to torture;
out of fear and pain
she told all about her husband:
how she had betrayed him
and taken away his clothes;
the story he had told her
about what happened to him and where he
went;
and how after she had taken his clothes
he'd never been seen in his land again.
She was quite certain
that this beast was Bisclavret.
The king demanded the clothes;
whether she wanted to or not
she sent home for them,

The Norse God Tyr Losing His Hand to the Bound Wolf, Fenrir. Danish illuminated manuscript. Royal Library, Copenhagen, Denmark.

Viewing the art: What parts of the selection does this scene remind you of?

255 During this time, *torture* was an acceptable means of gathering information. Sometimes testimony was not considered acceptable in court unless the witness had been tortured.

and had them brought to Bisclavret.
When they were put down in front of him
he didn't even seem to notice them;
the king's wise man—
the one who had advised him earlier—
said to him, "My lord, you're not doing it right.
This beast wouldn't, under any circumstances,
in order to get rid of his animal form,
put on his clothes in front of you;
you don't understand what this means:
he's just too ashamed to do it here.
Have him led to your chambers
and bring the clothes with him;
then we'll leave him alone for a while.
If he turns into a man, we'll know about it."
The king himself led the way
and closed all the doors on him.
After a while he went back,
taking two barons with him;
all three entered the king's chamber.
On the king's royal bed
they found the knight asleep.
The king ran to embrace him.
He hugged and kissed him again and again.
As soon as he had the chance,
the king gave him back all his lands;
he gave him more than I can tell.
He banished the wife,
chased her out of the country.
She went into exile with the knight
with whom she had betrayed her lord.
She had several children
who were widely known
for their appearance:
several women of the family
were actually born without noses,
and lived out their lives noseless.

The adventure that you have heard
really happened, no doubt about it.
The *lai* of Bisclavret was made
so it would be remembered forever.

Responding to Literature

Personal Response

Review the journal entry you made for the Reading Focus on page 800. How did you react to the changes Bisclavret underwent throughout the poem?

Analyzing Literature

Recall and Interpret

1. What arguments does the wife use in lines 32–52 to persuade the nobleman to divulge his secret? What do you think these arguments reveal about her character?
2. In what way does the wife betray her husband? Why do you think she does this?
3. Why does the king decide to bring the wolf back to his court?
4. How does Bisclavret revenge himself on his unfaithful wife?
5. What advice does the wise man offer to the king in lines 240–260?

Evaluate and Connect

6. Can you find any justification for the wife's actions in the poem? Explain your answer.
7. Would you describe the king as a wise and fair ruler? Explain.
8. In your opinion, is the wife's punishment just? Is it too severe? Give reasons for your answer.
9. The existence of werewolves is taken for granted in this narrative. How does this folk belief, or superstition, affect your appreciation of the poem?
10. Does this poem contain a **theme** or message for people today? If so, what is it?

Literary ELEMENTS

Suspense

Suspense is the quality in a story that makes the reader uncertain or tense about the outcome of events. In one kind of suspense, readers do not know what will happen next. In a second type, readers either know the plot or can make a reliable prediction about the general outcome, but they still wonder *how* the events will unfold.

1. At several strategic places in the poem, the narrator interrupts the story to address the reader directly (line 185, for example). In your opinion, do these intrusions help or hinder the suspense? Explain.
2. Does the wise man's speech in lines 240–260 create suspense? If so, how?

- See **Literary Terms Handbook,** p. R12.

Extending Your Response

Literature and Writing

Analyzing Character Motivation A character's **motivation** is the set of reasons he or she acts in a certain way. In a brief essay, identify the motivation of each of the three main characters: Bisclavret, his wife, and the king. Which character's motives do you find the most realistic or believable? The most praiseworthy? The most blameworthy? Support your answers with specific details.

Listening and Speaking

The Werewolf in Movies Use a movie or video guide to identify one or two appropriately rated movies that feature werewolves. Rent the videos or borrow them from a library. Join with a small group to watch the movies. Then hold a roundtable discussion comparing and contrasting the movie stories with "Bisclavret."

Save your work for your portfolio.

MEDIA connection

Web Site

During the Middle Ages, many people lived in castles. Today living in castles is not so common, but you can visit castles on the Internet.

Burghausen Castle

Address: http://www.teleport.com/~ludwig/1info.htm

Our family feels hands down that one of the most authentic, realistic, and wonderful castles that we have experienced is Burghausen Castle in beautiful southern Germany (Bavaria). It is over a kilometer in length, has six courtyards, several moats with wooden drawbridges, a Kemenate (Ladies' Bower), a Durnitz (Knights' Hall), and of course the Duke's residence.

Burghausen Castle.

It is very easy to get lost in daydreams as you meander through each courtyard. You can visualize the medieval activity: the craftsmen working on leather, the blacksmith shoeing horses, women looking over fruits and vegetables while watching their children play, etc. Yet as you venture further, at times you feel the cold, the dark, the seriousness, and the mystery of the Middle Ages.

This castle seems not to be the usual tourist castle because today many families live within most of the courtyards. It is estimated that about 150 people currently live within the castle walls. They come and go as you are exploring; hence, the castle is still functional, alive and bustling with everyday activity. Kids are playing ball and hide-and-seek, riding bikes, and going off to school. Ladies are going off to work, tending to their flowers, gardens, and walkways, while men are fixing cars, shoveling snow, or relaxing and reading the newspaper outside. We felt thankful that these people were willing to share their castle with us.

Today the Free State of Bavaria owns the castle. Its operation is maintained by the City Office for the Maintenance of Castles and Lakes. It appears that great care and pride over hundreds of years have preserved this truly medieval castle. To us, not only is Burghausen Castle a piece of history and an architectural masterpiece, but it is still very much alive. It is welcoming, authentic, comfortable, beautiful, and yet mysterious.

Analyzing Media

1. How many courtyards does this castle contain? How many people live in the castle today?
2. Would you like to live in a castle? Discuss the pros and cons of castle life.

Before You Read

from the *Inferno* from the *Divine Comedy*

Meet Dante Alighieri

"Consider your origin; you were not born to live like brutes, but to follow virtue and knowledge."

As a young man, Dante was a public figure in his native Florence. In 1302 a rival group gained power, and Dante was banished from Florence and forced to live the rest of his life in exile. Ten years later, he took revenge in "Inferno," placing several of his old political enemies in hell, identifying them by name, and describing their sins and torments in graphic detail.

Much of Dante's love poetry was inspired by a beautiful young woman named Beatrice, whom he met only twice—in 1274 when he was nine years old and again nine years later. She became for him the symbol of ideal love, and in the *Divine Comedy* she represents divine revelation as she conducts Dante through paradise.

Dante was the first major writer to use the modern Italian language, instead of traditional Latin, in his major works. In doing so, he helped create a unified national culture in Italy.

Dante was born in 1265 and died in 1321.

Reading Focus

In your opinion, how should wrongdoing be treated?

Chart It! Create a chart showing four or five misdeeds with appropriate reactions to each.

Setting a Purpose Read to find out how Dante portrayed the punishment of wrongdoers in "Inferno."

Building Background

Did You Know?

Dante's epic, the *Divine Comedy,* is divided into three sections: "Inferno," "Purgatorio," and "Paradiso." The narrator is Dante himself, guided through the first two regions by the Roman poet Virgil, whom Dante admired greatly. Dante was a devout Christian. However, he attacked the corruption of the Roman Catholic Church of his time; in "Inferno" he even condemned seven popes to damnation.

Dante's Cosmology

The modern scientific concept of an immense universe containing billions of galaxies strewn across the vastness of empty space was unknown to Dante. He believed in a relatively small cosmos, with the earth at its center. Just beyond the visible stars was Heaven, where God presided on a throne, and Satan's domain in hell was at the core of the earth. Human beings were on the surface of the earth, poised between the two warring kingdoms that contested for possession of the human soul.

Last Judgement, detail from *Table of the Seven Deadly Sins.* Hieronymus Bosch (Netherlands, c. 1450–1516). Oil on wood. Museo del Prado, Madrid, Spain.

from the Inferno
from the Divine Comedy

Dante Alighieri

Translated by John Ciardi

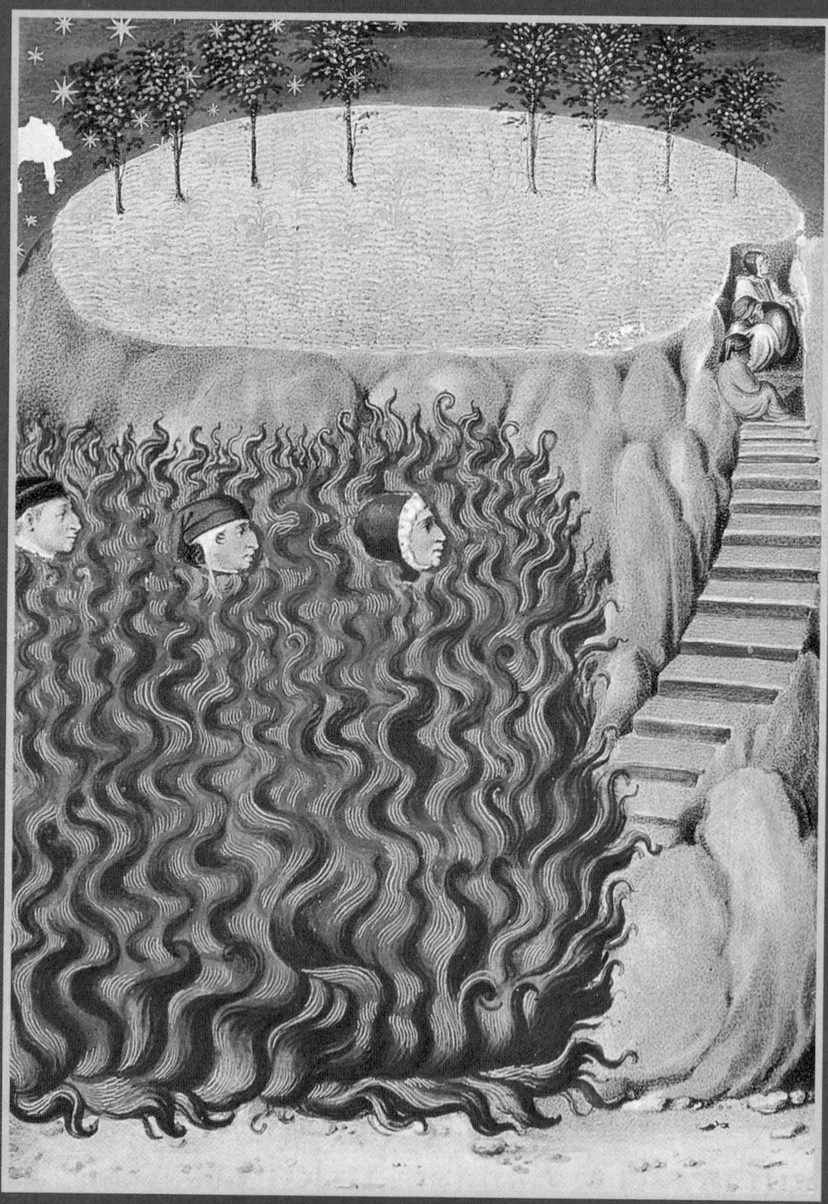

Inferno, Purgatory, and Paradise with the Poets, from *Divine Comedy.* 14th century, Italian illuminated manuscript. British Museum, London. What places can you identify in this painting? Explain.

Canto V

CIRCLE TWO . . . . *The Carnal*

The Poets enter the Second Circle. Here sits Minos, the dread and semi-bestial judge of the damned who assigns to each soul its eternal torment. They find themselves on a dark ledge swept by a great whirlwind, which spins within it the souls of the Carnal, whose sin was to abandon themselves to the tempest of their passions.

So we went down to the second ledge alone;
a smaller circle of so much greater pain
the voice of the damned rose in a bestial° moan.

There Minos sits, grinning, grotesque, and hale.°
He examines each lost soul as it arrives
and delivers his verdict with his coiling tail.

That is to say, when the ill-fated soul
appears before him it confesses all,
and that grim sorter of the dark and foul

decides which place in Hell shall be its end,
then wraps his twitching tail about himself
one coil for each degree it must descend.

The soul descends and others take its place:
each crowds in its turn to judgment, each confesses,
each hears its doom and falls away through space.

"O you who come into this camp of woe,"
cried Minos when he saw me turn away
without awaiting his judgment, "watch where you go

once you have entered here, and to whom you turn!
Do not be misled by that wide and easy passage!"°
And my Guide° to Him: "That is not your concern;

it is his fate to enter every door.
This has been willed where what is willed must be,
and is not yours to question. Say no more."

3 **bestial:** animal-like.

4 **hale:** healthy and vigorous—an ironic description, given the character of the place where Minos judges.

20 **wide and easy passage:** This phrase is a reference to the Book of Matthew in the Bible where Jesus warns that "wide is the gate, and broad is the way, that leadeth to destruction."

21 **Guide:** the Roman poet Virgil, also referred to as the Poet and the Master.

Now the choir of anguish, like a wound,
strikes through the tortured air. Now I have come
to Hell's full lamentation,° sound beyond sound.

I came to a place stripped bare of every light
and roaring on the naked dark like seas
wracked by a war of winds. Their hellish flight

of storm and counterstorm through time foregone,°
sweeps the souls of the damned before its charge.
Whirling and battering it drives them on,

and when they pass the ruined gap of Hell
through which we had come, their shrieks begin anew.
There they blaspheme° the power of God eternal.

And this, I learned, was the never ending flight
of those who sinned in the flesh, the carnal° and lusty
who betrayed reason to their appetite.

As the wings of wintering starlings bear them on
in their great wheeling° flights, just so the blast
wherries° these evil souls through time foregone.

Here, there, up, down, they whirl and, whirling, strain
with never a hope of hope to comfort them,
not of release, but even of less pain.

As cranes go over sounding their harsh cry,
leaving the long streak of their flight in air,
so come these spirits, wailing as they fly.

And watching their shadows lashed by wind, I cried:
"Master, what souls are these the very air
lashes with its black whips from side to side?"

"The first of these whose history you would know,"
he answered me, "was Empress of many tongues.
Mad sensuality corrupted her so

that to hide the guilt of her debauchery
she licensed all depravity alike,
and lust and law were one in her decree.

27 lamentation: wailing out of grief and pain.

31 time foregone: time past.

36 blaspheme (blas fēm′)**:** to insult or show a lack of reverence for God.

38 carnal: interested only in physical pleasure.

41 wheeling: to fly around in circles.

42 wherries: transports quickly, as in a light, low rowboat.

She is Semiramis° of whom the tale is told
how she married Ninus and succeeded him
to the throne of that wide land the Sultans° hold.

The other is Dido;° faithless to the ashes
of Sichaeus, she killed herself for love.
The next whom the eternal tempest lashes

is sense-drugged Cleopatra. See Helen° there,
from whom such ill arose. And great Achilles,°
who fought at last with love in the house of prayer.

And Paris. And Tristan."° As they whirled above
he pointed out more than a thousand shades
of those torn from the mortal life by love.

I stood there while my Teacher one by one
named the great knights and ladies of dim time;
and I was swept by pity and confusion.

At last I spoke: "Poet, I should be glad
to speak a word with those two swept together°
so lightly on the wind and still so sad."

And he to me: "Watch them. When next they pass,
call to them in the name of love that drives
and damns them here. In that name they will pause."

Thus, as soon as the wind in its wild course
brought them around, I called: "O wearied souls!
if none forbid it, pause and speak to us."

As mating doves that love calls to their nest
glide through the air with motionless raised wings,
borne by the sweet desire that fills each breast—

Just so those spirits turned on the torn sky
from the band where Dido whirls across the air;
such was the power of pity in my cry.

"O living creature, gracious, kind, and good,
going this pilgrimage through the sick night,
visiting us who stained the earth with blood,

58 Semiramis (sə mir′ ə mis): According to legend, Semiramis built Babylon. Her sin was her love affair with her own son.

60 Sultans: Muslim rulers of the area that was Babylon in Dante's day.

61 Dido: The queen of Carthage, unfaithful to the memory of her dead husband Sichaeus, fell in love with Aeneas; when he abandoned her, she killed herself.

64 Helen: the queen of Sparta. Helen left her husband Menelaus for **Paris** (line 67), the prince of Troy.

65 Achilles: In the Trojan War, the Greek hero Achilles fell so deeply in love with Polyxena, a Trojan, that he planned to switch sides. On his way to marry Polyxena, he was killed by Paris.

67 Tristan: In a famous love story of the Middle Ages, Tristan loved and died with Isolde, the wife of his uncle, King Mark.

74 those two swept together: The narrator sees Paolo and Francesca suffering together and wants to speak to them. In 1275 Francesca entered into a political marriage with Giovanni Malatesta. She fell in love with Giovanni's younger brother, Paolo, who was himself married. Their affair continued for several years, until Giovanni discovered them together and killed them.

were the King of Time° our friend, we would pray His peace
on you who have pitied us. As long as the wind
will let us pause, ask of us what you please.

The town where I was born lies by the shore
where the Po° descends into its ocean rest
with its attendant streams in one long murmur.

Love, which in gentlest hearts will soonest bloom
seized my lover with passion for that sweet body
from which I was torn unshriven° to my doom.

Love, which permits no loved one not to love,
took me so strongly with delight in him
that we are one in Hell, as we were above.

Love led us to one death. In the depths of Hell
Caïna° waits for him who took our lives."
This was the piteous tale they stopped to tell.

And when I had heard those world-offended lovers
I bowed my head. At last the Poet spoke:
"What painful thoughts are these your lowered brow
covers?"

When at length I answered, I began: "Alas!
What sweetest thoughts, what green and young desire
led these two lovers to this sorry pass."

Then turning to those spirits once again,
I said: "Francesca, what you suffer here
melts me to tears of pity and of pain.

But tell me: in the time of your sweet sighs
by what appearances found love the way
to lure you to his perilous paradise?"

And she: "The double grief of a lost bliss
is to recall its happy hour in pain.
Your Guide and Teacher knows the truth of this.

But if there is indeed a soul in Hell
to ask of the beginning of our love
out of his pity, I will weep and tell:

91 King of Time: God.

95 Po: Italy's longest river. It empties into the ocean at the northern end of the Adriatic Sea.

99 unshriven: In Roman Catholic belief, to die unshriven—without confessing one's sins and receiving God's forgiveness—means that the soul carries its sins into the afterlife.

104 Caïna: the ring of Hell reserved for people who commit treachery against their relatives.

Paolo and Francesca. Edward Charles Hallé (Great Britain, 1846–1919). Oil on canvas, 73½ x 48¼ in. Private collection.

Viewing the painting: What does the painting tell you about this couple's relationship?

On a day for dalliance° we read the rhyme
of Lancelot,° how love had mastered him.
We were alone with innocence and dim time.

Pause after pause that high old story drew
our eyes together while we blushed and paled;
but it was one soft passage overthrew

our caution and our hearts. For when we read
how her fond smile was kissed by such a lover,
he who is one with me alive and dead

breathed on my lips the tremor of his kiss.
That book, and he who wrote it, was a pander.°
That day we read no further." As she said this,

the other spirit, who stood by her, wept
so piteously, I felt my senses reel
and faint away with anguish. I was swept

by such a swoon as death is, and I fell,
as a corpse might fall, to the dead floor of Hell.

124 dalliance: wasting time in mindless pleasure; here, it means romantic love-making.

125 Lancelot: chief among the knights of the Round Table, he fell in love with King Arthur's wife.

134 pander: to deliberately appeal to people's self-indulgent side.

Canto XXXIV

NINTH CIRCLE: COCYTUS . . . . ***Compound Fraud***
ROUND FOUR: JUDECCA . . . . ***The Treacherous to Their Masters***

THE CENTER . . . . ***Satan***

As the Poets face the last depth, they see Satan in the distance, his great wings beating like a windmill. It is their beating that is the source of the icy wind of Cocytus, the exhalation of all evil. All about him in the ice are strewn the sinners of the last round. These are the *Treacherous to Their Masters.* It is impossible to speak to them, and the poets move on to observe Satan.

"On march the banners of the King of Hell,"
my Master said. "Toward us. Look straight ahead:
can you make him out at the core of the frozen shell?"

Like a whirling windmill seen afar at twilight,
or when a mist has risen from the ground—
just such an engine° rose upon my sight

stirring up such a wild and bitter wind
I cowered for shelter at my Master's back,
there being no other windbreak I could find.

I stood now where the souls of the last class
(with fear my verses tell it) were covered wholly;
they shone below the ice like straws in glass.

Some lie stretched out; others are fixed in place
upright, some on their heads, some on their soles;
another, like a bow, bends foot to face.

When we had gone so far across the ice
that it pleased my Guide to show me the foul creature
that once had worn the grace of Paradise,°

he made me stop, and, stepping aside, he said:
"Now see the face of Dis!° This is the place
where you must arm your soul against all dread."

Do not ask, Reader, how my blood ran cold
and my voice choked up with fear. I cannot write it:
this is a terror that cannot be told.

I did not die, and yet I lost life's breath:
imagine for yourself what I became,
deprived at once of both my life and death.

The Emperor of the Universe of Pain
jutted his upper chest above the ice;
and I am closer in size to the great mountain

the Titans° make around the central pit,
than they to his arms. Now, starting from this part,
imagine the whole that corresponds to it!

If he was once as beautiful as now
he is hideous, and still turned on his Maker,
well may he be the source of every woe!

6 engine: machine.

17–18 foul creature . . . Paradise: According to the Bible, Satan originally was the highest ranking and most beautiful of God's angels. (See also lines 34–35.)

20 Dis: Satan.

31 Titans: according to Greek mythology, a race of giants who ruled the earth until they were overthrown by Zeus and the other gods of Olympus. The speaker says that Satan is so huge that next to him the Titans look smaller than a human being would look next to a Titan.

With what a sense of awe I saw his head
towering above me! for it had three faces:
one was in front, and it was fiery red;

the other two, as weirdly wonderful,°
merged with it from the middle of each shoulder
to the point where all converged at the top of the skull;

the right was something between white and bile;°
the left was about the color one observes
on those who live along the banks of the Nile.

Under each head two wings rose terribly,
their span proportioned to so gross° a bird:
I never saw such sails upon the sea.

They were not feathers—their texture and their form
were like a bat's wings—and he beat them so
that three winds blew from him in one great storm:

it is these winds that freeze all Cocytus.
He wept from his six eyes, and down three chins
the tears ran mixed with bloody froth and pus.

In every mouth he worked a broken sinner
between his rake-like teeth. Thus he kept three
in eternal pain at his eternal dinner.

For the one in front the biting seemed to play
no part at all compared to the ripping: at times
the whole skin of his back was flayed° away.

"That soul that suffers most," explained my Guide,
"is Judas Iscariot,° he who kicks his legs
on the fiery chin and has his head inside.

Of the other two, who have their heads thrust forward,
the one who dangles down from the black face
is Brutus:° note how he writhes without a word.

And there, with the huge and sinewy arms, is the soul
of Cassius.—But the night is coming on
and we must go, for we have seen the whole."

40 **wonderful:** here, literally—filling a person with wonder or amazement.

43 **bile:** a fluid secreted by the liver, yellow or yellowish-green in color.

47 **gross:** of both large size and distasteful character.

60 **flayed:** having the skin ripped from it.

62 **Judas Iscariot:** one of Jesus' disciples. For a payment of thirty pieces of silver, he betrayed his master, showing the authorities where Jesus could be found and captured. Later, remorseful for this act, he hanged himself.

66 **Brutus:** a praetor (magistrate) in Rome. He and **Cassius** (line 68), once a general in the Roman army, led the plot to assassinate Julius Caesar in 44 B.C.

Then, as be bade, I clasped his neck, and he,
watching for a moment when the wings
were opened wide, reached over dexterously

and seized the shaggy coat of the king demon;
then grappling matted hair and frozen crusts
from one tuft to another, clambered down.

When we had reached the joint where the great thigh°
merges into the swelling of the haunch,
my Guide and Master, straining terribly,

turned his head to where his feet had been
and began to grip the hair as if he were climbing;
so that I thought we moved toward Hell again.

"Hold fast!" my Guide said, and his breath came shrill
with labor and exhaustion. "There is no way
but by such stairs to rise above such evil."

At last he climbed out through an opening
in the central rock, and he seated me on the rim;
then joined me with a nimble backward spring.

I looked up, thinking to see Lucifer°
as I had left him, and I saw instead
his legs projecting high into the air.

Now let all those whose dull minds are still vexed
by failure to understand what point it was
I had passed through, judge if I was perplexed.

"Get up. Up on your feet," my Master said.
"The sun already mounts to middle tierce,°
and a long road and hard climbing lie ahead."

It was no hall of state we had found there,
but a natural animal pit hollowed from rock
with a broken floor and a close and sunless air.

"Before I tear myself from the Abyss,"°
I said when I had risen, "O my Master,
explain to me my error in all this:

76 great thigh: The travelers are at Satan's hip.

88 Lucifer: light-bearer. The name is a reminder that Satan once had a place of honor among the angels of Heaven.

95 middle tierce: The Roman Catholic Church divided the day into canonical hours. Tierce (or terce) named the period from 6:00 A.M. to 9:00 A.M., so middle tierce would be about 7:30 A.M. As they have crossed Satan, the travelers have moved ahead half a day (it was twilight in line 68; see also line 120).

100 Abyss (ə bis′): a very deep gulf or pit. The Bible uses the term more specifically to refer to the hellish depths of the earth.

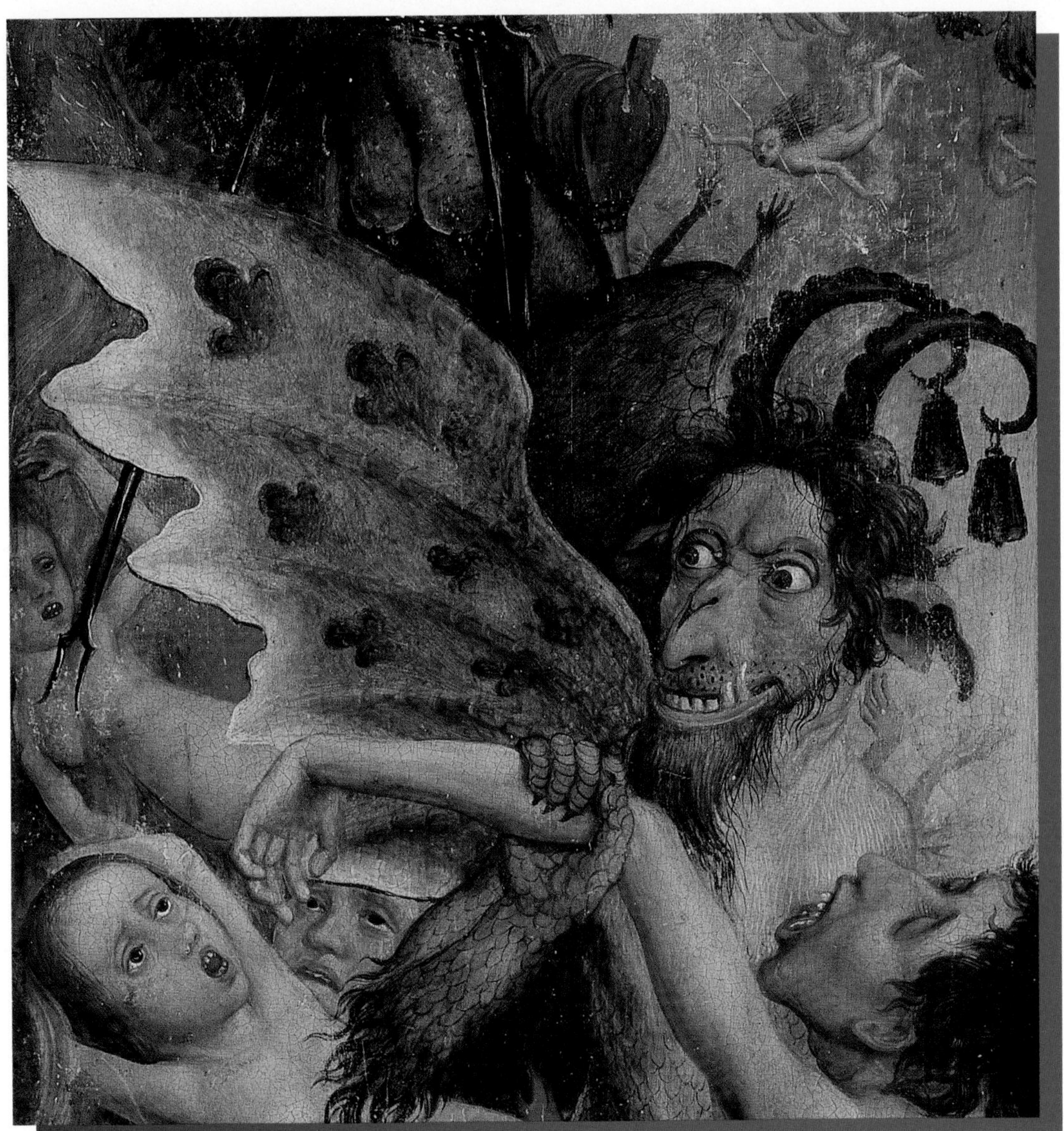

Hell (The Inferno), 15th century (detail). Flemish School. Oil on wood panel. Correr Civic Museum, Venice, Italy.
Viewing the painting: What qualities of Satan did this artist want to portray? Explain.

where is the ice? and Lucifer—how has he
been turned from top to bottom: and how can the sun
have gone from night to day so suddenly?"

And he to me: "You imagine you are still
on the other side of the center where I grasped
the shaggy flank of the Great Worm of Evil

which bores through the world—you *were* while I climbed down,
but when I turned myself about, you passed
the point to which all gravities are drawn.

You are under the other hemisphere where you stand;
the sky above us is the half opposed
to that which canopies the great dry land.

Under the midpoint of that other sky
the Man° who was born sinless and who lived
beyond all blemish, came to suffer and die.

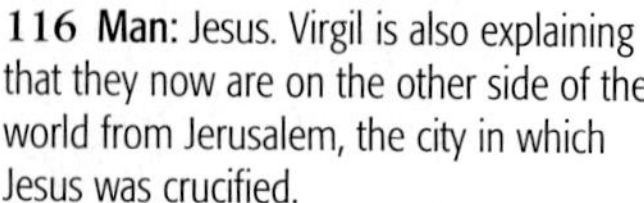

116 Man: Jesus. Virgil is also explaining that they now are on the other side of the world from Jerusalem, the city in which Jesus was crucified.

You have your feet upon a little sphere
which forms the other face of the Judecca.
There it is evening when it is morning here.

And this gross Fiend and Image of all Evil
who made a stairway for us with his hide
is pinched and prisoned in the ice-pack still.

On this side he plunged down from heaven's height,
and the land that spread here once hid in the sea
and fled North to our hemisphere for fright;

and it may be that moved by that same fear,
the one peak° that still rises on this side
fled upward leaving this great cavern here."

128 one peak: the Mount of Purgatory. In Roman Catholic belief, souls spend a time of suffering in Purgatory and thus are cleansed to enter Heaven.

Down there, beginning at the further bound
of Beelzebub's° dim tomb, there is a space
not known by sight, but only by the sound

131 Beelzebub: another name of Satan—literally, lord of the flies.

of a little stream° descending through the hollow
it has eroded from the massive stone
in its endlessly entwining lazy flow."

133 little stream: This may refer to the river Lethe (lē′ thē), the stream from which souls drank to forget the sorrows of their earthly lives. If so, Virgil may be suggesting that the stream carries memories of sin away from purified souls and into Hell.

My Guide and I crossed over and began
to mount that little known and lightless road
to ascend into the shining world again.

He first, I second, without thought of rest
we climbed the dark until we reached the point
where a round opening brought in sight the blest

and beauteous shining of the Heavenly cars.°
And we walked out once more beneath the Stars.

142 cars: chariots; figuratively, Dante is referring to the planets and stars.

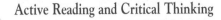

Responding to Literature

Personal Response

How did you react to the descriptions of the suffering sinners? Which description made the most vivid impression upon you? Why?

Analyzing Literature

Recall

1. In Canto V, what punishment do the souls suffer? For what sin?
2. What were Paolo and Francesca reading that led them astray?
3. At the beginning of Canto XXXIV, how are the sinners punished?
4. Who are the three sinners trapped in the mouths of Lucifer? Which sinner suffers most?
5. Before Dante and Virgil can leave hell, what ordeal must they undergo in lines 70–87 of Canto XXXIV?

Interpret

6. What is Dante's attitude toward the sinners in Canto V? Support your answer with examples from the selection.
7. How did the book that Paolo and Francesca read lead them into sin?
8. For what sin are the souls punished at the beginning of Canto XXXIV? How is this punishment appropriate for their particular sin?
9. What do the three sinners trapped in Lucifer's mouths all have in common? Why do you think Dante considered their sin to be so terrible?
10. Literally and allegorically (see page R1), what do Dante and Virgil struggle to overcome in lines 70–87 of Canto XXXIV?

Evalute and Connect

11. Do you think that the punishments described here are just? Explain your answer.
12. In your opinion, is Dante being presumptuous by including historical characters among the damned? Do you think he is "playing God"? Explain.
13. Look at the chart you made for the Reading Focus on page 811. What symbolic punishment might Dante have come up with for these misdeeds?
14. Paolo and Francesca blame their downfall on a book they read. Does this seem like a good excuse to you? Explain your answer.
15. Dante wrote for a European, Christian audience in the fourteenth century. Does his epic have a universal **theme** (see page R12) that is relevant today? If so, what might this message be?

Literary Criticism

Scholar Lawrence Baldassaro asserts that the *Divine Comedy* "depicts the pilgrim's [Dante's] vulnerability to sin dramatically . . . in the form of the pilgrim's . . . response to the sinners he encounters." Analyze the speaker-pilgrim's reaction to Francesca and Paolo's story. In your opinion, does it suggest that he identifies with them? Explain your answer in a paragraph, using passages from the text to support your ideas.

Literary ELEMENTS

Allegory

Allegory is a form of extended metaphor in which the events, actions, objects, and persons in a narrative represent moral qualities, universal struggles, or abstract ideas such as love, fear, or virtue. A popular allegorical subject throughout literary history has been that of the journey or quest, in which a hero, representing the human spirit, seeks a great treasure, representing knowledge or happiness. Virgil's *Aeneid* contains a number of allegorical episodes, which may have inspired Dante.

1. From the excerpts you have read, how would you describe Dante's allegorical purpose in writing the *Divine Comedy*?
2. What is the literal and symbolic meaning of Dante's and Virgil's journey through hell? What is the outcome of their quest?

- See **Literary Terms Handbook,** p. R1.

Literature and Writing

Writing About Literature

Evaluating Similes Elaborate similes usually play a prominent role in epic poetry. Dante relies heavily on the **simile,** a comparison using *like* or *as,* in his descriptions in "Inferno." In a few paragraphs, discuss the similes Dante uses in Canto V, lines 40–42, 46–48, and 82–84. What is being compared in each instance? How are these similes effective, especially when they are together?

Creative Writing

Writing a Scene for the *Divine Comedy* Imagine that you are on a tour of heaven and that you meet someone being rewarded for a virtuous life. Write a story narrating this encounter and identifying the reward. Follow Dante's lead in describing the scenery of the place and include your own reaction to hearing the virtuous soul's story.

Extending Your Response

Literature Groups

Political Freedom Dante wrote the *Divine Comedy,* in part, to express his political beliefs. He was banished from his beloved Florence for these beliefs and sentenced to death if he ever returned. Do you think it is ever wise or justifiable to forbid people to express their beliefs? Give reasons to support your opinions, and then share your views with another group.

Internet Connection

Compiling a Tourist Brochure Dante's native city of Florence is one of the most popular tourist destinations in Europe. Use the Internet to research the attractions of Florence. Then create a brochure, including notes about topics such as art, architecture, music, entertainment, and places to stay.

Listening and Speaking

Role-Playing a Debate In Canto XXXIV, Dante presents Brutus and Cassius as great sinners who betrayed their leader and benefactor, Julius Caesar. Shakespeare, however, makes Brutus the tragic hero of his play *Julius Caesar.* Get together with two partners. Using the play and other literary or historical sources, role-play a debate in which Brutus, Cassius, and Dante all present their points of view.

Save your work for your portfolio.

VOCABULARY • Prefixes

A prefix added to the beginning of a root word changes the meaning of the word. The prefix *out-* means "more than," "better than," or "in a manner that overpowers or defeats."

- *outdo*–to do more than expected
- *outwit*–to be smarter or more clever than an adversary
- *outrage*–an act that exceeds accepted limits of behavior
- *outnumber*–to be greater in number

PRACTICE Use your knowledge of the prefix *out-* to write a definition for each word below. Then write an original sentence using each word.

outlast	outshine
outgrow	outguess
outbid	outmaneuver
outstanding	outburst
outlive	outrank

Magazine Article

Living among the rugged mountains where southern France meets northern Spain, the Basque people have preserved a language and heritage unique in Europe.

from Europe's First Family: The Basques

by Thomas J. Abercrombie—*National Geographic,* November 1995

From road's end at Arantzazu Monastery, it's only a two-hour walk through fragrant forests of beech and pine to the high, stony pastures of Urbia. Yet the well-worn track leading to this high mountain valley crosses a dozen millennia.

In fields shielded from the chill north winds by the mile-high walls of the jagged Aitzkorri Range, Basque shepherds still summer their flocks, surrendering to a seasonal rhythm unbroken since Neolithic times.

Basques call their nation Euskal Herria, or "land of the Basque language." And it is their ancient mother tongue that truly unites them. It was spoken here 5,000 years ago, before the Indo-Europeans arrived and spread out across the continent.

Basques have looked to the sea for centuries. Their whaling camps stood on Labrador's stony shores long before the English arrived at Jamestown. Basque captains sailed the Atlantic with Columbus and carved the Pacific track of the famed Manila galleons.

The running of the bulls, part of the fiesta of San Fermin–held every summer since the thirteenth century.

Today more than half of Spain's 2.5 million Basques live in industrial towns and cities. And though Basques make up only about 5 percent of the population, they produce 10 percent of the country's exports.

The Basques' spirit of nationality is reflected in their many competitive sports. Jai alai (hī′ lī′), played today across the world, is a Basque invention. Each town has its *frontón,* or ball court, many sharing a wall with the village church.

Every Basque fishing village also has its own rowing team—13 powerful oarsmen and one on the rudder of the *trainera*—competing up and down the coast. The matches go back to the 12th century, when whalers, alerted by spotters on village watchtowers, raced out to hunt the giants that once breached along the coast. The fastest team got in the first harpoons.

Analyzing Media

1. Describe the sports that are popular with the Basques.
2. What elements of the Basque culture help to keep its people united? Discuss.

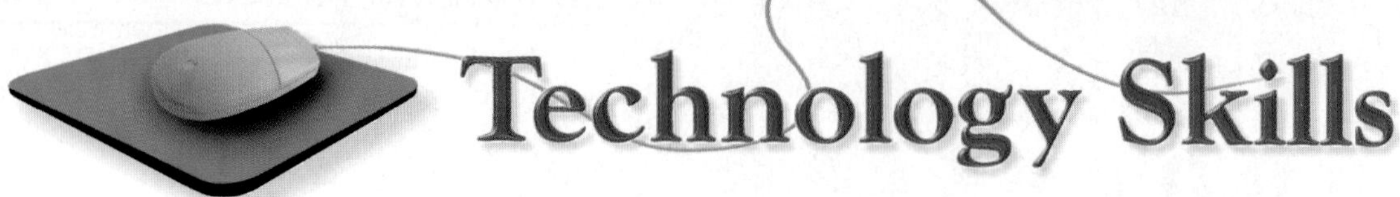

Technology Skills

E-mail: Communicating Across Cultures

Good communication can help you avoid misunderstandings and conflicts. However, effective communication can be difficult when crossing language and cultural barriers. Although e-mail lacks facial expressions, body language, and tone of voice, you should do your best to send clear and polite messages.

Other Cultures, Other Rules

Log on to the Internet, and do a search for information on the manners and accepted behavior in a few cultures other than your own. On your search engine, try using the keywords *customs* and *manners* along with the name of a culture (for example, Islamic, Latin American) or a country, region, or continent. Make a list of the do's and don'ts that you discover. For instance:

- Are handshakes expected? How about hugs and kisses? bows?
- Are women visitors expected to wear long sleeves or cover their hair?
- Is direct eye contact considered offensive?
- Are visitors expected to bring gifts? to stay a minimum amount of time?

These are a few of the subtleties that can affect international communication. Share your discoveries with your class, and learn what other students have discovered in their research.

TECHNOLOGY TIP

When you use a search engine, read the descriptors provided with the site names to avoid wasting time connecting with irrelevant sites. In looking for information on cultural differences, for example, you'll probably be referred to sites offering seminars in overseas customs and manners for business people who will be working abroad. You'll also be referred to book dealers who sell books on the topic. Skip over these and look for on-site information.

E-mail Etiquette

After you've familiarized yourself with some of the cultural differences in other countries, research those subtleties of communication you must consider when sending e-mail. Do a Web search on "e-mail etiquette." Download and print out the information you find. With your class, discuss any differences you discover in electronic etiquette from country to country.

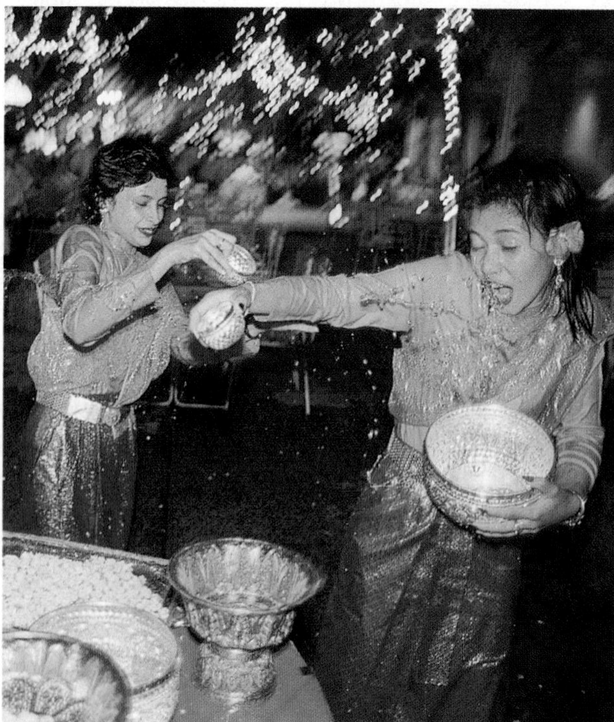

Thai women sprinkle water on each other in traditional celebration of the Thai New Year.

Maoris press noses in the customary greeting.

Find an Electronic Pen Pal

1. Conduct a Web search for high schools in countries around the world that have e-mail addresses. A good place to begin is the International Registry of Schools Online <http://web66.unm.edu/schools.html>.
2. With your teacher's approval, initiate e-mail communication with someone at the schools you find. It's probably best to begin with the head of the school, the English department head, or one of the teachers. Share some information about yourself and your goal while politely requesting that interested students get in contact with you by e-mail.
3. Once you've established contact with a student abroad, inquire about any possible cultural differences. To begin, you might ask about the educational system: How many days a week do students attend school? How many hours a day? How long is the school year? Do girls and boys go to the same schools? Is homework required? What is the average amount of time expected to be spent doing homework? What's a typical course of study for someone at your grade level? What kinds of extracurricular activities exist? Do many students have after-school jobs? What kinds of work are available?
4. Collaborate with an e-mail pal in creating a chart that will compare and contrast your schools or your daily lives. Each of you can share the results of your work with your classmates.
5. Save your e-mail correspondence. After several exchanges, read through your messages. Did you remember to practice the e-mail etiquette expected? What differences–minor or significant–did you discover about your own and your e-mail pal's ways of communicating?

TECHNOLOGY TIP

There are a number of Web sites devoted to helping young people find electronic pen pals around the world. Check with your teacher before using one of them, and remember to be cautious when corresponding with any stranger by e-mail. You can find online safety tips at <www.safeteens.com>.

ACTIVITIES

1. Continue your e-mail correspondence with one or more students abroad to learn more about daily life in another country.
2. Use the Internet to research student-exchange and other study-abroad programs. Make a list of those programs that interest you.

ITALY, c. 1348–1353

Before You Read

from the *Decameron: Federigo's Falcon*

Meet Giovanni Boccaccio

"To take pity on people in distress is a human quality which every man and woman should possess."

Giovanni Boccaccio (jō vä′ nē bō kä′ chō) has been called the father of modern fiction, because he was one of the first authors to write prose stories in a modern language.

Boccaccio grew up in the city-state of Florence. As a young man, he was sent to the kingdom of Naples to study business and law. There he experienced life among both the nobility and the prosperous middle class.

Upon returning to Florence, Boccaccio struggled financially, but he also served as an ambassador for the city and traveled widely. In 1350 he met the poet Petrarch. They inspired each other's literary work and together laid the foundations for Renaissance humanism in Europe. Like Dante before them, they wrote their best works in Italian, rather than in Latin, further raising the status of modern languages in literature. Boccaccio spent his last years in poverty and ill health.

Boccaccio was born in 1313 and died in 1375.

Reading Focus

What role, do you think, does chance or luck play in the achievement of happiness?

Journal In your journal, jot down some ideas about chance and human destiny. To what extent are we responsible for, or in control of, our own happiness?

Setting a Purpose Read to discover how much the happiness of the characters in the story is due to changes in fortune and how much is due to characters taking control of their own destiny.

Building Background

Did You Know?

In 1348 the city of Florence was suffering from an outbreak of the deadly bubonic plague. To avoid this highly contagious disease, many people fled to the countryside like the ten young people in the *Decameron*. To entertain each other during their retreat, they tell stories for ten days. The *Decameron* was Boccaccio's masterpiece and is one of the first prose story collections written in a modern language.

The Arno River, Florence.

Vocabulary Preview

revered (ri vērd′) *adj.* regarded as worthy of great honor; p. 830
chaste (chāst) *adj.* innocent; pure; p. 830
penuriously (pi noor′ ē əs lē) *adv.* in severe poverty; p. 830
extremity (iks trem′ ə tē) *n.* great danger or need; p. 830
presumption (pri zump′ shən) *n.* attitude or conduct that oversteps the bounds of propriety or courtesy; p. 832
contrary (kon′ trer ē) *adj.* unfavorable; p. 832

Melissa, c. 1523 (detail). Dosso Dossi (Italy). Oil on canvas. Galleria Borghese, Rome.

from the

Decameron

Federigo's Falcon

Giovanni Boccaccio
Translated by Richard Aldington

Filomena had ceased speaking, and the queen,[1] seeing that nobody was left to speak except Dioneo (who had his privilege)[2] and herself, began cheerfully as follows:

It is now my turn to speak, dearest ladies, and I shall gladly do so with a tale similar in part to the one before, not only that you may know the power of your beauty over the gentle heart, but because you may learn yourselves to be givers of rewards when fitting, without allowing Fortune[3] always to dispense them, since Fortune most often bestows them, not discreetly but lavishly.

1. The *queen* (or *king*) is the member of the group whose turn it is to preside over the day's storytelling.
2. *Dioneo* (dē ō nā′ ō) had the right to tell the last story in each day's group of stories.
3. *Fortune* means "fate" or "destiny."

You must know then that Coppo di Borghese Domenichi, who was and perhaps still is one of our fellow citizens, a man of great and revered authority in our days both from his manners and his virtues (far more than from nobility of blood), a most excellent person worthy of eternal fame, and in the fullness of his years delighted often to speak of past matters with his neighbors and other men. And this he could do better and more orderly and with a better memory and more ornate speech than anyone else.

Among other excellent things, he was wont[4] to say that in the past there was in Florence a young man named Federigo, the son of Messer Filippo Alberighi, renowned above all other young gentlemen of Tuscany[5] for his prowess in arms and his courtesy. Now, as most often happens to gentlemen, he fell in love with a lady named Monna Giovanna, in her time held to be one of the gayest[6] and most beautiful women ever known in Florence. To win her love, he went to jousts and tourneys, made and gave feasts, and spent his money without stint. But she, no less chaste than beautiful, cared nothing for the things he did for her nor for him who did them.

Now as Federigo was spending far beyond his means and getting nothing in, as easily happens, his wealth failed and he remained poor with nothing but a little farm, on whose produce he lived very penuriously, and one falcon which was among the best in the world. More in love than ever, but thinking he would never be able to live in the town any more as he desired, he went to Campi where his farm was. There he spent his time hawking,[7] asked nothing of anybody, and patiently endured his poverty.

Now while Federigo was in this extremity it happened one day that Monna Giovanna's husband fell ill, and seeing death come upon him, made his will. He was a very rich man and left his estate to a son who was already growing up. And then, since he had greatly loved Monna Giovanna, he made her his heir in case his son should die without legitimate children; and so died.

Monna Giovanna was now a widow, and as is customary with our women, she went with her son to spend the year in a country house she had near Federigo's farm. Now the boy happened to strike up a friendship with Federigo, and delighted in dogs and hawks. He often saw Federigo's falcon fly, and took such great delight in it that he very much wanted to have it, but did not dare ask for it, since he saw how much Federigo prized it.

4. *Wont* (wōnt) means accustomed.
5. *Tuscany* is an area in central Italy; its chief city is Florence.
6. *Gayest* means "liveliest, most high-spirited."
7. To go *hawking* is to hunt birds with a trained hawk (falcon).

The Journey of the Magi, c. 1460 (detail). Benozzo di Lesse di Sandro Gozzoli (Italy). Fresco. Palazzo Medici-Riccardi, Florence, Italy.

Vocabulary

revered (ri vērd′) *adj.* regarded as worthy of great honor
chaste (chāst) *adj.* innocent; pure
penuriously (pi noor′ ē əs lē) *adv.* in severe poverty
extremity (iks trem′ ə tē) *n.* great danger or need

While matters were in this state, the boy fell ill. His mother was very much grieved, as he was her only child and she loved him extremely. She spent the day beside him, trying to help him, and often asked him if there was anything he wanted, begging him to say so, for if it were possible to have it, she would try to get it for him. After she had many times made this offer, the boy said:

"Mother, if you can get me Federigo's falcon, I think I should soon be better."

The lady paused a little at this, and began to think what she should do. She knew that Federigo had loved her for a long time, and yet had never had one glance from her, and she said to herself:

"How can I send or go and ask for this falcon, which is, from what I hear, the best that ever flew, and moreover his support in life? How can I be so thoughtless as to take this away from a gentleman who has no other pleasure left in life?"

Although she knew she was certain to have the bird for the asking, she remained in embarrassed thought, not knowing what to say, and did not answer her son. But at length love for her child got the upper hand and she determined that to please him in whatever way it might be, she would not send, but go herself for it and bring it back to him. So she replied:

"Be comforted, my child, and try to get better somehow. I promise you that tomorrow morning I will go for it, and bring it to you."

The child was so delighted that he became a little better that same day. And on the morrow the lady took another woman to accompany her, and as if walking for exercise went to Federigo's cottage, and asked for him. Since it was not the weather for it, he had not been hawking for some days, and was in his garden employed in certain work there. When he heard that Monna Giovanna was asking for him at the door, he was greatly astonished, and ran there happily. When she saw him coming, she got up to greet him with womanly charm, and when Federigo had courteously saluted her, she said:

"How do you do, Federigo? I have come here to make amends for the damage you have suffered through me by loving me more than was needed. And in token of this, I intend to dine today familiarly with you and my companion here."

"Madonna," replied Federigo humbly, "I do not remember ever to have suffered any damage through you, but received so much good that if I was ever worth anything it was owing to your worth and the love I bore it. Your generous visit to me is so precious to me that I could spend again all that I have spent; but you have come to a poor host."

Did You Know?
Madonna is an Italian term of respect once used to address a lady. The term also is used as a name for the Virgin Mary.

So saying, he modestly took her into his house, and from there to his garden. Since there was nobody else to remain in her company, he said:

"Madonna, since there is nobody else, this good woman, the wife of this workman, will keep you company, while I go to set the table."

Now, although his poverty was extreme, he had never before realized what necessity he had fallen into by his foolish extravagance in spending his wealth. But he repented of it that morning when he could find nothing with which to do honor to the lady, for love of whom he had entertained vast numbers of men in the past. In his anguish he cursed himself and his fortune and ran up and down like a man out his senses, unable to find money or anything to pawn.[8] The hour was late and his

8. To *pawn* something is to deposit it with someone as security for a loan.

desire to honor the lady extreme, yet he would not apply to anyone else, even to his own workman; when suddenly his eye fell upon his falcon, perched on a bar in the sitting room. Having no one to whom he could appeal, he took the bird, and finding it plump, decided it would be food worthy such a lady. So, without further thought, he wrung its neck, made his little maid servant quickly pluck and prepare it, and put it on a spit to roast. He spread the table with the whitest napery,[9] of which he had some left, and returned to the lady in the garden with a cheerful face, saying that the meal he had been able to prepare for her was ready.

The lady and her companion arose and went to table, and there together with Federigo, who served it with the greatest devotion, they ate the good falcon, not knowing what it was. They left the table and spent some time in cheerful conversation, and the lady, thinking the time had now come to say what she had come for, spoke fairly[10] to Federigo as follows:

"Federigo, when you remember your former life and my chastity, which no doubt you considered harshness and cruelty, I have no doubt that you will be surprised at my presumption when you hear what I have come here for chiefly. But if you had children, through whom you could know the power of parental love, I am certain that you would to some extent excuse me.

"But, as you have no child, I have one, and I cannot escape the common laws of mothers. Compelled by their power, I have come to ask you—against my will, and against all good manners and duty—for a gift, which I know is something especially dear to you, and reasonably so, because I know your straitened[11] fortune has left you no other pleasure, no other recreation, no other consolation. This gift is your falcon, which has so fascinated my child that if I do not take it to him, I am afraid his present illness will grow so much worse that I may lose him. Therefore I beg you, not by the love you bear me (which holds you to nothing), but by your own nobleness, which has shown itself so much greater in all courteous usage than is wont in other men, that you will be pleased to give it to me, so that through this gift I may be able to say that I have saved my child's life, and thus be ever under an obligation to you."

When Federigo heard the lady's request and knew that he could not serve her, because he had given her the bird to eat, he began to weep in her presence, for he could not speak a word. The lady at first thought that his grief came from having to part with his good falcon, rather than from anything else, and she was almost on the point of retraction. But she remained firm and waited for Federigo's reply after his lamentation. And he said:

"Madonna, ever since it has pleased God that I should set my love upon you, I have felt that Fortune has been contrary to me in many things, and have grieved for it. But they are all light in comparison with what she has done to me now, and I shall never be at peace with her again when I reflect that you came to my poor house, which you never deigned to visit when it was rich, and asked me for a little gift, and Fortune has so acted that I cannot give it to you. Why this cannot be, I will briefly tell you.

"When I heard that you in your graciousness desired to dine with me and I thought of your excellence and your worthiness, I thought

9. *Napery* is another word for table linens—tablecloths, napkins, and so on.
10. Here, *fairly* describes a pleasant, charming way of speaking.
11. *Straitened* literally means "tightened"; here, it alludes to Federigo's fortune being almost used up.

Vocabulary

presumption (pri zump′ shən) *n.* attitude or conduct that oversteps the bounds of propriety or courtesy

contrary (kon′ trer ē) *adj.* unfavorable

April, from *Da Costa Book of Hours,* 1515. Simon Bening (Flanders). Illuminated manuscript page. The Pierpont Morgan Library, New York.

Viewing the painting: In what way does the scene in the painting reflect the setting of the story?

it right and fitting to honor you with the best food I could obtain; so, remembering the falcon you ask me for and its value, I thought it a meal worthy of you, and today you had it roasted on the dish and set forth as best I could. But now I see that you wanted the bird in another form, it is such a grief to me that I cannot serve you that I think I shall never be at peace again."

And after saying this, he showed her the feathers and the feet and the beak of the bird in proof. When the lady heard and saw all this, she first blamed him for having killed such a falcon to make a meal for a woman; and then she inwardly commended his greatness of soul which no poverty could or would be able to abate. But, having lost all hope of obtaining the falcon, and thus perhaps the health of her son, she departed sadly and returned to the child. Now, either from disappointment at not having the falcon or because his sickness must inevitably have led to it, the child died not many days later, to the mother's extreme grief.

Although she spent some time in tears and bitterness, yet, since she had been left very rich and was still young, her brothers often urged her to marry again. She did not want to do so, but as they kept on pressing her, she remembered the worthiness of Federigo and his last act of generosity, in killing such a falcon to do her honor.

"I will gladly submit to marriage when you please," she said to her brothers, "but if you want me to take a husband, I will take no man but Federigo degli Alberighi."

At this her brothers laughed at her, saying:

"Why, what are you talking about, you fool? Why do you want a man who hasn't a penny in the world?"

But she replied:

"Brothers, I know it is as you say, but I would rather have a man who needs money than money which needs a man."

Seeing her determination, the brothers, who knew Federigo's good qualities, did as she wanted, and gave her with all her wealth to him, in spite of his poverty. Federigo, finding that he had such a woman, whom he loved so much, with all her wealth to boot, as his wife, was more prudent with his money in the future, and ended his days happily with her.

Responding to Literature

Personal Response

Do you think Federigo acted wisely or foolishly in this story? Explain your answer.

Analyzing Literature

Recall and Interpret

1. How and why does Federigo squander his wealth?
2. Why does Monna want Federigo's falcon?
3. Why is killing the falcon such a great sacrifice for Federigo? What is **ironic** about his action?
4. What qualities does Monna discover in Federigo that later induce her to marry him?

Evaluate and Connect

5. Review the journal entry you made for the Reading Focus on page 828. To what extent is the outcome of this story due to fortune, and to what extent is it due to the characters taking control of their own destinies?
6. How might the outcome of the story have been different if Monna had told Federigo at the start of her visit that she had come for the falcon?
7. What is your assessment of Federigo's character? Do you admire him, or do you think he acts impulsively and allows people to take advantage of him? Explain.
8. From her behavior throughout the story and on her final decision, what values would you say are most important to Monna?

Literary Criticism

Many critics praise Boccaccio's skillful use of irony. At what points in "Federigo's Falcon" are the characters' actions ironic? How do those ironic actions help further the theme of the story? Analyze the irony of "Federigo's Falcon" in an essay, using details from the story to support your ideas.

Literary ELEMENTS

Theme

The **theme** of a story is the main idea or message that it conveys. All the details of a story point to the theme, which is usually an insight into human experience. Sometimes a theme is **directly stated** within the story, either by a narrator or another character. More often a theme is merely **implied** or suggested. The reader must figure out the theme from the story's details. Some literary works have more than one theme.

1. The narrator states one theme of "Federigo's Falcon" in the opening paragraph. What lesson does she **state** that her story will teach?
2. In Federigo's experiences, what theme is **implied** about a person's ability to control his or her own fate?

- See **Literary Terms Handbook**, p. R12.

Extending Your Response

Creative Writing

Composing a Modern Story Write an updated version of "Federigo's Falcon." In your story, make up modern-day equivalents for the jousts and tourneys, the falcons, and other elements of the original. Your characters may behave like those in the original story or in a more "modern" way.

Internet Connection

Exploring Falconry Falcons are swift and intelligent birds. Falconry, or the art of training falcons to hunt game, is still practiced throughout the world. Use the Internet to find out more about falcons and falconry and summarize your results in an oral report to the class.

Save your work for your portfolio.

Grammar Link

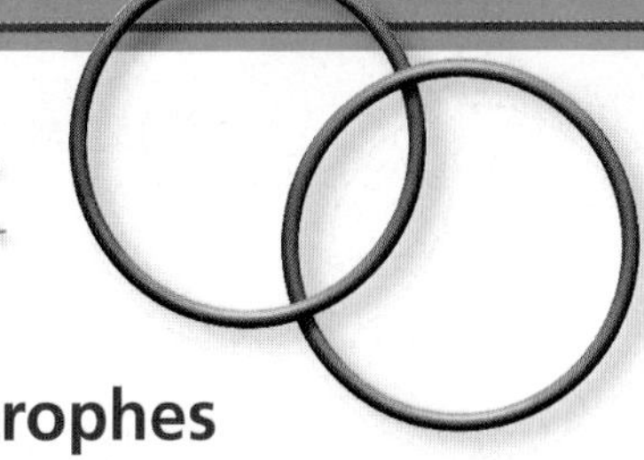

Missing or Misplaced Possessive Apostrophes

An important use of the apostrophe is to form the possessive of nouns and some pronouns. The general rule for forming the possessive of a singular noun is to add an apostrophe and *-s.*

Problem 1 Singular nouns that end in *s*

In the Decameron, *the deadly virus spread causes seven ladies and three gentlemen to leave Florence.*

Solution To make the possessive form of a singular noun ending in *s,* add an apostrophe and *-s*, except for ancient proper nouns that end in *s* (like *Jesus* or *Achilles*), add only an apostrophe.

In the Decameron, *the deadly virus's spread causes seven ladies and three gentlemen to leave Florence.*

Problem 2 Plural nouns ending in *s*

The small group passes ten days time by telling stories.

Solution If a plural noun ends in *s,* make it possessive by adding only an apostrophe.

The small group passes ten days' time by telling stories.

Problem 3 Plural nouns not ending in *s*

In the stories of the Decameron, *gentlemens good manners are highly valued.*

Solution If a plural noun does not end in *s,* add an apostrophe and *-s.*

In the stories of the Decameron, *gentlemen's good manners are highly valued.*

Problem 4 Pronouns

Now it is someones turn to tell the story of Federigo and his falcon.

Solution Form the possessive of an indefinite pronoun by adding an apostrophe and *-s.* Apostrophes are not used in possessive pronouns, such as *its, his,* or *hers.*

Now it is someone's turn to tell the story of Federigo and his falcon.

- For more about apostrophes, see **Language Handbook,** p. R50.

EXERCISE

If the sentence is correct, write *Correct* on your paper. If the sentence is incorrect, rewrite it to correct any missing or misplaced possessive apostrophes.

a. Titus' story from the *Decameron* takes place in Athens, Greece.

b. Titus, a young Roman who is studying philosophy, falls in love with his best friends fiancé, Sophronia.

c. Despite their families rage, Titus and Sophronia leave for Rome.

d. The rejected suitors despair leads him to Rome, where he is finally saved by his best friend.

SPAIN, 1605

Before You Read

from *Don Quixote*

Meet Miguel de Cervantes

"It can be said that all prose fiction is a variation on the theme of *Don Quixote*."

—*Lionel Trilling*

Miguel de Cervantes (mē gel′ dā sər vän′ tāz), the author of the first great novel of the Western world, was born in Alcalá, near Madrid. As a young soldier he lost the use of his left hand in the battle of Lepanto in 1571. On his journey home, he was captured by pirates and spent five years in captivity in North Africa before being ransomed and released.

Returning to Spain, Cervantes married and found a job as purchasing agent for the navy. The work was difficult; once he was excommunicated for seizing grain belonging to the Catholic Church.

Cervantes lived much of his life in poverty. His financial condition improved considerably, however, after the publication of *Don Quixote* met with popular success. The Spanish philosopher Miguel de Unamuno has remarked that Cervantes' novel embodies the spirit and genius of the Spanish people.

Cervantes was born in 1547 and died in 1616.

Reading Focus

What do you think would happen to someone who tried to live in the real world like a hero in a work of fiction?

Discuss With a group of classmates, discuss this question and the kinds of problems it could create.

Setting a Purpose Read to see how the author establishes a character who is both ridiculous and noble.

Building Background

The Medieval Code of Chivalry

The system of idealized manners and morals known as chivalry flourished in the literature of the medieval romance. It is based on a code of honor whereby a knight swears an oath that binds him to fidelity to God and king, dedication to his lady love, and service to all victims of oppression. By Cervantes' time, this tradition lived on only in literature. Cervantes' original intent was to mock the absurdities of the romances being written in his day, but in the process of writing *Don Quixote,* his narrative broadened and deepened to include the more serious themes and the complex character development we associate with the modern novel.

The First Modern Novel

A **novel** is a long fictional prose narrative containing a **plot,** or ordered sequence of events, that takes place in a specific **setting** and is concerned with **character** development and a statement of **theme.** What qualifies *Don Quixote* as the first modern novel in European literature is the complex, extended treatment of a single character whose quest unites all the episodes of the narrative into a coherent design.

Vocabulary Preview

interminable (in tur′ mi nə bəl) *adj.* having or seeming to have no end; p. 838

renown (ri noun′) *n.* a state of being widely acclaimed; p. 838

redress (ri dres′) *v.* to correct or compensate for a wrong or loss; p. 838

discourteous (dis kur′ tē əs) *adj.* impolite; p. 841

enmity (en′ mə tē) *n.* hatred or ill will; p. 843

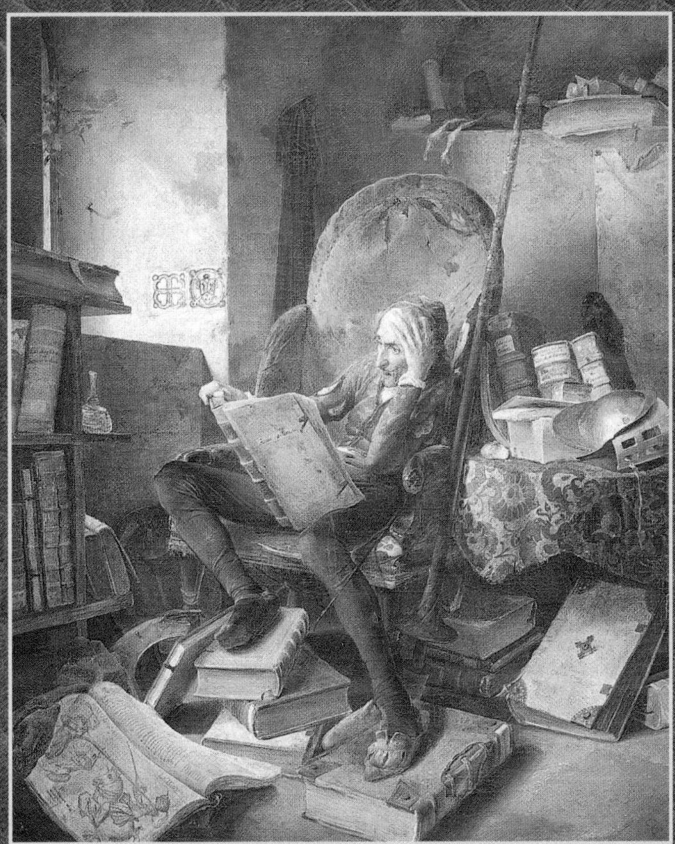

Don Quichote, im Lehnstuhl Lesend (Don Quixote Reading in His Easy Chair), 1834. Adolf Schroedter (Germany). Oil on canvas, 54.5 x 46 cm. National Gallery, Berlin. What do you think the man in the painting is like? Explain.

from Don Quixote

Miguel de Cervantes
Translated by J. M. Cohen

from Chapter I

Which treats of the quality and way of life of the famous knight Don Quixote de la Mancha.[1]

In a certain village in La Mancha, which I do not wish to name, there lived not long ago a gentleman—one of those who have always a lance in the rack, an ancient shield, a lean hack[2] and a greyhound for coursing. His habitual diet consisted of a stew, more beef than mutton, of hash most nights, boiled bones on Saturdays, lentils on Fridays, and a young pigeon as a Sunday treat; and on this he spent three-quarters of his income. The rest of it went on a fine cloth doublet,[3] velvet breeches and slippers for holidays, and a homespun suit of the best in which he decked himself on weekdays. His household consisted of a housekeeper of rather more than forty, a niece not yet twenty, and a lad for the field and market, who saddled his horse and wielded the pruning hook.

1. *La Mancha* is a region in south-central Spain.
2. Unlike a warhorse or a show horse, a *hack* is a horse used for transportation.
3. A *doublet* is a close-fitting jacket worn by men of this time.

Our gentleman was verging on fifty, of tough constitution, lean-bodied, thin-faced, a great early riser and a lover of hunting. They say that his surname was Quixada or Quesada—for there is some difference of opinion amongst authors on this point. However, by very reasonable conjecture we may take it that he was called Quexana. But this does not much concern our story; enough that we do not depart by so much as an inch from the truth in the telling of it.

The reader must know, then, that this gentleman, in the times when he had nothing to do—as was the case for most of the year—gave himself up to the reading of books of knight-errantry;[4] which he loved and enjoyed so much that he almost entirely forgot his hunting, and even the care of his estate. So odd and foolish, indeed, did he grow on this subject that he sold many acres of cornland to buy these books of chivalry[5] to read, and in this way brought home every one he could get. And of them all he considered none so good as the works of the famous Feliciano de Silva. For his brilliant style and those complicated sentences seemed to him very pearls, especially when he came upon those love passages and challenges frequently written in the manner of: "The reason for the unreason with which you treat my reason, so weakens my reason that with reason I complain of your beauty"; and also when he read: "The high heavens that with their stars divinely fortify you in your divinity and make you deserving of the desert that your greatness deserves."

These writings drove the poor knight out of his wits; and he passed sleepless nights trying to understand them and disentangle their meaning, though Aristotle[6] himself would never have unraveled or understood them, even if he had been resurrected for that sole purpose. He did not much like the wounds that Sir Belianis gave and received, for he imagined that his face and his whole body must have been covered with scars and marks, however skillful the surgeons who tended him. But, for all that, he admired the author for ending his book with the promise to continue with that interminable adventure, and often the desire seized him to take up the pen himself, and write the promised sequel for him. No doubt he would have done so, and perhaps successfully, if other greater and more persistent preoccupations had not prevented him.

In short, he so buried himself in his books that he spent the nights reading from twilight till daybreak and the days from dawn till dark; and so from little sleep and much reading, his brain dried up and he lost his wits. He filled his mind with all that he read in them, with enchantments, quarrels, battles, challenges, wounds, wooings, loves, torments and other impossible nonsense; and so deeply did he steep his imagination in the belief that all the fanciful stuff he read was true, that to his mind no history in the world was more authentic. . . .

In fact, now that he had utterly wrecked his reason he fell into the strangest fancy that ever a madman had in the whole world. He thought it fit and proper, both in order to increase his renown and to serve the state, to turn knight-errant and travel through the world with horse and armor in search of adventures, following in every way the practice of the knights-errant he had read of, redressing all manner of wrongs,

4. *Knights-errant* traveled about in search of adventure.

5. Medieval knights lived by a code of honorable behavior known as *chivalry.*

6. The Greek philosopher *Aristotle* (384–322 B.C.) was considered to possess one of the greatest minds of the ancient world.

Vocabulary

interminable (in tur′ mi nə bəl) *adj.* having or seeming to have no end
renown (ri noun′) *n.* a state of being widely acclaimed
redress (ri dres′) *v.* to correct or compensate for a wrong or loss

and exposing himself to chances and dangers, by the overcoming of which he might win eternal honor and renown. Already the poor man fancied himself crowned by the valor of his arm, at least with the empire of Trebizond; and so, carried away by the strange pleasure he derived from these agreeable thoughts, he hastened to translate his desires into action.

The first thing that he did was to clean some armor which had belonged to his ancestors, and had lain for ages forgotten in a corner, eaten with rust and covered with mold. But when he had cleaned and repaired it as best he could, he found that there was one great defect: the helmet was a simple headpiece without a visor. So he ingeniously made good this deficiency by fashioning out of pieces of pasteboard a kind of half-visor which, fitted to the helmet, gave the appearance of a complete headpiece. However, to see if it was strong enough to stand up to the risk of a sword cut, he took out his sword and gave it two strokes, the first of which demolished in a moment what had taken him a week to make. He was not too pleased at the ease with which he had destroyed it, and to safeguard himself against this danger, reconstructed the visor, putting some strips of iron inside, in such a way as to satisfy himself of his protection; and, not caring to make another trial of it, he accepted it as a fine jointed headpiece and put it into commission.

Next he went to inspect his hack, but though, through leanness, he had more quarters than there are pence in a groat,[7] and more blemishes than Gonella's horse, which was nothing but skin and bone, he appeared to our knight more than the equal of Alexander's Bucephalus and the Cid's Babieca.[8] He spent four days pondering what name to give him; for, he reflected, it would be wrong for the horse of so famous a knight, a horse so good in himself, to be without a famous name. Therefore he tried to fit him with one that would signify what he had been before his master turned knight-errant, and what he now was; for it was only right that as his master changed his profession, the horse should change his name for a sublime and high-sounding one, befitting the new order and the new calling he professed. So, after many names invented, struck out and rejected, amended, canceled and remade in his fanciful mind, he finally decided to call him Rocinante, a name which seemed to him grand and sonorous, and to express the common horse he had been before arriving at his present state: the first and foremost of all hacks in the world.

Having found so pleasing a name for his horse, he next decided to do the same for himself, and spent another eight days thinking about it. Finally he resolved to call himself Don Quixote. And that is no doubt why the authors of this true history, as we have said, assumed that his name must have been Quixada and not Quesada, as other authorities would have it. Yet he remembered that the valorous Amadis had not been content with his bare name, but had added the name of his kingdom and native country in order to make it famous, and styled himself Amadis of Gaul. So, like a good knight, he decided to add the name of his country to his own and call himself Don Quixote de la Mancha. Thus, he thought, he very clearly proclaimed his parentage and native land and honored it by taking his surname from it.

Now that his armor was clean, his helmet made into a complete headpiece, a name found for his horse, and he confirmed in his new title, it struck him that there was only one more thing to do: to find a lady to be enamored of. For a knight-errant without a lady is like a tree without leaves or fruit and a body without a soul. He said to himself again and again: "If I for my sins or by good luck were to meet with some giant hereabouts, as generally happens to

7. The *groat,* an old coin, was worth four pence (four pennies). Don Quixote's horse was so bony that it appeared to have more than four quarters (the part of an animal's body that includes a leg).

8. *Bucephalus* was the favorite horse of Alexander the Great (356–323 B.C.). *Babieca* was the horse of El Cid (Rodrigo Díaz de Vivar, 1040–1099), Spain's national hero.

knights-errant, and if I were to overthrow him in the encounter, or cut him down the middle or, in short, conquer him and make him surrender, would it not be well to have someone to whom I could send him as a present, so that he could enter and kneel down before my sweet lady and say in tones of humble submission: 'Lady, I am the giant Caraculiambro, lord of the island of Malindrania, whom the never-sufficiently-to-be-praised knight, Don Quixote de la Mancha, conquered in single combat and ordered to appear before your Grace, so that your Highness might dispose of me according to your will'?" Oh, how pleased our knight was when he had made up this speech, and even gladder when he found someone whom he could call his lady. It happened, it is believed, in this way: in a village near his there was a very good-looking farm girl, whom he had been taken with at one time, although she is supposed not to have known it or had proof of it. Her name was Aldonza Lorenzo, and she it was he thought fit to call the lady of his fancies; and, casting around for a name which should not be too far away from her own, yet suggest and imply a princess and great lady, he resolved to call her Dulcinea del Toboso—for she was a native of El Toboso—a name which seemed to him as musical, strange and significant as those others that he had devised for himself and his possessions.

Sancho Panza, 1859. Sir John Gilbert (Great Britain). Oil on canvas, 77 x 64 cm. Harris Museum and Art Gallery, Preston, Lancashire, UK.

Viewing the painting: Does this person look like a "young man of noble birth aspiring to knighthood"? Why or why not?

In spite of the arguments of his family and friends, Don Quixote is determined to live out his dream. Most knights-errant in books were accompanied by a squire–a young man of noble birth aspiring to knighthood. Don Quixote's squire is slightly different. . . .

from Chapter VII

Of the Second Expedition of our good knight Don Quixote de la Mancha.

All this while Don Quixote was plying a laborer, a neighbor of his and an honest man—if a poor man may be called honest—but without much salt in his brainpan. In the end, he talked to him so much, persuaded him so hard and gave him such promises that the poor yokel[9] made up his mind to go out with him and serve him as squire. Don Quixote told him, amongst other things, that he ought to feel well disposed to come with him, for some time or another an adventure might occur that would win him in the twinkling of an eye some isle, of

9. *Yokel* describes a naive or gullible inhabitant of a rural area or small town.

which he would leave him governor. These promises and others like them made Sancho Panza—for this was the laborer's name—leave his wife and children and take service as his neighbor's squire. Then Don Quixote set about raising money, and by selling one thing, pawning another, and making a bad bargain each time, he raised a reasonable sum. He also fixed himself up with a shield, which he borrowed from a friend, and patching up his broken helmet as best he could, he gave his squire Sancho notice of the day and the hour on which he proposed to set out, so that he should provide himself with all that was most needful; and he particularly told his squire to bring saddlebags. Sancho said that he would, and that he was also thinking of bringing a very fine ass he had, for he was not too good at much traveling on foot. At the mention of the ass Don Quixote hesitated a little, racking his brains to remember whether any knight-errant ever had a squire mounted on ass back; but no case came to his memory. But, for all that, he decided to let him take it, intending to provide him with a more proper mount at the earliest opportunity by unhorsing the first discourteous knight he should meet. He provided himself also with shirts and everything else he could, following the advice which the innkeeper had given him. And when all this was arranged and done, without Panza saying goodbye to his wife and children, or Don Quixote taking leave of his housekeeper and niece, they departed from the village one evening, quite unobserved, and rode so far that night that at daybreak they thought they were safe, and that even if anyone came out to search for them they would not be found.

Sancho Panza rode on his ass like a patriarch,[10] with his saddlebags and his leather bottle, and a great desire to see himself governor of the isle his master had promised him. It chanced that Don Quixote took the same route and struck the same track across the plain of Montiel as on his first expedition; but he traveled with less discomfort than before, as it was the hour of dawn, and the sun's rays, striking them obliquely, did not annoy them. . . .

10. A *patriarch* is the oldest and most respected male member of a family.

from Chapter VIII

Of the valorous Don Quixote's success in the dreadful and never before imagined Adventure of the Windmills, with other events worthy of happy record.

At that moment they caught sight of some thirty or forty windmills, which stand on that plain, and as soon as Don Quixote saw them he said to his squire: "Fortune is guiding our affairs better than we could have wished. Look over there, friend Sancho Panza, where more than thirty monstrous giants appear. I intend to do battle with them and take all their lives. With their spoils we will begin to get rich, for this is a fair war, and it is a great service to God to wipe such a wicked brood from the face of the earth."

"What giants?" asked Sancho Panza.

"Those you see there," replied his master, "with their long arms. Some giants have them about six miles long."

"Take care, your worship," said Sancho; "those things over there are not giants but windmills, and what seem to be their arms are the sails, which are whirled round in the wind and make the millstone turn."

"It is quite clear," replied Don Quixote, "that you are not experienced in this matter of adventures. They are giants, and if you are

Vocabulary
discourteous (dis kur′ tē əs) *adj.* impolite

Don Quixote and the Windmill. Francisco J. Torromé (Spain, flourished 1890–1908). Bonhams, London.

Viewing the painting: What do you suppose Sancho Panza is thinking in this picture?

afraid, go away and say your prayers, while I advance and engage them in fierce and unequal battle."

As he spoke, he dug his spurs into his steed Rocinante, paying not attention to his squire's shouted warning that beyond all doubt they were windmills and no giants he was advancing to attack. But he went on, so positive that they were giants that he neither listened to Sancho's cries nor noticed what they were, even when he got near them. Instead he went on shouting in a loud voice: "Do not fly, cowards, vile creatures, for it is one knight alone who assails you."

At that moment a slight wind arose, and the great sails began to move. At the sight of which Don Quixote shouted: "Though you wield more arms than the giant Briareus, you shall pay for it!" Saying this, he commended himself with all his soul to his Lady Dulcinea, beseeching her aid in his great peril. Then, covering himself with his shield and putting his lance in the rest, he urged Rocinante forward at a full gallop and attacked the nearest windmill, thrusting his lance into the sail. But the wind turned it with such violence that it shivered his weapon in pieces, dragging the horse and his rider with it, and sent the knight rolling badly injured across the plain. Sancho Panza rushed to his assistance as fast as his ass could trot, but when he came up he found that the knight could not stir. Such a shock had Rocinante given him in their fall.

"O my goodness!" cried Sancho. "Didn't I tell your worship to look what you were doing, for they were only windmills? Nobody could mistake them, unless he had windmills on the brain."

"Silence, friend Sancho," replied Don Quixote. "Matters of war are more subject than most to continual change. What is more,

Laura
from Canzoniere

Petrarch

Translated by Morris Bishop

She used to let her golden hair fly free
  For the wind to toy and tangle and molest;
  Her eyes were brighter than the radiant west.
  (Seldom they shine so now.) I used to see
Pity look out of those deep eyes on me.
  ("It was false pity," you would now protest.)
  I had love's tinder° heaped within my breast;
  What wonder that the flame burned furiously?
She did not walk in any mortal way,
  But with angelic progress;° when she spoke,
  Unearthly voices sang in unison.
She seemed divine among the dreary folk
  Of earth. You say she is not so today?
  Well, though the bow's unbent,° the wound bleeds on.

Canzoníere (kan zō nē′ ər): the Italian word for songs.

7 tinder: material used to start a fire.

10 progress: here, a forward movement.

14 unbent: An archer bends a bow into a curve before firing an arrow.

Lady at her Toilet, 1515 (detail). Giovanni Bellini (Italy). Oil on panel. Kunsthistorisches Museum, Vienna. Compare the woman in the painting to Laura. What similarities do you see? What differences?

Responding to Literature

Personal Response

Look over the list of phrases you wrote for the Reading Focus on page 846. What image of Laura do you have after reading this poem? Write your answer in your journal.

Analyzing Literature

Recall and Interpret

1. According to lines 1–4, how has Laura changed in appearance? What might be the reason for this change?
2. In lines 5–8, the poet says that he used to see pity when he looked into Laura's eyes. Do you think she really pitied him? Explain.
3. Is Laura depicted as human, divine, or both? Explain your answer.
4. The last line contains an **allusion** (see **Literary Terms Handbook,** page R1) to Cupid, the god of love in classical mythology, who shoots lovers with his arrows. Identify and explain the **metaphor** in line 14.

Evaluate and Connect

5. Identify the use of **personification** in lines 1–2. How effective are these lines in giving you an idea of Laura's personality? (See **Literary Terms Handbook,** page R9.)
6. What is your opinion of such descriptions as "Her eyes were brighter than the radiant west" (line 3)?
7. What is the function of the comments enclosed within parentheses (lines 4 and 6)? Explain their effectiveness.
8. What does this poem say about love, aging, and death? Do you agree or disagree with the speaker's sentiments? Explain your answer, citing details from the poem as support.

Literary ELEMENTS

The Petrarchan Sonnet

A **Petrarchan sonnet,** also called an **Italian sonnet,** is divided into a group of eight lines, called the **octave,** and a group of six lines, called the **sestet.** The **rhyme** scheme of the octave is *abba, abba.* The sestet may follow a number of different rhyme schemes. Among the most common patterns are *cde cde, cde dcd,* and *cdc dee.* In the Italian sonnet, the octave usually presents a single **theme** or main idea, and the sestet expands, contradicts, or develops it.

1. What is the main difference between the way Laura is described in the octave and in the sestet?
2. What is the main idea expressed in the octave? In the sestet?

- See **Literary Terms Handbook,** p. R11.

Extending Your Response

Writing About Literature

Analyzing Character Write a brief analysis of the character of Laura as the poet describes her. What kind of a person is she? Do you find her realistic or idealized? Answer these questions, citing evidence from the poem to support your conclusions.

Interdisciplinary Activity

Art: Creating a Renaissance Portfolio Together with a small group, research the painting, sculpture, and architecture of the Italian Renaissance. Use photocopies of illustrations in library reference works and art history magazines, as well as online resources from the Internet, to compile a Renaissance portfolio. Then share your work with the class as a whole.

Save your work for your portfolio.

Before You Read

Sonnet 8

Meet Louise Labé

"Do not criticize me, Ladies, if I have loved: if I have felt a thousand burning torches, a thousand travails, and a thousand times sharp pain."

Louise Labé (lo͞o ēz′ lä bā′) was known as *la belle cordière* ("the beautiful rope-maker") because her father was a rope-maker in the French city of Lyon. The middle class of sixteenth-century France usually valued education for its daughters only as a sign of social status. But Labé's father provided her with the same educational opportunities as his two sons. Her tutor, the poet Maurice Scève (who claimed to have discovered the lost tomb of Petrarch's Laura), urged her to read the works of Dante, Boccaccio, and Petrarch. Labé formed her own literary circle, which met in the garden of her home. She is reputed to have had a number of adventures, such as participating in a tournament in honor of King Henry II of France disguised as a man.

Labé was born around 1524 and died in 1566.

Reading Focus

In what ways can love be a bittersweet experience?

Journal In your journal describe occasions when you have felt mixed emotions of pleasure and pain, or joy and sadness, in relation to persons you cared about.

Setting a Purpose As you read, notice how the poet expresses her mixed feelings about being in love.

Building Background

Louise Labé and the Sonnet

In the typical Petrarchan love sonnet, the speaker is assumed to be a man yearning for an idealized lady who is aloof, inaccessible, and often indifferent to his love. The lady's beauty is praised in extravagant terms, but she is portrayed as a prized object rather than as a thinking and feeling subject. Louise Labé wrote within the Petrarchan tradition, but she provided her own perspective. She created a scandal by addressing her sonnets to her beloved, and she was criticized for writing love poetry from the woman's point of view.

Louise Labé's Feminism

Labé intended her poems to be read by knowledgeable readers who could appreciate the position she was taking in relation to the poetic conventions of her time. In the dedication to her single volume of poetry, she urged women to leave aside their domestic activities, fine clothes, and jewelry in order to rival men in pursuit of literature and culture. She considered the exaggerated praise of female beauty in the standard Petrarchan love sonnet superficial and insincere. She compared herself to the then recently rediscovered ancient Greek poet Sappho (see page 259), whose poems expressed a strong woman's voice.

Reading Further

If you enjoy reading Labé's "Sonnet 8," you might also enjoy the following:

Elegies and sonnets from *Louise Labé's Complete Works,* translated by Edith R. Farrell.

"My Familiar Dream" and "Nevermore," by Paul Verlaine, from *Treasury of French Love,* edited by Richard A. Branyon.

The Pained Heart, or 'Sigh No More, Ladies', 1868. Arthur Hughes (Great Britain). Oil on canvas, 94 x 110 cm. The Maas Gallery, London. What sort of mood do you think the younger woman is in? How could you compare this mood to the mood of the poem?

Sonnet 8

Louise Labé
Translated by Willis Barnstone

I live, I die, I burn myself and drown.
I am extremely hot in suffering cold:
my life is soft and hardness uncontrolled.
When I am happy, then I ache and frown.
Suddenly I am laughing while I cry
and in my pleasure I endure deep grief:
my joy remains and slips out like a thief.
Suddenly I am blooming and turn dry.
So Love inconstantly° leads me in vain
and when I think my sorrow has no end
unthinkingly I find I have no pain.
But when it seems that joy is in my reign
and an ecstatic hour is mine to spend,
He comes and I, in ancient grief, descend.

---

9 *Inconstantly* means "changing frequently" and "unpredictably."

Responding to Literature

Personal Response

Did you get a positive or negative feeling about love from reading this poem? Explain your answer in your journal.

Analyzing Literature

Recall and Interpret

1. An **oxymoron** (see page R9) is a figure of speech that combines seemingly contradictory words or meanings for effect, such as *cold sunlight.* What do the oxymorons in lines 1–8 suggest about being in love?
2. In your own words, explain the shift in thought between the **octave** and the **sestet** (see Sonnet, page R11).
3. To what or whom does the pronoun *He* refer in line 14?
4. How does the use of the word *ancient* in line 14 help to universalize the poet's message?

Evaluate and Connect

5. Review the journal entry you made for the Reading Focus on page 849. Do you think it is typical for a person in love to experience the radically opposite emotions expressed in this poem? Explain your answer.
6. In this poem, love is portrayed as a disturbing or unsettling force. Do you think this is necessarily the case, or do you think love can have a calming and peaceful effect? Explain your answer.
7. Louise Labé is sometimes considered an early feminist. Do you see any evidence of her feminism in this poem? Explain.
8. **Parallelism** is the use of phrases or sentences of similar construction or meaning placed side by side. In your opinion, how effective is the use of parallelism in this poem? Explain.

Literary ELEMENTS

Hyperbole

Hyperbole (hī pur′ bə lē) is intentional exaggeration, usually used to create emphasis or humor. Hyperbole is common in love poetry where the emotions of the lover and the desirable qualities of the beloved are expressed with heightened intensity.

1. State several of the hyperboles used in the octave in "Sonnet 8." How would you describe the overall effect of these hyperboles?
2. In the sestet, the poet switches from hyperbole to a more straightforward expression of her feelings. What is the effect of this change in style? In your opinion, does this shift enhance or diminish the overall impact of the poem?

- See **Literary Terms Handbook,** p. R6.

Extending Your Response

Writing About Literature

Analyzing Personification **Personification** is a figure of speech in which human qualities are attributed to objects, animals, or ideas. Write a brief essay analyzing the poet's personification of "joy" in lines 7 and 12 or "Love" in line 9. What human qualities are given to these two abstract ideas? What does this use of personification tell the reader about the poet's attitude toward life and human relationships? Give reasons to support your conclusions.

Literature Groups

Discussing Theme In a small group, discuss the theme or message conveyed in this poem. What statement do you think the poet is making about the experience of being in love? Is the theme affected by the fact that the poet is a woman? Provide reasons to support your opinions, and then share your views with the rest of the class.

Save your work for your portfolio.

ITALY, c. 1542

Before You Read

Sonnet 239

Meet Michelangelo Buonarroti

"[Michelangelo] says *things*, [other poets] say *words*."

—Francesco Berni

Many know Michelangelo Buonarroti (mī′ kal an′ je lō′ bwō′ när rô tē) as an artist of extraordinary talent, but few realize he was also an accomplished poet. Using a direct, simple style, he composed what many consider the greatest lyric poems of the sixteenth century. Yet Michelangelo never formally studied literature. Born into an impoverished family of noble origins, he settled on an artistic career to earn his living. At thirteen, he became an apprentice in a studio; ten years later he produced the world-famous "Pietà."

During his lifetime, Michelangelo composed over 300 poems on such subjects as mortal and divine love and eternal bliss. These works are characterized by complexity of thought, emotional intensity, and attention to form.

Michelangelo was born in 1475 and died in 1564.

Reading Focus

How would you choose to capture the beauty of someone you loved? Would you paint a picture, write a poem or play, or create a dance in honor of that person? Why would you choose that particular art form?

Quickwrite Spend two or three minutes quickwriting to explore your response to these questions.

Setting a Purpose Read to find out how one author would capture the beauty of his beloved.

Building Background

A Renaissance Woman

This poem was written for Vittoria Colonna (1492–1547). Born into a distinguished family, Colonna was one of the leading figures of her time, famous for her beauty and her wisdom. In 1518 the pope held a party in her honor, and the emperor visited her in Rome. She numbered many of Italy's most prominent writers and artists among her friends. A writer herself, Colonna wrote passionate poems about love and spiritual faith.

Many feel that Michelangelo composed his most ardent and tender love poems for Colonna. In some, he implores Colonna to help him become a better person; in others, written after her death, he conveys a deep yearning for her presence.

A Renaissance Man

Michelangelo was a master of painting, sculpture, architecture, and poetry. In the variety of his accomplishments he came close to fulfilling the Renaissance ideal of "the universal man." This concept, originally developed in Italy in the 1400s, is one of the dominant intellectual features of the period.

Renaissance humanists believed that humans should try to learn as much as possible and to be as skilled as possible in what they did. Along with their faith in human abilities came a belief that people had a duty to stretch their potential to the limit. The renowned architect, poet, and archeologist Leone Alberti (1404–1472) believed that a person could do anything through the power of will. He wrote that people were not born to lie down and rot in idleness, but to stand up and act.

Sonnet 239

Michelangelo

Translated by John Frederick Nims

My lady, how comes it about—what all can see
from long experience—that rough mountain stone
carved to a living form, survives its own
creator, who'll end as ashes in an urn?
Cause lesser than its effect. From which we learn
how nature is less than art, as well I know
whose many a lively statue proves it so,
which time and the tomb exempt, grant amnesty.
Mine then, the power to give us, you and me,
a long survival in—choose it—stone or color,
faces just like our own, exact and true.
Though we're dead a thousand years, still men can see
how beautiful you were; I, how much duller,
and yet how far from a fool in loving you.

Delphic Sibyl, detail from ceiling of the Sistine Chapel, c. 1508–1512. Michelangelo Buonarroti (Italy). Sistine Chapel, Vatican Palace, Vatican State. How does this painting illustrate Michelangelo's description of art in this sonnet?

Responding to Literature

Personal Response

Which lines from this poem did you find the most memorable?

Analyzing Literature

Recall and Interpret

1. What idea does the speaker express in the first **quatrain,** the first four lines, (see Sonnet, page R11) of this poem? Why might Michelangelo have chosen to express this idea in the form of a question?
2. What is less than art, according to the speaker? What proof does the speaker offer to support his conclusions?
3. According to lines 9–11, what will the speaker do to ensure his survival and that of his beloved?
4. In lines 12–14, what attitude toward his own appearance and personality does the speaker express?

Evaluate and Connect

5. Do you agree with the **theme,** or central message, of this poem? Why or why not?
6. Would you classify this sonnet as a love poem? Explain your answer, using details from the poem for support.
7. What thoughts and feelings about his own work does Michelangelo convey in this poem?
8. Do you think most Americans would share Michelangelo's attitude toward art? Explain your answer, citing examples from the media or personal experience for support.

End Rhyme

Rhyme is the repetition of accented vowel sounds and any succeeding sounds in words that appear close to each other in a poem. With **end rhyme,** the rhymes occur at the ends of lines. Translators must decide whether to try to produce a rhymed translation at all, and if so, whether to try to duplicate the rhyme scheme of the original.

1. How does the end rhyme in "Sonnet 239" contribute to the overall effect of the poem?
2. The pattern of end rhyme in this poem changes from the octave to the sestet. In your opinion, what impact does this shift have on the poem?

- See **Literary Terms Handbook,** page R3.

Extending Your Response

Creative Writing

Write a Love Poem Refer to the Reading Focus on page 852. Then write a poem in which you describe the appearance and characteristics of someone you love and tell what you might do to preserve these qualities for posterity. In composing your poem, try to use poetic devices found in "Sonnet 239" such as **end rhyme** and **alliteration** (see page R3).

Interdisciplinary Activity

Art History: Michelangelo's Work In addition to being a poet, Michelangelo was famous as an artist and architect. Research one field in which he worked–painting, sculpture, or architecture–to find out the significance of his contribution in that area. Prepare an illustrated report on your findings.

Save your work for your portfolio.

COMPARING selections

Laura and *Sonnet 8* and *Sonnet 239*

COMPARE **ATTITUDES**

Discuss The speakers in Petrarch's "Laura" and Michelangelo's "Sonnet 239" are each in love with a lady, but they express their love very differently. Think about the attitude that each speaker expresses and, together with a small group, consider the following questions:

- In your opinion, which speaker expresses greater love of his lady? Provide supporting details from the poem.
- How is the mood or atmosphere of Petrarch's sonnet different from the mood in Michelangelo's sonnet?
- What is different about the style that each speaker employs to describe his lady?

COMPARE **RESPONSES**

Write In the last lines of their sonnets, Petrarch and Labé both portray the emotion of being in love as painful. In "Laura," Petrarch calls love a bleeding wound, and in "Sonnet 8," Labé says that to be in love is to descend into "ancient grief." Which poem do you think makes a better or more convincing case for the conclusion that love is painful? State your opinion in a brief essay, supplying reasons and examples from both poems to support your view. If you wish, you might refer to twentieth-century songs and poems that echo the poets' sentiments.

The Pained Heart, or 'Sigh No More, Ladies', 1868 (detail).

COMPARE **CUSTOMS**

Investigate The sonnets of Petrarch, Labé, and Michelangelo arose from courtly traditions in which writing poetry was considered a noble pastime. Use library resources or the Internet to find out more about people's attitudes in Italy, France, and other European countries during the Renaissance toward reading and writing poetry. What subjects and styles were popular in each country? If possible, find the names of several Renaissance poets. What prizes could good poets win? Share your findings in an oral report to the class. Before presenting your report, you may wish to summarize your information and notes on a chart.

Writing Workshop

Expository Writing: Research Paper

A research paper begins with a writer's curiosity. The writer sets out to learn about something he or she does not know, and the paper reports the writer's discoveries. Reading a work of literature can spark a person's curiosity about many subjects, including the author's life and culture. **In this workshop, you will write a research paper on an author or a culture that produced a work of literature you have enjoyed.**

- As you write your research paper, refer to **Writing Handbook,** pp. R58–R69.

EVALUATION RUBRIC

By the time you complete this Writing Workshop, you will have

- developed a clear and focused thesis statement
- supported the thesis statement with facts gathered from research
- concluded with a paragraph that ties together your main ideas
- presented a research paper that is free of errors in grammar, usage, and mechanics

The Writing Process

PREWRITING

PREWRITING TIP

Before choosing your final topic, check the library and the Internet to make sure that there is enough information available. You will need to be able to find a number of articles and books on the topic.

Explore ideas

Choose a selection from this unit that you especially enjoyed reading. Think about how the selection might reflect aspects of the author's life or culture. For example, consider how the selection might

- have parallels in the events of the writer's life or times
- provide examples of values widely held within the culture
- reflect the culture's view of the world and of people's place in the world

You might also check articles on the author or the work in literary reference books, such as *Benét's Reader's Encyclopedia,* to get ideas for topics.

Consider your purpose and audience

The purpose of a research paper is to convey information, but you also want to capture and hold your audience's interest. Try to think of an intriguing angle on your topic.

Gather information

To guide your research, write *what, where, when, why,* and *how* questions that you want to find answers to. For example, if you have chosen to write about the connection between Dante's life and his poetry, you might consider questions similar to these:

- Was Beatrice modeled on a woman in Dante's life?
- How did Dante know so much about these different aspects of human experience?
- Is Dante the main character in the *Divine Comedy?*

To find answers to your questions, search reference books, periodicals, computer databases, and nonfiction books.

Take notes

As you investigate your topic, keep a working bibliography. When you find a useful source, record the publishing data on a three-by-five-inch index card and number the card. You can record different data for different kinds of sources. Paraphrase, summarize, or quote useful information on another note card and record the source's number from the bibliography card.

Develop a thesis statement

As you research answers to your questions, you'll probably refine your ideas about your topic. Review your notes and draw a conclusion about your topic. Write a sentence that states your **thesis**–the central idea you will focus on–and try to prove it in your paper. If necessary, do further research to find more support for your thesis.

STUDENT MODEL

Despite the fact that Dante Alighieri lived an external life of enormous tragedy and change, he became a deeply learned man who produced one of the greatest works in Western literature, the *Divine Comedy*.

Complete Student Model on p. R119.

Create an outline

Use your note cards and your thesis statement to create an outline for your paper. Sort out the note cards that support your thesis statement. Group the note cards on similar topics together and arrange the groups in a logical order. Use each group as a main topic in your outline. Your outline is a plan for the body of your paper, which should expand upon and provide support for your thesis statement.

STUDENT MODEL

Outline form

I. Main topic
    A. Subtopic
    B. Subtopic

II. Main topic
    A. Subtopic
    B. Subtopic

I. Tragedies and changes in Dante's life
    A. Falls in love with Beatrice, who dies prematurely, causing Dante enoromous grief
    B. Elected to political office, but due to political turmoil is exiled and forced to leave Florence

II. Literary pursuits and accomplishments in Dante's life
    A. After Beatrice's death, embarks on a period of intense study and learning
    B. During his exile, writes the *Divine Comedy*, which reflects many of his life experiences

Complete Student Model on p. R119.

DRAFTING

DRAFTING TIP

When you include information from your notes in your draft, write the note card number immediately after it. This numbering will make it easier to credit your sources and compile your final bibliography.

Get your reader's attention

Develop an opening paragraph that introduces your topic in a way that grabs your reader's attention. You might use a quote, an example, or an anecdote as an opener to lead up to your thesis statement.

Write your draft

As you draft, use your outline as a guide for the body of your paper. Write at least one paragraph for each main topic in your outline. Remember that each paragraph should have a topic sentence that is supported by relevant details. Write a conclusion for your paper that restates your thesis in a different way, recounts your main points, or provides a final thought-provoking idea.

STUDENT MODEL

Dante was exiled from Florence in 1302, charged with crimes against the Republic. The charges were mostly made up; nevertheless, when Dante failed to answer them, the situation grew worse. A second sentence soon followed the first: If Dante ever returned to his home, he was to be captured immediately and burned alive. Dante never saw his home again.

Complete Student Model on p. R119.

REVISING

REVISING TIP

Make your paper more effective by deleting details that do not support your thesis.

You may be able to make sentences or paragraphs flow more smoothly by changing their order.

Evaluate your work

After setting your draft aside for a while, reread it with a fresh eye. Mark any passages that are confusing, unclear, vague, or off track.

Have a writing conference

Work with a revision partner, and read your research reports to each other. Use the **Rubric for Revising** as a guide and offer suggestions for improving each other's work. As you revise, be sure to credit your sources.

RUBRIC FOR REVISING

Your revised research paper should have

- ☑ a well-defined thesis statement
- ☑ quotations that support your thesis
- ☑ effective organization, including a topic sentence for each paragraph
- ☑ transitions that connect ideas smoothly and logically
- ☑ a concluding paragraph that researches well documented information, such as facts, and ties together main ideas

Your revised research paper should be free of

- ☑ information used without acknowledgement of its source
- ☑ inaccurate or incorrect citations for sources used
- ☑ information that does not relate to your thesis
- ☑ errors in grammar, usage, and mechanics

STUDENT MODEL

extensive ^mainly northern

He began a period of ^travel ^in ^Italy. ~~It was not an easy period in his life.~~ These were ~~difficult~~ years for him.

not easy

Complete Student Model on p. R119.

EDITING/PROOFREADING

PROOFREADING TIP

Use the **Proofreading Checklist** on the inside back cover to help you catch and correct mistakes. Make a clean copy of your final report.

Grammar Hint

Use an apostrophe and an *s* to form the possessive of a singular noun. Use an apostrophe alone to form the possessive of a plural noun that ends in *s*.

INCORRECT: *Poet's life experiences often influence their writing.*

CORRECT: *Poets' life experiences often influence their writing.*

- For more on forming possessives, see **Language Handbook,** p. R25

STUDENT MODEL

In his Comedy, Dante is himself the ~~mane~~ main char-acter. "He writes in the first person so the reader can identify and deeply understand the truths he wished to share about the meaning of life and mans' relationship with the Creator." ("Dantes Inferno," n.pag.). As he had done in his erlier poems, he wrote the *Divine comedy* in Italian instead of the customery Latin.

Complete Student Model on p. R119.

Complete Student Model

For a complete version of the model developed in this workshop, refer to **Writing Workshop Models**, p. R119.

PUBLISHING/PRESENTING

Usually, research papers are presented in a formal way. Often they are bound in a folder with a cover sheet that gives the title of the paper and the writer's name. If you bind your report, you might add it to the school library. You could also present your report orally to the class.

PRESENTING TIP

Depending on your subject, you might add a time line or a map to your paper.

Reflecting

The Peruvian writer Mario Vargas Llosa has said that even the most inventive writers can only tell stories based on their own stories. Does the research you did for your paper support this statement?

Read your report one last time. In your journal or writer's notebook, jot down ideas for improvement to put into effect in your next research paper.

Save your work for your portfolio.

Continuity and Change

Since 1800 Europeans, more than any other peoples, have united the world into a single global system. They have done this partly through military, economic, and technological innovation, and partly through simple numbers. Between the mid-1800s and mid-1900s, over 60 million people left Europe. These people stamped the Americas, Australia, and parts of Africa and Asia with European culture.

- *Europeans carried their languages around the globe. Today more native speakers of English, Spanish, and Portuguese live outside of Europe than within it.*
- *Europeans spread ideas that reshaped how people think. Emigrants and missionaries made Christianity into the first religion to have followers around the world. Scholars and politicians developed concepts—democracy, capitalism, socialism, nationalism—that revolutionized societies around the world. Artists developed the modern style in painting and music.*
- *With the development of items as diverse as cement, automobiles, and penicillin, European scientists and inventors have transformed the world.*

Hamnoy, Norway.

Vienna, Austria.

Europe

- **1804** Napoleon Bonaparte is emperor of France
- **1814–1815** European diplomats negotiate a peace settlement at Vienna
- **1821** Greeks begin war for independence
- **1824** Composer Ludwig von Beethoven completes his Ninth Symphony
- **1830** Belgium declares independence from the Netherlands
- **1845** Potato blight starts a five-year famine in Ireland

1800 — **1825** — **1850**

World

- **1808** Spanish colonies in the Americas begin winning independence
- **c. 1818** Zulus begin conquests in southeastern Africa
- **1825–1830** Java War, between Indonesians and Dutch colonialists
- **1835** Dutch-speaking Boer colonists begin Great Trek to escape British rule in southern Africa

Literary Forms

Over the past two centuries, European writers have steadily expanded the range of topics, viewpoints, and styles in literature.

- James Joyce, Albert Camus, and others experimented with new types of novels. Writers eliminated plots, added multiple points of view, and presented events in nonchronological order.
- Poets generally moved away from the carefully structured patterns of rhymes and the number of stressed syllables in each line. Instead, they wrote poetry that sounded more like everyday speech.
- Drama flourished in the mid-1800s, as writers such as Henrik Ibsen and Anton Chekhov portrayed the contradictions in everyday life. By the 1950s and 1960s, Eugene Ionesco, Samuel Beckett, and others featured characters leading disoriented lives that had no ultimate meaning. In short, these characters led lives that were *absurd,* a term used to describe these plays.
- Writers developed the modern short story in the mid-1800s. The form fit well into the new magazines marketed to the growing market of literate readers. Writers such as Guy de Maupassant presented believable, well-constructed plots. Others, such as Nikolay Gogol, wrote more mysterious, dream-like tales.

European Community flag.

Modern Europe

1. Modern European society has been shaped by exciting—and sometimes disturbing—experiences. In a small group, create a list of three historical developments that transformed modern Europe.
2. In a small group, discuss effects that important historical developments had on European movements in art, music, and literature. Include details from the Part Introduction to support your ideas.

Still from production of Samuel Beckett's play *Happy Days*.

GERMANY, 1827

Before You Read

The Lorelei

Meet Heinrich Heine

"I . . . am essentially an enthusiast—one so moved by an ideal as to sacrifice himself for it."

Heinrich Heine (hīn′ rikн hī′ nə) came from a Jewish family in Düsseldorf. He began his literary career while studying law at German universities. In 1831 he left Germany, attracted by the recent liberal revolution in France. He received a warm welcome in French literary circles and became friends with many writers and political figures.

Heine is best known for his lyrical poems, which brought a new tone of irony and skepticism to German literature. In his time, however, these earned him as much condemnation as praise. As he grew older, financial and health problems increasingly burdened him. From age fifty, paralysis and partial blindness left him confined to what he called a "mattress-grave." However, during his remaining eight years he created many of his finest poems. His last request, appropriately, was for paper and pencil.

Heine was born in 1797 and died in 1856.

Reading Focus

Think of a time when a beautiful sound or sight made you lose track of what was going on around you.

Quickwrite Write for one or two minutes in your journal about this experience.

Setting a Purpose Read Heine's poem for a legend about dangerously beautiful music.

Building Background

Watery Temptress

The Lorelei (lôr′ ə lī′), on the bank of the Rhine River, is a large rock that produces an echo. It became associated with a legend about the spirit of a woman who would lure boatmen to their deaths with her beautiful singing. The woman had drowned herself in the river because of an unfaithful lover.

Heine's poem based on this legend first appeared in his most famous volume, the *Book of Songs.* Like much of his early verse, it was influenced by the Romantic writers' fascination with folk songs. "The Lorelei" has been set to music by more than twenty-five composers. It became so popular that the anti-Semitic Nazis, who controlled Germany during the 1930s and early 1940s, did not remove it from schoolbooks after they banned Heine's works because he was Jewish. Instead, editors described it as "a popular folk song, author unknown."

Reading Further

If you enjoy reading "The Lorelei," you might wish to sample the following:

Poems from *Homecoming* from *Songs of Love and Grief,* translated by Walter W. Arndt.

Jewish Stories and Hebrew Melodies, by Heinrich Heine.

Heinrich Heine

Translated by Aaron Kramer

I cannot explain the sadness
That's fallen on my breast.
An old, old fable haunts me,
And will not let me rest.

The air grows cool in the twilight,
And softly the Rhine flows on;
The peak of a mountain sparkles
Beneath the setting sun.

More lovely than a vision,
A girl sits high up there;
Her golden jewelry glistens,
She combs her golden hair.

With a comb of gold she combs it,
And sings an evensong;°
The wonderful melody reaches
A boat, as it sails along.

The boatman hears, with an anguish
More wild than was ever known;
He's blind to the rocks around him;
His eyes are for her alone.

—At last the waves devoured
The boat, and the boatman's cry;
And this she did with her singing,
The golden Lorelei.

The Siren, 1879. Charles Landelle (France). Oil on canvas. Russell-Cotes Art Gallery and Museum, Bournemouth, UK.

---

14 *Evensong* is a prayerful song sung late in the afternoon.

Responding to Literature

Personal Response

Which images from this poem linger in your mind? Share your response with the class.

Analyzing Literature

Recall and Interpret

1. What is the "old, old fable" that has been troubling the speaker?
2. What is the **setting**–the place and the time–of the legend that the speaker tells (see **Literary Terms Handbook,** page R11)?
3. What actions does the girl in the legend perform? Do you think that she is a real person? Explain your answer.
4. What happens to the boatman as he passes the girl on the rock? Why does he meet this fate?

Evaluate and Connect

5. Why might Heine have chosen to use several golden images in the poem?
6. A **symbol** is an object or action that stands for something else in addition to itself (see **Literary Terms Handbook,** page R12). What do you think the girl's singing symbolizes?
7. What, do you think, is the reason that "The Lorelei" became so popular in Germany?
8. Does "The Lorelei" remind you of any other poems or songs that you know? Explain.

Literary Criticism

"Most of [Heine's] early poems," argues Robert C. Holub, "deal with the theme of unrequited love . . . Their outstanding feature is the turn or ironic twist which frequently concludes a poem. The reader is lulled into a false sense of security when he or she encounters the familiar imagery . . . But in the final lines Heine calls this imagery–and the ideology behind it–into question with a note of discord or ironic distancing." In a brief essay, explain how this statement applies to "The Lorelei."

Literary ELEMENTS

Rhyme

Words **rhyme** when their accented syllables and all the letters that follow sound the same. The word *yearning* rhymes with *burning,* and *berate* rhymes with *fate.* When words sound similar but do not rhyme exactly (like *alone* and *belong*), they are called **half-rhymes** or **slant rhymes.** Rhyme can add to the pleasure of reading poetry and can also help link lines in a poem together. Literary scholars use letters to indicate a poem's rhyme scheme, or the pattern of rhymes that occur at the ends of lines (for example, *aabb* or *abab*).

1. What is the rhyme scheme of "The Lorelei"?
2. Identify a half-rhyme in this translation of the poem.

- See **Literary Terms Handbook,** p. R10.

Extending Your Response

Creative Writing

Poem In the Reading Focus on page 868, you were asked to describe a time when you became completely distracted by a beautiful sound or sight. Why did it have such an effect on you? Write a brief poem based on this experience. Use vivid imagery to help convey your feelings to the reader.

Interdisciplinary Activity

Music: Setting Heine's poem has been set to music by many different composers. Bring to class a recording of music that you think would make a good setting for the poem. Consider the rhythm and imagery of the poem as you select the music. After playing the recording for the class, explain why you chose it.

Save your work for your portfolio.

INTERDISCIPLINARY GEOGRAPHY CONNECTION

The Rhine

NORTH SEA
NETHERLANDS
BELGIUM
Rhine River
GERMANY
LUXEMBOURG
LIECHTENSTEIN
FRANCE
SWITZERLAND
AUSTRIA
ITALY

The Rhine and its dramatic path, sometimes between immense gorges, have been the stuff of legend since before Julius Caesar bridged the river in 55 and 53 B.C. In Heinrich Heine's poem "The Lorelei," you read about a beautiful singing maiden who sits atop a cliff over the Rhine and lures sailors and their ships to destruction. Lorelei is the name of an actual rock on the right bank of the Rhine that looms nearly 440 feet above the river. The rock and the reefs below present a real danger to passing ships. The Lorelei is one of countless examples of the role the Rhine has played in the romance, history, and legends of Germany and Europe. For many, the mere mention of the Rhine sparks the imagination.

The Rhine rises in two head streams high in the Swiss Alps. It flows generally north and west, through Germany and the Netherlands, for 865 miles until it reaches the North Sea. Linked by canals to other major rivers in Western Europe, the Rhine is one of Europe's most important commercial waterways. Many German manufacturing and industrial cities are located along the Rhine, adding to the importance of the river for shipping and transportation. It is also a major source of hydroelectric power.

North of Mainz, Germany, the Rhine winds its way between mountain peaks crowned with castles. This section of the Rhine—known as the Rhine Gorge—is perhaps the most picturesque view of the river. There are castles—both ruined and restored—on most stretches of the Rhine. From these strategically placed posts, feudal lords could keep watch over the traffic on the river as well as defend their land. Today, this section of the river is a major tourist attraction.

The Rhine has been both a link and a barrier between peoples and nations for centuries. Today, as Europe struggles toward economic unity and political cooperation, a multinational effort to clean up the river is underway.

Activity

1. Using a current map of Europe, locate the Rhine and trace its path from Switzerland through Germany. Then write a clear set of directions a ship captain could follow to find his or her way "down" the river. Note that there will be places on the map, and therefore in your set of directions, where the river divides. Be sure to use the compass points east, west, south, and north in your directions.
2. Find out more about the extensive river trade on the Rhine. You might consider questions such as: What products are shipped on its waters? What towns along the Rhine are key shipping ports? What physical features of the Rhine make it valuable or hazardous for commerce? Present your findings in an oral report to the class.

FRANCE, 1853

Before You Read

Russia 1812 from *The Expiation*

Meet Victor Hugo

"The excessive, the immense are the natural domain of Victor Hugo; he moves in it as if in his native atmosphere." —*Charles Baudelaire*

Victor Hugo (hū′ gō) was a remarkably versatile and prolific writer. According to some accounts, he would write a hundred lines of verse or twenty pages of prose each morning. A leader of the Romantic movement, which emphasized emotion and imagination rather than reason, Hugo introduced important innovations in French poetry. Outside of France, he is best known for his two major novels, *The Hunchback of Notre Dame* and *Les Misérables*.

Hugo believed that writers should play an active role in society. Many of his finest works date from the 1850s and 1860s, when he lived in exile because he opposed the rule of Napoleon III. He returned home a national hero after a new republican government came to power in 1870. His funeral fifteen years later was attended by two million people, including delegates from every European country.

Hugo was born in 1802 and died in 1885.

Reading Focus

Think of war footage that you have seen in movies or on television. What images can you recall?

Share Ideas Share your response with the class.

Setting a Purpose Read Hugo's vivid portrayal of an important event in military history.

Building Background

Napoleon in Russia

"Russia 1812" is excerpted from *The Expiation,* a narrative poem about the career of Napoleon Bonaparte. At the time he wrote the poem, Victor Hugo was living in exile, having fled Paris after Napoleon's nephew came to power as Napoleon III. Hugo had mixed feelings about his subject. He considered Napoleon Bonaparte (Napoleon I) both a hero and a tyrant. In the poem, he tried to show how the emperor's political crime of seizing power illegally was paid for, or "expiated," by his eventual downfall.

Napoleon still controlled much of Europe when he led his Grand Army to Russia in 1812. He expected a quick battlefield victory against Czar Alexander I, but the Russians chose a strategy of retreat, drawing the French deep into their territory. Napoleon entered Moscow, which the Russians had abandoned, in mid-September. But the Russians set fire to their own capital, forcing the French to retreat from the ruined city. Only fragments of the Grand Army made it back to France, after struggling through fierce winter cold and endless attacks by the Russians. This disastrous campaign emboldened Napoleon's enemies throughout Europe. Within two years, he was forced to abdicate and go into exile.

Reading Further

If you enjoy reading "Russia 1812," you might also enjoy these works:

Les Misérables, by Victor Hugo. Many critics consider this social novel Hugo's finest work.

With Napoleon in Russia, by Armand de Caulaincourt. A first-hand account of the invasion and the disastrous retreat, by one of Napoleon's generals.

Napoleon's Retreat From Moscow. Adolf Northen (Germany, 1828–1876). Private collection.

Russia 1812
from The Expiation

Victor Hugo
Translated by Robert Lowell

The snow fell, and its power was multiplied.
For the first time the Eagle° bowed its head—
dark days! Slowly the Emperor returned—
behind him Moscow! Its onion domes° still burned.
The snow rained down in blizzards—rained and froze.
Past each white waste a further white waste rose.
None recognized the captains or the flags.
Yesterday the Grand Army, today its dregs!
No one could tell the vanguard° from the flanks.°

2 **Eagle:** Napoleon, who took the eagle as his standard. Napoleon required his troops to swear by this standard that they would conquer or die.

4 **onion domes:** domes of Eastern Orthodox churches.

9 **vanguard:** the front division of an army. **flanks:** an army's sides.

The snow! The hurt men struggled from the ranks,
hid in the bellies of dead horse, in stacks
of shattered caissons.° By the bivouacs,°
one saw the picket° dying at his post,
still standing in his saddle, white with frost,
the stone lips frozen to the bugle's mouth!
Bullets and grapeshot° mingled with the snow,
that hailed . . . The Guard, surprised at shivering, march
in a dream now; ice rimes° the gray mustache.
The snow falls, always snow! The driving mire
submerges; men, trapped in that white empire,
have no more bread and march on barefoot—gaps!
They were no longer living men and troops,
but a dream drifting in a fog, a mystery,
mourners parading under the black sky.
The solitude, vast, terrible to the eye,
was like a mute avenger everywhere,
as snowfall, floating through the quiet air,
buried the huge army in a huge shroud.°
Could anyone leave this kingdom? A crowd—

12 **caissons** (kā′ sənz): chests that hold ammunition or carts for ammunition. **bivouacs:** temporary encampments.

13 **picket:** here, a sentry.

16 **grapeshot:** small metal balls fired from cannons.

18 **rime:** to cover with ice.

28 **shroud:** a sheet in which a corpse is wrapped before burial.

The Remains of the Grande Armée on the Retreat from Russia, 1890. Carl Röchling (Germany, 1855–1920). Color print after a gouache. AKG London.

Viewing the painting: How would you describe the mood of this painting? How is it similar to the mood of the poem at this point?

each man, obsessed with dying, was alone.
Men slept—and died! The beaten mob sludged on,
ditching the guns to burn their carriages.
Two foes. The North, the Czar. The North was worse.
In hollows where the snow was piling up,
one saw whole regiments fallen asleep.
Attila's° dawn, Cannaes of Hannibal!°
The army marching to its funeral!
Litters, wounded, the dead, deserters—swarm,
crushing the bridges down to cross a stream.
They went to sleep ten thousand, woke up four.°
Ney,° bringing up the former army's rear,
hacked his horse loose from three disputing Cossacks . . .
All night, the *qui vive?*° The alert! Attacks;
retreats! White ghosts would wrench away our guns,
or we would see dim, terrible squadrons,
circles of steel, whirlpools of savages,
rush sabering through the camp like dervishes.°
And in this way, whole armies died at night.

The Emperor was there, standing—he saw.
This oak already trembling from the axe,
watched his glories drop from him branch by branch:
chiefs, soldiers. Each one had his turn and chance—
they died! Some lived. These still believed his star,
and kept their watch. They loved the man of war,
this small man with his hands behind his back,
whose shadow, moving to and fro, was black
behind the lighted tent. Still believing, they
accused their destiny of *lèse-majesté*.°
His misfortune had mounted on their back.
The man of glory shook. Cold stupefied
him, then suddenly he felt terrified.
Being without belief, he turned to God:
"God of armies, is this the end?" he cried.
And then at last the expiation° came,
as he heard someone call him by his name,
someone half-lost in shadow, who said, "No,
Napoleon." Napoleon understood,
restless, bareheaded, leaden, as he stood
before his butchered legions in the snow.

36 **Attila:** ruler of the Huns (c. 406–453). Called "the Scourge of God," he plagued both the Roman and Byzantine empires. **Hannibal:** the Carthaginian general (247–183 B.C.) also fought against Rome. Hugo suggests that the winter (the North) gave Napoleon as much trouble as Attila and Hannibal gave ancient Rome.

40 **ten thousand, woke up four:** Napoleon's losses during this trek might have been as many as 500,000 soldiers (in an army of 600,000 to 700,000).

41 **Ney** (nā): Napoleon's second in command during this campaign.

43 ***qui vive*** (kē vēv): "long live who?" is the challenge of a sentry in French (similar to "who goes there?").

47 **dervishes:** a sect of Islam that is known for the whirling dances performed (sometimes with sabers, or swords) in religious ceremonies.

58 ***lèse-majesté*** (lez′ ma′ zhes tā′): the crime of insulting a ruler. Here, it is the weather that has committed the crime against Napoleon.

64 **expiation** (eks′ pē ā′ shən): making up for a wicked act.

Responding to Literature

Personal Response

How did you feel about the soldiers described in this poem? Jot down your response in your journal.

Analyzing Literature

Recall and Interpret

1. What is happening as the selection begins?
2. Which images in the poem suggest the extreme cold?
3. What metaphor is used to describe Napoleon as his army is being destroyed?
4. Whose thoughts and feelings are described in the poem? Whose thoughts and feelings are left out?
5. How do you interpret Napoleon's reaction to the voice that says this is not the end?

Evaluate and Connect

6. **Tone** is the attitude that a speaker takes toward the audience, a subject, or a character (see page R12). What is the speaker's tone in "Russia 1812"?
7. Why might Hugo have chosen to repeat the word *snow* so many times in the poem?
8. Do you think that Hugo's portrait of Napoleon is sympathetic or unsympathetic? Explain.
9. In your opinion, does Hugo glamorize war in this poem? Why or why not?
10. In the Reading Focus on page 872, you were asked to recall images from war footage. How do these images compare with the images in Hugo's poem?

Literary ELEMENTS

Antagonist

In a literary work, the **antagonist** is the person or force opposing the protagonist, or central character. The antagonist may be an individual, a group of people, a force in nature, or a social force such as racial and class prejudice. In "Russia 1812," Hugo identifies two protagonists: the cold winter and the czar's army.

1. How do you interpret the speaker's remark that the "North" was a worse foe than the czar?
2. Do you think the Russian troops are portrayed as evil in the poem, or simply as the opponents of Napoleon's army? Explain your response.

- See **Literary Terms Handbook,** p. R1.

Extending Your Response

Creative Writing

Diary Imagine that you are one of the soldiers in Napoleon's army. Write a diary entry revealing your thoughts and feelings about Napoleon, your opponents, and the merciless Russian winter. Use details from Hugo's poem and make up details about your personal situation (for example, you might describe being wounded or fleeing from the enemy).

Performing

Oral Reading In a small group, perform a round-robin reading of "Russia 1812." You might divide up the poem so that each student reads one long passage, or you might alternate every few lines. Before you begin reading, go over the poem together to clarify any unfamiliar words or phrases.

Save your work for your portfolio.

Literature FOCUS

Modernism

Shock and Scandal In this unit, you will read the play *A Doll's House*, written by the Norwegian dramatist Henrik Ibsen, who is generally considered the founder of modern prose drama. To modern sensibilities, Ibsen's play may not seem scandalous. However, when it was first performed in the late 1800s, it sent shock waves through the audience. What was it about Ibsen's play that caused the audience to gasp? What "modernist" techniques on stage resulted in what one critic called "a new order of experience in the theater"?

Prior to Ibsen's *A Doll's House,* theatergoers were used to seeing plays with a traditional plot structure, with each scene constructed specifically toward a predictable climax and equally predictable resolution. Such a structure was rejected by the playwrights, writers, and artists influenced by Modernism. As you read *A Doll's House,* notice how Ibsen conceals the traditional plot structure in carefully developed stage directions. The result on stage is the realistic and deceptively simple presentation of a few related scenes in the life of a husband and wife. The framework, with which today's audience is very familiar, was a bold innovation for which the early twentieth-century audience was unprepared.

A New Tradition Modernism, in general, reflects a sharp break with all tradition. One critic even called Modernism "the tradition of the new." In addition to technical experimentation, modernist playwrights, writers, and artists in the first half of the twentieth century were interested in the irrational or inexplicable, as well as in the workings of the unconscious mind. Many of these modernist interests were influenced by the psychology of Sigmund Freud, the creator of psychoanalysis (see page 325).

Just as Ibsen's *A Doll's House* provided a new order of experience in the theater, Freud's theories of the normal and abnormal mind opened up a new order of experience in psychology and literature. Modernist writers such as Virginia Woolf *(To the Lighthouse)* and James Joyce *(Finnegan's Wake),* for example, rejected traditional narrative form and experimented with stream of consciousness, a narrative technique that mimics the mind's flow of thoughts and feelings.

Modernists also rejected the moralizing of traditional literature. Instead of making sure the audience or reader learned a lesson, modernists presented circumstances of the human condition and the questions relating to that condition. As Ibsen himself said, "A dramatist's business is not to answer questions, but merely to ask them."

Variation II. Paul Klee (Switzerland, 1879–1940). Bauhaus Archive, Tiergarten, Berlin, Germany.

Before You Read

A Doll's House

Meet Henrik Ibsen

"It was a long time before I realized that to be a poet is, most of all, to see."

Henrik Ibsen (hən′ rik′ ib′ sən) came from a small town in southern Norway. When he was a boy, his father went bankrupt and the family fell into poverty. Ibsen left home at fifteen to study medicine, but he soon turned his attention to directing and writing for the theater. His early works failed to win over audiences. Frustrated, he moved to Italy in 1864. Over the next few years he wrote two verse plays, *Brand* and *Peer Gynt*, that finally established his reputation. However, Ibsen did not return to Norway to live until 1891.

Despite the success of his verse plays, Ibsen felt that a different style was needed for the stage. He began a series of prose plays exploring controversial social issues. The most famous of these, *A Doll's House*, stunned audiences when it premiered in 1879. Ibsen was one of the founders of modern realistic drama. He influenced writers throughout Europe, including George Bernard Shaw and James Joyce.

Henrik Ibsen was born in 1828 and died in 1906.

Reading Focus

Which three qualities or conditions do you think are most important for a good marriage? Why do you think these qualities or conditions are so important?

Survey It! Pose this question to five friends or relatives. As they respond, take notes on what they say. After you have spoken to all your respondents, write a summary of your findings. When you are finished, present the results of your survey to the class.

Setting a Purpose Read Henrik Ibsen's "A Doll's House" to see how an apparently happy marriage is affected by secrets and deception.

Building Background

Husbands and Wives

The issue of women's roles in society is at the forefront of *A Doll's House.* During the nineteenth century, middle-class women were expected to center their lives around the home. Social customs and laws encouraged wives to be completely dependent on their husbands. In an essay published in 1855, British novelist George Eliot (the pen name of Marian Evans) argued that this domestic arrangement harmed men as well as women. She pointed out that a man of genius might waste his talent to support "a woman who can understand none of his secret yearnings, who is fit for nothing but to sit in her drawing-room like a doll-Madonna in her shrine."

Vocabulary Preview

indiscreet (in′ dis krēt′) *adj.* lacking in good judgment; p. 886

rash (rash) *adj.* resulting from undue haste or a lack of planning or caution; p. 893

slander (slan′ dər) *v.* to damage another's reputation through the spreading of lies or false charges; p. 904

resolutely (rez′ ə lo͞ot′ lē) *adv.* with firm determination; p. 905

unperturbed (un′ pər turbd′) *adj.* not greatly disturbed in mind; calm; p. 928

A Doll's House

Henrik Ibsen
Translated by Rolf Fjelde

Cast of Characters

Torvald Helmer, a lawyer

Nora, his wife

Dr. Rank

Mrs. Linde

Nils Krogstad, a bank clerk

The Helmers' Three Small Children

Anne-Marie, their nurse

Helene, a maid

A Delivery Boy

The action takes place in HELMER's residence.

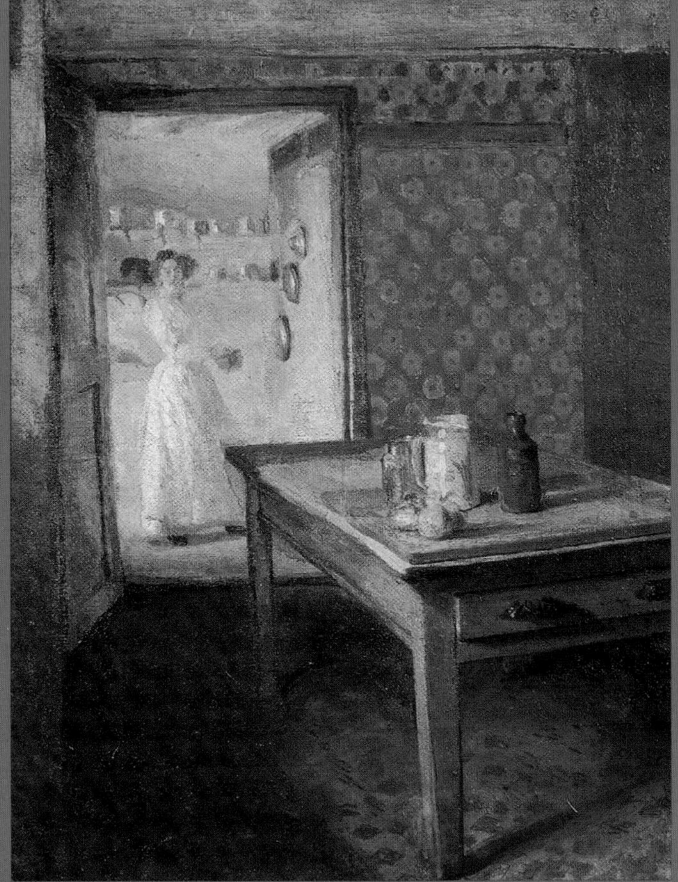

The Kitchen, 1902. Duncan Grant (Great Britain). Oil on canvas, 50.8 x 40.6 cm. Tate Gallery, London.

ACT I

[*A comfortable room, tastefully but not expensively furnished. A door to the right in the back wall leads to the entryway; another to the left leads to* HELMER's *study. Between these doors, a piano. Midway in the left-hand wall a door, and farther back a window. Near the window a round table with an armchair and a small sofa. In the right-hand wall, toward the rear, a door, and nearer the foreground a porcelain stove with two armchairs and a rocking chair beside it. Between the stove and the side door, a small table. Engravings on the walls. An étagère with china figures and other small art objects; a small bookcase with richly bound books; the floor carpeted; a fire burning in the stove. It is a winter day.*

A bell rings in the entryway; shortly after we hear the door being unlocked. NORA *comes into the room, humming happily to herself; she is wearing street clothes and carries an armload of packages, which she puts down on the table to the right. She has left the hall door open; and through it a* DELIVERY BOY *is seen, holding a Christmas tree and a basket, which he gives to the* MAID *who let them in.*]

NORA. Hide the tree well, Helene. The children mustn't get a glimpse of it till this evening, after it's trimmed. [*To the* DELIVERY BOY, *taking out her purse.*] How much?

DELIVERY BOY. Fifty, ma'am.

NORA. There's a crown. No, keep the change. [*The* BOY *thanks her and leaves.* NORA *shuts the door. She laughs softly to herself while taking off her street things. Drawing a bag of macaroons from her pocket, she eats a couple, then steals over and listens at her husband's study door.*] Yes, he's home. [*Hums again as she moves to the table right.*]

HELMER. [*From the study.*] Is that my little lark twittering out there?

NORA. [*Busy opening some packages.*] Yes, it is.

HELMER. Is that my squirrel rummaging around?

NORA. Yes!

HELMER. When did my squirrel get in?

NORA. Just now. [*Putting the macaroon bag in her pocket and wiping her mouth.*] Do come in, Torvald, and see what I've bought.

HELMER. Can't be disturbed. [*After a moment he opens the door and peers in, pen in hand.*] Bought, you say? All that there? Has the little spendthrift been out throwing money around again?

NORA. Oh, but Torvald, this year we really should let ourselves go a bit. It's the first Christmas we haven't had to economize.

HELMER. But you know we can't go squandering.

NORA. Oh yes, Torvald, we can squander a little now. Can't we? Just a tiny, wee bit. Now that you've got a big salary and are going to make piles and piles of money.

HELMER. Yes—starting New Year's. But then it's a full three months till the raise comes through.

NORA. Pooh! We can borrow that long.

HELMER. Nora! [*Goes over and playfully takes her by the ear.*] Are your scatterbrains off again? What if today I borrowed a thousand crowns, and you squandered them over Christmas week, and then on New Year's Eve a roof tile fell on my head, and I lay there—

NORA. [*Putting her hand on his mouth.*] Oh! Don't say such things!

HELMER. Yes, but what if it happened—then what?

NORA. If anything so awful happened, then it just wouldn't matter if I had debts or not.

HELMER. Well, but the people I'd borrowed from?

NORA. Them? Who cares about them! They're strangers.

HELMER. Nora, Nora, how like a woman! No, but seriously, Nora, you know what I think about that. No debts! Never borrow! Something of freedom's lost—and something of beauty, too—from a home that's founded on borrowing and debt. We've made a brave stand up to now, the two of us; and we'll go right on like that the little while we have to.

NORA. [*Going toward the stove.*] Yes, whatever you say, Torvald.

HELMER. [*Following her.*] Now, now, the little lark's wings mustn't droop. Come on, don't be a sulky squirrel. [*Taking out his wallet.*] Nora, guess what I have here.

NORA. [*Turning quickly.*] Money!

HELMER. There, see. [*Hands her some notes.*] Good grief, I know how costs go up in a house at Christmastime.

NORA. Ten—twenty—thirty—forty. Oh, thank you, Torvald; I can manage no end on this.

HELMER. You really will have to.

NORA. Oh yes, I promise I will! But come here so I can show you everything I bought. And so cheap! Look, new clothes for Ivar here—and a sword. Here a horse and a trumpet for Bob. And a doll and a doll's bed here for Emmy; they're nothing much, but she'll tear them to bits in no time anyway. And here I have dress material and handkerchiefs for the maids. Old Anne-Marie really deserves something more.

HELMER. And what's in that package there?

NORA. [*With a cry.*] Torvald, no! You can't see that till tonight!

HELMER. I see. But tell me now, you little prodigal,[1] what have you thought of for yourself?

NORA. For myself? Oh, I don't want anything at all.

HELMER. Of course you do. Tell me just what—within reason—you'd most like to have.

NORA. I honestly don't know. Oh, listen, Torvald—

HELMER. Well?

NORA. [*Fumbling at his coat buttons, without looking at him.*] If you want to give me something, then maybe you could—you could—

HELMER. Come on, out with it.

NORA. [*Hurriedly.*] You could give me money, Torvald. No more than you think you can spare; then one of these days I'll buy something with it.

HELMER. But Nora—

NORA. Oh, please, Torvald darling, do that! I beg you, please. Then I could hang the bills in pretty gilt paper on the Christmas tree. Wouldn't that be fun?

1. Here, a ***prodigal*** (prod′ i gəl) refers to a person who spends or gives lavishly and foolishly.

HELMER. What are those little birds called that always fly through their fortunes?

NORA. Oh yes, spendthrifts; I know all that. But let's do as I say, Torvald; then I'll have time to decide what I really need most. That's very sensible, isn't it?

HELMER. [*Smiling.*] Yes, very—that is, if you actually hung onto the money I give you, and you actually used it to buy yourself something. But it goes for the house and for all sorts of foolish things, and then I only have to lay out some more.

NORA. Oh, but Torvald—

HELMER. Don't deny it, my dear little Nora. [*Putting his arm around her waist.*] Spendthrifts are sweet, but they use up a frightful amount of money. It's incredible what it costs a man to feed such birds.

NORA. Oh, how can you say that! Really, I save everything I can.

HELMER. [*Laughing.*] Yes, that's the truth. Everything you can. But that's nothing at all.

NORA. [*Humming, with a smile of quiet satisfaction.*] Hm, if you only knew what expenses we larks and squirrels have, Torvald.

HELMER. You're an odd little one. Exactly the way your father was. You're never at a loss for scaring up money; but the moment you have it, it runs right out through your fingers; you never know what you've done with it. Well, one takes you as you are. It's deep in your blood. Yes, these things are hereditary, Nora.

NORA. Ah, I could wish I'd inherited many of Papa's qualities.

HELMER. And I couldn't wish you anything but just what you are, my sweet little lark. But wait; it seems to me you have a very—what should I call it?—a very suspicious look today—

NORA. I do?

HELMER. You certainly do. Look me straight in the eye.

NORA. [*Looking at him.*] Well?

HELMER. [*Shaking an admonitory finger.*] Surely my sweet tooth hasn't been running riot in town today, has she?

NORA. No. Why do you imagine that?

HELMER. My sweet tooth really didn't make a little detour through the confectioner's?

NORA. No, I assure you, Torvald—

HELMER. Hasn't nibbled some pastry?

NORA. No, not at all.

HELMER. Not even munched a macaroon or two?

NORA. No, Torvald, I assure you, really—

HELMER. There, there now. Of course I'm only joking.

NORA. [*Going to the table, right.*] You know I could never think of going against you.

HELMER. No, I understand that; and you *have* given me your word. [*Going over to her.*] Well, you keep your little Christmas secrets to yourself, Nora darling. I expect they'll come to light this evening, when the tree is lit.

At Dinner, 1914. Zinaida Evgnievna Serebryakova (Russia). Oil on canvas. Pushkin Museum, Moscow.

Viewing the painting: Describe the children's facial expressions. Is this how you imagine Nora's children? Explain.

NORA. Did you remember to ask Dr. Rank?

HELMER. No. But there's no need for that; it's assumed he'll be dining with us. All the same, I'll ask him when he stops by here this morning. I've ordered some fine wine. Nora, you can't imagine how I'm looking forward to this evening.

NORA. So am I. And what fun for the children, Torvald!

HELMER. Ah, it's so gratifying to know that one's gotten a safe, secure job, and with a comfortable salary. It's a great satisfaction, isn't it?

NORA. Oh, it's wonderful!

HELMER. Remember last Christmas? Three whole weeks before, you shut yourself in every evening till long after midnight, making flowers for the Christmas tree, and all the other decorations to surprise us. Ugh, that was the dullest time I've ever lived through.

NORA. It wasn't at all dull for me.

HELMER. [*Smiling.*] But the outcome *was* pretty sorry, Nora.

NORA. Oh, don't tease me with that again. How could I help it that the cat came in and tore everything to shreds.

HELMER. No, poor thing, you certainly couldn't. You wanted so much to please us all, and that's what counts. But it's just as well that the hard times are past.

NORA. Yes, it's really wonderful.

HELMER. Now I don't have to sit here alone, boring myself, and you don't have to tire your precious eyes and your fair little delicate hands—

NORA. [*Clapping her hands.*] No, is it really true, Torvald, I don't have to? Oh, how wonderfully lovely to hear! [*Taking his arm.*] Now I'll tell you just how I've thought we should plan things. Right after Christmas— [*The doorbell rings.*] Oh, the bell. [*Straightening the room up a bit.*] Somebody would have to come. What a bore!

HELMER. I'm not at home to visitors, don't forget.

MAID. [*From the hall doorway.*] Ma'am, a lady to see you—

NORA. All right, let her come in.

MAID. [*To* HELMER.] And the doctor's just come too.

HELMER. Did he go right to my study?

MAID. Yes, he did.

[*HELMER goes into his room. The* MAID *shows in* MRS. LINDE, *dressed in traveling clothes, and shuts the door after her.*]

MRS. LINDE. [*In a dispirited and somewhat hesitant voice.*] Hello, Nora.

NORA. [*Uncertain.*] Hello—

MRS. LINDE. You don't recognize me.

NORA. No, I don't know—but wait, I think—[*Exclaiming.*] What! Kristine! Is it really you?

MRS. LINDE. Yes, it's me.

NORA. Kristine! To think I didn't recognize you. But then, how could I? [*More quietly.*] How you've changed, Kristine!

MRS. LINDE. Yes, no doubt I have. In nine—ten long years.

NORA. Is it so long since we met! Yes, it's all of that. Oh, these last eight years have been a happy time, believe me. And so now you've come in to town, too. Made the long trip in the winter. That took courage.

MRS. LINDE. I just got here by ship this morning.

NORA. To enjoy yourself over Christmas, of course. Oh, how lovely! Yes, enjoy ourselves, we'll do that. But take your coat off. You're not still cold? [*Helping her.*] There now, let's get cozy here by the stove. No, the easy chair there! I'll take the rocker here. [*Seizing her hands.*] Yes, now you have your old look again; it was only in that first moment. You're a bit more pale, Kristine—and maybe a bit thinner.

MRS. LINDE. And much, much older, Nora.

NORA. Yes, perhaps a bit older; a tiny, tiny bit; not much at all. [*Stopping short; suddenly serious.*] Oh, but thoughtless me, to sit here, chattering away. Sweet, good Kristine, can you forgive me?

MRS. LINDE. What do you mean, Nora?

NORA. [*Softly.*] Poor Kristine, you've become a widow.

MRS. LINDE. Yes, three years ago.

NORA. Oh, I knew it, of course; I read it in the papers. Oh, Kristine, you must believe me; I often thought of writing you then, but I kept postponing it, and something always interfered.

MRS. LINDE. Nora dear, I understand completely.

NORA. No, it was awful of me, Kristine. You poor thing, how much you must have gone through. And he left you nothing?

MRS. LINDE. No.

NORA. And no children?

MRS. LINDE. No.

NORA. Nothing at all, then?

MRS. LINDE. Not even a sense of loss to feed on.

NORA. [*Looking incredulously at her.*] But Kristine, how could that be?

MRS. LINDE. [*Smiling wearily and smoothing her hair.*] Oh, sometimes it happens, Nora.

NORA. So completely alone. How terribly hard that must be for you. I have three lovely children. You can't see them now; they're out with the maid. But now you must tell me everything—

MRS. LINDE. No, no, no, tell me about yourself.

NORA. No, you begin. Today I don't want to be selfish. I want to think only of you today. But there *is* something I must tell you. Did you hear of the wonderful luck we had recently?

MRS. LINDE. No, what's that?

NORA. My husband's been made manager in the bank, just think!

MRS. LINDE. Your husband? How marvelous!

NORA. Isn't it? Being a lawyer is such an uncertain living, you know, especially if one won't touch any cases that aren't clean and decent. And of course Torvald would never do that, and I'm with him completely there. Oh, we're simply delighted, believe me! He'll join the bank right after New Year's and start getting a huge salary and lots of commissions. From now on we can live quite differently—just as we want. Oh, Kristine, I feel so light and happy! Won't it be lovely to have stacks of money and not a care in the world?

MRS. LINDE. Well, anyway, it would be lovely to have enough for necessities.

NORA. No, not just for necessities, but stacks and stacks of money!

MRS. LINDE. [*Smiling.*] Nora, Nora, aren't you sensible yet? Back in school you were such a free spender.

NORA. [*With a quiet laugh.*] Yes, that's what Torvald still says. [*Shaking her finger.*] But "Nora, Nora" isn't as silly as you all think. Really, we've been in no position for me to go squandering. We've had to work, both of us.

MRS. LINDE. You too?

NORA. Yes, at odd jobs—needlework, crocheting, embroidery, and such— [*Casually.*] and other things too. You remember that Torvald left the department when we were married? There was no chance of promotion in his office, and of course he needed to earn more money. But that first year he drove himself terribly. He took on all kinds of extra work that kept him going morning and night. It wore him down, and then he fell deathly ill. The doctors said it was essential for him to travel south.

MRS. LINDE. Yes, didn't you spend a whole year in Italy?

NORA. That's right. It wasn't easy to get away, you know. Ivar had just been born. But of course we had to go. Oh, that was a beautiful trip, and it saved Torvald's life. But it cost a frightful sum, Kristine.

MRS. LINDE. I can well imagine.

NORA. Four thousand, eight hundred crowns it cost. That's really a lot of money.

MRS. LINDE. But it's lucky you had it when you needed it.

NORA. Well, as it was, we got it from Papa.

MRS. LINDE. I see. It was just about the time your father died.

NORA. Yes, just about then. And, you know, I couldn't make that trip out to nurse him. I had to stay here, expecting Ivar any moment, and with my poor sick Torvald to care for. Dearest Papa, I never saw him again, Kristine. Oh, that was the worst time I've known in all my marriage.

MRS. LINDE. I know how you loved him. And then you went off to Italy?

NORA. Yes. We had the means now, and the doctors urged us. So we left a month after.

MRS. LINDE. And your husband came back completely cured?

NORA. Sound as a drum![2]

MRS. LINDE. But—the doctor?

NORA. Who?

MRS. LINDE. I thought the maid said he was a doctor, the man who came in with me.

NORA. Yes, that was Dr. Rank—but he's not making a sick call. He's our closest friend, and he stops by at least once a day. No, Torvald hasn't had a sick moment since, and the children are fit and strong, and I am, too. [*Jumping up and clapping her hands.*] Oh, dear God, Kristine, what a lovely thing to live and be happy! But how disgusting of me—I'm talking of nothing but my own affairs. [*Sits on a stool close by* KRISTINE, *arms resting across her knees.*] Oh, don't be angry with me! Tell me, is it

2. A person who is *sound as a drum* is very healthy.

really true that you weren't in love with your husband? Why did you marry him, then?

MRS. LINDE. My mother was still alive, but bedridden and helpless—and I had my two younger brothers to look after. In all conscience, I didn't think I could turn him down.

NORA. No, you were right there. But was he rich at the time?

MRS. LINDE. He was very well off, I'd say. But the business was shaky, Nora. When he died, it all fell apart, and nothing was left.

NORA. And then—?

MRS. LINDE. Yes, so I had to scrape up a living with a little shop and a little teaching and whatever else I could find. The last three years have been like one endless workday without a rest for me. Now it's over, Nora. My poor mother doesn't need me, for she's passed on. Nor the boys, either; they're working now and can take care of themselves.

NORA. How free you must feel—

MRS. LINDE. No—only unspeakably empty. Nothing to live for now. [*Standing up anxiously.*] That's why I couldn't take it any longer out in that desolate hole. Maybe here it'll be easier to find something to do and keep my mind occupied. If I could only be lucky enough to get a steady job, some office work—

NORA. Oh, but Kristine, that's so dreadfully tiring, and you already look so tired. It would be much better for you if you could go off to a bathing resort.

MRS. LINDE. [*Going toward the window.*] I have no father to give me travel money, Nora.

NORA. [*Rising.*] Oh, don't be angry with me.

MRS. LINDE. [*Going to her.*] Nora dear, don't you be angry with me. The worst of my kind of situation is all the bitterness that's stored away. No one to work for, and yet you're always having to snap up your opportunities. You have to live; and so you grow selfish. When you told me the happy change in your lot, do you know I was delighted less for your sakes than for mine?

NORA. How so? Oh, I see. You think maybe Torvald could do something for you.

MRS. LINDE. Yes, that's what I thought.

NORA. And he will, Kristine! Just leave it to me; I'll bring it up so delicately—find something attractive to humor him with. Oh, I'm so eager to help you.

MRS. LINDE. How very kind of you, Nora, to be so concerned over me—doubly kind, considering you really know so little of life's burdens yourself.

NORA. I—? I know so little—?

MRS. LINDE. [*Smiling.*] Well, my heavens—a little needlework and such—Nora, you're just a child.

NORA. [*Tossing her head and pacing the floor.*] You don't have to act so superior.

MRS. LINDE. Oh?

NORA. You're just like the others. You all think I'm incapable of anything serious—

MRS. LINDE. Come now—

NORA. That I've never had to face the raw world.

MRS. LINDE. Nora dear, you've just been telling me all your troubles.

NORA. Hm! Trivia! [*Quietly.*] I haven't told you the big thing.

MRS. LINDE. Big thing? What do you mean?

NORA. You look down on me so, Kristine, but you shouldn't. You're proud that you worked so long and hard for your mother.

MRS. LINDE. I don't look down on a soul. But it *is* true: I'm proud—and happy, too—to think it was given to me to make my mother's last days almost free of care.

NORA. And you're also proud thinking of what you've done for your brothers.

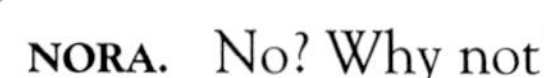

MRS. LINDE. I feel I've a right to be.

NORA. I agree. But listen to this, Kristine—I've also got something to be proud and happy for.

MRS. LINDE. I don't doubt it. But whatever do you mean?

NORA. Not so loud. What if Torvald heard! He mustn't, not for anything in the world. Nobody must know, Kristine. No one but you.

MRS. LINDE. But what is it, then?

NORA. Come here. [*Drawing her down beside her on the sofa.*] It's true—I've also got something to be proud and happy for. I'm the one who saved Torvald's life.

MRS. LINDE. Saved—? Saved how?

NORA. I told you about the trip to Italy. Torvald never would have lived if he hadn't gone south—

MRS. LINDE. Of course; your father gave you the means—

NORA. [*Smiling.*] That's what Torvald and all the rest think, but—

MRS. LINDE. But—?

NORA. Papa didn't give us a pin. I was the one who raised the money.

MRS. LINDE. You? That whole amount?

NORA. Four thousand, eight hundred crowns. What do you say to that?

MRS. LINDE. But Nora, how was it possible? Did you win the lottery?

NORA. [*Disdainfully.*] The lottery? Pooh! No art to that.

MRS. LINDE. But where did you get it from then?

NORA. [*Humming, with a mysterious smile.*] Hmm, tra-la-la-la.

MRS. LINDE. Because you couldn't have borrowed it.

NORA. No? Why not?

MRS. LINDE. A wife can't borrow without her husband's consent.

NORA. [*Tossing her head.*] Oh, but a wife with a little business sense, a wife who knows how to manage—

MRS. LINDE. Nora, I simply don't understand—

NORA. You don't have to. Whoever said I *borrowed* the money? I could have gotten it other ways. [*Throwing herself back on the sofa.*] I could have gotten it from some admirer or other. After all, a girl with my ravishing appeal—

MRS. LINDE. You lunatic.

NORA. I'll bet you're eaten up with curiosity, Kristine.

MRS. LINDE. Now listen here, Nora—you haven't done something indiscreet?

NORA. [*Sitting up again.*] Is it indiscreet to save your husband's life?

MRS. LINDE. I think it's indiscreet that without his knowledge you—

NORA. But that's the point: he mustn't know! My Lord, can't you understand? He mustn't ever know the close call he had. It was to *me* the doctors came to say his life was in danger—that nothing could save him but a stay in the south. Didn't I try strategy then! I began talking about how lovely it would be for me to travel abroad like other young wives; I begged and I cried; I told him please to remember my condition, to be kind and indulge me; and then I dropped a hint that he could easily take out a loan. But at that, Kristine, he nearly exploded. He said I was frivolous, and it was his duty as man of the house not to indulge me in whims and fancies—as I think he called them. Aha, I thought, now you'll just have to be saved—and that's when I saw my chance.

Vocabulary

indiscreet (in′ dis krēt′) *adj.* lacking in good judgment

you hear, Torvald; do it! You don't know how this can harm us.

HELMER. Too late.

NORA. Yes, too late.

HELMER. Nora dear, I can forgive you this panic, even though basically you're insulting me. Yes, you are! Or isn't it an insult to think that *I* should be afraid of a courtroom hack's revenge? But I forgive you anyway, because this shows so beautifully how much you love me. [*Takes her in his arms.*] This is the way it should be, my darling Nora. Whatever comes, you'll see: when it really counts, I have strength and courage enough as a man to take on the whole weight myself.

NORA. [*Terrified.*] What do you mean by that?

HELMER. The whole weight, I said.

NORA. [*Resolutely.*] No, never in all the world.

HELMER. Good. So we'll share it, Nora, as man and wife. That's as it should be. [*Fondling her.*] Are you happy now? There, there, there—not these frightened dove's eyes. It's nothing at all but empty fantasies— Now you should run through your tarantella and practice your tambourine. I'll go to the inner office and shut both doors, so I won't hear a thing; you can make all the noise you like. [*Turning in the doorway.*] And when Rank comes, just tell him where he can find me. [*He nods to her and goes with his papers into the study, closing the door.*]

NORA. [*Standing as though rooted, dazed with fright, in a whisper.*] He really could do it. He will do it. He'll do it in spite of everything. No, not that, never, never! Anything but that! Escape! A way out— [*The doorbell rings.*] Dr. Rank! Anything but that! Anything, whatever it is! [*Her hands pass over her face, smoothing it; she pulls herself together, goes over and opens the hall door.* DR. RANK *stands outside, hanging his fur coat up. During the following scene, it begins getting dark.*]

NORA. Hello, Dr. Rank. I recognized your ring. But you mustn't go in to Torvald yet; I believe he's working.

RANK. And you?

NORA. For you, I always have an hour to spare—you know that. [*He has entered, and she shuts the door after him.*]

RANK. Many thanks. I'll make use of these hours while I can.

NORA. What do you mean by that? While you can?

RANK. Does that disturb you?

NORA. Well, it's such an odd phrase. Is anything going to happen?

RANK. What's going to happen is what I've been expecting so long—but I honestly didn't think it would come so soon.

NORA. [*Gripping his arm.*] What is it you've found out? Dr. Rank, you have to tell me!

RANK. [*Sitting by the stove.*] It's all over with me. There's nothing to be done about it.

NORA. [*Breathing easier.*] Is it you—then—?

RANK. Who else? There's no point in lying to one's self. I'm the most miserable of all my patients, Mrs. Helmer. These past few days I've been auditing my internal accounts. Bankrupt! Within a month I'll probably be laid out and rotting in the churchyard.

NORA. Oh, what a horrible thing to say.

RANK. The thing itself is horrible. But the worst of it is all the other horror before it's over. There's only one final examination left; when I'm finished with that, I'll know about when my disintegration will begin. There's something I want to say. Helmer with his sensitivity has such a sharp distaste for anything ugly. I don't want him near my sickroom.

NORA. Oh, but Dr. Rank—

Vocabulary

resolutely (rez′ ə lo͞ot′ lē) *adv.* with firm determination

RANK. I won't have him in there. Under no condition. I'll lock my door to him— As soon as I'm completely sure of the worst, I'll send you my calling card marked with a black cross, and you'll know then the wreck has started to come apart.

NORA. No, today you're completely unreasonable. And I wanted you so much to be in a really good humor.

RANK. With death up my sleeve? And then to suffer this way for somebody else's sins. Is there any justice in that? And in every single family, in some way or another, this inevitable retribution of nature goes on—

NORA. [*Her hands pressed over her ears.*] Oh, stuff! Cheer up! Please—be gay!

RANK. Yes, I'd just as soon laugh at it all. My poor, innocent spine, serving time for my father's gay army days.

NORA. [*By the table, left.*] He was so infatuated with asparagus tips and *pâté de foie gras*,[6] wasn't that it?

RANK. Yes—and with truffles.[7]

NORA. Truffles, yes. And then with oysters, I suppose?

RANK. Yes, tons of oysters, naturally.

NORA. And then the port[8] and champagne to go with it. It's so sad that all these delectable things have to strike at our bones.

RANK. Especially when they strike at the unhappy bones that never shared in the fun.

NORA. Ah, that's the saddest of all.

RANK. [*Looks searchingly at her.*] Hm.

NORA. [*After a moment.*] Why did you smile?

RANK. No, it was you who laughed.

NORA. No, it was you who smiled, Dr. Rank!

RANK. [*Getting up.*] You're even a bigger tease than I'd thought.

NORA. I'm full of wild ideas today.

RANK. That's obvious.

NORA. [*Putting both hands on his shoulders.*] Dear, dear Dr. Rank, you'll never die for Torvald and me.

RANK. Oh, that loss you'll easily get over. Those who go away are soon forgotten.

NORA. [*Looks fearfully at him.*] You believe that?

RANK. One makes new connections, and then—

NORA. Who makes new connections?

RANK. Both you and Torvald will when I'm gone. I'd say you're well under way already. What was that Mrs. Linde doing here last evening?

NORA. Oh, come—you can't be jealous of poor Kristine?

RANK. Oh yes, I am. She'll be my successor here in the house. When I'm down under, that woman will probably—

NORA. Shh! Not so loud. She's right in there.

RANK. Today as well. So you see.

NORA. Only to sew on my dress. Good gracious, how unreasonable you are. [*Sitting on the sofa.*] Be nice now, Dr. Rank. Tomorrow you'll see how beautifully I'll dance; and you can imagine then that I'm dancing only for you—yes, and of course for Torvald, too—that's understood. [*Takes various items out of the carton.*] Dr. Rank, sit over here and I'll show you something.

RANK. [*Sitting.*] What's that?

NORA. Look here. Look.

RANK. Silk stockings.

NORA. Flesh-colored. Aren't they lovely? Now it's so dark here, but tomorrow— No, no,

---

6. *Pâté de foie gras* (pat ā′ də fwä grä′) is made of finely chopped or pureed goose liver, sometimes seasoned with truffles and fat pork.
7. *Truffles* are dark, wrinkled fungi that grow underground and are highly prized for their flavor.
8. *Port* is a sweet, rich wine.

Head of a Woman. Gustav Klimt (Austria, 1862–1918). Sketch. Neue Galerie, Linz, Austria.

Viewing the drawing: Why might the artist have chosen to leave out certain details in this drawing? How might Ibsen have used the same technique in his play?

no, just look at the feet. Oh well, you might as well look at the rest.

RANK. Hm—

NORA. Why do you look so critical? Don't you believe they'll fit?

RANK. I've never had any chance to form an opinion on that.

NORA. [*Glancing at him a moment.*] Shame on you. [*Hits him lightly on the ear with the stockings.*] That's for you. [*Puts them away again.*]

RANK. And what other splendors am I going to see now?

NORA. Not the least bit more, because you've been naughty. [*She hums a little and rummages among her things.*]

RANK. [*After a short silence.*] When I sit here together with you like this, completely easy and open, then I don't know—I simply can't imagine—whatever would have become of me if I'd never come into this house.

NORA. [*Smiling.*] Yes, I really think you feel completely at ease with us.

RANK. [*More quietly, staring straight ahead.*] And then to have to go away from it all—

NORA. Nonsense, you're not going away.

RANK. [*His voice unchanged.*] —and not even be able to leave some poor show of gratitude behind, scarcely a fleeting regret—no more than a vacant place that anyone can fill.

NORA. And if I asked you now for—? No—

RANK. For what?

NORA. For a great proof of your friendship—

RANK. Yes, yes?

NORA. No, I mean—for an exceptionally big favor—

RANK. Would you really, for once, make me so happy?

NORA. Oh, you haven't the vaguest idea what it is.

RANK. All right, then tell me.

NORA. No, but I can't, Dr. Rank—it's all out of reason. It's advice and help, too—and a favor—

RANK. So much the better. I can't fathom what you're hinting at. Just speak out. Don't you trust me?

NORA. Of course. More than anyone else. You're my best and truest friend, I'm sure. That's why I want to talk to you. All right, then, Dr. Rank: there's something you can help me prevent. You know how deeply, how inexpressibly dearly Torvald loves me; he'd never hesitate a second to give up his life for me.

RANK. [*Leaning close to her.*] Nora—do you think he's the only one—

NORA. [*With a slight start.*] Who—?

RANK. Who'd gladly give up his life for you.

NORA. [*Heavily.*] I see.

RANK. I swore to myself you should know this before I'm gone. I'll never find a better chance. Yes, Nora, now you know. And also you know now that you can trust me beyond anyone else.

NORA. [*Rising, natural and calm.*] Let me by.

RANK. [*Making room for her, but still sitting.*] Nora—

NORA. [*In the hall doorway.*] Helene, bring the lamp in. [*Goes over to the stove.*] Ah, dear Dr. Rank, that was really mean of you.

RANK. [*Getting up.*] That I've loved you just as deeply as somebody else? Was *that* mean?

NORA. No, but that you came out and told me. That was quite unnecessary—

RANK. What do you mean? Have you known—?

[*The* MAID *comes in with the lamp, sets it on the table, and goes out again.*]

RANK. Nora—Mrs. Helmer—I'm asking you: have you known about it?

NORA. Oh, how can I tell what I know or don't know? Really, I don't know what to say—

Why did you have to be so clumsy, Dr. Rank! Everything was so good.

RANK. Well, in any case, you now have the knowledge that my body and soul are at your command. So won't you speak out?

NORA. [*Looking at him.*] After that?

RANK. Please, just let me know what it is.

NORA. You can't know anything now.

RANK. I have to. You mustn't punish me like this. Give me the chance to do whatever is humanly possible for you.

NORA. Now there's nothing you can do for me. Besides, actually, I don't need any help. You'll see—it's only my fantasies. That's what it is. Of course! [*Sits in the rocker, looks at him, and smiles.*] What a nice one you are, Dr. Rank. Aren't you a little bit ashamed, now that the lamp is here?

RANK. No, not exactly. But perhaps I'd better go—for good?

NORA. No, you certainly can't do that. You must come here just as you always have. You know Torvald can't do without you.

RANK. Yes, but *you?*

NORA. You know how much I enjoy it when you're here.

RANK. That's precisely what threw me off. You're a mystery to me. So many times I've felt you'd almost rather be with me than with Helmer.

NORA. Yes—you see, there are some people that one loves most and other people that one would almost prefer being with.

RANK. Yes, there's something to that.

NORA. When I was back home, of course I loved Papa most. But I always thought it was so much fun when I could sneak down to the maids' quarters, because they never tried to improve me, and it was always so amusing, the way they talked to each other.

RANK. Aha, so it's *their* place that I've filled.

NORA. [*Jumping up and going to him.*] Oh, dear, sweet Dr. Rank, that's not what I meant at all. But you can understand that with Torvald it's just the same as with Papa—

[*The* MAID *enters from the hall.*]

MAID. Ma'am—please! [*She whispers to* NORA *and hands her a calling card.*]

NORA. [*Glancing at the card.*] Ah! [*Slips it into her pocket.*]

RANK. Anything wrong?

NORA. No, no, not at all. It's only some—it's my new dress—

RANK. Really? But—there's your dress.

NORA. Oh, that. But this is another one—I ordered it—Torvald mustn't know—

RANK. Ah, now we have the big secret.

NORA. That's right. Just go in with him—he's back in the inner study. Keep him there as long as—

RANK. Don't worry. He won't get away. [*Goes into the study.*]

NORA. [*To the* MAID.] And he's standing waiting in the kitchen?

MAID. Yes, he came up by the back stairs.

NORA. But didn't you tell him somebody was here?

MAID. Yes, but that didn't do any good.

NORA. He won't leave?

MAID. No, he won't go till he's talked with you, ma'am.

NORA. Let him come in, then—but quietly. Helene, don't breathe a word about this. It's a surprise for my husband.

MAID. Yes, yes, I understand— [*Goes out.*]

NORA. This horror—it's going to happen. No, no, no, it can't happen, it mustn't. [*She goes and bolts* HELMER*'s door. The* MAID *opens the hall door for* KROGSTAD *and shuts it behind him. He is dressed for travel in a fur coat, boots, and a fur cap.*]

NORA. [*Going toward him.*] Talk softly. My husband's home.

KROGSTAD. Well, good for him.

NORA. What do you want?

KROGSTAD. Some information.

NORA. Hurry up, then. What is it?

Portrait of Dr. Daniel Jacobson, 1909. Edvard Munch (Norway). Oil on canvas, 204 x 111.5 cm. Munch Museet, Oslo, Norway.

Viewing the painting: What do you think this man is like? How is he comparable to characters in the story?

KROGSTAD. You know, of course, that I got my notice.

NORA. I couldn't prevent it, Mr. Krogstad. I fought for you to the bitter end, but nothing worked.

KROGSTAD. Does your husband's love for you run so thin? He knows everything I can expose you to, and all the same he dares to—

NORA. How can you imagine he knows anything about this?

KROGSTAD. Ah, no—I can't imagine it either, now. It's not at all like my fine Torvald Helmer to have so much guts—

NORA. Mr. Krogstad, I demand respect for my husband!

KROGSTAD. Why, of course—all due respect. But since the lady's keeping it so carefully hidden, may I presume to ask if you're also a bit better informed than yesterday about what you've actually done?

NORA. More than you ever could teach me.

KROGSTAD. Yes, I *am* such an awful lawyer.

NORA. What is it you want from me?

KROGSTAD. Just a glimpse of how you are, Mrs. Helmer. I've been thinking about you all day long. A cashier, a night-court scribbler, a—well, a type like me also has a little of what they call a heart, you know.

NORA. Then show it. Think of my children.

KROGSTAD. Did you or your husband ever think of mine? But never mind. I simply wanted to tell you that you don't need to take this thing too seriously. For the present, I'm not proceeding with any action.

NORA. Oh no, really! Well—I knew that.

KROGSTAD. Everything can be settled in a friendly spirit. It doesn't have to get around town at all; it can stay just among us three.

NORA. My husband must never know anything of this.

KROGSTAD. How can you manage that? Perhaps you can pay me the balance?

NORA. No, not right now.

KROGSTAD. Or you know some way of raising the money in a day or two?

NORA. No way that I'm willing to use.

KROGSTAD. Well, it wouldn't have done you any good, anyway. If you stood in front of me with a fistful of bills, you still couldn't buy your signature back.

NORA. Then tell me what you're going to do with it.

KROGSTAD. I'll just hold onto it—keep it on file. There's no outsider who'll even get wind of it. So if you've been thinking of taking some desperate step—

NORA. I have.

KROGSTAD. Been thinking of running away from home—

NORA. I have!

KROGSTAD. Or even of something worse—

NORA. How could you guess that?

KROGSTAD. You can drop those thoughts.

NORA. How could you guess I was thinking of *that?*

KROGSTAD. Most of us think about *that* at first. I thought about it too, but I discovered I hadn't the courage—

NORA. [*Lifelessly.*] I don't either.

KROGSTAD. [*Relieved.*] That's true, you haven't the courage? You too?

NORA. I don't have it—I don't have it.

KROGSTAD. It would be terribly stupid, anyway. After that first storm at home blows out, why, then— I have here in my pocket a letter for your husband—

NORA. Telling everything?

KROGSTAD. As charitably as possible.

NORA. [*Quickly.*] He mustn't ever get that letter. Tear it up. I'll find some way to get money.

KROGSTAD. Beg pardon, Mrs. Helmer, but I think I just told you—

NORA. Oh, I don't mean the money I owe you. Let me know how much you want from my husband, and I'll manage it.

KROGSTAD. I don't want any money from your husband.

NORA. What do you want, then?

KROGSTAD. I'll tell you what. I want to recoup, Mrs. Helmer; I want to get on in the world—and there's where your husband can help me. For a year and a half I've kept myself clean of anything disreputable—all that time struggling with the worst conditions; but I was satisfied, working my way up step by step. Now I've been written right off, and I'm just not in the mood to come crawling back. I tell you, I want to move on. I want to get back in the bank—in a better position. Your husband can set up a job for me—

NORA. He'll never do that!

KROGSTAD. He'll do it. I know him. He won't dare breathe a word of protest. And once I'm in there together with him, you just wait and see! Inside of a year, I'll be the manager's right-hand man. It'll be Nils Krogstad, not Torvald Helmer, who runs the bank.

NORA. You'll never see the day!

KROGSTAD. Maybe you think you can—

NORA. I have the courage now—for *that.*

KROGSTAD. Oh, you don't scare me. A smart, spoiled lady like you—

NORA. You'll see; you'll see!

KROGSTAD. Under the ice, maybe? Down in the freezing, coal-black water? There, till you float up in the spring, ugly, unrecognizable, with your hair falling out—

NORA. You don't frighten me.

KROGSTAD. Nor do you frighten me. One doesn't do these things, Mrs. Helmer. Besides, what good would it be? I'd still have him safe in my pocket.

NORA. Afterwards? When I'm no longer—?

KROGSTAD. Are you forgetting that *I'll* be in control then over your final reputation? [*NORA stands speechless, staring at him.*] Good; now I've warned you. Don't do anything stupid. When Helmer's read my letter, I'll be waiting for his reply. And bear in mind that it's your husband himself who's forced me back to my old ways. I'll never forgive him for that. Good-bye, Mrs. Helmer. [*He goes out through the hall.*]

NORA. [*Goes to the hall door, opens it a crack, and listens.*] He's gone. Didn't leave the letter. Oh no, no, that's impossible too! [*Opening the door more and more.*] What's that? He's standing outside—not going downstairs. He's thinking it over? Maybe he'll—? [*A letter falls in the mailbox; then KROGSTAD's footsteps are heard, dying away down a flight of stairs. NORA gives a muffled cry and runs over toward the sofa table. A short pause.*] In the mailbox. [*Slips warily over to the hall door.*] It's lying there. Torvald, Torvald—now we're lost!

MRS. LINDE. [*Entering with the costume from the room, left.*] There now, I can't see anything else to mend. Perhaps you'd like to try—

NORA. [*In a hoarse whisper.*] Kristine, come here.

MRS. LINDE. [*Tossing the dress on the sofa.*] What's wrong? You look upset.

NORA. Come here. See that letter? *There!* Look—through the glass in the mailbox.

MRS. LINDE. Yes, yes, I see it.

NORA. That letter's from Krogstad—

MRS. LINDE. Nora—it's Krogstad who loaned you the money!

NORA. Yes, and now Torvald will find out everything.

MRS. LINDE. Believe me, Nora, it's best for both of you.

NORA. There's more you don't know. I forged a name.

MRS. LINDE. But for heaven's sake—?

NORA. I only want to tell you that, Kristine, so that you can be my witness.

MRS. LINDE. Witness? Why should I—?

NORA. If I should go out of my mind—it could easily happen—

MRS. LINDE. Nora!

NORA. Or anything else occurred—so I couldn't be present here—

MRS. LINDE. Nora, Nora, you aren't yourself at all!

NORA. And someone should try to take on the whole weight, all of the guilt, you follow me—

MRS. LINDE. Yes, of course, but why do you think—?

NORA. Then you're the witness that it isn't true, Kristine. I'm very much myself; my mind right now is perfectly clear; and I'm telling you: nobody else has known about this; I alone did everything. Remember that.

MRS. LINDE. I will. But I don't understand all this.

NORA. Oh, how could you ever understand it? It's the miracle now that's going to take place.

MRS. LINDE. The miracle?

NORA. Yes, the miracle. But it's so awful, Kristine. It mustn't take place, not for anything in the world.

MRS. LINDE. I'm going right over and talk with Krogstad.

NORA. Don't go near him; he'll do you some terrible harm!

MRS. LINDE. There was a time once when he'd gladly have done anything for me.

NORA. He?

MRS. LINDE. Where does he live?

NORA. Oh, how do I know? Yes. [*Searches in her pocket.*] Here's his card. But the letter, the letter—!

HELMER. [*From the study, knocking on the door.*] Nora!

NORA. [*With a cry of fear.*] Oh! What is it? What do you want?

HELMER. Now, now, don't be so frightened. We're not coming in. You locked the door—are you trying on the dress?

NORA. Yes, I'm trying it. I'll look just beautiful, Torvald.

MRS. LINDE. [*Who has read the card.*] He's living right around the corner.

NORA. Yes, but what's the use? We're lost. The letter's in the box.

MRS. LINDE. And your husband has the key?

NORA. Yes, always.

MRS. LINDE. Krogstad can ask for his letter back unread; he can find some excuse—

NORA. But it's just this time that Torvald usually—

MRS. LINDE. Stall him. Keep him in there. I'll be back as quick as I can. [*She hurries out through the hall entrance.*]

NORA. [*Goes to* HELMER*'s door, opens it, and peers in.*] Torvald!

HELMER. [*From the inner study.*] Well—does one dare set foot in one's own living room at last? Come on, Rank, now we'll get a look—[*In the doorway.*] But what's this?

NORA. What, Torvald dear?

HELMER. Rank had me expecting some grand masquerade.

RANK. [*In the doorway.*] That was my impression, but I must have been wrong.

NORA. No one can admire me in my splendor—not till tomorrow.

HELMER. But Nora dear, you look so exhausted. Have you practiced too hard?

NORA. No, I haven't practiced at all yet.

HELMER. You know, it's necessary—

NORA. Oh, it's absolutely necessary, Torvald. But I can't get anywhere without your help. I've forgotten the whole thing completely.

HELMER. Ah, we'll soon take care of that.

NORA. Yes, take care of me, Torvald, please! Promise me that? Oh, I'm so nervous. That big party— You must give up everything this evening for me. No business—don't even touch your pen. Yes? Dear Torvald, promise?

HELMER. It's a promise. Tonight I'm totally at your service—you little helpless thing. Hm—but first there's one thing I want to— [*Goes toward the hall door.*]

NORA. What are you looking for?

HELMER. Just to see if there's any mail.

NORA. No, no, don't do that, Torvald!

HELMER. Now what?

NORA. Torvald, please. There isn't any.

HELMER. Let me look, though. [*Starts out.* NORA*, at the piano, strikes the first notes of the tarantella.* HELMER*, at the door, stops.*] Aha!

NORA. I can't dance tomorrow if I don't practice with you.

HELMER. [*Going over to her.*] Nora dear, are you really so frightened?

NORA. Yes, so terribly frightened. Let me practice right now; there's still time before dinner. Oh, sit down and play for me, Torvald. Direct me. Teach me, the way you always have.

HELMER. Gladly, if it's what you want. [*Sits at the piano.*]

NORA. [*Snatches the tambourine up from the box, then a long, varicolored shawl, which she throws around herself, whereupon she springs forward and cries out.*] Play for me now! Now I'll dance!

[HELMER *plays and* NORA *dances.* RANK *stands behind* HELMER *at the piano and looks on.*]

HELMER. [*As he plays.*] Slower. Slow down.

NORA. Can't change it.

HELMER. Not so violent, Nora!

NORA. Has to be just like this.

HELMER. [*Stopping.*] No, no, that won't do at all.

MRS. LINDE. [*Standing dumbfounded at the door.*] Ah—!

NORA. [*Still dancing.*] See what fun, Kristine!

HELMER. But Nora darling, you dance as if your life were at stake.

NORA. And it is.

HELMER. Rank, stop! This is pure madness. Stop it, I say!

NORA. [*Laughing and swinging her tambourine.*] Isn't that what I told you?

RANK. Let me play for her.

HELMER. [*Getting up.*] Yes, go on. I can teach her more easily then.

[RANK *sits at the piano and plays;* NORA *dances more and more wildly.* HELMER *has stationed himself by the stove and repeatedly gives her directions; she seems not to hear them; her hair loosens and falls over her shoulders; she does not notice, but goes on dancing.* MRS. LINDE *enters.*]

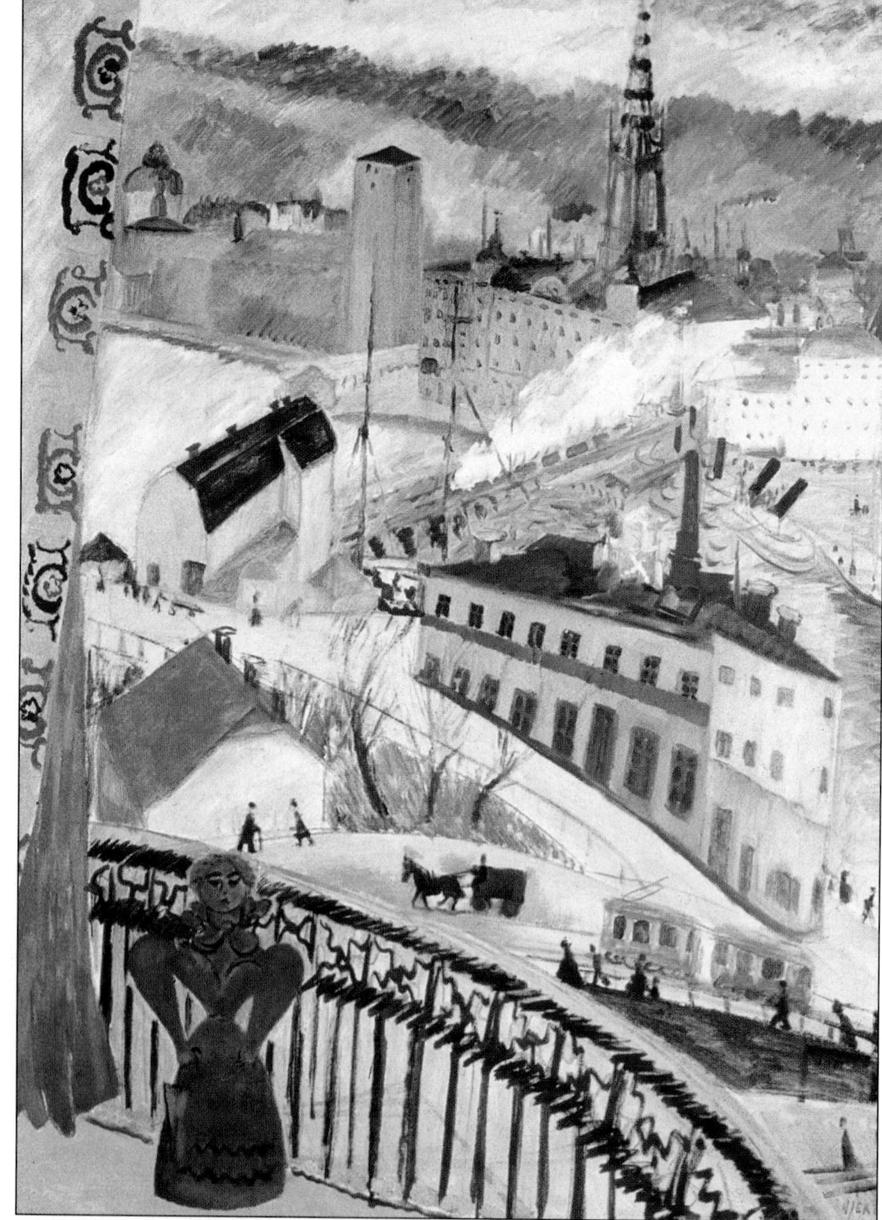

View of Slussen in Winter. Sigrid Hjertén-Grünewald (Sweden, 1885–1948). Gouache on paper. Moderna Museet, Stockholm, Sweden.

Viewing the painting: What effect does the composition create in this painting? In what ways might it remind you of Nora's position in the play?

[*RANK breaks off playing, and NORA halts abruptly.*]

HELMER. [*Going over to her.*] I never would have believed it. You've forgotten everything I taught you.

NORA. [*Throwing away the tambourine.*] You see for yourself.

HELMER. Well, there's certainly room for instruction here.

NORA. Yes, you see how important it is. You've got to teach me to the very last minute. Promise me that, Torvald?

HELMER. You can bet on it.

NORA. You mustn't, either today or tomorrow, think about anything else but me; you mustn't open any letters—or the mailbox—

HELMER. Ah, it's still the fear of that man—

NORA. Oh yes, yes, that too.

HELMER. Nora, it's written all over you—there's already a letter from him out there.

NORA. I don't know. I guess so. But you mustn't read such things now; there mustn't be anything ugly between us before it's all over.

RANK. [*Quietly to HELMER.*] You shouldn't deny her.

HELMER. [*Putting his arm around her.*] The child can have her way. But tomorrow night, after you've danced—

NORA. Then you'll be free.

MAID. [*In the doorway, right.*] Ma'am, dinner is served.

NORA. We'll be wanting champagne, Helene.

MAID. Very good, ma'am. [*Goes out.*]

HELMER. So—a regular banquet, hm?

NORA. Yes, a banquet—champagne till daybreak! [*Calling out.*] And some macaroons, Helene. Heaps of them—just this once.

HELMER. [*Taking her hands.*] Now, now, now—no hysterics. Be my own little lark again.

NORA. Oh, I will soon enough. But go on in—and you, Dr. Rank. Kristine, help me put up my hair.

RANK. [*Whispering, as they go.*] There's nothing wrong—really wrong, is there?

HELMER. Oh, of course not. It's nothing more than this childish anxiety I was telling you about. [*They go out, right.*]

NORA. Well?

MRS. LINDE. Left town.

NORA. I could see by your face.

MRS. LINDE. He'll be home tomorrow evening. I wrote him a note.

NORA. You shouldn't have. Don't try to stop anything now. After all, it's a wonderful joy, this waiting here for the miracle.

MRS. LINDE. What is it you're waiting for?

NORA. Oh, you can't understand that. Go in to them; I'll be along in a moment.

[*MRS. LINDE goes into the dining room. NORA stands a short while as if composing herself; then she looks at her watch.*]

NORA. Five. Seven hours to midnight. Twenty-four hours to the midnight after, and then the tarantella's done. Seven and twenty-four? Thirty-one hours to live.

HELMER. [*In the doorway, right.*] What's become of the little lark?

NORA. [*Going toward him with open arms.*] Here's your lark!

Responding to Literature

Personal Response

What went through your mind as you finished reading Act II? Share your response with a classmate.

Analyzing Literature

Recall and Interpret

1. Why does Nora like to spend time with Dr. Rank? Why does she change her mind about asking for his help?
2. What reason does Torvald give for disliking Mr. Krogstad? What do his comments about Krogstad suggest about his own character?
3. How have Krogstad's plans changed in Act II? What does Nora hint she will do to thwart his plans?
4. How does Mrs. Linde propose to help Nora? Why does she think she might be able to influence Krogstad?
5. What miracle is Nora waiting for? Why might she expect it?

Evaluate and Connect

6. Do you think Mrs. Linde has good reason to be nervous about Nora's relationship with Dr. Rank? Why or why not?
7. A **symbol** is an object or action that stands for something else in addition to itself (see page R12). Explain the symbolic meaning of an object or action in Act II.
8. Dr. Rank complains to Nora that he is paying for his father's sins. In what way might Nora be paying for her father's mistakes?
9. **Suspense** is the tension or excitement that a reader feels about what will happen next in a story (see page R12). How did Ibsen build suspense at the end of this act?
10. What other fictional character does Nora most remind you of? Why?

Literary ELEMENTS

Conflict

The basis of a story's plot is **conflict**–a struggle between opposing forces. An **external conflict** exists when a character struggles against some outside force, such as another character, a force of nature, or society. An **internal conflict** is a struggle within a character. For example, guilt is an internal conflict between a character's own actions and moral beliefs. Most works of literature, especially longer ones, have more than one conflict.

1. Describe a conflict between Nora and Torvald in Act II.
2. Describe an internal conflict within Nora in Act II.

- See **Literary Terms Handbook,** p. R2.

Extending Your Response

Creative Writing

In the Mail Write a letter from Krogstad to Torvald in which he informs his former friend about Nora's forgery. Think about the tone he might use in the letter. Would he openly threaten Torvald or merely hint at the consequences if he doesn't get his job back? What justification, if any, would he provide for revealing the truth about Nora?

Literature Groups

Saving Nora Suppose that Nora came to you for advice. How do you think she should respond to Krogstad's threat? As you discuss this question in your group, consider the possible actions she could take and their likely consequences. When you are finished, vote on the best course of action for her.

Save your work for your portfolio.

A Doll's House

ACT III

[Same scene. The table, with chairs around it, has been moved to the center of the room. A lamp on the table is lit. The hall door stands open. Dance music drifts down from the floor above. MRS. LINDE *sits at the table, absently paging through a book, trying to read, but apparently unable to focus her thoughts. Once or twice she pauses, tensely listening for a sound at the outer entrance.]*

MRS. LINDE. [*Glancing at her watch.*] Not yet—and there's hardly any time left. If only he's not— [*Listening again.*] Ah, there he is. [*She goes out in the hall and cautiously opens the outer door. Quiet footsteps are heard on the stairs. She whispers:*] Come in. Nobody's here.

KROGSTAD. [*In the doorway.*] I found a note from you at home. What's back of all this?

MRS. LINDE. I just *had* to talk to you.

KROGSTAD. Oh? And it just *had* to be here in this house?

MRS. LINDE. At my place it was impossible; my room hasn't a private entrance. Come in; we're all alone. The maid's asleep, and the Helmers are at the dance upstairs.

KROGSTAD. [*Entering the room.*] Well, well, the Helmers are dancing tonight? Really?

MRS. LINDE. Yes, why not?

KROGSTAD. How true—why not?

MRS. LINDE. All right, Krogstad, let's talk.

KROGSTAD. Do we two have anything more to talk about?

MRS. LINDE. We have a great deal to talk about.

KROGSTAD. I wouldn't have thought so.

MRS. LINDE. No, because you've never understood me, really.

KROGSTAD. Was there anything more to understand—except what's all too common in life? A calculating woman throws over a man the moment a better catch comes by.

MRS. LINDE. You think I'm so thoroughly calculating? You think I broke it off lightly?

KROGSTAD. Didn't you?

MRS. LINDE. Nils—is that what you really thought?

KROGSTAD. If you cared, then why did you write me the way you did?

MRS. LINDE. What else could I do? If I had to break off with you, then it was my job as well to root out everything you felt for me.

KROGSTAD. [*Wringing his hands.*] So that was it. And this—all this, simply for money!

MRS. LINDE. Don't forget I had a helpless mother and two small brothers. We couldn't wait for you, Nils; you had such a long road ahead of you then.

KROGSTAD. That may be; but you still hadn't the right to abandon me for somebody else's sake.

MRS. LINDE. Yes—I don't know. So many, many times I've asked myself if I did have that right.

KROGSTAD. [*More softly.*] When I lost you, it was as if all the solid ground dissolved from under my feet. Look at me; I'm a half-drowned man now, hanging onto a wreck.

MRS. LINDE. Help may be near.

KROGSTAD. It was near—but then you came and blocked it off.

MRS. LINDE. Without my knowing it, Nils. Today for the first time I learned that it's you I'm replacing at the bank.

KROGSTAD. All right—I believe you. But now that you know, will you step aside?

MRS. LINDE. No, because that wouldn't benefit you in the slightest.

KROGSTAD. Not "benefit" me, hm! I'd step aside anyway.

MRS. LINDE. I've learned to be realistic. Life and hard, bitter necessity have taught me that.

Fulfillment, c. 1905. Gustav Klimt (Austria). Tempera and watercolor. Osterreichische Galerie, Vienna, Austria.

Viewing the painting: In what ways do you think the content and mood of this painting match its title? Do you think any of the characters share this feeling at this point in the play? Explain.

like a dark cloud setting off our sunlit happiness. Well, maybe it's best this way. For him, at least. [*Standing still.*] And maybe for us too, Nora. Now we're thrown back on each other, completely. [*Embracing her.*] Oh you, my darling wife, how can I hold you close enough? You know what, Nora—time and again I've wished you were in some terrible danger, just so I could stake my life and soul and everything, for your sake.

NORA. [*Tearing herself away, her voice firm and decisive.*] Now you must read your mail, Torvald.

HELMER. No, no, not tonight. I want to stay with you, dearest.

NORA. With a dying friend on your mind?

HELMER. You're right. We've both had a shock. There's ugliness between us—these thoughts of death and corruption. We'll have to get free of them first. Until then—we'll stay apart.

NORA. [*Clinging about his neck.*] Torvald—good night! Good night!

HELMER. [*Kissing her on the cheek.*] Good night, little songbird. Sleep well, Nora. I'll be reading my mail now. [*He takes the letters into his room and shuts the door after him.*]

NORA. [*With bewildered glances, groping about, seizing* HELMER's *domino, throwing it around her, and speaking in short, hoarse, broken whispers.*] Never see him again. Never, never. [*Putting her shawl over her head.*] Never see the children either—them, too. Never, never. Oh, the freezing black water! The depths—down—Oh, I wish it were over— He has it now; he's reading it—now. Oh no, no, not yet. Torvald, good-bye, you and the children— [*She starts for the hall; as she does,* HELMER *throws open his door and stands with an open letter in his hand.*]

HELMER. Nora!

NORA. [*Screams.*] Oh—!

HELMER. What is this? You know what's in this letter?

NORA. Yes, I know. Let me go! Let me out!

HELMER. [*Holding her back.*] Where are you going?

NORA. [*Struggling to break loose.*] You can't save me, Torvald!

HELMER. [*Slumping back.*] True! Then it's true what he writes? How horrible! No, no, it's impossible—it can't be true.

NORA. It *is* true. I've loved you more than all this world.

HELMER. Ah, none of your slippery tricks.

NORA. [*Taking one step toward him.*] Torvald—!

HELMER. What *is* this you've blundered into!

NORA. Just let me loose. You're not going to suffer for my sake. You're not going to take on my guilt.

HELMER. No more playacting. [*Locks the hall door.*] You stay right here and give me a reckoning.[4] You understand what you've done? Answer! You understand?

NORA. [*Looking squarely at him, her face hardening.*] Yes. I'm beginning to understand everything now.

HELMER. [*Striding about.*] Oh, what an awful awakening! In all these eight years—she who was my pride and joy—a hypocrite, a liar—worse, worse—a criminal! How infinitely disgusting it all is! The shame! [NORA *says nothing and goes on looking straight at him. He stops in front of her.*] I should have suspected something of the kind. I should have known. All your father's flimsy values— Be still! All your father's flimsy values have come out in you. No religion, no morals, no sense of duty— Oh, how I'm punished for letting him off! I did it for your sake, and you repay me like this.

NORA. Yes, like this.

HELMER. Now you've wrecked all my happiness—ruined my whole future. Oh, it's awful to

4. At a *reckoning,* accounts are summed up or settled.

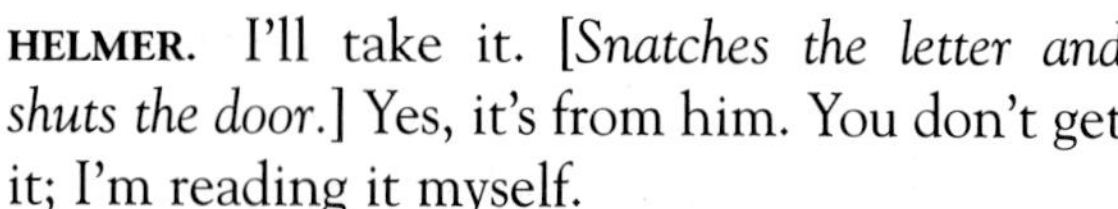

think of. I'm in a cheap little grafter's[5] hands; he can do anything he wants with me, ask for anything, play with me like a puppet—and I can't breathe a word. I'll be swept down miserably into the depths on account of a featherbrained woman.

NORA. When I'm gone from this world, you'll be free.

HELMER. Oh, quit posing. Your father had a mess of those speeches too. What good would that ever do me if you were gone from this world, as you say? Not the slightest. He can still make the whole thing known; and if he does, I could be falsely suspected as your accomplice. They might even think that I was behind it—that I put you up to it. And all that I can thank you for—you that I've coddled the whole of our marriage. Can you see now what you've done to me?

NORA. [*Icily calm.*] Yes.

HELMER. It's so incredible, I just can't grasp it. But we'll have to patch up whatever we can. Take off the shawl. I said, take it off! I've got to appease him somehow or other. The thing has to be hushed up at any cost. And as for you and me, it's got to seem like everything between us is just as it was—to the outside world, that is. You'll go right on living in this house, of course. But you can't be allowed to bring up the children; I don't dare trust you with them— Oh, to have to say this to someone I've loved so much! Well, that's done with. From now on happiness doesn't matter; all that matters is saving the bits and pieces, the appearance— [*The doorbell rings.* HELMER *starts.*] What's that? And so late. Maybe the worst—? You think he'd—? Hide, Nora! Say you're sick. [NORA *remains standing motionless.* HELMER *goes and opens the door.*]

MAID. [*Half dressed, in the hall.*] A letter for Mrs. Helmer.

5. A *grafter* (or *grifter*) is a person who attempts to acquire money in dishonest or questionable ways.

HELMER. I'll take it. [*Snatches the letter and shuts the door.*] Yes, it's from him. You don't get it; I'm reading it myself.

NORA. Then read it.

HELMER. [*By the lamp.*] I hardly dare. We may be ruined, you and I. But—I've got to know. [*Rips open the letter, skims through a few lines, glances at an enclosure, then cries out joyfully.*] Nora! [NORA *looks inquiringly at him.*] Nora! Wait—better check it again— Yes, yes, it's true. I'm saved. Nora, I'm saved!

NORA. And I?

HELMER. You too, of course. We're both saved, both of us. Look. He's sent back your note. He says he's sorry and ashamed—that a happy development in his life—oh, who cares what he says! Nora, we're saved! No one can hurt you. Oh, Nora, Nora—but first, this ugliness all has to go. Let me see— [*Takes a look at the note.*] No, I don't want to see it; I want the whole thing to fade like a dream. [*Tears the note and both letters to pieces, throws them into the stove and watches them burn.*] There—now there's nothing left— He wrote that since Christmas Eve you— Oh, they must have been three terrible days for you, Nora.

NORA. I fought a hard fight.

HELMER. And suffered pain and saw no escape but— No, we're not going to dwell on anything unpleasant. We'll just be grateful and keep on repeating: it's over now, it's over! You hear me, Nora? You don't seem to realize—it's over. What's it mean—that frozen look? Oh, poor little Nora, I understand. You can't believe I've forgiven you. But I have, Nora; I swear I have. I know that what you did, you did out of love for me.

NORA. That's true.

HELMER. You loved me the way a wife ought to love her husband. It's simply the means that you couldn't judge. But you think I love you any the less for not knowing how to handle your affairs? No, no—just lean on me; I'll guide you and teach you. I wouldn't be a man if this feminine helplessness didn't make you twice as attractive to me. You mustn't mind those sharp words I said—that was all in the first confusion of thinking my world had collapsed. I've forgiven you, Nora; I swear I've forgiven you.

NORA. My thanks for your forgiveness. [*She goes out through the door, right.*]

HELMER. No, wait— [*Peers in.*] What are you doing in there?

NORA. [*Inside.*] Getting out of my costume.

HELMER. [*By the open door.*] Yes, do that. Try to calm yourself and collect your thoughts again, my frightened little songbird. You can rest easy now; I've got wide wings to shelter you with. [*Walking about close by the door.*] How snug and nice our home is, Nora. You're safe here; I'll keep you like a hunted dove I've rescued out of a hawk's claws. I'll bring peace to your poor, shuddering heart. Gradually it'll happen, Nora; you'll see. Tomorrow all this will look different to you; then everything will be as it was. I won't have to go on repeating I forgive you; you'll feel it for yourself. How can you imagine I'd ever conceivably want to disown you—or even blame you in any way? Ah, you don't know a man's heart, Nora. For a man there's something indescribably sweet and satisfying in knowing he's forgiven his wife—and forgiven her out of a full and open heart. It's as if she belongs to him in two ways now: in a sense he's given her fresh into the world again, and she's become his wife and his child as well. From now on that's what you'll be to me—you little, bewildered, helpless thing. Don't be afraid of anything, Nora; just open your heart to me, and I'll be conscience and will to you both—[*NORA enters in her regular clothes.*] What's this? Not in bed? You've changed your dress?

NORA. Yes, Torvald, I've changed my dress.

HELMER. But why now, so late?

NORA. Tonight I'm not sleeping.

HELMER. But Nora dear—

NORA. [*Looking at her watch.*] It's still not so very late. Sit down, Torvald; we have a lot to talk over. [*She sits at one side of the table.*]

HELMER. Nora—what is this? That hard expression—

NORA. Sit down. This'll take some time. I have a lot to say.

HELMER. [*Sitting at the table directly opposite her.*] You worry me, Nora. And I don't understand you.

NORA. No, that's exactly it. You don't understand me. And I've never understood you either—until tonight. No, don't interrupt. You can just listen to what I say. We're closing out accounts, Torvald.

HELMER. How do you mean that?

NORA. [*After a short pause.*] Doesn't anything strike you about our sitting here like this?

HELMER. What's that?

NORA. We've been married now eight years. Doesn't it occur to you that this is the first time we two, you and I, man and wife, have ever talked seriously together?

HELMER. What do you mean—seriously?

NORA. In eight whole years—longer even—right from our first acquaintance, we've never exchanged a serious word on any serious thing.

HELMER. You mean I should constantly go and involve you in problems you couldn't possibly help me with?

NORA. I'm not talking of problems. I'm saying that we've never sat down seriously together and tried to get to the bottom of anything.

HELMER. But dearest, what good would that ever do you?

NORA. That's the point right there: you've never understood me. I've been wronged greatly, Torvald—first by Papa, and then by you.

HELMER. What! By us—the two people who've loved you more than anyone else?

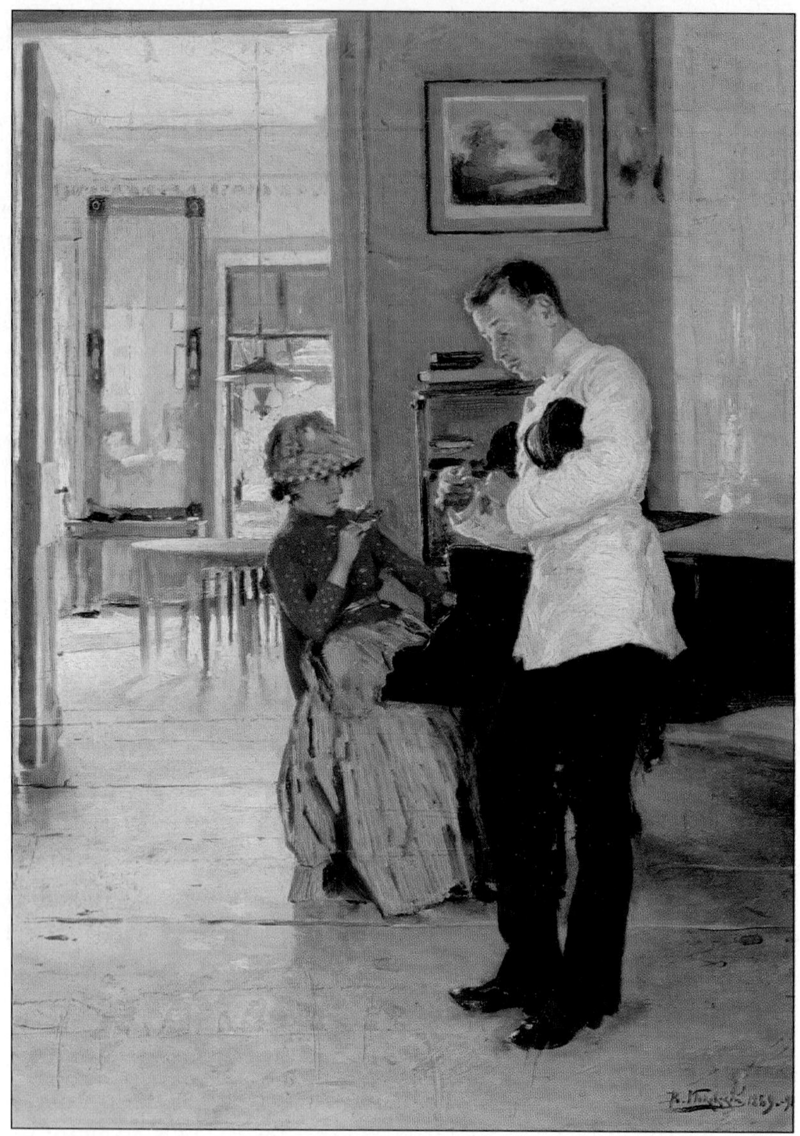

Explanation, 1889. Vladimir Jegorovitsch Makovsky (Russia). Oil on canvas, 53 x 39.5 cm. Tretyakov Gallery, Moscow.

Viewing the painting: How does the artist create a feeling of tension in this painting? How does Ibsen create tension in the play?

NORA. [*Shaking her head.*] You never loved me. You've thought it fun to be in love with me, that's all.

HELMER. Nora, what a thing to say!

NORA. Yes, it's true now, Torvald. When I lived at home with Papa, he told me all his opinions, so I had the same ones too; or if they were different I hid them, since he wouldn't have cared for that. He used to call me his doll-child, and he played with me the way I played with my dolls. Then I came into your house—

HELMER. How can you speak of our marriage like that?

NORA. [*Unperturbed.*] I mean, then I went from Papa's hands into yours. You arranged

Vocabulary

unperturbed (un′ pər turbd′) *adj.* not greatly disturbed in mind; calm everything to your own taste, and so I got the same taste as you—or I pretended to; I can't remember. I guess a little of both, first one, then the other. Now when I look back, it seems as if I'd lived here like a beggar—just from hand to mouth. I've lived by doing tricks for you, Torvald. But that's the way you wanted it. It's a great sin what you and Papa did to me. You're to blame that nothing's become of me.

HELMER. Nora, how unfair and ungrateful you are! Haven't you been happy here?

NORA. No, never. I thought so—but I never have.

HELMER. Not—not happy!

NORA. No, only lighthearted. And you've always been so kind to me. But our home's been nothing but a playpen. I've been your doll-wife here, just as at home I was Papa's doll-child. And in turn the children have been my dolls. I thought it was fun when you played with me, just as they thought it fun when I played with them. That's been our marriage, Torvald.

HELMER. There's some truth in what you're saying—under all the raving exaggeration. But it'll all be different after this. Playtime's over; now for the schooling.

NORA. Whose schooling—mine or the children's?

HELMER. Both yours and the children's, dearest.

NORA. Oh, Torvald, you're not the man to teach me to be a good wife to you.

HELMER. And you can say that?

NORA. And I—how am I equipped to bring up children?

HELMER. Nora!

NORA. Didn't you say a moment ago that that was no job to trust me with?

HELMER. In a flare of temper! Why fasten on that?

NORA. Yes, but you were so very right. I'm not up to the job. There's another job I have to do first. I have to try to educate myself. You can't help me with that. I've got to do it alone. And that's why I'm leaving you now.

HELMER. [*Jumping up.*] What's that?

NORA. I have to stand completely alone, if I'm ever going to discover myself and the world out there. So I can't go on living with you.

HELMER. Nora, Nora!

NORA. I want to leave right away. Kristine should put me up for the night—

HELMER. You're insane! You've no right! I forbid you!

NORA. From here on, there's no use forbidding me anything. I'll take with me whatever is mine. I don't want a thing from you, either now or later.

HELMER. What kind of madness is this!

NORA. Tomorrow I'm going home—I mean, home where I came from. It'll be easier up there to find something to do.

HELMER. Oh, you blind, incompetent child!

NORA. I must learn to be competent, Torvald.

HELMER. Abandon your home, your husband, your children! And you're not even thinking what people will say.

NORA. I can't be concerned about that. I only know how essential this is.

HELMER. Oh, its outrageous. So you'll run out like this on your most sacred vows.

NORA. What do you think are my most sacred vows?

HELMER. And I have to tell you that! Aren't they your duties to your husband and children?

NORA. I have other duties equally sacred.

HELMER. That isn't true. What duties are they?

NORA. Duties to myself.

HELMER. Before all else, you're a wife and a mother.

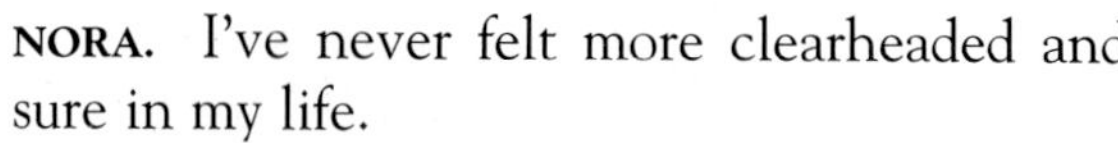

NORA. I don't believe in that anymore. I believe that, before all else, I'm a human being, no less than you—or anyway, I ought to try to become one. I know the majority thinks you're right, Torvald, and plenty of books agree with you, too. But I can't go on believing what the majority says, or what's written in books. I have to think over these things myself and try to understand them.

HELMER. Why can't you understand your place in your own home? On a point like that, isn't there one everlasting guide you can turn to? Where's your religion?

NORA. Oh, Torvald, I'm really not sure what religion is.

HELMER. What—?

NORA. I only know what the minister said when I was confirmed. He told me religion was this thing and that. When I get clear and away by myself, I'll go into that problem too. I'll see if what the minister said was right, or, in any case, if it's right for me.

HELMER. A young woman your age shouldn't talk like that. If religion can't move you, I can try to rouse your conscience. You do have some moral feeling? Or, tell me—has that gone too?

NORA. It's not easy to answer that, Torvald. I simply don't know. I'm all confused about these things. I just know I see them so differently from you. I find out, for one thing, that the law's not at all what I'd thought—but I can't get it through my head that the law is fair. A woman hasn't a right to protect her dying father or save her husband's life! I can't believe that.

HELMER. You talk like a child. You don't know anything of the world you live in.

NORA. No, I don't. But now I'll begin to learn for myself. I'll try to discover who's right, the world or I.

HELMER. Nora, you're sick; you've got a fever. I almost think you're out of your head.

NORA. I've never felt more clearheaded and sure in my life.

HELMER. And—clearheaded and sure—you're leaving your husband and children?

NORA. Yes.

HELMER. Then there's only one possible reason.

NORA. What?

HELMER. You no longer love me.

NORA. No. That's exactly it.

HELMER. Nora! You can't be serious!

NORA. Oh, this is so hard, Torvald—you've been so kind to me always. But I can't help it. I don't love you anymore.

HELMER. [*Struggling for composure.*] Are you also clearheaded and sure about that?

NORA. Yes, completely. That's why I can't go on staying here.

HELMER. Can you tell me what I did to lose your love?

NORA. Yes, I can tell you. It was this evening when the miraculous thing didn't come—then I knew you weren't the man I'd imagined.

HELMER. Be more explicit; I don't follow you.

NORA. I've waited now so patiently eight long years—for, my Lord, I know miracles don't come every day. Then this crisis broke over me, and such a certainty filled me: *now* the miraculous event would occur. While Krogstad's letter was lying out there, I never for an instant dreamed that you could give in to his terms. I was so utterly sure you'd say to him: go on, tell your tale to the whole wide world. And when he'd done that—

HELMER. Yes, what then? When I'd delivered my own wife into shame and disgrace—!

NORA. When he'd done that, I was so utterly sure that you'd step forward, take the blame on yourself and say: I am the guilty one.

HELMER. Nora—!

NORA. You're thinking I'd never accept such a sacrifice from you? No, of course not. But what good would my protests be against you? That was the miracle I was waiting for, in terror and hope. And to stave that off, I would have taken my life.

HELMER. I'd gladly work for you day and night, Nora—and take on pain and deprivation. But there's no one who gives up honor for love.

NORA. Millions of women have done just that.

HELMER. Oh, you think and talk like a silly child.

NORA. Perhaps. But you neither think nor talk like the man I could join myself to. When your big fright was over—and it wasn't from any threat against me, only for what might damage you—when all the danger was past, for you it was just as if nothing had happened. I was exactly the same, your little lark, your doll, that you'd have to handle with double care now that I'd turned out so brittle and frail. [*Gets up.*] Torvald—in that instant it dawned on me that for eight years I've been living here with a stranger, and that I'd even conceived three children—oh, I can't stand the thought of it! I could tear myself to bits.

HELMER. [*Heavily.*] I see. There's a gulf that's opened between us—that's clear. Oh, but Nora, can't we bridge it somehow?

NORA. The way I am now, I'm no wife for you.

HELMER. I have the strength to make myself over.

NORA. Maybe—if your doll gets taken away.

HELMER. But to part! To part from you! No, Nora, no—I can't imagine it.

NORA. [*Going out, right.*] All the more reason why it has to be. [*She reenters with her coat and a small overnight bag, which she puts on a chair by the table.*]

HELMER. Nora, Nora, not now! Wait till tomorrow.

NORA. I can't spend the night in a strange man's room.

HELMER. But couldn't we live here like brother and sister—

NORA. You know very well how long that would last. [*Throws her shawl about her.*] Good-bye, Torvald. I won't look in on the children. I know they're in better hands than mine. The way I am now, I'm no use to them.

HELMER. But someday, Nora—someday—?

NORA. How can I tell? I haven't the least idea what'll become of me.

HELMER. But you're my wife, now and wherever you go.

NORA. Listen, Torvald—I've heard that when a wife deserts her husband's house just as I'm doing, then the law frees him from all responsibility. In any case, I'm freeing you from being responsible. Don't feel yourself bound, any more than I will. There has to be absolute freedom for us both. Here, take your ring back. Give me mine.

HELMER. That too?

NORA. That too.

HELMER. There it is.

NORA. Good. Well, now it's all over. I'm putting the keys here. The maids know all about keeping up the house—better than I do. Tomorrow, after I've left town, Kristine will stop by to pack up everything that's mine from home. I'd like those things shipped up to me.

HELMER. Over! All over! Nora, won't you ever think about me?

NORA. I'm sure I'll think of you often, and about the children and the house here.

HELMER. May I write you?

NORA. No—never. You're not to do that.

HELMER. Oh, but let me send you—

NORA. Nothing. Nothing.

HELMER. Or help you if you need it.

A Street at Night. Aron Gerle (Sweden, 1860–1930). Oil on canvas, 95.5 x 122 cm. Private collection.

Viewing the painting: How does the artist create the mood in this painting? Is it similar to the mood of the play at this point?

NORA. No. I accept nothing from strangers.

HELMER. Nora—can I never be more than a stranger to you?

NORA. [*Picking up the overnight bag.*] Ah, Torvald—it would take the greatest miracle of all—

HELMER. Tell me the greatest miracle!

NORA. You and I both would have to transform ourselves to the point that— Oh, Torvald, I've stopped believing in miracles.

HELMER. But I'll believe. Tell me! Transform ourselves to the point that—?

NORA. That our living together could be a true marriage. [*She goes out down the hall.*]

HELMER. [*Sinks down on a chair by the door, face buried in his hands.*] Nora! Nora! [*Looking about and rising.*] Empty. She's gone. [*A sudden hope leaps in him.*] The greatest miracle—?

[*From below, the sound of a door slamming shut.*]

Responding to Literature

Personal Response

Were you surprised by the outcome of this play? Jot down your response in your notebook.

Analyzing Literature

Recall

1. Why does Mrs. Linde offer to marry Krogstad?
2. Why does Dr. Rank visit Nora and Torvald after the party?
3. How does Torvald plan to respond to Krogstad's first letter?
4. What does Torvald learn from Krogstad's second letter?
5. What decision does Nora make in the end?

Interpret

6. Why do you think Mrs. Linde believes that Krogstad is "good at heart"?
7. How deeply is Torvald affected by the news about Dr. Rank? Explain what led you to this conclusion.
8. **Irony** is a contrast between what is believed or expected and what actually exists or occurs (see **Literary Terms Handbook,** page R6). What is ironic about Torvald's demand that Nora stop "playacting" after he reads Krogstad's first letter?
9. What does Torvald believe will happen when he declares that he and Nora are safe?
10. Why does Nora feel that her final decision is necessary?

Evaluate and Connect

11. Do you think that Mrs. Linde and Krogstad are likely to have a good marriage? Why or why not?
12. Do you agree with Mrs. Linde that Krogstad should let Torvald find out the truth about Nora's forgery? Explain.
13. Would the play have ended happily if Torvald showed support for Nora after reading Krogstad's first letter? Why or why not?
14. A **theme** is a message or idea about life that is implied or stated in a literary work (see **Literary Terms Handbook,** page R12). How would you state the main theme of this play?
15. Do you think that *A Doll's House* could be set in contemporary Western society? Why or why not?

Literary Criticism

According to one critic, Ibsen "used dialogue, commonplace events, and symbolism to explore the elusiveness of self-knowledge and the restrictive nature of traditional morality." Do you think these are the central themes of *A Doll's House*? Do you agree that Ibsen uses dialogue, commonplace events, and symbolism to explore these themes? Present your answer in an essay, using details from the play to support your answer.

Literary ELEMENTS

Plot

A **plot** is the sequence of related events in a story. Many works of fiction follow a traditional plot structure that consists of four elements. In the **exposition,** characters are introduced, the setting is described, and the main conflict is established. Further complications develop in the **rising action,** making the conflict more difficult to resolve. Eventually the story reaches its **climax**—an event, decision, or discovery that determines the story's outcome. This point of greatest interest and intensity is followed by the **resolution,** in which conflicts are resolved, and the story is brought to a close.

1. Describe a complication that occurs in the rising action of *A Doll's House.*
2. What is the play's climax?
3. How is the main conflict resolved in the resolution?

- See **Literary Terms Handbook,** p. R9.

Literature and Writing

Writing About Literature

Review Would you recommend *A Doll's House* to a friend? Write a review of the play in which you analyze its strengths and weaknesses. Include a brief plot summary. You might wish to discuss literary elements such as characterization, irony, and conflict. Use quotes from the play to support your opinions.

Personal Writing

Standing Alone Describe a time when you had to act or think independently. For example, you might have solved a problem without help from your parents, or you might have disagreed with friends about an important issue. How did people respond to your independence from them? What did you learn about yourself?

Extending Your Response

Learning for Life

Casting Call Suppose that you are a casting director for a theater company planning to perform *A Doll's House.* Write a memo about the casting requirements for one of the characters. Describe that character's appearance and personality traits. Discuss whether the character is static or undergoes significant change in the course of the play.

Literature Groups

Nora's Awakening Do you find Nora's assertion of independence in Act III believable? Did Ibsen provide evidence earlier in the play that she is capable of taking such bold action? Discuss these questions in your group. When you are finished, share your conclusions with the class.

Performing

Staged Reading Choose a scene from the play to perform with a small group. As you rehearse, discuss different ways of delivering the dialogue. Before giving your performance, describe the set design and props you would use in a full production.

Reading Further

If you enjoyed reading *A Doll's House,* you might also enjoy these other plays by Ibsen:

An Enemy of the People, a study of a victim with a destructive streak.

Hedda Gabler, an intense study of an ambitious woman.

Save your work for your portfolio.

VOCABULARY • Idioms

Suffixes are groups of letters that can be added to words to change the part of speech. Here are a few common suffixes:

noun-forming: -dom (freedom), -ery (bakery), -ion (intention), -ment (contentment)

adjective-forming: -able (laughable), -ful (hopeful), -ic (allergic), -ous (poisonous)

adverb-forming: -ly (fairly)

- For more about suffixes, see **Language Handbook,** Spelling, pp. R55–R56.

PRACTICE Add a suffix to change each word as instructed. Check your answers (including the spelling) in a dictionary.

1. Make *pride* an adjective.
2. Make *confine* a noun.
3. Make *frequent* an adverb.
4. Make *rely* an adjective.
5. Make *locate* a noun.

LISTENING, SPEAKING, and VIEWING

Critical Viewing of a Play

As you read Ibsen's *A Doll's House,* you learned about the characters and plot by reading the dialogue and stage directions. You developed ideas about Nora and Torvald, and about the central and related conflicts. You may still be thinking about the themes or issues the play raises about marriage, identity, and individuality.

Now imagine yourself viewing a stage, video, or film performance of *A Doll's House.* What elements besides character, plot, conflict, or theme might you need to consider to analyze and evaluate the performance? The following guidelines might help you critically view a play.

First, look at the set.

- Does the set effectively transport you to the time and place of the story?
- Do the lighting, sound effects, props, and costumes help set the mood and draw you into the play? What is most noteworthy about these elements?

Think about the acting.

- Do the actors make the characters come to life? For example, do you believe you are watching *Nora* sneak a macaroon from her bag, or are you aware that you are watching an actress *playing* Nora?
- How does the way the dialogue is spoken by the actors add to the characterization and the main events in the plot?
- Is the acting strong enough to make you care about what happens in the story?

Evaluate the complete production.

- Did the setting and dialogue remain faithful to the original? If not, how did they differ?
- Did the performance hold your attention?
- What held your attention most effectively–the acting, the plot, or something else about the play?
- What was your overall response to the play?
- Did you find the ending satisfying? Why or why not?
- What did you learn about the characters, yourself, and the human condition from viewing this play?
- Do you think that viewing the play instead of reading it had any effect on what you learned? In what way?

ACTIVITY

As a class, watch a video of a short play or, if possible, attend a performance of a play. Afterward, break into small groups and conduct a discussion of the performance. Use the bulleted questions on this page to guide your discussion. As a group, write a critical review of the performance and share it with the rest of the class.

RUSSIA, 1885

Before You Read

How Much Land Does a Man Need?

Meet Leo Tolstoy

"There is no greatness where there is not simplicity, goodness, and truth."

When he was an old man, Leo Tolstoy sometimes made visitors uncomfortable; it often seemed as if he could read their minds. His profound psychological insight is also apparent in his fiction. One of Russia's greatest novelists, Tolstoy was a master at portraying how people think and feel.

Tolstoy came from an aristocratic family. He wrote his first two books while serving as an officer in the Russian army. In his early thirties, he married and settled down on his estate. He spent the next fifteen years working on the novels *War and Peace* and *Anna Karenina*. Then a spiritual crisis led him to renounce these realistic masterpieces. For a while, he wrote only nonfiction works about religion and morality. Eventually he returned to fiction. Many of his late works are moral tales written in a simplified style. By the end of his life, Tolstoy was revered throughout the world as an artist and a thinker.

Leo Tolstoy was born in 1828 and died in 1910.

Reading Focus

Think of a time when you wanted more of something than you really needed.

Quickwrite Write a paragraph describing this experience.

Setting a Purpose Read this story to see how a man is affected by his desire for land.

Building Background

Tolstoy's Moral Teachings

Inspired by the religious faith of Russian peasants, Tolstoy underwent a spiritual awakening in his early fifties. However, he came to reject the doctrines of the Russian Orthodox Church. In a series of essays, Tolstoy set forth a new system of beliefs based on the Gospels. He stressed the importance of pacifism, simple living, and self-improvement through physical work. He eventually gave up all claim to his extensive land holdings, believing it was wrong to own property. Tolstoy's ideas of civil disobedience and passive resistance had a great impact on the young Mahatma Gandhi, who used them to lead the people of India to independence from Great Britain.

Peasants and Land

Tolstoy, although an aristocrat, sympathized with the peasant class. Until 1861, under a system called serfdom, Russian peasants lived in virtual slavery. A serf literally belonged to the land: if a landowner sold a hundred acres, for example, the serfs working that land were sold along with it. Serfs had few legal rights—they could not leave the land, change jobs, or even marry without the landowner's permission. After the abolition of serfdom they were supposed to receive enough land to live on, but landowners and local authorities made sure they received only the smallest or least productive plots.

Vocabulary Preview

disparage (dis par′ ij) *v.* to speak badly of; p. 937
trespass (tres′ pəs) *v.* to illegally enter property; p. 939
arable (ar′ ə bəl) *adj.* fit for growing crops; p. 941
prostrate (pros′ trāt) *adj.* stretched out with one's face on the ground, usually in adoration or submission; p. 944

Ploughing the Field, 1871. M. K. Klodt von Juergensburg (Russia). State Russian Museum, Moscow.

How Much Land Does a Man Need?

Leo Tolstoy

Translated by Louise and Aylmer Maude

I

An elder sister came to visit her younger sister in the country. The elder was married to a tradesman in town, the younger to a peasant in the village. As the sisters sat over their tea talking, the elder began to boast of the advantages of town life: saying how comfortably they lived there, how well they dressed, what fine clothes her children wore, what good things they ate and drank, and how she went to the theater, promenades, and entertainments.

The younger sister was piqued, and in turn disparaged the life of a tradesman, and stood up for that of a peasant.

"I would not change my way of life for yours," said she. "We may live roughly, but at least we are free from anxiety. You live in better style than we do, but though you often earn more than you need, you are very likely to lose all you have. You know the proverb, 'Loss and gain are brothers twain.' It often happens that

Vocabulary

disparage (dis par′ ij) *v.* to speak badly of

people who are wealthy one day are begging their bread the next. Our way is safer. Though a peasant's life is not a fat one, it is a long one. We shall never grow rich, but we shall always have enough to eat."

The elder sister said sneeringly:

"Enough? Yes, if you like to share with the pigs and the calves! What do you know of elegance or manners! However much your goodman may slave, you will die as you are living—on a dung heap—and your children the same."

"Well, what of that?" replied the younger. "Of course our work is rough and coarse. But, on the other hand, it is sure, and we need not bow to any one. But you, in your towns, are surrounded by temptations; today all may be right, but tomorrow the Evil One[1] may tempt your husband with cards, wine, or women, and all will go to ruin. Don't such things happen often enough?"

Pakhom, the master of the house, was lying on the top of the stove and he listened to the women's chatter.

"It is perfectly true," thought he. "Busy as we are from childhood tilling mother earth, we peasants have no time to let any nonsense settle in our heads. Our only trouble is that we haven't land enough. If I had plenty of land, I shouldn't fear the Devil himself!"

The women finished their tea, chatted a while about dress, and then cleared away the tea-things and lay down to sleep.

But the Devil had been sitting behind the stove, and had heard all that was said. He was pleased that the peasant's wife had led her husband into boasting, and that he had said that if he had plenty of land he would not fear the Devil himself.

"All right," thought the Devil. "We will have a tussle. I'll give you land enough; and by means of that land I will get you into my power."

1. The *Evil One* is the Devil.

II

Close to the village there lived a lady, a small landowner who had an estate of about three hundred acres. She had always lived on good terms with the peasants until she engaged as her steward an old soldier, who took to burdening the people with fines. However careful Pakhom tried to be, it happened again and again that now a horse of his got among the lady's oats, now a cow strayed into her garden, now his calves found their way into her meadows—and he always had to pay a fine.

Pakhom paid up, but grumbled, and going home in a temper, was rough with his family. All through that summer, Pakhom had much trouble because of this steward, and he was even glad when winter came and the cattle had to be stabled. Though he grudged the fodder when they could no longer graze on the pasture-land, at least he was free from anxiety about them.

In the winter the news got about that the lady was going to sell her land and that the keeper of the inn on the high road was bargaining for it. When the peasants heard this they were very much alarmed.

"Well," thought they, "if the innkeeper gets the land, he will worry us with fines worse than the lady's steward. We all depend on that estate."

So the peasants went on behalf of their commune,[2] and asked the lady not to sell the land to the innkeeper, offering her a better price for it themselves. The lady agreed to let them have it. Then the peasants tried to arrange for the commune to buy the whole estate, so that it might be held by them all in common. They met twice to discuss it, but could not settle the matter; the Evil One sowed discord among them and they could not agree. So they decided to buy the land individually, each according to

2. In some rural areas, farmers organize into *communes* for mutual support. Members of the commune also may own or use property or equipment in common.

his means; and the lady agreed to this plan as she had to the other.

Presently Pakhom heard that a neighbor of his was buying fifty acres, and that the lady had consented to accept one half in cash and to wait a year for the other half. Pakhom felt envious.

"Look at that," thought he, "the land is all being sold, and I shall get none of it." So he spoke to his wife.

"Other people are buying," said he, "and we must also buy twenty acres or so. Life is becoming impossible. That steward is simply crushing us with his fines."

So they put their heads together and considered how they could manage to buy it. They had one hundred rubles laid by. They sold a colt and one half of their bees, hired out one of their sons as a laborer and took his wages in advance; borrowed the rest from a brother-in-law, and so scraped together half the purchase money.

Did You Know?
The *ruble* is the basic unit of Russian currency.

Having done this, Pakhom chose out a farm of forty acres, some of it wooded, and went to the lady to bargain for it. They came to an agreement, and he shook hands with her upon it and paid her a deposit in advance. Then they went to town and signed the deeds; he paying half the price down, and undertaking to pay the remainder within two years.

So now Pakhom had land of his own. He borrowed seed, and sowed it on the land he had bought. The harvest was a good one, and within a year he had managed to pay off his debts both to the lady and to his brother-in-law. So he became a landowner, ploughing and sowing his own land, making hay on his own land, cutting his own trees, and feeding his cattle on his own pasture. When he went out to plough his fields, or to look at his growing corn, or at his grass-meadows, his heart would fill with joy. The grass that grew and the flowers that bloomed there seemed to him unlike any that grew elsewhere. Formerly, when he had passed by that land, it had appeared the same as any other land, but now it seemed quite different.

III

So Pakhom was well-contented, and everything would have been right if the neighboring peasants would only not have trespassed on his corn-fields and meadows. He appealed to them most civilly, but they still went on: now the communal herdsmen would let the village cows stray into his meadows, then horses from the night pasture would get among his corn. Pakhom turned them out again and again, and forgave their owners, and for a long time he forbore to prosecute any one. But at last he lost patience and complained to the district court. He knew it was the peasants' want of land, and no evil intent on their part, that caused the trouble, but he thought:

"I cannot go on overlooking it or they will destroy all I have. They must be taught a lesson."

So he had them up, gave them one lesson, and then another, and two or three of the peasants were fined. After a time Pakhom's neighbors began to bear him a grudge for this, and would now and then let their cattle on to his land on purpose. One peasant even got into Pakhom's wood at night and cut down five young lime trees for their bark. Pakhom passing through the wood one day noticed something white. He came nearer and saw the stripped trunks lying on the ground, and close by stood the stumps where the trees had been. Pakhom was furious.

Vocabulary
trespass (tres′ pəs) *v.* to illegally enter property

The Wheat Harvest, 1914. Zinaida Evgnievna Serebryakova (Russia). Oil sketch. Private collection.

Viewing the painting: What do you think these peasants' lives are like? How might they be similar to the peasants in the story?

"If he had only cut one here and there it would have been bad enough," thought Pakhom, "but the rascal has actually cut down a whole clump. If I could only find out who did this, I would pay him out."[3]

He racked his brains as to who it could be. Finally he decided: "It must be Simon—no one else could have done it." So he went to Simon's homestead to have a look round, but he found nothing, and only had an angry scene. However, he now felt more certain than ever that Simon had done it, and he lodged a complaint. Simon was summoned. The case was tried, and retried, and at the end of it all Simon was acquitted, there being no evidence against him. Pakhom felt still more aggrieved, and let his anger loose upon the elder and the judges.

"You let thieves grease your palms," said he. "If you were honest folk yourselves you would not let a thief go free."

So Pakhom quarrelled with the judges and with his neighbors. Threats to burn his building began to be uttered. So though Pakhom had more land, his place in the commune was much worse than before.

About this time a rumor got about that many people were moving to new parts.

"There's no need for me to leave my land," thought Pakhom. "But some of the others might leave our village and then there would be more room for us. I would take over their land myself and make my estate a bit bigger. I could then live more at ease. As it is, I am still too cramped to be comfortable."

One day Pakhom was sitting at home when a peasant, passing through the village, happened to call in. He was allowed to stay the night, and supper was given him. Pakhom had a talk with this peasant and asked him where he came from. The stranger answered that he came from beyond the Volga,[4] where he had been working. One word led to another, and the man went on to say that many people were settling in those parts. He told how some people from his village had settled there. They had joined the commune, and had had twenty-five acres per man granted them. The land was so good, he said, that the rye sown on it grew as high as a horse, and so thick that five cuts of a sickle made a sheaf. One peasant, he said, had brought nothing with him but his bare hands, and now he had six horses and two cows of his own.

Pakhom's heart kindled with desire. He thought:

"Why should I suffer in this narrow hole, if one can live so well elsewhere? I will sell my land and my homestead here, and with the money I will start afresh over there and get everything new. In this crowded place one is always having trouble. But I must first go and find out all about it myself."

3. To *pay him out* means that Pakhom wants to hurt the person for the wrong he has done.
4. The *Volga* is a river in western Russia.

Towards summer he got ready and started. He went down the Volga on a steamer to Samara,[5] then walked another three hundred miles on foot, and at last reached the place. It was just as the stranger had said. The peasants had plenty of land: every man had twenty-five acres of communal land given him for his use, and any one who had money could buy, besides, at two shillings an acre as much good freehold[6] land as he wanted.

Having found out all he wished to know, Pakhom returned home as autumn came on, and began selling off his belongings. He sold his land at a profit, sold his homestead and all his cattle, and withdrew from membership of the commune. He only waited till the spring, and then started with his family for the new settlement.

IV

As soon as Pakhom and his family reached their new abode, he applied for admission into the commune of a large village. He stood treat to the elders and obtained the necessary documents. Five shares of communal land were given him for his own and his sons' use: that is to say—125 acres (not all together, but in different fields) besides the use of the communal pasture. Pakhom put up the buildings he needed, and bought cattle. Of the communal land alone he had three times as much as at his former home, and the land was good cornland. He was ten times better off than he had been. He had plenty of arable land and pasturage, and could keep as many head of cattle as he liked.

At first, in the bustle of building and settling down, Pakhom was pleased with it all, but when he got used to it he began to think that even here he had not enough land. The first year, he sowed wheat on his share of the communal land and had a good crop. He wanted to go on sowing wheat, but had not enough communal land for the purpose, and what he had already used was not available; for in those parts wheat is only sown on virgin soil or on fallow land.[7] It is sown for one or two years, and then the land lies fallow till it is again overgrown with prairie grass. There were many who wanted such land and there was not enough for all; so that people quarrelled about it. Those who were better off wanted it for growing wheat, and those who were poor wanted it to let to dealers, so that they might raise money to pay their taxes. Pakhom wanted to sow more wheat, so he rented land from a dealer for a year. He sowed much wheat and had a fine crop, but the land was too far from the village—the wheat had to be carted more than ten miles. After a time Pakhom noticed that some peasant-dealers were living on separate farms and were growing wealthy; and he thought:

"If I were to buy some freehold land and have a homestead on it, it would be a different thing altogether. Then it would all be nice and compact."

The question of buying freehold land recurred to him again and again.

He went on in the same way for three years, renting land and sowing wheat. The seasons turned out well and the crops were good, so that he began to lay money by. He might have gone on living contentedly, but he grew tired of having to rent other people's land every year, and having to scramble for it. Wherever there was good land to be had, the peasants would rush for it and it was taken up at once, so that unless you were sharp about it you got none. It happened in the third year that he and a dealer together

5. *Samara* is a city on the Volga.

6. Pakhom could purchase and then sell *freehold* land to anyone he liked.

7. *Virgin soil* is land that has never been farmed; *fallow land* is land that is being rested after producing a harvest.

Vocabulary

arable (ar′ ə bəl) *adj.* fit for growing crops

rented a piece of pasture land from some peasants; and they had already ploughed it up, when there was some dispute and the peasants went to law about it, and things fell out so that the labor was all lost.

"If it were my own land," thought Pakhom, "I should be independent, and there would not be all this unpleasantness."

So Pakhom began looking out for land which he could buy; and he came across a peasant who had bought thirteen hundred acres, but having got into difficulties was willing to sell again cheap. Pakhom bargained and haggled with him, and at last they settled the price at 1,500 rubles, part in cash and part to be paid later. They had all but clinched the matter when a passing dealer happened to stop at Pakhom's one day to get a feed for his horses. He drank tea with Pakhom and they had a talk. The dealer said that he was just returning from the land of the Bashkirs,[8] far away, where he had bought thirteen thousand acres of land, all for 1,000 rubles. Pakhom questioned him further, and the tradesman said:

"All one need do is to make friends with the chiefs. I gave away about one hundred rubles worth of silk robes and carpets, besides a case of tea, and I gave wine to those who would drink it; and I got the land for less than a penny an acre." And he showed Pakhom the title-deeds, saying:

"The land lies near a river, and the whole prairie is virgin soil."

Pakhom plied him with questions, and the tradesman said:

"There is more land there than you could cover if you walked a year, and it all belongs to the Bashkirs. They are as simple as sheep, and land can be got almost for nothing."

"There now," thought Pakhom, "with my one thousand rubles, why should I get only thirteen hundred acres, and saddle myself with a debt besides? If I take it out there, I can get more than ten times as much for the money."

8. The *Bashkirs* (bäsh′ kērs) are a nomadic people of western Russia.

V

Pakhom inquired how to get to the place, and as soon as the tradesman had left him, he prepared to go there himself. He left his wife to look after the homestead, and started on his journey taking his man[9] with him. They stopped at a town on their way and bought a case of tea, some wine, and other presents, as the tradesman had advised. On and on they went until they had gone more than three hundred miles, and on the seventh day they came to a place where the Bashkirs had pitched their tents. It was all just as the tradesman had said. The people lived on the steppes,[10] by a river, in felt-covered tents. They neither tilled the ground, nor ate bread. Their cattle and horses grazed in herds on the steppe. The colts were tethered behind the tents, and the mares were driven to them twice a day. The mares were milked, and from the milk kumiss[11] was made. It was the women who prepared kumiss, and they also made cheese. As far as the men were concerned, drinking kumiss and tea, eating mutton, and playing on their pipes, was all they cared about. They were all stout and merry, and all the summer long they never thought of doing any work. They were quite ignorant, and knew no Russian, but were good-natured enough.

As soon as they saw Pakhom, they came out of their tents and gathered round their visitor. An interpreter was found, and Pakhom told them he had come about some land. The Bashkirs seemed very glad; they took Pakhom and led him into one of the best tents, where they made him sit on some down cushions placed on a carpet, while they sat round him. They gave him some tea and kumiss, and had a sheep killed, and gave him mutton to eat. Pakhom took presents out of his cart and distributed them among the Bashkirs, and divided the tea amongst them. The Bashkirs were

9. Pakhom's *man* is his male servant.

10. *Steppes* are vast land areas and are usually level and treeless.

11. *Kumiss* (koo′ mis) is a beverage made from fermented horse milk.

IX

Pakhom went straight towards the hillock, but he now walked with difficulty. He was done up with the heat, his bare feet were cut and bruised, and his legs began to fail. He longed to rest, but it was impossible if he meant to get back before sunset. The sun waits for no man, and it was sinking lower and lower.

"Oh dear," he thought, "if only I have not blundered trying for too much! What if I am too late?"

He looked towards the hillock and at the sun. He was still far from his goal, and the sun was already near the rim.

Pakhom walked on and on; it was very hard walking but he went quicker and quicker. He pressed on, but was still far from the place. He began running, threw away his coat, his boots, his flask, and his cap, and kept only the spade which he used as a support.

"What shall I do?" he thought again, "I have grasped too much and ruined the whole affair. I can't get there before the sun sets."

And this fear made him still more breathless. Pakhom went on running, his soaking shirt and trousers stuck to him and his mouth was parched. His breast was working like a blacksmith's bellows, his heart was beating like a hammer, and his legs were giving way as if they did not belong to him. Pakhom was seized with terror lest he should die of the strain.

Though afraid of death, he could not stop. "After having run all that way they will call me a fool if I stop now," thought he. And he ran on and on, and drew near and heard the Bashkirs yelling and shouting to him, and their cries inflamed his heart still more. He gathered his last strength and ran on.

The sun was close to the rim, and cloaked in mist looked large, and red as blood. Now, yes now, it was about to set! The sun was quite low, but he was also quite near his aim. Pakhom could already see the people on the hillock waving their arms to hurry him up. He could see the fox-fur cap on the ground and the money on it, and the chief sitting on the ground holding his sides. And Pakhom remembered his dream.

"There is plenty of land," thought he, "but will God let me live on it? I have lost my life, I have lost my life! I shall never reach that spot!"

Pakhom looked at the sun, which had reached the earth: one side of it had already disappeared. With all his remaining strength he rushed on, bending his body forward so that his legs could hardly follow fast enough to keep him from falling. Just as he reached the hillock it suddenly grew dark. He looked up—the sun had already set! He gave a cry: "All my labor has been in vain," thought he, and was about to stop, but he heard the Bashkirs still shouting, and remembered that though to him, from below, the sun seemed to have set, they on the hillock could still see it. He took a long breath and ran up the hillock. It was still light there. He reached the top and saw the cap. Before it sat the chief laughing and holding his sides. Again Pakhom remembered his dream, and he uttered a cry: his legs gave way beneath him, he fell forward and reached the cap with his hands.

"Ah, that's a fine fellow!" exclaimed the chief. "He has gained much land!"

Pakhom's servant came running up and tried to raise him, but he saw that blood was flowing from his mouth. Pakhom was dead!

The Bashkirs clicked their tongues to show their pity.

His servant picked up the spade and dug a grave long enough for Pakhom to lie in, and buried him in it. Six feet from his head to his heels was all he needed.

Responding to Literature

Personal Response

Did you feel sorry for Pakhom at the end of this story? Explain why or why not to a classmate.

Analyzing Literature

Recall and Interpret

1. What boast does Pakhom make at the beginning of the story?
2. What are the factors that prompt Pakhom to buy his first piece of land?
3. How does Pakhom come to learn of other opportunities to acquire land?
4. What dream does Pakhom have in the land of the Bashkirs?
5. What arrangement does the Bashkir chief agree to make with Pakhom?
6. Why is the Devil pleased that Pakhom makes his boast?
7. How does Pakhom's purchase change his relations with other peasants?
8. Is the information Pakhom is given about acquiring land misleading? Explain.
9. How do you interpret Pakhom's dream?
10. Why does the arrangement the Bashkir chief makes with Pakhom lead to Pakhom's death?

Evaluate and Connect

11. In your opinion, does Pakhom realize his mistake before he dies? Explain.
12. **Situational irony** exists when the reality of a situation is different than what it appears to be (see **Literary Terms Handbook,** page R6). Describe an example of situational irony in the story.
13. Which elements of this story do you think are fantastic and which ones are realistic?
14. What kind of audience do you think Tolstoy was trying to reach with this story?
15. In the Reading Focus on page 936, you were asked to describe a time when you wanted more of something than you really needed. Compare your thoughts on that occasion with Pakhom's thoughts in the story.

Literary Criticism

"Tolstoy," suggests Edward Wasiolek, "promoted unconscious and unreflective living–whether in domestic or military life–and showed that intentional and conscious life results in sterility and defeat." Do you think this statement applies to "How Much Land Does a Man Need"? Why or why not? Present your answer in an essay.

Literary ELEMENTS

Dramatic Irony

Irony is a conflict between reality and appearance or expectations. **Dramatic irony** occurs when the reader or audience knows something that a character does not know. This technique can add to one's enjoyment of a literary work, much as one might enjoy knowing a secret in real life. Dramatic irony can also generate suspense about when the character will find out the truth.

1. What is the dramatic irony of Tolstoy's story?
2. How does the dramatic irony affect the level of suspense in the story?
3. Would this story be as interesting without the dramatic irony? Why or why not?

- See **Literary Terms Handbook,** p. R6.

Extending Your Response

Creative Writing

Dialogue Tolstoy opens his story with a conversation between Pakhom's wife and her sister. Write a dialogue in which the two women discuss Pakhom's death. If you like, you can include the Devil's comments as he overhears their discussion.

Writing About Literature

An Appropriate Setting Tolstoy, like most successful writers, knew how to reach his intended audience. Consider the audience for whom the story about Pakhom was intended. In a paragraph or two, describe the setting and explain its relevance to Tolstoy's readers.

Performing

Land Hunger Pretend that you are the chief of the Bashkirs planning a memorandum for your followers. Write two or three paragraphs in which you counsel your people against the vice of greed. Include references to Pakhom, his bargaining, and his ultimate fate. Deliver your instructions orally to members of your group. Then invite the group's comments on how convincing your counsel was.

Interdisciplinary Connection

Geography How much has Russian agriculture changed since Tolstoy's time? Note the facts about agriculture presented in "How Much Land Does a Man Need?" Then research modern Russian agriculture to find out what has changed. Consider factors such as crops, livestock, technology, and land ownership. Make a chart to display the similarities and differences between the time periods.

Literature Groups

Moral What lesson did Tolstoy want to teach with this story? In a small group, come up with a statement of the story's moral. Discuss how each event in the story supports this moral. When you are finished, share your moral statement with the class.

Reading Further

If you enjoyed reading "How Much Land Does a Man Need?" you might also enjoy the following:

The Death of Ivan Ilych and Other Stories, translated by Aylmer Maude and J. D. Duff.

Save your work for your portfolio.

Skill Minilesson

VOCABULARY • Idioms

Sometimes groups of words, when taken together, have a meaning that is different from the meanings of the individual words. These expressions are called idioms. Here are some of the idioms in "How Much Land Does a Man Need?"

put their heads together
pay him out
racked his brains
grease your palms
lay money by
fell out
high time

Usually, the more conversational a writer's style, the greater the number of idioms that will appear in the writing.

PRACTICE Use your knowledge of idioms to define the following idioms. (Hint: All of them act as verbs.)

chew out
fight fire with fire
let the cat out of the bag
stand on one's own two feet
talk back

RUSSIA, 1889

Before You Read

The Bet

Meet Anton Chekhov

"Gloomy people . . . always write merry things, while the cheerful depress people with their writings. And I am a cheerful man."

Anton Chekhov (chek′ ôf) grew up in southern Russia. When he was sixteen, his father went bankrupt and moved the family to Moscow. Chekhov stayed behind until he finished school. "There was no childhood in my childhood," he wrote later. A scholarship to study medicine in Moscow reunited him with his family. To help support them, he wrote comic fictional sketches for magazines and newspapers. He became widely popular as a humorist.

The grandson of serfs, Chekhov hated pretentiousness. He refused to get involved with politics, but he was often busy with humanitarian work. At age forty, he married the actress Olga Knipper, despite having already been diagnosed with tuberculosis. In his remaining few years, he concentrated on writing plays.

Chekhov was born in 1860 and died in 1904.

Reading Focus

How do you think a long period of isolation from other people would affect you?

Share Ideas Share your response with the class.

Setting a Purpose Read this story to see how a man is altered by solitude.

Building Background

Chekhov's Artistry

Chekhov claimed that his medical training had a great influence on his literary work because it taught him to be an objective observer. His goal was to depict life truthfully. Unlike Tolstoy, he believed that writers should avoid trying to teach moral lessons in their fiction: "The artist is not meant to be a judge of his characters and what they say; his only job is to be an impartial witness." Chekhov emphasized character and atmosphere over action. Indeed, it is often said that nothing happens in his stories and plays. Although a story such as "The Bet" shows that he could create a suspenseful plot, many of his finest works are uneventful or anticlimactic. Chekhov's genius was in revealing how ordinary events can have an impact on people's lives.

Reading Further

If you enjoy reading "The Bet," the following stories might also be of interest to you:

"Surgery," "The Milksop," and "The Darling" from *Anton Chekhov: Selected Stories,* translated by Ann Dunnigan.

Vocabulary Preview

humane (hū mān′) *adj.* marked by compassion, sympathy, or consideration for humans or animals; p. 952

compulsory (kəm pul′ sər ē) *adj.* mandatory; enforced; p. 952

indiscriminately (in′ dis krim′ ə nit lē) *adv.* randomly; haphazardly; p. 954

emaciated (i mā′ shē āt′ id) *adj.* thin and feeble; p. 955

renounce (ri nouns′) *v.* to give up, refuse, or resign, usually by formal declaration; p. 956

THE BET

Anton Chekhov
Translated by Constance Garnett

I

IT WAS A DARK AUTUMN NIGHT. THE OLD BANKER WAS WALKING up and down his study and remembering how, fifteen years before, he had given a party one autumn evening. There had been many clever men there, and there had been interesting conversations. Among other things they had talked of capital punishment. The majority of the guests, among whom were many journalists and intellectual men, disapproved of the death penalty.

The Artist's Dinner Party, 1903. Viggo Johansen (Denmark). Oil on canvas. National Museum, Stockholm, Sweden.

They considered that form of punishment out of date, immoral, and unsuitable for Christian States. In the opinion of some of them the death penalty ought to be replaced everywhere by imprisonment for life.

"I don't agree with you," said their host the banker. "I have not tried either the death penalty or imprisonment for life, but if one may judge *à priori*,[1] the death penalty is more moral and more humane than imprisonment for life. Capital punishment kills a man at once, but lifelong imprisonment kills him slowly. Which executioner is the more humane, he who kills you in a few minutes or he who drags the life out of you in the course of many years?"

"Both are equally immoral," observed one of the guests, "for they both have the same object—to take away life. The State is not God. It has not the right to take away what it cannot restore when it wants to."

Among the guests was a young lawyer, a young man of five-and-twenty. When he was asked his opinion, he said:

"The death sentence and the life sentence are equally immoral, but if I had to choose between the death penalty and imprisonment for life, I would certainly choose the second. To live anyhow is better than not at all."

A lively discussion arose. The banker, who was younger and more nervous in those days,[2] was suddenly carried away by excitement; he struck the table with his fist and shouted at the young man:

"It's not true! I'll bet you two millions you wouldn't stay in solitary confinement for five years."

"If you mean that in earnest," said the young man, "I'll take a bet, but I would stay not five but fifteen years."

"Fifteen? Done!" cried the banker. "Gentlemen, I stake two millions!"

"Agreed! You stake your millions and I stake my freedom!" said the young man.

And this wild, senseless bet was carried out! The banker, spoiled and frivolous, with millions beyond his reckoning, was delighted at the bet. At supper he made fun of the young man, and said:

"Think better of it, young man, while there is still time. To me two millions are a trifle, but you are losing three or four of the best years of your life. I say three or four, because you won't stay longer. Don't forget either, you unhappy man, that voluntary confinement is a great deal harder to bear than compulsory. The thought that you have the right to step out in liberty at any moment will poison your whole existence in prison. I am sorry for you."

And now the banker, walking to and fro, remembered all this, and asked himself: "What was the object of that bet? What is the good of that man's losing fifteen years of his life and my throwing away two millions? Can it prove that the death penalty is better or worse than imprisonment for life? No, no. It was all nonsensical and meaningless. On my part it was the caprice of a pampered man, and on his part simple greed for money. . . ."

Then he remembered what followed that evening. It was decided that the young man should spend the years of his captivity under the strictest supervision in one of the lodges in the banker's garden. It was agreed that for fifteen years he should not be free to cross the threshold of the lodge, to see human beings, to hear the human voice, or to receive letters and newspapers. He was allowed to have a musical

1. *À priori* (ā′ prī ôr′ ī) is a Latin term referring to reasoning based on ideas that are assumed to be true.
2. Even as he grew old, however, the banker continued to take risks with his money.

Vocabulary

humane (hū mān′) *adj.* marked by compassion, sympathy, or consideration for humans or animals

compulsory (kəm pul′ sər ē) *adj.* mandatory; enforced

Evening in the Ukraine, 1878. Arkhip Ivanovich Kuindzhi (Russia). Oil on canvas, 81 x 163 cm. State Russian Museum, St. Petersburg.

Viewing the painting: In what ways might the setting of this painting be similar to the setting of the story?

instrument and books, and was allowed to write letters, to drink wine, and to smoke. By the terms of the agreement, the only relations he could have with the outer world were by a little window made purposely for that object. He might have anything he wanted—books, music, wine, and so on—in any quantity he desired by writing an order, but could only receive them through the window. The agreement provided for every detail and every trifle that would make his imprisonment strictly solitary, and bound the young man to stay there *exactly* fifteen years, beginning from twelve o'clock of November 14, 1870, and ending at twelve o'clock of November 14, 1885. The slightest attempt on his part to break the conditions, if only two minutes before the end, released the banker from the obligation to pay him two millions.

For the first year of his confinement, as far as one could judge from his brief notes, the prisoner suffered severely from loneliness and depression. The sounds of the piano could be heard continually day and night from his lodge. He refused wine and tobacco. Wine, he wrote, excites the desires, and desires are the worst foes of the prisoner; and besides, nothing could be more dreary than drinking good wine and seeing no one. And tobacco spoilt the air of his room. In the first year the books he sent for were principally of a light character; novels with a complicated love plot, sensational and fantastic stories, and so on.

In the second year the piano was silent in the lodge, and the prisoner asked only for the classics. In the fifth year music was audible again, and the prisoner asked for wine. Those who watched him through the window said that all that year he spent doing nothing but eating and drinking and lying on his bed, frequently yawning and angrily talking to himself. He did not read books. Sometimes at night he would sit down to write; he would spend hours writing, and in the morning tear up all that he had written. More than once he could be heard crying.

In the second half of the sixth year the prisoner began zealously studying languages, philosophy, and history. He threw himself eagerly into these studies—so much so that the banker had enough to do to get him the books he ordered. In the course of four years some six hundred volumes were procured at his request. It was during this period that the banker received the following letter from his prisoner:

"My dear Jailer, I write you these lines in six languages. Show them to people who know the languages. Let them read them. If they find not one mistake I implore you to fire a shot in the garden. That shot will show me that my efforts have not been thrown away. The geniuses of all ages and of all lands speak different languages, but the same flame burns in them all. Oh, if you only knew what unearthly happiness my soul feels now from being able to understand them!" The prisoner's desire was fulfilled. The banker ordered two shots to be fired in the garden.

Then after the tenth year, the prisoner sat immovably at the table and read nothing but the Gospel. It seemed strange to the banker that a man who in four years had mastered six hundred learned volumes should waste nearly a year over one thin book easy of comprehension. Theology and histories of religion followed the Gospels.

In the last two years of his confinement the prisoner read an immense quantity of books quite indiscriminately. At one time he was busy with the natural sciences, then he would ask for Byron or Shakespeare. There were notes in which he demanded at the same time books on chemistry, and a manual of medicine, and a novel, and some treatise on philosophy or theology. His reading suggested a man swimming in the sea among the wreckage of his ship, and trying to save his life by greedily clutching first at one spar and then at another.

II

The old banker remembered all this, and thought:

"Tomorrow at twelve o'clock he will regain his freedom. By our agreement I ought to pay him two millions. If I do pay him, it is all over with me: I shall be utterly ruined."

Fifteen years before, his millions had been beyond his reckoning; now he was afraid to ask himself which were greater, his debts or his assets. Desperate gambling on the Stock Exchange, wild speculation, and the excitability which he could not get over even in advancing years, had by degrees led to the decline of his fortune, and the proud, fearless, self-confident millionaire had become a banker of middling rank, trembling at every rise and fall in his investments. "Cursed bet!" muttered the old man, clutching his head in despair. "Why didn't the man die? He is only forty now. He will take my last penny from me, he will marry, will enjoy life, will gamble on the Exchange; while I shall look at him with envy like a beggar, and hear from him every day the same sentence: 'I am indebted to you for the happiness of my life, let me help you!' No, it is too much! The one means of being saved from bankruptcy and disgrace is the death of that man!"

It struck three o'clock, the banker listened; everyone was asleep in the house, and nothing could be heard outside but the rustling of the chilled trees. Trying to make no noise, he took from a fireproof safe the key of the door which had not been opened for fifteen years, put on his overcoat, and went out of the house.

It was dark and cold in the garden. Rain was falling. A damp cutting wind was racing about the garden, howling and giving the trees no rest. The banker strained his eyes, but could see neither the earth nor the white statues, nor the lodge, nor the trees. Going to the spot where the lodge stood, he twice called the watchman.

Vocabulary

indiscriminately (in′ dis krim′ ə nit lē) *adv.* randomly; haphazardly

No answer followed. Evidently the watchman had sought shelter from the weather, and was now asleep somewhere either in the kitchen or in the greenhouse.

"If I had the pluck to carry out my intention," thought the old man, "suspicion would fall first upon the watchman."

He felt in the darkness for the steps and the door, and went into the entry of the lodge. Then he groped his way into a little passage and lighted a match. There was not a soul there. There was a bedstead with no bedding on it, and in the corner there was a dark cast-iron stove. The seals on the door leading to the prisoner's rooms were intact.

When the match went out the old man, trembling with emotion, peeped through the little window. A candle was burning dimly in the prisoner's room. He was sitting at the table. Nothing could be seen but his back, the hair on his head, and his hands. Open books were lying on the table, on the two easy chairs, and on the carpet near the table.

Five minutes passed and the prisoner did not once stir. Fifteen years' imprisonment had taught him to sit still. The banker tapped at the window with his finger, and the prisoner made no movement whatever in response. Then the banker cautiously broke the seals off the door and put the key in the keyhole. The rusty lock gave a grating sound and the door creaked. The banker expected to hear at once footsteps and a cry of astonishment, but three minutes passed and it was as quiet as ever in the room. He made up his mind to go in.

At the table a man unlike ordinary people was sitting motionless. He was a skeleton with the skin drawn tight over his bones, with long curls like a woman's, and a shaggy beard. His face was yellow with an earthy tint in it, his cheeks were hollow, his back long and narrow, and the hand on which his shaggy head was propped was so thin and delicate that it was dreadful to look at it. His hair was already streaked with silver, and seeing his emaciated, aged-looking face, no one would have believed that he was only forty. He was asleep. . . . In front of his bowed head there lay on the table a sheet of paper on which there was something written in fine handwriting.

"Poor creature!" thought the banker, "he is asleep and most likely dreaming of the millions. And I have only to take this half-dead man, throw him on the bed, stifle him a little with the pillow, and the most conscientious expert would find no sign of a violent death. But let us first read what he has written here. . . ."

The banker took the page from the table and read as follows:

"Tomorrow at twelve o'clock I regain my freedom and the right to associate with other men, but before I leave this room and see the sunshine, I think it necessary to say a few words to you. With a clear conscience I tell you, as before God, who beholds me, that I despise freedom and life and health, and all that in your books is called the good things of the world.

"For fifteen years I have been intently studying earthly life. It is true I have not seen the earth nor men, but in your books I have drunk fragrant wine, I have sung songs, I have hunted stags and wild boars in the forests, have loved women. . . . Beauties as ethereal as clouds, created by the magic of your poets and geniuses, have visited me at night, and have whispered in my ears wonderful tales that have set my brain in a whirl. In your books I have climbed to the peaks of Elburz and Mont Blanc, and from there I have seen the sun rise and have watched it at evening flood the sky, the ocean, and the mountaintops with gold and crimson. I have watched from there the lightning flashing over my head and cleaving the storm clouds. I have seen green forests, fields, rivers, lakes,

Vocabulary

emaciated (i mā′ shē āt id) *adj.* thin and feeble

towns. I have heard the singing of the sirens, and the strains of the shepherds' pipes; I have touched the wings of comely devils who flew down to converse with me of God. . . . In your books I have flung myself into the bottomless pit, performed miracles, slain, burned towns, preached new religions, conquered whole kingdoms. . . .

"Your books have given me wisdom. All that the unresting thought of man has created in the ages is compressed into a small compass in my brain. I know that I am wiser than all of you.

"And I despise your books, I despise wisdom and the blessings of this world. It is all worthless, fleeting, illusory, and deceptive, like a mirage. You may be proud, wise, and fine, but death will wipe you off the face of the earth as though you were no more than mice burrowing under the floor, and your posterity, your history, your immortal geniuses will burn or freeze together with the earthly globe.

"You have lost your reason and taken the wrong path. You have taken lies for truth, and hideousness for beauty. You would marvel if, owing to strange events of some sorts, frogs and lizards suddenly grew on apple and orange trees instead of fruit, or if roses began to smell like a sweating horse; so I marvel at you who exchange heaven for earth. I don't want to understand you.

"To prove to you in action how I despise all that you live by, I renounce the two millions of which I once dreamed as of paradise and which now I despise. To deprive myself of the right to the money I shall go out from here five hours before the time fixed, and so break the compact. . . ."

Kitchen Window. Francis Hamel (Great Britain, b. 1963). Oil on panel, 60.9 x 60.9 cm. John Martin of London.

Viewing the painting: Why might the artist have chosen this point of view in the painting? In what ways does it remind you of the point of view in the story?

When the banker had read this he laid the page on the table, kissed the strange man on the head, and went out of the lodge, weeping. At no other time, even when he had lost heavily on the Stock Exchange, had he felt so great a contempt for himself. When he got home he lay on his bed, but his tears and emotion kept him for hours from sleeping.

Next morning the watchmen ran in with pale faces, and told him they had seen the man who lived in the lodge climb out of the window into the garden, go to the gate, and disappear. The banker went at once with the servants to the lodge and made sure of the flight of his prisoner. To avoid arousing unnecessary talk, he took from the table the writing in which the millions were renounced, and when he got home locked it up in the fireproof safe.

Vocabulary

renounce (ri nouns′) *v.* to give up, refuse, or resign, usually by formal declaration

Responding to Literature

Personal Response

Were you surprised by the outcome of the story? Explain why or why not to a classmate.

Analyzing Literature

Recall

1. What issue do the guests debate at the banker's party?
2. What are the terms of the lawyer's imprisonment?
3. How has the banker's life changed during the lawyer's imprisonment?
4. Why does the banker go into the lodge where the lawyer is imprisoned?

Interpret

5. According to the banker's remarks about the death penalty, what does he seem to value most in life?
6. In your opinion, which is the most difficult period of the lawyer's imprisonment, and which is the least difficult? Explain.
7. Why does the banker feel such contempt for himself after reading the lawyer's letter?

Evaluate and Connect

8. **Motivation** is the reason or reasons behind a character's actions (see page R8). What, do you think, motivates the lawyer to stay in solitary confinement until the very last day?
9. In your opinion, did the lawyer really find wisdom during his imprisonment? Explain.
10. In the Reading Focus on page 950, you were asked to imagine how you would be affected by a long period of isolation. Compare your response with the lawyer's experience.

Literary Criticism

According to one critic, "the theme of life's meaninglessness recurs often in [Chekhov's] later work, along with a healthy skepticism–but never cynicism–toward the possible fulfillment of human hopes." In your opinion, is life's meaninglessness a central theme of "The Bet"? What attitude toward human hopes does Chekhov convey in the story? Present your answer in an essay.

Literary ELEMENTS

Character

A **character** is an individual who takes part in the action of a literary work. Most plots focus on one or several **main characters;** the rest are known as **minor characters.** A **flat character** has only one or two dominant traits. **Round characters** are more fully developed; like real people, there are many sides to their personalities. Characters who change significantly as the plot unfolds are called **dynamic characters. Static characters** remain essentially the same, even though their outward circumstances might change. For example, a character who experiences great hardship but remains cheerful throughout a story is a static character.

1. Is the banker a flat or round character? Explain your answer.
2. Is the lawyer a static or dynamic character? Explain your answer.

- See **Literary Terms Handbook,** p. R2.

Extending Your Response

Writing About Literature

Analyze Plot Imagine that you have been asked to write a screenplay based on "The Bet." Analyze the plot of the story, identifying the **exposition, rising action, climax,** and **resolution** (see page R9). Then explain how you would present these elements in your screenplay.

Literature Groups

Discuss Ending Did you find the ending of "The Bet" believable? How else might Chekhov have resolved the story's conflict? Discuss these questions in your group, using details from the story to support your opinions. Share your conclusions with the class.

ITALY, 1925

Before You Read

War

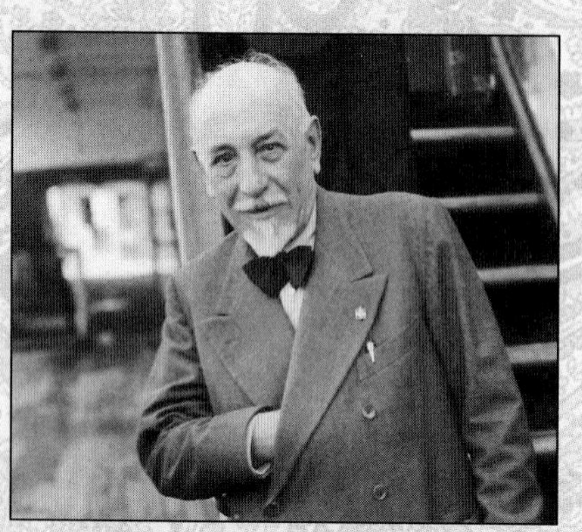

Meet Luigi Pirandello

"My art is full of bitter compassion for all those who deceive themselves."

Luigi Pirandello (lo͞o ē′ jē pir′ ən del′ ō) grew up on the island of Sicily in Italy. His father wanted him to study business, but he was more interested in literature and language. After earning a doctorate, Pirandello moved to Rome and married the daughter of his father's business associate. He published volumes of poetry and short stories. In 1903 the destruction of his family's sulfur mine left him devastated financially. Then his wife had a mental breakdown and eventually had to be institutionalized.

To escape from his troubles, Pirandello immersed himself more deeply in his writing. He had moderate success with his novels and short stories. In 1921 he wrote the play *Six Characters in Search of an Author*, which soon made him internationally famous. He was awarded the 1934 Nobel Prize for Literature in recognition of his great influence on modern theater.

Luigi Pirandello was born in 1867 and died in 1936.

Reading Focus

Why do people sometimes deceive themselves about their abilities, beliefs, or feelings?

Discuss Share your thoughts with a classmate.

Setting a Purpose As you read this story, notice how the characters interpret their situation.

Building Background

Pirandello's Philosophical Themes

In his preface to *Six Characters in Search of an Author,* Pirandello said that he had the "misfortune" of being a philosophical writer. Many of his works raise questions about the relationship between appearance and reality and between madness and sanity. Pirandello believed that people develop their identities in an attempt to bring stability to life, which is constantly changing. These "fictions we create for ourselves" are not always up to the task. Pirandello often portrayed the crisis that individuals experience after they begin to question the way they view themselves. Some critics have suggested that Pirandello's observations of his wife's mental illness deepened his interest in the problem of identity.

Vocabulary Preview

discrimination (dis krim′ ə nā′ shən) *n.* making a difference in treatment or favor on some basis other than individual merit; p. 960

console (kən sōl′) *v.* to alleviate a person's grief, sense of loss, or trouble; to comfort; p. 960

pettiness (pet′ ē nəs) *n.* a focus on unimportant or small-minded details; p. 961

disillusion (dis′ i lo͞o′ zhən) *n.* the state of being freed from misleading images or naïve trust; p. 961

contract (kən trakt′) *v.* to draw together; to wrinkle up; p. 961

distorted (dis tôrt′ id) *adj.* twisted out of a normal or original shape or condition; p. 961

Literature and Writing

Writing About Literature

Analyze Characterization In a short story, there is limited space in which to develop characters. Write an analysis of Pirandello's characterization of the fat man, the wife, or the husband. Discuss how character development in the story relies on the character's words and actions, the statements others make about the character, and the narrator's direct comments about the character.

Personal Writing

Describe an Experience Think of a time when you mourned the loss of someone–a relative, friend, or public figure whom you admired. How did you feel when you first heard about this person's death? How did your feelings change over time? What helped you to accept your loss? What advice would you offer to people in mourning? Write several paragraphs in response to these questions.

Extending Your Response

Literature Group

Evaluate a Speech The fat man dismisses the other passengers' talk of their suffering as nonsense. Do you think that we should dismiss the speech in which he explains why he isn't mourning his son, or does he express some valid thoughts? Discuss this question in your group. When you are finished, share your conclusions with the class.

Interdisciplinary Activity

Art: Depict a Scene The **setting** of "War" is important because it brings strangers together in a way that encourages them to talk (see page R11). Create a drawing, painting, or diorama that depicts the carriage in which the action takes place. Make sure that your artwork is consistent with details in the story.

Learning for Life

Interview Pirandello's story shows the anguish that parents often feel when their children go off to war. Interview someone in your neighborhood whose child served in the military. Ask the person how he or she dealt with fears for their child's safety. Read excerpts from the interview to the class.

Reading Further

If you enjoyed reading "War," the following might be of interest to you:

"The Plays on the Stage" from *Luigi Pirandello,* by Renate Matthaei.

"So It Is (If You Think So)" from *Six Characters in Search of an Author and Other Plays,* translated by Mark Musa.

Save your work for your portfolio.

VOCABULARY • Latin Prefixes

A prefix is a group of letters that can be added at the beginning of a word to change the meaning of the word. The Latin prefixes *con-* and *dis-* are in several vocabulary words in "War."

con-, "together; with"–implies physical or mental closeness, as in *concur* and *conform*

dis-, "apart; from"–suggests negative thoughts, feelings, or actions, as in *discredit* and *disenchant*

PRACTICE The literal meaning of a prefix may not appear in a particular word's dictionary definition, but it will probably be strongly implied.

1. Write an original sentence for each of the following words.

   console discrimination disillusionment

2. What is the difference between *contracted* and *distracted?* between *distorted* and *contorted?*

FRANCE, 1930

Before You Read

Two Memories of Sido

Meet Colette

"Instead of receding far from me through the gates of death, [Sido] has revealed herself more vividly to me as I grow older."

Sidonie-Gabrielle Colette (known simply as Colette) grew up in the French countryside. At twenty, she married and moved to Paris. She did not plan on a literary career, but her husband encouraged her to write a series of semiautobiographical novels (which he claimed to have written himself). After divorcing him, Colette performed in music halls while continuing to write fiction and journalism. A second marriage also ended in divorce. Her third husband, Maurice Goudeket, proved a faithful and loving companion.

Colette is widely admired for her precise style, her evocative descriptions of nature, and her insight into relations between men and women. She was a controversial figure; scandals erupted over her behavior as well as her writings. Toward the end of her life, however, she received many high honors from the French literary establishment.

Colette was born in 1873 and died in 1954.

Reading Focus

What do you think you will be like when you are old?

Journal Jot down a response in your journal.

Setting a Purpose Read this selection to discover how the author's mother deals with old age.

Building Background

A Mother's Influence

Colette's memoirs offer an endearing portrait of her mother, Sidonie, who showed a deep respect for everything that "germinates, blossoms, or flies." Sido (sē dō′), as Colette called her, was not a typical farm wife. Her unconventional views about religion and morality had a great influence on Colette. Once, when Colette brought home a bouquet that she had "blessed" on the Virgin Mary's altar, Sido laughed and asked, "Don't you think it was *already* blessed?" Sido taught Colette how to read before the age of three. Until her death, Sido continued to advise and encourage Colette about her writing.

Reading Further

You might enjoy these other works by Colette:

"The Captain" from *Earthly Paradise: An Autobiography Drawn from Her Lifelong Writings,* edited by Robert Phelps.

"Grape Harvest," "The Halt," "The Judge," and "The Sick Child" from *The Collected Stories of Colette,* edited by Robert Phelps.

Vocabulary Preview

undaunted (un dôn′ tid) *adj.* courageously firm or resolute, especially in the face of danger or difficulty; not discouraged; p. 966

respite (res′ pit) *n.* period of temporary relief, rest, or delay; p. 967

defiance (di fī′ əns) *n.* an act of resistance; p. 968

ecstasy (ek′ stə sē) *n.* a state of overwhelming emotion, especially rapturous delight; p. 968

Two Memories of Sido

from Earthly Paradise

Colette

Translated by Una Vincenzo Troubridge and Enid McCleod

The time came . . .

The time came when all her strength left her. She was amazed beyond measure and would not believe it. Whenever I arrived from Paris to see her, as soon as we were alone in the afternoon in her little house, she had always some sin to confess to me. On one occasion she turned up the hem of her dress, rolled her stocking down over her shin, and displayed a purple bruise, the skin nearly broken.

"Just look at that!"

"What on earth have you done to yourself this time, Mother?"

She opened wide eyes, full of innocence and embarrassment.

"You wouldn't believe it, but I fell downstairs!"

"How do you mean—'fell'?"

"Just what I said. I fell, for no reason. I was going downstairs and I fell. I can't understand it."

"Were you going down too quickly?"

"Too quickly? What do you call too quickly? I was going down quickly. Have I time to go downstairs majestically like the Sun King?[1] And if that were all . . . But look at this!"

On her pretty arm, still so young above the faded hand, was a scald forming a large blister.

"Oh goodness! Whatever's that!"

"My footwarmer."

"The old copper footwarmer? The one that holds five quarts?"

"That's the one. Can I trust anything, when that footwarmer has known me for forty years? I can't imagine what possessed it, it was boiling fast, I went to take it off the fire, and crack, something gave in my wrist. I was lucky to get nothing worse than the blister. But what a thing to happen! After that I let the cupboard alone. . . ."

Café, 1949. Tsuguharu Leonard Foujita (Japan). 76 x 64 cm. Musée National d'Art Moderne, Paris.

1. Louis XIV (1638–1715), King of France, was known as the *Sun King.*

She broke off, blushing furiously.

"What cupboard?" I demanded severely.

My mother fenced, tossing her head as though I were trying to put her on a lead.

"Oh, nothing! No cupboard at all!"

"Mother! I shall get cross!"

"Since I've said, 'I let the cupboard alone,' can't you do the same for my sake? The cupboard hasn't moved from its place, has it? So, shut up about it!"

The cupboard was a massive object of old walnut, almost as broad as it was high, with no carving save the circular hole made by a Prussian bullet that had entered by the right-hand door and passed out through the back panel.

"Do you want it moved from the landing, Mother?"

An expression like that of a young she-cat, false and glittery, appeared on her wrinkled face.

"I? No, it seems to me all right there—let it stay where it is!"

All the same, my doctor brother and I agreed that we must be on the watch. He saw my mother every day, since she had followed him and lived in the same village, and he looked after her with a passionate devotion which he hid. She fought against all her ills with amazing elasticity, forgot them, baffled them, inflicted on them signal if temporary defeats, recovered, during entire days, her vanished strength; and the sound of her battles, whenever I spent a few days with her, could be heard all over the house till I was irresistibly reminded of a terrier tackling a rat.

At five o'clock in the morning I would be awakened by the clank of a full bucket being set down in the kitchen sink immediately opposite my room.

"What are you doing with that bucket, Mother? Couldn't you wait until Josephine arrives?"

And out I hurried. But the fire was already blazing, fed with dry wood. The milk was boiling on the blue-tiled charcoal stove. Nearby, a bar of chocolate was melting in a little water for my breakfast, and, seated squarely in her cane[2] armchair, my mother was grinding the fragrant coffee which she roasted herself. The morning hours were always kind to her. She wore their rosy colors in her cheeks. Flushed with a brief return to health, she would gaze at the rising sun, while the church bell rang for early Mass, and rejoice at having tasted, while we still slept, so many forbidden fruits.

The forbidden fruits were the overheavy bucket drawn up from the well, the firewood split with a billhook on an oaken block, the spade, the mattock, and above all the double steps propped against the gable[3] window of the woodhouse. There were the climbing vine whose shoots she trained up to the gable windows of the attic, the flowery spikes of the too-tall lilacs, the dizzy cat that had to be rescued from the ridge of the roof. All the accomplices of her old existence as a plump and sturdy little woman, all the minor rustic[4] divinities who once obeyed her and made her so proud of doing without servants, now assumed the appearance and position of adversaries. But they reckoned without that love of combat which my mother was to keep till the end of her life. At seventy-one, dawn still found her undaunted, if not always undamaged. Burnt by the fire, cut with the pruning knife, soaked by melting snow or spilled water, she had always managed to

2. *Cane* furniture is made by weaving the hollow woody stems of reeds.
3. A *gable* is a triangular corner in a roof.
4. The narrator describes the plants and the cat as being almost godlike in importance in this country *(rustic)* setting.

Vocabulary

undaunted (un dôn′ tid) *adj.* courageously firm or resolute, especially in the face of danger or difficulty; not discouraged

A Woman Sitting at Her Writing Desk. Anna Ancher (Denmark). Oil on canvas, 48.5 x 39.5 cm. Private collection.

Viewing the painting: How would you describe this woman? In what ways might she remind you of Colette or Sido?

enjoy her best moments of independence before the earliest risers had opened their shutters. She was able to tell us of the cats' awakening, of what was going on in the nests, of news gleaned,[5] together with the morning's milk and the warm loaf, from the milkmaid and the baker's girl, the record in fact of the birth of a new day.

It was not until one morning when I found the kitchen unwarmed, and the blue enamel saucepan hanging on the wall, that I felt my mother's end to be near. Her illness knew many respites, during which the fire flared up again on the hearth, and the smell of fresh bread and melting chocolate stole under the door together with the cat's impatient paw. These respites were periods of unexpected alarms. My mother and the big walnut cupboard were discovered together in a heap at the foot of the stairs, she having determined to transport it in secret from the upper landing to the ground floor. Whereupon my elder brother insisted that my mother should keep still and that an old servant should sleep in the little house. But how could an old servant prevail against a vital energy so youthful and mischievous that it contrived to tempt and lead astray a body already half fettered[6] by death? My brother, returning before sunrise from attending a distant patient, one day caught my mother red-handed in the most wanton[7] of crimes. Dressed in her nightgown, but wearing heavy gardening sabots,[8] her little gray septuagenarian's plait of hair[9] turning up like a scorpion's tail on the nape of her neck, one foot firmly planted on the crosspiece of the

5. *Gleaned* means "gathered."

6. *Fettered* means "chained" or "shackled."
7. Anything done in a *wanton* way displays mischief–and, sometimes, cruelty.
8. *Sabots* (sa bōz′) is French for wooden shoes.
9. A *septuagenarian* (sep′ to͞o ə jə nār′ ē ən) is a person in his or her seventies; a *plait of hair* is a braid.

Vocabulary

respite (res′ pit) *n.* period of temporary relief, rest, or delay beech trestle, her back bent in the attitude of the expert jobber,[10] my mother, rejuvenated by an indescribable expression of guilty enjoyment, in defiance of all her promises and of the freezing morning dew, was sawing logs in her own yard.

"Sir, you ask me . . ."

> "Sir,
>
> "You ask me to come and spend a week with you, which means I would be near my daughter, whom I adore. You who live with her know how rarely I see her, how much her presence delights me, and I'm touched that you should ask me to come and see her. All the same I'm not going to accept your kind invitation, for the time being at any rate. The reason is that my pink cactus is probably going to flower. It's a very rare plant I've been given, and I'm told that in our climate it flowers only once every four years. Now, I am already a very old woman, and if I went away when my pink cactus is about to flower, I am certain I shouldn't see it flower again.
>
> "So I beg you, sir, to accept my sincere thanks and my regrets, together with my kind regards."

This note, signed "*Sidonie Colette, née*[11] *Landoy*," was written by my mother to one of my husbands, the second. A year later she died, at the age of seventy-seven.

Whenever I feel myself inferior to everything about me, threatened by my own mediocrity, frightened by the discovery that a muscle is losing its strength, a desire its power, or a pain the keen edge of its bite, I can still hold up my head and say to myself: "I am the daughter of the woman who wrote that letter—that letter and so many more that I have kept. This one tells me in ten lines that at the age of seventy-six she was planning journeys and undertaking them, but that waiting for the possible bursting into bloom of a tropical flower held everything up and silenced even her heart, made for love. I am the daughter of a woman who, in a mean, close-fisted, confined little place, opened her village home to stray cats, tramps, and pregnant servant girls. I am the daughter of a woman who many a time, when she was in despair at not having enough money for others, ran through the wind-whipped snow to cry from door to door, at the houses of the rich, that a child had just been born in a poverty-stricken home to parents whose feeble, empty hands had no swaddling clothes[12] for it. Let me not forget that I am the daughter of a woman who bent her head, trembling, between the blades of a cactus, her wrinkled face full of ecstasy over the promise of a flower, a woman who herself never ceased to flower, untiringly, during three quarters of a century."

10. The mother would bend in the position of an expert woodcutter, one foot braced on the horizontal piece of a bench made of beech wood.
11. *Née* (nā) is French for "born" and is used to identify a married woman's maiden name.
12. *Swaddling clothes* are narrow strips of cloth wrapped around an infant to restrict its movement.

Vocabulary

defiance (di fī′ əns) *n.* an act of resistance
ecstasy (ek′ stə sē) *n.* a state of overwhelming emotion, especially rapturous delight

Responding to Literature

Personal Response

What adjectives come to mind when you think of Sido? Share your response with the class.

Analyzing Literature

Recall and Interpret

1. What "sins" does Sido confess to Colette? Why is she having these experiences?
2. What does Sido like to do in the morning? Why do you think Colette describes these activities as "forbidden fruits"?
3. Why does Sido insist on doing things that put her in danger?
4. Why does Sido turn down an invitation from Colette's husband? What does her decision reveal about her?
5. Why does Colette value her memories of Sido?

Evaluate and Connect

6. Should Colette and her brother have taken stronger measures to protect Sido from injury? Why or why not?
7. How would you characterize Colette's relationship with her mother?
8. Do you think that Colette idealizes Sido in her memoirs? Explain.
9. What else would you like to find out about Sido?
10. In the Reading Focus on page 964, you were asked to predict what you will be like in your old age. How does Colette's portrait of Sido affect your ideas about aging?

Literary Criticism

"[It] is only with respect to Sido," writes Sylvie Romanowski, "that Colette brings any metaphysical or religious dimensions into her writings . . . [Sido's] superior understanding of nature and people . . . [comes] from . . . her reverent respect towards the holiness of all life." Do you agree that Colette's portrait of Sido has a religious dimension? Explain your answer in a brief essay.

Literary ELEMENTS

Characterization

The methods that a writer uses to reveal a character's personality are referred to as **characterization.** In **direct characterization,** the writer makes direct comments about the character's personality. **Indirect characterization** requires the reader to draw conclusions about the character based on evidence in the story. This evidence might include the character's words, thoughts, and actions, and the comments and thoughts of other characters.

1. What methods does Colette use to reveal Sido's personality?
2. Do you think that Colette's characterization of Sido is effective? Why or why not?

- See **Literary Terms Handbook,** p. R2.

Extending Your Response

Personal Writing

Character Sketch Think of a relative or friend whom you feel particularly close to. Write a character sketch that reveals why this person is so special. Include an anecdote about him or her. Try to use both direct and indirect characterization to give a vivid impression of your subject.

Performing

Readers Theater The scenes in "Two Memories of Sido" are rich with a variety of experiences and emotions. Use them as the basis for episodes of readers theater. Each actor takes the role of a person in the memoir (with one person playing the narrator) and reads the dialogue as though playing that character on stage. Give your performance for the class.

Save your work for your portfolio.

AUSTRIA, 1906

Before You Read

The Panther

Meet Rainer Maria Rilke

"Art is a thing that is too big and too heavy for a single life and even those who have reached a ripe old age are only beginners."

Rainer Maria Rilke (rī′ nər mä rē′ ä ril′ kə) was born in Prague, then part of the Austrian Empire, now the capital of the Czech Republic. He spoke, and usually wrote, in German. Despite Rilke's poor health, his parents enrolled him in military school. He emerged from this experience determined to become a writer.

Rilke traveled throughout Europe, spending long periods in Germany, France, and Switzerland. While visiting a patron at Duino Castle in northern Italy, he began a series of poems exploring the mysteries of life and death. He struggled with his *Duino Elegies* for ten years. Then in 1922, he had a creative breakthrough that allowed him to complete the elegies and write another series of poems called *Sonnets to Orpheus*. These works established his reputation as one of the greatest modern poets.

Rainer Maria Rilke was born in 1875 and died in 1926.

Reading Focus

What do you think it would feel like to be physically confined for a long period?

Quickwrite Jot down your thoughts in your journal.

Setting a Purpose Read this poem to discover a description of a caged panther.

Building Background

The Panther

Rilke's wife was a former student of the great French sculptor Auguste Rodin. In 1902 Rilke went to Paris to write a book about Rodin. Rilke was impressed with the artist's commitment to his work as well as his ability to capture the essence of a being or object. During this period, Rilke began to write poems with the solidity of sculpture. In his *Dinggedichte* ("thing-poems"), he offers exacting descriptions of animals, landscapes, works of art, and physical objects. The speaker's feelings are usually left unstated, yet Rilke was able to suggest them by focusing on the visible world. "The Panther," or "Der Panther" in German, describes a caged animal in a Paris park. On the next page, you will see the poem in English and the original German. He published it in the book *New Poems*, which many critics consider his first mature work.

Prague

Prague, Rilke's birthplace, is now the capital of the Czech Republic. As capital of the prosperous kingdom of Bohemia, it became one of Europe's most beautiful cities, and saw the premiere of important works by such composers as Mozart and Dvorak. It has been home to writers in Czech, like Jaroslav Hasek, and German, like Franz Kafka. Prague native Vaclav Havel, a playwright who served four years in prison for anti-communist activities, became Czechoslovakia's first president after the return of democracy in 1989.

Reading Further

If you enjoy reading "The Panther," you might also be interested in reading the following:

"Duino Elegies and The Sonnets to Orpheus" from *Ahead of All Parting: The Selected Poetry and Prose of Rainer Maria Rilke,* translated by Stephen Mitchell.

The Panther

Rainer Maria Rilke

Translated by Stephen Mitchell

Last Refuge. Yvonne Delvo (Great Britain, b. 1910). Oil on canvas. Private collection.

In the Jardin des Plantes, Paris

His vision, from the constantly passing bars
has grown so weary that it cannot hold
anything else. It seems to him there are
a thousand bars; and behind the bars, no world.

As he paces in cramped circles, over and over,
the movement of his powerful soft strides
is like a ritual dance around a center
in which a mighty will stands paralyzed.

Only at times, the curtain of the pupils
lifts, quietly—. An image enters in,
rushes down through the tensed, arrested muscles,
plunges into the heart and is gone.

Im Jardin des Plantes, Paris

Sein Blick ist vom Vorübergehn der Stäbe
so müd geworden, daβ er nichts mehr hält.
Ihm ist, als ob es tausend Stäbe gäbe
und hinter tausend Stäben keine Welt.

Der weiche Gang geschmeidig starker Schritte,
der sich im allerkleinsten Kreise dreht,
ist wie ein Tanz von Kraft um eine Mitte,
in der betäubt ein groβer Wille steht.

Nur manchmal schiebt der Vorhang der Pupille
sich lautlos auf—. Dann geht ein Bild hinein,
geht durch der Glieder angespannte Stille—
und hört im Herzen auf zu sein.

Responding to Literature

Personal Response

What images from this poem linger in your mind? Share your response with the class.

Analyzing Literature

Recall and Interpret

1. Why has the panther's vision grown weary?
2. How much awareness does the panther generally have of the world outside his cage?
3. What are the panther's movements compared to in the second stanza?
4. How would you explain the panther's reaction in the third stanza?

Evaluate and Connect

5. A **symbol** is an object or action that stands for something else in addition to itself (see page R12). What might the panther in this poem symbolize?
6. Does the poem offer a sympathetic view of the panther? Why or why not?
7. **Style** is a writer's distinctive manner of expression (see page R12). How would you describe the style of Rilke's poem?
8. In the Reading Focus on page 970, you were asked to imagine how a long period of physical confinement would affect you. Compare your response with the panther's behavior in Rilke's poem.

Literary Criticism

The poet W. H. Auden sums up Rilke's contributions as follows: "Rilke's most immediate and obvious influence has been upon diction and imagery." Rilke, Auden adds, conveys ideas with "physical rather than intellectual symbols . . . Rilke thinks of the human in terms of the non-human." Why do you think Auden singles out Rilke's diction and imagery for praise? What idea about humankind might Rilke be conveying through the image of the panther? Write an essay answering these questions.

Literary ELEMENTS

Mood

Mood is the overall feeling that a work of literature creates for readers. For example, a comedy about young lovers might have a joyous or romantic mood. *Mood* is a broader term than *tone,* which refers specifically to the attitude of the speaker or narrator. All of the elements of literature can contribute toward a work's mood.

1. What adjective would you use to describe the mood of "The Panther"?
2. Which literary elements help create this mood?

- See **Literary Terms Handbook,** p. R7.

Extending Your Response

Writing About Literature

Comparison Write one or two paragraphs comparing "The Panther" with another poem about an animal. What is the mood of each poem? How realistically are the animals portrayed in them? Do the animals come across as characters, or are they more like objects? What insights do these poems offer about the natural world?

Literature Groups

Prison or Preservation? Do you think it is good to keep animals in zoos? What effect does confinement have on the welfare of animals? How can zoos benefit society or the natural world? Discuss these questions in your group. Then consider whether Rilke's poem supports or contradicts your opinion.

Save your work for your portfolio.

Reading & Thinking Skills

Understanding Denotation and Connotation

> "Hey, isn't this place kind of cramped?" Luis asked. Tim looked around at his new studio apartment.
>
> "Well, I guess it is small," Tim replied. Tim's sister Tina disagreed with both of their assessments. "It is the perfect size for a first apartment—nice and compact."

Luis, Tim, and Tina use different words to describe the size of Tim's studio apartment. All three are basically acknowledging that the apartment is small, but Luis's remark seems critical, while Tina's seems approving. The words *cramped, small,* and *compact* have the same **denotation,** or explicit meaning. They all describe something limited in size. Each of the words, however, has a different **connotation,** or meaning that goes beyond the simple, literal definition. Connotations are the feelings and values commonly associated with a word. Connotation is an important feature of everyday language. The words *baseball* and *apple pie* have concrete meanings, or denotations. However, they have a world of connotations associated with them–patriotism, the Fourth of July, home, picnics, good times. In the excerpt above, for example, the word *cramped* has a negative connotation. It suggests a confined space. The word *compact* has a positive connotation. It implies something handy and convenient.

In his poem "The Panther," Rilke uses the connotations of words to create a powerful image of a caged animal. Words such as *paces, cramped, ritual, tensed,* and *arrested* suggest anger, frustration, power, dignity, and hopelessness.

Although you can look in the dictionary to get a sense of a word's connotation, the meaning suggested by a phrase is often difficult to determine. In order to understand a poet's meaning, read slowly and let the words roll around in your mind and on your tongue. What images do the words create? What feelings do they stir in you? Use the context to help you grasp the connotations of words.

- For more about denotation and connotation, see **Reading Handbook,** p. R81.

ACTIVITY

Reread the middle stanza of Rilke's poem "The Panther." Then answer the questions below.

> **As he paces in cramped circles, over and over,**
> **the movement of his powerful soft strides**
> **is like a ritual dance around a center**
> **in which a mighty will stands paralyzed.**

1. Which words have a positive connotation? Which words have a negative connotation?
2. What images or feelings does this stanza evoke? How does Rilke use connotation to create them?

RUSSIA, c. 1923

Before You Read

Lot's Wife

Meet Anna Akhmatova

"Fate did not leave anything out for me. Everything anyone could possibly experience fell to my lot."

Anna Akhmatova (uk mä′ tə və) is revered in Russia as a great poet and a symbol of integrity. She achieved early fame for her love poems, which are intimate yet highly sophisticated. Throughout her career, she remained a personal poet, even as she confronted the horrors of war and totalitarianism.

The communists executed Akhmatova's former husband in 1921. Akhmatova herself became politically suspect. Her son was imprisoned, and she also lost friends and colleagues to state persecution. Akhmatova wrote about Stalin's reign of terror in a cycle of poems called *Requiem*. She and a few trusted friends had to memorize this masterpiece—writing it down would have been much too dangerous. Toward the end of her life, the government eased its restrictions on Akhmatova and allowed some of her works to be published.

Anna Akhmatova was born in 1888 and died in 1966.

Reading Focus

How would you react if you were forced to leave your home? Why would you react that way?

Quickwrite Jot down a response in your journal. Be sure to include reasons for your reaction.

Setting a Purpose Read Anna Akhmatova's poem to see how a woman's attachment to her native town affects her destiny.

Building Background

Lot's Wife

The story of Lot and his wife comes from the Bible. According to Genesis 19, God sent his angels to Sodom after hearing of the town's wickedness. Lot was the only virtuous man they found living there. The angels told him to flee with his family, warning them to avert their eyes from Sodom. However, Lot's wife looked back at the burning city and was turned into a pillar of salt.

Akhmatova wrote "Lot's Wife" sometime between 1922 and 1924. During this period, she sometimes used biblical and literary allusions to suggest themes that could not be discussed openly. Although she suffered greatly under communism, Akhmatova had strong feelings for her homeland. In one poem, she criticized Russians who emigrated after the revolution: "I'm not of those who left their country / For wolves to tear it limb from limb."

On the following page, you will see "Lot's Wife" in English as well as in the original Russian. The Russian version appears in the Cyrillic alphabet. This alphabet was developed by the Christian missionary St. Cyril in the ninth century. It was based on the Greek alphabet, but many letters were added or changed to reflect the different sounds of the Slavic languages.

Reading Further

If you enjoy reading "Lot's Wife," you might also enjoy these poems:

Poems of Akhmatova, translated by Stanley Kunitz and Max Hayward.

Lot's Wife

Anna Akhmatova
Translated by Richard Wilbur

The just° man followed then his angel guide
Where he strode on the black highway, hulking
and bright;
But a wild grief in his wife's bosom cried,
Look back, it is not too late for a last sight

Of the red towers of your native Sodom, the square
Where once you sang, the gardens you shall mourn,
And the tall house with empty windows where
You loved your husband and your babes were born.

She turned, and looking on the bitter view
Her eyes were welded shut by mortal pain;
Into transparent salt her body grew,
And her quick feet were rooted in the plain.

Who would waste tears upon her? Is she not
The least of our losses, this unhappy wife?
Yet in my heart she will not be forgot
Who, for a single glance, gave up her life.

1 The Bible describes Lot as *just;* that is, morally upright.

Lot and His Daughters Leaving Sodom. Louis de Caullery (Flanders, c. 1580–1621). Oil on canvas. Rafael Valls Gallery, London.

И праведник шел за посланником Бога,
Огромный и светлый, по черной горе.
Но громко жене говорила тревога:
Не поздно, ты можешь еще посмотреть

На красные башни родного Содома,
На площадь, где пела, на двор, где пряла,
На окна пустые высокого дома,
Где милому мужу детей родила.

Взглянула,—и, скованы смертною болю,
Глаза ее больше смотреть не могли;
И сделалось тело прозрачною солью,
И быстрые ноги к земле приросли.

Кто женщину эту оплакивать будет?
Не меньшей ли мнится она из утрат?
Лишь сердце мое никогда не забудет
Отдавшую жизнь за единственный взгляд.

Responding to Literature

Personal Response

Which lines from this poem did you find most interesting or moving? Share your response with a small group of classmates.

Analyzing Literature

Recall and Interpret

1. What actions and feelings are described in the first stanza of the poem?
2. According to the speaker in the poem, what motivates Lot's wife to look back at Sodom?
3. How is she transformed after she looks back? How quickly does the change happen?
4. Why will the speaker always remember Lot's wife?

Evaluate and Connect

5. Are the memories the wife has of Sodom mostly positive or mostly negative? Explain your answer, citing details from the poem.
6. How does the poem's **imagery** (see page R6) help us understand why Lot's wife feels so strongly about Sodom?
7. According to the last stanza, what does the poem's speaker seem to value most?
8. What events in the world today force individuals to flee their homelands as Lot and his wife did?

Literary Criticism

According to one critic, "[Akhmatova] refused to emigrate, . . . knowing instinctively, . . . that for a poet to leave his or her native land is tantamount to a death worse than physical death. She did not hesitate to criticize those who had left their country in its worst hour." In the poem, what does the speaker's reaction to the fate of Lot's wife suggest about Akhmatova's attitude toward Russia and Russians who left the country? Present your answer in an essay.

Literary ELEMENTS

Tone

When we speak, we often give away our feelings through our tone of voice. In a literary work, **tone** is the attitude that a writer takes toward the audience, a subject, or a character. For example, a narrator might use an angry tone to describe an evil character and an amused tone to describe a good-hearted character who makes mistakes. Tone is conveyed through the writer's choice of words and details.

1. What is the speaker's tone in stanza 2 of "Lot's Wife"?
2. What tone does the speaker use in discussing the wife?

- See **Literary Terms Handbook,** p. R12.

Extending Your Response

Creative Writing

Eulogy Suppose that you were a friend or relative of Lot's wife. Write a eulogy to deliver at her memorial service. In the speech, describe what happened to her as she was being led away from Sodom. Offer your opinion about why she looked back at the town and draw a moral or lesson from this fateful move.

Literature Groups

Discussion In the Reading Focus on page 974, you were asked how you would react if you were forced to leave your home. Compare responses in a small group. Discuss how Lot's wife might have overcome her grief. When you are finished, share your conclusions with the class.

Save your work for your portfolio.

Before You Read

Lot's Wife

Meet Wisława Szymborska

"I borrow weighty words, / then labor heavily so that they may seem light."

For many years, Wisława Szymborska (vis lä′ vä shim bôr′ skä) has been well known in Poland; her poems have inspired rock lyrics and even a motion picture. She became internationally famous when she won the Nobel Prize for Literature in 1996. Yet she avoids literary conferences and other public events, preferring the company of a few friends in her small apartment. Her image is a modest one. She walks around in old coats and sweaters, and she enjoys collecting postcards.

Szymborska has lived in the city of Cracow since she was eight. Early in her career, she conformed to official literary doctrines in order to get her work published. She soon rejected this approach, although she never directly confronted her country's communist government. "Of course life crosses politics, but my poems are strictly not political," she says. "They are more about people and life."

Wisława Szymborska was born in 1923.

Reading Focus

Think of three things that you did today. Can you explain what motivated you to do those things?

Chart It! Use a chart like the one shown below to record your response.

Action	Motivation

Setting a Purpose Read this poem to discover what motivated the speaker to do what she did.

Building Background

Wit and Insight

In her poetry, Szymborska develops fascinating insights from observations of everyday life. One critic has praised her as a "master at recognizing the importance of the insignificant." Many of her poems focus on seemingly mundane activities, such as bodybuilding contests, removing and putting on clothes, writing a résumé, or peeling an onion. Even when addressing more serious topics, Szymborska writes with humor and subtle irony. For example, in a poem about death, she chides this supposedly omnipotent force for not being able to dig a grave or make a coffin, things "that are part of its trade."

The Rescue of Lot (detail). Wood engraving after an illustration by Gustave Doré.

Reading Further

If you enjoy reading "Lot's Wife," you may enjoy the following collection of Szymborska's poems:

"From *The End and the Beginning* 1993" from *View with a Grain of Sand,* translated by Stanislaw Baránczak and Clare Cavanagh.

Lot's Wife

Wisława Szymborska
Translated by Adam Czerniawski

I looked back supposedly curious.
But besides curiosity I might have had other reasons.
I looked back regretting the silver dish.
Through carelessness—tying a sandal strap.
In order not to keep staring at the righteous nape°
of my husband, Lot.
Because of sudden conviction that had I died
he wouldn't have stopped.
Being humble yet disobedient.
Listening for pursuers.
Touched with silence, hoping God had changed His mind.
Our two daughters were already disappearing beyond the hilltop.

I felt my age. Distance,
futility of wandering. Drowsiness.
I looked back when setting down the bundle.
I looked back in terror where to step next.
My path suddenly teeming with snakes,
spiders, field mice and baby vultures.
Now neither good nor evil—just everything living
crawled and hopped in crowded panic.
I looked back in desolation.°
Ashamed of running away in stealth.°
Wanting to scream, to turn back.
Or only when a gust of wind
untied my hair and lifted up my skirts.

I had a feeling they were watching from the walls of Sodom
with bursts of hearty laughter again and again.
I looked back in anger.
To savor their perdition.°

---

5 The *nape* is the back of the neck.

21 When describing emotions, *desolation* names a grief so deep that it leaves a person feeling empty and lost.

22 *In stealth* means in secret.

29 *Perdition* means complete destruction and suggests eternal damnation.

I looked back willessly.
It was only a rock slipping, growling beneath me.
It was a crevice suddenly cut my way off.
A hamster trotted on the edge on two paws
and then it was we both looked back.

No, no. I ran on,
I crawled and I soared
until darkness crashed from heaven
and with it hot gravel and dead birds.
Losing breath I often swerved.
If anyone saw me, would have thought I was dancing.
Conceivably, my eyes were open.

La Madonne Ronde, 1935. Tamara de Lempicka (Poland). Oil on wood, diameter: 34 cm. Musée Departemental de l'Oise, Beauvais, France.

Viewing the painting: How would you describe the expression on this woman's face? How might you compare her to Lot's wife?

Responding to Literature

Personal Response

Which lines in the poem did you find humorous? Discuss your response with the class.

Analyzing Literature

Recall and Interpret

1. What explanation have people offered for why Lot's wife looked back at Sodom? How does she respond to this explanation?
2. On the basis of lines 5–8, how do you think Lot's wife feels about her husband?
3. How might her thoughts about the residents of Sodom have motivated her to look back?
4. What sort of memories does Lot's wife have of Sodom in this poem? What phrases from the poem show her feelings?
5. What is your interpretation of the last stanza (lines 35–41) of the poem? Cite details from the poem to support your answer.

Evaluate and Connect

6. Do you think that Lot's wife understands exactly what made her look back? Explain.
7. **Style** is a writer's distinctive manner of expression (see **Literary Terms Handbook,** page R12). How would you describe Szymborska's style in this poem?
8. Do you consider "Lot's Wife" to be a religious poem? Explain your answer, citing details from the poem.
9. What aspect of human life do you think the poet was trying to deal with in "Lot's Wife"?
10. What would you say is the dominant mood that Szymborska is trying to convey in this poem?

Literary ELEMENTS

Speaker

The **speaker** of a poem is the voice that talks to the reader. Sometimes the speaker is a disembodied voice–someone you cannot identify as a specific person. Speakers can also have distinct identities, like characters. In either case, one should not assume that the speaker and the poet are identical. A speaker who is clearly different from the poet is called a **persona.** Szymborska used the persona of a famous biblical character in "Lot's Wife."

1. How much sympathy did you feel for the speaker as you read "Lot's Wife"?
2. What adjective, do you think, best describes the speaker?

- See **Literary Terms Handbook,** p. R11.

Extending Your Response

Personal Writing

Compare Experiences In the Reading Focus on page 977, you were asked to explain the motivation for three things you did today. Were you able to provide one reason for each action, or did you have trouble pinning down your motivation? In a paragraph or two, compare one of these experiences with the experience of Lot's wife.

Literature Groups

Analyze Motivation With your group, go over the reasons that Lot's wife offers for her glance back at Sodom. Which of them seems the most plausible? Discuss this question, and then take a vote. Share the results with the class.

Save your work for your portfolio.

COMPARING selections

Lot's Wife and *Lot's Wife*

COMPARE **RESPONSES**

Discuss In a small group, compare your response to Akhmatova's and Szymborska's poems about Lot's wife. Discuss the following questions:

- Which poem did you find more interesting? Why?
- Who is the speaker in each poem?
- Which poem offers a more sympathetic view of Lot's wife?
- How does the persona of the speaker affect the impact of the poem?
- In your opinion, which poem more accurately presents the thoughts and feelings of Lot's wife?
- Which poem seems more relevant to your own experiences of looking back at something you left behind?

COMPARE **REPRESENTATION**

Investigate The story of Lot and his wife has long been a popular subject for artists. Search the Internet or the art section of the library to find a painting or drawing inspired by this episode from the Bible. Compare how Lot's wife is represented in this artwork with her portrayal in the two poems. Which of the two poems would the artwork you selected best illustrate?

COMPARE **STYLES**

Analyze Write a paragraph comparing the styles of Akhmatova's and Szymborska's poems. Use examples from each poem to support your analysis. You might wish to focus on one or more of the following elements:

- imagery
- tone
- rhythm
- rhyme

Lot and His Daughters Leaving Sodom (detail).

PORTUGAL, 1944

Before You Read

In the terrible night

Meet Fernando Pessoa

"Ever since I was a small child I felt driven to create a fictitious world around me and to surround myself with friends and acquaintances who never existed."

Fernando Pessoa (pə sō′ ä) is generally considered Portugal's finest modern poet. He wrote poetry and criticism under about twenty different names, including his real name. These masks allowed him to give voice to the various personalities he sensed within himself.

Pessoa was born in Lisbon, Portugal's capital. His father died in 1893. His stepfather was a diplomat in South Africa, and Pessoa spent most of his childhood there, where he learned to speak and write English fluently. After returning to Lisbon, he worked as a translator. Although he was respected by fellow writers and intellectuals, Pessoa led an isolated existence, with no close relationships outside of his immediate family. He published three books of poetry in English and only one in Portuguese. Much of his work was published after his death.

Pessoa was born in 1888 and died in 1935.

Reading Focus

What are some ways in which a person's future can be limited by his or her past?

Share Ideas Discuss this question with a classmate.

Setting a Purpose Read this poem to see how the speaker views his past.

Building Background

Pessoa's Personalities

Pessoa was not the only modernist poet who experimented with different voices, but few went as far as he did. Each of his alter egos has a distinct writing style and point of view. He even created biographies for them. Pessoa chose to call these personalities "heteronyms" rather than pseudonyms. He explained that a pseudonym is merely a different name for an author, but that heteronyms were names for the author's different personalities.

Pessoa credited "In the terrible night" ("Na noite terrivel") to Alvaro de Campos, a poet who writes in free verse. De Campos comes across as a lonely, self-doubting figure; Pessoa said that de Campos's personality was very similar to his own.

Like many Portuguese writers, Pessoa studied English literature and wrote excellent English. But he was also a master of Portuguese verse. You might like to compare the original version of the last three lines of "Na noite terrivel" with those in the English translation on page 984.

Nesta noite em que não durmo, e o sossego me cerca
Como uma verdade de que não partilho
E lá for a o luar, como a esperança que não tenho, é
invisível p'ra mim.

Reading Further

If you enjoy reading "In the terrible night," you might also be interested in the following poetry by Pessoa:

The Keeper of Sheep, translated by Edwin Honig and Susan M. Brown.

El Corredor (The Corridor), 1976. Manuel Lopez Villasenor (Spain). Mixed media on canvas.

In the terrible night

Fernando Pessoa
Translated by Jonathan Griffin

In the terrible night, natural substance of all nights,
In the night of insomnia, natural substance of all my nights,
I remember, awake in tossing drowsiness,
I remember what I've done and what I might have done in life.
I remember, and an anguish
Spreads all through me like a physical chill or a fear,
The irreparable of my past—this is the real corpse.
All the other corpses may very well be illusion.
All the dead may be alive somewhere else,
All my own past moments may be existing somewhere
In the illusion of space and time,
In the falsity of elapsing.°

---

12 *Elapsing* means "slipping away," almost always referring to something abstract, such as time.

But what I was not, what I did not do, what I did not even dream;
What only now I see I ought to have done,
What only now I clearly see I ought to have been—
This is what is dead beyond all the Gods,
This—and it was, after all, the best of me—is what not even the Gods bring to life . . .

If at a certain point
I had turned to the left instead of to the right;
If at a certain moment
I had said yes instead of no, or no instead of yes;
If in a certain conversation
I had hit on the phrases which only now, in this half-sleep, I elaborate—

If all this had been so,
I would be different today, and perhaps the whole universe
Would be insensibly° brought to be different as well.

But I did not turn in the direction which is irreparably lost,°
Not turn or even think of turning, and only now I perceive it;
But I did not say no or say yes, and only now see what I didn't say;
But the phrases I failed to say surge up in me at present, all of them,
Clear, inevitable, natural,
The conversation gathered in conclusively,
The whole matter resolved . . .
But only now what never was, nor indeed shall be, hurts.

What I have missed definitely holds no sort of hope
In any sort of metaphysical system.°
Maybe I could bring what I have dreamed to some other world,
But could I bring to another world the things I forgot to dream?
These, yes, the dreams going begging, are the real corpse.
I bury it in my heart for ever, for all time, for all universes,

In this night when I can't sleep and peace encircles me
Like a truth which I've no share in,
And the moonlight outside, like a hope I do not have, is invisible to me.

---

26 *Insensibly,* here, means "without being aware."

27 *Irreparably lost* means that the loss cannot be made up or recovered.

36 A *metaphysical system* is a philosophical system that explains how and why things exist.

Responding to Literature

Personal Response

What feelings did this poem stir up in you? Share your response with the class.

Analyzing Literature

Recall and Interpret

1. What does the speaker say that he finds himself thinking about at night?
2. What effect do these thoughts have on the speaker? What emotions do they recall?
3. How do you interpret the statement "The irreparable of my past–this is the real corpse"?
4. How does the speaker seem to view his present life? Does he appear to be pessimistic or optimistic?

Evaluate and Connect

5. **Mood** is the overall feeling or atmosphere of a literary work (see page R7). How would you describe the mood of this poem?
6. Why might the thoughts expressed in this poem be particularly troubling to someone afflicted with insomnia?
7. In the Reading Focus on page 982, you were asked how a person's future can be limited by his or her past. Compare your conclusions with the speaker's thoughts in this poem.
8. After reading this poem, what thoughts did you have about the speaker's life?

Literary Criticism

"[When] Pessoa wrote as Campos . . . ," noted one scholar, "two contrary impulses [emerged]. The first . . . conveys a feverish desire to be everything and everyone . . . The second impulse is toward a state of isolation and a sense of nothingness." Do you think these two impulses are evident in "In the terrible night"? Explain your answer in a discussion with a small group of classmates.

Literary ELEMENTS

Rhythm

A poem's **rhythm** is the pattern of beats created by the arrangement of syllables. In metrical verse, the rhythm is mainly produced by a regular pattern of stressed and unstressed syllables. This pattern of stresses is called the **meter** of the poem. Poets can also create rhythm through repetition, parallelism, rhyme, and other literary techniques. **Free verse,** which does not have a regular meter, often follows the rhythm of natural speech.

1. Is the rhythm of "In the terrible night" consistent? Explain your answer.
2. What literary techniques help create the rhythm of this poem?

- See **Literary Terms Handbook,** p. R10.

Extending Your Response

Personal Writing

Looking Back What do you most regret not doing in the past? If you had taken this action, how might your life be different now? Write a paragraph about your missed opportunity.

Literature Groups

Analyzing Logic Does the speaker of "In the terrible night" express his thoughts in a logical manner, or can you find errors in his reasoning? In your group, analyze the poem to see whether the statements in it are generally logical. Share your conclusions with the class.

Save your work for your portfolio.

Before You Read

Gather Not Gold and Precious Stones

Meet Edith Södergran

"I do not write poems, I create myself, my poems are for me the way to myself."

Edith Södergran (sō′ dər gran) grew up in Finland, which was then part of the Russian Empire. Her family belonged to Finland's Swedish-speaking minority. When she was fifteen, her father died of tuberculosis. Södergran soon discovered that she also had this disease. She spent long periods at Finnish and Swiss treatment centers, where she learned about new trends in European literature. Her first volume of poetry came out in 1916. The book received mixed reviews; critics objected to her unconventional techniques and frank portrayal of a love affair.

Södergran and her mother lost all their money during the Bolshevik Revolution of 1917. They moved into a poorly heated house, which worsened Södergran's health. Although she continued to mature as a poet, few people appreciated her work during her lifetime. She is now regarded as an important innovator in Scandinavian literature.

Edith Södergran was born in 1892 and died in 1923.

Reading Focus

Can money buy happiness?

Share Ideas Discuss your response with the class.

Setting a Purpose Read this poem to find out the author's beliefs about wealth and spirituality.

Building Background

An Uncompromising Poet

Södergran once wrote of a former lover, "You sought a woman / and found a soul–You are disappointed." In her poetry as well as her personal life, she refused to conform to expectations. Södergran first aroused controversy by writing in free verse instead of traditional meters. After studying the works of German philosopher Friedrich Nietzsche, she began to write poems in which she defied her illness by portraying herself as a superior being. Later she fell under the influence of Rudolf Steiner, an Austrian writer who urged people to rise above material concerns so that they could perceive the true, spiritual nature of the universe.

Swedish and Finnish

For many years, Sweden and Finland were united. Today 93 percent of Finland's population speaks Finnish–a non-Indo-European language distantly related to Turkish and Hungarian–and 6 percent speaks Swedish. When Finland gained independence from Russia in 1919, the constitution recognized both as official languages. Finns of Swedish descent who have made outstanding contributions to the country include the world-famous composer Jean Sibelius, and Carl Mannerheim, who led Finland's armies against Russian invaders in 1939. On the following page, you will see Södergran's poem in both English and the original Swedish, "Samlen Icke Guld och Ädelstenar."

Reading Further

If you enjoy reading "Gather Not Gold and Precious Stones," you might also be interested in the following:

Edith Södergran: Love and Solitude, Selected Poems 1916–1923, translated by Stina Katchadourian.

Responding to Literature

Personal Response

Which lines in this poem made the biggest impression on you? Briefly explain why in your journal.

Analyzing Literature

Recall and Interpret

1. What is the speaker's overall impression of the world? How has he formed this impression?
2. A **symbol** is an object or action that stands for something else in addition to itself (see **Literary Terms Handbook,** page R12). What do you think bread symbolizes in the poem?
3. Who do you think are the friends the poet refers to in line 16 of the poem?
4. What is the "great struggle" the poet refers to? What has the speaker gained from his participation in the struggle?

Evaluate and Connect

5. What struggle, do you think, is the speaker engaged in? What leads you to this conclusion?
6. Which details in the poem help make the speaker's message more personal?
7. What adjective would you use to describe the speaker in this poem? Explain why.
8. Do you agree with the way the speaker seems to view the world? Explain.

Literary ELEMENTS

Free Verse

Free verse is poetry that does not follow a regular meter or rhyme scheme. Although poets who write free verse ignore traditional rules, they can use techniques such as **repetition** and **alliteration** to create patterns in their poems. Many poets find it easier to write in an informal, conversational tone when they choose free verse over standard meters. Such a tone was especially important for Hikmet, who hoped to reach a broad audience with his message.

1. What examples of repetition can you find in Hikmet's poem?
2. Describe a technique that Hikmet used to create shifts in the rhythm of his poem.

- See **Literary Terms Handbook,** p. R5.

Extending Your Response

Personal Writing

Connections In the Reading Focus on page 994, you were asked to discuss ways in which you are connected to people around the world. Write a newspaper editorial explaining the importance of one of these connections. Try to make your personality come across in the editorial by using an informal tone and including interesting details.

Performing

Oral Reading Read "The World, My Friends" aloud in a small group. Before you begin, think about how you can reflect the poem's rhythm in your reading. For example, you might choose to have each line recited by a different reader, or you might combine your voices to add emphasis to certain passages.

Save your work for your portfolio.

The Art of Translation

The Dream of a Common Language

Most of the European Union has been able to adopt a single currency, but it still has eleven official languages, a record-keeper's nightmare. At the United Nations, every word spoken at an official meeting must be translated and printed in six languages, at an estimated cost of hundreds of millions of dollars a year. Why can't Europe–and the rest of the world–agree on a single language for all international communication?

For centuries, many people have promoted the idea of adopting one language for use in international communication. Simple, easy-to-learn languages have been invented for just that purpose, with Esperanto being the best known. But nations cannot agree on a single international language, either an existing one, or a new one. Why do Europeans–and the rest of the world–resist a proposal that could save so much time, effort, money, and misunderstanding?

Prototype for new European Union coin.

Welcome

Albanian	Misardhje
Basque	Ongi-etorri
Bulgarian	Добрѐ дошьл
Danish	Velkommen
Dutch	Welkom
Esperanto	Bonveno
French	Bienvenue
German	Willkommen
Hungarian	Isten hozott
Irish Gaelic	Fáilte
Italian	Benvenuto
Norwegian	Velkommen
Polish	Witajcie
Portuguese	Bem-vindo
Russian	Добрó пожáловать
Serbian	Dobro si došao
Slovenian	Dobrodôšel
Spanish	Bienvenido
Swedish	Välkommen

Resistance to an International Language

Europe is a small continent–not much larger than the United States–but its people are divided into many nations and speak about sixty different languages. The political and cultural differences among Europeans have played a part in igniting two world wars in this century. Not surprisingly, Europe has been the center of the Esperanto movement, whose proponents believe that international understanding and tolerance would be furthered if everyone spoke the same language.

Although Esperanto has been the most successful of the languages invented for international use, it has failed to catch on. In the early twentieth century, as nationalism grew in Europe, many governments viewed the Esperanto movement as a threat to their national identity and goals. Esperanto faced competition from national languages as well as other invented languages.

Since World War II, English has become the international language of commerce, science, and technology because English-speakers have dominated those fields. Even so, the world's nations have not adopted English as the single official language for international forums. Many governments equate adopting a language with allowing one culture to dominate others. According to this view, language equals control.

The issue of cultural domination would seem to strengthen the case for adopting a neutral, invented language; however, many people object to invented languages on principle. They claim that invented languages lack the richness, vitality, and expressiveness that existing languages have built up. They resist giving up a "natural" language for an "artificial" one.

What's Special About One's Own Language?

Each of the world's languages has evolved over a long period of time, and each reflects the history and the culture of its speakers. Each language contains many words and expressions that have gained associations and feelings (connotations) specific to a given culture. Such aspects of a language cannot be easily translated, or imported into an invented language.

Many English words, for example, have connotations that either are lacking or are different in other languages. Take the word *red,* for instance. In English, the word is associated with blood, passion, and anger, as in the expression "seeing red." In Russian, on the other hand, the word red connotes beauty, and the name *Red Square* suggests beautiful architecture. In Russian, a "red girl" is a beautiful girl. In Chinese, the word *red* is associated with joy and celebration.

English, like other languages, contains thousands of idioms that are culture specific and are difficult, if not impossible, to translate. An *idiom* is an expression that has a meaning other than its literal one, such as "barking up the wrong tree." An idiom such as "bringing coals to Newcastle," which is based on British geography and industry, would be meaningless if translated literally into another language.

Each language has so many culture-specific elements that it helps define its speakers to the world and to themselves. Take away a people's language, and you take away part of their being. A Welsh proverb expresses this idea: "A nation without a language is a nation without a heart."

RESPOND

1. What idioms do you use that might be difficult to translate into another language?
2. Which do you think is a better solution to the international language problem—the use of an existing language or an invented one? Why?
3. Do you have any vocabulary that has special meaning for you and close friends or family? Think about how this private language evolved and why you use it. Share some of the words and their meanings with the class.

ROMANIA, 1958

Before You Read

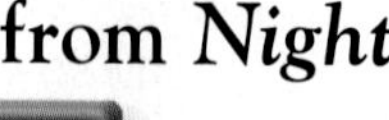

from *Night*

Reading Focus

What do you know about the Holocaust? How have you learned this information?

Share Ideas Discuss your response with a small group of classmates.

Setting a Purpose In this selection, the author describes his first days in Buchenwald, a Nazi concentration camp in Germany.

Meet Elie Wiesel

"Never shall I forget that night, the first night in camp, which has turned my life into one long night."

Elie Wiesel (el′ ē vē zel′) lived in Sighet, Romania until 1944, when Nazi soldiers rounded up the town's Jews for extermination. Wiesel was fifteen at the time. Somehow, he survived two concentration camps, but his parents and younger sister were among the millions who died there. After his camp was liberated, Wiesel went to France and became a journalist. Eventually he settled in the United States.

Wiesel waited ten years to write about the Holocaust because he felt that words could not describe such an event. His first book, *Night*, is considered one of the most powerful works of Holocaust literature. This semiautobiographical account is based on his experiences in the camps, an ordeal that shook his faith in his religion. Wiesel has written many other books about the Holocaust and Jewish life. In recognition of his commitment to speak out against violence and oppression, he was awarded the Nobel Prize for Peace in 1986.

Elie Wiesel was born in 1928.

Building Background

Wiesel's Nightmarish Journey

The Wiesel family was transported by train to Auschwitz, a large complex of concentration camps in the southern part of Poland. About 800,000 Jews died there, including Elie Wiesel's mother and sister. Wiesel and his father were chosen to work as slave laborers. Later, they were transferred to Buchenwald, a camp within Germany that sent prisoners to work in nearby weapons plants.

Unlike Auschwitz, Buchenwald did not have gas chambers for killing prisoners. However, many of the prisoners at Buchenwald died from disease, exhaustion, beatings, and executions. As the United States army neared Buchenwald in April 1945, the prisoners rose up in revolt and liberated the camp. Wiesel said in *Night* that when he first had a chance to look at himself in a mirror, he was shocked to see a corpse gazing back at him.

Vocabulary Preview

plaintive (plān′ tiv) *adj.* expressive of suffering or distress; p. 1002

beseeching (bi sēch′ ing) *adj.* in a begging or pleading manner; p. 1002

truncheon (trun′ chən) *n.* a billy club; p. 1005

spasmodically (spaz mod′ ik lē) *adv.* in an irregular or fitful manner; p. 1005

We Are the Living. Alfred Tibor (Hungary, b. 1920). Marble, height: 48 in. The Columbus Museum of Art, OH.

from Night

Elie Wiesel

At the gate of the camp, SS officers[1] were waiting for us. They counted us. Then we were directed to the assembly place. Orders were given us through loudspeakers:

"Form fives!" "Form groups of a hundred!" "Five paces forward!"

I held onto my father's hand—the old, familiar fear: not to lose him.

Right next to us the high chimney of the crematory[2] oven rose up. It no longer made any impression on us. It scarcely attracted our attention.

An established inmate of Buchenwald told us that we should have a shower and then we could go into the blocks. The idea of having a hot bath fascinated me. My father was silent. He was breathing heavily beside me.

"Father," I said. "Only another moment more. Soon we can lie down—in a bed. You can rest. . . ."

He did not answer. I was so exhausted myself that his silence left me indifferent. My only wish was to take a bath as quickly as possible and lie down in a bed.

1. *SS officers* were a unit of Nazi soldiers in charge of policing the concentration camps, among other things.
2. A *crematory* is a furnace for burning dead bodies.

But it was not easy to reach the showers. Hundreds of prisoners were crowding there. The guards were unable to keep any order. They struck out right and left with no apparent result. Others, without the strength to push or even to stand up, had sat down in the snow. My father wanted to do the same. He groaned.

"I can't go on. . . . This is the end. . . . I'm going to die here. . . ."

He dragged me toward a hillock of snow from which emerged human shapes and ragged pieces of blanket.

"Leave me," he said to me. "I can't go on. . . . Have mercy on me. . . . I'll wait here until we can get into the baths. . . . You can come and find me."

I could have wept with rage. Having lived through so much, suffered so much, could I leave my father to die now? Now, when we could have a good hot bath and lie down?

"Father!" I screamed. "Father! Get up from here! Immediately! You're killing yourself. . . ."

I seized him by the arm. He continued to groan.

"Don't shout, son. . . . Take pity on your old father. . . . Leave me to rest here. . . . Just for a bit, I'm so tired . . . at the end of my strength. . . ."

He had become like a child, weak, timid, vulnerable.

"Father," I said. "You can't stay here."

I showed him the corpses all around him; they too had wanted to rest here.

"I can see them, son. I can see them all right. Let them sleep. It's so long since they closed their eyes. . . . They are exhausted . . . exhausted. . . ."

His voice was tender.

I yelled against the wind:

"They'll never wake again! Never! Don't you understand?"

For a long time this argument went on. I felt that I was not arguing with him, but with death itself, with the death that he had already chosen.

The sirens began to wail. An alert. The lights went out throughout the camp. The guards drove us toward the blocks. In a flash, there was no one left on the assembly place. We were only too glad not to have had to stay outside longer in the icy wind. We let ourselves sink down onto the planks. The beds were in several tiers. The cauldrons of soup at the entrance attracted no one. To sleep, that was all that mattered.

It was daytime when I awoke. And then I remembered that I had a father. Since the alert, I had followed the crowd without troubling about him. I had known that he was at the end, on the brink of death, and yet I had abandoned him.

I went to look for him.

But at the same moment this thought came into my mind: "Don't let me find him! If only I could get rid of this dead weight, so that I could use all my strength to struggle for my own survival, and only worry about myself." Immediately I felt ashamed of myself, ashamed forever.

I walked for hours without finding him. Then I came to the block where they were giving out black "coffee." The men were lining up and fighting.

A plaintive, beseeching voice caught me in the spine:

"Eliezer . . . my son . . . bring me . . . a drop of coffee. . . ."

I ran to him.

"Father! I've been looking for you for so long. . . . Where were you? Did you sleep? . . . How do you feel?"

He was burning with fever. Like a wild beast, I cleared a way for myself to the coffee

Vocabulary

plaintive (plān′ tiv) *adj.* expressive of suffering or distress

beseeching (bi sēch′ ing) *adj.* in a begging or pleading manner cauldron. And I managed to carry back a cupful. I had a sip. The rest was for him. I can't forget the light of thankfulness in his eyes while he gulped it down—an animal gratitude. With those few gulps of hot water, I probably brought him more satisfaction than I had done during my whole childhood.

He was lying on a plank, livid, his lips pale and dried up, shaken by tremors. I could not stay by him for long. Orders had been given to clear the place for cleaning. Only the sick could stay.

We stayed outside for five hours. Soup was given out. As soon as we were allowed to go back to the blocks, I ran to my father.

"Have you had anything to eat?"

"No."

"Why not?"

"They didn't give us anything . . . they said that if we were ill we should die soon anyway and it would be a pity to waste the food. I can't go on any more. . . ."

I gave him what was left of my soup. But it was with a heavy heart. I felt that I was giving it up to him against my will. No better than Rabbi Eliahou's son[3] had I withstood the test.

He grew weaker day by day, his gaze veiled, his face the color of dead leaves. On the third day after our arrival at Buchenwald, everyone had to go to the showers. Even the sick, who had to go through last.

On the way back from the baths, we had to wait outside for a long time. They had not yet finished cleaning the blocks.

Seeing my father in the distance, I ran to meet him. He went by me like a ghost, passed me without stopping, without looking at me. I called to him. He did not come back. I ran after him:

"Father, where are you running to?"

He looked at me for a moment, and his gaze was distant, visionary; it was the face of someone else. A moment only and on he ran again.

Struck down with dysentery, my father lay in his bunk, five other invalids with him. I sat by his side, watching him, not daring to believe that he could escape death again. Nevertheless, I did all I could to give him hope.

Suddenly, he raised himself on his bunk and put his feverish lips to my ear:

"Eliezer . . . I must tell you where to find the gold and the money I buried . . . in the cellar. . . . You know. . . ."

He began to talk faster and faster, as though he were afraid he would not have time to tell me. I tried to explain to him that this was not the end, that we would go back to the house together, but he would not listen to me. He could no longer listen to me. He was exhausted. A trickle of saliva, mingled with blood, was running from between his lips. He had closed his eyes. His breath was coming in gasps.

For a ration of bread, I managed to change beds with a prisoner in my father's bunk. In the afternoon the doctor came. I went and told him that my father was very ill.

"Bring him here!"

I explained that he could not stand up. But the doctor refused to listen to anything. Somehow, I brought my father to him. He stared at him, then questioned him in a clipped voice:

"What do you want?"

"My father's ill," I answered for him. "Dysentery . . ."

"Dysentery? That's not my business. I'm a surgeon. Go on! Make room for the others."

Protests did no good.

"I can't go on, son. . . . Take me back to my bunk. . . ."

I took him back and helped him to lie down. He was shivering.

"Try and sleep a bit, father. Try to go to sleep. . . ."

His breathing was labored, thick. He kept his eyes shut. Yet I was convinced that he

3. Earlier, Eliezer had witnessed *Rabbi Eliahou's son* purposefully leaving his father behind to die. Eliezer had prayed for the strength never to betray his own father in this way.

could see everything, that now he could see the truth in all things.

Another doctor came to the block. But my father would not get up. He knew that it was useless.

Besides, this doctor had only come to finish off the sick. I could hear him shouting at them that they were lazy and just wanted to stay in bed. I felt like leaping at his throat, strangling him. But I no longer had the courage or the strength. I was riveted to my father's deathbed. My hands hurt, I was clenching them so hard. Oh, to strangle the doctor and the others! To burn the whole world! My father's murderers! But the cry stayed in my throat.

When I came back from the bread distribution, I found my father weeping like a child:

"Son, they keep hitting me!"

"Who?"

I thought he was delirious.

"Him, the Frenchman . . . and the Pole . . . they were hitting me."

Another wound to the heart, another hate, another reason for living lost.

"Eliezer . . . Eliezer . . . tell them not to hit me. . . . I haven't done anything. . . . Why do they keep hitting me?"

I began to abuse his neighbors. They laughed at me. I promised them bread, soup. They laughed. Then they got angry; they could not stand my father any longer, they said, because he was now unable to drag himself outside to relieve himself.

The following day he complained that they had taken his ration of bread.

"While you were asleep?"

"No. I wasn't asleep. They jumped on top of me. They snatched my bread . . . and they hit me . . . again. . . . I can't stand any more, son . . . a drop of water. . . ."

I knew that he must not drink. But he pleaded with me for so long that I gave in. Water was the worst poison he could have, but what else could I do for him? With water, without water, it would all be over soon anyway. . . .

"You, at least, have some mercy on me. . . ."

Have mercy on him! I, his only son!

A week went by like this.

"This is your father, isn't it?" asked the head of the block.

"Yes."

"He's very ill."

"The doctor won't do anything for him."

"The doctor *can't* do anything for him, now. And neither can you."

Don't Forget, 1964. Chaim Goldberg (Poland). Oil on linen, 96 x 78 in. Spertus Jewish Museum, Chicago.

Viewing the painting: Describe the composition of the painting. In what ways does it reflect its title and this selection?

He put his great hairy hand on my shoulder and added:

"Listen to me, boy. Don't forget that you're in a concentration camp. Here, every man has to fight for himself and not think of anyone else. Even of his father. Here, there are no fathers, no brothers, no friends. Everyone lives and dies for himself alone. I'll give you a sound piece of advice—don't give your ration of bread and soup to your old father. There's nothing you can do for him. And you're killing yourself. Instead, you ought to be having his ration."

I listened to him without interrupting. He was right, I thought in the most secret region of my heart, but I dared not admit it. It's too late to save your old father, I said to myself. You ought to be having two rations of bread, two rations of soup. . . .

Only a fraction of a second, but I felt guilty. I ran to find a little soup to give my father. But he did not want it. All he wanted was water.

"Don't drink water . . . have some soup. . . ."

"I'm burning . . . why are you being so unkind to me, my son? Some water. . . ."

I brought him some water. Then I left the block for roll call. But I turned around and came back again. I lay down on the top bunk. Invalids were allowed to stay in the block. So I would be an invalid myself. I would not leave my father.

There was silence all round now, broken only by groans. In front of the block, the SS were giving orders. An officer passed by the beds. My father begged me:

"My son, some water. . . . I'm burning. . . . My stomach. . . ."

"Quiet, over there!" yelled the officer.

"Eliezer," went on my father, "some water. . . ."

The officer came up to him and shouted at him to be quiet. But my father did not hear him. He went on calling me. The officer dealt him a violent blow on the head with his truncheon.

I did not move. I was afraid. My body was afraid of also receiving a blow.

Then my father made a rattling noise and it was my name: "Eliezer."

I could see that he was still breathing—spasmodically.

I did not move.

When I got down after roll call, I could see his lips trembling as he murmured something. Bending over him, I stayed gazing at him for over an hour, engraving into myself the picture of his blood-stained face, his shattered skull.

Then I had to go to bed. I climbed into my bunk, above my father, who was still alive. It was January 28, 1945.

I awoke on January 29 at dawn. In my father's place lay another invalid. They must have taken him away before dawn and carried him to the crematory. He may still have been breathing.

There were no prayers at his grave. No candles were lit to his memory. His last word was my name. A summons, to which I did not respond.

I did not weep, and it pained me that I could not weep. But I had no more tears. And, in the depths of my being, in the recesses of my weakened conscience, could I have searched it, I might perhaps have found something like—free at last!

Vocabulary

truncheon (trun′ chən) *n.* a billy club

spasmodically (spaz mod′ ik lē) *adv.* in an irregular or fitful manner

Responding to Literature

Personal Response

What detail or incident in this selection did you find most disturbing? Share your response with the class.

Analyzing Literature

Recall

1. How does Wiesel's father react when told that he should shower after arriving at Buchenwald?
2. What does Wiesel do the next morning when he realizes that he has become separated from his father?
3. How do other inmates treat the father after he comes down with dysentery?
4. What advice does the head of the block offer Wiesel?
5. How does Wiesel's father die?

Interpret

6. Why does Wiesel insist that his father follow him to the showers?
7. An **internal conflict** is a struggle within a character (see **Literary Terms Handbook,** page R2). What internal conflict does Wiesel experience on the morning after he arrives at Buchenwald?
8. Why do the other inmates behave as they do toward the father?
9. Why does Wiesel feel guilty after the head of the block offers him advice?
10. Why does Wiesel say that his father's last word was a summons "to which I did not respond"?

Evaluate and Connect

11. **Foreshadowing** occurs when a writer provides hints about what will happen in a story (see **Literary Terms Handbook,** page R5). What details foreshadow the death of Wiesel's father?
12. Do you think that Wiesel's guilty feelings about his father are justified? Why or why not?
13. The term **realism** describes a kind of writing in which life is depicted without sentimentality or idealization (see **Literary Terms Handbook,** page R10). What details or incidents in the selection help make it realistic?
14. What question would you like to ask Wiesel about the events described in this selection?
15. What do you think you would have done in Wiesel's place?

Literary ELEMENTS

Autobiography

An **autobiography** is an account of a person's life written by that person. The author selects which events to write about according to the purpose of the autobiography. Some autobiographies cover the subject's entire life, presenting a general self-portrait. Others focus on a particular experience or the author's relationship with another person. Autobiographies are usually not as objective as other forms of nonfiction, such as history books. However, they may provide a more intimate and moving portrayal of people and events from the past.

1. How might this selection be different if it were written by someone other than Wiesel?
2. Based on this selection from *Night,* what purpose or purposes did Wiesel have in writing the book?

- See **Literary Terms Handbook,** p. R1.

Literature and Writing

Writing About Literature

Examining Information As he describes his personal experiences in *Night,* Wiesel offers important historical information. In the selection, locate specific details that Wiesel provides about life in Buchenwald. Write a summary of your findings and then specify what additional information you would like to know about Buchenwald.

Personal Writing

Editorial What is the difference between being proud of your own ethnic background and hating people from different backgrounds? Write a newspaper editorial about this question. You may want to refer to the Holocaust in order to make your point.

Extending Your Response

Literature Groups

Compare Sources In the Reading Focus on page 1000, you were asked how you have learned information about the Holocaust. In your group, compare the selection from *Night* with other sources of information, such as novels, history books, fictional films, and documentaries. Summarize your observations for the class.

Internet Connection

Explore Controversy Although the Holocaust occurred over half a century ago, it continues to inspire controversy throughout the world. Do an Internet search to find out current issues related to the Holocaust. You might begin by typing *Holocaust* or *Auschwitz* into a search engine. Share your findings with the class.

Learning for Life

Plans for Healing The prisoners who survived Nazi concentration camps suffered from disease, malnutrition, injuries, and psychological trauma. With a partner, research ways of addressing one or more of these problems. Identify what kind of professionals would be helpful for the survivors and list concrete steps survivors could take to work toward healing.

Reading Further

If you found this selection from *Night* interesting, the following books might also be of interest to you:

Night, by Elie Wiesel.

From the Kingdom of Memory, by Elie Wiesel, a collection of essays and speeches, including his Nobel lecture.

Save your work for your portfolio.

VOCABULARY • Antonyms

Antonyms are words that have opposite meanings. Each of the following words from *Night* is paired with an antonym.

fascinated	repelled
indifferent	interested
timid	bold
ashamed	proud

One word may have many antonyms. The word that a writer chooses may depend upon the shade of meaning or the mental image that he or she wants to create.

PRACTICE Choose the vocabulary word that is the best antonym for each of the following words. Use a dictionary to check your work, if you wish.

regularly
boastful
happy

POLAND, 1937

Before You Read

Encounter

Meet Czesław Miłosz

"A poet carries his land within him. I never left Poland."

Czesław Miłosz (chezh′ lôv mē′ lôsh) was born in an ethnically mixed area that became part of Poland after the fall of the Russian Empire. He published his first volume of poetry at age twenty-one. During the Nazi occupation of Poland, he remained in the country, participating in the resistance movement as a writer calling for freedom. After World War II, the Polish government appointed him to positions in the foreign service. However, by 1951 he could no longer ignore the abuses of the Communist regime. He defected to the West and eventually settled in the United States, where he became a professor of Slavic literature. In 1980 he won the Nobel Prize for Literature.

Miłosz's writing is generally restrained, even when he addresses tragic events. He is often described as a philosophical poet because of his fascination with moral issues and the nature of existence and identity. In addition to poetry, he has written critical essays and novels.

Czesław Miłosz was born in 1911.

Reading Focus

What have you learned from observing or thinking about nature?

Discuss Discuss your response with the class.

Setting a Purpose Read this poem for the author's reflections on a fleeting encounter with nature at sunrise.

Building Background

Nature and the Countryside

Miłosz has written many superb descriptions of landscapes. As a boy, he wanted to become a naturalist, and this interest carried over into his poetry: "The forests, the valleys and the rivers which I saw in my childhood possess for me a strong evocative force." Miłosz draws a sharp distinction between an attachment to one's homeland and extreme forms of nationalism that encourage ethnic hatred. He also refuses to idealize nature. According to Miłosz, American writers tend to emphasize the beauty and wisdom of nature, whereas he feels "that nature is extremely cruel, or at least indifferent."

The Spirit of a Nation

In 1951 Miłosz chose to live and write in exile rather than in a Poland under Russian domination. In this he followed a tradition that developed in the nineteenth century. By 1795 Poland, once one of Europe's most powerful states, had been conquered and divided up by its Russian and German neighbors. Not until 1918 did an independent Poland appear again on the map of Europe. Throughout the period of foreign rule, the nation's spirit was kept alive by poets and writers, often living in exile in western Europe. Many of them, like the novelist Henryk Sienkiewicz, who was awarded a Nobel Prize in 1905, did not live to see a free Poland, but their work kept hope and the memory of liberty alive for a divided and oppressed people. On the following page, you will see Miłosz's poem as "Encounter" in English and as "Spotkanie," in Polish.

Reading Further

If you enjoy reading "Encounter," you might also be interested in the following:

"The World" from *The Collected Poems,* by Czesław Miłosz.

Encounter

Czesław Miłosz

Translated by the author and Lillian Vallee

Winter Sunday in Dalecarlia, 1899. Gustaf Ankarcrona (Sweden).

We were riding through frozen fields in a wagon at dawn.
A red wing rose in the darkness.

And suddenly a hare ran across the road.
One of us pointed to it with his hand.

That was long ago. Today neither of them is alive,
Not the hare, nor the man who made the gesture.

O my love, where are they, where are they going
The flash of a hand, streak of movement, rustle of pebbles.
I ask not out of sorrow, but in wonder.

Jechaliśmy przed świtem po zamarzłych polach,
Czerwone skrzydło wstawało, jeszcze noc.

I zając przebiegł nagle tuż przed nami,
A jeden z nas pokazał go ręką.

To było dawno. Dzisiaj już nie żyją
Ni zając, ani ten co go wskazywał.

Miłości moja, gdzież są, dokąd idą
Błysk ręki, linia biegu, szelest grud—
Nie z żalu pytam, ale z zamyślenia.

Responding to Literature

Personal Response

What were your thoughts as you finished reading this poem? Jot them down in your journal.

Analyzing Literature

Recall and Interpret

1. **Setting** is the time and place in which the events of a literary work occur (see **Literary Terms Handbook,** page R11). What is the setting chosen by Miłosz for "Encounter"?
2. Describe the encounter that is referred to in the poem's title.
3. When did this encounter take place? What has happened since the encounter took place?
4. What does the speaker say he is asking about "in wonder" in the last stanza?

Evaluate and Connect

5. Do you think that the encounter described in the poem was important to the speaker at the time it occurred? Why or why not?
6. What would you guess is the relationship between the speaker and the man who made the gesture? Explain your answer.
7. Why might Miłosz have decided to address this poem to a silent listener?
8. In the Reading Focus on page 1008, you were asked what you have learned from nature. Compare this insight with the speaker's reflections in "Encounter."

Literary Criticism

Scholars Leonard Nathan and Arthur Quinn assert that "Encounter" is "full of the very regret that the speaker tries to deny." What is that regret? Do you agree that the speaker tries to deny it? Discuss your answers with a small group of classmates.

Literary ELEMENTS

Lyric Poetry

In **lyric poetry,** the speaker expresses personal thoughts and feelings. Lyric poems are usually brief. They may describe incidents, but their main emphasis is on conveying emotions rather than telling a story. The term *lyric* comes from *lyre,* a stringed instrument that Greek poets used to accompany their singing. Although poets now seldom sing their poems to the accompaniment of music, lyric poems often have a songlike quality.

1. What personal thoughts and feelings does the speaker of "Encounter" express?
2. Which lines seem the most songlike to you? Explain why.

- See **Literary Terms Handbook,** p. R7.

Extending Your Response

Creative Writing

Write a Lyric Poem Nature is a common subject of lyric poetry. Write a lyric poem about an encounter with a wild animal or an experience in a natural setting. Try to select a few vivid images to express your thoughts and feelings in the poem.

Learning for Life

An Illustration for "Encounter" If you were publishing "Encounter" in a magazine, what sort of illustration might accompany it? Either draw an illustration for the poem or bring in a photocopy of artwork that you think would make a good illustration. Explain to the class which images in the poem inspired your choice.

Save your work for your portfolio.

Radio Transcript

History is a lot more than stories about people who lived long ago. It's always happening, all around us. Read to find out about the historical event.

Berlin Wall Crumbles

from *We Interrupt This Broadcast,* by Joe Garner

BILL KURTIS It was a wall that literally split a city in two, dividing families from friends, east from west, and communism from capitalism. The Berlin Wall was erected in 1961 by an East German government determined to stop the mass exodus of its citizens into West Berlin . . . but by the late 1980s, Communist regimes throughout Eastern Europe had begun to fall apart. By 1989, neighboring Czechoslovakia had turned to democracy and began allowing East German citizens free passage into West Germany, rendering the wall obsolete. Then, on November 9, 1989, East Berlin officially announced that its borders to West Germany would be opened for private trips abroad. Within hours, thousands of jubilant citizens from both East and West Berlin began massing at the wall to celebrate, freely crossing into what had been forbidden territory for nearly three decades. The end of the Berlin Wall was at hand.

ANNOUNCER'S VOICE Berlin's famous freedom bell rang out over the newly opened border. *[crowd noises]*

VOICE OF EYEWITNESS

I. I climbed over the wall and come and walked, uh, through the Brandenburg Gate.

II. I jumped over the wall.

III. It's a great feeling.

IV. I'm happy. You know, I have been dreaming of this for years.

ANNOUNCER'S VOICE After twenty-eight years, the east German government has thrown open the nation's prison-like Berlin Wall, and thousands of East and West Germans have been partying on the wall ever since *[sound of people whooping and yelling]*, some chipping away at sections of the twenty-mile long wall.

BILL KURTIS The next day, November 10, 1989, the final demolition of the Berlin Wall began, this time symbolizing the demise of Communist regimes throughout Eastern Europe.

Analyzing Media

1. What did the Berlin Wall, and its destruction, come to symbolize?
2. Imagine you were an East Berliner. Based on this report, how do you think you would have reacted to the fall of the Wall?

FRANCE, 1942

Before You Read

The Myth of Sisyphus

Meet Albert Camus

"The remarkable thing in man is not that he despairs, but that he overcomes or forgets despair."

Albert Camus (al bār′ ka mo͞o′) grew up in a poor household in Algeria, which at the time was a French colony. His father was killed in World War I soon after Camus's birth. His mother, an illiterate cleaning woman, raised the family. At seventeen, Camus was diagnosed with tuberculosis. This severe illness may have encouraged his preoccupation with death, but it did not stop him from pursuing his dream of becoming a writer.

In the 1930s, Camus moved to Paris where he wrote for several left-wing papers. By the end of World War II, he was already famous for his first novel, *The Stranger*, and a collection of philosophical essays called *The Myth of Sisyphus*. In the 1950s, he was widely seen as a controversial spokesman for his generation. Three years before his life was cut short by an automobile accident, he won the Nobel Prize for Literature.

Camus was born in 1913 and died in 1960.

Reading Focus

How can work give meaning to a person's life?

Quickwrite Jot down a response in your journal.

Setting a Purpose Read this essay for Camus's interpretation of a myth about endless labor.

Building Background

The Absurd

In *The Myth of Sisyphus,* Camus addressed the problems that arise from the concept of the absurd, a philosophical term referring to the idea that human life has no inherent meaning. Camus argued that the absurd does not justify despair. Once people come to recognize that the world is essentially meaningless, they can begin to make choices that give meaning to their lives. In this influential essay, Camus interprets a Greek myth about a man who offends the gods. Sisyphus was an ancient Greek trickster figure who chained up Death when it came for him. Eventually, however, he was condemned forever to push a huge stone up a hill, only to have it roll back every time he neared the top.

Reading Further

If you enjoy *The Myth of Sisyphus* you might also enjoy the following:

"Notebook I" from *Notebooks 1935–1942,* by Albert Camus.

"Reading Albert Camus" from *Understanding Albert Camus,* by David R. Ellison.

Vocabulary Preview

prudent (pro͞od′ ənt) *adj.* sensible; sound in judgment; p. 1013
chastise (chas tīz′) *v.* to condemn or punish severely; p. 1014
scorn (skôrn) *n.* disrespect; p. 1014
fidelity (fi del′ ə tē) *n.* faithfulness; p. 1015
negate (ni gāt′) *v.* to make ineffective or powerless; p. 1015

The Myth of Sisyphus

Albert Camus

Translated by Justin O'Brien

Sisyphos (Sisyphus), 1920. Franz von Stuck (Austria). Oil on canvas. Katharina Büttiker Collection, Galerie Wühre 9–Art Deco, Zurich, Switzerland.

THE GODS HAD CONDEMNED SISYPHUS to ceaselessly rolling a rock to the top of a mountain, whence the stone would fall back of its own weight. They had thought with some reason that there is no more dreadful punishment than futile and hopeless labor.

If one believes Homer, Sisyphus was the wisest and most prudent of mortals. According to another tradition, however, he was disposed to practice the profession of highwayman. I see no contradiction in this. Opinions differ as to the reasons why he became the futile laborer of the underworld. To begin with, he is accused of a certain levity[1] in regard to the gods. He stole their secrets. Aegina, the daughter of Aesopus, was carried off by Jupiter. The father was shocked by that disappearance and complained to Sisyphus. He, who knew of the abduction, offered to tell about it on condition that Aesopus would give water to the citadel of Corinth.[2] To the celestial thunderbolts he preferred the benediction[3] of water. He was punished for this in the underworld. Homer tells us also that Sisyphus had put Death in chains. Pluto could not endure the sight of his deserted, silent empire. He dispatched the god of war, who liberated Death from the hands of her conqueror.

It is said also that Sisyphus, being near to death, rashly wanted to test his wife's love. He

1. *Levity,* a lack of seriousness, borders on mocking disrespect.

2. According to Greek mythology, Sisyphus was the king of the city of *Corinth;* a *citadel* is a city's most important fort.

3. Here, *benediction* is something that causes goodness or well-being.

Vocabulary

prudent (pro͞od′ ənt) *adj.* sensible; sound in judgment ordered her to cast his unburied body into the middle of the public square. Sisyphus woke up in the underworld. And there, annoyed by an obedience so contrary to human love, he obtained from Pluto permission to return to earth in order to chastise his wife. But when he had seen again the face of this world, enjoyed water and sun, warm stones and the sea, he no longer wanted to go back to the infernal darkness. Recalls, signs of anger, warnings were of no avail. Many years more he lived facing the curve of the gulf, the sparkling sea, and the smiles of earth. A decree of the gods was necessary. Mercury came and seized the impudent man by the collar and, snatching him from his joys, led him forcibly back to the underworld, where his rock was ready for him.

You have already grasped that Sisyphus is the absurd hero. He *is*, as much through his passions as through his torture. His scorn of the gods, his hatred of death, and his passion for life won him that unspeakable penalty in which the whole being is exerted toward accomplishing nothing. This is the price that must be paid for the passions of this earth. Nothing is told us about Sisyphus in the underworld. Myths are made for the imagination to breathe life into them. As for this myth, one sees merely the whole effort of a body straining to raise the huge stone, to roll it and push it up a slope a hundred times over; one sees the face screwed up, the cheek tight against the stone, the shoulder bracing the clay-covered mass, the foot wedging it, the fresh start with arms outstretched, the wholly human security of two earth-clotted hands. At the very end of his long effort measured by skyless space and time without depth, the purpose is achieved. Then Sisyphus watches the stone rush down in a few moments toward that lower world whence he will have to push it up again toward the summit. He goes back down to the plain.

It is during that return, that pause, that Sisyphus interests me. A face that toils so close to stones is already stone itself! I see that man going back down with a heavy yet measured step toward the torment of which he will never know the end. That hour like a breathing space which returns as surely as his suffering, that is the hour of consciousness. At each of those moments when he leaves the heights and gradually sinks toward the lairs of the gods, he is superior to his fate. He is stronger than his rock.

If this myth is tragic, that is because its hero is conscious. Where would his torture be, indeed, if at every step the hope of succeeding upheld him? The workman of today works every day in his life at the same tasks, and this fate is no less absurd. But it is tragic only at the rare moments when it becomes conscious. Sisyphus, proletarian[4] of the gods, powerless and rebellious, knows the whole extent of his wretched condition: it is what he thinks of during his descent. The lucidity that was to constitute his torture at the same time crowns his victory. There is no fate that cannot be surmounted by scorn.

If the descent is thus sometimes performed in sorrow, it can also take place in joy. This word is not too much. Again I fancy Sisyphus returning toward his rock, and the sorrow was in the beginning. When the images of earth cling too tightly to memory, when the call of happiness becomes too insistent, it happens that melancholy rises in man's heart: this is the rock's victory, this is the rock itself. The boundless grief is too heavy to bear. These are our nights of Gethsemane.[5] But crushing

4. A *proletarian* is an industrial wage-earner.
5. According to the Bible, *Gethsemane* (geth sem′ ə nē) is the olive grove where Jesus Christ contemplated his possible death on the eve of his arrest.

Vocabulary

chastise (chas tīz′) *v.* to condemn or punish severely
scorn (skôrn) *n.* disrespect

truths perish from being acknowledged. Thus, Oedipus[6] at the outset obeys fate without knowing it. But from the moment he knows, his tragedy begins. Yet at the same moment, blind and desperate, he realizes that the only bond linking him to the world is the cool hand of a girl. Then a tremendous remark rings out: "Despite so many ordeals, my advanced age and the nobility of my soul make me conclude that all is well." Sophocles' Oedipus, like Dostoyevsky's[7] Kirilov, thus gives the recipe for the absurd victory. Ancient wisdom confirms modern heroism.

One does not discover the absurd without being tempted to write a manual of happiness. "What! by such narrow ways—?" There is but one world, however. Happiness and the absurd are two sons of the same earth. They are inseparable. It would be a mistake to say that happiness necessarily springs from the absurd discovery. It happens as well that the feeling of the absurd springs from happiness. "I conclude that all is well," says Oedipus, and that remark is sacred. It echoes in the wild and limited universe of man. It teaches that all is not, has not been, exhausted. It drives out of this world a god who had come into it with dissatisfaction and a preference for futile sufferings. It makes of fate a human matter, which must be settled among men.

All Sisyphus' silent joy is contained therein. His fate belongs to him. His rock is his thing. Likewise, the absurd man, when he contemplates his torment, silences all the idols. In the universe suddenly restored to its silence, the myriad wondering little voices of the earth rise up. Unconscious, secret calls, invitations from all the faces, they are the necessary reverse and price of victory. There is no sun without shadow, and it is essential to know the night. The absurd man says yes and his effort will henceforth be unceasing. If there is a personal fate, there is no higher destiny, or at least there is but one which he concludes is inevitable and despicable. For the rest, he knows himself to be the master of his days. At that subtle moment when man glances backward over his life, Sisyphus returning toward his rock, in that slight pivoting he contemplates that series of unrelated actions which becomes his fate, created by him, combined under his memory's eye and soon sealed by his death. Thus, convinced of the wholly human origin of all that is human, a blind man eager to see who knows that the night has no end, he is still on the go. The rock is still rolling.

I leave Sisyphus at the foot of the mountain! One always finds one's burden again. But Sisyphus teaches the higher fidelity that negates the gods and raises rocks. He too concludes that all is well. This universe henceforth without a master seems to him neither sterile nor futile. Each atom of that stone, each mineral flake of that night-filled mountain, in itself forms a world. The struggle itself toward the heights is enough to fill a man's heart. One must imagine Sisyphus happy.

6. *Oedipus* is a character from Greek mythology who fulfilled a prophesy by unknowingly killing his father and marrying his mother. The Greek dramatist Sophocles wrote a series of plays about him, which end with a blind Oedipus being led by his daughter (pages 263–322).
7. Russian writer Fyodor *Dostoyevsky* (dos′ tə yef′ skē) wrote about a character named Kirilov who commits suicide in an attempt to prove that there is no God to control his actions.

Vocabulary

fidelity (fi del′ ə tē) *n.* faithfulness

negate (ni gāt′) *v.* to make ineffective or powerless

Responding to Literature

Personal Response

What surprised you the most about Camus's interpretation of the myth of Sisyphus? Share your response with the class.

Analyzing Literature

Recall and Interpret

1. What explanations are offered for Sisyphus's punishment in the second and third paragraphs?
2. Why does Camus consider Sisyphus an absurd hero?
3. What opportunity becomes available to Sisyphus when the stone rolls down the slope?
4. How do you interpret Camus's statement that there is "no fate that cannot be surmounted by scorn"?
5. Why does Camus feel that Sisyphus's descent down the slope can be joyous?

Evaluate and Connect

6. A **symbol** is an object or action that stands for something in addition to itself (see page R12). What might the rock symbolize in Camus's interpretation of the myth?
7. Do you think that Camus's ideas are compatible with a religious view of the world? Explain.
8. In the Reading Focus on page 1012, you were asked how work can give meaning to a person's life. Compare your response with what Camus says about Sisyphus's labor.
9. Which idea in the essay is most relevant to your own life? Explain.
10. Why might Camus have written an essay like this during World War II?

Literary Criticism

Scholar Roy Pickett suggestes that readers are more likely to be moved by the absurd hero than the hero of legend because the absurd hero is vulnerable, aware of his vulnerability, and yet continues to act. Write an essay explaining why you agree or disagree with Pickett's statement. Use the character of Sisyphus as your main example.

Literary ELEMENTS

Persuasion

One of the purposes of writing can be to persuade. **Persuasion** is an attempt to convince readers to think or act in a certain way. Philosophical essays generally appeal to the reader's intellect through logic and evidence. Other forms of persuasive writing, such as political speeches and advertisements, may rely more on emotional appeals to win over the reader.

1. What does Camus try to persuade readers to think or do in his essay?
2. In your opinion, which part of Camus's argument is most effective, and which part is least effective? Explain your answer.

- See **Literary Terms Handbook,** p. R9.

Extending Your Response

Writing About Literature

Comparison In his discussion of Sisyphus as an absurd hero, Camus compares him to the tragic hero Oedipus (see page 263). Write one or two paragraphs comparing Sisyphus to another hero in a fictional work or in real life. What qualities do they have in common? How has each hero overcome the circumstances forced upon him or her?

Literature Groups

Happy Struggle? Camus ends his essay with the claim that "One must imagine Sisyphus happy." How would you interpret this statement? Do you think that the essay offers convincing support for the statement? Discuss these questions in your group. When you are finished, share your conclusions with the class.

Save your work for your portfolio.

Before You Read

Freedom to Breathe

Meet Aleksandr Solzhenitsyn

"Lies can prevail against much in this world, but never against art."

Aleksandr Solzhenitsyn (sōl′ zhə nēt′ sən) grew up in poverty. After earning degrees in philology, mathematics, and physics, he became a teacher. During World War II, he served in the artillery, rising to the rank of captain. Late in the war, however, he wrote some letters in which he criticized Communist dictator Joseph Stalin. For this he was arrested and sent to Siberia for more than ten years. He wrote of his experiences there in his first novel, published in 1962.

The authorities soon clamped down on Solzhenitsyn again, but in 1970 he won the Nobel Prize for Literature. Four years later, the government denounced his latest book, an account of the Siberian prison camps, and deported him. He took refuge in the United States, where he continued to write novels and nonfiction. In 1994 he returned to Russia, having outlasted the Communist regime.

Aleksandr Solzhenitsyn was born in 1918.

Reading Focus

What images come to mind when you think of the word *freedom?*

Quickwrite Jot down a response in your journal.

Setting a Purpose Read this prose poem to learn about the speaker's impressions of freedom.

Building Background

The Gulag

In 1919 the Communist Party established a system of forced labor camps known as the Gulag. The system expanded dramatically during Stalin's dictatorship: between 1934 and 1947, at least ten million people were sent to the Gulag. Besides ordinary criminals, they included political dissidents, peasants who resisted the seizure of their farms, and people merely suspected of opposing the government. Many were executed, and many more died from disease and malnutrition. Solzhenitsyn's greatest nonfiction work, *The Gulag Archipelago*—for which he was expelled from Russia—is based on his own experiences and the testimony of other inmates. He claimed that all Russians bore some responsibility for the Gulag: "We didn't love freedom enough."

Reading Further

If you enjoy reading "Freedom to Breathe," you might enjoy *One Day in the Life of Ivan Denisovich,* a masterpiece of Russian fiction, depicting life in a Stalinist camp.

Apple Trees in Bloom, 1904. Kazimir Severinovich Malevich (Russia).

Freedom to Breathe

Aleksandr Solzhenitsyn
Translated by Michael Glenny

L'Envol, 1968–1971. Marc Chagall (Russia, 1887–1985). Oil on canvas, 125 x 90 cm. Private collection.

A SHOWER FELL IN THE NIGHT and now dark clouds drift across the sky, occasionally sprinkling a fine film of rain.

I stand under an apple tree in blossom and I breathe. Not only the apple tree but the grass round it glistens with moisture; words cannot describe the sweet fragrance that pervades the air. I inhale as deeply as I can, and the aroma invades my whole being; I breathe with my eyes open, I breathe with my eyes closed—I cannot say which gives me the greater pleasure.

This, I believe, is the single most precious freedom that prison takes away from us: the freedom to breathe freely, as I now can. No food on earth, no wine, not even a woman's kiss is sweeter to me than this air steeped in the fragrance of flowers, of moisture and freshness.

No matter that this is only a tiny garden, hemmed in by five-story houses like cages in a zoo. I cease to hear the motorcycles backfiring, radios whining, the burble of loudspeakers. As long as there is fresh air to breathe under an apple tree after a shower, we may survive a little longer.

Responding to Literature

Personal Response

What memories did this selection bring back for you? Share your response with a classmate.

Analyzing Literature

Recall and Interpret

1. **Setting** is the time and place of events in a literary work (see **Literary Terms Handbook,** page R11). How would you describe the setting of "Freedom to Breathe"?
2. Why do the flowers and grass smell so fragrant?
3. What, in your opinion, is the meaning of the statement that the freedom to breathe freely "is the single most precious freedom that prison takes away from us"?
4. How do you interpret the last sentence in the selection? Support your answer with details from the selection.

Evaluate and Connect

5. What can we infer has happened to the speaker in the past?
6. Why might Solzhenitsyn have included the details about setting in the last paragraph?
7. **Tone** is the attitude that a speaker takes toward the audience, a subject, or a character (see **Literary Terms Handbook,** page R12). What is the speaker's tone in "Freedom to Breathe"?
8. In the Reading Focus on page 1017, you were asked which images you associate with the word *freedom.* Compare your images with the ones in Solzhenitsyn's poem.

Literary ELEMENTS

Prose Poem

A **prose poem** is a short prose composition that uses rhythm, imagery, and other poetic devices to express an idea or emotion. Unlike metrical and free verse, prose poetry does not have line breaks; instead, the sentences appear in standard paragraph form. A prose poem allows the writer to express a poetical idea without following the usual rules of poetic form.

1. What is the central idea or emotion expressed in "Freedom to Breathe"?
2. What poetic devices does Solzhenitsyn use to express this idea in prose?

- See **Literary Terms Handbook,** p. R10.

Extending Your Response

Creative Writing

Prose Poem In "Freedom to Breathe," the speaker's description of a physical sensation leads to a message about freedom. Write a prose poem of your own to express a feeling or idea about freedom. You may wish to use **repetition** (see **Literary Terms Handbook,** page R10) to give your prose poem a strong rhythm.

Literature Groups

Defending Rights Solzhenitsyn has said that the Russian people should have done more to prevent abuses during the Soviet period. What actions might students take to defend freedom under a dictatorship? Discuss this question in your group. When you are finished, share your conclusions with the class.

Save your work for your portfolio.

Writing Workshop

Persuasive Writing: Personal Response

What is the meaning of life? How should resources be shared? Can equality exist alongside difference? These kinds of political, social, or philosophical questions give rise to many different opinions. In a world of multiple points of view, one of the best ways to get others to view an issue as you do is through writing. **In this workshop, you will write a persuasive essay in which you take a position on an issue raised in a work of literature.**

- As you write your persuasive essay, refer to **Writing Handbook,** pp. R58–R63.

Evaluation Rubric

By the time you complete this Writing Workshop, you will have

- explained an issue raised in a literary work
- developed a position statement that takes a stand on the issue
- supported your position with examples, anecdotes, or other kinds of elaboration
- considered opposing viewpoints
- called your readers to action
- presented an essay that is free of errors in grammar, usage, and mechanics

The Writing Process

PREWRITING

PREWRITING TIP

Choose a work of literature that treats an issue you have strong opinions about.

Explore ideas

Review the selections you have read in the second part of Unit Five and consider some of the issues that they raise. For example, you might consider the following issues:

- a woman's need and right to be respected as a human being, as depicted in *A Doll's House*
- the debate over capital punishment, an issue introduced in "The Bet"
- the judgments about life and death made by the prisoner in "The Bet"
- the conflict between love of family and love of country, as portrayed in "War"
- the philosophical question about the meaning of life in "The Myth of Sisyphus"

State your position and gather support

A position is an opinion on an issue. Think about the issue you have chosen and then write a clear statement of your position. Make a list of reasons, arguments, or evidence to support your opinion.

Consider your purpose and audience

Your main purpose is to persuade readers that your position is reasonable. You also may want to convince them to adopt your position or to take a specific action. To make your readers more receptive to your ideas, think of ways to relate the literature or the issue to their experiences and interests.

Make a plan

Use your position statement and your list of reasons, arguments, or evidence to plan your essay. Follow the basic essay structure of introduction, body, and conclusion.

		STUDENT MODEL
Introduction	Identify the issue raised in the work to which you are responding. Clearly state your position on the issue.	In the essay "The Myth of Sisyphus," Albert Camus compares people who recognize the pointlessness of human life to Sisyphus, a person in Greek mythology who was condemned to ceaselessly roll a rock to the top of a mountain. We must not allow ourselves to think that we are like Sisyphus. We are not prisoners of our fate.
Body	Present your reasons, arguments, or evidence.	Sisyphus can't do anything about his situation, so he changes his attitude. We can do something about our circumstances if they make us miserable or unhappy. We can find creative ways to cope with our situations instead of feeling like we're victims.
Conclusion	Restate your position and leave the reader with a final thought or a call to action.	You're not trapped in the mythology of ancient Greece. If you don't like your circumstances, today you can work to change them.

Complete Student Model on p. R121.

DRAFTING

DRAFTING TIP

Focus on getting your ideas down. You can improve your choice of words, add transitions, and further refine your writing later.

State your opinions firmly

To persuade your readers, you need to appear convinced of your argument yourself. Stand by your convictions. State what you think clearly and forcefully.

STUDENT MODEL

Camus writes that "there is no fate that cannot be surmounted by scorn." Despising a situation, though, isn't the only way to rise above it. Some people find other ways of surmounting the obstacles in their lives. They gain control of their destinies and take action to alter the course of their lives.

Complete Student Model on p. R121.

Write your draft

As you draft your essay, use your plan as a guide but don't hesitate to include additional reasons or arguments as you think of them.

REVISING

REVISING TIP

When you revise, you may need to delete as many words and sentences as you add. Begin by deleting the phrases "I think" and "I believe." Just give your opinions directly.

Evaluate your work

To begin revising, read your draft to make sure it fits your purpose and audience. Then use the **Rubric for Revising** as a guide and mark any weak spots that you want to strengthen.

Have a writing conference

Read your draft to a partner or small group. Use your audience's reactions to help you evaluate and revise your work.

RUBRIC FOR REVISING

Your revised personal response should have

- ☑ a well-defined position statement
- ☑ convincing evidence and reasons to support and elaborate on your position statement
- ☑ a brief presentation of opposing viewpoints
- ☑ logical organization of ideas and clear transitions
- ☑ a compelling closing statement or call to action

Your revised personal response should be free of

- ☑ biased statements that weaken your argument
- ☑ factual errors that mislead your audience
- ☑ errors in grammar, usage, and mechanics

STUDENT MODEL

I [would] ~~think I'd like to~~ change the ~~central~~ statement Camus makes [about scorning fate.] I would say, "There is no fate that cannot be surmounted by trying."

Complete Student Model on p. R121.

EDITING/PROOFREADING

Examine your revised draft closely to find and correct errors in grammar, spelling, usage, and mechanics. You might also ask a classmate to proofread your essay and circle errors.

PROOFREADING TIP

Use the **Proofreading Checklist** on the inside back cover of this book to help you catch mistakes.

Grammar Hint

Be sure to use the correct comparative and superlative forms of modifiers. For short adjectives, add *-er* to form the comparative and *-est* to form the superlative. Use *more* and *most* for modifiers of three or more syllables.

INCORRECT: *Changing your fate makes you more happy than enduring it does.*

CORRECT: *Changing your fate makes you happier than enduring it does.*

Complete Student Model

For a complete version of the model developed in this workshop, refer to **Writing Workshop Models**, p. R121.

STUDENT MODEL

Camus says that Sisyphus has created his own fate. That's only partly true, since the gods have condemned him to ceaselessly rolling the rock to the top of the mountain. We are ~~more~~ luckier than Sisyphus ~~on account of~~ because we actually do get to create our fate.

Complete Student Model on p. R121.

PUBLISHING/PRESENTING

You might submit your essay to the student newspaper or literary magazine. You also might use your essay as the starting point for a panel discussion or a debate.

PRESENTING TIP

If you intend to use your essay in a debate, memorize the most important points so that you can refer to them easily.

Reflecting

Reflect on the experience of writing a persuasive essay in response to a work of literature by answering these questions in your journal. What do you like best about your essay? What was the hardest part of writing it? What did you gain from your writing conference?

Save your work for your portfolio.

Unit Assessment

Personal Response

1. Which of the selections in Unit 5 did you find the most moving or inspiring?
2. Which selections in this unit did you enjoy the most? Which selections did you not care for? Explain your responses and tell which elements of the selections helped create your responses.
3. What did you learn about the relationship between different cultures and the literature written about them? What elements in these selections helped you to bridge any gaps of time and culture?
4. What suggestions would you make to someone who is interested in learning about the literature and culture of Europe?

Analyzing Literature

The literature of Europe takes many different forms, including epics, plays, short stories, and poetry. Write several paragraphs in which you select one of these forms and explore at least one of the following elements in detail:

- literary elements
- theme
- language
- form

Refer to at least two of the selections you have read in the unit to support your opinion. You might conclude your analysis by stating which of the selections was your favorite and why you feel that way.

Evaluate and Set Goals

Evaluate

1. Make a list of three things you contributed to the class as you worked through this unit.
2. What aspect of this unit was the most challenging for you?
   - How did you approach this task?
   - What was the result?
3. How would you assess your work in this unit, using the following scale? Give at least two reasons for your assessment.
   4 = outstanding **3** = good **2** = fair **1** = weak

Set Goals

1. Set a goal to work toward while reading Unit 6. Try to focus on improving a skill area such as listening and speaking or critical thinking.
2. Discuss your goal with your teacher.
3. Write down steps that you will take to achieve your goal.
4. Plan checkpoints at which you will stop and assess your progress toward that goal.
5. Record your goal and checkpoints. Then refer to them periodically to keep yourself on track.

BUILD YOUR PORTFOLIO

Select Look over the writing that you did in this unit and select two pieces to include in your portfolio. Use the following questions to help you decide:

- Which piece was the most fun to write?
- Which piece challenged you the most?
- Which one led you to new discoveries as you wrote?
- Which do you consider your best work?

Reflect Include explanatory notes with the pieces you chose. Use these questions as a guide:

- What did you learn from the process of writing each one?
- What are the strengths and weaknesses of the piece?
- How might you revise the piece to make it stronger?

Reading on Your Own

If you have enjoyed the literature in this unit, you might also be interested in the following books.

The Metamorphosis
by Franz Kafka
A young man wakes one morning to find himself transformed into a wriggling insect. He must deal with alienation from family, friends, and society, who are repulsed by his metamorphosis.

Cyrano de Bergerac
by Edmond Rostand He is a courageous soldier, an astonishing wit, and a romantic poet; however, he has a huge nose. Can any woman ever love him? This is the story of Cyrano's search for a true love based on feelings and not appearances. This well-loved classic was introduced to the London stage in 1898.

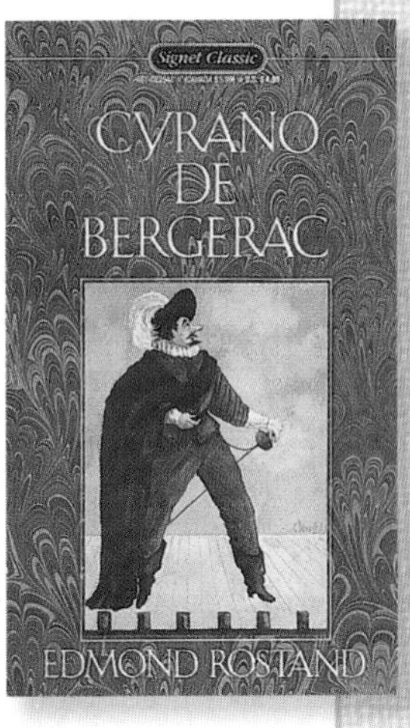

Anton Chekhov: Five Plays
translated by Ronald Hingley In some of his best plays, Chekhov explores the reality of Russian life in the late nineteenth century with humor, compassion, and a profound understanding of human nature. The plays included are *Ivanov, The Seagull, Uncle Vanya, Three Sisters,* and *The Cherry Orchard.*

The Ramsay Scallop
by Frances Temple
In 1299, a young couple, reluctantly betrothed to each other, make a pilgrimage to Spain from England. On the way, they share stories and songs with other travelers while learning to love and trust one another. The author is obviously indebted to *The Canterbury Tales* for the story's structure.

The Tempest
by William Shakespeare A duke and his daughter are exiled to an island occupied only by the spirit Ariel and the beast Caliban. Using magic, the duke regains his dukedom and wins his daughter a princely husband. This well-constructed and entertaining comedy was written in 1611.

Standardized Test Practice

The passage below is followed by five questions based on its content. Select the best answer and write the corresponding letter on your paper.

Frederic Bastiat (1801–1850) was a French economist, statesman, author, and philosopher. This excerpt from his essay "That Which is Seen and That Which is Not Seen" (1850) discusses some of the reasons he believes that the government should not intervene in institutions such as the arts.

There is certainly much to be said on both sides of this question. It may be said, in favor of the system of voting supplies for this purpose, that the arts enlarge, elevate, and harmonize the soul of a nation; that they divert it from too great an absorption in material occupations, encourage in it a love for the beautiful, and thus act favourably on its manners, customs, morals, and even on its industry.

It may be asked, what would become of music in France without her Italian theatre and her Conservatoire; of the dramatic art without her Theatre-Francais; of painting and sculpture, without our collections, galleries, and museums? It might even be asked, whether, without centralization, and consequently the support of fine arts, that exquisite taste would be developed which is the noble appendage of French labour, and which introduces its productions to the whole world? In the face of such results, would it not be the height of imprudence to renounce this moderate contribution from all her citizens, which, in fact, in the eyes of Europe, realizes their superiority and their glory?

To these and many other reasons, whose force I do not dispute, arguments no less forcible may be opposed. It might, first of all, be said, that there is a question of distributive justice in it. Does the right of the legislator extend to abridging the wages of the artisan, for the sake of adding to the profits of the artist? M. Lamartine said, "If you cease to support the theatre, where will you stop? Will you not necessarily be led to withdraw your support from your colleges, your museums, your institutes, and your libraries?" It might be answered, if you desire to support everything which is good and useful, where will you stop? Will you not necessarily be led to form a civil list for agriculture, industry, commerce, benevolence, education? Then, is it certain that government aid favours the progress of art?

This question is far from being settled, and we see very well that the theatres which prosper are those which depend upon their own resources. Moreover, if we come to higher considerations, we may observe, that wants and desires arise, the one from the other, and originate in regions which are more and more refined in proportion as the public wealth allows of their being satisfied; that Government ought not to take part in this correspondence, because in a certain condition of present fortune it could not by taxation stimulate the arts of necessity, without checking those of luxury, and thus interrupting the natural course of civilization. I may observe, that these artificial transpositions of wants, tastes, labour, and population, place the people in a precarious and dangerous position, without any solid basis.

These are some of the reasons alleged by the adversaries of State intervention in what concerns the order in which citizens think their wants and desires should be satisfied, and to which, consequently, their activity should be directed. I am, I confess, one of those who think that choice and impulse ought to come from below and not from above, from the citizen and not from the legislator; and the opposite doctrine appears to me to tend to the destruction of liberty and of human dignity.

1 According to the passage, the author believes that artistic institutions should

(A) find support from individuals rather than from the government
(B) merge with colleges and libraries
(C) try to increase profit for artists
(D) close so that citizens can focus on labour and industry
(E) renounce the opinions and preferences of moderate citizens

2 In paragraph 2, the author asks a series of hypothetical questions in order to

(A) propose that from an economic viewpoint, France would be better off if those individuals whose lives were devoted to art would focus their efforts on labour and industry
(B) show some of the arguments in favor of government support of the arts
(C) suggest reasons that France's artistic institutions are poorly regarded by the rest of Europe
(D) convince the reader that M. Lamartine should be named Minister of the Arts
(E) list the only artistic institutions he considered worthy of government support

3 Which of the following best expresses the author's tone in this passage?

(A) disinterested and confused
(B) passionate and inflammatory
(C) opinionated and obstinate
(D) annoyed and indignant
(E) contemplative and objective

4 In line 61, "checking" most nearly means

(A) evaluating
(B) boosting
(C) examining
(D) diminishing
(E) completing

5 The author uses the phrase "choice and impulse ought to come from below and not from above" (lines 75–76) to suggest that

(A) there should be a vote to determine which artistic institutions should receive government support
(B) eliminating government support for the arts will also eliminate the dignity and liberty of France's citizens
(C) support for the arts should come from individual citizens rather than from the government
(D) the government should tax the poor to support the arts
(E) if the government supports the arts, it will have to support many other worthy institutions as well

STOP

Turtle Sounds, 1986. David Dawangyumptewa (Hopi/United States). Watercolor, 23 x 30 in. Coconino Center for the Arts, Flagstaff, AZ.

UNIT SIX

The Americas

3000 B.C.–Present

Antigua América, novia sumergida, . . .
al salir del la selva hacia el alto vacío de los dioses . . .

Ancient America, bride in her veil of sea, . . .
from the jungle's edges to the rare height of gods . . .

—Pablo Neruda

The Land and Its People

The two connecting continents of North and South America stretch 11,000 miles from north to south, passing through many different climatic and ecological zones. The peoples of the Americas, isolated from the rest of the world, developed unique civilizations. Corn, domesticated in Mexico and Ecuador about 3500 B.C.*, allowed hunters and gatherers to settle into village life. About 1,000 years later, the domestication of the potato offered the same opportunity to the people of ancient Peru.*

America's first settlers arrived perhaps 30,000 years ago. They adapted to local conditions, from the icefields of northern Canada to the rain forests of Brazil. The Olmec, Maya, and Toltec civilizations of Mexico and Central America excelled in architecture, art, mathematics, and astronomy. The Aztecs in Mexico and the Incas in Peru built on these achievements and for a time controlled vast empires. Yet the Spanish conquistadors, aided by their superior technology and by the resentment of the conquered peoples of the empires, overthrew the Aztecs and Incas in a short time. Over the next centuries, the cultures of the colonizers influenced, and were influenced by, the indigenous cultures, producing a unique hybrid culture.

Ballplayer, Maya ceramic, A.D. 700–900.

Quechua woman with llamas, Cuzco, Peru.

Active Reading Strategies

Reading the Time Line

1. Around 2200 B.C., Ireland was at the beginning of the Bronze Age. About how many years later did South Americans begin working in gold?
2. When Spanish conquistador Hernan de Cortés defeated the Aztecs, about how many years had the Aztec city of Tenochtitlan been in existence? (See time line, page 1033.)

The Americas

- **c. 3000** First known pottery in America, in Ecuador
- **c. 2800** First farming villages in Amazon basin
- **c. 2500** Permanent villages forming in Mesoamerica
- **c. 2000** Inuit live in the Arctic
- **c. 1800** Ceremonial centers in Peru

3000 B.C. — **2250 B.C.** — **1500 B.C.**

World

- **c. 3000** Mesopotamians develop cuneiform writing
- **c. 2650** Step pyramid built at Saqqara, Egypt
- **c. 2500–1700** Indus Valley civilization thrives
- **c. 2200** Beginning of Bronze Age in Ireland
- **c. 1894–1595** First Babylonian Dynasty
- **c. 1600** Chinese develop bronze technology

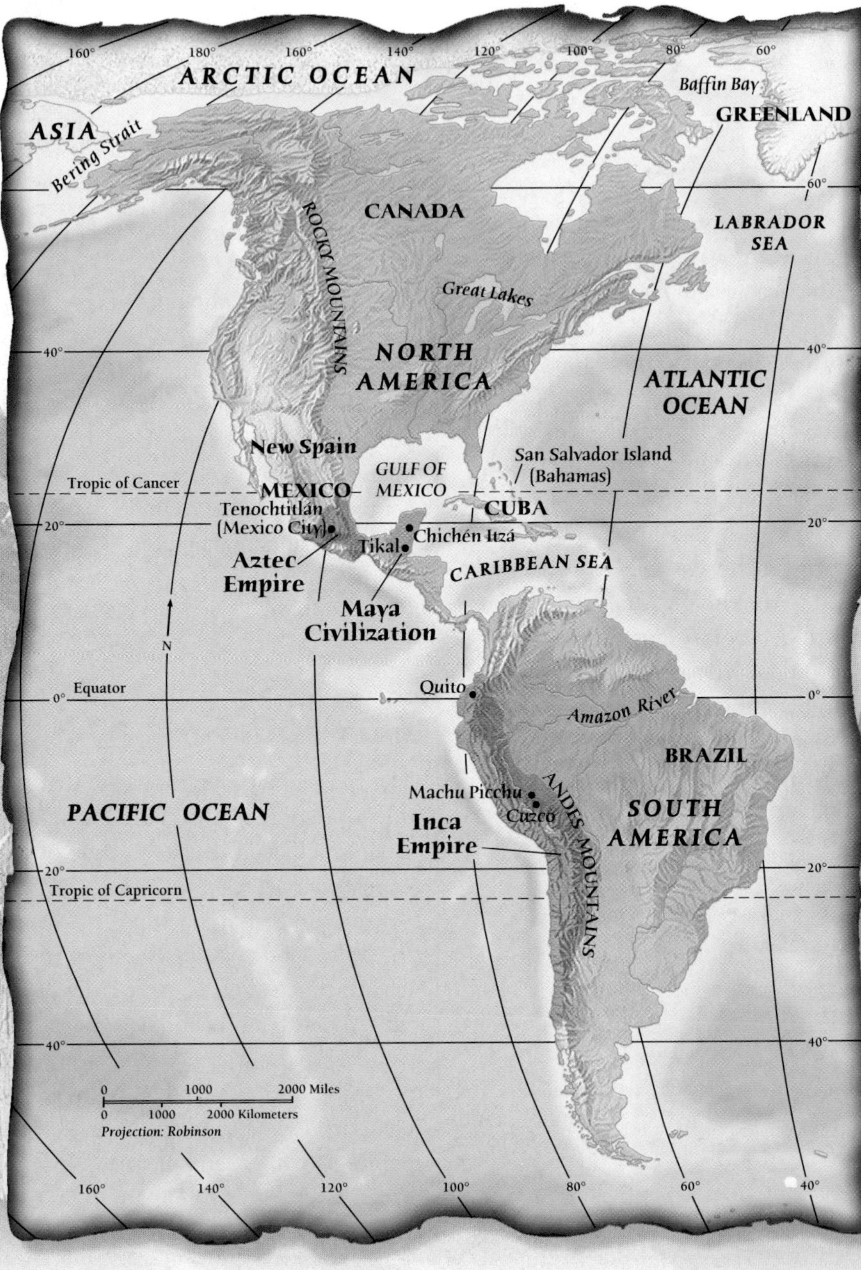

ARCTIC OCEAN
Baffin Bay
GREENLAND
ASIA
Bering Strait
CANADA
ROCKY MOUNTAINS
LABRADOR SEA
Great Lakes
NORTH AMERICA
ATLANTIC OCEAN
New Spain
GULF OF MEXICO
San Salvador Island (Bahamas)
Tropic of Cancer
MEXICO
Tenochtitlán (Mexico City)
CUBA
Chichén Itzá
Tikal
Aztec Empire
CARIBBEAN SEA
Maya Civilization
N
Equator
Quito
Amazon River
BRAZIL
Machu Picchu
Cuzco
ANDES MOUNTAINS
PACIFIC OCEAN
Inca Empire
SOUTH AMERICA
Tropic of Capricorn
0 1000 2000 Miles
0 1000 2000 Kilometers
Projection: Robinson
160° 180° 160° 140° 120° 100° 80° 60°
60° 40° 20° 0° 20° 40°
160° 140° 120° 100° 80° 60° 40°

c. 1200–400 Olmec civilization flourishes

c. 800–400 Chavín, first Andes civilization, at its peak

c. 750 First working in gold in South America

c. 200 B.C.–A.D. 1000 Arawak Indians reach West Indies from South America

c. 200 Hopewell period begins in North America

1500 B.C. — **750 B.C.** — **1 B.C.**

c. 1500 Iron Age begins in Asia Minor

c. 1100–900 First Chinese dictionary created

776 First Olympic games, Greece

586 Babylonians destroy Jerusalem and exile Jews

c. 563 Siddhartha Gautama, founder of Buddhism, is born

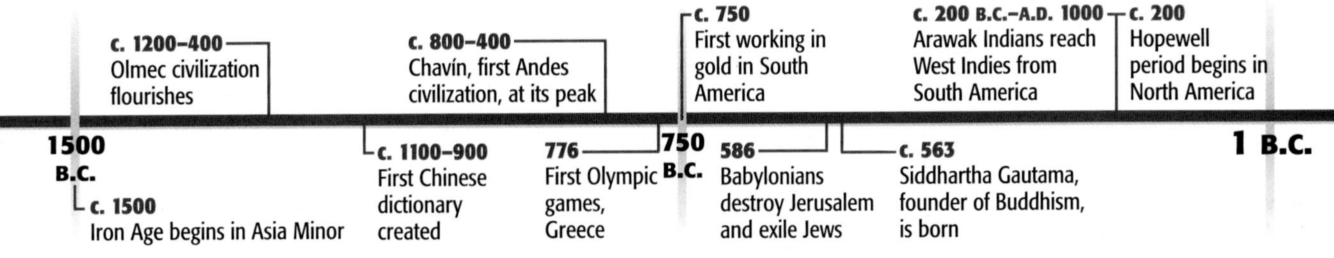

How People Lived

Hunters and Farmers

The oldest and the most widespread lifestyle found among the native Americans was that of nomadic hunters. In North America, groups moved with the seasons, following bison or caribou, or traveling to lake areas to trap migrating ducks and geese. In the winter, people lived on dried food. Along the northwest coast, where fish were abundant, people were able to establish permanent settlements, leading to the striking artistic achievements of such groups as the Haida and Tlingit.

The domestication of such vegetables as corn, squash, and beans led to the rise of farming-based societies. With the growth of farming, more groups established permanent towns and villages—although hunting remained an important food resource for most groups. Permanent homes and a more secure food supply allowed peoples such as the Natchez to develop complex societies and artistic forms.

Olmec colossal head, Jalapa, Mexico.

The arrival of the Europeans had a major effect on the cultures of the earlier settlers. The reintroduction of the horse—exterminated by early American hunters—revolutionized transportation. The production of furs and other raw materials expanded, as people sought items to trade for European manufactured goods.

Lakota Plains dress.

City Builders

The Maya, Aztec, and Inca are the best known of the urban-oriented civilizations of early America. Other groups included the Olmec, the Toltec, and the Zapotec.

Cities such as Tenochtitlan of the Aztec, Tikal of the Maya, and Cuzco of the Inca rivaled the size and magnificence of other great cities of the world in their time. Their temples and palaces are still among the wonders of the world. Supported by a stable food supply and the tribute paid by conquered peoples, a complex social structure—controlled by priests and nobles—evolved, and produced great works of art. Rulers encouraged foreign trade, and merchants traveled far afield in search of gold and precious stones.

The Americas

- **c. 1** Moche pyramids constructed, Peru
- **c. 150** Pyramid of the Sun constructed at Teotihuacán, Mexico
- **c. 600–900** Maya civilization at its peak in Central America
- **700** First Pueblo period starts in southwestern North America
- **750** Teotihuacán abandoned

1 A.D. — 450 — 900

World

- **312** Christianity legalized in Roman Empire
- **476** Last Roman Emperor in the west deposed
- **c. 610** Muhammad, founder of Islam, begins preaching
- **711** Islamic armies invade Spain

What People Believed

Divine Beings and Human Sacrifice

The people of the early Americas had a number of different belief systems, but they shared common factors. Often a group believed that one deity had created the earth and all its inhabitants but was not involved in everyday life.

In Central America, the Aztecs' need for religious sacrificial victims, and in South America, the Incas' ever increasing need for more territory, kept their large armies constantly at war. Some common characteristics of these and other Central and South American religions include the following:

- The central role of priests, who acted as intermediaries between the people and their gods
- Blood sacrifice, carried the furthest in the Aztec culture
- Worship of many gods and goddesses who represented natural forces and elements, such as the sun, moon, rain, and corn
- Construction of imposing temples
- An elaborate ceremonial year, marked by many processions and rituals

Totem pole, Sitka, Alaska.

Carmel Mission, Carmel, California.

The Merging of Traditions

Although the Europeans converted many Indians to Christianity, elements of ancient practices have survived, notably among the Maya Indians of Guatemala. There, Catholic practices took the place of many features of pre-Columbian religions: large churches on the town square replaced earlier temples, images of Catholic saints replaced representations of the ancient gods and goddesses, and the cross took the place of the ancient Maya World Tree.

Such survivals are found in many areas. According to legend, Our Lady of Guadalupe, the patron saint of Mexico, first appeared to an Aztec Indian in 1531. Elements of pre-Columbian earth and moon worship have been incorporated into the festivities and pilgrimages honoring her.

900 — 1350 — 1800

- **c. 1000** Leif Ericson leads first European landing in North America
- **1099** Crusaders capture Jerusalem
- **1215** English barons force king to sign the Magna Carta
- **1279** Mongols begin rule over China
- **c. 1325–1350** Aztecs found Tenochtitlan (now Mexico City)
- **1492** Christopher Columbus reaches America
- **1497–1498** Vasco da Gama sails around Africa on way to India
- **1521** Spanish conquistador Hernan de Cortés defeats the Aztecs
- **1653** Shah Jahan completes Taj Mahal

Arts and Entertainment

Pottery and Ceramics

The tradition of pottery-making in the Americas is over 5,000 years old; the earliest known examples, from Ecuador, have been dated to about 3200 B.C. Most pottery was made by the coil method and was shaped into bowls, vases, and spouted jars. The Moche culture, which flourished on the north coast of Peru from the first to the ninth centuries, excelled at making vessels in the shape of animals and human heads. These portrait jars, some of them depictions of Moche rulers, were executed with exceptional naturalism and skill.

Moche vase, 7th century. Lima, Peru.

Architecture

Ceremonial pyramids topped by temples were constructed throughout Central and South America. Some of the most elaborate were constructed by the Maya, who must be ranked among history's greatest builders. The Maya had little technology—they built their cities using only stone and bone tools—but they had great ingenuity. Many Maya temples were built on top of artifical mounds. Each building consisted of three parts: a massive base, a series of terraces or stairs, and a temple on top, usually single-storied. In later years, sometimes a palace occupied the place of the temple. The entire building was covered with white stucco and then brilliantly decorated. Often the interior was painted with frescoes.

Along the Arctic coast, the Inuit developed a perfectly-designed shelter, the igloo, using nothing more than snow and ice. In the Andes mountains, the Incas built entire cities from huge blocks of granite, putting the stones together so skillfully that a knife blade will not fit between them.

Critical Thinking

Connecting Cultures

1. Create a list of some of the main purposes behind architecture of the early Americas.
2. What main purposes does architecture serve in the United States today? Share your ideas in a group discussion.

Reclining Chac-Mool figure and Kukulcan Pyramid at Chichen Itza, Yucatan.

Viewing the glyphs: Besides using the alphabetic system shown on the opposite page, the Maya combined symbols in a number of ways. These characters illustrate five different ways to write the Maya word for "jaguar." Why do you think it took investigators such a long time to realize that these symbols made up a writing system?

modern Mayan language. But in 1952, a Russian scholar named Yuri Knorosov, who had never even seen a Maya ruin, showed that Maya writing reflects spoken language. Using Landa's "alphabet" and modern Mayan dictionaries, Knorosov showed that the Maya script consists of both symbols that express ideas and symbols that express sounds.

The ancient scribes organized the glyphs into blocks placed in horizontal and vertical rows. In each block, they wrote one or more glyphs. As the example above shows, a block might include a logogram (a glyph that represents a whole word), a logogram combined with phonetic signs (signs representing the sounds of syllables), or just phonetic signs.

Since Knorosov's discovery, scholars have unlocked the meaning of many more glyphs. In so doing, they have disproved the belief that the glyphs primarily record astronomical and mythological events. Many actually describe the history of the Maya kings—their birth, accession to the throne, marriages, children, military conquests, participation in bloodletting rites and human sacrifice, and deaths. This new information shattered the long-cherished view of the ancient Maya as a peaceful, star-gazing people. They were, we now know, constantly at war and capable of great cruelty toward their enemies. Yet they also developed a very rich and sophisticated culture.

Deciphering Other Ancient Scripts

Maya hieroglyphic writing is not the only ancient script that long eluded scholars. Egyptian hieroglyphic writing—a complex script with many similarities to Maya writing—also proved difficult to crack. As ancient Egyptian culture died out, and with it knowledge of Egyptian writing (the last example of ancient Egyptian writing is from A.D. 394), people began entertaining the mistaken notion that it was picture writing. This belief persisted until 1822, when a young Frenchman named Jean François Champollion proved the glyphs are largely phonetic, or based on the sounds of the spoken language. In so doing, he paved the way for the breaking of other early scripts, which scholars now realize all have phonetic components.

RESPOND

1. What steps might you take in trying to figure out an inscription in an unknown language?
2. What is your impression of the glyphs used to spell the word *jaguar?* What, in your opinion, are the strengths and drawbacks of each type of glyph?
3. Compare Maya hieroglyphic writing with Egyptian writing. Which script do you think would be the most difficult to decipher? Why?

Before You Read

from the Popol Vuh

Reading Focus

What stories have you heard about the creation of human beings?

Share Ideas In a small group, discuss how these stories reflect religious or cultural beliefs.

Setting a Purpose Read the following selection to enjoy a creation myth of the Maya.

Building Background

Popol Vuh

The Popol Vuh (pō pəl vu′), or "Council Book," is an important source of information about the history and culture of the ancient Maya. It was written in Quiché (kē chā′), a language spoken by a group of Maya living in Guatemala. The Quiché people believed that the Popol Vuh made it possible for their leaders to see into the future. The book contains stories about mythological heroes and an account of how the gods created humans. It also relates the history of the Quiché up to the Spanish conquest, around 1550.

We are fortunate that the Popol Vuh has survived. Christian missionaries burned almost all of the Maya hieroglyphic books, but some Christian-trained Maya wrote down the Popol Vuh in the Roman alphabet to preserve part of their traditional culture. Around 1700 a friar named Francisco Ximénez copied their version and translated it into Spanish. All modern editions of the Popol Vuh are based on his copy.

The Ancient Maya

The Maya created one of the most advanced societies of pre-Columbian America. At the height of their power, they occupied more than forty cities in southern Mexico, Guatemala, and northern Belize. Their civilization was at its peak between A.D. 250 and 900. Working with stone tools, they built pyramids, temples, and palaces. These structures were ornamented with carvings and hieroglyphic writing. In addition to their art and architecture, the Maya were experts in astronomy and mathematics.

Rollout of Mayan Cylindrical Vase. c. A.D. 700–900, Maya culture. Vase height: 20 cm. Private collection.

Vocabulary Preview

conceive (kən sēv′) *v.* to cause to begin; to originate; p. 1041
warble (wôr′ bəl) *v.* to sing with rapid variations, or changes, in pitch; p. 1042
immobile (i mō′ bil) *adj.* incapable of movement, motionless; p. 1042
sustain (sə stān′) *v.* to perform actions that keep something in existence; p. 1042

from the

Popol Vuh

Creation Hymn

Translated by Ralph Nelson

BEFORE THE WORLD WAS CREATED, Calm and Silence were the great kings that ruled. Nothing existed, there was nothing. Things had not yet been drawn together, the face of the earth was unseen. There was only motionless sea, and a great emptiness of sky. There were no men anywhere, or animals, no birds or fish, no crabs. Trees, stones, caves, grass, forests, none of these existed yet. There was nothing that could roar or run, nothing that could tremble or cry in the air. Flatness and emptiness, only the sea, alone and breathless. It was night; silence stood in the dark.

In this darkness the Creators waited, the Maker, Tepeu, Gucumatz, the Forefathers.[1] They were there in this emptiness, hidden under green and blue feathers, alone and surrounded with light. They are the same as wisdom. They are the ones who can conceive and bring forth a child from nothingness. And the time had come. The Creators were bent deep around talk in the darkness. They argued, worried, sighed over what was to be. They planned the growth of the thickets, how things would crawl and jump, the birth of man. They planned the whole creation, arguing each point until their words and thoughts crystallized and became the same thing. Heart of Heaven was there, and in the darkness the creation was planned.

Then let the emptiness fill! they said. Let the water weave its way downward so the earth can show its face! Let the light break on the ridges, let the sky fill up with the yellow light of dawn! Let our glory be a man walking on a path through the trees! "Earth!" the Creators called. They called only once, and it was there, from a mist, from a cloud of dust, the mountains appeared instantly. At this single word the groves of cypresses and pines sent out shoots, rivulets ran freely between the round hills. The Creators were struck by the beauty and exclaimed, "It will be a creation that will mount the darkness!"

The Creators then asked, "Will this silence reign under the trees forever?" Suddenly there were the Guardians of the Woods, the small animals, the little mensprites[2] of the mountains, deer, birds, jaguars, snakes, Guardians of the Thickets. Then the Creators gave these creatures homes: "You, deer, you will walk on all fours among greenness, and sleep in the

1. The reference to the *Maker . . . Forefathers,* in Maya mythology, concerns the deities who created life on Earth.

2. *Mensprites* (men′ sprīts′) are small, often mischievous, supernatural beings similar to elves.

Vocabulary

conceive (kən sēv′) *v.* to cause to begin; to originate fields on the shoulders of the rivers, or in the cover of ravines. Keep company with the thicket and the pasture, but go to the woods to mate. You, birds, take the air. Go live in the trees and vines, make nests there and mate there, fill the air with your children. They spoke to each creature in turn, assigning each a place, and the birds and animals, snakes and jaguars, went looking for their nests and homes.

With their places established, the Forefathers asked them to speak. "Cry, warble, call!" the Creators told them. "Each of you in your own language. Speak to us!" But a great din arose from their throats. "No!" cried the Creators, "Call our names, raise our names with your voices, Huracan, Chipi-Caculha, Raxa-Caculha, Heart of Heaven, Heart of Earth, Creator, Maker, Forefathers,[3] let your praise fall like rain!" But the birds and animals could not speak like men. The noise only rose in pitch. They could only scream and hiss and cackle. The birds and animals were deaf to each other's words, they were mute in the name of the Creators. When the Creators saw this, they knew that something must be done. They spoke to the jaguar and the turkey and the others, and said, "We have changed our minds. Because you cannot talk, you shall be destroyed. You may keep your places, your nests in the trees, your homes by the rivers, but since you cannot call our names, we will create more obedient creatures who will. Your destiny has been changed: your flesh will be torn." The animals of the earth were sacrificed, condemned to be killed and eaten.

"We need to try again! Dawn draws near!" And the Creators tried again, using clay to make man's flesh. But instantly they saw that it would come to nothing. It was a soft thing, it melted away. Immobile, without strength, it could not even turn its head to look behind. Its vision was runny, it spoke with a mind of mud. It melted into the water. The Creators knew that these creatures would never have sons, and their destruction was as quick as their creation.

Young Maize God. c. A.D. 775, Maya culture. Copan Temple 22, Honduras. Stone. British Museum, London.

"But what can we do?" they cried. "Who will worship and sustain us?" Again they bent their heads together. At last they decided to go to the soothsayers, the Grandparents of the Day and the Dawn. The old man was the one who could tell the future by throwing beans. The old woman was divine, a priestess and sorceress. They talked also with the Master of Emeralds, the sculptor who carves beautiful jewelry and gourds. The Creators asked them about making men out of wood. "What do you think?" they asked, "will men of wood worship us? Throw your red beans,

3. *Huracan . . . Forefathers* are all Maya deities.

Vocabulary

warble (wôr′ bəl) *v.* to sing with rapid variations, or changes, in pitch
immobile (i mō′ bil) *adj.* incapable of movement, motionless
sustain (sə stān′) *v.* to perform actions that keep something in existence

decide if we should make men by carving their eyes and mouth on a stick of wood."

The soothsayers squatted down and threw the beans and grains of corn. "Fate! Creature!" the old man and woman called, "Get together, beans, lock each other in your arms, speak to us! Tell us if the Creators should carve the wood. Tell us if men carved of sticks will worship and sustain us when the light comes. Beans, fate, creature! Come together, take each other! Heart of Heaven, let the truth be spoken!" Everything then stopped. The corn lay quiet with their message, the soothsayers squatted unmoving. Then the old ones spoke: "The voices of the wooden men shall echo across the earth!"

Instantly, the wooden figures were made. They were slender and looked like men. They cooked and washed in the river, they hunted in the forest with their dogs, they brought down the trees to plant corn. They had sons and daughters, and soon were everywhere on the earth. But the men of wood did not have souls or minds, and they wandered aimlessly. When they spoke, their faces were blank, their hands and feet were weak. They were without blood's flower, no moisture, no flesh, dry and yellow, and they no longer remembered Heart of Heaven. And since those who had made them and cared for them did not enter their thoughts, they were reduced to splinters. First, a flood was loosed on the wooden men by Heart of Heaven, a heavy resin[4] fell from the sky. The eagle flashed down out of the heavens to gouge out their eyes, the vampire bat winged in to claim their heads, the tapir[5] came to break and mangle their bones, and the jaguar, always waiting, took his chance. Heart of Heaven was not remembered, and the face of the earth was darkened; black rain fell day and night.

Then everything began to rise up against the wooden men. Sticks, pots and pans, large and small animals, everything. "You have eaten us, and now we shall eat you," said the birds and the dogs that were kept to be eaten.

The grinding stones spoke in rage: "What torture you caused us! Crush, crush, dawn and dusk our faces went crush, crush, crush! Now you are not men, it's our turn to grind you."

The hunting dogs spoke: "We hunted for you and guarded your house, but did you feed us? Did you think that we liked staying out in the rain? You were too busy for us, and kept a stick ready in case we came near your food. Why didn't you think about your future? But it's too late now, because the sticks are going to be between our teeth!" The dogs leaped on the stick men, knocking them down, tearing their faces.

The griddles and pots attacked them: "Oh, the pain and suffering you have caused us! Our mouths blackened with soot, our faces blackened. Every day you threw us on the fire as if we felt no pain! Now you shall feel the same burning!"

The wooden men were trapped. The firestones hurled themselves at the wooden men that ran past them, crashing into their heads. Splintering and burning, shrinking from blows, scurrying and falling, they ran looking for safety. Some climbed to the tops of the houses, but the houses tossed them from their backs. Some tried to climb trees; the trees threw them down. The caverns closed their mouths to those who tried to enter, and the wooden men were destroyed. Only a few, with mouths and faces mangled, escaped the spears of water and the splintering blows. Most of them became monkeys.

4. *Resin* (rez′ in) is the yellow or brown sticky substance secreted by certain trees.

5. The *tapir* (tā′ pər) is a hoofed, plant-eating mammal. Tapirs are native to the tropics of southeastern Asia and the Americas. Though pig-like in appearance, tapirs are related to horses.

Responding to Literature

Personal Response

What thoughts went through your mind as you finished reading this selection? Jot down a response in your journal.

Analyzing Literature

Recall and Interpret

1. How do the Creators fill the emptiness and silence of the world?
2. Why do the Creators need human beings?
3. What happens when the Creators first attempt to make human beings from clay?
4. In what ways are the wooden humans superior to the clay humans? What are their shortcomings?
5. Why do the Creators destroy the wooden humans?

Evaluate and Connect

6. **Imagery** is language that appeals to the senses (see page R6). Provide examples of imagery that appeals to the senses of sight, hearing, and touch.
7. In your opinion, do the Creators behave cruelly toward the wooden humans? Explain.
8. Which incident in this selection surprised you the most? Why?
9. What might this selection reveal about the moral values of the Maya?
10. In the Reading Focus on page 1040, you were asked to discuss stories you have heard about the creation of humans. Compare this selection with one of those stories.

Literary Criticism

Scholar Ralph Nelson points out that while many Western cultures have long held the belief that the natural world can be understood only through "objectification," or a "stepping back," the ancient Maya held a very different belief. On the basis of this selection from the Popol Vuh, how would you say the Maya viewed nature and humankind's place in it? Share your ideas in a discussion with your classmates.

Literary ELEMENTS

Myth

A **myth** is a traditional story that explains some aspect of human society or the natural world. Myths reflect the religious beliefs of a particular people. They often depict the actions of gods and heroes. Creation myths, such as the one in this selection from the Popol Vuh, explain the origin of the world and its inhabitants.

1. What aspect of the natural world is explained at the end of this selection?
2. What part of the creation story remains unresolved by the end of this selection?

- See **Literary Terms Handbook,** p. R8.

Extending Your Response

Creative Writing

Dialogue When the Creators are unsure about how to create humans, the aged soothsayers assure them that "The voices of the wooden men shall echo across the earth!" Write a dialogue between the Creators and the soothsayers after the wooden men turn out to be failures. How might the soothsayers try to defend their prophesy?

Performing

Puppet Show With a small group, perform a puppet show based on one of the episodes in this selection. For example, you might perform the scene where the Creators visit the soothsayers. You might model your puppets in the style of the Maya art that you see in this part.

Save your work for your portfolio.

MEDIA connection

Newspaper Article

Cracking the code of Maya writing changed many assumptions about Maya civilization. This newspaper article shows that theories about the earliest writing system may need to be changed too.

Egypt discovery may be earliest proof of writing

by Vijay Joshi—Associated Press, December 15, 1998

CAIRO–Clay tablets uncovered in southern Egypt from the tomb of a king named Scorpion may represent the earliest known writing by humankind, an archaeologist said Tuesday.

If confirmed, the discovery would rank among the greatest ever in the search for the origins of the written word.

Gunter Dreyer, head of the German Archaeological Institute, said the tablets record linen and oil deliveries made about 5,300 years ago as tithe to King Scorpion I.

He said that the tablets have been carbon-dated with certainty to between 3300 B.C. and 3200 B.C.

The discovery throws open for debate a widely held belief among historians that the first people to write were the Sumerians of the Mesopotamian civilization sometime before 3000 B.C. The exact date of Sumerian writing remains in doubt.

The Egyptian writings—in the form of line drawings

of animals, plants, and mountains—are the first evidence that hieroglyphics developed gradually.

Since 1985, Dreyer and his team have unearthed about 300 pieces of written material on clay tablets barely bigger than postage stamps and clay jars and vases with ink impressions.

Two-thirds of the tablets have been deciphered as accounts of linen and oil delivered to King Scorpion as taxes, short notes, numbers, lists of kings' names, and names of institutions.

Although the records are made up of symbols, they are considered true writing because each symbol stands for a consonant and makes up syllables. For example, the city named Ba-set was written by putting together a throne, known as "ba," and a stork, "set."

Apart from the academic question of who wrote first, Dreyer said, the writings prove that early Egyptian society was much more developed than previously thought.

Analyzing Media

1. How long ago were these newly discovered writings made? How big are the tablets on which the writing appears?
2. What does this latest discovery of ancient writing suggest to you about the history of human beings? Do you think hieroglyphics could be used as a writing system today? Explain.

The Coyote

As you will learn in reading "Coyote Finishes His Work" and "That Place Where Ghosts of Salmon Jump," Coyote plays many different roles in Native American mythology and folklore. Whether creator, teacher, hero, or trickster, Coyote is celebrated in a great number of stories throughout Native American oral tradition. In these stories, Coyote exhibits a variety of traits (foolishness, cleverness, playfulness, wisdom, strength, resourcefulness) all of which Coyote uses—sometimes accidentally—to "set the world right."

In the natural world, the coyote is a member of *Canidae*, or the dog family, and is also called prairie wolf, brush wolf, or little wolf. The name *coyote* comes from the Aztec word *coyotl*. Found from Alaska to Costa Rica, the coyote especially thrives on the North American plains. During the twentieth century, the coyote expanded its range—replacing the wolf—to include parts of the eastern United States, including New England. Weighing twenty to fifty pounds, the coyote is about the size of a medium-sized collie dog. One of its distinguishing features is its tail, carried straight out behind. Smaller than the wolf, it requires less food and can hide more easily.

Generally a nocturnal animal, the coyote scavenges and hunts alone or in relays with other coyotes. They run on their toes and for long distances to catch rodents, rabbits, and other prey. Their slight build helps them reach speeds of up to forty miles per hour. At night, the coyote also performs a serenade composed of mournful howls and short yaps. To those unaccustomed to its sound, the coyote's howl is eerie and frightening, but to farmers it is simply annoying. Farmers consider coyotes to be pests because they sometimes kill livestock and destroy crops—coyotes seem to enjoy watermelon almost as much as humans do!

Coyotes live in burrows and sometimes mate for life. Their pups are generally born in litters of six or more in the spring; both parents care for the pups until the fall. As they grow, the pups' buff and white fur will become long and coarse. The fur on their legs will be more reddish in color, and their black-tipped tails will get bushy. Other species related to the coyote are the jackal, the gray wolf, and the red wolf.

Activity

Find out more about the habitat and habits of the coyote. Find information about the impact of the human population on the habitats of the coyote. Create a collage that combines the different kinds of information that you gather. Display your collage in the classroom.

Before You Read

Coyote Finishes His Work

Reading Focus

What qualities do you associate with the coyote?

Word Web With a small group, fill in a word web such as the one below. Discuss how you formed this impression of coyotes.

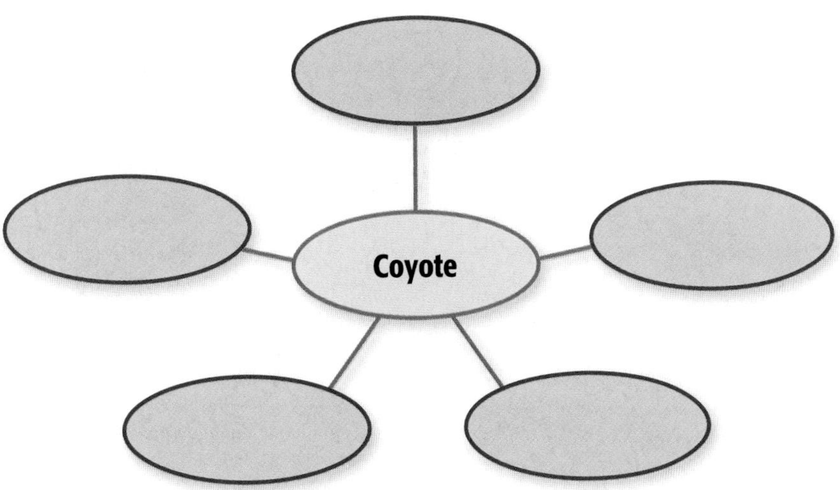

Setting a Purpose Read this tale for a portrait of a trickster called Coyote.

Building Background

Native American Religion

In traditional Native American communities, there is often no sharp distinction between the spiritual and the secular. Folktales are often told for entertainment, but they also communicate religious meaning. Even the most routine activities—putting on shoes, for example—may be accompanied by prayers or ceremonies.

Native American religion has always been extremely diverse, with each community maintaining its own set of beliefs and rituals. Yet some basic religious concepts are widely shared. The supernatural world is generally thought to include many different gods and spirits. They are led by a supreme being, usually a sky god. Other supernatural beings are associated with the earth, wind, plants, animals, and specific locations such as mountains and streams. In addition to religious ceremonies and prayers, visions offer a means for humans to interact with the spirit world.

The Coyote Trickster

Native American folklore is full of animal and human tricksters. The most familiar one is called Coyote. His character varies from story to story. At times extremely clever, he can also be a clown. He never shows concern for others, yet his selfish actions often end up benefiting them. Some creation myths give him a prominent role because his disruptive behavior helps transform the world into its present state.

Reading Further

If you enjoy "Coyote Finishes His Work," you might want to read the following:

"Glooscap and the Baby," "The Spirit Wife," "The End of the World," and "Deer Hunter and White Corn Maiden" from *Favorite Folktales from Around the World,* edited by Jane Yolen.

Coyote Finishes His Work

Retold by Barry Lopez

Brush Poppers, 1984. Jaune Quick-to-See Smith (Flathead/Shoshone/Cree/United States). Pastel on paper, 30 x 22 in. Marilyn Butler Gallery, Santa Fe, NM.

FROM THE VERY BEGINNING, COYOTE was traveling around all over the earth. He did many wonderful things when he went along. He killed the monsters and the evil spirits that preyed on the people. He made the Indians, and put them out in tribes all over the world because Old Man Above wanted the earth to be inhabited all over, not just in one or two places.

He gave all the people different names and taught them different languages. This is why Indians live all over the country now and speak in different ways.

He taught the people how to eat and how to hunt the buffalo and catch eagles. He taught them what roots to eat and how to make a good lodge and what to wear. He taught them how to dance. Sometimes he made mistakes, and even though he was wise and powerful, he did many foolish things. But that was his way.

Coyote liked to play tricks. He thought about himself all the time, and told everyone he was a great warrior, but he was not. Sometimes he would go too far with some trick and get someone killed. Other times, he would have a trick played on himself by someone else. He got killed this way so many times that Fox and the birds got tired of bringing him back to life. Another way he got in trouble was trying to do what someone else did. This is how he came to be called Imitator.

Coyote was ugly too. The girls did not like him. But he was smart. He could change himself around and trick the women. Coyote got the girls when he wanted.

One time, Coyote had done everything he could think of and was traveling from one place to another place, looking for other things that needed to be done. Old Man saw him going along and said to himself, "Coyote has now done almost everything he is capable of doing. His work is almost done. It is time to bring him back to the place where he started."

So Great Spirit[1] came down and traveled in the shape of an old man. He met Coyote.

1. *Great Spirit* is the creator; in this case, it is Old Man Above.

Coyote said, "I am Coyote. Who are you?"

Old Man said, "I am Chief of the earth. It was I who sent you to set the world right."

"No," Coyote said, "you never sent me. I don't know you. If you are the Chief, take that lake over there and move it to the side of that mountain."

"No. If you are Coyote, let me see you do it."

Coyote did it.

"Now, move it back."

Coyote tried, but he could not do it. He thought this was strange. He tried again, but he could not do it.

Chief moved the lake back.

Coyote said, "Now I know you are the Chief."

Old Man said, "Your work is finished, Coyote. You have traveled far and done much good. Now you will go to where I have prepared a home for you."

Then Coyote disappeared. Now no one knows where he is anymore.

Old Man got ready to leave, too. He said to the Indians, "I will send messages to the earth by the spirits of the people who reach me but whose time to die has not yet come. They will carry messages to you from time to time. When their spirits come back into their bodies, they will revive and tell you their experiences.

"Coyote and myself, we will not be seen again until Earth-woman[2] is very old. Then we shall return to earth, for it will require a change by that time. Coyote will come along first, and when you see him you will know I am coming. When I come along, all the spirits of the dead will be with me. There will be no more Other Side Camp.[3] All the people will live together. Earth-mother will go back to her first shape and live as a mother among her children. Then things will be made right."

Now they are waiting for Coyote.

2. *Earth-woman* is Earth personified as a woman and, figuratively, the mother of all people.
3. *Other Side Camp* is a place where the spirits of the dead reside.

Responding to Literature

Personal Response

Which details or incidents in this story did you find most interesting? Explain why in your journal.

Analyzing Literature

Recall and Interpret

1. What are some of the wonderful things that Coyote has accomplished in his travels?
2. In what ways was Coyote foolish? On whom did he depend to rescue him when his foolishness went too far?
3. Why does Old Man finally make the decision to send Coyote away from the world?
4. According to this story, how will the world be different when Old Man returns?

Evaluate and Connect

5. To what extent, do you think, does the Old Man seem to guide Coyote's actions?
6. **Myths** often suggest the values that are important to a people (see **Literary Terms Handbook,** page R8). What values held by Native Americans can you infer from this myth?
7. In the Reading Focus on page 1047, you were asked which qualities you associate with the coyote. Compare your response with the qualities that Coyote displays in this myth.
8. What other story that you have read does this myth most remind you of? Explain why.

Literary ELEMENTS

Trickster Figures

Every folklore tradition has its **trickster figures.** They represent that part of human nature that wants to break rules and stir up trouble. Tricksters try to outwit people, animals, and even gods. Although they are generally self-centered, we may admire them for their cunning and ability to overcome obstacles. Tricksters do not always get what they want; in many tales, their greed makes it easy for them to be tricked by others.

1. Do you admire Coyote for his trickery? Why or why not?
2. Overall, do you think Coyote is a force for good or evil?

- See **Literary Terms Handbook,** p. R13.

Extending Your Response

Creative Writing

Trickster Tale Write a brief folktale of your own in which a trickster figure serves as the main character. You may wish to use a character you have read about, such as Coyote. If you wish, you may make up your own trickster figure. When you are finished, read the tale aloud in a small group.

Interdisciplinary Activity

Art: Cartoon Create a cartoon of three or four panels that illustrates one of the incidents in "Coyote Finishes His Work." If possible, use dialogue from the selection in your cartoon. Before you begin, you might wish to look at cartoon strips in a newspaper to see the different ways in which artists draw animal figures.

Save your work for your portfolio.

Before You Read

UNITED STATES, 1996

That Place Where Ghosts of Salmon Jump

Meet Sherman Alexie

"Imagination is the only weapon on the reservation."

Sherman Alexie, a Spokane/Coeur d'Alene Indian, grew up on the Spokane Indian Reservation. Alexie took refuge from a difficult family life in books; by the fifth grade he had read every volume in his school library. He began to write poems and stories while attending Washington State University.

Most of Alexie's work is set on the reservation. He writes about Indians (he prefers this term to Native Americans) with understanding, affection, and a sense of humor. Alexie's published work includes *The Summer of Black Widows* (poetry), *The Lone Ranger and Tonto Fistfight in Heaven* (short stories), and *Smoke Signals* (a screenplay). Critics have praised his ability to merge the mythical past with the present. Alexie loves to puncture stereotypes: "I want to change the world. For one minute, for an hour, forever . . . I want to write books and make films that will change the world's perception of Indians."

Sherman Alexie was born in 1966.

Reading Focus

How can anger be put to good use?

Quickwrite Jot down a response to this question in your journal.

Setting a Purpose Read this poem to see how Coyote and the speaker deal with their anger.

Building Background

The Spokane Falls

For thousands of years, the Spokane and other native peoples lived along the Spokane River and its falls, which they considered sacred. They depended on the river's enormous salmon population for food. Late in the nineteenth century, the U.S. government removed the Spokane to a reservation about sixty miles from the falls. Dams were built on the river to generate electricity. Soon a railroad yard, sawmills, and factories sprang up around the falls, creating heavy pollution that killed off the salmon. In the 1960s, the city of Spokane began taking steps to clean up the river. City officials reclaimed industrial land near the falls and converted it into a park. Their efforts have helped restore some of the river's beauty.

Spokane Indians at the Spokane River, photographed by Edward S. Curtis, c. 1910.

That Place Where Ghosts of Salmon Jump

Sherman Alexie

Coyote was alone and angry because he could not find love.
Coyote was alone and angry because he demanded a wife

from the Spokane, the Coeur d'Alene, the Palouse, all those tribes
camped on the edge of the Spokane River, and received only laughter.

So Coyote rose up with his powerful and senseless magic
and smashed a paw across the water, which broke the river bottom

in two, which created rain that lasted for forty days and nights,
which created Spokane Falls, that place where salmon traveled

more suddenly than Coyote imagined, that place where salmon swam
larger than any white man dreamed. Coyote, I know you broke

the river because of love, and pretended it was all done by your design.
Coyote, you're a liar and I don't trust you. I never have

but I do trust all the stories the grandmothers told me.
They said the Falls were built because of your unrequited love

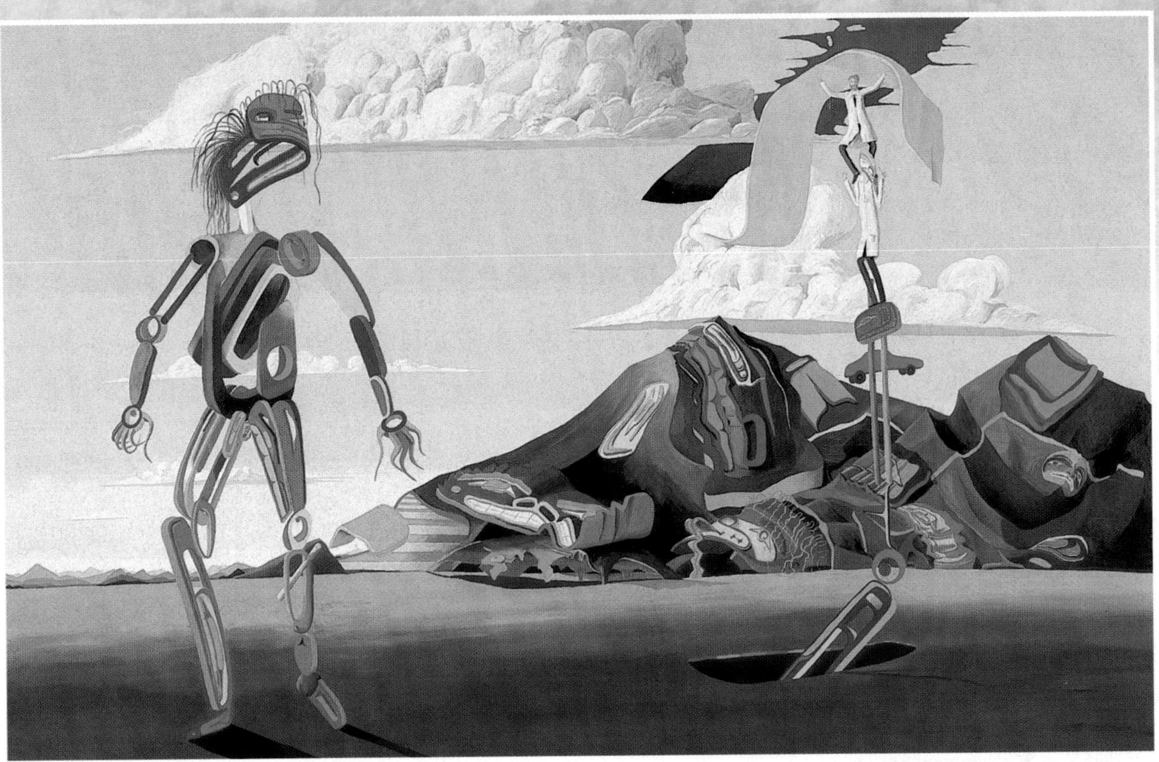

Red Man Watching White Man Trying to Fix Hole in Sky, 1990. Laurence Paul (Coast Salish/Okanagan/Canada). Acrylic on canvas, 142.24 x 226.06 cm. Canadian Museum of Civilization, Hull, Quebec, Canada.

and I can understand that rage, Coyote. We can all understand
but look at the Falls now and tell me what you see. Look

at the Falls now, if you can see beyond all of the concrete
the white man has built here. Look at all of this

and tell me that concrete ever equals love. Coyote,
these white men sometimes forget to love their own mothers

so how could they love this river which gave birth
to a thousand lifetimes of salmon? How could they love

these Falls, which have fallen farther, which sit dry
and quiet as a graveyard now? These Falls are that place

where ghosts of salmon jump, where ghosts of women mourn
their children who will never find their way back home,

where I stand now and search for any kind of love,
where I sing softly, under my breath, alone and angry.

Responding to Literature

Personal Response

What thoughts did you have while reading this poem? Share your response with a classmate.

Analyzing Literature

Recall and Interpret

1. Why was it that Coyote "smashed a paw across the water"?
2. Why might Coyote have pretended that he created the Spokane Falls on purpose?
3. How does the speaker feel about Coyote?
4. According to the speaker, what effect has the building of dams had on the Falls?
5. Whom, do you think, is the speaker referring to in line 26 when he speaks of the "children who will never find their way back home"?

Evaluate and Connect

6. The speaker says that he understands Coyote's rage. Do you understand the feelings that the speaker expresses? Why or why not?
7. A **symbol** is an object or action that stands for something else in addition to itself (see **Literary Terms Handbook,** page R12). What does concrete symbolize in the poem?
8. What does the poem suggest about the nature of creativity?
9. In the Reading Focus on page 1051, you were asked how anger can be put to good use. What insight into this issue did you get from reading the poem?
10. What good things might come from building a dam?

Literary ELEMENTS

Repetition

Repetition is the recurrence of sounds, words, phrases, lines, or stanzas in a literary work. Authors may use repetition to help unify a work. They may also use it to create a musical or rhythmic effect, or to emphasize an idea. **Rhyme, parallelism** (repetition of phrases with the same grammatical structure), and **alliteration** (repetition of initial consonant sounds) are types of repetition.

1. Identify an example of parallelism in "That Place Where Ghosts of Salmon Jump."
2. Which words does Alexie repeat in the poem to emphasize an idea?

- See **Literary Terms Handbook,** p. R10.

Extending Your Response

Writing About Literature

Myth Myths deal with imaginary events set in the distant past. Write a paragraph analyzing how Alexie uses myth in "That Place Where Ghosts of Salmon Jump" to comment on contemporary problems. Discuss the techniques that allow him to link present and past in the poem.

Performing

Oral Reading In a small group, perform a round-robin reading of "That Place Where Ghosts of Salmon Jump." You might alternate readers every two lines or divide up the poem into larger passages. Think about how you can use your voice to capture the poem's rhythm.

Save your work for your portfolio.

COMPARING *selections*

Coyote Finishes His Work and That Place Where Ghosts of Salmon Jump

COMPARE **RESPONSES**

Discuss In a small group, compare your responses to "Coyote Finishes His Work" and "That Place Where Ghosts of Salmon Jump." Discuss the following questions:

- Which selection did you find more interesting? Why?
- Which selection offers a more sympathetic portrayal of Coyote?
- What human faults does each selection attribute to Coyote?
- Which selection expresses a view of the world that is closer to your own?

COMPARE **CULTURES**

Investigate Both of these selections relate Native American myths about Coyote. With a partner, find a myth about a trickster figure from another culture. You might look up African folktales, such as the ones about Anansi, the spider, and trickster tales about hares and tortoises. Compare this myth with the Coyote myths and discuss how their differences might reflect cultural values or experiences.

COMPARE **EXPERIENCES**

Write Write a paragraph comparing the experiences of Coyote in the two selections. As you prepare to write, consider the following:

- what achievements are accomplished by Coyote
- his motivation
- how he interacts with humans and other characters

Brush Poppers, 1984 (detail).

MEDIA connection

Television Transcript

As an up-and-coming writer and filmmaker, Sherman Alexie often speaks to the media. Here, a television news correspondent, Thalia Assuras, discusses with Alexie his ability to mix humor with gritty reality.

Sending Smoke Signals

CBS News Sunday Morning, December 6, 1998

ASSURAS He makes people laugh. That, claims 32-year-old Sherman Alexie, is his greatest accomplishment. But he is not a standup comic. He is a poet, novelist, and, most recently, a filmmaker. His is the often lonely voice of a modern American Indian who fled the reservation where he grew up to live in the city. Yet his humor comes jumping through.

ALEXIE That's the only way people will listen to me and not run away screaming, or not get angry or not turn off because they don't want to hear what I'm saying, is if I'm funny. People listen to anything if you're funny.

ASSURAS Alexie is now adapting [his latest novel] to the screen and will direct the film, something new for him. Some scenes will be shot beneath Seattle's Alaskan Way viaduct where the city's homeless gather. Many of them are Indians.

Were you worried that you might end up here?

ALEXIE Oh yeah. My whole life has been a flight away from poverty. Even from a young age I thought, I don't want this to ever happen to me. I want to get away from this. So, it's always been a fear. It's still a fear.

I write about social problems [on the reservation]. Many people don't want that dirty laundry to be aired. Sometimes in focusing on the bad parts about what I write about, they neglect to see that there's a lot of love and humor and joy in the books as well.

Still from the film *Smoke Signals*.

ASSURAS Alexie says he intends to foster authentic images of his contemporaries in every medium open to him. He begins from his own experience.

ALEXIE Survival equals anger times imagination. Imagination is the only weapon on the reservation. Imagination is the politics of dreams. Imagine a spring with water that mends broken bones. Imagine a drum which wraps itself around your heart. Imagine a story that puts wood in the fireplace.

Analyzing Media

1. Do you agree with Alexie's thoughts on humor?
2. How powerful do you think imagination can be?

Grammar Link

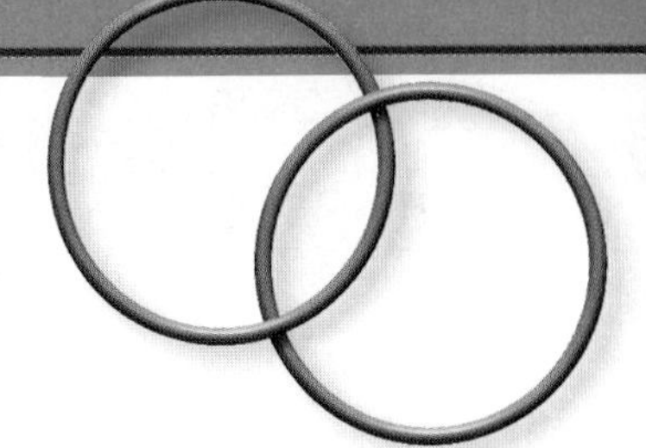

Misplaced or Dangling Modifiers

The position of a modifier—a word or phrase that describes something—determines what it modifies. For example, "Coyote tricked the girls in disguise." Who was disguised? If it was Coyote who was disguised, then the modifying phrase should make this clear. The easiest way to do this is to restructure the sentence. "In disguise, Coyote tricked the girls."

A **misplaced modifier** is one that is in the wrong place and, therefore, describes the wrong thing. A **dangling modifier** is one that is meant to modify a word or phrase, but that word or phrase is not present in the sentence. Such a modifier "dangles," attaching itself to nothing.

Misplacing a modifier or leaving one dangling is a common mistake that is easy to correct if you stop to think about what you are saying.

Problem 1 A misplaced modifier
Great Spirit met Coyote disguised as an old man.

Solution Place the modifier as close as possible to the word it modifies.
Disguised as an old man, Great Spirit met Coyote.

Problem 2 A dangling modifier
Smashing the water, the place was created.
Returning after many years, all the people will live together.

Solution Rewrite the sentence to include a noun or pronoun to which the dangling phrase clearly refers.
Smashing the water, Coyote created the place.
Returning after many years, Coyote and Old Man will gather the people together.

- For more on misplaced or dangling modifiers, see **Language Handbook,** p. R24.

EXERCISE

Correct the misplaced or dangling modifiers in these sentences.

1. Vicious dogs frighten people with big sharp teeth.
2. Drifting in the sky, Rachel saw puffy white clouds.
3. The man on the bicycle jumped the curb racing down the street.
4. By practicing every night, the song was easily learned.
5. Rushing through the grocery store, the shopping was quickly finished.

ITALY, 1492

Before You Read

from *The Voyage of Christopher Columbus*

Meet Christopher Columbus

"I was dumbfounded by the sight of so much beauty, and find myself unable to describe it adequately."

A native of the Italian port city of Genoa, Christopher Columbus went to sea at a young age. By his early thirties, he became determined to reach Asia by going west from Europe. After the Portuguese king turned down his proposal, King Ferdinand and Queen Isabella of Spain kept him waiting for seven years before they agreed to fund an expedition. In 1492 he crossed the Atlantic Ocean and explored several Caribbean islands.

On his next two voyages, Columbus established the first European settlement in the New World and reached the mainland of South America. He lost royal support after his fourth voyage, perhaps for having failed to find a route to the East. Columbus was not the first European to reach the Americas; the Vikings arrived there five hundred years earlier. However, he began an age of exploration, conquest, and cultural exchange that changed the world.

Columbus was born in 1451 and died in 1506.

Reading Focus

What is your opinion of Columbus's achievements?

Discuss Share your response with the class.

Setting a Purpose Read this selection for Columbus's account of his arrival in the New World.

Building Background

Columbus the Voyager

Columbus did not set out to "prove that the Earth was round"—all educated Europeans of his time knew that it was. But previous explorers had kept in sight of land, progressing slowly along every turn of the coastline. Columbus's great achievement as an explorer was in setting straight out across the ocean to see what was there.

Compass and navigational tools, 16th century.

It is hard to say for certain what drove Columbus to make the journey. Certainly he expected to make money, and an eventual royal grant of one tenth of the profits of the gold mines on Hispaniola did make him prosperous (although not fabulously wealthy). But his religious faith was an important factor as well. Toward the end of his life, he came to believe that he had been divinely appointed to spread Christianity and that his voyages were bringing him ever closer to "the rivers of Paradise."

Vocabulary Preview

coercion (kō ur′ shən) *n.* force, repression; p. 1060
tedious (tē′ dē əs) *adj.* tiresome because of length or dullness; boring; p. 1061
veer (vēr) *v.* to change direction or course; p. 1064

from The Voyage of Christopher Columbus

Christopher Columbus
Translated by John Cummins

Santa Maria, 1939. André Bauchant (France). Oil on canvas, 73 x 100 cm. Private collection.

Thursday, 11 October. Course WSW.[1] A heavy sea, the roughest in the whole voyage so far. We saw petrels,[2] and a green reed close to the ship, and then a big green fish of a kind which does not stray far from the shoals.[3] On the Pinta they saw a cane and a stick, and they picked up another little piece of wood which seemed to have been worked with an iron tool; also a piece of cane and another plant which grows on land, and a little board. On the Niña too they saw signs of land, and a thorn branch laden with red fruits, apparently newly cut. We were all filled with joy and relief at these signs. Sailed twenty-eight and a half leagues before sunset. After sunset I resumed our original course westward, sailing at about nine knots. By two o'clock in the morning we had sailed about sixty-eight miles, or twenty-two and a half leagues.

When everyone aboard was together for the *Salve Regina,*[4] which all seamen say or sing in their fashion, I talked to the men about the grace which God had shown us by bringing us

1. *WSW* is the abbreviation for West-South-West, one point on a mariner's compass.
2. *Petrels* (pe′ trəlz) are seabirds that can fly far from land.
3. *Shoals* (shōlz) are sandbanks or sandbars that make the water shallow.
4. *Salve Regina* (Latin for "Hail Holy Queen") is a prayer addressed to Mary, the mother of Jesus.

in safety, with fair winds and no obstacles, and by comforting us with signs which were more plentiful every day. I urged them to keep a good watch and reminded them that in the first article of the sailing instructions issued to each ship in the Canaries[5] I gave orders not to sail at night after we had reached a point seven hundred leagues from there; I was sailing on because of everyone's great desire to sight land. I warned them to keep a good lookout in the bows and told them that I would give a silk doublet[6] to the man who first sighted land, as well as the prize of 10,000 *maravedis*[7] promised by Your Majesties.

I was on the poop deck at ten o'clock in the evening when I saw a light. It was so indistinct that I could not be sure it was land, but I called Pedro Gutiérrez, the Butler of the King's Table, and told him to look at what I thought was a light. He looked, and saw it. I also told Rodrigo Sánchez de Segovia, Your Majesties' observer on board, but he saw nothing because he was standing in the wrong place. After I had told them, the light appeared once or twice more, like a wax candle rising and falling. Only a few people thought it was a sign of land, but I was sure we were close to a landfall.

Then the Pinta, being faster and in the lead, sighted land and made the signal as I had ordered. The first man to sight land was called Rodrigo de Triana. The land appeared two hours after midnight, about two leagues away. We furled all sail except the *treo*, the mainsail with no bonnets, and jogged off and on until Friday morning, when we came to an island. We saw naked people, and I went ashore in a boat with armed men, taking Martín Alonso Pinzón and his brother Vicente Yáñez, captain of the Niña. I took the royal standard, and the captains each took a banner with the Green Cross which each of my ships carries as a device, with the letters F and Y, surmounted by a crown, at each end of the cross.

Did You Know?
A *device* is a symbolic design, or emblem, often accompanied by a motto. Heralds—official messengers—carried a device to identify the noble family that they represented.

When we stepped ashore we saw fine green trees, streams everywhere and different kinds of fruit. I called to the two captains to jump ashore with the rest, who included Rodrigo de Escobedo, secretary of the fleet, and Rodrigo Sánchez de Segovia, asking them to bear solemn witness that in the presence of them all I was taking possession of this island for their Lord and Lady the King and Queen, and I made the necessary declarations which are set down at greater length in the written testimonies.

Soon many of the islanders gathered round us. I could see that they were people who would be more easily converted to our Holy Faith by love than by coercion, and wishing them to look on us with friendship I gave some of them red bonnets and glass beads which they hung round their necks, and many other things of small value, at which they were so delighted and so eager to please us that we could not believe it. Later they swam out to the boats to bring us parrots and balls of cotton thread and darts, and many other things, exchanging them for such objects as glass beads and hawk bells. They took anything, and gave willingly whatever they had.

5. The *Canaries* are the Canary Islands. Owned by Spain, the Canaries are located in the Atlantic Ocean about seventy miles west of North Africa.
6. A *doublet* is a man's close-fitting jacket.
7. A *maravedi* (mä rä vä′ dē) was a Spanish gold coin.

Vocabulary
coercion (kō ur′ shən) *n.* force, repression

However, they appeared to me to be a very poor people in all respects. They go about as naked as the day they were born, even the women, though I saw only one, who was quite young. All the men I saw were quite young, none older than thirty, all well built, finely bodied and handsome in the face. Their hair is coarse, almost like a horse's tail, and short; they wear it short, cut over the brow, except a few strands of hair hanging down uncut at the back.

Some paint themselves with black, some with the color of the Canary Islanders, neither black nor white, others with white, others with red, others with whatever they can find. Some have only their face painted, others their whole body, others just their eyes or nose. They carry no weapons, and are ignorant of them; when I showed them some swords they took them by the blade and cut themselves. They have no iron; their darts are just sticks without an iron head, though some of them have a fish tooth or something else at the tip.

They are all the same size, of good stature, dignified and well formed. I saw some with scars on their bodies, and made signs to ask about them, and they indicated to me that people from other islands nearby came to capture them and they defended themselves. I thought, and still think, that people from the mainland come here to take them prisoner. They must be good servants, and intelligent, for I can see that they quickly repeat everything said to them. I believe they would readily become Christians; it appeared to me that they have no religion. With God's will, I will take six of them with me for Your Majesties when I leave this place, so that they may learn Spanish.

I saw no animals on the island, only parrots.

Saturday, 13 October. In the early morning many of the islanders came to the beach, all young, as I have said, tall and handsome, their hair not curly, but flowing and thick, like horsehair. They are all broader in the forehead and head than any people I have ever seen, with fine, large eyes. None of them is black; they are rather the same color as the folk on the Canary Islands, which is what one might expect, this island being on the same latitude as Hierro in the Canaries, which lies due E. Their legs are very straight, and they are all the same height, not stout in the belly but well shaped. They came out to the ship in *almadías* made from a tree trunk, like a long boat, all of a piece, wonderfully shaped in the way of this land, some big enough to carry forty or fifty men, others smaller, with only one man. They row them with paddles like a baker's shovel, very swiftly, and if the boat overturns they all jump into the sea to turn it over again and bale it out with gourds. They brought us balls of cotton thread and parrots and darts and other little things which it would be tedious to list, and exchanged everything for whatever we offered them.

I kept my eyes open and tried to find out if there was any gold, and I saw that some of them had a little piece hanging from a hole in their nose. I gathered from their signs that if one goes south, or around the south side of the island, there is a king with great jars full of it, enormous amounts. I tried to persuade them to go there, but I saw that the idea was not to their liking.

I decided to wait until tomorrow and then to set off to the southwest, for many of them seemed to be saying that there is land to the S and SW and NW, and that the people from the NW often come to attack them, and continue to the SW in search of gold and precious stones. This island is large and very flat, with green trees and plenty of water; there is a large lake in the middle, no mountains, and everything is green and a delight to the eye. The people are very gentle; they are so eager for our things that if we refuse to give them something without getting

Vocabulary

tedious (tē′ dē əs) *adj.* tiresome because of length or dullness; boring

Sandy Island, The Grenadines, West Indies.

something in exchange they seize what they can and jump into the water with it. But they will give whatever they have for anything one gives them; they even bargained for pieces of broken plate and broken glasses. I saw them take three Portuguese *ceotís*, the equivalent of one Castilian *blanca*,[8] for sixteen balls of cotton which must have contained more than an *arroba*[9] of thread. I had forbidden anyone to take this, except that I had given orders to take it all for Your Majesties if it was in sufficient quantity. It grows on this island, though in the little time available I could not swear to this, and the gold they wear hanging from their noses is also from the island, but so as not to waste time I wish to set off to see if I can reach the island of Cipango.

It is now after nightfall and they have all gone ashore in their *almadías*.

Sunday, 14 October. I gave orders at daybreak for the small boat of the Santa María and the boats of the two caravels to be got ready, and went along the coast to the northeast to examine the eastward part of the island, and the villages, of which I saw two or three. The people kept coming down to the beach, calling to us and giving thanks to God. Some brought us water, some food; others, seeing that I did not wish to go ashore, swam out to us, and we understood them to be asking if we had come from Heaven. One old man climbed into the boat, and the others, men and women, kept shouting, "Come and see the men who have come from Heaven; bring them food and drink."

Many men and women came, each bringing something and giving thanks to God, throwing themselves on the ground and raising their hands in the air. They called to us to go ashore, but I was afraid of a great reef which encircles the whole island, though between it and the shore there is a deep harbor big enough to hold every ship in Christendom, with a very narrow entrance channel. There are certainly shoals within this reef, but the sea inside it is as calm as a millpond.

I bestirred myself to explore all this this morning so as to be able to give Your Majesties a description of it all, and also of a possible site for a fort. I saw a piece of land which is virtually

8. *Ceotís* (thā ō tēs′) and *blanca* (blän′ kä) are coins. *Castilian,* often used as a synonym for "Spanish," refers to Castile, a large region of central Spain.
9. An *arroba* (ä rō′ bä) is a unit of measurement equal to about twenty-five pounds.

an island; there are six houses on it, and it could be converted into an island with a couple of days' work, although I do not see the necessity. These people have little knowledge of fighting, as Your Majesties will see from the seven I have had captured to take away with us so as to teach them our language and return them, unless Your Majesties' orders are that they all be taken to Spain or held captive on the island itself, for with fifty men one could keep the whole population in subjection and make them do whatever one wanted.

Near the islet I have described there are groves of the most beautiful trees I ever saw; so green, with their leaves like those in Castile in April and May. There is also plenty of water. I explored the whole harbor, and then returned to the ship and set sail. I saw so many islands that I could not decide which to go to first. The men I had captured told me by signs that there are so many that they cannot be counted; they gave me the names of over a hundred. I therefore looked for the largest, and decided to sail for it, which is what I am doing now. It must be about five leagues from this island of San Salvador.[10] Some of the others are nearer, some further away. They are all very flat and fertile, with no mountains, and they are all populated and make war on one another, though these people are very simple, and very finely made.

Monday, 15 October. Last night I lay to[11] for fear of approaching land to anchor before morning, not knowing if the coast was free from shoals, and intending to increase sail at dawn. The distance was more than five leagues, nearer seven, and the tide set us back, so that it would be around noon when I reached the island. I found that the arm of the island nearest San Salvador runs N–S, and is five leagues long, and the other, along which I sailed, runs E–W for over ten leagues.

From this island I sighted another larger one to the west, so I increased sail to press on all day until nightfall, for otherwise I could not have reached the western cape. I named this island Santa María de la Concepción. I anchored off the western cape just before sunset to find out if there was any gold there. The prisoners I took on San Salvador kept telling me that the people of this island wore great gold bracelets and legbands, but I thought it was all invention to enable them to escape. However, my intention being not to pass by any island without taking possession of it, although taking possession of one might be taken to serve for them all, I anchored and remained there until today, Tuesday.

At daybreak I armed the boats and went ashore. There were numerous people, naked and similar to those on San Salvador. They let us go about on the island and gave us whatever I asked for. The wind was strengthening from the southeast, so I decided not to linger, but set off to return to the ship. A large *almadía* was alongside the Niña, and one of the men from San Salvador who was aboard the caravel jumped into the sea and went off in it (another had jumped overboard the previous night). Our boat set off after the *almadía,* which paddled away so fast that no boat ever built could have outpaced it, even with a considerable start. Anyway, it reached the shore and they abandoned it. Some of my men landed in pursuit, and the islanders all fled like chickens. The *almadía* was taken back on board the Niña.

By now another small *almadía* was approaching the Niña from a different headland with one man in it who had come to barter a ball of cotton. He did not want to come aboard, so some of the sailors jumped into the sea and captured him. I saw all this from the deck of the sterncastle,[12]

10. *San Salvador* (sän säl′ və dor) is one of the islands of the Bahamas in the Caribbean Sea. It is believed to be the place where Columbus first landed, on October 12, 1492.

11. *Lay to* means "kept the ship in place at sea with the front facing toward the wind."

12. The *sterncastle* is part of the upper deck toward the stern, or rear of a ship.

so I sent for him; I gave him a red bonnet and put a few little green glass beads on his arm and hung two bells from his ears. I had him put back in his *almadía*, which had also been taken aboard the ship's boat, and sent him back ashore. I then made sail to go to the other large island which I could see to the westward, and I ordered the other *almadía* which the Niña was towing astern[13] to be set adrift.

When the man to whom I had given gifts, refusing his ball of cotton, reached the shore I saw that all the others came up to him. He was amazed and thought that we were good people and that the other who had escaped was being taken with us because he had done us some harm. That was my purpose in giving him presents and letting him go: to make them think well of us, so that when Your Majesties send someone else here he may be well received. All the things I gave him would not be worth four *maravedis* if you put them together.

I set sail, then, at about ten o'clock with the wind SE, veering southerly, to cross to this other island. It is very large, and all the men from San Salvador tell me by signs that there is a lot of gold, which the people wear as bracelets and leg-bands, and in their ears and noses, and round their necks.

From the island of Santa María to this new one is nine and a half leagues, almost due W, and all this part of the island runs from NW to SE. There appears to be at least thirty leagues of coast on this side, very flat, without a hill anywhere, like San Salvador and Santa María. There are sandy beaches all the way, except that there are some underwater rocks near the shoreline, making it necessary to take care when anchoring and not to anchor close inshore, although the water is very clear and one can see the bottom. Two lombard[14] shots from shore all around these islands one can find no bottom.

The islands are very green and lush, with sweet breezes, and there may be many things here which I do not know about, because rather than lingering I wish to explore and investigate many islands in search of gold. As these people tell me by signs that the folk wear it on their arms and legs—and it is gold they mean, for I showed them some pieces of my own—with God's help I cannot fail to find the source of it.

Halfway between these two islands, Santa María and this larger one which I am calling Fernandina, we found a man alone in an *almadía* making the same crossing as ourselves. He had a piece of bread as big as his fist, a calabash[15] of water, a piece of red earth, powdered and kneaded, and a few dried leaves which must be something of importance to these people, because they brought me some in San Salvador. He also had a small basket with a little string of glass beads and two *blancas*, so I knew that he had come from San Salvador and called at Santa María on his way to Fernandina. He came alongside the ship and I let him come aboard at his request. I also made him bring his *almadía* on board with him. I let him keep all the things he had with him, and ordered him to be given bread and honey, and something to drink. I am going to take him to Fernandina and give him all his possessions so that he will give a good report of us, in order that when Your Majesties, with the grace of God, send men back to this place they will be received with honor, and we will be given whatever the island has to offer.

13. Here, *astern* means "behind."

14. A *lombard* was a type of cannon.

15. A *calabash* is a dried gourd used as a container.

Vocabulary

veer (vēr) *v.* to change direction or course

Responding to Literature

Personal Response

What thoughts went through your mind as you finished reading this selection? Write a response in your journal.

Analyzing Literature

Recall

1. What leads Columbus to believe that he is nearing land?
2. What is the first thing that Columbus does when he lands on San Salvador?
3. What step does Columbus take to ensure that the islanders learn Spanish?
4. What is Columbus's general impression of the islanders?
5. Why does Columbus give presents to some islanders?

Interpret

6. Why do you think Columbus emphasizes to his men that they are nearing land?
7. What do Columbus's actions suggest about his intentions regarding the islanders?
8. Why might Columbus be interested in having the islanders learn Spanish?
9. In your opinion, to what extent does Columbus's impression of the islanders affect his behavior toward them?
10. What does Columbus's explanation of his presents to the islanders reveal about his character?

Evaluate and Connect

11. **Motivation** is the reason or reasons behind a character's actions (see page R8). Which of the reasons behind Columbus's actions do you find most admirable, and which do you find least admirable?
12. What do you think you might have done differently if you were in Columbus's position?
13. Do you think that Columbus gives a fair and accurate portrayal of the islanders? Explain your response.
14. What would you like to find out about the islanders that isn't explained in Columbus's journal?
15. In the Reading Focus on page 1058, you were asked about your opinion regarding Columbus's achievements. How has reading this selection influenced that opinion?

Literary ELEMENTS

Journal

A **journal** is a personal record of experiences, ideas, and reflections that is kept on a regular basis. Like letters, journals are a form of autobiographical writing. Writers often use journals to record thoughts and details that they may later use in their literary work. Although many people use journals as a way of exploring their feelings in private, some journals are intended for publication or to be read by a specific audience.

1. What audience did Columbus have in mind when he was writing his journal?
2. How might Columbus's descriptions in the journal have been influenced by his intended audience?

- See **Literary Terms Handbook,** p. R16.

Signature and monogram of Christopher Columbus.

Literature and Writing

Writing About Literature

Analyze Diction Write a paragraph analyzing the words in Columbus's descriptions of the islanders. Discuss the words' positive or negative **connotations** (see page R2). Which words would you avoid using in a narrative of this historical encounter?

Creative Writing

Another Perspective Imagine that you are one of the sailors with Columbus's expedition. Write a journal entry about one of the incidents that Columbus describes in the selection. Use details from Columbus's journal, but offer your own thoughts and feelings about the incident.

Extending Your Response

Literature Groups

Remembering Columbus Five centuries after his voyage, Columbus remains a controversial figure. In a small group, discuss how you normally observe Columbus Day. How do you think that Columbus's arrival in America should be celebrated? What are some appropriate ways to commemorate this event? Share your conclusions with the class.

Learning for Life

Memo Imagine that you are an advisor to King Ferdinand and Queen Isabella. Write a memo in response to Columbus's journal. Do you think that Columbus offers a reliable account of his voyage? Should the king and queen fund more expeditions to the New World? Use quotations and refer to specific passages from the selection.

Interdisciplinary Activity

Science: Discovering Food Columbus's voyage began an exchange of food sources that transformed the diets of people around the world. With a partner, research a crop that originated in the New World. Find out how this plant was introduced to Europeans and how it affected their nutrition. Bring to class a recipe for a European dish that uses the food as an ingredient.

Reading Further

If you would like to find out more about voyages of exploration, the following book might interest you:

The Account: Alvar Núñez Cabeza de Vaca's Relación.

Save your work for your portfolio.

VOCABULARY • Analogies

Analogies are comparisons based on relationships between words. Some analogies are based on synonyms. In this type, both words have similar meanings and are the same part of speech.

hasten : hurry :: jog : trot

Hasten and *hurry* both mean "to move quickly"; *jog* and *trot* both suggest running at a controlled pace.

To finish an analogy, decide on the relationship of the first two words. Then apply that relationship to the second set of words.

PRACTICE Choose the pair that best completes each analogy.

1. rouse : awaken ::
   a. hypnotize : trance
   b. climb : ascend
   c. animate : repress
   d. invigorate : faint
   e. scale : rock

2. deceive : dupe ::
   a. mislead : reveal
   b. tutor : outwit
   c. enhance : diminish
   d. falsify : trick
   e. instruct : enlighten

- For more on analogies, see **Communications Skills Handbook,** p. R77.

Before You Read

Discoveries

MEXICO, 1992

Meet Eduardo Langagne

"There is little difference between the words of yesterday and today. Nevertheless, we look for something in them that can't be learned."

Born in Mexico City, Eduardo Langagne (ed wär′ dō län′ gan′ yə) is an award-winning writer. In college he studied dentistry, music, and film. He is the founder of a number of literary magazines. He has published several books of original writings as well as translations of Bulgarian poetry.

Eduardo Langagne was born in 1952.

Reading Focus

Think of some discoveries you have made about yourself and about the people who are important to you.

Journal Describe one of these discoveries in your journal.

Setting a Purpose In the following poem, the speaker reflects on a personal discovery.

Building Background

Amerigo Vespucci

While Christopher Columbus has long been credited with making the existence of the Americas known throughout Europe, it was another Italian mariner, Amerigo Vespucci, for whom the continents are named. Born in Florence, Vespucci went to Spain as an employee of that city's famous Medici Bank. There he helped to equip Columbus's expeditions. Later he made two important voyages of his own, during the years 1499–1502. On the first voyage he became the first European to see the Amazon River; the second took him further south, where he was the first European to see the Rio de la Plata. The discovery of these great rivers, and the vast extent of land between them, made it clear to Europeans that the Americas were not merely a string of islands on the way to Asia, but entire continents of their own. It was for this contribution that in 1507 the German mapmaker Herman Waldseemüller proposed the name "America" for the New World.

Caravels

Vespucci's Spanish and Portuguese contemporaries sailed in vessels called caravels. The Portuguese, whose expeditions usually traveled south along the coast of Africa, developed the vessels to sail windward along the coast, but they were also capable of sailing at high speeds, taking explorers to the New World. At least two of the ships in which Columbus sailed to the Americas were caravels.

Although the design of the caravel changed over the years, a typical caravel of Columbus's time would be a relatively wide ship. Approximately eighty feet long, caravels had two or three masts bearing triangular sails.

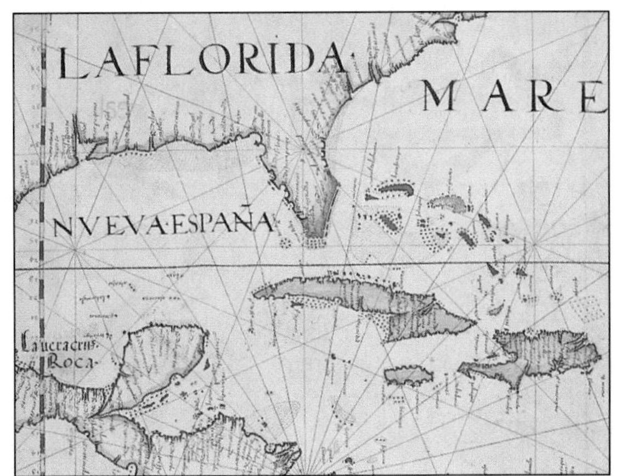

Map of the Gulf of Mexico. From the *Portolan Atlas,* 1565.

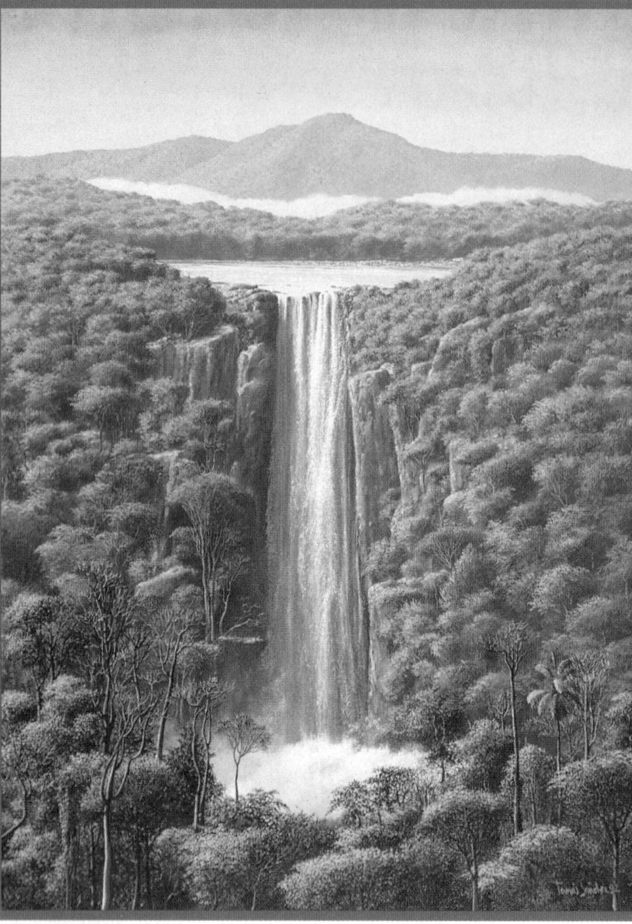

Caída de las aguas (Waterfall), 1992. Tomás Sánchez (Cuba). Tempera on heavy Arches paper, 76.5 x 58 cm. Private collection.

Discoveries

Eduardo Langagne

columbus did not discover this woman
nor do her eyes resemble caravels
vespucci never mapped her hair
no lookout ever shouted land-ho at sight of her—
although gulls do fly
        near
            her body
and on her continent the sun rises every day—
this woman was not discovered by columbus
nevertheless she was in the west
she was an unknown place
and to find her
it was necessary to spend a long time traveling
with a blue solitude in one's head

Responding to Literature

Personal Response

Which images from this poem linger in your mind? Share your response with a classmate.

Analyzing Literature

Recall and Interpret

1. What contrast does the speaker set up in the first four lines of the poem?
2. In what way is the woman referred to in the poem similar to the New World?
3. What do you think the poet is trying to say in the last two lines of the poem?

Evaluate and Connect

4. An **extended metaphor** is a metaphor that is sustained for several lines or all throughout a poem. Describe the extended metaphor that is used in "Discoveries."
5. **Tone** is the attitude that a speaker takes toward the audience, a subject, or a character (see page R12). How would you describe the tone of this poem?
6. In the Reading Focus on page 1067, you were asked to describe a personal discovery. Compare your experience to the discovery that Langagne portrays in his poem.

Literary ELEMENTS

Allusion

An **allusion** is a reference to a well-known person, place, or event from history, literature, or religion. Allusions enrich our reading experience by adding additional layers of meaning. In "Discoveries," Eduardo Langagne alludes to people, places, and events in the history of the exploration of the New World.

1. What do you think Langagne alludes to in the last two lines of the poem?
2. What do the allusions in the poem suggest about love?

- See **Literary Terms Handbook,** p. R1.

Extending Your Response

Writing About Literature

Analyze Metaphor Do you think that the extended metaphor Langagne uses in "Discoveries" is effective? Write a paragraph in which you give your response to this question. Use quotations from the poem to support your analysis. Then exchange papers with the other students in your group and discuss your opinions.

Interdisciplinary Activity

Art: Collage In "Discoveries," Langagne combines imagery in surprising ways. Create a collage based on this varied imagery. For your materials, you might wish to use clippings from current newspapers and magazines combined with photocopies of illustrations from books about the exploration and colonization of the New World. You may wish to display your collage in the classroom.

Save your work for your portfolio.

COMPARING selections

from *The Voyage of Christopher Columbus* **and** Discoveries

DISCUSS **RESPONSES**

In a small group, compare your response to these two selections about discoveries. Discuss the following questions:

- What do the writers of each selection discover?
- How might each writer's life have been different if he had not made his discovery?
- How would you compare the impacts of the discoveries?
- What might the authors say to each other if they met?

COMPARE **MOODS**

The journal entry and "Discoveries" are in different genres. Do they also express different moods? Write a paragraph comparing the moods of the selections. Consider the following questions in your comparison:

- How do the writers feel about the discoveries they have made?
- How do the writers use language to convey their feelings and establish a mood?

Fleet of Ships (detail), from *The Lives of Portuguese Viceroys in India.* 1558, Portuguese illuminated manuscript.

COMPARE **SETTINGS**

The setting plays an important role in each of these selections. With a partner, look for a painting or photograph that could be used to illustrate each of them. You might decide on an abstract painting or a photograph of a Caribbean landscape. Show your selection to the class and explain why you think it is appropriate for both selections. Be prepared to discuss and evaluate the selections of other students.

LISTENING, SPEAKING, and VIEWING

Critiquing Media Coverage

Eduardo Langagne uses poetry to express his feelings about love and the search for love. While subjective feelings and personal attitudes are appropriate in poetry, they are not always appropriate in other kinds of writing. For example, the best news reports–in the newspaper, on television, or on the Internet–are factual and objective. Instead of trying to persuade you toward a particular point of view, the best media coverage should simply provide the information you need to make up your own mind.

But how do you determine whether a news report is factual, complete, and responsible? To be able to critique the media coverage of any particular issue or event, watch and listen to news reports with these questions in mind:

Is the report biased toward one side or the other?

- Consider whether the reporter or the reporter's employer has a direct interest in the issue.
- Consider the sources for the material being reported.
- Ask yourself whether any side of the story is being underreported or ignored. What haven't you been told?

Are the report's claims backed up by specific evidence?

- Notice whether eyewitnesses are interviewed, primary documents are cited, and concrete facts are referenced. The use of specific evidence gives a report more legitimacy.
- Compare the amount of specific evidence to the amount of generalization, opinion, and speculation. The best reports stress facts over opinions.

Is the evidence reliable and relevant to the situation?

- Think about whether all the information given is relevant. Unnecessary details may distract from the main point of the story. Expert opinions and statistics should relate directly to the topic under discussion.
- Consider whether witnesses are biased.
- Consider whether the facts presented can be verified or confirmed by other reliable sources, such as encyclopedias, journals, or reputable news organizations.

ACTIVITY

With a group, choose a current event or political issue that is receiving national media attention. Then assign people to gather newspaper or magazine articles, videotapes of or notes on television reports, and Internet accounts of the event or issue. Together, compare and critique the media coverage. Use the questions provided above to evaluate the sources. Which source has the best coverage, and which has the worst. Then write a paragraph or two explaining your conclusions. Share your writing with classmates.

Technology Skills

Citing Electronic Sources

If you use the Internet when conducting research for a report on literature, art, or another subject in the humanities, use the following guidelines for citing your sources and preparing your bibliography or works-cited list. These guidelines are based on the style recommended by the Modern Language Association (MLA). The American Psychological Association (APA) and American Medical Association (AMA) guidelines, which differ somewhat, may be used when writing about scientific subjects, but check with your teacher first and use the guidelines he or she prefers.

The information in each works-cited entry should appear in the order listed below, but note that no source will include every item listed. The box on the next page provides sample entries you may use as models.

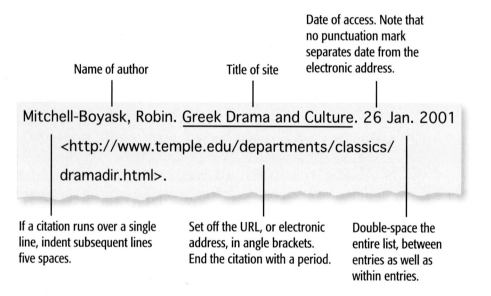

Name of author — **Title of site** — **Date of access. Note that no punctuation mark separates date from the electronic address.**

Mitchell-Boyask, Robin. Greek Drama and Culture. 26 Jan. 2001
     <http://www.temple.edu/departments/classics/
     dramadir.html>.

If a citation runs over a single line, indent subsequent lines five spaces.

Set off the URL, or electronic address, in angle brackets. End the citation with a period.

Double-space the entire list, between entries as well as within entries.

1. **Name** of author, editor, or translator of the source (last name first), followed by an abbreviation such as *ed.* or *trans.*, if appropriate
2. **Title**
- of a poem, short story, article, or other short work (in quotation marks)
- of a book (underlined)
- of a scholarly project, database, periodical, or site (underlined). If a personal or professional site has no title, use a description, such as *Home page* (with no underlining or quotation marks)
3. **Name** of editor or translator (if relevant and if not cited earlier), preceded by abbreviation such as *Ed.* or *Trans.*

TECHNOLOGY TIP

Since Web sites change frequently, be sure to print out any pages that you use for your research and that you will need to include in your list of works cited.

4. **Publication information**

- date of latest posting and institution or organization sponsoring the site
- place and date of an original version
- version number, volume number, or other identifying number
- reference to pages, paragraphs, or sections used (such as *pp. 47–52* or *pars. 1–14*)

3. For a posting to a **discussion list,** the name of the list and the description *Online posting*

4. Date when the researcher accessed the source

5. Electronic address, or URL, of the source (in angle brackets)

- For more on documenting sources, see **Writing Handbook,** pages R64–R69.

SAMPLE ENTRIES FOR LIST OF WORKS CITED

Professional Site

De Imperatoribus Romanis: An Online Encyclopedia of Roman Emperors. Salve Regina University. 25 Aug. 1996 <http://www.salve.edu/~dimaiom/deimprom.html>.

Personal Site

Mitchell-Boyask, Robin. Greek Drama and Culture. 26 Jan. 2001 <http://www.temple.edu/departments/classics/dramadir.html>.

Book

Homer. Iliad. Trans. A. T. Murray. London, 1924. Perseus Project. 21 Jan. 1999 <http://www.perseus.tufts.edu/cgibin/text?lookup= hom.+il.+1.1>.

Poem

Bevington, L. S. "Cloud-Climbing." Poems, Lyrics, and Sonnets. Ed. Perry Willett. London: Eliot Stock, 1882. 6 Jan. 2001 <http://www.indiana.edu/~letrs/vwwp/bevington/bevpoems.html>.

Article in a Reference Database

"Sonnet." Concise Columbia Electronic Encyclopedia. 2000. Infonautics. 26 Jan. 2001 <http://www.encyclopedia.com>.

Article in a Journal

Fox, Robert Elliot. "Shaping an African American Literary Canon." Postmodern Culture 9.1 (Sept. 1996): 19 pars. 23 Feb. 1999 <http://www.iath.virginia.edu/pmc/998/9.1.r_fox.html>.

Article in a Magazine

Bennehum, David S. "Coming of Age in Cyberspace." Atlantic Unbound (28 Oct. 1998). 26 Jan. 2001 <http://www.theatlantic.com/unbound/digicult/dc981028.htm>.

Posting to a Discussion List

Renshaw, Scott. "Review of *William Shakespeare's Romeo and Juliet.*" Online posting. 28 Oct. 1996. Usenet. 4 Nov. 1996 <http://www.usenet.com>.

EXERCISES

1. Think of a topic for a research paper. Then do a Web search for information relating to your topic. Find a significant fact from each of at least six electronic sources and write the citation you would use for that information. You might work with a partner to choose a topic. Then compare information and citations after completing your research independently.

2. With a small group, do a Web search for organizations other than the MLA that offer style guides for citing electronic sources. For instance, you might search for the guidelines provided by the Alliance for Computers and Writing or for the American Psychological Association (APA). What differences in citation style do you see?

MEXICO, c. 1690

Before You Read

Sonnet 145

Meet Sor Juana Inés de la Cruz

"Have [women] not a rational soul as men do? Well, then, why cannot a woman profit by the privilege of enlightenment as they do?"

Sor Juana Inés de la Cruz (sôr hwä′ nä ē nās′ dā lä kruz′), the first major writer of European descent born in America, began reading at age three. She was so eager to learn that when she was eight she asked her parents to let her disguise herself as a boy so she could attend the University of Mexico. Unfortunately, women had almost no opportunity to pursue education in colonial Mexico. Sor Juana made her way to the viceroy's court in Mexico City, where she impressed many with her knowledge and poetic talent. When she was seventeen, she decided to become a nun so that she could concentrate on her studies.

For about two decades, Sor Juana wrote poems and plays in the convent. She also read widely and performed scientific experiments. However, her pursuit of knowledge was disapproved of by many. In the early 1690s, she became involved in a controversial argument with some prominent church figures. Although she defended her opinions—and her right to express them—with vigor, criticism continued. Angered by the authorities' unyielding opposition, she decided to stop writing altogether. Sor Juana sold her books and research materials and gave the money to the poor. Then she devoted herself to caring for the sick. She died while nursing the victims of an epidemic.

Sor Juana was born in 1651 and died in 1695.

Reading Focus

Have you ever felt surprised or uncomfortable about your own image in a photograph? Why did your own image make you feel that way?

Quickwrite Jot down a response in your journal.

Setting a Purpose In the following poem, the speaker reflects on a portrait of herself.

Building Background

Sor Juana's Poetry

Many critics consider Sor Juana Inés de la Cruz the finest lyric poet from colonial Latin America. Her contemporary admirers called her the "Tenth Muse." She began to build this reputation at the viceroy's court, where she often composed poems for social or political occasions. She also wrote religious, philosophical, and love poems. She always maintained that women were intellectually equal to men–a controversial view at the time.

Sor Juana wrote a number of poems about portraits. In "Sonnet 145," she addresses a painting of herself. Her modesty is reflected in the poem's full title: "She attempts to minimize the praise occasioned by a portrait of herself inscribed by truth, which she calls passion."

Reading Further

You might enjoy the following anthology:

Sor Juana Inés de la Cruz: Poems, Protest, and a Dream is a bilingual anthology, translated by Margaret Sayers Peden.

Arcángel, 1748. Fray Miguel de Herrera (Mexico).

Portrait of Sor Juana Inés de la Cruz. Mexican School. Oil on canvas, 41½ x 32½ in. Philadelphia Museum of Art.

Sonnet 145

Sor Juana Inés de la Cruz
Translated by Margaret Sayers Peden

This that you gaze on, colorful deceit,
that so immodestly displays art's favors,°
with its fallacious° arguments of colors
is to the senses cunning counterfeit,
this on which kindness practiced to delete
from cruel years accumulated horrors,
constraining time to mitigate° its rigors,
and thus oblivion and age defeat,
is but an artifice,° a sop° to vanity,
is but a flower by the breezes bowed,
is but a ploy to counter destiny,
is but a foolish labor, ill-employed,
is but a fancy, and, as all may see,
is but cadaver, ashes, shadow, void.

2 **art's favors:** here, applied decorations of little value.

3 **fallacious** (fə lā′ shəs): erroneous or misleading.

7 **mitigate** (mi′ tə gāt′): to lessen.

9 **artifice** (är′ tə fis): ingenious deception. **sop:** a bribe.

Responding to Literature

Personal Response

What ideas or insights did you gain from reading the poem? Jot down your ideas in your journal. Then share your response with the class.

Analyzing Literature

Recall and Interpret

1. What does the phrase "fallacious arguments of colors" in line 3 of the sonnet refer to?
2. According to lines 5–8, what elements have been left out of the portrait?
3. Why do you think Sor Juana refers to the portrait as a "ploy to counter destiny"?

Evaluate and Connect

4. A **metaphor** is a comparison of two things that have some quality in common (see **Literary Terms Handbook,** page R7). Which metaphors in the poem suggest that the portrait, like its subject, will not last forever?
5. **Tone** is the attitude that a speaker takes toward the audience, a subject, or a character (see **Literary Terms Handbook,** page R12). How would you describe the speaker's tone toward the painting? Support your answer with details from the poem.
6. In the Reading Focus on page 1074, you were asked to describe your reaction to a photograph of yourself. Compare your feelings at the time with the feelings of the poem's speaker.

Rhyme

Words **rhyme** when their accented syllables and all the letters that follow sound the same. The word *bake* rhymes with *shake,* and *tickle* rhymes with *pickle.* When words sound similar but do not rhyme exactly, they are called half-rhymes or slant rhymes. *Bake-baste* and *tickle-buckle* are examples. Scholars use letters to indicate a poem's rhyme scheme, or the pattern of rhymes that occur at the ends of lines (for example, *aabb* or *abab*).

1. What is the rhyme scheme of "Sonnet 145"?
2. Identify a half-rhyme in this translation of the poem.

- See **Literary Terms Handbook,** p. R10.

Extending Your Response

Creative Writing

Poem Many poems have been inspired by works of art. Write a brief poem about an image that you have seen in a painting or photograph. Use vivid, precise words and plenty of sensory details to bring the scene to life for your readers. Then get together with a group of your classmates for a poetry reading. If possible, bring to the reading the image that inspired your poem. Once you have read your poem aloud, invite constructive criticism from your audience.

Literature Groups

Compare In a small group, compare "Sonnet 145" with a European sonnet written in the Renaissance period. (You might like to use Petrarch's "Laura," on page 847 of this book.) Discuss the style and theme of each poem. When you are finished, share your conclusions with the class.

Save your work for your portfolio.

EDITING/PROOFREADING

Use the **Proofreading Checklist** on the inside back cover of this book to help you find and correct errors in grammar, usage, mechanics, and spelling. Read your essay several times, looking for one type of error each time.

PROOFREADING TIP

To catch spelling mistakes, look at each word individually.

Grammar Hint

Modifying words and phrases should be as close as possible to the sentence elements they modify. A misplaced modifier seems to be modifying the wrong sentence element.

MISPLACED MODIFIER: *An island hoping for freedom, José Martí wrote about Cuba.*

CORRECT: *José Martí wrote about Cuba, an island hoping for freedom.*

- For more on misplaced modifiers, see **Language Handbook**, p. R24.

STUDENT MODEL

```
Fleeing there doomed city the poem describe too
people. Although the husband in the poem appears to
leave without turning back the wife can not.
```

Complete Student Model on p. R122.

Complete Student Model

For a complete version of the model developed in this workshop, refer to **Writing Workshop Models**, p. R122.

PUBLISHING/PRESENTING

Consider presenting your essay to the class by reading it aloud or by duplicating copies for your classmates to read. Afterwards, invite people to use your points of comparison as a springboard for discussion.

PRESENTING TIP

You might begin an oral presentation by reading passages from the two works of literature you have compared.

Reflecting

In the future, you might be required to write comparison-and-contrast essays in other subject areas. By comparing works of literature, what did you discover that may be helpful to you later? What might you do differently the next time you write a comparison-and-contrast essay?

Save your work for your portfolio.

The Land and Its People

North and South America have undergone great changes during the past 200 years. Between 1776 and 1828, most of the Americas won independence from England, Spain, and Portugal. Canada, once ruled by Great Britain, became self-governing in 1867.

Though the slave trade was gradually outlawed, traders brought nearly two million enslaved Africans into the Americas during the 1800s. By the late 1800s, the number of Native Americans was increasing, and immigration from Europe added more than 14 million people to the population. As a result, the Americas include perhaps the world's most diverse population.

Geography has seldom been an ally in the settlement of the region. The tropical rain forests play a vital role in the Earth's ecosystem but are of little use for growing crops. Deadly storms sweep the Caribbean. Canada has long, cold winters and a short growing season. Facing numerous challenges, the people of the Americas continue to create a New World.

Chateau Frontenac, Quebec City.

English Harbor, Antigua.

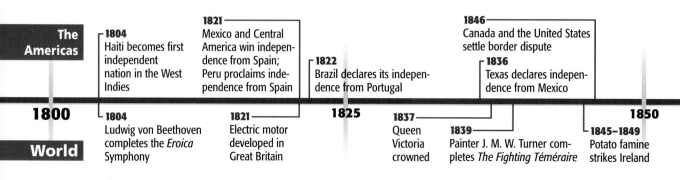

The Americas

- **1804** Haiti becomes first independent nation in the West Indies
- **1821** Mexico and Central America win independence from Spain; Peru proclaims independence from Spain
- **1822** Brazil declares its independence from Portugal
- **1836** Texas declares independence from Mexico
- **1846** Canada and the United States settle border dispute

1800 — **1825** — **1850**

World

- **1804** Ludwig von Beethoven completes the *Eroica* Symphony
- **1821** Electric motor developed in Great Britain
- **1837** Queen Victoria crowned
- **1839** Painter J. M. W. Turner completes *The Fighting Téméraire*
- **1845–1849** Potato famine strikes Ireland

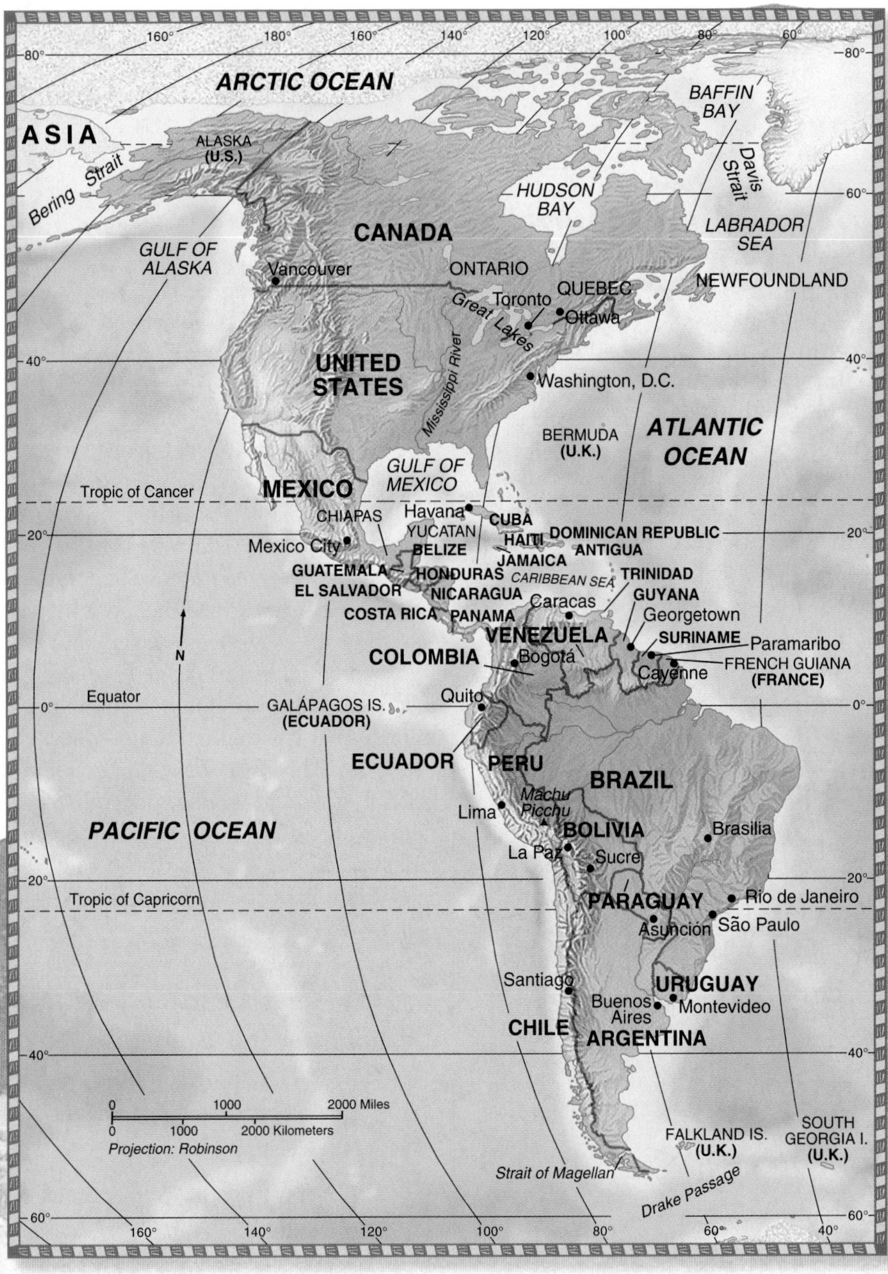

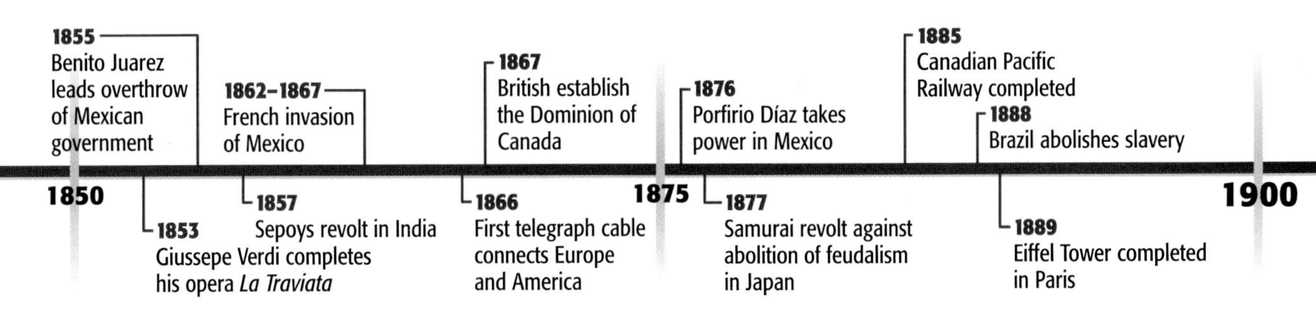
1855
Benito Juarez leads overthrow of Mexican government
1862–1867
French invasion of Mexico
1867
British establish the Dominion of Canada
1876
Porfirio Díaz takes power in Mexico
1885
Canadian Pacific Railway completed
1888
Brazil abolishes slavery
1850
1875
1900
1853
Giussepe Verdi completes his opera *La Traviata*
1857
Sepoys revolt in India
1866
First telegraph cable connects Europe and America
1877
Samurai revolt against abolition of feudalism in Japan
1889
Eiffel Tower completed in Paris

How People Live

City Life

In 1940, 65 percent of the people in Latin America lived in rural areas and 35 percent lived in the cities. By 1998 those figures had more than reversed: less than 30 percent lived in the countryside and more than 70 percent lived in the cities. Four Latin American cities rank among the world's largest: Mexico City; São Paulo and Rio de Janeiro, Brazil; and Buenos Aires, Argentina.

As in most of the world, people continue to leave rural areas to settle in cities. Cities offer schools, job opportunities, and the benefits of technology. Women, even more than men, find that cities are places of opportunity. In rural areas, women often confront customs that limit their options. In cities, women have a better chance of finding their own income and sense of independence.

Paseo de la Reforma, Mexico City.

A Diversity of Peoples

The first immigrants to the Americas came from Asia, crossing the land bridge between Alaska and Siberia tens of thousands of years ago. People from around the world have joined them since. With independence, settlers from all over Europe joined the earlier Spanish, British, and Portuguese immigrants. People of African descent, once slavery was abolished, were free to move about and settle where they wished. And since the late nineteenth century, Asian people have again settled in the region; in 1990 Alberto Fujimori was elected president of Peru. The dynamic and continuing intermingling of cultural traditions that has resulted has produced its own cultural tradition. Throughout the Americas, people question the old ways and look for new solutions to old problems. Many people feel respect and affection for their ancestral homelands, but throughout the hemisphere, people think of themselves first as Americans.

Telephone booth, Buenos Aires.

Active Reading Strategies

Reading the Time Line

1. In 1804, Ludwig von Beethoven composed the *Eroica* Symphony. What country became independent that same year?
2. List these events in the correct time order including the years they occurred: major oil deposits discovered in the Gulf of Mexico; Mexican Revolution begins; Mexico wins independence; Cuba gains independence.

The Americas

- 1902 Cuba gains independence
- 1910 Mexican Revolution begins
- 1912 European immigrants to Argentina top 300,000
- 1921 Diego Rivera begins work on his first mural in Mexico
- 1930–1945 Heitor Villa-Lobos composes *Bachianas Brasileiras*
- 1944 Juan Peron comes to power in Argentina

1901 — 1925 — 1950

World

- Composer Sergey Rachmaninoff completes his Second Piano Concerto
- 1904 Russia completes the Trans-Siberian Railroad
- 1914–1918 World War I
- 1931 Japan invades China
- 1936 First regular television broadcasts begin in Great Britain
- 1948 State of Israel proclaimed

Modern Languages

The most widely spoken languages in the Americas today are European languages: English in Canada and the United States, French in Canada, Portuguese in Brazil, and Spanish almost everywhere else. In addition, over 800 Native American languages are spoken. Several Native American languages have over a million speakers.

- In Mexico over 7.4 million people speak some Indian language, including Nahuatl, the language of the Aztecs.
- In Guatemala 3.9 million people speak one of the Mayan languages.
- In Peru more than 4 million people speak Quechua, the language of the Incas. This number is growing.
- In Paraguay about 4.4 million people speak some version of Guaraní.
- In Bolivia nearly 2 million people speak Aymara and nearly 3 million speak Quechua.

French Canadians

Cross from central Canada into Quebec province, and you may think you have entered another country. The street signs and advertisements are in French, as are the daily newspapers. All but one of the television and radio stations are broadcast in French, and all official business is conducted in French. Quebec City was founded by French explorers in 1608, and the province was a part of France until that country's defeat by the British in 1763. About 80 percent of the people in Quebec are of French ancestry. Some advocate separation from Canada and the formation of an independent nation.

Street sign, Quebec City.

Market, Chinchero, Peru.

Critical Thinking

The Modern Americas

1. In a small group, discuss the literature of the modern Americas, focusing on how it reflects the region's rich ethnic diversity.
2. In a group discussion, explain two concerns or challenges that face writers and speakers of minority languages.

MEXICO, c. 1965

Before You Read

The Luck of Teodoro Méndez Acúbal

Meet Rosario Castellanos

"Laughter is the most immediate form of freeing ourselves from that which oppresses us the most, of distancing ourselves from that which imprisons us!"

Rosario Castellanos (rō sä′ rē ō kä stā yä′ nōs) grew up on a plantation near Comitán, a village in the Chiapas region of southern Mexico. She published her first poems while studying philosophy in Mexico City. After receiving her master's degree, she returned to Chiapas to learn more about the culture of the Chamula group of Maya living there. In her fiction, Castellanos often focused on relations between the Chamulas and the landowners. She believed that Mexican women and the Chamulas suffered from similar forms of oppression.

During the 1960s, Castellanos lectured at universities in the United States and Mexico. She was appointed Mexico's ambassador to Israel in 1971. While carrying out her diplomatic responsibilities, she continued to write and teach. Castellanos died in a household accident at age forty-nine.

Rosario Castellanos was born in 1925 and died in 1974.

Reading Focus

Think of a time when you mistakenly assumed something bad about another person, or when someone did that to you. What were the consequences of that assumption?

Journal Briefly describe the experience in your journal.

Setting a Purpose Read this story to see how a stroke of luck changes a character's life.

Building Background

Native Americans in Chiapas

"The Luck of Teodoro Méndez Acúbal" is set in Chiapas, which was once a center of Maya civilization. Many of its inhabitants are descended, either completely or partly, from the Maya. Over the centuries, conflicts have broken out between the Maya and landowners in Chiapas. Many Maya were deprived of their land in the nineteenth century, when Mexico gained its independence from Spain. Racial, class, and language barriers have made it difficult for them to achieve an adequate standard of living.

Vocabulary Preview

propriety (prə prī′ ə tē) *n.* conformity to what is acceptable in conduct or speech; p. 1097

condescending (kon′ di sen′ ding) *adj.* characterized by an air of superiority or smugness; p. 1097

disdain (dis dān′) *n.* an attitude of scorn or contempt for those considered inferior; p. 1097

diligence (dil′ ə jəns) *n.* persistent hard work; alertness; p. 1097

Pre-Columbian Maya bowl with glyph decoration.

The Luck of Teodoro Méndez Acúbal

Rosario Castellanos
Translated by Myralyn F. Allgood

Walking along the streets of Jobel (with his eyes cast downward as custom dictates for those of his humble station), Teodoro Méndez Acúbal spotted a coin. All but lost in the dust, caked with mud, worn from years of use, it had been ignored by the white *caxlanes*.[1] For the *caxlanes* walk with their heads held high. Moved by pride, they contemplate from afar the important matters that absorb them.

La union (The Union), c. 1923. Diego Rivera (Mexico). Mural. Court of Fiestas, West Wall, Secretaria de Educacion Publica, Mexico City. What different types of people does this mural depict? Why might the artist have chosen to place these people in this way?

1. ***Caxlanes*** **(käs lä′ nās) are the dominant socioeconomic class in Chiapas, which has a large Maya population.**

Teodoro stopped, more out of disbelief than greed. Kneeling as if to fasten one of his sandals, he waited until no one was looking to pick up what he had found. He hid it quickly in the folds of his sash.

He stood again, swaying, overcome by a kind of dizziness. Weak-kneed and dry-mouthed, his eyes blurred as he felt his heart pounding, pulsing between his eyebrows.

Staggering from side to side as if in a drunken stupor, Teodoro began to make his way down the street. From time to time the passersby had to push him aside to avoid bumping into him. But Teodoro's spirit was too troubled to be bothered by what was going on around him. The coin, hidden in his sash, had transformed him into another man—a stronger man than before, it is true. But also more fearful.

He stepped off the path that led to his village and sat down on a fallen log. Could this be all a dream? Pale with anxiety, Teodoro's hands felt his sash. Yes, there it was—firm and round—the precious coin. Teodoro unwrapped it, moistened it with his breath and saliva and rubbed it against his clothing. On the metal (it had to be silver, judging from its whitish color) the outline of a profile appeared. Majestic. And around the edge, letters, numbers, and signs. Calculating its weight, testing it with his teeth, listening to its ring, Teodoro was able—at last—to determine its value.

And so, with this stroke of fortune, he had become rich. Richer than the owner of great flocks of sheep or vast stretches of cornfields. He was as rich as . . . as a *caxlán*. And Teodoro was amazed that the color of his skin had not changed.

The images of the members of his family (his wife, his three children, his aging parents) struggled to invade Teodoro's reverie. But he dispelled them with an air of displeasure. He saw no reason to tell anyone about his discovery, much less share it. He worked to maintain his household. That's as it should be; it's the custom, an obligation. But as for this stroke of fortune, it was his. Exclusively his.

And so, when Teodoro arrived at his hut and sat down by the fire to eat, he did not speak. His own silence made him uncomfortable, as if being quiet were a way of mocking everyone else. To punish himself he allowed his feelings of loneliness to grow within him, along with his shame. Teodoro was a man set apart, stifled by his secret. Moreover, this anguish produced physical discomfort—a cramp in the pit of his stomach, a chill deep in the marrow of his bones. Why suffer all this, when with a word the pain would disappear? To keep himself from uttering it, Teodoro grasped his sash and felt the lump there, made by the metal.

During the sleepless night, Teodoro talked to himself: what shall I buy? Before now he had never wanted things. So convinced was he that they were beyond his reach that he passed them by without a thought, without the slightest curiosity. And now he wasn't about to consider necessities—a blanket, a machete, a hat. No. These are things to be bought with wages. But Méndez Acúbal had not earned this coin. It was his luck, an outright gift. It was given to him so he could play with it, so he could waste it, so he could have something impractical and beautiful.

Teodoro had no idea about prices. On his next trip to Jobel, he began to notice the dealings of buyers and sellers. Both appeared to be calm. The one feigning lack of interest, the other the desire to please, they spoke of pesos and centavos,[2] of pounds and measures, of many other things that whirled about in Teodoro's head, making no sense at all.

Exhausted, Teodoro abandoned the struggle and took refuge in a delightful notion: with his silver coin he could buy anything he wanted.

2. *Pesos and centavos* (sen tä′ vōs) are coins used as currency in some Latin American countries. One hundred centavos equal one peso.

Virgin of Guadalupe. c. 19th century, Mexico.

Viewing the painting: What values do you think the Virgin of Guadalupe might represent?

Months went by before Teodoro made his irrevocable selection. It was a clay figurine, a small statue of the Virgin.[3] It was also a real find, because the figure lay in the midst of a clutter of objects that decorated the window of a store. From that time on, Teodoro hovered around it like a lover. Hours and hours went by. And always he was there, standing like a sentinel beside the window.

Don Agustín Velasco, the merchant, watched him with his tiny squinting eyes (eyes of a hawk, his mother would say) from inside the store.

3. *Virgin* refers to Mary, the mother of Jesus.

Even before Teodoro acquired the custom of appearing in front of his establishment, the Indian's features had attracted the attention of Don Agustín. No Ladino[4] could help but notice a Chamula[5] walking on the sidewalks (reserved for the *caxlanes*), and less so when he walked as slowly as if out for a stroll. It was unusual for this to happen, and Don Agustín had not even considered it possible. But he now had to admit that things might go further: an Indian was also capable of daring to stand before a window contemplating the display, not just with the assurance of one who can appreciate it, but with the bold insolence of one who comes to buy.

Don Agustín's thin, yellowish face grimaced in a gesture of scorn. For an Indian to go to Guadalupe Street to shop for candles for his saints, or whiskey for his festivals, or tools for his work is acceptable. The people who deal with them have neither illustrious lineage nor family names; they have no fortunes and therefore work at demeaning jobs. For an Indian to enter a pharmacy to ask for healing powders or liquid potions or miraculous ointments can be tolerated. After all, pharmacists belong to the middle-class families that wish to move upward and mingle with their betters, and that is why it's good for the Indians to humble them by frequenting their places of business.

But for an Indian to position himself so firmly in front of a jewelry store—no ordinary jewelry store at that, but the one belonging to Don Agustín Velasco, descendant of conquistadors, well received in the best circles, appreciated by his colleagues—was, at the very least, unfathomable. Unless . . .

A terrible thought began to gnaw at him. What if the boldness of this Chamula was based

4. *Ladino,* in the dialect of Chiapas, refers to an individual of mixed Maya and Spanish heritage. Ladinos make up the middle class.

5. *Chamula* (chä mo͞o′ lä) are a group of pure Maya heritage, who make up the least privileged socioeconomic class.

on the strength of his tribe? It wouldn't be the first time, the salesman admitted bitterly. Rumors . . . where had he heard rumors of revolt? Quickly Don Agustín tried to recall the places he had visited in the past few days: the Bishop's Palace, the Casino, the meeting at Doña Romelia Ochoa's house.

What foolishness! Don Agustín smiled, silently laughing at himself. How right Bishop Manuel Oropeza had been when he said that every sin has its punishment. And Don Agustín, who rigorously abstained from alcohol, tobacco, and women, was still a slave to one bad habit: gossip.

Slyly he made himself a part of conversations in doorways, in the market, even in the Cathedral. Don Agustín was the first to hear a rumor, to sniff out the scandals, and he longed for shared confidences, for secrets to guard and for intrigues to plot.

And at night, after supper (of thick chocolate provided by his anxious, worn-out mother), Don Agustín made a habit of attending a gathering of some sort. There they talked and entertained each other with stories. About love affairs, feuds over inheritances, sudden and unexplained fortunes, duels. For several nights the conversation had revolved around one topic: Indian uprisings. Everyone present had been witness, participant, victim, or victor in one or another. They recalled details of those they had seen. Terrible images that made Don Agustín tremble: fifteen thousand Chamulas ready for war, besieging Ciudad Real.[6] Haciendas plundered, men killed, women (no, no, we must not think of these things), women . . . in the end, violated.

Did You Know?
In Latin America, *hacienda* generally refers to a large ranch, farm, or plantation, especially to the main building or owner's residence.

Victory always fell on the side of the *caxlanes* (anything else would have been inconceivable), but at such a price, such loss.

Is experience worth anything? Judging by the Indian standing at the window of his jewelry store, no. The inhabitants of Ciudad Real, caught up in their daily routines and interests, forgot the past, which should serve as a lesson to them, and went about their business as if no danger threatened. Don Agustín was horrified by such an irresponsible attitude. The security of his life was so fragile that all it took was the face of a Chamula, seen through a glass, to shatter it completely.

Don Agustín looked out again into the street hoping to find the Indian no longer present. But Méndez Acúbal remained there still, motionless and attentive.

The passersby walked near him without any sign of surprise or alarm. This consoling fact (and the familiar sounds that came from the back of the house) restored Don Agustín's sense of tranquility. He could no longer justify his fears. Events like the one at Cancuc, like Pedro Díaz Cuscat's siege of Jobel, and Pajarito's threats[7]—those couldn't happen again. These were different times, more secure for decent people.

And besides, who was going to provide arms, who was going to lead the rebels? The Indian who was here, with his nose pressed against the window of the jewelry store, was alone. And if things got out of hand, no one was to blame but the townspeople themselves. No one was going to respect them if they themselves were not worthy of respect. Don Agustín disapproved of his fellow citizens' conduct, as if he had been betrayed by them.

They say that some—not many, thank God—even shake hands with the Indians. Indians—what a race of thieves!

6. *Ciudad Real* (sü däd′ rā äl′) is a city in Chiapas.

7. *[Cancuc . . . Pajarito's threats]* are references to conflicts involving Maya and people of European descent.

The thought left a peculiarly painful taste in Don Agustín's mouth. Not only from a sense of propriety, as entrenched in him as in anyone else in his profession, but from a special circumstance.

Don Agustín did not have the courage to admit it, but what tormented him was the suspicion that he was himself insignificant. And to make matters worse, his mother confirmed his suspicions in many ways. Her attitude toward this, her only child (son of Saint Anne,[8] she used to say), born when he was more a bother than a comfort, was one of Christian resignation. The "boy"—his mother and the servants continued to call him that in spite of the fact that Don Agustín was past forty—was very shy, cowardly, and passive. How many business deals had slipped through his fingers! And how many of those he did make resulted in nothing but failure! The Velasco fortune had dwindled considerably since Don Agustín took charge of things. And as for the prestige of the firm, it was maintained with great difficulty, and only because of the respect his late father, still mourned by mother and son, instilled in everyone.

But what could one expect from a wimp, an "overgrown child"? Don Agustín's mother shook her head sighing. And she kept on with her wheedling, her prudery, her condescending comments, for this was her way of expressing disdain.

Instinctively, the shopkeeper knew that he had before him the opportunity to prove his courage to others and himself. His zeal, his keen insight, would be evident to everyone. One simple word—thief—had given him the clue: the man with his nose pressed against the glass of his jewelry store was a thief. No doubt about it. Besides, the case was not uncommon. Don Agustín could think of countless anecdotes of robberies and even worse crimes attributed to the Indians.

Satisfied with his deductions, Don Agustín didn't settle for merely preparing a defense. His sense of racial, class, and professional solidarity obliged him to share his suspicions with the other merchants, and together they went to the police. The neighborhood was prepared, thanks to the diligence of Don Agustín.

But the person responsible for those precautions suddenly disappeared from sight. After a few weeks he appeared again in his customary spot and in the same posture: standing guard. Because Teodoro didn't dare go in. No Chamula had ever attempted such a bold act. If he were to risk being the first, surely they would throw him out into the street before his lice had a chance to escape into the establishment. But, if by remotest chance they didn't eject him, and if they allowed him to remain inside the store long enough to discuss the matter, Teodoro wouldn't know how to express his desires. He could neither understand nor speak Spanish. And so, to unclog his ears, to loosen his tongue, he had been drinking Indian whiskey. The liquor had instilled in him a sense of power. His blood flowed, hot and fast, through his veins. The ease with which he moved his muscles dictated his actions. As if in a dream, he crossed the threshold of the jewelry store. But the cool dampness and the still, musty air inside brought him abruptly back to reality with a shock of terror. From a jewelry case the flashing eye of a diamond stared at him threateningly.

8. *Saint Anne* was the mother of Mary, mother of Jesus.

Vocabulary

propriety (prə prī′ ə tē) *n.* conformity to what is acceptable in conduct or speech
condescending (kon′ də sen′ ding) *adj.* characterized by an air of superiority or smugness
disdain (dis dān′) *n.* an attitude of scorn or contempt for those considered inferior
diligence (dil′ ə jəns) *n.* persistent hard work; alertness

Ranchos Orilleros, 1932. José Cúneo (Uruguay). Oil on burlap, 24¼ x 36 in. Private collection.

Viewing the painting: How might this landscape suggest Teodoro's state of mind at the end of the story? Explain.

"May I help you, Chamula? What would you like?"

By repeating such pleasantries, Don Agustín sought to gain time. At the same time his hands searched for the gun he kept in the counter drawer. The Indian's silence frightened him more than any threat. He dared not raise his eyes until he had the gun in his hand.

The look he encountered paralyzed him. A gaze of surprise, of reproach. Why was the Indian staring at him like that? Don Agustín wasn't the one at fault. He was an honest man, he had never harmed anyone. And it appeared that he would be the first victim of these Indians who had suddenly set themselves up as judges! Here was his executioner, coming toward him with his fingers searching the folds of his sash, soon to draw forth who knows what instrument of death.

Don Agustín clutched the gun but could not fire. He cried out to the police for help.

When Teodoro tried to get away, he couldn't, because a crowd had gathered in the doorway of the store blocking his path. Shouts, gestures, angry faces. The police seized the Indian, questioned him, searched him. When the silver coin appeared in the folds of his sash, a shout of triumph arose from the crowd. Don Agustín excitedly held up the coin for all to see. The shouting exhilarated him.

"Thief, thief!"

Teodoro Méndez Acúbal was taken to jail. Since the charges against him were not unusual, no one was in a hurry to gather the facts of the case. His file grew yellow with age on the shelves of the police department.

Responding to Literature

Personal Response

How did you react to the story's ending? Why do you think you responded in that way? Share your response with the class.

Analyzing Literature

Recall

1. According to the narrator, why does Teodoro find a coin that the caxlanes failed to notice?
2. How does the coin affect Teodoro's feelings about himself?
3. What does Teodoro decide to purchase with the coin?
4. Why does Don Agustín grow suspicious of Teodoro?
5. What happens when Teodoro finally goes into the store?

Interpret

6. What does the explanation of how Teodoro found the coin suggest about relations between Chamulas and caxlanes in Jobel?
7. **Hyperbole** is a figure of speech in which exaggeration is used for emphasis or comic effect (see **Literary Terms Handbook,** page R6). Identify an example of hyperbole in the description of Teodoro's reaction to his good luck.
8. In your opinion, what does Teodoro's purchasing decision suggest about him?
9. How does Don Agustín's family background influence his feelings regarding the Chamulas?
10. How does Don Agustín misunderstand Teodoro's actions after he enters the store?

Evaluate and Connect

11. What, if anything, did you find humorous in this story? Explain your answer.
12. Why might the author have chosen to describe Don Agustín's relationship with his mother?
13. The **climax** is the point of greatest interest or emotional intensity in a narrative (see **Literary Terms Handbook,** page R2). What is the climax of this story?
14. Do you think that Teodoro is idealized in the story or portrayed realistically? Explain.
15. In the Reading Focus on page 1092, you were asked to describe a time when you mistakenly assumed something bad about another person, or vice versa. Compare this experience with Don Agustín's assumption about Teodoro.

Literary ELEMENTS

Dramatic Irony

Dramatic irony occurs when the reader or audience of a literary work knows something that a character does not know. Writers sometimes use this technique for comic effect, encouraging us to laugh at the character's mistakes. Dramatic irony can also be used to generate suspense or increase our sympathy for a character who is about to make a fateful error. For example, in Sophocles' tragedy *Oedipus the King* (page 263), Oedipus issues a harsh condemnation of a crime that he unknowingly committed.

1. What dramatic irony in "The Luck of Teodoro Méndez Acúbal" develops from Don Agustín's fear of Teodoro?
2. What dramatic irony occurs at the end of the story? How did this irony affect your response to the ending? Explain.

- See **Literary Terms Handbook,** p. R6.

Literature and Writing

Writing About Literature

Analyze Narration Write one or two paragraphs about the narration of "The Luck of Teodoro Méndez Acúbal." First identify the story's point of view. Then describe the narrator's attitude toward Teodoro, Don Agustín, and the town they live in. Use evidence from the story to support your analysis.

Creative Writing

Letter from Prison Write a letter from Teodoro to his family, explaining how he wound up in prison and why he didn't tell them about finding the coin. Do you think he would understand why Don Agustín was afraid of him? What might he have learned from this experience?

Extending Your Response

Literature Groups

Analyze Character Is Don Agustín an evil character, or do his actions result from weakness and ignorance? Discuss this question in your group. Refer to specific passages in the story to support your opinion. When you are finished, take a vote and announce the results to the class.

Listening and Speaking

Interview Imagine that you are a reporter for a Jobel newspaper. Role-play an interview with Teodoro or Don Agustín after their encounter in the jewelry store. Before you begin, go over the story together with your partner and discuss the interview subject's character traits and motivation.

Learning for Life

Community Relations How would you try to improve relations between the Chamulas and the Ladinos of Jobel? With a partner, draw up a list of steps that should be taken. Explain how your plan might have prevented Teodoro from winding up in prison.

Reading Further

If you enjoyed reading this story by Rosario Castellanos, the following selections of her work might interest you: "First Elegy," "A Palm Tree," and "Silence Concerning an Ancient Stone" from *The Muse in Mexico: A Mid-Century Miscellany,* edited by Thomas Mabry Cranfill.

Save your work for your portfolio.

VOCABULARY • Synonyms and Shades of Meaning

Some synonyms can be used interchangeably without sacrificing precision of meaning. *Glad* and *happy* are examples. Other synonyms, while they have similar meanings, differ in nuance. Nuance is a subtle difference or shade of meaning. For example, *rebellion* implies an open resistance that is often unsuccessful. *Uprising* implies a brief, limited, and often ineffective rebellion. *Revolution* applies to a successful rebellion that brings about a major change.

PRACTICE Each of the adjectives below shares the meaning "intelligent." Consult a dictionary to learn the nuances or shades of meaning that distinguish one from another. Then write an original sentence for each word illustrating the nuance it conveys.

1. wise
2. clever
3. shrewd
4. cunning

Vo•cab•u•lar•y Skills

New Words in English

What do the seemingly dissimilar words *modem, contra, perestroika,* and *CAT scan* have in common? They are all recent words that have come into the English vocabulary. Some are from new technology, such as the terms *modem* and *CAT scan.* Some are from other languages, such as the word *contra* from Spanish and the word *perestroika* from Russian. The English language has been evolving since well before Shakespeare's time and continues to evolve today, giving us the words we'll need to communicate in the years to come.

Despite the explosion of new words that are created by the demands of new technology, science, ideas, and innovations, the evolution of a language is a slow process. Changes usually aren't even noticed until decades or centuries later. Fifty or one hundred years in the future, what new words in the English language do you think will illustrate the changes that are occurring now? Clues to those changes will be found not only in new words–such as *aerobics, simulcast,* and *Internet*–but also in existing words with new meanings, in acronyms, and in slang.

The existing word *network,* for example, has a new meaning due to innovations in computer technology. Other existing words that have new meanings include *rap* and *mouse.* The word *rap,* for example, means "to knock." Today, *rap* also refers to a particular style of music. *Mouse* is the word for a small rodent. Today, however, it more usually refers to a device used to manipulate words and images on a computer screen.

Acronyms, words formed from the initial or first letters in a series of words, are yet another way new words enter the English language. The medical term *CAT scan,* for example, contains an acronym for "computerized axial tomography."

Every generation makes its own contribution of new words and meanings through the invention and use of slang–the popular and informal expressions you and your friends use every day. When your parents were teenagers, they might have described something wonderful as "groovy," "far out," or "heavy." What words and expressions do you and your friends use to describe something wonderful?

Ever evolving, language changes as the world changes. New words and meanings are invented to name and describe any new aspect of culture–from innovations in medical science, computer technology, and space exploration, to social behavior and trends.

ACTIVITY

With a partner, create a log that helps you keep track of some of the changes in the English language. Divide your log into sections labeled "New Words," "Existing Words with New Meanings," and "Current Slang." Listen for new words, meanings, acronyms, and slang when you read, listen to television or radio, or talk with your friends. Then, whenever you come across a word that fits one of these categories, add the word and its definition to your log.

MEXICO, 1957

Before You Read

The Window

Meet Jaime Torres Bodet

"Torres Bodet's endeavor was always to avoid divorcing art from life."

—*Sonja Karsen, critic and translator*

Jaime Torres Bodet (hī′ mā tō′ rās bō det′) juggled two careers: he was a distinguished public servant as well as a writer. He led a successful campaign against illiteracy in Mexico. As director general of UNESCO, he promoted educational programs throughout the world. Torres Bodet also served as a diplomat and Mexico's minister of foreign affairs. He felt that these positions helped his writing because they kept him involved in the concerns of other people.

Torres Bodet's mother used to read French literature to him when he was a boy. He became fluent in French, and his own poetry was influenced by French literary movements such as surrealism. He published over twenty volumes of poetry, six novels, a book of short stories, and many critical studies. In 1966 he was honored with the Mexican National Prize for Literature. He spent his last years writing about his experiences as a statesman.

Jaime Torres Bodet was born in 1902 and died in 1974.

Reading Focus

Why might people choose to lead solitary lives?

List Ideas With a partner, write down at least five reasons why people might want to live alone.

Setting a Purpose Read this poem to learn the speaker's views about solitude.

Building Background

Surrealism

In the first few decades of the twentieth century, France was the literary and artistic center of the world. One of the most influential literary movements produced there was surrealism. Originating in the early 1920s, surrealism was a reaction to the devastating effects of World War I. The war had supposedly been conducted by sensible, practical people, yet it left much of the continent in ruins and planted the seeds of the even more devastating Second World War.

In reaction, surrealist artists and writers downplayed the importance of rational thought and emphasized the unconscious. They created pictures from random images and wrote poems that ignored rules of structure and language, in an effort to reach a higher truth. André Breton, one of the movement's leaders, said surrealism was born of "an unlimited faith in the genius of youth." Eighty years after that birth, the surrealist approach, with its questioning of the very nature of reality, is still influential throughout the world.

UNESCO

Torres Bodet was the second director general of the United Nations Educational, Scientific, and Cultural Organization, serving from 1948 to 1952. This organization, founded in November of 1945, has as its objective the promotion of peace and security in the world by emphasizing education and the exchange of information among nations. UNESCO has 186 member countries.

Reading Further

If you enjoy "The Window," you may want to read the following: "Living" and "Labyrinth" from *Twentieth-Century Latin American Poetry,* edited by Stephen Tapscott.

Interior with Alarm Clock, 1928. Rufino Tamayo (Mexico). Oil on canvas. Private collection.

The Window

Jaime Torres Bodet

Translated by George Kearns

You closed the window. And it was
the world,
the world that wanted to enter,
all at once,
the world that gave that great shout,
that great, deep, rough cry
you did not want to hear—and now
will never call to you again as it called
today,
asking your mercy!

The whole of life was in that cry:
the wind, the sea, the land
with its poles and its tropics,
the unreachable skies,
the ripened grain in the resounding
wheat field,
the thick heat above the wine presses,
dawn on the mountains, shadowy woods,
parched lips stuck together longing for
cool water condensed in pools,
and all pleasures, all sufferings,
all loves, all hates,
were in this day, anxiously
asking your mercy . . .

But you were afraid of life.
And you remained alone,
behind the closed and silent window,
not understanding that the world
calls to a man
only once that way, and with that
kind of cry,
with that great, rough, hoarse cry!

Responding to Literature

Personal Response

What person or literary character did this poem remind you of? Jot down a response in your journal. Then share your response with a classmate.

Analyzing Literature

Recall and Interpret

1. According to the speaker in the poem, what makes up "the whole of life"?
2. How do you interpret the speaker's remark that the world was "asking your mercy"?
3. Why did the subject of the poem refuse to answer this call? In your opinion, what might have made the subject feel this way?
4. In your opinion, how might the subject of the poem have lost a unique opportunity? Support your answer with details from the poem.

Evaluate and Connect

5. Which of the poem's details suggesting "the whole of life" have the strongest appeal for you? Explain your answer.
6. **Tone** is the attitude that the speaker takes toward the audience, the subject, or the character (see page R12) that he is discussing. How would you describe the tone that the speaker uses in addressing the subject of this poem?
7. What opportunity in your life do you most regret not taking?

Literary Criticism

Scholar Sonja Karsen observes that the poetry of Torres Bodet often expresses a "desire to overcome man's isolation in the twentieth century." Do you see evidence of that desire in "The Window"? Write a paragraph discussing the theme of the poem in your own words.

Literary ELEMENTS

Extended Metaphor

A metaphor is a figure of speech that compares two things without using *like* or *as*. Sometimes the comparison is stated directly (for example, "the horse was a comet streaking through the sky"); in other metaphors, the comparison is implied. An **extended metaphor** is a comparison that runs through several lines or is developed throughout a poem. For example, if a man is compared to a bird, the speaker might go on to describe his nose as a beak and his hands as claws.

1. What is compared to the closing of a window in "The Window"?
2. Is the comparison in this extended metaphor implied or stated directly?

- See **Literary Terms Handbook,** p. R7.

Extending Your Response

Creative Writing

Response Write a dialogue in which the subject of "The Window" responds to the statements made by the speaker. Is this person really afraid of life, or was there some other reason for remaining alone? Before you begin, go over the list you wrote down for the Reading Focus on page 1102. Read your completed dialogue aloud to a group of classmates and encourage their constructive criticism.

Learning for Life

Overcoming Shyness Many people shut themselves away from others because of shyness. In a small group, discuss ways to encourage shy people to overcome their fears. Write down at least three suggestions and share them with the class.

Save your work for your portfolio.

Television Transcript

One of the greatest archaeological events of the twentieth century was the discovery of Machu Picchu. This Inca city, isolated deep in the mountains of the Andes, was forgotten and lay buried in the jungle for four hundred years.

In Search of History: Lost City of the Incas

A&E Television Network, 1996

Narrator: The year is 1911. Hiram Bingham, a professor of history at Yale University, hacks his way through dense jungles in southeastern Peru, following vague rumors of a lost city hidden deep in the Andes. Above him are 9,000-foot peaks; before him, the deadly torrents of the Urubamba River. Yet Bingham perseveres. Guided by a local Indian, he begins to climb up a nearly vertical mountain. By afternoon, he is among the clouds, on a narrow ridge which runs along the mountain's top. The natives call this ridge the Great Peak—in their language, *Machu Picchu.*

Quoting Hiram Bingham: Suddenly, we found ourselves standing in front of the finest and most interesting structures in ancient America. It seemed like an unbelievable dream. What could this place be? Would anyone believe what I had found?

Narrator: Over the years that followed, Bingham and other archaeologists excavated five square miles of ruins at Machu Picchu. Despite its remote location, the place Bingham discovered has become one of the most popular tourist destinations in the world. Slowly, scholars are filling in pieces of the Machu Picchu puzzle. And incredible as it may seem, they believe that it was not one of the Inca empire's most important cities.

Dr. Richard Burger, Director, Peabody Museum at Yale University: At Machu Picchu there was only a population that, at its peak, would have been in the hundreds, perhaps something on the order of five or six hundred. I believe that the site was a royal estate, that it was a place where the Inca elite would go to get away from Cuzco when the weather was unfavorable up in the capital.

Narrator: Was Machu Picchu a playground for the emperor and his court? Or was it a solemn place of worship, as many believe? Perhaps it was both.

Analyzing Media

1. What might have been some possible reasons for Bingham's search for the lost city?
2. Why might the Incas have abandoned Machu Picchu?

CHILE, 1958

Before You Read

Horses

Meet Pablo Neruda

"If you ask what my poetry is, I must confess that I don't know; but if you'll ask my poetry, it will tell you who I am."

As a boy growing up in southern Chile, Pablo Neruda (pä′ blō nā ro͞o′ dä) immersed himself in literature. He received encouragement from the poet Gabriela Mistral, who later became the first Chilean to win a Nobel Prize. Neruda began publishing poems when he was fifteen. By his early twenties, he was already one of Chile's most popular poets.

Unable to support himself from his writing, Neruda took a series of diplomatic positions in Asia and Europe. His experiences during the Spanish Civil War made him deeply committed to left-wing politics. After returning to Chile, he joined the Communist Party and won election to the senate. However, he soon had to go abroad for several years because his harsh criticism angered the president. In 1971 he became the second Chilean to win the Nobel Prize for Literature.

Neruda was born in 1904 and died in 1973.

Reading Focus

What qualities do you associate with horses?

Discuss With a small group, make a list of all the qualities of horses that come to mind.

Setting a Purpose Read to see how the sight of horses affects one man.

Building Background

Neruda's Poetry

Pablo Neruda wrote about fifty volumes of poetry in a career that spanned half a century. He wrote in different styles. Some of his poems are dense, highly experimental works; others are simple and direct. Neruda wrote epic poetry in which he reinterpreted the history of Latin America. He could also narrow his scope considerably; in his book *Elementary Odes,* he wrote about common objects such as onions and scissors. Uniting the different phases of his career are his love for the people and landscape of Chile, his exuberance, and the freshness of his imagery. Many critics regard Neruda as the most important Latin American poet of the twentieth century.

People and Places

Neruda had a natural gift for writing poetry. But beyond this gift, his travels and the people he met inspired him to continue and improve. When he was at school in the small town of Temuco, he met the poet Gabriela Mistral, a teacher there. Later to win a Nobel Prize herself, she encouraged the young Neruda to write. A few years later, Neruda entered Chile's diplomatic service. Although at first he was paid little or nothing, he was able to travel and to study other cultures. Eventually he met the Spanish poet Federico Garcia Lorca, who praised his work. He served as consul in Mexico, where he studied that country's ancient civilizations. His visit to the once lost city of Machu Picchu inspired what is often considered his greatest work. Some of Neruda's best work—even after he had established himself as a poet—was produced in the house he built, filled with mementos from a lifetime of travel, beside the Pacific Ocean.

HORSES

Pablo Neruda

Translated by Alastair Reid

The Small Yellow Horses, 1912. Franz Marc (Germany). Staatsgalerie, Stuttgart, Germany.

It was from the window I saw the horses.

I was in Berlin, in winter. The light
was without light, the sky skyless.

The air white like a moistened loaf.

From my window, I could see a deserted arena,
a circle bitten out by the teeth of winter.

All at once, led out by a man,
ten horses were stepping into the snow.

Emerging, they had scarcely rippled into existence
like flame, than they filled the whole world of my eyes,
empty till now. Faultless, flaming,
they stepped like ten gods on broad, clean hooves,
their manes recalling a dream of pure grace.

Their rumps were globes, were oranges.

Their color was amber and honey, was on fire.

Their necks were towers
carved from the stone of pride,
and in their furious eyes, sheer energy
showed itself, a prisoner inside them.

And there, in the silence, at the midpoint of the day, in a dirty, disgruntled winter,
the horses' intense presence was blood,
was rhythm, was the beckoning Grail° of being.

I saw, I saw, and, seeing, I came to life.
There was the unwitting fountain, the dance of gold, the sky,
the fire that sprang to life in beautiful things.

I have obliterated that gloomy Berlin winter.

I shall not forget the light from these horses.

---

23 In legend, the *Grail,* or cup used by Jesus at the Last Supper, was sought by Arthurian knights during a long, difficult quest.

Landscape with Wild Horses, 1941. Carlos Enriquez (Cuba). Oil on composition board, 17½ x 23⅝ in. The Museum of Modern Art, New York.

Viewing the painting: How is this landscape different from the one described in the poem? How is it similar?

Responding to Literature

Personal Response

What thoughts went through your mind as you finished reading this poem? Share your response with the class.

Analyzing Literature

Recall and Interpret

1. What is the scene that the speaker is describing in the first six lines of the poem?
2. Why do you think the horses are being led outside?
3. In your opinion, what do lines 22–23 of the poem mean? Explain.
4. What effect does the sight of the horses have on the speaker?

Evaluate and Connect

5. **Mood** is the overall feeling or atmosphere of a literary work (see page R7). What mood is established early in the poem? At what point does it change?
6. Why might Neruda have chosen to set this poem in the city rather than the countryside?
7. **Style** is a writer's distinctive manner of expression–not *what* is said, but *how* it is said (see page R12). What aspect of Neruda's style in this poem made the biggest impression on you?
8. In the Reading Focus on page 1106, you were asked what qualities you associate with horses. Which phrases in the speaker's description of horses match your own thoughts?

Literary Criticism

Scholar René de Costa asserts that many of Neruda's poems "ac[t] as a kind of magnifiying lens for the reader, helping him to see the importance of humble things." How does de Costa's statement apply to "Horses"? Dicuss your opinion with a small group.

Literary ELEMENTS

Figurative Language

The term **figurative language** refers to expressions that are meant to be interpreted imaginatively rather than literally. Metaphor, simile, and personification are the most common types of figurative language. Although these literary elements may appear in all forms of writing and speech, they are especially important in poetry.

1. What simile is used to describe the winter air in Berlin?
2. Identify a metaphor used to describe the horses.
3. Identify an example of personification in the poem.

- See **Literary Terms Handbook,** p.R4.

Extending Your Response

Personal Writing

Description Describe a personal experience you have had that reminds you of the speaker's experience in Neruda's poem. For example, you might write about an encounter with an animal or describe how the winter light affects your mood. Try to use figurative language to make your description vivid.

Performing

Oral Reading With a small group, perform an oral reading of "Horses." You may wish to alternate lines or to divide up the poem into larger passages. Before you begin reading, go over the poem together to clarify any difficult phrases.

Save your work for your portfolio.

ARGENTINA, 1966

Before You Read

The Night Face Up

Meet Julio Cortázar

"A certain type of story is the product of a trancelike condition."

Julio Cortázar (hōō′ lē ō kôr tä′ sär) grew up in Buenos Aires, Argentina. In his youth he was especially fond of reading fantasy and poetry. He worked as a teacher and translator in Argentina until, at age thirty-seven, his opposition to the dictatorship of Juan Perón led him to seek a new home in France. He supported himself by translating for a United Nations organization based in Paris.

Cortázar published his first collection of short stories in 1951, the year he left Argentina. He won acclaim as a novelist as well as a short-story writer. *Hopscotch*, which he published in 1963, is one of the most important modern Latin American novels. Cortázar loved using experimental literary techniques. His narratives often shift back and forth through time and space, challenging the laws of nature and logic.

Cortázar was born in 1914 and died in 1984.

Reading Focus

What is the most lifelike dream you have ever had?

Quickwrite Briefly describe the dream in your journal.

Setting a Purpose Read about a strange mingling of dreams and reality in Cortázar's story.

Building Background

The Ancient Aztecs

In "The Night Face Up," Cortázar explores a frightening aspect of the Aztec culture. During the fifteenth century, the Aztecs came to dominate what is now central and southern Mexico. Their society was highly organized, with the state controlling all religious, economic, and social activities. Aztec religious worship included the ritual sacrifice of humans. In one form of sacrifice, priests would cut out the beating hearts of victims on temple altars. Afterwards, the bodies were thrown down the high temple steps. Most of the sacrificial victims were prisoners of war or subject peoples of the Aztec Empire. Not surprisingly, the Aztecs failed to gain the loyalty of these subject peoples, who helped Spanish invaders destroy the empire in 1521.

Vocabulary Preview

solace (sol′ is) *n.* a source of relief; mental or spiritual comfort; p. 1112

lucid (lōō′ sid) *adj.* having full use of one's faculties; clear-headed; p. 1112

supplication (sup′ lə kā′ shən) *n.* humble entreaty; prayer of request; p. 1114

beneficent (bə nef′ ə sənt) *adj.* doing or producing good; p. 1114

consecrated (kon′ sə krā′ tid) *adj.* made or declared sacred; devoted to a religious purpose; p. 1115

Detail from Aztec codex.

Crash in Pthalo Green, 1984. Carlos Almaraz (Mexico). Oil on canvas, 122 x 183 cm. Los Angeles County Museum of Art.

The Night Face Up

Julio Cortázar
Translated by Paul Blackburn

Halfway down the long hotel vestibule,[1] he thought that probably he was going to be late, and hurried on into the street to get out his motorcycle from the corner where the next-door superintendent let him keep it. On the jewelry store at the corner he read that it was ten to nine; he had time to spare. The sun filtered through the tall downtown buildings, and he—because for himself, for just going along thinking, he did not have a name—he swung onto the machine, savoring the idea of the ride. The motor whirred between his legs, and a cool wind whipped his pants legs.

He let the ministries[2] zip past (the pink, the white), and a series of stores on the main street, their windows flashing. Now he was beginning the most pleasant part of the run, the real ride: a long street bordered with trees, very little traffic, with spacious villas[3] whose gardens rambled all the way down to the sidewalks, which were barely indicated by low hedges. A bit inattentive perhaps, but tooling along on the right side of the street, he allowed himself to be carried away by the freshness, by the weightless contraction of this hardly begun day. This involuntary relaxation, possibly, kept him from preventing the accident. When he saw that the woman standing on the corner had rushed into the crosswalk while he still had the green light, it was already somewhat too late for a simple solution. He braked hard with foot and hand, wrenching himself to the

1. A *vestibule* (ves′ tə būl′) is a small passage or hall between the outer door and the interior of a building.
2. *Ministries,* here, are government office buildings.
3. *Villas* are urban homes with a yard and garden space.

left; he heard the woman scream, and at the collision his vision went. It was like falling asleep all at once.

He came to abruptly. Four or five young men were getting him out from under the cycle. He felt the taste of salt and blood, one knee hurt, and when they hoisted him up he yelped, he couldn't bear the pressure on his right arm. Voices which did not seem to belong to the faces hanging above him encouraged him cheerfully with jokes and assurances. His single solace was to hear someone else confirm that the lights indeed had been in his favor. He asked about the woman, trying to keep down the nausea which was edging up into his throat. While they carried him face up to a nearby pharmacy, he learned that the cause of the accident had gotten only a few scrapes on the legs. "Nah, you barely got her at all, but when ya hit, the impact made the machine jump and flop on its side . . ." Opinions, recollections of other smashups, take it easy, work him in shoulders first, there, that's fine, and someone in a dustcoat giving him a swallow of something soothing in the shadowy interior of the small local pharmacy.

Within five minutes the police ambulance arrived, and they lifted him onto a cushioned stretcher. It was a relief for him to be able to lie out flat. Completely lucid, but realizing that he was suffering the effects of a terrible shock, he gave his information to the officer riding in the ambulance with him. The arm almost didn't hurt; blood dripped down from a cut over the eyebrow all over his face. He licked his lips once or twice to drink it. He felt pretty good, it had been an accident, tough luck; stay quiet a few weeks, nothing worse. The guard said that the motorcycle didn't seem badly racked up. "Why should it," he replied. "It all landed on top of me." They both laughed, and when they got to the hospital, the guard shook his hand and wished him luck. Now the nausea was coming back little by little; meanwhile they were pushing him on a wheeled stretcher toward a pavilion[4] further back, rolling along under trees full of birds, he shut his eyes and wished he were asleep or chloroformed.[5] But they kept him for a good while in a room with that hospital smell, filling out a form, getting his clothes off, and dressing him in a stiff, grayish smock. They moved his arm carefully, it didn't hurt him. The nurses were constantly making wisecracks, and if it hadn't been for the stomach contractions he would have felt fine, almost happy.

They got him over to X ray, and twenty minutes later, with the still-damp negative lying on his chest like a black tombstone, they pushed him into surgery. Someone tall and thin in white came over and began to look at the X rays. A woman's hands were arranging his head, he felt that they were moving him from one stretcher to another. The man in white came over to him again, smiling, something gleamed in his right hand. He patted his cheek and made a sign to someone stationed behind.

It was unusual as a dream because it was full of smells, and he never dreamed smells. First a marshy smell, there to the left of the trail the swamps began already, the quaking bogs from which no one ever returned. But the reek lifted, and instead there came a dark, fresh composite fragrance, like the night under which he

4. A *pavilion,* here, is an extension of a main building, such as a hospital.

5. *Chloroformed* (klôr′ ə fôrmd) means "rendered unconscious through the use of chloroform, a sweet-smelling, colorless liquid."

Vocabulary

solace (sol′ is) *n.* a source of relief; mental or spiritual comfort

lucid (lo͞o′ sid) *adj.* having full use of one's faculties; clear-headed moved, in flight from the Aztecs. And it was all so natural, he had to run from the Aztecs who had set out on their manhunt, and his sole chance was to find a place to hide in the deepest part of the forest, taking care not to lose the narrow trail which only they, the Motecas,[6] knew.

What tormented him the most was the odor, as though, notwithstanding the absolute acceptance of the dream, there was something which resisted that which was not habitual, which until that point had not participated in the game. "It smells of war," he thought, his hand going instinctively to the stone knife which was tucked at an angle into his girdle of woven wool. An unexpected sound made him crouch suddenly stock-still and shaking. To be afraid was nothing strange, there was plenty of fear in his dreams. He waited, covered by the branches of a shrub and the starless night. Far off, probably on the other side of the big lake, they'd be lighting the bivouac[7] fires; that part of the sky had a reddish glare. The sound was not repeated. It had been like a broken limb. Maybe an animal that, like himself, was escaping from the smell of war. He stood erect slowly, sniffing the air. Not a sound could be heard, but the fear was still following, as was the smell, that cloying incense of the war of the blossom. He had to press forward, to stay out of the bogs and get to the heart of the forest. Groping uncertainly through the dark, stooping every other moment to touch the packed earth of the trail, he took a few steps. He would have liked to have broken into a run, but the gurgling fens lapped on either side of him. On the path and in darkness, he took his bearings. Then he caught a horrible blast of that foul smell he was most afraid of, and leaped forward desperately.

History of Religions I, 1950. Diego Rivera (Mexico). Museo Nacional de Arte, Mexico City.

Viewing the mural: Which scene from the story might this painting reflect?

6. *Motecas* are another Native American culture of central Mexico.
7. A *bivouac* (biv′ o͞o ak′) is a temporary military encampment.

"You're going to fall off the bed," said the patient next to him. "Stop bouncing around, old buddy."

He opened his eyes and it was afternoon, the sun already low in the oversized windows of the long ward. While trying to smile at his neighbor, he detached himself almost physically from the final scene of the nightmare. His arm, in a plaster cast, hung suspended from an apparatus with weights and pulleys. He felt thirsty, as though he'd been running for miles, but they didn't want to give him much water, barely enough to moisten his lips and make a mouthful. The fever was winning slowly and he would have been able to sleep again, but he was enjoying the pleasure of keeping awake, eyes half-closed, listening to the other patients' conversation, answering a question from time to time. He saw a little white pushcart come up beside the bed, a blond nurse rubbed the front of his thigh with alcohol and stuck him with a fat needle connected to a tube which ran up to a bottle filled with a milky, opalescent liquid. A young intern arrived with some metal and leather apparatus which he adjusted to fit onto the good arm to check something or other. Night fell, and the fever went along dragging him down softly to a state in which things seemed embossed as through opera glasses,[8] they were real and soft and, at the same time, vaguely distasteful; like sitting in a boring movie and thinking that, well, still, it'd be worse out in the street, and staying.

A cup of a marvelous golden broth came, smelling of leeks, celery and parsley. A small hunk of bread, more precious than a whole banquet, found itself crumbling little by little. His arm hardly hurt him at all, and only in the eyebrow where they'd taken stitches a quick, hot pain sizzled occasionally. When the big windows across the way turned to smudges of dark blue, he thought it would not be difficult for him to sleep. Still on his back so a little uncomfortable, running his tongue out over his hot, too-dry lips, he tasted the broth still, and with a sigh of bliss, he let himself drift off.

First there was a confusion, as of one drawing all his sensations, for that moment blunted or muddled, into himself. He realized that he was running in pitch darkness, although, above, the sky crisscrossed with treetops was less black than the rest. "The trail," he thought, "I've gotten off the trail." His feet sank into a bed of leaves and mud, and then he couldn't take a step that the branches of shrubs did not whiplash against his ribs and legs. Out of breath, knowing despite the darkness and silence that he was surrounded, he crouched down to listen. Maybe the trail was very near, with the first daylight he would be able to see it again. Nothing now could help him to find it. The hand that had unconsciously gripped the haft of the dagger climbed like a fen scorpion up to his neck where the protecting amulet[9] hung. Barely moving his lips, he mumbled the supplication of the corn which brings about the beneficent moons, and the prayer to Her Very Highness,[10] to the distributor of all Motecan possessions. At the same time he felt his ankles sinking deeper into the mud, and the waiting in the darkness of the obscure grove of live oak grew intolerable to him. The war of the blossom had started at the beginning of the moon and had been going on for three days and three nights now. If he managed to hide in the depths of the forest, getting off the trail further up past the marsh country, perhaps the warriors wouldn't follow his track. He

8. *Opera glasses* are small, lightweight binoculars.

9. An *amulet* is an object worn to bring good fortune or to protect against disease or misfortune.

10. *Her Very Highness* is an apparent reference to a Motecan deity.

Vocabulary

supplication (sup′ lə kā′ shən) *n.* humble entreaty; prayer of request

beneficent (bə nef′ ə sənt) *adj.* doing or producing good thought of the many prisoners they'd already taken. But the number didn't count, only the consecrated period. The hunt would continue until the priests gave the sign to return. Everything had its number and its limit, and it was within the sacred period, and he on the other side from the hunters.

He heard the cries and leaped up, knife in hand. As if the sky were aflame on the horizon, he saw torches moving among the branches, very near him. The smell of war was unbearable, and when the first enemy jumped him, leaped at his throat, he felt an almost-pleasure in sinking the stone blade flat to the haft into his chest. The lights were already around him, the happy cries. He managed to cut the air once or twice, then a rope snared him from behind.

"It's the fever," the man in the next bed said. "The same thing happened to me when they operated on my duodenum.[11] Take some water, you'll see, you'll sleep all right."

Laid next to the night from which he came back, the tepid shadow of the ward seemed delicious to him. A violet lamp kept watch high on the far wall like a guardian eye. You could hear coughing, deep breathing, once in a while a conversation in whispers. Everything was pleasant and secure, without the chase, no . . . But he didn't want to go on thinking about the nightmare. There were lots of things to amuse himself with. He began to look at the cast on his arm, and the pulleys that held it so comfortably in the air. They'd left a bottle of mineral water on the night table beside him. He put the neck of the bottle to his mouth and drank it like a precious liqueur. He could now make out the different shapes in the ward, the thirty beds, the closets with glass doors. He guessed that his fever was down, his face felt cool. The cut over the eyebrow barely hurt at all, like a recollection. He saw himself leaving the hotel again, wheeling out the cycle. Who'd have thought that it would end like this? He tried to fix the moment of the accident exactly, and it got him very angry to notice that there was a void there, an emptiness he could not manage to fill. Between the impact and the moment that they picked him up off the pavement, the passing out or what went on, there was nothing he could see. And at the same time he had the feeling that this void, this nothingness, had lasted an eternity. No, not even time, more as if, in this void, he had passed across something, or had run back immense distances. The shock, the brutal dashing against

Selva con rama (Jungle with Branches), c. 1995. María Eugenia Terrazas (Chile). Watercolor, 70 x 60 cm. Private collection.

Viewing the painting: How does this painting appeal to the senses? Does the story appeal in a similar way? Explain.

11. The *duodenum* (do͞o′ ə dē′ nəm) is part of the small intestine.

Vocabulary

consecrated (kon′ sə krā′ tid) *adj.* made or declared sacred; devoted to a religious purpose

the pavement. Anyway, he had felt an immense relief in coming out of the black pit while the people were lifting him off the ground. With pain in the broken arm, blood from the split eyebrow, contusion on the knee; with all that, a relief in returning to daylight, to the day, and to feel sustained and attended. That was weird. Someday he'd ask the doctor at the office about that. Now sleep began to take over again, to pull him slowly down. The pillow was so soft, and the coolness of the mineral water in his fevered throat. The violet light of the lamp up there was beginning to get dimmer and dimmer.

As he was sleeping on his back, the position in which he came to did not surprise him, but on the other hand the damp smell, the smell of oozing rock, blocked his throat and forced him to understand. Open the eyes and look in all directions, hopeless. He was surrounded by an absolute darkness. Tried to get up and felt ropes pinning his wrists and ankles. He was staked to the ground on a floor of dank, icy stone slabs. The cold bit into his naked back, his legs. Dully, he tried to touch the amulet with his chin and found they had stripped him of it. Now he was lost, no prayer could save him from the final . . . From afar off, as though filtering through the rock of the dungeon, he heard the great kettledrums of the feast. They had carried him to the temple, he was in the underground cells of Teocalli itself, awaiting his turn.

Did You Know?
Teocalli was the chief temple in Tenochtitlán, the Aztec capital.

He heard a yell, a hoarse yell that rocked off the walls. Another yell, ending in a moan. It was he who was screaming in the darkness, he was screaming because he was alive, his whole body with that cry fended off what was coming, the inevitable end. He thought of his friends filling up the other dungeons, and of those already walking up the stairs of the sacrifice. He uttered another choked cry, he could barely open his mouth, his jaws were twisted back as if with a rope and a stick, and once in a while they would open slowly with an endless exertion, as if they were made of rubber. The creaking of the wooden latches jolted him like a whip. Rent, writhing, he fought to rid himself of the cords sinking into his flesh. His right arm, the strongest, strained until the pain became unbearable and he had to give up. He watched the double door open, and the smell of the torches reached him before the light did. Barely girdled by the ceremonial loincloths, the priests' acolytes[12] moved in his direction, looking at him with contempt. Lights reflected off the sweaty torsos and off the black hair dressed with feathers. The cords went slack, and in their place the grappling of hot hands, hard as bronze; he felt himself lifted, still face up, and jerked along by the four acolytes who carried him down the passageway. The torchbearers went ahead, indistinctly lighting up the corridor with its dripping walls and a ceiling so low that the acolytes had to duck their heads. Now they were taking him out, taking him out, it was the end. Face up, under a mile of living rock which, for a succession of moments, was lit up by a glimmer of torchlight. When the stars came out up there instead of the roof and the great terraced steps rose before him, on fire with cries and dances, it would be the end. The passage was never going to end, but now it was beginning to end, he would see suddenly the open sky full of stars, but not yet, they trundled him along endlessly in the reddish shadow, hauling him roughly along and he did not want that, but how to stop it if they had torn off the amulet, his real heart, the life-center.

In a single jump he came out into the hospital night, to the high, gentle, bare ceiling, to

12. *Acolytes* (ak′ ə līts′) are individuals who assist a priest at religious services.

When Greek

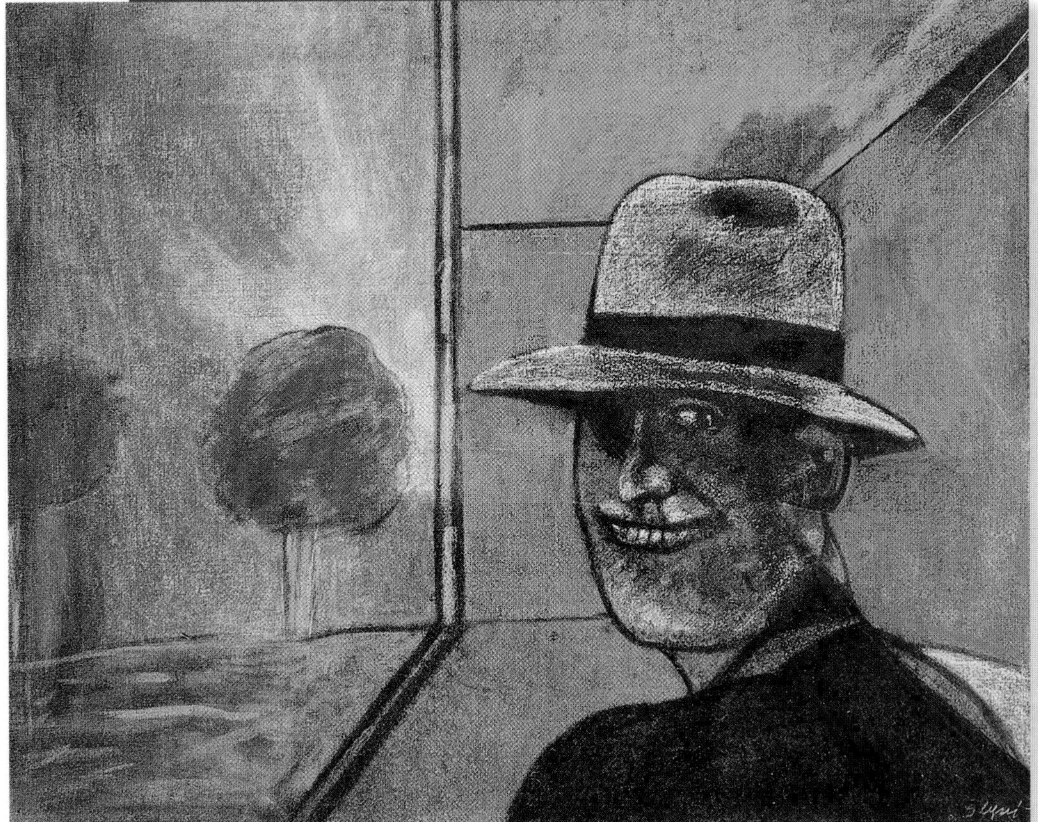

Alegria—Alegria! Antonio Seguí (Argentina, b. 1934). Oil on canvas, 65.4 x 81.3 cm. Private collection.

Meets Greek

Samuel Selvon

One morning Ramkilawansingh (after this, we calling this man Ram) was making a study of the notice boards along Westbourne Grove what does advertise rooms to let. Every now and then he writing down an address or a telephone number, though most of the time his eyes colliding up with *No Colors, Please*, or *Sorry, No Kolors*.

"Red, white and blue, all out but you," Ram was humming a little ditty what children say when they playing whoop. Just as he get down by Bradley's Corner he met Fraser.

"You look like a man who looking for a place to live," Fraser say.

"You look like a man who could tell me the right place to go," Ram say.

"You try down by Ladbroke Grove?" Fraser ask.

"I don't want to go down in that criminal area," Ram say, "at least, not until they find the man who kill Kelso."

"Then you will never live in the Grove," Fraser say.

"You are a contact man,"[1] Ram say, "which part you think I could get a room, boy?"

Fraser scratch his head. "I know of a landlord up the road who vow that he ain't ever taking anybody who come from the West Indies. But he don't mind taking Indians. He wouldn't know the difference when he see you is a Indian . . . them English people so foolish they believe every Indian come from India."

"You think I stand a chance?" Ram ask.

"Sure, you stand a chance. All you have to do is put on a turban."

"I never wear a turban in my life; I am a born Trinidadian, a real Creole. All the same, you best hads give me the address, I will pass around there later."

So Fraser give him the address, and Ram went on reading a few more boards, but he got discourage after a while and went to see the landlord.

The first thing the landlord ask him was: "What part of the world do you come from?"

"I am an Untouchable[2] from the heart of India," Ram say. "I am looking for a single room. I dwelt on the banks of the Ganges. Not too expensive."

"But you are not in your national garments," the landlord say.

"When you are in Rome," Ram say, making it sound like an original statement, "do as the Romans do."

Did You Know?
The *Ganges* (gan′ jēz) is India's major river. It is sacred to followers of the Hindu religion.

While the landlord sizing up Ram, an Indian tenant come up the steps to go inside. This fellar was Chandrilaboodoo (after this, we calling this man Chan) and he had a big beard with a hair net over it, and he was wearing a turban. When he see Ram, he clasp his hands with the palms touching across his chest by way of greeting.

The old Ram catch on quick and do the same thing.

"*Acha, Hindustani,*"[3] Chan say.

"*Acha, pilau, papadom, chickenvindaloo,*"[4] Ram say desperately, hoping for the best.

Chan nod his head, say good morning to the landlord and went inside.

"That was a narrow shave," Ram thought, "I have to watch out for that man."

"That was Mr. Chan," the landlord say, "he is the only other Indian tenant I have at the moment. I have a single room for two pounds. Are you a student?"

"Who is not a student?" Ram say, getting into the mood of the thing. "Man is for ever studying ways and means until he passes into the hands of Allah."

Well, to cut a long story short, Ram get a room on the first floor, right next door to Chan, and he move in that same evening.

But as the days going by, Ram had to live like cat-and-mouse with Chan. Every time he see Chan, he have to hide in case this man start up this Hindustani talk again, or start to ask him questions about Mother India. In fact, it begin to get on Ram nerves, and he decide that he had to do something.

"This house too small for the two of we," Ram say to himself, "one will have to go."

So Ram went down in the basement to see the landlord.

1. A *contact man* is someone who has useful information that is not common knowledge.
2. An *Untouchable* is a member of the lowest caste (hereditary social group) in India.
3. *Acha Hindustani* (ä′ chä hin′ do͞o stä′ nē) is a traditional greeting.
4. *Pilau* (pi′ lou), *papadom* (pä′ pä dom), and *chicken vindaloo* (vin′ də lo͞o) are three traditional Indian foods.

La grande ville–ville bleu, 1949. Antonio Bandeira (Brazil). Oil on canvas, 60 x 81 cm. Private collection.

Viewing the painting: How might this scene resemble the area in which Ram went to live? Explain.

"I have the powers of the Occult,"[5] Ram say, "and I have come to warn you of this man Chan. He is not a good tenant. He keeps the bathroom dirty, he does not tidy up his room at all, and he is always chanting and saying his prayers loudly and disturbing the other tenants."

"I have had no complaints," the landlord say.

"But I am living next door to him," Ram say, "and if I concentrate my powers I can see through the wall. That man is a menace, and the best thing you can do is to give him notice. You have a good house here and it would be a pity to let one man spoil it for the other tenants."

"I will have a word with him about it," the landlord say.

Well, the next evening Ram was in his room when he hear a knock at the door. He run in the corner quick and stand upon his head, and say, "Come in."

The landlord come in.

"I am just practicing my yogurt," Ram say.

"I have had a word with Mr. Chan," the landlord say, "and I have reason to suspect that you have deceived me. You are not from India, you are from the West Indies."

Ram turn right-side up. "I am a citizen of the world," he say.

"You are flying false colors,"[6] the landlord say. "You do not burn incense like Mr. Chan, you do not dress like Mr. Chan, and you do not talk like Mr. Chan."

"Give me a break, old man," Ram say, falling back on the good old West Indian dialect.

"It is too late. You have already started to make trouble. You must go."

Well, the very next week find Ram out scouting again, giving the boards a perusal, and who he should chance to meet but Fraser.

He start to tell Fraser how life hard, how he had to keep dodging from this Chan fellar all the time, and it was pure torture.

"Listen," Fraser say, "you don't mean a big fellar with a beard, and he always wearing a turban?"

"That sound like him," Ram say. "You know him?"

"Know him!" Fraser say. "Man, that is a fellar from Jamaica who I send to that house to get a room!"

5. *Powers of the Occult* are supernatural abilities to reveal secret knowledge.

6. *Flying false colors* means engaging in deception.

Vocabulary

dialect (dī′ ə lekt′) *n.* a regional variety of a language distinguished by nonstandard features of vocabulary, grammar, and pronunciation

perusal (pə ro͞o′ zəl) *n.* the act of reading in detail or examining carefully

Responding to Literature

Personal Response

Were you surprised by the outcome of the story? Explain why or why not to a classmate.

Analyzing Literature

Recall and Interpret

1. Why has Ram had difficulty finding a place to live?
2. What advice does Fraser offer to Ram? Why does Ram refuse to fully follow his advice?
3. Who is Chan? Why does Ram feel threatened by him?
4. What happens when Ram tries to get Chan kicked out of the house?
5. What does Ram find out from Fraser at the end of the story? How might this information have helped him if he had learned it earlier?

Evaluate and Connect

6. An **internal conflict** is a struggle within a character (see page R2). Describe an internal conflict within Ram.
7. Did you find Ram to be a sympathetic character? Why or why not?
8. **Situational irony** exists when the outcome of a situation is completely different from what is expected (see page R6). Identify an example of situational irony in this story.
9. **Tone** is the attitude that a narrator takes toward the reader, a subject, or a character (see page R12). What adjective would you use to describe the narrator's tone in this story?
10. Which ethnic groups have you encountered or heard of who faced problems in your community similar to the ones that Ram faces in the story?

Literary ELEMENTS

Dialect

Dialect is a version of a language spoken by members of a particular region or social group. For example, Cockney is an English dialect spoken by working-class residents of East London. In "When Greek Meets Greek," much of the dialogue and narration is written in a Caribbean English dialect. Dialects of the same language may differ from one another in pronunciation, vocabulary, and grammar.

1. Provide an example of dialect in "When Greek Meets Greek" that differs in grammar from Standard English.
2. Why might Selvon have chosen to use dialect in this story?

- See **Literary Terms Handbook,** p. R3.

Extending Your Response

Literature Groups

Discuss In the Reading Focus on page 1128, you were asked whether you would be likely to live among Americans if you moved to a foreign country. Do you think that Ram would prefer to live among other West Indians or would rather assimilate into British society? Discuss this question in a small group and then share your conclusions with the class.

Creative Writing

Caribbean Correspondence Write a letter from Ram to his family in Trinidad. Describe his experiences as an immigrant, referring to details and incidents from Selvon's story. You may wish to write about a more successful attempt of Ram's to find a place to live.

Save your work for your portfolio.

Literature FOCUS

Magic Realism

When reading Gabriel García Márquez's short story "The Handsomest Drowned Man in the World," you will encounter a world in which events of everyday life are fused with unexpected and, often, inexplicable details. For example, in the story, a drowned man who has been found on the beach is carried to a nearby house. After villagers place the body of the dead man on the floor, they realize there is barely enough room in the house for him! The villagers conclude that "maybe the ability to keep on growing after death was part of the nature of certain drowned men." The combination of realistic, unexpected, and inexplicable details are a few of the distinguishing trademarks of **magic realism**—a style of writing of which García Márquez is considered a master. The style is often regarded as a regional trend, restricted to Latin American writers. Some literary critics, however, consider magic realism a literary form that transcends regional boundaries. They contend that it is a major component of post-modernist fiction and point out that such diverse writers as Toni Morrison, Günter Grass, and Salman Rushdie have produced works containing elements of magic realism.

Literary works that are considered magic realist usually have a strong narrative—in other words, a story to tell. Often, this story sounds a great deal like myth. Read the following excerpt from "The Handsomest Drowned Man in the World":

That was how they came to hold the most splendid funeral they could conceive of for an abandoned drowned man. Some women who had gone to get flowers in the neighboring villages returned with other women who could not believe what they had been told, and those women went back for more flowers when they saw the dead man, and they brought more and more until there were so many flowers and so many people that it was hard to walk about.

What details or elements suggest myth to you?

Not only does the excerpt offer an explanation of an event, but it also elevates the drowned man to mythic proportions. The drowned man isn't simply handsome, he is the *handsomest* drowned man ever. Also notice the way the second sentence in this excerpt repeats and expands upon one idea, creating the impression of the story growing larger and larger—until it is larger than life itself.

In addition to myth, elements of dream and folklore usually appear in works of magic realism. These elements are often combined with the realistic events and details of everyday life. As you read "The Handsomest Drowned Man in the World," be prepared to have your idea of what is real enriched by the imaginative powers of magic realism.

El encuentro (The Encounter), 1962. Remedios Varo (Spain). Oil on Masonite, 64 x 44.5 cm. Private collection.

Before You Read

The Handsomest Drowned Man in the World

Meet Gabriel García Márquez

"There's not a single line in all my work that does not have a basis in reality. The problem is that Caribbean reality resembles the wildest imagination."

Gabriel García Márquez (gä′ brē′ el gär sē′ ä mär′ kez) spent his early childhood in Aracataca, a village near the Caribbean coast of Colombia. He began to write fiction when he was nineteen. He worked as a journalist in Colombia until, in 1955, a story he wrote exposing government corruption prompted Colombia's dictator to close down the paper. After living in various cities in Europe and the Americas, he chose Mexico City as his home.

García Márquez became famous in 1967 with the publication of *One Hundred Years of Solitude*, which is considered a masterpiece of magic realism. In more recent novels, he has continued to use innovative techniques to explore myths, history, and politics. He was awarded the Nobel Prize for Literature in 1982.

Gabriel García Márquez was born in 1928.

Reading Focus

Think of a time when you were moved by something beautiful or heroic. How did it affect your feelings about your own life?

Quickwrite Write for two minutes in response to this question.

Setting a Purpose Read this story to see how villagers react when they encounter a most unusual man.

Building Background

Childhood Influences

Gabriel García Márquez has usually taken the life and customs–and the legends–of Colombia's coastal region as his subject. Many of his novels and stories are set in Macondo, a fictional version of the village where he grew up. His native region provided him with material for his writing as well as a distinct way of viewing the world. "In the Caribbean, we are capable of believing anything," García Márquez once said. "I think that gives us an open-mindedness to look beyond apparent reality."

According to García Márquez, he modeled many of his characters on his grandparents "because I knew how they talked, how they behaved." His grandfather, a retired colonel, told the boy stories of his own experiences in the fierce civil war Colombians call "the War of a Thousand Days" (1899–1902). His grandmother, on the other hand, told the boy stories, based on the region's folklore, of ghosts and omens and mysterious happenings. From his grandmother, García Márquez learned the art of "saying incredible things with a completely unperturbed face."

Vocabulary Preview

haggard (hag′ ərd) *adj.* worn or wasted as from hunger; p. 1136

virile (vir′ əl) *adj.* masculine; p. 1136

frivolity (fri vol′ ə tē) *n.* silliness; p. 1137

improvise (im′ prə vīz′) *v.* to create to meet an unexpected need; p. 1137

discreet (dis krēt′) *adj.* quietly thoughtful; p. 1139

The Handsomest Drowned Man in the World

Gabriel García Márquez
Translated by Gregory Rabassa and J. S. Bernstein

The first children who saw the dark and slinky bulge approaching through the sea let themselves think it was an enemy ship. Then they saw it had no flags or masts and they thought it was a whale. But when it was washed up on the beach, they removed the clumps of seaweed, the jellyfish tentacles, and the remains of fish and flotsam,[1] and only then did they see that it was a drowned man.

They had been playing with him all afternoon, burying him in the sand and digging him up again, when someone chanced to see them and spread the alarm in the village. The men who carried him to the nearest house noticed that he weighed more than any dead man they had ever known, almost as much as a horse, and they said to each other that maybe he'd been floating too long and the water had got into his bones. When they laid him on the floor they said he'd been taller than all other men because there was barely enough room for him in the house, but they thought that maybe the ability to keep on growing after death was part of the nature of certain drowned men. He had the smell of the sea about him and only his shape gave one to suppose that it was the corpse of a human being, because the skin was covered with a crust of mud and scales.

They did not even have to clean off his face to know that the dead man was a stranger. The village was made up of only twenty-odd wooden houses that had stone courtyards with no flowers and which were spread about on the end of a desertlike cape. There was so little land that mothers always went about with the fear that the wind would carry off their children and the few dead that the years had caused among them had to be thrown off the cliffs. But the sea was calm and bountiful and all the men fit into seven boats. So when they found the drowned man they simply had to look at one another to see that they were all there.

That night they did not go out to work at sea. While the men went to find out if anyone was missing in neighboring villages, the women stayed behind to care for the drowned man. They took the mud off with grass swabs, they removed the underwater stones entangled in his hair, and they scraped the crust off with tools used for scaling fish. As they were doing that they noticed that the vegetation on him came from faraway oceans and deep water and that his clothes were in tatters, as if he had sailed through labyrinths of coral.[2] They noticed too that he bore his death with pride, for he did not

1. *Flotsam* is the floating wreckage of a ship or its cargo.

2. *Coral,* formed from the skeletal deposits of marine animals, can form reefs that extend for hundreds of miles.

have the lonely look of other drowned men who came out of the sea or that haggard, needy look of men who drowned in rivers. But only when they finished cleaning him off did they become aware of the kind of man he was and it left them breathless. Not only was he the tallest, strongest, most virile, and best built man they had ever seen, but even though they were looking at him there was no room for him in their imagination.

They could not find a bed in the village large enough to lay him on nor was there a table solid enough to use for his wake. The tallest men's holiday pants would not fit him, not the fattest ones' Sunday shirts, nor the shoes of the one with the biggest feet. Fascinated by his huge size and his beauty, the women then decided to make him some pants from a large piece of sail and a shirt from some bridal brabant[3] linen so that he could continue through his death with dignity. As they sewed, sitting in a circle and gazing at the corpse between stitches, it seemed to them that the wind had never been so steady nor the sea so restless as on that night and they supposed that the change had something to do with the dead man. They thought that if that magnificent man had lived in the village, his house would have had the widest doors, the highest ceiling, and the strongest floor, his bedstead would have been made from a midship frame held together by iron bolts, and his wife would have been the happiest woman. They thought that he would have had so much authority that he could have drawn fish out of the sea simply by calling their names and that he would have put so much work into his land that springs would have burst forth from among the rocks so that he would have been able to plant flowers on the cliffs. They secretly compared him to their own men, thinking that for all their lives theirs were incapable of doing what he could do in one night, and they ended up dismissing them deep in their hearts as the weakest, meanest, and most useless creatures on earth. They were wandering through that maze of fantasy when the oldest woman, who as the oldest had looked upon the drowned man with more compassion than passion, sighed:

"He has the face of someone called Esteban."

It was true. Most of them had only to take another look at him to see that he could not have any other name. The more stubborn among them, who were the youngest, still lived for a few hours with the illusion that when they put his clothes on and he lay among the flowers in patent leather shoes his name might be Lautaro. But it was a vain illusion. There had not been enough canvas, the poorly cut and worse sewn pants were too tight, and the hidden strength of his heart popped the buttons on his shirt. After midnight the whistling of the wind died down and the sea fell into its Wednesday drowsiness. The silence put an end to any last doubts: he was Esteban. The women who had dressed him, who had combed his hair, had cut his nails and shaved him were unable to hold back a shudder of pity when they had to resign themselves to his being dragged along the ground. It was then that they understood how unhappy he must have been with that huge body since it bothered him even after death. They could see him in life, condemned to going through doors sideways, cracking his head on crossbeams, remaining on his feet during visits, not knowing what to do with his soft, pink, sea lion hands while the lady of the house looked for her most resistant chair and begged him, frightened to death, sit here, Esteban, please, and he, leaning against the wall, smiling, don't bother, ma'am, I'm fine where I am, his heels raw and his back roasted

3. *Brabant* is a region in western Europe known for its textiles.

Vocabulary

haggard (hag′ ərd) *adj.* worn or wasted as from hunger
virile (vir′ əl) *adj.* masculine

Regreso del lunauta (Return of the Astronaut), 1969. Raquel Forner (Argentina). Oil on canvas, 160 x 120 cm. National Air and Space Museum, Smithsonian Institution, Washington, DC.

Viewing the painting: What do you think is happening in this painting? How might its composition remind you of the events in the story?

from having done the same thing so many times whenever he paid a visit, don't bother, ma'am, I'm fine where I am, just to avoid the embarrassment of breaking up the chair, and never knowing perhaps that the ones who said don't go, Esteban, at least wait till the coffee's ready, were the ones who later on would whisper the big boob finally left, how nice, the handsome fool has gone. That was what the women were thinking beside the body a little before dawn. Later, when they covered his face with a handkerchief so that the light would not bother him, he looked so forever dead, so defenseless, so much like their men that the first furrows of tears opened in their hearts. It was one of the younger ones who began the weeping. The others, coming to, went from sighs to wails, and the more they sobbed the more they felt like weeping, because the drowned man was becoming all the more Esteban for them, and so they wept so much, for he was the most destitute, most peaceful, and most obliging man on earth, poor Esteban. So when the men returned with the news that the drowned man was not from the neighboring villages either, the women felt an opening of jubilation in the midst of their tears.

"Praise the Lord," they sighed, "he's ours!"

The men thought the fuss was only womanish frivolity. Fatigued because of the difficult nighttime inquiries, all they wanted was to get rid of the bother of the newcomer once and for all before the sun grew strong on that arid, windless day. They improvised a litter with the remains of foremasts and gaffs,[4] tying it together with rigging so that it would bear the weight of the body until they reached the cliffs. They wanted to tie the anchor from a cargo ship to him so that he would sink easily into the deepest waves, where fish are blind and divers die of nostalgia,[5] and bad currents would not bring him back to shore, as had happened with other bodies. But the more they hurried, the more the women thought of ways to waste time. They walked about like startled hens, pecking with the sea charms on their breasts, some interfering on one side to put a scapular[6] of the good wind on the drowned

4. *Gaffs* are hooks for lifting heavy fish.
5. *Nostalgia* is a reference to the effects that changes in atmospheric pressure may have on deep-sea divers; symptoms include depression and disorientation.
6. A *scapular* is a small badge worn around the neck as a sign of religious devotion.

Vocabulary
frivolity (fri vol′ ə tē) *n.* silliness
improvise (im′ prə vīz′) *v.* to create to meet an unexpected need

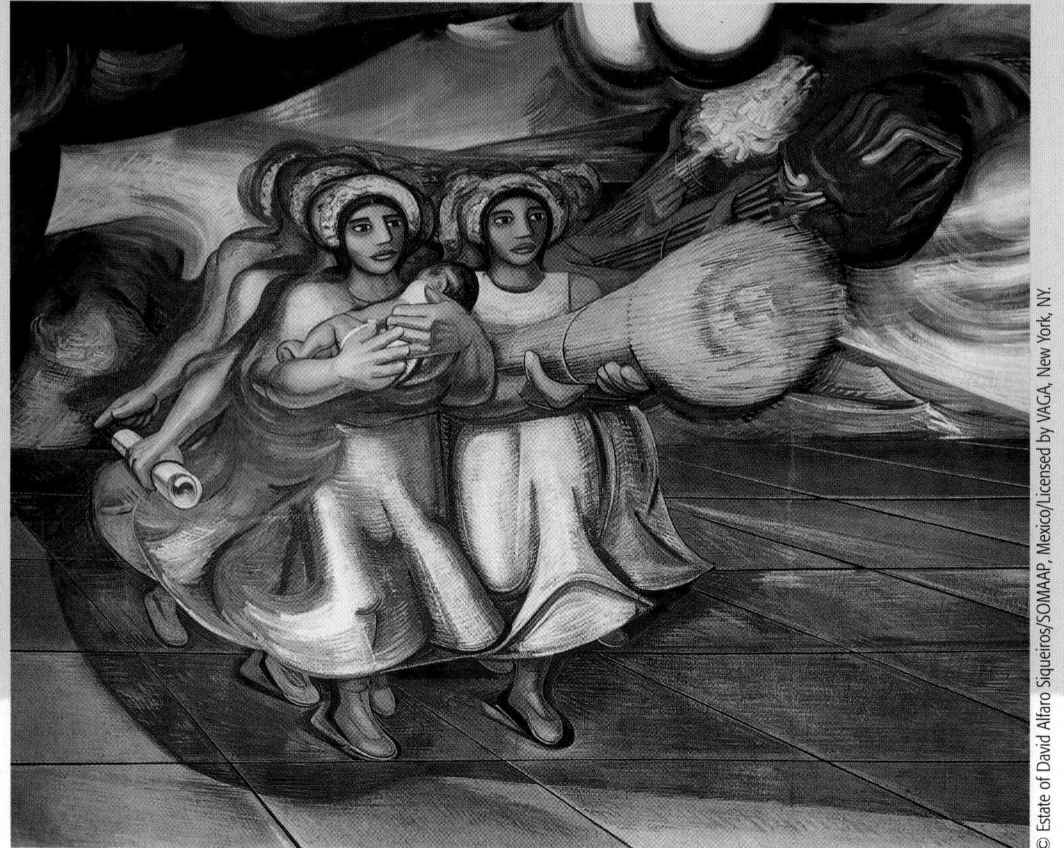

Women in Procession, detail from *For Complete Social Security of All Mexicans.* David Alfaro Siqueiros (Mexico, 1896–1974). Mural. Hospital de la Raza, Mexico City.

Viewing the mural: How would you describe these women? In what ways do they remind you of the women in the story?

man, some on the other side to put a wrist compass on him, and after a great deal of *get away from there, woman, stay out of the way, look, you almost made me fall on top of the dead man,* the men began to feel mistrust in their livers and started grumbling about why so many main-altar decorations for a stranger, because no matter how many nails and holy-water jars he had on him, the sharks would chew him all the same, but the women kept piling on their junk relics, running back and forth, stumbling, while they released in sighs what they did not in tears, so that the men finally exploded with *since when has there ever been such a fuss over a drifting corpse, a drowned nobody, a piece of cold Wednesday meat.* One of the women, mortified by so much lack of care, then removed the handkerchief from the dead man's face and the men were left breathless too.

He was Esteban. It was not necessary to repeat it for them to recognize him. If they had been told Sir Walter Raleigh,[7] even they might have been impressed with his gringo accent, the macaw on his shoulder, his cannibal-killing blunderbuss,[8] but there could be only one Esteban in the world and there he was, stretched out like a sperm whale, shoeless, wearing the pants of an undersized child, and with those stony nails that had to be cut with a knife. They only had to take the handkerchief off his face to see that he was ashamed, that it was not his fault that he was so big or so heavy or so handsome, and if he had known that this was going to happen, he would have looked for

7. *Sir Walter Raleigh* was a British sailor who explored South America in the sixteenth century.
8. A *blunderbuss* is a short rifle with a broad muzzle.

a more discreet place to drown in, seriously, I even would have tied the anchor off a galleon around my neck and staggered off a cliff like someone who doesn't like things in order not to be upsetting people now with this Wednesday dead body, as you people say, in order not to be bothering anyone with this filthy piece of cold meat that doesn't have anything to do with me. There was so much truth in his manner that even the most mistrustful men, the ones who felt the bitterness of endless nights at sea fearing that their women would tire of dreaming about them and begin to dream of drowned men, even they and others who were harder still shuddered in the marrow of their bones at Esteban's sincerity.

That was how they came to hold the most splendid funeral they could conceive of for an abandoned drowned man. Some women who had gone to get flowers in the neighboring villages returned with other women who could not believe what they had been told, and those women went back for more flowers when they saw the dead man, and they brought more and more until there were so many flowers and so many people that it was hard to walk about. At the final moment it pained them to return him to the waters as an orphan and they chose a father and mother from among the best people, and aunts and uncles and cousins, so that through him all the inhabitants of the village became kinsmen. Some sailors who heard the weeping from a distance went off course and people heard of one who had himself tied to the mainmast, remembering ancient fables about sirens.[9] While they fought for the privilege of carrying him on their shoulders along the steep escarpment by the cliffs, men and women became aware for the first time of the desolation of their streets, the dryness of their courtyards, the narrowness of their dreams as they faced the splendor and beauty of their drowned man. They let him go without an anchor so that he could come back if he wished and whenever he wished, and they all held their breath for the fraction of centuries the body took to fall into the abyss. They did not need to look at one another to realize that they were no longer all present, that they would never be. But they also knew that everything would be different from then on, that their houses would have wider doors, higher ceilings, and stronger floors so that Esteban's memory could go everywhere without bumping into beams and so that no one in the future would dare whisper the big boob finally died, too bad, the handsome fool has finally died, because they were going to paint their house fronts gay colors to make Esteban's memory eternal and they were going to break their backs digging for springs among the stones and planting flowers on the cliffs so that in future years at dawn the passengers on great liners would awaken, suffocated by the smell of gardens on the high seas, and the captain would have to come down from the bridge in his dress uniform, with his astrolabe,[10] his pole star, and his row of war medals and, pointing to the promontory of roses on the horizon, he would say in fourteen languages, look there, where the wind is so peaceful now that it's gone to sleep beneath the beds, over there, where the sun's so bright that the sunflowers don't know which way to turn, yes, over there, that's Esteban's village.

9. *[Tied . . . sirens]* refers to the *Odyssey,* in which Odysseus has himself tied to the mast so that he can navigate safely past the sirens (legendary enchantresses whose singing charmed sailors into jumping overboard).

10. An *astrolabe* (as′ trə lāb′) is a device used to observe and calculate the position of celestial bodies.

Vocabulary

discreet (dis krēt′) *adj.* quietly thoughtful

Responding to Literature

Personal Response

Did you find this story to be humorous or serious? Share your response with the class.

Analyzing Literature

Recall

1. What do the children think at the time they first notice Esteban's body?
2. What is unusual about the appearance of Esteban?
3. What do the women think about as they are sewing Esteban's clothes?
4. How do the men feel about Esteban before the handkerchief is removed from his face?
5. What changes do the villagers want to make in honor of Esteban?

Interpret

6. How is the children's reaction to Esteban different from the reaction of the adults?
7. Do you think the description of Esteban's face and body is realistic or magical?
8. What do the fantasies of the women suggest about them?
9. Why do the men change their opinion of Esteban after the handkerchief is removed?
10. A **theme** is a message or idea about life that is implied or stated in a literary work (see **Literary Terms Handbook,** page R12). In your opinion, what theme is implied in the description of changes that will be made in the village?

Evaluate and Connect

11. A story's **point of view** is the vantage point from which that story is told (see **Literary Terms Handbook,** page R9). What is the point of view of this story?
12. An **allusion** is a reference to a well-known person, place, or event from history, literature, or religion. Identify an allusion in the story and explain what it suggests to you.
13. Why might García Márquez have decided not to name the village and its inhabitants?
14. In the Reading Focus on page 1134, you were asked how your feelings about your own life were affected by something beautiful or heroic. Compare this experience with how the villagers are changed at the end of the story.
15. In what ways are the villagers similar to people you know?

Hyperbole

Hyperbole is a figure of speech in which exaggeration is used for emphasis or comic effect. It can be an effective way to express a feeling or perception. For example, the phrase "sweating buckets" suggests how one feels when perspiring heavily. In "The Handsomest Drowned Man in the World," there are several exaggerated statements, even if one accepts the description of Esteban's size as literal truth. When the women are sewing Esteban's clothes, for example, they think that he "would have had so much authority that he could have drawn fish out of the sea simply by calling their names."

1. Find another example of hyperbole in "The Handsomest Drowned Man in the World."
2. What, do you think, was García Márquez's purpose in using hyperbole?

- See **Literary Terms Handbook,** p. R6.

Literature and Writing

Writing About Literature

Analyze Setting Write one or two paragraphs about the story's setting. Begin with a description of the time and place in which the action occurs. Then discuss why the setting is important to the story. What role does it play in the plot? How does it help us understand the feelings and actions of the villagers?

Creative Writing

Sermon Write a sermon for Esteban's funeral. Discuss how Esteban arrived at the village and the effect he has had on the people living there. Conclude your sermon with comforting words that will help the mourners get over their grief.

Extending Your Response

Literature Groups

Analyze Style García Márquez is one of the best-known practitioners of magic realism, a literary style that combines fantastic events with realistic details. In your group, discuss which elements of the story are fantastic. How is the author's portrayal of these elements different from what one might find in a myth or folktale? Share your conclusions with the class.

Listening and Speaking

Role-Play García Márquez usually describes how groups react to Esteban rather than treating the villagers as individuals. With a partner, role-play a conversation between a husband and wife. Before you begin, go over the story together and notice the different concerns that men and women have about Esteban.

Learning for Life

Brochure At Esteban's funeral, the villagers imagine that passengers on ocean liners crossing the Caribbean will someday notice the aroma from their flower gardens. In a small group, create a brochure to attract tourists to "Esteban's village." Use descriptions and drawings or photographs inspired by details in the story.

Save your work for your portfolio.

VOCABULARY • Multiple-Meaning Words

Have you ever read a word and thought that you understood its meaning, only to realize later that it meant something quite different? Many words have multiple meanings. *Cross,* for example, means "annoyed" or "angry" in this story, but a person might *cross* a river or wear a small *cross* on a necklace. Each meaning of *cross* is very different.

PRACTICE If you suspect that a word has a meaning other than the one you know, check a dictionary.

1. *Cross* has even more meanings than the three mentioned here. Use a dictionary to find two additional meanings of *cross.* Then write an original sentence for each meaning.
2. Give two meanings for each of the following words: *called, free, lie, pound,* and *rose.*

CANADA, 1956

Before You Read

Day of the Butterfly

Meet Alice Munro

"I'm not an intellectual writer. I'm very, very excited by what you might call the surface of life . . ."

Alice Munro comes from a rural community in Canada. She began to write in her early teens and sold her first short story while attending college. After her marriage, she found that her literary ambitions often conflicted with family responsibilities. Although she went through periods of depression, her "incredible stubbornness" allowed her to continue writing.

It took Munro twelve years to complete her first volume of stories, *Dance of the Happy Shades*. She has received critical acclaim for this and subsequent books. Many of her stories are about misfits or people who feel isolated in some way. Known for her realistic descriptions, Munro believes that it is important "to get at the exact tone or texture of how things are." In 1990 she won the Canada Council Molson prize for her "outstanding lifetime contribution to the cultural and intellectual life of Canada."

Alice Munro was born in 1931.

Reading Focus

What are the most important factors that have influenced your choice of friends at school?

Discuss In a small group of classmates, discuss your response to this question.

Setting a Purpose Notice how the narrator's feelings toward an unpopular girl change during the course of this story.

Building Background

The World of Munro's Fiction

Munro grew up on a farm on the outskirts of Wingham, a small town in the rolling farmland of southern Ontario. Most of her stories are set in this region—where her family has lived since the 1850s—and are loosely based on her experiences there. She remembers the residents of Wingham as practical-minded people who disapproved of ambition and considered reading a waste of time. Even now, Munro says, her relatives generally consider her writing "a very meaningless, useless type of work." Although she felt alienated from this environment as a teenager, she appreciates the rich material it offers for her fiction. Munro lived in Vancouver and Victoria for twenty years while raising her family. She returned to Ontario in 1972 and today lives on a farm there—twenty miles from Wingham—with her second husband. "I love the landscape so much—more than love it. It's something I know so thoroughly I don't want to detach from it."

Vocabulary Preview

cryptically (krip′ tik lē) *adv.* secretly or mysteriously; p. 1144

self-possessed (self′ pə zest′) *adj.* in control of oneself; p. 1144

loiter (loi′ tər) *v.* to move along aimlessly, with frequent pauses, p. 1145

supplementary (sup′ lə men′ tər ē) *adj.* extra or additional; p. 1147

exalted (ig zôlt′ əd) *adj.* raised above the ordinary; p. 1149

Day of the Butterfly

Alice Munro

Still Closer, 1995. Daniel Nevins (United States). Oil, acrylic, collage on wood, 51 x 39 in. Private collection. What type of relationship do you think these girls have? Explain.

I do not remember when Myra Sayla came to town, though she must have been in our class at school for two or three years. I start remembering her in the last year, when her little brother Jimmy Sayla was in Grade One. Jimmy Sayla was not used to going to the bathroom by himself and he would have to come to the Grade Six door and ask for Myra and she would take him downstairs. Quite often he would not get to Myra in time and there would be a big dark stain on his little button-on cotton pants. Then Myra had to come and ask the teacher: "Please may I take my brother home, he has wet himself?"

That was what she said the first time and everybody in the front seats heard her—though Myra's voice was the lightest singsong—and there was a muted giggling which alerted the rest of the class. Our teacher, a cold gentle girl who wore glasses with thin gold rims and in the stiff solicitude of certain poses resembled a giraffe, wrote something on a piece of paper and showed it to Myra. And Myra recited uncertainly: "My brother has had an accident, please, teacher."

Everybody knew of Jimmy Sayla's shame and at recess (if he was not being kept in, as he often was, for doing something he shouldn't in school) he did not dare go out on the school grounds, where the other little boys, and some bigger ones, were waiting to chase him and corner him against the back fence and thrash him with tree branches. He had to stay with Myra. But at our school there were the two sides, the Boys' Side and the Girls' Side, and it was believed that if you so much as stepped on the side that was not your own you might easily get the strap. Jimmy could not go out on the Girls' Side and Myra could not go out on the Boys' Side, and no one was allowed to stay in the school unless it was raining or snowing. So Myra and Jimmy spent every recess standing in the little back porch between the two sides. Perhaps they watched the baseball games, the tag and skipping and building of leaf houses in the fall and snow forts in the winter; perhaps they did not watch at all. Whenever you happened to look at them their heads were slightly bent, their narrow bodies hunched in, quite still. They had long smooth oval faces, melancholy and discreet—dark, oily, shining hair. The little boy's was long, clipped at home, and Myra's was worn in heavy braids coiled on top of her head so that she looked, from a distance, as if she was wearing a turban too big for her. Over their dark eyes the lids were never fully raised; they had a weary look. But it was more than that. They were like children in a medieval painting, they were like small figures carved of wood, for worship or magic, with faces smooth and aged, and meekly, cryptically uncommunicative.

Most of the teachers at our school had been teaching for a long time and at recess they would disappear into the teachers' room and not bother us. But our own teacher, the young woman of the fragile gold-rimmed glasses, was apt to watch us from a window and sometimes come out, looking brisk and uncomfortable, to stop a fight among the little girls or start a running game among the big ones, who had been huddled together playing Truth or Secrets. One day she came out and called, "Girls in Grade Six, I want to talk to you!" She smiled persuasively, earnestly, and with dreadful unease, showing fine gold rims around her teeth. She said, "There is a girl in Grade Six called Myra Sayla. She *is* in your grade, isn't she?"

We mumbled. But there was a coo from Gladys Healey. "Yes, Miss Darling!"

"Well, why is she never playing with the rest of you? Every day I see her standing in the back porch, never playing. Do you think she looks very happy standing back there? Do you think you would be very happy, if *you* were left back there?"

Nobody answered; we faced Miss Darling, all respectful, self-possessed, and bored with the unreality of her question. Then Gladys said, "Myra can't come out with us, Miss Darling. Myra has to look after her little brother!"

"Oh," said Miss Darling dubiously. "Well you ought to try to be nicer to her anyway. Don't you think so? Don't you? You will try to be nicer, won't you? I *know* you will." Poor Miss Darling! Her campaigns were soon confused, her persuasions turned to bleating and uncertain pleas.

When she had gone Gladys Healey said softly, "You will try to be nicer, won't you? I *know* you will!" and then drawing her lip back over her big teeth she yelled exuberantly, "I don't care if it rains or freezes." She went through the whole verse and ended it with a

Vocabulary

cryptically (krip′ tik lē) *adv.* secretly or mysteriously

self-possessed (self′ pə zest′) *adj.* in control of oneself spectacular twirl of her Royal Stuart tartan skirt. Mr. Healey ran a Dry Goods and Ladies' Wear, and his daughter's leadership in our class was partly due to her flashing plaid skirts and organdy blouses and velvet jackets with brass buttons, but also to her early-maturing bust and the fine brutal force of her personality. Now we all began to imitate Miss Darling.

We had not paid much attention to Myra before this. But now a game was developed; it started with saying, "Let's be nice to Myra!" Then we would walk up to her in formal groups of three or four and at a signal, say together, "Hel-lo Myra, Hello My-ra!" and follow up with something like, "What do you wash your hair in, Myra, it's so nice and shiny, My-ra." "Oh she washes it in cod-liver oil, don't you, Myra, she washes it in cod-liver oil, can't you smell it?"

I felt a great pleasurable rush of self-conscious benevolence. . . .

And to tell the truth there was a smell about Myra, but it was a rotten-sweetish smell as of bad fruit. That was what the Saylas did, kept a little fruit store. Her father sat all day on a stool by the window, with his shirt open over his swelling stomach and tufts of black hair showing around his belly button; he chewed garlic. But if you went into the store it was Mrs. Sayla who came to wait on you, appearing silently between the limp print curtains hung across the back of the store. Her hair was crimped in black waves and she smiled with her full lips held together, stretched as far as they would go; she told you the price in a little rapping voice, daring you to challenge her and, when you did not, handed you the bag of fruit with open mockery in her eyes.

One morning in the winter I was walking up the school hill very early; a neighbor had given me a ride into town. I lived about half a mile out of town, on a farm, and I should not have been going to the town school at all, but to a country school nearby where there were half a dozen pupils and a teacher a little demented since her change of life. But my mother, who was an ambitious woman, had prevailed on the town trustees to accept me and my father to pay the extra tuition, and I went to school in town. I was the only one in the class who carried a lunch pail and ate peanut-butter sandwiches in the high, bare, mustard-colored cloakroom, the only one who had to wear rubber boots in the spring, when the roads were heavy with mud. I felt a little danger, on account of this; but I could not tell exactly what it was.

I saw Myra and Jimmy ahead of me on the hill; they always went to school very early—sometimes so early that they had to stand outside waiting for the janitor to open the door. They were walking slowly, and now and then Myra half turned around. I had often loitered in that way, wanting to walk with some important girl who was behind me, and not quite daring to stop and wait. Now it occurred to me that Myra might be doing this with me. I did not know what to do. I could not afford to be seen walking with her, and I did not even want to—but, on the other hand, the flattery of those humble, hopeful turnings was not lost on me. A role was shaping for me that I could not resist playing. I felt a great pleasurable rush of self-conscious benevolence; before I thought what I was doing I called, "Myra! Hey, Myra, wait up, I got some

Vocabulary
loiter (loi′ tər) *v.* to move along aimlessly, with frequent pauses

Cracker Jack!" and I quickened my pace as she stopped.

Myra waited, but she did not look at me; she waited in the withdrawn and rigid attitude with which she always met us. Perhaps she thought I was playing a trick on her, perhaps she expected me to run past and throw an empty Cracker Jack box in her face. And I opened the box and held it out to her. She took a little. Jimmy ducked behind her coat and would not take any when I offered the box to him.

"He's shy," I said reassuringly. "A lot of little kids are shy like that. He'll probably grow out of it."

"Yes," said Myra.

"I have a brother four," I said. "He's awfully shy." He wasn't. "Have some more Cracker Jack," I said. "I used to eat Cracker Jack all the time but I don't any more. I think it's bad for your complexion."

There was a silence.

"Do you like Art?" said Myra faintly.

"No. I like Social Studies and Spelling and Health."

"I like Art and Arithmetic." Myra could add and multiply in her head faster than anyone else in the class.

"I wish I was as good as you. In Arithmetic," I said, and felt magnanimous.

"But I am no good at Spelling," said Myra. "I make the most mistakes, I'll fail maybe." She did not sound unhappy about this, but pleased to have such a thing to say. She kept her head turned away from me staring at the dirty snowbanks along Victoria Street, and as she talked she made a sound as if she was wetting her lips with her tongue.

"You won't fail," I said. "You are too good in Arithmetic. What are you going to be when you grow up?"

She looked bewildered. "I will help my mother," she said. "And work in the store."

"Well I am going to be an airplane hostess," I said. "But don't mention it to anybody. I haven't told many people."

"No, I won't," said Myra. "Do you read Steve Canyon in the paper?"

"Yes." It was queer to think that Myra, too, read the comics, or that she did anything at all, apart from her role at the school. "Do you read Rip Kirby?"

"Do you read Orphan Annie?"

"Do you read Betsy and the Boys?"

"You haven't had hardly any Cracker Jack," I said. "Have some. Take a whole handful."

Myra looked into the box. "There's a prize in there," she said. She pulled it out. It was a brooch,[1] a little tin butterfly, painted gold with bits of colored glass stuck onto it to look like jewels. She held it in her brown hand, smiling slightly.

I said, "Do you like that?"

Myra said, "I like them blue stones. Blue stones are sapphires."

"I know. My birthstone is sapphire. What is your birthstone?"

"I don't know."

"When is your birthday?"

"July."

"Then yours is ruby."

"I like sapphire better," said Myra. "I like yours." She handed me the brooch.

"You keep it," I said. "Finders keepers."

Myra kept holding it out, as if she did not know what I meant. "Finders keepers," I said.

"It was your Cracker Jack," said Myra, scared and solemn. "You bought it."

"Well you found it."

"No—" said Myra.

"Go on!" I said. "Here, I'll *give* it to you." I took the brooch from her and pushed it back into her hand.

We were both surprised. We looked at each other; I flushed but Myra did not. I realized the pledge as our fingers touched; I was panicky, but *all right*. I thought, I can come early and walk with her other mornings. I can go and talk to her at recess. Why not? *Why not?*

---

1. A *brooch* (brōch) is an ornamental pin.

Myra put the brooch in her pocket. She said, "I can wear it on my good dress. My good dress is blue."

I knew it would be. Myra wore out her good dresses at school. Even in midwinter among the plaid wool skirts and serge tunics, she glimmered sadly in sky-blue taffeta, in dusty turquoise crepe, a grown woman's dress made over, weighted by a big bow at the V of the neck and folding empty over Myra's narrow chest.

And I was glad she had not put it on. If someone asked her where she got it, and she told them, what would I say?

Vegetation. Tamas Galambos (Hungary, b. 1939). Oil on canvas. Private collection.

Viewing the painting: What do butterflies, like this one, make you think of? In what ways does it suggest the butterfly in the story?

It was the day after this, or the week after, that Myra did not come to school. Often she was kept at home to help. But this time she did not come back. For a week, then two weeks, her desk was empty. Then we had a moving day at school and Myra's books were taken out of her desk and put on a shelf in the closet. Miss Darling said, "We'll find a seat when she comes back." And she stopped calling Myra's name when she took attendance.

Jimmy Sayla did not come to school either, having no one to take him to the bathroom.

In the fourth week or the fifth, that Myra had been away, Gladys Healey came to school and said, "Do you know what—Myra Sayla is sick in the hospital."

It was true. Gladys Healey had an aunt who was a nurse. Gladys put up her hand in the middle of Spelling and told Miss Darling. "I thought you might like to know," she said. "Oh yes," said Miss Darling. "I do know."

"What has she got?" we said to Gladys.

And Gladys said, "Akemia,[2] or something. And she has blood transfusions." She said to Miss Darling, "My aunt is a nurse."

So Miss Darling had the whole class write Myra a letter, in which everybody said, "Dear Myra, We are all writing you a letter. We hope you will soon be better and be back to school, Yours truly. . . ." And Miss Darling said, "I've thought of something. Who would like to go up to the hospital and visit Myra on the twentieth of March, for a birthday party?"

I said, "Her birthday's in July."

"I know," said Miss Darling. "It's the twentieth of July. So this year she could have it on the twentieth of March, because she's sick."

"But her *birthday* is in July."

"Because she's sick," said Miss Darling, with a warning shrillness. "The cook at the hospital would make a cake and you could all give a little present, twenty-five cents or so. It would have to be between two and four, because that's visiting hours. And we couldn't all go, it'd be too many. So who wants to go and who wants to stay here and do supplementary reading?"

We all put up our hands. Miss Darling got out the spelling records and picked out the first

2. *Akemia* is a mispronounciation of *leukemia,* which is a form of cancer that affects the blood.

Vocabulary

supplementary (sup′ lə men′ tər ē) *adj.* extra or additional fifteen, twelve girls and three boys. Then the three boys did not want to go so she picked out the next three girls. And I do not know when it was, but I think it was probably at this moment that the birthday party of Myra Sayla became fashionable.

Perhaps it was because Gladys Healey had an aunt who was a nurse, perhaps it was the excitement of sickness and hospitals, or simply the fact that Myra was so entirely, impressively set free of all the rules and conditions of our lives. We began to talk of her as if she were something we owned, and her party became a cause; with womanly heaviness we discussed it at recess, and decided that twenty-five cents was too low.

We all went up to the hospital on a sunny afternoon when the snow was melting, carrying our presents, and a nurse led us upstairs, single file, and down a hall past half-closed doors and dim conversations. She and Miss Darling kept saying, "Sh-sh," but we were going on tiptoe anyway; our hospital demeanor was perfect.

At this small country hospital there was no children's ward, and Myra was not really a child; they had put her in with two gray old women. A nurse was putting screens around them as we came in.

Myra was sitting up in bed, in a bulky stiff hospital gown. Her hair was down, the long braids falling over her shoulders and down the coverlet. But her face was the same, always the same.

She had been told something about the party, Miss Darling said, so the surprise would not upset her; but it seemed she had not believed, or had not understood what it was. She watched us as she used to watch in the school grounds when we played.

"Well, here we are!" said Miss Darling. "Here we are!"

And we said, "Happy birthday, Myra! Hello, Myra, happy birthday!" Myra said, "My birthday is in July." Her voice was lighter than ever, drifting, expressionless.

"Never mind when it is, really," said Miss Darling. "Pretend it's now! How old are you, Myra?"

"Eleven," Myra said. "In July."

Then we all took off our coats and emerged in our party dresses, and laid our presents, in their pale flowery wrappings, on Myra's bed. Some of our mothers had made immense, complicated bows of fine satin ribbon, some of them had even taped on little bouquets of imitation roses and lilies of the valley. "Here Myra," we said, "here Myra, happy birthday." Myra did not look at us, but at the ribbons, pink and blue and speckled with silver, and the miniature bouquets; they pleased her, as the butterfly had done. An innocent look came into her face, a partial, private smile.

"Open them, Myra," said Miss Darling. "They're for you!"

Myra gathered the presents around her, fingering them, with this smile, and a cautious realization, an unexpected pride. She said, "Saturday I'm going to London[3] to St. Joseph's Hospital."

"That's where my mother was at," somebody said. "We went and saw her. They've got all nuns there."

"My father's sister is a nun," said Myra calmly.

She began to unwrap the presents, with an air that not even Gladys could have bettered, folding the tissue paper and the ribbons, and drawing out books and puzzles and cutouts as if they were all prizes she had won. Miss Darling said that maybe she should say thank you, and the person's name with every gift she opened, to make sure she knew whom it was from, and so Myra said, "Thank you, Mary Louise, thank you, Carol," and when she came to mine she said, "Thank you, Helen." Everyone explained their presents to her and there was talking and excitement and a little gaiety, which Myra presided over, though she was not gay. A cake was

3. *London* is a city in southeast Ontario, Canada.

brought in with *Happy Birthday* Myra written on it, pink on white, and eleven candles. Miss Darling lit the candles and we all sang Happy Birthday to You, and cried, "Make a wish, Myra, make a wish—" and Myra blew them out. Then we all had cake and strawberry ice cream.

At four o'clock a buzzer sounded and the nurse took out what was left of the cake, and the dirty dishes, and we put on our coats to go home. Everybody said, "Good-bye, Myra," and Myra sat in the bed watching us go, her back straight, not supported by any pillow, her hands resting on the gifts. But at the door I heard her call; she called, "Helen!" Only a couple of the others heard; Miss Darling did not hear, she had gone out ahead. I went back to the bed.

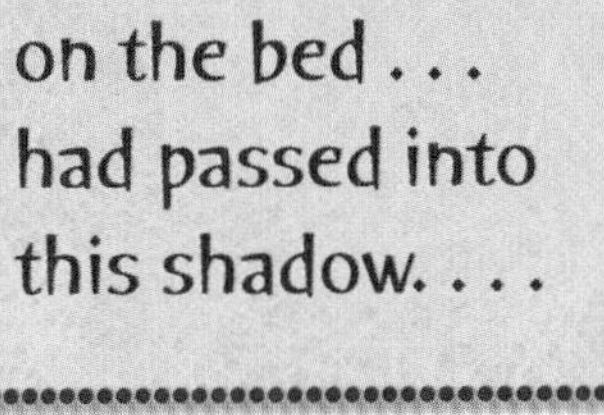
All the presents on the bed . . . had passed into this shadow. . . .

Myra said, "I got too many things. You take something."

"What?" I said. "It's for your birthday. You always get a lot at a birthday."

"Well you take something," Myra said. She picked up a leatherette case with a mirror in it, a comb and a nail file and a natural lipstick and a small handkerchief edged with gold thread. I had noticed it before. "You take that," she said.

"Don't you want it?"

"You take it." She put it into my hand. Our fingers touched again.

"When I come back from London," Myra said, "you can come and play at my place after school."

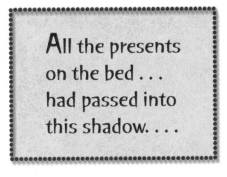

"Okay," I said. Outside the hospital window there was a clear carrying sound of somebody playing in the street, maybe chasing with the last snowballs of the year. This sound made Myra, her triumph and her bounty, and most of all her future in which she had found this place for me, turn shadowy, turn dark. All the presents on the bed, the folded paper and ribbons, those guilt-tinged offerings, had passed into this shadow, they were no longer innocent objects to be touched, exchanged, accepted without danger. I didn't want to take the case now but I could not think how to get out of it, what lie to tell. I'll give it away, I thought, I won't ever play with it. I would let my little brother pull it apart.

The nurse came back, carrying a glass of chocolate milk.

"What's the matter, didn't you hear the buzzer?"

So I was released, set free by the barriers which now closed about Myra, her unknown, exalted, ether-smelling hospital world, and by the treachery of my own heart. "Well thank you," I said. "Thank you for the thing. Good-bye."

Did Myra ever say good-bye? Not likely. She sat in her high bed, her delicate brown neck, rising out of a hospital gown too big for her, her brown carved face immune to treachery, her offering perhaps already forgotten, prepared to be set apart for legendary uses, as she was even in the back porch at school.

Vocabulary
exalted (ig zôlt′ əd) *adj.* raised above the ordinary

Responding to Literature

Personal Response

What opinions do you have about the relationship between Myra and the narrator? Share your response with a small group of classmates.

Analyzing Literature

Recall

1. Why is Myra unpopular with the other girls at school?
2. Why does Helen start a conversation with Myra on the way to school?
3. What gift does Helen give to Myra?
4. How does Myra's reputation in class change after she goes into the hospital?
5. Why does Myra call Helen back to her bed after the others have left?

Interpret

6. Why do Myra's classmates begin to tease her after ignoring her for so long?
7. Why might Helen be more sympathetic toward Myra than the other girls?
8. Do you think that Helen has decided to become Myra's friend when she gives her the gift? Why or why not?
9. Why do you think Miss Darling makes up an excuse for the students to visit Myra in the hospital?
10. Why is Helen so eager to be "set free" at the end of the story?

Evaluate and Connect

11. In what way is Myra like a butterfly?
12. Why might Munro have decided to narrate this story from the **first-person point of view** (see **Literary Terms Handbook,** page R9)?
13. **Irony** is a contrast between what is believed or expected and what actually exists or occurs (see **Literary Terms Handbook,** page R6). Identify an example of irony in the story.
14. Do you sympathize with Helen at the end of the story? Why or why not?
15. In the Reading Focus on page 1142, you were asked to discuss factors that have influenced your choice of friends at school. Which of these factors influence Helen's relationship with Myra?

Literary Criticism

Scholar Coral Ann Howells points out that in Munro's early stories "[t]here is always the sense of ordinary surfaces covering over some secret or scandal which threatens to collapse them." What "secret" in "Day of the Butterfly" threatens to shatter the children's comfortable world? What point or points about life does Munro make by revealing that secret? In an essay, analyze the theme of the story, using evidence from the text to support your ideas.

Literary ELEMENTS

Characterization

Characterization refers to the methods that a writer uses to reveal a character's personality. **Direct characterization** occurs when the narrator makes comments about personality traits. For example, the narrator might simply state that a character is lazy or absent-minded. **Indirect characterization** requires readers to draw their own conclusions about a character based on evidence in the story. This evidence might include descriptions of the character's appearance, words, thoughts, and actions, and the comments and thoughts of other characters.

1. Identify an example of direct characterization in "Day of the Butterfly."
2. How does Munro use indirect characterization to suggest that Myra has changed since going into the hospital?

- See **Literary Terms Handbook,** p. R2.

Literature and Writing

Writing About Literature

Compare Do you find it surprising that Helen and Myra would be drawn together? Write a paragraph in which you compare and contrast the two girls. You might wish to consider their family circumstances, their relations with other classmates, their interests, and their hopes for the future.

Personal Writing

Description Have you ever felt embarrassed to be seen with someone? Maybe it was a younger sibling or a friend who was unpopular with your other friends. Write a description of this experience. Then compare your feelings at the time with Helen's fear of being seen with Myra.

Extending Your Response

Literature Groups

Guilty or Not? At the end of the story, Helen refers to Myra's presents as "guilt-tinged offerings." Do you agree that the other girls feel guilty about their treatment of Myra, or do you think Helen is projecting her own feelings onto them? Discuss this question in your group, using evidence from the story to support your opinion. Share your conclusions with the class.

Listening and Speaking

Descriptive Details Read one of the descriptive passages in the story aloud to a classmate. Ask your partner to note down interesting details as you read. Then take notes as your partner reads another descriptive passage. Discuss why Munro might have included these details and how they contribute to the story.

Performing

Resolve Conflict The teasing of Myra ends only when she becomes ill. Could it have stopped sooner? Role-play the situation in a small group, and try to come up with one or two solutions to resolve the conflict. Share your suggestions with the class.

Reading Further

If you enjoyed reading this story, the following story by Alice Munro might be of interest to you:

"Dance of the Happy Shades" from *Dance of the Happy Shades,* Munro's first collection of stories, which includes "Day of the Butterfly."

Save your work for your portfolio.

VOCABULARY • Antonym Analogies

Some analogies are based on antonym relationships:

weak : strong :: full : empty

Strong is the opposite of *weak,* and *empty* is the opposite of *full.*

PRACTICE Choose the pair that best completes each analogy. Check definitions in the dictionary.

- For more on analogies, see **Communications Skills Handbook,** p. R77.

1. loiter : hurry ::
   a. muted : loud
   b. river : tree
   c. region : area
   d. huge : house
   e. green : blue

2. uncommunicative : talkative ::
   a. close : nearby
   b. teacher : instructor
   c. automobile : airplane
   d. benevolence : cruelty
   e. reading : writing

Before You Read

Mushrooms

Meet Margaret Atwood

"You can't write poetry unless you're willing to immerse yourself in language—not just in words, but in words of a certain potency. It's like learning a foreign language."

Margaret Atwood grew up in Toronto and taught English and Creative Writing before becoming a full-time writer. She has always had a taste for offbeat subjects. When she was a young child, she wrote a novel about ants. In high school, she created an opera about synthetic fabrics for her home economics class. "I sometimes get interested in stories," she once said, "because I notice a sort of blank—why hasn't anyone written about this? *Can* it be written about? Do I dare to write it?"

Atwood has published novels, short-story collections, and over a dozen books of poetry. Her criticism has influenced how many Canadians view their own literature. A superb craftsperson, Atwood often raises controversial issues in her work. Her best-known novel, *The Handmaid's Tale,* is set in an oppressive future society where women are treated as slaves.

Margaret Atwood was born in 1939.

Reading Focus

Do you think of mushrooms as ugly or beautiful?

Share Ideas Share your response with a classmate.

Setting a Purpose Read this poem to discover the speaker's thoughts about mushrooms.

Building Background

Atwood on Nature

Until she reached age eleven, Margaret Atwood spent about half of each year in Canada's northern wilderness, where her father conducted research on insects. Many of her poems focus on the constantly changing natural world, which she contrasts with the fixed creations of human society. Atwood traces this interest back to her childhood experiences: "My father is an entomologist and he used to bring home these 'things' in one form, they would go through some mysterious process and emerge as something else. So metamorphosis was familiar to me at an early age. Later on I studied chemistry and botany and zoology, and if I hadn't been a writer I'd have gone on with that." Atwood believes that the struggle to survive in nature is a theme that runs throughout Canadian literature.

Reading Further

If you enjoy the poem "Mushrooms," you might want to read the following poem by Atwood:

"You Begin" from *Selected Poems II: Poems Selected and New 1976–1986.*

Lac Monroe, Mont Tremblant Provincial Park, Quebec.

Mushrooms

Margaret Atwood

In this moist season,
mist on the lake and thunder
afternoons in the distance

they ooze up through the earth
during the night,
like bubbles, like tiny
bright red balloons
filling with water;
a sound below sound, the thumbs of rubber
gloves turned softly inside out.

In the mornings, there is the leaf mold
starred with nipples,
with cool white fish gills,
leathery purple brains,
fist-sized suns dulled to the color of embers,
poisonous moons, pale yellow.

ii

Where do they come from?

For each thunderstorm that travels
overhead there's another storm
that moves parallel in the ground.
Struck lightning is where they meet.

Underfoot there's a cloud of rootlets,
shed hairs or a bundle of loose threads
blown slowly through the midsoil.
These are their flowers, these fingers
reaching through darkness to the sky,
these eyeblinks
that burst and powder the air with spores.

iii

They feed in shade, on half-leaves
as they return to water,
on slowly melting logs,
deadwood. They glow
in the dark sometimes. They taste
of rotten meat or cloves
or cooking steak or bruised
lips or new snow.

iv

It isn't only
for food I hunt them
but for the hunt and because
they smell of death and the waxy
skins of the newborn,
flesh into earth into flesh.

Here is the handful
of shadow I have brought back to you:
this decay, this hope, this mouthful of dirt, this poetry.

"Listen, Mariana. Do you mind just letting me read in peace?"

"You're unpleasant to everyone. That's terrible, Lucia. You fight with Mom, you fight with Dad. With *everyone*." Mariana lets out a deep sigh. "You give your parents nothing but trouble, Lucia."

"Mariana, I wish you'd just drop dead, okay?"

"You're horrible, Lucia, horrible! You don't say to anyone that you wish they would drop dead, not to your worst enemy, and certainly not to your own sister."

"That's it, now start to cry, so that afterwards they will scream at me and say that I torture you."

"Afterwards? When afterwards? Do you know exactly *when* Mom will be back?"

"Just afterwards." Lucia has gone back to reading *Mediocre Man*. "Afterwards is afterwards." She lifts her eyes and frowns as if she were meditating on something very important. "The future, I mean."

"What future? You said Mom would be back very soon."

Lucia shakes her head in resignation and goes back to her book.

"Yes, of course, she'll be back very soon."

"No. Yes, of course, no. Is she coming back very soon or isn't she coming back very soon?"

Lucia glares at Mariana; then she seems to remember something and smiles briefly.

"And anyway what does it matter?" She shrugs her shoulders.

"What do you mean, what does it matter? You don't know what you're saying, do you? If someone comes home very soon, it means she comes home very soon, doesn't it?"

"*If* someone comes home, yes."

"What?"

"I just said that *if* someone comes home, then yes. Will you please let me read?"

"You're a cow, that's what you are! What you really want is for Mom never to come home again!"

Lucia closes the book and lays it down on the bed. She sighs.

"It has nothing to do with my wanting it or not," she explains. "What I'm saying is that it simply doesn't matter if Mom is here or there."

"What do you mean, there?"

"Just there; anywhere; it's all the same."

"Why the same?"

Lucia rests her chin on both her hands and stares gravely at Mariana.

"Listen, Mariana," she says, "I've got something to tell you. Mom doesn't exist."

Mariana jumps.

"Don't be stupid, okay?" she says, trying to look calm. "You know Mom doesn't like you saying stupid things like that."

"They're not stupid things. Anyway, who cares what Mom says, if Mom doesn't exist?"

"Lu, I'm telling you for the last time: I-don't-like-you-say-ing-stu-pid-things, okay?"

"Look, Mariana," Lucia says in a tired tone of voice. "I'm not making it up; there's a whole theory about it, a book."

"What does it say, the book?"

"What I just said. That nothing really exists. That we imagine the world."

"*What* do we imagine about the world?"

"Everything."

"You just want to frighten me, Lucia. Books don't say things like that. What does it say, eh? For real."

"I've told you a thousand times. The desk, see? There isn't really a desk there, you just imagine there's a desk. Understand? You, now, this very minute, imagine that you're inside a

Vocabulary

meditate (med′ ə tāt′) *v.* to focus one's thoughts on; reflect or ponder over

resignation (rez′ ig nā′ shən) *n.* unresisting acceptance

gravely (grāv′ lē) *adv.* in a serious or dignified manner

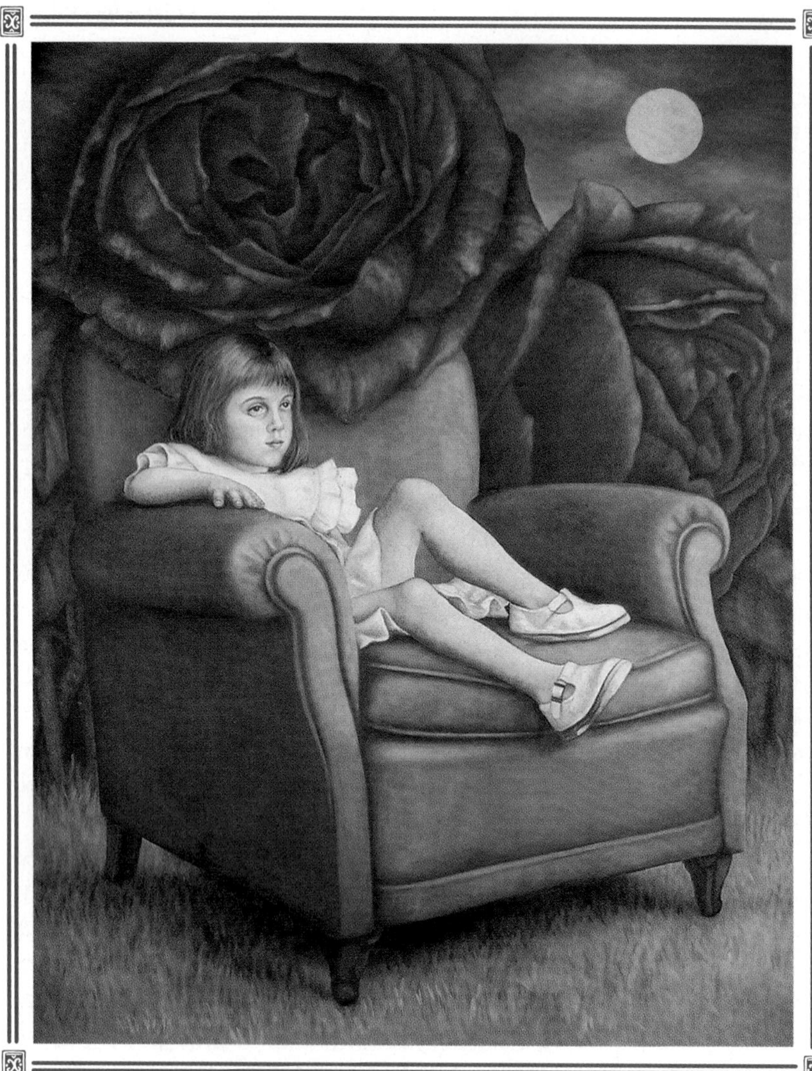

Hace mucho tiempo (It's Been a Long Time), 1995. Alicia Carletti (Argentina). Oil on canvas, 100 x 80 cm. Zurbaran Galeria, Buenos Aires, Argentina.

Viewing the painting: What character in the story does this girl remind you of? Explain.

room, sitting on the bed, talking to me, and you imagine that somewhere else, far away, is Mom. That's why you want Mom to come back. But those places don't really exist, there is no here or far away. It's all inside your head. You are imagining it all."

"And you?"

"I what?"

"There's you, see?" Mariana says with sudden joy. "You can't imagine the desk in the same exact place that I imagine it, can you?"

"You've got it all wrong, Mariana sweetheart. You just don't understand, as usual. It's not that both of us imagine that the desk is in the same place: it's that *you imagine* that both of us imagine that the desk is in the same place."

"No, no, no, no. *You* got it all wrong. Each of us doesn't imagine things on our own, and one can't guess what the other is imagining. You *talk* about what you imagine. I say to you: how many pictures are there in this room? And I say to myself: there are three pictures in this room. And at exactly the same time you tell me that there are three pictures in this room. That means that the three pictures are here, that we see them, not that we imagine them. Because two people can't imagine the same thing at the same time."

"Two can't, that's true."

"What do you mean?"

"I'm saying that *two* people can't."

"I don't understand what you're saying."

"I'm saying that you are also imagining *me*, Mariana."

"You're lying, you're lying! You're the biggest liar in the whole world! I hate you, Lucia. Don't you see? If I'm imagining you, how come you know I'm imagining you?"

"I *don't* know, I don't *anything*. You are just making me up, Mariana. You've made up a person called Lucia, who's your sister, and who knows you've made her up. That's all."

"No, come on, Lu. Say it's not true. What about the book?"

"What book?"

"The book that talks about all this."

"That talks about what?"

"About things not really existing."

"Ah, the book . . . The book is also imagined by you."

"That's a lie, Lucia, a lie! I could never imagine a book like that. I never know about things like that, don't you understand, Lu? I could never imagine something as complicated as that."

"But my poor Mariana, that book is nothing compared to the other things you've imagined. Think of History and the Law of Gravity and Maths and all the books ever written in the world and Aspirins, and the telegraph and planes. Do you realize what you've done?"

"No, Lucia, no, please. Everyone knows about those things. Look. If I bring a lot of people into this room, and I say when I count up to three, we all point to the radio at the same time, then you'll see. We'll all point in the same direction. Let's play at that, Lu, please, come on; let's play at pointing at things. Please."

"But are you stupid or what? I'm telling you that *you* are the one who's imagining all the people in the world."

"I don't believe you. You say that just to frighten me. I can't imagine all the people in the world. What about Mom? What about Dad?"

"Them too."

"Then I'm all alone, Lu!"

"Absolutely. All alone."

"That's a lie, that's a lie! Say that you're lying! You're just saying that to frighten me, right? Sure. Because everything's here. The beds, the desk, the chairs. I can see them, I can touch them if I want to. Say yes, Lu. So that everything's like before."

"But why do you want me to say yes, if anyway it will be *you* imagining that *I* am saying yes?"

"Always me? So there's no one but *me* in the world?"

"Right."

"And you?"

"As I said, you're imagining me."

"I don't want to imagine any more, Lu. I'm afraid. I'm really frightened, Lu. How much longer till Mom comes home?"

Mariana leans out of the window. Mom, come back soon, she begs. But she no longer knows to whom she's begging, or why. She shuts her eyes and the world disappears; she opens them, and it appears again. Everything, everything, everything. If she can't think about her mother, she won't have a mother any more. And if she can't think about the sky, the sky . . . And dogs and clouds and God. Too many things to think about all at once, all on her own. And why she, alone? Why *she* alone in the universe? When you know about it, it's so difficult. Suddenly she might forget about the sun or her house or Lucia. Or worse, she might remember Lucia, but a mad Lucia coming to kill her with a gun in her hand. And now she realizes at least how dangerous all this is. Because if she can't stop herself thinking about it, then Lucia will really be like that, crazy, and kill her. And then there won't be anyone left to imagine all those things. The trees will disappear and the desk and thunderstorms. The color red will disappear and all the countries in the world. And the blue sky and the sky at night and the sparrows and the lions in Africa and the earth itself and singing songs. And no one will ever know that, once, a girl called Mariana invented a very complicated place to which she gave the name of Universe.

Responding to Literature

Personal Response

What went through your mind as you finished reading this story? Share your response with the class.

Analyzing Literature

Recall and Interpret

1. What question does Mariana keep asking her sister Lucia? How does Lucia react to this question?
2. What imaginary images of Lucia suggest that Mariana has conflicting feelings toward her?
3. According to Lucia, why doesn't it matter whether her mother is coming home soon?
4. How does Mariana try to refute Lucia's argument? What claim does Lucia make in response?
5. Why does Mariana become so frightened by the theory that Lucia explains to her?

Evaluate and Connect

6. **Motivation** is the reason or reasons behind a character's actions (see **Literary Terms Handbook,** page R8). What motivates Lucia to tell her theory to Mariana?
7. Which character did you find the most sympathetic? Why?
8. Do you think Lucia is really trying to offer an accurate version of Berkeley's ideas about existence? Explain your answer, citing details from the story for support.
9. In the Reading Focus on page 1156, you were asked to describe the loneliest situation you could imagine. Compare the description you wrote in your journal with Mariana's thoughts about her own situation at the end of the story.
10. What is your reaction to Lucia's explanation of reality?

Literary ELEMENTS

Conflict

The basis of a story's plot is **conflict**—a struggle between opposing forces. An **external conflict** exists when a character struggles against some outside force, such as another character, a force of nature, or society. An **internal conflict** is a struggle within a character. For example, when a character struggles to make a difficult decision, he or she is experiencing internal conflict. Stories often involve more than one conflict.

1. Describe an external conflict in "Bishop Berkeley or Mariana of the Universe."
2. Describe an internal conflict in the story.

- See **Literary Terms Handbook,** p. R2.

Extending Your Response

Creative Writing

Ending Write a new ending for the story that shows what happens when Mariana and Lucia's mother comes home. Does Mariana continue to believe that she has imagined the universe? What does the mother say to Lucia after finding out about the philosophy lesson that she gave Mariana?

Literature Groups

Analyze Character Do you find Mariana's reaction to her sister's theory plausible? Discuss this question in a small group. Refer to specific passages in the story to support your opinion. When you are finished, share your conclusions with the class.

Save your work for your portfolio.

Before You Read

A Canary's Ideas

Meet Joaquim Maria Machado de Assis

"If the novelist's mission were to copy facts the way they are in reality, art would be worthless; memory would substitute for imagination."

Joaquim Maria Machado de Assis (wä kēm′ mä rē′ ä mə chä′ dō dā ä sēs′) received only an elementary school education. In addition to his other disadvantages, he was afflicted with stuttering, eye problems, and epilepsy. But he made up for his lack of education, spending hours at the library. He taught himself French and English.

Machado de Assis entered the printing trade at age seventeen. Through his work, he met some important literary figures who helped launch his career as a writer. After he turned forty, he began to publish the witty, although pessimistic, novels and short stories which earned him popular as well as critical success. He was the founder and first president of Brazil's Academy of Letters. By the time of his death, he was acknowledged as his country's outstanding literary and intellectual figure.

Joaquim Maria Machado de Assis was born in 1839 and died in 1908.

Reading Focus

If someone asked you to describe the world in two or three sentences, what would you say?

Quickwrite Jot down a response in your journal.

Setting a Purpose Read this story to discover how experience changes one character's ideas about the world.

Building Background

Ahead of His Time

There is nothing conventional about Machado de Assis's mature works. In a period dominated by faith in progress, he explored the irrational nature of human beings and the absurdity of life, anticipating the concerns of many twentieth-century writers. His experiments with literary techniques also distinguish him as a man ahead of his time. For example, he often used unreliable narrators who depart from chronological order in telling their stories. Machado de Assis was willing to abandon the illusion of realism to capture the inner lives of his characters.

Reading Further

If you enjoy reading this story, you might enjoy the following collection:

"Education of a Stuffed Shirt: A Dialogue" from *The Psychiatrist and Other Stories,* by Joaquim Maria Machado de Assis.

Vocabulary Preview

austere (ôs tēr′) *adj.* stern and cold in appearance or manner; somber; p. 1164

inherent (in hēr′ ənt) *adj.* forming an essential part of someone or something; firmly established by nature or habit; p. 1164

banal (bə nal′) *adj.* lacking originality, freshness, or novelty; p. 1164

phenomenon (fə nom′ ə non′) *n.* observable fact or subject of scientific study; remarkable event or occurrence; p. 1166

presumptuous (pri zump′ cho͞o əs) *adj.* excessively bold or arrogant; taking liberties; p. 1167

cursory (kur′ sər ē) *adj.* hasty and not thorough; superficial; p. 1167

A Canary's Ideas

Joaquim Maria Machado de Assis
Translated by Jack Schmitt and Lorie Ishimatsu

A MAN BY THE NAME OF MACEDO, WHO HAD a fancy for ornithology,[1] related to some friends an incident so extraordinary that no one took him seriously. Some came to believe he had lost his mind. Here is a summary of his narration.

At the beginning of last month, as I was walking down the street, a carriage darted past me and nearly knocked me to the ground. I escaped by quickly side-stepping into a secondhand shop. Neither the racket of the horse and carriage nor my entrance stirred the proprietor, dozing in a folding chair at the back of the shop. He was a man of shabby appearance: his beard was the color of dirty straw, and his head was covered by a tattered cap which probably had not found a buyer. One could not guess that there was any story behind him, as there could have been behind some of the objects he sold, nor could one sense in him that austere, disillusioned sadness inherent in the objects which were remnants of past lives.

The shop was dark and crowded with the sort of old, bent, broken, tarnished, rusted articles ordinarily found in secondhand shops, and everything was in that state of semidisorder befitting such an establishment. This assortment of articles, though banal, was interesting. Pots without lids, lids without pots, buttons, shoes, locks, a black shirt, straw hats, fur hats, picture frames, binoculars, dress coats, a fencing foil,[2] a stuffed dog, a pair of slippers, gloves, nondescript vases, epaulets, a velvet satchel, two hatracks, a slingshot, a thermometer, chairs, a

1. *Ornithology* (or′ nə thäl′ ə jē) is a branch of science dealing with the study of birds.

2. A *fencing foil* is a light sword.

Vocabulary

austere (ôs tēr′) *adj.* stern and cold in appearance or manner; somber
inherent (in hēr′ ənt) *adj.* forming an essential part of someone or something; firmly established by nature or habit
banal (bə nal′) *adj.* lacking originality, freshness, or novelty

Dialogue of Two Poets Disguised as Birds, 1988. Alfredo Castañeda (Mexico). Oil on canvas, 40 x 50 cm. Galería de Arte Mexicano, Mexico City. Why do you think this artist chose to "disguise" these poets as birds? How do they remind you of characters in the story?

lithographed portrait by the late Sisson, a backgammon board, two wire masks for some future Carnival[3]—all this and more, which I either did not see or do not remember, filled the shop in the area around the door, propped up, hung, or displayed in glass cases as old as the objects inside them. Further inside the shop were many objects of similar appearance. Predominant were the large objects—chests of drawers, chairs, and beds—some of which were stacked on top of others which were lost in the darkness.

I was about to leave, when I saw a cage hanging in the doorway. It was as old as everything else in the shop, and I expected it to be empty so it would fit in with the general appearance of desolation. However, it wasn't empty. Inside, a canary was hopping about. The bird's color, liveliness, and charm added a note of life and youth to that heap of wreckage. It was the last passenger of some wrecked ship, who had arrived in the shop as complete and happy as it had originally been. As soon as I looked at the bird, it began to hop up and down, from perch to perch, as if it meant to tell me that a ray of sunshine was frolicking in the midst of that cemetery. I'm using this image to describe the canary only because I'm speaking to rhetorical people, but the truth is that the canary thought about neither cemetery nor sun, according to what it told me later. Along with the pleasure the sight of the bird brought me, I felt indignation regarding its destiny and softly murmured these bitter words:

"What detestable owner had the nerve to rid himself of this bird for a few cents? Or what indifferent soul, not wishing to keep his late master's pet, gave it away to some child, who sold it so he could make a bet on a soccer game?"

The canary, sitting on top of its perch, trilled this reply:

"Whoever you may be, you're certainly not in your right mind. I had no detestable owner, nor was I given to any child to sell. Those are the delusions of a sick person. Go and get yourself cured, my friend . . ."

3. *Carnival,* traditionally, is a festival held before Lent, the Christian season of penitence. Carnivals include feasting, dances, and masquerades.

"What?" I interrupted, not having had time to become astonished. "So your master didn't sell you to this shop? It wasn't misery or laziness that brought you, like a ray of sunshine, to this cemetery?"

"I don't know what you mean by 'sunshine' or 'cemetery.' If the canaries you've seen use the first of those names, so much the better, because it sounds pretty, but really, I'm sure you're confused."

"Excuse me, but you couldn't have come here by chance, all alone. Has your master always been that man sitting over there?"

"What master? That man over there is my servant. He gives me food and water every day, so regularly that if I were to pay him for his services, it would be no small sum, but canaries don't pay their servants. In fact, since the world belongs to canaries, it would be extravagant for them to pay for what is already in the world."

Astonished by these answers, I didn't know what to marvel at more—the language or the ideas. The language, even though it entered my ears as human speech, was uttered by the bird in the form of charming trills. I looked all around me so I could determine if I were awake and saw that the street was the same, and the shop was the same dark, sad, musty place. The canary, moving from side to side, was waiting for me to speak. I then asked if it were lonely for the infinite blue space . . .

"But, my dear man," trilled the canary, "what does 'infinite blue space' mean?"

"But, pardon me, what do you think of this world? What is the world to you?"

"The world," retorted the canary, with a certain professorial air, "is a secondhand shop with a small rectangular bamboo cage hanging from a nail. The canary is lord of the cage it lives in and the shop that surrounds it. Beyond that, everything is illusion and deception."

With this, the old man woke up and approached me, dragging his feet. He asked me if I wanted to buy the canary. I asked if he had acquired it in the same way he had acquired the rest of the objects he sold and learned that he had bought it from a barber, along with a set of razors.

"The razors are in very good condition," he said.

"I only want the canary."

I paid for it, ordered a huge, circular cage of wood and wire, and had it placed on the veranda of my house so the bird could see the garden, the fountain, and a bit of blue sky.

It was my intention to do a lengthy study of this phenomenon, without saying anything to anyone until I could astound the world with my extraordinary discovery. I began by alphabetizing the canary's language in order to study its structure, its relation to music, the bird's appreciation of aesthetics,[4] its ideas and recollections. When this philological[5] and psychological analysis was done, I entered specifically into the study of canaries: their origin, their early history, the geology and flora of the Canary Islands, the bird's knowledge of navigation, and so forth. We conversed for hours while I took notes, and it waited, hopped about, and trilled.

As I have no family other than two servants, I ordered them not to interrupt me, even to deliver a letter or an urgent telegram or to inform me of an important visitor. Since

4. *Aesthetics* (es thet′ iks) is a branch of philosophy dealing with the nature of beauty and art, as well as their creation and appreciation.

5. *Philological* (fil′ ə loj′ i kəl) means "of or relating to philology, the comparative study of languages, including their origins, developments, and interrelationships."

Vocabulary

phenomenon (fə nom′ ə non′) *n.* observable fact or subject of scientific study; remarkable event or occurrence they both knew about my scientific pursuits, they found my orders perfectly natural and did not suspect that the canary and I understood each other.

Needless to say, I slept little, woke up two or three times each night, wandered about aimlessly, and felt feverish. Finally, I returned to my work in order to reread, add, and emend.[6] I corrected more than one observation, either because I had misunderstood something or because the bird had not expressed it clearly. The definition of the world was one of these. Three weeks after the canary's entrance into my home, I asked it to repeat to me its definition of the world.

"The world," it answered, "is a sufficiently broad garden with a fountain in the middle, flowers, shrubbery, some grass, clear air, and a bit of blue up above. The canary, lord of the world, lives in a spacious cage, white and circular, from which it looks out on the rest of the world. Everything else is illusion and deception."

The language of my treatise[7] also suffered some modifications, and I saw that certain conclusions which had seemed simple were actually presumptuous. I still could not write the paper I was to send to the National Museum, the Historical Institute, and the German universities, not due to a lack of material but because I first had to put together all my observations and test their validity. During the last few days, I neither left the house, answered letters, nor wanted to hear from friends or relatives. The canary was everything to me. One of the servants had the job of cleaning the bird's cage and giving it food and water every morning. The bird said nothing to him, as if it knew the man was completely lacking in scientific background. Besides, the service was no more than cursory, as the servant was not a bird lover.

One Saturday I awoke ill, my head and back aching. The doctor ordered complete rest. I was suffering from an excess of studying and was not to read or even think, nor was I even to know what was going on in the city or the rest of the outside world. I remained in this condition for five days. On the sixth day I got up, and only then did I find out that the canary, while under the servant's care, had flown out of its cage. My first impulse was to strangle the servant—I was choking with indignation and collapsed into my chair, speechless and bewildered. The guilty man defended himself, swearing he had been careful, but the wily bird had nevertheless managed to escape.

"But didn't you search for it?"

"Yes, I did, sir. First it flew up to the roof, and I followed it. It flew to a tree, and then who knows where it hid itself? I've been asking around since yesterday. I asked the neighbors and the local farmers, but no one has seen the bird."

I suffered immensely. Fortunately, the fatigue left me within a few hours, and I was soon able to go out to the veranda and the garden. There was no sign of the canary. I ran everywhere, making inquiries and posting announcements, all to no avail. I had already gathered my notes together to write my paper, even though it would be disjointed and incomplete, when I happened to visit a friend who had one of the largest and most beautiful estates on the outskirts of town. We were taking a stroll before dinner when this question was trilled to me:

"Greetings, Senhor Macedo, where have you been since you disappeared?"

6. To *emend* is to correct a text.

7. A *treatise* (trē′ tis) is a book or essay that examines a topic thoroughly and systematically.

Vocabulary

presumptuous (pri zump′ chōō əs) *adj.* excessively bold or arrogant; taking liberties

cursory (kur′ sə rē) *adj.* hasty and not thorough; superficial

Paisaje (Landscape). Juan Cardenas (Colombia, b. 1939). Oil on linen, 50 x 65 cm. Private collection.
Viewing the painting: What kind of mood does the artist create in this painting? How does it remind you of the story?

It was the canary, perched on the branch of a tree. You can imagine how I reacted and what I said to the bird. My friend presumed I was mad, but the opinions of friends are of no importance to me. I spoke tenderly to the canary and asked it to come home and continue our conversations in that world of ours, composed of a garden, a fountain, a veranda, and a white circular cage.

"What garden? What fountain?"

"The world, my dear bird."

"What world? I see you haven't lost any of your annoying professorial habits. The world," it solemnly concluded, "is an infinite blue space, with the sun up above."

Indignant, I replied that if I were to believe what it said, the world could be anything—it had even been a secondhand shop . . .

"A secondhand shop?" it trilled to its heart's content. "But is there really such a thing as a secondhand shop?"

Responding to Literature

Personal Response

What in the selection did you find amusing? Share your response with the class.

Analyzing Literature

Recall and Interpret

1. Where does Macedo find the canary? Why is he surprised to find it in such a place?
2. How does the canary first define the world? How does this idea conflict with Macedo's assumptions about the canary?
3. Why does Macedo bring the canary home with him? What new idea of the world does the canary express in Macedo's home?
4. What idea of the world does the canary express when Macedo finds it on his friend's estate? In your opinion, has the canary changed since it left Macedo's home? Why or why not?

Evaluate and Connect

5. Which do you find more surprising, the canary's ideas or Macedo's reactions? Explain.
6. In a **satire,** the writer ridicules human flaws, ideas, social customs, or institutions in order to change society (see **Literary Terms Handbook,** page R11). What aspect of human nature might Machado de Assis have wanted to satirize in this story?
7. In the Reading Focus on page 1163, you were asked to write a brief description of the world. How much does the environment in which you live affect your description? Explain.
8. What ideas about the world have you heard of that remind you of the canary's ideas?

Literary ELEMENTS

Unreliable Narrator

An **unreliable narrator** is a narrator whose account of events is faulty or distorted in some way. Some unreliable narrators intentionally mislead readers. Others fail to understand the true meaning of the events they describe. For example, if a story is narrated by a small child, he or she might misinterpret the behavior of adult characters. Many stories with unreliable narrators are written in the first person.

1. How does the author hint at the beginning of the story that Macedo is an unreliable narrator?
2. Identify another passage or detail in the story that suggests that Macedo is unreliable.

- See **Literary Terms Handbook,** p. R13.

Extending Your Response

Creative Writing

Definition The canary in Machado de Assis's story defines the world on the basis of its own limited experiences. Write a brief definition of the world from the perspective of another animal or insect. Make sure that your definition reflects the typical environment or experiences of such a creature.

Literature Groups

Analyze Character Do you agree with some of Macedo's friends that he has lost his mind? Discuss this question in a small group, using evidence from the story to support your opinion. When you are finished, take a vote and announce the results to the class.

Save your work for your portfolio.

COMPARING *selections*

Bishop Berkeley or Mariana of the Universe and A CANARY'S IDEAS

COMPARE EXPERIENCES

Both stories have protagonists whose understanding of reality is challenged by the ideas of another character. In a small group, compare and contrast the following:

- how Lucia and the canary are prompted to express their ideas about the world
- Lucia's attitude toward Mariana and the canary's attitude toward Macedo
- how Mariana and Macedo initially react to the ideas of Lucia and the canary
- the effect that the ideas ultimately have on Mariana and Macedo

COMPARE RESPONSES

With a classmate, compare your responses to the two selections. Discuss the following questions:

- Which story did you find more amusing? Why?
- Which protagonist did you most identify with, Mariana or Macedo? Give reasons for your choice.
- Whose ideas do you find most provocative, the canary's or Lucia's? Explain with examples from the stories.

COMPARE STYLES

Write a paragraph comparing the styles of Heker and Machado de Assis in the two stories. Use examples from each story to support your analysis. You might wish to focus on one or more of the following elements:

- point of view
- tone
- theme
- characterization
- setting
- conflict

Paisaje (Landscape) (detail).

Reading & Thinking Skills

Synthesizing

When you combine existing things or ideas to create something new, you are synthesizing. **Synthesizing** is an important thinking skill, because when you synthesize, you can rearrange information and arrive at a richer, more complete understanding. For example, visualize a place that you know very well, such as your bedroom. If you rearranged the furniture and other objects in your room, those elements would be placed in different positions than before. After the rearrangement, you can look at each piece of furniture and each object from a different angle and position. Not only have you created something new, but you may also have improved the way in which the room works for you. You may have greater appreciation for the space and see it as a unique and interesting place.

The process of synthesizing works in a similar way. It includes activities such as compiling, modifying, designing, and rearranging ideas found in a piece of writing. Any time you look for patterns or connections among parts of a story or other piece of writing and put those parts together in a new way, you are synthesizing.

In "A Canary's Ideas," for example, the narrator makes an initial assumption about the canary, as well as about the canary's past and present life. The canary, who can talk, states matter-of-factly to the narrator that "the world is a secondhand shop with a small rectangular bamboo cage hanging from a nail. The canary is lord of the cage it lives in and the shop that surrounds it. Beyond that, everything is illusion and deception." The narrator, who buys the canary, then goes on to relate the conversations he and the bird share, including the bird's changing perception of the world. Once you understand the pattern of these ideas and events, you can anticipate and appreciate the story's theme of changing perceptions of the world–and how those perceptions are dependent upon perspective.

- For more about comprehension strategies, see **Reading Handbook,** pp. R82–R87.

ACTIVITY

Reread the story "A Canary's Ideas." In a small group, discuss the pattern of ideas and events that the author presents. Then write a brief essay explaining how the story engages the narrator *and the reader* in the skill of synthesizing. In writing your essay, you might consider the following questions:

- What is the narrator's initial assumption about the canary?
- What role does the canary play in the narrator's rearrangement of ideas?
- What role do the narrator and the canary play in the reader's rearrangement of ideas?
- What information is modified or rearranged? Why?
- How do the canary, narrator, and reader change their perceptions of the world?

JAMAICA, 1986

Before You Read

Love Orange

Meet Olive Senior

"I want people to know that 'literature' can be created out of the fabric of our everyday lives, that our stories are as worth telling as those of Shakespeare."

Olive Senior was born in a poor village in western Jamaica. One of ten children, she spent long periods living with her mother's relatives after she turned four. This arrangement allowed her to get a good education and escape poverty. However, she felt isolated among her urban, middle-class relatives. She took an interest in writing when she was in high school, and after graduating she was hired by a Jamaican newspaper. Later she studied journalism in Canada.

Senior is a highly regarded poet and short-story writer. She has also written studies of Jamaican culture and the role of women in the Caribbean. Her work is influenced by the oral culture of her parents' village, where people told stories in the African tradition. One critic has said that her stories "might serve as a kind of laboratory for examining Jamaican speech."

Olive Senior was born in 1943.

Reading Focus

Many children grow up believing in the tooth fairy, who supposedly leaves money under a child's pillow in exchange for a baby tooth that has fallen out. Think of a childhood belief that you no longer accept as true. What effect did this belief once have on you?

Discuss Discuss your response with a small group of classmates.

Setting a Purpose In this story, a child's ideas about love are tested by experience.

Building Background

Jamaica

Jamaica (approximately the size of Connecticut) is the third largest island in the Caribbean. Its rugged, mountainous landscape is covered with green forests. When Columbus first saw it in 1494, he wrote that it was the most beautiful island in the world.

Jamaica's people are mostly of African heritage, with some Asian and European elements. The country has a strong sense of national unity, as expressed in its motto, "Out of Many, One People." Farming occupies the largest number of people, but mining and tourism are also important.

Christianity, in various denominations, is the religion of the vast majority of Jamaicans. There are also beliefs, such as Pocomania, based on a combination of Christian and traditional African beliefs.

Vocabulary Preview

finite (fī′ nīt) *adj.* having definite or definable limits; p. 1174

audacity (ô das′ ə tē) *n.* recklessly bold behavior or attitude; p. 1174

obscure (əb skyoor′) *v.* to make dark, dim, or indistinct; cloud; p. 1175

oblique (ə blēk′) *adj.* indirect; vague; p. 1175

potency (pōt′ ən sē) *n.* power to achieve a particular result; p. 1176

Girl with Orange. Gerard Sekoto (South Africa, 1913–1993). Oil on canvas, 47 x 39.5 cm. Johannesburg Art Gallery, South Africa.

Love Orange

Olive Senior

Work out your own salvation with fear and trembling.

Philippians[1]

Somewhere between the repetition of Sunday School lessons and the broken doll which the lady sent me one Christmas I lost what it was to be happy. But I didn't know it then even though in dreams I would lie with my face broken like the doll's in the pink tissue of a shoebox coffin. For I was at the age where no one asked me for commitment and I had a phrase which I used like a talisman.[2] When strangers came or lightning flashed, I would lie in the dust under my grandfather's vast bed and hug the dog, whispering "our worlds wait outside" and be happy.

Once I set out to find the worlds outside, the horizon was wide and the rim of the far mountains beckoned. I was happy when they found me in time for bed and a warm supper, for the skies, I discovered, were the same shade of China blue as the one intact eye of the doll. "Experience can wait," I whispered to the dog, "death too."

I knew all about death then because in dreams I had been there. I also knew a great deal about love. Love, I thought, was like an orange, a fixed and sharply defined amount, limited, finite. Each person had this amount of love to distribute as he may. If one had many people to love then the segments for each person would be smaller and eventually love, like patience, would be exhausted. That is why I preferred to live with my grandparents then since they had fewer people to love than my parents and so my portion of their love-orange would be larger.

My own love-orange I jealously guarded. Whenever I thought of love I could feel it in my hand, large and round and brightly colored, intact and spotless. I had moments of indecision when I wanted to distribute the orange but each time I would grow afraid of the audacity of such commitment. Sometimes, in a moment of rare passion, I would extend the orange to the dog or my grandmother but would quickly withdraw my hand each time. For without looking I would feel in its place the doll crawling into my hand and nestling there and I would run into the garden and be sick. I would see its face as it lay in the pink tissue of a shoebox tied with ribbons beside the stocking hanging on the bedpost and I would clutch my orange tighter, thinking that I had better save it for the day when occasions like this would arise again and I would need the entire orange to overcome the feelings which arose each time I thought of the doll.

I could not let my grandmother know about my being sick because she never understood about the doll. For years I had dreamed of exchanging homemade dolls with button eyes and ink faces for a plaster doll with blue eyes and limbs that moved. All that December I haunted my grandmother's clothes closet until beneath the dresses I discovered the box smelling faintly of camphor[3] and without looking I knew that it came from Miss Evangeline's toy shop and that it would therefore be a marvel. But the doll

1. *Philippians* (fi lip′ ē ənz) refers to a book of the Bible containing a letter of spiritual advice written by St. Paul to the people of Philippi, a Greek town.
2. A *talisman* (tal′ is mən) is an object believed to avert evil and bring good fortune.
3. *Camphor* is a fragrant compound made from the bark of the camphor tree. It is often hung in clothes closets to repel moths.

Vocabulary

finite (fī′ nīt) *adj.* having definite or definable limits
audacity (ô das′ ə tē) *n.* recklessly bold behavior or attitude

beside the Christmas stocking, huge in a billowing dress and petticoats, had half a face and a finger missing. "It can be mended," my grandmother said, "I can make it as good as new. 'Why throw away a good thing?' Miss Evangeline said as she gave it to me."

But I could no longer hear I could no longer see for the one China blue eye and the missing finger that obscured my vision. And after that I never opened a box again and I never waited up for Christmas. And although I buried the box beneath the allamanda tree the doll rose up again and again, in my throat, like a sickness to be got rid of from the body, and I felt as if I too were half a person who could lay down in the shoebox and sleep forever. But on awakening from these moments, I could find safely clutched in my hands the orange, conjured up from some deep part of myself, and I would hug the dog saying "our worlds wait outside."

That summer I saw more clearly the worlds that awaited. It was filled with many deaths that seemed to tie all the strands of my life together and which bore some oblique relationship to both the orange and the doll.

The first to die was a friend of my grandparents who lived nearby. I sometimes played with her grandchildren at her house when I was allowed to, but each time she had appeared only as a phantom, come on the scene silently, her feet shod in cotton stockings rolled down to her ankles, thrust into a pair of her son's broken-down slippers. In all the years I had known her I had never heard her say anything but whisper softly; her whole presence was a whisper. She seemed to appear from the cracks of the house, the ceiling, anywhere, she made so little noise in her coming, this tiny, delicate, slightly absurd old woman who lived for us only in the secret and mysterious prison of the aged.

When she died it meant nothing to me, I could think then only of my death which I saw nightly in dreams but I could not conceive of her in the flesh, to miss her or to weep tears.

The funeral that afternoon was 5:00 P.M. on a hot summer's day. My grandmother dressed me all in white and I trailed down the road behind her, my corseted and whaleboned[4] grandmother lumbering from side to side in a black romaine dress now shiny in the sunlight, bobbing over her head a huge black umbrella. My grandfather stepped high in shiny black shoes and a shiny black suit ahead of her. Bringing up the rear, I skipped lightly on the gravel, clutching in my hand a new, shiny, bright and bouncy red rubber ball. For me, the funeral, any occasion to get out of the house was a holiday, like breaking suddenly from a dark tunnel into the sunlight where gardens of butterflies waited.

They had dug a grave in the red clay by the side of the road. The house was filled with people. I followed my grandparents and the dead woman's children into the room where they had laid her out, unsmiling, her nostrils stuffed with cotton. I stood in the shadows where no one saw me, filled with the smell of something I had never felt before, like a smell rising from the earth itself which no sunlight, no butterflies, no sweetness could combat. "Miss Aggie, Miss Aggie," I said silently to the dead old woman and suddenly I knew that if I gave her my orange to take into the unknown with her it would be safe, a secret between me and one who could return no more. I gripped the red ball tightly in my hands and it became transformed into the rough texture of an orange; I tasted it on my tongue, smelled the fragrance.

4. A *corseted and whaleboned* woman is wearing a close-fitting undergarment reinforced with whalebone to hold its shape.

Vocabulary

obscure (əb skyoor′) *v.* to make dark, dim, or indistinct; cloud

oblique (ə blēk′) *adj.* indirect; vague

As my grandmother knelt to pray I crept forward and gently placed between Miss Aggie's closed hands the love-orange, smiled because we knew each other and nothing would be able to touch either of us. But as I crept away my grandmother lifted her head from her hands and gasped when she saw the ball. She swiftly retrieved it while the others still prayed and hid it in her voluminous skirt. But when she sent me home, in anger, on the way the love-orange appeared comforting in my hand, and I went into the empty house and crept under my grandfather's bed and dreamt of worlds outside.

The next time I saw with greater clarity the vastness of this world outside. I was asked to visit some new neighbors and read to their son. He was very old, I thought, and he sat in the sunshine all day, his head covered with a calico skull cap. He couldn't see very clearly and my grandmother said he had a brain tumor and would perhaps die. Nevertheless I read to him and worried about all the knowledge that would be lost if he did not live. For every morning he would take down from a shelf a huge Atlas and together we would travel the cities of the world to which he had been. I was very happy and the names of these cities secretly rolled off my tongue all day. I wanted very much to give him my orange but held back. I was not yet sure if he were a whole person, if he would not recover and need me less and so the whole orange would be wasted. So I did not tell him about it. And then he went off with his parents to England, for an operation, my grandmother said, and he came back only as ashes held on the plane by his mother. When I went to the church this time there was no coffin, only his mother holding this tiny box which was so like the shoe box of the doll that I was sure there was some connection which I could not grasp but I thought, if they bury this box then the broken doll cannot rise again.

But the doll rose up one more time because soon my grandmother lay dying. My mother had taken me away when she fell too ill and brought me back to my grandmother's house, even darker and more silent now, this one last time. I went into the room where she lay and she held out a weak hand to me, she couldn't speak so she followed me with her eyes and I couldn't bear it. "Grandma," I said quickly, searching for something to say, something that would save her, "Grandma, you can have my whole orange," and I placed it in the bed beside her hand. But she kept on dying and I knew then that the orange had no potency, that love could not create miracles. "Orange," my grandmother spoke for the last time trying to make connections that she did not see, "orange. . . . . ?" and my mother took me out of the room as my grandmother died. "At least," my mother said, "at least you could have told her that you loved her, she waited for it."

"But . . ." I started to say and bit my tongue, for nobody, not then or ever could understand about the orange. And in leaving my grandmother's house, the dark tunnel of my childhood, I slammed the car door hard on my fingers and as my hand closed over the breaking bones, felt nothing.

Vocabulary

potency (pōt′ ən sē) *n.* power to achieve a particular result

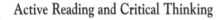

Responding to Literature

Personal Response

How did you react to the story's ending? Share your response with a classmate.

Analyzing Literature

Recall and Interpret

1. What does the narrator tell herself when she is frightened or unhappy? How do you interpret this saying?
2. What idea does the narrator have about love?
3. Why is the narrator sickened by the doll her grandmother has given her?
4. What does the narrator hope will happen when she places the love orange on her grandmother's bed?
5. How do you explain the narrator's final act?

Evaluate and Connect

6. **Irony** is a contrast between what is believed or expected and what actually exists or occurs (see page R6). Identify an example of irony in "Love Orange."
7. A **symbol** is an object or action that stands for something else in addition to itself (see page R12). What does the doll symbolize in the story?
8. Why might Olive Senior have chosen to include the quotation from the Bible at the beginning of this story?
9. In your opinion, is the narrator neglected by her grandparents? Why or why not?
10. Do you think that love is powerful or powerless? Explain your response.

Literary **ELEMENTS**

Description

Description is writing that creates a clear image in the reader's mind of an appearance, feeling, or action. Good descriptive writing appeals to the senses through imagery. Senior uses visual imagery such as "My grandfather stepped high in shiny black shoes and a shiny black suit." The use of figurative language and precise verbs, adjectives, and adverbs can also help make a description vivid.

1. What kind of imagery did Senior use to describe the friend of the narrator's grandparents?
2. What figurative language did Senior use to describe an important idea in the story?

- See **Literary Terms Handbook,** p. R3.

Extending Your Response

Personal Writing

Growing Pains In the Reading Focus on page 1172, you were asked to discuss a childhood belief that you no longer accept as true. How did you come to reject this belief? Were you upset at the time? Write a paragraph comparing your experience with the narrator's disillusionment at the end of "Love Orange."

Literature Groups

Discuss Do you think that the narrator would have undergone a similar crisis if she had been living with her parents rather than her grandparents? Discuss this question in your group. When you are finished, share your response with the class.

Save your work for your portfolio.

MEDIA connection

Web Site

In the summer of 1997, a replica of John Cabot's ship, the *Matthew*, sailed from England to Newfoundland to commemorate the five hundredth anniversary of Cabot's voyage. These excerpts are from the ship's Internet logbook.

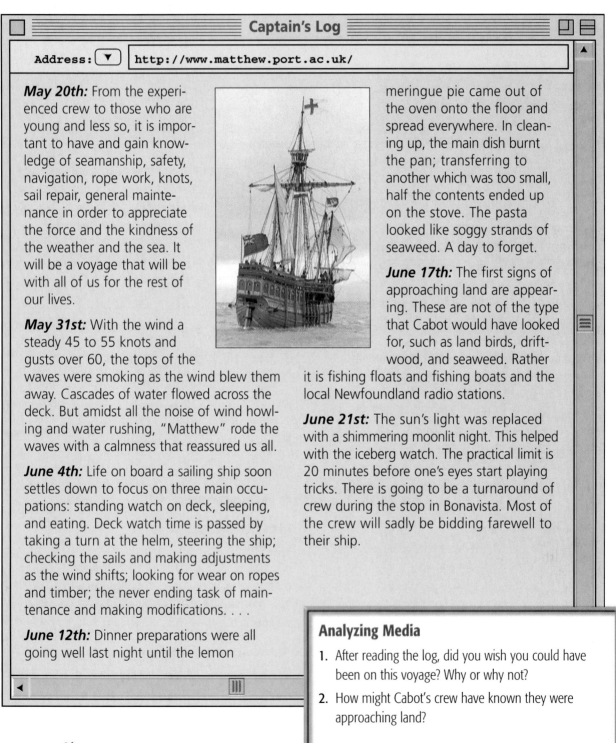

Captain's Log

Address: http://www.matthew.port.ac.uk/

May 20th: From the experienced crew to those who are young and less so, it is important to have and gain knowledge of seamanship, safety, navigation, rope work, knots, sail repair, general maintenance in order to appreciate the force and the kindness of the weather and the sea. It will be a voyage that will be with all of us for the rest of our lives.

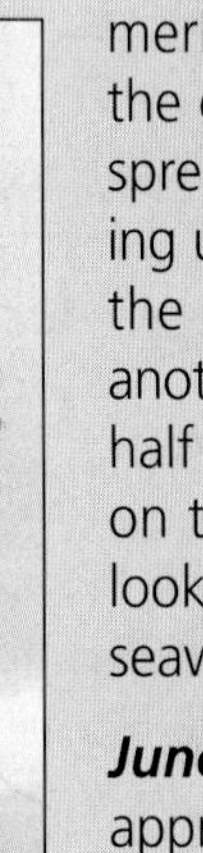

May 31st: With the wind a steady 45 to 55 knots and gusts over 60, the tops of the waves were smoking as the wind blew them away. Cascades of water flowed across the deck. But amidst all the noise of wind howling and water rushing, "Matthew" rode the waves with a calmness that reassured us all.

June 4th: Life on board a sailing ship soon settles down to focus on three main occupations: standing watch on deck, sleeping, and eating. Deck watch time is passed by taking a turn at the helm, steering the ship; checking the sails and making adjustments as the wind shifts; looking for wear on ropes and timber; the never ending task of maintenance and making modifications. . . .

June 12th: Dinner preparations were all going well last night until the lemon meringue pie came out of the oven onto the floor and spread everywhere. In cleaning up, the main dish burnt the pan; transferring to another which was too small, half the contents ended up on the stove. The pasta looked like soggy strands of seaweed. A day to forget.

June 17th: The first signs of approaching land are appearing. These are not of the type that Cabot would have looked for, such as land birds, driftwood, and seaweed. Rather it is fishing floats and fishing boats and the local Newfoundland radio stations.

June 21st: The sun's light was replaced with a shimmering moonlit night. This helped with the iceberg watch. The practical limit is 20 minutes before one's eyes start playing tricks. There is going to be a turnaround of crew during the stop in Bonavista. Most of the crew will sadly be bidding farewell to their ship.

Analyzing Media

1. After reading the log, did you wish you could have been on this voyage? Why or why not?
2. How might Cabot's crew have known they were approaching land?

Before You Read

A Walk to the Jetty from *Annie John*

Meet Jamaica Kincaid

"Everyone thought I had a way with words, but it came out as a sharp tongue. No one expected anything from me at all."

Jamaica Kincaid was born on the Caribbean island of Antigua. Her parents were unable to send her to a university, so at age seventeen she moved to the United States in search of better opportunities. Kincaid took classes while holding down various jobs. Eventually she came to the attention of *New Yorker* magazine editor William Shawn, who was amused by her comments about American culture. He hired her as a staff writer and later began publishing her fiction.

Kincaid is widely praised for her poetic literary style and her insight into relationships between parents and children. Much of her work is autobiographical. Although she admits that she has been "incredibly lucky" in her personal life, she refuses to write happy endings. "I think life is difficult," Kincaid has said. "I am interested in pursuing a truth, and the truth often seems to be not happiness but its opposite."

Jamaica Kincaid was born in 1949.

Reading Focus

How do you think you would feel if you were about to leave home to attend college or find work? How do you think you would deal with those feelings?

Journal Write a few paragraphs in your journal explaining your response to these questions.

Setting a Purpose Read this selection to discover how one teenager says good-bye to her parents and the island where she was raised.

Building Background

Annie John

The selection you will read is excerpted from the last chapter of *Annie John,* a coming-of-age novel about a girl growing up on the small (108 square miles) eastern Caribbean island of Antigua (an tē′ gə). In the early chapters, young Annie is constantly with her mother, helping with the shopping and housework. They even wear clothing made from the same cloth. However, the mother distances herself from Annie when she enters puberty. Resentful over the loss of their intimacy, Annie begins to rebel against her mother, whom she still loves. After she turns seventeen, Annie decides to move to England and study for a nursing career. Kincaid portrays Annie's confused feelings about her mother and her own identity by focusing on the mundane aspects of life.

Research

Use the library or the Internet to research the geography and culture of Antigua, Annie John's homeland. As you read "A Walk to the Jetty," keep in mind what you have learned about the land and people of this Caribbean island.

Vocabulary Preview

pasteurization (pas′ chə rə zā′ shən) *n.* subjecting a food, especially milk, to a temperature high enough to destroy disease-producing bacteria without altering the composition of the product; p. 1183

guffaw (gu fô′) *n.* loud or boisterous burst of laughter; p. 1183

stupor (sto͞o′ pər) *n.* dulled mental state often as a result of shock or stress; daze; p. 1185

A Walk to the Jetty:

My mother had arranged with a stevedore[1] to take my trunk to the jetty ahead of me. At ten o'clock on the dot, I was dressed, and we set off for the jetty. An hour after that, I would board a launch that would take me out to sea, where I then would board the ship. Starting out, as if for old time's sake and without giving it a thought, we lined up in the old way: I walking between my mother and my father. I loomed way above my father and could see the top of his head. We must have made a strange sight: a grown girl all dressed up in the middle of a morning, in the middle of the week, walking in step in the middle between her two parents, for people we didn't know stared at us. It was all of half an hour's walk from our house to the jetty, but I was passing through most of the years of my life. We passed by the house where Miss Dulcie, the seamstress that I had been apprenticed to for a time, lived, and just as I was passing by, a wave of bad feeling for her came over me, because I suddenly remembered that the months I spent with her all she had me do was sweep the floor, which was always full of threads and pins and needles, and I never seemed to sweep it clean enough to please her. Then she would send me to the store to buy buttons or thread, though I was only allowed to do this if I was given a sample of the button or thread, and then she would find fault even though they were an exact match of the samples she had given me. And all the while she said to me, "A girl like you will never learn to sew properly, you know." At the time, I don't suppose I minded it, because it was customary to treat the first-year apprentice with such scorn, but now I placed on the dustheap of my life Miss Dulcie and everything that I had had to do with her.

We were soon on the road that I had taken to school, to church, to Sunday school, to choir practice, to Brownie meetings, to Girl Guide meetings, to meet a friend. I was five years old when I first walked on this road unaccompanied by someone to hold my hand. My mother had placed three pennies in my little basket, which was a duplicate of her bigger basket, and sent me to the chemist's shop[2] to buy a pennyworth of senna leaves, a pennyworth of eucalyptus leaves, and a pennyworth of camphor.[3] She then instructed me on what side of the road to walk, where to make a turn, where to cross, how to look carefully before I crossed, and if I met anyone that I knew to politely pass greetings and keep on my way. I was wearing a freshly ironed yellow dress that had printed on it scenes of acrobats flying through the air and swinging on a trapeze. I had just had a bath, and after it, instead of powdering me with my baby-smelling talcum powder, my mother had, as a special favor, let me use her own talcum powder, which smelled quite perfumy and came in a can that had painted on it people going out to dinner in nineteenth-century London and was called Mazie. How it pleased me to walk out the door and bend my head down to sniff at myself and see that I smelled just like my mother. I went to the chemist's shop, and he had to come from behind the counter and bend down to hear

1. A *stevedore* (stē′ və dôr′) is one who works at or is responsible for loading and unloading ships in port.

2. A *chemist's shop* is a pharmacy, in British usage.

3. *Senna leaves, eucalyptus* (ū′ kə lip′ təs) *leaves,* and *camphor* are plant products used for medicinal purposes.

from Annie John

Jamaica Kincaid

Good Old Days, 1990. Shakito (Antigua). Acrylic. Private collection. How is this scene similar to what you imagine the setting of the story to be?

what it was that I wanted to buy, my voice was so little and timid then. I went back just the way I had come, and when I walked into the yard and presented my basket with its three packages to my mother, her eyes filled with tears and she swooped me up and held me high in the air and said that I was wonderful and good and that there would never be anybody better. If I had just conquered Persia,[4] she couldn't have been more proud of me.

We passed by our church—the church in which I had been christened and received and

4. The phrase *conquered Persia* means "accomplished an extraordinary feat." The allusion is to Alexander the Great, who vanquished the Persian Empire in the fourth century B.C.

had sung in the junior choir. We passed by a house in which a girl I used to like and was sure I couldn't live without had lived. Once, when she had mumps, I went to visit her against my mother's wishes, and we sat on her bed and ate the cure of roasted, buttered sweet potatoes that had been placed on her swollen jaws, held there by a piece of white cloth. I don't know how, but my mother found out about it, and I don't know how, but she put an end to our friendship. Shortly after, the girl moved with her family across the sea to somewhere else. We passed the doll store, where I would go with my mother when I was little and point out the doll I wanted that year for Christmas. We passed the store where I bought the much-fought-over shoes I wore to church to be received in. We passed the bank. On my sixth birthday, I was given, among other things, the present of a sixpence. My mother and I then went to this bank, and with the sixpence I opened my own savings account. I was given a little gray book with my name in big letters on it, and in the balance column it said "6d." Every Saturday morning after that, I was given a sixpence—later a shilling, and later a two-and-sixpence piece—and I would take it to the bank for deposit. I had never been allowed to withdraw even a farthing from my bank account until just a few weeks before I was to leave; then the whole account was closed out, and I received from the bank the sum of six pounds ten shillings and two and a half pence.

We passed the office of the doctor who told my mother three times that I did not need glasses, that if my eyes were feeling weak a glass of carrot juice a day would make them strong again. This happened when I was eight. And so every day at recess I would run to my school gate and meet my mother, who was waiting for me with a glass of juice from carrots she had just grated and then squeezed, and I would drink it and then run back to meet my chums. I knew there was nothing at all wrong with my eyes, but I had recently read a story in *The Schoolgirl's Own Annual* in which the heroine, a girl a few years older than I was then, cut such a figure to my mind with the way she was always adjusting her small, round, horn-rimmed glasses that I felt I must have a pair exactly like them. When it became clear that I didn't need glasses, I began to complain about the glare of the sun being too much for my eyes, and I walked around with my hands shielding them—especially in my mother's presence. My mother then bought for me a pair of sunglasses with the exact horn-rimmed frames I wanted, and how I enjoyed the gestures of blowing on the lenses, wiping them with the hem of my uniform, adjusting the glasses when they slipped down my nose, and just removing them from their case and putting them on. In three weeks, I grew tired of them and they found a nice resting place in a drawer, along with some other things that at one time or another I couldn't live without.

We passed the store that sold only grooming aids, all imported from England. This store had in it a large porcelain dog—white, with black spots all over and a red ribbon of satin tied around its neck. The dog sat in front of a white porcelain bowl that was always filled with fresh water, and it sat in such a way that it looked as if it had just taken a long drink. When I was a small child, I would ask my mother, if ever we were near this store, to please take me to see the dog, and I would stand in front of it, bent over slightly, my hands resting on my knees, and stare at it and stare at it. I thought this dog more beautiful and more real than any actual dog I had ever seen or any actual dog I would ever see. I must have outgrown my interest in the dog, for when it disappeared I never asked what became of it. We passed the library, and if there was anything on this walk that I might have wept over leaving, this most surely would have been the thing. My mother had been a member of the library long before I was born.

And since she took me everywhere with her when I was quite little, when she went to the library she took me along there, too. I would sit in her lap very quietly as she read books that she did not want to take home with her. I could not read the words yet, but just the way they looked on the page was interesting to me. Once, a book she was reading had a large picture of a man in it, and when I asked her who he was she told me that he was Louis Pasteur[5] and that the book was about his life. It stuck in my mind, because she said it was because of him that she boiled my milk to purify it before I was allowed to drink it, that it was his idea, and that that was why the process was called pasteurization. One of the things I had put away in my mother's old trunk in which she kept all my childhood things was my library card. At that moment, I owed sevenpence in overdue fees.

As I passed by all these places, it was as if I were in a dream, for I didn't notice the people coming and going in and out of them, I didn't feel my feet touch ground, I didn't even feel my own body—I just saw these places as if they were hanging in the air, not having top or bottom, and as if I had gone in and out of them all in the same moment. The sun was bright; the sky was blue and just above my head. We then arrived at the jetty.

My heart now beat fast, and no matter how hard I tried, I couldn't keep my mouth from falling open and my nostrils from spreading to the ends of my face. My old fear of slipping between the boards of the jetty and falling into the dark-green water where the dark-green eels lived came over me. When my father's stomach started to go bad, the doctor had recommended a walk every evening right after he ate his dinner. Sometimes he would take me with him. When he took me with him, we usually went to the jetty, and there he would sit and talk to the night watchman about cricket[6] or some other thing that didn't interest me, because it was not personal; they didn't talk about their wives, or their children, or their parents, or about any of their likes and dislikes. They talked about things in such a strange way, and I didn't see what they found funny, but sometimes they made each other laugh so much that their guffaws would bound out to sea and send back an echo. I was always sorry when we got to the jetty and saw that the night watchman on duty was the one he enjoyed speaking to; it was like being locked up in a book filled with numbers and diagrams and what-ifs. For the thing about not being able to understand and enjoy what they were saying was I had nothing to take my mind off my fear of slipping in between the boards of the jetty.

Now, too, I had nothing to take my mind off what was happening to me. My mother and my father—I was leaving them forever. My home on an island—I was leaving it forever. What to make of everything? I felt a familiar hollow space inside. I felt I was being held down against my will. I felt I was burning up from head to toe. I felt that someone was tearing me up into little pieces and soon I would be able to see all the little pieces as they floated out into nothing in the deep blue sea. I didn't know whether to laugh or cry. I could see that it would be better not to think too

5. *Louis Pasteur* was a nineteenth-century French chemist who invented the process known as pasteurization.

6. *Cricket* is a bat-and-ball game popular throughout the West Indies.

Vocabulary

pasteurization (pas′ chə rə zā′ shən) *n.* subjecting a food, especially milk, to a temperature high enough to destroy disease-producing bacteria without altering the composition of the product

guffaw (gu fô′) *n.* loud or boisterous burst of laughter clearly about any one thing. The launch was being made ready to take me, along with some other passengers, out to the ship that was anchored in the sea. My father paid our fares, and we joined a line of people waiting to board. My mother checked my bag to make sure that I had my passport, the money she had given me, and a sheet of paper placed between some pages in my Bible on which were written the names of the relatives—people I had not known existed—with whom I would live in England. Across from the jetty was a wharf, and some stevedores were loading and unloading barges. I don't know why seeing that struck me so, but suddenly a wave of strong feeling came over me, and my heart swelled with a great gladness as the words "I shall never see this again" spilled out inside me. But then, just as quickly, my heart shriveled up and the words "I shall never see this again" stabbed at me. I don't know what stopped me from falling in a heap at my parents' feet.

When we were all on board, the launch headed out to sea. Away from the jetty, the water became the customary blue, and the launch left a wide path in it that looked like a road. I passed by sounds and smells that were so familiar that I had long ago stopped paying any attention to them. But now here they were, and the ever-present "I shall never see this again" bobbed up and down inside me. There was the sound of the seagull diving down into the water and coming up with something silverish in its mouth. There was the smell of the sea and the sight of small pieces of rubbish floating around in it. There were boats filled with fishermen coming in early. There was the sound of their voices as they shouted greetings to each other. There was the hot sun, there was the blue sea, there was the blue sky. Not very far away, there was the white sand of the shore, with the run-down houses all crowded in next to each other, for in some places only poor people lived near the shore. I was seated in the launch between my parents, and when I realized that I was gripping their hands tightly I

Heading for Shore, c. 1990. Shakito (Antigua). Acrylic. Private collection.

Viewing the painting: What elements of this painting remind you of the way the speaker feels in the story?

glanced quickly to see if they were looking at me with scorn, for I felt sure that they must have known of my never-see-this-again feelings. But instead my father kissed me on the forehead and my mother kissed me on the mouth, and they both gave over their hands to me, so that I could grip them as much as I wanted. I was on the verge of feeling that it had all been a mistake, but I remembered that I wasn't a child anymore, and that now when I made up my mind about something I had to see it through. At that moment, we came to the ship, and that was that.

The good-byes had to be quick, the captain said. My mother introduced herself to him and then introduced me. She told him to keep an eye on me, for I had never gone this far away from home on my own. She gave him a letter to pass on to the captain of the next ship that I would board in Barbados.[7] They walked me to my cabin, a small space that I would share with someone else—a woman I did not know. I had never before slept in a room with someone I did not know. My father kissed me good-bye and told me to be good and to write home often. After he said this, he looked at me, then looked at the floor and swung his left foot, then looked at me again. I could see that he wanted to say something else, something that he had never said to me before, but then he just turned and walked away. My mother said, "Well," and then she threw her arms around me. Big tears streamed down her face, and it must have been that—for I could not bear to see my mother cry—which started me crying, too. She then tightened her arms around me and held me to her close, so that I felt that I couldn't breathe. With that, my tears dried up and I was suddenly on my guard. "What does she want now?" I said to myself. Still holding me close to her, she said, in a voice that raked across my skin, "It doesn't matter what you do or where you go, I'll always be your mother and this will always be your home."

I dragged myself away from her and backed off a little, and then I shook myself, as if to wake myself out of a stupor. We looked at each other for a long time with smiles on our faces, but I know the opposite of that was in my heart. As if responding to some invisible cue, we both said, at the very same moment, "Well." Then my mother turned around and walked out the cabin door. I stood there for I don't know how long, and then I remembered that it was customary to stand on deck and wave to your relatives who were returning to shore. From the deck, I could not see my father, but I could see my mother facing the ship, her eyes searching to pick me out. I removed from my bag a red cotton handkerchief that she had earlier given me for this purpose, and I waved it wildly in the air. Recognizing me immediately, she waved back just as wildly, and we continued to do this until she became just a dot in the matchbox-size launch swallowed up in the big blue sea.

I went back to my cabin and lay down on my berth. Everything trembled as if it had a spring at its very center. I could hear the small waves lap-lapping around the ship. They made an unexpected sound, as if a vessel filled with liquid had been placed on its side and now was slowly emptying out.

7. *Barbados* (bär bā′ dōz) is the easternmost island of the West Indies in the Caribbean Sea.

Vocabulary

stupor (sto͞o′ pər) *n.* dulled mental state often as a result of shock or stress; daze

Responding to Literature

Personal Response

What memories were stirred up in you as you read this selection? Write your response in your journal. Then share your response with a classmate.

Analyzing Literature

Recall

1. How have Annie's feelings about Miss Dulcie changed since she was her apprentice?
2. What happened when Annie returned from her first unaccompanied walk on the road?
3. What does Annie recall about her walks to the jetty as a child?
4. What conflicting emotions does Annie experience on the launch?
5. What does Annie's mother tell her when she says good-bye?

Interpret

6. What does the change in Annie's feelings about Miss Dulcie suggest about her?
7. From Annie's description of her first unaccompanied walk, how would you describe the relationship between Annie and her mother when Annie was little?
8. What parallel does Annie draw between her trips to the jetty as a child and the present moment?
9. Why does Annie suspect that her parents might be looking at her with scorn on the launch?
10. Why does Annie become wary of her mother when they are saying good-bye?

Evaluate and Connect

11. An **internal conflict** is a struggle within a character (see page R2). Identify an internal conflict in this selection.
12. Why do you think Annie notices things that she had long ignored as she rides on the launch? Support your answers with details from the story.
13. Why might Kincaid have chosen to end her book with a **metaphor** that describes how the waves sound? (See **Literary Terms Handbook,** p. R7.)
14. Do you think Annie seems mature enough to live on her own? Why or why not? Explain, citing details from the story for support.
15. In the Reading Focus on page 1179, you were asked to predict how you would feel if you were about to leave home. Compare the response you wrote in your journal with Annie's feelings about leaving her home island of Antigua.

Literary Criticism

In an analysis of *Annie John,* scholar Laura Niesen de Abruna suggests that the daughter's relationship with the mother is similar to the daughter's relationship with her "motherland," or homeland. Do you agree? In a group discussion, explain your ideas. Then present your group's ideas to the entire class.

Literary ELEMENTS

Flashback

In a **flashback,** the narrator interrupts the action of a literary work to present a scene that took place at an earlier time. Kincaid uses this technique to show how Annie was "passing through most of the years of my life" in her half-hour walk to the jetty. Flashbacks allow writers to fill in background information about characters and events. Writers can also draw parallels between the past and present by interrupting the chronological flow of a narrative.

1. On page 1182, Annie describes her experiences with eyeglasses. What does this flashback reveal about her character?
2. Why might Kincaid have included the flashback on page 1183 that describes Annie's walks to the jetty with her father?

- See **Literary Terms Handbook,** p. R5.

Literature and Writing

Writing About Literature

Analyze Technique Choose a scene or passage from the selection that you found especially moving or interesting. Write a paragraph analyzing the techniques that Kincaid used in it. You might wish to consider one or more of the following literary elements: imagery, setting, mood, parallelism, repetition, characterization, point of view.

Personal Writing

Description As she is passing the library, Annie remarks that "if there was anything on this walk that I might have wept over leaving, this most surely would have been the thing." What place would you miss the most if you moved far away? Describe the place and explain why you are so attached to it.

Extending Your Response

Literature Groups

Discuss Relationships In a small group, discuss the way each parent says good-bye to Annie on the ship. Consider how their words and actions might suggest differences in their relationship with her. When you are finished, share your conclusions with the class.

Learning for Life

Letter Suppose that Annie asked you to write a letter of recommendation to a nursing school in England. Which character traits would you emphasize in your letter? What incidents in her past suggest that she would be a good student? After you write the letter, read it aloud in a small group.

Interdisciplinary Activity

Social Studies: Investigate Setting *Annie John* is set on the Caribbean island of Antigua. With a partner, do research to find out information about the island's culture, its economic opportunities, or its historical ties to England. Share your findings with the class and discuss potential problems that Annie might face as she adjusts to English life.

Reading Further

If you enjoyed reading this selection, the following by Jamaica Kincaid might be of interest to you:

"At Last" and "What I Have Been Doing Lately" from *At the Bottom of the River,* Kincaid's first published work.

Save your work for your portfolio.

VOCABULARY • Etymology

As you have learned, English vocabulary has been influenced by many different sources. Some words have been incorporated directly from other languages. Some words have come directly from the names of people. For example, *maverick* refers to a person who defies traditional rules or customs. The term derives from Samuel Maverick, a nineteenth-century American rancher, who refused to brand his cattle for identification.

PRACTICE Consult a dictionary to learn the origins of the following words based on the names of historical persons.

Use what you learn to describe the individual briefly. Then write an original sentence using the word.

1. chauvinism *(n.)*
2. silhouette *(n.)*
3. guppy *(n.)*
4. diesel *(n.)*
5. macadamized *(adj.)*
6. cardigan *(n.)*

UNITED STATES, c. 1992

Before You Read

Fishing

Meet Joy Harjo

"Writing helped me give voice to turn around a terrible silence that was killing me."

Joy Harjo was born in Tulsa, Oklahoma. A member of the Muskogee (Creek) people, she is also descended from Cherokee, French, and Irish ancestors. Harjo did not have a traditional Creek upbringing, but she considers that part of her heritage the foundation of her writing: "I know when I write there is an old Creek within me that often participates."

Harjo studied painting in high school and in her first few years of college. When she was about twenty-two, she became interested in poetry. She switched to a creative-writing major because her poetry "was taking on more magical qualities than my painting. I could say more when I wrote." Many of her poems focus on the history and contemporary problems of Native Americans. In addition to writing poetry, she has worked on screenplays and has taught at various universities. She performs poems and plays saxophone with a band called Poetic Justice.

Joy Harjo was born in 1951.

Reading Focus

What things do you do that make you think of a friend or relative who is far away?

Share Ideas Share your response with a small group of classmates.

Setting a Purpose In the following poem, the speaker finds an imaginative way of keeping a promise to go fishing with an old friend.

Building Background

Harjo and Oklahoma

Until the early nineteenth century, the Muskogee, or Creek, people lived in settled agricultural towns in the southern areas of present-day Georgia and Alabama. Traditionally, the women raised crops while the men hunted and fished. The Creeks lost much of their land after being defeated by the United States in the Creek War of 1813–1814. (Harjo's great-great-grandfather, Menawha, helped lead the fighting against the United States troops.)

In the 1830s, almost all of the Muskogee were forced to move to the western area that had been set aside by the United States government for Native Americans from east of the Mississippi. This area, called Indian Territory, later became the state of Oklahoma. Harjo sees Oklahoma as "my mother, my motherland. I am connected psychically; there is a birth cord that connects me. But I don't live there and don't know that I ever will. It's too familiar, and too painful."

Reading Further

If you enjoy reading this selection, the following might be of interest to you:

"Perhaps the World Ends Here," "Fooling God," and "The Feathers" from *Reinventing the Enemy's Language: Contemporary Native Women's Writing of North America,* an anthology edited by Joy Harjo, Gloria Bird, and others.

Fishing

Joy Harjo

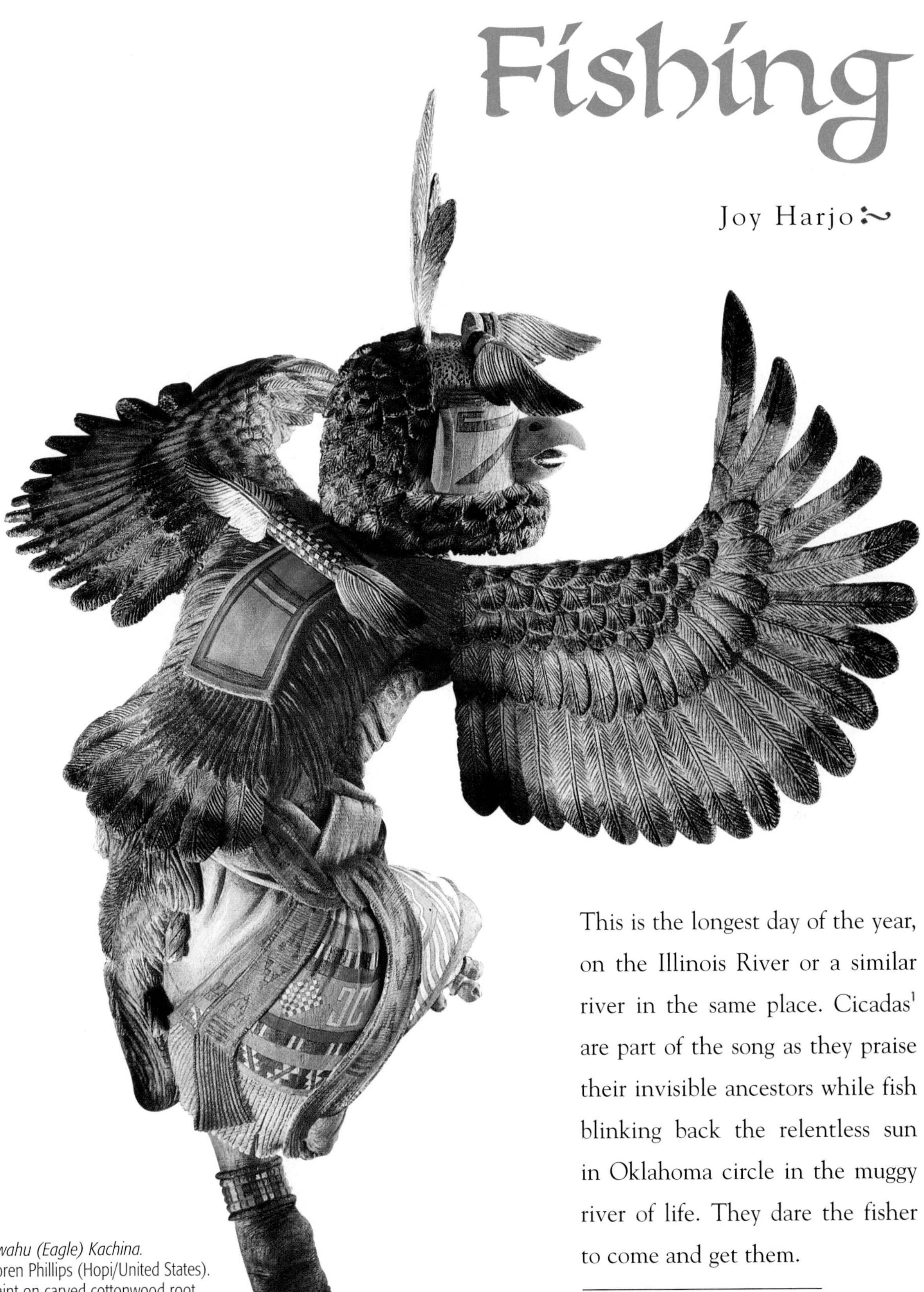

Kwahu (Eagle) Kachina.
Loren Phillips (Hopi/United States). Paint on carved cottonwood root. Gallery 10, Carefree, AZ. What do you think this sculpture represents?

This is the longest day of the year, on the Illinois River or a similar river in the same place. Cicadas[1] are part of the song as they praise their invisible ancestors while fish blinking back the relentless sun in Oklahoma circle in the muggy river of life. They dare the fisher to come and get them.

1. *Cicadas* (si kā′ dəz) are large insects that make a loud, shrill, buzzing sound.

Fishing

Fish too anticipate the game of fishing. Their ancestors perfected the moves, sent down stories that appear as electrical impulses when sunlight hits water. The hook carries great symbology in the coming of age, and is crucial to the making of warriors. The greatest warriors are those who dangle a human for hours on a string, break sacred water for the profanity of air, then snap fiercely back into pearly molecules that describe fishness.

They smell me as I walk the banks with fishing pole, night crawlers[2] and a promise I made to that old friend Louis to fish with him this summer. This is the only place I can keep that promise, inside a poem as familiar to him as the banks of his favorite fishing place. I try not to let the fish see me see them as they look for his tracks on the soft earth made of fossils and ashes. I hear the burble of fish talk: *When is that old Creek coming back? He was the one we loved to tease most, we liked his songs and once in a while he gave us a good run.*

Last night I dreamed I tried to die. I was going to look for Louis. It was rather comical. I worked hard to muster my last breath, then lay down in the summer, along the banks of the last mythic river, my pole and tackle box next to me. What I thought was my last breath floated off as a cloud making an umbrella of grief over my relatives. How embarrassing when the next breath came, and then the next. I reeled in one after another, as if I'd caught a bucket of suckers[3] instead of bass. I guess it wasn't my time, I explained, and went fishing anyway as a liar and I know most fishers to be liars most of the time. Even Louis when it came to fishing, or even dying.

The leap between the sacred and profane is as thin as fishing line, and is part of the mystery on this river of life, as is the way our people continue to make warriors in the strangest of times. I save this part of the poem for the fish camp next to the oldest spirits whose dogs bark to greet visitors. It's near Louis's favorite spot, where the wisest and fattest fish laze. I'll meet him there.

A few weeks before he died I wrote my friend the Muscogee poet, Louis Oliver, a promise that I would go fishing with him in Oklahoma that summer. Fishing to Louis was holy communion.

The struggle of the universe is exemplified in the sport. Yet it's possible to find the answer to every question with the right pole, the right place on the river.

As I mailed the letter I had a strange feeling the letter would never reach him. That cloud of illogic hovered over me for a few days.

When I was informed of his death I knew I had to keep that promise.

This is how I kept it.

---

2. *Night crawlers* are large earthworms found on the soil surface after dark. They are prized as fish bait.

3. *Suckers* are a group of toothless freshwater fish, not valued by fishers.

Responding to Literature

Personal Response

What new insights or ideas did you gain from reading this poem? Write a few paragraphs in your journal to answer this question. Then share your response with a classmate.

Analyzing Literature

Recall and Interpret

1. What has the speaker promised Louis?
2. Why is a poem the only place where the speaker can keep this promise?
3. Why did the speaker try to die in her dream? Why might she describe this dream as comical?
4. How do you interpret the speaker's remark that the "leap between the sacred and profane is as thin as a fishing line"? Support your interpretation with details from the poem.

Evaluate and Connect

5. Is the poem set in a real place or in an imaginary place? Explain your response.
6. **Personification** is a figure of speech that gives human characteristics to an object, animal, or idea (see page R9). Identify an example of personification in the poem.
7. In your opinion, could the first part of this poem stand on its own, without the sentences in italic type that explain the background? Why or why not?
8. In the Reading Focus on page 1188, you were asked what things you do that make you think of someone far away. How does the speaker's imaginary trip compare with what you do?

Literary ELEMENTS

Prose Poem

A **prose poem** is a short prose composition that uses rhythm, imagery, and other poetic devices to express an idea or emotion. Unlike metrical and free verse, prose poetry does not have line breaks; instead, the sentences appear in paragraphs with a right-hand margin. This genre was developed in the nineteenth century by the French poets Charles Baudelaire and Arthur Rimbaud.

1. What is the central idea or emotion expressed in "Fishing"?
2. What poetic devices does Harjo use to express this idea?

- See **Literary Terms Handbook,** p. R10.

Extending Your Response

Writing About Literature

Analyze Theme According to the poem's speaker, the "struggle of the universe is exemplified" in fishing. Write a paragraph analyzing how this theme is developed in the poem. What sort of spiritual or philosophical ideas does the speaker associate with the sport?

Literature Groups

Discuss Do you think that the speaker has come to accept Louis's death or that she is still in mourning? Discuss this question in your group. Use specific evidence from the poem to support your opinion. When you are finished, share your conclusions with the class.

Save your work for your portfolio.

Writing Workshop

Personal Writing: Personal Essay

Throughout this year, you have sampled the literature of the world. You've read about the experiences, hopes, dreams, fears, and imaginings of people near and far. In the years to come, your own world of experience will broaden. What do you imagine, or hope, your life will be like in the future? **In this workshop, you will write a personal essay about where you would like to be in ten years.** In a personal essay, you express your thoughts, opinions, or feelings about a topic relating to yourself.

- As you write your personal essay, refer to the **Writing Handbook**, pp. R58–R69.

EVALUATION RUBRIC

By the time you complete this Writing Workshop, you will have

- begun by introducing the topic of where you will be in ten years
- organized your ideas in a way that is easy to follow
- used details to make your descriptions come alive
- presented a personal essay that is free of errors in grammar, usage, and mechanics

The Writing Process

PREWRITING

PREWRITING TIP

Freewriting is a good method for generating ideas about your future. Let your mind wander and jot down ideas as they come to you.

Explore ideas

There are many ways to interpret the topic "Where I'd Like to Be in Ten Years." For example, you might base your essay on your answers to questions such as the following:

- Where in the world would I like to be living in ten years?
- What kind of person would I like to be?
- What kind of work would I like to be doing?
- What would I like to be studying?
- How would I like to be spending my free time?
- What kinds of people do I hope to know?

You might create a cluster diagram to explore ideas. Let your imagination run in any direction. You might come up with a number of goals and dreams to choose from.

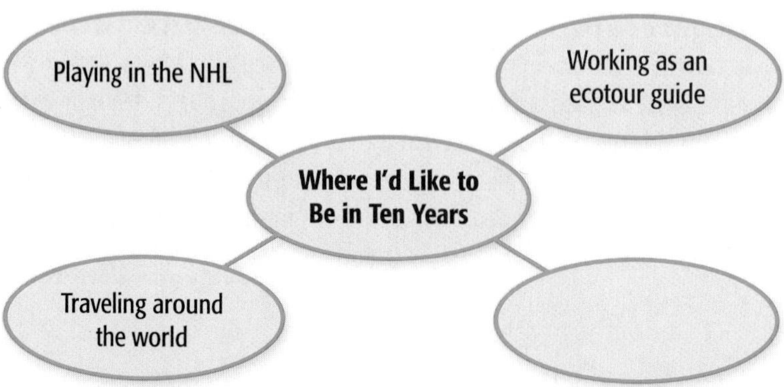

Reading on Your Own

If you have enjoyed the literature in this unit, you might also be interested in the following books.

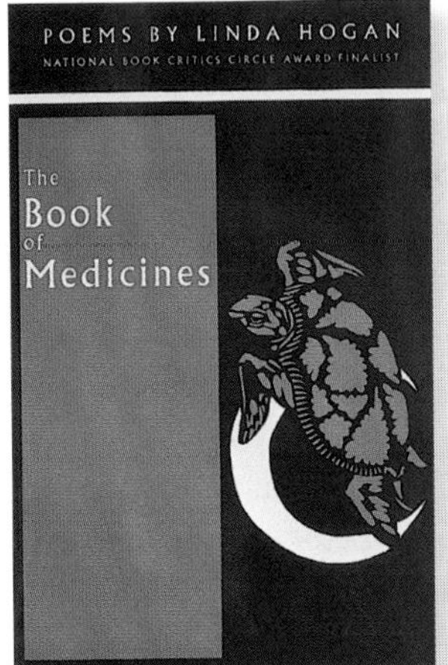

The Book of Medicines
by Linda Hogan Hogan writes forceful poems exploring the relationships among her Native American people, the land, and animals. Hogan's prose works include *Dwellings: A Spiritual History of the Living World* and *Solar Storms,* a novel.

Bless Me, Ultima
by Rudolfo A. Anaya In New Mexico, a magical healer befriends a socially isolated boy and helps him confront the past while facing the future. Ultima, a "curandera," and Antonio are the central figures in this coming-of-age novel.

The Heights of Macchu Picchu
by Pablo Neruda, translated by Nathaniel Tarn Considered one of Neruda's greatest poetic works, *The Heights of Macchu Picchu* recounts twelve phases of a man's spiritual and physical journey, arriving ultimately at the lost Inca city of Macchu Picchu in Peru.

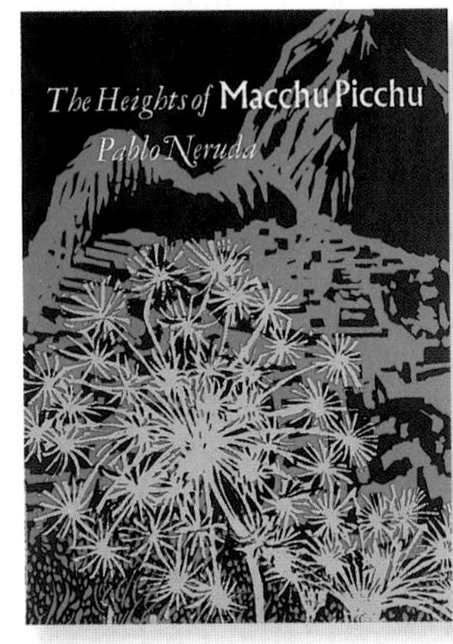

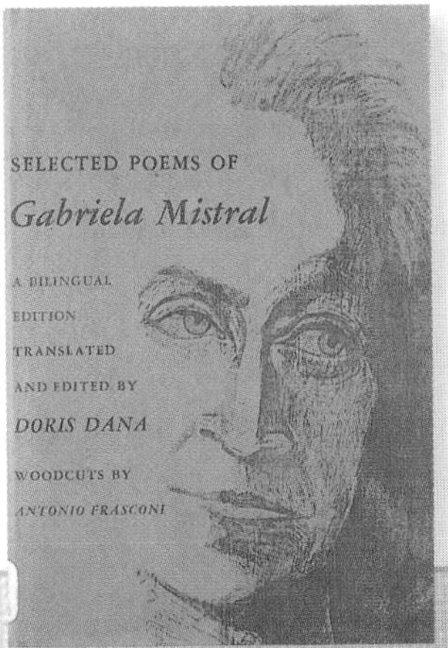

Selected Poems
by Gabriela Mistral These poems of love, pain, and hope, by the first Latin American writer to receive the Nobel Prize for literature, are translated by the American poet Doris Dana, who was awarded Chile's Order of Merit (that country's highest honor) for her work. For more poetry and prose by this author, you may want to look for *A Gabriela Mistral Reader,* edited by Marjorie Agosin and translated by Maria Jacketti.

Standardized Test Practice

The passage below is followed by five questions based on its content. Select the best answer and write the corresponding letter on your paper.

This selection was adapted from an essay written in 1996 by a professor of American Government.

Much has been written about the dissemination of information, particularly with regard to the news media. Long gone are the days when news traveled a circuitous path, one person at a time, from first-hand observer to friend, to neighbor, to co-worker, across the country. No longer must the news of the day travel by means of these second- and third-hand accounts. Rather, now a team of reporters and cameras can capture and interpret the news from hundreds of regions around the globe.

This more rapid connection between people and current events has created an entire industry—the news media. These are the television and radio stations, newspapers, and magazines that endeavor to carry the news of the day. Much has been written about the role of the news media, and the need for accuracy in reporting.

Though the various media may seem like little more than a means to transport information, upon closer examination news reporting is really an attempt at objective storytelling. It's a fact of life that when a person hears a story or witnesses an event, his or her own knowledge, skills, and interests dictate what about the experience is memorable. A teacher, for instance, will learn of a major news event and consider, perhaps, how the event could be used best to teach a particular lesson. A businessperson might well look at the same event and focus on its economic implications. If you ask both persons to explain the event's significance a week later, you should expect to receive two distinct accounts. Many critics have used this inevitable side-effect of human nature as evidence for their claim that media reports cannot be trusted.

A second consideration must enter into any discussion of the accurate dissemination of news. Consider if you will a corporation that has created a worldwide network of television stations, radio outlets, newspapers, and magazines. The corporation will, in all probability, place its limited personnel and its technologically advanced but often hard-to-move equipment in key positions throughout the world—regions from which news comes that will interest the largest number of viewers and readers. If an unexpected and newsworthy event occurs in a place where the corporation has not positioned its resources, will the story be told? Probably it will, but the presence or absence of cameras and other advanced technologies may determine how that story will be presented to the public, and an inevitable result of this location of resources is that some important news items may be relayed more slowly and in less noticeable formats than others.

Should we then distrust the news media? Perhaps it would be more accurate to say that as consumers we must educate ourselves about the media just as we would about any other product. For as viewers and readers of electronic and print media we are, in fact, consumers. We are paying for a product, and the product for which the most people pay will be the one to flourish. If we accept that the use of personnel and technologies vary, and if we understand that individual journalists, news writers, and reporters cannot be totally objective, it behooves each of us to make it our responsibility to seek out news from a variety of diverse sources, keeping in mind that each time a story is told, it is told from a different point of view.

1 The author's primary purpose in the passage is to

(A) criticize the news media for irresponsible reporting
(B) encourage individual citizens to take responsibility for seeking out balanced reporting from the news media
(C) argue that journalists are inclined to put their own opinions and interests aside in order to report the news accurately
(D) inspire students to consider careers in the news media
(E) describe the ways in which a news story might be ignored

2 In line 5, the word <u>circuitous</u> most nearly means

(A) round
(B) electrical
(C) indirect
(D) speedy
(E) second-hand

3 With which of these statements about the news media would the author be **most** likely to agree?

(A) Journalists would be more likely to report the news with greater objectivity if they had access to modern technology.
(B) Television stations should broadcast reports that are of the greatest interest to the most people.
(C) It is the public's responsibility to seek out balanced reporting by trying to find all sides of a story.
(D) Some regions are not newsworthy and need not be covered by the media.
(E) The news media always report the news in an even-handed and unbiased manner.

4 According to the author, the increasing importance of the media is largely due to the fact that

(A) people now have a greater interest in current events than before
(B) people are generally more highly educated than in the past
(C) developments in technology have improved the ability to share information
(D) news is more important to businesses than it was in the past
(E) journalists have become more responsible for the stories they write

5 The author mentions a "side-effect of human nature" (lines 41–42) in order to describe the tendency to

(A) describe events from one's own point of view
(B) fear what one does not understand.
(C) disagree with the personal opinions in the news media.
(D) pass information from one person to another
(E) rely more and more on information technology

Reference Section

Literary Terms Handbook

A

Act A major unit of a drama or play.

See also DRAMA.

Allegory The use of events, actions, objects, and persons in a narrative to represent moral qualities, universal struggles, or abstract ideas such as love, fear, or virtue. An allegory may be as brief as a metaphor, or it may be the basis for an entire novel. Virgil's *Aeneid* contains a number of allegorical episodes.

See page 823.

Alliteration The repetition of sounds, especially consonant sounds, at the beginning of words. For example, in line 13 of "Night of Sine," the *s* sound is repeated:

What do they say so secretly to the stars?

See page 1127.
See also SOUND DEVICES.

Allusion A reference to a well-known person, place, or event from history, literature, or religion. Allusions enrich the reading experience by adding another dimension of meaning. The title of "By Any Other Name" is an allusion to a line from Shakespeare's *Romeo and Juliet.*

See pages 388 and 1069.

Analogy A comparison made between two things to show how one is like the other. An analogy often explains something unfamiliar or abstract by comparing it to something familiar or concrete. In "Jade Flower Palace," Tu Fu draws an analogy between the inevitable effect of time on the palace and its effect on human life.

See page 542.

Anecdote A brief story giving an amusing, insightful look at a single incident or event.

Antagonist In a literary work, the person or force opposing the **protagonist,** or central character. The antagonist may be an individual, a group of people, a force of nature, or a social force such as racial and class prejudice. In "The Prisoner Who Wore Glasses," Warden Hannetjie is the antagonist.

See page 876.
See also PROTAGONIST.

Antithesis The balanced contrast of two phrases or ideas, as in "Creation Hymn" from the Rig Veda. Through antithesis, authors help emphasize important ideas:

Their cord was extended across. Was there below?
Was there above? There were seed-placers;
There were powers. There was impulse
Beneath; there was giving-forth above.

See page 450.

Aphorism. See MAXIM.

Assonance The repetition of similar vowel sounds, especially in a line of poetry. The repeated *a* sound in "the fl*a*sh of a h*a*nd" from "Encounter" is assonance.

See also SOUND DEVICES.

Atmosphere The dominant mood or feeling in a literary work. Writers create atmosphere through details of setting such as time, place, and weather.

See also MOOD.

Author's purpose An author's reasons for creating a literary work. These may include a desire to entertain readers, to inform or explain, or to express feelings, impressions, and opinions. The author's purpose in "The Immortality of Writers" was to emphasize the lasting importance of literature.

See pages 93, 397, and 620.

Autobiography The story of a person's life written by that person. Since autobiographies generally stress the author's personal views, they are often not as objective as other forms of nonfiction, such as history books. Some works, such as "A Walk to the Jetty," are partially autobiographical.

See also MEMOIR.
See pages 190, 550, 753, and 1006.

B–C

Biography A nonfiction narrative of a person's life, written by someone other than that person.

Canto From the Italian word for *song,* a subdivision in a long poem such as Dante's *Divine Comedy.*

Character A person, animal, or presence in a literary work. Characters may be **major** or **minor,** depending on their importance to the work. Characters may be described as flat or round. A **flat character** reveals only one personality trait; a **round character** shows varied and sometimes contradictory traits. In "The Doll's House," Lena Logan is a flat character; Kezia Burnell is a round character. Characters may also be classified as **static** or **dynamic.** A static character remains the same throughout the story. A dynamic character changes. Aunt Beryl in "The Doll's House" is a static character; Else Kelvey's character is dynamic.

See pages 155, 700, and 957.

Characterization The methods a writer uses to develop the personality of a character. With **direct characterization,** the writer makes direct statements about a character's personality, simply stating that a character is shy or selfish. **Indirect characterization** requires readers to draw their own conclusions about a character, based on evidence from the story. This evidence might include the character's appearance, words, thoughts, actions, and the comments and thoughts of other characters.

See pages 524, 969, and 1150.

Chorus A performer or group of performers whose function is to comment on the action that has just occurred in a drama and to sing and dance between scenes. The chorus serves as a bridge between the actors and the audience. Often an element in ancient Greek drama, the chorus is also found in other dramatic traditions, as in *The Damask Drum,* a Noh drama.

See page 284.

Climax The point of greatest interest or emotional intensity in a literary work. The climax of "The Luck of Teodoro Méndez Acúbal" occurs when Don Agustin calls for the police.

See also DRAMATIC STRUCTURE, PLOT.

Comparative literature The study of literatures of different cultures in order to examine the relationships between them. Significant similarities between works suggest how one culture influences another. Significant differences help point out the defining characteristics of each culture. Examining the similarities and differences between the flood story in Genesis and in the *Epic of Gilgamesh* would be an example of comparative literature.

See page 440.

Conflict A struggle between two opposing forces in the plot of a story. An **external conflict** exists when a character struggles against an outside force, such as another person or the rules of society. An **internal conflict** occurs within the mind of a character who is torn between opposing feelings or goals. Many characters experience both external and internal conflicts.

See pages 532, 656, 916, and 1162.

Connotation The unspoken or unwritten meanings associated with a word beyond its literal definition, or *denotation.* Paying attention to the connotations of words is often helpful in understanding literature that deals with abstract concepts or includes many abstract words. Words like *peered* and *blood-red* in "The Wagon" carry an eerie and foreboding connotation.

See page 499 and R81.

Consonance The repetition of consonant sounds within or at the ends of nonrhyming words. For example, notice the sounds in "Better to Live, Licinius":

to take in sail when it swells in a wind that's a
little too kind

See page 1127.

See also SOUND DEVICES.

Couplet Two consecutive rhymed lines of poetry that follow the same rhythmic pattern. The last two lines of a Shakespearean sonnet are often a couplet.

Crisis. See DRAMATIC STRUCTURE.

D

Denotation. See CONNOTATION.

Description Writing that creates a clear image of an appearance, feeling, or action. Good descriptive writing appeals to the senses through imagery. The use of figurative language and precise verbs, adjectives, and adverbs can also help make a description vivid.

See pages 179 and 1177.
See also VERISIMILITUDE.

Dialect A version of a language spoken by people in a particular region or social group. For example, Cockney is an English dialect spoken by working-class residents of East London. Dialects of the same language may differ from one another in pronunciation, vocabulary, and grammar.

See page 1132.

Dialogue Conversation between characters in a literary work.

Diary A work in which a person keeps an informal record of events in his or her life. Unlike a **journal,** a diary is most often a simple, spontaneous account of daily life.

See also JOURNAL.

Drama A story that is written to be acted out in front of an audience; also called a play or stage play. For example, Ibsen's *A Doll's House* is a drama.

See also DRAMATIC CONVENTION, DRAMATIC STRUCTURE, NOH, STAGE DIRECTIONS, TRAGEDY.

Dramatic convention An unrealistic device that a playwright uses to present a story on stage and that the audience accepts as realistic. Audiences at Noh plays accept, for example, the convention of male actors playing female roles. They also accept unrealistic shifts in time.

See page 638.

Dramatic structure The way information is presented in a play. Common elements in dramatic structure are **exposition,** or revelation of important background; **rising action,** which adds complications to the plot; **climax** (the **turning point** or **crisis**), the moment of greatest emotional intensity or suspense; **falling action,** which unravels the complications; and **resolution,** which resolves them or brings them to a close.

E

Elegy A poem on the themes of loss, sadness, or human mortality and their emotional consequences. Poets in all times and cultures have written elegies. "Elegy for a Woman of No Importance" is a modern example of this ancient poetic form.

See page 473.

End rhyme The repetition of sound in the syllables at the end of lines that appear close to each other in a poem. The following lines from "Sonnet 239" contain end rhyme.

nature is less than art as well I know
whose many a lively statue proves it so

See page 739, 854.
See also RHYME.

Enjambment The running over of a sentence from one line of a poem to the next. Enjambment enables poets to express a thought or image within the structure of the line, as well as extend it to the next line(s), while still maintaining unity of thought. Enjambment occurs in the following lines from "The Lorelei."

The wonderful melody reaches
A boat, as it sails along.

See page 471.

Epic A long narrative poem about a larger-than-life hero who embodies the values of his or her people.

Many earlier epics, such as *Gilgamesh,* were composed orally and preserved by storytellers before being written down. Such oral epics, or **folk epics,** may be developed in different versions as they are passed along from generation to generation. **Literary epics,** such as Virgil's *Aeneid,* are composed as written texts, although they are often modeled on oral epic poetry. An **epic hero** is a legendary, larger-than-life figure whose adventures form the core of the poem. Many epics share standard characteristics known as **epic conventions.** These include an **invocation,** or formal plea, to a deity for inspiration; **epithets,** something like nicknames, such as "the swift runner Achilles"; **epic similes,** which are longer and more elaborate than typical similes; and a set **rhythm** or **metrical structure.**

See pages 86, 211, 227, 245, 506, and 797.

Epigram. See MAXIM.

Epigraph A quotation that occurs at the beginning of a literary work and highlights a theme. "Love Orange" begins with a quotation from the New Testament that alludes to fear; the narrator is fearful that her supply of love will be exhausted if she does not use it carefully.

See page 668.

Epiphany A sudden, unexpected moment of insight. In "Pulse of the Land," the American experiences an epiphany when he finally realizes the extreme difficulty with which the children obtained the water he had taken for granted.

See page 469.

Essay A short piece of literary nonfiction devoted to a single topic from a limited viewpoint. For example, "The Myth of Sisyphus," by Albert Camus, gives the author's modern interpretation of the ancient Greek myth. Essays may be classified as **formal** or **informal.** Formal essays include **expository essays,** which offer information about a topic, and **persuasive essays,** which promote an opinion or position. Informal essays include **personal essays,** such as the memoir.

See pages 12–13.

Exaggeration An overstatement for the purpose of emphasis.

See page 660.
See also HYPERBOLE.

F

Fable A brief folktale, often using animals or inanimate objects as characters, told to teach a specific lesson or moral. In some fables, such as those of Aesop, the lesson or moral is stated explicitly. In other fables, the reader must infer the lesson based on what happens in the story. In "The Oak and the Reed" the moral must be inferred.

See pages 252 and 631.

Fairy tale A type of folktale that features supernatural elements, such as spirits, talking animals, and magic.

Fantasy A work that takes place in an unreal world and features incredible characters and events.

Fiction A narrative written in prose in which the situations and characters are invented by the writer. **Novels, short stories, folktales, fairy tales, fables,** and other forms of made-up stories come under the umbrella of fiction.

Figurative language Language used for descriptive effect in order to convey ideas or emotions. Figurative expressions, while not literally descriptive, express an aspect of the subject beyond the literal level.

See pages 649 and 1109.
See also FIGURES OF SPEECH.

Figures of speech A word or expression that is not meant to be taken literally. A **simile** uses the word *like* or *as* to compare two seemingly unlike things. A **metaphor** compares two or more different things and reveals something they have in common without using the words *like* or *as.* **Personification** involves giving human form or characteristics to an animal, object, or idea. **Figurative language,** which expresses a truth beyond the literal level, also includes symbols. The poem "Horses" contains several figures of speech. "The air white like a moistened loaf" is a simile. "They filled the whole world of my eyes" is a metaphor, and the reference to "the teeth of winter" is personification.

See pages 21 and 714.

Flashback An interruption in the plot of a literary work to relate a scene from an earlier time. A writer may use this device in order to give the reader background information or to create tension or contrast. In "When Heaven and Earth Changed Places," Le Ly Hayslip uses this technique to recall her father's tenderness and concern for her.

See pages 743 and 1186.

Foil A character whose personality traits are unlike, and best understood in contrast to, another character. For example, one character may be clever, while the foil may be bumbling. In "Day of the Butterfly," Gladys Healey, the prime antagonist, is a foil for Helen, the narrator.

See page 844.

Folktale A story that has been passed down from one generation to the next by word of mouth. Folktales do not have a known author, although they are often retold by authors for audiences from different times and cultures. They generally reflect the values of the societies that preserve them. Most folktales are simple narratives told for entertainment, although they might also teach moral values. **Animal trickster tales,** like "The Story of the Dress That Sang," are a common form of folktale in Africa. The **escape tale,** which is closely related to the trickster tale, involves a character who escapes a difficult situation by creating a problematic condition for another character.

See page 74.
See also FABLE.

Foreshadowing The use of clues by the author to prepare readers for events that will happen in a story. Much like eerie background music in a horror film, foreshadowing helps build suspense and draws the reader into the plot. In "The Weed," Angoori's singing foreshadows the outcome of the story.

See page 626.

Form The arrangement of words and lines in a poem. Form also refers to other types of poetry, such as a sonnet or an elegy. Form can also be used as a synonym for **genre.**

Formal speech A speech whose main purpose is to persuade, although it may also inform and entertain. There are four main types of formal speech: legal, political, ceremonial, and religious.

See page 332.

Frame story A story that surrounds another story or that serves to link several stories together. This technique is common in both ancient and modern writing. Some literary works, such as the *Decameron*, have frames that bind together many different stories.

See page 125.

Free verse Poetry that does not follow a regular meter or rhyme scheme. Although poets who write free verse ignore traditional rules, they use techniques such as repetition and alliteration to create musical patterns in their poems.

See pages 166, 997, and 1122.

G–H

Genre The category to which a literary work belongs. Examples of genre include drama, the epic, the short story, and lyric poetry.

Haiku A Japanese poetry form consisting of seventeen syllables arranged in three lines. The first and third lines have five syllables each, and the middle line has seven.

See page 640.

Historical context The time and place in which a literary work was written, including the traditions, customs, beliefs, and values of that time and place. *Don Quixote,* for example, is set in sixteenth-century Spain, and contrasts the chivalry idealized in literature with the reality of that time.

See page 446.

Historical fiction Fiction set in a past time period that actually existed. Some works of historical fiction include actual historical characters. Writers may have these characters reenacting actual events, or they may have them act in unhistorical ways. Historical fiction may also contain characters that are entirely the product of the author's imagination. However, the author should conduct extensive research on the historical period so that the characters he or she creates hold attitudes and beliefs similar to those of real people at that time.

See page 113.

Humor The quality of a literary work intended to be funny or amusing, although it can also be an important tool of persuasion. There are three basic types of humor. **Humor of situation** develops from the plot of a literary work, which may contain exaggerated or unexpected events, such as "A Canary's Ideas." **Humor of character** uses exaggerated personalities to make us laugh at the flaws of human nature, such as "Anansi's Fishing Expedition." **Humor of language** may include wordplay, verbal irony, exaggeration, or sarcasm.

See page 63.

Hymn A lyric poem or song addressed to a divine being. The term is also applied to a section of a longer religious poem. The selection from the Popol Vuh is a hymn.

Hyperbole Intentional exaggeration, usually used to create emphasis or humor. Notice the hyperbole in these lines from Mao Tse-tung's "The Long March."

We looked lightly on the ten thousand peaks
and ten thousand rivers.

See pages 851 and 1140.

I

Imagery Descriptive language that appeals to one or more of the five senses: sight, hearing, touch, taste, and smell. This use of sensory detail helps to create an emotional response in the reader. Because people usually rely on sight more than the other senses, most imagery is visual, but imagery can also help readers hear sounds, feel textures, smell aromas (as in Solzhenitsyn's "Freedom to Breathe") and taste foods.

No food on earth, no wine, not even a woman's kiss is sweeter to me than this air steeped in the fragrance of flowers, of moisture and freshness.

Imagery appears in all descriptive writing, but it is especially important in poetry.

See pages 21, 41, 148, 260, 384, 571, 606, 646, 690, 988, and 1155.

Implied comparison A comparison that is suggested rather than directly stated. The implied comparison is conveyed by connecting the images in a new or unexpected way, rather than by indicating that one image *is* the other (metaphor) or is *like* the other (simile). In "You Are Now Entering the Human Heart," the author implies a comparison between the workings of the literal and the symbolic human heart.

See page 643.

Irony A conflict between reality and appearance or expectations. **Dramatic irony** occurs when the reader or audience or reader knows something that a character does not know. In "The Story of Pyramus and Thisbe," the reader knows that Thisbe is merely hiding when Pyramus believes that she is dead. **Situational irony** occurs when what actually happens is the opposite of what is expected or appropriate. In "Federigo's Falcon," the hero gives the falcon to the lady as a meal, not knowing she has come to ask for it as a gift for her son. **Verbal irony** occurs when a writer or speaker says one thing but really means its opposite. It might occur when a person responds to a disappointment with an expression like "That's great."

See pages 67, 323, 948, and 1099.

J–L

Journal A personal record of experiences, ideas, and reflections that is kept on a regular basis. A journal is often begun with the intention of keeping a record of a significant time or series of events. Like letters, journals are a form of autobiographical or personal writing.

See pages 611 and 1065.
See also DIARY.

Legend A story about extraordinary deeds, often based to some extent on historical fact.

See also EPIC, MYTH.

Legendary heroes Idealized figures, sometimes based on real people, who embody qualities admired by the cultural group to which they belong. The adventures and accomplishments of these heroes are preserved in legends or tales that are handed down from generation to generation. Achilles is a legendary hero.

See page 432.

Lyric poetry Poetry in which the speaker expresses personal thoughts and feelings. Lyric poems may describe incidents, but their main emphasis is on conveying emotions rather than telling a story. The term *lyric* comes from *lyre,* a stringed instrument that Greek poets used to accompany their singing. This tradition has continued for centuries; troubador poems like "The Lark" were often sung to musical accompaniment. Few lyric poets today sing their work accompanied by a guitar, but the term *lyric poetry* is still very much in use.

See pages 358, 1010.
See also ODE, ELEGY, SONNET.

M

Magic realism A prose fiction style that originated in Europe and is now especially associated with Latin American writers, such as Gabriel García Márquez. In a magic realist work, figures from history, mythology, literature, and dreams may appear and play a part in everyday life. The rules of everyday life itself change: characters may suddenly travel great distances in space or time. Magic realism differs from **surrealism** in its emphasis on the intrusion of fantastic elements into normal life.

See page 1133.

Maxim A short saying that contains a general truth or gives practical advice. Philosophers have often used maxims to share advice, particularly about morality and behavior, as Lao Tzu does in the *Tao Te Ching.* Since maxims tend to be easy to remember, they often remain in circulation for centuries. Also known as sayings, adages, aphorisms, and proverbs, these brief statements are at their most memorable when they express a truth with wit, fresh imagery, and penetrating insight.

See pages 468 and 592.

Memoir A type of narrative nonfiction that presents the story of a period in the writer's life and is usually written from the first-person point of view. A memoir often emphasizes the writer's thoughts and feelings, his or her relationships with other people, or the impact of significant historical events on his or her life. "Two Memories of Sido" and *Out of Africa* are memoirs.

See also AUTOBIOGRAPHY, DIARY, JOURNAL.

Metaphor A figure of speech that makes a comparison between two seemingly unlike things without using the words *as* or *like.* An **extended metaphor** compares two unlike things point by point throughout a paragraph, a stanza, or an entire piece of writing.

See page 536, 1104.

Meter or **Metrical structure.** See RHYTHM.

Modernism A literary style developed in the late nineteenth century that reflected a break with existing tradition. In addition to technical experimentation, modern playwrights, writers, and artists in the first half of the twentieth century were interested in the irrational or inexplicable, as well as in the workings of the unconscious mind. "Bishop Berkeley or Mariana of the Universe" displays modernist characteristics.

See page 877.

Mood The overall feeling that a work of literature creates for readers. For example, a comedy about young lovers might have a joyous or romantic mood. **Mood** is a broader term than **tone,** which refers specifically to the attitude of the speaker or narrator. It also differs from **atmosphere,** which is concerned mainly with the physical qualities that contribute to a mood, such as time, place, and weather.

See pages 610 and 972.
See also ATMOSPHERE, TONE.

Moral A practical lesson about right and wrong conduct, often in an instructive story, such as a fable ("The Dog and the Wolf") or a parable.

See page 513.
See also FABLE.

Motif A word, character, image, metaphor, or idea that recurs in a work or in several works of literature.

Motivation The reason or reasons behind a character's actions. A character's motivation may be stated directly, or the reader may have to infer motivation from details in the story. Characters are often motivated by a combination of factors.

See page 134.

Myth A traditional story that explains some aspect of human life or the natural world. Myths reflect the religious beliefs of a particular people. They often depict the actions of gods or heroes. Ovid's *Metamorphosis* retells a great number of Greek and Roman myths. **Creation myths** explain the origin of the world and its inhabitants.

See pages 78, 770, and 1044.

N

Narrative Any work of literature that tells a story. Narratives may be fiction or nonfiction, prose or poetry. A **narrative poem** has characters and a plot that centers on conflict. **Epic poems,** such as the *Iliad* and the *Aeneid* are long narrative poems that recount the deeds of an epic hero. "Russia 1812" is an example of narrative poetry.

See page 365.
See also AUTOBIOGRAPHY, BIOGRAPHY, ESSAY, FLASHBACK, MEMOIR.

Narrator The person that tells a story. A **first-person narrator** tells the story as he or she experiences it, using the pronoun *I*. The reader sees everything through that character's eyes and experiences events and people as the narrator does, for example, in "The Iguana." A **third-person narrator,** on the other hand, tells the story from outside and does not use the pronoun *I*. In some cases, the third-person narrator is **limited** to revealing the thoughts and feelings of only one character; in other cases, the narrator is all-knowing, or **omniscient.**

See page 729.

Noh A highly stylized form of Japanese drama that originated in the Middle Ages. *The Damask Drum* is a Noh drama.

Nonfiction The broadest category of literature. It includes **autobiographies, biographies, journals, memoirs, diaries,** letters, **essays,** speeches, travelogues, news articles, reports, and many more types of writing.

Novel A long fictional prose narrative containing a **plot,** or ordered sequence of events that takes place in a specific **setting** and is concerned with **character** development and a statement of **theme,** or message. Forerunners of the novel include verse epics and romances, as well as loosely connected story collections such as Boccaccio's *Decameron.* Cervantes' *Don Quixote* is generally considered the first modern novel in European literature.

See page 836.

O

Ode A lyric poem with an elevated style and an exalted or enthusiastic tone. At first, most odes were written to glorify a public figure or commemorate an important event. The Roman poet Horace developed an ode that was more personal and meditative.

See page 354.
See also LYRIC POETRY.

Onomatopoeia A word whose sound suggests its meaning, for example *swoosh* or *crackle.*

See also SOUND DEVICES.

Oral tradition Oral literature was a way of recording the past, glorifying leaders, and teaching morals and traditions to young people. Literature in most of the world began in this way. In West Africa the *griot*–or professional storyteller–committed the stories and family histories to memory and recited verses.

See pages 37 and 419.
See also EPIC, FABLE, FOLKTALE, TRICKSTER.

Oxymoron A term made of two words that contradict each other, for example, jumbo shrimp.

See page 851.

P

Paradox An apparent contradiction that actually reflects reality. For example, Catullus writes "I couldn't like you if you were the best of women / or stop loving you, no matter what you do."

Parallelism The use of a series of similar words, phrases, or lines. Writers employ this technique to emphasize an idea or emotion, to create a sense of unity or balance in a literary work, or for musical effect. Hugo uses parallelism in the following lines:

Past each white waste a further white waste rose.

See pages 183, and 597.

Parody The humorous imitation of a particular writing style, often intended as a criticism of that style but somethimes done simply for humor.

See page 844.

Persona The speaker in a poem who is clearly a different person from the poet.

See also SPEAKER.

Personification The attribution of human qualities or thoughts to an animal, object, or idea. Poets use this device to highlight an idea or to create striking descriptions. In Choudhury's poem, "The Sun Witness," the sun is personified.

See pages 163, 475, 675, and 992.

Persuasion Writing that attempts to convince readers to think or act in a certain way. Philosophical essays sometimes appeal to the reader's intellect through logic and evidence and–as in the *Analects*–sometimes giving rules and examples. Political speeches and advertisements may rely more on emotional appeals.

See page 1016.

Plot The sequence of events in a story. Most plots deal with a problem and develop around a **conflict,** a struggle between opposing forces. An **external conflict** is a struggle between a character and an outside force, such as another character, society, nature, or fate. An **internal conflict** takes place within the mind of a character who struggles with opposing feelings. **Exposition** introduces the story's characters, setting, and conflict. **Rising action** develops the conflict with complications. **Climax** is the emotional high point of the story. **Falling action** shows what happens after the climax. **Resolution** shows how the conflict is resolved.

See pages 1 and 933.
See also FICTION.

Poetry Rhythmic and often rhymed writing that appeals to the emotions and the imagination through **imagery** and **figures of speech.**

See also EPIC, FREE VERSE, IMAGERY, LYRIC POETRY, RHYME, RHYTHM, SONNET.

Point of view The standpoint from which a story is told. In **first-person point of view,** the narrator is a character in the story, and uses the words *I* and *me* to tell the story. In **third-person point of view,** the narrator is someone who stands outside the story and describes the characters and action. **Third-person omniscient point of view** means that the narrator knows everything that goes on–including the thoughts and feelings of every character. If the narrator describes events as only one character perceives them, the point of view is called **third person limited.**

See pages 1, 10, and 1118.
See also NARRATOR.

Prose poem A short prose composition that uses rhythm, imagery, and other poetic devices to express an idea or emotion. Unlike metrical and **free verse,** prose poetry does not have line breaks; instead, the sentences appear in standard paragraph form. A prose poem allows the writer to express a poetic idea without following the usual rules of poetic form.

See pages 566, 672, 1019, and 1191.

Protagonist The main character in a literary work. The **antagonist** is the opposing character. In "The Prisoner Who Wore Glasses," Brille is the protagonist.

See page 762.
See also ANTAGONIST, TRAGEDY.

R

Realism Any accurate and detailed description in a literary work. The term is used more specifically to describe a movement of late-nineteenth- and early-twentieth-century writers. The Realists sought to depict life objectively, without sentimentality or idealization. They usually focused on the problems of middle- and lower-class people. Their work is often filled with details based on careful observation of everyday life. Chekhov, Tolstoy, and Ibsen are considered realists.

See page 962.

Repetition The recurrence of sounds, words, phrases, lines, or stanzas in a literary work. Authors may use repetition to help unify a work. They may also use it to create a musical or rhythmic effect, or to emphasize an idea. **Rhyme, parallelism,** and **alliteration** are types of repetition.

See pages 26 and 1054.

Renga A chain of poems written by several poets. One poet would write the first three lines of a 5-7-5-7-7 syllable-line tanka, and a second poet would complete the **tanka.** Another poet would begin the next tanka, or link, in the renga. The first three lines, or hokku, of the renga became an independent verse form that was eventually known as **haiku.**

See also HAIKU, TANKA.

Resolution. See DRAMATIC STRUCTURE, PLOT.

Rhyme The repetition of sounds in words that appear close to each other in a poem. Words **rhyme** when their accented vowels and all the letters that follow sound the same. For example, the word *borrow* rhymes with *tomorrow,* and *sincere* rhymes with *fear.* **Internal rhyme** occurs within lines of poetry. **End rhyme** occurs at the ends of lines. Letters are used to designate **rhyme scheme** or the pattern of end rhyme. A different letter of the alphabet signals each new rhyme (for example, *aabbcc* or *ababcdcd*). When words sound similar but do not rhyme exactly (like *jackal* and *buckle*), they are called **half rhymes** or **slant rhymes.** Notice the rhyme scheme in the following lines from the Rubáiyát:

Awake! for Morning in the Bowl of Night *a*
Has flung the Stone that puts the Stars to Flight: *a*
And Lo! the Hunter of the East has caught *b*
The Sultan's Turret in a Noose of Light. *a*

See pages 21, 255, 463, 870, and 1076.

Rhythm The pattern of sound created by the arrangement of stressed and unstressed syllables in a line. Rhythm can be regular or irregular. **Meter** is a regular pattern of stressed and unstressed syllables that sets the overall rhythm of certain poems. The basic unit in measuring rhythm is the **foot,** which usually contains one stressed syllable marked with (ʹ) and one or more unstressed syllables marked with (˘). **Free verse,** which does not have a regular meter, often follows the rhythm of natural speech.

See pages 20, 735, and 985.

Ruba'i A Persian word meaning "quatrain," or four-line verse.

See page 460.

S

Sacred texts Writings like the Tanakh or the Qur'an that are revered as holy or are closely linked to religion or religious ritual. These texts, which are sometimes called scriptures, are often regarded as divine revelations, directly communicated from God to human beings on a specific occasion.

See page 434.

Sarcasm. See IRONY.

Satire Writing that comments humorously on human flaws, ideas, social customs, or institutions in order to change them. The purpose of satire is to persuade, although satires can only be effective if they are also entertaining. In order to get his or her point across, a satirist might use such literary techniques as irony, exaggeration, parody, and understatement. For example, *Don Quixote* satirizes stories that idealize chivalry.

See page 175.

Scene A subdivision of an act in a play.

Setting The time and place in which the events of a literary work occur. The elements of setting may include geographical location, historical period, season of the year, time of day, and the beliefs and customs of a society. Setting can help establish the mood of a story. It can also influence the way characters think and behave. In some instances, the setting is not important; the story remains the same even if the setting changes. Other stories are closely tied to a particular setting.

See pages 50, 601, and 722.
See also HISTORICAL CONTEXT.

Short story A short, fictional prose narrative. It has many of the same elements as a novel but on a smaller scale. "The Night Face Up" is a short story.

Simile A figure of speech that uses *like* or *as* to compare two things. "The moonlight outside like a hope I do not have" is a simile from "In the terrible night."

See also FIGURES OF SPEECH.

Sonnet A fourteen-line lyric poem developed in Italy during the Renaissance. A **Petrarchan sonnet,** also called an **Italian sonnet,** is divided into a group of eight lines, called the **octave,** and a group of six lines, called the **sestet.** The **rhyme scheme** of the octave is *abba, abba.* The sestet may follow a number of different rhyme schemes. Among the most common patterns are *cde cde, cde dcd,* and *cdc dee.* In the Italian sonnet, the octave usually presents a single **theme** or main idea, and the sestet expands, contradicts, or develops it. A **Shakespearean sonnet,** sometimes called an **English sonnet,** has three **quatrains** (groups of four lines), which are followed by a rhymed **couplet** of two lines. The **rhyme scheme** is as follows: *abab, cdcd, efef, gg.* A Shakespearean sonnet retains the break in thought between octave and sestet, but forcefully states the theme, or sometimes inverts the **theme,** in the concluding couplet. Michelangelo used a variation of the sonnet form in his "Sonnet 239."

See page 848.

Sound devices A technique in which writers use the sound of words for effect. The most used sound devices include **alliteration,** the repetition of consonant sounds at the beginnings of words; **consonance,** the repetition of consonant sounds within words or at the ends of words; **assonance,** the repetition of vowel sounds; and **onomatopoeia,** the use of a word or phrase, such as *buzz* or *fizzle,* that imitates or suggests the sound of what it describes.

Speaker The voice that talks to the reader or to the person whom the work addresses. In some poems the speaker has a distinct identity, like a character in a story. One should never assume that the speaker and the writer are identical. A speaker who is clearly different from the writer, as in "The River Merchant's Wife," is called a **persona.**

See pages 20, 55, 350, 483, and 980.
See also NARRATOR.

Stage directions Notes in the text of a play that describe the appearance and movements of the characters, as well as the sets, costumes, and lighting. Stage directions serve primarily as instructions for the cast and crew of a theatrical production, but they also help readers imagine the action of the play.

See page 899.

Stanza A group of lines that form a unit in a poem. "Love Does Not Know Secrets" is divided into stanzas.

See page 20.

Stereotype A character who is not presented as an individual, but as an embodiment of traits and mannerisms supposedly shared by all members of a group.

Structure The particular order or pattern a writer uses to present ideas. Narratives commonly follow a chronological order, while the structure of persuasive or expository writing may vary. Listing detailed information, using cause and effect, or describing a problem and offering a solution are some other ways a writer can present a topic.

Style The expressive qualities that distinguish an author's work, including word choice and the length and arrangement of sentences, as well as the use of figurative language and imagery. Style can reveal an author's attitude and purpose in writing.

See also AUTHOR'S PURPOSE, FIGURATIVE LANGUAGE, IMAGERY, TONE.

Surprise ending An unexpected plot twist at the end of a story. The ending might surprise readers because the author provides ambiguous clues or withholds important information. A surprise ending is most effective when it adds to the meaning of a story rather than merely overturning the reader's expectations. "When Greek Meets Greek" has this kind of surprise ending.

See page 111.

Surrealism A literary and artistic style that originated in Europe in the 1920s. Typically, surrealist works feature ordinary people and objects brought together in strange and unexpected ways, or bizarre and impossible events treated as if they were normal, as in "Half a Day." Surrealism differs from **magic realism** in its emphasis on what surrealists see as the strangeness in "normal" life.

See page 1102.

Suspense The tension or excitement that a reader feels about what will happen next in a story. Writers often create suspense by raising questions in the reader's mind about the outcome of a conflict. Suspense is especially important in the **plot** of an adventure or mystery story.

See pages 144, 562, and 809.

Symbol A person, place, or thing that stands for something else in addition to itself. Some literary symbols have meanings that are widely understood. A rushing river, for example, often symbolizes the passing of time, just as sunrise often symbolizes rebirth or hope. In "Fishing," Joy Harjo uses fishing as a symbol for the struggle of the universe.

See pages 566, 709, and 1079.

T

Tanka An unrhymed Japanese verse form that consists of five lines. The first and third lines have five syllables each; the other lines have seven syllables each.

See page 608.
See also HAIKU, RENGA.

Theme The main idea or message that a poem or story conveys. All the details point to the theme, which is usually an insight into human experience. Sometimes a theme is **directly stated,** either by a narrator or another character. More often a theme is **implied** or suggested. The reader must figure out the theme from the work's details. Many literary works have more than one theme.

See pages 1, 19, 479, and 834.

Tone The attitude that a writer takes toward the audience, a subject, or a character. For example, a narrator might use an angry tone to describe an evil character and an amused tone to describe a good-hearted character who makes mistakes. Tone is conveyed through the writer's choice of words and details. Cavafy conveys a nostalgic, pessimistic tone in this way in "The Trojans."

See page 976.

Tragedy A play in which the main character is brought to ruin or suffers a great sorrow. In Greek tragedy, the main character is a person of dignified or heroic stature. He or she may be a victim of outside forces, but usually the character's downfall is at least partly caused by a flaw or error in judgment, often called the **tragic flaw.** According to the Greek philosopher Aristotle, the purpose of tragedy is to arouse pity (through identification with the main character) and fear (through dread at the possibility of sharing the main character's tragic flaw) in the audience as the main character's terrible fate unfolds.

See page 298.
See also DRAMA.

Trickster figures Characters that represent that part of human nature that wants to break rules and stir up trouble. Tricksters try to outwit people, animals, and even gods. Although they are generally self-centered, we may admire them for their cunning and ability to overcome obstacles. Trickster figures are most commonly depicted in animal form. Almost every folklore tradition has its own trickster figures, such as West Africa's Anansi.

See pages 1047 and 1050.

Turning point. See DRAMATIC STRUCTURE.

U

Understatement Language that emphasizes the importance of something by treating it as unimportant.

See also HYPERBOLE.

Unreliable narrator A narrator whose account of events is faulty or distorted in some way. Some unreliable narrators intentionally mislead readers. Others fail to understand the true meaning of the events they describe. For example, if a story is narrated by a small child, he or she might misinterpret the behavior of adult characters. Most stories with unreliable narrators are written in the first person.

See page 1169.
See also NARRATOR.

V

Verisimilitude The illusion of reality, often achieved by presenting concrete, detailed descriptions. In his account of the burning of Rome, Tacitus uses dramatic factual details to give the impression that he was an eyewitness, although he was not.

See page 458.

W

Wit A type of humor that relies especially on innovative observation and clever word play. For example, wit is a key element in "A Canary's Ideas."

Language Handbook

Troubleshooter

The Troubleshooter will help you recognize and correct errors that you might make in your writing.

Sentence Fragment

Problem: A fragment that lacks a subject

The snow is very deep. (Is hard to shovel.) *frag*

Solution: Add a subject to the fragment to make it a complete sentence.

The snow is very deep. It is hard to shovel.

Problem: A fragment that lacks a complete verb

The marathon winner received her awards. (A trophy and a check.) *frag*

The speaker addressed the unruly audience. (Nobody listening to him.) *frag*

Solution A: Add a complete verb or a helping verb and other words as needed to make the sentence complete.

The marathon winner received her awards. A trophy and a check were presented to her.

The speaker addressed the unruly audience. Nobody was listening to him.

Solution B: Combine the fragment with another sentence. Add a comma to set off a nonessential appositive or a comma and a conjunction to separate two main clauses in a compound sentence.

The marathon winner received her awards, a trophy and a check.

The speaker addressed the unruly audience, but nobody was listening to him.

Problem: A fragment that is a subordinate clause

Our teacher was late for school. Because she had a flat tire on the way. *frag*

I am eating spaghetti. Which is one of my favorite foods. *frag*

Solution A: Combine the fragment with another sentence. Add a comma to set off a nonessential clause.

Our teacher was late for school because she had a flat tire on the way.

I am eating spaghetti, which is one of my favorite foods.

Solution B: Rewrite the fragment as a complete sentence, eliminating the subordinating conjunction or the relative pronoun and adding a subject or other words necessary to make a complete thought.

Our teacher was late for school. She had a flat tire on the way.

I am eating spaghetti. It is one of my favorite foods.

Problem: A fragment that lacks both a subject and a verb

Kendra traveled all day and arrived in town. At nine o'clock. *frag*

Solution: Combine the fragment with another sentence.

Kendra traveled all day and arrived in town at nine o'clock.

Rule of Thumb: Sentence fragments can make your writing hard to understand. Be sure to check that every sentence has a subject and a verb.

Run-on Sentence

Problem: Comma splice—two main clauses separated by only a comma

We had dinner at a Chinese restaurant, I liked the cashew chicken. *run-on*

Solution A: Replace the comma with an end mark of punctuation, such as a period or a question mark, and begin the new sentence with a capital letter.

We had dinner at a Chinese restaurant. I liked the cashew chicken.

Solution B: Place a semicolon between the two main clauses.

We had dinner at a Chinese restaurant; I liked the cashew chicken.

Solution C: Add a coordinating conjunction after the comma.

We had dinner at a Chinese restaurant, and I liked the cashew chicken.

Problem: Two main clauses with no punctuation between them

The hurricane headed out to sea then it turned back toward land. *run-on*

Solution A: Separate the main clauses with an end mark of punctuation, such as a period or a question mark, and begin the second sentence with a capital letter.

The hurricane headed out to sea. Then it turned back toward land.

Solution B: Separate the main clauses with a semicolon.

The hurricane headed out to sea; then it turned back toward land.

Solution C: Add a comma and a coordinating conjunction between the main clauses.

The hurricane headed out to sea, but then it turned back toward land.

Problem: Two main clauses with no comma before the coordinating conjunction

I went to the mall on Saturday and my sister went with me. *run-on*

Solution: Add a comma before the coordinating conjunction to separate the two main clauses.

I went to the mall on Saturday, and my sister went with me.

Rule of Thumb: It often helps to have someone else read your writing to see if it is clear. Since you know what the sentences are supposed to mean, you might miss the need for punctuation.

Lack of Subject-Verb Agreement

Problem: A subject that is separated from the verb by an intervening prepositional phrase

The herd of wild horses (sweep) across the plains. *agr*

Even the youngest horses in the herd (keeps) up with the rest. *agr*

Solution: Make the verb agree with the subject, not with the object of a preposition. The subject of a sentence is never the object of a preposition.

The herd of wild horses sweeps across the plains.

Even the youngest horses in the herd keep up with the rest.

Problem: A predicate nominative that differs in number from the subject

Those three actors (is) the entire cast of the play. *agr*

The entire cast of the play (are) those three actors. *agr*

Solution: Ignore the predicate nominative, and make the verb agree with the subject of the sentence.

Those three actors are the entire cast of the play.

The entire cast of the play is those three actors.

Problem: A subject that follows the verb

In this cage (lives) six gerbils. *agr*

There (goes) two of them now. *agr*

Solution: In an inverted sentence, look for the subject *after* the verb. Then make sure the verb agrees with the subject.

In this cage live six gerbils.

There go two of them now.

Rule of Thumb: Reversing the order of an inverted sentence might help you decide on the correct verb form: "Six gerbils live in this cage."

Problem: A collective noun as the subject

The school band practice two days a week. *agr*

The group has different opinions on the subject. *agr*

Solution A: If the collective noun refers to a group as a whole, use a singular verb.

The school band practices two days a week.

Solution B: If the collective noun refers to each member of a group individually, use a plural verb.

The group have different opinions on the subject.

Problem: A noun of amount as the subject

Twenty dollars are the price they advertised. *agr*

Five one-dollar bills is in my wallet. *agr*

Solution: Determine whether the noun of amount refers to one unit and is therefore singular, or whether it refers to a number of individual units and is therefore plural.

Twenty dollars is the price they advertised.

Five one-dollar bills are in my wallet.

Problem: A compound subject that is joined by *and*

Macaroni and cheese are his favorite meal. *agr*

Vegetables and meat loaf is in the refrigerator. *agr*

Solution A: If the parts of the compound subject belong to one unit or if both parts refer to the same person or thing, use a singular verb.

Macaroni and cheese is his favorite meal.

Solution B: If the parts of the compound subject do not belong to one unit or if they refer to different people or things, use a plural verb.

Vegetables and meat loaf are in the refrigerator.

Problem: A compound subject that is joined by *or* or *nor*

Neither those cats nor that dog belong to me. *agr*

Solution: Make the verb agree with the subject that is closer to it.

Neither those cats nor that dog belongs to me.

Problem: A compound subject that is preceded by *many a, every,* or *each*

Every boy and girl here (live) in the neighborhood. *agr*

Solution: When *many a, every,* or *each* precedes a compound subject, the subject is considered singular. Use a singular verb.

Every boy and girl here lives in the neighborhood.

Problem: A subject that is separated from the verb by an intervening expression

Jermaine's dog, as well as Andrea's parrot, (do) a lot of tricks. *agr*

Solution: Certain intervening expressions, such as those beginning with *as well as, in addition to,* and *together with,* do not change the number of the subject. Ignore such expressions between a subject and its verb, and make the verb agree with the subject.

Jermaine's dog, as well as Andrea's parrot, does a lot of tricks.

Problem: An indefinite pronoun as the subject

Each of the activities (are) open to the public. *agr*

Solution: Determine whether the indefinite pronoun is singular or plural, and make the verb agree with it. Some indefinite pronouns are singular–*another, anyone, everyone, one, each, either, neither, anything, everything, something,* and *somebody.* Some are plural–*both, many, few, several,* and *others.* Some can be singular or plural–*some, all, any, more, most,* and *none*–depending on the noun to which they refer.

Each of the activities is open to the public.

Lack of Pronoun-Antecedent Agreement

Problem: A singular antecedent that can be either male or female

A family doctor sometimes refers (his) patient to a specialist. *ant*

Solution A: Traditionally, a masculine pronoun was used to refer to an antecedent that might be either male or female. This usage ignores or excludes females. Reword the sentence to use *he or she, him or her,* and so on.

A family doctor sometimes refers his or her patient to a specialist.

Solution B: Reword the sentence so that both the antecedent and the pronoun are plural.

Family doctors sometimes refer their patients to specialists.

Solution C: Reword the sentence to eliminate the pronoun.

A family doctor sometimes refers a patient to a specialist.

Problem: A second-person pronoun that refers to a third-person antecedent

Sarah is going to a school that trains (you) to repair computers. *ant*

Solution A: Use the appropriate third-person pronoun.

Sarah is going to a school that trains her to repair computers.

Solution B: Use an appropriate noun instead of a pronoun.

Sarah is going to a school that trains people to repair computers.

Problem: A singular indefinite pronoun as an antecedent

Neither of the boys brought (their) sleeping bag. *ant*

Solution: *Another, any, every, one, each, either, neither, anything, everything, something,* and *somebody* are singular; they therefore require singular personal pronouns even when followed by a prepositional phrase that contains a plural noun.

Neither of the boys brought his sleeping bag.

> **Rule of Thumb:** To help yourself remember that pronouns such as *each, either, every,* and *neither* are singular, think *each one, either one, every one,* and *neither one.*

Lack of Clear Pronoun Reference [Unclear Antecedent]

Problem: A pronoun reference that is weak or vague

The sculptor was carving, (which) we admired. *ref*

A flock of birds roosted in that tree last year, and (it) was very noisy. *ref*

Solution A: Rewrite the sentence, adding a clear antecedent for the pronoun.

The sculptor was carving a statue of a bear, which we admired.

Solution B: Rewrite the sentence, substituting a noun for the pronoun.

A flock of birds roosted in that tree last year, and their chattering was very noisy.

Problem: A pronoun that could refer to more than one antecedent

Roberto and his grandfather caught six fish, and he cleaned them all. *ref*

The toxic waste the factory dumped in the river made the people avoid it. *ref*

Solution A: Rewrite the sentence, substituting a noun for the pronoun.

Roberto and his grandfather caught six fish, and Roberto cleaned them all.

Solution B: Rewrite the sentence, making the antecedent of the pronoun clear.

The people avoided the river because of the toxic waste the factory dumped in it.

Problem: The indefinite use of *you* or *they*

The movie's characters seem so real that you get caught up in the story. *ref*

In New Orleans they have a Mardi Gras celebration every year. *ref*

Solution A: Rewrite the sentence, substituting a noun for the pronoun.

The movie's characters seem so real that the audience gets caught up in the story.

Solution B: Rewrite the sentence, eliminating the pronoun entirely.

The city of New Orleans has a Mardi Gras celebration every year.

Shift in Pronoun

Problem: An incorrect shift in person between two pronouns

I like to sit next to the window, where you can enjoy the scenery. *pro*

Eduardo and Lily are learning to search the World Wide Web, where you can find information on many topics. *pro*

When you surf the Web, one might come up with inaccurate data. *pro*

Solution A: Replace the incorrect pronoun with a pronoun that agrees with its antecedent.

I like to sit next to the window, where I can enjoy the scenery.

Eduardo and Lily are learning to search the World Wide Web, where they can find information on many topics.

When you surf the Web, you might come up with inaccurate data.

Solution B: Replace the pronoun with an appropriate noun.

Eduardo and Lily are learning to search the World Wide Web, where students can find information on many topics.

Shift in Verb Tense

Problem: An unnecessary shift in tense

Laurent goes across town by bus and worked at his job all afternoon. *shift t*

When the clock struck twelve, Cinderella's coach turns back into a pumpkin. *shift t*

Solution: When two or more events occur at the same time, be sure to use the same verb tense to describe each event.

Laurent goes across town by bus and works at his job all afternoon.

When the clock struck twelve, Cinderella's coach turned back into a pumpkin.

Problem: A lack of correct shift in tenses to show that one event precedes or follows another

By the time my aunt finally got here, we waited for an hour. *shift t*

Solution: When two events have occurred at different times in the past, shift from the past tense to the past perfect tense to indicate that one action began and ended before another past action began.

By the time my aunt finally got here, we had waited for an hour.

Rule of Thumb: When you need to use more than one verb tense in a sentence, it may help to first jot down the sequence of events you're writing about. Be clear in your mind which action happened first.

Incorrect Verb Tense or Form

Problem: An incorrect or missing verb ending

Have you ever (milk) a cow? *tense*

I did two months ago, when I (visit) my uncle's farm. *tense*

Solution: Add *-ed* to a regular verb to form the past participle and the past tense.

Have you ever milked a cow?

I did two months ago, when I visited my uncle's farm.

Problem: An improperly formed irregular verb

Jon (seeked) advice from all his friends. *tense*

Sheila nearly (freezed) before we built a warm fire. *tense*

Solution: Irregular verbs form their past and past participles in some way other than by adding *-ed.* Memorize these forms, or look them up in a dictionary.

Jon sought advice from all his friends.

Sheila nearly froze before we built a warm fire.

Problem: Confusion between the past form and the past participle

We've (went) to that beach many times. *tense*

Haskell has (chose) the bike he wants. *tense*

Solution: Use the past participle of an irregular verb, not the past form, when you use the auxiliary verb *have.*

We've gone to that beach many times.

Haskell has chosen the bike he wants.

Problem: Improper use of the past participle

He (begun) his assignment. *tense*

The tardy bell (rung) before I got through the door. *tense*

Solution A: The past participle of an irregular verb cannot stand alone as a verb. Add a form of the auxiliary verb *have* to the past participle to form a complete verb.

He has begun his assignment.

The tardy bell had rung before I got through the door.

Solution B: Replace the past participle with the past form of the verb.

He began his assignment.

The tardy bell rang before I got through the door.

Misplaced or Dangling Modifier

Problem: A misplaced modifier

Jungle cats frighten many people with big teeth and claws. *mod*

Floating over the park, Megan saw a red balloon. *mod*

The boy on the skateboard jumped the curb racing down the street. *mod*

Solution: Modifiers that modify the wrong word or that seem to modify more than one idea in a sentence are called misplaced modifiers. Move the misplaced phrase as close as possible to the word or words it modifies.

With big teeth and claws, jungle cats frighten many people.

Megan saw a red balloon floating over the park.

Racing down the street, the boy on the skateboard jumped the curb.

Problem: Incorrect placement of the adverb *only*

Juana only goes to movies on the weekend. *mod*

Solution: Place the adverb *only* immediately before the word or group of words it modifies.

Only Juana goes to movies on the weekend.

Juana goes only to movies on the weekend.

Juana goes to movies only on the weekend.

Rule of Thumb: Note that each time *only* is moved, the meaning of the sentence changes. Check to be sure that your sentence conveys your intended meaning.

Problem: A dangling modifier

Walking through the museum, the paintings were from many different countries. *mod*

By studying every night, the examination was easily passed. *mod*

Solution: Rewrite the sentence, adding a noun to which the dangling phrase clearly refers. Often you will have to add other words or change the form of the verb to complete the meaning of the sentence.

Walking through the museum, Arthur noticed paintings from many different countries.

By studying every night, the student passed the examination easily.

Missing or Misplaced Possessive Apostrophe

Problem: Singular nouns

That womans daughter is Doris best friend. *poss*

Solution: Use an apostrophe and -*s* to form the possessive of a singular noun or a proper name, even if the noun ends in *s*.

That woman's daughter is Doris's best friend.

Problem: Plural nouns ending in -*s*

Her twin daughters jackets are just alike. *poss*

Solution: Use an apostrophe alone to form the possessive of a plural noun that ends in -*s*.

Her twin daughters' jackets are just alike.

Problem: Plural nouns not ending in -*s*

This store carries a good selection of mens suits. *poss*

Solution: Use an apostrophe and -*s* to form the possessive of a plural noun that does not end in -*s*.

This store carries a good selection of men's suits.

Problem: Pronouns

In this organization everyones opinion counts. *poss*

Are these skates your's or her's? *poss*

Solution A: Use an apostrophe and *-s* to form the possessive of a singular indefinite pronoun.

In this organization everyone's opinion counts.

Solution B: Do not use an apostrophe with any of the possessive personal pronouns.

Are these skates yours or hers?

Problem: Confusion between *its* and *it's*

Its a long way from your house to mine. *cont*

The airplane had ice on it's wings. *poss*

Solution A: Use an apostrophe to form the contraction of *it is.*

It's a long way from your house to mine.

Solution B: Do not use an apostrophe to form the possessive of *it.*

The airplane had ice on its wings.

Missing Commas with Nonessential Elements

Problem: Missing commas with nonessential participles or participial phrases

Sonya exhausted from her long trip went to bed early. *com*

Solution: Determine whether the participle or participial phrase is essential to the meaning of the sentence or not. If it is not essential, set off the phrase with commas.

Sonya, exhausted from her long trip, went to bed early.

Problem: Missing commas with nonessential adjective clauses

My oldest cousin who visits us every summer is one grade ahead of me in school. com

Solution: Determine whether the clause is essential to the meaning of the sentence or not. If it is not essential, set off the clause with commas.

My oldest cousin, who visits us every summer, is one grade ahead of me in school.

Problem: Missing commas with nonessential appositives

In Chaco Canyon a site in New Mexico we saw the ruins of huge structures built by the Anasazi. com

Solution: Determine whether the appositive is essential to the meaning of the sentence or not. If it is not essential, set off the appositive with commas.

In Chaco Canyon, a site in New Mexico, we saw the ruins of huge structures built by the Anasazi.

Rule of Thumb: To determine whether a word, phrase, or clause is essential, try reading the sentence without it.

Problem: Missing commas with interjections and parenthetical expressions

Judith as you know will be sixteen tomorrow. com

Hey don't forget to bring the ice cream. com

Solution: Set off the interjection or parenthetical expression with commas.

Judith, as you know, will be sixteen tomorrow.

Hey, don't forget to bring the ice cream.

Missing Commas in a Series

Problem: Missing commas in a series of words, phrases, or clauses

Last summer Hideki visited relatives in Tokyo Kyoto and Kobe. *ꝺ com*

We followed the trail along the river across a wooden bridge and up a steep hill. *ꝺ com*

Alex dribbled the ball then he passed it to Dominic and Dominic scored the goal. *ꝺ com*

The library is open for people who want a book to read people who are looking for specific information and people who need a quiet place to study. *ꝺ com*

The little boy complained whined and cried until his mother picked him up. *ꝺ com*

Solution: When there are three or more elements in a series, use a comma after each element, including the element that precedes a conjunction.

Last summer Hideki visited relatives in Tokyo, Kyoto, and Kobe.

We followed the trail along the river, across a wooden bridge, and up a steep hill.

Alex dribbled the ball, then he passed it to Dominic, and Dominic scored the goal.

The library is open for people who want a book to read, people who are looking for specific information, and people who need a quiet place to study.

The little boy complained, whined, and cried until his mother picked him up.

Rule of Thumb: When you're having difficulty with a rule of usage, try rewriting the rule in your own words. Then check with your teacher to be sure you have grasped the concept.

Troublesome Words

This section will help you choose between words that are often confusing. It will also alert you to avoid certain words and expressions in school or business writing.

a, an

Use the article *an* when the word that follows begins with a vowel sound. Use *a* when the word that follows begins with a consonant sound.	**An** exercise mat lay in **a** corner of the room.
Use the article *a* when the word that follows begins with a sounded *h* or a *u* with the long sound ("yew"). Use *an* when the word that follows begins with an unsounded *h* or a *u* with the short sound.	**A** hungry family will not wait **an** hour for dinner. **An** umpire wears **a** uniform.

a lot, alot

The expression *a lot* means "a large amount" or "a great deal" (as in "I like him a lot") and should always be written as two words. Some authorities discourage its use in formal English.	**A lot** of people arrived early for the big game. **Many** people arrived early for the big game.

accept, except

Accept is a verb meaning "to receive" or "to agree to." *Except* is occasionally used as a verb, but more often it is used as a preposition meaning "but."	Sally will **accept** the award. Everybody was invited **except** Bob.

affect, effect

Affect is a verb meaning "to cause a change in" or "to influence." *Effect* as a verb means "to bring about or accomplish." As a noun, *effect* means "result" or "that which has been brought about."	Incorrect answers will **affect** your test score. Diligent study will **effect** a rise in your test score. Diligent study will have a good **effect** on your test score.

ain't

Ain't is never used in formal speaking or writing unless you are quoting the exact words of a character or real person. Instead of using *ain't,* say or write *am not, is not,* or use contractions: *I'm not, she's not, she isn't, they aren't.*	Cassandra **is not** going to the dance.

all ready, already

All ready, written as two words, is an adjective phrase that means "completely ready." *Already,* written as one word, is an adverb that means "before" or "by this time."

By the time supper was **all ready,** the guests had **already** arrived.

all right, alright

The expression *all right* should be written as two words.

Let's see if the man who fell down is **all right.**

Rule of Thumb: Dictionaries are good guides to the usage of a word. Even though some dictionaries do list the single word *alright,* they indicate that it is not a preferred spelling.

all together, altogether

All together means "in a group." *Altogether* is an adverb meaning "completely" or "on the whole."

They worked on the project **all together.**

Their work was **altogether** excellent.

amount, number

Use *amount* to refer to a quantity that cannot be counted. Use *number* to refer to things that can be counted.

A great **amount** of water went over the falls.

A great **number** of logs went over the falls.

Rule of Thumb: Use *amount* to refer to fluids, materials, and gases.

anxious, eager

Anxious means "uneasy or worried about some event or situation." *Eager* means "having a keen interest" or "feeling impatient for something expected."

Gus is **anxious** about the outcome of the difficult test.

Berta is **eager** to see her grades because she knows she did well.

a while, awhile

An article and a noun form the expression *a while.* Often the preposition *in* or *for* precedes *a while,* forming a prepositional phrase. The single word *awhile* is an adverb.

He'll arrive in **a while.** He'll work for **a while.**

He'll work **awhile** after he arrives.

being as, being that

Although the expressions *being as* and *being that* sometimes replace *because* or *since* in informal conversation, you should always avoid them in formal speaking and writing.

Because she made excellent grades, Sylvia skipped a year in school.

Since Carlos is already at home, let's visit him there.

beside, besides

Beside means "next to." *Besides* means "moreover" or "in addition to."

Clark sat **beside** me at dinner.

Besides having a fine dinner, we also ate dessert.

between, among

Use *between* when comparing one person or thing with another person or thing or with an entire group. Use *among* to show a relationship in which more than two persons or things are considered as a group.

He had to choose **between** the movie and the play.

What are the differences **between** a woodpecker and other birds?

There are differences **among** various kinds of birds.

bring, take

Bring means "to carry from a distant place to a closer one." *Take* means "to carry from a nearby place to a more distant one."

Bring me a copy of the newspaper when you come here tomorrow.

The cab will **take** you to the airport from here.

can, may

Can implies the ability to do something. *May* implies permission to do something or the possibility of doing it.

You **may** go to the movie if you **can** pay the price of a ticket.

Rule of Thumb: Although *can* is sometimes used in place of *may* in informal speech, you should distinguish between them when speaking and writing formally.

can't hardly, can't scarcely

Can't hardly and *can't scarcely* are considered double negatives, since *hardly* and *scarcely* by themselves have a negative meaning. Do not use *hardly* and *scarcely* with *not* or *-n't.*

Tamara **can hardly** reach the shelf.

Gabriel **can scarcely** believe he won the contest.

capital, capitol

Use *capital* to refer to the city that is the center of government of a state or country, to money or other assets, or to a capital letter. Use *capitol* to refer to the building in which a state or national legislature meets.

Our class took a trip to Washington, D.C., the nation's **capital.**

We toured the **capitol,** where the legislature was in session.

complement, compliment

A *complement* is something that makes a thing complete. A *compliment* is an expression of praise or admiration.

The CD-ROM is the **complement** of the textbook.

The teacher's **compliment** pleased Jade.

compose, comprise

Compose means "to form by putting together." *Comprise* means "to contain, embrace."

Water is **composed** of hydrogen and oxygen.

The United States **comprises** fifty states.

continual, continuous

Continual describes repetitive action with pauses. *Continuous* describes an action that continues with no interruption in space or time.

Whenever we get together, Jorge and I have **continual** discussions about science.

My interest in the subject has been **continuous** for as long as I can remember.

could of, might of, must of, should of, would of

The helping verb *have,* not the preposition *of,* should follow *could, might, must, should,* or *would.*

Midori **could have** climbed the rope if she had tried.

Isabel **must have** heard that song before.

different from, different than

The expression *different from* is generally preferred to *different than.*

Chess is **different from** checkers.

emigrate, immigrate

Emigrate means "to leave one country to settle in another." Use *from* with *emigrate. Immigrate* means "to enter a country in order to live there permanently." Use *to* or *into* with *immigrate.*

Nikolai plans to **emigrate** from the Ukraine.

Nikolai plans to **immigrate** to the United States.

Rule of Thumb: Remember that the *e-* in *emigrate* comes from *ex-* ("out of"); the *im-* in *immigrate* comes from *in-* ("into").

ensure, assure, insure

Ensure means to make sure of something, to guarantee it. *Assure* means to reassure someone, to remove doubt. *Insure* means to cover something with insurance or to secure it.

Please take action to **ensure** the prompt arrival of the package.

Can you **assure** me that everything has been taken care of?

You must **insure** the car before you can drive it.

farther, further

Farther refers to physical distance. *Further* refers to time or degree.

Now the comet is moving **farther** and **farther** away from Earth.

Think **further** back in time and see what you can remember.

There is nothing **further** to say.

fewer, less

Fewer is generally used to refer to things or qualities that can be counted. *Less* is generally used to refer to things or qualities that cannot be counted. In addition, *less* is sometimes used with figures that are regarded as single amounts or single quantities.

Fewer people attended the movie this week than last week.

There is **less** water in this swimming pool than in the one at school.

You can eat lunch at this restaurant for **less** than ten dollars. [The money is treated as a single sum, not as individual dollars.]

good, well

Good is often used as an adjective meaning "pleasing" or "able." *Well* may be used as an adverb of manner telling how ably something is done or as an adjective meaning "in good health."

This meal tastes **good.** [adjective after a linking verb]

Claudia swims **well.** [adverb of manner]

Because José has the flu, he is not **well** enough to come to school. [adjective meaning "in good health"]

had of

The word *of* should not be used between *had* and a past participle.

I wish I **had seen** that television show.

hanged, hung

When your meaning is "put to death by hanging," use *hanged* in the past tense. In all other cases, use *hung.*

Many countries **hanged** convicted murderers in the nineteenth century.

Rachel **hung** her hat on the peg.

in, into

Use *in* when you mean "inside" or "within." Use *into* to indicate movement or direction from outside to a point within.

Melissa is already **in** the theater.

I hurried **into** the theater because it was nearly time for the play to begin.

irregardless, regardless

Both the prefix *ir-* and suffix *-less* have negative meanings. When they are used together, they produce a double negative, which is incorrect. Therefore, you should use *regardless* rather than *irregardless.*

Riad listens to whatever people say, **regardless** of their opinions.

learn, teach

Learn means "to gain knowledge." *Teach* means "to instruct" or "to give knowledge to."

Emil **learns** well from his professor.

Mr. Musser **teaches** us our spelling lessons.

leave, let

Leave means "to go away; depart." *Let* means "to allow" or "to permit." With the word *alone* you may use either *let* or *leave.*

Francesca wanted to **leave** the party.

Ryugen **lets** me use his CDs.

Leave me alone. **Let** me alone.

lend, loan

Lend is a verb. *Loan* is a noun. Although *loan* is sometimes used informally as a verb, *lend* is preferable.

I will **lend** you my calculator if you return it tomorrow.

Thank you for the **loan.**

like, as

Use *like,* a preposition, to introduce a prepositional phrase. Use *as,* a subordinating conjunction, to introduce a subordinate clause. Many authorities believe that *like* should not be used before a clause in formal English.

Werner looks **like** his brother.

Mildred baby-sits tonight, **as** she always does on Fridays.

Rule of Thumb: *As* can be a preposition in some cases, as in *He posed as a secret agent.*

loose, lose

Use the adjective *loose* (lōōs) when you mean "free," "not firmly attached," or "not fitting tightly." Use the verb *lose* (lōōz) when you mean "to have no longer," "to misplace," or "to fail to win."

In spite of the city's leash laws, Miguel lets his dog run **loose.**

Marlene doesn't want to **lose** another set of keys.

passed, past

Passed is the past and the past participle form of *pass. Past* is used as a noun, an adjective, a preposition, or an adverb.

The blue car **passed** the bicycle. [verb]

History is a study of events in the **past.** [noun]

Ian took a long vacation this **past** summer. [adjective]

The grocery store is just **past** the gas station. [preposition]

The puppies woke up when their mother walked **past.** [adverb]

precede, proceed

Use *precede* when you mean "to go or come before." Use *proceed* when you mean "to continue" or "to move along."

July **precedes** August.

The line of customers will **proceed** slowly.

principal, principle

Principal, as an adjective, means "the most important or first in rank." As a noun, it is the title of the head of a school. *Principle* is a noun that means "a fundamental truth or general law."

My **principal** objection to the TV set is its price.

The school **principal** fully supports our club's activities.

My research project was set up according to strict scientific **principles.**

raise, rise

The verb *raise* means "to cause to move upward" or "to lift up." It always takes an object. The verb *rise* means "to get up" or "to go up." It is an intransitive verb and never takes an object.

The soldiers **raise** the flag at dawn every morning.

Your temperature will **rise** if you do vigorous exercise.

reason . . . is that, because

Because means "for the reason that." Therefore, do not use *because* after *reason . . . is.* Use either *reason . . . is that* or *because* alone.

The **reason** there is no baseball game today **is that** it is raining.

There is no baseball game today **because** it is raining.

respectfully, respectively

Use *respectfully* to mean "with respect." Use *respectively* to mean "in the order named."

Saul spoke **respectfully** to his boss.

Gareth and Alice are third and fourth in line, **respectively.**

says, said

Says is the present-tense, third-person singular form of the verb *say. Said* is the past tense of *say.* Do not use *says* when you are referring to the past.

Sebastian **says** he is going downtown.

Yesterday Sebastian **said** he was going downtown.

sit, set

Sit means "to be seated." It rarely takes an object. *Set* means "to put" or "to place," and it generally takes an object. When *set* is used to mean "the sun is going down," it does not take an object.

Sara is going to **sit** on the park bench.

Set the groceries down on the kitchen table.

The sun **set** at seven o'clock this evening.

than, then

Than is a conjunction. Use it in comparisons. *Then* is an adverb used to mean "soon afterward," "the time mentioned," "at another time," "for that reason," "in that case," and "besides."

The task is more complex **than** you think it is.

Alicia is better at math **than** Claudio is.

Rashad will go to the party, and **then** I will join him.

By **then** you will be very hungry.

Andres was only five years old **then.**

If you can't answer the question, **then** Sheila will.

their, they're, there

Their is the possessive form of *they. They're* is the contraction of *they are. There* means "in that place." *There* is also sometimes used as an interjection, expressing a sense of completion.

It's **their** business, not ours.

Ask them whether **they're** going to join us.

You will find your book **there** on your desk.

There!

to, too, two

Use *to* when you mean "in the direction of." Also, use *to* before a verb to form an infinitive. Use *too* when you mean "also" or "excessively." *Two* is the number that comes after one.

We will drive **to** the mall.

I need **to** buy new shoes.

My brother will come along, **too.**

I bought only **two** ice cream cones.

toward, towards

These words are interchangeable; as prepositions, they both mean "in the direction of."

She drove **toward** her house.

She drove **towards** her house.

where . . . at

Do not use *at* after a question with *where.*

Where are my keys?

whereas, while

Both *whereas* and *while* can be used as conjunctions meaning "although." *Whereas* also means "it being the fact that." *While* can be used as a conjunction indicating a period of time.

I spent the afternoon at work, **whereas** you went swimming.

Miryam's brother and sister like vanilla, **while** she prefers chocolate.

Whereas everyone is in agreement, we can adjourn this meeting.

Roberto reviewed the lesson **while** Marisela finished her research paper.

Rule of Thumb: The conjunction *whereas* is usually reserved for very formal usage.

who, whom

Use the nominative case pronoun *who* for the subject.

Who knocked on the door?

Tell me **who** can solve this problem. [subject of the noun clause]

Who do you think can solve the problem?

Rule of Thumb: When a question contains an interrupting expression such as *do you think,* it helps to omit the interrupting phrase to determine whether to use *who* or *whom.*

Use the objective pronoun *whom* for the direct or indirect object of a verb or the object of a verbal.

Whom are you describing? [direct object]

They gave **whom** the award? [indirect object]

Giovanni told me **whom** he saw. [direct object of the verb *saw*]

Whom does the teacher want to nominate for student council? [object of the verbal *to nominate*]

Rule of Thumb: When speaking informally, people often use *who* instead of *whom* in sentences like *Who are you describing?* In writing and formal speech, distinguish between *who* and *whom.*

Use the objective pronoun *whom* for the object of a preposition.

Giovanni is a person with **whom** I have much in common. [object of the preposition *with*]

Grammar Glossary

This glossary will help you quickly locate information on parts of speech and sentence structure.

A

Abstract noun. *See* Noun chart.

Action verb. *See* Verb.

Active voice. *See* Voice.

Adjective A word that modifies a noun or pronoun by limiting its meaning. An adjective may answer one of these questions: *What kind? Which one? How many? How much?* Adjectives appear in various positions in a sentence. (The *exciting* story held my attention. That story is *exciting.*)

Many adjectives have different forms to indicate **degree of comparison.** *(happy, happier, happiest)*

The **positive degree** is the simple form of the adjective. *(strong, much)*

The **comparative degree** compares two persons, places, things, or ideas. *(stronger, more)*

The **superlative degree** compares more than two persons, places, things, or ideas. *(strongest, most)*

A **predicate adjective** follows a linking verb and further identifies the subject. (The animals are *hungry.*)

A **noun used as an adjective** answers one of these questions: *What kind? Which one?* (*government* building, *physics* lesson) In some cases possessive nouns are used as adjectives. (*Asa's* car)

A **proper adjective** is formed from a proper noun and begins with a capital letter. Proper adjectives are often created by using the following suffixes: *-an, -ian, -n, -ese,* and *-ish.* *(Indonesian)*

Adjective clause. *See* Clause chart.

Adverb A word that modifies a verb, an adjective, or another adverb by making its meaning more specific. Adverbs answer the questions *How? When? Where?* and *To what degree?* When modifying a verb, an adverb may appear in various positions in a sentence. (The cattle disappeared *rapidly* over the hill. *Suddenly,* not a single one was in sight.) When modifying an adjective or another adverb, an adverb appears directly before the modified word. (The cowboy was *quite* annoyed that he had to find them.) The negatives *no, not,* and the contraction *-n't* are adverbs. (Nakia's score was *no* better than mine.) Other negative words, such as *nowhere, hardly,* and *never,* can function as adverbs of time, place, and degree. (I *never* imagined that they would win the game.)

Some adverbs have different forms to indicate degree of comparison. *(slowly, more slowly, most slowly)*

The **comparative** form of an adverb compares two actions. *(more quickly, better)*

The **superlative** form compares three or more actions. *(most quickly, best)*

Adverb clause. *See* Clause chart.

Antecedent. *See* Pronoun.

Appositive A noun or a pronoun placed next to another noun or pronoun to identify or give additional information about it. (My cousin *Lonnie* is going to Guatemala this summer.)

Appositive phrase. *See* Phrase.

Article The adjective *a, an,* or *the.*

Indefinite articles (*a* and *an*) refer to one of a general group of persons, places, or things. (We saw *a* fish.)

The **definite article** *(the)* indicates that the noun is a specific person, place, or thing. (It swam under *the* log.)

Auxiliary verb. *See* Verb.

B

Base form. *See* Verb tense.

C

Clause A group of words that has a subject and a predicate and is used as part of a sentence. Clauses fall into two categories: *main clauses*, which are also called *independent clauses*, and *subordinate clauses*, which are also called *dependent clauses*.

A **main clause** has a subject and a predicate and can stand alone as a sentence. There must be at least one main clause in every sentence. *(I can't wait to see your new dog. I will arrive in a few minutes.)*

A **subordinate clause** has a subject and a predicate, but it cannot stand alone as a sentence. A subordinate clause makes sense only when attached to a main clause. Many subordinate clauses begin with subordinating conjunctions or relative pronouns. (Ethan got a high grade *because he was well prepared*.) The chart on this page shows the main types of subordinate clauses.

Collective noun. *See* Noun chart.

Common noun. *See* Noun chart.

Comparative. *See* Adjective, Adverb.

Complement A word or phrase that completes the meaning of a verb. The four basic kinds of complements are *direct objects*, *indirect objects*, *object complements*, and *subject complements*.

A **direct object** answers the question *What?* or *Whom?* after an action verb. (Hiro likes his *job* and his *car.* Hiro brings *me* to school every day.)

An **indirect object** answers the question *To whom? For whom? To what?* or *For what?* after an action verb. (Adebesi gave the *museum* an authentic Nigerian drum.)

An **object complement** answers the question *What?* after a direct object. An object complement is a noun, a pronoun, or an adjective that completes the meaning of a direct object by identifying or describing it. (We elected her *chairperson* of the committee. Our group considers the award *ours*. Angela finds science *fascinating*.)

A **subject complement** follows a subject and a linking verb. It identifies or describes a subject. The two kinds of subject complements are *predicate nominatives* and *predicate adjectives*.

A **predicate nominative** is a noun or pronoun that follows a linking verb and gives more information about the subject. (Those three students are *athletes*. The guard is *he*.)

A **predicate adjective** is an adjective that follows a linking verb and gives more information about the subject. (Laura is *athletic*. Your painting looks *finished* to me.)

Complex sentence. *See* Sentence.

Compound-complex sentence. *See* Sentence.

Compound sentence. *See* Sentence.

Conjunction A word that joins single words or groups of words.

A **coordinating conjunction** *(and, but, or, nor, for, yet)* joins words or groups of words that are equal in grammatical

TYPES OF SUBORDINATE CLAUSES			
Clause	**Function**	**Example**	**Begins with . . .**
Adjective clause	Modifies a noun or pronoun in the main clause	The story *that I just read* is by Amy Tan.	A relative pronoun such as *that, which, who, whom,* or *whose*
Adverb clause	Modifies a verb, an adjective, or an adverb in the main clause	Beryl went to the movie *after she finished studying.*	A subordinating conjunction such as *after, although, because, if, since, when,* or *where*
Noun clause	Serves as a subject, an object, or a predicate nominative in the main clause	*Whoever writes a great deal* often draws on personal experience.	Words such as *how, that, what, whatever, when, where, which, who, whom, whoever, whose,* or *why*

importance. (Toshio *and* Linda entered their projects in the science fair.)

Correlative conjunctions *(both . . . and, just as . . . so, not only . . . but also, either . . . or, neither . . . nor)* work in pairs to join words and groups of words of equal importance. (Rosa *not only* won the race *but also* set a new school record.)

A **subordinating conjunction** *(after, although, as soon as, because, before, if, in order that, since, than, though, until, when, while)* joins a dependent idea or clause to a main clause. (We should leave *as soon as* we can get ready.)

Conjunctive adverb An adverb used to clarify the relationship between clauses of a compound sentence. (The team lost the game last night; *consequently*, they will not play in the tournament.)

Coordinating conjunction. *See* Conjunction.

Correlative conjunction. *See* Conjunction.

D

Definite article. *See* Article.

Demonstrative pronoun. *See* Pronoun.

Direct object. *See* Complement.

Emphatic form. *See* Verb tense.

Future tense. *See* Verb tense.

Gerund A verb form that ends in *-ing* and is used as a noun. A gerund may function as a subject, an object of a verb, or the object of a preposition. (*Studying* is not my favorite way to spend an evening. However, I have improved my grades by *studying*.)

Gerund phrase. *See* Phrase.

Indirect object. *See* Complement.

Infinitive A verb form that begins with the word *to* and functions as a noun, an adjective, or an adverb. (We were happy *to leave. To compose* was her ambition.) When *to* precedes a verb, it is not a preposition but instead signals an infinitive.

Infinitive phrase. *See* Phrase.

Intensive pronoun. *See* Pronoun.

Interjection A word or phrase that expresses emotion or exclamation. An interjection has no grammatical connection to other words in the sentence. Commas follow mild interjections; exclamation points follow stronger ones. (*Oh*, I forgot. *Wow!*)

Interrogative pronoun. *See* Pronoun.

Intransitive verb. *See* Verb.

Inverted order In a sentence written in *inverted order,* the predicate comes before the subject. Some sentences are written in inverted order for variety or special emphasis. (In the very center of the clearing *stood* a *deer*.) The subject also generally follows the predicate in a sentence that begins with *there* or *here.* (There *were* several *deer* beside the stream. Here *comes* the *bus* now.) Questions, or interrogative sentences, are generally written in inverted order. In many questions, an auxiliary verb precedes the subject and the main verb follows it. (*Has Edwin announced* the contest results?) Questions that begin with *who* or *what* follow normal word order.

Irregular verb. *See* Verb tense.

Linking verb. *See* Verb.

Main clause. *See* Clause.

Nominative pronoun. *See* Pronoun chart.

Noun A word that names a person, a place, a thing, or an idea. The chart on the next page shows the main types of nouns.

Noun clause. *See* Clause chart.

Noun of direct address. *See* Noun chart.

Number A noun, pronoun, or verb is *singular* in number if it refers to one, *plural* if it refers to more than one.

Objective pronoun. *See* Pronoun.

Mechanics

Capitalization

This section will help you recognize and use correct capitalization in sentences.

Rule	Example
Capitalize the first word in any sentence, including a direct quotation that is a sentence. Capitalize a sentence in parentheses unless it is included in another sentence.	He said, "We should leave now." We were looking for Laurel Avenue, where we thought Juanita lived. (There was no Laurel Avenue.)
Always capitalize the pronoun *I* no matter where it appears in the sentence.	No matter where I live, I'll always remember my home at the edge of the desert.
Capitalize proper nouns, including these: **a.** names of individuals, personal titles used in direct address, and personal titles preceding a name or describing a relationship	Robert Penn Warren; Class President Iris Mura; Uncle Bill
b. names of ethnic groups, national groups, political parties and their members, and languages	African Americans; Hopi; the Democratic Party; a Republican; Vietnamese
c. names of organizations, institutions, companies, monuments, bridges, buildings, and other structures	Red Cross; North Carolina State University; the Museum of Science and Industry; Microsoft; Vietnam Memorial; Golden Gate Bridge
d. trade names and names of documents, awards, and laws	Macintosh; the Constitution of the United States; Nobel Prize; the Fifth Amendment
e. geographical terms and regions or localities	Lake Superior; Main Street; Palisades Park; North Dakota; the Northwest
f. names of planets and other heavenly bodies	Earth; Mars
g. names of ships, planes, trains, and spacecraft	USS *Enterprise;* the *Orient Express; Apollo 13*
h. names of most historical events, eras, calendar items, and religious items	World War One; Middle Ages; Saturday; Judaism; Methodists; Bible; Yom Kippur; God

Rule of Thumb: Since people do not always speak in complete sentences, written dialogue may contain sentence fragments. In dialogue, capitalize the first word of each fragment and each complete sentence. For example: "Late for class," Ferris mumbled.

Rule	Example
i. titles of literary works, publications, works of art, and musical compositions	"Sound of Thunder"; *New Yorker*; *Little Dancer*; *Concerto for Orchestra*
j. specific names of school courses	Algebra I
Rule of Thumb: Do not capitalize the names of subjects (He studied *algebra.*) or seasons of the year (Ian enjoys *winter.*)	
Capitalize proper adjectives (adjectives formed from proper nouns).	Spanish rice; Vidalia onions; Freudian theory; Buddhist meditation

Punctuation

This section will help you use these elements of punctuation correctly.

Rule	Example
Use a **period** at the end of a declarative sentence or an imperative sentence (a polite command).	His lecture was fascinating. Please take your seats.
Use an **exclamation point** to show strong feeling or after a forceful command.	Oh, no! What a disaster! Listen to me!
Use a **question mark** to indicate a direct question.	Is it time for class?
Use a **colon** a. to introduce a list (especially after words such as *these,* or *as follows*) and to introduce material that explains, illustrates, or restates previous material	Toni Morrison's works include the following novels: *The Bluest Eye*, *Song of Solomon*, and *Beloved*. We must say it again: the customer is always right.
Rule of Thumb: Do not use a colon between the verb and its complement. A colon must follow a complete sentence.	
b. to introduce a long or formal quotation	In *Richard III*, the title character says: "Now is the winter of our discontent / Made glorious summer by this sun of York. . . ."
c. in precise time measurements, biblical chapter and verse references, and business letter salutations	12:45 P.M. 9:24 A.M. 2 Sam. 14:13–14 Eccles. 2:16 Dear Mrs. Clay: Dear Sir:

Rule	Example
Use a **semicolon**	
a. to separate main clauses that are not joined by a coordinating conjunction	Tipping is considered proper at a restaurant; the rate is between fifteen and twenty percent.
b. to separate main clauses joined by a conjunctive adverb or by *for example* or *that is*	Herman Melville's earlier novels were fairly simple adventure stories; however, in his later works, he dealt with more complex themes.
c. to separate the items in a series when these items contain commas	Three signers of the Declaration of Independence were Thomas Jefferson, who wrote the document; Benjamin Franklin, who discovered that lightning consisted of electricity; and George Washington, who became our first president.
d. to separate two main clauses joined by a coordinating conjunction when such clauses already contain several commas	Manny, who traveled all the way from Fairbanks, Alaska, attended the reunion; but Teri, a local resident, did not.
Use a **comma**	
a. between the main clauses of a compound sentence	The snow is already three feet deep, and it is still coming down.
b. to separate three or more words, phrases, or clauses in a series	Jefferson, Franklin, and Washington were three signers of the Declaration of Independence.
c. between coordinate modifiers	Sally is a shrewd, witty person.
d. to set off parenthetical expressions, interjections, and conjunctive adverbs	We might, in fact, go to the beach tomorrow. Oh, what a good idea! We spent all our money yesterday; consequently, we will stay home today.
e. to set off direct quotations	"My vacation," said Jana, "was great."
f. to set off long introductory prepositional phrases	From their hammocks in the trees, the hunters watched the boars.

Rule of Thumb: Use a comma after a short introductory prepositional phrase only if the sentence would be misleading without it.

Rule	Example
g. to set off nonessential words, clauses, and phrases, such as	
–adverbial clauses	Because I'm going to Mexico this summer, I need to work on my Spanish.
–adjective clauses	Alejo Carpentier, who wrote *The Lost Steps,* was born in Havana in 1904.
–participles and participial phrases	Joe, laughing, showed me the comic strip. Dashing along the sidewalk, I caught the bus.
–infinitive phrases	I didn't like that film very much, to tell the truth.
–prepositional phrases	The novel, from beginning to end, bored and depressed me.
–appositives and appositive phrases	Maxine Hong Kingston, an author and university lecturer, won the National Book Award for *China Men.*

Rule of Thumb: Nonessential elements can be removed without changing the meaning of the sentence.

Rule	Example
h. to set off an antithetical phrase	Daffodils, not crocuses, are my favorite flowers.
i. to set off a title after a person's name	Angela López, Ph.D. Lou Wright, Chairman of the Board
j. to separate the various parts of an address, a geographical term, or a date	Bend, Oregon May 3, 1999 Monday, June 14 Stanford, KY 40484
k. after the salutation of an informal letter and after the closing of all letters	Dear Marie, Yours truly,
l. to set off parts of a reference that direct the reader to the exact source	That is from Rudolfo Anaya's *Tortuga,* page 212.
m. to set off words or names used in direct address and in tag questions	Gerald, did you bring the thermos? You remember his name, don't you?

Rule	Example
Use a **dash** to signal a change in thought or to emphasize a parenthetical comment.	Julie was unhappy—actually she was devastated—when she lost her new bracelet. Izanami's voice was cheerful—more like it had been in happier days.
Rule of Thumb: A good test of the correct use of dashes is to delete the information that the dashes set off. If the remaining sentence retains its basic meaning, then the dashes were properly used. If the remaining sentence has lost crucial information, then the dashes were improperly used.	
Use **parentheses** to set off supplemental material. Punctuate within the parentheses only if the punctuation is part of the parenthetical expression.	The Maya (who lived in Mexico and Central America) built remarkable stone structures. The Maya built remarkable stone structures. (They lived in Mexico and Central America.) We crept along the hallway (why were we so afraid?) until we reached the door at the end.
Use **quotation marks** **a.** to enclose a direct quotation, as follows:	Secretary of State Madeleine Albright called her job "a great privilege."
When a quotation is interrupted, use two sets of quotation marks.	"One difference was apparent from the outset," a World War II news analyst said of radio. "It was the first time the peoples of the world could hear a war actually breaking out."
Use single quotation marks for a quotation within a quotation.	Ursula Le Guin wrote, "'Happens all the time,' says Coyote. 'That's what myths do. They happen all the time.'"
In writing dialogue, begin a new paragraph and use a new set of quotation marks every time the speaker changes.	"How about luncheon tomorrow?" "I'm afraid that's impossible." "How about dinner tomorrow evening?"
b. to enclose titles of short works, such as stories, poems, essays, articles, chapters, and songs	"Why I Live at the P.O." is a story by Eudora Welty.

Rule	Example
c. to enclose unfamiliar slang terms and unusual expressions	"Fuzzy logic" is a term applied to certain mathematical processes.

Rule of Thumb: A good way to tell whether question marks and exclamation points go inside or outside quotation marks is to take the direct quotation out of the sentence and see how it would be punctuated if it stood alone. If it would end with a question mark or exclamation point, then that mark of punctuation should go within the quotation marks. If the new sentence would end with a period, then the question mark or exclamation point should go outside the quotation marks.

Rule	Example
Use **italics**	
a. for titles of books, lengthy poems, plays, films, television series, paintings and sculptures, long musical compositions, court cases, names of newspapers and magazines, ships, trains, airplanes, and spacecraft (Italicize and capitalize *a, an,* and *the* at the beginning of a title only when they are part of the title.)	*Star Wars* [film]; *Under Milk Wood* [play] *Man at the Crossroads* [painting] *Discover* [magazine] *Apollo 13* [spacecraft] *Air Force One* [airplane] *The Lost Steps* [book] the *Los Angeles Times* [newspaper]
b. for foreign words and expressions that are not used frequently in English	He came up with the perfect word, the *mot juste.*
c. for words, letters, and numerals used to represent themselves	In that sentence, use *adapt*, not *adopt*. There is no *6* in this list.
Use an **apostrophe**	
a. for a possessive form, as follows: Add an apostrophe and *-s* to all singular indefinite pronouns, singular nouns, plural nouns not ending in *-s,* and compound nouns. Add only an apostrophe to a plural noun that ends in *-s.*	someone's jacket; California's coastline; the women's books; the boss's desk my brother-in-law's computer; the Chief of Police's office; the race car driver's accident the waves' continuous motion
If two or more persons possess something jointly, use the possessive form for the last person named. If they possess it individually, use the possessive form for each one's name.	Penn and Teller's magic act Romeo and Juliet's problem Picasso's and Braque's cubist paintings Ford's and Chrysler's minivans

Rule	Example
b. to express amounts of money or time that modify a noun	twenty dollars' worth; one day's vacation (You can use a hyphenated adjective instead: a one-day vacation.)
c. in place of omitted letters or numerals	it's [it is, it has] the floods of '97
d. to form the plural of letters, numerals, symbols, and words used to represent themselves (use an apostrophe and -*s*)	*9*'s *x*'s and *y*'s *#*'s
Use a **hyphen** **a.** after any prefix joined to a proper noun or proper adjective	mid-Atlantic post-Impressionist
b. after the prefixes *all-*, *ex-*, and *self-* joined to any noun or adjective; after the prefix *anti-* when it joins a word beginning with *i;* after the prefix *vice-* (except in *vice president*); and to avoid confusion between words that begin with *re-* and look like another word	ex-teammate self-taught anti-imperialist vice-principal re-view the picture review the book re-lay the flooring relay the message
Rule of Thumb: Remember that the prefix *anti-* requires a hyphen when followed by a word that begins with *i* in order to prevent spelling words with two successive *i*'s. Otherwise, *anti* does not require a hyphen, except before a capitalized word.	
c. in a compound adjective that precedes a noun	a five-year-old car her mud-encrusted boat
d. in any spelled-out cardinal or ordinal numbers up to *ninety-nine* or *ninety-ninth* and with a fraction used as an adjective	fifty-six seventy-first three-quarters majority
e. to divide a word at the end of a line between syllables	com-plete hang-man big-gest search-ing

Abbreviations

This section will help you learn how to use abbreviations, which are shortened forms of words.

Rule	Example
Use only one period if an abbreviation occurs at the end of a sentence. If the sentence ends with a question mark or exclamation point, use the period and the second mark of punctuation.	I called Terika Harvey, M.D. Have you ever been outside the U.S.A.? This temple was built around 1000 B.C.!
Capitalize abbreviations of proper nouns and abbreviations related to historical dates.	Edward R. Murrow First Ave. 1000 B.C. A.D. 502 C.E. 502
Use all capital letters and no periods for abbreviations that are pronounced letter by letter or as words.	NAFTA FBI NATO YWCA NAACP NBA UN CIA AFL-CIO
When addressing mail, use the U.S. Post Office abbreviations (two capital letters, no periods).	AK (Alaska) CT (Connecticut) HI (Hawaii) ME (Maine) MA (Massachusetts) TX (Texas)
Use abbreviations for some personal titles.	Ms. Goodwin; Gen. Anderson; Dr. Julia Marshall
Abbreviate units of measure used with numerals in technical or scientific writing, but not in ordinary prose. Use a period after an abbreviation of an English unit of measure, but not after a metric unit.	ft. (foot) g (gram) gal. (gallon) m (meter) in. (inch) mm (millimeter)

Rule of Thumb: In a letter it is appropriate to use a state abbreviation in the address. In other forms of writing, such as expository writing, spell out the name of a state.

Numbers and Numerals

This section will help you understand when to use numerals and when to spell out numbers.

Rule	Example
In general, spell out cardinal and ordinal numbers that can be written in one or two words.	More than three thousand people came to the lecture by physicist Stephen Hawking.
Spell out any number that occurs at the beginning of a sentence.	Two hundred eighty-one books have been added to the library.
In general, use numerals (numbers expressed in figures) to express numbers that would be written in more than two words. Extremely large numbers are often expressed as a numeral followed by the word *million* or *billion.*	The library has recently added 281 new books to its collection. The department store chain had a first-quarter income of $32.3 million.
If related numbers appear in the same sentence, use all numerals.	Of the 124 hotels and motels in the resort area, more than 100 have their own restaurant.
Use numerals to express amounts of money, decimals, and percentages.	$2.53 21.5 students per class 0.6% 12 percent
Use numerals to express the year and day in a date and to express the precise time with the abbreviations *A.M.* and *P.M.*	Robert was born January 17, 1979. Yemane has a job interview on March 4 at 9:00 A.M.
Spell out a number to express a century when the word *century* is used, or a decade when the century is clear from the context. When a century and a decade are expressed as a single unit, use numerals followed by *-s.*	In the twentieth century, many things changed, especially during the sixties. Some people look back upon the 1950s with nostalgia.
Use numerals for streets and avenues numbered above ten and for all house, apartment, and room numbers.	411 Eighth Avenue 310 West 72nd Street Room 205 Apartment 2H
Use numerals to express page, paragraph, stanza, and line numbers.	See page 325, paragraph 2, for that information. In stanza 4, lines 19, 21, and 23 rhyme.

Spelling

The following basic rules, examples, and exceptions will help you master the spelling of many words.

ie and *ei*

Many writers find the rules for certain combinations of letters, like *ie* and *ei,* difficult to remember. One helpful learning strategy is to develop a rhyme to remember a rule. Look at the following rhyme for the *ie* and *ei* rule.

Rule	Example
Put *i* before *e,* except after *c,* or when sounded like *a,* as in *neighbor* and *weigh.*	relief, thief, piece, brief receipt, deceit, perceive sleigh, deign, heir, rein, beige, vein

EXCEPTIONS: seize, leisure, weird, height, either, forfeit, protein, counterfeit, sleight.

-cede, -ceed, and *-sede*

Because various combinations of letters in English are sometimes pronounced the same way, it is often easy to make slight spelling errors. Except for the exceptions below, spell the *sēd* sound at the end of words as *cede:*

precede **accede** **intercede**

EXCEPTION: One word uses *-sede* to spell the final *sēd* sound: supersede.

EXCEPTION: Three words use *-ceed* to spell the final *sēd* sound: proceed, exceed, succeed.

Unstressed vowels

Notice the vowel sound in the second syllable of the word *or-i-gin.* This is the unstressed vowel sound; dictionary pronunciation spellings use the *schwa* symbol (ə) to indicate it. Because any of several vowels can be used to spell this sound, you might find yourself uncertain about which vowel to use. Try thinking of a related word in which the syllable containing the vowel sound is stressed.

Unknown Spelling	Related Word	Correct Spelling
dram_tize	dram**a**tic	dram**a**tize
rev_rence	rev**e**re	rev**e**rence
simil_r	simil**a**rity	simil**a**r
distr_bution	distr**i**bute	distr**i**bution

Adding prefixes

When adding a prefix to a word, keep the original spelling of the word. If the prefix forms a double letter, keep both letters.

dis + count = discount
ir + responsible = irresponsible
mis + spell = misspell

Suffixes and the silent *e*

Many English words end in a silent letter *e.* Sometimes the *e* is dropped when a suffix is added. When adding a suffix that begins with a consonant to a word that ends in silent *e,* keep the *e.*

hope + ful = hopeful
arrange + ment = arrangement

COMMON EXCEPTIONS: awe + ful = awful; judge + ment = judgment

When adding the suffix *-y* or a suffix that begins with a vowel to a word that ends in silent *e,* usually drop the *e.*

shade + y = shady
force + ible = forcible

COMMON EXCEPTION: mile + age = mileage

When adding a suffix that begins with *a* or *o* to a word that ends in *ce* or *ge,* keep the *e* so the word will retain the soft *c* or *g* sound.

peace + able = peaceable
manage + able = manageable
courage + ous = courageous

When adding a suffix that begins with a vowel to a word that ends in *ee* or *oe,* keep the *e.*

foresee + able = foreseeable
flee + ing = fleeing
tiptoe + ing = tiptoeing

Suffixes and the final *y*

When adding a suffix to a word that ends in a consonant + *y,* change the *y* to *i* unless the suffix begins with *i.* Keep the *y* in a word that ends in a vowel + *y.*

try + ed = tried
stay + ing = staying
copy + ing = copying
fry + ed = fried
display + ed = displayed
joy + ous = joyous

Doubling the final consonant

When adding a suffix to a word that ends in a consonant, double the final consonant if it is preceded by a single vowel and the word is one syllable, if the accent is on the last syllable and remains there even after the suffix is added, or if the word is made up of a prefix and a one-syllable word.

shop + ing = shopping
compel + ing = compelling
misstep + ed = misstepped
stop + age = stoppage
concur + ent = concurrent
reset + ing = resetting

Do not double the final consonant if the accent is not on the last syllable or if the accent shifts when the suffix is added. Also do not double the final consonant if it is preceded by two vowels or by another consonant. If the word ends in a consonant and the suffix begins with a consonant, do not double the final consonant.

develop + ing = developing
swoop + ing = swooping
remind + ed = reminded
travel + ing = traveling
rain + ing = raining
faith + ful = faithful

Adding *-ly* and *-ness*

When adding *-ly* to a word that ends in a single *l,* keep the *l,* but when the word ends in a double *l,* drop one *l.* When adding *-ness* to a word that ends in *n,* keep the *n.*

ideal + ly = ideally
full + ly = fully
mean + ness = meanness
real + ly = really
dull + ly = dully
keen + ness = keenness

Forming compound words

When joining a word that ends in a consonant to a word that begins with a consonant, keep both consonants.

rain + fall = rainfall
key + board = keyboard
year + book = yearbook
stair + case = staircase

Forming plurals

English words form plurals in many ways. Most nouns simply add *-s.* The following chart shows other ways of forming plural nouns and some common exceptions to the pattern.

GENERAL RULES FOR FORMING PLURALS		
If a noun ends in	**Rule**	**Example**
ch, s, sh, x, z	add *-es*	church, churches
a consonant + *y*	change *y* to *i* and add *-es*	baby, babies
o or a vowel + *y*	add only *-s*	radio, radios day, days
a consonant + *o* common exceptions	generally add *-es* but sometimes add only *-s*	tomato, tomatoes halo, halos
f or *ff* common exceptions	add *-s* change *f* to *v* and add *-es*	reef, reefs; riff, riffs leaf, leaves
lf	change *f* to *v* and add *-es*	shelf, shelves
fe	change *f* to *v* and add *-s*	life, lives

A few plurals are exceptions to the rules in the previous chart, but they are easy to remember. The following chart lists these plurals and some examples.

SPECIAL RULES FOR FORMING PLURALS	
Rule	**Example**
To form the plural of proper names and one-word compound nouns, follow the general rules for plurals.	López, Lópezes Farraday, Farradays newspaper, newspapers
To form the plural of hyphenated compound nouns or compound nouns of more than one word, make the most important word plural.	father-in-law, fathers-in-law oil well, oil wells attorney general, attorneys general
Some nouns have unusual plural forms.	woman, women mouse, mice ox, oxen
Some nouns have the same singular and plural forms.	sheep deer series

Writing Handbook

The Writing Process

The writing process consists of five stages that take you from choosing a topic to presenting a finished piece of writing. These stages are *prewriting*, *drafting*, *revising*, *editing/proofreading*, and *publishing/presenting*. You do not need to follow them in a strict order but can move back and forth among them as your ideas develop. For example, before revising your first draft, you might present it to a friend in order to get feedback; or you might go back to prewriting in order to rethink your topic or gather more information.

The Writing Process

Prewriting

In the prewriting stage, you explore topic ideas, choose a topic, gather information, and begin to organize your material.

Exploring ideas

Ask yourself the following questions before you begin exploring topic ideas.

- What is my general purpose? Am I writing to fulfill an assignment? Am I writing for a personal reason?
- What audience do I have in mind? My teacher? My classmates? Younger children? The general public?
- What do my purpose and audience determine about the length of my paper? the kinds of topics that are appropriate? the tone and language of my writing (formal or informal; serious or light; objective or personal)?

Once you have given some thought to these questions, the following techniques can help you find a topic to write about.

- Scan your memory for interesting, funny, or moving personal experiences.
- Flip through a variety of magazines and newspapers.
- Browse through a library catalog.
- Brainstorm for topics with a group of classmates.

Choosing a topic

When you have several possible topics in mind, ask yourself these questions about each one.

- Is this a topic that I am interested in?
- Does it fulfill my assignment or my own purpose for writing?
- Is it appropriate for the length of paper I plan to write? Would I need to narrow or broaden this topic?
- Do I know enough about this topic, or can I find enough information?

Gathering information

How you gather your information will depend upon the kind of paper you are writing.

If you are writing a personal essay, all of the information may come from your own experiences and feelings. Try one or both of the following techniques.

- Freewriting Set a time limit of ten minutes, and write down everything that comes to mind on your topic. You might want to list your thoughts and images under general headings or make a cluster diagram.
- Discussion Talk about your topic with one or more people. Take notes on your ideas as they come to you. Encourage your listeners to ask you questions.

If you are writing a report or a persuasive essay, you will probably need to locate pertinent factual information and take notes on it. You may consult library resources, such as books, magazines, and newspapers, as well as the Internet and other on-line resources. You may also choose to interview people with experience or specialized knowledge related to your topic. (See Research Paper Writing, pp. R64–R69.)

Organizing your material

Determine the main points, subtopics, or events you will be writing about, and choose a general order in which to present them.

Sometimes the best order will be self-evident. For example, a biography usually calls for chronological order, and a description of a place may lend itself to spatial order, such as from near to far or from low to high. For other kinds of writing, such as science reports, you may need to experiment to find the best order.

After deciding on the general order, make a rough outline. It can be as simple as a list, or it can include headings and subheadings.

Drafting

In the drafting stage, use your notes and outline to write a rough version of your paper. Drafting is an opportunity to explore and develop your ideas.

Tips for drafting

- You might want to write your draft very quickly, capturing the rapid flow of your ideas; or you might wish to work more slowly, rethinking and revising as you write. Choose the approach that works better for you.
- Whether you work quickly or slowly, don't focus on details. Concentrate on developing the main ideas. At this stage, just circle or annotate minor points that need more work.
- Keep your purpose in mind, and use your outline as a general guideline. At the same time, try to stay flexible. If part of your outline doesn't work, omit it. If better ideas occur to you as you write, feel free to change your direction.

Revising

After you have finished your first draft, set it aside for a while. Then reread it, and look for ways to improve and refine it. This is the point at which peer review can be most helpful.

Using peer review

Ask one or more of your classmates to read your draft. Here are some specific ways in which you can direct their responses.

- Have readers tell you in their own words what they have read. If you do not hear your ideas restated, you will want to revise for clarity.
- Ask readers to tell you what parts of your writing they liked best and why. You may want to expand those elements when you revise.
- Discuss the ideas in your writing with your readers. Have them share their own ideas about the topic. Include in your revision any new insights you gain.
- Ask readers for their suggestions in specific areas, such as organization, word choice, or examples.

You may want to take notes on your readers' suggestions so you will have a handy reference as you revise. Finally, weigh your peer responses carefully. Compare them with your own insights. Use what is most helpful to write the revised draft.

Editing/Proofreading

In the editing stage, you polish your revised draft and proofread it for errors in grammar and spelling. Use this proofreading checklist to help you check for errors, and use the proofreading symbols in the chart below to mark places that need corrections.

- ☑ **Have I avoided run-on sentences and sentence fragments and punctuated sentences correctly?**
- ☑ **Have I used every word correctly, including plurals, possessives, and frequently confused words?**
- ☑ **Do verbs and subjects agree? Are verb tenses correct?**
- ☑ **Do pronouns refer clearly to their antecedents and agree with them in person, number, and gender?**
- ☑ **Have I used adverb and adjective forms and modifying phrases correctly?**
- ☑ **Have I spelled every word correctly, and checked the unfamiliar ones in a dictionary?**

Proofreading Symbols

Symbol	Example	Meaning
⊙	Lieut⊙Brown	Insert a period.
∧	No one came∧the party. (to)	Insert a letter or a word.
≡	I enjoyed paris.	Capitalize a letter.
/	The Class ran a bake sale.	Make a capital letter lowercase.
⁀ ‿	The campers are home sick.	Close up a space.
(sp)	They visited (N.Y.) (sp)	Spell out.
∧ ∧ (, ;)	Sue, please come; I need your help.	Insert a comma or a semicolon.
∩∪	He enjoyed feild day.	Transpose the position of letters or words.
#	alltogether	Insert a space.
℘	We went to to Boston.	Delete letters or words.
∨ ∨ ∨	She asked, "Who's coming?"	Insert quotation marks or an apostrophe.
/=/	mid January	Insert a hyphen.
¶	"Where?" asked Karl. ¶ "Over there," said Ray.	Begin a new paragraph.

Publishing/Presenting

There are a number of ways you can share your work. You could publish it in a magazine, a class anthology, or another publication, or read your writing aloud to a group. You could also join a writer's group and read one another's works.

Writing Modes

Writing may be classified as expository, descriptive, narrative, or persuasive. Each of these classifications, or modes, has its own purpose.

Expository Writing

Expository writing explains and compares. There are six types of expository writing. The kind of essay you write depends on your goal.

As you write an expository piece, use the checklist shown here as a guide.

- ☑ **Does my opening contain attention-grabbing details or intriguing questions to hook the reader?**
- ☑ **Are my explanations complete, clear, and accurate?**
- ☑ **Have I presented information in a logical order?**
- ☑ **Have I included specific, relevant details?**
- ☑ **Have I defined any unfamiliar terms and concepts?**
- ☑ **Have I made comparisons clear and logical?**
- ☑ **Have I used language and details appropriate for my intended audience?**

Type	Definition	Example
Process explanation	Explains how something happens, works, or is done, using step-by-step organization	How the human brain stores memories
Cause and effect	Identifies the causes and/or effects of something and examines the relationship between causes and effects	Causes of skin cancer
Comparison and contrast	Examines similarities and differences to find relationships and draw conclusions	The safety features of U.S. cars compared with those of imported models
Definition	Explains a term or concept by listing and examining its qualities and characteristics	The "Trail of Tears"
Classification	Organizes subjects into categories and examines the qualities or characteristics of those categories	Kinds of snakes native to this area
Problem and solution	Examines aspects of a complex problem and explores or proposes possible solutions	Providing community-wide access to parks and playgrounds

Descriptive Writing

Good descriptive writing creates word pictures of people, places, things, and experiences. It includes carefully chosen details that appeal to the reader's senses. Descriptive passages are a part of many kinds of writing, including novels, short stories, informative essays, biographies, poems, and persuasive speeches.

Use this checklist when you write a descriptive passage.

- ☑ Did I use an introduction that grabbed the reader?
- ☑ Were the images I used clear and striking?
- ☑ Did I organize details carefully and consistently?
- ☑ Did I use exact, energetic verbs to enliven my description?
- ☑ Did I write from a vantage point that makes sense?
- ☑ Have I used precise, vivid word choices?
- ☑ Have I created a strong, unified impression?

Narrative Writing

A narrative, whether fictional or nonfictional, tells a story. Narratives include novels and short stories as well as biographies, memoirs, narrative poems, and histories. Narratives typically include a setting, characters, and a plot, which revolves around a conflict of some sort.

As you write your narrative, use this checklist as a guide.

- ☑ Did I introduce characters, setting, plot, and conflict?
- ☑ Did I include descriptions and dialogue appropriate for the characters–whether fictional or nonfictional?
- ☑ Did I present a clear and consistent point of view?
- ☑ Is the conflict or complication interesting to my audience?
- ☑ Did I use mood, foreshadowing, or dialogue to move the story along?
- ☑ Is the writing vivid and expressive?
- ☑ Did I end in a way that satisfies my audience?

Persuasive Writing

Persuasive writing expresses a writer's opinion and tries to make readers agree with it, change their own opinion, and perhaps even take action. Effective persuasive writing uses strong, reliable evidence to support the claims. Persuasive writing is used in newspaper editorials, letters of complaint, advertisements, product evaluations, and many other applications.

This checklist offers a guide for writing a persuasive piece.

- ☑ Is my position stated in a clear thesis statement?
- ☑ Is the supporting evidence convincing?
- ☑ Have I anticipated and responded to opposing viewpoints?
- ☑ Are my facts and opinions relevant and credible?
- ☑ Does the conclusion relate to the evidence?
- ☑ Is the tone appropriate?
- ☑ Have I used strong, specific words to support my argument?
- ☑ Did I end with a strong call to action?

Research Paper Writing

A research paper presents the findings and conclusions of an inquiry into primary and secondary sources. Unlike personal essays in which you present your own thoughts and feelings, a research paper requires that you go beyond personal experience to search for facts, gather data, and evaluate evidence in order to draw a conclusion.

Types of Research Papers

Research papers can take many forms. Some of the most common approaches to writing a research paper are listed below. In some cases you might combine approaches, perhaps by evaluating the research of others and then conducting original research.

- A **summary** explores a topic by summing up the opinions of other writers. The author of the paper does not express an opinion about the subject.
- An **evaluative paper** states an opinion and backs it up with evidence found in primary and secondary sources.
- An **original paper** involves research that leads to new insights or information about the topic.

Making a plan

- Schedule ample time for your research. A good research paper can't be written in a weekend. Sketch out a schedule that allows several weeks for the completion of your paper.
- Select a general topic that interests and motivates you.
- Do some preliminary research to build background and identify available resources.
- To set a clear path for research, generate three to seven research questions to answer first. In trying to answer these questions, you will discover other questions. Let your central idea guide you in selecting questions–the answers will emerge later in the course of your research.
- Refine and/or focus the topic as appropriate.
- Examine the topic. Look at the material from various points of view. Don't worry if some angles lead to dead ends. At this point just try to think critically about the topic from several perspectives.

Choosing and evaluating sources

Kinds of sources There are two kinds of sources–primary and secondary.

A **primary source** is a firsthand account of an event–an account by someone who has actually experienced or observed the event–for example, the slave narrative written by Olaudah Equiano.

A **secondary source** is one written by a person who has done extensive research on the topic and who has interpreted primary sources. Although most sources on a topic will be secondary, make use of primary sources when they are available.

Criteria for evaluation Examine sources critically. As you search for sources, select those that are authoritative and timely.

- Choose those authors who have written widely on a subject and whose work in their field is recognized.
- Use articles from well-respected newspapers or scholarly journals; do not use material from popular magazines unless it can be verified in another source.
- Try to find the most recently published information on your topic.
- Be especially careful in evaluating on-line sources. Anyone can create a Web site; therefore, the information found in such a source is not always reliable. Before using information from on-line sources, apply the criteria identified for print materials.

Because every source you use is written by a person with particular interests, knowledge, and values, be alert to the author's perspective. Try to get sources that approach your topic from various points of view.

Preparing a working bibliography

A working bibliography is a record of the books, articles, and other sources you will consult for your paper. For each source you find, follow these steps:

1. Skim it to see if it has any useful information. Also look at tables of contents, indexes, chapter titles, and graphic aids to efficiently locate information.
2. If it does, record on an index card all the information needed for compiling the list of works. Be sure to include the author's name and the title.
3. Number your cards in the upper right-hand corner so you can keep them in order. You can also write yourself notes on the cards.

See the sample cards below for a book, a magazine, and an on-line article.

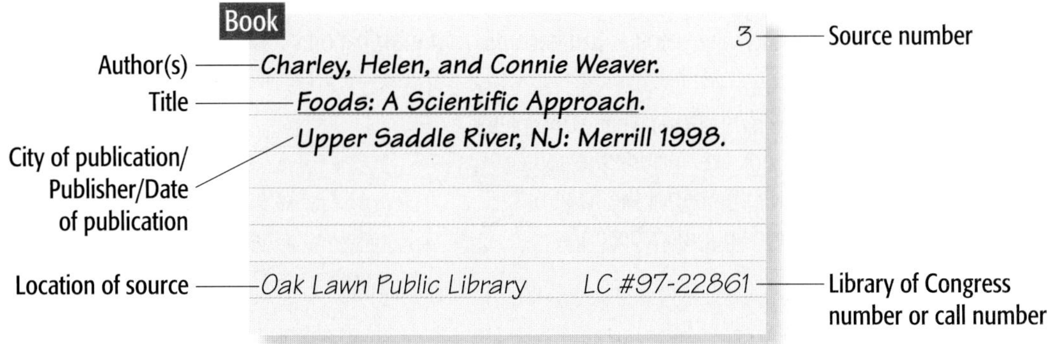

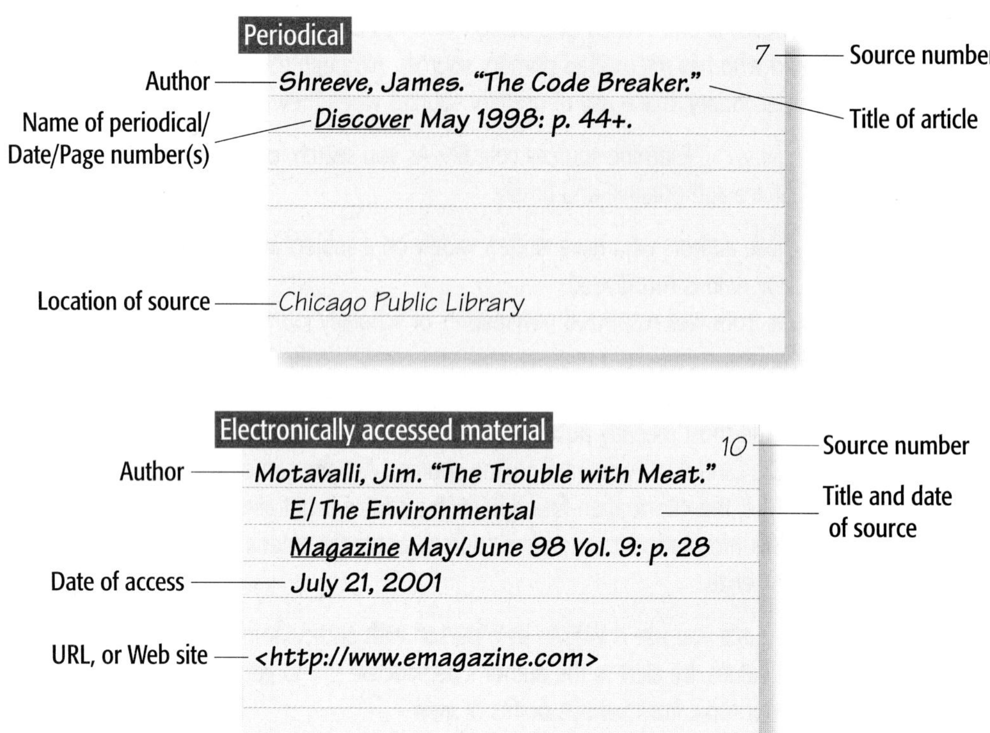

Taking careful notes

Use index cards when you take notes, and follow these guidelines:

- As you find information that you can use, note it on a card.
- In the upper right-hand corner of the note card, write the number of the source from the working bibliography.
- Place any exact words from the source in quotation marks.
- If you jot your own thoughts down on note cards, initial them so you can distinguish your own opinions from those that come from other sources.

> **Important** Avoid plagiarism. Plagiarism is using someone else's ideas or statements and presenting them as your own. Even when unintentional, plagiarism is a serious offense. Keep clearly documented notes so you know where you found each piece of information.

The card at the right shows what a completed note card will look like. Include the source number and the number of the page on which you found your information.

10
E. coli bacteria have become more widespread in the past thirty years. Eating infected food can result in hemolytic uremic syndrome (HUS), a condition that is life threatening.
"Meat-borne pathogens like Salmonella entenditis can be traced to 'factory farms.'"
p. 29

Developing an outline

Organize your note cards to develop a working outline.

- As you take notes, look for ways to classify the facts and ideas you find. For example, look for similar features, such as two facts about the role of an individual in a historical event, or two causes of the same effect.
- Begin to group the note cards as you classify them. As you make decisions on how to organize your cards, you are developing the headings you need to write a working outline.
- If some cards do not fit with any others, set them aside. Later you can decide whether to keep or discard them.

The following partial outline is based on chronological development. Note that in an outline, you cannot have a single subheading. If you have a *I,* you must have a *II;* if you have an *A,* you must have a *B,* and so on.

Sample Outline

Women in the Workplace

I. Prior to World War II

  A. Factors limiting women's employment outside the home

  B. Types of jobs assigned to women

  C. Percentage of women in the work force

II. From 1945 to 1975

  A. Factors promoting women's employment outside the home

  B. Continuing limitations

    1. Gender-specific job titles (secretary vs. executive assistant)

    2. Salary discrepancies for identical work by men and women

Writing a thesis statement

- To develop a thesis statement, rewrite your central idea into a concise, tightly focused sentence that describes your topic and your approach to it. Even though this thesis statement may change slightly in later stages of your writing process, it will provide a clear direction for your writing.
- The kind of thesis statement you use will depend upon the type of paper you write: summary, evaluative, original, or a combination of two or more types.

After you have made an outline and written a thesis statement, you are ready to proceed with drafting. As you draft your paper, be sure to document the information you include.

Documenting sources

The information in your research paper must be properly documented. By citing your sources accurately, you acknowledge those people whose ideas you are using. You do not have to cite the source of common knowledge, such as that the Andes are in South America or that the Magna Carta was signed in 1215. Widely known proverbs, famous quotations, and simple definitions are also considered common knowledge.

In-text citations The Modern Language Association (MLA) recommends using citations in the text of your writing that refer readers to a list of works cited at the end of the paper. The citation should appear at the end of the quotation or other material. The chart below shows the MLA style of documenting various sources.

Type of Source	Citation Style
Author named in text "According to M. Harte, . . ."	Page number in parentheses (52)
Author not named in text	Author's last name and page number in parentheses (Coogan 322)
More than one author is cited	Name all in text or authors' names and page number in parentheses (Lee, Sanford, Berlig 234)
No author listed	Title and page number in parentheses ("Lively Bacteria" 64)
More than one work in list by same author	Include words from title in reference (Sutford "Planetary Threat")
Quotation from another work	Use "qtd. in" (qtd. in Coogan 320)
Work from anthology	Cite author, not anthology editor
Novels; plays; poems	Page and chapter (43, ch. 8); part and line number (2:12–14); act and scene plus line number, if applicable (3.2:11–18)
Multivolume work	Include volume number (Durand 2:167)

Note: For material accessed on CD-ROM or on-line databases, follow the style of in-text references for print materials. See below for the style of their inclusion in works cited.

Compiling a list of works cited

At the end of your text, provide an alphabetized list of works cited.

- Include complete publishing information for each source.
- Cite only those sources from which you actually used information.
- Arrange entries in alphabetical order according to the author's (or editor's) last name. Write the last name first.
- If an entry runs more than one line, indent five spaces every line after the first.

WORKS CITED

One author — Barber, Elizabeth Wayland. *Women's Work: The First 20,000 Years.* New York: Norton, 1995. — Book

Bolz, Diane M. "Women and Flight." *Smithsonian* July 1997: 90+. — Magazine

Two or more authors — Brown, Clair, and Joseph A. Pechman. *Gender in the Workplace.* Washington, D.C.: Brookings, 1987. — Reverse only the first author's name.

No author given — "The Convention on the Elimination of All Forms of Discrimination Against Women." United Nations Division for Advancement of Women. 9 Mar. 2001 <http://www.un.org/womenwatch/daw/cedaw/conven.htm>. — Alphabetize by title, disregarding the word *a, an,* or *the* at the beginning of a title.

Online source — Rosie the Riveter: Women Join the Workforce. 4 Dec. 1999 American Airpower Heritage Museum. 1 Feb. 2001 <http://www.airpowermuseum.org/trrosier.html>. — Include sponsor of the site, date of access, and URL.

More than one work by an author — Ware, Susan. *Letter to the World: Seven Women Who Shaped the American Century.* New York: Norton, 1998.

---. *Modern American Women: A Documentary History.* Belmont, California: Wadsworth, 1988. — Use three hyphens followed by a period in place of the author's last name.

Note: Titles of books and magazines are in italic type or underlined; titles of articles are placed in quotation marks.

Preparing a manuscript

Follow the guidelines of the Modern Language Association when you prepare the final copy of your research paper.

- **Heading** On separate lines in the upper left-hand corner of the first page, include your name, your teacher's name, the course name, and the date.
- **Title** Center the title on the line below the heading.
- **Numbering** Number the pages one-half inch from the top of the page in the right-hand corner. Write your last name before each page number after the first page.
- **Spacing** Use double-spacing throughout.
- **Margins** Leave one-inch margins on all sides of every page.

Business and Technical Writing

Business and technical writing are kinds of expository writing that explain information and processes to people within various professions.

Business writing includes documents such as letters, memorandums, reports, briefs, proposals, and articles for business publications. Business writing must be clear, concise, accurate, and correct in usage.

Technical writing is expository writing that informs readers about specialized areas of science and technology, such as anthropology, biology, chemistry, computer science, engineering, electronics, and psychology. Technical writing is practical and objective, focusing on the technical content rather than on the author's perspective on the subject. Technical writing encompasses user guides and manuals, data sheets describing software or equipment, operator's manuals, business reports, and writing for newsletters in fields such as business, health, and science.

Writing a business letter

- Use proper business letter form.
- Whenever possible, address your letter to a specific person.
- Explain exactly what you are requesting in a businesslike tone.

The letter below illustrates the block form, a popular style for a business letter.

Alan Shephard High School
123 Washington Way
Oak Center, IL 60308
August 27, 20__

Carol Bosley

TV Channel 2
1 Merchandise Mart
Chicago, IL 60602

Dear Ms. Bosley:

On March 15, Alan Shephard High School will have its semiannual career day. We cordially invite you to address the students on the career of broadcast journalism.

The program is scheduled for 2 P.M. We anticipate that you will speak for twenty to thirty minutes with an additional time for questions. We are inviting two other speakers in the areas of business and science. If the time conflicts with other commitments you may have, we will be happy to adjust our schedule.

We would appreciate your prompt response to Dr. Harry Belding, Principal. The school phone number is 708-536-9887, or you may respond by E-mail to shephard@ilsch.edu.

Yours truly,

Peter Bianco

Sentence completion

Sentence completion items provide a sentence with one or two blanks and ask you to select the word or pair of words that best fits in the blank(s).

Start by reading the sentence and filling in your own word to replace the blank. Look for words that show how the word in the blank is related to the rest of the sentence–*and, but, since, therefore, although.* Then pick the word from the answer choices that is closest in meaning to your word. If you have trouble coming up with a specific word to fill in the blank, try to determine whether the word should be positive or negative. If you can eliminate even one answer choice, take a guess at the answer.

Reading comprehension

In Reading Comprehension, a series of questions follows each passage.

Read the passages quickly and spend your time working on the questions. You get points for answering questions correctly, not for reading passages thoroughly. Briefly summarize the passage. This will help you answer questions based on the passage as a whole. For specific questions based on details, return to the passage. Reading Comprehension is like an open-book test; you are expected to look at the passage while answering the questions. Finally, if you can eliminate even one answer choice, take a guess at the answer.

Analogies

Nearly half of the items on the verbal sections of the PSAT and SAT-I are designed to test your vocabulary. Therefore, the more words you know, the higher your score will be. Refer to pages R78–R81 of the **Reading Handbook** for information on how to build your vocabulary.

One type of vocabulary-based question is the analogy, which tests your ability to grasp the relationships between concepts. The best way to pinpoint the relationship is to connect the words in a simple sentence that defines one of the words. Some of the most common relationships seen on the PSAT and the SAT-I are shown below.

Relationship	Example
Cause and effect	heat : perspiration :: sadness : tears
A person to the normal action of that person	comedian : amuse :: journalist : write
An object to its normal function	telescope : magnify :: aircraft : fly
User to tool	teacher : book :: carpenter : hammer
Degree	terrified : frightened :: destitute : poor
Object to characteristic	water : wet :: brick : hard
Class to subclass (or subclass to class)	grain : rye :: music : rap

Reading Handbook

The Reading Process

Being an active reader is a very important part of being a lifelong learner. It is also an ongoing task. Good reading skills build on each other, overlap, and spiral around in much the same way that a winding staircase goes round and round while leading you to a higher place.

This handbook is designed to help you find and use the tools you'll need before, during, and after reading.

Vocabulary Development

Word identification and vocabulary skills are key building blocks in reading and in the comprehension process. By learning to use a variety of strategies to build your word skills and vocabulary, you will become a stronger reader.

Using context to determine meaning

The very best way to expand and extend your vocabulary is to read widely, listen carefully, and participate in a rich variety of discussions. When reading on your own, though, you can often figure out the meanings of new words by looking at their **context,** the other words and sentences that surround them. For example:

> *Contiguous* countries, such as the United States and Canada, usually have border patrols.

Although you may not know the meaning of *contiguous,* you can figure out from the phrase *such as the United States and Canada* that the word means "adjoining."

Tips for Using Context

- **Look for clues such as**
  - –a synonym or an explanation of the unknown word in the sentence.
    *Elise's shop specialized in **millinery,** or **hats for women.***
  - –a reference to what the word is or is not like.
    *An **archaeologist,** like a **historian,** deals with the past.*
  - –a general topic associated with the word.
    *The **cooking** teacher discussed the best way to **braise** meat.*
  - –a description or action associated with the word.
    *He used the **hoe** to **dig** up the garden.*
- **Predict a possible meaning.**

- **Determine whether the meaning makes sense in terms of the whole passage.**
- **Be aware the writer may be using**
  –a word with **multiple meanings.**
    Some of the group will play games; others will attend a play.
  –**figurative language,** such as **similes,** which use *like* or *as* to compare two unlike things, and **metaphors,** which compare two unlike things without using *like* or *as.*
    The leaves rustled like silk as they drifted to the ground. (simile)
    The bullets of rain pelted the sidewalk. (metaphor)
  –**idioms,** expressions that have a meaning apart from the literal one.
    I'm just pulling your leg is an idiom used about joking with someone.
    Hint: If you come across an idiom with an unfamiliar meaning, look in the dictionary under the main word in the phrase. Many dictionaries list idioms after the definitions.
  –**technical vocabulary,** words that require an understanding of the specific terms of a specialized field.
    Be sure to clean your **mouse** *from time to time to make the* **cursor** *move smoothly.*

● For more on figurative language, see **Literary Terms Handbook,** p. R4.

Using word parts and word origins

Another way to determine the meaning of a word is to take the word itself apart. If you understand the meaning of the **base,** or **root,** part of a word and also know the meanings of key syllables added either to the beginning or end of the base word, you can usually figure out what the word means.

Word Part	Definition	Example
Base or root	the most basic part of a word	*voc* means "call" *Convoke* means "call together."
Prefix	a syllable placed before a base word to change or add to its meaning	*inter-* means "between" *Intervene* means "come between."
Suffix	a syllable placed after a base word to create a new meaning	*-less* means "without" *Hopeless* means without hope

Word origins Since Latin, Greek, and Anglo-Saxon roots are the basis for much of our English vocabulary, having some background in one of these languages can be a useful vocabulary tool. For example, *astronomy* comes from the Greek root *astro,* which means "relating to the stars." *Stellar* also has a meaning referring to stars, but its origin is Latin. Knowing root words in other languages can help you determine meanings, derivations, and spellings in English.

Using vocabulary references

Dictionaries A dictionary provides the meaning or meanings of a word. Look at the sample dictionary entry below to see what other information it provides.

Forms of the word

Usage label

Part of speech

Numbered definitions

Examples of use

Idioms

Synonyms

Origin (etymology)

help (help) **helped** or *(archaic)* **holp, helped** or *(archaic)* **hol-pen, help-ing.** *v.t.* **1.** to provide with support, as in the performance of a task; be of service to: *He helped his brother paint the room.* ▲ also used elliptically with a preposition or adverb: *He helped the old woman up the stairs.* **2.** to enable (someone or something) to accomplish a goal or achieve a desired effect: *The coach's advice helped the team to win.* **3.** to provide with sustenance or relief, as in time of need or distress; succor: *The Red Cross helped the flood victims.* **4.** to promote or contribute to; further. *The medication helped his recovery.* **5.** to be useful or profitable to; be of advantage to: *It might help you if you read the book.* **6.** to improve or remedy: *Nothing really helped his sinus condition.* **7.** to prevent; stop: *I can't help his rudeness.* **8.** to refrain from; avoid: *I couldn't help smiling when I heard the story.* **9.** to wait on or serve (often with *to*): *The clerk helped us. The hostess helped him to the dessert.* **10. cannot help but.** *Informal* cannot but. **11. so help me (God).** oath of affirmation. **12. to help oneself to.** to take or appropriate: *The thief helped himself to all the jewels.* *–v.i.* to provide support, as in the performance of a task; be of service. *–n.* **1.** act of providing support, service, or sustenance. **2.** source of support, service, or sustenance. **3.** person or group of persons hired to work for another or others. **4.** means of improving, remedying, or preventing. [Old English *helpan* to aid, succor, benefit.] **Syn.** *v.t.* **1. Help, aid, assist** mean to support in a useful way. **Help** is the most common word and means to give support in response to a known or expressed need or for a definite purpose: *Everyone helped to make the school fair a success.* **Aid** means to give relief in times of distress or difficulty: *It is the duty of rich nations to aid the poor.* **Assist** means to serve another person in the performance of his task in a secondary capacity: *The secretary assists the officer by taking care of his correspondence.*

Thesauruses These references provide synonyms and often antonyms. Some dictionaries and thesauruses are available on CD-ROM and on the Internet.

Glossaries Many textbooks and technical works contain condensed dictionaries that provide an alphabetical listing of words used in the text and their specific definitions. The example on page R81 is from a social studies textbook.

Glossary

A

abolitionist 1800s reformer who worked to end slavery (p. 342)
acid rain acid precipitation in the form of rain (p. 1016)
agribusiness large farming operation that includes the cultivation, processing, storage, and distribution of farm products (p. 869)
amendment alteration to the Constitution (p. 160)
amnesty act of a government by which pardon is granted to an individual or groups of persons (p. 445)
anarchism a belief in no direct government authority over society (p. 531)
anarchist one who opposes all forms of government (p. 616)

Identifying word relationships

Determining the relationships of words to each other also aids comprehension. Some special word relationships include analogies, synonyms, antonyms, denotation, and connotation.

- **Denotation** A denotation expresses the exact meaning of a word. A word may have more than one denotation, but all of its denotations will be listed in the dictionary. Notice, for example, all the denotations for the word *help* listed in the dictionary entry on page R80.
- **Connotation** Connotation refers to an emotion or an underlying value that accompanies a word's dictionary meaning. When the word *leper* is used, you know that the word refers to someone suffering from a specific disease, but its connotation includes feelings of disgust or pity and suggests separation from familiar surroundings.

TRY THE STRATEGIES

Play a game of Word Clues. Each player chooses a word that has been used in class in the past two weeks and coins a nonsense word to represent it. Player One writes a sentence on the board using his or her nonsense word in an appropriate context. Players who can identify the word from the context raise their hands. Each scores five points for a correct identification. If no one is able to identify the word, Player One supplies a synonym or antonym for it. Players who identify the word correctly after the second clue score three points. If no one identifies the word, Player One gets a one-point penalty and the next player repeats the procedure. When time is up, the player with the most points wins.

Comprehension Strategies

Reading comprehension means understanding–deriving meaning from–what you have read. Using a variety of strategies can help you improve your comprehension and make reading more interesting and more fun.

Previewing

Before beginning a selection, it's helpful to **preview** what you are about to read.

- **Read** the title, headings, and subheadings of the selection.
- **Look** at the illustrations and notice how the text is organized.
- **Skim** the selection; that is, take a quick glance at the whole thing.
- **Decide** what the author's purpose might be.
- **Predict** what the selection will be about.
- **Set a purpose** for your reading.

Establishing a purpose for reading

To get the greatest benefit from what you read, you should **establish a purpose for reading.** Some purposes for reading are

- to enjoy
- to find information, to discover
- to interpret
- to follow directions or take action
- to be persuaded about an issue
- to appreciate a writer's craft
- to find models for your own writing

Vary your reading strategies to fit the different purposes you have when you read. If you are reading for entertainment, you might read quickly, but if you read to gather information or follow directions, you might read more slowly, take notes, construct a graphic organizer, or reread sections of text.

TRY THE STRATEGIES

Look through a newspaper or a magazine at home or at the library. Preview three or four articles using the strategies listed under Previewing. Then decide what your purpose for reading would be for each of the articles selected. Which of the articles should you read slowly? Which might you read quickly? In a small group, discuss your purposes for reading and why your reading speed would differ from article to article.

Drawing on personal background

Good reading is an interactive process between the writer and each different person reading a selection. Even the youngest child has a body of information and personal experiences which are important and uniquely his or her own. When you draw on your personal background, combining it with the words on a page, you create meaning in a selection. Drawing on this personal background is also called **activating prior knowledge.** To expand and extend your prior knowledge, share it in active classroom discussions.

Ask yourself questions like these:

- What do I know about this topic?
- What familiar places have similar settings?
- What experiences have I had that compare or contrast with what I am reading?
- What characters from life or literature remind me of the characters or narrator in the selection?

Making and verifying predictions

As you read, take educated guesses about story events and outcomes; that is, **make predictions** before and during reading. Using your prior knowledge and the information you have gathered in your preview, you can predict what you will learn or what might happen in a selection. Then use information you gather as you read to adjust or **verify your predictions.** Have you ever read a mystery, decided who committed the crime, and then changed your mind as more clues emerged? You were adjusting your predictions. Or did you shriek with delight or smile smugly when you found out you guessed the murderer? You were verifying your predictions. Careful predictions and verifications increase your comprehension of a selection.

TRY THE STRATEGIES

Find a selection from your social studies or science textbook. First, preview the title, illustrations, and available headings and subheadings to determine what the piece might be about or what might happen. On your own paper, write your predictions about what you will read. Then, as you read, revise your predictions based on new information and your own background or prior knowledge.

Monitoring and modifying reading strategies

No matter what your purpose for reading, your most important task is to understand what you have read. Try having a conversation with yourself as you work through a selection. **Check,** or **monitor, your understanding,** using the following strategies:

- Summarize
- Clarify
- Ask questions
- Predict what will come next

This might be done once or twice in an easy, entertaining selection, or after every paragraph in a nonfiction selection, dense with new concepts.

One way of questioning yourself is to pretend that you are the teacher trying to determine if your students have understood the main ideas of a selection. What questions would you ask? Be sure that you can answer those questions before you read on.

Tips for Monitoring Understanding

- Reread.
- Make a graphic organizer, such as a chart or a diagram, to help sort out your thoughts.
- Consult other sources, including text resources, teachers and other students.
- Write comments or questions on another piece of paper for later review or discussion.

Use or modify whatever strategy fits your learning style, but don't settle for not understanding. Be an active reader.

Visualizing

Try to form a mental picture of scenes, characters, and events as you read. Use the details and descriptions the author gives you. According to your imagination and the text, what do the characters look like? What does the setting look like? Can you picture the steps in a process when you read nonfiction? If you can **visualize** what you read, selections will be more interesting. When someone reads aloud to you, try sketching what you're hearing–you'll be more likely to recall it later.

Constructing graphic organizers

Graphic organizers help you reconstruct ideas in a visual way, so you can remember them later on. You might make a **chart** or **diagram,** showing the information the author provides.

Venn diagrams When mapping out a comparison-and-contrast text structure, you can use a Venn diagram. The outer portions of the circles will show how two characters, ideas, or items contrast, or are different, and the overlapping part will show how they are similar, or compare them.

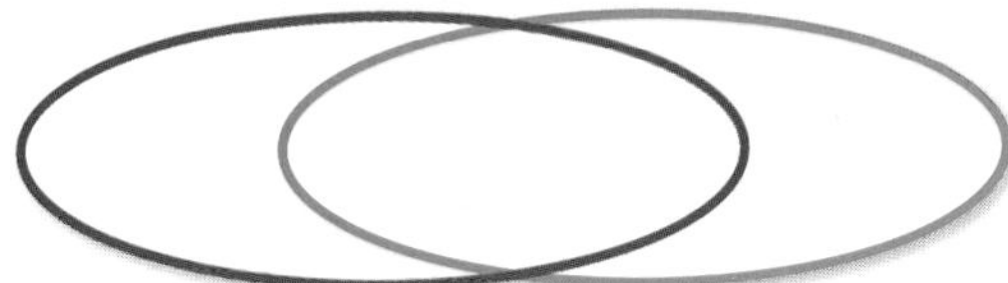

Flow charts To help you keep track of the sequence of events, use a flow chart. Arrange ideas or events in their logical, sequential order. Then draw arrows between your ideas to indicate how one idea or event flows into another. Look at the following flow chart to see how you can map out story events in chronological order or show cause and effect relationships.

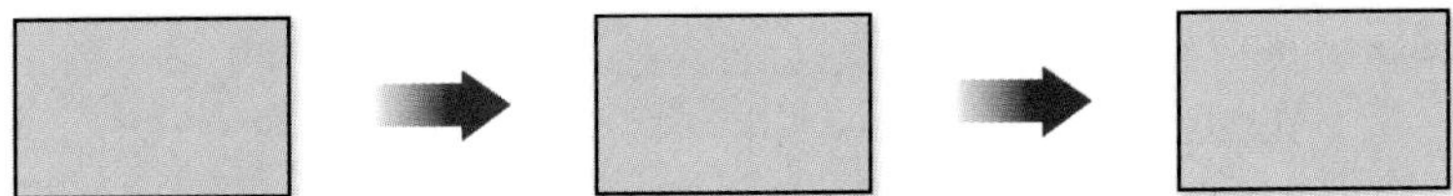

Web To help you determine a main idea and supporting details, use a web. Surround the main idea with examples or supporting details. Then create additional circles, branching off from the supporting details, to add related thoughts.

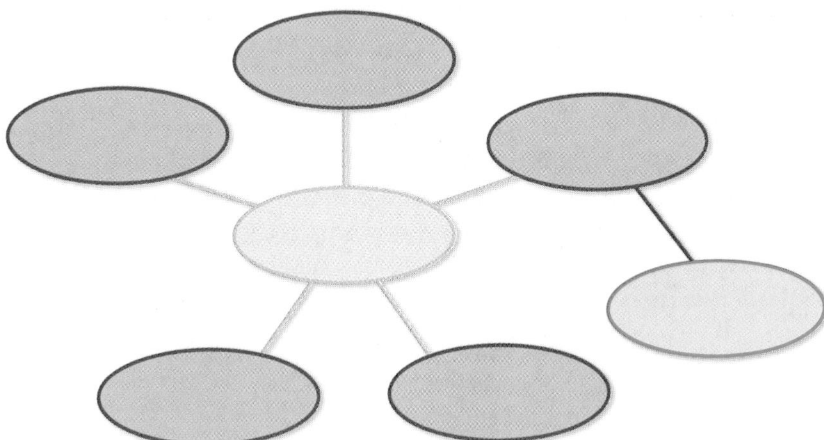

READING HANDBOOK

Analyzing text structures

Writers organize their written work in various ways, depending on their topic and purpose. Finding and analyzing that pattern of organization or **text structure** helps you to understand what an author is trying to say. Here are three important ways that writers structure or organize text:

Kind of Organization	Purpose	Clues
Comparison and contrast	To determine similarities and differences	Words and phrases like *similarly, on the other hand, in contrast to, but, however*
Cause and effect	To explore the reasons for something and to examine the results of events or actions	Words and phrases like *because* and *as a result*
Chronological order	To present events in time order	Words and phrases like *first, next, then, later,* and *finally*

Writers may embed one kind of structure within another, but it is usually possible to identify one main pattern of organization that will help you discover an author's purpose and will focus your attention on the important ideas in the selection.

Read the following example. Analyze the text structure used.

Two high school athletes who have attracted the attention of state high school tennis fans are Cleo Whittington and Tessa Levine. Two great players could hardly be more different. Cleo is a left-hander who depends on her lightning serve and ground strokes to overpower her opponents. Tessa is right-handed, hits her backhand with two hands, and outlasts other players with an endless stream of smooth shots as if she were a human backboard. Cleo displays her emotions, while Tessa is known for her blank expression on the court.

Cleo was born in Jamaica, but she and her family moved here when she was in eighth grade. Although she had not played tennis in Jamaica, she seemed to have been born with a tennis racquet in her hand. In her freshman year, she tried out for the tennis team. After one month, she was moved to the varsity team because no other freshman girls offered her competition.

Tessa, on the other hand, grew up playing tennis with her family. She began playing in tournaments at age nine. Her goal has always been to make a name for herself as a tennis pro.

Throughout their years in high school, Cleo and Tessa have been friendly rivals. Both were delighted when they were chosen to represent their school in the Regional Junior Championship Tournament at Forest Park on Long Island.

What is the basic text structure of the previous paragraphs? How do you know? What words help you to see the structure? How could you show this information on a graphic organizer?

TRY THE STRATEGIES

Find a selection in your literature, social studies, or science textbook and determine its text structure. Look for important clues. Use the chart on page R86 to help you in your determination.

Interpreting graphic aids

Graphic aids provide an opportunity to see and analyze information at a glance. Some effective graphic aids include maps, charts, tables, and diagrams. To interpret any of these graphic aids, you need to understand how the information presented is organized.

Reading a map Maps are flat representations of land, with other features included. A **compass rose** helps a reader to determine direction. A **legend** explains the map's symbols, while a **scale** shows the relationship of the map size to the land represented. A map may show physical features, political divisions, or historical data.

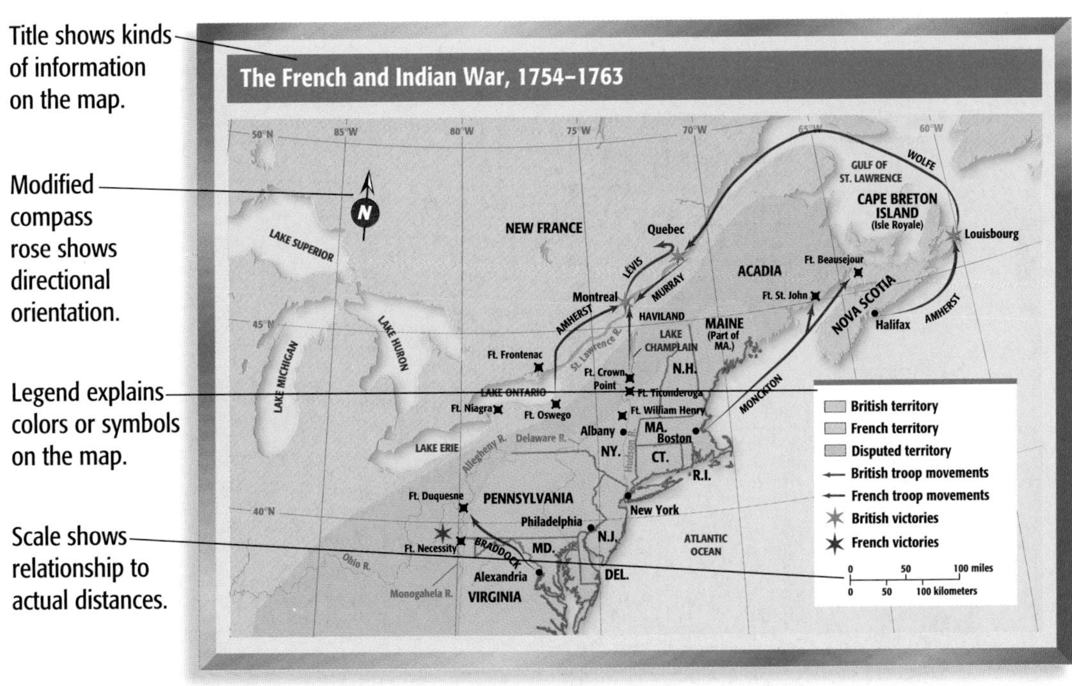

Refer to the map to answer these questions. What route did British General Wolfe take to reach Quebec? Where did the French secure victories?

Reading a chart Charts help you compare and analyze information. In charts or tables, information is presented in rows and columns.

Video Rentals and Sales (in millions)		
Year	Video Rental	Video Sales
1986	$3,308	$810
1987	$4,168	$1,004
1988	$5,210	$1,483
1989	$6,096	$2,240
1990	$6,645	$2,800

Title of chart
Column heads
Data

Between which two years did video rentals make the biggest jump? What conclusions can you draw about video sales over the five years from 1986 to 1990? Based on the trend shown on this chart, how might you expect the number of video rentals to have changed over the next five years, to 1995?

Reading a graph The relationship between two or more elements can be shown in a graph, using dots, bars, or lines. Look at the title of the graph and the labels. Be sure you understand what they mean. The labels on the bottom of line graphs tell you what each vertical line represents. In this case, the lines represent different years, and the vertical labels refer to thousands of automobiles. The source, shown below the graph, tells you where the data comes from. The title of this graph tells you that you will be comparing auto sales in the years from 1920 to 1929.

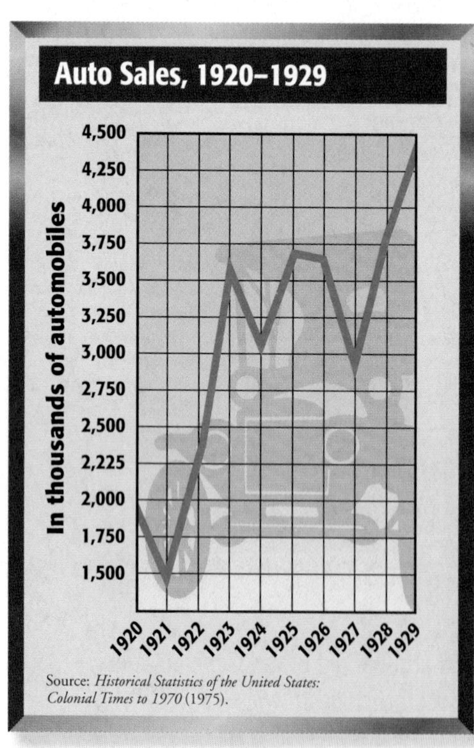

Source: *Historical Statistics of the United States: Colonial Times to 1970* (1975).

In what year were auto sales the lowest? How many cars were sold in 1925?

Reading a diagram A diagram illustrates the parts of an item. You might see a diagram of a bicycle, for instance, with arrows identifying the name of each part. Diagrams can also illustrate how a process functions. The diagram below illustrates how heat energy is turned into electricity.

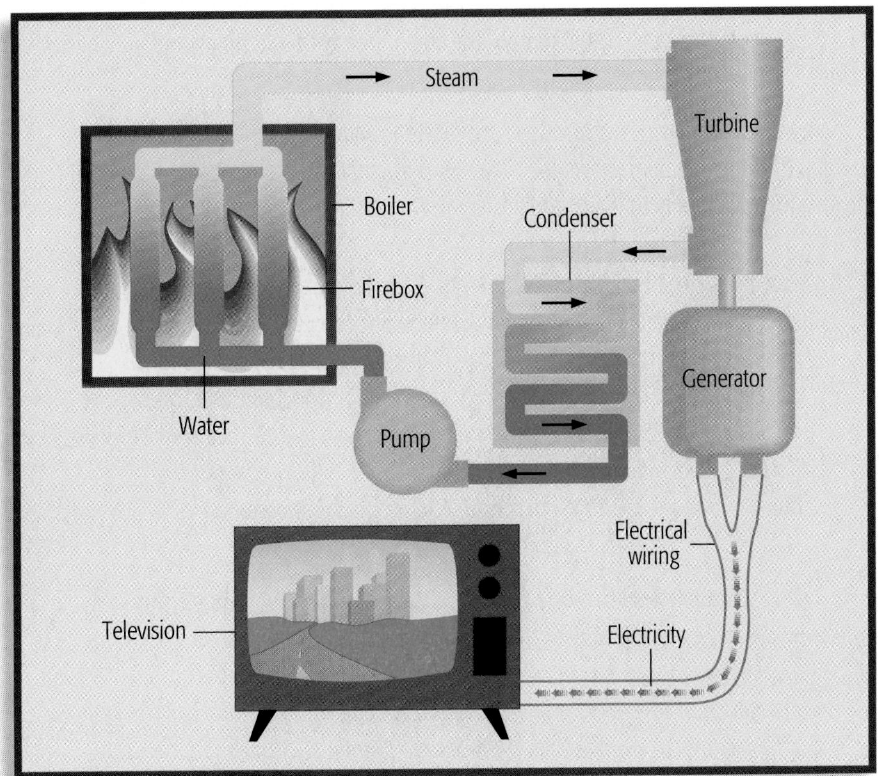

TRY THE STRATEGIES

In your social studies or science text, locate a section that uses a graphic aid. What kind of information is presented graphically? Read and interpret the information using the graphic aid, and then, on your paper, explain why the visual representation successfully presents the material.

Sequencing

The order in which thoughts are arranged is called **sequence.** A good sequence is logical, given the ideas presented. Three common forms of sequencing are

- Chronological order
- Spatial order
- Order of importance

Recognizing the sequence of something is particularly important when **following complex written directions.** If a written sequence is illogical or incomplete, or if you fail to precisely follow steps in a given order, you may be unable to complete an important task such as taking a test or locating a destination when driving a car.

Identifying main ideas and supporting details

As you read, it is important to identify the **main idea** of a paragraph or passage. Works of fiction and nonfiction can express one or more main ideas. In a single paragraph, the main idea will be the thought that organizes that paragraph and around which all other sentences are built. Some writers directly state the main idea in a topic sentence, while others imply the main idea with examples and other clues.

Read a paragraph carefully. Then decide if one sentence states the main, organizing thought, or if that thought is implied. Once you identify the main idea, you can use the **supporting details** to learn additional information about the main idea.

The next big breakthrough in fighting lung cancer may be as simple as a beam of light. **Doctors are now experimenting with lasers to kill tumors in patients.** *The new treatment is called photodynamic therapy. Most patients prefer the new treatment to the old style of operation. It's faster, less frightening for the patient, and even costs less. The method is still being studied, but the early results hold promise. One study showed a success rate of almost eighty percent.*

Main idea — Supporting details

The treatment works like photosynthesis in plants, using light to set off a chemical reaction. *First the patient is injected with a drug that is sensitive to light. The drug travels through the bloodstream to cancerous cells. Then a scope is slid into the lung, where it emits a red-light laser. The light causes the drug to change into a form of oxygen that inflames the tumor. As the cancer cells die, they fall away from the lung like dead skin.*

Main idea — Chronological order — Supporting details

Paraphrasing

When you **paraphrase,** you put something you've read into your own words. You might paraphrase just the main ideas, or you might retell an entire story in your own words. You need to understand something thoroughly in order to put it into your own words, so paraphrasing is a useful strategy for reviewing and for judging if you've understood what you've read.

- **Original** Doctors are now experimenting with lasers to kill tumors in patients. The new treatment is called photodynamic therapy. Most patients prefer the new treatment to the old style of operation. It's faster, less frightening for the patient, and even costs less. The method is still being studied, but the early results hold promise.
- **Paraphrase** Patients are enjoying a new experimental laser therapy used to treat tumors. It's not scary, it's quicker and cheaper, and it seems to work.

Summarizing

When you **summarize** you relate the main ideas of a selection in a logical sequence and in your own words. You are combining three skills in one. To create a good summary, include all the main ideas. Answer who, what, where, why, how, and when if that information is included in the passage. Do not include anything that is not important. A good summary can be easily understood by someone who has not read the whole text or selection. If you're not sure if an idea is a main idea or a detail, try taking it out of your summary. Does your summary still sound complete?

Look at the following summary of the passage on photodynamic therapy.

> There's a new photodynamic laser treatment that kills tumors and is quicker and cheaper than surgery. Patients like the therapy, and studies indicate that it works. Like photosynthesis in plants, the treatment uses light to set off a chemical reaction. The laser triggers a drug that kills the cancer cells and makes the tumor fall away.

TRY THE STRATEGIES

Read "Life in Benin" on page 90 of your text. On separate paper, list the main ideas of the selection. Under each main idea, list the major supporting details that explain it. Use this information to write a summary of what you have read. Be sure that you do not use the writer's words. Paraphrase the writer's ideas in your own words.

Drawing and supporting inferences

Authors don't always directly state what they want you to understand in a selection. By providing clues and interesting details, they imply certain information. Whenever readers combine those clues with their own background and knowledge, they are drawing an inference. An **inference** involves using your reason and experience to come up with an idea, based on what an author implies or suggests. The following active reading behaviors help you infer:

- **Predicting** When you predict what a story will be about, or guess what will happen next, you are drawing an inference.
- **Drawing conclusions** A conclusion is a general statement you can make and explain with reasoning, or with supporting details from a text. If you read a story describing a sport where five players bounce a ball and throw it through a hoop, you may conclude that the sport is basketball.
- **Making generalizations** When readers make generalizations, they draw an inference that can apply to more than one item or group. This inference has a more general scope than a prediction or a conclusion. If you read articles

about how the Sioux people revere the crane and how the Cherokee believe strongly in protecting our natural resources, you might generalize that Native Americans respect nature.

What is most important when drawing inferences is to be sure that you have accurately based your guesses on supporting details from the text, as well as on your own knowledge. If you cannot point to a place in the selection to help back up your inference, you may need to rethink your guess.

Having walked home from school in a cool rain, Patricia trudged inside and tossed her wet coat on the throw rug. Her umbrella stood dripping in the entryway. "Patty, did you shut the front door?" her father called from his study down the hall. "Yes, Dad," she replied, and slowly moved back to pull the door closed. Her father was always checking up on her. Then she turned on the TV in the living room and went to the kitchen to make a snack. Patricia removed the mustard, lettuce, and bologna from the refrigerator and began looking for the bread. The theme song of her favorite afternoon TV show enticed her back into the living room.

At the first commercial break, Patricia decided to take a nice hot bath. In the bathroom off the back hallway, she turned on the tub faucet and tested the water several times with two fingers to make sure it was the correct temperature. Over the rush of the faucet she could hear the laugh track on TV, and she returned to the living room sofa.

It wasn't long before the phone rang. Patricia's best friend, Trudy, had a lengthy story to tell about that new boy from Idaho. Patricia sat watching TV and yawning and nodding at Trudy's story, feeling glad that she hadn't a worry in the world.

It wasn't until she noticed her dog's wet paws that a growing awareness came over her. Just then she heard her father's booming voice.

What inferences might you draw from the paragraphs above? What supporting details would support your inferences? Can you make a prediction or draw a conclusion from the information given? Is there enough information to support a generalization? Why or why not?

TRY THE STRATEGIES

Together with several other students, silently read several pages from a selection none of you has previously read. On your own paper, write down any inferences you can draw from the material you read. Compare your inferences within your group.

Using study strategies

All students face important studying tasks. Finding the right strategy will depend on the task you face. You may need to study for a quiz or a test, or make a class presentation with a group or by yourself. In each case you will want to pick the strategy which is most efficient and which helps you to organize and remember the material you need. Some useful study strategies include:

- **Skimming and scanning** If you want to refresh your memory about a passage you've read or get a general overview of new material, **skim** the pages by glancing quickly over the entire selection. It will focus your attention on the main ideas and the author's purpose. If you need to go back and find a particular piece of information, **scan** the selection, looking for key words or phrases that will point you to the specific information you need. You don't need to look at the whole selection. As you scan, look for section headings or terms in **boldfaced** type.
- **Using and creating study guides** It is often helpful to use end of chapter questions to guide you while you read. You can also create your own guide by turning headings and subheadings into questions to answer as you read. Don't forget to consider captions underneath illustrations when thinking up questions to help focus your attention. Use the guide to help you review aloud or silently.
- **Reviewing** Active readers go back over selections again and again. They combine their notes, outlines, and study guides to provide themselves with different ways of approaching the same information. The more you review information from different angles, the better you'll recall it when you need to.
- **Using KWL** A KWL is a good device for charting expository information. Make three columns on a page. Label the first column *What I Know,* the second column *What I Want to Know,* and the third column *What I Learned.* You can also add more columns to record places where you found information and places where you can look for more information.

TRY THE STRATEGIES

Skim a few chapters in a history textbook to find examples of comparison and contrast, chronological order, and cause and effect. Make graphic organizers to create a visual presentation of the ideas you have just read. Use these organizers to study the material.

For more about study strategies, see **Communications Skills Handbook,** pp. R74–R77.

Reading silently for sustained periods

What things keep you on track when you read? Do you need total silence to concentrate well, or does some soft background music help you stay focused? Whatever your preference, it is important to avoid distractions or interruptions when you have to read silently for any length of time.

Tips for Reading Silently

- Be sure you're comfortable, but not too comfortable.
- Once your external surroundings are set, it's important to maintain your concentration and check your comprehension regularly.
- Using a study guide or a concept web can help you get through difficult nonfiction passages. Your teacher may provide a guide, or you can use questions from the end of the material to guide you.
- When you read fiction, a story map or other graphic organizer will help you stay focused on the important elements of the selection.
- Take regular breaks when you need them, and vary your reading rate with the demands of the text.

TRY THE STRATEGIES

Choose one or more longer selections in this book. Block out a period of time during which you won't be interrupted. Make sure you are in a comfortable spot where you can concentrate. Read silently until you finish the selection. Then use the **Responding to Literature** questions that follow the selection to monitor your comprehension.

Reading Across Texts and Cultures

One of the most important student tasks is to read widely and to integrate information from different sources to create new knowledge. Throughout this text you have read both classic and contemporary works, looking at themes from different perspectives, from different cultures, and for different purposes. As a citizen of the world, and not just your own country, you have examined world literature through the eyes of history and with a view toward the future. Every time you discussed a selection, interpreted a theme, or analyzed a writer's purpose, you created new knowledge for yourself and your classmates.

Reading in varied sources

Depending on the type of source material they are creating, writers may use a variety of styles and settings to tell the same story or cover the same subject. Each source gives specific information in a particular way. For instance, if you were researching the American artist Georgia O'Keeffe, you might first locate some basic facts about her in a book on art history. A biography might give you additional details about her life. Then, if you searched her personal writings, such as letters and diaries, you would collect information from the artist's own perspective. Whatever sources you use, it's important to be able to organize and evaluate information, combining or synthesizing what you learn from varied sources to create something for your own purposes.

For instance, to learn about the history of your hometown or region, you might read and refer to a variety of texts:

- Consult a **map** to discover the boundaries and relative positions of the geographical features of your town.
- Look up **diaries** and **journals** of long-time and former residents to gain valuable insights into different times and places.
- Find **speeches** made in the town on special occasions. These recorded public comments can showcase the style of the orator, as well as provide information about a topic, an area, or a group of people.
- Refer to the Internet and other **electronic media** that can lead you to a variety of sources and allow you to find a broader base of information about a subject.
- Try to find old **letters, memoranda, newspapers, magazines,** and **textbooks** that may provide valuable information not generally available in other sources.
- Ask a librarian or the curator of a local museum about **special collections** of posters or other resources that might offer information on your subject.

Read the following paragraphs from two kinds of primary sources. Then answer the questions that follow.

> Lincoln used to go to bed ordinarily [between] ten and eleven o'clock, unless he happened to be kept up by important news, in which case he would frequently remain at the War Department till one or two. He rose early. When he lived in the country at the Soldiers' Home, he would be up and dressed, eat his breakfast (which was extremely frugal, an egg, a piece of toast, coffee, etc.), and ride into Washington, all before eight o'clock. In the winter at the White House he was not quite so early.
>
> *—John Hay, one of Lincoln's private secretaries*

Four score and seven years ago our fathers brought forth on this continent, a new nation, conceived in Liberty, and dedicated to the proposition that all men are created equal.

Now we are engaged in a great civil war, testing whether that nation, or any nation so conceived and so dedicated, can long endure. We are met on a battlefield of that war. We have come to dedicate a portion of that field, as a final resting place for those who gave their lives that that nation might live. . . .

But in a larger sense, we can not dedicate—we can not consecrate—we can not hallow—this ground. The brave men, living and dead, who struggled here, have consecrated it, far above our poor power to add or detract. . . . It is rather for us to be here dedicated to the great task remaining before us—that from these honored dead we take increased devotion to that cause for which they gave the last full measure of devotion—that we here highly resolve that these dead shall not have died in vain—that this nation, under God, shall have a new birth of freedom—and that government of the people, by the people, for the people, shall not perish from the earth.

—Abraham Lincoln, from his address delivered at the dedication of the cemetery at Gettysburg, November 19, 1863

Which source would be better to use in a report on Lincoln as president of the United States? Which source would be better to use in a report on Abraham Lincoln's private life? How does reading across these texts provide a more complete picture of Abraham Lincoln?

TRY THE STRATEGIES

With a partner, select a topic that interests you, and research it in several kinds of sources. Compare the information from each source. Then organize and combine your information to present it to the class in some new form.

Recognizing distinctive and shared characteristics of cultures

When reading literature from different world cultures, you will find common themes about human nature. You will also see the ways in which distinctive characteristics of cultures increase your appreciation of those themes while enriching the understanding, knowledge, and enjoyment you have for your own roots. Fairytales, for example, often have counterparts in different cultures, so reading an Egyptian, a Native American, and an Asian version of "Cinderella" enhances your understanding of the story and also shows you the beauty and subtleties of different cultural traditions. Notice the similarities and differences in the elements of the Cinderella story in the four cultures charted at the top of page R97.

Culture	Heroine	Supernatural elements	Special clothing	Outcome
American/ European	Cinderella, mistreated stepchild	Fairy godmother	Glass slippers	Marries the prince
Zuni (Native American)	Turkey girl, turkey herder	Sacred turkeys	White doeskin robes	Returns to rags because she breaks her promise
Egyptian	Rhodopis, Greek slave girl	Falcon	Rose-red slippers	Marries the Pharaoh
Hmong (Asian)	Jouanah, despised stepchild	Dead mother's spirit	Special sandals	Finds love and happiness

Literary Response

Whenever you share your thoughts and feelings about something you've read, you are responding to text. Since we are all different people, though, we respond in different ways. Everyone has a learning style. Some learn best when speaking and writing, while others enjoy moving around or creating something artistic. What you do when you read can take different forms. Some responses to reading can include discussions, journals, oral interpretations, and dramatizations.

Responding to informational and aesthetic elements

You respond to what you read with both your mind and your emotions. To respond intellectually, think about whether ideas are logical and well supported. To respond emotionally, ask yourself how you feel about a selection.

Tips for Interpreting and Responding to Literature

- **Discuss** what you have read and share your views of the selections with your teacher and other students in the class.
- **Keep a journal** about what you read. Record your thoughts, feelings, or what you have learned in a journal. Write down what impresses you as well as what questions you have.
- **Read aloud** to yourself or with others. Poetry and drama make particularly good read-aloud materials, but even nonfiction passages can become clearer if troublesome passages are read orally.
- **Take part in dramatizations** and **oral interpretations.** Present characters through actions and dialogue. Use your voice, facial expressions, and body language to convey meaning. A **readers theater** is one kind of dramatic presentation in which students take different parts and read through a play or other fictional work.

Using text elements to defend personal interpretations

Whatever your response to a selection or your interpretation of a theme, you must be sure to use elements of the text to support those responses and interpretations. You need to provide details given by the writer to back up your interpretation. If you can't provide those text proofs, you may need to rethink your response.

Often you are asked to write about the selections you read. It is not enough to say, "I really liked the main character." You must know why you liked him or her. Look for specific descriptions. What did you find interesting about a story's setting? What details created certain feelings in you?

Comparing personal responses with authoritative views

Critics' reviews may encourage you to read a book, see a film, or attend a performance. They may also warn you that whatever is reviewed is not acceptable entertainment or is not valued by the reviewer.

Ask yourself the following questions:

- Would I go to a movie if it got a bad review from critics?
- Would I read a book if a reviewer said that it was a waste of time?
- Do I ever disagree with reviewers?

Deciding whether or not to value a review depends on the credibility of the reviewer, and also on your own personal viewpoints and feelings. Be sure that as you read authoritative reviews, you determine if the writer's opinions are supported with adequate and accurate details. Read the following model.

Review of *Life Is Beautiful*

Playing a game within the Holocaust

Italy's Roberto Benigni, like many great clowns, has his serious side: a Don Quixote or Joseph K. thumping inside the chest of this bumptious little Puck. But who could have dreamed that dark side would blossom out with the poignant and powerful results Benigni gets in his new film, *Life Is Beautiful*? Set in World War II Italy during the Holocaust—with much of its action laid in a notably grim concentration camp—*Life Is Beautiful* is a deeply moving blend of cold terror and rapturous hilarity. Lovingly crafted by Italy's top comedian and most popular filmmaker, it's that rare comedy that takes on a daring and ambitious subject and proves worthy of it.

In the movie, which he also cowrote and directed—Benigni plays a frenziedly high-spirited Italian Jewish bookseller named Guido, an elfin, Chaplinesque figure who leads a fairytale existence with his wife and young son, until the Nazis occupy Italy in 1943 after their ally Mussolini has been ousted—and the mass internment of Italy's Jews begins.

. . . Seeking to protect his son, Giosue, from fear and despair, the previously madcap Guido embarks on an improbable deception. With the collusion of his fellow inmates, he hides Giosue from the guards and persuades the little boy that the imprisonment is all a holiday game, in which the pretend "prisoners" vie with each other to win points for a grand prize: a huge army tank. . . . It's a dangerous game—both for Guido and the audience—and we're never sure, right up until the last moments, whether it will end comically or tragically. Or, possibly, both.

The movie divides seamlessly into two parts: romantic lightness and gathering dark. The early, merrier part of *Life* shows bouncy Guido's arrival in Arezzo, a real-life Tuscan town, and his comical-lyrical wooing of Dora. . . . Having achieved their hearts' desire, Guido and Dora settle into what would normally be their happy-ever-after coda. But instead, darkness falls. And it falls so believably—with such well-observed portrayals of the social erosion that overtook Italy after the 1938 Racial Laws and the 1943 Nazi occupation—that we're never jarred too far from the history beneath Benigni's fairytale.

Like the other Guido, Benigni is an artist trying, but with more success, to create delight in the face of pain and catastrophe, to distract both Giosue and us from the darkness. When he cuts capers during the romantic comedy first half with Dora, we laugh. And we laugh later in the camp too, but with a salting of tears and anguish.

—Michael Wilmington, *Chicago Tribune* movie critic

If you have seen the film, answer these questions:

- Is the review positive or negative?
- What does the reviewer like best about the film?
- Do you agree with the reviewer's evaluation? Why or why not?
- If you disagree with the reviewer, what do you think the reviewer failed to recognize in the film that might have influenced what he or she wrote?

If you have not seen the film, answer these questions:

- Based on this review, would you go to see this film? Why or why not?
- What evidence can you find that the reviewer is reliable?
- Does he or she back up his or her opinions with facts?

TRY THE STRATEGIES

In the weekend newspaper or on the Internet, find and evaluate a review of a recent film. If you have not seen the film, would the review influence you to see it? If you have seen the film, in what ways do you agree with the review? Explain.

Analysis and Evaluation

Active readers want to go beyond a simple understanding of the words on a page. They want to do more than recall information or interpret thoughts and ideas. When you read, you will want to read critically, forming opinions about characters and ideas and making judgments using your own prior knowledge and information from the text.

Analyzing characteristics of texts

To be a critical reader and thinker, start by analyzing the characteristics of the text. Some text characteristics can include:

- **Structure** Writers use patterns of organization to clearly present main ideas or themes. By figuring out what text structure a writer has used–for instance, chronological order, comparison-contrast, or cause and effect–you can better understand a writer's message. Look at the structure to unlock the meaning.
- **Word choices** Writers select words according to their connotations, which carry emotional or implied meanings, as well as their denotations, or dictionary meanings. A writer who uses the words *blabbed, tattled,* or *gossiped* to describe what someone said has a different attitude from a writer who uses the words *reported, narrated,* or *documented.* Looking at word choices helps you determine the writer's attitude about a topic and establishes a general mood within a piece of writing.
- **Intended audience** Most selections are written with a specific audience in mind. A speech at a pep rally would have a different style from one given by a diplomat at the United Nations. Similarly, writers must know their audiences in order to write material that is appropriate and interesting to the people who will read it.

As you read, look for the structure and word choices a writer uses to characterize his or her writing. Determine the intended audience for each selection you read.

Evaluating the credibility of sources

Would you take an article on nuclear fission seriously if you knew it was written by a comedic actor? If you need to rely on accurate information, it helps to know who wrote the selection and if that writer is qualified to speak with authority. How did the writer become informed?

Tips for Determining Credibility of a Source

- Look at the possible motivation of the writer. (If a reporter, for instance, writes an article about the rise in crime rate, you might find the story believable. If you found out, though, that the reporter has a close relative who is a police officer, and who wants a raise in pay, you might begin to question the truth, or credibility, of the article.)

- Check on the background of the writer. Do some research on the Internet, for example, to discover whether the writer is an authority in his or her field. Writers sometimes slant the facts in their work to convince readers to agree with them.
- Look at the statements the writer makes. Is the information fact or opinion? Can the writer's statements be proved by other sources?
- Consider the publication in which an article appears. Is it a well-known journal or respected newspaper?
- Ask the opinion of a librarian or teacher–someone who is likely to be familiar with a particular writer.

Look at the model below and think about the writer's motive or purpose.

> Do you need a flu shot but you're not crazy about being stuck with a needle? Imagine getting vaccinated with a simple nasal spray. Sound too good to be true? Scientists at a California company have created a spray mist that works as a vaccine for influenza. The spray contains a mild strain of a live virus. The virus, which can survive in the cool temperature of the nose and throat but not in the warmer areas of the body, causes the immune system to respond with infection-fighting activity in the nose and throat, where flu germs often attack. Several studies have proved that the spray works. So why get jabbed when you can get the same effect from a light mist? Your arm will thank you for it!

Has the writer included mostly factual statements or opinions? How can you tell?

How would it affect your opinion about this story if the author were

- president of the company that is marketing the new nasal spray vaccine?
- a medical expert on viruses?
- a student who saw the new product on a television news magazine program?

TRY THE STRATEGIES

Read the selection from *Night,* on page 1001 of your text. Is this author credible? How do you know? Can you determine the author's motive for writing the selection? Is the information in the selection fact or opinion?

Analyzing logical arguments and modes of reasoning

When you analyze works you've read, ask yourself whether the reasoning behind the writer's views are logical. Two kinds of logical reasoning are

Inductive Reasoning By observing a limited number of particular cases, a reader arrives at a general or universal statement. This logic moves from the specific to the general.

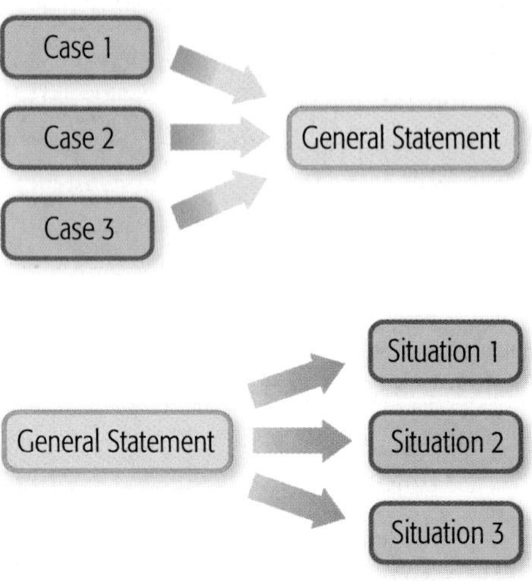

Deductive Reasoning This logic moves from that which is general to that which is specific. The reader takes a general statement and, through reasoning, applies it to specific situations.

Identifying errors in logic

Whether reading an editorial, listening to a speech, or evaluating a commercial, watch out for these errors in logic:

- **Bare assertion** A claim is made and is not backed up with reasons.
  Go-Car-Go is the best gas on the market.
- **Oversimplifying** One cause or solution is given for a situation without the consideration of other factors.
  Annice wouldn't be so tired if she got to bed on time.
- **Begging the question** The writer assumes in a statement or definition the very point to be proved. Another name for this fallacy is circular reasoning.
  Teenagers cannot be trusted because they are irresponsible.
- **Either/or reasoning** This fallacy consists in reducing all options to two extremes.
  If you don't approve of capitalism, you must be a Communist.
- **Red herring** A side issue is introduced that distracts from the issue under discussion.
  You won't like that play. The lead actor owns that terrible restaurant on Third Street.

Sometimes writers neglect to support their arguments with facts, relying instead on opinions or generalizations. If ideas are not supported with facts, reasoning can become cloudy. When you interpret speeches and other persuasive writing, be sure to question the logic of the writer to determine whether the reasoning is faulty.

Analyzing bias and persuasive techniques

A writer shows a **bias** when he or she demonstrates a strong, personal, and sometimes unreasonable opinion. A writer who shows bias is inclined to a particular way of thinking. Editorials, documentaries, and advertisements commonly show bias. Writers use **persuasive techniques** when they try, through their writing, to get readers to believe a certain thing or to act in a particular way. A writer may have a strong personal bias and yet compose a persuasive essay that is logical and well supported. On the other hand, writers can be less than accurate in order to be persuasive. As a good reader, you'll need to judge whether a writer's bias influences his or her writing in negative or positive ways.

Look at some ways writers can misuse evidence in order to persuade:

- **Impressing with large numbers** Sometimes called the bandwagon appeal, this kind of argument relies on large numbers or references to *everybody* to be convincing.
  Over 5,000,000 satisfied customers have bought our product.
  Everybody raves about the new sports utility vehicle.
- **Irrelevant appeals to authority** An authority can only provide evidence in his or her own field. Dr. Joyce Brothers, for example, is not a competent authority in the field of breakfast cereals.
  Dr. Joyce Brothers says you won't be disappointed in the taste of Munchy Crunchies.
- **Appeal to popular sentiment** Some speakers or writers associate the point they are making with an item that enjoys popular appeal.
  Brushing with Toothful Polish is as important as drinking bottled water.

How well does the following paragraph persuade?

> There really is no need to build a new high school in our town. Another new school would only mean higher taxes for everyone. With all the new families moving into our community, it would be better to build more shopping malls. That would provide more jobs. Teachers have always been able to handle thirty or thirty-five students in a classroom. Besides, residents who no longer have children in school should not have to pay for all this fancy education. Vote "No" on the school referendum.

What bias does the writer show? With a partner, analyze the logic of the author's persuasive technique. How well are the writer's ideas supported?

TRY THE STRATEGIES

Find and read an editorial in the local newspaper. On your own paper, write a brief analysis of the writer's persuasive techniques. What kind of reasoning did the writer use? Was the writer biased?

Inquiry and Research

Asking and answering questions is at the very heart of being a good reader. You will need to read actively in order to research a topic assigned by a teacher. More often, you will need to generate an interesting, relevant, and researchable question on your own and locate appropriate print and nonprint information from a wide variety of sources. Then categorize that information, evaluate it, and organize it in a new way in order to produce some kind of research project for a specific audience. Finally, draw conclusions about your original research question. These conclusions may lead you to other areas for further inquiry.

It sounds like a lot, but when you generate a question of strong interest to you, the process is fun and very worthwhile.

Generating relevant and interesting questions for research

Finding a good research question or topic is a very important first step and deserves your careful attention. Whether you are researching an assigned topic or a topic you have selected, start by generating questions.

Tips for Generating Research Questions

- Think of a question or topic of interest to you.
- Choose a question that helps you focus your study on one main idea.
- Be sure your question is not too broad or too narrow.
  Too broad: How can we be ecologically more responsible?
  Better: What have Americans done in the last five years to preserve the Amazon rain forest?

Locating appropriate print and nonprint information

In your research, try to use a variety of sources. Because different sources present information in different ways, your research project will be more interesting and balanced when you read in a variety of sources. The following are some helpful print sources for research:

- **Textbooks** Texts include any book used as a basis for instruction or a source of information.
- **Book indices** A book index contains an alphabetical listing of books. Some book indices list books on specific subjects; others are more general. For example, H. W. Wilson's *Cumulative Book Index* lists hardcover and paperback books of fiction and nonfiction. Other indices list a variety of resources.
- **Periodicals** Magazines and journals are periodicals, publications issued at regular intervals, but less frequently than daily. One way of locating information in magazines is to use the *Readers' Guide to Periodical Literature.* This guide is available in print form in most libraries. Here is a subject entry from the *Readers' Guide*:

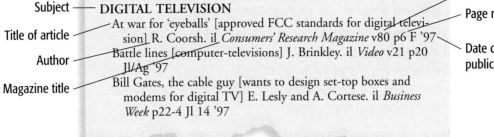

Subject — DIGITAL TELEVISION
Title of article — At war for 'eyeballs' [approved FCC standards for digital television] R. Coorsh. il *Consumers' Research Magazine* v80 p6 F '97 — Volume number; Page number(s); Date of publication
Author — Battle lines [computer-televisions] J. Brinkley. il *Video* v21 p20 Jl/Ag '97
Magazine title — Bill Gates, the cable guy [wants to design set-top boxes and modems for digital TV] E. Lesly and A. Cortese. il *Business Week* p22-4 Jl 14 '97

- **Technical manuals** A manual is a guide or handbook intended to give instruction on how to perform a task or operate something. A vehicle owner's manual might give information on how to operate and service a car.
- **Reference books** These books include encyclopedias and almanacs, and are books used to locate specific pieces of information.
- **Electronic encyclopedias, databases, and the Internet** There are many ways to locate extensive information using your computer. Infotrac®, for instance, acts as an on-line readers guide. CD-ROM encyclopedias can provide easy access to all subjects.
- **Nonprint information** This includes anything that is not written down. Some good nonprint sources of information are films, videos, and recorded interviews.

Organizing and converting information

As you gather information from different sources, taking careful notes, you'll need to think about how to **synthesize** the information, that is, convert it into a unified whole, as well as how to change it into a form your audience will easily understand and that will meet your assignment guidelines.

First, ask yourself what you want your audience to know. Then, think about a pattern of organization, a structure that will best show your main ideas. You might ask yourself questions like the following:

- When comparing items or ideas, what graphic aids can I use?
- When showing the reasons something happened and the effects of certain actions, what text structure would be best?
- How can I briefly and clearly show important information to my audience?
- Would an illustration or even a cartoon help to make a certain point?

TRY THE STRATEGIES

Read a nonfiction selection from your text. Based on a topic in the selection, create a question you would use as a focus for a research paper. Determine what kinds of sources you would use to gather information. Then plan how you would organize the material, including the graphic aids. Share your research plan with the class.

Adapting researched material for presentation

How should you present the material you've gathered? Before you decide, think about your audience and purpose. Who will receive this information? What is your purpose? When you change the information you've located in order to tell or show someone else, you are adapting your research material for presentation. There are many options you might consider:

- Written or oral report
- Interview
- Debate
- Dramatic presentation

For more on publishing/presenting, see **Writing Handbook,** p. R61.

Drawing conclusions from gathered information

After you've spent considerable time looking at a research question, you will certainly form opinions about your topic. A conclusion is a general statement that you'll make about the information you have found. It is important to explain your conclusions with good reasons and with supporting details from your sources.

Read the following excerpts and the conclusion that follows:

> Many scientists believe that acid deposition contributes to deforestation and soil degradation. It is known to dramatically accelerate the deterioration of buildings, including landmarks such as the Acropolis in Athens, the Taj Mahal in India, and the Statue of Liberty in New York City.
>
> —*National Geographic Information Central*

> It is not only plants and animals that suffer when the air is polluted. Buildings, sculptures, paintings, metal, glass, paper, leather, textiles, and rubber all deteriorate rapidly if exposed to sulphur dioxide, nitrogen oxides, or ozone.
>
> —*Norwegian Pollution Control Authority*

> The chemical content of acid rain is in itself dangerous to fish and other freshwater organisms. Another, equally important reason why fish populations are depleted, impoverished, or, as is often the case, wiped out altogether, is that acid water leaches toxic aluminum from the soils and bedrock. . . .
>
> —*Green Issues*

Conclusion: If acid rain is not controlled, both natural resources and art treasures may be lost to future generations.

Tips for Drawing Conclusions

- Don't try to twist the facts to match your original idea.
- Don't make sweeping generalizations that go beyond the facts you've gathered.
- Be prepared to adjust your original question to reflect the information you've located. Recognize that your conclusions might be different from what you originally thought they might be.
- Be sure to accurately record where you've gotten your information.
- Never present as your own ideas that aren't yours.
- Cite sources completely. If you're using a quote from someone, or if you want to present an idea taken from another source, be sure to use the proper notations.

TRY THE STRATEGIES

Read three or four articles about the same topic or current event. Compare the information and take careful notes. Then decide how you could organize and convert your information to support a reasonable conclusion, drawn from your reading.

● For more on citing sources and conducting research, see **Writing Handbook,** pp. R64–R69.

Writing Workshop Models

The following Writing Workshop Models are complete versions of the student models developed in the Writing Workshops at the end of each part in this book. Use these models as examples of how one student might have responded to the assignments in the Writing Workshops.

Unit 1, Part 1, pages 94–97

Narrative Writing: Autobiographical Incident

What a Chicken!

When I was in second grade, my whole class performed a play called *James and the Giant Peach.* It was based on Roald Dahl's famous book for children. Doing a play can be fun for everyone. But when you are shy, as I was, doing a play can also be a form of torture. That was how it was for me until I learned how to help myself.

I had the part of Aunt Sponge, who was not a main character but who had far more lines than I thought I could possibly deliver. "I'm too shy for this part," I thought to myself. "Why did Mrs. Wu give it to me?"

Mrs. Wu must have wondered that herself. "This will never do! I can't hear you!" she called at me during rehearsals as I stood up on stage, embarrassed that my voice was cracking with nervousness. It seemed as if I was the only one in my whole class who could not say the lines loudly enough. After being prompted, I would try to bring my volume up to what I thought was just about shouting, and still Mrs. Wu would remind me, "Louder, Lauren!"

As if that weren't enough, I was having trouble remembering all those lines. Too often the girl playing Aunt Spiker would whisper to me, "Oh no, you skipped a line, right here!" I was miserable.

On one particular day, when I seemed to be forgetting more than half my lines, when Aunt Spiker was losing her patience prompting me so often, and when Mrs. Wu was shouting over and over, "Louder!" I felt my face go crimson. Then I felt tears getting ready to fall. I tried to stop them, but I couldn't. I was embarrassed, and most of all, I wanted to quit. Of course, in second grade, there is no such thing as quitting the class play.

I went home, and I talked to my mother about what had happened. She gave me a hug and then some important advice that I used in the performance as well as in the last few rehearsals. "Just relax," she said. Of course, that advice wouldn't have helped by itself. But she added, "When there are people watching, even Mrs. Wu, just look at them and think of them as chickens." Mother even crunched up her arms, chicken-like, and flapped them, so I'd get the idea. She walked around the kitchen clucking and pecking. I laughed.

The funny thing was that this advice worked. It must have relaxed me to turn Mrs. Wu, the kids who were watching, and later the whole audience into silly, squawking, soon-to-be-eaten birds. Of course, what also helped was that I did, finally, memorize all my lines. On the night of the performance, my mother whispered her advice to me right before I went on stage, and that helped too. I walked onto that stage feeling pretty confident.

Halfway through the performance, however, I was late for an entrance, and then I missed a line. There was a second of silence that felt as if it lasted a year.

Luckily Aunt Spiker, who knew the play cold, whispered the line to me. I looked out at the audience, saw more than one hundred chickens, and then said the line perfectly. After that, I didn't miss another entrance or line, and I even started to feel comfortable. At one point I looked around. I realized that everybody was having fun—and that even included me.

At the end of the performance, my family hurried back stage and congratulated me. Mrs. Wu shook my hand and smiled warmly at me. Over and over I heard "You did a great job!" and "Great play!" Best of all, from somewhere deep inside myself, I felt successful. I had not chickened out. Instead, I had sort of let the chickens in.

Unit 1, Part 2, pages 192–195

Descriptive Writing: Travel Article

Going Back in Time at Bandelier

Bandelier National Monument, located forty-five miles west of Santa Fe, New Mexico, and only a few miles from Los Alamos, is not hard to reach. However, not every visitor to New Mexico, or even every resident, is lucky enough to discover Bandelier.

Why should you visit this national monument that so few people outside of the Southwest have heard of? For one thing, you will instantly be in another place and time. For another, you will be in a beautiful, sun-baked landscape filled with the smell of pine. Finally, you will walk or hike some of the most interesting and inviting trails anywhere in this country.

Bandelier is the site of a series of historic cultures. Ancient hunter-gatherers lived here. Later, perhaps two thousand years ago, the Anasazi made it their home. About eight hundred years ago, a large number of people migrated to this site, probably from Chaco Canyon or the Four Corners region.

The drama of Bandelier doesn't really come from knowing who lived there, though. It comes from walking quietly and respectfully through the awesome remains of these people's lives. There are caves, cliff dwellings, and ancient pueblos. There are petroglyphs, and there is at least one ceremonial cave. Bandelier has been called one of the most important sites in the Southwest. It is a must-see for any lover of the past.

From the moment you get out of the car and head off on a trail, you will be in a completely different time and place. As you follow dusty paths with cliffs at your side, you will first be struck by how incredibly dry the air can be. The hot air doesn't seem to have a drop of moisture left. It can get so dry, in fact, that it almost feels sharp. If you're not used to it, your mouth will feel scratchy and your eyes will burn. This sensation will increase as the day wears on and dust covers your skin. Yet as you hike, you will gaze out at beautiful cottonwood and box elders that cover the canyon floor. The yucca, cholla, and other desert plants hang from the canyon walls. At the mesa tops, you will see both pinyon pines and junipers.

As you hike, you will see how the ten-thousand-foot peaks of the Jemez Mountains surround you. They enclose this piece of the past and seem to seal it off. After a while, you will catch your first breathtaking views of Tyuonyi. It is a circular three-story pueblo, built in the 1300s, that contained more than four hundred rooms. You will see other mysterious dwellings scooped out of the soft volcanic rock on the base of the canyon. You will also see multistory dwellings—America's first apartment houses.

In 1880, when Adolph Bandelier, who was a Swiss-born anthropologist, saw the ruins of these dwellings for the first time, he said this was "the grandest thing I ever saw." You may say the same thing. Visit Bandelier National Monument and find out.

Unit 2, Part 1, pages 334–337

Creative Writing: A Dramatic Scene

The City Mouse and the Country Mouse

COUNTRY MOUSE (*opening the door to her small but cozy home*): Lucinda, I'm so glad you're here.
CITY MOUSE (*elegantly dressed; she struts condescendingly as she enters*): Well, Pat, I'm glad I could come.
COUNTRY MOUSE: I hope you had a good journey.
CITY MOUSE (*sighing and snooty*): Oh, it was just tolerable. But I've had to fire my coachmen again. Good help is SO hard to find.
COUNTRY MOUSE: Well, you can rest yourself here. And I've got everything ready to refresh you. Won't you take a seat at my table?
CITY MOUSE: Ah, gladly, Pat. Thank you.
COUNTRY MOUSE (*Offering simple dishes, she attends courteously to her guest. The furniture is plain but sturdy and well cared for. The windows are bare but clean, revealing the lush countryside.*): Lucinda, I would be so honored if you would try this homemade farm cheese. And here is some white bread. And we have the best water here right from the tap; it's so clean and fresh. I kept it cold for you in this pitcher!
CITY MOUSE (*smiles, chats, as she eats*): I do appreciate this. I am rather hungry. How have you been?
COUNTRY MOUSE: All is well, as you can see. I love this quiet country life.
CITY MOUSE: Do you? I would miss the city.
COUNTRY MOUSE: Oh, Lucinda, you're so different from me. I'm glad I left the city years ago.
CITY MOUSE: Really, I suppose you're right, my dear. I do so love living in the palace.
COUNTRY MOUSE: Well, everything I need is right here. I'm content.
CITY MOUSE: You know, you really ought to visit the palace, though. Tell you what. Why not return with me? We can have our evening meal there!
COUNTRY MOUSE: That's very kind, Lucinda. Um . . . well . . . of course. I'd be glad to have dinner at your home. Do I need to change my clothes?
CITY MOUSE: Well— (*hesitates and sizes up the country mouse*) No . . . no . . . you're fine, I suppose.
COUNTRY MOUSE: Well then, let me just clear this table, and we'll be off. (*bustles about cleaning up after the simple lunch of bread, cheese, and water. Meanwhile, City Mouse relaxes or lounges. She watches as Country Mouse works.*)
CITY MOUSE (*after a bit of time*): Well, let's be off.
(*The scene changes. The mice are now in an elegant dining room of the palace. On the dining room table are the remains of an elegant dinner.*)
COUNTRY MOUSE: Oh, I've never seen anything quite like this.
CITY MOUSE (*with a superior tone of voice*): Really? I eat like this every day. Here, try this French bread, baked by Chef Pierre today, and dip it in a bit of that olive oil first.
COUNTRY MOUSE (*Following orders, she does what City Mouse says.*): Ummm . . . good . . .
CITY MOUSE: Oh yes, and here is some of the finest ham in the world. Oh, and do try those imported goat cheeses. Don't forget the arugula and fresh chive salad either. (*half giddy now*) We must get our vitamins!
COUNTRY MOUSE (*following orders again*): Yes, it's all so good.
CITY MOUSE: Oh, and here is the finest tea in the world, imported from Ceylon.
COUNTRY MOUSE: Thank you, Lu—
(*A snappy, barking lapdog runs in.*)
COUNTRY MOUSE (*scurrying to a mouse hole in fear*): Lucinda, help! Help!
(*The mice both hide; the dog disappears; the mice come back.*)
CITY MOUSE: Oh, that was nothing, Pat. Happens all the time—
(*In runs a beautiful, pampered Siamese cat.*)
COUNTRY MOUSE (*running to the mouse hole again, screaming again*): Help! Help!
(*They hide again. The cat leaves. They attempt to resume their meal, but Country Mouse is shaken.*)

CITY MOUSE: Pat, don't be such a scaredy-mouse!
COUNTRY MOUSE: I'm just not used to—
(*A whole group of servants enters. While the mice hide, the servants take away all the food, every single crumb.*)
CITY MOUSE: Well, Pat, forgive the slight interruption. That's it till tomorrow. Hope you enjoyed the meal.
COUNTRY MOUSE: I did, Lucinda, thank you. But . . . I think I need to go back to my little home and my plain food.
(*Stagehands hold this banner: MORAL: It is better to have peace than plenty.*)

Unit 2, Part 2, pages 400–403

Narrative Writing: An Eyewitness Account

Monarch Madness

Last year during February vacation, my family and I went to visit my grandmother, who lives in Toluca, a city just west of Mexico City. This was my first time in Mexico, and I enjoyed almost everything that we did there. Most of all, however, I enjoyed a trip we took to a nearby place called Angangueo. There we saw the greatest show on Earth: the migration of the monarch butterflies.

Before we went, Grandma gave us a little bit of background. She told us that Angangueo is the home of a monarch butterfly sanctuary. Every winter, butterflies make the long journey to Angangueo from North America. Some travel as far as eighteen hundred miles. Perhaps even more amazing, every year the butterflies come back to the very same place. Most of these butterflies live two years, which means they make this trip twice.

Our trip to the sanctuary began with a ride in a flatbed truck up a rural mountainside. Several trucks and buses were also making the trip up the bumpy, narrow road. We sat in the truck with several other Mexican families. Everyone seemed happy and expectant. Still, none of us were prepared for the great thrill that awaited us.

Once we got within a quarter-mile of the sanctuary, we became part of a whole army of people hiking the final distance to the sanctuary at the top of the mountain. The last part of the climb took us through a congested area of stands where busy merchants were selling butterfly souvenirs, frying fragrant meats, making spicy tamales and empanadas, and selling ice cold green and pink drinks. The cool beverages were too tantalizing to resist, because we had all become thirsty from our long journey in the hot sun. The cold drinks gave us the energy and enthusiasm we needed to reach the entrance of the reserve.

At first, we spotted a few small groups of monarchs flying in the air overhead, clustering on the grass, or sitting together in a bush. Never having seen as many as five or ten monarchs together, we thought this was a big deal. But by the time we had climbed just ten feet higher into the sanctuary, we began to see a vast sea of orange. Butterflies covered entire trees, weighing down their branches. They filled the sky—a blizzard of butterflies. They alighted on tourists' arms and heads, including my own, and were crushed under our feet, despite everyone's best efforts to avoid stepping on them.

My binoculars brought into focus whole tree trunks and boughs that were covered on every square inch with monarchs. Individual butterflies would have come into close view, except for the fact that the monarchs were all on top of one another, the way bees swarm in a hive or termites in a nest form a dense mass of insect bodies. As I looked through my binoculars, I repeatedly found myself exclaiming out loud—and often to no one! My family was scattered on all parts of trail, oohing and aahing.

If I had to guess how many monarchs I saw in just that one day, I would say millions. I would guess, though I do not know this, that some trees held ten thousand or more. And I would say that seeing those monarchs was just as thrilling and memorable as seeing a million diamonds all sparkling under a bright blue sky.

Unit 3, Part 1, pages 484–487

Personal Writing: Reflective Essay

Reflections on "The Death of Enkidu" from the *Epic of Gilgamesh*

The excerpts from the *Epic of Gilgamesh* in our textbook are a moving—sometimes confusing—account of some of Gilgamesh's adventures following the death of his dear friend Enkidu. This selection is not always easy to read. From the very beginning, when Enkidu relates his dream, there seemed to be far too many details and strange names to take in. As I reread, however, I started to understand the feelings and ideas conveyed in these tales. I started to realize that I was reading heartfelt and moving reflections on life and death. Although they come from such a different time and place, they are still so very human.

My confusion began on the first page. On that page, Enkidu speaks. First he talks about killing Humbaba and cutting down a forest, which I thought were probably good things to do, since Enkidu brags about them. Then Enkidu starts talking about a dream. I expected there to be some relationship between this dream and the actions of killing and cutting, but I didn't find that. Instead, I got lost in a sea of details ranging from a description of some "somber-faced man-bird" to the Queen of Darkness, and from the god of cattle to Belit-Sheri and the book of death. This was all too much for me to understand on the first reading, so I went back over it. When I reread, I was able to see that the dream was relating one set of the details but that the killing of Humbaba and the cutting down of the forest had happened before the dream. It wasn't until another rereading that I finally realized that the dream about Enkidu's coming death was sent to him by the gods as a warning. Furthermore, his death was a punishment from the gods for killing Humbaba and cutting down the forest.

Some other parts of this narrative also went by me on the first reading. Between the time Gilgamesh sets out to find Utnapishtim and the time he encounters him, there are so many details! I also became confused about who exactly Gilgamesh was. The Man-Scorpion tells his mate that "this one who comes to us now is flesh of the gods." But later, the Man-Scorpion says to Gilgamesh that "no man born of woman has done what you have asked, no mortal man has gone into the mountains. . . ." This seems to suggest that Gilgamesh is not a god but a brave and noble mortal.

As my understanding of the details of the story deepened on rereading, my understanding of the characters' deep feelings increased. The passages in which Gilgamesh mourns Enkidu and reflects on his mortality became all the more powerful. For example, I was struck by the heartfelt sorrow of Gilgamesh's words: "I wept for [Enkidu] seven days and nights till the worm fastened on him. Because of my brother I am afraid of death, because of my brother I stray through the wilderness and cannot rest."

By the time I had reread twice, I felt the horrible disappointment that Gilgamesh must have felt when even someone immortal could give him no hope for immortality. When Utnapishtim says flat out, "There is no permanence" (meaning there is no immortality for mortals), I almost wished he would have told the suffering Gilgamesh some comforting myth instead. But the truth is as cold and hard as stone. Utnapishtim repeats, ". . . there is no permanence. The sleeping and the dead, how alike they are, they are like painted death." In this way, he indicates that just as all mortals must sleep, all mortals must die.

As I reflect on my readings, I see that this epic is dense and difficult, especially since it does not contain stories familiar to me (except the one about the flood). I think the names of gods and places could slow down any reader. Yet, I also now believe that this tale is worth time and effort. This story reminded me that all humans, in all times and places, need comfort when loved ones die and that all humans search—sometimes desperately—for meanings to explain their own existence on this Earth.

Unit 3, Part 2, pages 572–575

Persuasive Writing: Critical Review

"The Weed"

"The Weed" by Amrita Pritam is a stirring short story that explores the traditional roles of women in Indian culture and raises thought-provoking issues about love. Much of the short story reads like a fascinating interview between the narrator (a well-educated Indian woman from a city) and Angoori (a young Indian bride from a village). The narrator begins the story by providing background information on Angoori's prearranged marriage to Prabhati, a much older man. The remaining part of the story mainly consists of a conversation between the two women. Through their spoken words, Pritam does a marvelous job of bringing the characters to life. Pritam is a master at dialogue and characterization.

"What are you wearing, Angoori?". . . "Want to learn?" . . . "Why do you want to write? To write letters? To whom?" Like any expert interviewer, the narrator of "The Weed" is curious and attentive. She asks probing questions that lead Angoori to talk about herself in an honest and open way. Through Angoori's responses, we can picture her dazzling presence and discover her true feelings toward the cultural values of her traditional upbringing. For example, Angoori says, "It's a sin for women to read," but then later confesses that she wants to be taught reading and writing. The narrator also encourages Angoori to talk about how prearranged marriages are practiced in her village.

In addition, Pritam's skill in weaving the telling of a folktale into the dialogue adds an enchanting dimension to the short story and further develops the characterization of Angoori. As the narrator and Angoori continue their discussion about relationships and marriage, Angoori explains how a man tricks a woman into falling in love with him: "See, what happens is that a man makes the girl eat a weed and then she starts loving him." The moral lesson of the tale is that women should resist romantic attractions. For Angoori, this lesson about forbidden love takes on real-life meaning, and she must suffer the consequences.

Finally, Pritam successfully adds a poetic touch to the dialogue that reveals a deeply emotional side to Angoori's character. Toward the end of the story, Angoori recites these lyrics to the narrator, who listens sympathetically:

> Four months of winter reign in my heart;
> My heart shivers, O my love.
> Four months of summer, wind shimmers in the sun.
> Four months come the rains; clouds tremble in the sky.

Although some people might find these lines a bit sappy or melodramatic, I think they succeed in capturing Angoori's romantic feelings.

"The Weed" does not read like a love story from a TV soap opera in which characters speak in cliches. Pritam's varied use of dialogue—the language of everyday speech, highlights from a folktale, a stanza of verse—is highly original and reveals the personalities of two memorable women. Pick up a copy of this short story at your library and read what Angoori and the narrator have to say about love and cultural values.

Unit 4, Part 1, pages 676–679

Expository Writing: Feature Story

The Japanese Tea Ceremony

If you want to understand traditional Japanese culture, look no further than the tea ceremony. There's a whole lot more to this action than slipping bags into teacups, pouring in some boiling water, and drinking a hot beverage. In fact, nowhere else in the world is tea drunk in quite this way. That is because the Japanese tea ceremony is really not about tea.

The tea ceremony is about the spirit of *wabi. Wabi* is a Japanese word that does not have an exact English translation. Roughly, it means tranquility and serenity, or an attitude toward life that results when one's state of mind is tranquil and serene. The tea ceremony also incorporates the ideas of purity, harmony, and elegant simplicity. It is an art form and a kind of meditation.

An essential part of the tea ceremony is that host and guest give each other every consideration. Another word for this concept is respect. This respect requires careful behavior. It also requires recognition of the philosophy of *ichigo-ichie,* which literally means "one cup, one moment." In short, it means one chance: This is one chance that may not come again. Therefore, both guest and host have the responsibility to put everything they can into the tea ceremony. The guest recognizes what an honor it is to be invited to such a ceremony, and the host spends days going over all the details to make sure that the ceremony will be perfect.

Sometimes the tearoom is inside a teahouse, which is located away from the home and in the garden. The guests are first shown into a waiting room. If there is more than one guest, they choose one of their group to be the main guest. Just before receiving the guests, the host cleans his hands and mouth. Then the host welcomes the guest with a wordless bow. The host then leads them (main guest first) toward the tea-room, and the guests purify their hands and mouth. The movement into the tearoom is symbolic: It is a moment of leaving the outer world for an inner one. Another way to look at this part of the ceremony is that the participants leave the purely physical world to enter a more spiritual state.

At the tea ceremony, each guest is given a meal, often with three courses. The first course includes rice, miso soup, and pickled vegetables. The second consists of seafood and mountain food. Fragrant things, followed by a sweet, are served last. Everything is served and eaten with great care, and all actions are performed in a certain order. Then the host asks his guests to wait in the dining room, garden, or other place.

At this point, the host may remove or change the decorative objects in the room. The room is swept. Flowers are arranged. Finally, items related to making the tea, many of which are art objects, are arranged.

Sometimes a gong will call the guests back to the teahouse or tearoom. When they enter, with the main guest first, each guest admires such objects as the tea kettle and flowers.

There are more objects to admire during the tea ceremony. The host ladles hot water into the tea bowl and then scoops tea into the bowl with a tea scoop. Each guest, in order, raises the tea bowl and comments on its beauty. Then each guest drinks from the bowl, wipes the rim, and passes the bowl to the next person. After this, the host offers the tea container and tea scoop to his guests for close examination. The participants discuss the artistic features of these objects but may also chat about other appropriate topics.

Finally, the guests have a second tea, a thin tea. This moment is also transitional: They are preparing to leave the spiritual world. As guests do so, they express their respect for their host by complimenting the art of the ceremony. A complex and artistic expression of respect, unlike any other in the world, ends.

Unit 4, Part 2, pages 772–775

Business Writing: Letter of Application

5521 Plains Road
West Racine, WI 53405
January 19, 20__

Euro-American Intercultural Exchange, Inc.
402 West Broadway, Suite 1910
New York, NY 10003

Dear Sir or Madam:

I am a high school sophomore who would like to take part in your foreign exchange program for the coming school year. The country where I would most like to spend a school year abroad is Spain. I have been interested in this country ever since I first studied it in fifth grade. Since the seventh grade, I have been concentrating on studying the Spanish language and culture.

I believe several experiences have prepared me for your program. First, I have traveled before without my family, and I have even visited a foreign country. When our junior high school sponsored a trip to Venezuela, I was one of the first to sign up. The trip, which lasted eight days, gave me a realistic taste of being abroad. Although we had chaperones, all of us students had to deal with challenges such as new and different food, different currency, different customs, and a different language. Although some students became homesick or in some way frightened on this trip, I never did. In fact, I was sorry to see it end.

What makes me most suited as a foreign exchange student, however, is not my past experience with travel abroad, but my ability to get along with people and to accept their differences. I have an older brother and a younger sister, and I have to get along with both of them, and that's not easy. In my spare time, I babysit for children who range in ages from two to twelve. I was also elected a student council representative both this year and in my freshman year. I believe this shows that people who know me have confidence in me and think I can get along with others on the council. In addition, I performed volunteer community service last summer, helping in a daycare center. In my work at the center, I think I got along as well with the parents and staff as I did with the children.

I also recognize that going to live in someone else's home requires extra effort and thoughtfulness. Because all cultures have their own special customs and sensitivities, it will be important for me to communicate carefully and clearly and to ask about things I don't understand. At all times, I must also remember that I am a guest. I can't promise that I will be the best person ever to be an exchange student, but I do know that I am planning to try as hard as anyone ever has.

Finally, I would like to mention my foreign language skills. Ever since I began taking Spanish, I have had almost all A's and just a few B's. For the past year, I have been going to the language lab almost every day during study hall or after school in order to improve my conversational skills. My current teacher, Miss Nuñez, tells me I am showing great improvement. She has said that she feels confident that my Spanish language skills are good enough for me to spend a year in Spain.

In closing, let me say that I think I can adjust to this experience, benefit from it, and get along with others, including my host family. I also believe that I have the skills that will enable me to succeed both socially and academically.

Sincerely,

Margaret Belew

Expository Writing: Research Paper

Dante Alighieri: Love, Chaos, and Creativity

Dante Alighieri lived an external life of enormous tragedy and change. Although he never left his native Italy, he was exiled from his home in Florence. During a large portion of his adult life, he was seldom at home, seldom at ease, and seldom at rest. Despite these external changes, which included lost love, he became a deeply learned man who produced one of the greatest works in Western literature, the *Divine Comedy*.

Born in 1265, Dante was the son of a minor noble family in Florence. His mother died when he was young; his father remarried and had two more children. Though the family was not rich, Dante had access to a good education and was always passionate about learning. "The family's modest social standing did not prevent him from pursuing his studies, nor was he hindered in his effort to lead the life of a gentleman" ("Dante," *European* 411).

By all accounts, one of the most important moments of Dante's life occurred when he was just nine years old. At that time he met the woman who proved to be perhaps the most powerful force in his life and art. "According to the testimony of Boccaccio and others, the woman, called Bice, was the daughter of Folco Portinari of Florence. She later became the wife of the banker Simone de' Bardi. Dante called her Beatrice, the bringer of blessings, the one who brought bliss to all who looked upon her" ("Dante," *European* 411). Indeed, though Dante eventually married another woman, he idealized Beatrice. Her premature death was the cause of enormous grief in Dante's life.

Shortly after the death of Beatrice, Dante embarked on a period of intense study and learning. He determined to read the philosophical works of both Boethius and Cicero, and he admitted in the *Convivio*, published sometime between 1304 and 1307, that this reading was very difficult for him at first. Still, he kept at it. Also in the *Convivio*, Dante said:

> And as it may happen that a man looking for silver accidentally hits on gold . . . so I, seeking consolation [for the death of Beatrice] found not only a remedy for my sorrow but the language of authors and sciences and books; reflecting on which I judged that philosophy—the lady of these authors and sciences and books—was a very great thing. And I imagined it as a noble lady, whom I could not represent to myself in any attitude but one of compassion; with the result that my sense of truth . . . was so drawn to her that I could not take my eyes off her (Foster 35).

This quotation describes how love of Beatrice became transformed into love of philosophy and how this passion took over Dante's life.

Well before Dante wrote about the changes in his life, however, he became involved in the political life of Florence. To do so, he became a member, in 1295, of the physicians' guild. At that time, becoming a member of a guild was one of the few ways of being eligible for public office (*Dante: His Life* 14). The timing of this was disastrous, however. The Florence in which Dante grew up and lived was divided by feuding families, conspiracies, and factions. Neighborhood rivalries and private interests within families and between families often caused intrigue and plotting, if not outright turmoil. This turmoil reached a boiling point just as Dante took office. Because of this political turmoil, Dante was exiled from Florence in 1302. The charges were mostly made up; nevertheless, when Dante failed to answer them, the situation grew worse. A second sentence soon followed the first: If Dante ever returned to his home, he was to be captured immediately and burned alive. There is no evidence that Dante ever returned to Florence.

He began a period of extensive travel, mainly in the north of Italy. These were not easy years for him. "He followed more and less favorable opportunities, fulfilling diplomatic assignments, when he could find them, on behalf of lords who received him grudgingly and those who really opened their doors to him. He lived more or less like a courtier, spending his talent in the service of noblemen and sharing their hospitality with diplomats, soldiers, adventurers, buffoons, and men of every kind" (*Dante: His Life* 19–20). Of this period of time, Dante himself remarked, "Truly I have been a ship without a rudder, driven to many ports and river mouths and shores by the dry wind of miserable poverty…" (*Dante: His Life* 5).

Dante is believed to have written his greatest work, the *Divine Comedy*, during this time of exile. This work and others reflect some of Dante's life experiences, which included being a victim of treachery and cruelty, knowing the danger and humiliation of exile, feeling all the painful joys of love, and also knowing some political and artistic success. In his *Comedy*, Dante is himself the main character. "He writes in the first person so the reader can identify and deeply understand the truths he wished to share about the meaning of life and man's relationship with the Creator" (Dante's Inferno 2). As he had done in his earlier poems, he wrote the *Divine Comedy* in Italian instead of the customary Latin. "This was a bold step representing a new outlook on the potential of Italian prose and became a turning point for European poetry" ("Dante Alighieri," *Vita* 1).

Dante's reputation rests on the *Divine Comedy*, his final work, which he completed shortly before his death in 1321. Like Dante's life, this epic poem describes a difficult journey that has more than its share of disappointments, hardships, questions, and revelations. It ultimately ends happily (that is why it is called a "comedy")—more happily than Dante's own life did. A work of supreme beauty, learning, wisdom, and poetic mastery, it is the crowning achievement of Dante's full and courageous life.

Works Cited

"Dante Alighieri." *European Writers: Selected Authors.* Vol. I. Ed. George Stade. New York: Scribner, 1992. 411–415.

"Dante Alighieri." *Vita Nuova*. 5 June 1999 <http://www.vitanuova.com/dantebi.htm>.

Dante: His Life, His Work, His Times. Trans. Giuseppina T. Salvadori and Bernice L. Lewis. New York: American Heritage, 1968.

"Dante's Inferno." *StudyWorld*. 7 Feb. 2001 <http://www.studyworld.com/literature/novels/dantes_inferno.htm>.

Foster, Kenelm. "The Mind in Love: Dante's Philosophy." *Dante: A Collection of Critical Essays.* Ed. John Freccero. Englewood Cliffs, N.J.: Prentice-Hall, 1965. 43–60.

Unit 5, Part 2, pages 1020-1023

Persuasive Writing: Personal Response

"The Myth of Sisyphus"

Albert Camus's essay "The Myth of Sisyphus" raises a philosophical question about the meaning of life: How should a person respond to a cruel twist of fate? To answer this question, Camus draws upon the story of Sisyphus from Greek mythology. Sisyphus is doomed forever to roll a rock up a hill. Once the rock reaches the top, the rock rolls back down, and Sisyphus once again must perform this senseless task. Camus claims that by scorning this bleak situation, Sisyphus finds a way to rise above it. According to Camus, "There is no fate that cannot be surmounted by scorn." I would change the statement that Camus makes about scorning fate. I would say, "There is no fate that cannot be surmounted by trying."

In support of my position, I would like to present two real-life examples. Both Christopher Reeve and Florence Griffith Joyner have shown that "trying" to overcome unfortunate predicaments can bring personal success and fulfillment.

The actor Christopher Reeve, well known for his movie role as Superman, suffered a horrible fate that changed his life forever. In 1995 he was thrown from a horse. This riding accident left him paralyzed from the neck down, but Christopher Reeve holds fast to his dream that some day he will be able to walk again. Despite his physical disabilities, he has directed a film made for cable TV, and he raises funds for people with spinal cord injuries. Unlike Camus's version of Sisyphus, Christopher Reeve faces the limitations and frustrations of his life with optimism and courage, rather than scorn. Christopher Reeve sums up his winning attitude: "I think a hero is an ordinary individual who finds strength to persevere and endure in spite of overwhelming obstacles."

Florence Griffith Joyner, the famous Olympic runner who died in 1998 at the age of 38, also surmounted overwhelming obstacles. "FloJo," as she was nicknamed, grew up in large family that lived in a poverty-stricken neighborhood of Los Angeles. The circumstances of her childhood didn't favor her dreams of becoming a spectacular track star, but she beat the odds with her winning attitude. After her death, President Clinton remembered her outstanding achievements—both on and off the track: "Though she rose to the pinnacle of sports, she never forgot where she came from, devoting time and resources to helping children—especially those growing up in devastated neighborhoods—make the most of their talents."

Viewing unfortunate circumstances with contempt is not the best attitude to hold. We must not allow ourselves to think we are like Sisyphus. We are not prisoners of our fate. Like Christopher Reeve and Florence Griffith Joyner, we have can find creative and courageous ways of coping with difficult situations instead of feeling like victims. We can succeed in transforming a seemingly hopeless situation into a personal victory.

Unit 6, Part 1, pages 1080–1083

Expository Writing: Comparison-and-Contrast Essay

For Love of Home and Country

"Two Countries" by José Martí is a poem written by an exiled man who views his native country, Cuba, as being under the shadow of tyranny. "Lot's Wife" by Anna Akhmatova is also a poem about the agony of exile from one's homeland—in this case, the city of Sodom, whose destruction is described in the Bible. Both poems are highly emotional. Though the poems differ greatly in structure and point of view, they share at least one key image. They also both present active responses to the agony of exile.

Both poems express a love of homeland. "Two Countries" describes Cuba before it was liberated from Spanish rule. Martí, who is the speaker, says that Cuba in the grip of Spain is the same as darkness, night, and widowhood. As an exile from his country, Martí says, "My breast / Is empty, destroyed and empty / Where the heart lay." In exile, or without his country, he is as good as dead. "Lot's Wife" describes two people who are fleeing their doomed city. Although the husband in the poem appears to leave without turning to look back, the wife cannot. She loves her country so much she must have one last look.

The structure of the two poems is different. "Two Countries" is written in blank verse. It does not have regular stanzas. It uses the first-person point of view. "Lot's Wife" uses a traditional rhyming structure. It has traditional stanzas. It uses the third-person point of view.

Despite these differences, both poems share at least one key image—the color red. In "Two Countries," the bloodstained carnation is red. This red image is nearly synonymous with Cuba itself: Martí writes that Cuba holds the carnation. In "Lot's Wife," the red towers of Sodom echo those of Moscow's Red Square. Akhmatova's poem has been interpreted as a commentary on people who emigrated from Russia after the Bolshevik Revolution.

Both poems show active responses to the threat of exile. At first the speaker in "Two Countries" seems to be overwhelmed by his exile. But when "the candle's red flame flutters," he feels a "closeness" and opens windows. The patriotic spirit and the call to battle are still alive in him. Lot's wife also does not accept exile. She turns back, even though this causes her mental pain.

On the surface, the poems seem so different. "Two Countries" seems free form, dreamlike, and elusive, while "Lot's Wife" seems like a structured retelling of an old Biblical tale. Deeper down, however, both poems treat the same heartfelt theme: A person's country means everything, and the loss of one's country can bring despair.

Unit 6, Part 2, pages 1192–1195

Personal Writing: Personal Essay

Song of Myself

No one knows what the future will bring, but each of us can still have goals. My most important goals for my future relate to the most important part of my life: music. By the time ten years have passed, I hope to have completed my music education at a good school and have a career as a professional musician.

Although I play piano and enjoy sports and other hobbies, the guitar has been at the center of my life for more than three years now. I think the guitar is a versatile instrument, and I enjoy playing various styles of music on it, including classical. I feel happiest when I am playing guitar, especially if I am experimenting with new sounds or trying out new things I've never done before. I am also happiest when I am playing music with people who have similar musical tastes and abilities. That is why I bring my guitar almost everywhere I go.

Wherever I go, I hope to find rock musicians. My number one fantasy is that ten years from now I will be part of a famous band. Of course, I know how unlikely that is. If I am not a famous rock star in ten years, I would at least like to be a successful studio musician. I'd like to be regularly called in to back up other recording musicians. I'd also like to be called in to do work for films, television, and video. In ten years, when I reach the point in my life when I am working every day, I hope I am working at something that requires bringing my guitar along.

Because of my career goals, I hope to be living in the Los Angeles area or in metropolitan New York. Because both of these cities have great music scenes, I know I will be happy living in either place. If I do not manage to become a studio musician, I might find a satisfying day job in another field, but I would still have the opportunity to play in some good clubs on the weekends. I believe both New York and Los Angeles are filled with people who are passionate about their music and who find opportunities to play music, if not to make a living from it.

No matter where I end up, music has to be part of my life. If possible, I would like to live in a building or a neighborhood with other musicians. An ideal situation would be having a nearby place for rehearsing that I could share with other people who also need rehearsal space. I would also like to live where I can easily go to hear music. For example, if I lived in Manhattan, I would go everywhere from Carnegie Hall and Lincoln Center to the jazz clubs of the West Side and the Village. Hearing other musicians perform would be important to me. I know I would also be constantly hearing some fine street musicians. Although it is possible for me to get the music and CDs I want online, I also enjoy visiting good CD and music stores, which I know I would find in both Los Angeles and New York.

In short, I want music to be my life. Having music at the center of everything will affect all my choices: where I live, what I do, and how I spend my time. For me, music will always be the key.

Glossary

This glossary lists the vocabulary words found in the selections in this book. The definition given is for the word as it is used in the selection; you may wish to consult a dictionary for other meanings of these words. The key below is a guide to the pronunciation symbols used in each entry.

a	at	**ō**	hope	**ng**	sing
ā	ape	**ô**	fork, all	**th**	thin
ä	father	**oo**	wood, put	**th**	this
e	end	**o͞o**	fool	**zh**	treasure
ē	me	**oi**	oil	**ə**	ago, taken, pencil, lemon, circus
i	it	**ou**	out	**′**	indicates primary stress
ī	ice	**u**	up	**′**	indicates secondary stress
o	hot	**ū**	use		

A

abstain (ab stān′) *v.* to refrain with an effort of self-denial from a practice or action; p. 748

abstracted (ab strak′ tid) *adj.* preoccupied; absent-minded; p. 530

accomplice (ə kom′ plis) *n.* a participant in a crime or wrongdoing p. 760

acquittal (ə kwit′ əl) *n.* setting free from a criminal charge by verdict, sentence, or other legal process; p. 328

affront (ə frunt′) *n.* a deliberate insult; p. 84

animosity (an′ ə mos′ ə tē) *n.* ill will or resentment; p. 159

appease (ə pēz′) *v.* to make peace with through concessions; p. 396

arable (ar′ ə bəl) *adj.* fit for growing crops; p. 941

arid (ar′ id) *adj.* excessively dry; p. 520

askew (ə skū′) *adj.* crooked; at an angle; p. 6

assailant (ə sā′ lənt) *n.* attacker; p. 66

assiduously (ə sij′ o͞o əs lē) *adv.* attentively or busily; p. 655

attainment (ə tān′ mənt) *n.* an accomplishment; p. 511

audacity (ô das′ ə tē) *n.* recklessly bold behavior or attitude; p. 1174

austere (ôs tēr′) *adj.* stern and cold in appearance or manner; somber; p. 1164

austerity (ôs ter′ ə tē) *n.* a spiritual, morally strict act; p. 502

avail (ə vāl′) *n.* use or advantage; p. 110

avarice (av′ ər is) *n.* greed; p. 505

avenge (ə venj′) *v.* to take revenge for a wrong by punishing the wrongdoer; p. 752

B

banal (bə nal′) *adj.* lacking originality, freshness, or novelty; p. 1164

banish (ban′ ish) *v.* to drive away or remove by authority; p. 616

bashing (bash′ ing) *n.* a forceful blow; p. 152

bedlam (bed′ ləm) *n.* a state of uproar or confusion; p. 152

beneficent (bə nef′ ə sənt) *adj.* doing or producing good; p. 1114

beseeching (bi sēch′ ing) *adj.* in a begging or pleading manner; p. 1002

besiege (bi sēj′) *v.* to surround with hostile forces; p. 697

blandly (bland′ lē) *adv.* quietly; without concern; p. 84

boon (bo͞on) *adj.* convivial or sociable; p. 457

boorishness (boor′ ish nəs) *n.* rudeness and insensitivity; p. 664

braying (brā′ ing) *n.* the loud, harsh cry of a donkey; p. 728

bulwark (bool′ wərk) *n.* the side of a ship above the upper deck; p. 117

C

censure (sen′ shər) *v.* to find fault with and criticize; p. 330

chafe (chāf) *v.* to make sore or irritate by constant rubbing; p. 251

chaste (chāst) *adj.* innocent; pure; p. 830

chastise (chas tīz′) *v.* to punish, reprimand, or discipline severely; p. 616; to condemn or punish severely; p. 1014

clamor (klam′ ər) *n.* noisy shouting; p. 427

coax (kōks) *v.* to persuade by means of gentle urging or flattery; p. 140

coercion (kō ur′ shən) *n.* force, repression; p. 1060

coincide (kō′ in sīd′) *v.* to occupy the same place in space or time; p. 177

compound (kom′ pound) *n.* a fenced or walled-in area containing a group of buildings; p. 71

compulsory (kəm pul′ sər ē) *adj.* mandatory; enforced; p. 952

conceive (kən sēv′) *v.* to cause to begin; to originate; p. 1041

condescending (kon′ di sen′ ding) *adj.* characterized by an air of superiority or smugness; p. 1097

congealed (kən jēld′) *adj.* thickened; changed from a liquid to a solid state; p. 704

conjurer (kon′ jər ər) *n.* individual who practices magic; magician, juggler, snake charmer; p. 110

consecrate (kon′ sə krāt′) *v.* to induct into a permanent office through a religious rite; p. 138

consecrated (kon′ sə krāt id) *adj.* made or declared sacred; devoted to a religious purpose; p. 1115

console (kən sōl′) *v.* to alleviate a person's grief, sense of loss, or trouble; to comfort; p. 960

contract (kən trakt′) *v.* to draw together; to wrinkle up; p. 961

contrary (kon′ trer ē) *adj.* unfavorable; p. 832

counterrevolutionary (koun′ tər rev′ ə lo͞o′ shə ner′ ē) *n.* a person actively opposed to a government established by a revolution; p. 664

covenant (kuv′ ə nənt) *n.* a formal, solemn, and binding agreement; p. 437

cringing (krinj′ ing) *adj.* shrinking back, as if in fear; p. 697

cryptically (krip′ tik lē) *adv.* secretly or mysteriously; p. 1144

culinary (kə′ lə ner′ ē) *adj.* related to the kitchen or cooking; p. 539

cursory (kur′ sər ē) *adj.* hasty and not thorough; superficial; p. 1167

D

debar (di bär′) *v.* to shut out or exclude from doing something; p. 442

debauch (di bôch′) *v.* to corrupt; p. 90

defect (di fekt′) *v.* to desert one group or political entity for another; p. 752

defiance (di fī əns) *n.* an act of resistance; p. 968

deficiency (di fish′ ən sē) *n.* a shortage or lack of something essential; p. 653

demolition (dem′ ə lish′ ən) *n.* act of tearing down or breaking to pieces; destruction; p. 394

demur (di mur′) *n.* hesitation or objection; p. 519

denizen (den′ ə zən) *n.* inhabitant; p. 141

depraved (di prāvd′) *adj.* marked by evil; p. 396

derisively (di rī′ siv lē) *adv.* using ridicule or scorn to show contempt; p. 83

desist (di sist′) *v.* to cease to proceed or act; to stop; p. 160

detainee (di tān′ ē) *n.* a person held in custody especially for political reasons; p. 160

detractor (di trak′ tər) *n.* one who speaks ill of someone or something; p. 328

dialect (dī′ ə lekt′) *n.* a regional variety of a language distinguished by nonstandard features of vocabulary, grammar, and pronunciation; p. 1131

diffuse (di fūz′) *v.* to disperse; p. 91

diligence (dil′ ə jəns) *n.* persistent hard work; alertness; p. 1097

diligent (dil′ ə jənt) *adj.* characterized by steady, earnest, and energetic effort; p. 747

disciple (di sī′ pəl) *n.* one who accepts or assists in spreading the teachings of another; p. 625

discourteous (dis kur′ tē əs) *adj.* impolite; p. 841
discreet (dis krēt′) *adj.* quietly thoughtful; p. 1139
discreetly (dis krēt′ lē) *adv.* unnoticeably; p. 84
discrimination (dis krim′ ə nā′ shən) *n.* making a difference in treatment or favor on some basis other than individual merit; p. 960
disdain (dis dān′) *n.* an attitude of scorn or contempt for those considered inferior or unworthy; p. 1097
disillusion (dis′ i lo͞o′ zhən) *n.* the state of being freed from misleading images or naïve trust; p. 961
disparage (dis par′ ij) *v.* to speak badly of; p. 937
dispose (dis pōz′) *v.* to arrange or place in a particular position; p. 90
dissension (di sen′ shən) *n.* disagreement; discord; p. 66
distorted (dis tôrt′ id) *adj.* twisted out of a normal or original shape or condition; p. 961
dullard (dul′ ərd) *n.* a stupid or unimaginative person; p. 512

E

ecstasy (ek′ stə sē) *n.* a state of overwhelming emotion, especially rapturous delight; p. 968
emaciated (i mā′ shē āt′ id) *adj.* thin and feeble; p. 955
empathy (em′ pə thē) *n.* the understanding and entering into the feelings and experiences of another person; p. 747
endorse (en dôrs′) *v.* to inscribe with one's signature to show approval; p. 172
enmity (en′ me tē) *n.* hatred or ill will; p. 843
exalted (ig zôlt′ əd) *adj.* raised above the ordinary; p. 1149
extremity (iks trem′ ə tē) *n.* great danger or need; p. 830

F

faculty (fak′ əl tē) *n.* an inherent or natural ability; p. 330
fatuous (fach′ o͞o əs) *adj.* silly, foolish; p. 504
fettered (fet′ ərd) *adj.* chained; p. 521
fidelity (fi del′ ə tē) *n.* faithfulness; p. 1015
finite (fī′ nīt) *adj.* having definite or definable limits; p. 1174
firmament (fur′ mə ment) *n.* the sky; p. 427
flag (flag) *v.* to decline in interest or attraction; p. 707
formidable (for′ mi də bəl) *adj.* tending to inspire awe, wonder, or fear; p. 520
frantically (fran′ tik lē) *adv.* in a manner marked by fast and nervous activity; p. 759
frivolity (fri vol′ ə tē) *n.* silliness; p. 1137
frock (frok) n. a woman's dress; p. 172
fumble (fum′ bəl) *v.* to grope or handle clumsily; p. 174
furtively (fur′ tiv lē) *adv.* in a secretive manner; p. 652

G

galley (gal′ ē) *n.* the kitchen and cooking apparatus, especially of a ship or airplane; p. 117
gaunt (gônt) *adj.* excessively thin, as from suffering; p. 251; excessively thin and angular; p. 694
gesticulate (jes tik′ yə lāt′) *v.* to make gestures, especially when speaking; p. 614
glean (glēn) *v.* to pick up or gather grain left on the field after the reaping; p. 443
glower (glou′ər) *v.* to look or stare with sullen annoyance or anger; p. 47
granary (grā′ nər ē) *n.* storehouse; p. 73
gravely (grāv′ lē) *adv.* in a serious or dignified manner; p. 1159
guffaw (gu fô′) *n.* loud or boisterous burst of laughter; p. 1183

H

hack (hak) *v.* to use heavy blows to cut or chop in an irregular or unskillful manner; p. 60
haggard (hag′ ərd) *adj.* worn or wasted as from hunger; p. 1136
harangue (hə rang′) *v.* to make an angry, ranting speech; p. 667
heedless (hēd′ lis) *adj.* inconsiderate, thoughtless; p. 84
hoary (hôr′ ē) *adj.* extremely old or ancient; p. 555
hoist (hoist) *v.* to raise or pull up; p. 60
horde (hôrd) *n.* teeming crowd or throng; p. 110
hover (huv′ ər) *v.* to linger or remain nearby; p. 706
humane (hū mān′) *adj.* marked by compassion, sympathy, or consideration for humans or animals; p. 952

I

ideal (ī dē′ əl) *n.* goal; aim; p. 1158
immobile (i mō′ bil) *adj.* incapable of movement, motionless; p. 1042
immutable (i mū′ tə bəl) *adj.* unchanging; p. 720
impale (im pāl′) *v.* to pierce with a pointed object; p. 457
impassive (im pas′ iv) *adj.* giving no sign of feeling or emotion; p. 761
impede (im pēd′) *v.* to hinder; to interfere with or slow the progress of; p. 44
impervious (im pur′ vē əs) *adj.* not easily affected or disturbed; p. 554
impetuous (im pech′ o͞o əs) *adj.* impulsive; p. 18
implement (im′ plə mənt) *n.* tool, instrument, or utensil used to carry out tasks; p. 46
imploring (im plôr′ ing) *adj.* begging, or beseeching; p. 708
improvise (im′ prə vīz′) *v.* to create to meet an unexpected need; p. 1137
incantation (in′ kan tā′ shən) *n.* use of spells or verbal charms as part of a magic ritual; p. 422
increment (ing′ krə mənt) *n.* something gained or added in a series, usually at regular intervals; p. 541
indignantly (in dig′ nənt lē) *adv.* with dignified anger; aroused by unfair or mean actions or comments; p. 61
indiscreet (in′ dis krēt′) *adj.* lacking in good judgment; p. 886
indiscriminately (in′ dis krim′ ə nit lē) *adv.* randomly; haphazardly; p. 954
indolent (ind′ əl ənt) *adj.* lazy; p. 726
inexorable (i nek′ sər ə bəl) *adj.* relentless; unyielding; p. 554
ingratiating (in grā′ shē āt′ ing) *adj.* deliberately intending to win another's favor; p. 540
inherent (in hēr′ ənt) *adj.* forming an essential part of someone or something; firmly established by nature or habit; p. 1164
inordinate (in ôr′ də nit) *adj.* excessive; p. 503
inquisitive (in kwiz′ ə tiv) *adj.* curious about the affairs of others; p. 614
instinctively (in stingk′ tiv lē) *adv.* naturally or unconsciously; p. 624
insular (in′ sə lər) *adj.* characteristic of island people; especially, reflecting a narrow, isolated viewpoint; p. 546
interminable (in tur′ mi nə bəl) *adj.* having or seeming to have no end; p. 838
intertwined (in′ tər twīnd′) *adj.* twisted, woven, or interlaced together; p. 178
intimation (in′ ti mā′ shən) *n.* an indirect suggestion; p. 330
intransigence (in tran′ sə jəns) *n.* the state of being uncompromising; p. 654
irate (ī rāt′) *adj.* hot-tempered or angry; p. 188
issue (ish′ o͞o) *v.* to come forth; to emerge; p. 46

K

keen (kēn) *v.* to lament or mourn loudly; p. 162
knobbly (nob′ lē) *adj.* shaped like a knob; p. 151

L

lamentation (lam′ ən tā′ shən) *n.* act of mourning, crying, or wailing; p. 121
languor (lang′ gər) *n.* weakness or weariness of body or mind; p. 529
lanky (lang′ kē) *adj.* ungracefully tall and thin; p. 188
libation (lī bā′ shən) *n.* a liquid used in ceremonial drinking; p. 428
lilting (lil′ ting) *adj.* characterized by a rhythmical flow or cadence; p. 726
lithely (līth′ lē) *adv.* with flexibility and grace; easily; athletically; p. 117
loiter (loi′ tər) *v.* move along aimlessly, with frequent pauses, p. 1145
lucid (lo͞o′ sid) *adj.* having full use of one's faculties; clear-headed; p. 1112
luminous (lo͞o′ mə nəs) *adj.* emitting light; p. 17

M

malevolently (mə lev′ə lənt lē′) *adv.* in an intentionally harmful manner; p. 666
mediocre (mē′ dē ō′ kər) *adj.* of moderate or low quality; undistinguished; p. 1158
meditate (med′ ə tāt′) *v.* to focus one's thoughts on; reflect or ponder over; p. 1159; to quietly focus one's thoughts; p. 625
miasma (mī az′ mə) *n.* a heavy vaporous emanation or atmosphere; p. 560
monotony (mə not′ ən ē) *n.* sameness leading to boredom; lack of variety; p. 697

munificence (mū nif′ ə sens) *n.* great generosity; p. 396

N

nape (nāp) *n.* the back of the neck; p. 66
negate (ni gāt′) *v.* to make ineffective or powerless; p. 1015
nib (nib) *n.* pen point; p. 174
nullity (nul′ ə tē) *n.* a mere nothing; insignificance; p. 512

O

oblation (ob lā′ shən) *n.* religious sacrifice; p. 92
oblique (ə blēk′) *adj.* indirect; vague; p. 1175
obscure (əb skyoor′) *v.* to make dark, dim, or indistinct; cloud; p. 1175
odoriferous (ō′ də rif′ ər əs) *adj.* having or giving forth a scent; p. 91
ominous (om′ ə nəs) *adj.* foreboding or foreshadowing evil; p. 422

P

palpitation (pal′ pə tā′ shən) *n.* a rapid heartbeat; p. 559
pasteurization (pas′ chə rə zā′ shən) *n.* subjecting a food, especially milk, to a temperature high enough to destroy disease-producing bacteria without altering the composition of the product; p. 1183
peevishness (pē′ vish nəs) *n.* fretful temperament or mood marked by ill temper; p. 549
pensive (pen′ siv) *adj.* sadly or dreamily thoughtful; p. 529
penuriously (pi noor′ ē əs lē) *adv.* in severe poverty; p. 830
persist (pər sist′) *v.* to insist, as in repeating a statement; p. 7
perusal (pə ro͞o′ zəl) *n.* the act of reading in detail or examining carefully; p. 1131
pester (pes′ tər) *v.* to harass or annoy with petty irritations; p. 172
petrified (pe′ trə fīd) *adj.* paralyzed with fear or horror; p. 7
pettiness (pet′ ē nəs) *n.* a focus on unimportant or small-minded details; p. 961
phenomenon (fə nom′ ə non′) *n.* observable fact or subject of scientific study; remarkable event or occurrence; p. 1166
pilgrimage (pil′ grə mij) *n.* a journey taken by a disciple; p. 625
pivot (piv′ ət) *n.* a person, thing, or factor having a central role, function, or effect; p. 153
plaintive (plān′ tiv) *adj.* expressive of suffering or distress; p. 1002
plaintively (plān′ tiv lē) *adv.* in a manner expressing suffering or woe; p. 655
plausible (plô′ zə bəl) *adj.* appearing worthy of belief; p. 760
poignancy (poin′ yən cē) *n.* the quality of painfully affecting one's feelings; p. 503
populace (pop′ yə lis) *n.* the inhabitants of a place; p. 716
potency (pōt′ ən sē) *n.* power to achieve a particular result; p. 1176
precipitous (pri sip′ ə təs) *adj.* having very steep sides; p. 395
prelude (prel′ ūd) *n.* an event preceding and preparing for a more important matter; p. 759
prerogative (pri rog′ ə tiv) *n.* an exclusive or special right, power, or privilege; p. 527
presumption (pri zump′ shən) *n.* attitude or conduct that oversteps the bounds of propriety or courtesy; p. 832
presumptuous (pri zump′ cho͞o əs) *adj.* excessively bold or arrogant; taking liberties; p. 1167
primordial (prī môr′ dē əl) *adj.* ancient, from the beginning of time; p. 666
prodigy (prod′ ə jē) *n.* extraordinary person, thing, or deed; p. 454
profusion (prə fū′ zhən) *n.* extravagance; p. 90
propriety (prə prī′ ə tē) *n.* conformity to what is acceptable in conduct or speech; p. 1097
prostrate (pros′ trāt) *v.* to throw oneself face downward on the ground as a gesture of humility or submission; p. 443
prostrate (pros′ trāt) *adj.* lying flat; p. 177; stretched out with one's face on the ground, usually in adoration or submission; p. 944
provincial (prə vin′ shəl) *adj.* relating to or coming from a province; lacking sophistication and refinement; p. 546
provisions (prə vizh′ ənz) *n.* food supplies; p. 695
prudent (pro͞od′ ənt) *adj.* sensible; sound in judgment; p. 1013

pulsate (pul′ sāt) *v.* to throb or beat rhythmically; p. 18

pungent (pun′ jənt) *adj.* having a sharp or stinging quality, especially affecting the sense of taste or smell; p. 557

Q

quarry (kwôr′ ē) *n.* something that is sought or pursued; prey; p. 48

query (kwēr′ ē) *v.* to ask, especially with a desire for authoritative information; p. 122

queue (kū) *n.* waiting line; p. 187

R

rash (rash) *adj.* resulting from undue haste or a lack of planning or caution; p. 893

reactionary (rē ak′ shə ner′ ē) *adj.* supporting a return to a previous form of government; p. 666

rebuke (ri būk′) *v.* to criticize sharply; p. 138

recoil (ri koil′) *v.* to draw back, as in fear, horror, or surprise; p. 7

redress (ri dres′) *adj.* to correct or compensate for a wrong or loss; p. 838

refuse (ref′ ūs) *n.* trash, garbage; p. 110

renounce (ri nouns′) *v.* to give up, to abandon; p. 625; to give up, refuse, or resign, usually by formal declaration; p. 956

renown (ri noun′) *n.* a state of being widely acclaimed; p. 838

reproach (ri prōch′) *v.* to express disappointment for conduct that is blameworthy; p. 328; to charge with blame or fault for a wrongdoing; p. 616

reserve (ri zurv′) *n.* land set aside by the government for a specific purpose, such as wildlife preservation; p. 17

resignation (rez′ ig nā′ shən) *n.* unresisting acceptance; p. 1159

resilience (ri zil′ yens) *n.* ability to recover or adjust easily; p. 529

resolutely (rez′ ə lo͞ot′ lē) *adv.* with firm determination; p. 905

respite (res′ pit) *n.* period of temporary relief, rest, or delay; p. 967

retaliation (ri tal′ ē a′ shən) *n.* revenge; p. 143

retort (ri tort′) *v.* to reply in kind, especially with anger or with a witty or insulting response; p. 66

revered (ri vērd′) *adj.* regarded as worthy of great honor; p. 830

reverie (rev′ ər ē) *n.* the condition of being lost in thought; p. 717

rivulet (riv′ yə lət) *n.* a small stream; p. 531

ruse (ro͞oz) *n.* trick; p. 186

S

sabotage (sab′ ə tazh′) *v.* to cause damage for political reasons; p. 666

scholarship (skol′ ər ship′) *n.* academic achievement or knowledge; p. 511

scorn (skôrn) *n.* disrespect; p. 1014

scrutinize (skro͞ot′ ən īz) *v.* to examine with close attention to detail; p. 541

sedately (si dāt′ lē) *adv.* quietly; seriously; p. 548

self-possessed (self′ pə zest′) *adj.* in control of oneself; p. 1144

sentinel (sent′ ən əl) *n.* a person standing guard or keeping watch; p. 720

shirk (shurk) *v.* to evade or avoid one's duty; p. 539

sinister (sin′ is tər) *adj.* singularly evil; menacing; p. 396

slander (slan′ dər) *v.* to damage another's reputation through the spreading of lies or false charges; p. 904

sluice (slo͞os) *n.* floodgate; p. 431

solace (sol′ is) *n.* a source of relief; mental or spiritual comfort; p. 1112

spasmodically (spaz mod′ ik lē) *adv.* in an irregular or fitful manner; p. 1005

stealthily (stelth′ ə lē) *adv.* slowly and secretly; p. 444

stifled (stī′ fəld) *adj.* muffled or repressed; p. 178

stolid (stol′ id) *adj.* having or expressing little or no sensibility; unemotional; p. 115

stupefied (sto͞o′ pə fīd′) *adj.* groggy or insensible; p. 540

stupor (sto͞o′ pər) *n.* dulled mental state often as a result of shock or stress; daze; p. 1185

submerge (sub murj′) *v.* to go under water; p. 178

supplementary (sup′ lə men′ tər ē) *adj.* extra or additional; p. 1147

supplication (sup′ lə kā′ shən) *n.* humble entreaty; prayer of request; p. 1114

suppress (sə pres′) *v.* to keep secret; p. 18
surfeited (sur′ fi tid) *adj.* having overindulged, as with food; p. 728
sustain (sə stān′) *v.* to perform actions that keep something in existence; p. 1042

T

taint (tānt) *v.* to contaminate morally; to corrupt; p. 761
taut (tôt) *adj.* having no give or slack; tightly drawn; p. 178
tedious (tē′ dē əs) *adj.* tiresome because of length or dullness; boring; p. 1061
tepid (tep′ id) *adj.* moderately warm; lukewarm; p. 548
thicket (thik′ it) *n.* dense growth of shrubbery or small trees; p. 453
throng (thrông) *n.* crowding together of many persons; p. 110
titter (tit′ ər) *n.* a laugh; a snicker; p. 152
titter (tit′ ər) *v.* to laugh nervously; p. 707
toil (toil) *n.* fatiguing work or effort; p. 66
torrent (tôr′ ənt) *n.* enormous outpouring of rainwater; p. 139
trek (trek) *n.* a slow and difficult journey; p. 720
trespass (tres′ pəs) *v.* to illegally enter property; p. 939
trivial (triv′ ē əl) *adj.* commonplace; of little importance; p. 614
truncheon (trun′ chən) *n.* a billy club; p. 1005
tumult (to͞o′ məlt) *n.* noisy confusion; p. 456

U

ubiquitous (ū bik′ wə təs) *adj.* existing or being everywhere at the same time; p. 189
undaunted (un dôn′ tid) *adj.* courageously firm or resolute, especially in the face of danger or difficulty; not discouraged; p. 966
unmarred (un märd′) *adj.* unspoiled; p. 108
unperturbed (un′ pər turbd′) *adj.* not greatly disturbed in mind; calm; p. 928

V

veer (vēr) *v.* to change direction or course; p. 1064
vex (veks) *v.* to annoy; p. 71, 517
virile (vir′ əl) *adj.* masculine; p. 1136
virulent (vir′ yə lənt) *adj.* exceptionally severe and malicious; p. 189

W

warble (wôr′ bəl) *v.* to sing with rapid variations, or changes, in pitch; p. 1042
warder (wôr′ dər) *n.* a prison guard; p. 151
whitewash (hwīt′ wôsh) *v.* to apply a mixture of lime and water for whitening a surface; p. 173
winnow (win′ ō) *v.* to separate the grain from the chaff; p. 444
wizened (wiz′ ənd) *adj.* dry, shrunken, and wrinkled as a result of aging; p. 548

Spanish Glossary

A

abstain/abstenerse *v.* renunciar a algo o dejar de hacer algo mediante esfuerzo o sacrificio; p. 748

abstracted/abstraído *adj.* preocupado; distraído; absorto; p. 530

accomplice/cómplice *s.* quien participa en un crimen o maldad; p. 760

acquittal/absolución *s.* liberación de una acusación criminal mediante veredicto, sentencia u otro proceso legal; p. 328

affront/afrenta *s.* insulto deliberado; p. 84

animosity/animosidad *s.* mala voluntad o resentimiento; p. 159

appease/apaciguar *v.* lograr la paz mediante un acuerdo o concesión; p. 396

arable/arable *adj.* adecuado para la siembra y cultivo; p. 941

arid/árido *adj.* excesivamente seco; p. 520

askew/oblicuo *adj.* torcido; en ángulo; p. 6

assailant/asaltante *adj.* atacante; p. 66

assiduously/asiduamente *adv.* con puntualidad o juicio; p. 655

attainment/logro *s.* realización; consecución; p. 511

audacity/audacia *s.* actitud o comportamiento atrevido o valiente; p. 1174

austere/austero *adj.* frío o duro en apariencia o modales; sombrío; p. 1164

austerity/austeridad *s.* actitud espiritual o moral muy estricta; p. 502

avail/utilidad *s.* beneficio o ventaja; p. 110

avarice/avaricia *s.* codicia, p. 505

avenge/vindicar *v.* buscar venganza castigando a la persona que cometió la ofensa; p. 752

B

banal/trillado *adj.* que carece de originalidad, frescura o novedad; p. 1164

banish/desterrar *v.* expulsar o retirar de un lugar mediante la autoridad; p. 616

bashing/impacto *s.* golpe fuerte; p. 152

bedlam/batahola *s.* estado de confusión o estrépito; p. 152

beneficent/benéfico *adj.* que produce bien; p. 1114

beseeching/suplicante *adj.* que implora o ruega; p. 1002

besiege/sitiar *v.* rodear con fuerzas hostiles; p. 697

blandly/imperturbablemente *adv.* calladamente; sin interés; p. 84

boon/jovial *adj.* amigable o sociable; p. 457

boorishness/tosquedad *s.* rudeza o insensibilidad; p. 664

braying/rebuzno *s.* chillido o voz del asno; p. 728

bulwark/rompeolas *s.* lado del barco arriba de la plataforma superior; p. 117

C

censure/censurar *v.* encontrar una falla; criticar; p. 330

chafe/raspar *v.* irritar de tanto rozar o frotar; p. 251

chaste/casto *adj.* inocente; puro; p. 830

chastise/sancionar *v.* castigar, reprender o disciplinar severamente; p. 1014

clamor/clamor *s.* griterío; p. 427

coax/instar *v.* convencer o inducir con halagos; p. 140

coercion/coacción *s.* uso de la fuerza; represión; p. 1060

coincide/coincidir *v.* ocupar el mismo lugar en espacio o tiempo; p. 177

compound/recinto *s.* zona cercada o amurallada que contiene un grupo de edificios; p. 71

compulsory/imperativo *s.* obligatorio; p. 952

conceive/concebir *v.* hacer que comience; originar; p. 1041

condescending/condescendiente *adj.* con aire de superioridad; transigente; p. 1097

congealed/cuajado *adj.* endurecido; que cambió de estado sólido a líquido; p. 704

conjurer/prestidigitador *s.* individuo que practica la magia; mago; encantador de serpientes; p. 110

consecrate/bendecir *v.* realizar un rito religioso para inaugurar un negocio u oficina; p. 138

consecrated/consagrado *adj.* declarado sagrado; dedicado a un fin religioso; p. 1115

console/consolar *v.* aliviar el dolor o la angustia de una persona; calmar; p. 960

contract/contraer *v.* unir; encoger; p. 961

contrary/contrario *adj.* que no es favorable; p. 832

counterrevolutionary/contrarrevolucionario *s.* persona que se opone a un gobierno establecido mediante la rebelión; p. 664

covenant/convenio *s.* acuerdo formal y solemne; pacto; p. 437

cringing/contraído *adj.* que se retira o encoge; p. 697

cryptically/enigmáticamente *adv.* secreta o misteriosamente; p. 1144

culinary/culinario *adj.* relativo a la cocina; p. 539

cursory/superficial *adj.* de modo precipitado y a medio hacer; p. 1167

D

debar/privar *v.* negar o excluir; p. 442

debauch/viciar *v.* corromper; p. 90

defect/desertar *v.* abandonar un grupo o entidad política por otra; p. 752

defiance/desafío *s.* acto de resistencia; p. 968

deficiency/deficiencia *s.* falta o ausencia de algo esencial; p. 653

demolition/demolición *s.* acto de derribar o romper en pedazos; destrucción; p. 394

demur/vacilación *s.* duda u objeción; p. 519

denizen/morador *s.* habitante; residente; p. 141

depraved/depravado *adj.* corrupto; perverso; p. 396

derisively/burlonamente *adv.* que muestra desprecio mediante burla o ridículo; p. 83

desist/desistir *v.* dejar de hacer o actuar; detenerse; p. 160

detainee/detenido *s.* persona arrestada, sobre todo por razones políticas; p. 160

detractor/detractor *s.* quien critica o se opone; p. 328

dialect/dialecto *s.* variedad regional de un idioma que se distingue por características no reglamentarias de vocabulario, gramática y pronunciación; p. 1131

diffuse/difundir *v.* dispersar; p. 91

diligence/diligencia *s.* trabajo persistente y cuidadoso; esmero; p. 1097

diligent/diligente *adj.* que se esfuerza y tiene constancia; p. 747

disciple/discípulo *s.* quien comunica las enseñanzas de otro; p. 625

discourteous/descortés *adj.* de malos modales; p. 841

discreet/discreto *adj.* sensato; cuidadoso; p. 1139

discreetly/discretamente *adv.* sin hacerse notar; p. 84

discrimination/discriminación *s.* tratamiento diferente por hechos distintos a los méritos personales; p. 960

disdain/desdén *s.* actitud de desprecio hacia aquéllos que se consideran inferiores o sin valor; p. 1097

disillusion/desengañar *v.* liberar de ilusiones falsas; hacer perder la confianza; p. 961

disparage/desacreditar *v.* hablar mal de alguien o de algo; p. 937

dispose/disponer *v.* arreglar o colocar en determinada posición; p. 90

dissension/discordia *s.* desacuerdo; p. 66

distorted/deformado *adj.* torcido; que perdió su forma o condición normal u original; p. 961

dullard/idiota *s.* persona estúpida o sin imaginación; p. 512

E

ecstasy/éxtasis *s.* estado de gran emoción o entusiasmo; arrebato; p. 968

emaciated/enflaquecido *adj.* flaco y débil; p. 955

empathy/empatía *s.* entendimiento; comprensión de los sentimientos y experiencias de otra persona; p. 747

endorse/endosar *v.* firmar para demostrar aprobación; p. 172

enmity/enemistad *s.* odio o enfrentamiento; p. 843

exalted/elevado *adj.* por encima del nivel ordinario; p. 1149

extremity/apuro *s.* gran peligro o necesidad; p. 830

F

faculty/facultad *s.* habilidad inherente o natural; p. 330

fatuous/fatuo *adj.* tonto; necio; p. 504

fettered/encadenado *adj.* inmovilizado con cadenas; p. 521

fidelity/fidelidad *s.* lealtad; p. 1015

finite/finito *adj.* que tiene un punto final o límite definido; p. 1174

firmament/firmamento *s.* cielo; p. 427

flag/decaer *v.* perder interés o atractivo; p. 707

formidable/formidable *adj.* que inspira asombro, maravilla o temor; p. 520

frantically/frenéticamente *adv.* de modo nervioso y agitado; p. 759

frivolity/frivolidad *s.* tontería; p. 1137

frock/saya *s.* vestido de mujer; p. 172

fumble/torpemente *v.* andar o moverse a tropezones; p. 174

furtively/furtivamente *adv.* en secreto; p. 652

G

galley/fogón *s.* hornilla para cocinar, especialmente en un barco o en un avión; p. 117

gaunt/demacrado *adj.* excesivamente flaco, debido a problemas o sufrimientos; p. 251; excesivamente flaco y angular; p. 694

gesticulate/gesticular *v.* hacer gestos, especialmente al hablar; p. 614

glean/espigar *v.* recoger espigas después de la siega; p. 443

glower/mirar con ceño *v.* mirar con rabia o molestia; p. 47

granary/granero *s.* depósito; p. 73

gravely/gravemente *adv.* de modo serio o severo; p. 1159

guffaw/carcajada *s.* risotada; p. 1183

H

hack/tajar *v.* dar golpes fuertes para cortar o picar de modo disparejo; p. 60

haggard/macilento *adj.* desgastado debido al hambre; p. 1136

harangue/arengar *v.* dar un discurso furioso y vociferante; p. 667

heedless/desatento *adj.* que no demuestra consideración; descuidado; p. 84

hoary/remoto *adj.* extremadamente viejo o antiguo; p. 555

hoist/elevar *v.* alzar o levantar; p. 60

horde/horda *s.* multitud o tumulto de personas; p. 110

hover/revolotear *v.* rondar o permanecer en los alrededores; p. 706

humane/humano *adj.* que demuestra compasión o consideración por personas o animales; p. 952

I

ideal/ideal *s.* meta, objetivo; p. 1158

immobile/inmóvil *adj.* incapaz de moverse; estático; p. 1042

immutable/inmutable *adj.* que no cambia; p. 720

impale/empalar *v.* atravesar con un objeto puntiagudo; p. 457

impassive/impasible *adj.* indiferente; que no da signos de sentir emoción; p. 761

impede/impedir *v.* obstruir; entorpecer; p. 44

impervious/impenetrable *adj.* que no se deja afectar o molestar fácilmente; p. 554

impetuous/impetuoso *adj.* impulsivo; p. 18

implement/implemento *s.* herramienta, instrumento o utensilio que se usa para llevar a cabo una tarea; p. 46

imploring/implorante *adj.* que suplica o ruega; p. 708

improvise/improvisar *v.* crear algo para satisfacer una necesidad inesperada; p. 1137

incantation/encantamiento *s.* uso de hechizos o encantos verbales como parte de un ritual mágico; p. 422

increment/incremento *s.* algo que se gana o se agrega por etapas, por lo común a intervalos regulares; p. 541

indignantly/con indignación *adv.* que siente o demuestra rabia por una acción o comentario injusto o mal intencionado; p. 61

indiscreet/indiscreto *adj.* que carece de buen juicio; imprudente; p. 886

indiscriminately/indistintamente *adv.* al azar; sin un orden concreto; p. 954

indolent/indolente *adj.* perezoso; p. 726

inexorable/inexorable *adj.* inflexible; implacable; p. 554

ingratiating/congraciador *adj.* que busca ganarse aprecio o buena voluntad; p. 540

inherent/inherente *adj.* que hace parte esencial; firmemente establecido por naturaleza o hábito; p. 1164

inordinate/inmoderado *adj.* excesivo; p. 503

inquisitive/inquisitivo *adj.* curioso por los asuntos ajenos; p. 614

instinctively/instintivamente *adj.* de modo natural o inconsciente; p. 624

insular/insular *adj.* relativo a los habitantes de una isla; especialmente, actitud que refleja un punto de vista estrecho y limitado; p. 546

interminable/interminable *adj.* que parece no tener fin; p. 838

intertwined/entrelazado *adj.* enrollado, tejido o unido entre sí; p. 178

intimation/insinuación *s.* sugerencia indirecta; p. 330

intransigence/intransigencia *s.* estado de no querer ceder ni buscar un acuerdo; p. 654

irate/airado *adj.* furioso o colérico; p. 188

issue/emerger *v.* surgir; p. 46

K

keen/plañir *v.* lamentarse o llorar ruidosamente; p. 162

knobbly/nudoso *adj.* lleno de bultos o protuberancias; p. 151

L

lamentation/lamentación *s.* acto de lamentar, llorar o gemir; p. 121

languor/desfallecimiento *s.* debilidad o agotamiento del cuerpo o de la mente; p. 529

lanky/larguirucho *adj.* persona alta y flaca; p. 188

libation/libación *s.* bebida usada durante ceremonias; p. 428

lilting/melodioso *adj.* que tiene ritmo o cadencia; p. 726

lithely/flexiblemente *adv.* con flexibilidad y gracia; fácilmente; atléticamente; p. 117

loiter/remolonear *v.* moverse sin rumbo fijo haciendo pausas frecuentes; p. 1145

lucid/lúcido *adj.* que posee facultades mentales; sensato; p. 1112

luminous/luminoso *adj.* que emite luz; p. 17

M

malevolently/malignamente *adv.* con intención de hacer daño; de modo perverso; p. 666

mediocre/mediocre *adj.* de mediana o baja calidad; que no se distingue o sobresale; p. 1158

meditate/meditar *v.* reflexionar; pensar detenidamente; pp. 625 y 1159

miasma/miasma *s.* emanación de un vapor nocivo; p. 560

monotony/monotonía *s.* igualdad que conduce al aburrimiento; falta de variedad; p. 697

munificence/munificencia *s.* gran generosidad; p. 396

N

nape/nuca *s.* parte de atrás del cuello; cogote; p. 66

negate/anular *v.* hacer ineficaz o cancelar; p. 1015

nib/pluma *s.* bolígrafo; p. 174

nullity/nulidad *s.* insignificancia; p. 512

O

oblation/oblación *s.* sacrificio religioso; p. 92

oblique/ambiguo *adj.* indirecto; vago; p. 1175

obscure/ensombrecer *v.* obscurecer, opacar; enturbiar; p. 1175

odoriferous/odorífero *adj.* que tiene o emite un olor; p. 91

ominous/ominoso *adj.* siniestro; de mal agüero; p. 422

P

palpitation/palpitación *s.* latido rápido del corazón; p. 559

pasteurization/pasteurización *s.* someter un alimento, en particular la leche, a temperaturas altas para destruir bacterias nocivas sin alterar la composición del producto; p. 1183

peevishness/quisquillosidad *s.* temperamento irritable o mal carácter; p. 549

pensive/abstraído *adj.* pensativo, triste o soñador; p. 529

penuriously/miserablemente *adv.* de un modo extremadamente pobre; p. 830

persist/persistir *v.* insistir; repetir un comentario o conducta; p. 7

perusal/lectura cuidadosa *s.* acto de leer en detalle o de examinar cuidadosamente; p. 1131

pester/fastidiar *v.* molestar o perturbar con tonterías; p. 172

petrified/petrificado *adj.* paralizado del miedo o del asombro; p. 7

pettiness/mezquindad *s.* énfasis en detalles sin importancia; insignificancia; p. 961

phenomenon/fenómeno *s.* sujeto de estudio científico; suceso o acontecimiento extraordinario; p. 1166

pilgrimage/peregrinaje *s.* viaje realizado por un discípulo; p. 625

pivot/fundamental *s.* persona, cosa o factor que tiene un papel o función central; p. 153

plaintive/quejumbroso *adj.* que expresa sufrimiento o molestia; p. 1002

plaintively/quejumbrosamente *adv.* de un modo que expresa sufrimiento o desdicha; p. 655

plausible/verosímil *adj.* que se puede creer; factible; p. 760

poignancy/mordacidad *s.* conducta que hiere; p. 503

populace/población *s.* habitantes de un lugar; p. 716

potency/potencia *s.* poder para alcanzar un resultado concreto; p. 1176

precipitous/escarpado *adj.* que tiene lados muy empinados; p. 395

prelude/preludio *s.* preparativo o suceso anterior a otro más importante; preámbulo; p. 759

prerogative/prerrogativa *s.* derecho exclusivo o especial; poder o privilegio; p. 527

presumption/insolencia *s.* actitud o conducta que sobrepasa los límites de la cortesía; p. 832

presumptuous/presuntuoso *adj.* excesivamente atrevido o arrogante; p. 1167

primordial/primordial *adj.* fundamental; p. 666

prodigy/prodigio *s.* persona, cosa o hazaña extraordinaria; p. 454

profusion/profusión *s.* extravagancia; p. 90

propriety/decoro *s.* conducta que se ajusta a normas convencionales; p. 1097

prostrate/postrarse *v.* arrojarse al piso en gesto de humildad o sumisión; p. 443

prostrate/postrado *adj.* arrodillado con el rostro en el suelo, usualmente en gesto de adoración o sumisión; p. 944

provincial/provinciano *adj.* relacionado a provincia o procedente de ella; sin refinamiento; p. 546

provisions/provisiones *s.* abastacemientos; p. 695

prudent/prudente *adj.* sensible; sensato; p. 1013

pulsate/palpitar *v.* latir rítmicamente; p. 18

pungent/acre *adj.* que tiene un sabor u olor agudo o punzante; p. 557

Q

quarry/presa *s.* animal o cosa que se quiere atrapar; p. 48

query/inquirir *v.* preguntar, especialmente con una actitud autoritaria; p. 122

queue/cola *s.* fila de espera; p. 187

R

rash/apresurado *adj.* hecho a la carrera o sin cuidado; p. 893

reactionary/reaccionario *adj.* que respalda el regreso a una forma anterior de gobierno; p. 666

rebuke/reprender *v.* criticar agudamente; p. 138

recoil/retroceder *v.* retirarse, por miedo o sorpresa; p. 7

redress/resarcir *v.* corregir o compensar por una equivocación o pérdida; p. 838

refuse/desecho *s.* basura; p. 110

renounce/renunciar *v.* ceder, abandonar; p. 625; dimitir, por lo común mediante una declaración formal; p. 956

renown/renombre *s.* condición de ser ampliamente conocido o aclamado; p. 838

reproach/reprochar *v.* expresar disgusto por una conducta errónea; pp. 328 y 616

reserve/reserva *s.* tierra reservada por el gobierno para un propósito específico, tal como la preservación de animales y plantas; p. 17

resignation/resignación *s.* aceptación o conformismo; p. 1159

resilience/elasticidad *s.* capacidad de recuperarse o ajustarse fácilmente; p. 529

resolutely/resueltamente *adv.* con firmeza o determinación; p. 905

respite/respiro *s.* pausa o período de descanso o tranquilidad; p. 967

retaliation/represalia *s.* venganza; p. 143

retort/devolver un insulto *v.* responder con rabia a una ofensa verbal; p. 66

revered/venerado *adj.* que se considera digno de ser honrado; p. 830

reverie/ensueño *s.* abstracción; contemplación; p. 717

rivulet/riachuelo *s.* pequeño arroyo o quebrada; p. 531

ruse/artificio *s.* truco; p. 186

S

sabotage/sabotear *v.* causar daño por razones políticas; p. 666

scholarship/erudición *s.* conocimientos académicos o sabiduría; p. 511

scorn/desdén *s.* desprecio; p. 1014

scrutinize/escudriñar *v.* examinar con atención; indagar; p. 541

sedately/sosegadamente *adv.* calmadamente; seriamente; p. 548

self-possessed/sereno *adj.* que tiene control de sí mismo; p. 1144

sentinel/centinela *s.* vigilante; guardián; p. 720

shirk/eludir *v.* evadir o evitar un deber; p. 539

sinister/siniestro *adj.* maligno; amenazador; p. 396

slander/calumniar *v.* dañar una reputación difundiendo mentiras o acusaciones falsas; p. 904

sluice/esclusa *s.* compuerta; p. 431

solace/solaz *s.* fuente de consuelo; alivio mental o espiritual; p. 1112

spasmodically/espasmódicamente *adv.* de modo irregular o intermitente; p. 1005

stealthily/furtivamente *adv.* en secreto y lentamente; p. 444

stifled/reprimido *adj.* que se frena o abstiene; p. 178

stolid/impasible *adj.* que no expresa sensibilidad o emoción; p. 115

stupefied/estupefacto *adj.* atontado o desconcertado; p. 540

stupor/estupor *s.* actitud de asombro o atontamiento como resultado de un impacto emocional; sopor; p. 1185

submerge/sumergirse *v.* lanzarse debajo del agua; p. 178

supplementary/suplementario *adj.* adicional; p. 1147

supplication/súplica *s.* ruego o plegaria; p. 1114

suppress/reprimir *v.* mantener en secreto; ocultar; p. 18

surfeited/hartado *adj.* que comió en exageración; p. 728

sustain/sostener *v.* mantener algo que ya existe; p. 1042

T

taint/corromper *v.* contaminar moralmente; viciar; p. 761

taut/tenso *adj.* que no se relaja o cede; p. 178

tedious/tedioso *adj.* aburrido debido a su duración o tema; p. 1061

tepid/tibio *adj.* templado; p. 548

thicket/espesura *s.* lugar con muchos matorrales o vegetación espesa; p. 453

throng/gentío *s.* multitud, tumulto; p. 110

titter/reírse *v.* reírse con disimulo; p. 707

titter/risita *s.* risa disimulada o entre dientes; p. 152

toil/faena *s.* trabajo o esfuerzo pesado; p. 66

torrent/torrente *s.* lluvia fuerte; aguacero; p. 139

trek/jornada *s.* viaje largo y difícil; p. 720

trespass/entrar ilegalmente *v.* colarse a una propiedad ajena; p. 939

trivial/trivial *adj.* insignificante o de poca importancia; común; p. 614

truncheon/cachiporra *s.* vara del policía; p. 1015

tumult/tumulto *s.* confusión ruidosa; p. 456

U

ubiquitous/ubicuo *adj.* que existe o está en todas partes al mismo tiempo; p. 189

undaunted/intrépido *adj.* muy firme o resuelto, especialmente al enfrentar un peligro o dificultad; audaz; p. 966

unmarred/inmaculado *adj.* sin mancha ni daño; p. 108

unperturbed/inalterado *adj.* sereno; p. 928

V

veer/desviarse *v.* cambiar de dirección o curso; p. 1064

vex/fastidiar *v.* molestar; p. 71, 517

virile/viril *adj.* masculino; p. 1136

virulent/virulento *adj.* excepcionalmente severo o malicioso; p. 189

W

warble/trinar *v.* cantar con variaciones o cambios rápidos; p. 1042

warder/guardián *s.* vigilante de una prisión; p. 151

whitewash/blanquear *v.* aplicar una mezcla de cal y agua a una superficie; p. 173

winnow/bieldar *v.* separar el trigo de su cáscara o desperdicio; p. 444

wizened/marchito *adj.* seco y arrugado como resultado del paso de los años; p. 548

Index of Skills

References beginning with R refer to handbook pages.

Literary Concepts & Techniques

Reading & Thinking

Grammar and Language

Vocabulary

Writing

Listening, Speaking, and Viewing

Research and Study Skills

Media and Technology

Life Skills

Interdisciplinary Studies

Index of Authors & Titles

Index of Authors & Titles

Index of Authors & Titles

Index of Art and Artists

Acknowledgments

(continued from page ii)

Literature

Active Reading Models

"You Are Now Entering the Human Heart" by Janet Frame. Permission courtesy of Curtis Brown (Australia) Pty Ltd.

"The Iguana" from *Out of Africa* by Isak Dinesen. Copyright © 1937, 1938 by Random House, Inc. Copyright renewed 1965, 1966 by Rungstedlundfonden Foundation. Reprinted by permission of Random House, Inc.

"Night of Sine" from *Nocturnes* by L. S. Senghor. Copyright © Editions du Seuil, 1964. Reprinted by permission.

"Civilian and Soldier" by Wole Soyinka. Reprinted by permission of the author.

"The Prisoner Who Wore Glasses" from *Tales of Tenderness and Power,* published by William Heinemann in their African Writers Series. Copyright © The Estate of Bessie Head, 1989. Reprinted by permission of John Johnson, Ltd.

"The Return" from *Secret Lives.* Copyright © 1975 by Ngugi wa Thiong'o. Reprinted by permission of East African Educational Publishers.

"A House for Us" by Etidal Osman, from *Stories by Egyptian Women* by Marilyn Booth, published by Quartet Books in 1991. Reprinted by permission of the publisher.

Reprinted with the permission of Scribner, a Division of Simon & Schuster from *Kaffir Boy in America* by Mark Mathabane. Copyright © 1989 by Mark Mathabane.

Unit One

"The Immortality of Writers" from *Poetry of Asia,* reprinted by permission of Weatherhill, Inc.

"So Small Are the Flowers of Seamu" from *Love Poems of Ancient Egypt,* translated by Ezra Pound and Noel Stock. Copyright © 1960 by Ezra Pound, © 1962 by Noel Stock, © 1962 by New Directions. Reprinted by permission of New Directions Publishing Corp.

Excerpt from The Kamusi Project, www.cis.yale.edu, reprinted by permission of the Yale University Program in African Languages.

"Useful Swahili Words," www.glcom.com/hassan/swahili, reprinted by permission of Hassan Ali.

"Anansi's Fishing Expedition" from *The Cow-Tail Switch* by Harold Courlander. Copyright 1947, © 1974 by Harold Courlander. Reprinted by permission of Henry Holt and Company, Inc.

"Edju and the Two Friends" from *African Folktales,* selected and edited by Paul Radin. Copyright © 1964 by Bollingen Foundation. Reprinted by permission of Princeton University Press.

"Magic Words" reprinted by permission of Edward Fields.

Excerpt from "The Lion's Awakening" from *Sundiata: An Epic of Old Mali* by D. T. Niane. Copyright © 1965 by Longmans, Green & Co. Reprinted by permission of Addison Wesley Longman Ltd.

Excerpt from *Equiano's Travels,* abridged and edited by Paul Edwards. Copyright © 1967 by Paul Edwards. Reprint by permission of Heinemann Educational Publishers, a division of Reed Educational & Professional Publishing Ltd.

"Half a Day" from *The Time and the Place and Other Stories* by Naguib Mahfouz. Copyright © 1991 by the American University in Cairo Press. Reprinted by permission of Doubleday, a division of Random House, Inc.

"Tribal Scars" from *Tribal Scars and Other Stories* by Sembene Ousmane, translated by Len Ortzen. Copyright © 1962 Editions Presence Africaines. Reprinted by permission.

"The Voter" from *Girls at War and Other Stories* by Chinua Achebe. Copyright © 1972, 1973 by Chinua Achebe. Used by permission of Doubleday, a division of Random House, Inc.

"The Voter" from *Girls at War and Other Stories* by Chinua Achebe. Copyright © 1972 by Chinua Achebe. Reprinted by permission of Harold Ober Associates Incorporated.

"The Rain Came" by Grace Ogot, reprinted by permission of East African Educational Publishers.

Unit Two

"The Rage of Achilles" and "The Death of Hector" by Homer, from *The Iliad* by Homer, translated by Robert Fagles. Translation copyright © 1990 by Robert Fagles. Introduction and Notes copyright © 1990 by Bernard Knox. Used by permission of Viking Penguin, a division of Penguin Putnam Inc.

"Ask the Oracle" from Loxias' Page, www.classicspage.com, reprinted by permission of Andrew Wilson.

"The Oak and the Reed" from *La Fontaine: Selected Fables.* Translation copyright © 1979 by James Michie. Reprinted by permission of Penguin Books Ltd.

Excerpts from *Sappho: A Garland* by Jim Powell. Copyright © 1993 by Jim Powell. Reprinted by permission of Farrar, Straus & Giroux, Inc.

"Oedipus the King" from *Three Theban Plays by Sophocles,* translated by Robert Fagles. Translation copyright © 1982 by Robert Fagles. Used by permission of Viking Penguin, a division of Penguin Putnam Inc.

From *The Dialogues of Plato* by William Chase Greene, editor, from the translation of Benjamin Jowett. Copyright © 1927 by Horace Liveright, Inc., renewed 1954 by Liveright Publishing Corporation. Reprinted by permission of Liveright Publishing Corporation.

"The Hadrianic Baths: A Computer Reconstruction by Bill Rattenbury," reprinted by permission of the School of Architecture Property and Planning, University of Aukland, New Zealand.

"Better to Live, Licinius" from *The Odes and Epodes of Horace: A Modern English Verse Translation* by Joseph P. Clancy. Copyright © 1960 by The University of Chicago.

"At Last It's Come" (III 13) by Sulpicia, from *Latin and Elegaic Poetry.* Garland Reference Library of the Humanities, Vol. 1425. Copyright © 1995 by Diane J. Rayor and William W. Batstone. Reprinted by permission of Garland Publishing.

"The Story of Pyramus and Thisbe" from *Metamorphoses* by Ovid, translated by Rolfe Humphries. Copyright © 1955 Indiana University Press. Reprinted by permission of Indiana University Press.

Excerpt from *The Aeneid* by Virgil, translated by Robert Fitzgerald. Copyright © 1981, 1982 by Robert Fitzgerald. Reprinted by permission of Random House, Inc.

"The Trojans" from *The Complete Poems of Cavafy,* translated by Rae Dalven, copyright © 1961 and renewed 1989 by Rae Dalven, reprinted by permission of Harcourt Brace & Company.

Excerpt from *The Annals of Imperial Rome* by Tacitus, translated by Michael Grant (Penguin Classics 1956, revised edition 1959) copyright © Michael Grant Publications Ltd., 1956, 1959. Reprinted by permission of Penguin Books Ltd.

"Pather Tells Story with Simple Beauty" by Edward Guthman. *San Francisco Chronicle,* August 4, 1995. Copyright © 1995, *San Francisco Chronicle.* Reprinted by permission.

Unit Three

Excerpt from *The Epic of Gilgamesh,* translated by N. K. Sandars (Penguin Classics 1960, 2nd revised edition 1972) copyright © N. K. Sandars, 1960, 1964, 1972. Reprinted by permission of Penguin Books Ltd.

Genesis 6–9 and The Book of Ruth from *Tanakh: A New Translation of the Holy Scriptures.* Copyright © 1985 by The Jewish Publication Society. Reprinted by permission of The Jewish Publication Society.

"The Exordium" and "Daylight" from *The Koran,* translated by N. J. Dawood (Penguin Classics 1956, 3rd revised edition 1968) copyright © N. J. Dawood, 1956, 1959, 1966, 1968. Reprinted by permission of Penguin Books Ltd.

"The Second Voyage of Sindbad the Sailor" from *Tales From the Thousand and One Nights,* translated by N. J. Dawood (Penguin Classics, 1954, revised edition 1973). Translation copyright © N. J. Dawood, 1954, 1973. Reprinted by permission of Penguin Books Ltd.

"The A–Z of Camels" reprinted by permission of ArabNet.

"The Counsels of the Bird" reprinted by permission from *Teachings of Rumi: The Masnavi* (Octagon Press Ltd.; London).

"The Sound of Birds at Noon" by Dahlia Ravikovitch, translated by Chana Bloch and Ariel Bloch, from *The Window* (NY: Sheep Meadow Press, 1989).

"The Diameter of the Bomb" by Yehuda Amihai, from *The Selected Poetry of Yehuda Amihai,* edited and newly translated by Chana Bloch and Stephen Mitchell. Copyright © 1986 by Chana Bloch and Stephen Mitchell. Reprinted by permission of the University of California Press.

"Butterflies" by Fawziyya Abu Khalid from *The Literature of Modern Arabia,* copyright © 1988 by the King Sand University. Reprinted by permission of Kegan Paul International.

"Creation Hymn" from *The Rig Veda,* translated by Wendy Doniger O'Flaherty (Penguin Classics, 1981) copyright © Wendy Doniger O'Flaherty, 1981. Reprinted by permission of Penguin Books Ltd.

"Hundred Questions" from *The Mahabharata.* Copyright © 1978 by R. K. Narayan. Reprinted by permission of the Wallace Literary Agency, Inc.

"The Lion-Makers" from *The Panchatantra,* translated from the Sanskrit by Arthur W. Ryder. Copyright © 1956 by Mary E. and Winifred Ryder. Reprinted by permission of The University of Chicago Press.

"The Lark" by Bernart de Ventaforn, from *The Translations of Ezra Pound.* Reprinted by permission of New Directions Publishing Corp.

"Like the Sun" from *Under the Banyan Tree* by R. K. Narayan. Copyright © 1985 by R. K. Narayan. Reprinted by permission of Viking Penguin, a division of Penguin Putnam, Inc.

"By Any Other Name" from *Gifts of Passage* by Santha Rama Rau. Copyright ©1951 by Vasanthi Rama Rau Bowers. Copyright renewed. "By Any Other Name" originally appeared in the *New Yorker.* Reprinted by permission of HarperCollins Publishers, Inc.

"River Light" by Inoue Yasushi from *The Modern Japanese Prose Poem,* translated by Dennis Keene. Copyright © 1980 by Princeton University Press. Used by permission of the publisher.

Unit Four

31, 33, 29 from *Tao Te Ching by Lao Tzu, a New English Version with Forewards and Notes* by Stephen Mitchell. Translation copyright © 1988 by Stephen Mitchell. Reprinted by permission of HarperCollins Publishers, Inc.

"The River Merchant's Wife: A Letter" by Ezra Pound, from *Personae.* Copyright © 1926 by Ezra Pound. Reprinted by permission of New Directions Publishing Corp.

"A Good Hair Week in Mongolia" by Tim Cahill from *Outside,* April 1996. Reprinted by permission.

"'Jade Flower Palace' by Tu Fu" by Kenneth Rexroth, from *One Hundred Poems from the Chinese*. Copyright © 1971 by Kenneth Rexroth. Reprinted by permission of New Directions Publishing Corp.

"A World of Dew and Melting Snow" by Kobayashi Issa, "Four Views of Spring Rain" by Yosa Buson, "When I Went to Visit" by Ki Tsurayuki, "Forsaking the Mists" by Lady Ise, "Was It That I Went to Sleep" by Ono Komachi, and "Trailing on the Wind" by Priest Saigy¯o, from *The Penguin Book of Japanese Verse,* translated by Geoffrey Bowns and Anthony Thwaite (Penguin Books, 1964). Translation copyright © Geoffrey Bowns and Anthony Thwaite, 1964. Reprinted by permission of Penguin Books Ltd.

Excerpts from *The Pillow Book of Sei Shōnagon,* translated and edited by Ivan Morris. Copyright © 1991 by Columbia University Press. Reprinted with permission of the publisher.

"Green Willow" from *Mysterious Tales of Japan,* retold by Rafe Martin, text copyright © 1996 by Rafe Martin. Reprinted by permission of G. P. Putnam's Sons.

"Awakening the Dragon," by Shelagh Peirce. Reprinted by permission.

"Two Lies" from *Folk Tales from Korea.* Copyright © 1952, 1970, 1982 by Zong In-sob. Reprinted by permission of Hollym International.

"The Damask Drum" attributed to Seami, from *The No Plays of Japan.* Copyright © 1922 by Arthur Waley. Used by permission of Grove/ Atlantic.

"Poverty's Child" and "The Sun's Way" by Bashō, from *An Introduction to Haiku* by Harold G. Henderson. Copyright © 1958 by Harold G. Henderson. Reprinted by permission of Doubleday, a division of Random House, Inc.

"The Long March" from *Twentieth Century Chinese Poetry* by Kai-Yu Hsu, translated by Kai-yu Hsu. Translation copyright © 1963 by Kai-yu Hsu. Reprinted by permission of Doubleday, a division of Random House, Inc.

"Answer" by Bei Dao, translated by Donald Finkel with Chen Xueliang, and "Assembly Line" by Shu Ting, translated by Carolyn Kizer and Y. H. Zhao, from *A Splintered Mirror: Chinese Poetry from the Democracy Movement,* translated by Donald Finkel. Translation copyright © 1991 by Donald Finkel. Reprinted by permission of North Point Press, a division of Farrar, Straus & Giroux, Inc.

"The Jay" from *Palm-of-the-Hand Stories* by Yasunari Kawabata, translated by Lane Dunlop and J. Martin Holman. Translation copyright © 1988 by Lane Dunlop and J. Martin Holman. Reprinted by permission of North Point Press, a division of Farrar, Straus & Giroux, Inc.

"August River" by Pak Tu-jin and "Song of Peace" by Hwang Tonggyu, from *The Silence of Love: Twentieth-Century Korean*

Poetry, Peter H. Lee, ed. Copyright © 1997 by Peter H. Lee. (Honolulu: University of Hawaii, 1980).

"A Personal Opinion About Gray" by Tanikawa Shuntaro, from *62 Sonnets and Definitions.* Katydid Books, 1992.

"Riding the Ghan" copyright © 1997 Great Southern Railway. Reprinted by permission. All rights reserved.

"A Handful of Dates" from *The Wedding of Zein* by Tayeb Salih. Copyright © Tayeb Salih and Denys Johnson-Davies. Reprinted by permission of Heinemann Educational Publishers, a division of Reed Educational & Professional Publishing, Ltd.

"Full Moon Rhyme," "Rainforest," and "River Bend" by Judith Wright, from *A Human Pattern: Selected Poems* (ETT Imprint, Sydney 1995).

"Municipal Gum" by Oodgeroo of the tribe Noonuccal (formerly known as Kath Walker), in *My People,* 3rd Edition, 1990, published by Jacaranda Press.

"Clouds on the Sea" by Ruth Dallas, from *Fire in the Sea,* edited by Sue Cowing. Copyright © 1996 University of Hawai'i Press. Reprinted by permission.

"Fathers and Daughters" from *When Heaven and Earth Changed Places* by Le Ly Hayslip. copyright © 1989 by Le Ly Hayslip and Charles Jay Wurts. Reprinted by permission of Doubleday, a division of Random House, Inc.

Reprinted with the permission of The Free Press, a Division of Simon & Schuster from *Stay Alive, My Son* by Pin Yathay. Copyright © 1987 by Pin Yathay.

Excerpt from *Stay Alive, My Son,* copyright © 1987 by Pin Yathay. Reprinted by permission of the author.

"Ocean Facts" from www.ocean98.org, reprinted by permission of Ocean98.

"Tarroa" by Ulli Beier, "Islands" by Nicholas Hasluck, "Island" by Albert Wendt, from *Fire in the Sea,* edited by Sue Cowing. Copyright © 1996 University of Hawai'i Press. Reprinted by permission.

Unit Five

From *The Song of Roland* by Frederick Goldin, translator. Copyright © 1978 by W. W. Norton & Company, Inc. Reprinted by permission of W. W. Norton & Company, Inc.

"Burghausen Castle" from www.teleport.com/~ludwig, reprinted by permission of Debbie McCord.

From "Europe's First Family: The Basques" by Thomas J. Abercrombie, from *National Geographic,* November 1995. Reprinted by permission of the National Geographic Society.

From *The Divine Comedy* by Dante Alighieri, translated by John Ciardi. Translation copyright 1954, 1957, 1959, 1960, 1961, 1965, 1967, 1970 by the Ciardi Family Publishing Trust. Reprinted by permission of W. W. Norton & Company, Inc.

Excerpt from *Don Quixote* by Miguel de Cervantes, translated by J. M. Cohen (Penguin Classics, 1950) copyright © J. M. Cohen, 1950. Reprinted by permission of Penguin Books Ltd.

"Sonnet VIII" by Louise Labé, from *Book of Women Poets from Antiquity to Now, Revised Edition,* by Willis Barnstone and Aliki Barnstone, editors. Copyright © 1980, 1992 by Schocken Books Inc. Reprinted by permission of Schocken Books, distributed by Pantheon, a division of Random House, Inc.

"Sonnet 239" from *The Complete Poems of Michelangelo,* translated by John Frederick Nims. Copyright © 1998, The University of Chicago Press. Reprinted by permission.

"The Lorelei" from *The Poetry and Prose of Heinrich Heine,* edited by Frederick Ewen. Copyright © 1948 by the Citadel Press. Published by arrangement with Carol Publishing Group.

"Russia 1812" by Victor Hugo, translated by Robert Lowell, from *Imitations* by Robert Lowell. Copyright © 1959 by Robert Lowell. Copyright renewed © 1987 by Harriet, Sheridan and Caroline Lowell. Reprinted by permission of Farrar, Straus & Giroux, Inc.

"A Doll's House" from *The Complete Major Plays of Henrik Ibsen* by Henrik Ibsen, translated by Rolf Fjelde, translation copyright © 1965, 1970, 1978 by Rolf Fjelde. Used by permission of Dutton Signet, a division of Penguin Putnam Inc.

"War" from *The Medals and Other Stories* by Luigi Pirandello. Copyright © 1939 by E. P. Dutton & Co. Reprinted by permission of the Pirandello Estate and Toby Cole, Agent.

Excerpt from *Earthly Paradise* by Colette, edited by Robert Phelps. Translation copyright © 1966 and translation copyright renewed © 1994 by Farrar Straus & Giroux, Inc. Reprinted by permission of Farrar, Straus & Giroux, Inc.

"The Panther" from *The Selected Poetry of Rainer Maria Rilke* by Rainer Maria Rilke, translated by Stephen Mitchell. Translation copyright © 1982 by Stephen Mitchell. Reprinted by permission of Random House, Inc.

"Lot's Wife" translated by Richard Wilbur, from *Walking to Sleep, New Poems and Translations,* copyright © 1969 by Richard Wilbur, reprinted by permission of Harcourt Brace & Company.

"In the terrible night" from *Selected Poems* by Fernando Pessoa, translated by Jonathan Griffin (Penguin Books 1974, second edition 1982) copyright © L. M. Rosa. Translations copyright © Jonathan Griffin, 1974, 1982. Reprinted by permission of Penguin Books Ltd.

"The Guitar" reprinted from *Lorca and Jimenez: Selected Poems,* chosen and translated by Robert Bly, Beacon Press, 1973, 1997. Copyright © 1973, 1997 by Robert Bly. Reprinted with his permission.

"The World, My Friends, My Enemies, You and the Earth" from *Things I Didn't Know I Loved* by Nazim Hikmet, translated by Randy Blasing and Mutlu Konuk. Copyright © 1975 by Randy Blasing and Mutlu Konuk. Reprinted by permission of Persea Books, Inc.

Excerpt from *Night* by Elie Wiesel, translated by Stella Rodway. Copyright © 1960 by MacGibbon & Kee. Copyright renewed © 1988 by The Collins Publishing Group. Reprinted by permission of Hill and Wang, a division of Farrar, Straus & Giroux, Inc.

"Encounter" from *Bells in Winter* by Czesław Miłosz. Copyright © 1974, 1977, 1978 by Czesław Miłosz. Reprinted by permission of The Ecco Press.

"The Myth of Sisyphus" from *The Myth of Sisyphus and Other Essays* by Albert Camus, translated by Justin O'Brien. Copyright © 1955 by Alfred A. Knopf, reprinted by permission of Random House, Inc.

Unit Six

"Creation Hymn" from *Popol Vuh.* Copyright © 1974, 1976 by Ralph Nelson. Reprinted by permission of Houghton Mifflin Company. All rights reserved.

Excerpt from "Egypt discovery may be earliest proof of writing" by Vijay Joshi. Associated Press, December 15, 1998. Reprinted by permission of Associated Press.

"Coyote Finishes His Work" by Barry Lopez. Reprinted by permission of Universal Press Syndicate.

"That Place Where Ghosts of Salmon Jump" by Sherman Alexie, reprinted from *The Summer of Black Widows.* Copyright © 1996 by Sherman Alexie, by permission of Hanging Loose Press.

Excerpt from *The Voyage of Christopher Columbus* by John Cummins. Copyright © 1992 by John Cummins. Reprinted by permission of St. Martin's Press Incorporated.

"Sonnet 145" reprinted by permission of the publisher from *Sor Juana* by Octavio Paz, Cambridge, Mass.: Harvard University Press, copyright © 1988 by the President and Fellows of Harvard College.

"Two Countries" by José Martí in *José Martí: Major Poems,* edited and with an introduction by Philip S. Foner (New York: Holmes & Meier, 1982). Copyright © 1982 by Holmes & Meier Publishers, Inc. Reproduced with the permission of the publisher.

"The Luck of Teodoro Méndez Acúbal" from *Another Way to Be: Selected Works of Rosario Castellanos* by Rosario Castellanos. Copyright © 1990 by The University of Georgia Press.

"The Window" by Jaime Torres Bodet, translated by George Kearns. Reprinted by permission.

Excerpt from *In Search of History: Lost City of the Incas* Copyright © 1997 A&E Television Networks. Reprinted by permission.

"Horses" from *A New Decade (Poems: 1958–1967)* by Pablo Neruda. English translation copyright © 1969 by Alastair Reid. Used by permission of Grove/Atlantic.

"The Night Face Up" from *End of the Game and Other Stories* by Julio Cortazar, translated by Paul Blackburn. Copyright © 1963 by Random House, Inc. Reprinted by permission of Pantheon Books, a division of Random House, Inc.

"Fable" by Octavio Paz, from *Collected Poems 1957–1987.* Copyright © 1986 by Octavio Paz and Eliot Weinburger. Reprinted by permission of New Directions Publishing Corp.

"Spring over the City" by Anne Hébert, translated by Kathleen Weaver. Reprinted with the permission of General Publishing, 30 Lesmill Road, North York, Ontario.

"The Handsomest Drowned Man in the World" from *Leaf Storm and Other Stories* by Gabriel García Márquez and translated by Gregory Rabassa. Copyright © 1971 by Gabriel García Márquez. Reprinted by permission of HarperCollins Publishers, Inc.

"Day of the Butterfly" from *Dance of the Happy Shades.* Copyright © 1968 by Alice Munro. Published by McGraw-Hill Ryerson, Ltd. Reprinted by arrangement with the Virginia Barber Literary Agency. All rights reserved.

"Day of the Butterfly" from *Dance of the Happy Shades.* Copyright © 1968 by Alice Munro. Reprinted by permission of McGraw-Hill Ryerson, Ltd.

"Mushrooms" from *Selected Poems II: Poems Selected and New 1976–1986.* Copyright © 1987 by Margaret Atwood. Reprinted by permission of Houghton Mifflin Company. All rights reserved.

"Mushrooms" from *Selected Poems 1966–1984* by Margaret Atwood. Copyright © Margaret Atwood 1990. Reprinted by permission of Oxford University Press Canada.

"Shoes for the Rest of My Life" by Guadalupe Duenas, and "Bishop Berkeley or Mariana of the Universe" by Liliana Heker are reprinted with permission from the publisher of *Short Stories by Latin American Women,* edited by Celia Correas de Zapata (Houston: Arte Publico Press–University of Houston, 1990).

"A Canary's Ideas" from *The Devil's Church and Other Stories* by Joaquim Maria Machado de Assis, translated by Jack Schmitt and Lori Ishimatsu, copyright © 1977. By permission of the University of Texas Press.

"Love Orange," from *Summer Lightning and Other Stories* by Olive Senior. Copyright © 1986 by Olive Senior. Reprinted by permission of Addison Wesley Longman Ltd.

Excerpt from the Ship's Log of *Matthew,* reprinted by permission of the Matthew Society.

"A Walk to the Jetty" from *Annie John* by Jamaica Kincaid. Copyright © 1985 by Jamaica Kincaid. Reprinted by permission of Farrar, Straus & Giroux, Inc.

"Fishing" from *The Woman Who Fell From the Sky* by Joy Harjo. Copyright © 1994 by Joy Harjo. Reprinted by permission of W. W. Norton & Company, Inc.

Maps

Ortelius Design, Inc./GeoSystems Global Corp.

Photography

Abbreviation key: **AR**=Art Resource, New York; **BAL**=Bridgeman Art Library, London/New York; **CI**=Christie's Images; **CO**=CORBIS; **EL**=Erich Lessing; **GL**=Gamma Liaison; **GR**=Giraudon, Paris; **INBA**=Reproducción autorizada por el Instituto Nacional De Bellas Artes Y Literatura. ©2000 Reproducción autorizada por el Banco de México. Fiduciario en el Fideicomiso relativo a los Museos Diego Rivera y Frida Kahlo, Av. 5 de Mayo No. 2, Col. Centro, 06059, México, D.F.; **LPBC/AH**=book courtesy Little Professor Book Centers, photo by Aaron Haupt; **NGS**=National Geographic Society Image Collection; **SC**=Scala; **SIS**=Stock Illustration Source; **SO**=Sotheby's Picture Library, London; **SS**=SuperStock; **TSI**=Tony Stone Images; **TSM**=The Stock Market.

Cover (l)Stone of the Sun. Aztec calendar stone, diameter: 11½ ft. National Museum of Anthropology, Mexico City/Michel Zabe/AR, (r)Dance in Tehuantepec, 1928. Diego Rivera (Mexico). Oil on canvas, 199 x 162 cm. Private collection/IBNA/SO; **vii** (t to b)M. Courtney-Clark/Gamma-Liaison, GR/AR, BAL, Alain Evrard/GL, BAL, ©Estate of David Alfaro Siqueiros/SOMAAP, Mexico/Licensed by VAGA, New York, NY/Schalkwijk/AR; **viii** (l)BAL, (r) ©Africa Museum Tervuren, Belgium. Photo: R. Asselberghs; **ix** CI; **x** Arvind Vohora/In The Dark Ltd; **xi** CI; **xii** BAL; **xiii** Suad al-Attar/ICWA; **xiv** Freer Gallery of Art, Smithsonian Institution, Washington DC; **xv** ©1999 The Art Institute of Chicago. All Rights Reserved. Photograph by Robert Hashimoto; **xvi** Brooklyn Museum of Art, New York; **xviii** (l)CI/BAL, (r)Ali Miruku/SS; **xx** ©1999 Estate of Tamara de Lempicka/Artists Rights Society (ARS), New York/© Photos-Contact, Beauvais; **xxi** Jerry Jacka; **xxii** The Pierpont Morgan Library/AR; **xxiii** Jerry Jacka; **xxvi** CI; **xxvii** (l)Miramax Films/Shooting Star International, (r)Gordon Langsbury/Bruce Coleman, Inc.; **xxviii** (l)©1999 Artists Rights Society (ARS), New York/VEGAP, Madrid/CI, (r)CORBIS/Andrew Cowin/Travel Ink; **2** LPBC/AH; **4** N.Z.M./Key-Light Image Library; **5** Corbally Stourton Contemporary Art, London, UK/BAL; **8** BAL; **14** LPBC/AH; **16** Archive Photos; **17** Courtesy The Everard Read Gallery, Johannesburg, South Africa; **22–23** LPBC/AH; **24** Globe Photos; **25** Bruno Barbey/Magnum/PNI; **28–29** ©Africa Museum Tervuren, Belgium. Photo: R. Asselberghs; **30–37** (border)courtesy Joyce White; **30** (l)J.P. Fruchet-TCL/Masterfile, (r)Pictor/Uniphoto; **30–31** SS; **32** (background) Mike Malyszko/FPG, (l)Louvre Museum, Paris/Explorer/SS, (r)CI; **33** (t)Louvre Museum, Paris/GR/SS, (b)Victoria & Albert Museum, London/BAL; **34** (t)Jacksonville Museum of Contemporary Art, FL/SS, (c)Tim Courlas, (b)James L. Stanfield/NGS; **35** (t)British Museum, London, (b)Glen Allison/TSI; **36** CI; **37** (t)Jeffrey Ploskonka, (b)Jason Lauré; **38** British Museum, London/BAL; **39** CI; **40** Werner Forman Archive/AR; **42** Nicholas DeVore/TSI; **43, 46** Kuona Trust/In The Dark Ltd; **48** Stephen J. Krasemann/DRK Photo; **49** CO/Michael Boys; **52** ©C.A.A.C.–The Pigozzi Collection, Geneva; **53** Beth Hinckley/SS; **57** David Young-Wolff/Photo Edit; **58** BAL; **59** Daniel Riffet/TSI; **61** ©C.A.A.C.–The Pigozzi Collection, Geneva; **64** CI; **65, 70** ©C.A.A.C.–The Pigozzi Collection, Geneva; **71** *Ceremonial Costume of King Mbop.* Kuba

People, Zaire. Raffia fiber, cowrie shells, fur, copper, beads. The Newark Museum NJ/AR; **72** BAL; **76** Photographers Aspen/PNI; **77** *Red Bear Inua Mask.* National Museum of Natural History, Smithsonian Institution, Washington DC/SS; **79** The Newark Museum, NJ/AR; **80, 81** Jason Lauré; **82** ©1998 Detroit Institute of Arts; **83** Sam Abell/NGS; **84** Pierre-Alain Ferrazzini/Musée Barbier-Mueller, Genève; **88** Larry Moore/SIS; **89** (l)Royal Albert Memorial Musem, Exeter/BAL, (r)British Museum, London/BAL; **91** (l)BAL, (r)WK; **98–105** (border)The Newark Museum, NJ/AR; **98** (l)M. Courtney-Clark/GL, (r)David Austen/TSI; **98–99** Nicholas DeVore/TSI; 100 (background)Thierry Borredon/TSI, (l)CI, (r)Betty Press/Woodfin Camp & Associates/PNI; **101** (l)Chris Johns/NGS, (r)Kal Muller/Woodfin Camp & Associates/PNI; **102** (t)Hilarie Kavanagh/TSI, (b)Jack Vartoogian; **103** (l)photo by Herbert Lotz/courtesy Shona Sol Gallery, Sante Fe NM, (r)SS; **104** Glen Allison/TSI; **105** (t)CO/K.M. Westermann, (b)T. Charles Erickson/Theatre Pix; **106** Jean-Claude Aunos/GL; **107** SS; **108** Michel Renaudeau/GL; **109** University of Maryland Unversity College; **113** Photofest; **114** Andrea Renault/Globe Photos; **115** (background)Geoff Butler, (inset)Pierre-Alain Ferrazzini/Musée Barbier-Mueller, Genève; **119** BSDA, Dakar, Senegal; **122** Bogumil Jewsiewicki; **123** CI; **128** (l)Reuters/Brian Snyder/Archive Photos, (r)Picture Research Consultants and Archives; **129** Kuona Trust/In The Dark Ltd; **132** ©C.A.A.C.; **134** C.M. Hardt/GL; **136** (l)courtesy East African Educational Publishers, (r)Kuona Trust/In The Dark Ltd; **137** Kuona Trust/In The Dark Ltd; **140–141** CI; **146** (l)Frederic Reglain/GL, (r)CI; **147** Liliane Karnouk; **149** Robert Ellison/Black Star; **150** Michael Vaha/Heinemann Educational Publishers; **151** First Image; **152** Peter Magubane/NGS; **153** Etienne Bol; **155** file photo; **158** (t)Heinemann Educational Publishers, (b)CO/Jeffrey L. Rotman; **161** ©C.A.A.C.–The Pigozzi Collection, Geneva; **164** Louise Gubb/The Image Works;

165, 167 ©C.A.A.C.–The Pigozzi Collection, Geneva; **170, 171, 172** Arvind Vohora/In The Dark Ltd; **173** Amrit P. Singh; **174** Arvind Vohora/In The Dark Ltd; **176** MENA; **177** Liliane Karnouk; **181** CO/Fulvio Roiter; **183** *Woman's Kente Cloth* (detail). Asante peoples, Ghana. Rayon, 64½ x 33¾ in. The Newark Museum, NJ/AR; **184** William Campbell/Time Magazine; **185, 187** National Heritage and Cultural Studies Centre, University of Fort Hare, South Africa; **197** LPBC/AH; **200–201** CI; **202–209** (border)Tzovaras/AR; **202** (l)CI, (r)EL/AR; **202–203** WK; **204** (background)WK, (l)EL/AR, (r)CI; **205** (l)British Museum, London, (r)EL/AR; **206** (t)CI, (b)Louvre Museum, Paris/SS; **207** (t)Phyllis Picardi/Stock South/PNI, (b)Sheridan/Ancient Art & Architecture Collection; **208** Sheridan/Ancient Art & Architecture Collection; **209** (t)Sheridan/Ancient Art & Architecture Collection, (b)John Heimlich/Stock South/PNI; **210** Mauritshuis, The Hague, Holland/BAL/SS; **211** SC/AR; **213** GR/AR; **216** SC/AR; **219** CI; **223, 224, 228** SC/AR; **232** SS; **235** The National Museum, Athens/Philip Harrington/NGS; **236** GR/AR; **240** William Francis Warden Fund, Museum of Fine Arts, Boston; **243** Fitzwilliam Museum, University of Cambridge, UK/BAL; **244** CI; **248** BAL; **249** AKG London; **250** SC/AR; **251** AKG London; **253** GR/AR; **254, 256** SS; **257** (t)SC/AR, (b)Aaron Haupt; **258** BAL; **258–259** Aaron Haupt; **261** John Colm Leberg, 1997 Stratford Production; **262** (t)CO/Gianni Dagli Orti, (b)SC/AR; **263** Adolph and Esther Gottlieb Foundation; **266** BAL; **270** GR/AR; **273** BAL; **274** Tate Gallery, London/AR; **279** ©1998 Kate Rothko-Prizel & Christopher Rothko/Artists Rights Society (ARS), New York; **281** CI; **288** SS; **295** EL/AR; **302** CI; **307** Cylla von Tiedemann/Stratford Festival; **311** EL/AR; **316** Cylla von Tiedemann/Stratford Festival; **321, 325** BAL; **327, 329** SC/AR; **338–345** (border)GR/AR; **338** (l)H.P. Merten/TSM, (r)Archeological Museum, Florence, Italy/E.T. Archive, London/SS; **338–339** Robert Frerck/TSI; **340** (background)SS, (l)Michael Holford, (r)Jonathan Blair/NGS; **341** (l)Index/BAL, (r)Louvre Museum, Paris/Peter Willi/BAL; **342** (t)Tomb of Leopardi, Tarqina, Italy/Fratelli Alinari/SS, (b)CI; **343** (t)CI, (b)BAL; **344** (t)SC/AR, (b)SC/AR; **345** (t) Alinari/AR, (b) SC/AR; **346** Bill Rattenbury; **347** (l)Hulton Getty Collection/TSI, (r)Michael Holford; **349** Bradford City Art Gallery and Museum, England/SS; **352** EL/AR; **353** *Ships on Violent Sea,* from *Faits Des Romains.* c. 1340, Italian illuminated manscript. Collection of Royal Manuscripts, British Library, London; **355** Larry Moore/SIS; **357** SS; **359** SC/AR; **360** GR/AR; **363** SS; **367** CO/Roger Wood; **368** GR/AR;

371 National Trust Photographic Library/From the De Morgan Foundation; **375** BAL; **378** SS; **383** CI; **386** (t)Margot Granitsas Archives/The Image Works, (b)David Ball/TSM; **387** CI; **389** SS; **390** First Image; **392** GR/AR; **393** CO/Buddy Mays; **395** GR/AR; **405** (tl, c)Aaron Haupt, (tr, b)LPBC/AH; **408** Suad al-Attar/International Council for Women in the Arts; **410–417** (border)AR; **410** (l)Lisa Quinoes/Black Star/PNI, (r)CO/Nik Wheeler; **410–411** Josef Polleross/TSM; **412** (background)J. Polleros/TSM, (t)SC/AR, (b)Rene Burri/Magnum; **413** (t)British Library, London/BAL/SS, (b)SC/AR; **414** BAL; **415** CO/Hans Georg Roth; **416** ICWA; **417** (t)Institut d'Etudes Orientales, St. Petersburg, Russia/GR/SS, (b)The Lowe Art Museum, The University of Miami/SS; **419** E.T. Archive, London/SS; **420** BAL; **421** Steve McCurry/NGS; **423** Michael Holford; **424** O. Louis Mazzatent/NGS; **426** BAL; **427** Roy Gumpel/GL; **429** SS; **430** SC/AR; **433** Michael Holford; **435** Jewish Museum/AR; **437** CI; **438, 441, 444, 448** BAL; **449** GR/AR; **451** Larry Moore/SIS; **452** BAL; **453** Freer Gallery of Art, Smithsonian Institution, Washington DC; **454** Ned Gillette/TSM; **455** (t)Freer Gallery of Art, Smithsonian Institution, Washington DC, (b)James Carmichael/The Image Bank; **456, 457** Freer Gallery of Art, Smithsonian Institution, Washington DC; **459** BAL; **460** (l)BAL/AR, (r)Victoria & Albert Museum, London/AR; **461** Bonhams, London/BAL; **462** BAL; **465** AKG London; **466** SC/AR; **466–467** (background)SC/AR; **469** (t)Dina Gona, (b)International Council of Women in the Arts; **470** Gordon Langsbury/Bruce Coleman, Inc.; **472** Noah Satat/Animals Animals; **473** (l)file photo, (r)Ken Graham/TSI/PNI; **474** WK; **477** (l)Dina Gona, (r)Liliane Karnouk; **478** Tel Aviv Museum of Art; **482** Liliane Karnouk; **488–495** (border)BAL; **488** (l)Richard A. Cooke III/TSI, (r)Nicholas DeVore/TSI; **488–489** Chris Noble/TSI; **490** (background) WK, (t)Douglas T. Mesney/TSM, (b)David Ball/TSM; **491** (l)Peter Willi/BAL, (r)BAL; **492** (t)WK, (b)Lisa Kremer/GL; **493** (t)The Stapleton Collection/BAL, (b)David Ball/TSM; **494** Joel Simon/TSI; TSI; **495** Amrit P. Singh; **496, 497** BAL;

498 Werner Forman Archive/AR; **500** BAL; **501** The Pierpont Morgan Library/AR; **503, 504** BAL; **508** Michele & Tom Grimm/International Stock Photo; **509** (t)Lindsay Hebberd/Woodfin Camp & Associates, (b)Mike Yamashita/Woodfin Camp & Associates; **510** GR/AR; **511, 512** BAL; **514** Robert Frerck/TSI; **515** Mark Gamba/TSM; **516** CO/E.O. Hoppe; **517** file photo; **518** WK; **519** CI; **521** Anil A. Dave/Dinodia/Images of India; **522** file photo; **526** AP/Wide World Photos; **527** CI; **528** (l)Anthony Edgeworth/TSM, (r)V.H. Mishra/Dinodia/Images of India; **530** Mills College Art Museum with permission from Lalitha Lajmi; **532** Satish Parashar/Dinodia; **533** SO; **534** (t)cliché Bibliothèque nationale de France, (b)BAL; **535** BAL; **537** CI; **538** Kothari/GL; **541** file photo; **544** CO/UPI/Bettmann; **545** file photo; **549** courtesy Sanjay Bhattacharyya; **552** MENA; **553** SO; **554** Bill Lyons; **557** International Council for Women in the Arts; **558** Bill Lyons; **560** TIMOTCA, Laguna Beach CA; **564** (l)Sophie Bassouls/Sygma, (r)BAL; **565** The Nelson-Atkins Museum of Art, Kansas City MO (Purchase: Nelson Trust); **567** SO; **568** Photofest; **570** file photo; **577** LPBC/AH; **580–581** ©1999, The Art Institute of Chicago. All Rights Reserved. Photograph by Robert Hashimoto; **582–589** (border)CI; **582** (l)Keren Su/TSI, (r)Chad Ehlers/TSI; **582–583** George Disario/TSM; **584** (background)David Ball/TSM, (l)Cary Wolinsky/TSI, (r)CO/Michael S. Yamashita; World View/TSI; **586** (t)Victoria & Albert Museum, London/AR, (b)CO/Michael S. Yamashita; **587** Michele Burgess/TSM; **588** The Newark Museum, NJ/AR; AR; **589** First Image; **590** (l)Vanni/AR, (r)*Mountain Landscape.* Qing Dynasty, China. Jade, height: 17.5 cm. Gift of the Misses Alice and Nellie Morris, 1941.594/The Cleveland Museum of Art; **591** BAL; **594** Royal Ontario Museum ©ROM; **595** EL/AR; **596** Photograph ©1999, The Art Institute of Chicago, All Rights Reserved; **599** Sovfoto; **600** Gifts of J.H. Wade & Purchase from the J.H. Wade Fund by exchange, 1980.186/The Cleveland Museum of Art; **603** CI/BAL; **604** Sovfoto; **605** CI; **608** *Komachi Washes the Book,* from the series *Seven Elegant Episodes from the Life of the Poetess Ono no Komachi,* early 1810s, Edo period. Kikugawa Eizan (Japan). Color woodblock print, 38.2 x 25.4 cm. Gift of Mrs. Ralph King, 1943.30/The Cleveland Museum of Art; 609 Asian Art Museum of San Francisco/ The Avery Brundage Collection 1991.54.2; **611** The Newark Museum, NJ/AR; **613, 615** BAL; 617 CO/Dean Conger; **619** The Stapleton Collection/BAL; **622** Spencer Museum of Art, The University of Kansas; **623** Fenollosa-Weld Collection, Museum of Fine Arts, Boston; **626** CI; **628** Keren SU/FPG; **629, 630** Brooklyn Museum of Art, New York; **633** Guthrie/AR; **635** Museum of Fine Arts, Springfield MA, Raymond A. Bidwell Collection; **637** The Lowe Art Museum, The University of Miami, FL/SS; **638** Embroidery on silk ground with (beaten) gold leaf, sleeve to sleeve: 138 cm., neck-hem: 158.5 cm. John L. Severance Fund, 1974.36/The Cleveland Museum of Art; **640** CO/Asian Art & Archaeology, Inc.; **641** Photograph ©1999, The Art Institute of Chicago, All Rights Reserved; **642** BAL; **644** (t)CO/UPI/Bettmann, (b)BAL; **645** CI; **647** Frederic Reglain/GL; **648, 650** Charlesworth/Saba Press Photos; **651** Burt Glinn/Magnum Photos; **653** Photograph ©1999, The Art Institute of Chicago, All Rights Reserved; **658** Courtesy Hwang Tong-gyu; **659** David Portnoy/Black Star; **662** Bob Daemmrich/Stock Boston/PNI; **663** W.E. Garrett/NGS; **665** Courtesy Dr. Michael Sullivan, St. Catherine's College, Oxford University; **670** Kyodo News International; **671** Tom Maday/Photonica; **673** (t)ChinaStock, (b)Bruce Dale/NGS; **680–687** (border)courtesy Mary Schafer/photo by Aaron Haupt; **674** Alistair Berg/GL; **680** (l)Mitsuaki Iwago/Minden Pictures, (r)SS; **680–681** Tibor Bognar/TSM; **682** (background) Bushnell/Soifer/TSI, (l)Holden Clay/Pacific Stock, (r)Paul Chesley/TSI; **683** (b)Cilles Mermet/GL, (t)Art Wolfe/TSI; **684** (t)John Elk/TSI, (b)CI/SS; **685** Harvey Lloyd/TSM; **686** Shaun Egan/TSI; **687** (t)Gift of Sunday Reed, 1977/National Gallery of Australia, Canberra, (b)Don Smetzer/TSI; **689** SS; **691** Paul Souders Photography Worldwide; **692** J.K. Moir Collection, State Library of Victoria; **693, 694–695** BAL; **697** Bill Cardoni/GL; **698** BAL; **702** (l)Roger-Viollet/GL, (r)Christian Michaels/FPG; **703** BAL; **705** Eunice Harris/Photo Researchers; **706** ©1999 Artists Rights Society (ARS), New York/DACS, London/BAL; **712** CO/UPI/Bettmann; **713** Courtesy Smithsonian Institution Traveling Exhibition Service; **715** Courtesy Taynie Nuyda; **716–717** Lynn Funkhouser/GL; **718** Catherine Karnow/Woodfin Camp & Associates/PNI; **719** Robin Siegell/NGS; **723** Alain Evrard/GL; **724** MENA; **725** Bill Lyons; **726** CO/Peter Harholdt; **727** CO/WK; **731** Tom Bean/DRK Photo; **732** Courtesy Judith Wright; **733** Ray Juno/TSM; **734–735** Kevin Schafer/TSI; **736** (t)Penny Tweedie/Camera Press, (bl)courtesy The Otago Daily Times, (br)Paul Souders/TSI; **737** CO/Penny Tweedie; **738** Auckland Art Gallery Toi o Tamaki, New Zealand, gift of Mrs. Joyce Milligan in memory of Dr. R.R.D. Milligan, 1984. Reproduced with the permission of the artist's estate; **740** Courtesy Nguyen Thi Vinh; **741** Indochina Arts Partnership; **745** The Kobal Collection; **746** Alain Buu/GL; **747** Indochina Arts Partnership; **750** Courtesy Smithsonian Institution Traveling Exhibition Service; **755** Larry Moore/SIS; **756** Sophie Bassouls/Sygma; **757, 759** Monirith Chhea; **762** WK; **764** Rick Doyle/The Viesti Collection; **765** Courtesy Albert Wendt; **766** The Newark Museum, NJ/AR; **766–769** Carl Shaneff/Pacific Stock; **767** TIMOTCA, Laguna Beach CA; **768–769** Art Wolfe; **770** WK; **777** LPBC/AH; **780–781** Ali Miruku/SS; **782–789** (border)The Cummer Museum of Art and Gardens, Jacksonville FL/SS; **782** (l)Musée de la Reine, Bayeux, France/BAL/SS, (r)Victoria and Albert Museum, London/AR; **782–783** Stephen Studd/TSI; **784** (background)SS, (l)CI/BAL, (r)Kunsthistorisches Museum, Vienna, Austria/SS; **785** (t)SS, (b)Louvre Museum, Paris/SS; **786** (t)SO/BAL, (b)SS; **787** (t)EL/AR, (b)Ben Asen/Envision; **788** By Courtesy of The Board of Trustees of The Victoria and Albert Museum, London/BAL/SS; **789** (t)Phillips, The International Fine Art Auctioneers/BAL/SS, (b)British Library, London/AKG, Berlin/SS; **790** GR/AR; **791** SC/AR; **795** BAL; **796** AKG London; **800** (t)cliché Bibliothèque nationale de France, (b)GR/AR; **801** SS; **804** The Huntington Library, Art Collections, and Botanical Gardens, San Marino CA/SS; **807** BAL; **810** Bryan Peterson/TSM; **811** (t)Pitti Palace, Florence, Italty/E.T. Archive, London/SS, (b)Museo del Prado, Madrid, Spain/Lauros-GR/SS; **812** BAL; **816** CI; **821** SS; **825** Joanna B. Pinneo/Aurora; **826** Paul Chesley/NGS; **827** John Eastcott & Yvangs Momatiuk/NGS; **828** (l)EL/AR, (r)Joe Cornish/TSI; **829** Galleria Borghese, Rome, Italy/Canali PhotoBank, Milan/SS; **830** BAL; **831** Pushkin Museum of Fine Arts, Moscow/SS; **833** The Pierpont Morgan Library/AR; **836** Archive Photos; **837** AKG London; **840, 842** BAL; **846** E.T. Archive, London; **847** BAL; **849** AKG London; **850** BAL; **852** Palazzo Cancellaeria, Rome/Canali Photobank, Milan/SS; **853** SC/AR; **855** BAL; **860–867** (border)Whitford & Hughes, London/BAL; **860** (l)Chad Ehlers/TSI, (r)John Brooks/GL; **860–861** Bruce Stoddard/FPG; **862** (background)Travel Pix/FPG, (l)Jean Higgins/Envision, (r)Tim Gibson/Envision; **863** (l)TSM, (r)EL/AR; **864** Jim Cummins/FPG; **865** (t)©1999 Estate of Pablo Picasso/Artists Rights Society (ARS), New York/British Library, London/BAL, (b)©1999 Artists Rights Society (ARS), New York/ADAGP, Paris/AKG London; **866** Ken Ross/GL; **867** (t)Andreas Rudolf/TSI, (b)Chris Bennion/Theatre Pix; **868** CO/Library of Congress; **869** BAL; **871** CO/Andrew Cowin/Travel Ink; **872** Archive Photos; **873** SO; **874** AKG London; **877** ©1999 Artists Rights Society (ARS), New York/VG Bild-Kunst, Bonn/Bauhaus Archive/E.T. Archive, London/SS; **878** National Gallery, Oslo, Norway/BAL/SS; **879** Tate Gallery, London/AR; **882** ©Artists Rights Society (ARS), New York/ADAGP, Paris/BAL; **889** BAL; **892** ©1999 The Munch Museum/The Munch-Ellingsen Group/Artists Rights Society (ARS), New York/EL/AR; **897** SO; **902** ©1999 Artists Rights Society (ARS), New York/BONO, Oslo/BAL; **907** BAL; **910** ©1999 The Munch Museum/The Munch-Ellingsen Group/Artists Rights Society (ARS), New York/AR; **914, 918** BAL; **922** ©1999 The Munch Museum/The Munch-Ellingsen Group/Artists Rights Society (ARS), New York/BAL; **928** AKG London; **932** SO; **935** Larry Moore/SIS; **936** CO/Bettmann; **937** State Russian Museum, Moscow/SC/AR; **939** Mark Harwood/TSI; **940** AKG London; **945** CI; **950** Archive Photos; **951** ©1999 Artists Rights Society (ARS), New York/COPY-DAN, Copenhagen/BAL; **953, 956** BAL; **958** CO/UPI/Bettmann; **959, 963** BAL; **964** (l)CO/Bettmann, (r)Night-flower native to Jamaica. Henriette Gertruide Knip/Fitzwilliam Museum, University of Cambridge, UK/BAL; **965** ©1999 Artists Rights Society (ARS), New York/ADAGP, Paris/GR/AR; **967** ©1999 Artists Rights Society (ARS), New York/COPY-DAN, Copenhagen/SO; **970** Roger-Viollet/GL; **971** BAL; **974** Lenfilm Studios/Globe Photos; **975** BAL; **977** (l)Andre Zak/Sipa Press, (r)AKG London; **979** ©1999 Estate of Tamara de Lempicka/Artists Rights Society (ARS), New York/©Photos-Contact, Beauvais; **981** BAL; **982** Archives of Lisbon City Hall—Fernando Pessoa House; **983** Agnew & Sons, London/BAL; **986** Courtesy Stina Katchadourian; **987** ©1999 The Munch Museum/The Munch-Ellingsen Group/Artists Rights Society (ARS), New York/EL/AR; **989** GR/AR; **990** Popperfoto/Archive Photos; **991** BAL; **994** (t)courtesy Persea Books, (b)Retrograph Archive Limited, London, UK/BAL; **995, 996** BAL; **998** AP/Wide World Photos; **999** John D. Norman/TSM; **1000** Miriam Berkley; **1001** Courtesy Alfred Tibor; **1004** The Jewish Institute for the Arts, Inc.; **1006** BAL; **1008** Boleslaw Edelhajt/GL; **1009** SO; **1011** Eric Bouvet/GL; **1012** Roger-Viollet/GL; **1013** Courtesy Galerie Wühre 9—Art Deco, Zurich, Switzerland; **1017** (t)Vyto Starinskas/Rutland

Herald/Sygma, (b)State Russian Museum, St. Petersburg, Russia/BAL; **1018** ©1999 Artists Rights Society (ARS), New York/ADAGP, Paris/SO; **1025** LPBC/AH; **1028–1029** Coconino Center for the Arts, Flagstaff, AZ/Jerry Jacka; **1030–1037** (border)SEF/AR; **1030** (l)WK, (r)Laurie Platt Winfrey; **1030–1031** Art Wolfe; **1032** (background)David Barnes/TSM, (t)The Lowe Art Museum, The University of Miami, FL/SS, (b)AR; **1033** (t)Larry Ulrich/TSI, (b)SS; **1034** (t)Robert Frerck/TSM, (b)EL/AR; **1035** Cliff Hollenbeck/International Stock; **1036** AKG London; **1037** (t)Andrew Rakoczy/Photo Researchers, (b)Laurie Platt Winfrey; **1038** (t)SS, (b)D. Donne Bryant/AR; **1040, 1042** Justin Kerr; **1045** AP/Wide World Photos; **1046** Konrad Wothe/Minden Pictures; **1048** Jerry Jacka; **1051** (t)Marion Ettlinger/Outline, (b)Edward S. Curtis/NGS; **1053** Canadian Museum of Civilization, image number: S97-10761; **1055** Jerry Jacka; **1056** Miramax Films/Shooting Star International; **1058** (l)Metropolitan Museum of Art, New York/AKG Berlin/SS, (r)CO/Adam Woolfitt; **1059** ©1999 Artists Rights Society (ARS), New York/ADAGP, Paris/CI; **1060** Mary Evans Picture Library; **1062** James Frank/Stock Connection/PNI; **1065** Ken Welsh/BAL; **1067** (t)courtesy Eduardo Langagne, (b)Newberry Library, Chicago/SS; **1068** CI; **1070** The Pierpont Morgan Library/AR; **1071** Larry Moore/SIS; **1074** CI; **1075** CO/Philadelphia Museum of Art; **1077** (t)CO/Bettmann, (b)National Museum of Cuba, Havana/BAL; **1078** North Wind Picture Archive; **1084–1091** (border)Jian Chen/AR; **1084** (l)ZEFA/TSM, (r)WK; **1084–1085** Gene Peach/GL; **1086** (background)Jose Fuste Raga/TSM, (l)Alon Reininger/TSM, (r)CO/Hubert Stadler; **1087** (t)CO/Macduff Everton, (b)CI; **1088** (l)Schalkwijk/AR, (r)Andrew Klapatiuk/GL; **1089** (t)CO/Dave G. Houser, (b)WK; **1090** Heard Museum Shop, Phoenix AZ/Jerry Jacka; **1091** (t)Ray Juno/TSM, (b)WK; **1092** (t)Hans Beacham, (b)The Cummer Museum of Art and Gardens, Jacksonville FL/SS; **1093** INBA/Schalkwijk/AR; **1095** SS; **1096** Kal Muller/Woodfin Camp/PNI; **1098** CI/SS; **1102** Dominique Roger/UNESCO; **1103** AR; **1104** WK; **1106** Hulton Getty Collection/TSI; **1107** EL/AR; **1108** Photograph ©1999 The Museum of Modern Art, New York; **1110** (t)Goldberg/Sygma, (b)GR/AR; **1111** ©Estate of Carlos Almaraz/Los Angeles County Museum of Art, gift of the 1992 Collectors; **1112** GR/AR; **1113** INBA; **1114** GR/AR; **1115** (t)GR/AR, (b)Kactus Foto, Santiago, Chile/SS; **1116** (t)GR/AR, (b)Werner Forman Archive/AR; **1117** GR/AR; **1120** Marc Deville/GL; **1121** INBA/Schalkwijk/AR; **1124** Ulf Andersen/GL; **1125** BAL; **1126** CI/SS; **1128** file photo; **1129** CI; **1130** Tim Bieber/The Image Bank; **1131** CI; **1133** ©1999 Artists Rights Society (ARS), New York/VEGAP, Madrid/CI; **1134** Ulf Andersen/GL; **1137** National Air and Space Museum, Smithsonian Institution, Washington DC. NASM 5008, CAT NO 1975-0095; **1138** Schalkwijk/AR; **1142** Marion Ettlinger/Outline; **1143** SS; **1147** BAL/SS; **1152** (t)Wyatt Counts/Outline, (b)WK; **1153, 1154** Matt Meadows; **1156** Courtesy of the Harbourfront Reading Series, Toronto, Canada; **1157** INBA/CI; **1160** Zurbaran Galeria, Buenos Aires/SS; **1163** Nettie Lee Benson Latin American Collection, University of Texas at Austin; **1165** Courtesy Galería de Arte Mexicano, México; **1168** CI; **1170** CI; **1172** Courtesy Bently Quast/McClelland & Stewart Inc.; **1173** BAL; **1178** AP/Wide World Photos; **1179** Bob Wagner/Outline; **1181** Erol Samuel/SS; **1184** Private collection/Erol Samuel/SS; **1188** Hulleah Tsinhnahjinnie; **1189** Courtesy Gallery 10, Carefree AZ/Santa Fe NM/Jerry Jacka; **1197** (tl, tr, c)LPBC/AH, (b)Aaron Haupt.